The International Instit
And The Temple of
Graciously ~~~~~~

THE SECRET TEACHINGS OF CHINESE ENERGETIC MEDICINE: VOLUME 1

"ENERGETIC ANATOMY AND PHYSIOLOGY"

PROFESSOR JERRY ALAN JOHNSON, PH.D., D.T.C.M. (CHINA)

EDITED BY
DR. WILLIAM WELCH JR., D.T.C.M. (CHINA)

First published in March 2002 -
The International Institute of Medical Qigong
Pacific Grove, California 93950 U.S.A.
© 2002 Prof. Jerry Alan Johnson, Ph.D., D.T.C.M., D.M.Q. (China)

Revised Addition: March 2014 -
The International Institute of Medical Qigong Publishing House
Monterey, CA 93940 U.S.A.
© 2014 Prof. Jerry Alan Johnson, Ph.D., D.T.C.M., D.M.Q. (China)

All rights reserved under the International and Pan-American copyright conventions. No part of this publication may be reproduced, stored in a retrieval system, or transmitted in any form or by any means, electronic, mechanical, photocopying, recording or otherwise, without the prior written permission of the publisher (The International Institute of Medical Qigong). Reviewers may quote brief passages.

ISBN# 978-0-9915690-0-7
Printed in the United States of America.

Disclaimer:
Chinese Energetic Medicine (Medical Qigong Therapy) is not intended to replace orthodox Western Medicine, but rather to complement it. The meditations, practices, techniques and prescriptions described herein were effectively practiced in the government hospitals, Medical Universities, and Cancer Clinics of the People's Republic of China, up until the year 1999. Be the year 2000, the study and clinical application of Medical Qigong Therapy was suddenly terminated due to the political actions of the Falun Gong Qigong Schools.

The techniques described in the following text can be very powerful, and may in some cases be too mentally and physically demanding for some individuals. The readers should therefore use their own discretion and consult a Doctor of Medical Qigong Therapy, Acupuncturist, Medical Doctor, or mental health professional before engaging in these exercises and meditations. The author, the International Institute of Medical Qigong, and the publishers are neither liable or responsible to any person or entity with respect to any loss or damage caused, or alleged to be caused, directly or indirectly by reading or following the instructions for any condition, or interpreting information provided in this text. The treatments mentioned in this book are not meant to be used as symptomatic prescriptions. The treatment of specific organs, channels, channel points, and prescriptions must always be selected based on a thorough understanding of the origin of the patient's disease. If an ailment is severe, or if symptoms persist, please consult a medical professional immediately.

Throughout the text I will suggest that the doctor prescribe herbs for certain conditions along with Medical Qigong therapy. The Medical Qigong Treatments and Homework Prescription Exercises and Meditations assigned to patients sometimes require herbal prescriptions, as well as the regulation of the patient's diet and living environment. Herbal prescriptions will vary according to the patient's constitution, condition and specific illness, and must be prescribed only by a doctor or herbalist qualified to prescribe Chinese Medical Herbs. Each state in the U.S. has its own regulations and restrictions. Therefore, it is advisable for the reader to consult his or her own state medical board regarding the legalities and liabilities of the techniques described in this text.

Throughout the text I have used the term *doctor* when referring to professional practitioners of Traditional Chinese Medicine, as well as to those who use energetic medicine to treat patients. The word "doctor" means "to teach." I believe that the foremost duty of any doctor of medicine (Western or Chinese) should be as educator, to teach his or her patients the knowledge and skills for the pre-

TABLE OF CONTENTS

Foreword XXIV
Acknowledgments XXVI
Introduction XXVIII

SECTION I
FOUNDATIONS OF CHINESE ENERGETIC MEDICINE 1

CHAPTER 1 INTRODUCTION TO MEDICAL QIGONG 3
    Understanding the Concept of Qi 4
    The Five Realms of Energy 5
    Defining the Energy of Yin and Yang 7

    The History of Qigong and Chinese Medicine 8
        The Yellow Emperor (Huangdi) 8
        The Zhou Dynasty (1028-221 B.C.) 9
        The Qin Dynasty (221-206 B.C.) 11
        The Western Han Dynasty and Eastern Han Dynasties (206 B.C.-220 A.D.) ... 11
        The Three Kingdoms Period (220-280 A.D.) 12
        During the Jin Dynasty (265-420 A.D.) 13
        The Northern and Southern Dynasty Period (386-588 A.D.) 13
        The Sui Dynasty and Tang Dynasties (581-907 A.D.) 14
        The Song, Jin, and Yuan Dynasties (960-1368 A.D.) 14
        The Ming Dynasty and Qing (Manchu) Dynasties (1368-1911) 15
        The Republic of China (1912-1949 A.D.) 16
        The People's Republic of China (1949 A.D.-Present) 16

    History of Ancient Chinese Shaman Doctors: Wu Yi 18
        The Magical Powers of the Wu Yi 20
        Official Duties of the Wu Yi 20

    The Evolution of Chinese Medicine 29
        Qigong of the Imperial College 29
        Three Main Schools of Qigong 31
        The Body's Three Wei Qi Fields 33
        Medical Qigong Training in China 34
        Five Clinical Posts of Chinese Medicine 36
        Medical Qigong Examination and Clinical Qualifications in China 37
        Medical Qigong Training in the U. S. 37
        Medical Qigong Training in T.C.M. Colleges 39
        Traditional Chinese Medicine and Medical Qigong Therapy 40
        Acupuncture 41
        Herbology 44
        Chinese Massage Therapy 48
        Medical Qigong Therapy 50

    Learning Medical Qigong Therapy in China 52
        Changing Times in China for Medical Qigong Therapy 54

Chapter 2 Understanding Ancient Chinese Metaphysics 55
- The Energetic Formation of the Universe 56
- Shang Di (Highest God) 56

The Dao: The Way 58
- The Dao, Heaven, and Earth 59
- The Dao as the Zhong (Center) 60
- The Dao within the Body 60

The Wuji: Infinite Space 61
- Knowledge Stored within the Wuji 61
- Messages Within the Human Body 61
- Sending Messages 63
- The Perceptual Dimensions of the Wuji 63
- Penetrating the Infinite Perceptual Dimensions of the Wuji 64

Taiji: Great Ultimate 65
- Taiji Within the Human Body 66
- Yin and Yang Transformations 66

Sixiang: 4 Phases of Universal Qi 67
- From the Four Phases to the Bagua 69

Bagua: Eight Trigrams 70
- The Bagua, The Sun, and the Moon 71
- Bagua Energetic Manifestations 73
- Bagua Energetic Transformations 75
- Bagua Creative Formations 75

The Wu Xing: Five Elements 76
- The Five Element Cycles 76
- The Five Pure Lights 77

The Three Bodies and Three Worlds 79
- The Physical Body & Physical World 80
- The Energy Body & Energetic World 80
- Understanding The Energetic Realm 81
- The Spirit Body & Spirit World 82
- Understanding The Spirit Realm 82
- Overview 82

Energetic Formation of the Human Spirit 84
- The Embodiment of the Dao 84
- The Light of the "Dao" Inside 84
- Ling Shen: Supernatural Spirit 85
- The Ling Shen and Immortality 86
- Ling Qi: Supernatural Energy 87
- Shen Xian: Eternal Soul 88
- From Eternal Soul to Human Soul 88
- Energetic Manifestation of the Soul 89

Table of Contents

- Soul Travel 89
- The Yin and Yang Manifestations of the Eternal Soul 90

The Body's Original States 91
- Yin and Yang Spiritual States 92
- Cultivating and Refining Xing and Ming 92
- The Three Bodies and Three Births 93
- The First Birth (Yuan Jing) 93
- The Second Birth (Yuan Qi) 94
- The Third Birth (Yuan Shen) 94
- The Yuan Shen's Spiritual Manifestations 96
- The Wujing Shen (Five Essence Spirits) 97
- Original Mind & Prenatal Wujingshen 97
- Acquired Mind & Postnatal Wujingshen 98
- Introduction To Energetic Embryology 99

Introduction To Energetic Embryology 99
- The Body's Essence, Energy, and Spirit During Conception 99
- A Daoist Perspective Of Early Embryological Development 102
- Yin and Yang Fertilization 103
- Understanding Fetal Toxins 104
- The Embryo's Internal Channel Development Sequence 105
- The Creation of Yin & Yang Channels 105

The Five Element Jing Formation 105
- Water Jing Formation 106
- Fire Jing Formation 107
- Metal Jing Formation 107
- Wood Jing Formation 107
- Earth Jing Formation 107

Understanding The Body's Prenatal Jing, Qi, and Shen 108
- The Yuan Jing (Original Essence) 108
- The Yuan Qi (Original Energy) 108
- The Yuan Shen (Original Mind/Heart) 109
- The Extraordinary Vessels Of Creation 109

Overview Of The Ten Lunar Months Of Creation 110
- Month One 112
- The Uterus 112
- The Uterus and the Lower Dantian 113
- The Role of the Mother's Liver Channels 114
- Mother's Shen 114

- Month Two 115
- The Role of the Mother's Gall Bladder Channels 115
- Energetic Formation 115

- Month Three 116
- The Role of the Mother's Pericardium Channels 116

- Energetic Formation 116
- Tissue Formation 116

Month Four 117
- The Role of the Mother's Triple Burner Channels 117
- Water Jing Formation 117
- Tissue Formation 117

Month Five 118
- The Role of the Mother's Spleen Channels 118
- Fire Jing Formation 118
- Energetic Formation of the Five Orbs 118
- Tissue Formation 118

Month Six 119
- The Role of the Mother's Stomach Channels 119
- Metal Jing Formation 119
- Formation of the Six Storage Areas 119
- Formation of the Six Energetic Pitches 120
- Tissue Formation 120

Month Seven 121
- The Role of the Mother's Lung Channels 121
- Wood Jing Formation 121
- Seven Essential Stars 121
- The Body's Six Openings 122
- Tissue Formation 122

Month Eight 123
- The Role of the Mother's Large Intestine Channels 123
- Earth Jing Formation 123
- Tissue Formation 123

Month Nine 124
- The Role of the Mother's Kidney Channels 124
- Function of the Umbilical Cord 124
- Energetic Formation 124
- Tissue Formation 124

Month Ten 125
- The Role of the Mother's Urinary Bladder Channels 125
- Energetic Formation 125

Postnatal Energy Development 126
- Postnatal Channel Function 126
- The Child's Internal Energy Flow 127
- The Microcosmic Orbit Water Cycle 127
- A Child's Natural Psychic Tendencies 127

Congenital or Acquired Disorders 128
Congenital (Before-Birth) Disorders 128
Acquired (After-Birth) Diseases 128

Prenatal and Postnatal Energetic Patterns 129
The Ten Heavenly Stems 129
The Twelve Earthly Branches 131
Conception and the Body's Prenatal Ancestral Traits 133
Birth and the Patterns of Postnatal Energetic Cycles 134

Ancient Daoist Archetypes of the Human Soul 135
Taiyi (Great Unity) 136
Si Ming (Administrator of Destiny) 136
Wu Ying - The Regulator of the Hun 137
The Five Agents of Shang Ling 137
Bai Yuan, The Regulator of the Po 140
Xia Tao Kang (Below Healthy Peach) 141
The Ethereal Soul (Hun) & Corporeal Soul (Po) 142

The Hun: Three Ethereal Souls 142
Chinese Ideogram for the Hun 143
Functions of the Hun 143
The Spiritual Awareness of the Hun 147

The Po: Seven Corporeal Souls 148
Chinese Ideogram of the Po 148
Functions of the Po 148
The Spiritual Awareness of the Po 150
Negative Attributes of the Po 150

The Hun and Po and the Yuan Shen 152
The Hun, Po, Yuan Shen & Spirit Travel 153
The Internal Development Of The Five Limitations 154
Four Spiritual Paths of the Human Soul 155

The Twelve Embryonic Knots and Death Roots of the Womb 155
The Final Exit Of The Human Soul 156
Preparation for Death 157
"Picking Up One's Steps" 158
Overview 160

Chapter 3 Tissue Formation and Development 161
Internal Fascial Development and Energy Flow 161
The Three Types of Ancient Body Classifications 162
Yin & Yang Structural Formation 163
Yin and Yang Anatomical Aspects 164

The Body's Five Element Pattern 166
The Congenital Constitutions 168
Understanding Pattern (Li) & Energy (Qi) 168
Classification of the Five Element Physical Constitutions 169

- The Wood Element Constitution 170
  - The Wood Element Personality 170
  - Treatment For A Yin Wood Element Personality: 171
  - Treatment For A Yang Wood Element Personality: 171

- The Fire Element Constitution 172
  - The Fire Element Personality 172
  - Treatment for Yin Fire Element Personality: 173
  - Treatment for Yang Fire Element Personality: 173

- The Earth Element Constitution 174
  - The Earth Element Personality 174
  - Treatment for Yin Earth Element Personality: 175
  - Treatment for Yang Earth Element Personality: 175

- The Metal Element Constitution 176
  - The Metal Element Personality 176
  - Treatment for Yin Metal Element Personality: 177
  - Treatment for Yang Metal Element Personality: 177

- The Water Constitution 178
  - The Water Element Personality 178
  - Treatment for Yin Water Element Personality: 179
  - Treatment for Yang Water Element Personality: 179
  - Combined Element Constitutions 180

- Yin and Yang and the Yao Image 181
  - The Yao And Physical Anatomy 182
  - The Three Yao Regions Of The Body 184
  - Upper and Lower Hexagram Patterns 185
  - The Upper Hexagram Construction 186
  - The Lower Hexagram Construction 186
  - Therapeutic Use of the Yao Hexagrams 187
  - Herbs and the Yaos 188

- Identifying Introverted and Extroverted Structures 189
  - Introverted Structure 189
  - Extroverted Structure 189
  - Combined Structural Formations 190
  - Congenital and Acquired Energetic Patterns 190
  - Summary 191

Chapter 4 The Five Energies of the Human Body 193
- Cellular Vibration and the Five Energies of the Human Body 194

- Sound Energy Resonances 195
  - Sound Energy and the Human Body 198
  - The Anatomy of Listening 199
  - Balance, Listening, and Stimulation 199
  - The Anatomy of the Spoken Sound 200
  - Sound Therapy Through Emitted Qi 201

FIVE ANCIENT CHINESE PITCHES	201
PROJECTED SOUND	202
THREE MODALITIES OF SOUND THERAPY	203
MUSIC AND SOUND THERAPY	204
ENTRAINMENT AND SOUND THERAPY	204
THE FOUR ELEMENTS OF MUSIC THERAPY	205
THE FIVE TIMBRES OF THE VOICE	205
THERAPEUTIC EFFECTS OF SOUND	206
THE THERAPEUTIC USES OF ENTRAINMENT	206
THE THERAPEUTIC USES OF CHAOTIC RESONANCE	207
HARMFUL EFFECTS	207
THE HARMFUL EFFECTS OF ENTRAINMENT	207
THE HARMFUL EFFECTS OF CHAOTIC RESONANCE	208
MUSIC IN ANCIENT CHINA	209
SECONDARY ACOUSTIC BIOLOGICAL RESPONSE	209
WESTERN SOUND THERAPY	210

LIGHT ENERGY 211

BIOPHOTONS AND THE HUMAN BODY	211
LIGHT AND ENERGETIC FIELDS	211
LIGHT AND FOOD	212
LIGHT AND THE BODY'S DNA	212
THE BODY'S INTERNAL LIGHT	212
THE INTERNAL LIGHT OF THE BODY'S THREE DANTIAN CHAMBERS	214
LIGHT AND THE PHYSICAL REALM	214
LIGHT AND THE ENERGETIC REALM	215
LIGHT AND THE SPIRIT REALM	215
LIGHT AND AURA COLORS	216
COLOR VIBRATIONAL CLASSIFICATIONS	216
THE PHYSIOLOGY OF VISUAL PERCEPTION	218
THE ANATOMY OF SEEING AURAS	219
PROJECTING COLORED LIGHT	220
LIGHT THERAPY THROUGH EMITTED QI	220
USING HEALING COLOR IMAGERY	223
EXPOSURE TO EXTERNAL COLOR FIELDS	223
FOOD, COLOR, AND HEALING LIGHT	224
MAINTAINING THE DISTANCE & RANGE, ACCORDING TO FOCUSED CONCENTRATION	224
WESTERN LIGHT THERAPY	224

MAGNETIC ENERGY 225

MODERN RESEARCH ON MAGNETIC FIELDS	227
THE ELECTROMAGNETIC EFFECTS OF THE BODY'S TAIJI POLE	227
MAGNETIC THERAPY IN THE CLINIC	228
WESTERN MAGNETIC THERAPY	229

HEAT 229

THE ANCIENT DAOIST TEACHINGS OF THE BODY'S THREE FIRES	229
THE YIN FIRE AND YANG FIRE CATEGORIES	232
FUNCTION OF THE BODY'S SPIRIT FIRES	233
HEAT THERAPY THROUGH EMITTED QI	233
WESTERN HEAT THERAPY	234

DRY-HEAT THERAPY:	234
MOIST-HEAT THERAPY	234
ELECTRICITY	234
THE BODY'S PIEZOELECTRIC QUALITIES	235
ELECTRICAL THERAPY THROUGH EMITTED QI	236
WESTERN ELECTROTHERAPY	236

CHAPTER 5 THE TAIJI POLE AND THREE DANTIANS ... 237

THE TAIJI POLE	237
TAIJI POLE OF HEAVEN, EARTH, & MAN	238
INTERNAL ENERGY INTERACTIONS	239
SPIRITUAL MANIFESTATIONS	240
THE SUBTLE ENERGY OF THE TAIJI POLE	241
MASKS AND DEFENSE MECHANISMS SURROUNDING THE CENTER CORE	242
MEDITATING ON THE TAIJI POLE	243
ENERGIZING THE TAIJI POLE	244
ENERGIZING THE TAIJI POLE: STAGE #1	245
ENERGIZING THE TAIJI POLE: STAGE #2	246
ENERGIZING THE TAIJI POLE: STAGE #3	247

THE SIX EXTERNAL TRANSPERSONAL POINTS ... 248

ACTIVATING THE BODY'S TRANSPERSONAL POINTS	251
THE SOUL STAR (LING HUN XING)	252
ENERGETIC AWAKENING	252
THE EARTH STAR (DI XING)	253
ENERGETIC AWAKENING	253
ACTIVATING THE FIRST HEAVENLY AND EARTHLY TRANSPERSONAL POINTS	254
THE TAIJI POLE AND THE INTERNAL CHAKRA SYSTEM	256

MULTIDIMENSIONAL ENERGETIC REALMS OF THE CHAKRA SYSTEM ... 258

YIN AND YANG AND THE SEVEN INTERNAL CHAKRAS	259
A WOMAN'S ENERGETIC POLARITY	259
A MAN'S ENERGETIC POLARITY	259
COLOR AND SOUND	259
AWAKENING THE SEVEN CHAKRAS	260
THE NERVE PLEXUSES OF THE SEVEN INTERNAL CHAKRAS	260

FIRST CHAKRA ... 260

PHYSIOLOGICAL ASSOCIATIONS	261
THE FIRST PSYCHIC KNOT	261
BALANCED MANIFESTATION	262
PATHOLOGICAL MANIFESTATION	262
ENERGETIC AWAKENING	262
SPIRITUAL POWERS	262

SECOND CHAKRA ... 262

PHYSIOLOGICAL ASSOCIATIONS	263
BALANCED MANIFESTATION	263
PATHOLOGICAL MANIFESTATION	263
ENERGETIC AWAKENING	263
SPIRITUAL POWERS	263

Third Chakra 264
Physiological Associations 264
Balanced Manifestation 265
Pathological Manifestation 265
Energetic Awakening 265
Spiritual Powers 265

Fourth Chakra 266
Physiological Associations 266
Balanced Manifestation 266
Pathological Manifestation 266
The Second Psychic Knot 266
Energetic Awakening 266
Spiritual Powers 267

Fifth Chakra 267
Physiological Associations 267
Balanced Manifestation 268
Pathological Manifestation 268
Energetic Awakening 268
Spiritual Powers 268

Sixth Chakra 269
Physiological Associations 269
The Third Psychic Knot 269
Balanced Manifestation 269
Pathological Manifestation 269
Energetic Awakening 269
Spiritual Powers 270

Seventh Chakra 270
Physiological Associations 270
Balanced Manifestation 270
Pathological Manifestation 270
Energetic Awakening 270

The Taiji Pole, Chakras, and the Bridge Of Light 271

The Twelve Chakra Gates 273
Energetic Function 274
Opening And Closing A Chakra Gate 274
The Bottom Chakra Gate 274
The Second Chakra and Gates 274
The Third Chakra and Gates 275
The Fourth Chakra and Gates 275
The Fifth Chakra and Gates 275
The Sixth Chakra and Gates 275
The Seventh Chakra Gate 275
Precautions 275
The Twelve Earthly Branches and the Twelve Chakra Gates 276
Reconstructing A Damaged Chakra Gate 278
Energizing The Seven Chakras Through Stimulating The Twelve Gates 279

The Three Dantians 280
The Chinese Character for Dantian 280
The Energetic Functions of the Three Dantians 281
Ancient Daoist Alchemy 282
The Alchemical Cultivation of Jing, Qi, and Shen 283

The Lower Cinnabar Field: (Xia Dantian) 284
The Lower Dantian & Postnatal Jing 284
The Jing Gong (Essence Palace) 285
Kidney Jing And Reproductive Cycles 286
The Lower Dantian & Prenatal Jing 287
The Lower Dantian and Prenatal Qi 287
The Lower Dantian and Earth Qi 287
The Lower Dantian and Shen 288
The Lower Dantian and Kinesthetic Awareness 288
The Lower Dantian and Science 289
Lower Dantian Anatomical Location 289
The 9 Chambers of the Lower Dantian 294
Training of the Lower Dantian 294

The Middle Cinnabar Field: (Zhong Dantian) 295
The Middle Dantian and Jing 295
The Middle Dantian and Qi 296
Women and Middle Dantian Qi 296
The Middle Dantian and Shen 297
The Middle Dantian and Empathic Awareness 297
The Middle Dantian and Science 298
Middle Dantian Anatomical Location 298
The 9 Chambers of the Middle Dantian 301
Training of the Middle Dantian 302

The Upper Cinnabar Field: (Shang Dantian) 302
The Upper Dantian and Jing 303
The Upper Dantian and Qi 304
The Upper Dantian and Shen 304
The Upper Dantian and Intuitive Awareness 305
Five Spiritual Principles 305
The Upper Dantian and Science 306
Upper Dantian Anatomical Location 306
The 9 Chambers of the Upper Dantian 310
Training of the Upper Dantian 310
Daoist Meditations for Energizing 311
The Upper Dantian's Nine Palaces 311
The Seven Secret Portals of the Upper Dantian 315

The Dantian's Yin and Yang Energetic Chambers 316
The Lower Dantian 316
The Middle Dantian 316
The Upper Dantian 316

The Doctor's Projected Aura Fields and the Three Dantians 317
Red Qi Emitted Color 317
Green/Blue Qi Emitted Color 317
White Qi Emitted Color 317

The Moveable Bones Of the Three Dantians.................................. 318
The Lower Dantian - Sacral Rhythm 318
The Middle Dantian - Thoracic Rhythm 318
The Upper Dantian - Cranial Rhythm 318

Chapter 6 The Eight Extraordinary Vessels.......................... 319
The Body's Eight Extraordinary Vessels..319
The Vessel Formation Of Energetic Embryology 320
The Three-Dimensional Space of the Impregnated Egg.......................321
The Energetic Function of the Eight Extraordinary Vessels 322
The Eight Extraordinary Vessels and Medical Qigong Therapy 324
The Eight Extraordinary Vessels And The Medical Qigong Doctor ... 324
Clinical Indications and Uses 324
The Vessels Energetic Location 325
The Vessels Energetic Function 325
The Extraordinary Vessels and The Eight Confluent Points 326
Master - Coupled Point Combination 327
Same Side and Crossover Treatments 327
The Daoist Magic Square 328

Governing & Conception Vessels: Du & Ren Mai 329
The Governing Vessel: Du Mai 330
Development.. 330
Energetic Pathway 330
Clinical Manifestations 333
Pathological Manifestations 333
The Conception Vessel: Ren Mai 334
Development.. 334
Energetic Pathway 334
Clinical Manifestations 336
Pathological Manifestations 337

Thrusting & Belt Vessels: Chong Mai and Dai Mai 338
The Thrusting Vessels: Chong Mai 338
Development.. 338
Energetic Pathway 339
Clinical Manifestations 341
Pathological Manifestations 342
The Belt Vessel: Dai Mai 343
Development.. 343
Energetic Pathway 344
Clinical Manifestations 346
Pathological Manifestations 346

Yin & Yang Heel Vessels: Yin Qiao Mai & Yang Qiao Mai............... 347
The Yin Heel Vessel: Yin Qiao Mai 348
Development.. 348

- Energetic Pathway 348
- Clinical Manifestations 349
- Pathological Manifestations 349
- The Yang Heel Vessels: Yang Qiao Mai 351
- Development 351
- Energetic Pathway 351
- Clinical Manifestations 352
- Pathological Manifestations 352

- **Yin & Yang Linking Vessels: Yin Wei Mai & Yang Wei Mai** 354
  - The Yin Linking Vessel: Yin Wei Mai 354
  - Development 355
  - Energetic Pathway 355
  - Clinical Manifestations 356
  - Pathological Manifestations 356
  - The Yang Linking Vessels: Yang Wei Mai 357
  - Development 357
  - Energetic Pathway 358
  - Clinical Manifestations 359
  - Pathological Manifestations 359

- **The Eight Extraordinary Vessels and Twelve Primary Channels** 360
  - Personality Constitutions of the Eight Extraordinary Vessels 362
  - The Pathological Personality Type of the Governing and Yang Heel Vessels 362
  - The Pathological Personality Type of the Conception and Yin Heel Vessels 363
  - The Pathological Personality Type of the Belt and Yang Linking Vessels 363
  - The Pathological Personality Type of the Thrusting and Yin Linking Vessels ... 364
  - Daoist Alchemy and The Eight Extraordinary Vessels 365

Chapter 7 The Six Extraordinary Organs 369
- Introduction To Tissue Formation 369
- Chinese Characters for the Extraordinary Organs: Qi Heng Zhi Fu 369
- Functions of the Six Extraordinary Organs 370
- The Eight Extraordinary Vessels and Six Extraordinary Organs 371

- **The Uterus: Bao** 372
  - Chinese Character for Uterus 372
  - Function of the Uterus 372
  - The Bao (Uterus) and Ancient Daoist Internal Alchemy 374

- **The Brain: Nao** 375
  - Chinese Characters for Brain 375
  - The Brain as the Sea of Marrow 375
  - Main functions of the Brain 376
  - The Brain and Daoist Mysticism 376
  - The Brain and The Mind 377
  - The Brain According to Chinese Energetic Medicine 378
  - The Brain Receives, Records, and Maintains the Energy of Thought 378
  - Clinical Pathology and the Brain 378
  - The Brain Detects Emitted Qi 379
  - Scientific Controls 380
  - Four Major Changes Occurring in the Brain During Qigong Meditation 381

Western Medical Viewpoint	382
The Reptilian Brain	382
The Mammalian (Limbic) Brain	382
The Primate (Neocortex) Brain	383
Brain-Wave Patterns	383
Science, the Brain, and Memory	384

The Gall Bladder: Dan ... 385
- The Chinese Character for Gall Bladder ... 385
- Function Of The Gall Bladder ... 386
- The Gall Bladder Channel ... 386
- Ancient Daoist Mysticism and The "Gall Bladder" ... 387

The Marrow: Sui ... 388
- Chinese Characters for Marrow ... 388
- The Marrow and Jing ... 388
- Energetic Pathology & Marrow ... 388
- The Marrow and Daoist Mysticism ... 389
- Marrow and Western Medicine ... 389
- Red and White Blood Cells ... 389

The Bones: Gu ... 390
- Chinese Characters for Bones ... 390
- Bones and Marrow ... 390
- Pathology of the Bones ... 390
- Bones Produce Piezoelectric Charges ... 390
- Bones and Daoist Mysticism ... 392
- Western Medical Perspective ... 392

The Blood Vessels: Mai ... 393
- Chinese Characters for Blood ... 393
- Chinese Characters for Blood Vessels ... 393
- The Energetic Function Of Blood Vessels ... 394
- The Energetic Channels and Streams of the Blood Vessels ... 394
- The Energetic Pathways of the Blood Vessels ... 395
- Function of the Blood Vessels ... 396
- Pathology of the Blood Vessels ... 396
- The Blood Vessels and Ancient Daoist Mysticism ... 396
- Western Medical Perspective ... 397
- Circulatory System ... 397
- Three Circulatory Routes ... 399
- Systemic Circulation ... 399
- Pulmonary Circulation ... 399
- Fetal Circulation ... 400
- The Pulse ... 400

Chapter 8 The 12 Primary Organs, Channels & Collaterals ..401
- The Internal Organs and Chinese Internal Medicine ... 401
- Energetic Anatomy ... 402
- Energetic Physiology ... 402
- The Zang Fu Organs & Yin and Yang ... 404
- The Internal Organs & Five Elements ... 404

Internal Organs & the Vital Substances	405
The Internal Organs & the Tissues	407
The Internal Organs & the Emotions	407
The Internal Organs and their Original Spiritual States	408
The Internal Organs and Climate	409
The Internal Organs and their Sense Organ Openings	409
The Internal Organs and Taste	409
The Internal Organs and Sound	409
The Internal Organs and Color	409

Introduction to Channels — 410
- Classification of Channels — 413
- The Meridian Channels (Jing Mai) — 413
- The Collaterals (Luo Mai) — 414
- Muscle Tendon Channels (Jing Jin) — 416
- Cutaneous Regions: Pi Fu — 417

The Channels' Relationship to Qi and the Blood Heat Cycle — 418
- The Channel's Qi and Blood Reservoirs — 418
- The Channel System & Fascia Network — 419
- The Function of the Channels — 419
- The Centrifugal & Centripetal Flow of Channel Qi — 420
- Hun and Po Channel Influence — 422

The Twelve Primary Organs & Channels — 423
- "Gods Living In The Body?" — 423

The Gall Bladder: Dan — 425
- Ancient Gall Bladder Organ Teaching — 425
- Chinese Character for the Gall Bladder: Dan — 426
- The Gall Bladder Organ in Chinese Energetic Medicine — 426
- The Gall Bladder Channels — 427
- The Channels' Energy Flow — 429
- The Influence of Climate — 429
- The Influence of Taste, Color, and Sound — 429
- Gall Bladder Pathology — 429
- T.C.M. Patterns of Disharmony — 430
- The Gallbladder Organ in Western Medicine — 430
- Disorders of the Gall Bladder — 431

The Liver: Gan — 432
- Ancient Liver Organ Teaching — 432
- Chinese Character for the Liver: Gan — 433
- The Yin and Yang of the Liver — 434
- The Liver's Wood Jing Formation — 434
- The Liver in Chinese Medicine — 434
- Chinese Ideogram of the Hun — 437
- The Liver Channels — 438
- Channels' Energy Flow — 438
- The Influence of Climate — 439

Section	Page
The Influence of Taste, Color, and Sound	439
Liver Pathology	439
T.C.M. Patterns of Disharmony	440
The Liver in Western Medicine	443
Anatomy of the Liver	443
Bile Secretion	445
Physiology of the Liver	445
Common Disorders of the Liver	447

The Lungs: Fei 448

Section	Page
Ancient Lung Organ Teaching	448
Chinese Character for the Lung: Fei	449
The Yin and Yang of the Lungs	449
The Lungs' Metal Jing Formation	449
The Lungs in Chinese Medicine	450
The Lungs' Energetic Function	451
Chinese Ideogram of the Po	454
The Lung Channels	455
Channels' Energy Flow	456
The Influence of Climate	456
The Influence of Taste, Color, and Sound	456
Lung Pathology	456
T.C.M. Patterns of Disharmony	456
Anatomy of the Respiratory System	459
The Upper Respiratory System	460
The Nose: Nostrils and Nasal Cavity	460
The Pharynx	460
The Lower Respiratory System	460
The Larynx: Voice Box	460
The Trachea: Windpipe	460
The Bronchi	460
The Lungs in Western Medicine	461
Blood Supply to the Lungs	462
Respiration	463
Physiology of Respiration: Inhalation	463
Physiology of Respiration: Exhalation	463
Diaphragmatic & Costal Breathing	464
Respiratory Volumes	464
Respiratory Capacities	464
Common Disorders of the Lungs and Respiratory System	465

The Large Intestine: Da Chang 466

Section	Page
The Large Intestine in Chinese Medicine	467
The Large Intestine Channels	468
Channels' Energy Flow	469
The Influence of Climate	469
The Influence of Taste, Color, and Sound	469
Large Intestine Pathology	469
T.C.M. Patterns of Disharmony	469
The Large Intestine in Western Medicine	470
Physiology	472

The Stomach: Wei ... 473
- Chinese Character for the Stomach: Wei ... 473
- The Stomach in Chinese Medicine ... 474
- The Stomach Channels ... 476
- Channels' Energy Flow ... 476
- The Influence of Climate ... 476
- The Influence of Taste, Color, and Sound ... 476
- Stomach Pathology ... 476
- T.C.M. Patterns of Disharmony ... 477
- The Stomach in Western Medicine ... 478
- Physiology ... 479

The Spleen: Pi ... 480
- Ancient Spleen Organ Teaching ... 480
- Chinese Character for the Spleen: Pi ... 481
- The Yin and Yang of the Spleen ... 481
- The Spleen's Earth Jing Formation ... 482
- The Spleen And The Pancreas ... 482
- The Spleen in Chinese Medicine ... 484
- The Spleen and the Yi ... 486
- The Spleen Channels ... 487
- Channels' Energy Flow ... 487
- The Influence of Climate ... 489
- The Influence of Taste, Color, and Sound ... 489
- Spleen Pathology ... 489
- T.C.M. Patterns of Disharmony ... 490
- The Spleen in Western Medicine ... 493
- Physiology ... 493
- Common Disorders of the Spleen ... 494

The Heart: Xin ... 495
- Ancient Heart Organ Teaching ... 495
- The Spiritual Evolution of the Heart ... 496
- Chinese Character for Heart: Xin ... 496
- The Yin and Yang of the Heart ... 497
- The Heart's Fire Jing Formation ... 497
- The Heart in Ancient Chinese Medicine ... 497
- The Heart in Chinese Medicine ... 497
- Chinese Ideogram of the Shen ... 500
- The Six Transportations Of Shen ... 500
- The Heart Channels ... 501
- Channels' Energy Flow ... 501
- Qi & Blood Flow Within the Channels ... 502
- The Influence of Climate ... 502
- The Influence of Taste, Color, and Sound ... 502
- Heart Pathology ... 502
- T.C.M. Patterns of Disharmony ... 503
- The Heart in Western Medicine ... 506
- Anatomy of the Heart ... 507
- The Four Chambers of the Heart ... 507
- The Heartbeat: Cardiac Cycle ... 508

THE HEART'S ELECTRICAL SYSTEM	509
COMMON DISORDERS OF THE HEART	509

THE SMALL INTESTINE: XIAO CHANG 510

CHINESE CHARACTER FOR SMALL INTESTINE: XIAO CHANG	510
THE SMALL INTESTINE IN CHINESE MEDICINE	511
THE SMALL INTESTINE CHANNELS	511
CHANNELS' ENERGY FLOW	513
THE INFLUENCE OF CLIMATE	513
THE INFLUENCE OF TASTE, COLOR, AND SOUND	513
SMALL INTESTINE PATHOLOGY	513
T.C.M. PATTERNS OF DISHARMONY	513
THE SMALL INTESTINE IN WESTERN MEDICINE	515
PHYSIOLOGY	516

THE URINARY BLADDER: PANG GUANG 517

CHINESE CHARACTER FOR URINARY BLADDER: PANG GUANG	517
THE URINARY BLADDER IN CHINESE MEDICINE	518
THE URINARY BLADDER CHANNELS	520
CHANNELS' ENERGY FLOW	520
THE EIGHTEEN BACK-SHU POINTS	520
THE INFLUENCE OF CLIMATE	521
THE INFLUENCE OF TASTE, COLOR, AND SOUND	521
URINARY BLADDER PATHOLOGY	521
T.C.M. PATTERNS OF DISHARMONY	521
THE URINARY BLADDER IN WESTERN MEDICINE	522
PHYSIOLOGY	522

THE KIDNEY: SHEN 523

ANCIENT KIDNEY ORGAN TEACHING	523
CHINESE CHARACTER FOR THE KIDNEY: SHEN	524
THE YIN AND YANG OF THE KIDNEYS	525
THE KIDNEY'S WATER JING FORMATION	526
THE KIDNEYS IN CHINESE MEDICINE	526
CHINESE IDEOGRAM OF THE ZHI	529
THE KIDNEYS AND THE WILLPOWER	529
MEMORY	529
THE KIDNEY CHANNELS	530
CHANNELS' ENERGETIC FLOW	531
THE INFLUENCE OF CLIMATE	531
THE INFLUENCE OF TASTE, COLOR, AND SOUND	531
KIDNEY PATHOLOGY	531
T.C.M. PATTERNS OF DISHARMONY	532
THE KIDNEYS IN WESTERN MEDICINE	533
FILTERING FLUIDS FROM THE BLOODSTREAM	533
URINARY SYSTEM	533
ANATOMY OF THE KIDNEYS	533
THREE REGIONS OF THE KIDNEYS	534
NEPHRONS	535
THREE MAIN SECTIONS OF THE RENAL TUBULE	535
COMMON DISORDERS OF THE KIDNEYS	536

Pericardium: Xin Zhu 537
The Chinese Characters for Pericardium: Xin Zhu (Heart Master) 537
Ancient Pericardium Organ Teaching 538
The Pericardium in Chinese Energetic Medicine 539
The Pericardium Channels 539
Channels' Energy Flow 540
The Influence of Climate 541
The Influence of Taste, Color, and Sound 541
Pericardium Pathology 541
T.C.M. Patterns of Disharmony 541
The Pericardium in Western Medicine 541
Physiology 542

Triple Burners: San Jiao 543
Chinese Character for Triple Burners: San Jiao 543
The Triple Burners in Chinese Medicine 543
The Triple Burner Channels 546
Channels' Energy Flow 547
The Energetic Anatomy of the Triple Burners 547
The Body's Three Fires 549
The Influence of Climate 549
The Influence of Taste, Color, and Sound 549
Triple Burner Pathology 549
T.C.M. Patterns of Disharmony 550
The Triple Burners in Western Medicine 550

Understanding Internal Organ Pathology 551
Understanding Channel Pathology 551
The Four Causes of Channel Pathology 551
Differentiation by Channel Full/Excess and Empty/Deficient 552
Differentiation of Channel Patterns by Specific Channels 552

Summary of the Primary Channels 553
Root and Branch 553
The Daoist 12 Organs Hand Seal 553

Understanding Shadow Organs & Channels 555
Understanding The Shadow 555
The Shadow Organs and Channels 555
Training To Remove Shadow Organ Qi 556

Chapter 9 The Connecting Vessels, Divergent Channels, Muscle and Tendon Channels and Skin Zones 557
The Fifteen Connecting Vessels: Luo Mai 557
Translation of "Luo Mai" 557
Energetic Anatomy of the Luo Mai 558
Embryological Points of the Luo Mai 558
Transverse & Longitudinal Luo 559
Functions of the Luo Mai 559
Excess and Deficient Pathology 559

| Lou Mai Color Diagnosis | 560 |
| Point Location of the Fifteen Major Collaterals | 560 |

The Twelve Divergent Channels: Jing Bie 565
- Translation of "Jing Bie" 565
- Embryological Development 566
- Energetic Anatomy of the Jing Bie 566
- The Six Confluences 566
- Energetic Function of the Jing Bie 567
- Yin & Yang Divergent Channels 567

The Twelve Muscle and Tendon Channels: Jing Jin 569
- Translation of "Jing Jin" 569
- Embryological Development 570
- Energetic Anatomy of the Jing Jin 570
- Yin and Yang 570
- Clinical Application 570
- Diagnosis and Treatment Using The Muscle Tendon Channels ... 577

The Skin Zones: Pi Fu 578
- Origin of Name 578
- The Energetic Patterns of Skin 578
- The Skin Patterns of Blaschko's Lines 578
- The Skin Patterns of Langer's Lines 579
- The Skin Patterns of Dermatomes 579
- Energetic Function of the Skin 580
- Pathological Symptoms 580
- The Connective Tissue of the Twelve Skin Zones 581
- Clinical Diagnosis and the Twelve Skin Zones 584
- Palpating the Patient's Skin 584

Channel & Collateral Therapy 585
- Qi Extension and The Body's Channels 585
- The Depth of the Body's Channel Flow 586

Chapter 10 The Body's Energetic Points 587
- Introduction to Energetic Points 587
- The Translation of "Xue" 588

Historic Use of Energetic Points 588
- The Three Levels of Points 589
- The Formation of Energetic Points 590
- The Four Categories of Points 591
- A Points Energetic Gate 591
- Energetic Functions of Points 592
- Centrifugal and Centripetal Energy Flow 594
- Point Names 595

Classification of Energetic Points 596
- The Five Shu Points 596
- The 5 Shu Points, Yin and Yang Channels, and The Five Elements ... 596

The 16 Xi-Cleft (Accumulation) Points ... 599
The 12 Front-Mu (Alarm) Points ... 600
The 18 Back-Shu (Transporting) Points ... 600
The 15 Luo (Connecting) Points ... 600
The Twelve Entry Points ... 600
The Twelve Exit Points ... 601
The Eight Influential Points ... 602
The Eight Confluent Points ... 602
The 12 Yuan (Source) Points ... 603
The Points of the Four Seas ... 604
The Thirteen Ghost Points ... 605
The Ten Window of Heaven Points ... 607

Summary of Points ... 608
Scientific Research of Acupoints ... 608

Appendix 1 Chronology of Chinese Dynasties ... 610
Introduction ... 610

China's Pre-Dynasty Myths (5000-2436 B.C.) ... 610
The Reign of Fu Xi: 5000-4000 B.C. (Qing Di) Emperor of the East ... 610
The Reign of Shen Nong: 4000-3000 B.C. (Chi Di) of the South ... 610
The Reign of Huangdi: 2697-2599 B.C. (Huang Di) of the Center ... 610
The Reign of Shaohao: 2598-2514 B.C. (Bai Di) of the West ... 610
The Reign of Zhuanxu: 2514-2436 B.C. (Hei Di/Xuan Di) of the North ... 610

The Three Rulers Period (2357-2197 B.C.) ... 610
The Reign of Yao: 2357-2258 B.C. ... 610
The Reign of Shun: 2257-2208 B.C. ... 610
The Reign of Yu the Great: 2207-2197 B.C. ... 610

Dynasties of China (2207 B.C.- 1911 A.D.) ... 611

The Republic of China (1912-1949 A.D) ... 611

People's Republic of China (1949-Present) ... 611

Appendix 2 Medical Qigong Therapy Instruction 612
Introduction 612

Medical Qigong Therapy Classes 612
Medical Qigong Philosophy 613

The 1999 Medical Qigong Courses at the Five Branches T.C.M. College . 614
The 1999 Medical Qigong Clinic at the Five Branches T.C.M. College 614
The 1999 Medical Qigong Courses Taught at the Five Branches T.C.M. College . 615

The 2003 Medical Qigong Courses at the Five Element T.C.M. College ... 616
The 2003 Medical Qigong Clinic at the Five Element T.C.M. College 616
The 2003 Medical Qigong Courses Taught at the Five Element T.C.M. College 617

The 2005 Medical Qigong Courses at the Henan T.C.M. University 618

Doctor of Medical Qigong Therapy Graduate Directory 620
Doctor of Medical Qigong Therapy Graduating Classes 620
The Medical Qigong Doctor Qualifications 620
1997 DMQ Graduating Class 621
2003 DMQ Graduating Class 621
2004 DMQ Graduating Class 621
2006 DMQ Graduating Class 621
2009 DMQ Graduating Class 621
2012 DMQ Graduating Class 621

Master of Medical Qigong Therapy Graduate Directory 623
Master of Medical Qigong Therapy Graduating Classes 623
1997 MMQ Graduating Class 623
1999 MMQ Graduating Class 623
2000 MMQ Graduating Class 623
2001 MMQ Graduating Class 623
2002 MMQ Graduating Class 624
2003 MMQ Graduating Class 624
2004 MMQ Graduating Class 624
2005 MMQ Graduating Class 624
2006 MMQ Graduating Class 624
2007 MMQ Graduating Class 625
2008 MMQ Graduating Class 625
2010 MMQ Graduating Class 625
2011 MMQ Graduating Class 625

Glossary of Terms 626

Bibliography 657

Clinical References 671

About the Author 673

Foreword

The Magic of the New Edition

In the Westernization of China, some of the most ancient treasures that have survived the nightmare of the Cultural Revolution are now being honored. However, there is much in the way of ancient traditions, especially spiritual and shamanic, that are still being repressed due to the belief that these esoteric teachings are considered to be superstitious, and part of an old China; that today would be thought of as embarrassing and a "loss of face" to a modern superpower.

This parallels the fact that with the loss of ancient teachings, we are also losing important "ways of knowing." The modern trend to use more and more Western Medicine at the expense of other healing modalities, can also limit the value in different ways of approaching treatment.

This approach can eventually lose both the poetic and metaphoric power that is needed to inspire deep spiritual healing. For a truly modern person interested in using what works in assisting people, making use of the various world-views is truly increasing one's openness and resources. If your body heals, does it matter what belief or ritual might have been part of the process?

Consider that today, one can be walking down the steps of a church, and overhear a conversation between a Western Medical Doctor with a cold, and his Acupuncturist friend. The Medical Doctor is going on about the Rhinovirus attacking his nasal tissues, while his Acupuncturist friend is reminding him that his Weiqi (Protective Energy) is down because he did nothing about the internal Liver Fire he had previously warned him about. This discussion over the difference in clinical healing occurred after hearing a sermon about the Jesus they both worship, healing a person by casting out demons.

Could it be that whether it is a concern for pathogens, energy imbalances, or even the shamanic approach of casting out demons, could all of these healing approaches have something valuable to add to the treatment of a person? Why would anyone want to be limited in their clinical approach or healing modality?

Much of what you will encounter in these new books by Dr. Jerry Alan Johnson are from a world-view that is most ancient, and is currently being overlooked or suppressed. It is always easy to write off other approaches and methods as primitive and superstitious, without having to consider their effectiveness, and the real reasons that they have persisted through the passing of time.

Therefore, in order to comprehend and fully understand this ancient approach to Chinese Energetic Medicine, the reader is encouraged to have an open mind, and consider the depth and richness of this rare and unique teaching.

Lama Lar C. Short
Board of Directors, Five Branches University, California Graduate School of T.C.M.
Senior Lama of Grace Essence Mandala,
Author of: *Opening the Heart of Compassion; Body of Light;* and *The Way of Radiance.*

This massive compendium on Medical Qigong Therapy is a veritable encyclopedia on the subject. Dr. Jerry Alan Johnson's textbooks, well recognized and greatly revered, are in many ways the professional standard. Unlike many Traditional Chinese Medicine works, they also include numerous selections on the mind and emotional states, as well as on spiritual aspects of the practice, such as the soul and spirit, the stars, magical diagrams, and the *Yi Jing*.

They are a valuable resource on Qigong Therapy and practice, and contain information on numerous issues and problems. The scope is admirable, the execution with its many illustrations highly recommendable. These volumes are a treasure trove and serve well as a reference work for students and practitioners.

Dr. Livia Kohn, Ph.D.,
Professor of Religion and East Asian Studies
Boston University, United States
Author of *Taoist Meditation and Longevity Techniques; Early Chinese Mysticism; The Taoist Experience: An Anthology; Laughing at the Tao; Lao-tzu and the Tao-te-ching;* and *God of the Dao*

There are a number of excellent books on various aspects and methods of Qigong. However, there has not been, in English, a comprehensive exploration of Medical Qigong. Dr. Johnson has created a breakthrough work on Medical Qigong, which is a clear and useful revelation of the Medical Qigong curriculum at the Hai Dian University Medical Qigong College of Beijing, China, and an excellent synthesis of Medical Qigong Theory from throughout China. This textbook will very likely remain the definitive compendium of Medical Qigong in the West for many years, and become the foundation from which the field of Medical Qigong will evolve in Western society.

Dr. Roger Jahnke, O.M.D.
Chair, Department of Medical Qigong
Santa Barbara College of Oriental Medicine
Author of *The Healer Within: The Four Essential Self-Care Methods For Creating Optimal Health;* and *The Healing Promise of Qi.*

In 1994, I was honored to write the Preface for the two volumes of *The Essence of Internal Martial Arts*, which was published in France by Chariot d'Or. The Preface emphasized the originality of the explicit nature of these two incredible works by Dr. Jerry Alan Johnson, which have now become the primary reference material used in the domain of the Internal Martial Arts, within Chinese Kung Fu.

Today, I salute the publication of a *magnus opus*, with an exhaustive description of Chinese Medical Qigong Therapy. These volumes are a statement of the energetic treatments and clinical protocols which have found great hope in both curative and palliative Qigong. One would have expected such publications from Chinese experts, and yet to this day, no work of such amplitude has ever come forth, neither in China nor in the West.

Professor Jerry Alan Johnson's merit is to have brought forth the most complete traditional and particularly Daoist methods of Medical Qigong Therapy. This largely surpasses the structure of the simple outline of gymnastic health exercises, fully expanding toward the fields of physiology, psychology, and spirituality.

In addition, all of the therapeutic aspects of Medical Qigong are also evoked with respect to the particular needs of the practitioners of this discipline. We can add that the theoretical aspects of these works go largely beyond the simple framework of Traditional Chinese Medicine, reaching the esoteric, metaphysical and spiritual roots of this art.

Professor Gérard Edde, Ph.D.
Director of Daoist Studies,
L'Institut Dragon Celeste, France
Author of *Contes du Tao Sauvage; Le Chemin du Tao; Tao et Santé; Santé et Méditation dans l'énergétique Chinoise; Digiponcture Taoiste; Qigong de la Régénértion des Moelles; La Medicina Ayurvedica; Chakras y Salud: La Medicina Tantrica de los Centros de Energia; La Medecine Chinoise: Dietetique et phytotherapie*

Acknowledgments

In this special "Revised and Expanded Addition" of my original work entitled *Chinese Medical Qigong Therapy, Volume 1: Energetic Anatomy*, I would like to express my sincere gratitude to my many friends and colleagues who helped encourage and support me in rewriting this new five volume textbook series.

I will be forever indented to Dr. Pang Donghui, the Executive Deputy President of the Hai Dian Qigong College of Beijing, China, and to Li Fudong, D.T.C.M. the university's chief director of Medical Qigong Science, and his assistants, Lu Guohong, D.T.C.M. and Niu Yuhua, D.T.C.M. for their support and encouragement, and for sharing their innermost secrets on Medical Qigong Therapy and Chinese Energetic Medicine during my academic studies in 1995.

I am very grateful to Professor Teng Yingbo, D.T.C.M., president and secretary general of the Beijing Western District Qigong Science and Traditional Chinese Medicine Research Institute, for his constant support and openness in sharing the wealth of knowledge contained with the Institute's clinical modalities.

A special thanks to Doctor Bi Yongsheng, D.T.C.M.; Yu Wenping, D.T.C.M.; and the Shandong Provincial Qigong Association for their wealth of knowledge and enthusiastic support in sharing their clinical Qigong modalities, and to Dr. He Sihai, D.T.C.M., of the Zhe Jiang Qigong Hospital for his openness and kindness in sharing his knowledge.

A special thanks to Qigong Grandmaster Zheng Zhanding, D.T.C.M., for being my mentor, taking me under his powerful wing, and teaching me advanced Medical Qigong clinical modalities of energetic diagnosis and treatment therapies.

A special thanks to Medical Qigong Master Yu Yan Min D.T.C.M., for teaching me advanced esoteric sound therapy, and for supporting and encouraging my energetic and healing practice.

A special thanks to Qigong and Taiji Master Shifu Zhang Yufei for teaching, supporting, and encouraging my energetic and healing practice.

I am also indebted to Professor Zang Lu and doctors Xu Hongtao, D.T.C.M.; Ren Shuntu, D.T.C.M.; Xu Zongwei, D.T.C.M.; and the directors, teachers, interpreters and staff at the Xi Yuan Hospital of Traditional Chinese Medicine for their time, effort, knowledge and support during my 1993-1995 internship.

I am very grateful to Sun Shuchun, D.T.C.M., the Assistant Professor and Dean of the Beijing Academy of Acupuncture, Orthopedics, and Traumatology and the Hu Guo Si Hospital of Traditional Chinese Medicine for their time, effort, knowledge and support during my 1995 internship.

I would like to thank Professor Meng Xiantong and Tara Peng, D.M.Q., of the Beijing Chengjian Integrated Traditional Chinese Medicine and Western Medical Experts Clinic for sharing their knowledge of advanced clinical modalities, and for opening my eyes to the "ancient" world of esoteric medicine.

I am very grateful to Madame Wang Yan of the Beijing International Acupuncture Training Center, the Acupuncture Institute of China Academy of Traditional Chinese Medicine, and the World Health Organization Collaborating Center for Traditional Medicine for their years of support and for believing in me.

I would also like to thank President Yue Licui, D.T.C.M., of the World Academic Society of Medical Qigong and all my friends and colleagues at the Beijing College of Traditional Chinese Medicine for their years of help and support.

A special thanks to the Five Branches T.C.M.College, the Academy For Five Element Acupuncture, College and Clinic of T.C.M., and the He Nan University of T.C.M. for their encouragement and support. Also, special thanks to Professor Lu Shi Cai for his never-ending support in integrating the I.I.M.Q.'s Medical Qigong Programs at the He Nan University, and for his assistance in maintaining the high standards and clinical integrity of all the Medical Qigong classes.

Special thanks to the Mao Shan Monastery of Jiang Su Province, for sharing their wealth of knowledge. I would like to especially thank Abbot Cao Dao Zhang for his assistance in gathering ancient Daoist esoteric knowledge; to Fa Shi He Yu Hong, for sharing privileged information on esoteric Shang Qing training and exorcism. Special thanks to my teacher, Master Min Xian, a powerful Jing Shi and Talisman Master. Special thanks to Yue Shi Min

Guan and Professor Pan Yi De for sharing ancient Mao Shan history and esoteric Daoist Qigong.

Special thanks to the Longhu Shan Monastery of Jiang Xi Province, for sharing their wealth of knowledge. I would like to especially thank senior Abbot Zhang Jing Tao, the 65th Celestial Master, for his assistance in gathering ancient Daoist esoteric knowledge; and to my teacher, Grand Master Qiu Yusong of the Celestial Masters Mansion, for sharing the skills of creating talismans and invocations to bind evil spirits. He is a powerful exorcist and has been a guiding light in my spiritual growth. A special thanks to Master Zeng Guang Liang for sharing with me the most ancient healing skills of Long Hu Shan Daoism.

A special thanks to my good friend and Daoist brother, Father Michael Saso, for his invaluable contribution, encouragement and support. His years to intense study as a Professor and true scholar of ancient Daoist traditions helped enhance this textbook series.

A special thanks to my good friends and teachers Lama Lar and Paige Short of Grace Essence Fellow, for their invaluable contributions, encouragement, and loving support. Their years to intense dedication to embody the esoteric magical teachings of Padmasambhava and the Nyingma tradition have forever transformed my life. I will always remember those exciting times, sitting at the kitchen table, sharing esoteric teachings, and comparing notes between the Daoist and Nyingma energetic traditions.

A special thanks to my good friend and Daoist sister, Livia Kohn, Ph.D., for her invaluable contribution, encouragement and support. Her years to intense study as a Professor and true scholar of ancient Daoist traditions helped enhance this textbook series.

A special thanks to my Daoist brother, Professor Gerard Edde, Ph.D., for his invaluable contribution, encouragement, and support.

I would especially like to thank Dr. William Welch Jr., D.T.C.M., for his invaluable help and contribution in editing this textbook series, and Dr. John DeAnzo for his incredible support and friendship.

A special thanks to Jason Streetman for his incredible artwork. His unique skill and talent made several of the Medical Qigong Prescription Exercises more visually comprehensive.

A special thanks to Daniel Burton-Rose for his many painstaking hours of translating ancient Daoist Alchemical and Medical Texts, which enabled me to draw from more comprehensive resources.

Also, special thanks to Daoist Master Chang Jiun Li for his assistance in deciphering and expounding on several esoteric Daoist texts.

A special thanks to IIMQ graduate Dr. Bernard Shannon, D.T.C.M. and Professor Ma of the Defense Language Institute, in Monterey California for their many painstaking hours of providing translations and information on specific ancient Chinese Medical Texts. As a youth, Professor Ma served as one of the Official Librarians in Beijing, China, and had access to the Imperial Library, which contained several ancient unpublished medical texts. These texts were later destroyed by the Red Guard during the Cultural Revolution. Professor Ma's educated insight contributed extensive knowledge to the historical understanding of Ancient Chinese Medicine written in this textbook series.

A special thanks to Madhu Nair and Tomoko Koga for their many painstaking hours of translating ancient Japanese Medical Texts, which enabled me to draw from additional sources of ancient Chinese clinical records.

A special thanks to Jody Thomas Ho for his many painstaking hours of translating the French versions of ancient Chinese Medical Texts, which also enabled me to draw from more comprehensive and clinical resources.

A special thanks to Dr. Diego Sanmiquel, D.T.C.M., for his excellent work on designing the front and back cover of these five new volumes.

Above all, I would like to express my love, gratitude, and respect to my parents Antoinette and Lt. Cdr. (Rt.) Perry E. J. Johnson for their years of love, understanding, and encouragement. They have equally been my support and light in this present journey.

To my three beautiful daughters: Laura Marie, Leah Ann, and Hannah Daniel, whom I will always love, and will forever be honored and proud to be called their father.

And finally, to Erika Rosa Johnson, my "Forever Wife." Whom I will love forever, and am truly honored to be called her "Forever Husband."

INTRODUCTION

The following research presented in these five textbooks on *The Secret Teachings of Chinese Energetic Medicine*, has taken me a lifetime of study and investigation. This exploration into Chinese Energetic Medicine includes knowledge gathered from my personal clinical observations while treating patients here in the United States, as well as from treating patients in several of the People's Republic of China's Medical Universities, hospitals, and clinics in Beijing and Hunan.

In my life I have been fortunate enough to be introduced to several unique teachers, and have been honored to apprentice with several gifted masters of the "hidden" knowledge concealed within the obscure veil of Chinese esoteric medicine. This special teaching includes powerful healers originating from both Taiwan and the People's Republic of China.

Having procured several out-of-print texts written in the 1800's by Jesuit priests on the subject of ancient Chinese metaphysics and Daoist mysticism, my understanding of Chinese Energetic Medicine broadened enormously. Initially, all of the missing pieces slowly began to fit together, revealing a multidimensional form of healing, based on the microcosm and macrocosm of energetic and spiritual cause and effect.

The primary goal in releasing this esoteric knowledge to the public is twofold: First, to return to the Chinese people the lost riches of their ancient culture; and second, to provide an accurate historical foundation for modern energetic medicine, which has been lost or removed from current T.C.M. colleges and universities.

It has long been said that, "the proper study of Chinese Energetic Medicine involves the study of its ancient history." Therefore, the development of Traditional Chinese Medicine originated not only from generations of refined skills and sciences, but also from its ancient culture and beliefs as well.

In their most early stages, the knowledge of science and magic were indistinguishable, and it was difficult to differentiate between them. There is an old expression that states, "the only difference between occult magic and science is time."

This is why, after centuries of extensive energetic study, the founders of ancient Chinese Energetic Medicine made immense contributions to the scientific fields of Clinical Medicine, Pharmacology, and Chemistry.

Chinese Energetic Medicine, as an applied science, has an ancient history submerged in esoteric magic and Daoist Shamanism. This is why the ancient Chinese approach in explaining medical concepts is generally expressed through a three dimensional convergence, seeing the physical body as an energetic hologram, and observing the physical, energetic, and spiritual aspects of the tissues. By stimulating any one of these three energetic properties, an individual will in effect influence the other two, and begin to initiate either a healing or diseased condition. Diagnosis and treatment is therefore approached in a nonlinear progression, working holographically towards the health and healing of the multidimensional person.

Western Medicine, however, is taught to view the physical body on a two dimensional level, as a completed progression of cause and effect, separating the reactions of the tissues from the effects of the mind and emotions, as well as from universal and environmental influences. Though this attitude is gradually changing within the Western scientific and medical community, this change has been slow to reach the population at large.

In order to help the Western mind understand Chinese Energetic Medicine, this five volume textbook series was written with the goal of comprehensive instruction, combined with practical clinical application. It embraces the concepts of both Traditional Chinese Medicine, in particular Chinese Medical Qigong Therapy, as well as the energetic study of ancient Chinese Medicine as found in Daoist Shamanism.

The understanding of Chinese Energetic Medicine in the West has been hampered by the lack of accessibility to the "ancient" knowledge that has been handed down from master to student through centuries of secrecy. Through gross manipulation of source materials, the history and theory of "modern" Traditional Chinese Medicine was rewritten to reflect the interests of the Communist Party. Therefore, edited versions subject to the censorship of metaphysical ideas due to political influence, and the "cleaning up" for scientific respectability have been introduced to the public as the acceptable norm.

My hope in writing this five volume textbook series is to "reinstate" the energetic and spiritual principles originally contained within ancient Pre-Communist Chinese Energetic Medicine. Therefore, this entire textbook series provides a basic understanding of the complex energetic structure, theory, and practical application of ancient Chinese Energetic Medicine:

It is important for the reader to understand, that ancient Chinese Medical Terminology is extremely subjective and metaphoric, and is traditionally used to describe the many aspects of the human body through physical, energetic, and spiritual (Heart/Mind) domains of existence. Many technical terms in Traditional Chinese Medicine have numerous meanings, depending on the context of the subject and from which discipline they originate (i.e., Daoist or Buddhist).

Much of the obscure terminology existing in Chinese Energetic Medicine comes directly from ancient shamanistic sources. Therefore these terminologies can sometimes be extremely vague in their explanations, yet deeply profound in their true meanings.

When appropriate, throughout this entire textbook series, I have chosen to periodically use the term "Divine" for expressing the energy of the Dao, or of God. This will help the reader comprehend the original context in which the terminology arose.

Also for the sake of clarity, special Chinese terms are capitalized along with the English words for which ancient Chinese Energetic Medicine assigns a special meaning. Such words include, but are not limited to, Gall Bladder, Small Intestine, Spleen, Pericardium, Urinary Bladder, Liver, etc. When you see words such as Blood, Heart, and Marrow capitalized, assume that their meaning

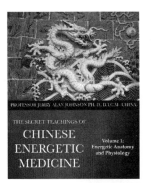

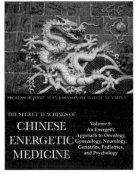

differs from that ascribed to by Western Medicine. For example, in Traditional Chinese Medicine, the word Marrow does not refer only to bone marrow as it is traditionally recognized in the West, but rather describes the energetic substance which is the common matrix of bones, bone marrow, the brain, and spinal cord. Non-capitalized terms retain their traditional Western meanings.

Historically, many of the terms originally used to describe the natural forces of Nature existing within Heaven, Earth, and Man, were personalized and referred to as "gods" or "spirits" by

"Religious Daoism." This was done purposely in order to compete with the colorful deities imported by the Buddhists into China from India. Therefore, when reading this textbook, the reader should not become confused or alarmed by certain terminologies describing "deities" which govern specific energetic principles. For example, when reading the section on the Human Soul, the title "Lords of the Three Dantians" implies the fact that the soul has three primary, separate, yet interconnected energetic properties rooted and sustained within each of the Three Dantians.

In China, many of the Medical Qigong Doctors and masters with whom I have trained asked me to keep these advanced energetic and spiritual theories in confidence, for fear of governmental reprisal. Currently, due to the Chinese government's response to the Falun Gong Qigong Association's political activities, many of the Medical Qigong Colleges and clinics have been closed. Therefore, I have decided to openly share these ancient energetic theories concerning the interactions of the body, mind, spirit, soul, and divine, without revealing my sources.

Finally, within this textbook series, I have included years of extensive research from several sources:

- **The Daoist Systems:** I have included information from ancient Daoist Energetic Medicine and advanced spiritual disciplines of the Bei Ji (Northern Pole Star) Daoist sect, from Wu-Dang Shan; the Tian Shi (Celestial Master) Daoist Sect from Long-Hu Shan; and the Shangqing (Upper Clarity) Daoist sect, from the Mao-Shan.
- **The Buddhist Systems:** I have included information from ancient Buddhist Energetic Medicine and advanced spiritual disciplines from the Shaolin Monastery teachings, Tantric Buddhism, and Orthodox Buddhism.
- **The Tibetan Tantric and Bon Systems:** I have included information from ancient Tibetan Buddhist Energetic Medicine and advanced spiritual disciplines from several Tibetan Monastery teachings, including the Tibetan Tantric, and Tibetan Bon shamanic traditions.

To quote one of my teachers, "Sanjiao Gui Yi" ("The three teachings make a whole person"). Meaning that through exposure to the esoteric knowledge contained within all three energetic and spiritual sources, the individual can become a more complete human being.

In writing and presenting these five volumes on Chinese Energetic Medicine to the public, I hope to condense the diverse fields of ancient energetic healing into a comprehensive medical compendium for the Western mind to understand. With this goal in mind, I have found it necessary to repeat information in certain sections in order to emphasize important information for increased comprehension.

Professor Jerry Alan Johnson, Ph.D., D.T.C.M.
Monterey, California - March, 2014

"When the Spiritual Powers
are passed on and transmitted,
they can no longer
be turned back!

If they are turned back,
they cannot be transmitted;
and their moving powers
will be forever lost to the universe!

In order to fulfill destiny,
man should go beyond
that which is near at hand,
and consider it as trifling!

One should make public,
upon tablets of jade,
that which was hidden and concealed
in treasuries and storehouses!

Study it from Sunrise until Sunset,
and thus make known
the precious mechanisms
of the Universe."

Huangdi Neijing
(The Yellow Emperor's Canon of Internal Medicine)

Section I
Foundations of Chinese Energetic Medicine

Chapter 1
Introduction to Chinese Energetic Medicine

Introduction To Life Force Energy

More than 5000 years ago, the ancient Chinese masters of Energetic Healing came to the understanding that everything is composed of the same ethereal substance, which they called "Qi" (pronounced "chee"). These ancient masters observed that there is a oneness and wholeness in all existence and that everything is energetically interconnected as one body through Qi.

The most ancient Chinese Character used for "Qi," appeared on the Shang Dynasty (1600-1028 B.C.) Oracle Bones and on the Zhou Dynasty (1028-221 B.C.) Bronze Inscriptions, as three horizontal lines. This ancient character originally depicted a "mist that rises from the Earth in order to form clouds" (Figure 1.1). This unique ideographic was retained until the early Western Zhou Dynasty (1066-770 B.C.), and was also used to indicate Heat Waves that rise from the heated surface of the Earth (and later used to describe exhaled breath that can be seen on a cold day).

In the clinic, Traditional Chinese Medical Diagnosis is primarily based on understanding the internal transformations of the body's Qi. This is because the ancient Chinese believed that all physical transformations happened under the guidance and influence of Qi.

In Daoist Alchemy, disciples are traditionally taught that when the Original Energy (Yuan Qi) is radiant and still, it is called Spirit (Shen); as it flows into movement it is called Breath (Qi); as it coagulates and condenses itself, it is called Essence (Jing).

According to the *Daodejing*, within the entire Universe, there is but one Primordial Breath (Yuan Qi). It is from this inexhaustible reservoir, that all things derive their existence. The Birth, Aging and Death of all things within Heaven, Earth and Man, including Planets and Stars, Mountains and Oceans, Forests and Deserts, Plants and Animals, are all caused by and formed out of Qi. Although energy may appear to take on many different patterns and forms, all things in Nature, and in fact all things in the Universe, are intrinsically woven together so that we are, quite literally, all symbiotically "One" via the system of Qi.

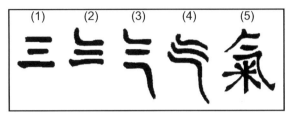

Figure 1.1. From the most ancient to modern Chinese characters for "Qi"

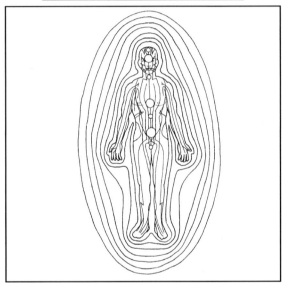

Figure 1.2. The body's Qi radiates from the tissues in order to form the external Wei Qi fields.

Qi is vibrating in constant energetic motion within all things. It is the catalyst for everything to relate and interrelate within the universe. The ancient Chinese believed that the Qi of Yin and Yang fills the "Great Void" (Wuji), enveloping all things and leaving nothing outside its boundary.

In modern times, the laws of physics have demonstrated that matter and energy are interchangeable and that matter is simply another form of energy. Matter is constantly vibrating in the form of particles or wave forms; it is constantly changing, either affecting or interacting with energy. Energy is inherent in the living human body, and the human body is sustained by energy (Figure 1.2).

The ancient Chinese mastered specific techniques to balance the body's energy (Qi), in order to live in harmony with the ever changing environmental (Earth Qi) and universal (Heaven Qi) energetic fields. Chinese Energetic Medicine maintains that when living things start to lose their Qi, they lose their vitality. An ancient Daoist saying states, "Life comes into beginning because Qi is amassed; when Qi is scattered, the person dies."

Qi is stored within the human body in the form of energetic pools, creating the energetic matrix of the internal organs. From these internal pools, the body's life-force energy flows in the form of rivers and streams. These special energetic rivers and streams extend throughout the human body, creating its various energetic vessels, channels, and collateral pathways.

UNDERSTANDING THE CONCEPT OF QI

While the concept of Qi in Chinese Energetic Medicine may seem complicated, it is actually quite simple. Matter progresses to energy, and energy progresses to spirit, and vice-versa. Qi is considered the medium, or bridge, between matter and spirit.

Qi has mass, the same way that smoke or vapor has mass. Therefore, Qi as energy can manifest within the human body through three primary levels:

- **Physically as Matter:** At this level, Qi energetically manifests through the physical matrix or sacred geometry (form) of a specific object (e.g., the construction of the body's cells and tissues). Within the human body, it manifests in the various forms of Essence, Marrow, Blood, and Body Fluid.
- **Energetically as Resonant Vibrations:** At this level, Qi energetically manifests through heat, sound, light, and electromagnetic fields resonating within the physical matrix of a specific object.
- **Spiritually as Divine Light:** At this level, Qi energetically manifests through subtle vibrations which contain "messages" (i.e., thoughts and feelings) resonating within the specific object's energetic field. Daoist priests teach that these energetic "messages" extend through infinite space (Wuji) to the Dao (Figure 1.3).

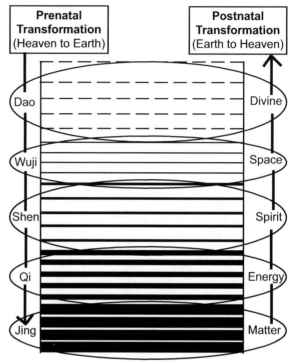

Figure 1.3. The Five Energetic Fields

Through observation and study, Chinese Qigong (Energy Skill) Masters discovered that each internal organ within the human body has a different function and a different speed of energetic vibration. By tracing the energetic pathways of Qi through each internal organ, and observing its affect on bodily functions, the Chinese developed the basic theories upon which Traditional Chinese Medical practice was founded. For thousands of years, Chinese Medicine has successfully cured serious illnesses by stimulating the body's Qi in very specific ways.

Through the study and practice of Medical Qigong, one can cultivate an awareness of internal energy and its individual pathways, and can learn to influence and even control its subtle energetic power. Medical Qigong Practitioners use these skills to heal and strengthen the immune system, and to improve the function of various organ systems within the body. In the year 2000, China Healthways International estimated that in Beijing alone more than 1.3 million people practiced some form of Qigong every day; and in China as a whole, around 80 million people were practicing some form of Qigong.

Chapter 1: Introduction to Chinese Medicine

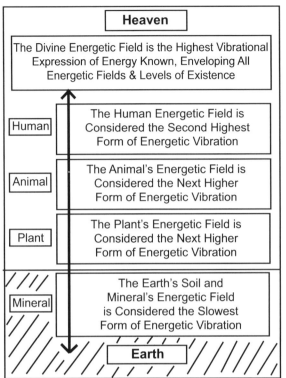

Figure 1.4. The Five Realms or manifestations of matter and energy

Figure 1.5. The Mineral Realm

Figure 1.6. The Plant Realm

THE FIVE REALMS OF ENERGY

The nature of energetic fields is still considered mysterious by most modern scientists. According to modern physics, energetic fields are more fundamental than matter. Energetic fields cannot be explained in terms of matter; rather, matter is explained in terms of the energy within the fields.

The ancient Daoist masters observed that Qi can be divided into five main realms (Mineral, Plant, Animal, Human, and Divine), each manifesting in various forms of matter and energy. Each energetic "form" draws from the energetic realm of the next, resonating and interacting with the Divine through the form's relationship within the Wuji (infinite space). With each increase in vibrational frequency, there is a corresponding increase in complexity, consciousness, and level of awareness. The Five Main Realms or manifestations of matter and energy are described as follows (Figure 1.4):

1. **The Realm of Minerals:** This is considered the lowest (densest and slowest) form of energetic vibration (Figure 1.5). Mineral particles divide, disintegrate, and eventually combine with the Elements of Wind/Air (Feng) and Water (Shui) to form the Earth's soil. Every particle in the soil still retains the original Primordial Qi of the Mineral, which interacts with the energy of the Divine.

2. **The Realm of Plants:** The energetic potential of the Mineral Realm is absorbed by the Plant Realm, being refined and organized into a more powerful energetic matrix. Thus the Plant Realm is considered the next higher form of energetic vibration (Figure 1.6). All of the Earth's vegetation (trees, bushes, flowers, herbs, plants) absorbs life-energy from the minerals' energetic field, increasing and multiplying the plant's energetic potential. Therefore, the plant's energetic field is considered the next ascension in energetic evolution

Figure 1.7. The Animal Realm

Figure 1.8. The Human Realm

towards the Divine Energetic Field. In this form of energetic manifestation, the energetic field of the plant has now combined with the energetic matrix of the minerals.

3. **The Realm of Animals:** The energetic potential of both the Mineral Realm and Plant Realm is absorbed by the Animal Realm, being refined and organized into a more powerful energetic matrix. Thus the Animal Realm is considered the next higher form of life-force energy (Figure 1.7). As the animal consumes and absorbs energy from the plant's energetic field, it further increases and multiplies its own energetic potential, bringing it one step closer towards the Divine Energetic Field. In this form of energetic manifestation, the energetic field of the animal is now combined with the energetic matrix of both the Plant Realm and Mineral Realm.

4. **The Realm of Man (Humanity):** The energetic potential of the Mineral, Plant, and Animal Realms are absorbed by the Human Realm, being refined and organized into an even more powerful energetic matrix. Because humans consume and absorb energy from all three preceding realms (Mineral, Plant, and Animal), their energetic potential is further increased and multiplied (Figure 1.8). This brings the human's own energetic potential one step closer towards the Divine Energetic Field. This is considered the second highest form of energetic vibration and life-force energy. Humans are unique in that, through diet, Qigong practice, prayer, and meditation, they can intentionally refine and enhance their own energetic potential.

5. **The Realm of the Divine:** This is the highest vibrational expression of energy known. As it envelops and becomes active within the human body, it further increases and multiplies the body's energetic potential, allowing mankind to attain Divine Consciousness.

All of these energetic fields originate from one source, and thus contain the vibrational resonance of the True Divine Life-Force. Knowing this, the ancient Daoists believed that it was possible to enhance the nutritional value of what they ate by adapting an attitude of deep respect for the plants and animals that give their life-force energy for their personal consumption. The blessing of food, and preparing food with a loving attitude, allows for the absorption of not only the vitamins and minerals contained therein, but also the absorption of the higher vibrations of the One True Divine Energy inherent in all things.

Once a Daoist disciple becomes aware of the Divine Energetic Field, he can begin to experience the refined vibrational energy fields of minerals, plants, animals, and human beings on an entirely different level. This increased awareness of the Divine Life-Force Energy strengthens the awareness of the disciple's own energetic fields. This in turn can deepen the conscious and unconscious energetic connection existing within the subtle energetic fields resonating between the disciple and minerals, plants, animals, humans, and the Divine. There is an ancient Chinese saying that states, "Consciousness sleeps in Minerals, dreams in Plants, begins to stir in Animals, and is awakened in Man."

Yang	Yang	Yin	Yin
Depicts the Bright, Sunny Side of a Hill or River Bank	Active	Passive	Depicts the Dark, Shady Side of a Hill or River Bank
	Creative	Receptive	
	Masculine	Feminine	
	Back	Front	
Sun Above the Horizon	Left	Right	A Covering Over Clouds
	Fire	Water	
	Hot	Cold	
Hill 陽	Dry	Wet	Hill 陰
	Hard	Soft	
Sun's Rays Shining Down	Light	Heavy	Mist above Clouds
	Bright	Dark	
○ Yang	Heaven	Earth	● Yin
	Sun	Moon	
	White	Black	

Figure 1.9. The Chart above shows the ancient Chinese Yang (Heaven) and Yin (Earth) Symbols: Yang is represented by White, and Yin is represented by Black. The center of the circle towards the right represents the Eternal Dao within the Wuji. Yin and Yang give birth to the Elements of Fire and Water, which give birth to Four Phases of universal energy (Great Yang, Lesser Yang, Great Yin and Lesser Yin). The Four Phases of energy create the Bagua (Eight Trigrams), which transform into the 64 Hexagrams of the Yi-Jing.

DEFINING THE ENERGY OF YIN & YANG

Each of the five energetic fields can be further divided into aspects of Yin and Yang. In Traditional Chinese Medicine, the theory of Yin and Yang Qi represents the duality of balance and harmony within the body, as well as within the universe. The Qi of Earth is Yin, while the Qi of Heaven is Yang.

The Chinese ideogram of Yin depicts the dark, shady side of a hill or river bank; Yang depicts the bright, sunny side of a hill or river bank (Figure 1.9). Yin exists within Yang, and Yang exists within Yin. Yang manifests as active, creative, masculine, hot, hard, light, Heaven, white and bright. Yin manifests as passive, receptive, feminine, cold, soft, dark, Earth, black and shadow.

Yin is dependent on Yang, and Yang is dependent on Yin. Thus, all things have a Yin and Yang aspects, which can be further subdivided into Yin and Yang. Yin and Yang mutually create each other, control each other, consume each other and transform each other. This dynamic balance of Yin and Yang constantly changes and transforms the body's life-force energy.

From an ancient Daoist perspective, the Dao creates the infinite space of the Wuji, which in turn creates the Yin and Yang energies of the Taiji, which give birth to further subdivisions of Yin and Yang, manifesting as four phases of universal energy (Great Yang, Lesser Yang, Great Yin and Lesser Yin). These four phases of universal energy form the energetic basis of the Prenatal and Postnatal transformations, manifested in the form of eight energetic actions. The eight energetic actions (also known as the Bagua) act as a template for all creation, and can further be manifested through the ever-changing energetic form of the 64 Hexagrams of the Yi-Jing (I-Ching).

The later symbol for Yin and Yang (which became popular in the Song Dynasty 960-1279 A.D.) still expresses the energetic concept of the Dao, the Wuji and the transforming energies of Yin and Yang. However, unless an individual has received competent instruction, the subtleties are easy to overlook.

Successful practitioners who trained and mastered the art of balancing the body's Yin-Yang energies were considered "Tian Shen" or "Xian," meaning "immortals." They were able to harmonize the body with the mind, the mind with the will, the will with the breath, the breath with the spirit, the spirit with motion, and finally, motion with the surrounding environment (Earth), the universe (Heaven), and the divine (Dao).

THE HISTORY OF QIGONG AND CHINESE MEDICINE

Energetic medicine developed in China over a span of thousands of years. Although the art and clinical skill of Chinese Medical Qigong is considered an integral and critical component of modern Traditional Chinese Medicine (T.C.M.), its historical origin can be traced back further than the invention of written language.

In ancient China, energetic medicine and all forms of healing were the exclusive domain of the tribal shamans. *Qigong ("Energy Skill")* was then known by other names, for example *Xingqi ("Aiding Qi Flow"), "Tuna" ("Exhalation and Inhalation"),* and *"Daoyin" ("Guiding and Stretching")*.

THE YELLOW EMPEROR (HUANGDI)

According to Chinese legend, the origination of ancient Daoist Magic, Esoteric Qigong practices, and Acupuncture has always been linked to Huang Di (the Yellow Emperor), whose surname was Gongsun (also called Xuanyuanshi after Xuanyuan Hill, the place of his birth). The Yellow Emperor ruled over a confederation of tribal clans in Northern China from approximately 2696-2598 B.C. (Figure 1.10).

The Yellow Emperor is said to have practiced Qigong breathing exercises and meditations, internal alchemy, herbology, and sexual alchemy, and lived to the age of 111 years old.

It is said that when he was passing Wind Mountain, on the road going East towards Green Mountain, the Yellow Emperor met the "Master of the Purple Chamber." It was here that the Yellow Emperor received the secret text known as the "Esoteric Writings of the Three Sovereigns." Through this secret text, the Yellow Emperor was able to summon hundreds of spirits.

According to the *Biographies of the Immortals*, written in the Han Dynasty (206 B.C.-220 A.D.), "the Yellow Emperor possessed many magical powers, and could summon, control, and order about various deities and spirit entities, through the use of magical talismans and other esoteric magical tools. It was said that the Yellow Emperor was personally known as "Xianyuan" (the

Figure 1.10. Huang Di (The Yellow Emperor) Inspired from the Original Artwork of Neal White

Figure 1.11. The Title Page of the *Huangdi Neijing* (Yellow Emperor's Canon of Internal Medicine)

"Original Immortal"), and ruled over hundreds of gods, who would all pay homage to him and service his every need and desire. Eventually, the Yellow Emperor ascended to Heaven at the foot of Mount Thorn, on the back of a large dragon."

There are a number of esoteric texts attributed to the magical teachings of the Yellow Emperor. These magical books are entitled:

- *The Yellow Emperor's Old Willow Divination by Dreams*
- *The Yellow Emperor's Inner Classics*
- *The Dietary Prescriptions of the Divine Agriculturist (Shen Nong) the Yellow Emperor*
- *Wondrous Mushrooms of the Yellow Emperor and His Various Disciples*
- *The Yellow Emperor's Classics of the Golden Bookcase and Jade Scales*

CHAPTER 1: INTRODUCTION TO CHINESE MEDICINE

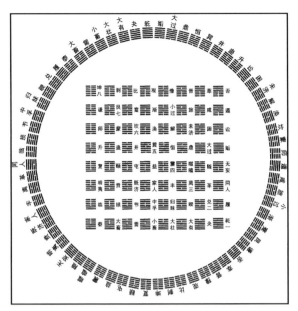

Figure 1.12. The 64 Hexagrams of the Yi-Jing

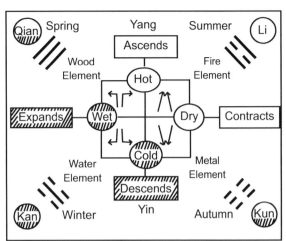

Figure 1.13. Four Main External Conditions

- *The Yellow Emperor's Canon of Internal Medicine*
- *The Yellow Emperor's and Three King's Techniques for Nourishing Yang*
- *The Massage of Huang Di and Qi Bo*

The belief that the original school of Magical Daoism is founded by the Yellow Emperor was actually common knowledge in China until the Chinese government moved to embrace Western Medicine, and sought to squelch any metaphysical knowledge or Daoist Magic pertaining to the root or origin of modern Traditional Chinese Medicine.

It was Huang Di's discourses on health and longevity with his chief medical advisors Qi Bo and Lei Gong, that were eventually compiled and recorded in twelve scrolls during the Warring States period. This work is known as the *Huang Di Nei Jing (Yellow Emperor's Canon of Internal Medicine)*, and is hailed as the foundation of all Chinese Energetic Medicine (i.e., Doctors of Acupuncture, Chinese Herbology, Medical Qigong Therapy, and Tuina Massage). In the *Huang Di Nei Jing*, there are eight sections that clearly mention Qigong therapy and principles of Medical Qigong Therapy (Figure 1.11).

One of the ministers of the Yellow Emperor (the founder of Chinese Medicine) was a Wu (Shaman Priest) named Zhu You. Zhu You practiced an ancient form of Qi Emission combined with Sacred Prayer Incantations while treating his patients. So effective was this method of treatment that the *Yellow Emperor's Classic of Internal Medicine* states that in ancient times most illnesses were treated according to Zhu You's Healing Methods. Practitioners of this method were known as professional "prayer healers," and were once widespread throughout ancient China.

THE ZHOU DYNASTY (1028-221 B.C.)

During the Zhou Dynasty (1028-221 B.C.), the ancient book of divination known as the *Yi-Jing (Book of Changes)* appeared publicly, and became the theoretical basis for all Qigong training (Figure 1.12). This was because, in ancient China there was no clear separation between the study of medicine and the study of divination. The study of the ever changing energies of Heaven, Earth and Man was essential to obtaining proper medical diagnosis:

- **Heaven's Qi:** Related to the study of Chinese Astrology, and the influence of the celestial energies of the Sun, Moon, and Stars.
- **Earth's Qi:** Related to the study of Feng Shui, and the influence of the energy of Wind and Water, brought about by the seasonal changes (Figure 1.13).
- **Man's Qi:** Related to the study of the Yi-Jing, and the 64 divination patterns, observed through the six lined oracular hexagrams.

The Yi-Jing was originally titled *Zhouyi (the Zhou Changes)*, and represents the foundation of Chinese culture, influencing the basic concepts of Traditional Chinese Medicine. It is rooted in the interaction of the Prenatal Bagua and Postnatal Bagua (Eight Trigrams).

In imperial China, the Yi-Jing had two distinct functions. First, it was studied as a classic compendium of ancient cosmic principles; second, it functioned as a divination text. Therefore, the ancient study of the Yi-Jing was divided into two main branches: Xiang-Shu (Images and Numbers), and Yi-Li (Philosophy and Logic).

The ancient Chinese believed that there was a unique energetic and spiritual connection between an individual's birth and the eight energetic fields manifesting within the eight directions of the Bagua (Figure 1.14). So important was this energetic relationship that the famous Han physician Sun Simao once said, "You cannot master medicine until you have studied the Yi-Jing." In fact, according to medical historian Yang Li, no doctor in Chinese medical history has ever studied the *Huangdi Neijing (The Yellow Emperor's Inner Canon)* without consulting the *Yi-Jing (Book of Changes)*.

During the Spring and Autumn (770-476 B.C.) and Warring States (475-221 B.C.) Periods, ancient China experienced an unprecedented academic and literary phenomenon known as the "contention of 100 schools of thought." This movement helped to further spread the development and refinement of Qigong. At this point in time, Qigong had already developed through its embryonic stage of being utilized for ancient rituals of worship, the development of hunting skills, and ceremonial dance.

The ancient Chinese began to extensively apply Qigong in the practice of medicine, and the first monograph combining both Qigong and medicine was written during the Warring States period in the *Huangdi Neijing (Yellow Emperor's Inner Canon)*. In the twelve scrolls were listed five therapeutic methods, the nine needles application, herbal decoctions, moxibustion, stone needling, massage and Dao Yin training (in which Qigong

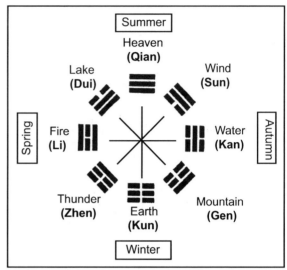

Figure 1.14. The Eight Energetic Fields Manifesting Within the Eight Directions of the Prenatal Bagua

is included). Also included within the twelve scrolls are basic theories and methods for applying Qigong training for health care (see Figure 1.11).

The *Huangdi Neijing* represents the first time in China's history that Qigong is introduced in a systematic and theoretical format. During this time period, many famous philosophers such as Laozi and Zhuangzi (the forefathers of Daoism), as well as Confucius, were all publicly recognized as great Qigong masters. According to the *Shi Ji* (Records of the Historian), the great physician Bian Que used Dao Yin and massage in treating diseases.

During the Warring States period, Laozi (Old Sage), to whom the *Daodejing* (The Way and Its Power) is attributed, was regarded as the preeminent Daoist philosopher. Therefore, the Daoists during this time period were known as Huang Lao Dao (The Way of the Yellow Emperor and the Old Sage).

Additionally, during the early years of the Warring States period, records of Qigong training methods and theory were compiled in the *Xing Qi Yu Pei Ming* (Jade Pendant Inscriptions of Qigong), and the *Zhou Yi Can Tong Qi* (Analogs of Principles of Changes Formulated in the Zhou Dynasty).

CHAPTER 1: INTRODUCTION TO CHINESE MEDICINE

Figure 1.15. The *Dao Yin Tu* postures from the King Ma Tomb

THE QIN DYNASTY (221-206 B.C.)

During this time period, the Qin Prime Minister Lu Buwei, compiled a text entitled *Spring and Autumn Book of Lu*. In this text, Lu Buwei compiled many of the ancient Daoist practices of "The Harmony of Heaven and Man," discoursing the effects of seasonal changes and other natural forces on the human body. The ancient Daoist book, *The Way of Cultivating Life*, which contains Dao Yin training, diet regulation, and sexual practices, became codified during this time.

THE WESTERN HAN DYNASTY AND EASTERN HAN DYNASTIES (206 B.C.-220 A.D.)

Many of the earliest known Medical Qigong prescription exercises were derived from martial applications and the movements of animals. In 1972, archaeologists began excavating the Mawangdui Han Dynasty tombs (206 B.C.-220 A.D.) in Hunan Province, and in one of the coffins uncovered a silk relic that portrayed drawings of Dao Yin postures (also known as the *Dao Yin Tu*) dating prior to the third century B.C.

This silk scroll is considered the first complete set of Qigong movements, and is commonly known as the "Dao Yin Breathing Drawings of the Han Dynasty." Contained in these forty-four an-

Figure 1.16. Zhang Zhongjing (150-210 A.D.)

cient Qigong Classic illustrations are descriptions of postural movements and the names of the diseases that they treat. Over half of these illustrated postures are of animal movements (Figure 1.15).

During the Han Dynasty, one famous physician named Zhang Zhongjing (Figure 1.16), mentioned in his book *Jin Kui Yao Lue (Synopsis of Prescriptions of the Golden Chamber)*, that Daoyin ("Guiding and Stretching"), Tuna ("Exhalation and Inhalation"), Massage, Acupuncture, and Moxibustion should be used to purge the body's channels, regulate the Yin and Yang, and treat illnesses.

Also during the Han Dynasty, the great physician and Daoist Alchemist Hua Tuo (Figure 1.17) created a set of systematic Dao Yin physical training known as the *Wuqinxi* (Five Animal Play). These five exercises mimic the various movements and gestures of the Deer, Bird, Ape, Tiger, and Bear (Figure 1.18). The initial goal of these five exercises is to help the practitioner improve his or her health and counteract disease, by opening the channels in order to cultivate Essence (Jing), Energy (Qi) and Spirit (Shen). Each of the Five Animals relate to a specific internal organ, for example:

- **The Deer Form:** stimulates and strengthens the function of the Liver and Gall Bladder, stretches and strengthens the legs, spine, and waist, and helps improve flexibility
- **The Bird Form:** stimulates and strengthens the function of the Heart and Small Intestine, improves balance, opens the joints, relieves congestion and helps cool the body
- **The Ape Form:** stimulates and strengthens the function of the Spleen and Stomach
- **The Tiger Form:** stimulates and strengthens the function of the Lungs and Large Intestine
- **The Bear Form:** stimulates and strengthens the function of the Kidneys and Urinary Bladder, develops rooted power, strengthens the Bones, and helps warm the body

During the end of the Han Dynasty, the Daoist master Wei Boyang wrote the classic *Zan Dong Ji (The Union of Three Equations)*, in which he discussed the inner alchemy of Qigong Breathing, Qi Transformation, and the Dual Cultivation of Sexual Practices. The *Tai Ping Jing (Classic of Great Peace)*, also written during this time period, summarized many of the traditional alchemical teachings from the Huang-Lao Daoist lineage.

Figure 1.17. Hua Tuo (110-207 A.D.)

Figure 1.19. Ji Kang (223–262 A.D.)

THE THREE KINGDOMS PERIOD (220-280 A.D.)

During the Three Kingdoms period, many people practiced Qigong, including several famous scholars, physicians, and alchemists. Daoist Master Ji Kang (Figure 1.19), was both a famous scholar and musician during the Wei Dynasty (220-265 A.D.). He wrote both the *Yang Sheng Lun (On Health Preservation)* and the *Da Nan Yang Sheng Lun (On Difficulties of Health Preservation)*, which described various Qigong exercises used for healing.

Figure 1.18. Hua Tuo's Five Animal Play

CHAPTER 1: INTRODUCTION TO CHINESE MEDICINE

Part of a Song Dynasty stone rubbing of Wang Xizhi's manuscript of the Huang Ting Jing (Yellow Court Classic)

Figure 1.20. The Huang Ting Jing (Yellow Court Classic)

Figure 1.21. Ge Hong (281-341 A.D.)

Figure 1.22. Tao Hongjing (456-536 A.D.)

DURING THE JIN DYNASTY (265-420 A.D.)

During The Jin Dynasty, the word "Qigong" ("Energy Skill") first appeared in the book *Jing Ming Zong Jiao Lu (Records of the Clear Bright Sect)*, written by a Daoist priest Xu Xun (239-374 A.D.).

Additionally, the important Daoist text, *Huang Ting Jing (Yellow Court Classic)* was first published during the Jin Dynasty, and caused the Daoist Nei Dan (Internal Elixir) School of thought to become the prevalent basis for all Qigong training (Figure 1.20). This text thoroughly explained the key components of esoteric Daoist alchemical practice, including the secret skill of gathering Internal Energy, and the regulation of the Three Dantians.

Ge Hong (Figure 1.21), another noted Daoist scholar, physician, and alchemist from the Eastern Jin Dynasty, wrote a milestone compendium of Daoist theory and practice. In his book *Bao Pu Zi (He Who Embraces the Uncarved Block)*, Ge Hong detailed specific techniques for developing physical longevity and spiritual immortality, using static Qigong exercises. This text is still regarded today as one of the most influential texts used in the development of Qigong practice.

THE NORTHERN AND SOUTHERN DYNASTY PERIOD (386-588 A.D.)

Tao Hongjing (Figure 1.22), a noted Daoist scholar and physician in the Southern Dynasty, compiled the ancient Daoist Qigong book, *Yang Xing Yan Ming Lu (The Record of Cultivating One's Nature and Longevity)*. It was during this period that the famous Daoist Qigong monograph *Huang Ting Nei Jing (Classic on Cultivation of the Internal Essence)* and an important Daoist Qigong reference book, *Huang Hai Jing (Cultivation of the Sea of Essence)* were compiled.

During the Southern Liang Dynasty (520-556 A.D.), the Indian Buddhist monk Da Mo (Bodhidharma) came to China teaching an unorthodox style of Tantric Buddhism. In 527 A.D., Da Mo traveled to the Shaolin temple of the Song Mountain, in Henan province, and introduced the famous Muscle/Tendon Changing and Marrow/Brain Washing Qigong Exercises, as well as the Buddha Palm training.

THE SUI DYNASTY AND TANG DYNASTIES (581-907 A.D.)

At the time of the Sui and Tang Dynasties, Qigong was extensively utilized in clinical application, including Laozi Qi Massage and various Qigong prescription exercises. Because of their effectiveness as powerful healing modalities, three medical classics were written recording these ancient Qigong protocols. The three books that included detailed Qigong training methods were: *Zhu Bing Yuan Hou Lun (General Treatise on the Causes and Symptoms of Disease), Bei Ji Qian Jin Yao Fang (One Thousand Golden Prescriptions for Emergencies)*, and *Wai Tai Mi Yao (The Medical Secrets of an Official)*.

The most famous physician and Daoist alchemist during the Tang Dynasty (618-907 A.D.), was Sun Simiao (Figure 1.23). A prolific author, clinician, and Daoist alchemist, he contributed much to the promotion of Chinese medicine and Qigong training. Although the first acupuncture charts were believed to be produced during the Han Dynasty (206 B.C.-220 A.D.), Sun Simiao is credited with drawing the first charts of the anterior, posterior, and lateral views of the body. These charts showed the Twelve Primary Channels in Five Element colors, with the Extraordinary Vessels drawn in a sixth color. This anatomical format is still being used today in all T.C.M. universities, colleges and clinics around the world. Sun Simiao is also credited with the introduction of the system of proportional measurement (called "cun"), which allows for accurate location of the channel points.

During this time period, an imperial physician named Chao Yuan Fang (Figure 1.24), included in his book, *Zhu Bing Yuan Hou Lum (A General Treatise on the Etiology and Symptomology of Various Diseases)*, 250 ways of enhancing the body's internal and external flow of energy with various forms of Qigong theory, techniques, and healing applications. In this special textbook, instead of advocating herbal prescriptions, it only lists Medical Qigong Therapy for the treatment of the diseases.

THE SONG, JIN, AND YUAN DYNASTIES (960-1368 A.D.)

During the Song, Jin, and Yuan Dynasties, there was an upsurge of interest in Daoist Nei Dan (Inter-

Figure 1.23. Sun Si Miao (590-682 A.D.)

Figure 1.24. Chao Yuan Fang (550-630 A.D.)

Figure 1.25. Su Shi (1037-1101 A.D.)

nal Alchemy), which is used as an integral part of Qigong exercises. Greater developments of fitness-oriented Qigong emerged as people began to pay special attention to the health and healing benefits of Qigong exercises and meditations. Su Shi (Figure 1.25), a famous writer of the Northern Song Dynasty (960-1127 A.D.), enthusiastically promoted the health

Figure 1.26. Zhou Dunyi (1017-1073 A.D.)

Figure 1.27. Zhu Xi (1130-1200 A.D.)

Figure 1.28. Zhang Boduan (987-1082 A.D.)

and healing effects of Qigong. Even today his ideas continue to influence the practice of Medical Qigong.

Also during this time period, a philosopher of the Northern Song Dynasty named Zhou Dunyi (Figure 1.26), and a philosopher of the Southern Song Dynasty named Zhu Xi (Figure 1.27), developed a Neo-Confucian-based Qigong. This Qigong system advocated the "Quiescence" theory of meditation and the study of the Tai Ji Tu Shuo (The Teaching of the Taiji Symbol).

Among the many Daoist masters whose works served to promote Qigong during this time period, was Zhang Boduan (Figure 1.28). His writings incorporated lucid explanations of advanced Daoist principles from the Quan Zhen (Complete Reality) School of Daoism. Among his writings, the most famous of his works are, *The Secret of the Opening the Passes, The Four-Hundred Character Treatise on the Golden Elixir,* and *Understanding Reality.*

THE MING DYNASTY AND QING (MANCHU) DYNASTIES (1368-1911)

During the Ming and Qing Dynasties, Qigong was extensively adopted by all physicians for the treatment of disease and health maintenance. In the early Ming Dynasty (1368-1644 A.D.), discussions on the effects and proper applications of Qigong were found in two medical textbooks. One textbook was written by Wang Lu entitled *Yi Jing Su Hui Ji (Recall of Medical Classics),* the other was written by Wan Jin entitled *Wan Mi Zhai Yi Shu Shi Zhong (Ten Medical Books of Wan Mi Zhai).*

Figure 1.29. Li Shizhen (1518-1593 A.D.)

During the Ming Dynasty, the great physician, herbalist, and Qigong master Li Shizhen (Figure 1.29) extensively combined the use of Qigong with his clinical treatments. In his book, *Qi Jing Ba Mai Kao (Study On The Eight Extra Meridians),* he wrote, "The inner scenery and channels [of the human body] can be viewed only by those who reflect inwardly, illuminating the interior through meditation."

Figure 1.30. The Gujin Tushu Jicheng

Figure 1.31. The Zhang Shi Yi Tong

In the Qing Dynasty (1644-1911 A.D.), Dao Yin techniques were extensively mentioned in the famous medical opus known as *Gujin Tushu Jicheng (Collected Ancient and Modern Books)*, written by Chen Menglei (Figure 1.30).

Also during the Qing Dynasty, the *Zhang Shi Yi Tong (Zhang's Medical Experience)* compiled by the famous physician Zhang Lu, discussed Qi Deviations for the first time in Chinese history. (Figure 1.31).

THE REPUBLIC OF CHINA (1912-1949 A.D.)

During the Republic of China, China suffered from the effects of foreign invasion, as well as from corrupt imperialistic powers. The confusion and infighting between warlords wreaked havoc throughout the country, causing a halt in the development of both Qigong and Chinese Medicine.

THE PEOPLE'S REPUBLIC OF CHINA (1949 A.D.-PRESENT)

In 1953, Professor Liu Guizhen (Figure 1.32) compiled the *Qigong Liao Fa Shi Jian (Application of Qigong to Medical Practice)*, and the term "Qigong for Health" became popular among the Chinese people. In 1955, the first Qigong Sanitarium was created in the city of Tangshan (Hebei province), introducing Mecial Qigong Therapy to the public. By 1956, Medical Qigong workshops were established in Tangshan and Beidaihe in order to foster a select group of Qigong professionals. As a result, several institutes and clinics sprang up throughout the country. Medical Qigong Therapy won the support of the government, and in October of 1959,

Figure 1.32. Professor Liu Guizhen (1920-1983)

the First National Qigong Experience Exchange Conference sponsored by the Ministry of Public Health for the People's Republic of China was held in Beidaihe. Participants came from 64 Medical colleges and institutes, and 17 different provinces.

From 1966-1976, during the Great Proletarian Cultural Revolution, Chairman Mao Zedong dispatched the Red Guard to enforce the "Out with the Old in with the New" policy. During that time period, Chinese martial arts and Qigong training were strictly forbidden. Most practitioners either fled to Taiwan, went "underground" (denying any specific training or skill), or were sent to "reeducation" camps. Chairman Mao also issued a decree that all doctors of Chinese medicine should now study Western Medicine, and the practice of Chinese medicine was forbidden.

With fewer than 30,000 trained Western physicians in all of China, however, the Chinese were suddenly faced with a new problem. Lines of patients waiting for treatment at the various hospitals literally extended for miles. Doctors, constantly working seven days a week, were utterly exhausted. The state of medical care in China had now evolved into a serious health crisis.

During that time, one of Chairman Mao's cabinet members became sick with cancer (leukemia) and could not be healed by the Western medical protocols. He learned of a Qigong master hiding out in Beijing, and there he sought help and treatment. Within three months the cabinet member was completely healed. He reluctantly reported what had transpired to Chairman Mao, and that the healing had occurred not through Western Medicine, but through Qigong therapy and herbs. Noting the current health crisis, Chairman Mao reevaluated his policy and restriction of Chinese medicine, and initiated the widespread training of "barefoot doctors" of Traditional Chinese Medicine.

Immediately thereafter, the Chinese government began to focus attention on resurrecting the ancient treasure of Chinese medicine. Hospitals and clinics of Traditional Chinese Medicine once again began to flourish throughout China. In order to combat the current health crisis, the new government policy required every patient with a chronic health condition to be given a hospital pass. Each hospital pass consisted of a sheet of paper with 30 squares, each square represented a space for 30 wood-block chopped signatures.

Taiji and Qigong instructors were positioned in each park, and offered free instruction to the public. After each lesson, the master would chop the participant's hospital pass. In order to return to the hospital, the patient was required to have his or her sheet of paper completed with 30 individual chops from either the Qigong or Taiji master. Within a very short time, the health crisis was solved. This is why by the 1970's there were millions of people practicing Taijiquan and Qigong in parks throughout China.

In 1978, extensive research on Qigong was conducted using modern scientific techniques and equipment in Beijing and Shanghai. By 1998, there were several experimental bases established in Beijing, Nanjing, and Guangzhou for specific research into the energetic potential of Qigong training. At that time, Qigong was applied and studied in

Figure 1.33. The World Academic Society of Medical Qigong Official Seal

medicine, nuclear physics, industry, agriculture, engineering, and sports. Encouraging results were achieved in each of these fields. The Chinese government became extremely concerned about the future development of Medical Qigong and sought to promote it as a viable clinical modality.

In 1999, the study of Qigong took a sudden change in formal development. Due to the political antics of the fanatical Falun Gong "Qigong" organization, the Chinese government put a sudden halt to any and all Qigong practices. In the middle of the night, armed guards entered the various Medical Qigong colleges, laboratories, and clinics, removed all of the scientific equipment, and chained and padlocked the doors. Some Qigong doctors and instructors were held and interrogated, and several Medical Qigong hospitals and clinics throughout China were closed. All Qigong practice groups were dispersed. Even individuals practicing in the various parks were ordered to disband and the leaders were taken in for questioning.

As of 2013, only two Medical Qigong organizations are recognized by the People's Republic of China, and are allowed to work in the government-sponsored hospitals and clinics. These two organizations are the China Medical Qigong Association and the World Association of Medical Qigong. Additionally, most of the doctors from both organizations are former members of the World Academic Society of Medical Qigong (Figure 1.33).

To date, many of the Medical Qigong applications and prescription exercises that were taught to the author and were normally implemented in the Medical Qigong hospitals are no longer being taught to the public, or utilized in the various clinics.

HISTORY OF ANCIENT CHINESE SHAMAN DOCTORS: WU YI

It is important for the reader to understand that the most ancient roots of Chinese energetic medicine originated within the mystical realm of ancient Chinese shamanism (Wu). The Wu Yi (Shaman Healers) of ancient China were known as spirit mediums who have practiced divination, prayer, sacrifice, rainmaking, and healing. They were highly respected in the community, and were traditionally consulted regarding medical ailments, problems in relationships, spiritual disharmonies, and various occult practices.

The Wu Yi understood that the birth, existence, transformation, and death of everything in the universe happened under the influence of the energetic transformations of Qi. The major philosophical and spiritual basis for all Traditional Chinese Medicine owes its existence to shamanistic Daoism.

According to ancient Chinese belief, the founder of esoteric shamanistic Daoism (or Magical Daoism) was not Laozi (whose original name was Li Er), the keeper of the archives in the Zhou Court, but the Yellow Emperor (Huang Di), who was believed to have lived in China as early as 3,000 B.C. It is known by many ancient historians that the Yellow Emperor's Daoists Shengong and Qigong magical practices were legendary.

At the time of Laozi's birth (in the state of Chu) during the Qin Dynasty (221-206 B.C.), the reigning Emperor Qin Shi Huang was already a strong devotee of Daoist shamanistic magic. By the time Laozi was born, most of the ancient energetic practices had become commingled with the sage's teachings.

The Chinese character Wu translates as "magician, sorcerer, spirit medium, shaman, or doctor." Its ancient character was first recorded during the Shang Dynasty (1600-1028 B.C.). At that time, "Wu" could also be used to describe the magical workings of someone of either sex. The character Wu was sometimes used in such terms as "Wugu" (meaning "sorcery; cast harmful spells"), "Wushen" or "Shenwu" (meaning "wizard; sorcerer"), and "Wuxian" (meaning "immortal shaman").

Figure 1.34. The character "Wu" (Female Shaman)

During the late Zhou Dynasty (1028-221 B.C.), the term "Wu" was used to specify a "female shaman or sorceress;" and the term "Xi" was used to specify a "male shaman or sorcerer." Other sex-differentiated shaman names include the term "Nanwu" for a "male shaman, sorcerer, or wizard;" and the term Nüwu (also Wunü, Wupo, and Wuyu) for a "female shaman; sorceress; or witch"). In ancient China, two characters were eventually used to represent the Wu, one was used for men and the other for women.

- **The Female Wu (Xi):** Before 1,000 B.C., the majority of "Wu" were predominantly female. The ideograph for a female shaman consists of the character "Gong" (work) surrounded by two characters "Ren" (man or person). The upper horizontal stroke can also be translated as "above," or "Heaven;" while the lower horizontal stroke can be translated as "below," or "Earth." A complete translation can therefore be explained as "working to connect the energetic power of the unseen spirits within Heaven and Earth" (Figure 1.34).

The female Wu were directed to perform exorcisms annually, at specific times, while using specific fragrances to wash their bodies. In times of drought, the Wu priestesses (representing the Yin or feminine aspect of the Universal Order, to which clouds and rain belong) performed dances or offered specific prayers at the three tiered altars during the sacrifice for rain. In times of disaster and great calamity in the kingdom, the female Wu were also responsible for entreating the celestial immortals with incantations, wailing, and presenting special offerings, expressing

CHAPTER 1: INTRODUCTION TO CHINESE MEDICINE

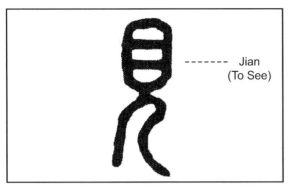

Figure 1.35. The ancient Chinese character "Jian," (the Imperial Seers, Invokers, and Conjurers)

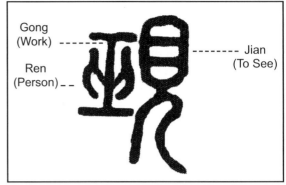

Figure 1.36. The character "Wu" (Male Shaman)

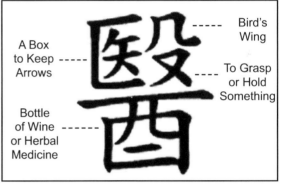

Figure 1.37. The Chinese Character "Yi" (Doctor)

the peoples' grief and distress. Additionally, whenever the emperor's consort paid a visit of condolence, the female Wu would walk before her with the female "Jian" (Figure 1.35). The Jian were magical invokers or conjurers, traditionally known as the Imperial Seers.

- **The Male Wu:** The male ideograph for Wu included the extra character "Jian" (meaning to "see") towards the right side of the ideograph, and depicted clairvoyant "seeing" (Figure 1.36). In ancient China, the male priest represented the Yang or masculine aspect of the Universal Order, to which the source of light, lucidity and brightness belong.

The male Wu's responsibility was to turn his attention towards the sacrifices and to invite spiritual immortals, calling and gathering them from the six directions of Heaven and Earth before the altar. In the winter (when spiritual entities dominate the Earth), the male Wu were responsible for purging and exorcising evil from the imperial halls. In the spring, the male Wu were responsible for calling celestial immortals for the prosperity of agriculture, averting demons or evil, and warding off disease.

Additionally, whenever the emperor paid a visit of condolence, the male Wu would walk before him with the male "Jian" (invokers or conjurers, also known the Imperial Seers). It is important to note, that it was not until the Han Dynasty (206 B.C. - 220 A.D.) that the terminology Wu Jian was later used to denote the combined metaphysical functions of both the Wu and the Jian.

During the later Zhou Dynasty (1028-221 B.C.) the character "Yi" (Doctor of Medicine) was sometimes used or substituted for "Wu" (Magician or Sorcerer) in order to denote specific Clinical Applications. At that time, the ancient Chinese Character for Doctor of Medicine (Yi), originally used the radical "Wu" as its bottom ideograph. Later, the bottom ideograph was substituted for the radical "Jiu" which translates as "a Bottle of Wine," denoting the medical application of special Herbs (Figure 1.37).

The Chinese character for Doctor of Medicine (Yi) is divided into three parts. The top left ideograph translates as, "to treat disease," and depicts a box or quiver containing arrows. Some historians have speculated that the quiver full of

19

arrows was used to perform an ancient type of minor surgery or acupuncture; others speculate that the arrows represented certain spiritual powers and were used to drive off evil influences, as well as heal diseases.

The top right ideograph depicts a bird's wing, and below is the image of a right hand, raised as if "to hold" or "to grasp something." In ancient China, the "White Crane Feather Fan" was traditionally used by Daoist shamans to drive out evil spirits and bring the dead back to life. Together, the image depicts a seat or table and something being held in the right hand to make quick actions. The bottom ideograph "Jiu" translates as "a bottle of wine." Certain historians speculate that the wine was used as an herbal medicine to anesthetize the patient before treatment, or to sterilize a wound.

THE MAGICAL POWERS OF THE WU YI

The ancient shaman-doctors (known as Wu Yi) were believed to possess special magical powers. They relied on their ability to cultivate the fundamental energetic forces of nature for healing, spinning webs of intrigue, secrecy and magic into every aspect of China's ancient culture. By controlling and utilizing Qi, the Wu Yi could communicate with the energetic forces of supernatural beings. Invisible spirits could be contacted, demons could be exorcized, and various diseases could be treated.

These ancient masters of supernatural energy were reported to be able to fly into the sky, journey underground, converse with animals, initiate the dance of power to conjure spiritual entities, control the power of the elements, possess extensive knowledge of herbs, excel in numerous healing arts, and initiate the magical "Dance of Power" (i.e., Star Stepping) in order to conjure spirit entities and control the powers of the various Elements.

Acting as intermediaries, the Wu Yi would utilize magical chants and incantations, herbal formulas, Qi and Shen emission, massage, point stimulation, various elaborate rituals, dancing, and healing prayers in order to initiate control over the Qi of nature and to intercede between their human patients and the supernatural world.

These ancient doctors also utilized the power of the spoken word in conjunction with strong imagination, visualization and powerful affirmation in order to perform their magical medicine. For example, when treating patients, the Wu Yi would often energetically journey into the spiritual realm through prayer and movement in order to diagnose the root cause of the patient's disease.

During the Shang Dynasty (1600 - 1028 B.C.), the Wu Yi rose to prominence, holding high social positions as oracles, sages, and judges. Oracle records inscribed on the back of tortoise shells and the leg bones of oxen explained how ancient kings and emperors of the Shang dynasty invoked the power of Heaven before embarking on journeys, hunting, building projects, royal burials and warfare. The oracle bones made a clear distinction between the "Spirits of Heaven" who control the weather, the "Spirits of Earth" who control nature, and the "Immortal Spirits" or "Demons" of the afterlife who control illness and the suffering of humanity.

Evidence from the oracle records suggests that these powerful Wu Yi were influential in counseling kings and emperors, who were themselves reluctant to initiate any military action without the advice of these powerful spiritual guides. Since the emperors were known as the "Sons of Heaven," and the Wu Yi were the standing messengers between the mysterious realms of Heaven and Earth, the Wu Yi wielded enormous social and political power. Many of the fundamental notions about the origin and treatment of disease in Traditional Chinese Medicine stemmed from the spiritual insights gathered by the Wu Yi who worked as advisers, diviners and healers.

OFFICIAL DUTIES OF THE WU YI

During the Zhou Dynasty (1028-221 B.C.), the special duties of the Wu Yi were specifically detailed, and any failure to perform an assigned task was often punishable by death. The six primary duties of the Wu Yi were as follows: Conjuring Spirits and Removing Malevolent Spirits, Spirit Travel and Dream Interpretation, Reading Omens, Rainmaking, Healing, and Celestial Divination (Figure 1.38):

CHAPTER 1: INTRODUCTION TO CHINESE MEDICINE

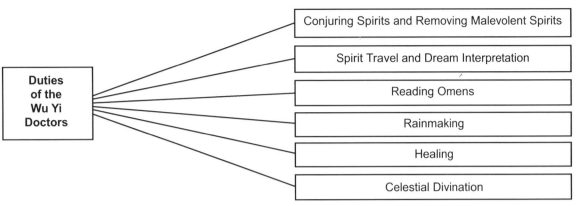

Figure 1.38. The Six Primary Duties of the Wu Yi Doctors

1. **Conjuring Spirits and Removing Malevolent Spirits:** The ancient Chinese believed that spirit beings could be summoned, controlled and dispatched to carry out tasks; or when needed, a spirit could be expelled by a qualified individual such as a Wu Yi. These energetic skills required the Wu Yi to either invite spiritual deities and immortals into the mortal realm to ask for knowledge, or to ask that they temporarily stay in the mortal realm to perform some service (i.e., as a protector). Additionally, the Wu Yi were sometimes summoned to remove malevolent spirits (Figure 1.39).

- **Conjuring Spiritual Deities and Immortals:** To connect with the spirit world, the Wu Yi would perform an Evocation, an Invocation, or an Necromancy:

    An Evocation: An evocation is the skill of conjuring a spiritual entity from another plane of existence, causing it to manifest as a visible entity in either the energetic plane or the physical plane. In an Evocation, the spirit entities were brought into the presence of the Wu Yi (never within his body), where they could be observed and communicated with. The spirit entities summoned in an evocation were not dead (Necromancy), but existed within other spiritual dimensions.

Figure 1.39. Spirit beings could be summoned, controlled, ordered, and dispatched by the Wu Yi.

VOLUME 1, SECTION 1: FOUNDATIONS OF CHINESE ENERGETIC MEDICINE

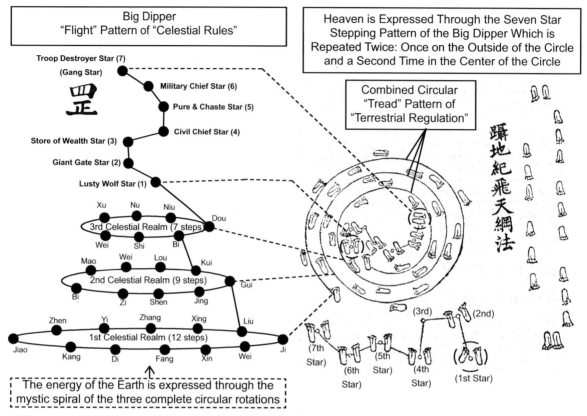

Figure 1.40. The "Steps of Yu," is used for invocation. This three dimensional pattern was originally used to demonstrate the energetic and spiritual union of Heaven and Earth. It magically reveals the combined circular "Tread" pattern of "Terrestrial Regulation" and the Big Dipper "Flight" pattern into the "Celestial Realm."

Invocation: An invocation occurs by allowing a benign spirit entity to inhabit his own body and speak through the Wu Yi. The power and prestige of the Wu Yi largely depended on the number of spirits he could voluntarily incarnate and control within his own body. This was sometimes achieved through the aide of magical songs, incantations, dances, drumming, and psychedelic herbs and mushrooms. Specific dances and Star Stepping (Figure 1.40) were commonly performed before entering into a trance to allow a spirit entity to enter the Wu Yi's body. Sometimes sand, flower, or ash writing divination was employed while the Wu Yi was in this trance state. "Channeling" is but one example of an invocation used to bring a foreign intelligence into the body.

Necromancy: Necromancy is the skill of calling forth spirits of the dead for revealing past, present and future events. A "medium" is an example of an individual skilled in contacting the dead.

- **Removing Malevolent Spirits:** The removal of spirit entities traditionally required the use of powerful Incantations (Zhou Yu), esoteric Hand Seals (Shou Jue), Magical Talismans (Fu Zhou). Other magical implements, such as the Seven-Star Sword, Holy Water, Red Cord, fire, incense, and "Bagua Mirrors" were also used to combat destructive spiritual forces (Figure 1.41).

Sometimes after a malevolent spirit had been bound, it was sealed within a special container (i.e. a magical double-gourd), transported, and then imprisoned within a secluded cave. The cave was then magically sealed and a "talisman of containment" was written and placed at the entrance of the cave.

2. **Spirit Travel and Dream Interpretation:** This energetic skill required the Wu Yi to transcend his normal conscious perceptions and senses, in order to observe and communicate with the spirit world. This was known in ancient times as having "Yin eyes." Individuals who possessed "Yin eyes" were able to see and talk to the spirits of the dead. The Wu Yi was occasionally required to administer "soul retrieval" to recover the life-force or soul qualities of an individual who had been damaged, lost, stolen, or was otherwise trapped within the Spirit World.

- The Wu Yi was required to spirit travel into the celestial realms of the cosmos, and to commune with the deities and immortals dwelling within the constellations. Other times, the Wu Yi's journey into the spirit world required him to travel underground and enter into the underworld, in order to rescue souls of the dead who had been abducted by malevolent spirits. Specific rites were performed to free the victim from the negative influences that had ensnared them, and to support and guide them back through the "Celestial Gate of Life."

- In ancient China, dreams were considered the carriers of omens, and the Daoist shamanic doctor was considered a "dream master" who could not only interpret these subconscious messages (akin to modern psychology), but could also travel into the dream world (lucid dreaming) to communicate with the spirit realm. When a Wu Yi consulted a tortoise shell about a particular dream, it had to be interpreted first thing in the morning or by the next evening (after sundown the divination had passed beyond the boundaries of the ritual).

The ancient Chinese also understood the principle of antithetical (reverse) dream interpretation, in which the true meaning of an individual's dream is sometimes just the opposite of what the images would normally suggest. This was known as "the dream life inverting the waking life."

3. **Reading Omens:** This special skill required

Figure 1.41. A Wu Yi removing a malevolent spirit

the Wu Yi to observe and interpret the changes occuring within the Earth (Feng Shui), and predict whether the courses of events were auspicious or destructive. The ancient Chinese believed that one's destiny could be revealed in omens and Auguries:

- **Omens:** An omen was seen as extremely meaningful, because it was specifically arranged for an individual by "higher" forces, and because everything within the cosmos (the energetic natures of Heaven, Earth and Man) was influenced through the Dao. It was also believed that spirits communicated through signs and symbols encountered in daily life.

The skill of reading omens set the foundation for divination in ancient China, thereby establishing an interest in the study of the *Yi-Jing* (Book of Changes), and Yarrow Stick Divination (Figure 1.42). The most common questions requiring the Wu Yi's omen reading skills involved matters of sacrifice, war, hunting, trips and future weather conditions.

- **Augury:** An Augury is an ancient practice that observes a particular energetic pattern at a precise moment in time, revealing the deeper nature of the universe and its manifest design. It is the skill of reading divinations from auspicious events or omens and interpreting these energetic patterns in the context of human destiny.

Auguries were used in the form of the examination of tea leaves and oracle bones (heating tortoise shells or ox shoulders), and the examination of celestial changes, cloud formations, weather conditions, sounds of water, and dreams.

- **Tortoise Shell Divination:** Tortoise shells were commonly used as tools of divination (Figure 1.43). It was believed that the tortoise was an ordained animal, capable of acting as an oracle. The top of the tortoise shell is round, representing Heaven; the bottom of the tortoise shell is square and flat, representing Earth. Together, both parts of the tortoise shell represent a microcosm of life as a whole. For use in omen reading, the tortoise shells were heated until they cracked. Each of the cracks were then interpreted by the Wu Yi according to the trigram patterns recorded in the Yi-Jing.

The ancient Chinese used four primary types of divination for revealing future events. These included the study of the energetic impressions created within the subtle and sometimes dynamic manifestations of the four primary powers of the Prenatal Bagua (the Qian, Kun, Li, and Kan Trigrams), described as follows (Figure 1.44):

- **Qian (Heavens) Trigram - Aeromancy:** This is the Study of the energy of the Winds, and the Qi of Heaven. This special type of divination reveals the future according to the energetic motion or impressions created within the air and wind. This study includes the observation of sudden changes occurring within the directions of the wind, mist, and cloud formations.

Clouds were considered highly significant when they appeared near the Sun or Moon, or in the shape of halos. Also noted were clouds bursting open, clouds displaying the formation of armies, dense clouds that covered the sky without shedding a drop of rain, as well as specific visions created within mist (fog) and clouds.

Figure 1.42. In ancient China, a Wu Yi was skilled in the art of reading Omens using Yarrow Sticks; which were commonly used as Oracles. Fifty Yarrow Stems were laid out according to the correspondences of Heaven, Earth, and Man. The Odd (Yang) and Even (Yin) residues of whole or broken stems, were then formed into Trigrams; and subsequently expanded into the specific Hexagrams of the Yi-Jing.

Figure 1.43. In ancient China, Tortoise Shells were traditionally used as an Augury for Divination; each crack represented a specific type of energetic change, or an approaching form of Destiny.

Careful attention was placed on the formation, movement and colors of mist and dew appearing at sunrise and sunset. Certain types of dew were considered very auspicious and were sometimes called "sweet dew," "celestial wine," or "honey dew" because they always represented luxurious growth and abundance.

Rainbows were considered to be like the wind, composed of both Yang and Yin, and an excellent means of investigating the will of the Dao. Their colors and times of appearance were intensely studied. Pale rainbows, for example, were always considered unfavorable omens.

The energetic skill used in performing Qian Trigram Divination also required the Wu Yi to observe and decipher the energetic changes in Heaven. The Wu Yi were believed to possess the ability to predict the course of events (whether they were auspicious or destructive), as well as to predict the course of a disease.

- **Kun (Earth) Trigram - Geomancy:** This is the study of the energy of the Earth. This special type of divination reveals the future according to both the energetic motion or impressions created within the Earth. This study includes the observation of sudden changes occurring within the ground, trembling noises, swelling and ground elevation, fissures, landslides, pits and other impressions suddenly created. Earthquakes generally revealed impending bloodshed, the destruction of crops, famine, plague and other evils, depending on the types of buildings that were destroyed and other circumstances (structures of tombs moving, etc.).

- **Li (Fire) Trigram - Pyromancy:** This is the study of the energy of Fire. This special type of divination reveals the future according to the energetic motion or impressions created within fire. This study includes the observation of sudden changes occurring within the direction of the fire or its smoke, specific sounds, colors, motions or patterns created within the fire or from its ashes, and specific visions created within the flames.

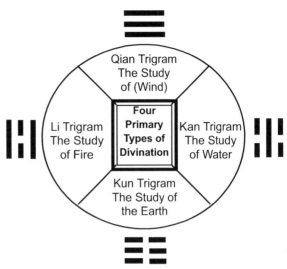

Figure 1.44. The ancient Chinese used four primary types of divinations for revealing future events.

- **Kan (Water) Trigram - Hydromancy:** This is the study of the energy of Water. This special type of divination reveals the future of things according to the energetic motion or impressions created within water. This study includes the observation of sudden changes occurring within the direction of the water, aquatic ebbing and flowing, increases and depressions, colors and specific visions created within water. If, for example, a brook or well suddenly dried up or changed its water color (especially if it became as red as blood or so foul that fish died), it was considered a particularly ill omen. However, if normally unclean water should suddenly become clear and clean, it was considered an auspicious omen. Additionally, gales, typhoons, and excessive rainfall that destroyed crops and caused floods were all considered ill omens.

4. **Rainmaking:** This energetic skill required the Wu Yi to summon and control the foundational powers within the universe. By embodying the ancient magical powers of the Bagua (Figure 1.45), the Wu Yi could summon and control the Four Powers of Heaven: Qian (Sky and Clouds), Dui (Lake, Mist, and Rain), Li (Fire), and Zhen (Thunder); and the Four Powers of Earth: Kun (Earth and Soil), Gen (Mountains), Kan (Water), and Xun (Wind).

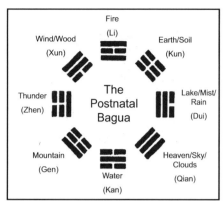

Figure 1.45. The Eight Powers of the Bagua Trigrams

One important power needed to ensure the kingdom's survival was the ability to create rain, avoiding drought and famine. The ancient Chinese believed that clouds and mist (fog) float between Heaven and Earth, and are the vapor of the Dao. They therefore saw clouds, mist and dew as containing the "Essence of the Primordial Vapor of the Dao," and sought to join with the subtle energy of the Dao, in order to summon or create rain.

One example of the Wu Yi's ability to control Nature was the skill of bringing rain, brought about in one of two ways: "Direct Influence" or "Indirect Influence," which are described as follows:

- **Direct Influence:** In the first approach, the "Elements" of the clouds and rain were summoned directly. A very powerful Wu Yi could call down thunder, rain, or even snow, and create rain clouds out of a clear sky. A less powerful Wu Yi had to extend his spirit into the sky and "call" the clouds and rain from a nearby area. Therefore, Direct Influence pertains to rain that was brought about through the control and manipulation of the natural forces of Heavenly Qi (i.e., controlling wind and clouds). The ability to have Direct Influence over the wind and clouds was proportional to the amount of cultivated Ling Qi (Spiritual Energy) and Ling Shen (Spiritual Mind) that the Wu Yi possessed. For example, if the Wu Yi's cultivated spiritual energy was powerful, he could extend his energy into the Heavens (sky), and begin to create/manifest rain clouds wherever he desired; if however, the Wu Yi's cultivated Spiritual Energy was only moderate, he would have to extend his spirit into the sky, locate the rain clouds, and use the wind to pull the rain clouds into the needed area.

Figure 1.46. The Wu Yi were known for their abilities to perform powerful magical healing.

- **Indirect Influence:** In the second approach, the Wu Yi would petition a Dragon God, Celestial Immortal, or Spirit Deity, asking and "persuading" the celestial powers to send rain. Therefore, Indirect Influence pertains to rain that was brought about through supplication. Having found favor with the Dao, and the Heavenly Spirits, the Wu Yi would set up an altar, offer sacrifices, and request a Celestial Spirit to be sanctioned to bring rain per the request of the people.

5. **Healing:** This energetic skill required the Wu Yi to treat and cure diseases (Figure 1.46). Healing was divided into three main approaches: Healing the Body, Healing the Energy, and Healing the Spirit.

- **Healing the Physical Body:** This energetic skill required the Wu Yi to use various types of Herbal Medicine, Medical Qigong, Acupuncture, Massage and Dietetics.

For the Wu Yi, herbs were associated with one of the Five Element energies, and their spiritual natures. The qualities of the herbs' special energies and spiritual natures were assimilated through drinking infusions in teas, soups, or wines; eating the herbs in either raw or cooked form; or by burning them and inhaling the smoke.

- **Healing the Energy Body:** This energetic skill required the Wu Yi to use special heat, sound, and color, in order to stimulate the patient's Energy Body.
- **Healing the Spiritual Body:** This energetic skill required the Wu Yi to use various types of magical rituals to access the patient's spiritual state. This special type of training traditionally required a basic understanding of psychological and emotional counseling skills, usually based on the patient's culture and spiritual belief system.

The ancient Chinese believed that occasionally illness was a result of malevolent spirits invading the body. In some instances black sorcerers and magicians were hired to harm people by inflicting illness. To combat such unethical energetic practices, the Wu Yi would use powerful counter-incantations, hand seals, and talismans.

It is also believed that fragments of the oracle Bones were sometimes shaped into needles and used to perform acupuncture for the treatment of demonic possession. This was traditionally accomplished by stimulating the "Thirteen Ghost Points," which are currently still used in Acupuncture Clinics for the treatment of mental illness.

6. **Celestial Divination:** This special skill required the Wu Yi to observe and decipher the energetic changes occuring within the Heavens (Sky). The ancient Chinese believed that peace and prosperity lay in following the "Will of Heaven," and that the phenomena occurring within the macrocosm of Heaven had parallels occurring within the microcosm of Man. By studying the astrological patterns of the night sky, it is said that the Wu Yi possessed the ability to predict the various courses of events, and whether they were auspicious or destructive (Astrology of Prediction), or predict the course of a disease (Astrology of Diagnosis).

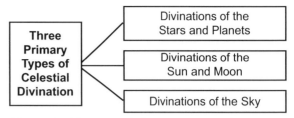

Figure 1.47. The ancient Chinese used three primary types of celestial divinations for revealing future events.

Figure 1.48. A Thunder and Lightning Storm

The official observation of nature was a statutory obligation in ancient China. Records gathered during the Han Dynasty (206 B.C.-220 A.D.) and mentioned in the *Shu King* (Canon of History), categorize celestial divination into three primary observations: divinations of the sky, divinations of the sun and moon, and divinations of the stars and planets (Figure 1.47). These three types of celestial divinations are described as follows:

- **Divinations of the Sky:** In order to derive messages from the sky, the Wu Yi studied strange or sudden changes occurring within the sky, such as changes in sky color, blood colored streams of light, voices resounding in the wind or air, and the appearance of thunder and lightning.

Thunder was always considered to be an auspicious phenomenon, unless it occurred without rain. Lightning (called the "Fire of Heaven"), was considered to be an instrument of the Dao, and was commonly believed to strike demons, evil men, and other objects (Figure 1.48).

The Wu Yi also believed that hail was produced when Yang and Yin collided. Therefore, hail was thought to be an inauspicious omen.

Figure 1.49. Cloud formations and haloes used to cast prophecies

The predictions of the type of evil omen, that was derived from the hail, differed according to the specific season in which it fell.

- **Divinations of the Sun and Moon:** In order to derive messages from the Sun and Moon, the Wu Yi studied energetic changes occurring during the times of an eclipse, the appearance of strange or sudden spots or protuberances on the Sun or Moon, specific colors of the haloes or circles around the Moon, and strange colorations surrounding these illuminations (Figure 1.49). According to the *Yuyang Qihun Qinji (Atmospheric Agents Causing Sunshine and Rain)*, the climatic changes revealed in the celestial movements, form and color of the clouds, force and direction of the winds, reveal the presence of auspicious times or inauspicious calamities.
- **Divinations of the Stars and Planets:** In order to derive messages from the stars and planets, the ancient Wu Yi studied changes in the aspects and brightness of the stars and planets, their conjunctions with the Sun and Moon, their position in the Heavens at the times of an eclipse, and circles occurring around the stars. Also important were subtle Colors and vibrations (such as Musical Tunes and other sounds) that were emitted by the Five Planets (Figure 1.50), and 28 Star Constellations. The movements of Comets through the Constellations, Falling Stars, and Meteor Showers were also important.

Figure 1.50. A Wu Yi worshipping "The Spirits of the Fives Planets" (Mercury, Venus, Mars, Jupiter and Saturn)

CHAPTER 1: INTRODUCTION TO CHINESE MEDICINE

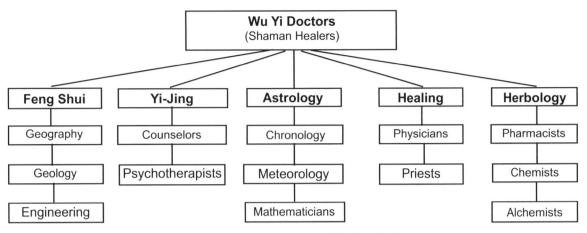

Figure 1.51. The Progression of Ancient Medicine

THE EVOLUTION OF CHINESE MEDICINE

As the Chinese civilization continued to expand, the theories and practice of medicine became more refined, formalized and recorded. The primary structure of Chinese Medicine was organized to reflect the energetic harmony and influential interactions between the energies of Heaven, Earth, and Man. This evolution transformed the healing arts developed by the Wu Yi into the various intellectual sciences and artisan skills. No longer considered primitive magical sorcerers, the Wu Yi became established in the new scientific world as Alchemists, Astronomers, Chemists, Physicians, Pharmacists, Counselors, Engineers, Mathematicians, etc. (Figure 1.51).

QIGONG OF THE IMPERIAL COLLEGE

Throughout China's vast medical history, therapeutic categories and specialties were classified into separate divisions or medical departments, also known as "Classes of Mastery" (Figure 1.52). The following is a brief synopsis of eight major changes occurring within the various medical departments of China's Imperial Colleges (Figure 1.53):

1. **Zhou Dynasty (1028-221 B.C.):** This was the first Imperial Dynasty to organize clinical medicine into separate divisions or medical departments.
2. **Northern Wei Dynasty of the Six Dynasties Period (386 A.D.-533 A.D.):** The Imperial Medical Colleges maintained four depart-

Figure 1.52. The Imperial Medical College

ments: Internal and External Medicine (including Surgery, Traumatology, Dermatology and Antiseptic Techniques); Acupuncture and Moxibustion; Massage and Tissue Manipulation; and Demonology.
3. **Tang Dynasty (618-907 A.D.):** The Imperial Medical Colleges maintained four departments: Medicine (Herbs and Diet); Acupuncture and Moxibustion; Massage and Tissue Manipulation; and Charms and Incantations.
4. **Song Dynasty (960-1279 A.D.):** The Imperial Medical Colleges maintained nine departments: Internal Medicine; War Wounds; Ophthalmology; Pediatrics; Obstetrics and Wind Diseases (including stroke); Fractures, Abscesses and Ulcers; Diseases of the Mouth,

VOLUME 1, SECTION 1: FOUNDATIONS OF CHINESE ENERGETIC MEDICINE

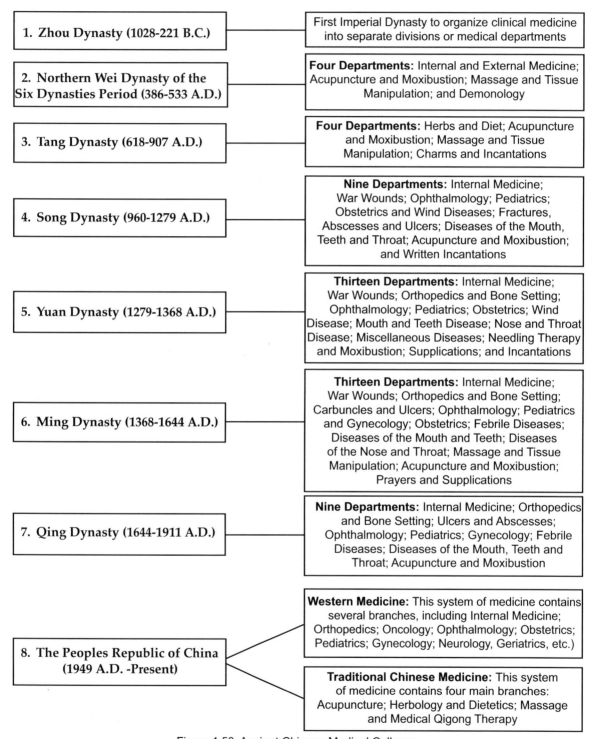

Figure 1.53. Ancient Chinese Medical Colleges

Teeth and Throat; Acupuncture and Moxibustion; and Written Incantations.
5. **Yuan Dynasty (1279-1368 A.D.):** The Imperial Medical Colleges maintained thirteen departments: Internal Medicine; War Wounds; Orthopedics and Bone Setting; Ophthalmology; Pediatrics; Obstetrics; Wind Diseases (including stroke); Diseases of the Mouth and Teeth; Diseases of the Nose and Throat; Miscellaneous Diseases; Acupuncture and Moxibustion; Prayers and Supplications; and Incantations.
6. **Ming Dynasty (1368-1644 A.D.):** The Imperial Medical Colleges maintained thirteen departments: Internal Medicine; War Wounds; Orthopedics and Bone Setting; Carbuncles and Ulcers; Ophthalmology; Pediatrics and Gynecology; Obstetrics; Febrile Diseases; Diseases of the Mouth and Teeth; Diseases of the Nose and Throat; Massage and Tissue Manipulation; Acupuncture and Moxibustion; Prayers and Supplications.
7. **Qing Dynasty (1644-1911 A.D.):** The Imperial Medical Colleges maintained nine departments: Internal Medicine; Orthopedics and Bone Setting; Ulcers and Abscesses; Ophthalmology; Pediatrics; Gynecology; Febrile Diseases; Diseases of the Mouth, Teeth and Throat; Acupuncture and Moxibustion.
8. **The Peoples Republic of China (1949 A.D.-Present):** Medical Colleges are now divided into two main tracks, each containing several departments: Western Medicine and Traditional Chinese Medicine, briefly described as follows:
- **Western Medicine:** This system of medicine contains several branches, including Internal Medicine; Orthopedics; Oncology; Ophthalmology; Obstetrics; Pediatrics; Gynecology; Neurology, Geriatrics, etc.
- **Traditional Chinese Medicine:** This system of medicine contains four main branches: Acupuncture (including Needling, Cupping, Bloodletting, Moxa Burning, and Magnet Healing); Herbology and Dietetics (including Nutritional Education; Teas and Soups; Tinctures and Wines; Oils, Balms, and Liniments; and Compresses, Powders, and Pills); Massage Therapy (including Scraping Therapy,

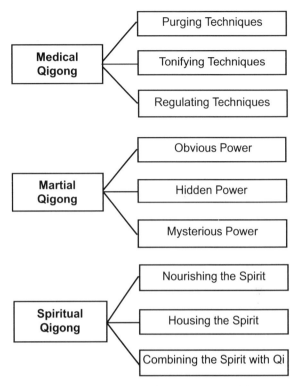

Figure 1.54. The Three Different Schools of Qigong

Tissue Manipulation and Traumatology, Bone Setting, Visceral Manipulation and Channel Point Therapy); and Medical Qigong Therapy (including Qi Emission Therapy, Prescription Exercises and Meditations, Qigong Massage, Sound Therapy, and Invisible Needle Therapy).

THREE MAIN SCHOOLS OF QIGONG

The term "Qigong" first appeared in the Jin Dynasty (265-420 A.D.) in a Daoist text entitled *"Records of the Clear Mirror of Religion"* by Xu Xun. Qi means "life-force energy" and Gong means "skill." Qigong is therefore the skillful practice of applying life-force energy.

In modern China, Qigong practice is divided into three main schools: Medical, Martial, and Spiritual. The three schools are all based on the same philosophical system and share many of the same meditations and techniques. They differ primarily in their initial focus and application. Students choose a specific school based on how they want to apply their Qigong training (Figure 1.54).

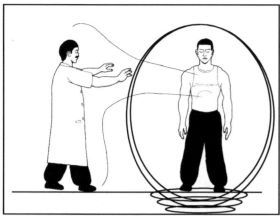

Figure 1.55. Medical Qigong Schools Focus on Purgation, Tonification and Regulation.

Figure 1.56. Martial Qigong Schools Focus on Building Speed, Endurance, Strength and Power.

Qigong training involves all of the individual's physical senses. Concentration is focused on the development of the individual's faculties of imagination, visualization, hearing, smelling, tasting, and touching, in addition to breathing, muscle relaxation and proper posture. Massage and movement are also used to develop and control the body's intrinsic energy. Studying Qigong requires not only comprehending the immeasurable wisdom gathered for Medical, Martial, or Spiritual development, but also studying the ancient Chinese culture inherent within these systems.

Briefly, each Qigong school focuses on one of the following specialties:

1. **The Medical Qigong Schools:** These schools train doctors and healers in special Qigong Therapies, used for health maintenance and longevity, disease prevention, and the diagnosis and treatment of diseases and disorders (Figure 1.55). The three primary modalities of Medical Qigong Therapy are described as follows:
   - **Purging Techniques:** Used to detoxify the body through the removal of pathogens
   - **Tonifying Techniques:** Used to strengthen the internal organs and organ systems, by adding to and increasing the body's Qi
   - **Regulating Techniques:** Used to balance the body's internal organs and organ systems, by regulating the Essence (Jing), Energy (Qi) and Spirit (Shen) contained within the tissues
2. **The Martial Qigong Schools:** These schools train warriors in specific strength, power, speed and endurance techniques needed for performing martial arts combat (Figure 1.56). The three primary stages of Martial Qigong applications include training Ming Jing (Obvious Power), An Jing (Hidden Power) and Hua Jing (Transforming Power), described as follows:
   - **Clear or Obvious Power (Ming Jing):** These specific techniques emphasize the training and conditioning of the muscles, strengthening the bone structure, and increasing the individual's overall stamina and root. This stage also includes such techniques as conditioning the body (arms, hands, legs, torso and head) to strengthen and toughen the tissues.
   - **Hidden or Secret Power (An Jing):** These specific techniques emphasize stretching and twisting the tendons and ligaments (known as Reeling and Pulling the Silk) to cultivate resonant vibration within the body for striking and issuing power.
   - **Changing or Transforming Power (Hua Jing):** These specific techniques emphasize the training and conditioning of the individual's mind and spirit. The focus in Hua Jing training is placed on acquiring and developing the Yi (imagination and intention) and Zhi (will power), needed to energetically project and utilize the power of the Shen (Spirit).
3. **The Spiritual Qigong Schools:** These schools train priests who seek spiritual transformation and enlightenment (known as Shen Ming or

Figure 1.57. Spiritual Qigong Schools Focus on Spiritual Transformation and Enlightenment.

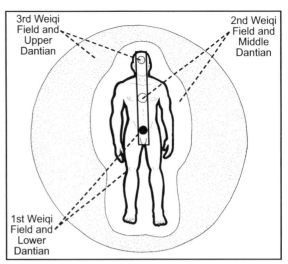

Figure 1.58. The Three External Wei Qi Fields

Spiritual Brightness). In China, the three primary spiritual schools, Daoism, Buddhism, and Confucianism, each have their own unique energetic approaches and Shengong (Spirit Skill) Techniques. These special techniques include meditations for "awakening" and "releasing," the disciple's Yuan Shen (Original Spirit). This is accomplished by cultivating the internal energy of the Prenatal Wujing Shen (i.e., the Original Virtues of the Five Essence Spirits).

When the Original Spirit (Yuan Shen) is fully developed, the disciple will acquire certain extraordinary powers and abilities, such as spirit travel and soul travel. The goal, is to achieve transformation and a state of enlightenment, and the student must take care not to be led astray by the glamor of extra powers. The three primary techniques of Spiritual Qigong training include the following (Figure 1.57):

- **Nourishing the Spirit (Shen):** These specific techniques emphasize strengthening and refining the power of the individual's Yuan Shen.
- **Housing the Shen:** These specific techniques emphasize disciplining the thoughts and emotions. This helps to relax and tranquilize the individual's Yuan Shen, and to increase receptivity to divine energy and guidance.
- **Combining the Shen with the Qi:** These specific techniques emphasize the coordination of the breath and intention for directing the Yuan Shen to guide the body's life-force energy.

THE BODY'S THREE WEI QI FIELDS

All living tissues generate an energetic field. In Medical Qigong Therapy, the body's external field of energy is called Wei Qi (pronounced "whey chee"), which translates as "protective/defensive energy." The observation and energetic manifestation of the body's Wei Qi field in Medical Qigong Therapy is slightly different than that of Traditional Chinese Medicine (T.C.M.). In classical T.C.M. texts, the Wei Qi field is seen to be limited to about an inch from the surface of the body, circulating within the tissues of the skin, tendons, and muscles. In Medical Qigong Therapy, however, the external Wei Qi field also includes the three layers of the body's subtle energy fields (Figure 1.58). These three Wei Qi fields originate from the center core (Taiji Pole) of the body. The energy of each of the internal organs radiate outside the body through the external tissues, and are reflected within these three energy fields, commonly seen as "auras."

The body's Lower Dantian is responsible for sustaining the defensive power of the first Wei Qi field. The Middle Dantian is responsible for sustaining the various colors and light images seen within the second Wei Qi field. The Upper Dantian is responsible for sustaining the thoughts and perceptions experienced within the third Wei Qi field (see Chapter 5). The three Wei Qi fields completely surround and protect the body's tissues from the external invasion of pathogens while constantly communicating and interacting with the subtle universal and environmental energetic fields.

The body's Wei Qi fields can be strengthened through the proper intake of food, air, drink, sleep, prayer and meditation. Consequently, the Wei Qi field will also diminish and weaken due to an insufficient intake of food, air, drink, sleep, prayer and meditation. In the clinic, in order to protect themselves, Medical Qigong doctors will occasionally visualize specific colors, lights and sounds in order to fortify their Wei Qi field.

Both internal and external pathogenic factors affect the structural formation of the Wei Qi. Internal pathogenic factors include suppressed emotional influences such as anger and grief from emotional traumas. External pathogenic factors include exposure to adverse environmental influences, especially when they are extreme (such as Cold, Damp, Dry, Heat, Fire, or Wind). Physical traumas can also affect the Wei Qi field.

Any negative interchange affects the Wei Qi by literally creating holes within the matrix of the individual's external energetic fields. Without proper attention, these holes leave the body vulnerable to invasion, and disease can begin to take root. When strong emotions become trapped and suppressed within the body's tissues, they become a form of toxic energy. As these unprocessed emotional stagnations continue to block the natural flow of Qi, they begin to create stagnant pools of toxic energy within the body's tissues.

Medical Qigong Therapy consists of specific techniques that use the knowledge of the body's internal and external energy fields to purge, tonify, and balance these energies. Medical Qigong Therapy offers patients a safe and effective way to rid themselves of toxic pathogens and years of painful emotions that can otherwise cause mental and physical illness. This special healing therapy combines breathing techniques with movement, creative visualization, and spiritual intention. All of these techniques are used in order to improve the patient's health and personal power. It also enables the patients to reclaim control over their own lives.

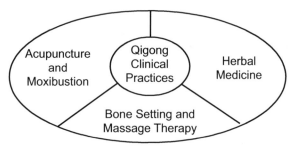

Figure 1.59. Qigong as a Foundation for all Chinese Clinical Practices.

MEDICAL QIGONG TRAINING IN CHINA

According to Professor Zhou Qianchuan, Qigong master and doctor of Traditional Chinese Medicine, all of the most famous Chinese doctors of Acupuncture and Moxibustion, Herbal Medicine, Bone Setting and Massage Therapy either practiced Qigong themselves or incorporated Qigong Therapy into their clinical practices (Figure 1.59).

There were numerous colleges of Traditional Chinese Medicine throughout China that focused on utilizing Medical Qigong Therapy (i.e., up until the year 1999). The majority of these schools supported the scientific study and expansion of Medical Qigong clinical applications along with Traditional Chinese Medicine treatments.

All of the major Traditional Chinese Medical colleges in China offered comprehensive, government-sponsored, three-year programs in Medical Qigong Therapy. These programs also included classes, labs, and seminars on Traditional Chinese Medical theory. The various courses included the "Foundations of Chinese Medicine for Internal Diseases" according to the *Huangdi Neijing (Yellow Emperor's Inner Canon)*: *Ling Shu (Magical Pivot)* and *Su Wen* (Essential Questions), and the *Nanjing (Canon of Perplexities)*. The Medical Qigong classes also included Energetic Anatomy and Physiology, Energetic Diagnosis and Symptomatology, Energetic Psychology, Qigong Pathology, Medical Qigong Therapy, as well as a survey of other related medical modalities. These other related modalities included Herbal Medicine, Acupuncture Therapy, and Chinese Massage. Classes of Western Anatomy and Physiology, Western Internal Diseases, and Health and Recovery were also required (Figure 1.60).

CHAPTER 1: INTRODUCTION TO CHINESE MEDICINE

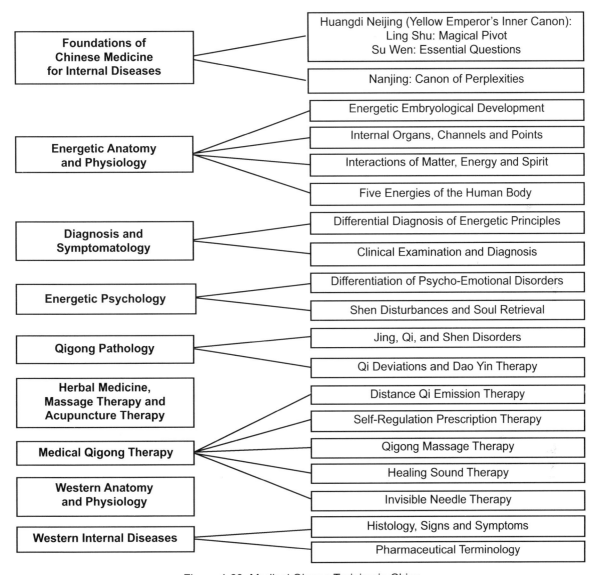

Figure 1.60. Medical Qigong Training in China

As part of the certification program, three to five training hours per day were required in addition to the standard six-day-a-week classroom curriculum. Course content, personal mastery of energy extension, and diagnostic techniques were rigorously tested each week. Upon completing the required courses and passing the final exams, the student received a graduate certificate.

Next, a six-month to one-year internship was required at a program-affiliated hospital or clinic. Upon successful completion of this internship, the intern was licensed by the People's Republic of China's Ministry of Health, as a Doctor of Traditional Chinese Medicine, specializing in Medical Qigong Therapy.

Each internship program was assigned a separate wing in select Chinese hospitals. Both inpatient and outpatient facilities were available to the public. Each wing had specific approaches to healing a patient, and its own unique set of ground rules for diagnosis and treatment.

FIVE CLINICAL POSTS OF CHINESE MEDICINE

After graduating from a local Medical University, a student can progress through five separate positions of Clinical Rank. These five distinct levels represent the clinical "pecking order" within each branch of Traditional Chinese Medicine in China today. The five distinct clinical positions are described as follows:

- **Intern Doctor:** The first position is that of an "Interning Doctor," whereby the newly graduated intern is responsible for refining his or her treatment skills under the strict guidance of a qualified, seasoned doctor.
- **Doctor:** The second position is that of a "Doctor," who is responsible for the treatment of all clinic patients. The doctor positions are generally filled by T.C.M. Medical College graduates who have spent a minimum of three years in clinical internship and practice.
- **Doctor in Charge (Clinic Director):** The next level is called a "Clinic Director" or "Doctor In-Charge," and denotes a senior position within the clinic. The Doctor In-Charge is responsible for the supervision of all the doctors and the interns. This position is usually obtained only after spending a minimum of five years in the hospital as an active clinical doctor.
- **Vice-Chief Doctor (Associate Professor):** The next position is that of a "Vice-Chief Doctor" or "Associate Professor," who has the responsibility of overseeing the Doctors In-Charge, as well as teaching, treating, and training other doctors. This position is usually obtained after spending a minimum of five to six years in the clinic as a Doctor In-Charge.
- **Chief Doctor (Professor):** The highest position in the hospital is called a "Chief Doctor," or "Professor." This position is responsible for overseeing the Vice-Chief Doctors, as well as publishing researched studies in order to pass on clinical knowledge to future generations. This position is usually obtained after a minimum of five to six years as a Vice-Chief Doctor and publishing several researched clinical records.

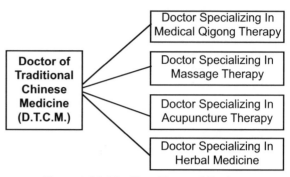

Figure 1.61. The Four Types of Doctors in Traditional Chinese Medicine

The licensing is reviewed and issued by the People's Republic of China's Ministry of Health. The doctor's skills are tested through oral, written, and practical examinations and a license is issued accordingly. In China, currently there are four divisions of training available for a Doctor of Traditional Chinese Medicine (D.T.C.M.). These four divisions are described as follows (Figure 1.61).

1. **Doctor of Acupuncture Therapy:** This doctor specializes in the five main modalities of Chinese Acupuncture: Needle Insertion, Cupping, Bloodletting, Moxa Burning, and Magnet Healing.
2. **Doctor of Herbal Medicine:** This doctor specializes in the five main modalities of Chinese Herbology: Nutritional Education; Formulating and Prescribing Teas and Soups; Tinctures and Wines; Oils, Balms, and Liniments; and Compresses, Powders and Pills.
3. **Doctor of Massage Therapy (D.M.T.):** This doctor specializes in the five main modalities of Chinese Massage and Tissue Alignment: Jie Gu-Bone Setting, Tui Na-Muscle Setting, Gua Sha-Tissue Scraping, An Mo-Visceral Manipulation, and Jing Point Therapy -Channel Point Manipulation.
4. **Doctor of Medical Qigong Therapy (D.M.Q.):** This doctor specializes in the five main modalities of Chinese Medical Qigong: Distance Qi Emission Therapy, Self-Regulation Prescription Therapy, Qigong Massage Therapy, Healing Sound Therapy, and Invisible Needle Therapy.

MEDICAL QIGONG EXAMINATION AND CLINICAL QUALIFICATIONS IN CHINA

At one time, there existed numerous Medical Qigong Colleges throughout China within various Traditional Chinese Medical Universities. Upon completing academic and clinical qualifications, Medical Qigong students had to pass five proficiency examinations before being allowed to graduate. After graduation, the students then entered specific Traditional Chinese Medical hospitals to complete their clinical internship for their doctorate.

The following five Medical Qigong Proficiency Examinations were used to determine the students' energetic potential. They were included in the final exams that each student was required to pass at the Hai Dian University in Beijing, China. At that time, they were commonly used throughout China by various Traditional Chinese Medical Universities in order to establish clinical standards. The five Proficiency Examinations include:

1. **Decreasing the alcohol content in a cup of wine:** Wine is poured into two cups on a table in front of the student. The student must then purge and reduce the alcohol content in one cup. The student may also be asked to increase the alcohol content in the second cup (this is achieved through transferring the alcohol from the first cup into the second cup) (Figure 1.62).
2. **Neutralizing the acid in a glass of water containing ascorbic acid:** A glass of water containing a dissolved Vitamin C tablet is placed on a table in front of the student. The student must purge the Vitamin C water, neutralizing its acidic content (Figure 1.64).
3. **Imprinting an image of the palm on an x-ray film:** A piece of x-ray film is wrapped with a towel and placed on a table in front of the student. The student must place his hand over the towel and emit Qi into the film. Once it has been developed, an image of the student's palm must be visible on the film (Figure 1.64).
4. **Changing the acidic component of red litmus paper:** A strip of red litmus paper is placed inside a glass flask, and floats in an acidic solution. The student must place his hand over the strip of red litmus paper and emit Qi into

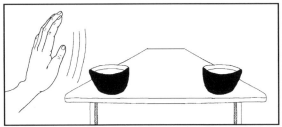

Figure 1.62. The test of decreasing the alcohol content in a cup of wine demonstrates the Medical Qigong Doctor's ability to energetically Purge.

Figure 1.63. The test of Neutralizing the acid in a glass of water to which a capsule of ascorbic acid has been added demonstrates the Qigong Doctor's ability to energetically Regulate.

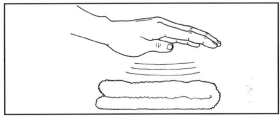

Figure 1.64. The test of imprinting an image of the palm on x-ray film demonstrates the Qigong Doctor's ability to energetically Tonify.

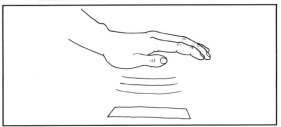

Figure 1.65. Changing the acidic component of the red litmus paper demonstrates the Qigong Doctor's ability to energetically transform.

the acidic solution, increasing or decreasing its acidic nature depending on the examining doctor's request (Figure 1.65).

5. **Changing the alkaline component of blue litmus paper:** A strip of blue litmus paper is placed inside a glass flask, and floats in an alkaline solution. The student must place his hand over the strip of blue litmus paper and emit Qi into the alkaline solution, increasing or decreasing its alkaline nature depending on the examining doctor's request (Figure 1.66).

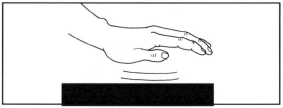

Figure 1.66. Changing the acidic component of the blue litmus paper demonstrates the Qigong Doctor's ability to energetically transform.

MEDICAL QIGONG TRAINING IN THE U. S.

Currently, the most clinically active and academically complete Medical Qigong schools operating within the United States stem from the International Institute of Medical Qigong (Figure 1.67), with several branches extending throughout North America, Belgium, Bermuda, Brazil, Canada, England, Guatemala, Ireland, and Sweden.

Programs are comprised of three to four years of classes in Medical Qigong Therapy, plus Clinical Internship. Also included are classes, labs, and seminars on Traditional Chinese Medical Theory, and the Foundations of Chinese Medicine for Internal Diseases according to *the Yellow Emperor's Inner Canon: Magical Pivot and Essential Questions*, and *the Canon of Perplexities*. All Medical Qigong programs include Energetic Anatomy and Physiology, Diagnosis and Symptomatology, Energetic Psychology, Qigong Pathology and Medical Qigong Therapy. Other related modalities include: a basic understanding of Herbal Medicine, Acupuncture Therapy, and Chinese Massage. Classes in Western Anatomy and Physiology, Western Internal Diseases, and Health and Recovery are also required.

The International Institute of Medical Qigong (I.I.M.Q.) was founded in 1985 by Professor Jerry Alan Johnson, Ph.D., D.T.C.M. (China). Since that time, under the direction of its founder, various branches of the I.I.M.Q. Clinical and Academic programs have extended throughout the world.

Because of its exceedingly high standards, in 1996, the I.I.M.Q. was established as a satellite school and an overseas branch of the Medical Qigong College at the Henan University of Traditional Chinese Medicine (Figure 1.68).

In 2012, the I.I.M.Q. became part of the academic teaching programs of the Tian Yun Gong (Temple of the Celestial Cloud) Daoist Temple (Figure 1.69).

Figure 1.67. The Official Logo of the International Institute of Medical Qigong

Figure 1.68. The Official Logo and Seal of the Henan University of Traditional Chinese Medicine

Figure 1.69. The Official Logo of the Tian Yun Gong (Temple of the Celestial Cloud)

Figure 1.70. The Five Branches Institute: College and Clinic of Traditional Chinese Medicine - 1999

Figure 1.71. Medical Qigong Doctors at the Academy For Five Element Acupuncture - 2003

MEDICAL QIGONG TRAINING IN T.C.M. COLLEGES

In the Spring of 1999, Professor Johnson accepted the position of Dean of Medical Qigong Science from the Five Branches Institute, College and Clinic of Traditional Chinese Medicine, in Santa Cruz, California. At the Five Branches College, Professor Johnson incorporated two programs from the I.I.M.Q. into the Five Branches T.C.M. Curriculum: A two year, 200 hour Medical Qigong Practitioner (M.Q.P.) certification program, and an ongoing Medical Qigong Clinic open to the public (Figure 1.70).

In May of 2003, Professor Johnson accepted the position of Dean of Medical Qigong Science from The Academy For Five Element Acupuncture, in Hallandale, Florida (Figure 1.71). At the Florida acupuncture college, Professor Johnson incorporated four programs from the I.I.M.Q. into the Five Element T.C.M. Curriculum: A 200 hour Medical Qigong Practitioner (M.Q.P.) certification program, A 500 hour Medical Qigong Therapist (M.Q.T.) certification program; A 1000 hour Master of Medical Qigong (M.M.Q.) certification program, and an ongoing Medical Qigong Clinic.

Additionally, in August of 2004, Professor Johnson implemented a 200 hour Medical Qigong Practitioner program within the Belgium College of Traditional Chinese Medicine, and in May of 2005, another 200 hour Medical Qigong Practitioner (M.Q.P.) certification program and ongoing Medical Qigong Clinic was started at the Acupuncture and Integrative Medicine College in Berkeley, California.

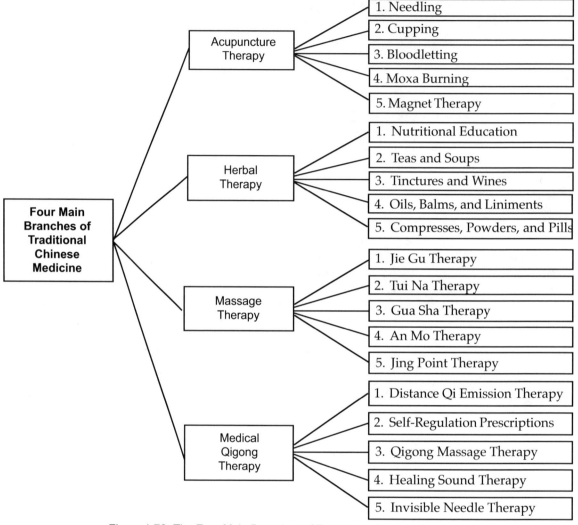

Figure 1.72. The Four Main Branches of Traditional Chinese Medicine

TRADITIONAL CHINESE MEDICINE AND MEDICAL QIGONG THERAPY

Medical Qigong therapy is the oldest of the four branches of Traditional Chinese Medicine, and provides the energetic foundation from which the other branches of T.C.M. (Acupuncture Therapy, Herbal Therapy, and Massage Therapy) originated. It is through the energetic understanding inherent in Medical Qigong practice that the other branches of Traditional Chinese Medicine become elevated to a spiritual path of self-realization and internal transformation (Figure 1.72).

Doctors of Traditional Chinese Medicine address the patients' physical, energetic, and spiritual needs simultaneously. According to the principles of Traditional Chinese Medicine, the root cause of all disease can be traced to a critical imbalance within the body's vital energies. Therefore, the best way to prevent or cure disease requires establishing a healthy energetic balance and harmony between the body's energy field and the forces of nature and the cosmos.

Traditional Chinese Medicine is divided into four branches of healing: Acupuncture, Herbology and Dietetics, Massage Therapy, and Medical Qigong Therapy. All of these four main branches are built on the same foundation of energetic diagnosis, known as the "Five Main Roots of Traditional Chinese Medicine." The Five Main Roots are the theoretical framework used for internal organ diagnosis, and are described as follows: Six Stages Theory, Five Element Theory, Eight Principles Theory, Triple Burners Theory, and Four Levels Theory.

ACUPUNCTURE

According to historical records, the use of stone (magnetic) acupuncture needles and herbal moxibustation in China dates as far back as the New Stone Age. Later, bone and bamboo needles were commonly used as acupuncture instruments (Figure 1.73). When the ancient Chinese began to use pottery, ceramic needles entered into the clinic, and were used to puncture certain shallow points on the skin.

The shapes, lengths and uses of "nine special needles" were written about during the Warring States Period (475-221 B.C.), and described in the *Huangdi Neijing*. These nine ancient needles are described as follows (Figure 1.74):

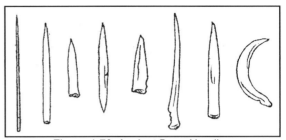

Figure 1.73. Ancient Bone Needles used in Acupuncture Treatments

- **Di Needles:** These needles are used for pressing
- **Rounded Needles:** These needles are used to massage certain points
- **Round and Sharp Needles:** These needles are used for quick puncturing
- **Chun Needles:** These needles are used for piercing shallow points
- **Sword Needles:** These needles are used for cutting and discharging pus
- **Sharp-pointed Needles:** These needles are used for bloodletting
- **Hair Needles:** These needles are used for a variety of applications
- **Long Needles:** These needles are used for puncturing thick muscles
- **Large Needles:** These needles are used for puncturing joints

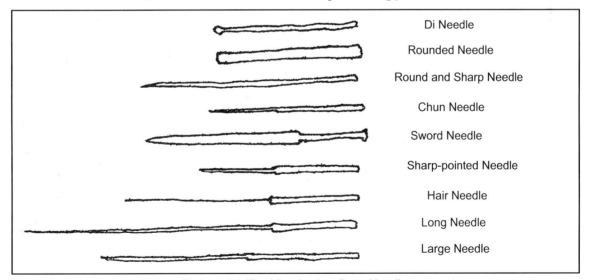

Figure 1.74. The Nine Ancient Bone Needles

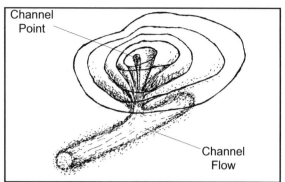

Figure 1.75. The energetic points can be seen as small energetic pools lying along the body's channels.

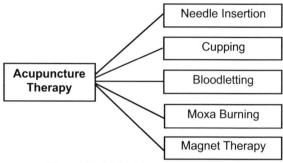

Figure 1.76. The Five Main Branches of Chinese Acupuncture Therapy

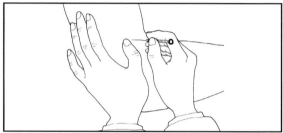

Figure 1.77. A doctor inserts an acupuncture needle into the patient's channel point. Acupuncture needles of various sizes are used to stimulate the energy flow for the tonification of Deficient Qi or the reduction of Excess Qi.

The specific application of these nine needles expanded the clinical practice and potential uses of Acupuncture Therapy. By inserting various types of needles into specific points, the Acupuncturist would manipulate the patient's Qi in order to achieve an overall energetic and physical balance. In an acute or emergency situation, the life threatening symptoms were treated first, after which the focus was redirected to disperse and remove stagnations, strengthen deficient conditions, and then return the patient's energetic fields and physical tissues back to a state of harmony.

The Acupuncture Points (Figure 1.75) are specific areas within the body and on the body's surface, where Qi emerges from deep energetic pools within the body's organs and tissues. Before inserting needles into a specific point, an Acupuncturist is required to first master the art of "De Qi" ("Reaching and Feeling Energy").

The Qi moves along specific pathways known as "Channels" and "Collaterals." A Primary Channel, takes its name from one of the Six Yin or Six Yang organs to which it energetically corresponds. Each organ has two channels, one located on each side of the body. The Collaterals are the smaller streams of Qi that branch away from the main Channel's energetic flow.

Often in Chinese Medical Diagrams, one will see abbreviations referring to specific energetic points. The names of these points are based upon the specific energetic function of the channel point and its exact location along the channel. For example, the first points located on each side of the body's Gall Bladder Channels, are traditionally known as the "Pupil Crevice," and clinically called "GB-1."

Some channels contain over 60 points, each numbered sequentially from beginning to end. These points are also given descriptive names according to their location and energetic affect upon the body when treated. The GB-1 points, for example, are located next to the eyes, on the outer canthus, level with the pupils, and are called Tongziliao, or "pupil's crevice/seam."

Acupuncture Therapy includes five major treatment techniques: Needling, Cupping, Bloodletting, Moxa Burning, and Magnet Healing, described as follows (Figure 1.76):

1. **Needle Insertion Therapy:** This utilizes Acupuncture Needles of various sizes that are inserted into Channel Points. These points are tiny areas where the Qi pools along the streams of an energy channel. The use of needles stimulates the nerves and energy flow to Tonify Deficient Qi or reduce Excess Qi (Figure 1.77).

2. **Cupping Therapy:** This utilizes glass, wooden, or clay cups that adhere to the patient's skin through suction. This suction drains and removes Pathogenic Qi via the body's pores. This technique can also be used to tonify specific areas of the body. This modality of treatment has been successfully combined with Bloodletting to treat acute sprains accompanied by Blood Stagnation (Figure 1.78).
3. **Bloodletting Therapy:** This is induced with instruments such as Blood Needles or Five and Seven Star Hammers, used to remove Toxic Qi, Blood Stagnation, Heat, and other pathogenic states. The hammer has five to seven sharp projections that pierce the skin. The doctor pricks the points and superficial channels to cause slight bleeding (sometimes called "Cutaneous Needle Puncturing"). The Acupuncturist diagnoses and then monitors the patient's condition by the different shades of blood brought to the surface of the skin. Trapped or diseased Blood (usually dark red or black) is released until a healthy color is observed (ruby red). This therapy is considered useful for treating nervous system disorders, physical trauma, and extremely serious febrile diseases (Figure 1.79).
4. **Moxa Burning Therapy:** This consists of three types of ignited Herbal Therapy: Rolled Moxa Sticks, Moxa Cones, and Moxa that is inserted on top of Acupuncture Needles (Figure 1.80). The moxa herb (mugwort) is held over specific channel points to infuse heat and Qi into specific body areas for tonification and improving immune function. This technique is also used to expel Cold in order to disperse Blood stagnation.
5. **Magnetic Therapy:** This utilizes magnetic patches or strips that are attached to various channel points or special ear points used to stimulate a response in the body's electromagnetic field. The magnets are applied to specific points for a period of 3 to 5 days, removed for one day, then reapplied. Whether used for tonification or sedation, this therapy facilitates the constant treatment of the channel points. Magnet Therapy has been used since the Tang Dynasty (618–907 A.D.) (Figure 1.81).

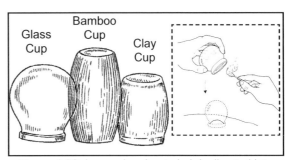

Figure 1.78. In cupping, heated air is directed into wooden, clay, or glass cups which are then placed on the patient's skin. The rapidly cooling air creates a suction force that pulls and removes pathogenic Qi to the body's surface and out the pores.

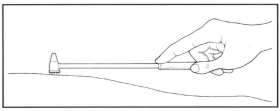

Figure 1.79. The doctor lightly taps the skin with a Five-Star Hammer that has five sharp projections used to pierce the skin and cause slight bleeding. The color of the patient's blood provides the doctor with information about the patient's condition.

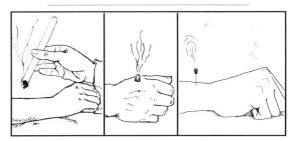

Figure 1.80. Rolled Moxa Sticks, Moxa Cones, and Moxa inserted on top of an Acupuncture Needle.

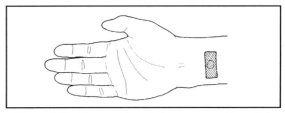

Figure 1.81. A magnetic patch is worn on the wrist. Magnets may be attached to various parts of the body or may be worn in shoes or wristbands.

HERBOLOGY

Herbal formulas have been used successfully to treat a variety of illnesses for over 5000 years (Figure 1.82). Much of the Chinese medical research on Pharmacology organized during the Qin (221-206 B.C.) and Han (206 B.C.-220 A.D.) Dynasties was recorded in the *Canon of Materia Medica of Shen Nong* (also known as the *Canon of Herbal Medicine*). In this text, it contained 252 plants, 67 animals, and 46 minerals, and included a brief description of the places of each herb's origin, secondary names, the specific forms and energetic properties of each herb, and the curative powers of each part of the plant, animal, or mineral.

Herbal medicine was the historical precursor of Pharmaceutical Medicines. Today, herbs still provide the source and inspiration for the majority of the Pharmaceuticals used in modern Western medicine, including those utilized for the treatment of viral and bacterial diseases, pain, tumors, chronic diseases, internal and external tissue regeneration, and many other infirmities.

Herbology is both a science and an art. An herbalist spends many years studying the herbs used to create herbal formulas. The herbalist must also understand the energetic effects of each individual herb, as well as the synergistic effects of herbal combinations and formulas.

Herbs can be used for tonifying, purging, dispersing, warming, cooling, nourishing the Yin, nourishing the Yang, and clearing heat, as well as for moving Qi, Blood, Phlegm, and Fluids within the body. They cause the Qi in the body to either ascend or descend, and primarily affect either the upper or the lower portions of the body. Thus, Chinese herbs are categorized according to the nature and effect that they produce on the Qi of the body.

Chinese Medicine prescribes specific parts of plants (flowers, leaves, stems, seeds, roots, bark, etc.) for particular medicinal purposes. Parts of trees, shrubs, herbs, vines, and flowers are selected for their specific energetic properties (hot, warm, neutral, cool, and cold) and taste (sour, bitter, sweet, pungent, and salty). These special properties either tonify or disperse Qi and Blood.

Figure 1.82. Herbology is both a science and an art

Chinese Herbology includes the cultivation and gathering of seeds, grains, fruits, flowers, leaves, barks, stems, and roots. Non-herbal components such as minerals, fish, animals, or insect parts are sometimes added to energetically enhance the herbs' healing effect.

Chinese herbs cure by energetically moving the Qi flowing within the channels. Each herb enters specific channels and affects different internal organs. Herbs are therefore an extremely powerful healing modality. A Chinese Herbalist can use herbs to either tonify (strengthen) and move the body's Qi and Blood, or eliminate heat and toxins from the Blood. When tailored to an individual's constitution, or combined into a formula for specific symptoms, herbs can be an invaluable aid in restoring and maintaining the health of the body. Taking an improper herb or herbal formula can have potentially harmful effects.

Chinese Herbal Therapy includes five major clinical applications: Nutritional Education (food and diet); Teas and Soups (Tang); Tinctures and Wines (Jin); Oils, Balms, and Liniments (You and Gao); and Compresses, Powders (San), and Pills (Wan), which are described as follows (Figure 1.83):

CHAPTER 1: INTRODUCTION TO CHINESE MEDICINE

1. **Nutritional Education:** This type of education is stressed in order to assist patients in choosing the best foods available for their body's nourishment. It is also used to increase to optimum health a particular organ system, as well as for the treatment of a specific condition and/or diseased state. Foods have many healing properties similar to herbs, and can be used as seasonal prescriptions. An old Chinese saying stresses the importance of diet by asking the question, "Are herbs food or food herbs?"

   During China's Six Dynasties period (420-581 A.D.), the main concern of a doctor was maintaining a patient's health by means of diet, herbal prescriptions and physical exercise. As a result, two types of medical literature developed in China: books that focused on nourishing life and the classics of diet.

2. **Teas and Soups:** These are water-based herbal formulas traditionally prepared from raw or processed herbal ingredients. Teas and soups are traditionally ingested for the treatment of internal and external disorders, whether acute or chronic in nature.

3. **Tinctures and Wines:** These are both alcohol-based herbal formulas.
   - **Tinctures** are concentrated alcohol-based formulas prepared from raw herbs that are used in small doses for treatment (similar to teas and soups).
   - **Wines** are traditionally applied externally to alleviate pain or ingested as a tonic, depending on the specific formula and the disease being treated.

4. **Oils, Balms, and Liniments:** These are oil-based herbal formulas usually applied externally for the treatment of muscle, tendon, and ligament trauma, to alleviate pain, disperse Excess Qi, or to draw Qi into specific areas for tonification.

5. **Compresses, Powders, and Pills:** These consist of herbs that have been pulverized into a powder.
   - **Compresses** are made into a paste or poultice and are then applied externally for the treatment of acute or chronic injuries.

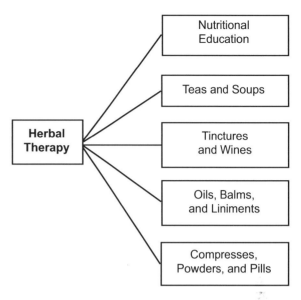

Figure 1.83. The Five Main Branches of Chinese Herbal Therapy

- **Powdered Herbs** can also be formed into teas, crackers, cakes, pastries and honey-based candies. They are ingested for internal organ tonification and rebalancing of the body's energy systems.
- **Pills** are herbs specifically prepared from traditional formulas, rolled into little balls, and orally ingested for the treatment of internal disorders.

SUPERIOR, MEDIUM AND INFERIOR HERBS

According to the ancient Daoist text *Redoubled Yang's Fifteen Discourses*, "all medicinal herbs are the flourishing emanations of mountains and waterways, the essential florescence of plants and trees. If one is willing to study them as essences, one can enliven the innate nature and destiny of others."

Virtually all plants and herbs have significant medicinal potential. Additionally, the ancient Wu Yi explored and documented the specific medicinal potentials of various animal and mineral substances. Over a period of 5,000 years, the Chinese materia medica has accumulated information on the medicinal uses of over 30,000 plant, animal, and mineral substances; of these about 3,000 are of primary clinical importance, while 300 remain in common everyday use.

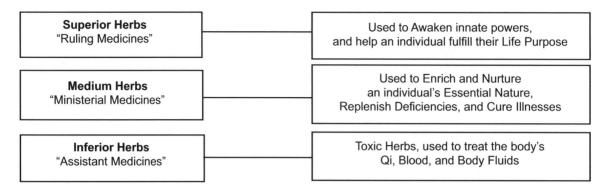

Figure 1.84. The Three Traditional Classes of Chinese Herbs (Materia Medica)

The ancient Wu Yi divided the Plant Kingdom into several different categories, based on the plant's essential qualities and the level at which these qualities influenced the body's Jing, Qi, and Shen. This method of categorization existed until the Song Dynasty (960-1279 A.D.). After observing the ability of plants to infuse new life into the sick, the Plant Kingdom was divided into three separate divisions: Superior Herbs (tonics), Common Herbs (slightly toxic), and Inferior Herbs (toxic). The three methods of categorization are described as follows(Figure 1.84):

- **Superior Herbs:** These special magical plants and substances appeared, either by their shape or color, to contain the most concentrated form of "soul substance," and could therefore be used to obtain immortality. Rather than simply restore health and promote longevity, the soul substance of these various magical plants immediately enveloped, penetrated, and permeated the body-moistures (i.e., blood, sweat, saliva, tears, etc.), and body-vapors, producing and enhancing the vital energy, vital odors, and vital colors of the tissues. Because they were specifically endowed with powerful Ling Shen ("Magical Spirit"), these special herbs were considered by the ancient Daoists to be the drugs of immortality.

According to ancient Daoist teaching, the plants that were believed to contain the greatest amount of soul-substance were those that grew in water and constantly absorbed moisture (like the "Fungus of Immortality"), or those that sprang up suddenly during a thunderstorm (like the "Red Cloud Herb").

Superior Herbs were believed to be able to "feed" and restore the individual's Jing, Qi, Shen, and especially the Prenatal Wu Jing Shen (original spirit energies of the Five Yin Organs). Specific herbal formulas (i.e., powders, pills, tinctures, elixirs, talismans, etc.) that contained the same qualities as Superior Herbs were commonly known as "Ling Yao" (drugs possessing Ling), Shen Yao (drugs containing Spirit Substance), or Xian Yao (drugs used by Immortals).

This category of herbs included 120 varieties of superior medicinal substances. They affect the circulation and collection of internal Qi and Shen, and they are usually taken in conjunction with specific exercises and meditations. Certain herbs are only suitable for the body when the individual has attained a high level of both internal and external development; in addition, other herbs are only effective if the common blockages in certain energetic pathways have already been opened.

Considered in ancient times as the "Ruling Medicines," these herbs are said to awaken our innate vital powers and help to fulfill our life purpose. Examples of Superior Herbs include the following:
1. Special Magic Mushrooms
2. Knotted Fungus
3. The leaves, resin, or roots of a "Thousand Year Old" - Pine, Fir, or Cypress Tree

CHAPTER 1: INTRODUCTION TO CHINESE MEDICINE

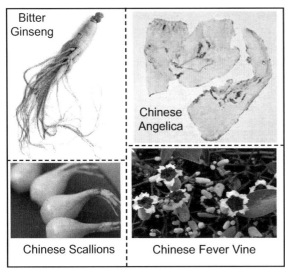

Figure 1.85. Medium (Ministerial) Herbs

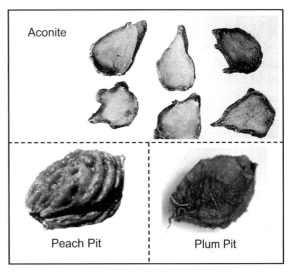

Figure 1.86. Inferior (Assistant) Herbs

4. The ancient large fruits or kernels of certain plum, pear, jujube, or Nai trees
5. The seeds of an ancient Cassia, Sesame, or Chinese Cinnamon Tree

All of these "Superior Herbs" were said to have an effect on the body's Jing, Qi, and Shen, by making the body light, preventing old age, prolonging life, forestalling hunger, and creating advanced spirit travel abilities.

- **Medium Herbs:** Considered in ancient times as "Ministerial Medicines," these special herbs are said to enrich and nurture the individual's character and essential nature, replenish deficiencies, and cure illnesses. These herbs, however, should not be taken over a long period of time (Figure 1.85).

This category of herbs included 120 varieties of moderate types of medicinal substances. Their curative properties are ideal for countering illness, strengthening the patient's constitution, helping to maintain general health, and strengthening the patient's immune system. Examples of Medium Herbs include the following:
1. Bitter Ginseng
2. Chinese Angelica
3. Scallions
4. Chinese Fever Vine

The Ming Dynasty physician Liao Zhong-Chun wrote in his classic herbal pharmacopeia: *Annotated Divine Husbandman's Classic of the Materia Medica (Shen-Nong Ben-Cao Jing Shu)*, "the Ministerial Plant *Paedaria foetida* controls extremely poisonous magical infections; expels malignancies and evil influences; dispels killer-demons, plague, and pestilence; and eliminates spirit possession."

- **Inferior Herbs:** Considered in ancient times as "Assistant Medicines," Inferior Herbs were used to remove disease, ward-off venomous insects, and drive away demonic influences. They are mostly toxic and must be taken with caution when used to treat an individual's disease (Figure 1.86). Inferior herbs were said to have a curative effect on the body's Qi, Blood, and Body Fluids. This category of herbs included 120 varieties of inferior types of medicinal substances.

Examples of Assistant Herbs include the following:
1. Aconite
2. Peach Pit
3. Plum Pit

VOLUME 1, SECTION 1: FOUNDATIONS OF CHINESE ENERGETIC MEDICINE

CHINESE MASSAGE THERAPY

Chinese Massage Therapy is a term used to describe all tissue manipulation techniques currently used in the People's Republic of China. In ancient China, during the Qin (221-206 B.C.) and Han (206 B.C.-220 A.D.) Dynasties, several books on the clinical use of Massage Therapy were compiled. During that time period, a ten-volume treatise, known as *The Massage of Huang Di and Qi Bo* was written, revealing the effective clinical applications of specific massage techniques.

The writings known as the *Prescriptions for 52 Cases* were unearthed in 1973, in a tomb from the Han Dynasty. This book included documentation of Massage Therapy used to treat and cure specific chronically diseased states and acute first aid.

By the Northern Wei Dynasty (386-533 A.D.), Massage Therapy had become part of the four official medical departments within China's Imperial Medical Colleges.

Chinese Massage Therapy consists of the external manipulation of the skin, muscles, tendons, joints, nerves, and inner fascia; and the internal manipulation of the body's organs and organ systems, as well as special tools used to stimulate the tissues (Figure 1.87).

As a clinical modality, Chinese Massage Therapy can be used either as a preventative treatment or to heal acute and chronic injuries. Historically it is the inspirational source of modern Swedish Massage, Shiatsu, Myofascial Trigger Point Therapy, Reflexology, Chiropractic Therapy, Osteopathy, and Neuromuscular Therapy.

Chinese Massage Therapy focuses on improving the structural alignment of the body and on healing soft-tissue injuries. By applying specific methods of tissue manipulation, obstructions in the channels' pathways can be removed, thus promoting and increasing the circulation of Qi and Blood. It also corrects deviant functions of the internal organs, nerves, and joints. These treatment modalities utilized in Chinese Massage are similar to those used in Chiropractic, Osteopathy, Western Physical Therapy, and Sports Massage Therapy.

Chinese Massage Therapy is divided into five different schools of instruction: Jie Gu, Tui Na, Gua Sha, An Mo, and Jing Point Therapy. Jie Gu, Tui Na,

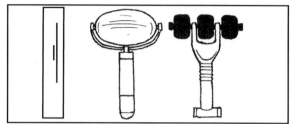

Figure 1.87. Ancient Chinese Massage Tools

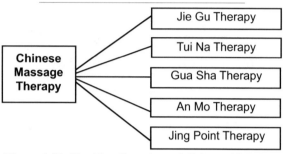

Figure 1.88. The Five Branches of Chinese Massage

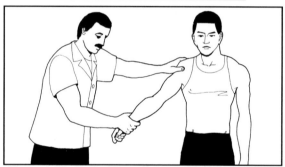

Figure 1.89. Jie Gu Therapy is used to set the bones and ligaments in order to unblock and release trapped junctions of Qi and Blood at the patient's joints.

and Gua Sha employ external tissue manipulations (Figure 1.88); these three external manipulations are used to treat the Bones, muscles, ligaments, and tendons, and also to treat fevers. An Mo and Jing Point Therapy utilize soft-tissue manipulation and are used primarily to treat disorders of the internal organs and energy pathways.

1. **Jie Gu Therapy:** This is used for bone setting and to adjust the patient's body alignment. The literal translation for Jie Gu is "Knotted Bone," which describes the art of manipulating the Bones and ligaments to unblock and release the trapped junctions of Blood and Qi in the channels at the patient's joints (Figure 1.89).

CHAPTER 1: INTRODUCTION TO CHINESE MEDICINE

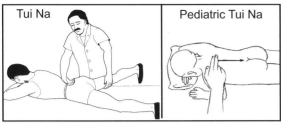

Figure 1.90. Tui Na Therapy is used to adjust the muscles and focuses on external tissue manipulation of the muscles and tendons in order to correct abnormal Qi circulation within the body's muscular system.

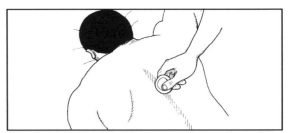

Figure 1.91. Gua Sha Therapy is commonly used for clearing heat, cooling the blood, removing stagnant Qi and Blood, and dissolving masses.

2. **Tui Na Therapy:** This focuses on external tissue manipulation and the adjustment of the muscles and tendons to correct abnormal Qi circulation within the body's muscular system. Tui Na is translated as "Push and Grasp," and was developed primarily for correcting the misalignment of the body's Bones and muscles due to traumatic physical injuries. The popular practice of "Reflexology" is historically rooted in the use of Tui Na Therapy in Chinese Pediatric Therapy (Figure 1.90).

3. **Gua Sha Therapy:** This is used to regulate febrile conditions, such as flu, cholera and malaria, and to treat trauma and musculoskeletal conditions. Gua is translated as "to Scrape or Scratch" and Sha is defined as "Cholera," or "sand-like maculae" (referring to the red discoloration that is raised on the skin by the application of scraping). This therapy focuses on external surface tissue scraping, usually on the posterior aspect of the neck and thoracic areas (Figure 1.91).

Gua Sha Therapy is commonly used for promoting Qi and Blood circulation, removing toxins, clearing heat, cooling the Blood, removing stagnation, and dissolving masses.

- **A Jade Scraper:** Either a spoon or utensil with smooth edges is used for purifying the Qi and transforming the Shen (Thoughts and Emotions).
- **Water Buffalo Horn:** This is commonly used for pulling heat and toxins from the patient's body (ceramic is used, but never glass or plastic).

4. **An Mo Therapy:** This is used for internal organ regulation. An Mo focuses primarily on Qi extension and soft-tissue and internal organ manipulation. Although the literal translation

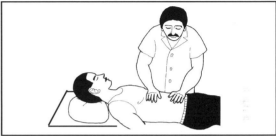

Figure 1.92. An Mo Therapy allows for internal visceral regulation and concentrates directly on treating specific Internal organ diseases.

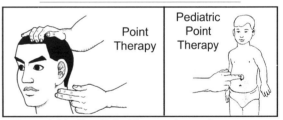

Figure 1.93. Jing Point Therapy is used to promote Qi and Blood circulation, balance the body's Yin and Yang energy, tonify weak organs, dredge the channels, and expel pathogenic factors.

means to "Press and Rub," this therapy focuses primarily on internal visceral manipulation, concentrating directly on the treatment of specific internal diseases (Figure 1.92).

5. **Jing Point Therapy:** This is employed for channel and internal organ regulation. Jing point therapy uses pressing, pinching, clapping, and tapping techniques on specific energetic points and energetic channels. These techniques are used to promote Qi and Blood circulation, balance the body's Yin and Yang energy, tonify weak organs, dredge the channels, and expel pathogenic factors (Figure 1.93).

Medical Qigong Therapy

Over the past two millennia, many doctors of Tradition Chinese Medicine, Daoist and Buddhist Monks and Priests, and Internal Martial Arts Masters have contributed to the expansion of Chinese Medical Qigong Therapy. The objectives for healing disease in Medical Qigong training are as follows:

- First, Purge and eliminate Internal Pathogenic Factors (the accumulation of excessive emotions such as anger, grief, worry, fear, etc.) as well as External Pathogenic Factors (the invasion of Cold, Hot, Damp, etc., from the environment).
- Second, Tonify and increase or decrease the patient's relative Qi levels, as needed to counteract the Deficient or Excess condition within the internal organs and channels.
- Third, Regulate and balance the patient's Yin and Yang energy, and bring the body back into harmony.

Medical Qigong Therapy consists of regulating the body's three external Wei Qi fields (physical, mental/emotional, and spiritual), and the four internal fields of life-force energy (Wind of Nurturing Qi, Sea of Blood, Sea of Marrow, and the center core Taiji Pole). Some of the most common diseases treated in Medical Qigong Clinics are: diabetes, arthritis, high blood pressure, breast and ovarian cysts and tumors, migraine headaches, fibromyalgia, insomnia, acute abdominal pain, prostatitis, irritable bowel syndrome, deep tissue obstruction, muscle atrophy, brain tumors, stroke, coma retrieval, and certain types of cancer. The Medical Qigong Therapy focuses on relieving pain, detoxifying the body of toxic emotions (e.g., excessive anger, fear, worry, etc.), correcting internal organ dysfunctions, and balancing excess or deficient Qi and Blood conditions.

Ancient Chinese Medical Qigong Therapy was divided into three levels of treatment, corresponding to Heaven, Earth, and Man. Which clinical methods and internal powers were used depended on the healer's own personal internal cultivation and understanding of energetic and spiritual principles. Medical Qigong Therapy is where the medical skills of treating patients and the energetic and spiritual intuitive skills of shamanism unite, creating a complete and balanced form of Energetic Medicine.

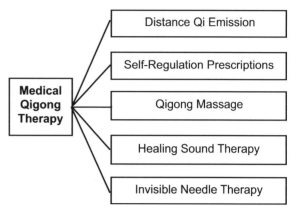

Figure 1.94. The Five Main Branches of Chinese Medical Qigong Therapy

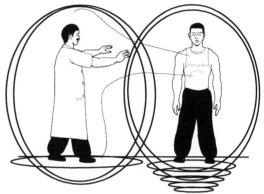

Figure 1.95. In Qi Emission Therapy, the Qigong doctor manipulates a patient's Qi by focusing on the energetic properties of the patient's channels, collaterals, and points from a distance of several inches, several feet, or even many miles.

Medical Qigong Therapy uses five major clinical modalities: Distance Qi Emission Therapy, Self-Regulation Prescriptions, Qigong Massage Therapy, Healing Sound Therapy, and Invisible Needle Therapy (Figure 1.94).

1. **Distance Qi Emission:** This requires the Qigong Doctor to make contact and transform a patient's Qi, by focusing on the energetic properties of his or her internal organs, channels, collaterals, and points, from a distance of several inches, several feet, or even many miles away (Figure 1.95).

CHAPTER 1: INTRODUCTION TO CHINESE MEDICINE

Figure 1.96. In Self-Regulation Prescriptions, the patients are required to self-regulate by performing Medical Qigong prescription exercises (postures, movements, breathing exercises, sounds, visualizations, etc.). Here the patient regulates his own Liver Qi.

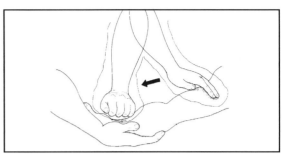

Figure 1.97. In Qigong Massage, the doctor softly dredges the patient's external channels in order to release stagnant energy from the internal channels, which serve as pathways for Qi transference.

2. **Self-Regulation Prescriptions:** These are Qigong exercises that include Dao Yin postures, movements, respiratory patterns, sound vibrations, and mental visualizations. Medical Qigong Prescription Exercises are given to patients to augment the benefits of a Medical Qigong treatment. Patients then use these Qigong techniques to regulate and maintain their own health between treatments, using various lying, sitting, standing and moving postures. The patients may also use their own spiritual belief system as a healing tool (Figure 1.96).

3. **Qigong Massage:** This is a soft-tissue regulation technique, that differs from the Tui Na or An Mo methods (Chinese Massage Therapy), in that the doctor's hand barely skims the patient's body, as lightly as a feather, never exceeding the pressure one would place on an eyeball. The light skimming action is used to dredge the patient's external channel Qi, causing energy to be released from the internal channels themselves, which serve as pathways for Qi transference (Figure 1.97).

4. **Healing Sound Therapy:** This is one of the most powerful tools used in Medical Qigong for breaking up energetic stagnations. It requires the doctor to project sound vibration deep into the patient's tissues. When the sound resonation penetrates the patient's body it causes massive chaotic vibrational patterns that disrupt the body's accepted "normal" en-

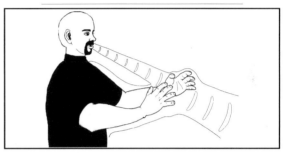

Figure 1.98. With Healing Sound Therapy, the doctor projects his or her voice deep into the patient's tissues, creating a vibrational resonance that purges the stagnant energy trapped deep within the viscera.

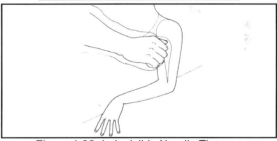

Figure 1.99. In Invisible Needle Therapy, the doctor visualizes inserting energetic acupuncture needles into the patient's channel points in order to stimulate the patient's Qi.

ergetic flow. This energetic disruption softens and liquifies the patient's stagnant Qi, making it easier to purge and disperse (Figure 1.98).

5. **Invisible Needle Therapy:** This involves the visualization of energetic needles of light being inserted into specific points on the patient's body. The needles of light are used to stimulate and direct the patient's Qi (Figure 1.99).

Learning Medical Qigong Therapy in China

In 1974 I began training in Traditional Chinese Medical Theory, Acupressure, Moxa, Herbology, Traumatology, Chinese Bone-Setting, Chinese Massage, Medical Qigong Therapy, as well as Martial Qigong (Energy Skill), Neigong (Internal Skill) and Shengong (Spirit Skill) training from my Northern Shaolin instructor. In 1978, after many years of intense private training, I become a Shifu (Master Teacher) of Mizongquan from the Ching Wu Kungfu Association of Hong Kong, and was also authorized as a Shifu from the Yang Family Tai Chi Chuan Association of Taiwan.

During that time period, I also began my formal clinical training, and worked as an apprentice of Acupuncture, Herbs and Medical Qigong Therapy under the private tutelage of Dr. Hyun Huh in an Acupuncture Clinic in Monterey California, from 1978 to 1981.

In 1981, I moved to Colorado, opened two Acupuncture Clinics, and ran two Kungfu Schools in the Colorado Springs area. At that time, I trained with two Chinese brothers who were well versed in both the internal and external aspects of Qigong, Neigong, and Shengong skill. I also trained with a Daoist Maoshan Priest.

I moved back to Monterey in 1984, and from 1986 to 1987 continued my internal training under the careful instruction of Daoist Master Fei.

By the time I first visited the People's Republic of China in 1993, I was well versed in all four branches of Chinese Medicine (i.e., Acupuncture, Herbology, Medical Qigong, and Massage). Having continually practiced for over 19 years at that time, and was an instructor in Martial, Medical, and Spiritual Qigong, Neigong, and Shengong training, and had successful ran three Acupuncture Clinics, and several Chinese Gongfu Schools.

While running the Acupuncture Clinics, one of my many "gifts" as a healer was acquired due to the extensive years of practicing "crushing-palm" training. This unique energetic ability enabled me to dissolve cysts and tumors. In many instances, I was even able to halt the growth of late-stage cancer, sending it into remission. The problem was, some

Figure 1.100. The Xi Yuan Hospital in 1993.

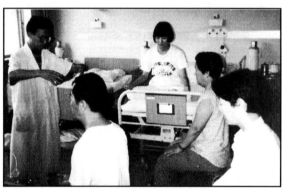

Figure 1.101. Treating patients at the Xi Yuan Hospital in 1993 with one of my colleges Doctor Xu Hongtao

of the tumors and cancers would eventually start to grow back. With no one in America familiar with this type of clinical treatment modality to talk to, I eventually traveled to China seeking help for my patients.

While in China, I entered into the Beijing International Acupuncture Training Center and Acupuncture Institute of China - Academy of Traditional Chinese Medicine. I went before a Review Board, passed the initial entry examination, and was admitted into the Xi Yuan Hospital as a visiting foreign doctor (Figure 1.100 and Figure 1.101). Within the first week, I had worked my way through the ranks, and was training with Professor Lu (the Chief Doctor) and the Associate Professor Dr. Xu Zong Wei (the Vice-Chief Doctor) of the Medical Qigong Division.

The Xi Yuan Hospital in Beijing, China, was at one time the academic and clinical equivalent of the Stanford Medical Center in the United States. It specialized in training interning doctors from several medical universities, and focused on the various clinical protocols utilized in all four distinct branches of Traditional Chinese Medicine: Acupuncture, Herbs and Nutrition, Medical Qigong, and Massage Therapy. The Medical Qigong Department at the Xi Yuan Hospital had their own wing, which extended throughout several floors, and included both Inpatient and Outpatient clinics. In addition, the Medical Qigong Department also maintained an active division of research scientists for clinical research. The scientists were specifically trained for gathering information on the healing effects of Qi Emission Therapy.

Because of my success in the Medical Qigong In-Patient and Out-Patient Clinics, I was invited to meet with the Director and Associate Director of the Medical Qigong College at the Hai Dian T.C.M. University (Figure 1.102 through Figure 1.104). At that time, the graduate students of the Medical Qigong College at Hai Dian University, all interned at the Xi Yuan Hospital in Beijing, China, for a period of 6 months to a year before being licensed as Doctors of Traditional Chinese Medicine through the government's Ministry of Health, which monitored the student programs.

Again, I went before a Review Board, was tested and evaluated, and allowed to enter the Hai Dian T.C.M. University as a visiting foreign doctor. After three months I returned home, continued my clinical practice, and then returned back to China in 1995 to complete my clinical studies at the Hai Dian University, and supervised clinical internship at the Xi Yuan Hospital. After graduating from the Hai Dian University, I received my Doctor of Traditional Chinese Medicine (D.T.C.M.) from the People's Republic of China's Ministry of Health.

In 1999, due to the extreme political actions of the Falun Gong Qigong Association, stern restraints on all Qigong activities were immediately applied throughout the country, especially to those Qigong Departments existing within the government hospitals and clinics in Beijing. As of 2014, the Hai Dian University closed, and the Medical Qigong departments of the Xi Yuan Hospital have

Figure 1.102. The Front Gate of the Hai Dian T.C.M. University in Beijing, China (1995)

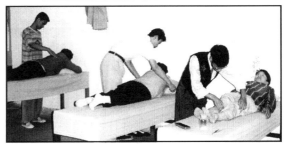

Figure 1.103. Students at the Medical Qigong College at the Hai Dian T.C.M. University in Beijing, China

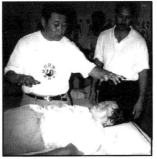 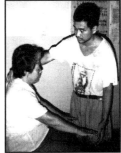

Figure 1.104. Dr. Lu Guo Hong (Director-R) and Dr. Niu Yu Hua (Associate Director-L) of the Medical Qigong College at Hai Dian University.

been extremely down-sized, reduced to only two small treatment rooms, one of which is currently being shared with the Tuina Massage Department.

The teaching and information contained within this Medical Qigong textbook series is no longer available in China. This is why the Henan University of Traditional Chinese Medicine accepted the International Institute of Medical Qigong as their "oversees" branch of the T.C.M. University.

Changing Times in China for Medical Qigong Therapy

Contained within this five volume Medical Qigong textbook series, is ancient knowledge and privileged information detailing how to effectively diagnose and energetically treat patients using Medical Qigong Therapy, as set forth by the Hai Dian ("Sea of Elixir") Medical Qigong College of Beijing, authorized through the Henan University of Traditional Chinese Medicine (Figure 1.105 and Figure 1.106).

Graduating students from the Medical Qigong College at Hai Dian University interned at the Xi Yuan Hospital for a period of 6 months to a year before being licensed as Doctors of Traditional Chinese Medicine through the government's Ministry of Health, which monitored the student programs.

By the year 1999, the study of Qigong had taken a sudden change in formal development. Due to the political actions and activities of the Falun Gong Qigong Schools, the Chinese government put a sudden halt to any and all Qigong practices. In the middle of the night, armed guards entered the various Medical Qigong colleges, laboratories, and clinics and removed all of the scientific equipment, and then chained and padlocked the doors. Some Qigong doctors and instructors were held and interrogated, and most Medical Qigong hospitals and clinics throughout China were closed. All practice groups of Qigong were dispersed. Even small, individual groups practicing in the various parks were ordered to disband and the leaders were taken in for questioning. Sadly, this closure also included that of the Medical Qigong college at the Hai Dian University. By the end of 2000, many of the Medical Qigong clinical application and prescription exercises that were considered to be common treatment protocols in the Medical Qigong hospitals were no longer being taught to the public, or utilized in the various clinics.

Even more shocking, is that the Medical Qigong treatment protocols have dramatically changed, as doctors in Beijing are no longer allowed to Purge, Tonify, and Regulate the patients' life-force energy. The new government treatment policy only allows them to emit Qi into the patient's body until they fall asleep.

Figure 1.105. The three representatives of the International Institute of Medical Qigong (I.I.M.Q.) (L) Richard Lee, Dr. Bernard Shannon (Executive Director), and Professor Jerry Alan Johnson (President & Founder), meet and sign papers with the Professor Lu Mei (Dean of International Education), from the Henan University of Traditional Chinese Medicine. At this historical meeting in 2005, the I.I.M.Q. officially accepted the post as the "Sister School" of the Henan T.C.M. University, and was authorized to represent the Henan University as its Overseas Medical Qigong College. At that time, Professor Johnson received the official government stamp from the P.R.C. as the Oversees Director of Medical Qigong Training from the Henan University of Traditional Chinese Medicine.

Figure 1.106. The Official Logo and Overseas Seal of the Henan University of Traditional Chinese Medicine

Therefore, the faculty and graduate students of the I.I.M.Q. have accepted the responsibility of teaching the same information and maintaining the same strict standards established by the former Hai Dian Medical Qigong College of Beijing, China. It is our hope that one day the Chinese government will loosen its restraints on Medical Qigong Therapy and actively return this great knowledge back to the Chinese people.

Chapter 2
Understanding Ancient Chinese Metaphysics

Introduction To The Energetic Realms

When I began my Clinical Internship at the Xi Yuan Hospital in Beijing, China, back in 1993, I became aware that most of the Chinese Medical Qigong Doctors that I spoke to had a different approach to understanding Western Anatomy and Physiology. For example, when I asked why more attention was not paid to the subject, I was told, "The perspective and priority we place on Gross Physical Anatomy and Physiology is quite different from yours -- Westerners only study "dead tissue" -- we study life, and are familiar with the living pools, rivers, and currents of Life-Force Energy, that can only be found in the living body."

Ancient Chinese Energetic Medicine teaches that when an individual dies, the energetic substance that gave the body life, returns back to its original source, and all that remains of the individual is a mass of lifeless tissue. In this model, the tangible and the energetic coexist in a binary, cohesive relationship (Figure 2.1). This is why, when studying Chinese Energetic Medicine, a Medical Qigong Doctor must understand the concept of "life-force energy" in order to comprehend, diagnose, treat, and prescribe the appropriate form of Qigong Therapy for the patient.

The concept of the energetic formation of the human body is new to Western thought, which has primarily focused on that which is physically tangible. The philosophical foundation of Traditional Chinese Medicine, on the other hand, includes the study of the entire human being, with all of the various aspects of the body's physical, mental, emotional, energetic, and spiritual components. This esoteric concept of Energetic Anatomy focuses not only on understanding the tangible physical form of human tissue, but also on comprehending the various contributing energies and energetic fields that affect and govern the body as well.

In China, Medical Qigong Doctors continually study the effects of these energies, as well as

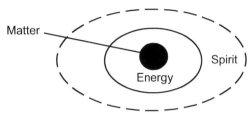

Figure 2.1. Matter - Energy - Spirit

their interrelationship with Heavenly and Earthly energetic influences.

In 1998, while visiting with friends at a local Medical Qigong Clinic in Beijing, I was fortunate to spend the entire day with a "founding father" of the World Academic Society of Medical Qigong. The Professor Meng Xiantong, and I spoke at great length about ancient Chinese Energetic Medicine, the energetic creation and formation of the tissues, the descent of the Eternal Soul (Shen Xian), and the creation of the Human Soul (Yuan Shen). I would like to now present this great grandmaster's gift of insight into ancient Daoist "forbidden knowledge" regarding energetic and spiritual transformations.

The first part of this chapter will explore early Chinese mystical understandings of the medical, energetic, and spiritual aspects of the formation of the universe. This will include the original concepts of the Dao (Divine), Wuji (Infinite Space), Taiji (Yin and Yang), Bagua (Eight Trigrams), Wu Xing (Five Phases) and the Three Worlds of matter, energy, and spirit.

The second part of this chapter will explore ancient Chinese mystical understandings of the medical, energetic, and spiritual aspects of the formation of the human body. This includes the ancient concepts of the Dao (Divine), Shen Ling (Supernatural Spirit), Zhi Yi Tian (the Will and Intent of Heaven), Shen Xian (Eternal Soul), Yuan Shen (Original Spirit), Wujingshen (Five Essence Spirits), Shen Zhi (the Acquired Personality), Energetic Embryology (from conception to birth), and the Three Bodies (Physical Body, Energy Body, and Spirit Body).

THE ENERGETIC FORMATION OF THE UNIVERSE

Throughout China's ancient history, there have been numerous theories and philosophies regarding the creation of the Universe, and the specific energetic components responsible for sustaining the creation of Heaven, Earth, and Man.

The following Daoist theory originated during the Spring and Autumn Period (770-476 B.C.) in ancient China, and was originally taught to me in secret by one of my Daoist teachers from mainland China, Master Wong. It is introduced here as part of the foundational knowledge that is essential for the disciple to understand before he begins a healing practice based on Chinese Energetic Medicine.

Studying Chinese Energetic Medicine requires not only comprehending the immeasurable wisdom gathered for ancient martial, medical, and spiritual development, but also studying the ancient Chinese culture which fostered these powerful energetic systems.

SHANG DI (HIGHEST GOD)

The prevailing opinion held by most scholars, is that during the Shang Dynasty Period (1600-1028 B.C.), the ancient Chinese believed in a Supreme Deity known as "Shang Di" ("Highest God"). This is based on ancient Oracle Bone Inscriptions that were found dating back to the Shang Dynasty. However, according to the *Classic of History*, yearly sacrifices were traditionally made to Shangdi by Emperor Shun (of the Three Rulers Period), even before the time of the Xia Dynasty (2205-1600 B.C.).

As the "Celestial Emperor" responsible for overseeing the creation of Heaven and Earth, Shangdi was especially regarded as an ultimate spiritual power by the ruling elite of the Huaxia during the Shang Dynasty. He was therefore believed to control victory in battle, the success or failure of every harvest, weather conditions such as the floods of the Yellow River, and the fate of the Imperial Kingdom. He was also believed to have ruled over a hierarchy of various gods responsible for controlling all of Nature, as well as the Spirits of the Underworld (Figure 2.2).

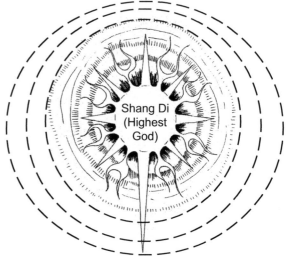

Figure 2.2. "Shang Di" ("Highest God")

Shang Di was believed to be the ultimate power, having dominion over all Human Fate. However, being a Supreme Deity, Shang Di stood aloof, and was indifferent to all mortal concerns. Any living ruler who sought favor with Shang Di could only intercede through the spiritual voice of his royal ancestors, who could themselves communicate directly with the Supreme Deity, because they had already passed into the Spirit World. Therefore, by presenting abundant and regular sacrificial offerings to the royal ancestors, Shang Di could inevitably be influenced and blessings could be obtained.

The communication between the Shang rulers and their royal ancestors was essential for the harmonious state of the government. All important decisions were accomplished via Divinations based on Oracle Readings. Originally, the Shang ruler would act as the Chief Priest, personally conducting Divinations and ancestral rites with the help of Court Priests. During these magical rituals, the Shang Ruler acted as the sole intermediary between the mortal and celestial realms.

During the late Shang Dynasty, the Shang rulers began to assert their direct control over the Celestial Realm (including Shang Di), claiming themselves to be "living gods." At this point in China's ancient history, the Celestial Realm remained a privileged world, accessible only to the ruling class.

During the Zhou Dynasty period (1028-221 B.C.), a new concept of the Supreme Deity emerged. The Supreme Deity was now named "Tian" (Heaven), and was perceived as an immanent god who manifestly intervened in all human affairs. Additionally, Tian subordinated the emperor and all of his subjects to a Universal Moral Law. All those living within the physical realm were now under "Tianming" ("Heaven's Mandate"). Although the emperor was now referred to as the "Son of Heaven," his right to rule remained contingent on his ability and willingness to uphold Heaven's Mandate.

During the Zhou Dynasty period, ancestral sacrifices took the form of communal feasts, celebrated in the presence of the ancestors. During these celebrations, the spirit of one of the ancestors would sometimes descend into the body of an individual who was chosen to receive the food offerings on behalf of the ancestral lineage.

During the Spring and Autumn Period (770 - 476 B.C.), the relationship between the living and the dead, from a Chinese perspective, once again underwent a major transformation. The spiritual emphasis was now placed on the specific "soul" of each individual and his or her fate in the afterlife. The reference to an individual's Hun (Ethereal Soul) and Po (Corporeal Soul) signaled the emergence of a dualistic conception of the postmortem "soul." The concept of a Supreme Being who acted as the judge of all human fate persisted, however this god was now commonly referred to as "Tian Di" (God of Heaven).

Towards the end of the Zhou Dynasty, during the Warring States Period (475 - 221 B.C.), many scholars, priests, and masters of the occult arts flocked to the various courts of powerful monarchs, offering esoteric knowledge and magical formulas that would enable the rulers to achieve both personal and political advantage. During this time period "Fangshi," "Masters of Occult Magic" who could personally interact with Tian Di, were prevalent throughout China.

During the Han Dynasty Period (206 B.C. - 220 A.D.), the concept of death and the afterlife once again underwent a profound transformation. When interacting with Tian Di, the spiritual emphasis was suddenly placed on Divine Judge-

Figure 2.3. In Religious Daoism, "Shang Di" ("Highest God") later became known as "Yuánshǐ Tiānzūn" ("The Original Lord of Heaven")

ment and Punishment. The spiritual dogma now included the existence of various celestial and terrestrial gods and spirit entities. Every man and woman should now be concerned with the afterlife procedures, occurring within the vast spiritual domain of the Underworld.

Increasingly, the ancient Chinese began to view their Mortal Destiny as being under the control of powerful gods. Illness and misfortune were commonly blamed on agitated ancestors who filed "Writs of Grievances from the Grave" with the Underworld Magistrates, and requested Divine Punishment for personal infractions.

The promise of salvation from mortal misery and infernal punishment prepared the ground work for the transplanting of Buddhism into China in the upcoming centuries after the fall of the Han Dynasty in 220 A.D. It was at this time that many of the terms used to describe the Daoist Natural Forces (existing within Heaven, Earth, and Man) were personalized and referred to as "gods" or "spirits" by "Religious Daoists." This was done in order to compete with the colorful deities imported into China through Buddhism from India. Eventually, Shang Di became known as Yuanshi Tianzun ("The Original Lord of Heaven") by the Religious Daoists (Figure 2.3).

THE DAO: THE WAY

The ancient Chinese character for "Dao" (The "Way") depicts a wise sage, with his hair unbound like a Wu (ancient shaman), walking a special "path," via a secret way, method, or principle (Figure 2.4). This special character was viewed by many ancient Daoists as a magical "teaching," containing the secret act of deliberately evoking something through magic ritual rather than a symbolic gesture. The special "path" shown in the character is associated with the three unique magical dance steps, used in ancient China for invoking spirits (traditionally the left "Yang" foot begins the ritual facing south, and moves towards the Eastern rising Sun). Therefore, the ideograph suggests that the specific action of each footstep is made by one who possesses privileged knowledge with directed purpose and intent.

The ancient meaning conveyed by this ideograph can be translated as "the Way that one comes to see and understand oneself in relationship to the universe (Heaven), environment (Earth), and the Divine." Originally, the study of the Dao in ancient China was not a religion, but a way and means of maintaining energetic harmony between this world (the Physical Realm) and the worlds beyond.

The meaning of "Dao" can also be translated as "the infinite spiritual approach to the natural way of the Divine." For the most part, it is the study of the most subtle realm and presence of the Divine Spirit that underlies all creation. According to ancient Daoist teachings, the energy and light pertaining to the infinite Dao is imprinted in every particle, and that whatever exists (i.e. all of creation) is simply an expression and manifestation of the Great Dao.

All Daoist priests say, that the "True Dao" is beyond human comprehension. It is nameless, formless, and beyond all description. According to the *Daode Jing (Scripture of the Dao and its Virtue)*,

"The Dao that can be told
Is not the Eternal Dao.
The Name that can be Named
is not the Eternal Name."

Figure 2.4. The Chinese Character "Dao" ("Way")

The ancient Daoists also believed that all life emerged from the Dao, and would someday dissolve back into its infinite energy. According to Guan Zi, the Prime Minister of the State of Qi, who lived during the Spring and Autumn Period (770-476 B.C.),

"The Dao has neither root nor stem,
no leaf nor flower,
but all ten thousand things
are born of and grow from it.

It comes to rest
in the Compassionate Heart.
In the Tranquil Mind and Harmonized Qi
is where the Dao abides."

Additionally, the famous Daoist Scholar Zhuangzi once stated,

"The Dao has reality and evidence,
but no action and no form.
It may be transmitted
but cannot be received.
It may be attained
but cannot be seen.
It exists by and through itself.
It existed before Heaven and Earth,
and indeed for all eternity.
It causes the gods to be divine
and the world to be produced.
It is above the zenith,
but it is not high.
It is beneath the lowest point
but it is not low.
Though prior to Heaven and Earth
it is not ancient.
Though older than the most ancient,
it is not old."

The subtle energy of the Dao exists within every single particle of "Mind;" the Mind being the organization of consciousness through which the Divine manifests its intentions. Therefore, the "Divine Mind" exists as an infinite ocean of subtle vibration, resonating within the infinite space of the Wuji, ranging from the "highest" levels of energetic pulse and vibration, to the slower vibrations of the gross material plane.

The ancient Daoists believed that before conception, an individual existed as an integral part of the Dao. That is, we were with the Divine, formless and undifferentiated, and not subject to the physical laws of birth, growth, decay, and death. At conception, we became less conscious of this connection. Therefore the "Way," refers to the journey of walking the road back to conscious wholeness and integration with the cosmic order of creation, and reconnecting with the Divine Light and eternal pulse of the Dao.

It is important to note that before the Later Han Dynasty (25-220 A.D.), the term "Dao" was commonly used by all ancient Chinese schools of esoteric thought to explain the origin of creation and the realm of Natural Magic. At that time, the term "Dao Jiao" was originally used to emphasize the secret transmissions of the "teaching of the Dao." The study of this esoteric magical training included the ancient texts of the *Four Classics of the Yellow Emperor*, the *Daodejing*, and the writings of *Zhuangzi*. After the Later Han Dynasty, the teachings of the ancient Daoist schools were eventually combined with the new developing political power of Chinese religion, and slowly became known as "Daoist Religion." The ancient term "Dao Jiao" was then retranslated to emphasize its political status as a "Daoist Religion."

THE DAO, HEAVEN, AND EARTH

Understanding the "Way" ("Dao"), is the key to maintaining harmony within the Three Realms of Heaven, Earth, and Man. In ancient China, the Daoists realized that the various realms of Heaven and Earth were beyond their control. Therefore, in order to attain health and longevity, Man was continually challenged to follow and adjust to the

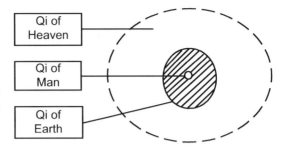

Figure 2.5. Each subtle realm fits into the other's energetic form, creating a multidimensional unity.

ever changing course of Nature. Perfect health and longevity depended on Man's correct behavior towards the "Way" ("Dao") of Heaven and Earth.

As all of Man's actions (i.e., eating, sleeping, working, resting, etc.) continued to adjust to the seasonal changes, he suddenly awakened to the subtle energetic rhythms of life that influenced his body. He began to understand that within its vast energetic sea, the Dao gives birth to two main energetic polarities, Yang (attributed to the celestial energies of Heaven) and Yin (assigned to the terrestrial energies of Earth). The Yang Qi of Heaven arises from the sea of Primordial Chaos, radiating down Celestial Qi from the Sun, Moon and Stars, with an active energetic quality. The Yin Qi of Earth, being passive, receives and energetically interacts with the Yang Qi of Heaven via the Soil, Wind, and Water, which contain and transform the Celestial Qi.

To the ancient Daoists, the concept of "Dao," could be better understood by observing its energetic influence in three subdivisions: the Dao of Heaven, the Dao of Earth, and the Dao of Man. Each of these three energetic realities can stand alone (i.e., act as a separate realm/world within itself), yet each will naturally fit into each other's energetic field, creating a multidimensional unity (Figure 2.5). For example, the energetic fields of Heaven (created from the energetic influences of the Sun, Moon, and Stars) envelop and affect the energetic fields of the Earth (causing energetic movement within the Soil, Wind, and Water); the energetic fields of the Earth in turn envelop and influence the energetic fields of Man (causing energetic movement within the body's Essence, Energy, and Spirit.

THE DAO AS THE ZHONG (CENTER)

The ancient Daoists believed that the energies of Heaven, Earth, and the infinite space of the Wuji compose the fundamental unity of the energetic matrix known as the "Primordial Dao." This sacred energy existed before the creation and evolution of all material existence. The "True Dao" was considered to energetically and spiritually exist as the "Zhong" (the "Center" or "Middle") of all things. Its supernatural force was believed to exist within the "center of the center" (i.e., the "space within the space"), and maintained its numinous existence throughout all time, resonating from deep within the infinite space of the Wuji (Infinite Void).

This subtle energy continually pulsed and "breathed" as a sacred energetic mist, that extended from the Infinite Void outward, interconnecting and blending its energetic field to all things existing within Heaven and Earth like a vast, endless net.

The ancient Daoists also believed that this sacred, vaporous energy also existed within the human body as its "Zhong Qi." It was through the whirling energetic vortex of this Zhong Qi that the energetic qualities of the body's Yin and Yang polarities were continually blended together.

THE DAO WITHIN THE BODY

As a microcosm, the human body takes the place of the Wuji, mediating between the energies of Heaven and Earth. Just as the infinite energy of the Wuji (i.e., the "Void") blends together the energies of Heaven (associated with the Qi of the Sun, Moon, Planets, and Stars) and Earth (associated with the Qi of the Soil, Water, and Wind), so too does the energy of the Breath of the Dao blend with and actively awakens the spiritual energy of Man (associated with the body's Original Essence, Energy, and Spirit).

This Divine interaction of Primordial Yin and Yang energy, produces and sustains the energetic fields of the disciple's Original Three Treasures (Yuan Jing, Yuan Qi, and Yuan Shen), which in turn act as the true human manifestation and expression of the physical, energetic and spiritual realms of existence.

Figure 2.6. An individual's energetic field is suspended between the two energy fields of Heaven and Earth.

The ancient Daoists extensively studied the functional relationship between the body's tissues, organs and organ systems, and their relationship with the energetic influences of Heaven, Earth, and Man. Because he was suspended between the energies of Heaven and Earth (Figure 2.6), once Man had become spiritually awakened, he could then consciously experience life as an energetic conduit, able to absorb, cultivate, and utilize (transmit or distribute) the infinite powers of Heaven and Earth.

To the ancient Daoists, the Three Treasures of Man (Essence, Energy and Spirit) were believed to have two fundamental properties, one half existed on Earth in tangible form (Yin), the other half existed in Heaven in spiritual form (Yang). The energetic awakening and harmonization of the Earthly half, enabled the disciple to summon the celestial energies of the Heavenly half. Through the union of Heaven (Yang) and Earth (Yin), the Daoist disciple could magically transform himself, and bring about an energetic and spiritual state of renewal. This magical transformation was accomplished by consciously directing and controlling the subtle energy that acted as a medium between matter and spirit.

THE WUJI: INFINITE SPACE

The ancient Chinese ideograms for Wuji are defined in Daoist Alchemy as "the infinite space embodied in-between matter, energy, and spirit." The character "Wu" translates as "Nothing or Without;" and the character "Ji" translates as "the Ultimate or Extreme." Together, the term "Wuji" translates as "Ultimate Emptiness," and describes the vast expansiveness of infinite space. In ancient China, this concept was symbolically represented by the formation of a never-ending image of a circle (Figure 2.7).

The Wuji is the state of no boundaries, the state of pure and complete oneness. Its essence is that of emptiness (as depicted by the empty circle).

The ancient Daoists believed that the Wuji, extending from the omnipresent energy of the Dao, was an infinite ocean of the most subtle vibrational resonance, existing like an invisible web. This was the original energetic matrix from which all the realms of creation and all the different energetic worlds were constructed. It was through the subtle energetic medium of the Wuji that the Divine manifested its infinite form.

The ancient Daoist Canon *Huainan Zi*, describes the existence of the Wuji and its subtle energetic state as follows:

> **"In ancient times,
> Before Heaven and Earth even existed,
> there were only images without form;
> Profound, opaque, vast, immobile,
> impalpable and still.
> There was a haziness,
> Infinite, unfathomable and abysmal.
> A vast deep
> to which no one knew the door."**

In esoteric Daoist alchemy, the Yang within Heaven corresponds to time, while the Yin within Earth corresponds to space. Through the quiescent state of deep meditation, the ancient Daoist masters were able to dissolve their physical energy into the infinite space of the Wuji, and reconnect with the Dao, transcending both time (Yang) and space (Yin). Through this stillness of Mind, the ancient Daoists realized the boundless ocean of subtle energy connected to everything contained within the infinite space of the Wuji.

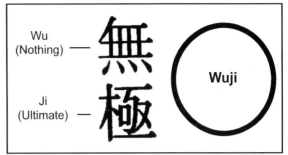

Figure 2.7. "Wuji" ("Ultimate Emptiness")

KNOWLEDGE STORED WITHIN THE WUJI

On the most fundamental level, all things are constructed of Qi (Energy), and are constantly vibrating, actively exchanging information through the Wuji's inexhaustible energetic field. All matter in the universe is interconnected by energetic waves contained within the Wuji's vast sea of Qi, which transcends the manifestations of time and space.

The stable state of matter depends on the dynamic interchange of subatomic particles flowing within the Wuji for its very existence. Similar to ripples on a pond, energetic waves are expressed by periodic oscillations, moving through the medium of the Wuji on a subatomic level. Each energetic wave is encoded with information.

The energetic field of the Wuji creates a vast medium, enabling the molecules to communicate with each other in oscillating frequencies. As molecules slow down, they give off radiation, and release encoded wave information about the history imprinted within the energetic field of a person, place or item.

MESSAGES WITHIN THE HUMAN BODY

In ancient China, the body's encoded "Bio-information" was traditionally known as "Xin Xi" or "the Message." It was believed that the subtle energies contained and expressed within these encoded Messages were not limited by the confines of space or time. Therefore "the Message" commonly referred to the imprinted information contained within and surrounding the body's tissues; as well as the information contained within the various energy fields that flowed into, away from, and within the infinite space of the Wuji.

In modern China, the study of the various forms and patterns of "Bio-information" is a natural part of understanding patient diagnosis in the Traditional Chinese Medical clinic. While at the Xiyuan Hospital in Beijing, China, I was told that because the body's "Chemical Messages" (i.e., the cell to cell communication occurring via the exchange of molecules) are considered to be primarily an energetic function of the Endocrine System, they are considered to be Yin Messages. And, because the body's "Electrical Messages" are expressed through energetic impulses and are considered to be primarily a function of the Nervous System, they are considered to be Yang Messages. Both of these types of energetic "Messages" are attributed to the Jing to Qi (Matter to Energy) interactions occurring within the body's tissues. However, the most subtle information contained within and surrounding the body's tissues occurs within the Qi to Shen (Energy to Mind/Spirit) interaction, which is usually overlooked in a Western Clinic.

This special type of Bio-information resonance contains subtle information that can be subdivided into five levels of energetic expression, described as follows (Figure 2.8):

- **Jing Expression:** This refers to information imprinted within matter, form, and patterns.
- **Qi Expression:** This refers to information imprinted within colors, sounds, and electromagnetic fields.
- **Shen Expression:** This refers to information imprinted within the spiritual field of the Mind (i.e., its Beliefs, Thoughts, and Feelings).
- **Wuji (Infinite Space) Expression:** This refers to information imprinted within the infinite field of limitless Space.
- **The Dao (Divine Energy) Expression:** This refers to the divine information and "awakened" awareness imprinted within the very core of all creation.

The infinite space of the Wuji records the vibrational resonance of every action (including all thoughts and emotions), as well as all patterns of light and sound. These energetic impressions are stored within the spiritual plane and exist as psychic impressions. To the trained Daoist disciple, they provide a kind of accessible filing system for

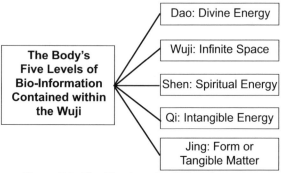

Figure 2.8. The Five Levels of Bio-information contained within the Wuji

information about past history, past lives, or even vital information that can be used for the examination of their own spiritual progress.

In order to access this type of subtle information, a Daoist disciple will go into deep meditation, and energetically stimulate his Niwan Palace, located within the third ventricle of the brain. This will energetically stimulate the disciple's hypothalamic limbic system, allowing him admittance into this subtle energetic field of knowledge and intuitive perception.

The body is composed of trillions upon trillions of energetic molecules. Each molecule is a hologram of ancestral particles, knowledge, and experiences that have existed throughout time and space, spanning our entire history as we know it. These molecules gather to form and create matter. They serve a specific purpose for life transitions and energetic interactions, and then dissolve and transform back into Qi and Shen. Each molecule stores energetic experiences that can be later accessed through spiritual intention.

In Daoist Energetic Embryology, as the molecules gather to form a fetus, energy and ancestral history are stored within the cells of the tissues. This energy is gathered via the environmental, universal, maternal, and paternal energetic fields.

By connecting to a person, place, or item's energetic field, a Daoist disciple is able to access specific information through an internal connection to the patterns and impressions contained within the item's energetic space. This allows the disciple to study and learn about the item's past history, and gain access to the information contained within the molecular structures of its energetic field.

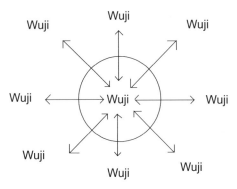

Figure 2.9. The Infinite Space of the Wuji

When performing esoteric Daoist alchemy, deep meditation energetically "opens" the disciple's internal receptivity to the subtle subconscious information contained within his Jing, Qi, and Shen. This "awakening" allows the disciple to access the hidden information and response patterns of the subconscious mind that have become trapped within his tissues, initially programmed by the Ego Mind (Acquired Personality). These "implanted" beliefs, serve as an automatic defence mechanism, and were subconsciously established into the disciple's psyche via the negative influence of the "cultural trance." Through continual meditation practice and repeated "awakenings," the disciple can eventually free himself from the initial programming and habitual patterns that are contrary to his true spiritual nature.

Sending Messages

In the T.C.M. Clinic, Medical Qigong Doctors access the knowledge needed to treat a patient's condition by remaining receptive to the subtle messages stored within his Jing, Qi, and Shen. When the Qigong Doctors emit healing energy into the patient, they are sending subtle healing messages encoded within the emitted Qi. When these imprinted messages are received by the patient's cells, the intended healing process is initiated.

The Perceptual Dimensions of the Wuji

Within the infinite energy of the Wuji, is the history of ancient knowledge that has been gathered and stored since the beginning of time. In Medical Qigong practice, accessing the knowledge

Figure 2.10. The Moon is 238,857 Miles from the Earth

of the infinite space of the Wuji is expressed both through internal and external dimensional perceptions, described as follows (Figure 2.9):

- **The Internal Perceptual Dimension of Wuji:** The infinite knowledge and subtle messages contained within the Wuji, are perceived through enveloping, penetrating, and descending deep into the energetic fields of a person, place, or object. Because this information is not limited by an object's material design or pattern, it can also be easily accessed when enveloping and penetrating the subtle energetic fields of the internal human form.

In Daoist Alchemical practice, the internal energetic field is seen as unlimited, boundless, and beyond all description. The term "Falling into the Wuji," describes the esoteric practice of releasing the Spirit Body from the Physical Body, and fusing with an item's energetic field. In Daoist alchemy, matter is described as consisting of more space than actual physical form, and its energetic properties can be infinitely divided. My teacher once informed me that within the human body there are trillions upon trillions of atoms. If you could expand just one of these atoms to the size of the Earth, the location of the next atom would be as far away as the distance of the Moon (Figure 2.10). This is how much space we have existing within the living tissues of the human body. This infinite amount of space is

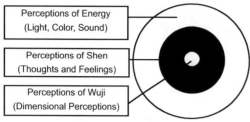

Figure 2.11. Wuji, Qi, and Shen, form a Trinity of Intuitive and Psychic Power.

why, contained within the energetic fields of the Wuji, there are infinite forms, sensations, and perceptions of consciousness.

- **The External Perceptual Dimension of Wuji:** In Daoist Alchemical practice, the external energetic field is also seen as unlimited, boundless, and beyond all description. Although it is unbound by the material, it contains all material things. It is the main energetic vehicle for all life, resonating through sound and light, and permeating everything in the universe.

In the practice of esoteric Daoist Alchemy, the infinite space of the Wuji is one of three universal principles (along with Qi and Shen), which are used for training and developing intuitive and psychic power (Figure 2.11). These three universal principles are also imprinted and manifest within the human soul, allowing divine thought to infuse and animate matter.

Penetrating the Infinite Perceptual Dimensions of the Wuji

Many Medical Qigong Doctors are taught special meditations that allow them to dissolve into the infinite space of the Wuji in order to obtain hidden information concerning various people, places, and things. The following example is a secret meditation taught to me by one of my teachers, and is traditionally used by Daoist priests in order to "Work" with the supernatural energies of sacred objects and sacred places.

- When working with a sacred object, begin by purifying its energy field, then place the sacred object onto the Altar Table.

  If however, you are working with a sacred place, begin by scanning and feeling the exact location of the most powerful energetic vortex

Figure 2.12. Separate Your Three Bodies

from which to sit and "dream" the history of the sacred place, and begin there.
- Next, sit in a relaxed, comfortable location, in order to act as an "observer."
- Then, drop into deep meditation, wherein you begin to activate the energetic fields of your Three Bodies (i.e., energetically "awaken" your Physical Body, Energy Body, and Spirit Body).
- Next, separate the energetic fields of your Three Bodies (Figure 2.12).
- Then, envelop and place the focus of your intention onto the sacred object (or sacred area). Begin to energetically intensify and separate the sacred object's (or sacred area's) three fields (i.e., its physical, energetic, and spiritual fields).
- Begin to increase this focused intention, by "raising" the energetic field. Continue to increase this projected energy until you are able to dissolve the sacred object (or sacred place) into the infinite space of the Wuji. This will allow both time and space to begin to energetically "open."
- After intensifying the energetic charge of the sacred object (or sacred place), quietly receive and observe the subtle manifestations of its imprinted story.
- Then, receive, absorb and ingest this energy into your Three Bodies.
- In order to end the meditation, gently dissolve and reunite your Three Bodies back into your physical form.

CHAPTER 2: UNDERSTANDING ANCIENT CHINESE METAPHYSICS

Figure 2.13. The Daoist Alchemist Wei Boyang

Figure 2.14. Wei Boyang creates the Immortal Elixir with Disciple Yu

Figure 2.15. The Chinese characters for "Taiji" (The "Great Ultimate")

TAIJI: GREAT ULTIMATE

The first record of the Taiji symbol was derived from the ancient book, *The Harmony In the Book of Changes*, written by Daoist Alchemist Wei Boyang (Figure 2.13) in the Eastern Han Dynasty (25 B.C.-225 A.D.). Wei Boyang is famous for his composition of the secret Daoist Immortal Elixir (Figure 2.14). His work talks about the *Yijing (Book of Changes)*, but in fact utilizes its lines and images to discuss the principles of compounding the Immortal Elixir. Knowing nothing about the Divine Elixir, worldly scholars have written several commentaries on it based on Yin and Yang theory, and have truly missed its esoteric meaning.

When deciphering the ancient Chinese characters for Taiji, the character "Tai" translates as "Highest" or "Greatest," and the character "Ji" translates as "Ultimate" or "Extreme." Together, the term "Taiji" can be translated as "the Great Ultimate," and represents the infinite, ultimate state of transformation (Yin transforming into Yang, and Yang transforming into Yin). Both Yin and Yang represent opposite yet complementary energetic qualities of all creation (Figure 2.15).

There is an ancient Daoist saying that states,

> **"The Dao Governs the True,
> and Yin and Yang are
> Transitory Manifestations of it."**

The reunion of Yin and Yang is necessary for the unified existence of all human life. Yang produces Energy and Yin produces Form. Therefore,

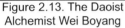

Yang Depicts the Bright Sunny Side of a Hill or River Bank	Yang	Yin	Yin Depicts the Dark Shady Side of a Hill or River Bank
	Active	Passive	
	Creative	Receptive	
	Masculine	Feminine	
Sun Above the Horizon	Back	Front	A Covering Over Clouds
	Left	Right	
	Fire	Water	
Hill or Mound	Hot	Cold	Hill or Mound
	Dry	Wet	
	Hard	Soft	
Sun's Rays Shining Down	Light	Heavy	Clouds Mist
	Bright	Dark	
Yang Fire	Heaven	Earth	Yin Water
	Sun	Moon	
	White	Black	
Yang Yao Line			Yin Yao Line

The Chinese Yang (Heaven) and Yin (Earth) Symbols: The Yang is represented by white, Yin is represented by black, and the center of the circle represents the Eternal Dao within the Wuji.

Figure 2.16. Yang and Yin

energetically, Taiji is considered to be the origin of change or movement, which initiates "creation."

The Chinese ideogram for Yang depicts the bright, sunny side of a hill or river bank; while Yin is depicted as the dark, shady side of a hill or river bank (Figure 2.16). Yin exists within Yang, and Yang within Yin. The dynamic balance of Yin and Yang constantly changes and transforms the body's life-force energy.

- Yang energetically manifests as active, creative, masculine, hot, hard, light, Heaven, Sun, white, and bright.

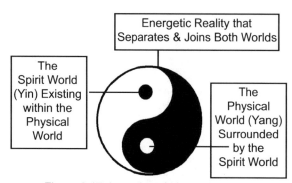

Figure 2.17. In ancient Chinese Alchemy, the two circles within the Yin and Yang symbol represented the mysterious existence of the Spirit World that exists within the Physical World; as well as the Physical World surrounded by the Spirit World. The center dividing line represents the Energetic World, and is considered to be the secret bridge that both separates and joins these two worlds.

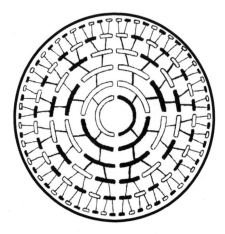

Figure 2.18. The ever-changing energy of Yin and Yang, is continually active within the human body

- Yin energetically manifests as passive, receptive, feminine, cold, soft, dark, Earth, Moon, black, and shadow.

All matter is composed of different relative proportions of Yin and Yang energy. Within the infinite space of the Wuji, both Yin and Yang energy gathers or disperses in order to balance the forces of Nature. To the ancient Daoists Alchemist, the theory of Yin and Yang energy represented the duality of balance and harmony within the human body, as well as within the universe itself.

The two circles within the Yin and Yang symbol represented the mysterious existence of the spirit world that lives within the physical world, as well as the physical world surrounded by the spirit world (Figure 2.17). The center dividing line represented the energetic world, considered the bridge that separated the two worlds.

TAIJI WITHIN THE HUMAN BODY

In ancient Chinese Medicine, the theory of Yin and Yang energy represents the duality of balance and harmony within the body, as well as within the universe. All comprehensions of Traditional Chinese Medical physiology, pathology and treatment can be expressed through the clinical understanding of Yin and Yang energetics).

In the Medical Qigong clinic, the body's tissues are understood to have energetic aspects that can be classified in terms of Yin and Yang. Every person has both Yin and Yang elements within them, but will tend to be predominantly one or the other in terms of personality, physique, life-style preferences, speech patterns and mannerisms. Within a general constitution, there will be more subtle patterns and fluctuations along the Yin and Yang continuum, as the body reacts to external and internal energetic movements. For example, when designing the patient's exercise program, diet, or herbal remedies, it is necessary to first determine whether the patient was predominantly Yin or Yang in constitution.

YIN AND YANG TRANSFORMATIONS

According to the basic foundational teachings of Daoist Alchemy, from the Wuji, the Dao creates Yin and Yang, which in turn gives birth to the Four Phases of Universal Energy (i.e., Great Yang, Lesser Yang, Great Yin and Lesser Yin). The Four Phases of Universal Energy give birth to the eight natural forces of the Bagua (Heaven, Thunder, Water, Mountain, Earth, Wind, Fire and Lake). These special Four Phases also create the energetic basis of the Prenatal and Postnatal transformations, manifested in the form of eight energetic actions via the Bagua. The eight energetic actions act as a template for all creation and can further be manifested through the ever-changing Yin and Yang energetic forms of the 64 Hexagrams of the Yi-Jing (Figure 2.18).

CHAPTER 2: UNDERSTANDING ANCIENT CHINESE METAPHYSICS

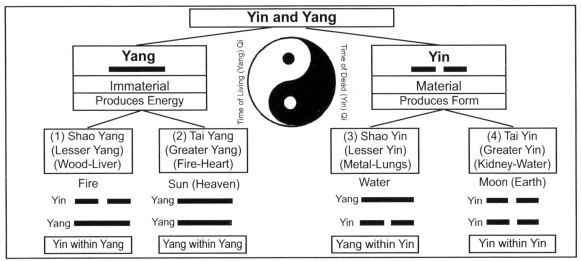

Figure 2.19. The energy of Yin and Yang gives birth to Sixiang (Four Phases) of Universal Energy

SIXIANG: 4 PHASES OF UNIVERSAL QI

The ancient Daoists understood that from the Wuji, the Dao creates the Yin and Yang of Taiji, which in turn gives birth to Sixiang (Four Phases) of universal energy (Figure 2.19). The ancient Daoist text *Huai Nan Zi ("The Masters of Huainan")* states,

> "The combined essence
> of Heaven and Earth
> become Yang and Yin;
> the concentrated essences
> of Yin and Yang
> gives birth to the Four Phases
> of universal energy;
> and the scattered essence
> of the Four Phases
> become the myriad creatures
> of the mundane physical world"

These four energetic phases (Lesser Yang, Great Yang, Lesser Yin, and Great Yin), create the great powers from which the ancient Daoist describe the Four Appearances (Si Xiang) of the celestial and terrestrial energetic transformations (i.e., the Four Principal Time Periods, Four Seasons, Four Directions, Four Quarters of Life, etc.).

In Daoist Alchemy, the Four Principal Time Periods (Zi, Mao, Wu, and You) facilitate the vigorous growth of internal energy, in harmony with the changes of energy in Nature. For example:

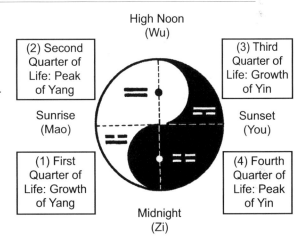

Figure 2.20. The Four Principle Time Periods

- **To Nourish The Qi:** Practice Qi Cultivation during Sunrise (Mao) and/or Sunset (You).
- **To Stabilize The Qi:** Practice Qi Cultivation during Midnight (Zi) and/or High Noon (Wu).

The following is a brief explanation of the Four Principal Time Periods that correspond to the Four Phases (Figure 2.20 and Figure 2.21):

1. **The Zi Time Period (Kidney-Water):** The Zi time period is at Midnight (between 11 p.m. – 1 a.m.), and corresponds to the Kidney's core energy. At Midnight (12:00 a.m.) the air is cool, and the energy naturally contracts and sinks. This time period is related to the peak

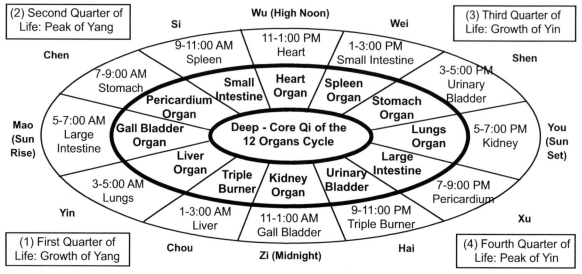

Figure 2.21. The Body's Superficial (External) and Deep (Internal) Energy Cycles
(The Four Principle Time Periods and based on the Deep - Core Qi of the 12 Organ Cycle)

of Yin cycle (12:00 a.m.) and the beginning of the Yang cycle (1:00 a.m.). It is associated with the energy of Tai Yin (Greater Yin), and is the perfect time period for gathering and storing the energy of the Yuan Qi (Original Energy). Because the Yuan Qi is the root of life, formed through the divine combination of the Primordial Yin and Yang, it is stored primarily in the Kidney's Water energy. During this time, the Yin aspect of the Kidney's energy is in full harmony, continuously combining and accumulating energy. Therefore, practicing Qi Cultivation meditations and exercises during this time period results in twice the effect with half the effort.

2. **The Mao Time Period (Liver-Wood):** The Mao time period is at Sunrise (between 5:00 a.m. – 7:00 a.m.), and corresponds to the Gall Bladder's core energy. As the Sun rises (6:00 a.m.), it warms the air in the Eastern direction increasing the temperature. This is considered to be the time period of the natural progressive energy of Shao Yang (Lesser Yang). During this time, the Liver's Yang energy is in full harmony, and the body is continuously combining and accumulating energy within the Gall Bladder. During the time of Sunrise, the Yang Qi of the body is in a state of expansion. Therefore, practicing Qi Cultivation meditations and exercises during this time period aids the vigorous growth of Yang.

3. **The Wu Time Period (Heart-Fire):** The Wu time period is at High Noon (between 11:00 a.m. – 1:00 p.m.), and corresponds to the Heart's core energy. At High Noon (12:00 p.m.), the air temperature increases, initiating the Yang processes of rising and expanding. This time period is related to the peak of the Yang cycle (12:00 p.m.) and the beginning of the Yin cycle (1:00 p.m.). This time period is thus associated with the growing energy of Tai Yang (Greater Yang). During this time, the Heart's energy is in full harmony, and is continuously accumulating energy. However, during this time period, the Yang energy peaks, then begins to wane rather than grow. Therefore, practicing Qi Cultivation meditations and exercises during this time period can also be used to help increase the growth of Yin energy and suppress hyperactive Yang energy.

4. **The You Time Period (Lung-Metal):** The You time period is at Sunset (between 5 p.m. – 7 p.m.), and corresponds to the Lung's core

energy. At dusk (6:00 p.m.), as the Sun begins to set, the energy of the environment turns from clear and radiant to dark. The heat in the air disperses and its volume diminishes and slowly withdraws. During this time, the energy of the Lungs is in full harmony, and is continuously combining and accumulating energy. This time period is associated with the gathering energy of Shao Yin (Lesser Yin). Therefore, practicing Qi Cultivation meditations and exercises during this time period nurtures and increases the Prenatal Yin Qi and the conservation and nourishment of Yang Qi.

From the Four Phases to the Bagua

The Four Phases of universal energy give birth to eight natural forces (Figure 2.22). These transformational forces are known in Daoist practices as the mystical powers of the Bagua (Eight Trigrams), and are categorized as: Heaven, Thunder, Water, Mountain, Earth, Wind, Fire, and Lake. Because of this, the Four Phases also form the energetic basis of all of the Prenatal and Postnatal transformations occurring within Heaven, Earth, and Man, which are traditionally manifested in the form of these eight energetic actions.

Because of this important observation, the study and understanding of the ever changing energies of Heaven, Earth, and Man was essential for obtaining proper medical diagnosis in ancient China:

- **Heaven's Qi:** Related to the study of Chinese Astrology, and the influence of the celestial energies of the Sun, Moon, Planets, and Stars.
- **Earth's Qi:** Related to the study of Feng Shui, and the influence of the energy of Wind and Water on the Soil (Earth), as brought about by the seasonal changes.
- **Man's Qi:** Related to the study of the Yi-Jing, and the 64 Divination Patterns, observed through the six lined oracular Hexagrams.

Eight Prenatal and Postnatal energetic patterns acted as a template for all creation, and could be further combined to form the ever-changing energetic patterns of the 64 Hexagrams of the *Yi-Jing*.

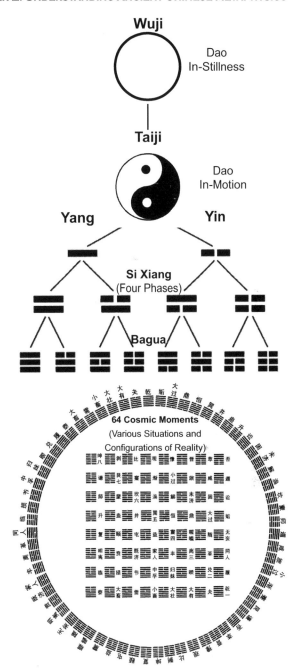

Figure 2.22. From Wuji (Dao in Stillness) comes the Yin and Yang of Taiji (Dao in Motion); From Taiji comes the Sixiang (Four Phases). The Sixiang give birth to the eight natural forces of Bagua (Eight Trigrams). The Yin and Yang transforming Bagua gives birth to the 64 Yi-Jing Divination Hexagrams.

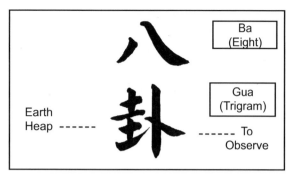

Figure 2.23. "Bagua" ("Eight Trigrams")

BAGUA: EIGHT TRIGRAMS

The term "Bagua" is commonly translated as "Eight Trigrams" (Figure 2.23). The Chinese character "Ba" translates as the number "Eight." The ideogram for "Gua" is composed of two symbols, on the right is the radical meaning "To Observe;" on the left is the radical "Gui" meaning "Earth Heap." In ancient China, the Gui was a special Earth Heap that was traditionally used to measure shadows and record segments of time. A "Gua" was therefore seen as an ancient symbol of "Divination," and was originally used for observing the movements of the Sun and Moon (Figure 2.24). Together, the term "Bagua" describes the eight important Daoist magical patterns used for depicting the basic powers and fundamental law of all energetic movement and transformation occurring within the Three Realms of Heaven, Man, Earth (Figure 2.25).

These eight energetic patterns are symbolized by joining combinations of Yin and Yang lines (known as a "Yao"), together. Traditionally, a Yin Yao is represented as a broken line (- -), and a Yang Yao is represented as a solid line (---). Each of the Eight Trigrams is composed of three Yao lines, constructed with either a Yin Yao, a Yang Yao, or a combination of both (Figure 2.26).

One ancient poem traditionally taught to Daoist disciples to help them memorize these special eight trigram patterns goes as follows:

**"Three Lines Heaven - Six Lines Earth.
Bowl Up Thunder - Bowl Down Mountain.
Middle Yin Fire - Middle Yang Water.
Broken Top Lake - Broken Bottom Wind."**

Figure 2.24. It is interesting to note, that the ancient Sundial of the Zhou Dynasty (1028-221 B.C.) was called a "Guibiao." At the rounded of a long tablet (called a "Gui") on an Earth Heap, was placed a gnomon (the pointer on a Sundial) known as a "Biao." The Biao was used to cast a shadow onto the Gui in order to reveal the exact time of day, season and year.

If you add the Chinese character for "Divining" (representing a divination-crack observed within a tortoise shell or bone) to the right of the Gui character, then you create the character for "Gua" (meaning Trigram or Hexagram).

Six lines are traditionally used because there are Six Moons (i.e., months) from the shortest shadow at Midsummer, until longest shadow at Midwinter; and then again 6 Moons/Months until next Midsummer.

Figure 2.25. The Prenatal Bagua

Figure 2.26. Yin and Yang Yao Trigram

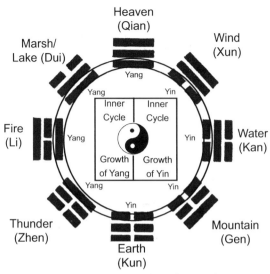

Figure 2.27. The Inner Yao Circle of the Prenatal Bagua Represents the Celestial Seasonal Yin and Yang Cycles of the Sun.

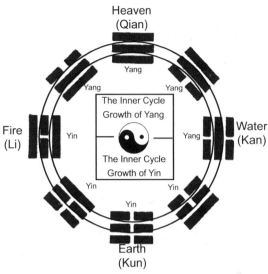

Figure 2.28. The Middle Yao Circle of the Prenatal Bagua Represents the Terrestrial Yin and Yang Cycles of each Earth day.

The Bagua, The Sun, and the Moon

When specifically observing the energetic cycles of the Sun and Moon through the Bagua patterns, each trigram "Yao" represented a basic unit of the Eight Trigrams, and had three meanings: Sunlight, Moonlight and the mutual projection of the Sun and Moon. The Yao Trigram itself was observed as the symbol of the energetic movement (both internal and external) of the Sun and Moon.

- **Year (Heaven and Earth):** The Inner Circle Yao Lines of the Prenatal Bagua configuration begins either with the extreme Heavenly Yang Trigram "Qian," located at the top; or with the extreme Earthly Yin Trigram "Kun," located at the bottom. These two transforming powers of Yin and Yang express the Sun's movement during the seasonal year (Figure 2.27).
- **Day (Fire and Water):** The Middle Circle Yao Lines of the Prenatal Bagua configuration begins either the Fire Yang Trigram "Li," located at the left side (Sunrise); or with the Water Yin Trigram "Kan," located at the right (Sunset). These two transforming powers of Fire and Water express the growth and decline of Yang and Yin during the Earth's rotation within each day and revolution within each year (Figure 2.28).

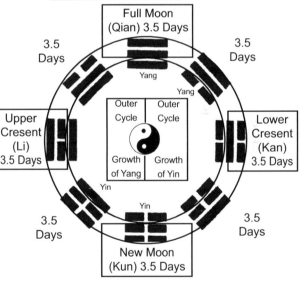

Figure 2.29. The Outer Circle (last Two Yao) of the Prenatal Bagua Represents the Celestial Yin and Yang Monthly Cycles of the Moon

- **Month (Moon):** The Outer Circle Yao lines of the Prenatal Bagua configuration are composed of both the middle and outer Yaos. It represents the transformation of Yin and Yang energy in the Moon's movement, which can be observed each lunar month (Figure 2.29).

VOLUME 1, SECTION 1: FOUNDATIONS OF CHINESE ENERGETIC MEDICINE

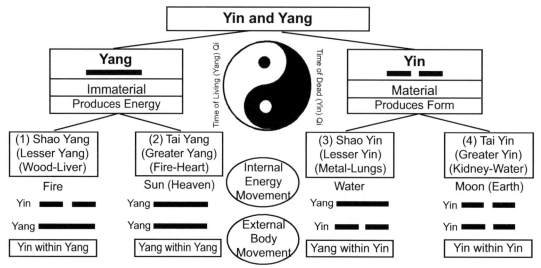

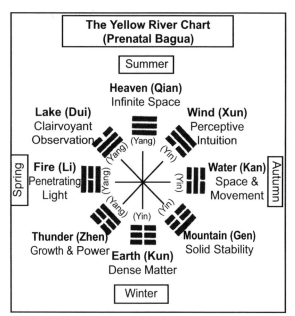

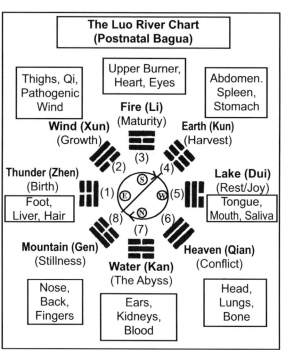

The Prenatal Bagua Trigrams
Eight Dimensions or Phases of Energy
Polar Opposites: Yin across from Yang.
This Cycle of Harmony relates to the
World of Thoughts and Ideas;
The Opposition of Energetic Forces;
and the Creation of All Phenomena.

The Postnatal Bagua Trigrams
The Energetic Cycles of Forces are the
External Manifestations of Divine Thought
(The World of Phenomena or Senses)

Figure 2.30. The Ancient Daoist Concept of Yin and Yang Expressing the Four Phases of Universal Energy and Manifesting Through the Prenatal and Postnatal Bagua Trigrams (Pre-Five Element Theory).

The Eight Trigrams	Heaven Qian	Mist, Rain Dui	Fire Li	Thunder Zhen	Earth Kun	Mountain Gen	Water Kan	Wind/Air Xun
Yang and Yin	Yang	Yang	Yang	Yang	Yin	Yin	Yin	Yin
General Principles	Creative	Reflective	Bright	Exciting	Receptive	Steady	Dark	Penetrating
	Activity	Weightless	Formed	Impetus	Passivity	Heaviness	Formless	Sensitivity
Principles of Nature	Immaterial	Evaporation	Solar Forces	Vitality	Material	Inertia	Lunar Forces	Assimilation
	Universal	Inorganic	Elementary	Organic	Universal	Inorganic	Elementary	Pervasiveness
	Formless	Changeability	Heat	Mobility	Form	Resistance	Cold	Organic
	Energy	Evaporation	Incandescence	Fertilization	Matter	Inertia	Fluidity	Gaseous
	Infinite Space	Clairvoyant Observation	Penetrating Light	Growth and Power	Dense Matter	Solid Stability	Space and Movement	Perceptive Intuition

Figure 2.31. The Bagua Trigram Powers According to the Universal Forces of Yin and Yang

BAGUA ENERGETIC MANIFESTATIONS

The Prenatal (Before Birth) Bagua and the Postnatal (After Birth) Bagua, as well as their energetic manifestations were extensively studied by the ancient Daoist for their hidden alchemical meanings (Figure 2.30). Because the Four Phases formed the energetic basis of all Prenatal and Postnatal transformations, it was believed that all movements of Heaven, Earth, and all living things, could be depicted by these special Bagua images:

- **The Prenatal Bagua (Yin - Spirit Realm Trigrams):** These special Bagua (attributed to Fu Xi) were defined as the Eight Dimensions (or Phases) of energetic polar opposites. This was the Cycle of Harmony that related to the World of Thoughts and Ideas. It manifested as the opposition of energetic forces, that were responsible for the creation of all phenomena. In this special energetic pattern, the Celestial Qi descends from Heaven into Earth, and represents harmony and balance occurring between the Five Elements.
- **The Postnatal Bagua (Yang - Human Realm Trigrams):** These special Bagua (attributed to King Wen) were defined as the energetic Cycle of Forces, that are observed as the external manifestations of Divine Thought within the World of Sensory Phenomena. In this special pattern, the Terrestrial Qi Ascends from Earth towards the Heavens, and denotes the destruction occurring between the Five Elements.

The Postnatal (After Birth) Bagua system depicts the creation of all phenomena and focuses on the fundamental principles of Earthly transformation. In this system, the trigrams are arranged according to the increasing or decreasing qualities of physical life (beginning at Zhen - Thunder, and following a clockwise progression). These Earthly principles represent a chronological and energetic sequence moving around the periphery of the Bagua circle, instead of matching powers through opposite polarity alignment as in the Prenatal Bagua system. The following are several "interpretations" used by Daoist mystics when studying the ever changing energetic patterns of life, expressed by the Bagua (Figure 2.31).

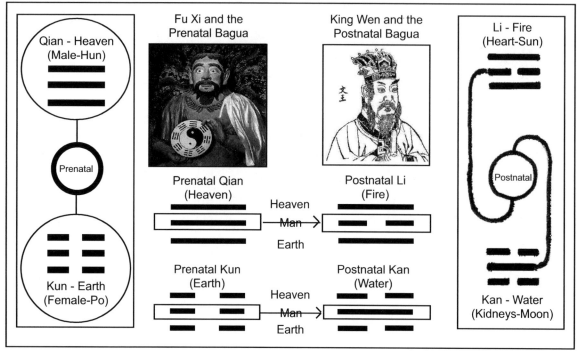

Figure 2.32. The ancient Daoist understanding of Prenatal and Postnatal Transformations. Together they are known as the Four Phases of Daoist Alchemy.

- **Thunder (Zhen) Exciting Birth:** Starting with Zhen, which represents Thunder, energy births forth as the exciting first impulse or creative stimulation of Qi; humans begin the progression of awakening consciousness.
- **Wind/Air (Xun) Penetrating Growth:** The Xun Trigram does not necessarily correspond to simply Wind as Air, rather it symbolizes the energy of emotion; expressing feelings and the inner development of pure transformation.
- **Fire (Li) Radiant Maturity:** The Li Trigram does not necessarily correspond to simply Fire, rather it symbolizes illuminated maturity, vitality and full development of self-consciousness, as well as clinging and possessiveness.
- **Earth (Kun) Receptive Harvest:** The Kun Trigram does not necessarily correspond to simply Earth, rather it symbolizes the state of openness, receptivity and fertility, which occurs after spiritual maturity has been attained.
- **Lake/Mist (Dui) Reflective Rest and Joy:** The Dui Trigram does not necessarily correspond to Lake/Mist as water, rather it symbolizes rest, contemplation, and joyful reflection.
- **Heaven (Qian) Creative Conflict:** The Qian Trigram does not necessarily correspond to Heaven as the cosmos, rather it symbolizes creative forces, and an accountable state of mind which must be acquired in order to truly possess divine purpose.
- **Water (Kan) The Dark Abyss:** The Kan Trigram does not necessarily correspond to Water, but denotes the greatest spiritual depth (maturity), as well as the danger of a bottomless abyss into which we may fall if we lose control of ourselves.
- **Mountain (Gen) Steady Stillness:** The Gen Trigram does not necessarily correspond to Mountain, rather it symbolizes quietness, inwardness, and solid completion, as well as mental stagnation or spiritual death.

BAGUA ENERGETIC TRANSFORMATIONS

The ancient Daoists believed that after an individual was born, his internal energy field immediately changed. The radiant Heavenly Qi, represented by the Qian Trigram (placed on top of Fu Xi's Prenatal Bagua pattern), was suddenly transformed from a pure Tai Yang state (depicted by three solid Yao lines), into a Shao Yang Fire Energy, represented by the Li Trigram (depicted as having one Yin Yao positioned in-between two Yang Yao lines). Additionally, the individual's spiritual connection with the Earth Qi, represented by the Kun Trigram (located on the bottom of Fu Xi's Prenatal Bagua pattern), also transformed from a pure Tai Yin state (depicted as three broken Yin Yao lines) into a type of Water Energy, represented by the Kan Trigram (depicted as having one Yang Yao positioned in-between two Yin Yao lines).

The primary goal of ancient Daoist Alchemy was to purify and refine the body's acquired Postnatal Qi, cultivate Prenatal Qi, and transform both energies into Ling Qi (Spiritualized Energy) and Shen Ling (Spiritualized Mind). This important cultivation practice was deemed necessary in order to create and establish the coveted Immortal Body.

Traditionally, a Daoist disciple would be taught how to transform his body's Postnatal Li (Fire) energetic state (traditionally placed on top of King Wen's Postnatal Bagua pattern), back into its original Prenatal "Qian" Heaven energetic state. Simultaneously, the disciple would also work to transform the energy of his body's Postnatal Kan (Water) energetic state (traditionally placed on the bottom of King Wen's Postnatal Bagua pattern), back into its original Prenatal Kun (Earth) energetic state (Figure 2.32). This continual Blending and Steaming cultivation practice was used to internally harmonize and transform the energy of Heaven and Earth, currently existing within the disciple's body.

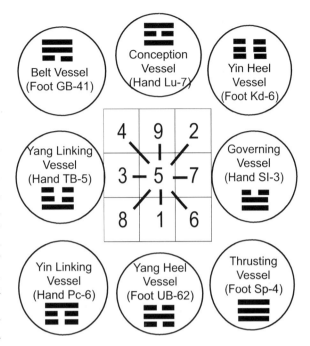

Figure 2.33. The Postnatal Eight Trigrams Form the Magic Square

BAGUA CREATIVE FORMATIONS

In modern Chinese Energetic Medicine, both the Prenatal and Postnatal Bagua energetic patterns are assigned to specific stages of cellular division, forming within the developing zygote (explained later in this chapter).

Additionally, each of the Eight Trigrams are assigned to one of the Eight Extraordinary Vessels responsible for fetal growth, causing specific areas of fetal tissue to develop. The Postnatal Bagua energetic pattern of the Eight Extraordinary Vessels is traditionally placed within the structural formation of the Daoist priest's "Magic Square" (Figure 2.33).

The ancient Clinical Applications of the Prenatal and Postnatal Eight Trigrams are addressed in *The Secret Teachings of Chinese Energetic Medicine: Volume 3*.

The Wu Xing: Five Elements

In the Chinese ideogram for "Wuxing," the character "Wu" translates as "Five," and the character "Xing" translates as "Movement, Process, Manifestation, or Phase." Therefore, the term "Wuxing" is traditionally translated as "Five Phases" or "Five Elements," and is considered an energetic template based on the study of five phases or processes of energetic manifestation and transformation (Figure 2.34). These special Five Element phases are traditionally known as Wood, Fire, Earth, Metal, and Water.

Figure 2.34. "Wuxing" ("Five Phases")

In ancient China, the five unique properties of the Five Elements were used to explain, classify, and characterize all natural phenomena of creation, such as their unique shape, movement, sound, color, taste, direction, force, and energetic function. In Chinese Energetic Medicine, each unique phase is also used in order to classify all tangible and intangible substances into five specific categories (e.g., five senses, five viscera, five emotions, five virtues, five flavors, five seasons, five phases of energetic transition, etc.); all of which can be used for clinical observation, study, diagnosis, and treatment. For example:

- **Wood Element Qi:** Is energetically defined as being Expansive, Sprouting, and Windy. It also corresponds to the East Direction, Green or Blue Color, Sour Taste, "Jue" (Me-E Tone) Sound, Rancid Smell, Virtue of Compassion, and the Emotion of Anger.
- **Fire Element Qi:** Is energetically defined as being Ascending, Blooming, and Hot. It also corresponds to the South Direction, Red Color, Bitter Taste, "Zhi" (So-G Tone) Sound, Scorched Smell, Virtue of Inner-Peace, and the Emotion of Excitement.
- **Earth Element Qi:** Is energetically defined as being Harmonizing, Ripening, and Damp. It also corresponds to the Center Direction, Yellow or Brown Color, Sweet Taste, "Gong" (Do-C Tone) Sound, Fragrant Smell, Virtue of Honesty, and the Emotion of Worry.
- **Metal Element Qi:** Is energetically defined as being Contracting, Withering, and Dry. It also corresponds to the West Direction, White or Clear Color, Pungent Taste, "Shang" (Re-D

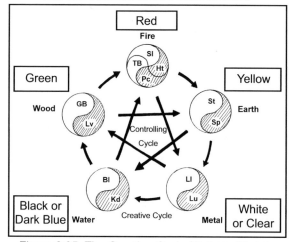

Figure 2.35. The Creating Cycle (Outside Circle), and the Controlling Cycle (Inside Circle)

Tone) Sound, Rotten Smell, Virtue of Trustful Integrity, and the Emotion of Grief
- **Water Element Qi:** Is energetically defined as being Descending, Dormant, and Cold. It also corresponds to the North Direction, Dark Blue or Black Color, Salty Taste, "Yu" (La-A Tone) Sound, Scorched Smell, Virtue of Wisdom, and the Emotion of Fear.

The Five Element Cycles

Traditionally, there are two main energetic cycles used in Five Element Theory to describe the various manifestations and interactions occurring within matter, energy, and spirit (Figure 2.35). These are traditionally known as the Creating Cycle, (one Element producing another) and the Controlling Cycle (one Element controlling another). To the ancient Daoists, all energy was in the process of either being created, controlled, or dissolving back into the infinite space from which it originated.

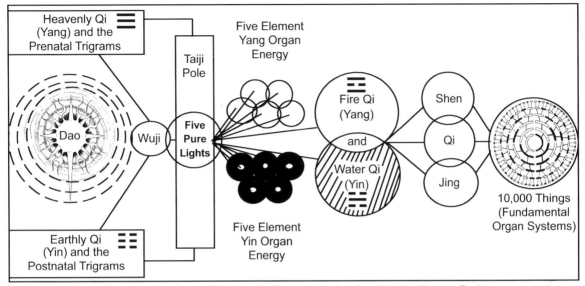

Figure 2.36. Stages of Energetic Transformation Forming the Human Body

The Five Pure Lights

The ancient Daoists believed that the energetic and spiritual components of the Five Elements originally existed as "Five Pure Lights," which emanated as a subtle expression of the "Primordial Luminosity" of the Dao. In ancient China, it was traditionally taught that the Original Nature of the "True" Five Elements, existed as pure radiant light, energetically pulsing from within the infinite space of the Wuji. According to ancient Daoist texts,

> **"When Yin and Yang divided,**
> **the Five Pure Lights shot forth;**
> **Spontaneously born from**
> **the infinite space of the Wuji,**
> **they appeared as rays of Divine light,**
> **that came before the creation of the world."**

The "Five Pure Lights" were considered the energies from which all other energies (including visible light) arose. As they transformed to become the various dimensions of existence (matter, energy, and spirit) they formed the different realms or worlds in which we now exist.

One of the Daoist teachers secretly told me, "For the uneducated, all matter appears as real. This is due to the individual's inability to recognize the subtle influences and effects of the Five Pure Lights in this realm. This subtle illusion of matter also extends to the "formless realms," and clouds the minds of the "unawakened." The five colors of the Five Pure Lights are the original source of the Five Elements. They are the underlying energetic and spiritual structures of both the external existence of the material world, and the internal existence of the individual's Mind. In seeing this, we perceive the Five Elements in their gross material form, but in all reality, the source of these Elements is the pure light of the eternal Dao."

My teacher then went on to explain that in Energetic Embryology, it is traditionally taught that at the time of conception, an individual's soul will begin the process of accumulating and harmonizing the various energies of the Five Elements in order to construct the various tissues of his or her physical body. As the energy of the Five Elements begin to construct the physical body, their original spiritual components establish an important relationship with the forming tissues. Internally, the Five Pure Lights begin to manifest into the Jing level of the body's organs, and inhabit the various channels, tissues, and fluids, which communicate externally via the five senses (Figure 2.36).

This interconnected communication creates a powerful way to energize the body's internal system. This is one of the main reasons why such meditations as "Eating the Five Sprouts" are diligently practiced in Daoist Alchemy, and are traditionally used in order to energetically build and fortify the tissues of the body. The interconnections of the various Five Element correspondences are therefore studied in great detail by a Daoist disciple, before beginning the internal construction of the "Immortal Fetus."

Within the human body, the energetic qualities of the Five Elements are divided into Yin (solid) and Yang (hollow) organ energies. These Five Element energies sustain the tissues and establish the foundation for all of the body's internal organ systems (e.g., digestive system, cardiovascular system, reproductive system, endocrine system, nervous system, etc.). The body's internal energetic states continually change, affected internally by thoughts and emotions, and externally by the various energetic changes in the temperatures of the seasons, and by weather.

Externally, an individual's energy field is influenced by four main transformational conditions. Each of these changes correspond to a specific Element, Trigram, season, color, taste, smell, sound, and energetic application. During each of the four Seasons, the Earth Qi causes the environmental energetic fields to rise, expand, sink, or contract, depending on the solar influence, for example (Figure 2.37):

- **Spring, the Wood/Wind Element:** This "Wind" energy manifests through conditions and temperatures of Hot (ascending Yang at the core) and Wet (expanding Yin at the peak).
- **Summer, the Fire Element:** This "Heat" energy manifests through conditions and temperatures of Hot (ascending Yang at the core) and Dry (contracting Yang at the peak).
- **Autumn, the Metal Element:** This "Dry" energy manifests through conditions and temperatures of Dry (contracting Yang at the core) and Cold (descending Yin at the peak).
- **Winter, the Water Element:** This "Cold" energy manifests through conditions and temperatures of Cold (descending Yin at the core) and Wet (expanding Yin at the peak).

To the ancient Daoists, the various energies

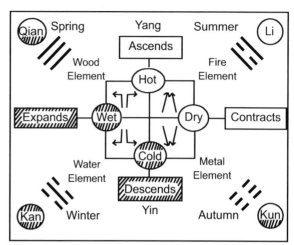

Figure 2.37. Four Main External Conditions

of the Five Elements were also at the effect of the celestial powers of the Sun and the Moon. For example, the High (Yang) and Low (Yin) energies of the ocean are manifested through the strength and power of its waves and currents, which are effected by the celestial power of the Moon. Likewise, the various internal currents and "seas" of the body respond to the energetic pull of the Moon, and carry their own energetic pulse that follows the rhythm of the body's own "high and low tides."

The Cold (Yin) and Hot (Yang) energies of the Earth are effected through the heat and light of the Sun's Radiance. Likewise, the energy of the various internal organs are at the effect of the radiant spiritual light of the Yuan Shen (Original Spirit), which is also affected by the quality of radiant light contained within the surrounding environment.

Because of the intense light and heat of the Sun, the energetic tides that flow during the day time and influence the human body, are fundamentally different from the energetic currents that flow during the night. Because these energetic currents always change, the ancient Daoists believed that the particular types of Yin, Yang, and Five Element energies that were manifesting during the exact year, month, day, and hour when a disciple took his "first breath" (known as the Four Pillars), would define his personality, and outline his particular fate during the course of their life.

THE THREE BODIES AND THREE WORLDS

To review, from the eternal Dao emerges the infinite space of the Wuji (the "Ultimate Emptiness"). From this quiescent energetic state (considered to be the "Dao in Stillness") comes the Yin and Yang of Taiji (considered to be the "Dao in Motion"). From the continual energetic interaction of the Taiji, comes the Sixiang (Four Phases), which give birth to the energies of the Four Seasons (Spring, Summer, Autumn, and Winter) and the eight natural forces of the Bagua. The continual Yin and Yang transformations occurring within the Bagua (Eight Trigrams), gives birth to the 64 Yi-Jing Divination Hexagrams, and manifest as the creative influence of the 10,000 Things (everything in existence). This energetic subdivision of matter, energy, and spirit create the foundation for the existence of worlds within worlds, separated by their different vibrational frequencies. Just as each person is intrinsically constructed of three unique bodies (i.e., a physical body, energy body and spirit body), so too are there three realms of external existence, manifesting as a physical realm, an energetic realm, and a spirit realm (Figure 2.38).

In the study of Chinese Energetic Medicine, it is essential that the student have a clear understanding of the subtle energetic matrix that creates and maintains each of his Three Bodies. This is because, all of the clinical treatments and special prescription exercises and meditations surrounding Chinese Energetic Medicine place its focus on aligning, healing, and utilizing the energetic fields of the Three Bodies.

The infinite space of the Wuji provides the energetic medium which joins both matter and spirit, as well as the energetic matrix through which all things exist (i.e., the 10,000 things). These energetic and spiritual fields are classified according to the specific characteristics and laws of universal cycles, that were set forth by the energetic and spiritual natures of the Bagua (Eight Trigrams) and the Wuxing (Five Elements) according to ancient Daoist understandings.

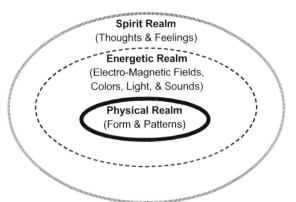

Figure 2.38. In the same manner that the human body is made of a Physical Body, Energy Body and Spirit Body, there is also a Physical Universe, Energetic Universe, and Spiritual Universe.

According to ancient Daoist teachings, every human soul is composed of and enveloped by Three Bodies (i.e., a Physical Body, an Energy Body, and a Spirit Body). Because these Three Bodies are intrinsically interlinked, they constantly influence the energetic fields of one another. By understanding and training these Three Bodies, a student of Chinese Energetic Medicine will be able to establish a deeper connection and more powerful influence over the various physical, energetic, and spiritual fields resonating within and without his body's tissues.

In Chinese Energetic Embryology, it is taught that while in the mother's womb, the human soul was initially enveloped within the luminous orb of its Spirit Body. The Energy Body was simultaneously constructed and formed within the subtle matrix of the Spirit Body during the gestation period. At this delicate time of internal growth, the Physical Body was continually constructed within the subtle matrix of both the Energy Body and Spirit Body. This important energetic interaction and transformation, allows the individual to live within the lower levels of creation (i.e., matter, form, and substance), yet simultaneously interact with the other "higher" realms of existence (e.g., dreams, thoughts, desires, etc.). All of the Three Bodies have substance, yet they simultaneously exist at different levels of vibration.

THE PHYSICAL BODY & PHYSICAL WORLD

In Chinese Energetic Medicine, the Physical Body (Figure 2.39) corresponds to Jing (Essence), the Lower Dantian, the energy of the Earth, and to Yin Qi. In this context, Jing is defined as the body's tangible essence, and can be best understood as being a morphogenic field of energy that creates and sustains the body's physical form. It is considered to be the lower vibrational frequency of the human energy matrix.

The Physical Body operates within the restrictive realm of the Physical World (the Realm of Matter), which has both form and substance, and is accessible through the ordinary senses. The Physical Body is also associated with slower vibrational resonance, wherein Qi congeals into dense pools of matter, form, and substance, and is subject to the laws of three dimensionality (i.e., it can only occupy one position in space). To the ancient Daoists, the Physical World simply appears to be solid, because it vibrates on the same frequency as matter. However, they understood that everything which exists in the Physical World also has an energetic and spiritual counterpart.

It is through the Physical Body, that an individual will express his personal thoughts and beliefs. Which create the various energetic patterns that continually manifest themselves through the vibrational resonance of the internal organs and tissues. Because every particle, atom, and cell of the Physical Body has its own unique energetic and spiritual counterpart, in order to rise above this lower realm of understanding, an individual must become "awakened" to the subtle energetic fields active and currently resonating within his Energy Body and Spirit Body.

While orienting from the Physical Body, an individual's level of experience is only accessible through his five ordinary senses, which expresses itself through various interactions with people, places, things, and events. Because this is the lower energetic plane of thought, individuals orienting through life from the realm of physical senses cannot detect the Spirit, which is beyond the Realm of Matter.

The Physical Earth has within its unique structure an Energetic Earth (the Earth as it exists within the realm of the Fourth Dimension), as well as a Spirit Earth (the Earth as it exists within the realm of the Fifth Dimension).

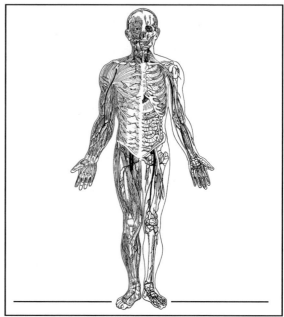

Figure 2.39. Jing: the "Physical" Body

THE ENERGY BODY & ENERGETIC WORLD

The Energy Body (Figure 2.40) corresponds to Qi (Energy and "Breath"), the Middle Dantian, the energy of "Man," and to Combined Yin and Yang Energy. Within the human body, it is the life-force energy (Qi) that maintains the quality and vital functional aspects of the Jing, and serves as a special energetic "womb" that is formed and contained within and around the Physical Body.

The Energy Body sustains the human body's energetic field, and is responsible for activating and maintaining the tissue's electromagnetic channel system. Because it distributes vitality throughout the tissues by energetic transference, it is considered to be the middle vibrational frequency of the human energetic matrix. The vibrational field of the Energy Body contains and sustains thoughts and emotions, and interacts with the vibrational fields of both the body's Jing (Essence) and Shen (Mind and Spirit).

The Energy Body exists within the Fourth Dimensional World, is associated with the Realm of Qi (energy and vibration), and is considered to be a polarized plane, simultaneously housing the forces of both Light and Darkness. This special realm is considered to be a hidden level of experi-

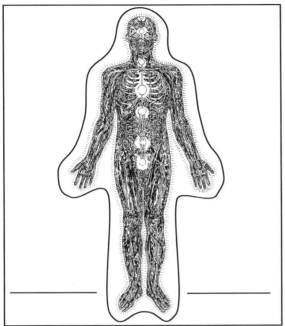

Figure 2.40. Qi: the "Energy" Body
(Inspired by the original artwork of Alex Grey)

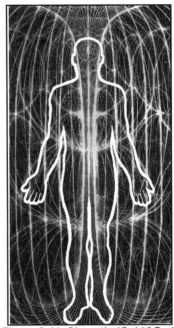

Figure 2.41. Shen: the "Spirit" Body
(Inspired by the original artwork of Alex Grey)

ence, that has form but no substance and substance but no form (e.g., energy, color, light, and sound).

It is through the Energy Body that an individual expresses his thoughts, feelings, passions, and desires. Because the Energy Body is composed of energetic matter, it is constructed via various frequencies and energetic pulses, resonating within the subtle matrix of the body's internal and external energy field. These electromagnetic fields are rooted and governed within the individual's Middle Dantian.

The Energy Body reflects the various internal conditions of the Physical Body. Even the smallest physical details occurring within the Physical Body's tissues are projected into the Energy Body, and observed within its subtle energetic fields.

Understanding The Energetic Realm

The Energetic World is also considered a type of Physical World, existing within an accelerated energetic state. It is considered to be a world that simultaneously exists at a higher level of vibration along side (and within) the physical matrix of the gross material world. The Energetic World cannot exist by itself, because its energetic field lives as an infinite malleable substance, constantly being programmed and shaped by thought and intention. Everything that exists within the Energetic World must have within itself a spiritual aspect, because energetic matter or substance cannot obtain shape or color unless it acquires it from the thoughts and intentions of the Mind (Spirit). These thoughts and intentions are continually being projected into the Energetic World via the Spirit World. Think of it like a mirror, which simply reflects and produces new shapes and forms according to the specific patterns that are continually being introduced into its energetic matrix. The Energetic World can therefore be conceived of as a mirror, upon which everything in the physical and spirit realms are mutually reflected. Likewise, both the physical realms and energetic realms also act as "mirrors" that reflect what is currently transpiring within the Spirit World.

Within the energetic and spirit worlds, every cell and particle feels and perceives. Therefore an individual who is "visiting" within this realm, is able to absorb the thoughts of others without the need for language. As such, communication takes place directly from cell to cell and mind to mind. Within both the energetic and spirit worlds, space is transcended and one can move their Energy Body instantly from one side of the Earth to the other. One can also be several places at once.

THE SPIRIT BODY & SPIRIT WORLD

The Spirit Body (Figure 2.41) corresponds to Shen (Mind, Thought, and Spirit), the Upper Dantian, the energy of the Heavens, and to Yang Qi. In this context, Shen is defined as the body's mind, thoughts, and spirit, which maintain and direct the body's life-force energy (Qi). It is the higher vibrational frequency of the human energetic matrix. The Shen is also the body's most subtle energetic field, which sustains and projects the vibrational resonances of the Mind. The Mind, in this context, refers to a process of awareness and consciousness that exists throughout the entire body, and is not merely limited to the Brain.

The Spirit Body exists within the Fifth Dimensional World, manifesting as thoughts, desires, and dreams. This is the level of experience that has neither form nor substance, and continually resonates at a higher and more subtle vibrational level than the Energetic World.

It is through the Spirit Body that an individual can express and manifest his internal thoughts and intentions into the external world. Therefore, the energy of the Spirit Body animates the body's life-force, and its subtle energetic field is continually rooted and governed within the Upper Dantian.

In Chinese Energetic Medicine, it is traditionally taught that there are two important aspects to the Spirit Body: The Lower (Yin) Spirit Body and the Higher (Yang) Spirit Body, described as follows:

- **The Lower (Yin) Spirit Body:** This subtle energy body has shape and form, and is traditionally observed as a bright white light.
- **The Higher (Yang) Spirit Body:** This subtle energy body is shapeless, and is traditionally observed as a radiant golden light.

UNDERSTANDING THE SPIRIT REALM

In the Spirit World, time and space are transcended. When traveling within the energetic and spiritual dimensions, everything manifests simply by focusing one's intention.

Manifestations occurring from the higher vibrational resonance of the Lower Spirit Worlds (that are extending into the lowest vibrational resonance of the Physical World), are defined by their energetic form and shape. This is because the Higher Spirit Worlds have shape (to a lesser degree), but are not limited to the confines of shaped forms. Therefore, the Spirit Realm is considered to be a world of unexpressed forms (i.e., a world of "thoughts and ideas").

OVERVIEW

The ancient Daoist understanding of the physical, energetic, and spiritual transformations occurring within the formation of the universe and the human body laid the foundation for their alchemical cultivation training, as well as for all modern Traditional Chinese Medicine practices. Although there is great variation in both the terminologies used and the spiritual practices associated with this knowledge, the practical clinical applications still contain the essence of the ancient Daoist theories behind them.

This is why, in the Medical Qigong Clinic, the treating doctor will always observe the transformations occurring within a patient's body from the perspective of the ever changing spiritual, energetic, and physical interactions occurring within the various cosmic (Heavenly) and environmental (Earthly) influences. This observation includes the interactions that transpire according to all of the aforementioned aspects: the Dao (Divine), Wuji (Infinite Space), Taiji (Yin and Yang), Bagua (Eight States), Wu Xing (Five Phases) the Three Worlds (Matter, Energy and Spirit), and the Three Bodies (Physical, Energetic, and Spirit).

To the ancient Daoists, each of the specialized exercises and meditations used in alchemical training represented three supernatural concepts of physical, energetic, and spiritual manifestation. These three important harmonies were traditionally classified as secret aspects of training the disciple's body, breath, and mind (Figure 2.42).

CHAPTER 2: UNDERSTANDING ANCIENT CHINESE METAPHYSICS

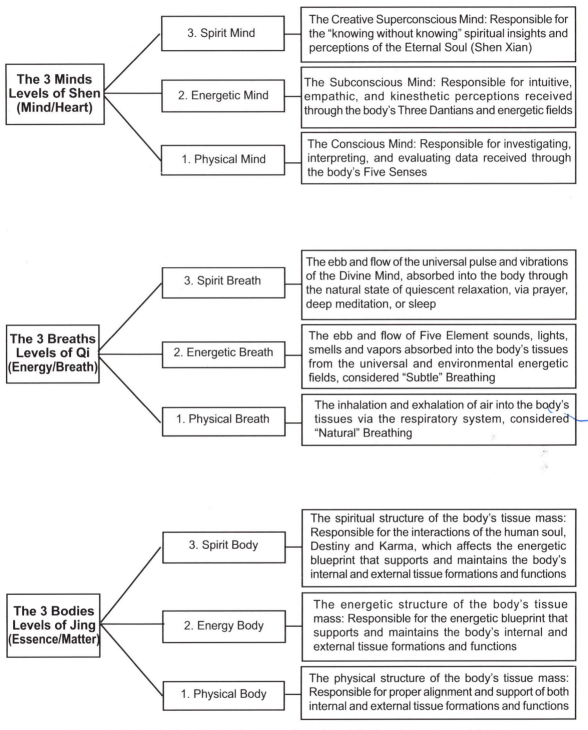

Figure 2.42. The Ancient Daoist Understanding of the 3 Bodies, 3 Breaths, and 3 Minds

Energetic Formation of the Human Spirit

Once a student understands the secret components of the Energetic Formation of the Universe, and is "awakened" to the experiences of his Three Bodies and how they interact within the Three Worlds, he will be open to uncovering and comprehending the "true" Energetic Formation of the Human Body.

Throughout China's ancient history, there have been numerous theories regarding the creation of "Heaven, Earth and Man" as well as the creation and formation of the human soul (sometimes known as the "Shen Xian" or "Immortal Spirit"). The concept of the energetic formation of the human body, mind and soul, as well as its spiritual evolution has spawned numerous philosophies and religions throughout the millennia. In Daoism, ancient symbols and metaphors are traditionally used to describe the various internal transformations of energy and spirit.

The following theory continues from the original teachings that I received from Master Wong in China, which were popular in ancient Daoism during the Spring and Autumn Period (770-476 B.C.). It is introduced here as part of the foundational knowledge that is essential for the disciple to understand before he begins a healing practice based on Chinese Energetic Medicine.

Studying Chinese Energetic Medicine requires not only comprehending the immeasurable wisdom gathered from ancient martial, medical, and spiritual development, but also studying the ancient Chinese culture which fostered these powerful energetic systems.

The Embodiment of the Dao

The ancient Daoists believed that the energetic and spiritual form of the Divine was a vibrant luminous fire, composed of an infinite number of Shen Ling (i.e., Supernatural Spirits, seen as "Gods" or "Deities,") that surrounded its center core (Figure 2.43). The Shen Ling emanate from the Dao as myriad rays of Divine fragments of light, and were sometimes called the "Sparks of the Supreme Fire."

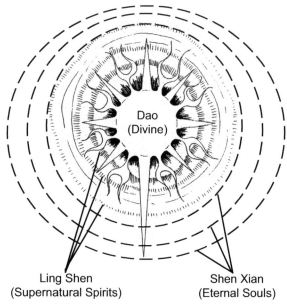

Figure 2.43. The Infinite Dao or Divine

The Shen Ling were also considered to be "Divine Messengers," and were surrounded by an infinite number of Shen Xian (Eternal Souls, or Immortal Spirits).

The Light of the "Dao" Inside

When the Eternal Dao begins to manifest its Divine Nature within the infinite space of the Wuji, its natural energetic Nature appears as a continual pulsating sound and radiant light, which dispels all darkness. Consequently, when the Eternal Dao begins to manifests its Divine Nature as a pure and tangible physical form inside the human body, its pulsating sound and radiant light appears within the individual's Spirit Body. Individuals who have continually cultivated this special spiritual light are traditionally known as spiritually enlightened beings (i.e., manifesting the spiritual light of a Saint or Immortal).

It is important to note that the Five Virtues (Compassion in the Liver, Inner-Peace in the Heart, Honesty in the Spleen, Integrity in the Lungs, and Wisdom in the Kidneys) are the original energetic and spiritual manifestations of the Five Pure Lights. This is why, according to ancient Daoist teaching, the "Virtues" are composed of subtle energetic and spiritual substances, known

CHAPTER 2: UNDERSTANDING ANCIENT CHINESE METAPHYSICS

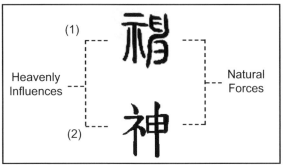

Figure 2.44. The Ancient "Shen" Character (1-Top) and the Modern "Shen" Character (2-Bottom)

Figure 2.45. "Ling," (Supernatural, Magical, Spiritual)

Figure 2.46. Ancient Daoist Wu (Shaman) Were known for their supernatural abilities.

as "Ling Qi" ("Spiritual Energy") and "Ling Shen" ("Spiritual Mind"). The Energy Body and Spirit Body are both composed from this subtle energetic and spiritual substance.

LING SHEN: SUPERNATURAL SPIRIT

The Chinese characters "Ling Shen" can be translated as the "Spiritual Mind," "Magical Mind," or "Supernatural Spirit," representing the living power of the Divine Spirit acting inside of the human body.

The word "Shen" translates as "Spirit; God, Deity; Spiritual, Supernatural; Awareness, Consciousness (Mind)." The Chinese ideogram for Shen is depicted by two characters: positioned on the right is a character representing the alternating expression of natural forces; positioned to the left is a character representing the unfolding of things under the authority and influence of Heaven. The ideograph depicts the heavenly influence that penetrates and instructs the core of the Heart, or "that which descends from the sky and passes through the body" (Figure 2.44).

The Chinese character "Ling" describes the spiritual quality of the Dao and is translated as "Supernatural or Magical." In contemporary religion, the Ling Shen is equivalent to the awakening spiritual power of the "Holy Spirit," and is responsible for extraordinary manifestations such as radiating Divine Light, supernatural healing, and miracles.

The ideograph for "Ling" consists of three special characters, each is described as follows (Figure 2.45):
- **Yu:** The top radical "Yu" translates as "Rain."
- **Kou:** The three squares located in the center of the character are three mouth radicals "Kou," which originally stood for "Calling for Rain."
- **Wu:** The bottom character "Wu" translates as "Magician, Shaman, or Sorcerer" (Figure 2.46).

Together, the three ideographs (Yu, Kou and Wu) depict the image of an ancient Wu (Shaman Priest) dancing, chanting and supplicating the Celestial Gods (Shen Ling) for Heavenly Blessings (rain).

At conception, the individual's Ling Shen (Supernatural Spirit) lowers its vibrational essence in order to combine with the sperm and ovum and form the human soul. It is this point in time, that the Soul, previously escorted by the Five Pure Lights, becomes the individual's Original Spirit (Yuan Shen).

THE LING SHEN AND IMMORTALITY

In ancient China, the Wu believed that the supernatural energy of the Dao also existed within the body of each individual, and within the Heavens ("as above - so below"). This living "River of God," or "Heart of the Dao," was located in the center core (Taiji Pole) of an individual, within the subtle spiritual field of the heart. This is why the Wu shamans were often represented as being partially divided (half in Heaven and half on Earth), becoming energetically and spiritually whole only when they were possessed by the other half of their celestial spirit.

The ancient Wu believed that through sacred prayer and meditation, the supernatural spiritual quality of an individual's Ling Shen (being spiritually Yin), would reconnect with the supernatural spiritual quality of the Dao (being spiritually Yang), and become energetically and spiritually whole again. This energetic and spiritual union allowed the Wu access to supernatural powers, allowing him or her the ability to influence Nature.

The primary goal of ancient Daoists Alchemy was to purify and refine the body's Postnatal Qi, cultivate Prenatal Qi, and transform both energies into Ling Qi (Spiritualized Energy) and Ling Shen (Spiritualized Mind). This important cultivation practice was necessary, in order to create and establish the Daoist Priest's Immortal Body.

According to ancient Maoshan teachings of the Shang Qing Daoist Sect, the Ling Shen (Spiritual Energy) of a person, place, or item can be gathered and ingested through the absorption of it's Jing (Essence), Xue (Blood), Qi (Breath and Energy), or Shen (Spirit). The more talented and magically skillful the disciple was at this specific task, the more powerful his own Ling Shen (Magical Spirit) would become. This special cultivation practice also included the ingestion and utilization of the subtle spiritual radiant light active within the body's Shen (Spirit). This advanced form of alchemical cultivation is sometimes known as Spirit Magic, and is used in order to absorb Ling Qi (Spirit Energy) into the disciple's body, via training his Ling Shen (Spiritual Mind).

The magical skill of training the Ling Shen is essentially accomplished through esoteric Qigong, using focused intention, imagination and powerful visualizations. This special type of training' eventually included such esoteric teachings as Dream Magic, Mineral and Plant Magic, Spirit Travel, and other secret Shengong methods. It is important to note that in ancient China, the word "Shengong" ("Spirit Skill") was also used to describe the magical function of absorbing the celestial energy and magical influences of the Sun, Moon, and Stars into the disciple's body. By absorbing and incorporating these celestial energies within their own bodies, the ancient Daoists believed that they could establish and maintain an extremely powerful energetic field.

To the ancient Daoists, mastering the Alchemical Transformations occurring within the Three Realms also involved the exploration, training, absorption, and transmutation of the Ling Qi (Spiritualized Energy) and Ling Shen (Spiritualized Mind) that originates from various energetic and spiritual interactions occurring within and around the spiritual realm of Matter. It focuses on the study of transmuting the body's Essence (Jing), Energy (Qi) and Spirit (Shen) originating from the divine forces responsible for the creation, transformation, and dissolution of all matter. The disciple's main goal in performing this type of External Alchemy was to systematically replace his body's internal energy with divine energy that was continually collected and absorbed via the Ling Shen (Spiritual Light) originating from special people (i.e., divine spirits, celestial immortals, and deities, etc.), Holy places, and sacred things (items that were replete with divine Ling Shen). It was also believed that this continual energetic absorption and spiritual transformation process alone could allow the disciple to eventually achieve a divine radiant state of Immortality.

In ancient China, the primary goal of creating and ingesting these various magical components was to eventually double the disciple's Ling Qi (Spiritual Energy) and his Ling Shen (i.e. the spiritual powers of the disciple's Mind). This increase in magical energy and spiritual power was needed in order to assist the disciple in reverting back to the spiritual Prenatal (Yuan) state of existence. It is while the disciple is "awake" within this "before-birth" state, that he is able to begin creating the energetic formation of the "Immortal Embryo."

This also included the mastery of the esoteric art of Chinese Astrology (Celestial Divination), Immortality (i.e., creating the Immortal Golden Light Body), and mastering the hidden power and magical influence that is contained within the energetic and spiritual realms of the Nine Levels of Heaven.

LING QI: SUPERNATURAL ENERGY

The Chinese Characters for "Ling Qi" can be translated as the "Spiritual Energy," "Magical Breath," or "Supernatural Breath," representing the living power of the Divine Breath acting inside of the human body (Figure 2.47). The ancient Chinese believed that before creation, an individual's Original Essence (Yuan Jing) was energetically formed out of Ling Qi.

In Daoist alchemy, Ling Qi is considered to be celestial particles of sacred light and sound, that resonate throughout the universe. Ling Qi is the spiritual energy that envelops and forms all things. The *Ancient Book of Lu* states that "even a blade of grass or clump of dirt contains Ling Qi." In order to connect with and perceive the Ling Qi contained within the environment, an individual must first cultivate his own personal Ling Qi.

Figure 2.47. The Chinese Characters for "Ling Qi" (Supernatural Breath, Magical/Spiritual Energy)

An individual's "Original Nature" or Yuan Shen, is developed through the Spiritual Energy (Ling Qi) and Spiritual Awareness (Ling Shen) that has been transformed from and united with, the Qi originating from the Heart. When the Heart's passions unite with the Original Nature, this is considered to be the true Union of Metal and Wood (i.e., the Dragon and Tiger Copulating).

In esoteric Daoist Alchemy, the fusion of all Four Celestial Animal's spiritual "root" energies is a pre-requisite for creating the true magical power of energetic manifestation. The root energies of the Green Dragon (Wood - Imagination) and the White Tiger (Metal - Feeling Sensation) must be combined in order to create and sustain the individual's Energy Body. The root energies of the Red Phoenix (Fire - Intention) and Black Turtle/Snake (Water - Attention) must be combined in order to create and sustain the individual's Spirit Body. Then, the combined energies of both the Energy Body and Spirit Body must be fused as one Qi in order to create the true internal power needed for energetic manifestation (Figure 2.48).

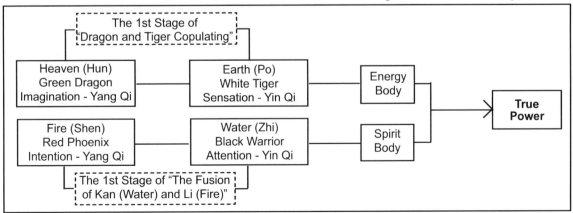

Figure 2.48. The "Root" energies of the Four Celestial Animals are required in order to create true power

SHEN XIAN: ETERNAL SOUL

The Eternal Soul (Shen Xian) has an infinite source of vitality, derived from the high-frequency resonating power of the Divine or Dao. The Eternal Soul's quest for knowledge and experience within the three realms (physical, energetic and spiritual) as a human spirit (Yuan Shen) has always been a topic of controversy and debate.

As previously mentioned, the Chinese ideogram for "Shen" can be translated as "Spirit; God, Deity; Spiritual, Supernatural; Awareness, Consciousness (Mind)." The Chinese ideogram for "Xian" can be translated as "Celestial Being, Immortal; Transcendent; Saint; Alchemist." It is depicted by two characters: positioned on the right is a character for "Mountain;" positioned to the left is a character depicting "Man." The ideograph depicts the "Immortals" said to have lived in ancient times, high in the sacred mountains of China. Together, Shen Xian can be translated as "Divine Transcendent," "God Spirit," or "Eternal Soul" (Figure 2.49).

The Shen Xian (Eternal Soul) is sometimes considered a component of the Divine Ling Shen (Divine Spirit Mind) that reincarnates. Because the Ling Shen is rooted in the light of the Divine, the Shen Xian is guided by the direction of the Shen Ling.

FROM ETERNAL SOUL TO HUMAN SOUL

From an ancient Daoist perspective, it is taught that the Shen Xian (Eternal Soul or "Immortal Spirit") living within the human body, was not initially created at the time of an individual's birth. Being a part of the Divine, all Shen Xian have existed since the beginning of time. Every birth is a rebirth of the Eternal Soul, which has already existed and will continue to reincarnate. The human body simply serves as an alchemical medium for the spiritual transformation of the Eternal Soul. It is through the external vehicle of the human body that the Eternal Soul radiates and expresses itself. As we continue to grow and change while living within the lower realms of creation, the human soul maintains its stability by constantly providing the energetic blueprints for overcoming hardships.

It is said that, once the Shen Xian (Eternal Soul) receives Heaven's Mandate (Tian Ming), to reincarnate, it will descend into the realm of matter and be absorbed into the mother's egg at the time

Figure 2.49. The Chinese Characters for "Shen Xian" (Immortal Soul, Eternal Spirit)

of conception. It will now live within the Earthly realm in the form of a "Yuan Shen," becoming the "Original Spirit" of this individual's Human Soul. Although it is spiritual in nature, the Shen Xian is also connected to the infinite space of the Wuji, and is considered to be a separate "entity," eternally existing apart from the body.

It is the Ling Qi (Spiritual Energy) of the Shen Xian that creates and sustains the Three Bodies (Physical Body, Energy Body, and Spirit Body), and roots them within the forming tissues. This special rooting enables the Three Bodies to interact with the ever-changing energetic fields actively transforming within the various realms of the Three Worlds.

During fetal development, the Shen Xian is rooted in the area of the individual's Heart and Middle Dantian by a silver cord, which itself is rooted within the body's center column of Divine Energy, traditionally known as the "Taiji Pole of Man." The human Taiji Pole is described as "emitting the True Spark of the Supreme Fire" (i.e., the Light of God), and is considered to be a divine fragment of the light of the Dao (hence its internal connection to the spiritual mind of the Ling Shen). It is from this divine resonating light, that the body's Taiji Pole becomes energized and all Three Dantians (Fields of Energy) become interconnected. The rooting of the Shen Xian into the physical body as a Human Soul (Yuan Shen) is, therefore considered the first manifestation of the divine source within the Human Body (Figure 2.50).

Whole-body consciousness is the main characteristic of the Shen Xian. The Shen Xian radiates its sacred light and divine influence through the physical, energetic, and spiritual domains of human existence. Without the interactive process of the Shen Xian, the body's spiritual energy would have no specific direction, and would remain in

CHAPTER 2: UNDERSTANDING ANCIENT CHINESE METAPHYSICS

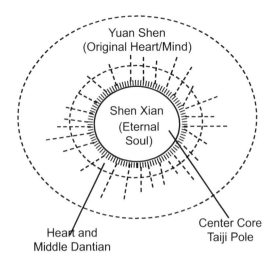

Figure 2.50. The Eternal Soul (Shen Xian) is energetically associated with the area of the Heart and Middle Dantian; which is also energetically rooted within the center core Taiji Pole.

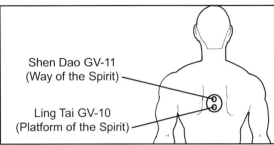

Figure 2.51. The Silver Cord is rooted in the Heart, and corresponds to the Ling Tai and Shen Dao areas

meaningless activity. The Shen Xian radiates its spiritual energy in all directions, and is therefore responsible for growth, formation, vitality and health manifesting throughout the human body.

ENERGETIC MANIFESTATION OF THE SOUL

The Shen Xian manifests its innate radiant qualities as spiritual insight, functioning through the physical form of the tissues. The Shen Xian is therefore expressed through the body's Yuan Shen (Original Spirit), and is interconnected to all parts of the body. In every individual, the light of the Shen Xian is revealed through the sparkle or "Shen" observed in their eyes.

Through the influence of the Shen Xian, all of the body's energetic processes seek wholeness. The Shen Xian knows exactly what is needed for health preservation and survival in every situation.

When conserved and amplified through spiritual practice, the energy of the Shen Xian reveals a bright radiant quality which permeates and penetrates the cells, tissues, organs, and external energy fields. These energetic fields create a strong luminous shield of energy capable of guarding the individual's body against an attack by hostile or pathogenic energy, by enabling it to:

- Ward off the invasion of external pathogens and harmful electromagnetic fields
- Ward off the negative influences of malevolent spirits
- Ward off ill intentions and spiritual malice projected unconsciously or deliberately by others
- Ward off the parasitic influences of demonic forces

SOUL TRAVEL

The ancient Daoists believed that in order to receive spiritual guidance and insight, every night the Shen Xian (Eternal Soul) would leave the physical body in the form of a "Soul Body" (i.e., the Spirit Body), departing from the physical body while in deep sleep. The silver cord, which is sometimes connected to the Spirit Body, is located at the fifth and sixth thoracic vertebrae. This physical area is the place on the spine where the silver cord lifts the Spirit Body when an individual Soul Travels (sometimes known as Astral Projection). This area also corresponds to the back of the Heart (Figure 2.51), located between Ling Tai GV-10 (Platform of the Spirit) and Shen Dao GV-11 (Way of the Spirit) areas.

The journey of the Shen Xian is based on the spiritual evolution of the individual. The individual's ability to sojourn into other dimensions of existence depends on his or her capability to relax and increase the level of vibrational frequency.

When an individual prays or meditates, his Yuan Shen (Original Spirit) reconnects with its Shen Xian (Eternal Soul), and consciously enters into a spiritual realm, wherein he will perceive the ideal of things (i.e., its intention and thought) rather than the things themselves. The individual no longer depends on the senses, but upon a clear inner-vision that perceives the whole picture. It is within this spiritual state that higher knowledge unfolds through divine intelligence, allowing all things to reveal their true nature.

THE YIN AND YANG MANIFESTATIONS OF THE ETERNAL SOUL

When referring to the special spiritual dynamics of the Eternal Soul (Shen Xian), the ancient Daoists focused on two primary energetic movements, described as follows (Figure 2.52):

1. **Prenatal Transformation (Heaven to Earth):** This special spiritual transformation pertains to the downward energetic movement of the Eternal Soul, as it journeys from the most subtle energy of the Dao, traveling through the infinite space of the Wuji. It then transforms from being a radiating celestial light, into a human soul; and finally comes to rest as the lower energetic form of the body's Original Spirit.

    As the Eternal Soul descends into the physical realm, the transformation of spiritual energy shifts from the highest to the lowest divine energetic frequencies, resulting in a corresponding decrease in consciousness.

    The lowest frequency creates matter and is the basis for prenatal transformations. At the higher energetic frequencies, the principles by which Qi operates are difficult to perceive if the individual's lower state of consciousness does not resonate in harmony with the information being presented. However, as energy slows down its resonance, it is more readily perceived by the five senses. This gives matter the quality of hardness, form, and smell, and also allows individuals to observe its energetic patterning.

2. **Postnatal Transformation (Earth to Heaven):** This pertains to the upward movement of the Original Spirit, as it frees itself from the gross physical realm and moves upward towards the higher energetic reunion and spiritual fusion with the Dao.

    As the Eternal Soul spirals upward, away from the physical realm, the transformation of the spiritual energy from the lowest level of consciousness to the highest divine energetic frequencies creates a highly evolved spiritual consciousness. In Daoist alchemical training, this is the primary goal of true transformation.

    Spiritual evolution involves a progressive opening of all the body's energy centers (i.e., Three Dantians, Energetic Gates, and Taiji Pole), until a

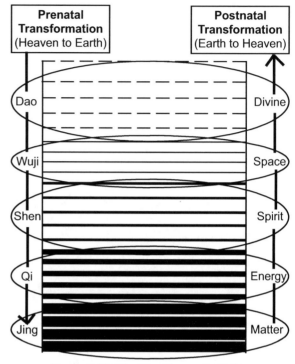

Figure 2.52. The Five Energetic Fields

state of absolute unity of body, energy, mind, and spirit is achieved. Once this awakened state is achieved, true enlightenment is attained.

In the evolutionary process of the soul, stability and change become as one, especially when there is a deep connection and internal commitment to integrated wholeness. The Eternal Soul serves as a pivotal point for the body's Jing (cells, tissues, organs, and organ systems), Qi (energy and breath), and Shen (internal thoughts and feelings), all of which express the multidimensional aspects of the individual's Original Spirit.

This is why, in the clinic, without a deep energetic and spiritual connection for transformation and change, a patient can suddenly experience a psychic splitting of his or her energies, and enter into a deep state of internal conflict. The part of the patient that is open to change, because it originally came into this realm for experiences via the Yuan Shen (Original Spirit), will experience a powerful resistance from the fear based part that demands stability and desires to maintain the denial system (i.e., the patient's willful Shen Zhi, or Acquired Mind).

CHAPTER 2: UNDERSTANDING ANCIENT CHINESE METAPHYSICS

THE BODY'S ORIGINAL STATES

In Chinese Energetic Medicine, in order to understand the various energetic states and transformations of the body's tissues, we must first begin by comprehending the true meaning of the Chinese word "Yuan." In Medical Qigong Therapy, the word "Yuan" is traditionally used to represent "Primary," "Original," "Innate," or "Pre-natal." It is expressed in Chinese Energetic Medicine to describe the esoteric transformations and manifestations occurring around an individual's Original Nature (Yuan Xing) and energy surrounding their personal Life/Destiny (Ming).

To the ancient Daoists, an individual's spiritual Nature (Xing) and his Ming (Life/Destiny) were closely connected (Figure 2.53), and were also associated with the energetic activities of his Original Essence (Yuan Jing), Original Energy (Yuan Qi), and Original Mind/Spirit (Yuan Shen).

It was believed that an individual's Destiny was given by Heaven at birth, and stored away in the Mingmen (Gate of Life/Destiny), located in-between the Kidneys (Figure 2.54). Therefore, it was also believed that the spiritual activation of an individual's Mingmen would awaken this spiritual spark of life, and release the hidden dynamic potential existing behind all of his thoughts and actions. Although the subtle impulses emanating from the individual's Ming are generally hidden from the conscious mind, through consistent quiescent meditation, a deeper understanding of this True Destiny can be intuitively discovered, accessed, and followed.

It is up to each individual to consciously and consistently act in accordance with their Ming throughout life. This action is based on the individual's conscious desire to remain congruent and in harmony with the "Will of Heaven." It is through this conscious action that an individual will develop true spiritual Virtue (De), and establish a healthy relationship with the Spirit World existing within the Three Realms of Heaven, Earth, and the Underworld.

One ancient Daoist teaching states, "When the Original Nature of All is realized, the disciple returns back to Non-being (Wu)." This deeper spiritual understanding, also allowed the students of Daoist Energetic Medicine to comprehend the true Nature of their Three Bodies, and the true origin of their Three Births.

Figure 2.53. The Chinese Characters for Xing (Nature) and Ming (Life-Destiny)

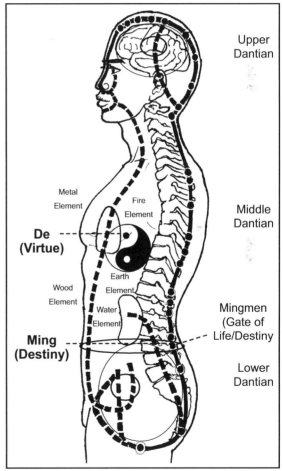

Figure 2.54. An individual's Destiny is spiritually stored in the energetic field of their Mingmen.

YIN AND YANG SPIRITUAL STATES

If we consider Xing (Nature) to be a Yin Spiritual State, and Ming (Destiny/Life) to be a Yang Spiritual State, then we would observe that the Yin Spirit (the Nature of the Heart) is powerless by itself. Because it has no energy on its own, this spiritual state cannot ascend into the higher spiritual realms.

The Yin Spiritual Nature of the Heart needs energy for its function and movement. Therefore practicing specific meditations and spiritual methods that only establish a relationship with one's Xing, will simply make minor changes in the Yin Spirit's characteristics, but no profound life-transforming spiritual changes will occur. This is why the ancient Daoists traditionally used the energy of Ming (the Primordial Qi of Life/Destiny) in order to establish a dynamic fusion with Xing (the Nature of the Heart). This energetic fusion transforms these two combined Yin and Yang states into a powerful Yang Spirit, which is held as the true spiritual root of the Immortal Fetus. Because of this dynamic energetic/spiritual fusion (i.e., Xing and Ming Copulating), the Immortal Fetus can manifest its true potential of evolving and sojourning into higher spiritual realms. Therefore, it is through the Copulation and spiritual fusion of the Energy of Ming with the Soul of Xing, that the True Essence of Daoist alchemical cultivation is created. According to the ancient writing of the *Huimingjing,*

> **"If you do not understand
> Xing (Nature) and Ming (Life/Destiny),
> then the Great Dao will not be achieved.**
>
> **Since ancient times,
> no sage has ever arrived at Sainthood
> without first cultivating and refining
> their Xing and Ming."**

It is interesting to note, that the Chinese characters meaning "to die," are written as "Lost Ming."

CULTIVATING AND REFINING XING AND MING

In Daoist Alchemy, the word "Cultivation" is defined as "mending and making whole that which is broken;" and the term "Refining" is defined as "using Fire to transform the Alchemical Agent." If there is Fire, but no Wind, the Fire will not burn; and if the Alchemical Agent does not have a place to stay and collect, it will disperse. Therefore, both Wind and Fire are simultaneously used together equally on the Alchemical Agent, in order to unite the Xing (Nature) of the Heart and the Ming (Life) of the Kidneys as One.

The Ming (Life/Destiny) is rooted in the Kidneys, and when the Kidneys move there is Water. The Xing (Nature) is rooted in the Heart, and when the Heart moves there is Fire.

Blowing Fire with Wind, changes the cultivated energy into the True Seed (Zhen Zhong). Through cultivating the True Seed, the disciple will then create the True Alchemical Agent.

In Daoist Energetic Embryology, it is taught that at the time of becoming pregnant, before a father and mother have yet given birth to a child, they first give birth to a sacred "Opening" (i.e., create a Sacred Space/Portal) allowing both Xing (Original Nature) and Ming (Life/Destiny) to manifest, become real, and reside inside the forming fetus. As these two sacred energies internally unite to become one, their energetic union radiates its glow outward, and becomes like a spark inside a stove.

Therefore, if the disciple gathers his Yuan Shen (Original Spirit) into this sacred "Opening," his Yuan Qi (Original Energy) will follow, and will spontaneously return back to its place of prenatal origin. Within a few months of cultivating and refining, the disciple should feel his Yuan Qi resonating, glowing, and turning inside the "Sacred Opening" (i.e., the Dantian). Once a disciple understands these Heavenly Inner-Workings of the True Dual Cultivation (i.e., the energetic fusion of Xing and Ming), he should train with a dedicated heart, attain the Great Dao, and allow his longevity to be everlasting.

In Daoist Alchemy, true energetic transformation depends upon "Spiritual Copulation." According to one of my Maoshan Daoist teachers, the true "Dual Cultivation" used in magical alchemy is the spiritual Copulation of the "Xing" of the Heart (i.e., its true/original spiritual nature) and the "Ming" of the Kidneys (i.e., the original Primordial Qi of Life and Destiny), combining inside the body and uniting as One. Because the ancient Daoist considered both Xing and Ming to be two separated parts of the Primordial (Prenatal) Unity, their internal cultivation was essential for obtaining alchemical transformation.

THE THREE BODIES AND THREE BIRTHS

According to ancient Daoist alchemical teachings, each individual has Three Bodies (i.e., a Physical Body, an Energy Body, and a Spirit Body), that manifest into the realm of matter through Three Births (a Physical Birth, an Energetic Birth, and a Spiritual Birth), described as follows (Figure 2.55):

THE FIRST BIRTH (YUAN JING)

An individual's First Birth is developed through the formation of the Physical Body, and is attributed to the energetic functions of the body's Original Essence (Yuan Jing), and the Lower Dantian; it also corresponds to the energies of the Moon and the Lunar Plexus.

It is important to understand, that in Daoist Alchemy, the Original Essence is the body's Generative Force (Jing Qi). This special type of energy is neither matter nor form, but considered to be an internal, luminous, vaporous kind of energy. The Generative Force energetically spreads throughout the entire body by way of the blood vessels, energetic channels, nerves, and internal fascia. When it remains within the body, it is the energetic vitality (Jing Qi) that supports and sustains human life. When it is discharged from the body, it transforms its energetic property to become the Generative Fluid (Reproductive Jing), responsible for creating new life.

The body's Original Essence is the innate, true energetic substance, through which the disciple's constitutional makeup, strength, and overall vitality originated and externally manifested. According to ancient Daoist teachings,

> "The Original Essence
> is devoid of form and matter.
> As soon as matter is generated,
> it cannot be used in Alchemical Cultivation
> as the Mother of the Elixir.
>
> Only when the Original Essence
> is combined with the energy
> of the Original Breath (Yuan Qi),
> is the Immortal Elixir created."

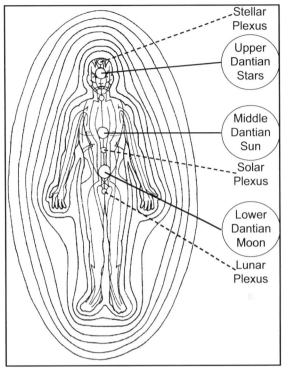

Figure 2.55. The Three Bodies and Three Births, correspond to the Three Dantians and the celestial energies of the Sun, Moon, and Stars.

In Daoist Alchemy, the Original Yang (Yuan Yang) is the same as the Original Essence (Yuan Jing), it has no form, and resides within the Original Breath (Yuan Qi). When the Original Essence receives any type of external stimuli, it moves, separates itself from the Original Breath, transforms from a "Generative Force" ("Jing Qi") into a "Generative Fluid" (Postnatal Jing) and becomes energetically active as the body's Postnatal Essence.

When the Original Essence is in its natural state, it is stored within the Five Yin and Six Yang Organs, existing as an energetic mist, still, and formless. As soon as a single thought arises from the Postnatal state, it immediately transforms it from a Prenatal state into a Postnatal state.

According to ancient Daoist teachings, "when Jing is abundant, the Qi is Full and the Shen is flourishing." It is during this time, that the disciple should begin the practice of "Lian Jing Hua Qi" ("Transforming Essence into Energy").

According to ancient Daoist teaching, the Vitality of the Generative Force (Jing Qi) is internally injured by the Seven Passions (i.e., intense anger, hate, delight, love, grief, fear, and desire), which energetically offset the delicate harmony of the Yuan Shen (Original Mind/Spirit).

THE SECOND BIRTH (YUAN QI)

An individual's Second Birth is developed through the formation of the Energy Body, and is attributed to the energetic functions of the body's Yuan Qi (Original Energy), and the Middle Dantian; it also corresponds to the energies of the Sun and the Solar Plexus (Yellow Court).

In Daoist Alchemy, the body's Yuan Qi is the original energy that radiates from the body and extends into the infinite space of the Wuji, to reconnect with the celestial realms of the eternal Dao. Therefore, it is the original motivational force that energetically links the Prenatal Jing (Yuan Jing) with the Prenatal Shen (Yuan Shen).

The Yuan Qi is the true force behind the activity of all the organs and energies in the body. It is closely related to the Mingmen (Gate of Life) and works to sustain the life of the body.

The energetic functioning of the Three Bodies depends upon the interaction of Yin and Yang Qi. Because the Yuan Qi is the root of life, formed through the divine combination of the Primordial Yin and Yang, it is stored primarily in the Kidney's Water energy. During conception, when the Yin and Yang energies of both parents interact within the womb, in the midst of the darkness there is a point of Divine living potential which comes forth from the Dao, emerging from the infinite space of the Wuji. This is what was known to the ancient Daoists as the "Primordial, True, Unified Generative Energy of Creation" or "Yuan Qi" ("Original Energy"). This special energy of creation enters into the sperm and ovum, fusing them as one. The ancient Daoist texts state, "formless, it produces form; immaterial, it produces substance. The internal organs, sense organs, and various parts of the body all naturally evolve because of this energy of creation, becoming complete." In other words, inside the mother's womb, it is the Yuan Qi (Original Energy) that causes the embryo to congeal and form, which then nourishes the embryo, and eventually causes it to become complete.

With its first cry, the infant comes in contact with the surrounding environmental energy. As the infant inhales, the Environmental Energy (or "Postnatal Qi"), mixes with the energy of the infant's Yuan Qi (Original Energy). The innate Prenatal Qi supports the tissues of the body, while the acquired Postnatal Qi supports the tissue's function. The Postnatal Qi depends on the Prenatal Qi to support the body's Respiratory System (breathing in and out), while the Prenatal Qi depends on the Postnatal Qi to nurture the body's Vascular System.

When the Physical Body is in a state of quiescent stillness, and the Generative Force (Jing Qi) is internally stabilized, then the Original Energy (Yuan Qi) and Spiritual Energy (Ling Qi) of the Water Element (stored within the Lower Dantian) will move upward, through the body, into the Upper Dantian of the head.

The ancient Daoists believed that the "Primordial Breath" (Yuan Qi), always energetically appeared as a blue-green light, residing as a luminous mist inside the Niwan Palace.

THE THIRD BIRTH (YUAN SHEN)

An individual's Third Birth is developed through the formation of the Spirit Body, and is attributed to the energetic functions and spiritual transformations of the body's Original Mind/Spirit (Yuan Shen), and the Upper Dantian; it also corresponds to the energies of the Stars and the Stellar Plexus.

The Upper Dantian is also the place where the Yuan Shen (Original Spirit) dissolves into the infinite space of the Wuji, in order to merge with the radiant light of the eternal Dao. The spiritual awareness associated with this supernatural union is beyond description, as this level of divine unity surpasses conceptual thought and words.

In Daoist Alchemy, there are two "Minds" or "Spiritual Natures," and a distinction is continually made between the cultivation and empowerment of either one or the other. The two Minds (i.e., the Original Mind and the Acquired Mind), are described as follows:

- **The Original Mind ("Yuan Shen"):** This virtuous spiritual state is traditionally known as the original divine influence the "Yuan Shen" ("Original Mind/Spirit"), that existed before conception.

  The ancient Daoists understood that the Original Spirit reveals itself as the Spiritual Vitality (Ling Qi) stored within each individual's Heart (Middle Dantian). It also energetically manifests itself through the two Niwan Palace branch channels that connect the body from the top of the head (Baihui) to the bottom of the feet (Figure 2.56).

  The dominating Virtue of the Shen (Heart/Mind) is the sense of Inner-Peace, propriety, and discriminating awareness (i.e., Justice). The Hun control the smooth flow of Qi throughout the body and are nourished by the Five Virtues of Kindness, Inner-Peace, Truthfulness, Integrity, and Wisdom. These Five Virtues give peace and clarity to the Heart/Mind, and allow the higher qualities of the Original Spirit (Yuan Shen) to override the selfish impulses of the Po (Corporeal Soul).

- **The Acquired Mind (Shen Zhi):** These are the emotional traits and survival influences of the acquired personality. Traditionally observed as the "Ren Xin" ("Man Heart"), this Postnatal state of ego expression is created after birth.

  All emotions have an effect on the Heart/Mind, which easily fall under the influence of the Po (the Seven Corporeal Souls), who are concerned with the body's survival. When the Po dominate the Heart/Mind, their overexaggerated self-concern gives rise to a chronic state of fear, sadness, worry, anger, and defensive arrogance. These negative emotions are sometimes called "the Five Thieves," because the chronic states of their negative influence drains the body's life-force.

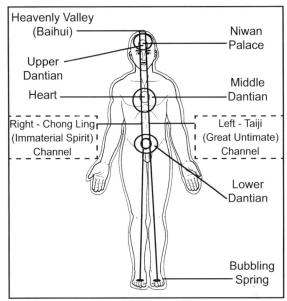

Figure 2.56. The two minor channels of the Niwan Palace connect from the top of the head, through the Heart, to the bottom of both feet.

During the initial stages of fetal development, although there is human form, there is no development of the individual's Acquired Mind, only the true, "Congenital Mind" (Yuan Shen) exists. The Yuan Shen ("Original Spirit or Original Mind") is considered to be the Yang aspect of the Human Soul.

As the Shen Xian (Eternal Soul) descends into the material world, it fuses the energetic and spiritual natures of the eternal Dao, Wuji, and Taiji, with the structural energetic natures of the Ba Gua and the Wu Xing (Five Elements). These energetic components combined and fused inside the body's living cells and tissue during the formation of the human Taiji Pole, which was created when the sperm penetrated the egg. As the various energies seek balance within themselves, the Three Bodies become internally established within the forming tissues (Figure 2.57).

When the mother's and father's Jing, Qi and Shen combine during conception, the energy of the Dao is drawn into the mother's womb in order to orchestrate the forming of the embryo. While in the womb, the fetus continues to transform and develop the accumulated Jing, Qi and Shen, while remaining in a state of quiescence.

The vibrational levels of the Eternal Soul must slow down to resonate with the frequencies of the lower dimensions in order to maintain physical form. This will allow the Eternal Soul to acquire experiences within the world of time and space as a human soul.

The ancient Daoists believed that we, as living organisms, are pure spirit, and that we have dressed ourselves with form via the Mind (Shen) in order to manifest as a part of creation. As we live within the Wuji, we are suspended between Heaven and Earth on the material plane and are affected by all universal and environmental energetic phenomena.

The ancient Daoists also believed that the Yuan Shen (the Original Soul's Mind or "Spirit") is expressed as the lower creative aspects of the Eternal Soul, upon which incarnate experiences will be recorded once it has been absorbed into the mother's egg upon conception. Sometimes described as the "feet of the Eternal Soul," the Yuan Shen represents the expressions of the Eternal Soul's personality, containing within itself the Divine consciousness. It also supervises the life and experiences of the individual's temporary Acquired Personality (the ego-personality developed through various "survival" experiences).

THE YUAN SHEN'S SPIRITUAL MANIFESTATIONS

The Eternal Soul (Shen Xian) radiates its spiritual light from the interior of the Taiji Pole, via the Yuan Shen (Original Spirit). This spiritual light also energetically crystallizes in order to form the individual's Spirit Body, which gradually becomes conscious and awakens into action, affecting the Energy Body and Physical Body's Jing, Qi and Shen (Mind). This special spiritual energy can be observed radiating from within an individual's eyes.

As the Spirit Body envelops both the Physical Body and Energy Body, its subtle communications are received through the individual's innermost thoughts, feeling sensations, and inspirations.

The body's Jing, Qi, and Shen are temporal, while being enveloped, fused, and housed in the

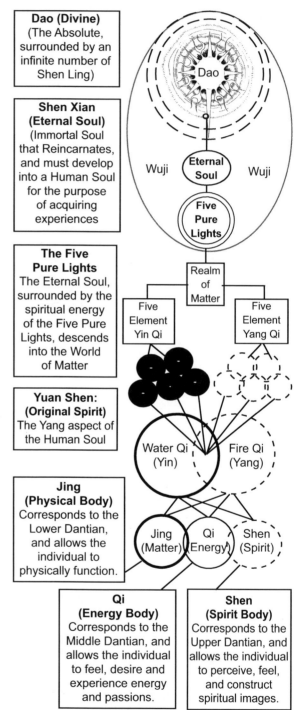

Figure 2.57. The Descent of the Soul into the Human Body

physical form. These Three Treasures (Jing, Qi and Shen) will eventually separate when the individual dies. The Jing and the Yin aspect of the Qi will dissolve back into the Earth, while the Yang aspect of the Qi and the Yuan Shen (Original Spirit) will ascend to Heaven along with the Shen Xian (Immortal Soul). The ancient Chinese believed that the Yuan Shen, being an expression of the Shen Xian, was a temporal part of the body. It simply played a role, like a stage actor, while it was on the Earth, in order to acquire various experiences.

THE WUJING SHEN (FIVE ESSENCE SPIRITS)

Once the energies of the fetus' Yin (Water-Ming) and Yang (Fire-Xing) divide and begin the work of internal tissue construction, the Spiritual Energy (Ling Qi) of the Five Pure Lights takes residence within the Five Yin Organs (Liver, Heart, Spleen, Lungs, and Kidneys). Upon taking residence, the Five Pure Lights begin gathering, absorbing, and utilizing the various energies radiating from the Heavens and Earth to sustain the tissues. These subtle energies are composed of Five Elements (Wood, Fire, Earth, Metal, and Water), and are needed in order to continue building the forming fetus's internal energetic fields (Figure 2.58). In Daoist Alchemy, these special energies are sometimes known as the Ling Qi (Spiritual Energy) of the individual's internal Virtues (De).

The Yuan Shen ("Original Mind/Spirit") is integrated and sustained by the embryo's "Five Spiritual Essences," or "Prenatal Wujingshen," which are in turn supported by the Qi and energetic fields of the Five Yin Organs.

The Yuan Shen is also rooted in the combined energies of the Jing (Essence), Qi (Energy), and Shen (Mind/Spirit) that the mother and father provided during the time of conception. It is important to note, that this combined Jing, Qi, and Shen also provides the energetic basis for the formation of the individual's "Acquired Mind," which is integrated and sustained after birth by his or her Postnatal "Emotional" Wujingshen.

The energetic states of the Five Elements differ in their specific spiritual manifestations, described as follows:

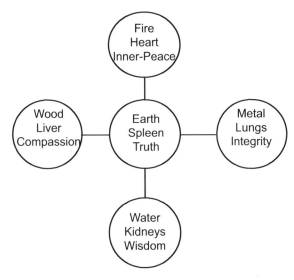

Figure 2.58. Once the energies of the fetus's Yin (Water-Ming) and Yang (Fire-Xing) divide and begin the work of internal tissue construction, the Ling Qi (Spiritual Energy) of the Five Pure Lights take residence within the Five Yin Organs, and become the individual's internal Virtues (De).

ORIGINAL MIND & PRENATAL WUJINGSHEN

These energetic states manifest as one or several of the spiritual virtues of compassion, inner-peace, truth, integrity, and wisdom. Energetically, the spiritual virtues of the Prenatal Wujingshen continually nourish and support each other.

When the spiritual virtues of the Prenatal Wujingshen nourish and support each other, they become integrated within the celestial design, causing the spiritual energies (Ling Qi) of the Five Elements to fuse as one energy. Therefore, the ancient Daoists believed that the cultivation of the Prenatal Wujingshen Virtues produced Immortal Sages; while the unbridled emotional state of the Postnatal Wujingshen only produced ordinary people, and inevitably lead to death.

In the ancient Daoist text *Understanding Reality*, the Chinese masters of esoteric magic wrote the following:

"When the Spiritual Energies of the Five Elements are assembled, the Great Dao may be attained."

97

The work of assembling the spiritual energies of the Five Elements requires the individual to constantly manifest the spiritual virtues of the Prenatal Wujingshen (Compassion, Inner-Peace, Truth, Integrity, and wisdom) in all situations. Especially those incidences that "trigger" the release of the programmed acquired emotional patterns of the Postnatal Wujingshen (i.e., anger, joy, worry, grief, and fear).

Acquired Mind & Postnatal Wujingshen

These energetic states manifest as one or several of the acquired emotional states of anger, excitement, worry, grief, or fear. The Acquired mental/emotional states of the Postnatal Wujingshen continually fight, attack, and overcome one another.

The Chinese phrase "Shen Zhi," can be translated as the "spirit's acquired will" or "Acquired Mind," and is considered to be the Yin aspect of the human soul. Traditionally, the Shen Zhi functions manifests in gathering and retrieving the knowledge and patterns acquired through the individual's experiences.

As the human soul descends into the "world of physical matter" it is temporarily expressed through an acquired Shen Zhi, also known as the acquired personality. The Shen Zhi experiences a myriad of emotions and desires, forming a unique personality characteristic that learns to interpret and interact within its environment for the sake of survival (Figure 2.59).

The Prenatal Wujingshen helps to create and support the spiritual virtues of the Yuan Shen, and in a similar fashion, the Postnatal Wujingshen helps to create and support the acquired thoughts and emotions of the Shen Zhi. At the moment of the infant's first cry, the ancient Daoists believed that the acquired conscious spirit (Shen Zhi) becomes activated as the Postnatal Qi enters into the opening of the mouth and nose and energetically merges with the baby's original spirit (Yuan Shen). The congenital Yuan Shen depends on the acquired Shen Zhi to exist, while the Shen Zhi depends on the Yuan Shen for effective awareness.

The ancient Daoists believed that the Shen Zhi's behavioral patterns are developed last, after all of the body's initial energetic and spiritual systems are intact and functioning. As the Shen Zhi is considered the lowest expression of the Divine within the individual, it is continually evolving, striving to become one with the human soul that resides within the Taiji Pole. It is believed that together the individual's Shen Zhi and Yuan Shen complete the Yin and Yang aspects of the human soul. Together, they gather the sum total of all thoughts, emotions, and experiences that the human soul accumulates from the moment of its first descent into matter at conception.

The various personality characteristics of each individual's Shen are sometimes described as "soul extensions" because they manifest within the individual's energetic field and tend to influence his or her behavior and perception. The Yuan Shen is influenced primarily by the Hun (Ethereal Soul) while the Shen Zhi is influenced primarily by the Po (Corporeal Soul).

Introduction To Energetic Embryology

In Chinese Medical Qigong Therapy, the study of the embryological development of the body's inner fascia and internal organ tissues illuminates many of the ideas about energy, health, and disease contained within Traditional Chinese Medicine.

The ancient Chinese doctors understood that the original energetic patterns created during prenatal tissue formation remain operative throughout adulthood. Afterbirth, the tissues and internal organs of the developing child continue to interrelate according to the energetic patterning that began during conception. As an embryo develops while in-utero, it passes through several stages of internal formation, causing it to recreate the energetic patterning of inherited ancestral traits. This type of energetic heredity sometimes manifests as a form of unconscious organic memory.

Essentially, the Yang Qi (+) of Heaven (i.e., the energy related to the Sun, Moon, and Stars) and the Yin Qi (-) of Earth (the environmental energy related to the Soil, Water and Wind) both produce powerful energetic fields that influence the formation of all life on the planet. The ancient Daoists believed that "Man" was energetically suspended between the two enormous fields of Heaven and Earth Qi. As the Yang energetic field of the Heavens radiates downward into the planet, and the Yin energetic field of the Earth's core extends upward through the soil, "Man" being suspended in-between these two powerful energetic fields is continually affected accordingly by both celestial and terrestrial interactions (Figure 259).

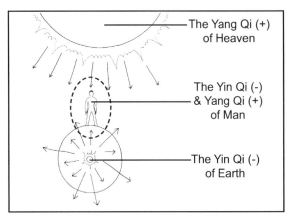

Figure 2.59. The human energetic field is suspended between the two energy fields of Heaven and Earth.

The Body's Essence, Energy, and Spirit During Conception

A myriad of energetic interactions begin at the moment of conception. The energies of Heaven and Earth, as well as those of the mother and father, all exert a powerful influence on the energetic state and patterning of the zygote. As these four energies condense upon impact and begin to form the nucleus of the cellular patterning of the new life, every part of the developing zygote is affected (Figure 2.60).

Figure 2.60. The blending of the energies of Heaven (Yang Qi) and Earth (Yin Qi) with the energies of the father (Yang Qi) and mother (Yin Qi) creates a fusion of Yin and Yang energies within the body's tissues and cells during creation. These energies are responsible, on a psychophysical level, for transferring talents and traits from generation to generation.

The ancient Daoists taught that at conception, as the fetus's body begins to form, the two spirits of the mother and father interlock. The energetic joining and spiritual fusion of the mother and father's Jing (Essence), Qi (Energy) and Shen (Heart/Mind) unite to form Prenatal Essence (Yuan Jing). This creative essence leads to the internal formation of the fetus's Kidneys (Lotus Bulb), Sea of Marrow, Spinal Cord (Lotus Stem) and Brain (Lotus Flower) (Figure 2.61).

During embryonic development, the Bones also begin to form the structural framework of the body, and the blood vessels begin to nourish the child's developing tissues. In the *Yellow Emperor's Classic of Internal Medicine* it is written,

> "When the Essence of Yin and Yang Qi Merges
> (i.e., the blending of the sperm and the egg),
> before the fetus changes into its dominant sex,
> the two Kidney Orbs grow first."

According to Professor Meng Xiantong, during this important time of internal transformation, the growth of the fetus progresses through the following energetic pattern:

> "Both Kidneys are formed
> like two halves of a "bean,"
> with the Yuan Qi (Original Energy)
> acting like a swirling mist between them,
> orchestrating the internal development.
>
> Out of these Lotus Bulbs (Kidneys),
> the Lotus Stem (Spinal Cord) extends upward
> to create the Lotus Flower (Brain).
> All of this transformation occurs
> within the dark murky waters of creation."

In ancient China, the left Kidney orb was at one time called the "True Kidney," while the right Kidney was considered to be the Mingmen (Gate of Life, Fate, or Destiny). The Mingmen is said to store the energy of the man's sperm essence, or the woman's egg essence (i.e., their Reproductive Postnatal Jing). During the Ming Dynasty (1368-1644 A.D.), the idea that the Mingmen Fire occupied the space between the two Kidneys became popular, and eventually this new theory dominated the way of Chinese medical thinking.

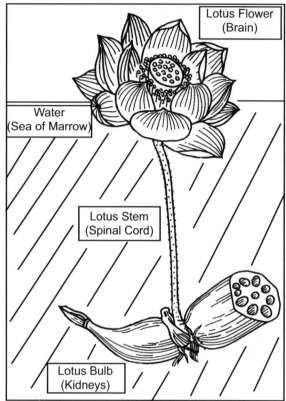

Figure 2.61. The Mother's and Father's Jing (Reproductive Essence) create the formation of the child's Kidneys (Lotus Bulb), Sea of Marrow, Spinal Cord (Lotus Stem), and Brain (Lotus Flower). (Inspired by the original artwork of Lilian Lai Bensky)

The *Yellow Emperor's Classic of Internal Medicine* states that a woman's physiology is dominated by Blood, which serves as the foundation of her menstrual cycle, fertility, pregnancy, and childbirth. It further states that man's physiology is dominated by Qi, which serves as the basis of his strength, fertility, endurance, and virility. Around the age of fourteen, a girl's Conception Vessel (Sea of Yin) grows to maturity and fully energizes her Xin (Heart), and her menses begin. Around the age of sixteen, a boy's Governing Vessel (Sea of Yang) becomes mature and fully energizes his Kidneys, and his body produces mature semen.

To the ancient Daoists, the body's Yuan Qi (Original Energy) is the representation of the energetic forces of Heaven and Earth as imprinted within the body's Yuan Jing (Original Essence) at the moment of conception. As the Yuan Shen (Original Spirit) rises from the Original Essence, it creates the internal polarity of the body's Yuan Yin and Yang Qi (which is associated with the Kidney's Original Energy). An old Daoist saying used in the Medical Qigong Clinic to describe the body's internal energetic formation states:

"When people are born,
Heaven gives them Jing and Shen,
which align to form the Mind;
Earth gives them Bones and Shape,
which unite to form the body.

When joined together,
these two sources of energy
cause human beings to develop.

When people die,
their Essence and Spirit
return back to Heaven;
and their Bones and Shape
return back to the Earth."

During birth, pairs of channels originating from the mother's internal organs carry Qi that creates and nourishes the baby at each stage of its development. Receiving its sustenance through the umbilical cord, the developing child's navel, Kidneys, and lower abdominal area become the collection points for its Prenatal Qi (i.e., the Yuan Qi is the energy that is collected and stored within the baby's body before it is born).

Every life begins with inherent strengths and weaknesses. Therefore, the ancient Daoists believed that a child's energetic constitution could be augmented while in-utero by using special energetic applications (i.e., diet, herbs, and certain Prenatal Qigong exercises and massage).

It was also believed that if a mother achieved orgasm during the time of conception, the child's energetic constitution would also become stronger. This strength in prenatal energy was due to a greater release of the combined energetic and spiritual forces of both parent's Jing, Qi, and Shen, as they enter into the physical tissues of the Uterus. As this released energy combined with the mother's receptive Lower Dantian, the forming zygote was allowed to experience maximum ener-

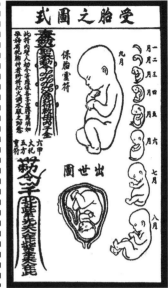

Diagram of the Various Forms of Fetal Conception

Spirit Talisman to Protect the Fetus
If the Fetus of a pregnant woman is attacked by an evil spirit, this Daoist Protective Talisman petitions the help of the Six Jia Spirit Generals to Transform Fire and Regulate Water within the pregnant mother. This is done in order to bring about a swift recovery, and secure the perfection of the Child currently forming within the Mother's womb.

Figure 2.62.. In ancient China, Daoist talismans were sometimes used as magical charms in order to insure safe and healthy fetal development.

getic potential. Likewise, it is also believed that if the mother did not achieve an orgasm during the time of conception, the child's energetic constitution could become relatively weaker.

Prenatal care is mandatory for the healthy formation of the embryo. Before cell division, the DNA mass must be duplicated exactly in order to transfer normal genetic characteristics on to the next generation. Although both parents contribute to the cellular DNA of the forming embryo, it is the mother who is solely responsible for contributing the mitochondrial DNA. Although heredity plays a large part in the transference of both parents' genetic history, a weakness in the mother's energy channels during the child's energetic formation can result in congenital toxins, or other problems that the fetus may acquire during one of the corresponding stages of its development. Because of this belief, in ancient China magical talismans were sometimes given to pregnant women in order to ward off pathogenic influences, protect the womb against evil spirits, and to secure the health and safety of the developing child (Figure 2.62).

A Daoist Perspective Of Early Embryological Development

The following is a modern correlation of an ancient Daoist perspective of embryological development, that was originally taught at the Hai Dian College of Traditional Chinese Medicine in 1995. It combines the modern Western anatomical understandings of fertilization and cell division with ancient Daoist teachings (Figure 2.63).

- **From Infinite Space (Wuji) At Conception:** In essence, all life arises directly from the ocean of Qi that exists within the infinite space of the Wuji. Similarly, a woman's Bao (Uterus) is considered to be the ocean of Qi from which all humanity is created; and, it also represents the infinite space of the Wuji, in terms of embryological development.
- **Within 36 Hours - the Great Ultimate (Taiji) Emerges:** As the sperm breaks through the cell membrane of the ovum, it loses its tail and transforms into the male pronucleus (Yang). Once the male pronucleus (Yang) joins the female pronucleus (Yin), the first cellular division occurs, and Wuji becomes Taiji. As both the Yin (female) and Yang (male) membranes of the two pronuclei fuse and then absorb into each other, and the zygote divides into "blastomeres." This energetic transformation causes the zygote to undergo its normal cellular division within 36 hours after fertilization.
- **Within 48 Hours - the Four Phases (Si Xiang) of Universal Energy Manifest:** The blastomeres further divide into several distinct layers (later becoming the body's various energetic organs and systems). Within 48 hours, the next cellular division occurs, manifesting the development of the Four Phases (Si Xiang) of Universal Energy.
- **Within 60 Hours - the Supernatural Powers of the Prenatal Bagua Manifest:** Within 60 hours after Conception, eight cells have developed and form what is known as a morula (a mass of blastomeres). According to Daoist belief, this energetic transformation relates to the eight energetic powers of the Prenatal Bagua configuration.

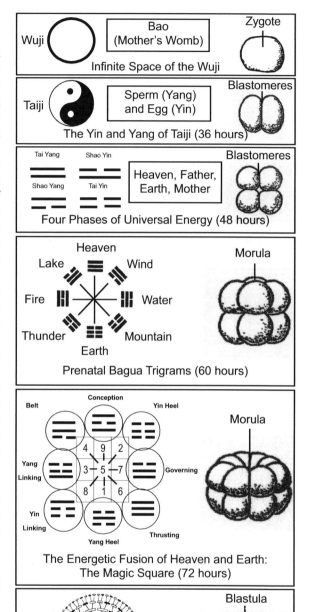

Figure 2.63. Embryological Development from an Ancient Daoist and Modern Medical Perspective

- **Within 72 Hours - the Bagua of Heaven and Earth Stabilize:** By the end of the third day (72 hours), there are sixteen cells, a microcosm functioning under the macrocosmic influence of the energetic fields of Heaven and Earth. This corresponds to the interactions of the Eight Prenatal and Eight Postnatal Bagua and the energetic cycles of the Magic Square.
- **After 5 Days - The Eternal Soul (Shen Xian) Has Found A Home:** After five days, the dense cluster of cells has developed into a hollow ball of cells known as a blastula and enters the uterine cavity. This completes the 64 Prenatal and Postnatal Bagua energetic formation of the Yi-Jing.

YIN AND YANG FERTILIZATION

Because both the father's sperm and the mother's egg consists of Jing (Essence), Qi (Energy), and Shen (Spirit), both parents energetically contribute to the baby's conception. The combination of Father and Mother energies is collectively known as Yuan Qi (Original/Prenatal Energy), and represents the energetic matrix from which all individuals are developed and maintained.

While studying synchronistic and coherent excitations in microtubules, Italian nanobiologist Ezio Insinna has proposed that centrioles (small tubular structures responsible for holding the cell structure in place) are virtually immortal oscillators or wave generators. Within the embryo, these energetic waves are set into motion by the father's Jing, Qi, and Shen when they fuse with the mother's Jing, Qi, and Shen. Once activated, they will continue to pulse throughout the life of the individual. During the first stage of the embryo's development, the centrioles' vibrational pattern begins at a particular frequency, affecting both cell formation and metabolism. This frequency changes as the child matures, producing corresponding changes in metabolism and cell formation.

The quality and quantity of Yuan Qi that the baby receives at conception depends on three main factors:
- **Jing - The Condition Of The Parent's Sperm And Egg:** This includes the purity and potency of the parents' genetic plasma.

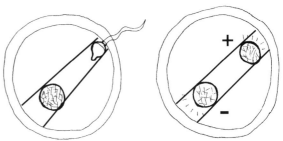

Figure 2.64. The human body is primarily composed of Water. The Jing of Man (sperm) and Woman (egg) unite within the uterine sea, in order to begin the formation of the zygote. The egg is polarized at the entry point of the sperm, creating the original polar axis known as the Human Taiji Pole. The energetic structure of the Taiji Pole determines the complex pattern of cellular division that will occur along its polar axis throughout the development of the fetus.

- **Qi - The Condition Of The Parents' Health And Vitality:** This includes the state of the parent's physical, mental, emotional, and spiritual relationship at the time of conception.
- **Shen - The Child's Destiny:** This includes the spiritual factors surrounding the conception (i.e., the personal Karma that was brought into this life by the incoming soul, and its energetic influence on the surrounding environment)

As the sperm containing the energetic patterns of the father's Jing, Qi and Shen, fertilizes the egg containing the energetic patterns of the mother's Jing, Qi and Shen, Heaven's Yang Qi and Earth's Yin Qi all blend together within the zygote. The swirling and blending of these four energies form energetic pools (which will later evolve into organs), rivers (which later evolve into channels), and streams (which later evolve into collaterals).

The instant the sperm penetrates the egg, it immediately produces a polar axis, that creates an energetic vortex within and around the zygote (similar to the energetic vortex created by the central axis of the Earth). This energetic vortex forms the central Taiji Pole of Man, by drawing Qi from Heaven and Earth into the zygote, allowing the Eternal Soul (Shen Xian) to enter into the fetus' forming body (Figure 2.64).

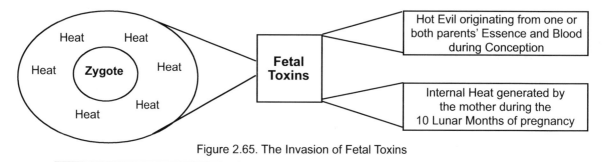

Figure 2.65. The Invasion of Fetal Toxins

Understanding Fetal Toxins

While internally forming within the uterus, sometimes an external invasion of Pathogenic Qi (known as "Fetal Toxins" in this context) can penetrate the growing zygote with latent heat. This pathogenic invasion can eventually cause diseases to appear during early fetal or childhood development. Once established, Fetal Toxins can manifest as either emotional or physical pathogenic patterns. This is why in the Chinese culture, it is extremely important for both parents, especially the mother, to strive towards strength and health at the time of conception and throughout the pregnancy. Pathogenic Toxins can be transferred to the embryo in-utero in one of two ways:

- **During Conception:** Either the mother or father can transfer toxins at the moment of conception. Toxins transferred from one or both parents can create an inherited toxicity due to a retention of "Hot Evil," originating from either of the parents' Essence and Blood.
- **During Pregnancy:** Internal Heat generated by the mother during pregnancy can lead to the development of Fetal Toxins. Toxins can be caused from either internal or external stresses placed on the mother due to suppressed emotions, poor diet, unbalanced life-style, overwork, or negative environmental influences (Figure 2.65).

During pregnancy, the fetus is perceptually aware of both light and sound, and also feels the mother's reaction to the surrounding environmental energy fields. The fetus is therefore strongly influenced by its mother's physical

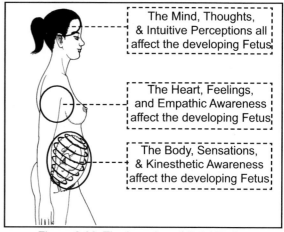

Figure 2.66. The Invasion of Fetal Toxins

activities, as well as her mental, emotional, and spiritual states.

According to "Fetal Education Training" provided in modern Traditional Chinese Medicine, it is necessary that the parents provide a harmonious and supportive environment for the mother and the unborn child in order to improve its physical, emotional, and mental health. In China, all Doctors of T.C.M. believe that Fetal Education is important to ensure optimum development of the child's Prenatal Essence (Yuan Jing), Energy (Yuan Qi), and Spirit (Yuan Shen). This viewpoint is validated by the fact that the mother's Mind, Heart, and Uterus are all directly connected via her internal channels, allowing abundant Qi and Blood to flow into the Uterus. Anything that influences the mother's mind, emotions, and spirit affects her Heart, travels to the Uterus, and can then affect the developing fetus (Figure 2.66).

THE EMBRYO'S INTERNAL CHANNEL DEVELOPMENT SEQUENCE

The following description of the Embryo's Internal Channel Developmental Sequence is only one of the many theories used in Chinese Energetic Embryology to describe the internal formation. The ancient Chinese did not have a comprehension of the body's cells and cellular division. However, many theories have postulated that the channels were energetically formed at the earliest stages of cell division, creating the foundational energy matrix for the developing fetus. The following theory was originally taught to me at the Hai Dian College of Traditional Chinese Medicine in Beijing, China as part of the Energetic Embryological course in 1995.

THE CREATION OF YIN & YANG CHANNELS

One ancient Daoist understanding of human creation is described and explained as follows:

**Once the Absolute has Divided,
The Clear Yang Qi Rises
Creating the images of Heaven;
At the same time,
the Opaque Yin Qi Descends,
creating the energetic forms of Earth."**

Meaning that, once the zygote experiences its first cellular division, Yang Qi begins to ascend and initiates the creation of the body's energetic and spiritual fields (i.e. the image of Heaven).

At the same time, the Yin energy begins to sink and initiates the creation of the physical fields of the body's organs and tissues (i.e., creating the energetic forms of Earth).

After the first cellular division, the fetus will begin the continual accumulation of the Five Element Energies within its forming internal structure. This is initiated in order to construct the fetus's developing physical, energetic, and spirit body. As the Five Element energies begin to construct the fetus's physical body, the energetic and spiritual components of the Five Pure Lights (i.e., spiritual manifestations of the Five Elements) begin to thicken the energetic mass (Yuan Jing). This helps to form the energetic matrix through which all of the body's internal organs and organ systems will function.

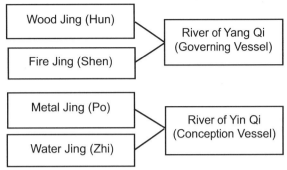

Figure 2.67. The Creative Process of the Body's Yin and Yang Formation

Within the forming fetus, the qualities of the Five Element Jing are further divided into Major Yang and Major Yin energetic components. These special Five Elemental energies are responsible for producing the core foundations of the Major Yang and Major Yin organ and channel systems.

For example, the Original Jing (Yuan Jing) of the Wood and Fire Element energies produce the bodies Major Yang Qi. It is believed that during this important transformation, the congenital Wood Jing Shen (Hun - Ethereal Soul) and congenital Fire Jing Shen (Heart-Mind/Spirit) influence the internal production and formation of the "River of Yang Qi," which manifests as the Governing Vessel (Figure 2.67).

At the same time, the Original Jing of the Metal and Water Element Energies will produce the bodies Major Yin Qi. During this important time of internal transformation, the congenital Metal Jing Shen (Po - Corporeal Soul) and congenital Water Jing Shen (Zhi - Innate Wisdom) will influence the energetic production and formation of the "River of Yin Qi," which manifests as the Conception Vessel.

THE FIVE ELEMENT JING FORMATION

Beginning in the fourth lunar month and continuing until the ninth lunar month, each of the Five Element's energetic natures (Xing) and their associated spiritual characteristics (Shen) will be progressively activated and developed within the fetus' body. The Prenatal Wujingshen (Five Essence Spirits) represents the most subtle level of energetic expression manifesting within the spiritual matrix of the human body.

Jing	Formation	Energetic Property	Disorders
Water Jing 4th Lunar Month	The Water Jing governs the genetic developmental aspect of the fetal growth, encompasses the fetus' unconscious reservoir of intuitive intelligence, will, and life-force energy, and relates to divine love, power, and spirit.	Harmonization of Kidney Yin and Yang Energy	Any faltering of Water Jing is associated with pervasive or subtle neurological disorders, as well as a predisposition to severe psychological disorders (e.g., schizophrenia). Water (Kidney) Jing Deficiency can cause retardation or Congenital Qi Deficiency (i.e., Deficiency in the Sea of Marrow). This, in turn, can lead to Down Syndrome, Attention Deficit Disorder (ADD) and other learning disabilities.
Fire Jing 5th Lunar Month	The Fire Jing promotes emotional and spiritual well-being by generating, controlling, protecting, integrating, dividing and harmonizing the internal energies of the fetus.	Harmonization of Fire and Water Energy	Any faltering of Fire Jing energy is associated with problems of right (Yin) and left (Yang) brain communication, such as internal imbalances between the rational male energy and intuitive female energy.
Metal Jing 6th Lunar Month	The Metal Jing stabilizes the sinews and connective tissues and governs the ability to form and maintain emotional bonding with others.	Harmonization of Corporeal Soul and Ethereal Soul for Interaction and Survival	Any faltering of the Metal Jing energy is associated with problems of emotional attachment such as autism.
Wood Jing 7th Lunar Month	The Wood Jing supervises the assertion and direction of the fetus' emotional and spiritual aspects.		Any faltering of the Wood Jing energy is associated with psychological problems such as passive-aggressive personality disorder.
Earth Jing 8th Lunar Month	The Earth Jing energy supervises the quality and maturation of the fetus' emotional and spiritual bonding and boundaries.	Integration of Intention to Direct Spiritual Forces	Any faltering of the Earth Jing energy is associated with problems of severe psychological disturbances, such as schizophrenia.

Figure 2.68. The Creative Process of the Body's Prenatal Jing Formation

The body's Yuan Jing (Original/Prenatal Essence) fastens the Shen (Mind/Heart) into place by fusing each spiritual aspect with a particular Yin organ system, thus creating a special pathway for physical and energetic expression. For this reason, any deficiency in Prenatal Jing formation can create Postnatal problems, as detailed in the following chart (Figure 2.68). The first Jing to enter its orb and begin its energetic function is the Water Jing.

WATER JING FORMATION

During the Fourth Lunar Month (16 weeks), the Water Jing energy governs the genetic developmental aspect of the fetal growth. This energy encompasses the fetus' unconscious reservoir of intuitive intelligence, will, and life-force energy. It also energetically relates to divine love, power, and the spirit (i.e., the mind-heart influence). Any faltering of the Water Jing energy (due to the influence of Fetal Toxins, stress, trauma, or malnutrition) is associated with both pervasive and subtle Neurological Disorders, as well as a predisposition to severe Psychological Disorders, such as Schizophrenia.

According to the *Huang Di Nei Jing - Ling Shu (The Yellow Emperor's Inner Classic - Spiritual Pivot),*

> **"When the Jing is complete,
> it gives birth to the formation
> of the Brain and Marrow.**
>
> **Then the Bones solidify,
> the Channels begin to nourish,
> the Muscles begin to strengthen,
> the Flesh begins to become a wall,
> the Skin begins to firm
> and the Hair begins to grow."**

Any Deficiency in Water (Kidney) Jing can cause retardation or Congenital Qi Deficiency (i.e., Deficiency in the Sea of Marrow), known in ancient China as the "Five Slows" (i.e., slow in standing, walking, speaking, growing teeth, and growing head hair). This, in turn, can lead to Down Syndrome, Attention Deficit Disorder (ADD), and other learning disabilities. These psychological disturbances may be evident at birth or may develop later on in life.

Fire Jing Formation

During the Fifth Lunar Month (20 weeks), the Fire Jing energy generates and controls, protects and integrates, as well as divides and harmonizes the fetus' internal energies.

Because it promotes emotional and spiritual well-being, any faltering of the Fire Jing energy is associated with problems of right (Yin - intuitive) and left (Yang - logical) Brain communication. This can sometimes result in internal imbalances occurring between the rational male and intuitive female energies of the mind/heart. These psychological disturbances may be evident at birth or may develop later on in life.

Metal Jing Formation

During the Sixth Lunar Month (24 weeks), the Metal Jing is established in the fetus' body, stabilizing the sinews and connective tissues. The Metal Jing energy is also responsible for fetal tissue and structural formation, and the ability to form and maintain emotional bonds.

Any faltering of the Metal Jing energy is associated with problems of emotional attachment, such as autism. These psychological disturbances may be evident at birth or may develop later on in life.

Wood Jing Formation

During the Seventh Lunar Month (28 weeks), the Wood Jing is beginning to be incorporated into the fetus' body. The Wood Jing energy governs the assertion and direction of the fetus' emotional and spiritual aspects. Any faltering of the Wood Jing energy is associated with psychological problems such as passive-aggressive personality disorder. These psychological disturbances may be evident at birth or may develop later on in life.

Earth Jing Formation

During the Eighth Lunar Month (32 weeks), the fetus receives the Zong Qi (the Energetic Breath of the Ancestors) from the mother's Spleen. This special energy has been collected from the Heavens (i.e., the Sun, Moon, Planets and Stars) and the Earth (i.e., the Soil, Water and Wind) and accumulates within the center of the mother's chest.

In Traditional Chinese Medicine, Zong Qi is sometimes known as "Essential Energy, Center Energy, Chest Energy, Gathering Energy, and Big Energy of the Chest." It is responsible for nourishing the Heart and Lungs, and it forms the basis for the involuntary functions of the heartbeat and respiration, as well as the heart's function of governing the Blood and Blood Vessels.

The Zong Qi ("Breath of the Ancestors") and the Yuan Qi (Original/Prenatal Energy) mutually assist and support each other. The Zong Qi flows downward to aid the Kidneys; while the Yuan Qi flows upward in order to aid in respiration, and assist in the formation of Zong Qi. The chest area where Zong Qi collects in the body is traditionally called the "Upper Sea of Qi" (CV-17).

During the Eighth Lunar Month, the Earth Jing begins to complete the formation of the skin. It also governs the quality and maturation of the fetus' emotional and spiritual bonding and boundaries.

Any faltering of the Earth Jing energy is associated with problems of severe psychological disturbances, such as schizophrenia, which may be evident at birth or develop later on in life.

Understanding The Body's Prenatal Jing, Qi, and Shen

Within the developing fetus, three important energies known in Daoist teachings as the "Three Treasures of Man," combine (Figure 2.69). These special energies are traditionally known as "Yuan Jing" (Original Essence), "Yuan Qi" (Original Energy), and "Yuan Shen" (Original Mind/Heart).

In modern times, there is much confusion about the Three Treasures and their energetic applications. Therefore, I have included some of the secret esoteric teachings that were passed down to me ("ear whispered"), from one of my Daoist Masters:

The Yuan Jing (Original Essence)

Although "Jing" (Essence) is the body's foundational substance responsible for nourishing the tissues, it is important to note that the body's "Yuan Jing" (Original or Prenatal "Essence") is not Reproductive Essence, which is considered to be Postnatal Essence.

The body's Yuan Jing is a primordial substance that is not born from a Postnatal state. It is the innate, true energetic substance, through which the body's constitutional makeup, strength, and overall vitality originated and externally manifested. According to ancient Daoist teachings, "the Original Essence is devoid of form and matter. As soon as matter is generated, it cannot be used in alchemical cultivation as the Mother of the Elixir. Only when the Original Essence is combined with the energy of the Original Breath (Yuan Qi), is the Immortal Elixir created."

In Daoist alchemy, the Original Yang (Yuan Yang) is the same as the Original Essence (Yuan Jing), it has no form, and resides within the Original Breath (Yuan Qi) as an energetic vapor. When the Original Essence receives any type of external stimuli, it moves, separates itself from the Original Breath, transforms from a "Generative Force" ("Jing Qi") into a "Generative Fluid" (Postnatal Jing) and becomes energetically active as the body's Postnatal Essence.

When the Original Essence is in its natural state, it is stored within the Five Yin and Six Yang Organs, existing as an energetic mist, still, and formless. As soon as a single thought arises from the Postnatal state, it immediately transforms it from a Prenatal state into a Postnatal state.

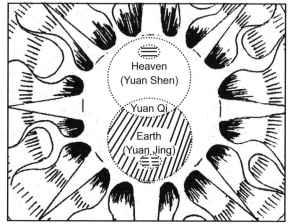

Figure 2.69. the Human Body's Three Treasures

According to ancient Daoist teachings, when Jing is abundant, the Qi is Full and the Shen is flourishing. It is only during this time that a disciple will begin the alchemical practice of "Lian Jing Hua Qi" ("Transforming Essence into Energy").

The Yuan Qi (Original Energy)

Sometimes called "Source Qi" in Traditional Chinese Medicine, the Yuan Qi (Original or Prenatal "Breath/Energy") is the foundation of all the other types of energy inside the body.

The Yuan Qi is closely linked with the Yuan Jing (Original or Prenatal Essence). Together, the Yuan Qi and Yuan Jing determine the body's overall health, vitality, stamina, and life span.

In Daoist Alchemy, the body's Yuan Qi is considered to be the original energy that radiates from the body and extends into the infinite space of the Wuji, to reconnect with the celestial realms of the eternal Dao. Therefore, it is the original motivational force that energetically links the Yuan Jing (Original Essence) with the Yuan Shen (Original Mind/Heart).

The Yuan Qi is the true force behind the activity of all the organs and energies in the body. It is closely related to the Mingmen (Gate of Life) and works to sustain the life of the body.

The body's Yuan Qi is also the catalytic agent needed for transforming food, air, and drink into Postnatal Qi, and also facilitates the production of Blood. Although the Yuan Qi is housed within the Lower Dantian, it also flows to all the internal organs and channels.

THE YUAN SHEN (ORIGINAL MIND/HEART)

The Yuan Shen (Original Mind/Heart) is the body's most subtle energetic field of sound and light, that can express and manifest an individual's internal thoughts, desires, dreams, and intentions into the external world. The Original Mind/Heart, in this context, refers to a process of awareness and consciousness that exists throughout the entire body, and extends into the surrounding environment, and is not merely limited to the Brain.

The Original Mind/Heart is connected to the eternal core of the Dao. It governs the body's tissues and energetic fields, energizes the Qi, and forms a solid connection of internal light and vibrational energy active within and without the tissues. The energy of the various internal organs are at the effect of the radiant spiritual light of the Yuan Shen (Original Mind/Heart), which is also affected by the quality of radiant light contained within the surrounding environment.

When the Yuan Shen is fully developed, an individual will naturally acquire certain extraordinary powers and psychic abilities, such as Clairvoyant Sight and Soul Travel (also known as "Astral Projection").

In Daoist alchemy, the innate spiritual power accessible to a disciple via his Yuan Shen, is represented by the intensity of this special light, and the number of energetic rings that surround the light's resonating core. Many years ago, one of my Daoist teachers explained that the degree of accumulated spiritual energy is reflected by the number of light circles developed within the body's core Taiji Pole.

The spiritual insights and psychic perceptions of an individual's Original Spirit (Yuan Shen) are integrated and sustained by the "Five Spiritual Essences" of the Prenatal Wujingshen, which are in turn housed and rooted within the energy of the Five Yin Organs. The Yuan Shen then becomes established and rooted in the combined Congenital Jing, Qi, and Shen that the mother and father provided upon conception. This combined Congenital energy also provides the basis for the formation of the "Acquired Mind" ("Shen Zhi" - developed personality, or "ego"), which is integrated and sustained after the child is born by the Postnatal Wujingshen.

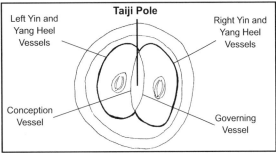

Figure 2.70. During the first cellular division, the field of energy in the polar axis is related to the Yuan Qi, from which the Conception and Governing Vessels form the seas of Yin and Yang energy. The Yin Heel and Yang Heel Vessels are also established during the first cellular division, forming the left and right sides. The development of the zygote's exterior is controlled by the Yang Linking Vessels. The development of the zygote's interior is controlled by the Yin Linking Vessels.

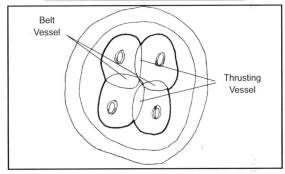

Figure 2.71. The second cellular division is associated with the development of the Belt Vessel and the Thrusting Vessel.

THE EXTRAORDINARY VESSELS OF CREATION

With the first cell division, the energetic polarization of the zygote determines a ventral and dorsal surface, which become the embryo's Conception and Governing Vessels, respectively (Figure 2.70). At this point, the Governing Vessel controls the cell divisions that eventually form the back of the body; while the Conception Vessel controls the cell divisions forming the front of the body.

This first cell division also establishes a right and left side. Here, the Heel Vessels control the balance of Yin and Yang energy development in the two sides of the body.

The Belt Vessel and Thrusting Vessels form at the time of the second cell division (Figure 2.71).

The four vessels formed at this point (Governing, Conception, Thrusting, and Belt Vessels) are interlinked for the production, circulation, and regulation of the body's Yuan Jing. With the formation of these first four vessels, the body's entire energetic system becomes established and is maintained.

During embryonic formation, the Yang Linking Vessels are responsible for the exterior development of the embryo, while the Yin Linking Vessels are responsible for the interior development.

Each of the Eight Extraordinary Vessels specific role in the development of the embryo is described as follows:

1. **The Governing Vessel (Du Mai):** Controls the development of the body's back.
2. **The Conception Vessel (Ren Mai):** Controls the development of the body's front.
3. **The Thrusting Vessels (Chong Mai):** Transport Qi through the center of the body, controls the center core, and regulates Blood.
4. **The Yang Heel Vessels (Yang Qiao Mai):** Control the development of the body's right and left Yang energy.
5. **The Yin Heel Vessels (Yin Qiao Mai):** Control the development of the body's right and left Yin energy.
6. **The Yang Linking Vessels (Yang Wei Mai):** Control the development of the Exterior of the body, and correlate to the energy of Heaven.
7. **The Yin Linking Vessels (Yin Wei Mai):** Control the development of the Interior of the body, and correlate to the energy of Earth.
8. **The Belt Vessel (Dai Mai):** Energetically binds all of the body's channels together.

The Eight Extraordinary Vessels form a vortex of energy at the center of the embryo's body centered in the area between what will become the left and right Kidneys. The Taiji Pole and Thrusting Vessels are at the center of this vortex and will form the Sea of Five Yin and Six Yang Organs, the Sea of Twelve Primary Channels, and the Sea of Blood. The body's Qi and Blood are energetically distributed through small channels or rivers of energy from the Taiji Pole and the Thrusting Vessels. This energetic vortex creates the energy for the growth of the embryo's physical form (Figure 2.72).

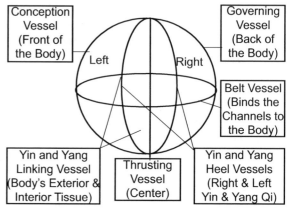

Figure 2.72. The Energetic Embryological Flow of the Eight Extraordinary Vessels

After the initial cell division is complete, the embryo's Yang channels and Yin channels begin the development and formation of the embryo's tissues and organs. Twenty main channels envelop the forming tissues, and are divided into two separate groups of energetic rivers. These special energetic rivers are traditionally known as the Eight Extraordinary Vessels and the Twelve Primary Channels. As the embryo develops into a fetus and continues to grow, these twenty channels will also continue to develop.

During the formation of the embryo, Nine Yang Channels begin to flow from the main Governing Vessel (Sea of Yang Qi), and form nine energetic rivers that are known as the Urinary Bladder, Gall Bladder, Stomach, Small Intestine, Triple Burner, Large Intestine, Yang Heel, Yang Linking, and Belt Channels. At this time, the Nine Yin Channels that flow from the main Conception Vessel (Sea of Yin Qi), will form the nine energetic rivers that are known as the Kidney, Liver, Spleen, Heart, Pericardium, Lung, Yin Heel, Yin Linking, and Thrusting Channels.

OVERVIEW OF THE TEN LUNAR MONTHS OF CREATION

The following description of the sequence of embryological development was presented by the Imperial Physician Chao Yuan Fang, who compiled the *Zhu Bing Yuan Hou Lun (Treatise on Causes and Symptoms of Diseases)* during the Sui Dynasty (581-618 A.D.). In this ancient Daoist model, pregnancy is measured in Ten Lunar Months spanning the forty weeks of a normal pregnancy (Figure 2.73).

CHAPTER 2: UNDERSTANDING ANCIENT CHINESE METAPHYSICS

The Ten Heavenly Stems Birth Cycle

甲	乙	丙	丁	戊	己	庚	辛	壬	癸
Jia Wood Yang (1)	Yi Wood Yin (2)	Bing Fire Yang (3)	Ding Fire Yin (4)	Wu Earth Yang (5)	Ji Earth Yin (6)	Gen Metal Yang (7)	Xin Metal Yin (8)	Ren Water Yang (9)	Gui Water Yin (10)
(E) Green Dragon		(S) Red Phoenix		(C) Golden Dragon		(W) White Tiger		(N) Black Warrior	

	Lunar Month	Mother's Channels	Channel's Energetic Influence	Internal Formation Activity of the Embryo and Fetus
Wood Element	Month (1) (4 Weeks) Embryo	Liver Channels (Foot Absolute Yin)	Responsible for Stopping the Menses, and providing the energy to nourish the growth of the embryo	The mother's Blood is transformed into Jing, and her Essence and Blood coagulate in her womb "Mingling, Clotting, Solidifying, and Rounding."
Wood Element	Month (2) (8 Weeks) Embryo	Gall Bladder Channels (Foot Lesser Yang)	Responsible for Saturating the Embryo, Uterus, and Placenta with Jing, causing the Embryonic Qi to transform into Amniotic Fluid	The Mesenteric Membrane Sac, Umbilical Cord, and Placenta form, and the embryo begins to take shape inside the uterine lining, developing basic structural features.
Fire Element	Month (3) (12 Weeks) Fetus	Pericardium Channels (Hand Absolute Yin)	Responsible for the amount of Jing and Shen in the vessels, channels, & collaterals of the forming fetus.	The fetus begins micro-movement; heartbeat can now be detected; the Hun & Po are active within the internal organs.
Fire Element	Month (4) (16 Weeks) Fetus	Triple Burner Channels (Hand Lesser Yang)	Responsible for the development of the fetus's inner fascia and connective tissues; and for stabilizing the Blood Vessels	The Yin Organs develop, and the Water Jing Qi governs the genetic development of the fetus, including the intuitive intelligence, will, and life-force energy.
Earth Element	Month (5) (20 Weeks) Fetus	Spleen Channels (Foot Greater Yin)	Responsible for directing the development & completion of the 4 limbs (i.e., both arms and legs).	The Five Agents enter the Five Yin Organs, and the Fire Jing Qi generates, controls, protects, integrates, divides, and harmonizes the fetus' internal energies.
Earth Element	Month (6) (24 Weeks) Fetus	Stomach Channels (Foot Bright Yang)	Responsible for establishing the fetus' muscles; and the 6 Pitches reside in the body's 6 Storage Areas	The Metal Jing Qi is responsible for fetal tissue and structural formation, and the ability to form and maintain emotional bonds with others.
Metal Element	Month (7) (28 Weeks) Fetus	Lung Channels (Hand Greater Yin)	Responsible for creating the Bones, Skin, and Hair; and the 7 Essential Stars open the fetus' orifices to let in the light of Heaven & Earth.	The Wood Jing Qi is responsible for the assertion and direction of the fetus' emotional and spiritual aspects.
Metal Element	Month (8) (32 Weeks) Fetus	Large Intestine Channels (Hand Bright Yang)	Responsible for completing the formation of the skin, harmonizing the Shen and quieting the breath.	The Earth Jing Qi governs the quality and maturation of the fetus' emotional and spiritual bonding and boundaries.
Water Element	Month (9) (36 Weeks) Fetus	Kidney Channels (Foot Lesser Yin)	Responsible for controlling the amount of Qi the fetus absorbs from the mother through the umbilicus	The 9 Internal Palaces within the 3 Dantians are created, and are established to keep the fetus' Yuan Jing, Qi, and Shen safe.
Water Element	Month (10) (40 Weeks) Fetus	Urinary Bladder Channels (Foot Greater Yang)	Responsible for energetically harmonizing the Jing, Qi, and Shen of all Yin and Yang Organs	The Qi of Heaven and Earth settle into the fetus' Lower Dantian in preparation for birth

Figure 2.73. Dr. Chao Yuan Fang's "Prenatal Energy Development" Chart

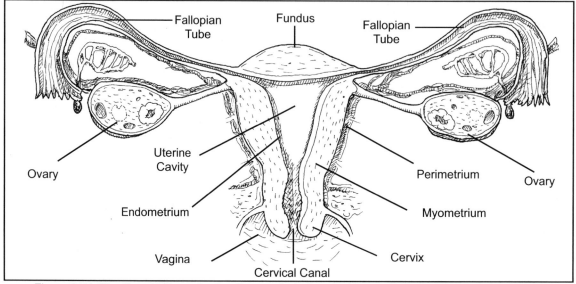

Figure 2.74. The Female Reproductive Organs, including the Uterus, Fallopian Tubes, and Ovaries. (Inspired by the original artwork of Dr. Frank H. Netter)

Month One

Once a young woman's Uterus becomes fully developed she begins her menstrual cycle. When an egg is released from her ovary pregnancy can occur, and fetal growth will follow (Figure 2.74).

The First Lunar Month of pregnancy is traditionally called the "Beginning of Form" Stage and refers to the internal formation of the Jing of the placenta. This stage also covers conception and early cell division and is described as the progression of "Mingling, Clotting, Solidifying, and Rounding."

The ancient Daoists believed that during this special time of growth, there is only Yuan Qi (Original Energy) active within the mother's womb. This special primal generative energy is responsible for the congealing and nurturing of the forming embryo, seeing it through to its completion.

During conception, when the Yin and Yang energies of both parents interact inside the womb, in the midst of the darkness, there is a point of Divine living potential which comes forth from the Dao, merging from out of the infinite space of the Wuji. This is what is known to the ancient Daoists as the "Primordial, True, Unified Generative Energy of Creation." This special energy of creation enters into the sperm and egg, fusing them as one. The ancient Daoist teachings state the following:

"Formless, it produces form; Immaterial, it produces substance. The internal organs, sense organs, and various parts of the body all evolve because of this energy of creation, becoming complete."

Within the mother's womb, it is the Primordial, True, Unified Generative Energy of Creation (Yuan Qi) that causes the embryo to congeal and form, then nourishes the embryo, and eventually causes it to become complete. At this beginning stage in development, although there is human form, there is no development of the Acquired Mind (Shen Zhi), only the true, Congenital/Original Mind (Yuan Shen) exists.

The Uterus

In Traditional Chinese Medicine, the physiological functions of a woman's Uterus is connected to her Heart, Liver, Spleen, Kidneys, Conception and Thrusting Vessels. The Uterus connects to the Kidneys (which provide the Uterus with Jing), the Conception Vessel (which provides the Uterus with Qi and nourishes the fetus), and the Thrusting Channel (which provides the Uterus with Blood).

When the Jing of the Kidneys is sufficient, the menstrual period will occur regularly, making

Figure 2.75. The Chinese Ideograph for "Bao," Uterus

pregnancy and fetal growth possible. The Qi and Blood of the Twelve Primary Channels pass into the Uterus through the Thrusting and Conception Vessels, affecting the amount of menstrual flow and its cycle.

Chinese Character for Uterus

The Chinese character that depicts the ideogram for "Bao" is composed of two images (Figure 2.75):

- **Bao:** The Chinese ideogram for "Bao" is composed of two images: the character to the left, "Ji" depicts the Chinese ideogram for "Body Tissue, Muscle or Flesh" (all of which are forms of connective tissue); the character on the right "Bao" means "To Wrap, Surround, and Encase" and refers to "a bag or sack."

Together these characters depict the Uterus and represent an embryo wrapped, protected, and contained inside the mother's abdomen. It is important to note, that in ancient China, the character for Bao was occasionally used to refer to the urinary bladder, placenta, or Uterus.

The Uterus and the Lower Dantian

It is important to realize that each individual was conceived inside the core of the Uterus, which is considered the center of a woman's Lower Dantian (Sea of Qi). Given its Yin nature and close proximity to the Earth, the Lower Dantian itself is considered a center of consciousness, and is more kinesthetic in its perceptive nature (Figure 2.76).

According to Daoist Inner Alchemy, the Earth Qi is gathered in the Uterus and Lower Dantian area. The Uterus is associated with the development of the fetus' forming tissues, allowing the Eternal Soul (Shen Xian) the ability to acquire a lower vibrational resonance in order to experience life on the gross physical realm.

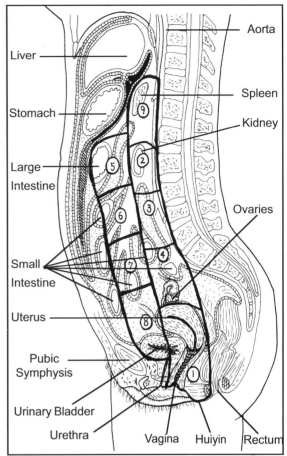

Figure 2.76. The Nine Chambers of the Lower Dantian in the female body. Each number encompasses the entire chamber. (Inspired by the artwork of Dr. Frank H. Netter)

The Prenatal quiescent state from which the fetus develops, translates to the same energetic state that can be acquired after birth through deep prayer, meditation, and sleep. Therefore, these three special methods are used to form the energetic foundation needed for recharging the body's Prenatal (Yuan) Jing, Qi, and Shen.

The Uterus and Lower Dantian are the major storage areas for the various types of Kidney energies (i.e., Qi of the ovaries). It is the place where Qi is housed, the body's Mingmen Fire is aroused, the Kidney Yin and Yang Qi is gathered, and the Yuan Qi (Original Energy) is stored. The Yuan Qi is the foundation of all the other types of Qi in the

VOLUME 1, SECTION 1: FOUNDATIONS OF CHINESE ENERGETIC MEDICINE

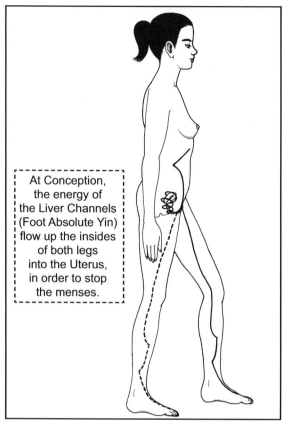

At Conception, the energy of the Liver Channels (Foot Absolute Yin) flow up the insides of both legs into the Uterus, in order to stop the menses.

Figure 2.77. The Mother's and Father's Essence (Jing), Energy (Qi), and Spirit (Shen) blend with Heaven and Earth energies during the fusion of the sperm and egg. During the First Lunar Month, the mother's Liver Channels stop her Menses and begin the Embryonic Growth Cycle.

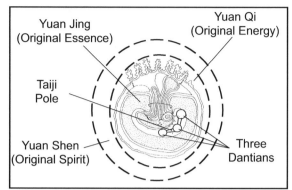

Figure 2.78. Sustained through the Umbilical Cord, the Embryo absorbs the mother's Blood, Essence, Energy, and Spirit.

body. Because it is closely linked with the Prenatal Essence (Yuan Jing), together, the Yuan Qi and Yuan Jing determine the bodies overall health, vitality, stamina, and life span.

THE ROLE OF THE MOTHER'S LIVER CHANNELS

At conception, the mother's Liver Channels (Figure 2.77) stop her menses, and the energy begins to nourish the growth of her embryo. During pregnancy, the mother's Blood is transformed into Jing (Essence), that continually nourishes both the mother's body, as well as the her forming embryo. The mother's Liver Channels cause Essence and Blood to coagulate in her womb. This Blood coagulation continues after the initial cellular division.

MOTHER'S SHEN

The mother's Shen (Mind/Spirit) becomes part of a threefold activity, described as follows:

- **Energizes The Creation Fluids:** First, the mother's Shen (Mind/Spirit) projects through the umbilical cord, sustaining and energizing the forming embryo's production of Jing, Qi, Shen, Blood, and Body Fluids (Figure 2.78).
- **Sustains The Embryo's Original Three Treasures:** Second, the mother's Shen (Mind/Spirit) influences the embryo's Yuan Jing (Original Essence) and Yuan Qi (Original Energy), as well as the formation of the embryo's Yuan Shen (Original Spirit).

  The embryo's Yuan Shen manifests as a multicolored light, which contains all of the inherited patterns and knowledge of both parent's lineage ancestors, including special talents, skills, and natural abilities. This special knowledge is stored deep within the embryo's forming cells, tissues, and consciousness, and will "awaken" once the right stimulus is applied.
- **Creates the Pregnancy "Glow:"** Third, the mother's Shen (Mind/Spirit) influences the embryo's Qi and Blood, and internally "Awakens" the embryo's Yuan Shen (Original Spirit) to manifest its radiant spiritual light. This special energetic light manifests through the mother's skin, and is commonly associated with the radiant "glow" observed shining through her eyes and energy field after conception.

CHAPTER 2: UNDERSTANDING ANCIENT CHINESE METAPHYSICS

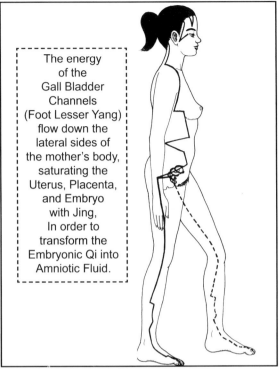

Figure 2.79. The Mother's Gall Bladder Channels saturate the embryo with Jing during the Second Lunar Month, causing the Embryonic Qi to transform into amniotic fluid. The embryo begins to take shape as the energetic boundaries, pools, spatial cavities, channels and collaterals, internal and external spiritual, energetic and physical forms begin to manifest.

MONTH TWO

The Second Lunar Month of pregnancy is traditionally called the "Beginning To Gel" Stage, and refers to the completion of the formation of the "first shape" of the embryo.

THE ROLE OF THE MOTHER'S GALL BLADDER CHANNELS

During the second four weeks, the mother's Gall Bladder Channels (Figure 2.79) are responsible for the development of the mesenteric membrane sac. The Gall Bladder Channels also saturate the embryo, Uterus, and placenta with Jing, causing the embryonic Qi to become denser until it transforms into a thick liquid (amniotic fluid).

This external (embryonic) fluid helps regulate the embryo's internal Body Fluids. The amniotic fluid that surrounds the embryo also acts as an en-

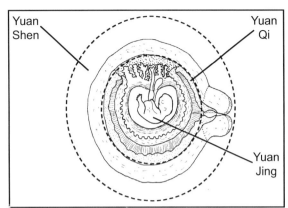

Figure 2.80. During the Second Lunar Month, the embryo begins to take shape as the energetic boundaries begin to form.

ergetic condenser, retaining and magnifying the Qi and Shen that is flowing into the mother's womb.

At this stage, the umbilical cord and placenta are now formed, and the embryo begins to take shape inside the uterine lining, developing basic structural features (Figure 2.80). Additionally, the Lungs, Liver, Kidneys, and major Blood Vessels are beginning to form.

ENERGETIC FORMATION

With the formation of the major Blood Vessels, the Yin and Yang Qi begin to occupy the embryo's channels. As the embryo's internal and external Yin and Yang energies actively balance themselves, the following occurs:
- The energy that will later coalesce into Lung Qi moves to the upper part of the body.
- The Original Qi (Yuan Qi) of the Kidneys begins to collect deep in the center of the body.
- The Earth Qi, absorbed by the embryo from the mother's exposure to the outside environment, begins to collect in the lower front and upper back areas of the embryo's body.

During embryonic formation, each distinct energy is naturally drawn to the appropriate area within the embryo's developing body, creating its own unique boundaries and pools of Qi. These pools and boundaries will later form the major internal organs and external tissues, in addition to the energetic spatial cavities that surround them.

The areas where the energetic pools settle and begin to create a balance within themselves are the precursors to the body's internal organ systems. During this creative process, internal movement creates tiny energetic currents, eddies, and whirlpools that flow throughout the entire body. As the energy shifts, seeking balance, the larger pools of energy begin to condense, forming the bones, spine, brain, internal organs, and skin.

Once the energetic pools and rivers have formed, then all of the currents and eddies simultaneously evolve in order to form the body's energetic channel and collateral systems. Throughout the developing tissues, these energetic currents will continue to move in accordance with the mother's respiratory patterns, up until the moment of the child's birth. After the baby's first breath, the energetic currents will begin to follow the rhythmic patterns of the child's own respiration.

As these currents continue to spiral within the forming channels, energetic points are established according to the body's subtle energetic blueprint. Some of these areas spiral outward to form energetic exit points, while others spiral inward in order to form energetic entry points.

Month Three

The Third Lunar Month of pregnancy is traditionally called the "Beginning Of The Pregnant Uterus" Stage. During this period, the embryo becomes a fetus and begins micro-movement. Its heartbeat can now be detected.

The Role of the Mother's Pericardium Channels

The mother's Pericardium Channels (Figure 2.81) control the presence and amount of Jing and Shen in the vessels, channels, and collaterals of the fetus. The Jing and Shen that flow from the mother into the fetus are rooted in the Qi of her Blood. The combination of the mother's Qi and Body Fluids purifies and cleanses the Shen of the fetus. This purifying action transforms into Heat, causing the fetus' Yang Qi to arouse the Hun (the body's Ethereal Soul) into life. During the third lunar month, the Prenatal Five Agents (Wu Jing Shen) begin to energetically awaken.

Energetic Formation

As the Prenatal Jing and Blood combine, the fetus' Shen (Mind/Heart) is further refined.

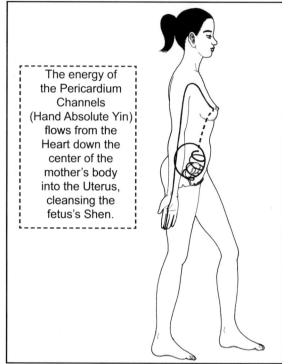

Figure 2.81. The Mother's Pericardium Channels govern the Third Lunar Month of creation. During this phase, the mother's Qi and body fluids purify and cleanse the fetus's Shen (Mind/Spirit). At this time, the Hun (Heaven) and the Po (Earth) are established within the fetus's internal organs.

The energy of the Pericardium Channels (Hand Absolute Yin) flows from the Heart down the center of the mother's body into the Uterus, cleansing the fetus's Shen.

During the Third Lunar Month, the Hun and Po "awaken." The energy of the Hun (Ethereal Soul) was sometimes referred to by the ancient Daoists as an aspect of the Ling Shen (Spiritual Mind/Heart), because they flow with the movement of the Blood. The energy of the Po (Corporeal Souls) was sometimes referred to as a Moving Shen, because they followed the movement of the Jing. Combined, the energetic functions of the Hun acting as a Spiritual Mind/Heart was considered to be the "active impulse," while the energetic functions of the Po, acting as a Moving Shen, was considered to be the "enabling mover" of the body's Jing, Qi, and Shen.

Tissue Formation

At the end of the third month, the internal organs, limbs, and external sex organs of the fetus are fully formed, and the nails have developed.

MONTH FOUR

During the Fourth Lunar Month, the mother's Triple Burner Channels, which are connected to the Yang Organs, stabilize the Blood Vessels of the fetus. At this stage, the Water Jing is beginning to be accepted by the fetus' body, enabling the development of the Yin Organs.

THE ROLE OF THE MOTHER'S TRIPLE BURNER CHANNELS

The mother's Triple Burner Channels (Figure 2.82) direct the development of the fetus's inner fascia and connective tissues. This process is referred to as "the development of Qi and Blood penetrating to the ears and eyes and circulating throughout the fetus' channels and connecting vessels."

During the Fourth Lunar Month, a doctor can tell from the mother's pulse whether she is having a boy or a girl. According to ancient Daoist teachings, "If the left pulse is lively, it is a Boy; if the right pulse is lively, it is a Girl; if both the left and right pulses are lively, she will have twins."

WATER JING FORMATION

Beginning in the Fourth Lunar Month and continuing through the Ninth Lunar Month, the energetic nature and spiritual characteristics of each of the Prenatal Wujingshen are progressively activated and developed within the fetus' body. The Jing of the Water Element is the first of the five Jing Shen (Essence Spirits) to energize the developing fetus, and become active in tissue formation. Although the Water Jing energy governs the genetic development of the fetus it also encompasses the fetus' unconscious reservoir of intuitive intelligence, will, and life-force energy; and relates to divine love, power, and spirit. Any faltering of the Water Jing Qi due to the influence of fetal toxins, stress, trauma or malnutrition, is associated with both pervasive and subtle neurological disorders, as well as a predisposition to severe psychological disorders.

During this time, any deficiency in Water (Kidney) Jing can cause retardation or Congenital Qi Deficiency (i.e., Deficiency in the Sea of Marrow). This, in turn, can lead to Down Syndrome, Attention Deficit Disorder (ADD) and learning disabilities. These psychological disturbances may be evident at birth or may develop later on in life.

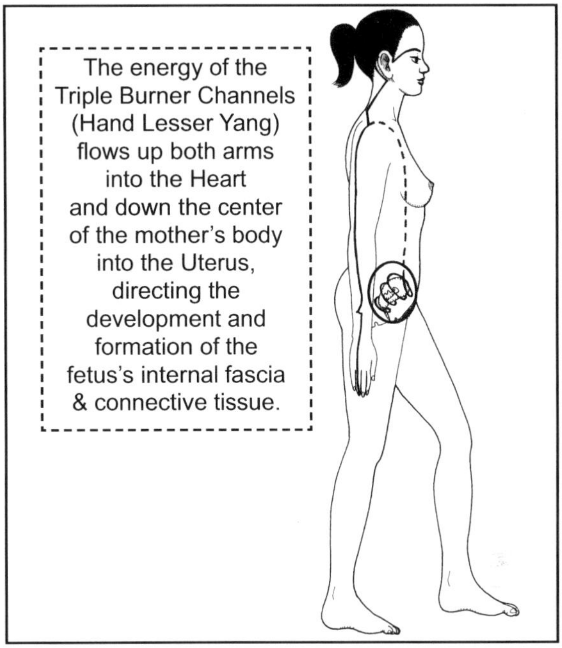

The energy of the Triple Burner Channels (Hand Lesser Yang) flows up both arms into the Heart and down the center of the mother's body into the Uterus, directing the development and formation of the fetus's internal fascia & connective tissue.

Figure 2.82. The Mother's Triple Burner Channels govern the Fourth Lunar Month of creation. At this time, the Water Jing (Essence) is accepted by the fetus' body..

TISSUE FORMATION

Through the later stages of fetal development, the embryo's relatively homogenous tissues transform into the more mature differentiated tissues of the fetus. The structures and boundaries of the maturing tissues (i.e., the muscles, Bones, and organs, etc.) are defined and maintained by the fetus' connective tissue (inner fascia). Accordingly, a very large part of the body consists of connective tissue and membranes functioning in order to support and define the body's internal and external structures.

As the different structures of the body are defined by fascial boundaries (which border each other), these same tissues and structures are woven together through a vast network of interpenetrating connective tissue that pervades the entire body. This internal network facilitates the body's inter-cellular communication. Because these structures connect to every part of the fetus' body, they form a vast energetic and physical system capable of regulating and transforming the body's Jing, Qi, and Shen.

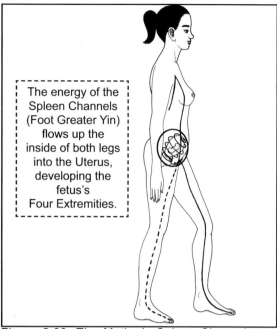

Figure 2.83. The Mother's Spleen Channels are responsible for the Fifth Lunar Month of creation. The development of the fetus' four limbs is completed. The Fire Jing is accepted by the fetus' body, and the Five Agents are distributed within the Five Yin Organs).

MONTH FIVE

During the Fifth Lunar Month, the mother's Spleen Channels (Figure 2.83) are responsible for completing the development of the four limbs. At this stage, the fetus begins to have its own respiratory movement. The Fire Jing is now accepted into the fetus's forming tissues, and begins creating internal energy that stabilizes the Qi of the Five Yin Organs (Liver, Heart, Spleen, Lungs, Kidneys).

THE ROLE OF THE MOTHER'S SPLEEN CHANNELS

The mother's Spleen Channels direct the development and completion of the four limbs.

FIRE JING FORMATION

During the Fifth Lunar Month, the Fire Jing Qi generates, controls, protects, integrates, divides, and harmonizes the fetus' internal energies.

Any faltering of the Fire Jing energy at this time is associated with problems of right (Yin) and left (Yang) Brain communication, such as internal imbalances between the rational male energy and

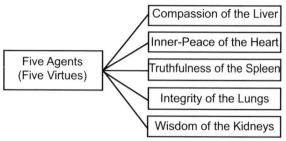

Figure 2.84. During the Fifth Lunar Month, the Five Agents are distributed into the Five Orbs

intuitive female energies. These psychological disturbances may be evident at birth or may develop later on in life.

ENERGETIC FORMATION OF THE FIVE ORBS

At this stage of development, the Prenatal Five Agents (i.e., the five spiritual virtues of the Five Pure Lights) are distributed to the Five Yin Organ Orbs, through the influence on the Middle Hun "Shang Ling" (see end of Chapter).

The Five Yin Organ Orbs include the internal cells, tissues and associated organs, as well as the organ's spatial cavity, associated Channels, Body Fluids, Jing, Qi, Blood, its Shen, and external energetic influence (sounds, colors, tastes, and smells). Additionally, the energetic Orb of each Yin Organ also includes the corresponding emotions and spiritual states that extended throughout the entire body, and are responsible for energetically influencing the organ itself. The Prenatal Five Agents are distributed as follows (Figure 2.84):

- The Virtue of Compassion to the Liver
- The Virtue of Inner-Peace to the Heart
- The Virtue of Truthfulness to the Spleen
- The Virtue of Integrity to the Lungs
- The Virtue of Wisdom to the Kidneys

The even distribution and balance of the Prenatal Five Agents allows the energetic nature of the Hun (Ethereal Soul) to stabilize itself within the fetus' organs, creating peace and order within the fetus' Yuan Shen (Original Mind/Spirit).

TISSUE FORMATION

At the end of the Fifth Lunar Month, the fetus' body systems develop rapidly. Its head is less disproportionate to the rest of its body, and the mother often feels the fetus's spontaneous movements.

CHAPTER 2: UNDERSTANDING ANCIENT CHINESE METAPHYSICS

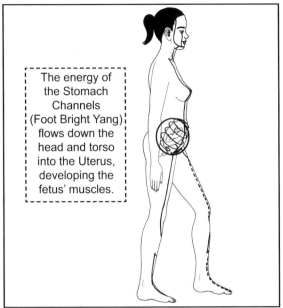

Figure 2.85. The Mother's Stomach Channels govern the Sixth Lunar Month of creation. At this time, the Six Pitches are established within the body's storage areas, and the Metal Jing is accepted by the fetus' body.

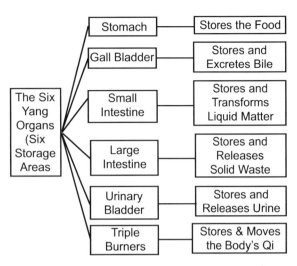

Figure 2.86. During the Sixth Lunar Month, the Yang Organs develop the Six Storage Areas.

MONTH SIX

During the Sixth Lunar Month, the mother's Stomach Channels govern the development of the fetus, and the Six Pitches ("Jue," "Zhi," "Gong," "Shang," "Yu," and "Xi") are established within its body's storage areas. At this stage, the Metal Jing is beginning to be accepted by the fetus' body.

THE ROLE OF THE MOTHER'S STOMACH CHANNELS

In the Sixth Lunar Month of creation, the mother's Stomach Channels begin to establish the fetus' muscles (Figure 2.85).

METAL JING FORMATION

During the Sixth Lunar Month, the Metal Jing is established in the fetus' body, and is responsible for fetal tissue and structural formation, stabilizing the fetus's internal sinews and connective tissues.

The Metal Jing energy is also responsible for the ability to form and maintain emotional bonds with others. Any faltering of the Metal Jing Qi is associated with problems of emotional attachment, such as autism. These psychological disturbances may be evident at birth or may develop later on in life.

FORMATION OF THE SIX STORAGE AREAS

During the Sixth Lunar Month, the Yang organs begin to develop (i.e., the Stomach, Gall Bladder, Small Intestine, Large Intestine, Urinary Bladder, and Triple Burners). The Six Storage Areas of the body's Yang organs are constantly filling and emptying. Each of the Yang organs receive, move, transform, digest, or excrete substances, described as follows (Figure 2.86):

1. **The Stomach Stores the Food.** This Yang Organ is responsible for receiving, storing, rotting, and ripening food.
2. **The Gall Bladder Stores and Excretes Bile.** This Yang Organ is responsible for storing and releasing bile into the Small Intestine.
3. **The Small Intestine Stores and Transforms Liquid Matter.** This Yang Organ receives, stores, transforms, and digests food and releases its waste products into the Large Intestine.
4. **The Large Intestine Stores the Solid Waste.** This Yang Organ receives, stores, and absorbs food and releases waste.
5. **The Urinary Bladder Stores and Releases the Urine.** This Yang Organ is responsible for receiving, storing, and releasing urine.
6. **The Triple Burners Store the Body's Qi.** These three areas of the body receive, store, absorb, and move Qi.

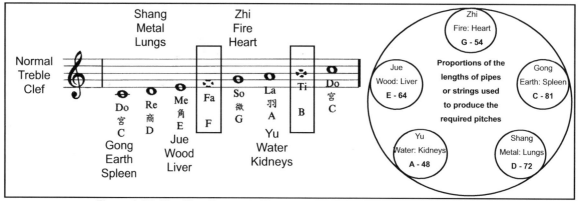

Figure 2.87. The Five Energetic Pitches and Their Corresponding Elements

FORMATION OF THE SIX ENERGETIC PITCHES

The Six Pitches are six specific tone resonances (i.e., musical notes) that vibrate within the body's internal organs, stimulating specific organ and tissue areas. Energetically, the Six Pitches nourish the body's Qi, and also support and stabilize the body's Lower Burner (see Triple Burners, Chapter 8).

The special vibrational sounds of the Six Pitches are established within the Six Yang Organs (i.e., the Six Storage Areas), and energetically correspond to the Heavenly Five Element Prenatal Sounds (Figure 2.87):

1. Heaven "Jue" (Wood Element)
2. Heaven "Zhi" (Fire Element)
3. Heaven "Gong" (Earth Element)
4. Heaven "Shang" (Metal Element)
5. Heaven "Yu" (Water Element)
6. Earth "Xi" (Fire Element)

The sixth note, "Xi," corresponds to the Earthly Postnatal Fire Element, and represents the vibrational sound of the Pericardium (i.e., the Heart Protector) and the Triple Burners.

It is important to note, that the Triple Burners (San Jiao) are considered to be a Yang Organ, and their associated Yin organ is the Pericardium. The Triple Burners are also known as the Triple Heaters and Triple Warmers, and are called the "Father of Yang Qi," because they are responsible for commanding the circulation of Yang Qi. In ancient China, the Triple Burners were conceptualized as being a large bowel that contained all of the body's internal organs (Figure 2.88)

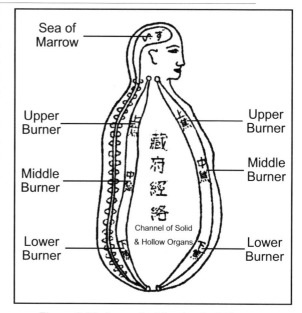

Figure 2.88. An ancient Anatomical Diagram of the Triple Burner (San Jiao) "Bowel".

The ancient Daoists used these Six Pitches for specific clinical treatments. For example, the "Yu" sound (i.e., the Water Element Pitch), was traditionally spoken in a low tone, in order to vibrate and influence the lower abdominal area; and was also used for the treatment of Kidney and Urinary Bladder problems.

TISSUE FORMATION

In the Sixth Lunar Month, the fetus' eyelids separate, the eyelashes form, and the skin becomes wrinkled.

Month Seven

The mother's Lung Channels govern the Seventh Lunar Month of creation. The Seven Essential Stars open the fetus' orifices to let in the light from Heaven and Earth. At this stage, the Wood Jing is beginning to be accepted by the fetus' body.

The Role of the Mother's Lung Channels

During the Seventh Lunar Month, the mother's Lung Channels create the bones, skin, and hair (Figure 2.89).

Wood Jing Formation

During the Seventh Lunar Month, the Wood Jing is beginning to be incorporated into the fetus' body. The Wood Jing energy governs the assertion and direction of the fetus' emotional and spiritual aspects. Any faltering of the Wood Jing energy is associated with psychological problems, such as passive-aggressive personality disorder. These psychological disturbances may be evident at birth or may develop later on in life.

Seven Essential Stars

In the Seventh Lunar Month, the fetus' Stomach and Intestines are stabilized, and the "Seven Essential Stars" open the body's upper orifices to absorb the light from Heaven and Earth. These special stars correspond to the celestial energies of the Sun, the Moon, and the Five Planets (Mars, Venus, Mercury, Saturn, and Jupiter). Each celestial star is associated with one of the body's upper orifices and a particular Element, described as follows (Figure 2.90):

- **The Right Ear:** Saturn - Earth Element
- **The Left Ear:** Jupiter - Wood Element
- **The Right Nostril:** Mars - Fire Element
- **The Left Nostril:** Venus - Metal Element
- **The Right Eye:** Moon - Celestial Yin (Water)
- **The Left Eye:** Sun - Celestial Yang (Fire)
- **The Mouth:** Mercury - Water Element

These seven special orifices serve as receiving and projecting energetic portals for the body's Jing (Essence), Qi (Energy), and Shen (Mind/Spirit). They also serve as subtle "messengers," by receiving and projecting the energies of the body's Five Yin Organs.

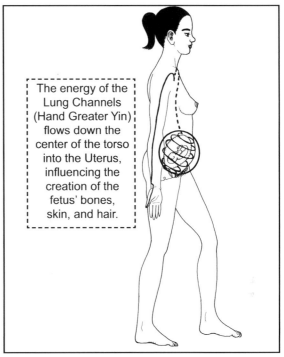

Figure 2.89. The Mother's Lung Channels govern the Seventh Lunar Month of creation. The Seven Essential Stars open the fetus' orifices to let in the light from Heaven and Earth. The Wood Jing is accepted by the fetus' body.

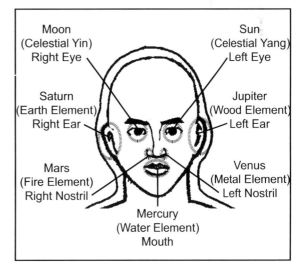

Figure 2.90. Each celestial star is associated with one of the body's upper orifices and a particular Element

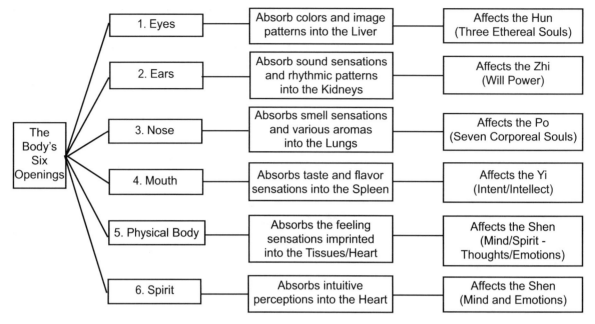

Figure 2.91. During the Seventh Lunar Month, the body's Six Openings are stimulated into energetic awakening.

According to ancient Daoist teaching, the Liver expresses itself through observation, the Heart through speech, the Spleen through taste, the Lungs through smell, and the Kidneys through hearing. These energetic messages are received by the body's Wujingshen (Five Essence Spirits), and are then emotionally as well as energetically interacted with, through the body's Six Openings.

THE BODY'S SIX OPENINGS

The energetic messages received through the body's Six Openings are described as follows (Figure 2.91):

1. **The Eyes:** Absorb colors and image patterns into the Liver, which affect the Hun (i.e., the Three Ethereal Souls).
2. **The Ears:** Absorb sound sensations and rhythmic patterns into the Kidneys, which affect the Zhi (Will Power).
3. **The Nose:** Absorbs smells and various aromas into the Lungs, which affect the Po (The Seven Corporeal Souls).
4. **The Mouth:** Absorbs tastes and flavor sensations into the Spleen, which affect the Yi (Intent/Intellect).
5. **The Physical Body:** Absorbs the feeling sensations imprinted into the tissues, which affect the Shen (Mind/Spirit), thoughts, and emotions.
6. **The Spirit:** Absorbs intuitive perceptions into the Heart, which also affect the Mind, thoughts, and emotions.

TISSUE FORMATION

During the Seventh Lunar Month, there is a substantial increase in the weight of the fetus, and its head and body are even more proportionate. At this point, the fetus can survive if born prematurely (between 27 and 28 weeks); however, its temperature regulation (a function of the hypothalamus) and the lungs' production of surfactant (a phospholipid substance important in controlling the surface tension of the air-liquid emulsion present in the lungs) is still inadequate.

CHAPTER 2: UNDERSTANDING ANCIENT CHINESE METAPHYSICS

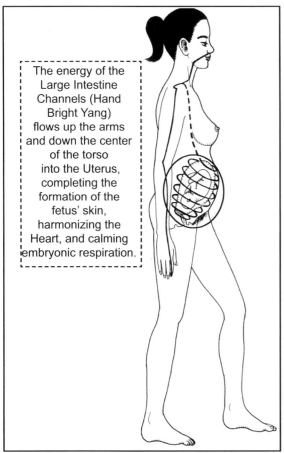

Figure 2.92. The Mother's Large Intestine Channels govern the Eighth Lunar Month of creation. At this stage, the Earth Jing is accepted by the fetus's body.

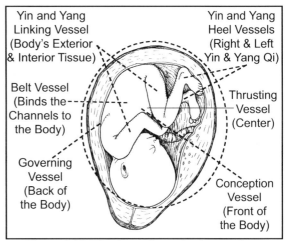

Figure 2.93. The tissue formation is complete, and the fetus assumes an upside-down position

MONTH EIGHT

The mother's Large Intestine Channels (Figure 2.92) govern the Eighth Lunar Month of creation. During this month, the mother's Large Intestine Channels complete the formation of the fetus' skin, harmonizing the Heart (the Shen) and quieting the breath. At this stage, the Earth Jing is accepted by the fetus' body.

THE ROLE OF THE MOTHER'S LARGE INTESTINE CHANNELS

The mother's Large Intestine Channels control the fetus' orifices. At this stage in development, the fetus' flesh is formed. The formation and consolidation of the fetus' Jing is now complete. The fetus' Zhen (True) Qi is now fully developed and circulates in the body's Extraordinary Vessels, Channels and Collaterals, nourishing the Yin and Yang organs, and fighting disease.

EARTH JING FORMATION

During the Eighth Lunar Month, the fetus receives the Zong (Essential) Qi from the mother's Spleen. Zong Qi is energy collected from Heaven and Earth which accumulates within the chest. At this stage, the Earth Jing is accepted by the fetus' body, completing the formation of the skin.

The Earth Jing energy governs the quality and maturation of the fetus' emotional and spiritual bonding and boundaries.

Any faltering of the Earth Jing energy is associated with problems of severe psychological disturbances, such as schizophrenia. These psychological disturbances may be evident at birth or develop later in life.

TISSUE FORMATION

At the end of the eighth month, the Bones of the fetus' head are soft, the skin is less wrinkled, and there is subcutaneous fat deposited throughout the body. If the fetus is a male, its testes will now descend into the scrotum.

At this stage, an energetic shift will occur and the baby will "drop." The fetus will normally assume an upside-down position in preparation for birth (Figure 2.93). If the fetus is born prematurely, its chances for survival are now much greater.

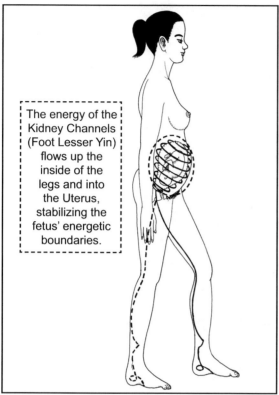

The energy of the Kidney Channels (Foot Lesser Yin) flows up the inside of the legs and into the Uterus, stabilizing the fetus' energetic boundaries.

Figure 2.94. The Mother's Kidney Channels govern the Ninth Lunar Month of creation. At this stage, all of the fetus' spatial cavities and energetic boundaries are now firmly established.

Month Nine

The mother's Kidney Channels (Figure 2.94) govern the Ninth Lunar Month of creation. At this stage, all of the fetus' spatial cavities and energetic boundaries are now firmly established.

The Role of the Mother's Kidney Channels

During the Ninth Lunar Month, the mother's Kidney Channels control the amount of energy the fetus absorbs from the mother through the umbilicus.

Function of the Umbilical Cord

The fetus absorbs Qi and the nutrition derived from the mother's Blood by way of the umbilical vein which connects to the fetus' Liver. From the Liver, nutrients are processed and absorbed into the Blood to be distributed throughout the fetus.

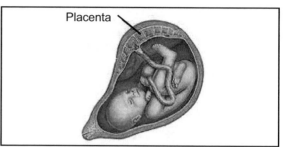

Figure 2.95. The umbilical cord attaches to the placenta from the abdomen of the fetus

The umbilical cord attaches to the placenta from the abdomen of the fetus (Figure 2.95). The placenta, which forms on the uterine wall after the first week of pregnancy, consists of tissues from both the mother and the embryo. Within the placenta, Qi and nutrients are transported from the mother's blood to the blood of the fetus. Although the circulation of the two come close, they never actually connect.

The function of the umbilical cord is to remove waste products and pass food, energy, and oxygen from the mother's bloodstream to the fetus. The mother's Kidney Channels regulate the flow of Qi and Shen into the fetus through the umbilical cord.

After the umbilical cord has been severed, the fetus' umbilical veins still remain. These umbilical veins eventually become the ligamentum teres that connect from the umbilicus, up along the interior surface of the abdominal wall, through the free margin of the falciform ligament to the right and left lobes of the Liver. This maintains the baby's connection between its Liver and its Lower Dantian (navel).

Energetic Formation

In the Ninth Lunar Month, the Nine Internal Palaces within the Three Dantians are created and established in order to keep the fetus' Yuan Jing, Yuan Qi and Yuan Shen safe. At this stage of energetic formation, all of the fetus' energetic spatial cavities (internal organ tissue chambers) and energetic boundaries are arranged to prepare the fetus for its birth.

Tissue Formation

In the Ninth Lunar Month, additional subcutaneous fat accumulates throughout the fetus' body. Externally, the fetus' fingernails will extend to the tips of the fingers and sometimes beyond.

CHAPTER 2: UNDERSTANDING ANCIENT CHINESE METAPHYSICS

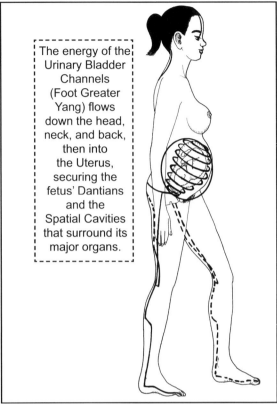

The energy of the Urinary Bladder Channels (Foot Greater Yang) flows down the head, neck, and back, then into the Uterus, securing the fetus' Dantians and the Spatial Cavities that surround its major organs.

Figure 2.96. The Mother's Urinary Bladder Channels govern the Tenth Lunar Month of creation. At this stage, the fetus' Dantians and the spatial cavities that surround the major organs are completely developed to maintain the safety of the fetus' Jing.

MONTH TEN

The mother's Urinary Bladder Channels (Figure 2.96) govern the Tenth Lunar Month of creation. At this stage, the baby's Dantians and the spatial cavities that surround the major organs are completely developed to maintain the safety of the fetus' Jing. Heaven and Earth Qi settle into the fetus' Lower Dantian in preparation for birth.

THE ROLE OF THE MOTHER'S URINARY BLADDER CHANNELS

During the Tenth Lunar Month, the mother's Urinary Bladder Channels harmonize all Five Yin Organs (Liver, Heart, Spleen, Lungs, and Kidneys) and Five Yang Organs (Gall Bladder, Small Intestine, Stomach, Large Intestine, and Urinary Bladder).

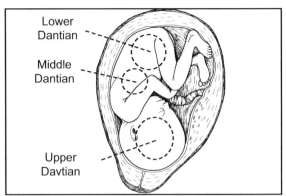

Figure 2.97. Heaven and Earth Qi settle into the fetus' Lower Dantian and the process of birth begins.

ENERGETIC FORMATION

After ten lunar months in the womb, the fetus' Three Dantians are fully established. Also, the energy of the Wujingshen are now active within the internal spatial cavities that surround the major organs. The internal spatial cavities are developed to maintain the safety of the fetus' Jing, Qi and Shen. The fetus is now ready to be released into the world.

The process of birth begins when Heaven Qi and Earth Qi settle into the fetus' Lower Dantian (Figure 2.97). The ancient Daoists described the birth transition as "a ripe melon falling off the stem," noting that the fetus breaks out of its amniotic sac and emerges head first towards the Earth, and its feet pointing towards the Heavens.

With its first cry, Yuan Qi is exhaled, and the infant comes in contact with the environmental air. As the infant inhales, the air (considered Postnatal Qi), mixes with the infant's innate primordial Original Energy (Yuan Qi). The ancient Daoists believed that the innate Prenatal Qi supports the tissues of the body, while the acquired Postnatal Qi supports the tissue's function. The Postnatal Qi depends on the Prenatal Qi to support the respiratory system (breathing in and out), while the Prenatal Qi depends on the Postnatal Qi to nurture the vascular system.

At the moment of the infant's first cry, the ancient Daoists also believed that the acquired spirit (Shen Zhi) enters into the opening and merges with the baby's primordial original spirit (Yuan Shen). The congenital Yuan Shen depends on the acquired Shen Zhi to survive, while the Shen Zhi depends on the Yuan Shen for awareness.

POSTNATAL ENERGY DEVELOPMENT

According to ancient Daoists teaching, the moment the baby cries (i.e., the child's first breath), the "sealed enclosure" of Prenatal Qi is broken, and the baby's Original (Yuan) Jing, Qi, and Shen divide into three separate energetic states. This energetic division causes the baby's original Fire (Yuan Shen) to separate from its original Water (Yuan Jing), and begins the Postnatal patterns of its energetic existence.

The ancient Daoists also believed that at the moment of birth, the energy of the postnatal Acquired Mind/Spirit (Shen Zhi) merges with the energy of the child's prenatal Original Spirit (Yuan Shen). Through this combination, the Original Spirit learns to depend on the Acquired Mind to survive within its new environment; while the Acquired Mind learns to depend on the intuitive perceptions of the Original Spirit for effective awareness.

The energy of the Po (Corporeal Soul) is responsible for the first physiological processes after birth, allowing the child's eyes to see, ears to hear, and Heart/Mind to perceive. The Po also govern the movements of the child's hands and feet, as well as its breathing patterns.

In the clinic, the Medical Qigong doctor studies the Ten Lunar Month process of fetal development in order to understand the original formation of the patient's physical and energetic structures. This knowledge also aides the doctor in comprehending the initial formation of the patient's Five Elemental Constitution.

POSTNATAL CHANNEL FUNCTION

During prenatal development, the Eight Extraordinary Vessels (see Chapter 6) are responsible for transporting, transforming, and producing Qi and Blood for the fetus, while the Twelve Primary Channels (see Chapter 8) are still in the process of gradual development. While in utero, the energetic activity generated from the fetus' Lower Dantian and Eight Extraordinary Vessels resonates throughout its body, creating tissue development.

Once the umbilical cord is severed, the primary focus of energy shifts from the Lower Dantian to the Middle Dantian (located in the baby's chest area).

In ancient China, it was believed that the energies of Preheaven (Yuan) Qi begin to combine with the acquired influences of the Postheaven

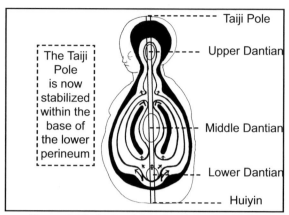

Figure 2.98. As the fetus develops, the Eight Extraordinary Vessels govern the postnatal development of the Twelve Primary Channels.

Qi within the child's chest. This internal blending and mixing is used to energetically activate the "genetic" potential previously stored within the forming child's Original (Yuan) Qi.

After birth, the baby is no longer receiving nourishment from its mother internally via the umbilical cord, but is now receiving external nourishment through breast-feeding, transforming it into Gu Qi (energy derived from air, food, and drink) through its Stomach and Spleen. Because Gu Qi is created within the baby's Stomach while it nurses, the development of the baby's Spleen and Stomach Qi is important. As the Gu Qi establishes itself within the baby's Stomach and Spleen, it helps to form Qi and Blood. The Qi and Blood then become energized and flows within the Twelve Primary Channels, nourishing the child's forming organs and tissues. This is also why the air, food, and drink that the mother consumes while she is breast-feeding will have a direct affect on the nursing baby's health.

The Twelve Primary Channels ("after-birth" channels) will now assume the responsibility of circulating Qi and Blood throughout the baby's entire physical and energetic structure. The Eight Extraordinary Vessels ("before-birth" channels) will now shift their energetic function from sustaining and directing tissue development, to regulating the baby's Channel Qi (Figure 2.98). Additionally, the Taiji Pole is now stabilized in the child's lower perineum area.

THE CHILD'S INTERNAL ENERGY FLOW

The resonant internal vibration of the baby's Taiji Pole (i.e., its energetic core) initiates a natural energetic expansion and contraction. This continual energetic pulse simultaneously affects the baby on five distinct levels: physical, energetic, mental, emotional, and spiritual.

In ancient China, it was taught that after birth the energetic pulsing resonating within a child's Taiji Pole acts as an internal spiralling vortex, connecting and harmonizing its internal and external energy fields. These special energy fields facilitate the subtle subconscious influences that lead to energetic and spiritual "awakenings," as well as "divine insights" that are used to guide and direct the individual's spiritual path throughout their life.

According to ancient Daoist teaching, harmonized physical growth will only occur when all Three Bodies (Physical Body, Energy Body, and Spirit Body) are in equilibrium. The physical body is generally the slowest to respond to growth and change. Matter does not move at the same rate as energy, or Mind; thus, the energy, mind, and spirit must wait patiently for the physical body to evolve before progressing as a whole.

THE MICROCOSMIC ORBIT WATER CYCLE

The term "Microcosmic Orbit" generally refers to the flow of energy moving through the Sea of Yang (Governing Vessel) and the Sea of Yin (Conception Vessel). One of the functions of the Microcosmic Orbit is to connect the energetic and spiritual centers of the body's Three Dantians.

According to ancient Daoist teachings, once a child has been born, the flow of its Microcosmic Orbit will naturally follow the energetic movements of the "Water Cycle" (Figure 2.99). In the Water Cycle movement, the energy will flow up the front of the body (Conception Vessel) and down the back (Governing Vessel), during normal respiration. This energetic movement naturally facilitates the child's spiritual, intuitive, and psychic perceptions.

This energetic pattern generally continues until the child reaches puberty; at which time the energy reverses its direction and begins to flow up the spine (Governing Vessel) and down the chest (Conception Vessel) in the direction of the "Fire Cycle." This shift in energetic direction is

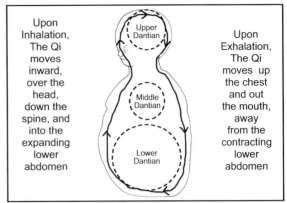

Figure 2.99. The Child's internal energy follows the pathway of the Microcosmic Orbit "Water Cycle."

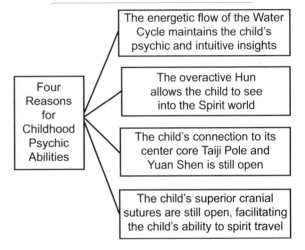

Figure 2.100. Children have a natural tendency towards psychic and intuitive insights.

facilitated by the child's cognitive development (Shen Zhi), and manifests their ability to suppress (control) their emotions and impulses. The time of the energetic reversal varies depending on the child's physical constitution, state of health, and its living environment.

A CHILD'S NATURAL PSYCHIC TENDENCIES

Children have a natural tendency towards psychic and intuitive insights due to a number of factors (Figure 2.100):

1. **Water Cycle Energy Flow:** The constant flow of energy moving through the child's Microcosmic Orbit Water Cycle, maintains the child's psychic and intuitive insights.

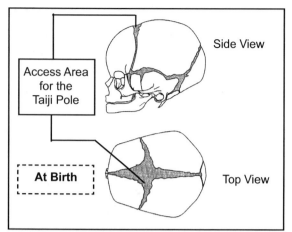

Figure 2.101. At birth, the baby's superior cranial sutures are completely open and susceptible to the vibrational resonance of the subtle energetic world.

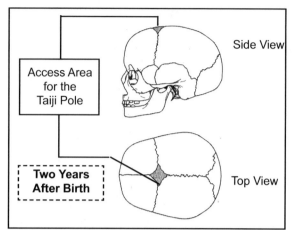

Figure 2.102. After two years, the baby's superior cranial sutures close, making the child less susceptible to the vibrational resonance of the subtle energetic world.

2. **An Overactive Hun (Ethereal Soul):** The overactive spiritual movements of its Hun (Ethereal Soul) going in and out of the child's body allows it to see energy, and observe occurrences happening within the Spirit World.
3. **A Powerful Connection To Its Taiji Pole:** The child's energetic connection to its internal Taiji Pole and Yuan Shen (Original Mind/Spirit) is still open, and subconsciously active. This allows the child to receive energy and information directly from its Eternal Soul.
4. **Its Fontanels Are Still Open:** The child's superior cranial sutures are still open, allowing its Taiji Pole to be more receptive to the vibrational resonance of the subtle energetic fields, hence facilitating the child's ability to spirit travel (Figure 2.101).

Following the Third Lunar Month after birth, the soft apertures (fontanels) in the baby's skull slowly start to close (Figure 2.102). The ancient Daoist teach that psychic and intuitive insights, as well as the ability to spirit travel, gradually wane as the baby's superior cranial sutures continue to close.

In ancient Tibetan Qigong practices (specifically those teachings used to prepare someone for death), the individual's superior cranial sutures are trained to once again become soft in order to facilitate the final exit of the Eternal Soul.

CONGENITAL OR ACQUIRED DISORDERS

Understanding the energetic process of fetal development provides the Medical Qigong Doctor with an overview of the internal components of tissues, organs, and channel function. This understanding is essential for diagnosing the causes of a disease, whether it is either congenital or acquired in origin. Unlike Western Medicine, Chinese Energetic Medicine treats the root of the illness and not just its manifested symptoms. Both congenital and acquired factors must be considered in every case. This is necessary, because both the origin and development of any disease can result from either a congenital or acquired source, or a combination of both.

CONGENITAL (BEFORE-BIRTH) DISORDERS

In the Medical Qigong Clinic, cases of Congenital Qi Deficiency or Congenital Disorders of Qi flow, are always treated by Tonifying (strengthening) the patient's internal organs and Eight Extraordinary Vessels. In some cases, it is necessary to first Purge the Pathogenic Qi from the Eight Extraordinary Vessels before Tonifying and Regulating the Prenatal Qi.

ACQUIRED (AFTER-BIRTH) DISEASES

Patients suffering from Acquired Diseases are treated by Purging, Tonifying, and Regulating according to the imbalance of Qi circulation occurring within the internal organs and the Twelve Primary Channels.

CHAPTER 2: UNDERSTANDING ANCIENT CHINESE METAPHYSICS

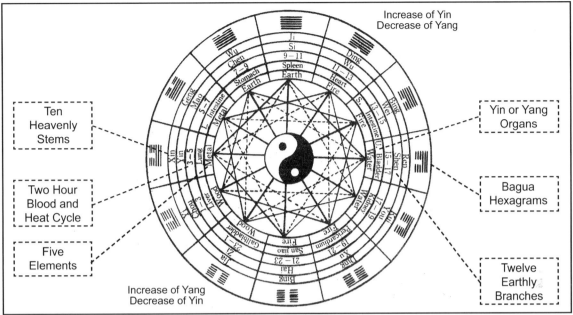

Figure 2.103. After birth, the Daily Qi, Blood, and Heat Cycle is constantly being influenced by the interactions of the Celestial and Environmental Energetic Fields. Taken from the ancient Daoist writings of Meng Xi, constructed during the Han Dynasty (206 B.C. - 220 A.D.).

PRENATAL AND POSTNATAL ENERGETIC PATTERNS

In ancient China, an individual's physical, energetic, and spiritual strengths and weaknesses, as well as his or her destiny were believed to be influenced by both Yang and Yin energetic patterns. The Prenatal energetic patterns were believed to originate at the moment of conception, and were considered to be Yang; while the Postnatal patterns were seen to originate at the moment of birth, and were considered to be Yin.

The ancient Chinese calculated the strength or weakness of an individual's Prenatal (congenital) and Postnatal (acquired) energetic patterns according to interactions of the Heavenly and Earthly energetic fields. These energetic and spiritual interactions were manifested through the influences of the Ten Heavenly Stems and the Twelve Earthly Branches, and were assigned to the 64 Hexagram patterns of the *Yijing* (Figure 2.103).

The Ten Heavenly Stems and the Twelve Earthly Branches are described as follows:

THE TEN HEAVENLY STEMS

As the internal organs develop within the forming fetus, the Ten Heavenly Stems are responsible for the Prenatal regulation of all Jing formation, growth, and internal power. They are relate to the energies of Heaven and are represented in "Man" as the Yin and Yang aspects of the Five Element organs of Wood, Fire, Earth, Metal, and Water.

The first and second stems correspond to the Wood Element, the third and forth stems correspond to the Fire Element, the fifth and sixth stems correspond to the Earth Element, the seventh and eighth stems correspond to the Metal Element, and the ninth and tenth stems correspond to the Water Element.

Originally, the ancient Daoists considered the Heaven Stems to correspond with the process of plant growth and farming activities. When corresponding to Energetic Embryology, each of the Ten Heavenly Stems represented a specific process in energetic growth and development.

The Ten Heavenly Stems

甲	乙	丙	丁	戊	己	庚	辛	壬	癸
Jia Wood Yang (E)	Yi Wood Yin (E)	Bing Fire Yang (S)	Ding Fire Yin (S)	Wu Earth Yang (C)	Ji Earth Yin (C)	Gen Metal Yang (W)	Xin Metal Yin (W)	Ren Water Yang (N)	Gui Water Yin (N)
Green Dragon		Red Phoenix		Golden Dragon		White Tiger		Black Turtle/Snake	

Figure 2.104. The Ten Heavenly Stems

The energy of each position is assigned to a specific Element, Color, and Animal (Figure 2.104); and is responsible for overseeing a specific spiritual transformation that occurs within the forming fetus. According to the Zheng Yi Daoist Priest's *Tai Shang Lao Jun's Imperial Proclamation for the Offering of Sacrifices Made by the Lu Holders*, the magical correspondences of the Ten Heavenly Stems are expressed in the following manner:

- **Jia (#1 Stem - Yang Wood) Position:** Corresponds to the Wood Element, and the energy of the Celestial Green Dragon. The 1st Heavenly Stem "Jia," originally meant "shell." It implied that all things on Earth originated out of shells (e.g., seeds, wombs, eggs, etc.), and that during the Spring time, these shells began to sprout (as all plant seeds do).

  The Yang Jia Moon is ruled by the "Yang Balanced." It is responsible for bringing balance to the embryo's Primordial Qi.

- **Yi (#2 Stem - Yin Wood) Position:** Corresponds to the Wood Element, and the energy of the Celestial Green Dragon. The 2nd Heavenly Stem "Yi," implies that all grass and trees are now starting to grow, with small leaves beginning to develop.

  The Yin Yi Moon is ruled by the "True Multitude." It is responsible for leading the Spirits of the embryo's Primordial Qi.

- **Bing (#3 Stem - Yang Fire) Position:** Corresponds to the Fire Element, and the energy of the Celestial Red Phoenix. The 3rd Heavenly Stem "Bing," suggests that all things are receiving light, and are obviously seen.

  The Yang Bing Moon is ruled by the "North Balanced." It is responsible for examining and watching over the fetus' Primordial Qi.

- **Ding (#4 Stem - Yin Fire) Position:** Corresponds to the Fire Element, and the energy of the Celestial Red Phoenix. The 4th Heavenly Stem "Ding," implies that grass and trees are now well grown and strong.

  The Yin Ding Moon is ruled by the "Deer Hall." It is responsible for bringing balance to the fetus' Primordial Qi

- **Wu (#5 Stem - Yang Earth) Position:** Corresponds to the Earth Element, and the energy of the Celestial Golden Dragon. The 5th Heavenly Stem "Wu," represents the luxuriant growth of all things.

  The Yang Wu Moon is ruled by the "Northern Mang" (a mountain in Henan). It is responsible for examining the fetus' Primordial Qi.

- **Ji (#6 Stem - Yin Earth) Position:** Corresponds to the Earth Element, and the energy of the Celestial Golden Dragon. The 6th Heavenly Stem "Ji," corresponds to energy increasing in quantity and in intensity, and expresses the meaning that all things are strongly rising up.

  The Yin Ji Moon is ruled by the "Roots of Bamboo." It is responsible for examining and watching over the fetus' Primordial Qi.

- **Gen (#7 Stem - Yang Metal) Position:** Corresponds to the Metal Element, and the energy of the Celestial White Tiger. The 7th Heavenly Stem "Gen," refers to taking on a new aspect of energy, which implies that it is time for Autumn harvesting.

The Twelve Earthly Branches

子	丑	寅	卯	辰	巳	午	未	申	酉	戌	亥
Zi	Chou	Yin	Mao	Chen	Si	Wu	Wei	Shen	You	Xu	Hai
Rat	Ox	Tiger	Rabbit	Dragon	Snake	Horse	Goat	Monkey	Rooster	Dog	Pig
Nov.	Dec.	Jan.	Feb.	March	April	May	June	July	Aug.	Sept.	Oct.
11-1am	1-3am	3-5am	5-7am	7-9am	9-11am	11-1pm	1-3pm	3-5pm	5-7pm	7-9pm	9-11pm
Midnight			Sunrise			High Noon			Sunset		

Figure 2.105. The Twelve Earthly Branches

The Yang Geng Moon is ruled by the "Mouth of the Jin" (a river in Hubei). It is responsible for observing and paying tribute to the fetus' Primordial Qi.

- **Xin (#8 Stem - Yin Metal) Position:** Corresponds to the Metal Element, and the energy of the Celestial White Tiger. The 8th Heavenly Stem "Xin," implies that all things are new after the harvesting.

  The Yin Xin Moon is ruled by the "True Multitude." It is responsible for leading all the Spirits of the Primordial Qi.

- **Ren (#9 Stem - Yang Water) Position:** Corresponds to the Water Element, and the energy of the Celestial Black Turtle/Snake. The 9th Heavenly Stem "Ren," refers to the understanding that the Yang of Nature is now beginning to withdraw into the Earth.

  The Yang Ren Moon is ruled by "that which is within one's communications with the throne." It is also responsible for leading the Spirits of the Primordial Qi.

- **Gui (#10 Stem - Yin Water) Position:** Corresponds to the Water Element, and the energy of the Celestial Black Turtle/Snake. The 10th Heavenly Stem "Kui," implies that new lives are breeding down underneath the Earth, and are waiting for new birth.

  The Yin Gui Moon is ruled by the "Jade Assembly." It is responsible for investigating the fetus' Primordial Qi.

THE TWELVE EARTHLY BRANCHES

The Twelve Earthly Branches (Figure 2.105) represents the ancient Chinese system of time, space, and Fate Calculation (known as "Ming Shu").

After birth, as the internal organs continue to develop within the forming baby, the Twelve Earthly Branches are responsible for the Postnatal interactions occurring within the universal (Heaven) and environmental (Earth) energetic fields. Therefore, when corresponding to Energetic Embryology, the Twelve Earthly Branches are Earth energies that represent the interactions of "Man," internally manifesting as the energy of the Twelve Primary Channels.

The ancient Daoists viewed the body as a small and complete universe unto itself and understood that the internal organs are influenced by the celestial movements of the Sun, Moon, planets, and stars. The Governing and Conception Vessels in particular are influenced by these Heavenly cycles.

According to ancient Daoist teachings, the day is divided into twelve separate time divisions. Each time division encompasses two hours and is named after one of the Twelve Earthly Branches. The ancient Daoists discovered that the body's Qi and Blood mirror the Earth's seasonal ebb and flow, energetically rising and falling like the lunar tides.

Each time period in the Twelve Earthly Branches system was regarded as having a specific influence on each of the body's twelve gates. The rhythmic variations of the waxing and waning of Qi and Blood was associated with the waxing and waning of Yin and Yang energy coursing through the body, as it circulated along the Microcosmic Orbit (Fire) cycle.

Each of the Twelve Earthly Branches also correspond to 12 important energetic stages, that naturally occur within Nature. For example:

- **The 1st Branch "Zi" (11pm-1am),** implies that seeds of plants and trees are ready to sprout when absorbing water.
- **The 2nd Branch "Chou" (1am-3am),** implies that sprouts are bending out of the earth surface.
- **The 3rd Branch "Yin" (3am-5am),** implies the out-of-earth grass and plants are stretching towards the sunlight.
- **The 4th Branch "Mao" (5am-7am),** implies that all things are thickly or densely grown.
- **The 5th Branch "Chen" (7am-9am),** implies that the Yang power within all things is being pushed to grow and develop.
- **The 6th Branch "Si" (9am-11am),** implies the full power of Yang arrives, and all things are in full development.
- **The 7th Branch "Wu" (11am-1pm),** implies the full growth of all things on Earth because of the full power of Yang (and the beginning of Yin in nature). It also implies the blending of Yin & Yang.
- **The 8th Branch "Wei" (1pm-3pm),** implies that fruits are ripening and are ready to taste.
- **The 9th Branch "Shen" (3pm-5pm),** implies that all things are well formed and developed.
- **The 10th Branch "You" (5pm-7pm),** implies that all things are starting to wither after ripening.
- **The 11th Branch "Xu" (7pm-9pm),** implies that all things are withering and dying out.
- **The 12th Branch "Hai" (9pm-11pm),** implies that all things are exposed to and surrounded by Yin, which now reaches its peak.

Within the Fire Cycle of the Microcosmic Orbit, there are Twelve Primary Channel points located along the Governing and Conception Vessels, which relate to the Twelve Earthly Branches and the waxing and waning of the Yin and Yang cycles of the Sun and Moon (Figure 2.106).

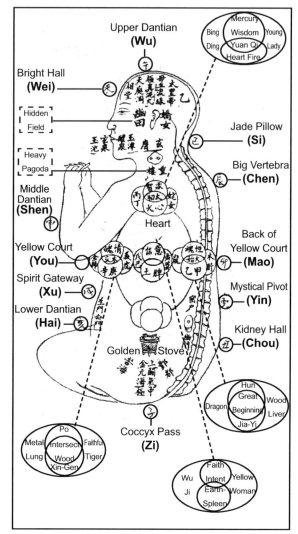

Figure 2.106. The Twelve Earthly Branch Relation with the Microcosmic Orbit (Common Daoist Names).

The power of Heaven affects the external energetic field of the Earth, which in turn affects the energetic movement of the body's internal energetic field. This special energetic movement was also depicted by the ancient Daoists through the "Bright Mirror of Spirit Alchemy" Chart.

Within the human body, the Fire Element phase of the Microcosmic Orbit was believed to start at the Zi Earthly Branch located at the Sheng Si Qiao area at the root of the penis in men (Huiyin area) and at the root of the vagina in women.

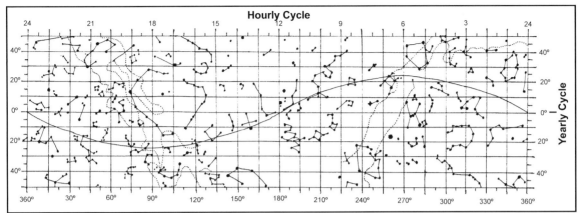

Figure 2.107. The Pathway of the Earth through the Twenty-Eight Constellations influences the fetus' Prenatal Jing (Essence), Qi (Energy), and Shen (Mind/Spirit) formation.

CONCEPTION AND THE BODY'S PRENATAL ANCESTRAL TRAITS

According to ancient Daoist teachings, the Prenatal energetic patterns of the human body are influenced by the time and place of the individual's conception (Figure 2.107). As a general rule, in order to determine the exact time (day) of conception, the ancient Daoists would count back forty weeks from the time of an individual's birth.

The time and place of conception, establishes the inherent strength or weakness of an individual's spiritual constitution, as well as their ancestral traits (food preferences, manner of dress, spiritual beliefs, affinity for certain cultures, and so on).

The ancient Daoists believed that, as the divine energy of the Five Pure Lights infuse the fetus' soul into its forming tissues, the energy of the Eternal Soul (Shen Xian) combines with the environmental spiritual influences of its surrounding geographic location (e.g., the Orient, Europe, North America, etc.). This infusion of geographic spiritual energy creates within the individual a predisposition towards specific ancestral traits and cultural attractions.

At conception and throughout pregnancy, the mother absorbs the natural environmental energy through respiration (breathing Qi through the mouth, nose, and pores), digestion (absorbing nutrients from the food and soil), and visual/auditory absorption (observing and experiencing the surrounding environment). The entire history of each cultural environment is encoded within the natural energetic fields contained within that environment. Therefore, an individual conceived in the Orient may find themselves unconsciously drawn to the social and cultural patterns and influences of that particular Asian population. This subconscious energetic attraction is considered a natural phenomenon, due to the subtle influences of the location's spiritual and ancestral fields. The subconscious energetic attraction can indirectly affect an individual in several ways, described as follows:

1. The natural environment surrounding the location of an individual at conception exerts a strong influence on his or her environmental preferences. This often manifests as a general preference or attraction to environmental patterns and locations similar to those at conception. People conceived by the ocean, for example, may find within themselves an unconscious need to live by the ocean. Likewise, people conceived in the mountains, valleys, tropics, or deserts, may find feelings of peace or ease envelop them when visiting such places.

2. The time of an individual's conception also exerts a strong influence. The energetic formation, strength and weaknesses of the fetus' internal organs are also determined by the positions of the Sun, Moon, and Stars at the moment of conception. These celestial energies affect on the fetus at the time of conception continue influencing the fetus' formation throughout the entire pregnancy.

BIRTH AND THE PATTERNS OF POSTNATAL ENERGETIC CYCLES

The ancient Chinese believed that after birth, the degree to which an individual can draw upon and absorb spiritual energy depended on his or her Karma (i.e., the energetic momentum of previous intentions, thoughts and actions which manifest as, or influence, their Destiny).

The Postnatal energetic patterns of the body are determined by the time and place of birth. The time and place of birth also mark the beginning of the individual's energetic "Biorhythm Cycles" (defined as an individual's physical, emotional, and intellectual cycles).

These Biorhythm Cycles are developed according to the energetic influence of the Heavens (position of the sun, moon, planets and stars), as well as the energetic influence of the Earth (i.e., geographic location: mountains, valleys, desert, ocean, etc.). This infusion of the Earth's geographic energy and Heaven's stellar energy creates within the individual a predisposition towards specific psychological traits.

The body's Biorhythms, which react to universal and environmental energetic fields, are divided into three distinct cycles and energy flows (Figure 2.108). Each rhythm follows a cyclical process of waxing and waning, creating times of physical, emotional, and intellectual peaks, as well as times of reflection and withdrawn behavior.

These three cycles begin at the moment of birth and continue with regularity until death. The conditions of the cycle are divided into positive (the first, waxing half) and negative (the second, waning half) attributes. Research indicates that these special rhythms influence the times during which many illnesses occur or worsen, as well as how fast a medication takes effect and how long the effect lasts.

The body's Biorhythms are but one small example of the profound influences that energetic cycles have on the physical, emotional, and intellectual properties of the human body. By understanding the energetic applications of these various cycles (including those influenced by the sun, moon, and stars), a Medical Qigong Doctor can more easily regulate and balance his patient's disharmonious Qi.

Additionally, by understanding the energetic potential of local seasonal changes, the Qigong doctor can direct the environmental energy of Earth to regulate and balance the patient's Qi.

Physical Cycle

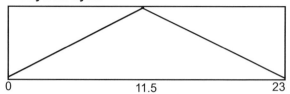

The Physical Cycle is 23 days long. The first 11.5 days are the positive side of the cycle, in which the individual experiences an increase in physical strength and endurance. The second 11.5 days are the negative side of the cycle, marked by a gradual decrease in the level of endurance, and a tendency towards fatigue.

Emotional Cycle

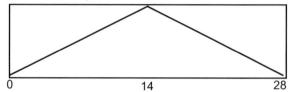

The Emotional Cycle is 28 days long. The first 14 days are the positive side of the cycle, in which the individual feels increasingly optimistic, cheerful, and cooperative. For the second 14 days, a negative stage of the cycle results in a tendency to be more moody, irritable, or pessimistic.

Intellectual Cycle

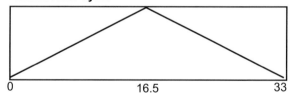

The Intellectual Cycle is 33 days long. The first 16.5 days are the positive side of the cycle, in which the individual experiences greater success in learning new material and pursuing creative, and intellectual activities. The next 16.5 days are the negative side of the cycle, in which the individual is encouraged to review old material rather than attempting to learn new concepts.

Figure 2.108. The physical, emotional, and intellectual cycles begin at birth.

CHAPTER 2: UNDERSTANDING ANCIENT CHINESE METAPHYSICS

Figure 2.109. The Lords of the Three Dantians

ANCIENT DAOIST ARCHETYPES OF THE HUMAN SOUL

Ancient Chinese medicine describes the Eternal Soul (Shen Xian) as consisting of three spiritual energies, called the "Lords of the Three Dantians" (Figure 2.109), which oversee the influences of the individual's Original Spirit (Yuan Shen). This terminology is metaphoric, in that, it is sometimes used to describe the various energetic aspects of the human soul (Shen Xian).

In esoteric Daoist Embryology, it is traditionally taught that once the Eternal Soul (Shen Xian) has established its residence within the forming embryo's Taiji Pole, it separates its Yin and Yang energy into three distinct spiritual aspects, as described within the *Daodejing*:

> "The Tao gives birth to One.
> One gives birth to Two.
> Two gives birth to Three.
> Three gives birth to all things."

These three spiritual aspects, oversee the various internal energies and powers of the body's Three Dantians. In Daoist alchemy, these three spiritual influences are secretly referred to as the "Lords of the Three Dantians," and are known as "Taiyi," "Si Ming," and "Xia Tao Kang." Traditionally, they are named according to their energetic function (Figure 2.110):

- **Taiyi:** translates as "Great Unity"
- **Si Ming:** translates as "Administrator of Destiny"
- **Xia Tao Kang:** translates as "Below Healthy Peach" (in ancient China, the "Peach" was symbolically used to represent "Life")

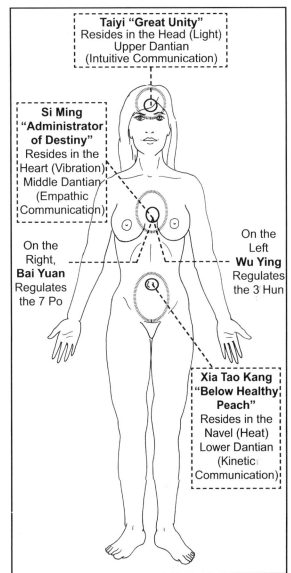

Figure 2.110. The Lords of the Three Dantians: Taiyi, Siming, and Xia Tao Kang

During conception, these three important spiritual energies are given to each individual from the Divine Source. They are physically incorporated inside the body's tissues in order to assist the human body in maintaining the spiritual residence of its own Original Spirit (Yuan Shen). These three important energies reside inside the innermost subtle aspects of the human body's energy field, and are described as follows:

TAIYI (GREAT UNITY)

Taiyi (Great Unity) resides within the Upper Dantian, in the head region, behind the Third Eye, inside the area known as the Niwan Palace (i.e., the Pineal Gland). The name "Taiyi," corresponds to the "Primordial Unity of Yin and Yang." According to religious Daoism, Taiyi's special palace is located within the Celestial Realm, and the Upper Dantian.

Taiyi is responsible for "Intuitive Communication," and is known as the "Lord of the Niwan Palace." He governs a multitude of the body's guardian and messenger spirits, and rules all the activities of the mind, including the spiritual potential of an individual's "enlightened" mind. According to Daoist teachings, when the celestial energy of the True Lord Taiyi is "awakened" and active within an individual's body, it causes his Original Spirit (Yuan Shen) to radiate a bright luminous light, which sometimes shines externally outside the body.

Taiyi is responsible for facilitating energetic and spiritual awareness, and he advocates personal spiritual growth and enlightenment (Figure 2.111). According to ancient Shangqing Scriptures, The True Lord Taiyi is sometimes known as the "Upper One." As the Celestial Emperor of the Niwan Palace, he is traditionally dressed in a radiant robe of scarlet brocade, radiates a Purple Vapor, and resides in the center of the Seven Stars of the Northern Dipper, located in the center of the Upper Dantian.

He is sometimes referred to as "The God of the Mysterious-Coagulated Heaven," and "The Infant of the Upper Prime." Internally, he watches over the realms of the face, eyes, ears, nose, mouth, tongue, teeth, and hair. Externally, he is responsible for scaring away the multitude of demons and evil spirits. Once every five days, the Three Hun come and pay respect to him and receive instruction."

SI MING (ADMINISTRATOR OF DESTINY)

The Si Ming (The Administrator of Destiny) resides within the Middle Dantian, in the region of the Heart, in the area known as the "Terrestrial Realm." He regulates the body's Qi, and is the source of the Shen (Mind/Heart) and its Empathic Communication.

Figure 2.111 The True Lord Taiyi

Si Ming challenges our reactions to various internal and external obstacles. Although Si Ming controls and maintains the residence of the Eternal Soul (i.e., located within the Scarlet Chamber of the heart), the body's Shen is free to make decisions that affect the individual's life and health based upon his own free-will. The interaction between the wants and desires of the individual's Shen Zhi (Acquired Personality) and his Yuan Shen (the nature of his Original Spirit) persistently challenge each other within the Shen (Mind/Heart). Inevitably, the individual's final decision will manifest through his thoughts and actions.

According to ancient Shangqing Scriptures, Si Ming (The Administrator of Destiny) is sometimes known as the "Middle One." As the "Cinnabar Sovereign of the Crimson Palace," he is dressed in a radiant robe of vermilion brocade, radiates a Red Vapor, and resides in the center of the Heart, located in the Middle Dantian.

Internally, he watches over the realms of the Five Yin Organs, Bones, Muscles, Blood, and flesh. Externally, he is responsible for scaring away the harmful effects of the various pathogenic influences. Under his direction, the Three Hun nurture the individual's internal light and pacify his spirit, so that he may obtain eternal life and perpetual youth. Once every three days, the Three Hun come and pay respect to Si Ming, and receive instruction.

According to ancient Daoist teachings, Si Ming also controls the spiritual energies (Ling Qi) of Wu Ying on the left side of the body, and Bai Yuan on the right side of the body, which affect the body's Jing, Qi, and Shen via the breath.

Figure 2.112. The Three Hun

WU YING - THE REGULATOR OF THE HUN

Si Ming also controls the spiritual energies of Wu Ying ("Without Excess"). Wu Ying regulates the Three Hun, the actions of the Yang Spirits of the body, the energy of all formless consciousness, and the various actions of the internal spirit of the Liver's Green Dragon.

The Spirit of "Wu Ying" occupies the left side of the body and regulates the disciple's ethereal "spiritual nature. According to ancient Daoist teachings, when meditating, the energy of the Hun can be directed to exit the body in the form of a Green Dragon (Figure 2.112), this is accomplished via a special energetic portal located on the left side of the rib-cage.

In ancient China, the Three Hun were traditionally known as "Tai Guang" ("Greatest Light"), "Shang Ling" ("Pleasant Soul") and "Yu Jing" ("Hidden Essence"), and are described as follows:

1. **Tai Guang (Greatest Light):** The Hun known as Tai Guang resides within the Upper Dantian and is situated in the cranial cavity (i.e., the Niwan Palace), located just below the Baihui GV-20 ("One Hundred Meetings") point. Tai Guang literally means "Greatest Light," and it is considered to be the highest expression of Yin and Yang energy harmonized within the human form. He is spiritually connected to the energy of the Upper Dantian and to Heaven, and strives for the highest development of physical, mental, emotional, and spiritual purity.

   Certain ancient Daoist texts refer to the spiritual energy of Tai Guang as a type of "Animal Hun." This is because this level of

Figure 2.113. The Five Agents

spiritual energy is commonly seen within both animals and humans.

2. **Shang Ling (Pleasant Soul):** The Hun known as Shang Ling resides within the Middle Dantian. He is situated in the Heart and the corresponding vessels, and is linked to the body's Five Agents. Shang Ling literally means "Pleasant Soul," and is considered to be transformed Yin energy. He is connected with the Middle Dantian and is the expression of the Hun concerned with universal compassion towards others. It is through the influence of the Hun Shang Ling, that the Five Virtues of each of the Five Agents are manifested.

   Certain ancient Daoist texts refer to the spiritual energy of Shang Ling as a type of "Vegetative Hun." This is because this level of spiritual energy is commonly seen within the plant, animal, and human realms.

The Five Agents of Shang Ling

Acting as the "inner-voice" of the Five Pure Lights, the spiritual natures of the Five Agents (Figure 2.113), influence our desires to be involved in a variety of positive social interests and responsibilities. Internally functioning as the individual's Prenatal Wujing Shen (i.e., the Five Essence Minds/Spirits) they are considered to be the original spiritual virtues that are linked to the

Yin Organ	Element	Congenital Agent	Acquired Emotion
Liver	Wood	Kindness	Anger
Heart	Fire	Order	Excitement
Spleen	Earth	Trust	Worry
Lungs	Metal	Integrity	Grief
Kidneys	Water	Wisdom	Fear

Figure 2.114. The Five Virtues of the Five Yin Organs

individual's moral character, contained within the energetic orbs of the Five Yin Organs (i.e., the Liver, Heart, Spleen, Lungs and Kidneys.)

The Spiritual Virtues of the Prenatal Wujingshen are Kindness, Inner-Peace (Order), Trust, Integrity, and Wisdom); the acquired thoughts, beliefs and emotional states of the Postnatal Wujingshen are Anger, Excitement, Worry, Grief, and Fear. Both of these energetic states are stored within the body's Five Yin Organs (Figure 2.114), and are expressed through either the positive (Yang) moral characteristics of the Prenatal Wujingshen (i.e., the Five Agents) or through the negative (Yin) experiences of the acquired Postnatal Wujingshen.

The Five Agents (i.e., the Hun, Shen, Yi, Po, and Zhi) are all stored within the energetic and spiritual fields of the body's Yuan Jing (Figure 2.115). Each of the Five Element energies that internally support the Five Agents (i.e., the Wood, Fire, Earth, Metal, and Water), encompass not only the various tissues of the physical body, but also all external phenomena existing within nature. These energies combine and recombine in infinite ways, in order to produce our manifested existence. The internal Yin and Yang descriptions of the internal Five Elements Virtues and emotional states are described as follows:

- **The Wood Agent (The Virtue of Kindness):** This Congenital Agent represents the Prenatal Virtuous State of love, compassion, benevolence, kindness, patience, and unselfish actions. It is spiritually connected to the "Hun" Agent and the Wood Element, and is housed within the Liver Orb. The Wood Element also affects the flow of energy moving within both the Liver and Gall Bladder organs and channels.

  The Wood Agent governs the energy of the

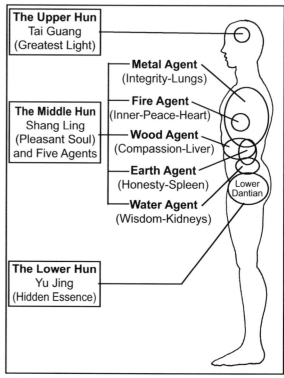

Figure 2.115. The Three Hun: Tai Guang (Greatest Light), Shang Ling (Pleasant Soul) and Yu Jing (Hidden Essence).

tendons, ligaments, small muscles, peripheral nerves, iris of the eyes, vision, tears, bile, nails, and external genitalia. After birth, through the influence of the Po, the Liver stores the acquired Postnatal emotions of frustration, irritability, stubbornness, anger, blame, rage, resentment, rudeness, impatience, jealousy, and depression.

When excess anger is eliminated through the influence of the Hun, the congenital energies of benevolence, compassion, and love for others begin to flourish and energetically radiate from the Liver Orb.

- **The Fire Agent (The Virtue of Inner-Peace):** This Congenital Agent fosters social harmony and represents the Prenatal Virtuous State of inner-peace, pleasure, joy, contentment, tranquility, order, forgiveness, and healthy boundary setting. It is spiritually connected to the "Shen" Agent and the Fire Element, and is housed within the Heart Orb. The Fire

Element also affects the Heart, Small Intestine, Pericardium and Triple Burners, as well as the flow of energy moving within each of these channels.

The Fire Agent governs the energy of the blood vessels, complexion, perspiration, and the tongue. After birth, through the influence of the Po, the Heart stores the acquired Postnatal emotions of nervousness, excitement, shock, anxiety, overexcitement, heartache, and mania.

Eliminating anxieties and excess nervousness allows the congenital energies of order, forgiveness, and inner-peace to be experienced. The environment is then conducive for contentment and orderliness, which allows self-esteem to grow through the influence of the Hun Agent.

- **The Earth Agent: The Virtue of Honesty.** This Congenital Agent represents the Prenatal Virtuous State of trust, faithfulness, honesty, openness, acceptance, and truthfulness. It is spiritually connected to the "Yi" Agent and the Earth Element, and is housed within the Spleen Orb. The Earth Element also affects the flow of energy moving within the Spleen and Stomach organs and channels.

The Earth Agent governs the energy of the large muscles, lymph, saliva secretions, mouth, lips, and taste. After birth, through the influence of the Po, the Spleen stores the acquired Postnatal emotions of worry, regret, remorse, obsessiveness, self-doubt, self-centeredness and suspicion.

Eliminating excess worry allows the congenital energies of trust and peace of mind to flourish through the influence of the Hun.

- **The Metal Agent: The Virtue of Integrity.** This Congenital Agent represents the Prenatal Virtuous State of integrity, honor, justice, righteousness, dignity, generosity and social responsibility. It is spiritually connected to the "Po" Agent and the Metal Element, and is housed within the Lungs Orb. The Metal Element also affects the flow of energy moving within the Lung and Large Intestine organs and channels.

The Metal Agent governs the energy of the skin and mucous membranes, body hair, nose, and the sense of smell. After birth, through the influence of the Po, the Lungs store the acquired Postnatal emotions of grief, sorrow, sadness, shame, disappointment, self-pity, guilt, and despair.

Once excess sorrow is relieved, the congenital energies of justice, righteousness, integrity, dignity, and social responsibility flourish under the influence of the Hun.

- **The Water Agent: The Virtue of Wisdom.** This Congenital Agent represents the Prenatal Virtuous State of wisdom, rationality, clear perception, self-understanding, and self-confidence. It is spiritually connected to the "Zhi" Agent and the Water Element, and is housed within the Kidneys Orb. The Water Element also affects the flow of energy moving within the Kidney and Urinary Bladder organs and channels.

The Water Agent governs the energy of the Brain, inner ear, hearing, spinal cord, cerebrospinal fluid, Bones, Bone Marrow, ovaries, testes, head and pubic hair, anus, urethra and sexual fluids. After birth, through the influence of the Po, the Kidneys store the acquired Postnatal emotions of fear, paranoia, terror, panic, horror, loneliness, and insecurity.

Once excess fear is eliminated, the congenital energies of the mind become rational and wise under the influence of the Hun.

3. **Yu Jing (Hidden Essence):** The Hun known as Yu Jing resides in the Lower Dantian. Yu Jing literally means "Hidden Essence." This Hun is considered mixed (or combined) Yin energy. He is connected to the Lower Dantian, and is associated with the energy of the Earth, the physical realm, and for producing our desire for enjoying life's clean pleasures, and experiencing the highest quality of living according to our a state of divine connection.

Certain ancient Daoist texts refer to the spiritual energy of Yu Jing as a type of "Human Hun." This is because this level of spiritual energy is only seen within human beings.

Figure 2.116. The Seven Po

BAI YUAN, THE REGULATOR OF THE PO

Si Ming also controls the spiritual energies of Bai Yuan ("Pure Origin"). Bai Yuan regulates the emotional energies of the Seven Po, the Yin Spirits of the body, considered to be the tangible consciousness. This includes the sensory perceptions received into the body through the seven apertures (the 2 eyes, 2 ears, 2 nostrils, and the 1 mouth), and the energy of the breath.

The Spirit of Bai Yuan occupies the right side of the body and regulates the disciple's "animal nature." According to ancient Daoist teachings, when meditating, the energy of the Seven Po (Corporeal Souls) can be directed to exit the body in the form of a White Tiger (Figure 2.116). This is accomplished via a special energetic portal located on the right side of the rib-cage.

The word Po is defined as "the soul of vigor, animation, or life." The energetic functions of the Po pertain to the individual's animal nature, his survival instincts, and passionate drives. The Po are emotional, and advocate experiencing life to its fullest measure. They are the Earthly aspects of the human soul. Being attached to the physical body, they are in a constant state of dying, and are considered to be the counterpart of the Hun.

The Po are housed originally within the Lungs, but also reside in seven specific areas in the body. According to ancient Daoist teachings, they are located inside the human body in-between the perineum and the top of the head, at the following locations (Figure 2.117):

1. **The Po of Life (Soul of Heaven):** This is considered the Po of the Upper Dantian. It is located below the Baihui (GV-20) point, within the Niwan Palace (Pineal Gland) of the Upper Dantian.

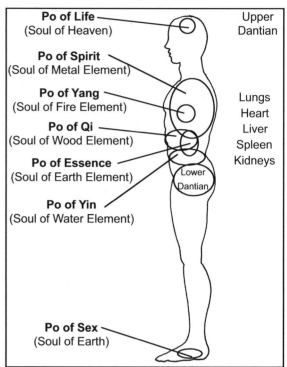

Figure 2.117. The Location of the Seven Po Inside the Human Body

2. **The Po of Qi (Soul of the Five Element Wood):** This is considered the Po of the Liver. It is located below the diaphragm, and manifests through the acquired emotions of frustration, irritability, stubbornness, anger, blame, rage, resentment, rudeness, impatience, jealousy, and depression. This Po is the counterpart to the Hun's Wood Agent (the Virtue of love, compassion, benevolence, kindness, patience, and unselfish actions).

3. **The Po of Yang (Soul of the Five Element Fire):** This is considered the Po of the Heart. It is located behind the Heart, anterior to the Taiji Pole. It manifests through the acquired emotions of nervousness, excitement, shock, anxiety, overexcitement, heartache, and mania. This Po is the counterpart to the Hun's Fire Agent (the Virtue of inner-peace, pleasure, joy, contentment, tranquility, order, forgiveness, and healthy boundary setting).

4. **The Po of Essence (Soul of the Five Element Earth):** This is considered the Po of the Spleen.

It is located at the midpoint of the Taiji Pole, and manifests through the acquired emotions of worry, regret, remorse, obsessiveness, self-doubt, self-centeredness and suspicion. This Po is the counterpart to the Hun's Earth Agent (the Virtue of trust, faithfulness, honesty, openness, acceptance, virtue, and truthfulness).

5. **The Po of Spirit (Soul of the Five Element Metal):** This is considered the Po of the Lungs. It is located posterior to the Tanzhong (CV-17) point inside the mediastinum near the Middle Dantian, and manifests through the acquired emotions of grief, sorrow, sadness, shame, disappointment, self-pity, guilt, and despair. This Po is the counterpart to the Hun's Metal Agent (the Virtue of integrity, honor, justice, righteousness, dignity, generosity, and social responsibility).

6. **The Po of Yin (Soul of the Five Element Water):** This is considered the Po of the Kidneys. It is located between the navel and the Taiji Pole, and manifests through the acquired emotions of fear, paranoia, terror, panic, horror, loneliness, and insecurity. This Po is the counterpart to the Hun's Water Agent (the Virtue of wisdom, rationality, clear perception, self-understanding, and self-confidence).

7. **The Po of Sex (Soul of Earth):** This is considered the Po of the Lower Dantian. It is the only one not located within the midline of the body. Instead, it is located at the bottom of the feet in the Yongquan (Kd-1) points. It is considered a neighbor of the Po of Essence because of its relationship and energetic connection to Earth.

XIA TAO KANG (BELOW HEALTHY PEACH)

The Third Lord of the Three Dantians is Xia Tao Kang ("Below Healthy Peach/Life"). He resides within the Lower Dantian (Figure 2.118), in the region of the navel, and in the area known as the "Water Realm" (sometimes known as the Underworld). He is responsible for procreation, and for the preservation of the body's Essence (Jing).

According to ancient Shangqing Scriptures, Xia Tao Kang (Below Healthy Peach), is sometimes

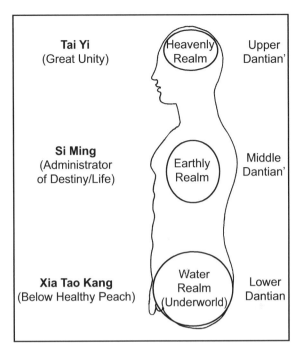

Figure 2.118. The energy of Xia Tao Kang Resides within the Lower Dantian

known as the "Lower One." Because he is also the "Primordial King of the Yellow Court," he is dressed in a radiant robe of yellow embroidered gauze, and resides in the center of the Lower Cinnabar Field (the Lower Dantian). In Daoist Magic Rituals, he is sometimes known as "The God of the Beginning-Radiance Essence," "The Glory of Primordial Yang," "The "Peach Child," and "The Immortal Embryo of the Lower Prime."

The Palace of the Cinnabar Field (sometimes known as the "Gate of Destiny" or "Deep Navel") is perfectly square, each side measuring one inch. A White Vapor surges from out of the center of the Palace of the Cinnabar Field and ascends upward into the Heavens.

Internally, he watches over the Body Fluids, Blood, Stomach, Intestines, and Urinary Bladder, as well as the external four limbs. Externally, he is responsible for removing all calamity and misfortune, and removing various evil influences. Three times each day, the Three Hun and Seven Po come and pay respect to Xia Tao Kang and receive instruction.

The Ethereal Soul (Hun) & Corporeal Soul (Po)

In Chinese Energetic Medicine, the internal dialogues that sometimes have an affect on a patient's psyche can be divided into either positive (Yang) or negative (Yin) influences. These unique influences are considered to be the internal characteristics (i.e., archetype manifestations) of the patient's Hun (Ethereal Soul) and Po (Corporeal Soul), energetically expressing themselves on a conscious level, and acting upon the individual's Shen (Mind/Heart).

These two major archetype systems, are regarded as spirit souls capable of exerting a positive or negative influence on a person's life, according to the nature of the individual's human soul. The positive or good internal influences are said to energetically manifest through the Hun and the Original Five Prenatal Virtues of its Five Agents; the negative or primal internal influences are said to energetically manifest through the Po, and the individual's acquired "wants and desires."

According to ancient Daoist Alchemy, an individual's Hun or Po can either motivate or hinder their personal spiritual growth and cultivation practice, as well as cause illness and even the demise of the body due to the suppression of unreleased emotional experiences.

The Hun (considered to be the influence of "Heaven") and the Po (considered to be the influence of "Earth") are both established within the fetus's internal organs at conception, yet they remain dormant until the Third Lunar Month after conception. This is because at the time of the Third Lunar Month, the fetus' internal organ Orbs are finally sufficiently formed in order to house, support, and maintain the spiritual energies of the Original/Prenatal Wujingshen. One ancient belief is that the Hun and Po, although residing in the fetus, frequently leave and return in order to gather and absorb celestial and environmental Qi. The Hun was said to naturally connect with Celestial Beings, as well as with the spirits of the Divine; while the Po was said to naturally connect with Nature Spirits and the various environmental energies.

Figure 2.119. The Three Hun (Ethereal Soul)

The Hun: Three Ethereal Souls

In the human body, an individual's Three Ethereal Souls are collectively referred to as the "Hun." The Hun are rooted within the Liver, specifically the Liver Yin and the Liver Blood, and represent spiritual consciousness. Traditionally, the Hun provide the energetic movement of the Mind/Heart, and are associated with the Qi of Heaven and the Virtues of the Five Agents.

Although Traditional Chinese Medicine often refers to the Hun as a single entity, the ancient Daoists have maintained that there are Three Hun since the Han Dynasty (206 B.C. - 220 A.D.). This was because, the Hun represent the body's internal energetic and spiritual activities operating at three levels of influence, which directly inspire and are inspired by the Shen (Mind/Heart).

The Three Hun originate from Heaven, and are considered to exist as a unique state of subtle, formless energy (Figure 2.119). They are therefore considered to be an important part of the spiritual aspects of an individual that can spirit travel. Upon the death of the individual's physical body, the spiritual essence of their Hun will ascend back into the Heavens.

Although they originally reside in the Liver Orb, the Hun also energetically express themselves from the various chambers of the Three Dantians (like a vaporous mist extending from the Liver and filling the body's three main fields of energy). The Hun are energetically associated with Yang Qi, the Heavenly Soul, bright light, constructive virtues, and transforming inspirations.

Chapter 2: Understanding Ancient Chinese Metaphysics

Chinese Ideogram for the Hun

The Chinese ideogram for the Hun has two parts. The character to the right represents the word "Gui," meaning "Ghost" or "Spirit." This character is depicted by the image of a head being suspended above a vaporous body; with an appendage symbolizing the whirlwind accompanying its movements.

The character to the left is the image for Clouds (Yun), seen as vapor rising from the Earth and gathering in the Heavens (Figure 2.120).

Together, the Hun character describes the easy movement of the ethereal spirit, as it freely moves within the tissues; like clouds following the will of the "Heavenly Breath moving within the celestial vault." From this ideogram we also get a distinct picture of the spirit (Hun) rising towards the Heavens.

According to Daoist teachings, the Eternal Soul (Shen Xian) is considered different from the Hun in both energetic and spiritual application. In this context, the Eternal Soul is seen as the more personal of the two, while the Hun are seen as more universal temperaments or archetypes.

Functions of the Hun

In both Daoist Alchemy and Chinese Energetic Medicine, the Hun are described as having eight primary functions, described as follows (Figure 2.121):

Figure 2.120. The Three Hun (Ethereal Soul)

1. **The Hun Control Sleep And Dreaming:** The Hun reside in the eyes during the day, and lodge in the Liver at night. When residing in the eyes, they see; when lodging in the Liver, they dream.

   Dreams are the roaming of the body's Hun. Because it is the nature of the Hun to wander, at night they must be anchored and rooted in the Liver. For this reason, the Liver Blood and Liver Yin must be strong. If the Liver Blood and Liver Yin are not strong, the Hun will wander and the person will dream too much, or have unpleasant dreams. Individuals who suffer from severe Yin Deficiency may experience a floating sensation just before falling asleep. This symptom is due to the Hun not being adequate-

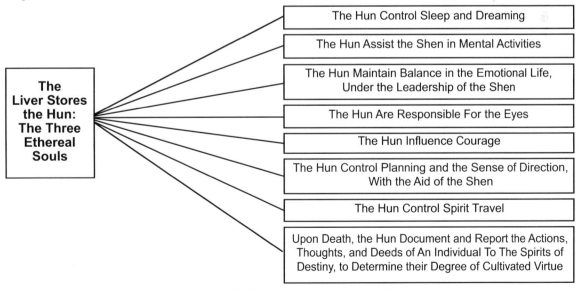

Figure 2.121. The Eight Functions of the Hun

ly rooted in the Individual's' Yin. If the body's Liver Yin is depleted, the Hun are deprived of their residence, resulting in such conditions as fear, excessive daydreaming, insomnia, and a lack of sense of direction or purpose in life (one of the main features of depression).

Dreams are an example of the information that is gathered during the Hun's out of body travels. The ancient Daoists believed that dreams were the wandering of the Hun into the various realms of the Spirit World. They also believed that when consistently trained, the body's Hun could instantaneously traverse the Nine Levels of Heaven or Nine Levels of Earth in order to communicate with various spirit entities. The Nine Levels of Heaven, are various spiritual realms which energetically exist within Heaven's nine celestial grids. In the lower levels of the celestial grids, there are enlightened beings coexisting with other spiritual entities. In the Nine Levels of Earth, there are various realms that energetically exist within Earth's nine energetic grids. In these Earthly realms, there exists the various dimensions of the animal, vegetable, and mineral realms, as well as various Nature Spirits.

It was believed that the ability to sojourn deep into these various spiritual dimensions each night and receive needed counsel and direction, was essential for every individual's spiritual growth (Figure 2.122).

According to the *Upper Scripture of Purple Texts Inscribed by the Spirits,* written by Daoist Master Yang Xi during the Jin Dynasty (265-420 A.D.),

*"The Hun should be secured,
for it is their nature to freely wander.
Once free of the body,
the Hun are subject to demonic attack,
or may become involved with other Hun spirits that are freely wandering about.*

*However, dreams that deal with "Transcended" or "Perfected" Beings indicate a healthy orientation on the part of the wandering Hun,
and should be encouraged."*

Figure 1.122. The individual's Hun would sojourn into the various Spiritual Worlds in order to receive needed counsel and direction.

The Hun also store the sum total of an individual's past experiences. The expressions of the Hun are manifested through images, symbols, and ideas from the divine, as well as through the energetic state of the Wuji. These images, symbols, and ideas are stored in the individual's mind, affecting his or her spiritual life. Without this important spiritual interaction, a patient's inner mental and spiritual life would become deficient in ideas, images, and dreams.

The Hun not only control the dreams, but they also initiate daydreaming and inspirational ideals, as well as assist in providing guidance and overall direction for the individual's life. The absence of these important dreams, objectives, and goals, results in the manifestation of internal feelings such as worthlessness and depression.

Traditionally, sleepwalking is associated with the Hun. When sleepwalking, the body's Shen is not active and functioning; instead, the Hun are moving the individual. This is why a common treatment for a patient who suffers from sleepwalking involves the emission of Qi into the patient's Hunmen UB-47 (Door of the Hun).

If the patient does not sleep well because the Hun are wandering, the Medical Qigong Doctor will sometimes prescribe sour and astringent herbs (i.e., Bai Shao, Mu Li, Suan Zao Ren) in order to affect the Liver and encourage the Hun to return back into the patient's body.

According to ancient Daoist teachings, the Po sometimes take an active role in sleep walking, especially when the sleep state involves violent actions (e.g., patients who thrash about, hurt people, or destroy things when they sleep).

Additionally, although the Po are generally confined to the body, they sometimes wander. According to the *Upper Scripture of Purple Texts Inscribed by the Spirits,* written by Daoist Master Yang Xi during the Jin Dynasty (265-420 A.D.),

"When the Po wander,
they join in lascivious embrace
with demons, spirit entities, and ghosts,
and provide the sexual content of dreams.

Therefore, the Po should not be allowed
to leave the body.
The Po must be controlled through the
visualization of the Four Celestial Animals
and other Spirit Guardians
who stand guard and are stationed
at any likely spirit exit point in the body.

2. **The Hun Assist The Shen In Mental Activities:** This relationship is very important, as the energy of both the Shen and the Hun must continually be coordinated. The Shen (Mind/Heart) is related to rational thinking and inspiration. Although the Hun give the Shen a sense of spiritual direction and project the energy of the Shen outward, the Shen must direct the Hun to "condense" in order to gather the Hun back inside the body.

    The Hun give the Shen its movement and purpose, encouraging the Shen to relate with people, socialize, and bond. The Hun, in turn need to be gathered and restrained by the Shen. If the Shen is weak and does not control the Hun, the Hun will excessively move about, resulting in having many ideas but never accomplishing anything, which internally leads to frustration.

    Because knowledge is dependent on the Hun's awareness, the Hun are considered to be the collectors of information. The Hun however, do not interpret, rationalize, or analyze the knowledge they collect; they pass on the information to the Shen, which is responsible for rational thinking, intuition, and inspiration. The Shen therefore help to distinguish between useful and irrelevant information.

    The Hun inspire us and give us dreams. That is why the words "movement," "coming and going," and "swimming" are often used in connection with the Hun. There is an interesting connection between the Hun controlling sleep and dreaming, and the Hun being rooted in the Liver Blood and Yin. The Hun's movement in and out of the Liver governs the free flow of Liver Qi, and the free flow of Liver Qi is a manifestation of the swimming energy of the Hun as it moves in and out of the tissues. Therefore, if the Liver Yin or Liver Blood is deficient, the Hun cannot move freely and the individual will experience restlessness (especially at night).

3. **The Hun Maintain Balance In The Emotional Life Under The Leadership of The Shen:** The Hun have a regulatory function closely related to the balance between Liver Blood (Yin) and Liver Qi (Yang). It is normal for everyone to experience various emotional states during their life. The Hun however, are responsible for maintaining a balance within these emotions. This important regulation process is needed in order to prevent excessive emotions from causing disease formation.

    The Postnatal Mind/Heart (Shen Zhi) discriminates, while the Hun does not. The relationship between the Shen and the Hun is very similar to the concepts of the conscious-mind and unconscious-mind in Jungian terms. The

Hun are a repository of images and archetypes connecting the (personal) subconscious mind with the collective unconscious. If the Hun are unsettled, then the Shen (consciousness) is cut off, confused, isolated, aimless, sterile, and without dreams.

The movement of ideas in the body has to be controlled, or it can lead to madness. Madness can occur to the degree that the Shen does not control the Hun, resulting in an uncontrolled amount of emotional, mental, and spiritual input (Figure 2.123). All of the energies and symbols coming through the Hun have to be integrated and assimilated, otherwise there can be serious mental illness and possibly psychosis.

One exception is in the case of young children, who are continually full of ideas, have active imaginations, and are also able to integrate and assimilate these energies and symbols at a phenomenal rate. In a child, the Hun are very active, and the Shen is not as restraining; so there is a continuous flow of energies streaming from the unconscious world of symbols into the child's consciousness without causing psychological problems.

Figure 2.123. Overstimulated Hun
Madness can occur to the degree that the Shen does not control the Hun

4. **The Hun Are Responsible For The Eyes:** When the Hun wander in through the eyes, the eyes can see. Therefore, the Hun give us both internal and external vision, and allow us to see mentally and spiritually.

5. **The Hun Influence Courage:** If the Hun are strong, an individual will become fearless, and can face many difficulties in life, while simultaneously taking the appropriate actions needed to overcome these obstacles.

    If however the Hun are deficient and weak, the individual will become timid and fearful. A patient with a weak Hun will have difficulty gathering information, making decisions, and lack courage. They will also become easily discouraged and/or apathetic.

6. **The Hun Control Planning and The Sense of Direction, With The Aid of The Shen:** If the Liver is strong while the Hun are firmly rooted, the individual will have a clear sense of direction.

    However, whenever there is a deficiency, the individual will experience mental and spiritual confusion about their role in life (i.e., what to do, what goals to set, why am I here, etc.), which can be clinically diagnosed as a symptom of Hun Disturbance known as the "Aimless Wandering of the Hun." This internal syndrome is a feature of clinical depression. During this type of deficiency, the patient feels timid, depressed, and confused. They also lack emotional expression and are usually too weak to even try to start a project (if they do make an attempt, they often cannot get past the initial decision making stage).

7. **The Hun Control Spirit Travel:** By housing the Shen, it is possible for the individual's Hun to consciously direct its own spirit travel (i.e., the journeying of the "Spirit Eyes" outside of the Physical Body). This type of traveling clairvoyance is different from the spirit travel that involves the individual's Spirit Body journeying outside the Physical Body (sometimes connected to the body by an energetic cord). In this type of spirit travel, the Hun, accompanied by the individual's consciousness, act as one unit, and is sometimes referred to as "the projection of the spirit-eyes." The clairvoyant vision of the spirit-eyes allows the doctor to know the exact location of the "spirit routes" travelled when the Hun leaves

the body. Otherwise, when the Hun begin to wander, an individual will "Shen-Out," and have no recollection of where he or she has been within the various spirit realms.

Because the Hun and Po are considered to be the influential expressions of the body's "True Spirit" (Yuan Shen), the ancient Daoists believed that in the presence of a serious disorder (i.e., physical, mental, emotional, or spiritual) the Hun would sometimes "fly away" (like startled birds in a yard). This sudden vacancy of the Hun would cause the body's Po (Corporeal Soul) to either stir about thoughtlessly in the absence of effective control (clinically known as "disassociation" or commonly called "spacing out"), or to become animalistic in nature and attack, freeze, or flee for the sake of survival.

8. **The Hun Leave The Body, and Ascend Back To Heaven At The Time of Death:** According to ancient Daoist teachings, upon death, an individual's Hun will exit the body through the Baihui at the top of the head, and ascend to the Big Dipper. While at the Big Dipper, the Hun will report all of the individual's actions, thoughts, and deeds, from his or her previous lifetime on Earth, to the celestial spirits that preside over the individual's destiny. The celestial spirits will then determine the degree to which the individual had cultivated virtue during that incarnation.

In Religious Daoism, it is taught that the reason why both (Black (Yin) and White (Yang) Spirit Guardians are used as Wuchang Escorts at the time of death, is because the human body contains both a Yang Ethereal Soul (Hun) and a Yin Corporeal Soul (Po). The Hun are connected and influenced by spirits of the celestial realm, and are responsible for spirit travel, dreaming, and spiritually "feeding" the individual's Original Spirit and Eternal Soul with divine inspiration and energy. The Po are the individual's spirit-soul that energetically "sticks" or clings to the physical body. The Po is connected and influenced by the spirits of the terrestrial realm, and are responsible for animal instinct and survival (i.e., fighting and reproduction), and for "feeding" the ego of the individual's Acquired Spirit (Shen Zhi).

When an individual dies, both Wuchang Spirit Guardians come to escort the spirit of the dead. One Wuchang is responsible for picking up and escorting the Hun, while the other is responsible for 'dispersing' the Po within the individual's dead corpse, by absorbing it. Then, the departed spirit is transported into the Underworld to await judgement.

THE SPIRITUAL AWARENESS OF THE HUN

The Hun spiritually and energetically respond to the energetic grids of Heaven (universal energetic fields). The stars and planets within these Heavenly grids exert an influence on the Hun causing each individual's body to react to certain astrological configurations (full moon, new moon, equinox and solstice). An individual's positive or negative emotional reactions are sometimes based on the affinity of the vibrational rate of the Hun with the energies of a particular astrological alignment.

The Hun are classified as Yang spirits; they can be cultivated and refined. Imagination, visualization, and positive affirmation in the form of prayer and incantations (Mantras), meditation, and Hand Seals (Mudras) are traditionally used to awaken and establish an active relationship with the Hun. Energetically, the Hun can be stimulated through the Hunmen UB-47 ("Gate to the Hun") points located on the back of the body below the shoulders. These points are used clinically to treat difficult or chronic disorders by regulating Liver Qi flow.

THE PO: SEVEN CORPOREAL SOULS

The Po are a composite of Seven Corporeal Souls, which originate from the Earth, are housed within the Lungs, and remain attached to the body until death (Figure 2.124). They reside in specific areas inside the body, located mostly between the base of the perineum and the top of the head.

The body's Corporeal Souls are traditionally referred to as the "Po," with the assumption that this term depicts all seven. Therefore in Traditional Chinese Medicine, doctors often refer to the Po as a singular entity stored within the Lungs.

The word Po is defined as "the soul of vigor, animation, or life." They are physical in nature, and are connected to the body's Jing and Qi. Because the Po are closely linked to the body's Jing (Essence), they are considered to be the "soul of the senses" (i.e., they manifest through the body's Essence in the form of hearing, sight, and tactile sensations)

The Seven Corporeal Souls are the Earthly aspects of energetic influence that is placed on the Human Soul, and are considered to be the counterparts of the Hun. Consequently, the energetic functions of the Po pertain to the individual's animal nature, and his or her survival instincts and drives. Within the human body, the Po passionately advocate experiencing life in its fullest measure. However, being attached to the physical body, they are in a constant state of dying.

CHINESE IDEOGRAM OF THE PO

The Chinese ideogram for the Po has two parts (Figure 2.125). The character to the right represents the word "Gui," meaning "Ghost" or "Spirit." This character is depicted by the image of a head being suspended above a vaporous body; with an appendage symbolizing the whirlwind accompanying its movements.

The character to the left is the image for the color White (Bai). In Daoist alchemy, the color white represents the Underworld or Realm of the Dead. Similar to the image of dried bones lying on the Earth. The Po are linked with a descending movement of Qi, and with the body's Jing. The Po are also said "to come and go, enter and exit," in association with the body's Jing.

Figure 2.124. The Seven Po are composed of the Seven Corporeal Souls.

Figure 2.125. The Chinese Character "Po" (Corporeal Soul, or White Soul)

FUNCTIONS OF THE PO

In both Daoist Alchemy and Chinese Energetic Medicine, the Po are described as having six primary functions, described as follows (Figure 2.126):

1. **The Po Are The Somatic Expressions Of The Human Soul:** The Po are related to the reflexive nervous system and limbic system (i.e., the "reptilian brain"). They manifest through the body's sensations of feeling, hearing, and sight. The Po have an impulsive tendency towards action, and correspond to the deep animal instincts within the Mind/Heart and cells.

   In Daoist Alchemy, our reflexes are said to be a Po reaction. The Po also provide us with the animal strength and resources necessary to mobilize the body and perform incredible feats of power. The "animal within" is driven

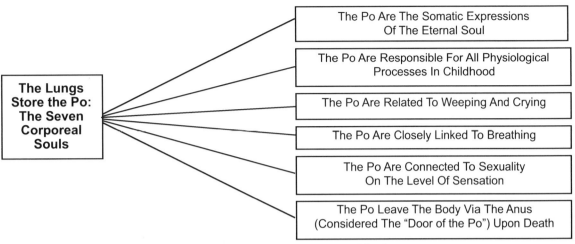

Figure 2.126. The Six Functions of the Po

by the Po. They are the manifestation of the body's Jing in the sphere of sensations and feelings. Just as the Hun provide an individual with the energetic movement for the Shen (Mind/Heart), the Po provide the individual with the energetic movement of the body's Jing (essence).

2. **The Po Are Responsible For All Physiological Processes During Childhood:** At conception, the energetic interactions of the body's transforming Jing not only create the embryo but also establish the Po within the tissues. In the beginning of childhood, the Po are responsible for the sensations of pain and itching brought about by "growing pains." The Po serve as the intermediary between the Essence (Jing) and the body's other vital substances.

3. **The Po Are Related To Weeping and Crying:** The connection between the Po and Lungs is very important from an emotional point of view. When the Po's movement in the Lungs is constricted, grief and sadness are suppressed within the chest through shallow breathing. Additionally, if a patient experiences a dull and depressed feeling within his chest upon waking, this is sometimes known as "the Shen Clinging to the Body," and refers to the patient's Shen being constricted by the excessive energy of the Po.

4. **The Po Are Closely Linked To Breathing:** The Po influence the sympathetic and parasympathetic nervous systems. Because the Po reside in the Lungs, all forms of Qigong Breathing Techniques and Daoist Breath Control Meditations are actually secret methods used to regulate the energy of the Po, calm the Shen (Mind/Heart), and allow an individual the ability to access the higher spiritual states of the Hun.

In ancient Daoist Alchemy, the movement of the breath was considered to be the energetic pulsation of the Po. With each emotional change, the body experiences a shift in its respiratory pattern. The quality of Qi and its circulation moving within the body's tissues, is dependent upon the type and method of breathing (i.e., its depth, speed, duration, and rhythm). To the ancient Daoists, in order to support the greatest longevity possible, it was important to utilize long, slow, and even breaths. The breath (air from Heaven) interacts with the Po in the Lungs, and plays a significant role in the Heaven-Man-Earth concept of balancing the emotions.

The Virtues (De) of the Lungs are righteousness and courage. These virtues give a person the drive and strength to do the "right thing" when the need arises. These virtues also manifest to promote good health, when a balanced energetic alignment with the Po is achieved (i.e., an alignment between the Lungs' breathing patterns and the Po is accomplished).

5. **The Po Are Connected To Sexuality On The Level Of Sensation:** The Po are linked to the basic animal instincts and perceptions of the body. Therefore, all instinctive sexual reactions and passions come under the authority of the Po. The Po provide the fundamental biological energy and are the source of biological needs and impulses. They are driven by basic instincts and urges, and their sole concern is the immediate satisfaction of biological needs and impulses (i.e., emotional and physical survival, reproductive urges, etc.). Most self-destructive behavior, such as an attraction to unhealthy and dangerous life-styles, is due to imbalances of the Po.

6. **The Po Leave The Body Via The Anus Upon Death:** Since the Corporeal Souls have a relationship with the Lungs and Large Intestine, the anus is considered the Po Men or "the Door of the Po." The anus acts as a doorway for the elimination of the waste products from the Five Yin Organs, by draining off impure liquids and waste. Upon death, the energy of the Po disintegrates and disperses into the Earth within a few days, descending out the body through the individual's anus.

THE SPIRITUAL AWARENESS OF THE PO

The Po are classified as Yin Spirits, and they can be controlled and refined through breathing exercises and quiescent meditations. When the fetus begins its movement, its Yin Qi tranquilizes the animal nature of the Po, which allows them to act as guardians of the fetus' body. Throughout the individual's life, the Po will help to develop his or her growth of consciousness. This is accomplished by providing various obstacles used to test the individual's faith and spiritual devotion. Many times the Po will work in conjunction with hostile external energetic forces in order to test the individual's spiritual endurance.

Energetically, the Po can be accessed through the Pohu (Door to the Po) UB-42 point located on the back of the body and between the shoulders. This special point is also used clinically to treat energetic imbalances of the Lungs.

The energetic nature of the Po responds to the energetic grids of the Earth, and can cause an individual to resonate in harmony or disharmony with certain ecological configurations (mountains, oceans, forests, valleys, etc.). For example, an individual's attraction to a particular environment, or a feeling of not belonging there, depend on the vibratory affinity (or lack thereof) between the individual's Po and the environmental energy of a particular area.

NEGATIVE ATTRIBUTES OF THE PO

The Po's animal nature is one of survival, and their energies can be directed towards self-preservation or self-destruction (i.e., devouring and robbing the body of its life-force energy). In ancient China, it was believed that the Po would sometimes desire to rejoin the damp, dark underground springs whose moist, heavy nature they share. Therefore, the Po would seek to undermine and rid themselves of the constraining human body that they were presently inhabiting. This was accomplished while their host was asleep and the Hun were spirit-traveling. The Po would beckon to passing ghosts and disease-demons, inviting them into the individual's body to take possession and work towards the destruction of the body.

Therefore, the Po were sometimes called the "Seven Animals," the "Seven Sentient Souls," or the "Seven Turbid Demons." When either afflicted or not kept in check, the animal nature of the seven Po quickly becomes restless and hostile. In this context, the Po were given different names by the ancient Daoists, in order to express the different negative thought forms and emotional states that were specific to each Corporeal Soul.

In order to influence and control them, each Po was said to have a particular emotional characteristic and phrase that it would whisper into the Shen (Mind/Heart) of an individual. The following are some examples and basic descriptions of the Po's Seven Turbid Demon natures (Figure 2.127), as written in the ancient Daoist text *Taishang Chu Sanshi Jiuchong Baoshen Jing (Great Highest Scripture For Protecting Life and Expelling the Three Death Bringers and Nine Worms)*:

Figure 2.127. The Po's Seven Turbid Demon Natures
(From the: *Taishang Chu Sanshi Jiuchong Baoshen Jing*)

1. **Fei Du (Flying Poison):** The Fei Du Po manifests itself through feelings of anger and rage. The indignation and wrath that it helps to generate can produce hostile, destructive, and violently aggressive reactions. This "Po of Anger," can cause an individual to suddenly explode with venomous thoughts and evil intentions.

2. **Chu Hui (Sprouting Filth):** The Chu Hui Po expresses itself through haughty behavior and feelings of pride and arrogance.

3. **Chou Fei (Stinking Lungs):** The Chou Fei Po manifests itself as hopelessness, and is often experienced as the "smells of death." It destroys hope and faith, and feeds on ignorance, which can lead to a sense of despair, spiritual apathy or inactivity. It emotionally expresses itself through feelings of victimization and martyrdom.

4. **Shi Kou (Corpse Dog):** The Shi Kou Po manifests itself through feelings of greed, envy, and selfishness. It emotionally expresses itself through feelings of selfish desires and covetous actions.

5. **Fu Shi (Fallen Arrow):** The Fu Shi Po manifests itself through feelings of intense lust and unbridled passion. It entices the individual by tempting or luring him or her into a desirable place or situation through unethical actions. It then creates distress in the form of guilt which generates shame. This spirit further creates anxiety and fear of being caught, discredited, dishonored, or disgraced, and then immediately generates the feeling that any attempt to correct the situation is fruitless. It also energetically manifests in the form of various addictions and compulsions.

6. **Que Yin (Yin Bird):** The Que Yin Po manifests itself by tormenting the individual with the various images and experiences of the unhealed "ghosts of their past." During this energetic assault, the Que Yin Po will cause an individual to experience extreme pain and severe anguish by obsessing over unresolved past emotional issues, present anxieties, and future fears. Also known as the "night tormentor," this Po it is especially active at night, commonly manifesting via nightmares, restless sleep, and insomnia.

7. **Tun Zei (Sipping Thief):** The Tun Zei Po manifests itself by stealing the individual's life-force energy, devouring it through negative judgements and bitter emotions such as jealousy, envy, and resentment.

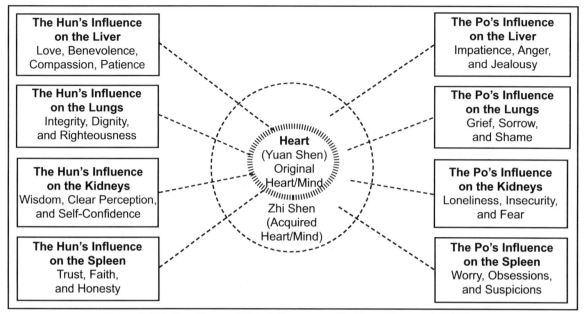

Figure 2.128. The Hun and Po's Influence on the Yuan Shen and Zhi Shen

THE HUN AND PO AND THE YUAN SHEN

According to ancient Daoist teachings, the Hun control the Yang Spirits in the body, the Po control the Yin Spirits in the body. The Hun is responsible for all formless consciousness, including the Three Treasures: Jing, Qi and Shen. Po is responsible for all tangible consciousness, including the perceptions of the Seven Orifices (i.e., the 2- eyes, 2- ears, 2- nostrils, and 1- mouth).

In esoteric Daoist Alchemy, the Yuan Shen (Original or Prenatal Mind/Heart) is considered to be a manifestation and expression of the Human Soul (Shen Xian); and is primarily affected by the energetic and spiritual influences of the Hun and Po. The combination of intuitive perceptions provided by the Hun (Yang Souls) and the Po (Yin Souls) create the foundational input for the body's Yuan Shen (Original Mind/Heart). It is through this special energetic input that the Yuan Shen organizes and controls the psycho-emotional aspect of the body's Five Yin Organs (Figure 2.128).

The ancient Daoist viewed the Shen (Mind/Heart) as the Emperor of the body; the Hun was considered to be the loyal Minister of Spiritual Council; and the Po was seen as a powerful Guardian General (Figure 2.129). If the Guardian General

Figure 2.129. The ancient Daoist Observation of the Shen (Emperor), Hun (Minister) and Po (General)

(Po) was left in control of the body, because it is only concerned with the body's survival, it would eventually start to dominate all of the individual's thoughts, emotions, and actions. This will create a clinical condition commonly referred to as "a Rebellious General Controlling a Weak Emperor."

Once the Guardian General (Po) dominates the individual's thoughts, emotions and actions, the individual's Acquired Mind (Shen Zhi) takes over, and they become overly concerned with their own personal survival. At this point, the individual becomes obsessed with the protection and maintenance of his or her ego based vanity.

In this context, the purpose of introducing a Spiritual Cultivation Practice to the patient, is to subdue and control the Rebellious General and transform his dominant will into a servant of the Emperor. Once the internal government is brought back into order, the strong and violent nature of the Po (General) will become subdued. Then, the wise guidance of the loyal Minister of Spiritual Council (Hun) can assist the Emperor (Shen) in continuing his virtuous walk with the Dao.

To the ancient Daoists, Virtue was the enlightened path that leads the individual's Shen back to the eternal Dao. Therefore, by cultivating virtue, the individual's consciousness becomes dominated by the spiritual council of the loyal Minister (Hun), who naturally produces healthy choices for the Yuan Shen.

When the Hun control the Energy Body and are nourished by the Five Virtues, the Energy Body then becomes a powerful spiritual vehicle for the Heart's Shen.

When the Heart's Shen is no longer dominated by the Yin and Yang souls (i.e., the subtle influences of the Hun and Po) and the destructive aspects of the acquired emotional states, the individual will naturally return back to an innate awareness of his connection to the universe (Wuji) and the Divine (Dao). This important spiritual state of balanced consciousness is sustained through consistent meditation and prayer.

The Hun, Po, Yuan Shen & Spirit Travel

After the initial separation of the Spirit Body (or "Dream Body") from their Physical Body, the type of spirit travel that the individual will experience will depend on their personal cultivation of Jing, Qi, and Shen.

If the individual's Shen leaves the body in a weakened state, it is traditionally referred to as a Yin Shen. This weakened Yin Shen must be protected. Although the Yin Shen is still part of the guiding influence of the Hun's external wanderings, it will naturally leave the body whenever an individual is weak, sick, in shock, or asleep. It can also leave the body during the early stages of meditation or Qigong practice, especially if

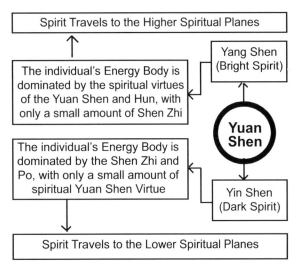

Figure 2.130. The Yuan Shen and Spirit Travel

the practitioner encounters blocks and obstacles within their unconscious mind.

The spirit travels of the Yin Shen are generally confined to the lower spiritual planes, and a scattered Yin Shen sometimes needs to be reclaimed through "Soul Retrieval." Once the Shen has been cultivated, refined, strengthened, fortified, and controlled through the proper development of the Energy Body, it is then referred to as a Yang Shen. The Yang Shen is sometimes referred to as a Shenming ("Bright Spirit" or "Spirit of Light"). According to ancient Daoist teachings, when the Spirit Body travels, the developed Yang Shen can transverse the upper realms of the Nine Levels of Heaven or the Nine Levels of Earth in an instant (Figure 2.130).

The terms Ling Qi ("Spirit Energy"), Ling Hun ("Spirit Soul") and Shen Ling ("Spirit Mind") are all ancient Daoist expressions used to describe the Yang Soul manifesting its effective power and spiritual influence, either while residing within an individual's body, or traveling outside of it in a disembodied energetic state.

The expression "Ling" (Supernatural, Spiritual, magical") is believed to be the true manifestation of the Human Soul. According to *The Book of Rites of the Senior Tai*, compiled by the Daoist Master Tai De during the Xia Dynasty (2205-1600 B.C.), the Shen Ling ("Spirit Mind") is historically believed to be the original spiritual state of existence for all living beings.

The Internal Development Of The Five Limitations

According to ancient Daoist teachings on Energetic Embryology,

> "As the Po Manifests - Jing Appears.
> Because of Jing - the Hun Manifests.
> The Hun causes the Birth of the Shen,
> Because of the Shen -
> Consciousness comes forth.
> Because of Consciousness -
> the Po is brought forth again."

The ancient Daoists believed that as the Human Soul (Yuan Shen) continued to live and work within the Physical World, it slowly began to lose its spiritual connection with the Dao. The subtle interconnections of the spiritual-self were eventually replaced with those of the sensory survival instincts, developed by the acquired self (with the help of the Po) for survival.

As the Eternal Soul (Shen Xian) enveloped itself within the Human Body's physical housing, its spiritual core becomes veiled by the illusionary existence of matter, space, and time. At this point in the individual's orientation and spiritual adjustment, the energetic fields of matter begin to dominate the individual's Yuan Shen (Original Spirit), giving rise to the birth and development of the individual's Shen Zhi (Acquired Personality).

According to ancient Daoist teachings, along with the individual's disconnection from their spiritual core and the development of the Shen Zhi, is also the development and formation of the belief in the Five Limitations. These Five Limitations inhibit the individual's personal power and potential, and are described as follows:

- **The Limitation To Accomplish:** The belief in the limitation of the individual's power and potential to accomplish all things.
- **The Limitation To Know:** The belief in the limitation of the individual's power and potential to know all things.
- **The Limitation To Live:** The limitation of the ability to utilize the individual's power and potential, by creating desire and attachment, thus giving rise to unceasing discontentment.
- **The Limitation Of Time:** The limitation of utilizing the individual's power and potential, by creating the illusion of time related life changes (e.g., birth, growth, maturation, waning and death).
- **The Limitation Of Life:** The limitation of utilizing the individual's free will, by creating Fate, thus binding an individual to the endless cycles of birth and death.

The development of the belief in the Five Limitations causes the individual's subtle connection to their Eternal Soul (Shen Xian) to "fall asleep," whereby allowing certain unique survival patterns to become initiated; facilitating the creation and development of the individual's acquired ego (Shen Zhi). The Shen Zhi's investment in emotional and mental survival, allows the acquired ego the ability to develop its unique personality.

The conscious state of the ego survival, operates through the individual's physical body via the five senses and analytical mind. The subconscious state of the ego operates through the individual's Spirit Body via the Dream State. When the individual is in a deep sleep or a meditative state, the ego retires into the Energy Body in the form of inner-awareness.

In order to reconnect with the divine, a spiritual "awakening" must occur, allowing the individual to remember and reexamine his lost spiritual state of existence. Once this "awakening" occurs, the individual must then come to the realization that he no longer needs to be attached to the acquired ego, acquired intellect, acquired memories, and acquired thought patterns. These four principles (acquired ego, intellect, memories, and thought patterns) constitute the medium through which the individual's consciousness and Shen Zhi act. It is the human consciousness that distinguishes the domain of man, separating him from the Mineral, Plant, and Animal Kingdoms.

An individual's relationship with his acquired ego, is considered to be the paradox of creation. Although the acquired ego energetically binds an individual to the Physical Realm of existence, it also allows for objective experiences. On the other hand, the acquired ego must also be completely eradicated in order to allow the individual the ability to reconnect with his True Self (Human Soul), and to begin experiencing true liberation through increased spiritual intuition.

Four Spiritual Paths of the Human Soul

The ancient Daoists believed that the true purpose for the Human Soul's journey into the Physical World was to evolve through four stages of spiritual transformation: the Path of Desire, the Path of Renunciation, the Path of Service and the Realization of Immortality (Figure 2.131). These four spiritual paths allow the individual to uncover and control the acquired patterns of the ego, to deepen the energetic and spiritual connections with the Heavenly and Earthly realms, and augment a relationship with the divine. These four spiritual paths are described as follows:

1. **The Path Of Desire:** The first challenge for the young Human Soul to overcome is the pursuit of the "Four Worms:" Pleasure, Wealth, Fame and Power. These four worms are said to eat away at the individual's spiritual growth. Each has its own inherited limitations and illusions, and none of them can ever be fully satisfied. These illusions, however, are considered to be necessary obstacles for the experience and development of young souls. As the soul matures, it will eventually overcome the fascination of the Path of Desire and seek something more fulfilling.

2. **The Path Of Renunciation:** The next stage that the Human Soul will experience is the Path of Renunciation. This entails avoiding any indulgences that interfere with the spiritual growth of the individual.

3. **The Path Of Service:** At this stage, the individual has overcome the fascinations of pleasure and success, and genuinely devotes himself to the role of service. As the individual continues to mature spiritually, however, he will eventually recognize that society is finite and that even patriotism, and all forms of social as well as communal activities cannot fully satisfy the Human Soul.

4. **The Realization Of Immortality:** At this final stage, the Human Soul understands "Infinite Beingness," experiencing and comprehending the infinite awareness and bliss present within his own core self. This realization allows the individual to feel and experience and deep connectedness with the divine and to all creation.

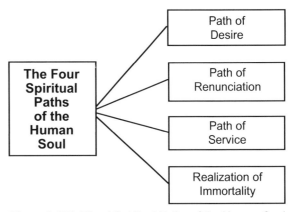

Figure 2.131. The 4 Spiritual Paths of the Human Soul

The Twelve Embryonic Knots and Death Roots of the Womb

According to the secret Daoist teachings of the Luo River Graph (Figure 2.132), the energy of Heaven is animated by clockwise (Yang) descending movements; while the energy of Earth is animated by counterclockwise (Yin) ascending movements. Therefore, the ancient Daoists believed that Man was formed through the energetic union of Yin and Yang Qi, created from the interactions of these opposing Heaven and Earth movements.

According to the ancient Daoist text, *The Book of the Superior Transformations of the Cinnabar Nine into the Essence of the Embryo*,

> "As the embryo develops,
> it receives the "Nine Breaths"
> of the Nine Primordial Heavens.
> These Nine Breaths are responsible
> for the spiralling transformations
> that occur during the process of
> Jing, Qi, and Shen embryonic development.
> Once all Heavenly Breaths are present,
> Birth occurs in the Tenth Lunar Month."

The Nine Breaths of the Nine Primordial Heavens, are various spiritual energies that exist within Heaven's Nine Celestial Realms. In the lower levels of the celestial realms, there are enlightened beings who coexist with other spiritual entities. Mankind is therefore believed to be the product of the energetic condensation of the spiritual breaths of these Nine Heavens, which

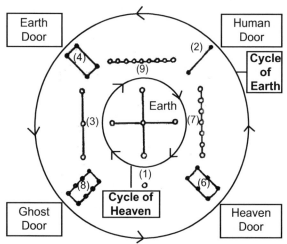

Figure 1.132. The Cycles of Heaven and Earth, According to the design of the Luo River Graph

are knotted and contained inside a person's Jing, transformed into spirit, and then formed into a human being.

In Daoist Alchemy, the progressive energetic development of the fetus during pregnancy is attributed to the intervention of a divine influx of spiralling Yin and Yang energy, known as the "Motion of the Nine Revolutions of Cinnabar."

During the time of pregnancy, as these Congenital Knots (twelve in number) begin to energetically form, they were considered by the ancient Daoists to be the "Death Roots Of The Womb." According to *The Book of the Superior Transformations of the Cinnabar Nine into the Essence of the Embryo*, an individual's life also contains a "Morbid Breath," and its energetic root is tightly formed into these twelve Embryonic Knots. Therefore, an individual also receives death at the same time that he or she receives life.

The ancient Daoists believed that these twelve embryonic knots have twelve nodules, and are divided into three groups of four, located within each of the Three Dantians. The three groups of four nodes are described as follows:

- **The Upper Four Nodules:** These special knots are located in the Upper Dantian, and are connected to the eyes, cheeks, and mouth.
- **The Middle Four Nodules:** These special knots are located in the internal viscera of the Middle Dantian, and are specifically connected to the Stomach, Small Intestine, and Large Intestine.
- **The Lower Four Nodules:** These special knots are located in the Lower Dantian, and are specifically connected to the Urinary Bladder, reproductive organs, anus, and feet.

The ancient Daoists believed that when an individual's Fate was cut short, it was because the Twelve Embryonic Knots became too tight, causing the Morbid Breath to become released.

THE FINAL EXIT OF THE HUMAN SOUL

From the most ancient times, the Chinese have considered death itself to be a temporary state of transition, which may be followed by the return of the Eternal Soul back to the Earth for additional "training." At the time of death, the individual will begin to release the accumulation of the Five Element energies that have amassed inside the body in order to constitute the energetic matrix of the individuals physical, energetic, and spirit bodies. As they slowly dissolve their attachment to the Three Body's energetic fields, each of the Five Element energies will disperse back into nature.

At the time of death, the Five Elements will begin to release their energetic attachment to the individual's Three Bodies, and the spiritual components of the Five Pure Lights (responsible for the energetic creation and formation of the prenatal tissues) will return back to their original energetic state, dissolving back into the infinite space of the Wuji. The individual's transforming Human Soul (Original Spirit or Yuan Shen) is then returned back to its original energetic form as a Ling Shen (Supernatural Spirit), and the Shen Xian (Eternal Soul) is released back into the infinite space of the Wuji, in order to reconnect with the divine. Once it has been released, the Ling Shen will go through a reprocessing time, before it is allowed to reincarnate back to Earth as a new form.

In a "normal" death-bed situation, just before the spirit separates itself from the decaying tissues of the Physical Body, the Yuan Shen (Human Soul) prepares itself for its final journey home. This internal transformation process, initiated by the spiritual energies of the dying person, is crucial.

PREPARATION FOR DEATH

At the time of death, it is important that the Human Soul disconnect itself from the energy fields of the Three Dantians and Three Bodies, and exit the patient's dying body.

When the Medical Qigong Doctor is assisting a terminally ill patient, treatment focuses primarily on purging stagnant spiritual energy from the patient's dying body. This spiritual purging is required in order to purify and cleanse the patient's Spirit Body. Once the energetic fields surrounding the Human Soul have been cleansed, and all physical, emotional, and spiritual attachments to this life have been released, the patient becomes peaceful. As the patient attains a sense of completion, he begins to welcome the final adventure of going home. At this time in his passing, he will traditionally receive the "Last Rites," performed by his priest or spiritual mentor.

The Medical Qigong Doctor will then encourage and lead the patient's Human Soul up the center core of their Taiji Pole, in order to leave the dying body through the top of the head (Baihui). According to ancient Daoist belief, souls that are more highly spiritually evolved will exit the body through the top of the head, while souls of lesser spiritual evolution will exit the body through lower portions of the body's physical structure. The energetic formation of a "Gui" (ghost) is said to emerge from the un-transformed energy of the Human Soul, manifested from the individual's Po (see Volume 2, Chapter 20).

The ancient Daoists considered death to be a separation of Yin and Yang energy. As an individual ages, for example, the Yin increases at the expense of the Yang, and death marks the total separation of the two. Likewise, the Human Soul also contains both elements of Yin and Yang. The Yin aspect of the soul is called a Gui (ghost) the Yang aspect of the soul is called a Shen (spirit).

Emanating from the Human Soul is the individual's Yuan Shen (Original Spirit/Mind). The Yuan Shen consists of Yang energetic substance and is associated with the body's Yuan Qi and the Hun of Heaven.

The individual's Gui consists of Yin energetic substance, and is associated with the Po and Earth. The union of the energetic and spiritual substances of the individual's Gui and Shen constitutes the matrix of his internal being, allowing for the connection and absorption of both universal and environmental Five Element energies. According to writings from Wei Liaoweng during the Yuan Dynasty (1279-1368 A.D.),

"The Hun joins and gathers Qi into a Mass, While the Po unites and consolidates it."

Therefore upon the death of the physical body, the Hun ascends, becoming a Shen and returns to Heaven; the Po descends becoming a Gui and returns to Earth. The energy of Tai Yi from the Upper Dantian, and Xia Tao Kang from the Lower Dantian, envelop the Eternal Soul stored in the Middle Dantian with Si Ming. These three spiritual energies (Tai Yi, Xia Tao Kang, and Si Ming) blend together, combining into one energy that completes the integration of the Human Soul (Figure 2.133).

The Human Soul then leaves the physical body as a shining Shenming ("Bright Spirit") and is escorted by the Five Pure Lights, to return back to the source from which it came. At this phase, the Eternal Soul (Shen Xian) will experience the judgements and subsequent consequences of all of the individual's actions and non-actions, when it existed on Earth in the form of a Human Soul.

However, if the individual's spirit still possesses a strong emotional attachment to unresolved issues that transpired while it was in human form, the unreleased energy of the Human Soul will not be able to elevate its lower vibrational resonance. If this occurs, the individual's spirit will become energetically stuck in the lower vibrational plane, and begin to wander the Earth in its Yin form as a Gui (ghost).

In ancient China, when an individual died, there was a ceremony traditionally performed by the family and a Daoist priest called a "Zhao Hun" or "The Calling of the Hun." This ritual was part of the Funeral Ceremony, and entailed someone (i.e., a relative or the deceased individual's mate) going

Spiritual Energy	Resides in	Associated Dantian	Purpose	
Tai Yi Great Divinity	the head as light	Upper Dantian (intuitive communication)	Governs the body's spirits, makes life shine forth, and encourages mankind to know the spirits of his or her Three Ethereal Souls	
Si Ming Administrator of Destiny	the Heart as vibration	Dantian Middle Dantian (empathic communication)	The Eternal Soul—regulates the primal energy of life (Qi) and is the source of emotions and the mind Controls the Wu Ying and Bai Yuan Spirits	Wu Ying (Without Essence), occupies the left side of the body and regulates the Three Hun (Ethereal Souls), associated with the Liver
				Bai Yuan (Pure Origin) occupies the right side of the body and regulates the Seven Po (Corporeal Souls), associated with the Lungs
Xia Tao Kang Below Healthy Peach (life)	the navel as heat	Lower Dantian (kinetic communication)	Preserves the root of the body's Essence (Jing)	

Figure 2.133. The patient's human soul resides in his or her Taiji Pole, and relates with Si Ming, the Administrator of Destiny. Upon the death of the physical body, the three Hun return to Heaven and the seven Po return to Earth, while the energy of Tai Yi and Xia Tao Kang envelop the Eternal Soul (stored in Si Ming) and combine into one energy. The human soul leaves the body through the particular gate (solar plexus, third eye, or top of the head) associated with the patient's degree of spiritual evolution, and returns through the tunnel of light to the divine.

to the roof of the deceased individual's house, and calling to the deceased person's Hun, begging it to return back into its body. It was believed that if the deceased individual's Hun did not return, then their Po would now begin its descent into the Earth, and the physical body's tissues would start to decay.

In order to insure that the deceased individual's Po would stay inside the decaying body after it had been buried (and that the spirit of the deceased individual would not come out to annoy the living) the relatives would seal all of the deceased individual's body orifices (exits). This was used in order to trap and seal the deceased individual's Po inside Physical Body. Traditionally, the orifices of the deceased individual's body were plugged with either jade or rice (depending on the family's financial status).

"Picking Up One's Steps"

In ancient China, it was believed that if an individual was about to prematurely die, and he suddenly saw his life flash before his eyes, it was the projected images of his Yuan Shen (Original Spirit). The individual's Yuan Shen quickly makes a fast review of all the good and bad deeds that have been committed during this visit to the material world. The ancient Daoists called this spiritual phenomena "Picking Up One's Steps."

In Religious Daoist practice, it is believed that all individuals have this unique experience right after their death, which allows them to understand exactly what the Three Judges of Death (i.e., The Judge of Heaven, The Judge of Earth, and The Judge of Water) will be reviewing when they pass sentence on their spirit soul. However, some individuals who suddenly suffer from a severe shock when faced with the potential of an unexpected death, accidentally visualize their whole lives within a couple of seconds. These earthly images are the last ones that the individual will see in his or her present reincarnation. After that, he or she will be judged and sentenced by the Three Judges of Death and will have to wait for the next cycle of reincarnation to begin again.

Chapter 2: Understanding Ancient Chinese Metaphysics

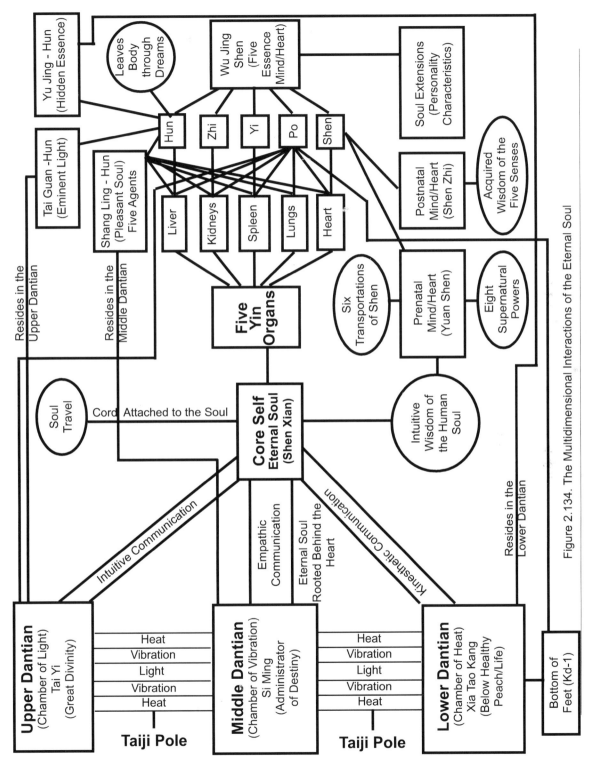

Figure 2.134. The Multidimensional Interactions of the Eternal Soul

Overview

One of the unique healing aspects of ancient Chinese Energetic Medicine, is that it addresses all facets of the individual's body, energy, and spirit. It explores in great detail the spiritual transformations that take place during the body's prenatal development, as well as the energetic relationship of fetal development, as it progresses towards the internal formation of the adult body. It also covers the energetic transformations that occur during the internal stages of the dying and after-death states.

Ancient Chinese Medicine further addresses the potential of spiritual involvement, as a cause or cure of specific psycho-physical diseases.

It is only through the complete and thorough study of an individual's physical, mental, emotional, energetic, and spiritual aspects, that a doctor of Medical Qigong Therapy will ascertain how, and when to treat a patient.

According to ancient Daoist teachings, every human is a multidimensional being, existing within three energetic fields, inside Three Worlds. Although the energetic forms of our Essence (Jing), Energy (Qi), and Mind/Spirit (Shen) compose our present personality, they also exist within three different dimensions of vibrational frequencies. These energetic fields overshadow and are interlinked together, by their corresponding relationships to the alchemical transformations that maintain their vitality and keep the human body alive.

The metaphysical abilities of the individual's Shen (Mind/Heart) are the spiritual manifestations of the Eternal Soul (Shen Xian). Once the Medical Qigong Doctor regulates his or her own spiritual life, these supernatural abilities become natural and internalized, giving way to the development of advanced diagnostic abilities.

A chart describing the internal interactions of the body's Eternal Soul with the energetic functions of the Three Dantians and Five Yin Organs' Wujingshen (Five Essence Spirits) is located at Figure 2.134.

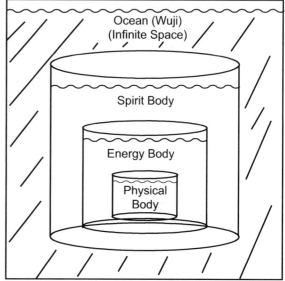

Figure 2.135. Jars of Water Floating Inside An Ocean

In ancient China, when a Daoist disciple was focusing on any form of meditation that required him to extend his Energy Body and Spirit Body away from his Physical Body, it was important that he first relax all Three Bodies, before releasing his Mind into these three energy fields. In order to comprehend this secret type of esoteric teaching, my teacher privately explained the following visual example, stating that our Three Bodies and their relationship to the Three Realms were similar to three jars of water floating inside an ocean (Figure 2.135):

*"You are composed of Three Bodies,
a Physical Body, an Energy Body,
and a Spirit Body.*

*Think of a jar of water
(your Physical Body)
existing inside a bigger jar of water
(your Energy Body),
contained inside an even bigger jar of water
(your Spirit Body),
residing inside a vast ocean
(the infinite space of the Wuji).*

*Once you are able to open and release
the contents of the last jar of water
(i.e., the Spirit Body), you are on your way
to True Enlightenment and Freedom."*

Chapter 3
Tissue Formation and Development

Internal Fascial Development and Energy Flow

After being generated within the body's internal organs, Qi is then distributed throughout the body's entire energetic network through the channels and collaterals, via the internal fascia. Each organ has its own layers of web-like fascia that covers, connects, protects, and nourishes its tissues. Fascia also forms the energetic chambers of the body's organs and channels, allowing Qi to flow between the fascial sheaths and along the internal channel systems.

According to the *American Medical Association Encyclopedia of Medicine*, "fascia is the fibrous connective tissue that surrounds many structures in the body (Figure 3.1). One layer of this special tissue, known as the superficial fascia, envelops the entire body just beneath the skin. Another layer, the deep fascia, encloses the muscles, forming a sheath for individual muscles, and also separates them into groups. The deep fascia also holds in place the body's internal organs, such as the Kidneys. The thick fascia in the palms of the hands and soles of the feet have a cushioning, protective function."

In Chinese Energetic Medicine, the fascia are commonly referred to as "Huang," meaning any membranous tissue. Its internal development is divided into two stages: Prenatal Fascia and Postnatal Fascia, described as follows:

- **The Prenatal Fascia:** This type of internal fascia is congenitally formed. It is "fixed" and determined by the combination of the parents' Yuan Jing, Yuan Qi, and Yuan Shen.
- **The Postnatal Fascia:** This type of internal fascia is acquired. It is formed through individual diet, exercise, and environmental stress.

Qi is stored within the tissues and inner fascial layers, where it envelops and protects the body's internal organs. Energy that has been stored within the body's organs is available through the fascia to nourish the body's Jing, Qi, and Shen.

The body consists of three tissue layers, described as follows (Figure 3.2):

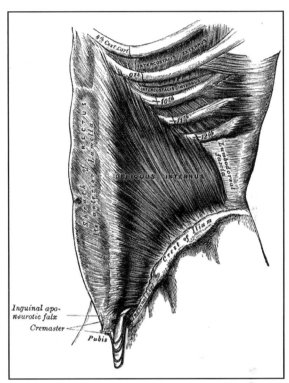

Figure 3.1 The Body's Inner Fascia
(Artwork from Gray's Anatomy)

Outermost Layer	Second Layer	Innermost Layer
Muscles and Skin where Weiqi circulates to protect the body from invasion of External Pathogens such as Cold, Damp, Wind, Heat	Fascia, Tendons, Ligaments, and Bones which assist in Transporting Qi to the Extremities	Internal Organs which Produce and Transform Qi
←——————————————————→		

Figure 3.2 The Three Tissue Layers of the Body

1. **Internal Organs:** The first and innermost layer is made of the internal organs which produce and transform Qi.
2. **Connective Tissue and Bones:** The second layer consists of the body's Connective Tissues (i.e., fascia, tendons, and ligaments) and Bones, which assist in transporting Qi to the extremities.
3. **Muscles and Skin:** The third and outermost layer of tissue consists of the muscles and skin, where Weiqi circulates to protect the organism from invasion of external pathogens such as Cold, Heat, Wind, and Dampness, etc.

In its various forms, the fascia is the basic connective element that weaves together all other body tissues. It is the internal fascia that ultimately determines and maintains the body's structure. This structure is in part an adaptation and response of the body's fascial network to the stresses of the external environment. Therefore, our internal and external constitutions are formed, in part, by conditions from the environment that affect the innermost layers of fascial development. For example, the internal fascia can form adhesions through trauma, infection, surgery, disease, or chronic muscular tension. These fascial adhesions restrict the flow of Qi and Blood to the tissues, thereby accelerating the aging process.

Modern Traditional Chinese Medicine divides the observation and diagnosis of the physical characteristics and patterns of the body's inner fascia into Yin and Yang structures and Five Elemental constitutions.

THE THREE TYPES OF ANCIENT BODY CLASSIFICATIONS

The ancient Wuyi (Shaman Doctors) taught three different ways of classifying and diagnosing the energetic patterns of an individual's body shape and tissue formation: Diagnosis According to Prenatal and Postnatal Influences, Diagnosis According to Five Element Influences, and Diagnosis According to Yin or Yang Influences. These three unique classifications are described as follows (Figure 3.3):

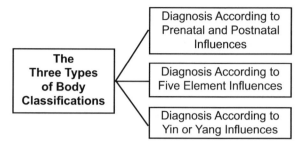

Figure 3.3 The ancient Wuyi (Shaman Doctors) taught three different ways of classifying and diagnosing the energetic patterns of an individual's body shape and tissue formation.

- **Diagnosis According to Prenatal and Postnatal Influences:** In this type of diagnosis, the shaman doctor observed the influence of the specific strengths or weaknesses initiated by both the patient's Prenatal and Postnatal constitutional formations.

  This type of diagnosis determined each patient's inclination towards specific congenital or acquired disease patterns.

- **Diagnosis According to Five Element Influences:** In this type of diagnosis, the shaman doctor observed the energetic formation and influence of the patient's Five Element Constitution.

  This type of diagnosis determined each Element's continual influence (balanced, excessive or deficient) on the patient's Jing, Qi, and Shen.

- **Diagnosis According to Yin or Yang Influences:** In this type of diagnosis, the shaman doctor observed the dominant Yin and Yang formation of the patient's constitution.

  This type of diagnosis determined the overall dominant energetically induced patterns of the patient's tissues (introverted, extroverted or balanced state).

To better comprehend the ancient Wuyi classification of the human body's physical development and structural formations, it is important to begin with an understanding of some of the basic principles of the human body according to ancient Daoist Alchemy.

CHAPTER 3: TISSUE FORMATION AND DEVELOPMENT

	Yang	Yin
Attributes	Active, Creative, Masculine, Fire, Hot, Heaven, Light	Passive, Receptive, Feminine, Water, Cold, Earth, Dark
Organs	The Six Hollow Yang Organs: Gall Bladder, Small Intestine, Stomach, Large Intestine, Urinary Bladder, and Triple Burners	The Five Solid Yin Organs: Liver, Heart, Spleen, Lungs, and Kidneys
Respiration	Exhalation	Inhalation
Time of Day	The 12 Hour Yang Cycle: From 11 p.m. (Before Midnight) to 11 a.m. (Before High Noon)	The 12 Hour Yin Cycle: From 11 a.m. (Before Noon) to 11 p.m. (Before Midnight)
Seasons	Spring and Summer	Autumn and Winter
Pathological Movement	Turbid Yang Flows Upward like Fire	Turbid Yin Flows Downward like Water
Normal Movement	Heavenly Yang Flows Downward From the Sky	Earthly Yin Flows Upward from the Soil

Figure 3.4 Yin and Yang Are the governing forces of the body.

YIN & YANG STRUCTURAL FORMATION

Ancient Daoist Alchemy teaches that the universe is composed of a duality of opposing forces or energies known as Yin and Yang. Everything in the natural world contains both Yin and Yang. Yin and Yang are interdependent; Yin cannot grow without Yang, and Yang cannot develop without Yin. The energetic transformation of Yin into Yang and Yang into Yin produces the various changes observed in matter and form.

Accordingly, Yin and Yang are also the principles governing all things within the human body. Life and death originate from the energies of Yin and Yang, and they are the forces that create all physiological change. In ancient Daoist Alchemy, the physical structure of the human body was divided into Yin and Yang organs, Yin and Yang substances, and Yin and Yang energetic functions (e.g., Qi that expands and flows outward is Yang, while Qi that contracts and flows inward is Yin).

Yin and Yang are in a constant state of waxing and waning (Figure 3.4). If this waxing and waning exceeds the body's natural energetic limitations and the body loses its dynamic equilibrium, deficiency

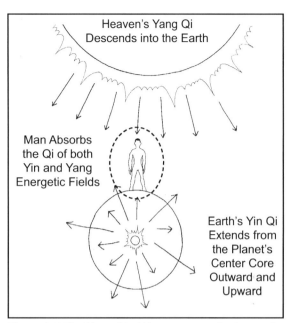

Figure 3.5 The Yang Qi of Heaven naturally descends, and the Yin Qi of the Earth naturally ascends.

or excess of either Yin or Yang will occur, leading to the development of abnormalities and illness.

Additionally, the Yin Qi of the Earth was believed to naturally ascend upward from the core of the planet (Figure 3.5). It was therefore believed that Earth Qi naturally enters into the body via the Kidney, Liver, and Spleen Channels of the legs, and moves upward through the body feeding and supporting the tissues. When Yin Qi becomes pathological, weak, turbid, or destructive, it reverses its energetic flow and moves downward, descending like cascading water. For example, descending Spleen Qi due to deficiency can cause tiredness, incontinence, diarrhea, edema or prolapse of the viscera.

Likewise, the Yang Qi of Heaven naturally descends downward, towards the core of the planet. For example, Heaven Qi enters the Stomach, Urinary Bladder and Gall Bladder Channels and flows downward into the Earth. When Yang Qi becomes pathological, weak or destructive, it reverses its energetic flow and ascends upward like the flames of a fire. For example, Rebellious Stomach Qi ascends upward, causing nausea and vomiting. Another example of pathogenic Yang Qi ascending would be the temperature of a rising fever.

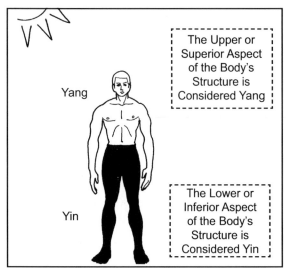

Figure 3.6. The top of the body's structure is Yang; the bottom portion of the body is Yin. Think of the Sun shining on the upper torso, illuminating the body from the head to the waist, while the lower torso, from the hips down toward the feet, is hidden in the shade.

YIN AND YANG ANATOMICAL ASPECTS

The ancient Wuyi (Shaman Doctors) of Chinese Energetic Medicine were among the first to develop a standardized system to describe the various anatomical features, locations and regions of the human body using Yin and Yang terminologies.

Similar to Western Anatomy, Chinese Energetic Medicine also divides the human body into anatomical planes. However, these classifications are divided into either Yin or Yang physical planes and anatomical directions.

These divisions aid the Medical Qigong Doctor in defining and categorizing the patient's tissues and body structure. They also assist him in determining the specific collection and type of energetic movement (i.e., if energy is moving into and Qi is coalescing within a predominantly Yin or Yang area of a patient's body).

The Yin and Yang structural aspects of Chinese Energetic Medicine are categorized as follows:
- The Cranial or Superior aspect (top half) of the body's structure is considered Yang; the Caudal or Inferior portion of the body (bottom half) is considered Yin (Figure 3.6)

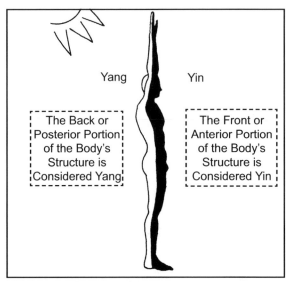

Figure 3.7. The back of the body's structure is Yang; while the front portion of the body is Yin. Think of the Sun shining on the back of the body, while the front of the body is kept in the shade.

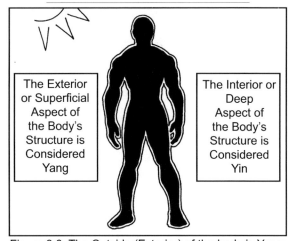

Figure 3.8. The Outside (Exterior) of the body is Yang; The deep (interior) portion of the body is Yin. Think of the Sun shining on the external surfaces of the body, while the internal organs remain in the dark.

- The Posterior or Dorsal portion (back side) of the body is considered Yang; the Anterior or Ventral portion (front side) is considered Yin (Figure 3.7)
- The Superficial aspect (Exterior) of the body is considered Yang; the Deep portion (Interior) of the body is considered Yin (Figure 3.8)

CHAPTER 3: TISSUE FORMATION AND DEVELOPMENT

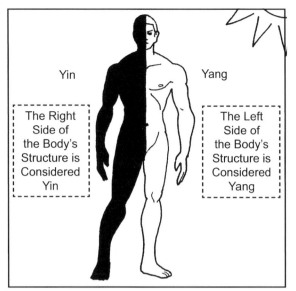

Figure 3.9. The left side of the body is Yang; While the right side of the body is Yin. Think of facing South in the morning, while practicing Medical Qigong Exercises. The Sun will rise in the East, illuminating and warming the left side (Yang) of the body; while the right side will remains in the cool shade (Yin).

- The Left side of the body is considered Yang; the Right side is considered Yin (Figure 3.9)
- The Lateral aspect (further from the center) of the body is considered Yang; the Medial portion (middle) is considered Yin (Figure 3.10)

These Yin and Yang structural aspects of Chinese Energetic Anatomy are defined in polar relationship to each other (Figure 3.11). It is important to remember this energetic point of relativity, when considering the anatomical aspects of Yin and Yang. In clinical observation, for example, Yin and Yang are mostly used to describe the dominant nature or quality of something (e.g., is it energetically Hot or Cold, Excess or Deficient). The most common mistake is to view Yin and Yang as representing the fixed nature of a particular person, place, or thing, rather than simply seeing it in its dominant energetic nature. The quality of an objects Yin and Yang nature are in a constant state of change, always waxing and waning. Two points of reference alone are not enough to

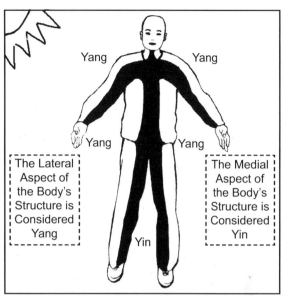

Figure 3.10. The further from the center of the body is Yang; the middle portion of the body is Yin. Think of the Sun shining on the furthest parts of the external tissues, while the center is still in the shade.

Yang	Yin
Superior (Upper)	Inferior (Lower)
Posterior (Back)	Anterior (Front)
Superficial (External)	Deep (Internal)
Left Side	Right Side
Lateral (Away from Center)	Medial (Middle)

Figure 3.11. The Yin and Yang Anatomical Aspects

sufficiently classify the many phases and stages of physical and energetic transformation. For example, day (Yang) can be further divided into Dawn (waxing Yang), Midday (peaking Yang), and Late Afternoon (waning Yang); while night (Yin) can be further divided into Late Afternoon (waxing Yin), Midnight (peaking Yin), and Dawn (waning Yin).

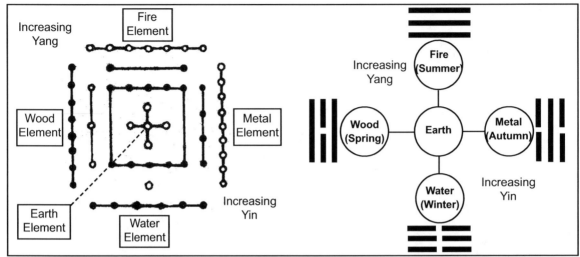

Figure 3.12. The Original Daoist Five Element Pattern - According to the Design of the Hetu River Graph

THE BODY'S FIVE ELEMENT PATTERN

The body contains the energetic attributes of Five Elements, sometimes translated as the Five Phases (Wu Xing). These special Five Element Qi (Wood, Fire, Earth, Metal, and Water), were traditionally used by the ancient Daoists in order to describe the energetic states of nature, and were originally introduced into ancient Chinese society via the special designs of the Hetu River Graph (Figure 3.12).

The ancient Daoists used the unique framework of the Five Elements in order to explain, classify, and characterize all natural phenomena. This Five Element categorization helped the ancient Daoists to understand the various movements of the Heavens and the different land forms of the Earth. It also helped them in comprehending the energetic workings of the ever changing human anatomy, physiology, and its psychology.

Each of the Five Element energies were used in order to describe the unique shapes, movements, tastes, sounds, colors, directions, forces, and energetic functions. For example:
- **Wood (Spring-Windy) Qi:** Describes an expansive period of growth, which generates abundant New Yang vitality.
- **Fire (Summer-Hot) Qi:** Describes an ascending period of expansion, which radiates outward with Full Yang energy.
- **Earth (Transition-Harmonizing) Qi:** Describes the in-between transitional period.

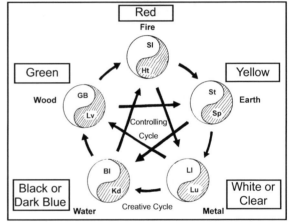

Figure 3.13. The Five Element (Wu Xing) Creating Cycle (Outside) and Controlling Cycle (Inside)

This Yin and Yang Balanced energy was sometimes viewed as a separate "season" known as "Late Summer" or "Long Summer," and was associated with Dampness.
- **Metal (Autumn-Dry) Qi:** Describes a contracting period of harvest and collection, with New Yin energy.
- **Water (Winter-Cold) Qi:** Describes a descending period of retreat, where stillness and storage pervade the Full Yin energy.

To the ancient Daoists, the Five Element energies painted a clear and natural image of the ever changing cycles of celestial and terrestrial Yin and

Chapter 3: Tissue Formation and Development

The Seven Toxic Internal Emotional States

Emotion			Associated Yin Organ	Description Of Emotional Characteristic	Energetic Manifestation
Xi (Joy)	禧		Heart	Over-Excitement, Mania	Slows Down and Relaxes the Qi
Nu (Anger)	怒		Liver	Irritation, Frustration, Resentment, Indignation, Anger, Rage, Fury	Causes Qi to Rise
Si (Worry)	思		Spleen and Lungs	Concern, Worry, Fret, Distress, Obsession, Torment	Causes Qi to Stagnate or Knot
You (Anxiety)	忧		Lungs	Excessive Thinking, Pensiveness, Anxiety	Obstructs & Knots the Flow of the Qi
Kong (Fear)	恐		Kidneys	Fear, Dread, Terror, Feeling Threatened or Intimidated	Causes Qi to Descend
Jing (Shock)	惊		Heart then Kidneys	Surprise, Fright, Alarm, Shock	Scatters and Deranges the Qi
Bei (Sadness)	悲		Lungs and Heart	Melancholy, Sadness, Sorrow, Grief	Disperses and Consumes the Qi

Figure 3.14. The Seven Emotions and their energetic manifestations within the human body

Yang Qi (see Volume 3, Chapter 24). Furthermore, each of these Five Element energies could be additionally separated into a Yin and Yang division, making a total of ten subdivisions (Figure 3.13):
- **Wood:** The Liver (Yin) and Gall Bladder (Yang) correspond to the Wood Element Qi;
- **Fire:** The Heart (Yin) and Small Intestine (Yang) correspond to the Fire Element Qi;
- **Earth:** The Spleen (Yin) and Stomach (Yang) correspond to the Earth Element Qi;
- **Metal:** The Lungs (Yin) and Large Intestine (Yang) correspond to the Metal Element Qi;
- **Water:** The Kidneys (Yin) and Urinary Bladder (Yang) correspond to the Water Element Qi.

These internal organ correspondences express the functional aspects of the Five Elements within the human body, as they interact with each other in order to promote and maintain life.

The Five Yin Organs (i.e., the Liver, Heart, Spleen, Lungs, and Kidneys) are all said to store the Jing (Essence) of the Five Elements, though they share this essence with their elementally paired Yang Organs. While the Yin Organs serve as repositories that gather and store the Jing of the Five Elements, the Five Yang Organs (Gall Bladder, Small Intestine, Stomach, Large Intestine, and Urinary Bladder) mobilize and utilize this gathered Jing in order to perform various functions specific to each organ (i.e., transforming, transporting, etc.).

The Five Yin Organs also store the Five Agents (i.e., the Original Five Virtues of the Five Pure Lights), and are more easily energetically disrupted by the Seven Emotions (Joy, Anger, Worry, Anxiety, Fear, Shock, and Sadness) than the Five Yang Organs. When in excess, the body's emotions can create an energetic imbalance, which in turn can cause a destructive physical pattern to occur within the body (Figure 3.14). An example of this toxic process is excessive anger leading to hypertension.

The emotions are said to be the motivational force behind energy transformation within each individual. However, people will have a different reaction to specific emotional changes based on their dominant Five Element Constitutional pattern.

The Congenital Constitutions

The energies of the Five Elements shape all aspects of a human being. Most individuals are born with a dominant Element pattern, which will determine that individual's physical, energetic, and psycho-emotional constitution. When excess or deficient, the body's emotions can create an energetic imbalance, which in turn can lead to a destructive physical pattern within the body.

Understanding Pattern (Li) & Energy (Qi)

The ancient Daoists believed that the two fundamental properties of Nature, "Li" (Pattern) and "Qi" (Energy), establish the foundation of all existence. Throughout the universe there can be no Qi without Li, nor Li without Qi. They also believed that Li (Pattern) was the Dao (Way) from which all Forms (Xing) from the Heavens above and the Earth below were originally organized. Therefore Li was considered to be the foundational roots from which all things were produced.

Qi (Energy) is the instrument that originally composed all Form within the Earth, and provided the tools and raw material from which all things are made. Therefore, all things must receive Li (cosmic and organic patterning) in their creative moment of coming into existence; and obtain their specific Nature and Form (Xing) through energy and matter.

The ancient Daoists believed that an individual's Li (Pattern) was molded through the assistance of the "Five Pure Lights," which were responsible for assisting the Eternal Soul (Shen Xian) in molding the Five Element Jing (the body's original Essence) into "Wu Cai" (Five Materials). While in-utero, these Five Materials began to manifest within the Physical Realm as five types of tissue formations (i.e., the physical manifestations of Wood Qi, Fire Qi, Earth Qi, Metal Qi, and Water Qi).

The previous chapter on energetic embryology described the different Five Element Jings (Essences) and how they enter the fetus via each of the mother's organs from the fourth to the eighth lunar month of pregnancy. Depending on the relative strength or weakness of the mother's internal organ energies during her pregnancy, the fetus will inherit a greater or lesser amount of Five Element Jing from the mother. If the mother's Liver energy is dominant, then the child will have a tendency to develop a Wood Element Constitution; if her Kidney energy is dominant, then the child develops a Water Element Constitution, and so forth.

Ancient Chinese Astrology states that the various Heavenly influences present at the time of conception and birth energetically influence the relative Five Element strengths and weaknesses inherent within a newborn's constitution. Thus, the Astrological influences at conception and birth as well as the prenatal maternal transmission of Jing, Qi, and Shen determine each person's Congenital Constitution.

After birth, the Prenatal Jing is cultivated and sustained through prayer, meditation, physical exercise, and sleep, which are described as follows:

- **In Prayer:** The Jing is given guidance, direction and purpose
- **In Meditation:** The Jing is refined
- **In Exercise:** The Jing is nourished, energized and cleansed through alternating Yin and Yang movements
- **In Sleep:** The Jing is replenished

The health of the Prenatal Jing determines the physical and energetic balance of the overall constitution, the level of vitality and resistance to disease, as well as the mental and emotional natures of the individual. The Prenatal Jing, with its unique balance of the Five Elements, becomes the foundation for an individual's Qi and Shen.

The congenital influence is, however, not absolute. Postnatal factors, such as diet, life-style, environmental influences, and internal belief structures all either support or undermine the health and balance of the individual's constitution. Thus, patients with congenital deficiencies can still improve their health by prayer, meditation, Medical Qigong, adequate sleep, proper diet and exercise, herbs, medicines, stress management, and other therapeutic modalities.

On the negative side, patients with strong inherited constitutions may still develop serious constitutional imbalances through intemperate lifestyles such as chronic stress, overwork, excessive sexual activity, or poor eating habits. Therefore, the doctor must consider both prenatal (congenital) and postnatal (acquired) constitutional factors to understand and differentiate between the patient's innate constitution and his current condition.

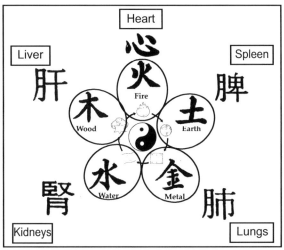

Figure 3.15. The Five Element Creative Cycle

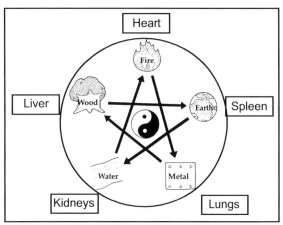

Figure 3.16. The Five Element Controlling Cycle

CLASSIFICATION OF THE FIVE ELEMENT PHYSICAL CONSTITUTIONS

Over the centuries, much has been written in Chinese medical literature about the Five Element Constitutions. For example, the Five Element Physical Constitutions are associated with the Five Yin Organs, and have numerous physical, energetic and spiritual correspondences (e.g., each Element is expressed through different emotions, colors, tastes, body types, illnesses and thought patterns).

Because each of the Five Element Constitutions has both a characteristic physical appearance and a corresponding psycho-emotional profile, through observing these special characteristics, the ancient Wuyi (Shaman Doctors) could determine a patient's Five Element Constitution. From this diagnosis, the doctor would then discover much about the balance or imbalance of the patient's physical and mental health.

In Traditional Chinese Medicine, an individual's body type and his or her psyche are closely intertwined. Physical aspects such as coloring, proportion, dominant tissue (muscle, fat, sinew, etc.), tone, movement, postural patterns, as well as general vitality, all express the patient's internal energetic and psycho-emotional matrices. This body type patterning reveals much about the patient's innate personality and acquired personality, as well as his or her emotional history.

Each of the Five Element Constitutions is subdivided into three categories: Yin Nature, Yang Nature, and Balanced Nature. The goal is to have a Balanced Nature, regardless of one's Element type. Since the Mind/Heart (Shen) is closely tied with the Jing and Qi, it is not enough to simply tell a patient how to change their personality in order to restore balance. The doctor must also work with a patient on all levels (i.e., physical, energetic, and spiritual) to help them restore balance. Specific healing methods are discussed at length in later chapters.

The doctor normally selects treatment principles based on the Five Element Creative (Figure 3.15) and Controlling (Figure 3.16) Cycles to help restore balance. For example, a patient with a Yin Wood Nature might tend to have weak or Deficient Wood Qi. Therapeutically, the doctor would choose one of the three following treatment methods:

1. Direct Tonification of the Wood Element
2. Tonification of the Water Element in accordance with the principle, "To nourish the child, strengthen the mother"
3. Disperse or reduce the Metal Element (Metal, the "grandmother," may be "Overcontrolling" Wood, the "grandson")

A patient with a Yang Wood Nature might tend to have Excess Wood Qi. In this case, the doctor would choose one of the two treatment methods:

1. A Purging method to reduce the Wood Element
2. Strengthen the Metal Element to control the Wood Element.

THE WOOD ELEMENT CONSTITUTION

The energetic Pattern (Li) and Form (Xing) of a Wood Element person is structurally shaped like a tree. According to ancient Daoist teachings, a Wood Element person can be identified by their "Three Longs:" Long Face, Long Body, and Long Fingers.

- **Long Face:** A Wood Element person has a small head and a long face; that is wide on top and narrow at the bottom.
- **Long Body:** They have a tall and sinewy body. They are bony with scant flesh, and have wide, slouching shoulders, small torsos, and a straight, flat back (Figure 3.17). Their dominant features include strong sinews.
- **Long Fingers:** They have well-proportioned, long, nicely formed hands and feet, with knotted joints. Their fingernails tend to have a normal convex curvature (Figure 3.18).
- **Complexion:** They usually have a subtle shade of green/blue in their complexion, and a solemn looking demeanor. This is because they are prone to anger, manifested by bulging, green veins.
- **Talking:** Their speech is blunt and short, with words sounding "thin," as though coming from the teeth.
- **Walking:** They walk with a noisy, marching gait, lifting the feet and letting them drop.
- **Season:** By nature, they enjoy the Spring and Summer seasons. This preference is due to the inherent vulnerabilities of their Wood Element Constitution, making them especially susceptible to pathogenic invasion and disease during the Autumn and Winter seasons.
- **Pattern (Li):** Their energetic pattern is a observed as a Rectangular shape
- **Energy (Qi):** Their energetic manifestation is expansive growth, and abundant vitality
- **Sound:** Their energetic sound is "Jue" (E).
- **Color:** Their energetic color is "Green-Blue."
- **Organ:** Their Yin dominant internal organ is the "Liver," which is paired with the Yang Gall Bladder organ.
- **Direction:** Their cardinal direction is East
- **Planet:** Their celestial planet is Jupiter

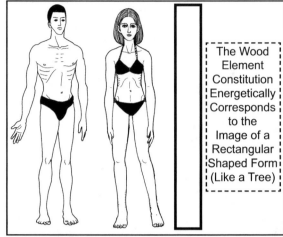

Figure 3.17. The Wood Constitution (Three Longs)

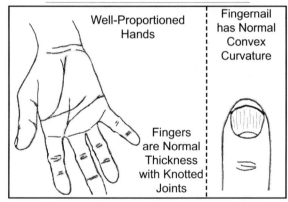

Figure 3.18. Wood Constitution Hand Features

THE WOOD ELEMENT PERSONALITY

The Wood Element personality can be categorized into three specific subdivisions, which are described as follows:

1. **A Balanced Wood Element Nature:** Predisposes individuals to be confident, strong, independent, and intuitive, with a clear understanding of themselves and their goals. They are patient, able to allow things to develop naturally, and express their personality in a relaxed and harmonious way. They are kind when communicating with others, creative, free-flowing in self-expression, and display merciful and unselfish traits when dealing with the needs of others. They are able to establish and maintain healthy and proper boundaries (Figure 3.19).

2. **A Yin Wood Element Nature:** Predisposes individuals to feel externally insecure and to be overcautious. They have a tendency to worry and have a weak sense of their own abilities and potential. They are unassertive and are unsure of their identities and life purpose. They also have difficulty expressing their egos and have weak boundaries. They are timid, lack confidence, and display considerable doubt (Figure 3.20).

TREATMENT FOR A YIN WOOD ELEMENT PERSONALITY:

Medical Qigong Treatment involves establishing a sense of inner strength and security, by teaching them self-trust and building self-esteem. These patients need to strengthen their boundaries, so that they no longer allow intrusion or domination from others. They also need to learn to trust in their own intuition, develop a greater degree of confidence, enhance their personal power, and find a stronger sense of spiritual growth.

3. **A Yang Wood Element Nature:** Predisposes individuals to manifest their internal insecurities through irritability and impatience. Such individuals are intolerant, rude, stubborn, selfish, and tend to expand their egos without consideration for others. They are domineering, angry, aggressive, and generally known as overachievers; however, they are easily frustrated and depressed. Their self-esteem is elevated by acquiring higher social, political or otherwise influential positions; or by bullying others (Figure 3.21).

TREATMENT FOR A YANG WOOD ELEMENT PERSONALITY:

Medical Qigong Treatment should focus on cultivating humility, reverence, and inner peace, as well as consciously blending and harmonizing with life by following the Dao. In situations of conflict, they need to learn to relax, slow down, and act out of stillness. These patients must learn to surrender to a higher will, and rely on their own spiritual intuition and inner direction. It is also important for them to learn to respect others.

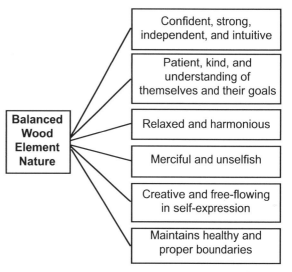

Figure 3.19. Balanced Wood Element Nature

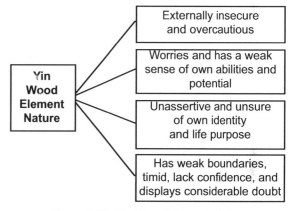

Figure 3.20. Yin Wood Element Nature

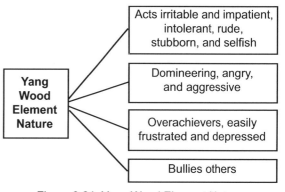

Figure 3.21. Yang Wood Element Nature

THE FIRE ELEMENT CONSTITUTION

The energetic Pattern (Li) and Form (Xing) of a Fire Element person is structurally shaped like a triangle. According to ancient Daoist teachings, a Fire Element person can be identified by their "Three Points:" Pointed Nose, Pointed Chin, and Pointed Head.

- **Pointed Nose:** A Fire Element person has a pointy nose, wide teeth, and curly or scanty hair, or no hair on top of their head.
- **Pointed Chin:** They have a thin face and pointy chin
- **Pointed Head:** They have a small pointy head, their face is round and full, and the hair is thin.
- **Plump Body:** Traditionally, a Fire Element person's body is shaped like a torch: pointy on top, narrow on the bottom, and flared in the middle. They usually have a medium build with sloping shoulders, broad paravertebral muscles, and a well-proportioned upper back, shoulders, buttocks, thighs and abdomen (Figure 3.22). They also have small hands and feet. Their dominant features include a strong circulatory system.
- **Long Fingers:** Their hands have a long-proportioned structure, with fingers that are long, slender and flexible. The finger tips are pointed, and fingernails tend to be long and narrow, with a very convex curvature from base to tip (Figure 3.23).
- **Complexion:** They usually have a subtle shade of red in their complexion, and their ears and neck turn crimson red when their temper is roused.
- **Talking:** Their voice is sharp and high-pitched, with a broken quality. The sounds seemingly come from the tongue.
- **Walking:** The Fire-type person is light-footed and walks at a hurried pace, dashing forward with the upper body swaying from side to side.
- **Season:** By nature, they enjoy the Spring and Summer seasons. This preference is due to the inherent vulnerabilities of their Fire Element Constitution, making them especially susceptible to pathogenic invasion and disease during the Autumn and Winter seasons.

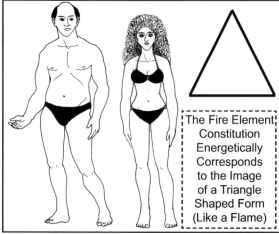

Figure 3.22. The Fire Constitution (Three Points)

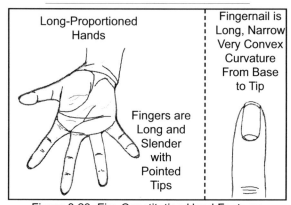

Figure 3.23. Fire Constitution Hand Features

- **Pattern (Li):** Their energetic pattern is a observed as a Triangle shape
- **Energy (Qi):** Their energetic manifestation is ascending, and expanding growth
- **Sound:** Their energetic sound is "Zhi" (G).
- **Color:** Their energetic color is "Red."
- **Organ:** Their Yin dominant internal organ is the "Heart," which is paired with the Yang Small Intestine organ.
- **Direction:** Their cardinal direction is South
- **Planet:** Their celestial planet is Mars

THE FIRE ELEMENT PERSONALITY

The Fire Element personality can be categorized into three subdivisions, which are described as follows:

1. **A Balanced Fire Element Nature:** Predisposes individuals to be trusting, open-minded, com-

placent, social, unconcerned about wealth, and fond of beauty. They love themselves and others and are very expressive of their affection. They are calm, peaceful, happy, lively, spontaneous, funny, and fun to be with (Figure 3.24).

2. **A Yin Fire Element Nature:** Predisposes individuals to be solemn and depressed. They usually lack interest in life and have a tendency to become isolated, feeling unloved and unlovable (Figure 3.25).

TREATMENT FOR YIN FIRE ELEMENT PERSONALITY:

Medical Qigong Treatment requires teaching them how to store and conserve their energy, avoid extremes and apply the principle of moderation to all aspects of their life. They also need to engage in activities that create personal enjoyment, and find simple pleasures that awaken their affection. Individuals of a Yin Fire Element Nature can further benefit from learning how to express their feelings, wants, and needs.

3. **A Yang Fire Element Nature:** Predisposes individuals to be arrogant, ignorant, and troublesome. They are restless and excitable, and tend to talk excessively. Individuals of a Yang Fire Element Nature are overenthusiastic, exaggerate often, and generally display foolish and careless behavior. They are socially and sexually overactive and seek every opportunity to assert themselves. These individuals are often overconfident, slightly lazy, irresponsible, and less than truthful. They can easily go from mania to exhaustion, and then burnout and become suicidal (e.g., bipolar disorder) (Figure 3.26).

TREATMENT FOR YANG FIRE ELEMENT PERSONALITY:

Medical Qigong Treatment requires teaching them to learn how to stop, slow down, and look for their contentment from within. They should balance their feelings of love with contemplation and wisdom, avoid over-enthusiasm, and allow their inner spirit to radiate through in a more steady and sober manner.

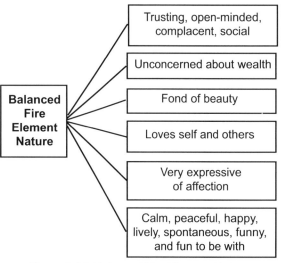

Figure 3.24. Balanced Fire Element Nature

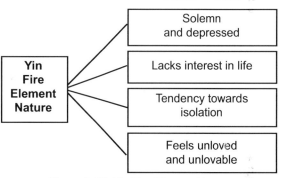

Figure 3.25. Yin Fire Element Nature

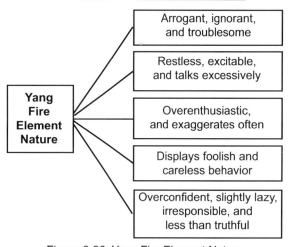

Figure 3.26. Yang Fire Element Nature

THE EARTH ELEMENT CONSTITUTION

The energetic Pattern (Li) and Form (Xing) of a Earth Element person is structurally shaped like a square. According to ancient Daoist teachings, an Earth Element person can be identified by their "Three Shorts:" Short Neck, Short Body, and Short Fingers.

- **Short Neck:** The Earth Element person has a short neck, a square face with big ears, and a bulbous nose shaped like a head of garlic. Their head is large, with a round shaped face, and wide jaw.
- **Short Body:** They are categorized as having excessive flesh, with upper and lower limbs mutually well-proportioned. They have well developed shoulders and back, large abdomen, strong thighs and calf muscles. Their muscles are strong and both the waist and back are thick, and they usually have a somewhat large body (Figure 3.27).
- **Short Fingers:** They have thick, pudgy, short fingers, and small, thick proportioned hands and feet. The fingernails also tend to be short and flat, with a slightly convex curvature and a triangular shape beginning at the nail base (Figure 3.28).
- **Complexion:** They usually have a subtle shade of yellow in their complexion, which turns into a withered yellow when the person is unhappy.
- **Talking:** Their speech is loud, with a low-pitched nasal tone.
- **Walking:** Their movements tend to be clumsy, and they walk with a heavy-footed gait, with every step solidly landing on the ground.
- **Season:** By nature, they enjoy the Autumn and Winter seasons. This preference is due to the inherent vulnerabilities of their Earth Element Constitution, making them especially susceptible to pathogenic invasion and disease during the Spring and Summer seasons.
- **Pattern (Li):** Their energetic pattern is a observed as a Square shape
- **Energy (Qi):** Their energetic manifestation is transitional, and expresses balance
- **Sound:** Their energetic sound is "Gong" (C).
- **Color:** Their energetic color is "Yellow."

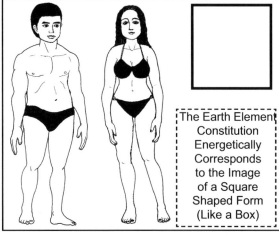

Figure 3.27. The Earth Constitution (Three Shorts)

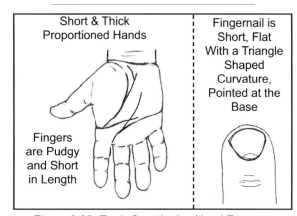

Figure 3.28. Earth Constitution Hand Features

- **Organ:** Their Yin dominant internal organ is the "Spleen," which is paired with the Yang Stomach organ.
- **Direction:** Their cardinal direction is Center
- **Planet:** Their celestial planet is Saturn

THE EARTH ELEMENT PERSONALITY

The Earth personality can be categorized into three subdivisions, which are described as follows:

1. **A Balanced Earth Element Nature:** Predisposes individuals to lead quiet, stable, and peaceful lives, unconcerned about fame or wealth. They are easygoing, calm, generous, forgiving, sincere, and unambitious. They usually have open minds and rarely live in fear or make excessive demands. Individuals of a Balanced Earth Element Nature are analytical,

logical and practical; and they use sound reasoning to communicate their opinions to others. They are adaptable to changing situations, and rarely use coercion to achieve power. They are kind and gentle with an earnest and well-mannered attitude. These individuals are pleasant, sweet, sympathetic, caring, and able to maintain healthy boundaries (Figure 3.29).
2. **A Yin Earth Element Nature:** Predisposes individuals to worry endlessly, becoming suspicious and self-centered. They think too much and rarely follow through with actions that manifest their decisions. Because they feel empty inside, they find it difficult to be nurturing to themselves and others (Figure 3.30).

Treatment for Yin Earth Element Personality:

Medical Qigong Treatment requires teaching them to learn how to let go of their inner feelings of worry and defensiveness. These individuals need to examine their assumptions, connect with their physical bodies, come out of their shells, and begin to live in the real world. They need to replace their negative thought patterns with positive affirmations, realistically look at their true potential and abilities, and learn how to take action and follow through.

3. **A Yang Earth Element Nature:** Predisposes individuals to cling to others. They are codependent, pushy, and possessive. Such individuals try to dominate in a passive-aggressive way while limiting the independence of others (Figure 3.31).

Treatment for Yang Earth Element Personality:

Medical Qigong Treatment consists of teaching them to develop their inner strength in order to control the feelings of fear, insecurity, and inner emptiness that make them want to hold on to others. They need to create and establish love as a source of security from within themselves. They need to learn how to be themselves regardless of the praise of others. They must learn to become emotionally independent.

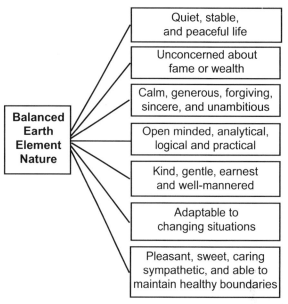

Figure 3.29. Balanced Earth Element Nature

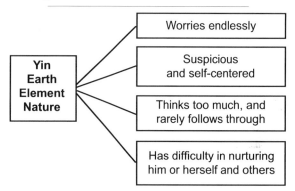

Figure 3.30. Yin Earth Element Nature

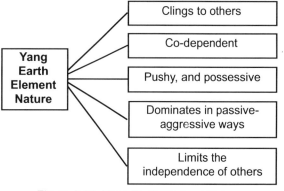

Figure 3.31. Yang Earth Element Nature

The Metal Element Constitution

The energetic Pattern (Li) and Form (Xing) of a Metal Element person is structurally shaped like a Ball. According to ancient Daoist teachings, a Metal Element person can be identified by their "Three Thins:" Thin Lips, Thin Eyelids, and Thin Skin.

- **Thin Lips:** The Metal Element person is attractive looking, with well defined, well distributed features. They usually have a small head, square-shaped face with a triangular jaw, and thin lips.
- **Thin Eyelids:** They have thin eyelids.
- **Thin Skin:** They have thin skin over their back and hands.
- **Athletic Body:** They have broad and square shoulders and upper back, flat abdomen, and a strong, muscular build (Figure 3.32).
- **Long Fingers:** Their hands generally have an oval shaped structure with a long palm, and fingers that are proportionally longer than the palm. The fingernails tend to be long with a rectangular curvature and sharp edges, and are slightly rounded at the nail base (Figure 3.33).
- **Complexion:** They usually have a subtle shade of white in their complexion, that turns pale when their tempers are aroused.
- **Talking:** Their voice is strong, bright, and clear as a bell, with the sounds coming from the throat. They are good with words and are persuasive communicators.
- **Walking:** Their gait is swift and light, and their movements are graceful and lively.
- **Season:** By nature, they enjoy the Autumn and Winter seasons. This preference is due to the inherent vulnerabilities of their Metal Element Constitution, making them especially susceptible to pathogenic invasion and disease during the Spring and Summer seasons.
- **Pattern (Li):** Their energetic pattern is observed as a Round (Oval) shape
- **Energy (Qi):** Their energetic manifestation is gathering, and cultivating vitality
- **Sound:** Their energetic sound is "Shang" (D).
- **Color:** Their energetic color is "White."
- **Organ:** Their Yin dominant internal organ is the "Lungs," which is paired with the Yang Large Intestine organ.

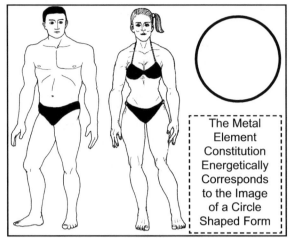

Figure 3.32. The Metal Constitution (Three Thins)

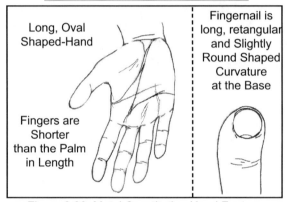

Figure 3.33. Metal Constitution Hand Features

- **Direction:** Their cardinal direction is West
- **Planet:** Their celestial planet is Venus

The Metal Element Personality

The Metal personality can be categorized into three subdivisions, which are described as follows:

1. **A Balanced Metal Element Nature:** Predisposes individuals to process grief, enabling them to let go of past emotional baggage. They believe that they cannot be in the present without cleaning up and being released from their past. They are able to gain knowledge and wisdom by gathering and releasing their emotional bonds while learning and growing from each experience of intimacy and connection. They participate fully in life and form new bonds without fear of loss. They are also generous, just, and bright (Figure 3.34).

2. **A Yin Metal Element Nature:** Predisposes individuals to have a difficult time creating lasting bonds. They are fearful of establishing new relationships due to past losses and emotional trauma. They avoid joining with others and withdraw from active social participation. Living in remorse, they grieve over lost opportunities and relationships. They become angry when they do not have things that others possess. They can be haughty, coldhearted, jealous, cunning, sneaky, and furtive. Covetous and socially isolated, they try to obtain happiness by possessing people, places and things (Figure 3.35).

TREATMENT FOR YIN METAL ELEMENT PERSONALITY:

Medical Qigong Treatment requires teaching them how to strengthen their physical body, as well as the energy of their Heart, Spleen, and Lower Dantian. They also need to strengthen their abilities to form close emotional bonds with people, reduce their fears of rejection and abandonment, and cultivate the strength, courage and ability to let go of their past hurts. They need to open themselves emotionally to experience the warmth and compassion of life.

3. **A Yang Metal Element Nature:** Predisposes individuals to suppress their emotions and hold on to grief. They are generally considered whiners and complainers, talking to others about their problems in order to unload grief and control the situation. They use new relationships as an emotional bandage to avoid the unprocessed grief of their past relationships. They are also overly meticulous, independent, and strong-willed (Figure 3.36).

TREATMENT FOR YANG METAL ELEMENT PERSONALITY:

Medical Qigong Treatment requires teaching them how to let go of the need to control and suppress their feelings, while allowing them to genuinely grieve over past wounds. They need to face the truth and be honest about their feelings, instead of selfishly using people and new relationships to cover up their grief. They also need to develop sympathy for the pain and sorrows of others and to put their own feelings of grief into a broader, healthier perspective.

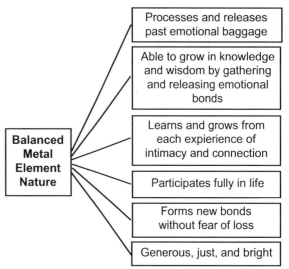

Figure 3.34. Balanced Metal Element Nature

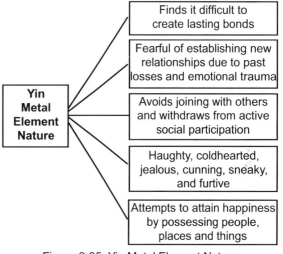

Figure 3.35. Yin Metal Element Nature

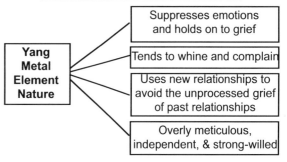

Figure 3.36. Yang Metal Element Nature

THE WATER CONSTITUTION

The energetic Pattern (Li) and Form (Xing) of a Water Element person is structurally shaped like a Curve. According to ancient Daoist teachings, a Water Element person can be identified by their "Three Thicks:" Thick Eyelids, Thick Jaw, and Thick Skin.

- **Thick Eyelids:** They have big eyes, thick eyebrows, and thick hair.
- **Thick Jaw:** Their face is large, fleshy, and round, wider at the base than the top; and they often have a double chin.
- **Thick Skin:** Both their face and body are full and chubby.
- **Large Body:** They usually have a large head, long upper back, large abdomen substantial body mass and unbalanced or uneven physical features (Figure 3.37).
- **Short Fingers:** Their hands generally have a short proportioned structure with short fingers. The fingernails tend to have a short convex curvature, with a trapezoidal shape beginning with the short side at the nail base (Figure 3.38).
- **Complexion:** They usually have a subtle shade of black in their complexion, which darkens when their temper is roused.
- **Talking:** They speaks with a relaxed, low tone, with the sounds coming from the throat.
- **Walking:** They walk slowly, with their feet dragging on the ground.
- **Season:** By nature, they enjoy the Autumn and Winter seasons. This preference is due to the inherent vulnerabilities of their Metal Element Constitution, making them especially susceptible to pathogenic invasion and disease during the Spring and Summer seasons.
- **Pattern (Li):** Their energetic pattern is a observed as an Wavy (Curve) shape
- **Energy (Qi):** Their energetic manifestation is stillness, and storing vitality
- **Sound:** Their energetic sound is "Yu" (A).
- **Color:** Their energetic color is "Black."
- **Organ:** Their Yin dominant internal organ is the "Kidneys," which is paired with the Yang Urinary Bladder organ.
- **Direction:** Their cardinal direction is North
- **Planet:** Their celestial planet is Mercury

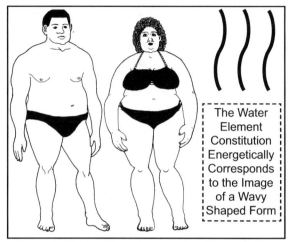

Figure 3.37. The Water Constitution (Three Thicks)

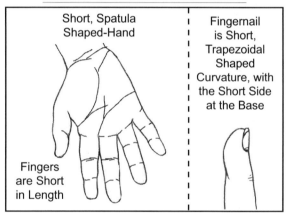

Figure 3.38. Water Constitution Hand Features

THE WATER ELEMENT PERSONALITY

The Water personality can be categorized into three subdivisions, which are described as follows:

1. **A Balanced Water Element Nature:** Predisposes individuals to be skilled negotiators who are not discouraged by difficulty and do not take foolish risks. They are sympathetic and loyal to their employers and their friends. They have a clear perspective and are sensitive and intuitive. They are powerful, tender, and soft. They have a firm will and know their boundaries and limitations. They are known for their inner strength and strong faith in themselves (Figure 3.39).

2. **A Yin Water Element Nature:** Predisposes individuals to lack spiritual, emotional, mental,

and physical energy. They give up on life and surrender the control of their own destiny's to inertia and external circumstances. They lack the determination to achieve their goals, doing everything halfheartedly, and becoming easily discouraged by difficult challenges (Figure 3.40).

TREATMENT FOR YIN WATER ELEMENT PERSONALITY:

Medical Qigong Treatment requires teaching them how to conserve and strengthen their energy by not reaching beyond their capacity. They need to learn to break down larger tasks into small sections that they can realistically complete. These individuals must learn how to follow their projects through to completion, and avoid procrastination. They also need to find the strength to overcome their fear of failure by learning to take action through the completion of their goals.

3. **A Yang Water Element Nature:** Predisposes individuals to be ambitious overachievers and to live under great stress. They lack consideration for others and can be reckless and foolhardy. They can also be greedy, ruthless, and cold-blooded. Seemingly modest, they can be insidious and sinister, concealing their true emotions by suppressing deeply rooted fears. Because they fear loss of control, they believe that their safety lies in their power and ability to dominate others. They habitually act in a self-serving manner and blame others for their problems (Figure 3.41).

TREATMENT FOR YANG WATER ELEMENT PERSONALITY:

Medical Qigong Treatment consists of teaching them to learn how to act from inner stillness and gain strength and courage from their true selves. It is essential that they learn to surrender their ego and trust in the processes of the divine. They need to learn how to gain consideration for themselves and others, as well as how to open their hearts and begin to love. They also need to emotionally and physically slow down and to balance their activities with rest.

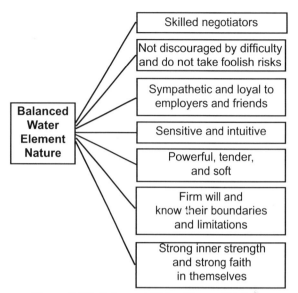

Figure 3.39. Balanced Water Element Nature

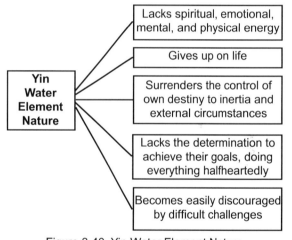

Figure 3.40. Yin Water Element Nature

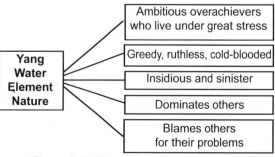

Figure 3.41. Yang Water Element Nature

COMBINED ELEMENT CONSTITUTIONS

Each of the Five Element Constitutions have an apparent external Form (Xing) and physical manifestation, as well as a hidden internal energetic pattern (Qi). Therefore, in the Medical Qigong Clinic, a patient's external physical structure serves as a visual guide to congenital and acquired patterning, balance, and internal organ interactions.

According to the Yellow Emperor's physician Shao Shi, the Five Element Constitutions consisted of both internal and external energetic forms based on the strength and energetic development of the individual's Jing, Qi, and Blood.

When traditionally applied within the Medical Qigong Clinic, a patient is first diagnosed according to his or her physical Five Element Constitution. For example, their "type" of physical body is determined by the dominant Wood, Fire, Earth, Metal, or Water Element Constitution pattern (Figure 3.42).

After determining the physical constitution, the patients are then classified in terms of their dominant Five Element Color: Green/Blue, Red, Yellow, White, or Black. This special Prenatal Color pattern allows the doctor to choose the specific light imagery that will most quickly influence the patient's tissues.

Next, the patients are further classified according to their dominant Five Element Tone: Jue, Gong, Zhi, Shang or Yu. These special Prenatal Notes allow the doctor to choose the specific sound patterns that will most quickly influence the patient's tissues.

Each of the Five Element patterns are observed and carefully studied, and clinically assessed according to their Excess, Deficient or Balanced energetic patterns.

It is important to note, that the Five Element Constitutions are guidelines which aid the Medical Qigong Doctor in evaluating the patient. These guidelines are not fixed, and the doctor is likely to encounter combinations of two or more of these Elements within one patient. Inevitably, this system of pattern diagnosis came to recognize twenty five (5 x 5) constitutional types.

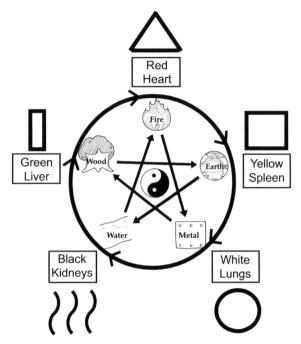

Figure 3.42. The Five Element Cycle

When several patterns from the Five Element Constitutions are noted within an individual's body, the multiple combinations may be due to a congenital and/or acquired influence. In such cases, the Medical Qigong doctor must evaluate the patient differentiating between their congenital and acquired tissue formations. For example, a woman who has large hips (Water), and a small chest and shoulders (Wood), probably inherited this structure from her parents. This woman's physical structure and personality would then be considered to be a combination of both Water and Wood (depending on which internal organ characteristic dominates).

A female patient who is a swimmer, on the other hand, may be congenitally Wood, but may have developed a dominant Metal upper physique through years of physical training. If, through intense physical activity, someone acquires a Metal physique, he or she may also acquire a Metal personality. This depends on the psychological predisposition rooted within his or her internal organs.

CHAPTER 3: TISSUE FORMATION AND DEVELOPMENT

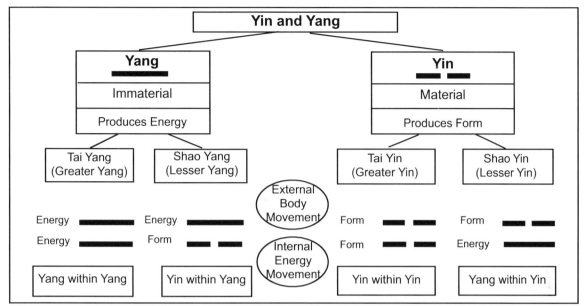

Figure 3.43. Yin and Yang Yao - Expressing the Four Phases of Universal Energy

YIN AND YANG AND THE YAO IMAGE

One ancient method of clinical diagnoses still used in China today for determining external abnormalities, requires an understanding of the "Yao" image and its energetic correspondence to a patient's physical anatomy. In order to better comprehend the complexity of this diagnostic and treatment modality, the doctor must first understand the energetic origin of the Yao images.

To the ancient Daoists, all matter was believed to be composed of different proportions of Yin and Yang energy (Figure 3.43). Within the infinite space of the Wuji, Yin and Yang energy continually gathers and disperses, giving rise to all forces and cycles of change in the universe. This interaction of Yin and Yang energy develops and transforms into four phases (or stages) of universal energy: Greater Yin, Lesser Yin, Greater Yang, and Lesser Yang. These four phases can be explained as follows (Figure 3.44):

1. **Greater Yin (Tai Yin)** is associated with Midnight and the New Moon phase. Modern physicists associate the Greater Yin with a weak nuclear force.
2. **Lesser Yin (Shao Yin)** is associated with Sunset and the Waning Moon phase. Modern physicists associate the Lesser Yin with a heavy force and gravity.

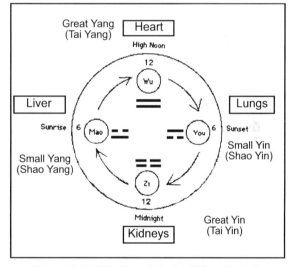

Figure 3.44. The Four Principal Time Periods

3. **Greater Yang (Tai Yang)** is associated with High Noon and the Full Moon phase. Modern physicists associate the Greater Yang with a strong nuclear force.
4. **Lesser Yang (Shao Yang)** is associated with Sunrise and the Waxing Moon phase. Modern physicists associate the Lesser Yang with electromagnetism and a light force.

Figure 3.45. This diagram shows a Hexagram composed of an upper and lower trigram. In this particular example, the upper trigram contains all Yin Yaos (symbolized by broken lines), while the lower trigram is composed of all Yang Yaos (symbolized by solid lines).

These four solar and lunar energetic phases transform themselves into the energies of the eight foundational trigrams, collectively known as the Bagua (Eight Trigrams). The Eight Trigrams further combine together in order to form sixty-four Hexagrams, and create the ancient binary system used in Daoist Divinational practices, applied within the ancient teachings of the *Yi-Jing (Book of Changes)*. The formation and patterning of these energetic powers (or stages) vary according to the composition of Yin and Yang expressed through the energetic symbols of the "Yao."

A Yao is a line that represents either Yin or Yang energy. The lines fall into two categories:
- **The Negative Yao:** is symbolized by broken lines (- -) and relates to Yin energy
- **The Positive Yao:** is symbolized by solid lines (---) and relates to Yang energy

When these lines are stacked in combinations of three, they form "Trigrams" (a group of three Yao lines). A Hexagram, or six Yao line, is formed when two pairs of Trigrams are joined. The Hexagram lines are arranged from bottom to top, with the first Yao beginning on the bottom (Figure 3.45).

THE YAO AND PHYSICAL ANATOMY

To the ancient Daoists, each trigram pattern indicated a specific energetic manifestation, and was associated with a special direction, Element, body part, and energetic action. The identity of the trigram also had a unique bearing on an individual's personal character, and the exact body part that was most likely to be adversely

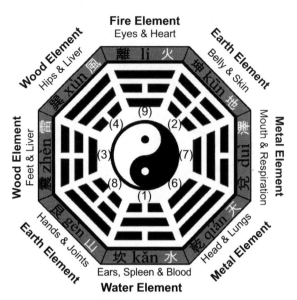

Figure 3.46. The Postnatal Eight Trigram Pattern

affected during the Four Principle Time Periods (see Figure 3.44).

Through understanding each trigram's energetic correspondence to a patient's physical anatomy, the ancient Wuyi (Shaman Doctors) could often predict the future state of an individual's health or illnesses. When used in clinical diagnosis, the esoteric meanings and implications of each trigram gave valuable clues as to how to create energetic balance (Figure 3.46 and Figure 3.47):

- **Qian (Three Lines - Heaven):** In the Postnatal Bagua Pattern, Qian is placed in the Northwest. It represents the Patriarch, and its Element is Metal (represented by the Lou Shu number 6). Its anatomical properties correspond to the energies of the head and the Lungs. Its related illness manifests as problems of the head and Lung region.

- **Kun (Six Lines - Earth):** In the Postnatal Bagua Pattern, Kun is placed in the Southwest. It represents the Matriarch, and its Element is Earth (represented by the Lou Shu number 2). Its anatomical properties correspond to the energies of the belly (stomach). Its related illness manifests as problems of the digestive system, skin, and sometimes the reproductive system.

CHAPTER 3: TISSUE FORMATION AND DEVELOPMENT

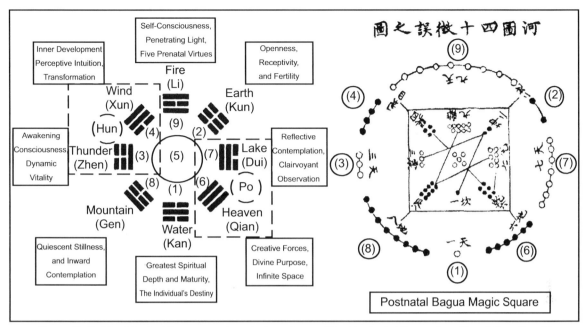

Figure 3.47. The Magical Square and esoteric pattern of the Postnatal Bagua Lou Shu (River Graph) (Relating to the Yang-Human Realm): Representing the Energetic Cycles of Forces that are the External Manifestation of Divine Thought (The World of Phenomena or Senses).

- **Zhen (Bowl Up - Thunder):** In the Postnatal Bagua Pattern, Zhen is placed in the East. It represents the first born male, and its Element is Wood (represented by the Lou Shu number 3). Its anatomical properties correspond to the energy of the feet. Its related illness manifests as injuries to the feet, as well as problems of the Liver.
- **Gen (Bowl Down - Mountain):** In the Postnatal Bagua Pattern, Zhen is placed in the Northeast. It represents the third born male, and its Element is Earth (represented by the Lou Shu number 8). Its anatomical properties correspond to the energy of the hands. Its related illness manifests as problems of the hands, joints, nose, and digestive system.
- **Li (Middle Yin - Fire):** In the Postnatal Bagua Pattern, Zhen is placed in the South. It represents the second born female, and its Element is Fire (represented by the Lou Shu number 9). Its anatomical properties correspond to the energies of the eyes. Its related illness manifests as problems of the eyes and Heart.

- **Kan (Middle Yang - Water):** In the Postnatal Bagua Pattern, Zhen is placed in the North. It represents the second born male, and its Element is Water (represented by the Lou Shu number 1). Its anatomical properties correspond to the energy of the ears. Its related illness manifests as problems of the ears, Spleen, and blood.
- **Dui (Broken Top - Lake):** In the Postnatal Bagua Pattern, Zhen is placed in the West. It represents the third born female, and its Element is Metal (represented by the Lou Shu number 7). Its anatomical properties correspond to the energy of the mouth. Its related illness manifests as problems of the mouth and respiratory system.
- **Xun (Broken Bottom - Wind):** In the Postnatal Bagua Pattern, Zhen is placed in the Southeast. It represents the first born female, and its Element is Wood (represented by the Lou Shu number 4). Its anatomical properties correspond to the energy of the hips. Its related illness manifests as problems of the hips, Urinary Bladder, and Liver.

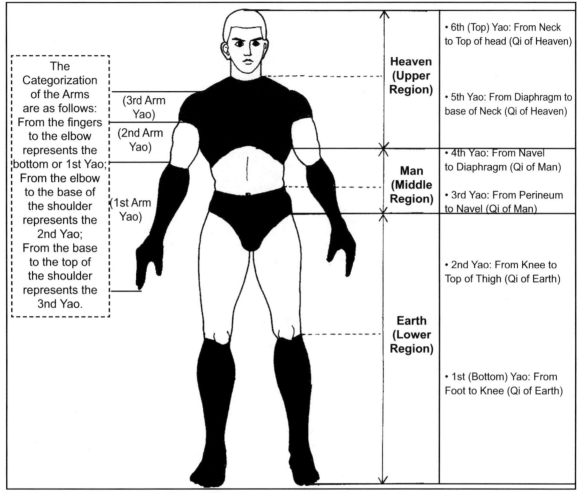

Figure 3.58. Yao Image and the Human Body

THE THREE YAO REGIONS OF THE BODY

The Yao Trigrams and their relationship to the body's physical and energetic structure can be utilized by the Medical Qigong Doctor for both diagnosis and treatment. According to the ancient Daoists, the human body is subdivided into three regions:
- **The Lower Region:** This area of the body pertains to the energy of the Earth;
- **The Middle Region:** This area of the body pertains to the energy of Man;
- **The Upper Region:** This area of the body pertains to the energy of Heaven.

Each of these three regions were further subdivided three more times. Each of the additional three subdivided levels contained the metaphysical aspect of the material, energetic and spiritual dimensions of Heaven (Shen: Spirit), Earth (Qi: Energy), and Man (Jing: Matter).

In one form of clinical application, the Medical Qigong Doctor will use the six Yao lines of a hexagram as a template for diagnosis, by overlaying the Yin and Yang patterns alongside the patient's body. The arrangement of Yao images assists the doctor in recognizing the patient's physical and energetic imbalances. This type of Yao image diagnosis has been used in China for centuries.

Each Yao corresponds to a different region of the human body, as well as a different aspect of Qi. The system of energetic Yao correspondence with the physical body is described as follows (Figure 3.58):

1. **The Two Bottom Yaos:** The two Yaos of the Lower Region of the body correspond physically to the feet and legs. They energetically manifest the body's receptive interactions with the Earth Qi, and the energy contained within the soil (including minerals and plants), water, and the energy introduced by wind into the environment.
   - The 1st (Bottom) Yao extends from the feet to the middle of the knees.
   - The 2nd Yao extends from the middle of the knees to the upper thighs.
2. **The Middle Two Yaos:** The two Yaos of the Middle Region of the body correspond physically to the lower and upper abdominal regions. They energetically manifest the body's receptive interactions with Human Qi (including the thoughts and emotional responses pertaining to people, places, and things).
   - The 3rd Yao extends from the perineum (i.e., the base of the Lower Dantian) to the navel.
   - The 4th Yao extends from the navel to the xiphoid process and the diaphragm (i.e., the base of the Middle Dantian and Yellow Court area).
3. **The Upper Two Yaos:** The two Yaos of the Upper Region of the body correspond physically to the upper chest, neck, and head regions, and energetically to the body's interaction with Heaven Qi, and the energetic influence of the Sun, Moon and Stars.
   - The 5th Yao extends from the xiphoid process of the diaphragm to the top of the manubrium at the base of the throat (i.e., the Heaven's Chimney).
   - The 6th (Top) Yao extends from the manubrium to the top of the head (Baihui).

In ancient China, the knowledge of hexagram diagnosis was used in order to explain the etiology, pathology, clinical manifestations, and treatment principles that were used to treat a patient's disease. By observing the physical body's relationship to the three energetic Yao divisions of Heaven, Earth, and Man, the ancient Wuyi (Shaman Doctors) were able to note specific changes occurring within the various regions of the patient's external tissues. Through this observation and study, the ancient doctors were able to determine the various energetic and emotional associations each patient carried within their tissues in relationship to the surrounding environment.

For example, if the Jing, Qi or Shen within a patient's Upper Yao was out of harmony with the Jing, Qi or Shen of his Middle or Lower Yao formation, the patient's energetic balance could be compromised. Such a patient was likely to experience some form of energetic disconnection with his body. In this example, if the Upper Yao is in a relatively Excess energetic condition, it could result in a Yang Qi manifestation (i.e., mental restlessness) due to an excess spiritual "Heaven" state. If the patient's Upper Yao was energetically Deficient, it could result in a Yin Qi manifestation (i.e., mentally tired) due to a deficient spiritual "Heaven" state.

Upper and Lower Hexagram Patterns

In addition to applying the previous Hexagram Diagnosis to assess the body's relationship to the energetic changes occurring within the realms of Heaven, Earth, and Man, the ancient Daoists also studied two additional Hexagram formations for clinical evaluation. These additional Hexagram formations were known as the "Upper Hexagram" and "Lower Hexagram" Patterns.

When using the Upper and Lower Hexagram Patterns for diagnosis and treatment, the ancient Daoists would further divide a patient's body into six Upper Yao and six Lower Yao formations. This unique energetic division was used to determine a patient's dominant emotional and energetic patterns, and additionally diagnosed where the patient's Qi was gathering, dispersing or stagnating.

In the Ming Dynasty (1368-1644), when referring to the clinical uses of the six Upper Yao and six Lower Yao formations, Professor Tang Rongchuan stated in his book *Detailed Explanations of the Application of the Book of Changes to Medicine*,

"In the clinical environment, the body may be divided into two different sets of Hexagram constructions for the purpose of making Clinical Diagnosis, Detecting Qi, and for performing Therapeutic Qigong Treatments."

The special relationship of Yao positioning also energetically corresponds to both the channel system and the body's nervous system. Any physical disorders located within these two special hexagram formations are generally expressed as symptoms manifesting within the extremities. For example, if Stagnant Qi or other abnormal conditions were found to occur in any particular part of the body, an imbalance of both internal and external Qi may be detected in either its corresponding Yao area, or within the specific Yao area of the body.

When using the Upper and Lower Hexagram Patterns for diagnosis and treatment, the body's upper torso, arms, neck, and head are divided into what is known as the Upper Hexagram partition; while the body's lower limbs and torso are divided into the Lower Hexagram partitions. In this model, the six Yao of the Upper Hexagram interlock with the six Yao of the Lower Hexagram at the chest and abdomen (Figure 3.59).

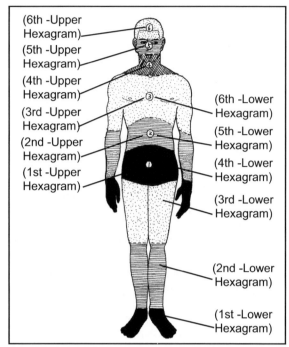

Figure 3.59. The Six Upper Hexagram and Six Lower Yao Hexagram Diagnostic Patterns

The Upper Hexagram Construction

The Upper Hexagram extends from the base of the perineum to the top of the head. The six Yaos are organized as follows:

1. **The 1st (Bottom) Yao:** This encompasses the area from the pubic region to the navel. Reproductive, digestive, and urinary tract diseases are found in this area.
2. **The 2nd Yao:** This encompasses the area from the navel to the xiphoid process. Digestion, elimination, the distribution of nutrients, pancreatic diseases, problems with the Kidneys, adrenal glands, Liver, and Spleen are all found in this area.
3. **The 3rd Yao:** This encompasses the area from the xiphoid process to the clavicles at the base of the throat. Respiratory and circulatory diseases are found in this area.
4. **The 4th Yao:** This encompasses the area from the clavicles at the base of the throat to the tip of the nose. Teeth, jaw, and thyroid diseases are found in this area.
5. **The 5th Yao:** This encompasses the area from the tip of the nose to the eyebrows. Sinus problems, frontal headaches, and ear, nose, and eye diseases are found in this area.
6. **The 6th (Top) Yao:** This encompasses the area from the eyebrows to the top of the head. Headaches, brain tumors, and upper cranial dysfunctions are found in this area.

The Lower Hexagram Construction

The lower hexagram extends from the bottom of the patient's feet to the base of the patient's throat. The six Yaos are organized as follows:

1. **The 1st (Bottom) Yao:** This encompasses the area from the bottom of each foot to the ankle. Foot, toe, and ankle problems are found in this area.
2. **The 2nd Yao:** This encompasses the area from the ankles to the knees. Shin splints and calf and ankle problems are found in this area.
3. **The 3rd Yao:** This encompasses the area from the knees to the pubic symphysis. Thigh, knee, and quadriceps problems are found in this area.
4. **The 4th Yao:** This encompasses the area from the pubic region to the navel. Reproductive, digestive, and urinary tract diseases are found in this area.
5. **The 5th Yao:** This encompasses the area from

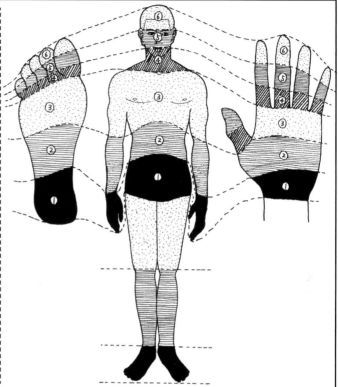

> The following diagram depicts the correspondence of the Yaos of the body with the Yaos of both the hands and feet.
>
> 6. **Top (Third) Joint of the Toes, and the Fingers:** Pertains to the top Yao, and the energy of Heaven
>
> 5. **Middle (Second) Joint of the Toes, and the Fingers:** Pertains to the 5th Yao, and the energy of Heaven
>
> 4. **Lower (First) Joint of the Toes, and the Fingers:** Pertains to the 4th Yao, and the energy of Man
>
> 3. **Ball of the Foot, and the Upper Palm:** Pertains to the 3rd Yao, and the energy of Man
>
> 2. **Instep of Foot, and the Mid-Palm with the Thumb:** Pertains to the 2nd Yao, and the energy of Earth
>
> 1. **Heel, and the Lower Palm:** Pertains to the 1st Yao, and the energy of Earth

Figure 3.60. The Therapeutic Use of the Yao Hexagrams

the navel to the xiphoid process. Digestion, elimination, the distribution of nutrients, pancreatic diseases, problems with the Kidneys, adrenal glands, Liver, and Spleen are all found in this area.

6. **The 6th (Top) Yao:** This encompasses the area from the xiphoid process to the clavicles at the base of the throat. Respiratory and circulatory diseases are found in this area.

THERAPEUTIC USE OF THE YAO HEXAGRAMS

When using the Yao Hexagram pattern formations, the entire body can be diagnosed and treated by simply focusing on one small area. For example, when Excess, Deficient, or Stagnant Qi occurs in one part of the body, the imbalance is detectable in that area or its corresponding region on the body's extremities. This ancient form of Chinese energetic diagnosis and treatment was also originally part of Pediatric Tuina, and is the historical root of what is popularly called "Reflexology" in the West today.

When the Yao images are superimposed onto the patient's body, the patient can be diagnosed according to the Yin and Yang energetic symptoms expressed. This diagnosis can be either through the patient's extremities (hands, forearms, arms, feet, shins, and thighs), or through the six divisions located on the patient's torso and head. A Yao hexagram can additionally be visualized on specific locations of the patient's body such as the face, nose, ears, hand, or foot for diagnosis. The base of the palm, for example, corresponds to the lower abdominal area and reproductive organs, and relates to the 1st Yao in the Hexagram applied to the hands. The six Yao areas of each hand provide a basis for diagnosis, treatment of diseases, and even for the perception and prediction of certain future diseases (Figure 3.60).

As an example of how a Medical Qigong Doctor can use the six Yaos of the body for clinical application, consider the following situation: an

VOLUME 1, SECTION 1: FOUNDATIONS OF CHINESE ENERGETIC MEDICINE

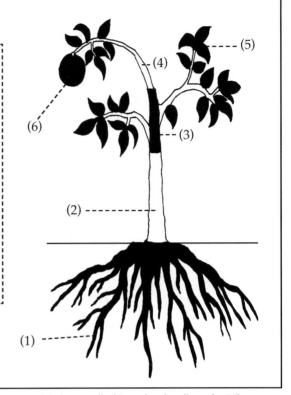

Figure 3.61. In ancient China, the Six Yao Hexagram image was also applied to using healing plant therapy

elderly patient with a problem in his prostate area pays a visit to the clinic. The prostate is located in the lower abdominal area, which is in the 1st Yao of the upper hexagram. Since the six Yao positions can be transferred to the hands and feet, the doctor knows that this particular Yao correlates with the 1st Yao of the foot. Therefore, the doctor may focus his or her attention on the foot as an energetic entry point into the patient's prostate area.

When dividing the foot into six Yaos, the Qigong doctor knows that the 1st Yao of the foot is the heel area. Therefore, in order to treat the prostate gland, the doctor will focus his or her treatment on the patient's heel and ankle area. Alternatively, the doctor could have chosen the 1st Yao area of the hand, which is considered the 1st Yao position of the arm. Thus, the 1st Yao of the hand corresponds to the prostate and urogenital area.

HERBS AND THE YAOS

According to ancient Daoist teaching, Herbs may also be classified and prescribed in accordance with the six Yao hexagram patterns. For example, with plants, the Yao correspondences are described as follows (Figure 3.61):

1. **Roots:** Correspond to the bottom or 1st Yao
2. **Stalk:** Corresponds to the 2nd Yao
3. **Upper stems:** Corresponds to the 3rd Yao
4. **Branches:** Correspond to the 4th Yao
5. **Leaves:** Correspond to the 5th Yao
6. **Flowers & Fruit:** Correspond to the 6th Yao

When plants are used as medicine, the part of the plant corresponding to the number and position of the Yao manifests its healing properties through a particular energetic action, such as Ascending, Descending, Floating, or Sinking Qi. For example, the Achyranthes Root (Niu Xi), corresponds to the 1st Yao, and leads heal-

CHAPTER 3: TISSUE FORMATION AND DEVELOPMENT

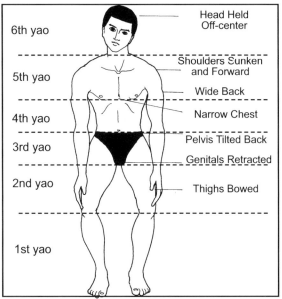

Figure 3.62. The Introverted Structure

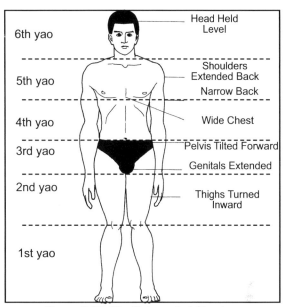

Figure 3.63. The Extroverted Structure

ing Qi downward; helping to heal the patient's lower back, knees and joints. The Chrysanthemum Flower (Ju Hua) on the other hand, corresponds to the top Yao, and leads healing Qi upward into the area of the patient's head and eyes.

IDENTIFYING INTROVERTED AND EXTROVERTED STRUCTURES

Qi flows through the matrix of the connective tissue and adapts to the postural and structural demands of the body by changing the density and direction of the body's connective tissues and inner fasciae. Any postural habit creates an imprinted tissue memory in the supporting connective tissue, as well as an energetic memory in the supporting channels of Qi. These imprints can result in introverted or extroverted postural structures.

Each introverted (Yin) and extroverted (Yang) postural structure has a predictable impact on the myofascial webbing, as well as on the emotional disposition. Emotions create changes in posture, Qi flow, and breathing patterns and conversely, can be influenced by them. The patient's breathing pattern, emotional state and Qi flow affect his or her posture. Primary structural patterns are determined by the patient's habitual posture, which is in turn a composite of habitual breathing patterns, Qi flow and emotional states. All chronic stress creates postural imprinting or tissue memory and a corresponding energetic memory in the supporting Qi field.

INTROVERTED STRUCTURE

In a patient with an introverted structure, the back (Yang) area is rounded, and the his or her muscle structure is usually well-developed. The front of the body (Yin), especially around the chest and Heart area, is retracted, resulting in a narrow chest. The patient's head is generally held off-center, and his or her shoulders are sunken and slightly forward. Additionally, the patient's pelvis is tilted back with the genitals retracted (posterior tilt). This introverted condition is commonly referred to as "extended Yang and retracted Yin" of the upper torso (Figure 3.62).

EXTROVERTED STRUCTURE

In a patient with an extroverted structure, the back (Yang) area is retracted, while the front of the patient's body is expanded (Yin) and overly exposed. The head is usually held vertically, the shoulders are slightly extended back and the chest is wide. Additionally, the patient's pelvis is tilted forward with genitals extended (anterior tilt). This extroverted condition is commonly referred to as "extended Yin and retracted Yang" of the upper back (Figure 3.63).

COMBINED STRUCTURAL FORMATIONS

As with the Five Element Constitutions, the introverted and extroverted structures provide guidelines for the Medical Qigong Doctor to evaluate the patient. These guidelines are not fixed, and the doctor is most likely to encounter combinations of introverted and extroverted structures in one patient. When two structures combine in an individual, the combination may be congenital or acquired in nature. Therefore the doctor must always differentiate between a patient's congenital and acquired tissue formations.

CONGENITAL AND ACQUIRED ENERGETIC PATTERNS

When a Medical Qigong Doctor is evaluating a patient's physical condition according to whether the patterns are congenital or acquired, he may ask specific questions. These questions are used to determine whether the condition was acquired through exposure to environmental pathogens, diet, trauma, occupation, or congenitally inherited and genetic in origin.

This information aids the doctor in obtaining a deeper understanding of the patient's condition, and in helping the patient reprogram any dysfunctional congenital or acquired cellular patterns, described as follows:

1. **Congenital Cellular Patterns and Disease:** According to Traditional Chinese Medicine, sometimes while in-utero, certain predispositions are energetically locked within the patient's Yuan Jing (Original Essence), and can be later released inside the body like a biological time-bomb. This is similar to the Western medical concept of genetic or inherited disease. The goal of Medical Qigong Therapy is to alter the toxic energetic pattern and to help the patient's body recognize that the energetic formation of the disease is a "mistake." Once these subtle energetic "awakenings" is achieved, the doctor will begin to stimulate the creative healing potential of the patient's Yuan Shen (Original Mind/Heart) as it expresses itself through the tissues.

   In order to reprogram these energetic patterns, the Medical Qigong Doctor will prescribe guided meditations that involve vivid imagination, colorful visualizations, and positive affirmations. These images are used to identify diseased patterns and to release and return them to the divine light.

   While in the presence of the divine light, the Xie (toxic) Qi can either be energetically transformed and recycled back to the patient as a form of healing energy, or be energetically disintegrated and scattered into the universe. That way when healing the diseased condition, the empty void left by the released energetic pattern is suddenly filled from within by the resonant expression of the patient's Yuan Shen (Original Mind/Heart). Patients with a family history of cancer, for example, can neutralize this tendency by correctly employing this type of Medical Qigong imagery.

2. **Acquired Cellular Patterns and Diseases:** These toxic patterns arise from either external exposure to pathogens, or the chronic suppression of emotions. The initial goal of the Medical Qigong Doctor is to assist the patient in discovering the origin of his or her present disease. The next step is to teach the patient to alter the toxic energetic patterns.

   In order to reprogram these dominant energetic patterns, the doctor will have the patient attempt to identify and eliminate all known external pathogenic factors. Next, the doctor will clinically Purge the patient's body, and eliminate all of the pathogens from the patient's energetic fields. Finally, the doctor will Tonify the patient's Righteous Qi, internal organ system, and Weiqi fields.

   The patient must additionally address all chronic patterns of emotional suppression. In order to reprogram these toxic patterns, the doctor will help the patient identify specific emotions related to the initial trauma from the patient's personal history. Then, the doctor will encourage the patient to release the suppressed energy through Medical Qigong exercises and prescription meditations. For example, a patient who has been experiencing severe headaches due to a stressful work or family environment will immediately benefit from this kind of energetic treatment.

Summary

By observing the patient's physical and structural development, the Medical Qigong Doctor will gain an understanding of the various strengths and weaknesses of the patient's internal organs and immune system.

The four patterns of physical development and structural formation described in this chapter (The Five Element Constitutions, the Yao Hexagram Formations, the Yin or Yang Structures, and the Congenital and Acquired Cellular Patterns) are summarized as follows (Figure 3.64):

1. **Five Element Constitution:** First, the doctor begins to diagnose the patient's physical body according to the Five Element Constitutions and the dominant Element. This helps the doctor to understand the condition of the patient's internal organs.
2. **The Upper And Lower Hexagram Pattern:** The doctor further divides the patient's body into six upper and lower Yao to determine the dominant energetic and emotional patterns (where the patient's Qi is gathering, collecting, and stagnating).

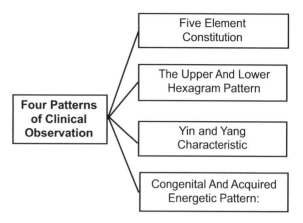

Figure 3.64. The Patterns of Physical Development Observed in the Medical Qigong Clinic

3. **Yin and Yang Characteristic:** The doctor evaluates the patient's external structure according to his or her body's Yin and Yang characteristics to understand whether the patient has a primarily introverted or extroverted physique.
4. **Congenital And Acquired Energetic Pattern:** The doctor determines whether the patient's condition is congenital, acquired, or a combination of both. This information helps the doctor understand the nature of the energetic and cellular patterns underlying the disease.

CHAPTER 4
THE FIVE ENERGIES OF THE HUMAN BODY

FIVE TYPES OF CELLULAR ENERGY

The study of various forms of Qi and energetic transformations has led to one of the greatest theories in physics - the Law of Conservation of Energy, which states:

> "Energy can neither be created or destroyed. It may be transformed from one form into another, but the total amount of energy in a given system never changes."

Physics defines four types of energy: Mechanical, Electromagnetic, Chemical and Thermal. All four types of energy interrelate and convert from one to another. Electricity, for example, can be converted into Sound, Light, Mechanical Energy, and Heat. Conversely, Sound, Light, Mechanical Energy, and Heat can all be reconverted into Electricity.

Western Science is philosophically rooted in the "Enlightenment" obtained from the 17th Century period of Western Europe. This knowledge is still, for the most part, founded on the scientific principles established by Sir Isaac Newton and Descartes, and relies heavily on logical and measurable scientific evidence and methods. This observation generally sees humanity as separate and relatively independent from the cycles and processes of nature and the environment, viewing energy as an impersonal and inanimate force. This antiquated Western scientific view, has led to the clinical separation of treatment methods used to individually target the experiences of a patient's body, mind, and spirit (mind/heart).

The ancient Daoists believed that all things were intimately connected in a vast unbroken harmony, existing within the eternal matrix of the Dao. They perceived human beings as a microcosm of the universe that surrounded them, with the same essential forces that motivated the macrocosm. This ancient view of energy is much more akin to the theories of quantum physics.

Both Daoist energetic theories and quantum physics hypothesize that energy cannot be studied

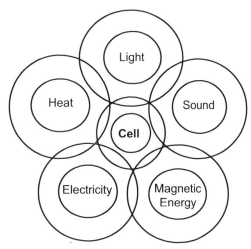

Figure 4.1. The Five Major Forms of Energy Active within the Human Body

without taking into account the mind's influence over it. Furthermore, as energy and matter are interchangeable, energetic behavior cannot be studied independently of matter.

From a Medical Qigong perspective, the entire human body is infused with energy from the environment, which is converted within the human organism. Light energy, for example, is absorbed, stored, and converted into various forms of energy within the tissues, similar to the way that plants absorb and convert light into chemical energy.

There are five major forms of energy active within the human body (Figure 4.1). Sound, Light, Magnetism, Heat, and Electricity envelop and sustain all of our internal experiences, as well as all of our interactions with the external world. These five energies not only sustain, govern and control our psychology and physiology, but also determine the subtle resonances of our energetic and spiritual fields.

In Medical Qigong Therapy, these energies are considered to be properties of the deeper spiritual reality that underlies and directs the body's physical reality. Therefore, in the Medical Qigong Clinic, these energies are considered in both the diagnosis and treatment of all illness.

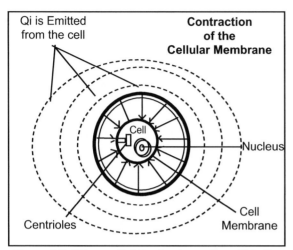

Figure 4.2. When a Cell Contracts, matter within the cell is released and transformed into energy.

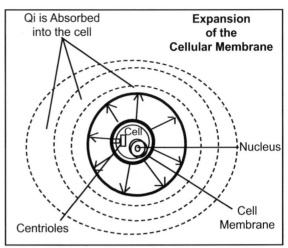

Figure 4.3. When a Cell Expands, energy is taken from outside the cell and transformed into matter within the cell.

Cellular Vibration and the Five Energies of the Human Body

The condition and level of the body's overall health, stems from the active patterns of cellular vibration within the tissues. The body's cells are constantly resonating, expanding and contracting with the cycles and flow of the body's Qi. Throughout this process of cellular expansion and contraction, matter (Jing) is continually being transformed into energy (Qi), and energy is continually being transformed back into matter.

When a cell contracts (known as "cellular exhalation"), matter within the cell is released and transformed into energy (Figure 4.2). When a cell expands (known as "cellular inhalation"), energy is taken from outside the cell and transformed into matter within the cell (Figure 4.3).

- **"Qi Excess:"** If a group of cells contract too much (e.g., due to stress, overwork, too much caffeine or other stimulants), an excessively large amount of energy is released from within the cells into the space surrounding the cells. This results in a condition clinically known as "Qi Excess," because more energy has been released than the body is able to utilize or process. Qi Excess can manifest through symptoms such as radiating heat.
- **"Qi Stagnation:"** The accumulated Qi surrounding the cells can also obstruct the body's energetic flow, resulting in a condition clinically known as "Qi Stagnation." Qi Stagnation can manifest through symptoms such as pain, inflammation and swelling.
- **"Qi Deficiency:"** Conversely, if a group of cells expand too much (e.g., due to obesity, sleeping, lethargy, or depression), a great amount of energy is absorbed from the space surrounding the cells, and is converted into matter within the cell. When too much matter is absorbed into the cell, an insufficiency of energy is created outside of the cells resulting in a condition clinically known as "Qi Deficiency." Qi Deficiency can manifest through symptoms such coldness, weakness, fatigue, and degenerative conditions.

Matter and energy rhythmically transform into each other within and around the cells. Constantly transforming back and forth, this cellular activity energetically influences the nearby cells, creating a sympathetic resonance that is unique to each type of tissue. The Daoist believe that the tissues, energies, and emotions connected to each internal organ is based on this concept of sympathetic resonance, and not on the Western classification of tissues and tissue functions.

Chinese Energetic Medicine approaches disease with the understanding that the energy and cellular function of the tissues must both be harmonized in order to initiate healing. Every cell of the body responds to and produces Sound, Light, Magnetic Energy, Electricity, and Heat. Therefore, all tissues and the functions of the body can be either positively or negatively influenced by the amount and quality of any one of the above five energies. The majority of celestial and environmental influences on the body (i.e., excluding the more subtle aspects of the Mind/Heart) can be explained in terms of these energies. The effect of each type of energy on the body is described as follows (Figure 4.4):

- **Sound:** When the body is exposed to any type of sound resonance, the tissues and cell structures are influenced by that particular frequency or combination of frequencies. Therefore, tone frequency can be used clinically to Purge energetic excess or stagnation conditions, and calm the nervous system.
- **Light:** All living cells emit units of light called "bio-photons." Emitted light affects cellular membranes, and can be used clinically to Tonify energetic deficiencies.
- **Magnetic Energy:** The body's cells carry electromagnetic fields containing positive (+) and negative (-) polarities that both attract and repel each other. This results in a magnetic pull between the body's various types of Qi, tissues, organs, and extremities. Specific magnetic fields can be created to either attract (Tonify), repel (Purge), unify (Regulate) and direct the Qi created from within the cells.
- **Heat:** The heat within the body causes increased electron movement, resulting in the generation of more heat at the cellular level. Heat is also created as a by-product of cellular metabolism and can be used to increase the activity of Qi and Tonify an energetic deficiency.
- **Electricity:** The electromagnetic energy in the cells is continuously generated through the biochemical transformations of food and air, and is circulated by the electromagnetic fields generated by the tissues. Examples of the electrical energy in the body are found in the bioelectrical impulses of the nervous system and heart.

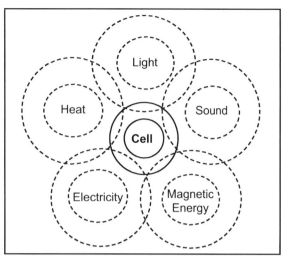

Figure 4.4. Each of the body's cells produces and responds to the vibrational resonance of Sound, Light, Heat, Magnetic and Electric sensations.

SOUND ENERGY RESONANCES

Audible sound has three main energetic characteristics: pulse, wave, and form. Every phenomenon, from molecular to cosmic, is the result of the combination and interaction of these three forces, described as follows:

- **Pulse:** The term "pulse" is used to describe the generating aspect of sound, arising from the energetic force of expansion and contraction. Energetically, the pulse is the fundamental field which simultaneously creates wave and form patterns.

  In musical terms, the pulse is expressed as the "beat" that is experienced in a repetitive series of identical, yet distinct, periodic short-duration stimuli. This type of rhythmical pulse is typically what listeners entrain to as they tap their foot or dance along with a piece of music.
- **Wave:** A sound "wave" is represented in the rising (expanding) and falling (contracting) rhythm of an energetic pulse. The original pulse is always contained within the wave.

  A sound wave's energetic properties and characteristics are often described in terms of Frequency, Wavelength, Wavenumber, Amplitude, Sound, Pressure, Intensity, Speed, and Direction.

Sound Image From Sand	Sound Image From Water
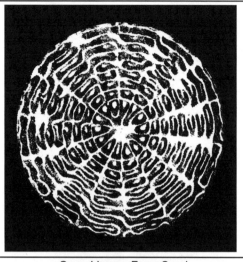	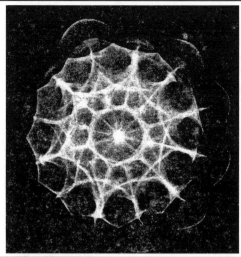
Sound Image From Sand	Sound Image From Water
	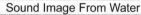

Figure 4.5. Dr. Hans Jenny's Sound Form Images (created from sand and water)

- **Form:** Sound "form" can be observed by subjecting matter to a continuous sound vibrational pattern. In the mid-1960's, research scientist Dr. Hans Jenny created sound form images by placing sand or water on a steel plate with a crystal sound oscillator attached to the bottom. The sound vibrated the steel plate and organized the matter placed on it into various forms and patterns (Figure 4.5 and Figure 4.6). Dr. Jenny's findings revealed that the sound pulse and waves were not the by-products of an unregulated chaos, but of dynamically ordered energetic patterns. Other research physicists have discovered similar phenomena using water, light, and subatomic particles in conjunction with sound vibration.

This extensive research on the various effects of sound on water, has great significance to the understanding of the subtle influences that sound, music, and speech have on the human body. Although the human body appears to be solid, it is roughly 75% liquid. The Blood is 92% water, the brain and muscles are 75 % water, and the bones are about 22 percent water.

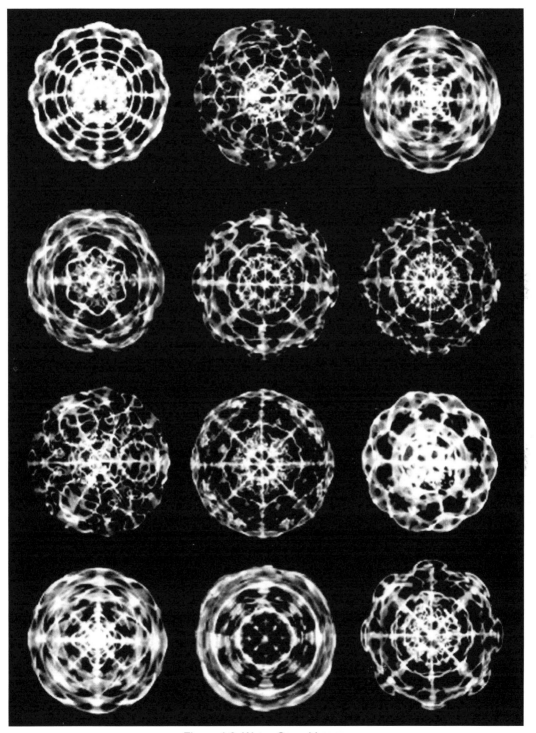

Figure 4.6. Water-Sound Images

Sound Energy and the Human Body

All of matter is a manifestation of vibration and wave function. Both the solid and liquid aspects of the body are organized and defined by underlying vibrational patterns, which maintain the body's structural form. Energetically, we are constructed of pulses (energetic fields), waves (energetic vibrations) and form (energetic particles).

Sound has a profound influence as an energetic code on the subtle body. Sound is capable of accessing consciousness and creating a link between matter and spirit. When the body is exposed to any type of sound resonance, the tissues and cell structures are affected by that particular frequency or combination of frequencies, which results in either an automatic positive or negative response.

The human body both receives and generates sound energy. These subtle sounds resonate from four distinct physical and energetic actions. The following subtle sounds are natural tones that resonate as a result of four physical energetic actions: breath, muscle movements, Qi movements and the subtle pulsating sounds of the center core Taiji Pole, which are described as follows (Figure 4.7):

1. **Breathing:** This physical action creates respiratory sound resonances, that follow the inhaled and exhaled air through the lungs, mouth, and nose. The condition of the five Yin Organs are naturally reflected by the body's respiratory patterns, described as follows:
   - **The Liver:** By grunting, screaming, and sighing
   - **The Heart:** By laughing and cooing
   - **The Spleen:** By singing, whistling, humming, gurgling, belching, and hiccuping
   - **The Lungs:** By yawning, sneezing, sniffing, panting, sighing, sobbing, and crying
   - **The Kidneys:** By groaning, whining, moaning, yelping, gasping, and shivering
2. **Muscle Movements:** This physical action creates somatic and visceral sound resonances. These include the clicking of the joints, the beating of the heart, the movement of the blood flowing through the veins and vessels, and the gurgling of the stomach and intestines.
3. **Qi Movements:** Energy can produce a more subtle type of sound resonance. For example,

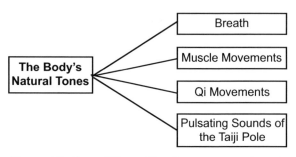

Figure 4.7. Natural Tones That Resonate as a Result of Four Physical Energetic Actions

when Liver Yang, Liver Fire, or Liver Wind rise, a high-pitched tone is heard in the ears. When the Kidney Yin is deficient, this sound is dull, like rushing wind.

Additionally, in advanced stages of Daoist Alchemy, the movement of the Qi within a disciples body will create what is traditionally known as the "Inner Sound." Because all matter is composed of energy, all living things have a sound quality to them. The whole universe and everything in it, is derived from sound.

In Daoist Alchemy, the "Inner Sound" is traditionally heard by all disciples during deep meditation practice. It is sometimes described as a sacred current, vibrating as a rhythmical stream of life within the disciple's body. The internal resonance of the disciple's "Inner Sound" is considered to be a sacred vibration, manifesting as the internal experience of his Yuan Shen (Original Mind/Heart). It is a combination of the most subtle energetic forms of inner music and inner light, spiritually resonating within the disciple's Three Bodies.

4. **Energy Pulsating:** The energy within the body's center core Taiji Pole creates the most subtle sound vibrations within the human body. These vibrations resonating from deep within the body's Taiji Pole, manifest as three distinct pulsating sounds. They are produced when the current of energy pulsating within the Taiji Pole interacts with the body's Upper, Middle, and Lower Dantians. These sounds can be heard when an individual is in deep meditation.

THE ANATOMY OF LISTENING

Although the human body is capable of hearing, the ability to perceive and listen energetically is quite different. In this case, sounds must be both perceived by the ear as well as analyzed and decoded by the Brain.

The basic anatomy of the ear consists of three main structures, described as follows (Figure 4.8):

- **The Outer Ear:** The external area of the ear is responsible for collecting and channeling sound. It is composed of the Ear Lobe (i.e., the Auricle or Pinna), and the Ear Canal (the External Auditory Meatus). Both structures funnel sound waves towards the Ear Drum (Tympanic Membrane), allowing it to vibrate. The Ear Lobe is also responsible for protecting the Ear Drum from damage. Modified sweat glands in the Ear Canal form ear wax.

- **The Middle Ear:** The middle area of the ear is responsible for converting sound energy into mechanical energy, amplifying it, and then transferring it on to the next inner chamber.

    The Middle Ear is an air filled space, located in the Temporal Bone of the skull. Air pressure is equalized in this space via the Eustachian Tube, which drains into the back of the nose and throat (i.e., the Nasopharynx area).

    There are three small Ossicles bones (i.e., the Malleus, Incus, and Stapes) that are located adjacent to the Tympanic Membrane. They are attached like a chain to the Tympanic Membrane, and convert sound waves that vibrate the membrane into mechanical vibrations.

- **The Inner Ear:** The internal part of the ear is responsible for both auditory and vestibular stimulation. It has two main functions; the first is hearing and the second is balance.

BALANCE, LISTENING, AND STIMULATION

According to French Otolaryngologist Dr. Alfred Tomatis, there are three main functions of the ear: Balance, Listening and Stimulation, described as follows (Figure 4.9):

- **Balance:** This involves the ear's function of maintaining equilibrium, tissue symmetry, and the integration of motor and sensory information. Of the three main components to the ear, only the Inner Ear is responsible for balance.

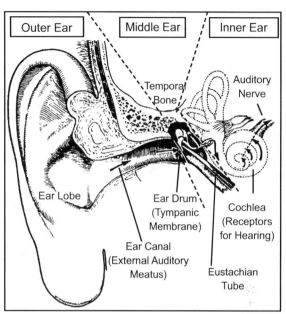

Figure 4.8. The three main structures of the Ear (Inspired by the original artwork of Wynn Kapit)

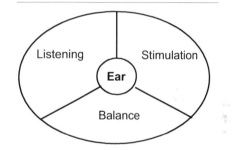

Figure 4.9. The Three Main Functions of the Ear

The body's balance is a choreographed arrangement, that takes sensory information from a variety of organs and integrates it in order to tell the body where it is in relation to gravity and the energetic fields of the Earth.

When regulating the body's balance, information from the vestibular system of the Inner Ear is sent to the brainstem, cerebellum, and spinal cord. Any abnormal vestibular signals causes the body to try and compensate by making adjustments in the body's posture (torso and limbs), as well as making changes in eye movement to adjust sight input into the brain.

- **Listening:** Anytime you make an effort to hear, it involves the ear's function of analyzing and

decoding vibrations from both outside the body (Cochlea), and inside the body (Vestibular). This allows an individual to audibly perceive external sounds (such as language) and recreate them using the vocal cords.
- **Stimulation:** This involves the ear's function of stimulating the Central Nervous System and the cortex of the brain. The ear is connected to the 10th Cranial Nerve (i.e., the Vagus Nerve) which affects the heart, larynx, bronchi, and intestinal tract.

According to ancient Daoist teaching, there are two types of sound stimulation that will affect an individuals listening: Turbid Sound and Clean Sound, described as follows:

Turbid (Yin) Sound Stimulation: This type of sound is toxic to the body, resulting in both physical and energetic fatigue to the listener.

Clean (Yang) Sound Stimulation: This type of sound is beneficial to the body, resulting in energetically stimulating and charging the listener's Central Nervous System, and the cortex of the brain.

The Anatomy of the Spoken Sound

Energetically, spoken sound is the result of a powerful spiritual interaction and energetic fusion involving the Brain (Kidney Water) and Heart (Heart Fire). It is therefore important for the Shen to guide and direct the spoken sound, as the projected voice is a direct manifestation of the individual's spirit and life-force energy.

In human physiology, the body creates sound vibration by controlling the flow of air as it passes through the larynx in the throat. The larynx, which is located in the upper part of the trachea, contains the vocal cords, which consist of two strong bands of elastic tissue (another form of fascia) that are stretched across the larynx. The stream of exhaled air is transformed into controlled sound vibration by regulating the amount of tension placed on the elastic membranes of the vocal cords. With the exhalation, Qi is released from the diaphragm, lungs, trachea and bronchi, and is modified and refined by the action of the larynx.

As the air is forced through the membranous folds of the larynx, a small amount of pressure

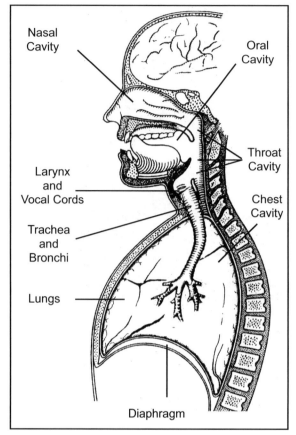

Figure 4.10. The Mechanics of Sound Creation

builds up behind the closed membranes of the vocal cords and causes them to vibrate. This vibration creates controlled waves of sound that resonate within and around the body (Figure 4.10). These sound waves are further amplified through the primary "resonators" (consisting of the nasal, oral and throat cavities), and the secondary "resonators" (consisting of the chest cavities and chest Bones). The emitted sound is further shaped and augmented through primary "articulators" (consisting of the lips, teeth, gum ridges, hard palate, soft palate, tongue, and uvula).

The resonating surfaces of the body's tissues act as initial vibrators of sound. Bone, cartilage, membrane and muscle have the potential of serving as living amplifiers and conductors. Thus, the structure and density of the body's tissues modify and enhance the quality of emitted sound. The harder the surface of the tissue, the stronger the energetic resonance. It is for this reason that the sounds made by a patient (language, moaning, etc.) create an accurate and detailed map of the individual's internal physical structure. In addition to using sound as a diagnostic modality, the Medical Qigong Doctor is also able to use emitted sound for a variety of therapeutic purposes.

SOUND THERAPY THROUGH EMITTED QI

As sound waves vibrate through the body, the liquid crystalline structures of the tissues transform the vibration into pulsed currents. These currents are then conducted throughout the body to various structures, organs and glands, according to the frequency and amplitude of the incoming wave signal. As the tissues change and transform due to the influence of sound wave vibrations, it automatically creates a corresponding change in the function and flow of energy in the body. Thus, sound vibrations have a profound effect on psychology, physiology, and the flow of the body's internal energy. Sound and tone resonation have been used for centuries as effective healing tools and are currently used as an integral part of modern Qigong Medicine.

Recent research on molecular water patterns has confirmed what the ancient Chinese sages have known for millennia, that the vibrational patterns of sound can disrupt the tissues' energetic patterns and can initiate a new energetic pattern. Depending on the type of projected sound vibration, the new pattern can either be healthy or destructive.

During extensive experimentations, a drop of water was subjected to the vibrational patterns of specific sounds. At a certain pitch, the drop of water's entire structure dissolved and immediately created (and maintained) an entirely different energetic pattern. Each time the sound pattern was altered, it initiated a chaotic energetic resonance into the water-drop form, causing the water-drop to disperse and reshape itself in accordance with the new projected sound pattern.

FIVE ANCIENT CHINESE PITCHES

For centuries in China, patients have used sound therapy to heal certain parts of the body. Used in this way, sound therapy stimulates the flow of Qi and Blood to move into and/or away from specific internal organs and tissues. This new movement of Qi and Blood is used to increase health and energetic balance within the patient. The primary healing sounds relate to the Five Agents, the Five Element aspects of the patient's internal organs, and to the Chinese Pentatonic Scale.

The Chinese Pentatonic Scale is essentially five energetic pitches, placed within a rotating circle, with no fixed starting or ending point (Figure 4.11). In music terminology, there is no fixed "tonic" note (i.e., the first tone of a scale) used in order to start the scale. This gives the energetic pattern of the melody a type of floating quality to its musical structure.

The non-tempered Chinese Pentatonic Scale causes the listener to become more energetically alive and alert, to the ever shifting and sometimes disharmonious musical patterns resonating about him. The listener must continue to internally reconcile the disharmonious tones, as if forced to bring the slight dissonance between the tones that are stimulating the left and right hemispheres of the brain into balance. This type of musical regulation process is inherently alchemical in nature, in the sense that he must transmute two disharmonious forces into a third tone-entity, by way of focused internal centering.

The following describes each of the Five Tones, their energetic correspondences, their secret military manifestations revealed in Feng Jiao Divination, their Five Element Pattern, and their associated internal organ system:

- **Gong -C- (The Tone of Princes):** This sound corresponds to the rumbling of "Thunder in Autumn;" its secret military divination reveals that the army is of good accord, and both soldiers and officers agree; its Element is Earth; and its Internal Organ is the Spleen.
- **Shang - D - (The Tone of Ministers):** This sound corresponds to the "Peals of Thunder in Autumn;" its secret military divination reveals great victory in battles, and strong

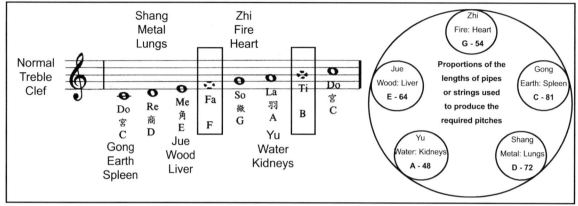

Figure 4.11. The Five Energetic Pitches and Their Corresponding Elements

soldiers; its Element is Metal; and its Internal Organ is the Lungs.

- **Jue -E- (The Tone of People):** This sound corresponds to the "Violent Winds of Summer;" its secret military divination reveals that the army is troubled, and the soldiers lose courage; its Element is Wood; and its Internal Organ is the Liver.
- **Zhi - G- (The Tone of Affairs):** This sound corresponds to "The Lightning Flashes in Autumn;" its secret military divination reveals that the army is restless and irritated, and the soldiers are tired; its Element is Fire; and its Internal Organ is the Heart.
- **Yu -A- (The Tone of Beings):** This sound corresponds to "The Cloudburst in Spring and Summer;" its secret military divination reveals that the soldiers are soft and there will be no glory in battle; its Element is Water; and its Internal Organ is the Kidneys.

It is said that within this underlying Five Phase Pentatonic scale, every single note contains the vibration of all the rest, yet each has an individual participatory "consciousness" within its energetic field.

Projected Sound

The Medical Qigong Doctor can project powerful sound vibrations by focusing on the middle of all three Dantians, at the center of his Taiji Pole. With intention and focused concentration, the doctor can vibrate specific internal organs and combine these energies with the Qi of the Dantians to project powerful sound vibrations in order to treat a patient. Traditionally, a Medical Qigong Doctor is trained to practice Vibrating Sound Therapy according to the following four methods:

1. **Audible Toning:** By audibly toning the healing sounds, the doctor can fill his energetic field with a solid "tangible" healing sound vibration. This audible energetic field of sound is then projected into his patient's tissues. Audible sound resonance is considered to be a Jing level of energetic projection, and is generally used when the patient is emotionally armored or not energetically sensitive.

2. **Slightly Audible Toning:** By using slightly audibly healing tones (also known as "Whispering Sound Therapy"), the doctor can project and release a type of emotional vibration into the patient's tissues. In this method, the doctor will begin by internally focusing his mind on the healing sound. As this internal sound fills the doctor's energetic field, it is then emitted into the patient's body. To increase the energetic intensity of the sound projection, the doctor needs only to increase the mind's intention and the pressure of his exhalation. Slightly audible sound resonance is considered a Qi level energy projection, and is generally used when the patient is energetically sensitive.

3. **Inaudible Toning:** By projecting the healing sounds with breath, in conjunction with focused mental intention (also known as

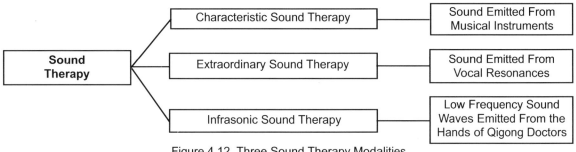

Figure 4.12. Three Sound Therapy Modalities

"Breath Incantation"), the doctor can initiate deep yet subtle vibrations inside the patient's body. In this method, the doctor will begin by internally focusing his mind on the healing sound. As this internal sound fills the doctor's energetic field, it is then emitted into the patient's body through soft exhalation. To increase the intensity of the energetic sound projection, the doctor needs only to increase his mind's intention, and focus the vibration resonating deeper into the patient's tissues. Inaudible sound resonation is considered a Shen level energy projection, and is used when the patient is energetically sensitive.

4. **Combined Toning:** In this special method, both the doctor and patient simultaneously resonate the sound in order to enhance the synchronization of both their energy fields. As the doctor resonates his own internal organ sound along with the participating patient, the sound and energy patterns can be modulated as needed. Sometimes the doctor will combine color with the emitted sound in order to increase the sound's effect on the patient's tissues. This combined sound resonation is used in cases of extreme armoring, in which the patient first needs to be brought to a state where he can feel his tissues vibrating.

THREE MODALITIES OF SOUND THERAPY

The healing sounds used by Medical Qigong Doctors are effective because they are based on an understanding of the multidimensional influence of sound on the human structure. The modulated nature of sound pulsation affects the energetic structures which shape and maintain the patient's physical structure. Once the patient's energetic structures have been disturbed, the body must immediately begin a reconstructive process, creating new energetic patterns to restructure and heal the tissues.

In 1996, I spent quite some time studying privately with a Daoist Master of Esoteric Sound Therapy named Yu Yan Min. Master Min explained that in ancient China, music was commonly used for Trance Induction, Summoning Spirits, Sex Magic, and Healing Wounds. When applied in the clinical setting, there were traditionally three main methods of Sound Therapy used for healing application. These three main methods are described as follows (Figure 4.12):

1. **Characteristic Sound Therapy:** This refers to the sound produced by musical instruments (flute, guitar, piano, drum, etc.) and their effects on the subconscious mind. This type of instrumental musical energy creates specific physical, emotional, and spiritual states in both the listener and within the energetic fields of the surrounding environment.

2. **Extraordinary Sound Therapy:** This refers to the vocal resonances used in chanting, prayer, and singing. Such techniques include the Daoist Six-Word Healing Sound Method, Zhuang Zi's Breath Listening Method, and Lao Zi's Sound-Voice Method. This type of sound therapy uses the individual's cultivated internal energy to produce sound with focused intention and enhanced visualization. It is also practiced in conjunction with breathing techniques that are guided by the practitioners Yuan Shen (Original Heart/Mind). All of these energetic techniques are internally combined

in order to achieve a powerful physiological and psychological transformational state.

3. **Infrasonic Sound Therapy:** This refers to the low frequency sound waves emitted from the hands of Medical Qigong Doctors. These chaotic low frequency sound waves are inaudible to the human ear, and are a vibrational by-product of the intense amount of Qi focused in a Medical Qigong Doctor's hands. This subtle yet powerful infrasonic sound resonance affects the central nervous system and alters the body's neurophysiological functions. Extensive research performed by Richard H. Lee of the Chi Institute in San Clemente, California, as well as research performed by the Beijing College of Traditional Chinese Medicine and the Department of Natural Science in Beijing, China, confirms that all humans have a very high degree of acoustic activity in the subsonic range below 20 Hertz (infrasonic). This subsonic level of sound vibration is the "hum" of human energy, similar to the alpha rhythm of an EEG.

In the clinic, Medical Qigong Doctors may combine Characteristic, Extraordinary, and Infrasonic Sound Therapies into one treatment modality, in order to facilitate a deeper and more thorough energetic transformation within their patient's tissues. The choice of which sound prescriptions to apply varies according to each patient's cultural upbringing, religious beliefs, emotional temperament, and appreciation of energetic healing modalities.

Music and Sound Therapy

Since ancient times, masters of Chinese Energetic Medicine have known that musical patterns can affect an individual's health, character, morality, and consciousness. In one ancient Daoist text, it is written that "each sound has something that it disturbs, calls, and causes to come." Because of this supernatural energetic principle, it was written in the *Book of History*, that the ancient Daoists traditionally used the power of music to tame wild animals, change the natural order of the world, provoke drought, or alter the course of the seasons.

When notes are specifically arranged into rhythmical and melodic patterns, they can produce either a positive or negative effect on the body's physical, energetic, and spiritual fields. One of the books written in the *Daoist Treaties on Ceremonial Usages,* entitled *The Book of Music,* states that an individual's passions should be restrained by means of music.

The importance that the ancient Daoists placed on sound and music as necessary to harmonizing the forces of Nature is found in many ancient texts, including the Confucian Classics, where the great sage advised that Musical Rites be performed regularly, in order to prevent beasts from going wild and to avert natural catastrophes.

Entrainment and Sound Therapy

The powerful effects of music are largely due to what is known as "entrainment." Entrainment is a principle in physics in which the stronger vibrations of one object (in this case, the musical instrument or voice) will cause the weaker vibrations of another object (the tissue cells) to change and begin oscillating at the same rate as the stronger object. Thus, the melody and rhythm of music can positively or negatively entrain an individual's body, mind, and spirit by affecting the rhythms of his or her subtle energetic fields.

Another effect of music on the body's tissues is that of destabilizing pre-existing physical and energetic patterns by temporarily introducing a new and more powerful sound vibration. Any exposure to powerful sound resonation disturbs the body's energetic field and disrupts the individual's pre-existing established patterns. This energetic disruption is known in Medical Qigong Therapy as "Chaotic Resonance." The principle of Chaotic Resonance can be applied therapeutically to disperse harmful physical and energetic patterns before the introduction of beneficial healing patterns. Similarly, unconscious exposure to fields of Chaotic Resonance can also disrupt the body's natural pattern and rhythms.

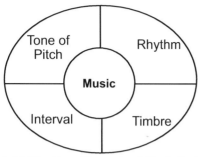

Figure 4.13. The Four Elements of Music that Induce a Physiological and Psychological Effect on the Body

THE FOUR ELEMENTS OF MUSIC THERAPY

Research has shown that the elements of music that induce a physiological and psychological effect on the body are: Rhythm, Tone or Pitch, Interval, and Timbre, described as follows (Figure 4.13):

- **Rhythm:** This is the energetic beat and pulse. It has the most immediate and intense effect on the body, especially affecting the individual's pulse rate, skin temperature, blood pressure, muscle tension, emotions and brain-wave activity.
- **Tone or Pitch:** This is the specific rate of vibration that determines different notes.
- **Interval:** This is the distance between the notes, and creates the melody, as well as the harmony.
- **Timbre:** This is the specific quality and "color" ("Energetic Nature") of the sound that is produced from an instrument or a voice. In ancient China, the voice was traditionally divided into five basic timbres, each related to the energetic natures of the Five Elements.

THE FIVE TIMBRES OF THE VOICE

In music, Timbre is also known as the tone quality manifesting through psychoacoustic sound. Likewise, the quality of an individual's voice has its own unique musical note or tone that distinguishes different types of sound production.

In simple terms, Timbre is what makes a particular musical sound different from another, even when they have the same pitch and volume. For example, there is the difference between a guitar and a piano playing the same note at the same volume. Experienced musicians are able to distinguish between different instruments based on their varied Timbres, even if those instruments are playing notes at the same pitch and volume.

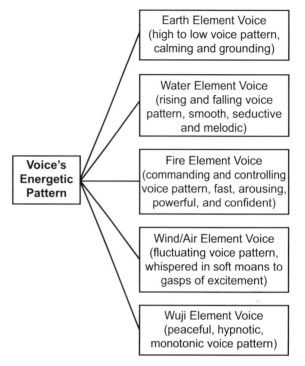

Figure 4.14. The seductive patterns of the voice

In ancient China, the energetic qualities of an individual's voice was divided into five primary Elements. According to Daoist teachings, the energy of each of these Five Element voices can be combined to create a symphony of living sounds and energetic breathing rhythms, which can sometimes be used for seduction and trance induction. Each energetic activity of the Five Element voices manifests a specific type of energy inside the listener's tissues, for example (Figure 4.14):

- **The Earth Element Voice:** The energy of this Element moves within the listener's body like a slow falling leaf. Its deep, high to low energetic voice pattern is used to calm, ground, and solidify. Often pausing or stopping, the Earth voice relaxes, and awakens the listener's feelings of trust and respect.
- **The Water Element Voice:** The energy of this Element moves within the listener's body like a seductive melody. Its smooth energetic nature rises and falls, and it is used to carry the listener's emotions into higher realms of excitement. The Water voice is intoxicating,

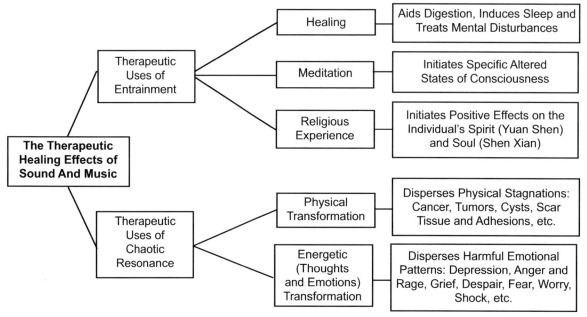

Figure 4.15. The Therapeutic Healing Effects of Sound and Music

tempting, soothing, healing, gathering, and harmonizing.

- **The Fire Element Voice:** The energy of this Element moves within the listener's body in a bold consuming pattern. The Fire voice is a spoken manifestation of energetic power and confidence, and it is used to command and control. The Fire voice is fast, arousing, exciting, horrifying, and awakening.
- **The Wind/Air Element Voice:** The energy of this Element moves within the listener's body in a fluctuating pattern. Whispered in enticing sounds that resonate from soft moans to gasps of excitement, the Wind voice is used energetically to move, inspire, and encourage. It uplifts the listener and carries him or her to the higher realms of emotional awareness.
- **The Wuji Element Voice:** The energy of this Element expands and dissolves the patterns of Qi and Shen within the listener's body. Usually spoken in a hypnotic, monotonic manner, the Wuji voice is energetically used for dispersing, and it is peaceful and liberating in nature. This voice is often used to energetically carry the listener back to his or her original spiritual nature (Yuan Shen).

THERAPEUTIC EFFECTS OF SOUND

Sound, music and vocal harmonics have always been acknowledged as a powerful medium for emotional enhancement. Scientific studies have shown that plants grow faster, trees produce sweeter fruit, cows produce more milk and patients recover quicker when they are exposed to soft, mellow music. The therapeutic healing applications of music and sound can be divided into two main categories: the therapeutic uses of Entrainment, and the therapeutic uses of Chaotic Resonance (Figure 4.15):

The Therapeutic Uses of Entrainment

The energetic principle of Entrainment can be applied therapeutically to induce healing, meditation and religious experience, and is described as follows:

- **Healing:** Vocal harmonics have been shown to physiologically create changes in heartbeat, respiration, and brain-wave patterns. Sounds and tones stimulate the cerebral centers creating a wide range of results including enhanced memory retention, facilitating certain emotions, stimulating creative inspirations, treating mental disturbances, aiding digestion, and inducing sleep.

- **Meditation:** Music and sound can initiate specific altered states of consciousness by influencing and directing the body's internal biorhythms and frequencies. When used as a healing modality, music and sound can cause subtle shifts and frequency coherence within the listener's Brain, Heart and internal organ systems. Examples range from Shamanic Trance to various other altered states.
- **Religious Experience:** For centuries, music and sound have been used to help people transcend the physical and social planes of awareness and enter into the archetypal realm of the spirit. The ancient Chinese Wu Yi (Shaman Doctors) would traditionally use music and sound to initiate positive effects on the listener's Spirit (Yuan Shen) and Eternal Soul (Shen Xian).

The Therapeutic Uses of Chaotic Resonance

The principle of Chaotic Resonance can be applied therapeutically to induce physical transformation and energetic transformation (effecting the thoughts and emotions), described as follows:
- **Physical Transformation:** Sound Therapy is often applied to disperse a wide variety of physical stagnations. This is because of the susceptibility of the body's tissues to vibrational resonance. In Medical Qigong Therapy, Chaotic Resonance is generally used in cases of stagnation to break up the cellular and energetic accumulations held within the liquid matrix of the body (see Volume 3, Chapter 39). Physical stagnations that have been proven to be especially responsive to Medical Qigong Sound Therapy include: cancer, tumors, cysts, scar tissue and fascial adhesions. Modern Sound Therapy treatment protocols include the use of sound to break up kidney stones and gallstones (shock-wave lithotripsy), and the use of ultrasound to relieve sore muscles.
- **Energetic (Thoughts and Emotions) Transformation:** The principle of Chaotic Resonance can be applied to disperse harmful energetic and emotional patterns. Examples include using Chaotic Resonance in the treatment of depression, anger, rage, grief, despair, fear, worry and shock.

Harmful Effects

The improper or unconscious exposure to music and sound can damage or imbalance the individual's physical, energetic, or spiritual well being. The harmful effects of music and sound can be divided into two main categories: the harmful effects of Entrainment, and the harmful effects of Chaotic Resonance (Figure 4.16):

The Harmful Effects of Entrainment

The harmful effects of Entrainment can be observed when exposure to music or sound creates an unhealthy or unnatural pattern of resonance within the body's tissues and energetic fields. Modern research has shown diseases and emotions to possess specific vibrational frequency patterns, which can be accidently triggered by chronic exposure to any strong detrimental vibrational field.

The harmful effects of Entrainment are generally due to exposure to music or sound that is extreme in nature (too loud, too fast, too slow, etc.), or out of harmony with the body's natural frequencies. Examples include jackhammers, sirens, car horns, heavy machinery, heavy metal music, fast aerobic or trance dance music, and depressing musical compositions such as funeral marches. Such exposure can negatively affect the listener's physical, energetic, and spiritual health.
- **Physical:** Entrainment can have a negative effect on the body's physiology when the dominant vibration to which the listener is exposed creates patterns detrimental to proper cell and tissue structure. Examples of the harmful physical effects of Entrainment include:
    1. A physical weakening of the muscles.
    2. Psychophysiological deterioration (syncopated rhythms).
    3. Uncontrollable cellular proliferation.
    4. Epileptic seizures in energetically hypersensitive individuals (certain rhythms).
- **Energetic (Thoughts and Emotions):** Entrainment can have a negative effect on the energetic field of the body by inciting toxic thoughts and emotions. This effect can be created with either harmful musical tones and patterns, or through disturbing lyrics that affect the listener's sub-

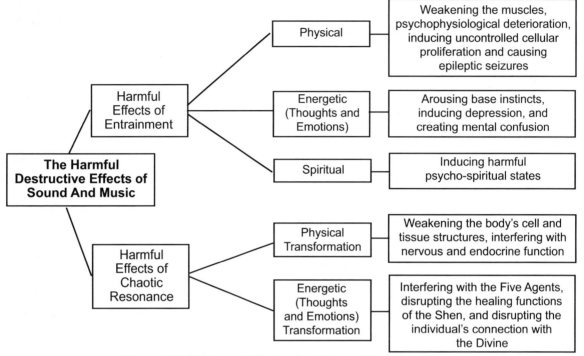

Figure 4.16. The Harmful Destructive Effects of Sound and Music

conscious mind. Some examples of the harmful energetic effects of entrainment include:

1. Arousing base instincts (aggression, and destructive behavior).
2. Inducing states of depression or melancholy.
3. Creating mental confusion.

- **Spiritual:** The physical and energetic effects of Entrainment, in combination with the more subtle vibrations of will and intent, can negatively influence an individual's spiritual field by inducing harmful psycho-spiritual states.

The Harmful Effects of Chaotic Resonance

The harmful effects of Chaotic Resonance are observed when exposure to music or sound interferes with the body's physical structures or energetic patterns.

- **Physical:** Chaotic Resonance can have a negative effect on the body's physiology when it interferes with an individual's normal internal rhythms. When these rhythms are disrupted, the ability of the body's systems to properly interact is compromised, resulting in general weakness, or specific tissue malfunction. Examples of the harmful physiological effects of chaotic resonance include:

1. Weakening the body's cell and tissue structures.
2. Interfering with the proper functioning of the body's electrical (nervous system) and chemical (endocrine system) communication systems.

- **Energetic and Spiritual:** The energetic and spiritual field patterns exist on a more subtle level, and are therefore more sensitive and susceptible to the effects of Chaotic Resonance. Examples of the harmful effects of Chaotic Resonance on an individual's energetic and spiritual fields include:

1. Interfering with the proper spiritual functioning of the Five Agents.
2. Disrupting the natural healing functions of the individual's Shen.
3. Disrupting the individual's connection to the Divine.

Music in Ancient China

The ancient Daoists believed that music was the basis of everything; that all things, including the human body, were molded according to the music performed within its substance. According to this theory, a Primordial Sound emitted from a central spiritual source created the entire physical universe. According to one ancient Zhengyi Daoist Text:

**Before the sacred sounds were heard,
the stars were not in their place,
when suddenly the Yuan Qi
from the Three Regions gushed forth,
producing the Eight Notes of Harmony.**

**These sacred sounds coagulated
in the center of the Wuji,
as billowing clouds,
constantly intermingling,
spinning and turning
above the Purple Heavens.**

**Now floating, now sinking,
in accordance with the natural,
being neither smoke nor dust,
neither vapors nor steam,
they formed characters
ten thousand yards square
resounding with the Eight Notes,
expressing the essence
of the Three Energies,
and the subtle manifestations
of the Five Elements.**

Masters of Chinese Energetic Medicine have known for centuries that musical patterns can affect an individual's health, character, morality and consciousness. This is why "Sacred Sounds" have been used for healing and various spiritual endeavors throughout the ages (in combination with postures, rhythmic movements and chants).

Music was also believed to have a powerful social and political influence. Confucius once stated that if the music of a kingdom changed, then its society would alter itself accordingly.

In ancient China, music therapy was focused on harmonizing the Five Elements within the body's Yin and Yang organs, and was also used in Feng Shui training to regulate mind and body imbalances stemming from seasonal changes. During autumn, for example, when dryness is prevalent and there is a transition from warm to cool, music was used to help stabilize the body in relation to the changing external conditions.

Secondary Acoustic Biological Response

The following information was presented at the World Academic Society of Medical Qigong Conference in Beijing, China by my friend and college Professor Lu Yan Fang:

The frequency of sound is measured by the number of oscillations a sound wave makes in one second, called a hertz (Hz). Most individuals can consciously hear frequencies vibrating between the ranges of 30 Hz. to 20,000 Hz. Secondary sounds, however, are those sound vibrations that resonate outside of the hearing range of the human ear. One fascinating observation about secondary sounds is that they can travel long distances with little attenuation or distortion.

Secondary sounds were first discovered and scientifically measured during the 1930's. However, it was not until the 1960's that secondary sound started generating attention.

Initial studies regarding the biological effects of secondary sound on human tissue revealed that exposure to certain ranges of secondary sounds consistently caused damage to the structure and function of the human body. After laboratory studies showed that strong secondary sounds (beyond 150 dB) were harmful to biological tissues, the American Environmental Protection Agency (E.P.A.) began to set strict standards for secondary sounds released within the environment. These studies also concluded that secondary sounds vibrating below 130 dB were not harmful to the body.

To date, there have been few studies that have examined how secondary sounds affect the biological processes of the human tissues; nor has there been much investigation into the production of secondary sounds by the human body. The small amount of the scientific information that is available comes from the Peoples Republic of China, or is classified U.S. Military research.

In 1983, a study began in the Peoples Republic of China, which included the investigation of more than 70 famous Medical Qigong masters. In this study, it was discovered that the human body actually emits a secondary sound signal. The average frequency emitted by the Qigong Masters measured in the secondary sound region of about 10 Hz.

In 1984, more than 100 repeated lab experiments revealed identical results of frequency distribution. Based on an analysis of these results, the first infrasonic Medical Qigong machines were constructed. These machines used electroacoustic technology to simulate the low frequency signal emitted by the Medical Qigong masters, and further increased the intensity of the signal. In the two years that followed, many clinical trials were performed incorporating the use of the "Infratonic Qigong Machine." Several hospitals (1,134 patients), and several animal studies were included. All tests revealed that weak secondary sounds can be beneficial to the human body. It was also discovered that infrasonic sound could be used as a basic substitute for Medical Qigong Qi emission therapy, which opened an exciting new door for medical science.

The Infratonic Qigong Machine can also have significant treatment value by promoting circulation, regulating Qi and Blood, opening the body's channel systems, and relieving pain.

A Qigong master is not alone in his or her ability to emit secondary acoustical signals, as most individuals can be taught to generate a similar energetic pattern. The human body is a receptor of secondary acoustical signals. It produces, delivers, emits, receives and controls various forms of low frequency energy. Very early in the development of Traditional Chinese Medicine, the effects of secondary acoustic signals had been demonstrated. Medical Qigong Therapy, Acupuncture, and Chinese Therapeutic Massage Therapy all use aspects of this type of low frequency stimulation to influence the human body.

WESTERN SOUND THERAPY

Sound Therapy is also being used in contemporary Western Medicine, and we have hardly begun to tap into its full healing potential. The following are some examples of clinical research applied to Music Therapy according to Wikipedia:

- **Stroke Therapy:** Recent studies have examined the effect of music therapy on stroke patients when combined with Traditional Western Therapy. One study found the incorporation of music with therapeutic upper extremity exercises gave patients more positive emotional effects than exercise alone.
- **Heart Disease:** According to a 2009 Cochrane Review of 23 clinical trials, some music may reduce heart rate, respiratory rate, and blood pressure in patients with coronary heart disease. Benefits included a decrease in blood pressure, heart rate, and levels of anxiety in heart patients.
- **Neurological Disorders:** Music therapy has showed effectiveness in treating symptoms of many disorders, including schizophrenia, amnesia, dementia and Alzheimer's, Parkinson's disease, mood disorders such as depression, aphasia and similar speech disorders, and Tourette's syndrome, among others.
- **Depression:** Music therapy has been found to have numerous significant outcomes for patients with major depressive disorders. One study found that listening to soft, sedative music for only 30 minutes a day for two weeks led to significantly improved global depressive scores, and improved scores on individual depressive sub-scales. Like many of the other studies mentioned, the effects were seen to be cumulative over the time period studied – that is, longer treatment led to increased improvement.
- **Ultrasound Therapy:** Used for treating sore muscles and back injuries.
- **Shock-wave Lithotripsy Therapy:** Used for treating kidney stones and calcified gallstones.
- **Postoperative Healing:**

LIGHT ENERGY

Quantum theory arose from the concept that atoms absorb and emit light in quanta (portions or units of energy). A quantum is the smallest known indivisible unit in which waves of information and energy are either absorbed or emitted. A quantum of light is known as a photon, while a quantum of electricity is known as an electron.

Figure 4.17. Plant Leaves Emitting Biophotons

Matter and the transformation of matter can be viewed as a result of light (photons) interacting with atoms and molecules. All matter absorbs, stores, produces, and transmits light. Matter and light are fundamentally inseparable. Matter is simply a denser form of energy and consciousness. All life on Earth, whether plant, animal, or human, is dependent upon light and its miraculous qualities for existence.

BIOPHOTONS AND THE HUMAN BODY

All living cells emit units of light called "Biophotons." A Biophoton is a photon of non-thermal origin in the visible and ultraviolet spectrum, that is emitted from a biological system. The emission of Biophotons is technically a type of "bioluminescence" (Figure 4.17).

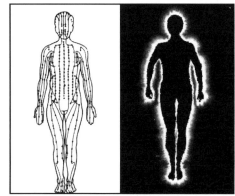

Figure 4.18. The Human Body Emitting Biophotons

Biophoton emissions radiate from the internal organs, as well as from the body's surface tissues, to create the body's auric field (Figure 4.18).

Over 50 years ago, Soviet scientists discovered that light carries biological information. In a 1995 documentary shown on Swiss/Italian television, Dr. Fritz-Albert Popp showed cells actually talking to each other in short and long bursts of light, similar in pattern to that of Morse code.

This interaction of light on the body's tissues and within the body's internal organs has a profound healing effect, especially when activated by the Qi emission from a Medical Qigong Doctor (Figure 4.19). When muscles or nerves are activated by the energy generated via Medical Qigong Therapy or Medical Qigong Exercises, the intensity of the biophoton emission increases. Studies performed on the healing potential of light and color therapies have repeatedly demonstrated their clinical efficacy. Like sound resonance, light therapy is also being researched further as an addition to modern clinical medicine.

Figure 4.19. A Medical Qigong Doctor Emitting Healing Light

LIGHT AND ENERGETIC FIELDS

Research has shown that all living things emit a permanent current of photons, extending beyond the organism. The number of photons emitted are determined by the organism's position on the evolutionary scale, the more complex the organism, the fewer the photons being emitted. For example:
- Plants and animals generally emit 100 photons per square centimeter per second, at a wavelength of 200 to 800 nanometers. This corresponds to a very high frequency of electromagnetic wave.

- Humans normally emit only 10 photons per square centimeter per second, at a wavelength of 200 to 800 nanometers. This corresponds to a lower frequency of electromagnetic wave.

LIGHT AND FOOD

While studying photosynthesis, in which plants use light as their primary source of energy, Dr. Popp observed that as humans consume plant foods, they absorb and store the photons present within the plant structure (Figure 4.20). As the food is digested, it is metabolized into nutrients, carbon dioxide, water, and light that had been stored from the Sun and was present during the plant's photosynthesis. The human body naturally absorbs and utilizes the nutrients and water, stores the light's electromagnetic waves, and removes the carbon dioxide. Once the energy of these photons is absorbed into the cells and tissues, it is distributed over the entire spectrum of the body's electromagnetic frequencies, adding to the energy present in all the molecules of the body. The most essential storehouse of light, and the major source of biophoton emission, is the body's DNA.

LIGHT AND THE BODY'S DNA

Dr. Popp discovered that DNA is capable of sending out a large range of light frequencies, and that these frequencies produce various energetic effects within the body. The DNA acts as a master tuning fork, releasing specific frequencies that cause certain molecules within the tissues to resonate. This active resonation acts as a feedback system of communication through energetic waves which encode and transfer information. Dr. Popp reasoned that if the DNA is responsible for storing light, it would naturally be responsible for emitting more light once it was unwound.

Research conducted by Dr. Popp in 1970 revealed that compounds that are carcinogenic absorbed UV light, which then changed their DNA energetic frequency. Dr. Popp's research also confirmed that carcinogens reacted only to the light at a specific 380 nanometer wavelength. Further biological laboratory experiments showed that if you can blast a cell with UV light so that 99% of the cell is destroyed (including the DNA), you can almost entirely repair the damage in a

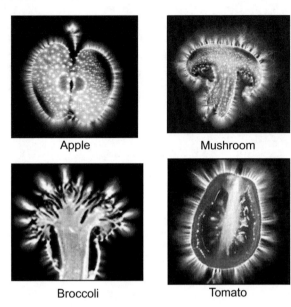

Figure 4.20. Food Emitting Biophotons

single day by illuminating the cell with the same wavelength at a very weak intensity. This type of "photo-repair" works most efficiently at 380 nanometers, the very same wavelength to which the cancer causing compounds react.

Dr. Popp realized that the body must have some type of light that is responsible for photo-repair, and that a cancerous compound therefore causes cancer because it permanently blocks this light and scrambles its signal preventing photo-repair from happening.

THE BODY'S INTERNAL LIGHT

The body both absorbs and projects light energy. According to ancient Daoist teachings, the Divine Light that entered into the forming tissues at the time of conception, continues to reside within the body's Taiji Pole throughout an individual's life. During a clinical treatment, this sacred light internally responds and reacts to the Medical Qigong Doctor's emitted healing light energy. The emitted light and colors are then absorbed into the patient's body, causing the energies of Heaven and Earth to fuse inside the patient's internal tissues. This subtle energetic interaction helps to facilitate the body's internal healing process.

CHAPTER 4: THE FIVE ENERGIES OF THE HUMAN BODY

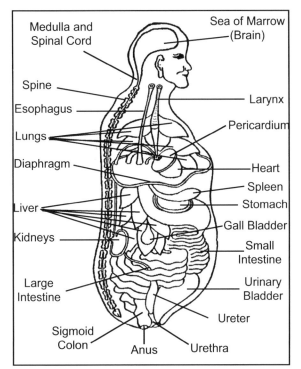

Figure 4.21. The Ancient "Chart of Inner Lights"

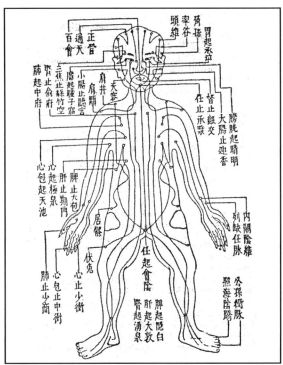

Figure 4.22. The Ancient "Chart of the Halls of Light"

In 1989, Russian research scientist Professor Kaznacheev proved that channels of light exist within the human body. These unique channels of light correspond to the ancient Chinese channel system currently being taught in all Traditional Chinese Medical Colleges today. Professor Kaznacheev further showed that these lines of energetic light operated like mighty rivers of information, flowing in and around the body's tissues in order to create an energetic grid along which light quanta move.

In Traditional Chinese Medicine, one of the most ancient illustrations used to depict the internal organs and the energetic routes of the body's fluids was a Daoist Chart called "The Chart of Inner Lights," sometimes known as "The Chart For Visualizing the True Ones." Ancient Daoist Charts such as these were traditionally used to depict the body's internal organ systems, along with their energetic "guardians," who were sometimes referred to as the "Radiant Ones Residing within the Organs." In these ancient charts, the body's internal organs and its internal organ systems were traditionally referred to as "Orbs of Light" or "Spheres of Energetic Influence" (Figure 4.21).

Additionally, the ancient Daoist illustrations that were used to depict the body's energetic channels were traditionally called "The Charts of the Halls of Light." These famous charts were extensively studied by the Daoist adepts, because they showed the disciples the unique pathways along which the body's energy moved, gathered, and pooled (Figure 4.22). Many times these esoteric maps contained detailed illustrations of the secret pathways that were used by the ancient sages for special energetic transformation and cultivation.

According to esoteric teachings revealed within these special charts, it was the energetic cultivation and awakening of the Yuan Shen (Original Heart/Mind) from within the Daoist adept's body that was responsible for transforming his internal energy into light and radiating it outside his tissues. It was believed that at the higher levels of spiritual cultivation, this illuminating spiritual light would eventually radiate from within his physical body and could then be seen by others.

THE INTERNAL LIGHT OF THE BODY'S THREE DANTIAN CHAMBERS

A "Dantian" is considered to be one of three powerful energetic chambers or fields that are located within the center core of the body. In ancient Daoist Alchemy, it was originally taught that light could be energetically cultivated and stored within the internal chambers of the body's Three Dantians, described as follows:

- **The Upper Dantian:** This energetic field is traditionally called the "Peak of Yang Qi," and is considered to be the energetic doorway to the chamber of Heavenly or Divine Light. In Daoist Alchemy, White Light is traditionally cultivated within the center of the Upper Dantian, where spiritual energy is released into the infinite space of the Wuji. During cultivation practice, once the energy of the White Light manifests, it is drawn down the center core Taiji Pole and rooted into the center of the disciple's Lower Dantian. By using inner vision to focus the eyes on the center core of the body, the White Light energy will begin to vibrate and can then be drawn downward from the Upper Dantian into the Lower Dantian.
- **The Middle Dantian:** This energetic field is traditionally called the "Blending of Yin and Yang Qi," and is considered to be the location of transforming Yin and Yang energy. In Daoist Alchemy, the Middle Dantian contains the spiritual light of the Yuan Shen (Original Heart/Mind), which forms the energetic basis of all human interactions and relationships.
- **The Lower Dantian:** This energetic field is traditionally called the "Peak of Yin Qi," and is considered to be the body's most direct connection to the energy of the Earth. In Daoist Alchemy, accumulated Earth Qi is generally stored as a ball of glowing golden energy within the center of the Lower Dantian.

The ancient Daoists were taught that with proper Qigong training and time, the Postnatal Qi circulating up the body's Governing (Yang) Vessel and down the Conception (Yin) Vessel will eventually awaken the Prenatal Qi stored within the Brain (Figure 4.23). This powerful energetic

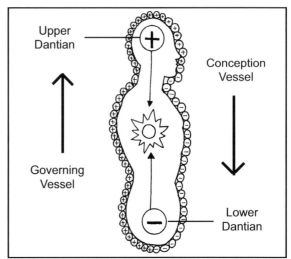

Figure 4.23. White Light resonating from within the body's Taiji Pole and Three Dantians.

awakening will cause the cultivated Qi to suddenly manifest a full integration of Yin and Yang energy, which manifests as a shimmering white light glowing from in the center of the Upper Dantian. This illuminating glow will suddenly radiate outside the body, and is universally depicted in pictures of saints, prophets and celestial beings.

LIGHT AND THE PHYSICAL REALM

In the study of the energetic properties of light, we would be remiss to leave out the various effects of light within the Three Realms (Physical, Energetic, Spirit Realm). The following was taught to me by Daoist Master Wang in Beijing China in 1993.

The light of the Physical World is governed by the energy of the Sun. This type of external light manifests as electromagnetic waves and particles, creating energetic fields that ripple throughout space in all directions. These energetic fields of light can be observed via our physical sense of sight.

The eyes, acting as light receptors, observe the different details that manifest as light particles collide with the various surfaces and then bounce back to reflect their unique shapes, colors, sizes, etc. The Brain records the data as the light manifests both the heat and colors that are being projected through visible and invisible color spectrums. At one end of the color spectrum is

Chapter 4: The Five Energies Of The Human Body

Level of Spiritual Light	Dimension of Existence	Source of Light	Manifestation of Light
(4th Level) Highest Level	Light Existing Within the Higher Spirit World	Higher Spiritual Light develops from the fusion of the Individual's Heart and Mind with the eternal light of the Divine	Higher Spiritual Light is not associated with the concept of "Seeing," but with "Illumination"
(3rd Level) Higher Level	Light Existing Within the Lower Spirit World	Lower Spiritual Light exists as a continuation of light stemming from both the Energetic World and the projected energetic frequencies of the Spirit World	Lower Spiritual Light manifests through the individual's Spiritual Consciousness
(2nd Level) Middle Level	Light Existing Within the Energetic World	The Light of the Energetic World Extends from the Vibration of each Atom, Molecule and Cell	Nothing is lit by reflection each Individual's Mind (Thought and Emotion) Creates Light
(1st Level) Lowest Level	Light of the Physical World	The Light of the Physical World is Governed by the Energy of the Sun	Light Vibrations Collide with Various Surfaces and Reflect Shapes, Colors, Sizes, Etc.

Figure 4.24. The Energetic Dimensions of Light

infrared light, capable of thermodynamic manifestation (giving off heat). At the other end of the color spectrum is ultraviolet light, which gives off no heat, but enables photosynthesis (the absorption of light) in plants and is the mechanism for suntans in humans.

Light And the Energetic Realm

The light existing within the Energetic World is different from the light existing within the Physical World. All of the planes and sub-planes of the Energetic World are internally illuminated from within, instead of reflecting what has been projected onto them. This special light has two main aspects, described as follows (Figure 4.24):

1. In the Energetic World, nothing is lit by reflection. Here the source of light is the very high frequency vibration of each atom, molecule and cell. This is a living light that is connected to, and essentially linked with shapes, sounds and consciousness.
2. The Energetic World is a world of conscious thought and emotional energy. The brighter an individual's energetic light, the greater the feeling of satisfaction that he or she experiences. When clear and unobstructed, this higher vibrational resonance produces a feeling of euphoria within an individual's body.

Light And The Spirit Realm

Beyond the light of the Energetic World exists the Lower Spiritual Light and the Higher Spiritual Light, described as follows:

1. The Lower Spiritual Light forms a continuum with the Energetic Light, and corresponds to the lower frequencies of the Spirit World. When internally awakened, the Lower Spiritual Light manifests through the individual's Spiritual Consciousness.
2. The Higher Spiritual Light is not associated with the ability of "seeing," but rather with the spiritual presence of "illumination." This is considered to be the true spiritual perception of "Oneness," which comes from the fusion of an individual's Yuan Shen (Original Heart/Mind) with the Divine Mind. It energetically manifests within a superluminal (faster than light) state of existence.

LIGHT AND AURA COLORS

An "Aura" is a field of luminous energy that surrounds all living things (people, animals and plants), and to a lesser degree, all inanimate objects. The energetic field of an Aura is traditionally categorized in the various shades of seven primary colors: Red, Orange, Yellow, Green, Blue, Indigo, and Violet. These various colors are in a constant state of energetic flux, changing their shades and patterns with each shift of an individual's thoughts and emotions. This is why Aura colors will sometimes appear in the form of waves or patterns of energy (for example: colors that are evenly layered, blotchy, or combined together).

Whether spontaneously manifesting through an individual's natural energetic skills, or acquired through consistent Qigong practice, in ancient Daoist teachings, the perception of seeing Auras always corresponded to the energetic "awakening" of the disciple's Yintang (or "Third Eye") area.

In the clinic, these unique colors are observed continually changing and blending within and around each patient's Second Weiqi field, usually about a foot from their physical body (Figure 4.25). This visual energetic field is associated with the patient's Energy Body, manifesting the current mental and emotional states of his or her internal organs. According to ancient Daoist teachings, through great spiritual cultivation, the various colors of the body's aura will eventually transform into a luminous white to golden light halo, that will be observed surrounding the head of the priest just before he becomes an immortal.

In the Medical Qigong Clinic, the energetic state of a patient's Auras serves as a visual measurement of the state of their physical health. When diagnosing a patient's Aura field, it may sometimes be observed in the energetic form of a transparent or opaque flow of Qi or as masses of different densities and colors. This manifested energetic field may be used as a basis for determining the location and features of specific diseases.

Each Yin and Yang organ has its own signature color vibration. When the energy of an organ is healthy, the Qi color is clean, clear, and lucid. When an organ is diseased, its Qi becomes dark gray and turbid. These colors reveal whether an

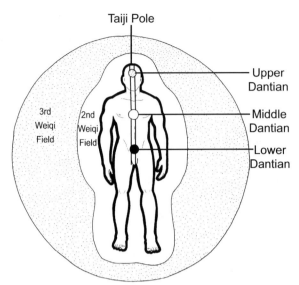

Figure 4.25. The Body's Aura is Composed of Numerous Interacting Fields of Energy

organ is in an abnormal condition and to what extent it has been affected.

To a Medical Qigong Doctor, the human aura is both an energy field and a reflection of the subtle life-force energies active within the human body. These energies are continually affected by our surroundings and our personal life style. The patient's Aura reflects his or her health, character, mental activity, and emotional state. It also exposes the internal conditions of a latent disease, often long before the onset of its symptoms.

COLOR VIBRATIONAL CLASSIFICATIONS

The visible light spectrum is measured in nanometers (nm). A nanometer is one billionth of a meter. Colors are divided into approximately 700 bandwidths (or wavelengths) ranging from 290 to 990 nm. The variety of shifting colors can be interpreted according to their density and tone. The preceding chart displays the color frequency correlation in nanometers (Figure 4.26). All living organisms vibrate at a frequency with a wavelength between 300-2,000 nanometers. Specific colors emanate consistent frequencies and wave forms. The slower frequencies register in the infrared light spectrum, while the highest vibrational frequencies register in the ultraviolet light spectrum.

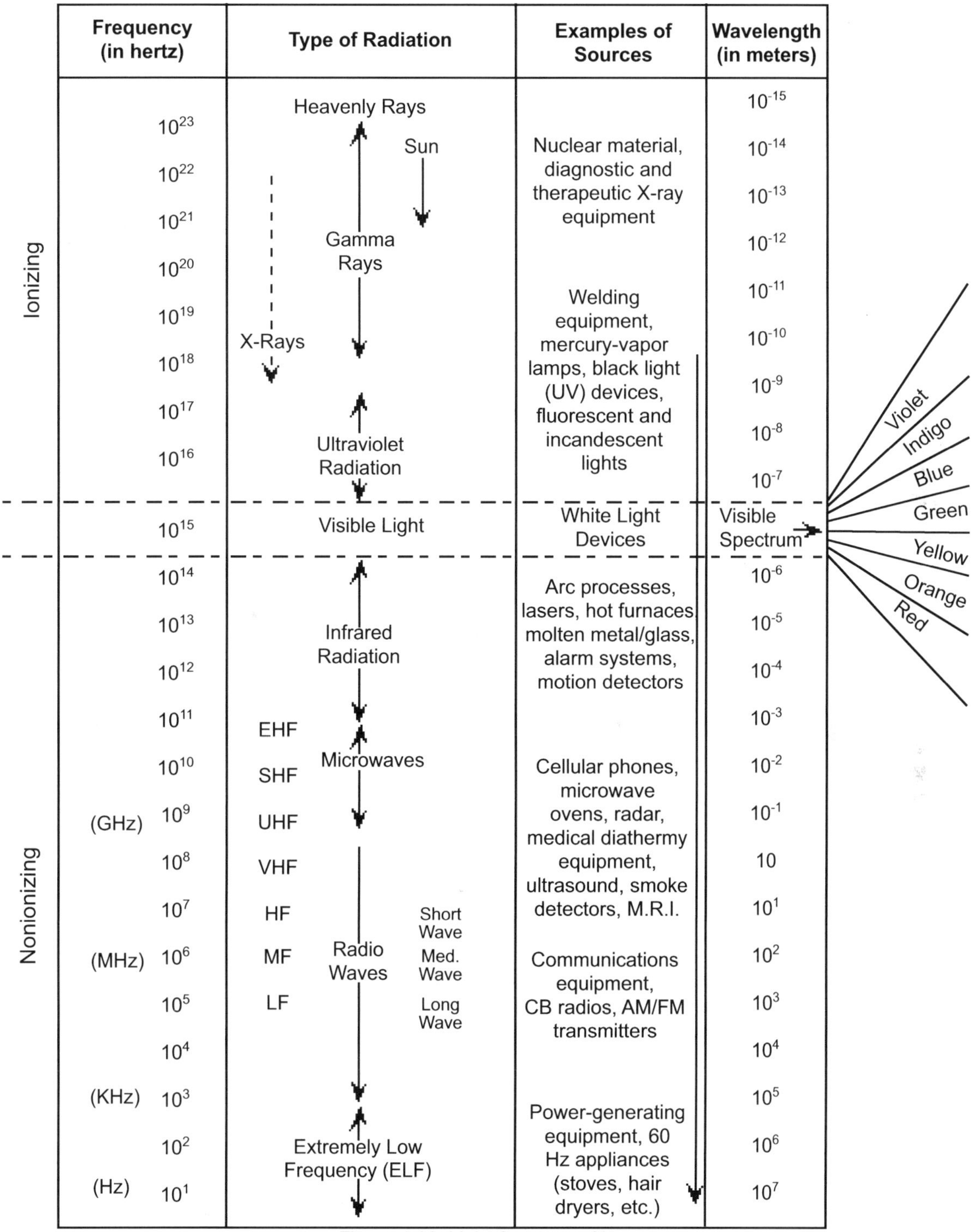

CHAPTER 4: THE FIVE ENERGIES OF THE HUMAN BODY

Frequency (in hertz)	Type of Radiation	Examples of Sources	Wavelength (in meters)
Ionizing			
10^{23}	Heavenly Rays ↑	Nuclear material, diagnostic and therapeutic X-ray equipment	10^{-15}
10^{22}	Sun ↓		10^{-14}
10^{21}			10^{-13}
10^{20}	Gamma Rays		10^{-12}
10^{19}		Welding equipment, mercury-vapor lamps, black light (UV) devices, fluorescent and incandescent lights	10^{-11}
10^{18}	X-Rays ↓		10^{-10}
10^{17}	↑		10^{-9}
10^{16}	Ultraviolet Radiation ↓		10^{-8}
			10^{-7}
10^{15}	Visible Light	White Light Devices	Visible Spectrum →
Nonionizing			
10^{14}	↑	Arc processes, lasers, hot furnaces, molten metal/glass, alarm systems, motion detectors	10^{-6}
10^{13}	Infrared Radiation		10^{-5}
10^{12}	↓		10^{-4}
10^{11}	EHF ↑		10^{-3}
10^{10}	SHF Microwaves	Cellular phones, microwave ovens, radar, medical diathermy equipment, ultrasound, smoke detectors, M.R.I.	10^{-2}
(GHz) 10^9	UHF ↓		10^{-1}
10^8	VHF		10
10^7	HF — Short Wave		10^1
(MHz) 10^6	MF — Radio Waves — Med. Wave	Communications equipment, CB radios, AM/FM transmitters	10^2
10^5	LF — Long Wave		10^3
10^4			10^4
(KHz) 10^3	↓	Power-generating equipment, 60 Hz appliances (stoves, hair dryers, etc.)	10^5
10^2	↑ Extremely Low Frequency (ELF)		10^6
(Hz) 10^1	↓		10^7

Visible spectrum: Violet, Indigo, Blue, Green, Yellow, Orange, Red

Figure 4.26. Light Spectrum Chart

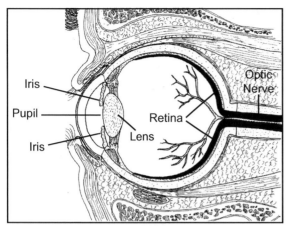

Figure 4.27. The surrounding aperture known as the "iris" expands and contracts around the pupil according to various types of stimulation. (Inspired by the original artwork of Wynn Kapit)

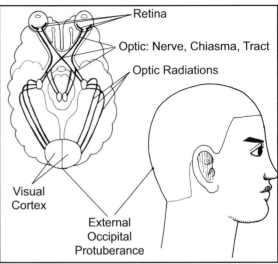

Figure 4.28. As light enters the pupils, it converges on the retina at the back of the eye, creating a reversed image in two dimensions. (Inspired by the original artwork of Wynn Kapit)

THE PHYSIOLOGY OF VISUAL PERCEPTION

The surrounding aperture of the eye, known as the "iris," expands and contracts around the pupil according to various energetic stimulations (Figure 4.27). As light enters the pupils, it converges on the retina at the back of the eye, creating a reversed image in two dimensions. These images are converted into electrical impulses that travel through the optic chiasm to various parts of the visual centers at the back of the Brain where they are then reversed and interpreted (Figure 4.28).

There are two types of nerve cell receptors located within the retina. These nerve cell receptors are known as Rod Cells and Cone Cells, described as follows (Figure 4.29):

- **Rod Cells (Nighttime Vision):** The rods are responsible for nighttime vision; they discern the shadows between light and darkness, shape and movement. The rods are more numerous, and are more sensitive than the cones. However, they are not sensitive to color.
- **Cone Cells (Daytime Vision):** The cones are responsible for daytime vision, provide the eye's with color sensitivity, and can distinguish between 7,500,000 different hues. However, if even a single set of these color receptive cones is missing from the retina, an individual will be unable to distinguish most colors and can be classified as "color blind."

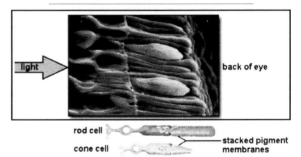

Figure 4.29. Rods And Cones

On average, the cone receptors have three light sensitive pigments, which respond to the "Red" cones (64%), "Green" cones (32%), and "Blue" cones (2%), based on measured response curve.

The cones are responsible for all high resolution vision. During daylight vision, the cone cells adapt and adjust much more rapidly to the ever changing light levels. Like all neurons, the cones fire to produce an electrical impulse on the nerve fiber and then must reset to fire again. Therefore, the eye continually moves in order to keep the light from a specific object of interest falling directly onto the fovea centralis area, where the bulk of the cones reside.

THE ANATOMY OF SEEING AURAS

Through the energetic stimulation and physical dilation of the occipital lobe of the Brain, an individual will begin to develop the unique visual ability of seeing Auras. The word "aura" literally means "breeze" manifesting as shimmering layers of luminous colored energy that circulate around and penetrate into the physical body. These colors are part of the body's biophoton emissions, which is radiant light energy that emanates from all living systems. These colors are constantly in motion, reflecting thoughts, feelings, emotional patterns, and environmental influences.

Seeing Auras is a visual phenomenon which commonly occurs after many hours of regular Qigong training. However, this ability to see the external energy field is not limited to Medical Qigong training, as many people are born with this ability.

In the beginning stages of aura observation, the Medical Qigong Doctor may see energy coming off his or her patient's body like steam. Later however, brilliant, luminous colors will become visible. According to modern research, in the beginning stages the doctor is observing the infrared and ultraviolet radiation color patterns emitted by a patient's tissues. The infrared spectrum is just below the average person's visual spectrum, while the ultraviolet is just above the average visual spectrum. By stimulating and dilating the occipital lobe, the visual spectrum expands to include the infrared and ultraviolet frequencies, allowing the doctor to observe a much greater range of color.

Remember that the rod and cone cells are scattered at the back of the eye, where the image of the observed item is formed. The occipital lobe, along with help from the ventral (upper) and dorsal (side) streams of energy, help to process optical information (Figure 4.30). Rod cells respond to the amount of ambient light, and are responsible for our low-light vision and the overall brightness of what we see. In contrast, cone cells are receptive to one of three main wavelengths of light - red, green or blue. As these cells fire to produce an electrical impulse on the nerve fiber, the brain assigns another level of the corresponding color to

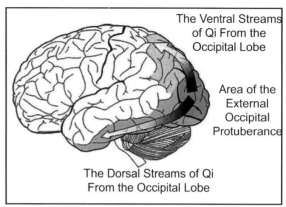

Figure 4.30. The Stimulation of the Occipital Lobe

that area of the image, at the brightness dictated by the rod cells.

It has been my personal observation that students who possess a large bump on the back of the cranium, specifically between the channel points GV-16 and GV-17, begin to see auras at a very early stage. These points are below and just above the external occipital protuberance and surround the internal branches of the occipital arteries, veins, and nerves. When energy fills this area, it stimulates and vibrates these nerves and arteries which causes the visual receptors of the Brain to perceive phenomena at a faster rate. This has the subjective effect of slowing down time.

These subtle perceptions are all possible due to the dilation of the occipital membranes. To maintain this dilation, the doctor must remain calm and relaxed. Any tension brought about by stress only diminishes this ability. Auras are generally seen through the peripheral field of vision, using the rods rather than the cones of the eyes. The rods are more sensitive to the low light levels than are the cones, which are more sensitive to color.

If the doctor begins to stare at any particular object, focused concentration will contract the occipital membranes, causing tension and pressure which can inhibit the dilation process. The secret in maintaining this altered state of observation is to anchor the mind deep into the ground. By focusing the mind on a specific point, the attention can be shifted to receiving and observing auras, or to extending energy without distraction.

Projecting Colored Light

In the clinic, when a Medical Qigong Doctor connects with the Divine just before performing an energetic healing, he will first absorb massive quantities of divine light into his center core Taiji Pole. While absorbing the Divine light, the energy will immediately prism into multicolored beams of Qi. These transformed colors are not only absorbed into the body in order to strengthen the doctor's internal organs, but will also be projected outside the doctor's body via Qi Emission Therapy in order to heal his patient (Figure 4.31).

Traditionally, Medical Qigong Doctors project energy of different colors by first gathering Divine light into their body via the Taiji Pole. They then place their focus on releasing this Divine Light by either projecting it through their hands, or releasing it via visualizing the Divine Light projecting from their Yintang (Third Eye) area into the patient's internal organs, channels, and tissues.

In order to cultivate this special energetic ability, the Medical Qigong Doctors are traditionally taught important Inner-Vision Techniques that connect their Yuan Shen (Original Heart/Mind) with the proper color required for stimulating the patient's energetic healing. One special technique that allows the healing color to naturally develop within the doctor's body before projecting it into a patient, requires the doctor to mentally place the focus of his eyes towards the back of his head.

While maintaining this focused intention, a specific color will suddenly be observed in the back of the mind. This special color is then projected out of the doctor's body into the patient's tissues. It is important to note, that this visualization technique is only practiced after first connecting with and enveloping the patient's energetic field.

Light Therapy Through Emitted Qi

In China, doctors of Traditional Chinese Medicine have discovered that Light Therapy is a powerful clinical tool that can be effectively used for treating certain diseases. This is due to the fact that projected light is able to penetrate deep into the tissues and interact with the patients' internal energetic fields. In the Medical Qigong Clinic,

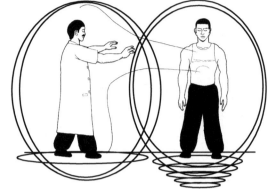

Figure 4.31. Qi Emission Therapy

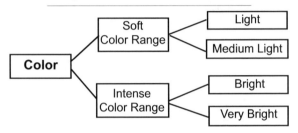

Figure 4.32. The Four Levels of Energetic Projection of Colored Light

the emitted colored light acts as a catalyst used to bring specific aspects of the patient's subconscious thoughts and feelings to the surface.

In order to treat a patient with Emitted Light Therapy, a Medical Qigong Doctor will first focus his intention on seeing, hearing and feeling the energy of a specific color. By visualizing this specific color, the doctor is activating a particular aspect of the light energy within his own body. The doctor will then focus on projecting this healthy colored light into the patient's organs, channels, and organ systems.

Energetic color therapy traditionally utilizes eight different healing colors, ranging from low frequency (red) to high frequency (violet) and white. These energetic projections are associated with the colors emanating from the body's Taiji Pole and range from dark to lighter color bands.

When projecting healing colors, it is important to note that there are four levels, or intensities, of color gradations within each color band (Figure 4.32). In the Soft Color range, there are two levels: a light and a medium-light color, both of which are

Chapter 4: The Five Energies Of The Human Body

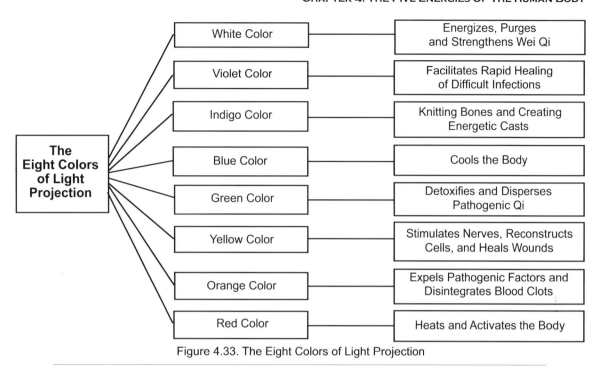

Figure 4.33. The Eight Colors of Light Projection

used for gentle, less potent projections (usually for healing and cleansing wounds). Medium-light Color projections are especially effective for treating young children and the elderly. In the Intense Color range, there are also two levels of intensity: a bright and a very bright color range, both of which are used for full-force projection (for destroying cells and pathogenic factors, or for stabilizing a deficient organ or organ area). The bright color is initially used to begin with; later, the very bright color is used as the patient's strength increases.

Research in China has demonstrated that the use of color in Medical Qigong treatments can effectively change a patient's pulse rate, body rhythms, and depth of breathing. Medical Qigong doctors traditionally modulate, and switch energetic color projections during a treatment. To avoid overstimulating the patient's tissues, the doctor will start with a lighter shade of color projection, then gradually increase the color's intensity until the desired affect is obtained.

Medical Qigong Therapy uses the following eight colors for energetic projection: Red, Orange, Yellow, Green, Blue, Indigo (Dark Blue), Violet, and White. Based on the modern understanding of the prismatic division of light, color projection is categorized and described as follows (Figure 4.33):

1. **The Red Color:** This color has the longest wavelength of the visible colors, and is associated with physical and material forces. It simultaneously heats and activates the body. The color red improves blood circulation and can be used to stimulate the Small Intestine, Heart, Triple Burners and Pericardium organs and channels, as well as energize the body's Fire Element Qi. Red can sometimes be used to repair the body's tissues, Tonify Blood Deficiency, increase cellular growth, increase blood pressure, and increase the body's metabolic rate. Additionally, the color red can be used to vitalize the body's tissues, Blood, and the skeletal system. It can also be used for treating paralysis, broken Bones, and both internal and external wounds. The color red engenders strength, courage, passion and sensuality, and it counteracts depression, worry, and fear. It can have a positive influence in cases of debility and Blood disorders.

Contraindications: The doctor must avoid using red colored Qi when treating patients who have hypertension, external bleeding, or when women are menstruating. The use of the color red is strictly prohibited in cases of Excess Heart Fire.

Generally, the color pink is used to tonify the Heart in cases where the color red is too strong. Pink can also be used in small doses to relax and neutralize aggressive behavior, however, prolonged exposure will cause irritability, aggression and emotional distress.

2. **The Orange Color:** This color expels pathogenic factors and is often used for treating cysts and for disintegrating blood clots. The color orange can also be used to stimulate the Spleen and Stomach organs and channels. It is associated with both Qi (energy) and Zhi (wisdom), and is considered to be a powerful tonic. The color orange engenders self-confidence, determination and optimism, and stimulates the visual expression of ideas.

Contraindications: The doctor must avoid projecting orange colored Qi into the Brain, eyes, or Heart of the patient. The color orange is extremely potent and may cause tissue damage when used improperly or in excess.

3. **The Yellow Color:** This color stimulates the nerves, reconstructs cells, and heals wounds. Yellow or Orange-Yellow can be used to stimulate the Stomach and Spleen organs and channels, as well as the body's pancreas, digestive system and nervous system. The yellow color can be used to energize the body's Earth Element Qi. Yellow is also used in the treatment of skin rashes. The color yellow revitalizes and stimulates the Shen (spirit) and assists the mind in creating thoughts and visualizations. It engenders optimism, happiness, and a balanced outlook on life.

4. **The Green Color:** This color is soothing to the nerves and can be used as a tonic for the Heart. It can also be used to detoxify and disperse pathogenic Qi. Green can stimulate the Liver and Gall Bladder organs and channels, and energize the body's Wood Element Qi. The color green is associated with harmony and compassion, and engenders peace, sympathy, and kindness.

Green is also used in combination with other colors. For example, shades of green are sometimes combined with shades of orange for treating tumors. Green color vibration is generally not as powerful as orange and may be used on elderly patients, young children, or for a more gentle healing session.

5. **The Blue Color:** This light color cools the body and is beneficial in soothing and calming anxiety. The light blue color can be used to stimulate the Urinary Bladder and Kidney organs and channels, as well as the body's reproductive system, skeletal system, throat, and thyroid gland. Light blue can also be used to energize the body's Water Element Qi. The light blue color can be used as a mild anesthetic, and is also excellent for relieving inflammation, insomnia, headache, and fever. Additionally, the light blue color is used for slowing the metabolism, lowering blood pressure, perspiration, respiration and brain-wave activity. It is a spiritual color that engenders truth, devotion, serenity, peace, and religious aspirations.

6. **The Indigo Color:** This dark blue color has a deep penetrating property. It is generally used for knitting Bones, treating eye diseases, insomnia, mental disorders, nervous disorders, and for creating "energetic casts" (enveloping wounds and encapsulating specific internal organs). The dark blue indigo color can also be used to stimulate the Urinary Bladder and Kidney organs and channels, as well as the body's skeletal system, reproductive system, and pineal gland. The dark blue color can also be used to energize the body's Water Element Qi. The color indigo is a spiritual color that engenders inspiration and artistic creativity.

7. **The Violet (Reddish-Blue) Color:** This color has the shortest wavelength of all visible colors and is associated with spirituality, mysticism, intuition, psychic abilities, and enlightenment. It is known for its purifying force, which facilitates the rapid healing of difficult infections, such as pneumonia. It is also excellent for treating nervous disorders, mental diseases, neurosis, neuralgia, and epilepsy. Because of its ability to energetically dissolve into the Wuji, the color

violet can sometimes be used to dissolve brain tumors (when used in short durations during treatment and then immediately removed).

8. **The White Color:** This color is a fusion of all other colors, and thus the most neutral. White is associated with purity, and is the most common color of light used by Medical Qigong doctors. It is useful for calming the mind, or for placing a protective field around the body or around a specific internal organ. White can be used to stimulate the Large Intestine and Lung organs and channels, as well as the body's respiratory system. The white color can also be used to energize the body's Metal Element Qi.

Using Healing Color Imagery

Medical Qigong Homework Exercises that emphasize meditating on specific colors can be prescribed in order to assist a patient in his healing (Figure 4.34). During these types of treatments, the patient is instructed to visualize a specific organ color, while the Qigong Doctor projects that same type of color into his body and energetic fields. The patient may later be asked to repeat the visualization as a Medical Qigong Homework prescription exercise. This treatment technique has successfully been used for Tonifying, Regulating, or Purging all the body's major organs, and is often combined with Healing Sound Therapy.

When using colors in therapeutic imagery, the patients are encouraged to first visualize the diseased organ as being dull, dark, and impure in color. For example, in cases of Liver Heat, patients might imagine a dull, turbid brownish-green tinged with red; for a Heart imbalance, the red color may be first imagined as a dull, weak or darkish red, tinged with brownish-red or purplish-red (like the color of stagnant Blood).

The patient is instructed to begin the meditation by inhaling and imagining a pure, vibrant color flowing into his body from the Heavens, energizing and cleansing his tissues, internal channels, and organ systems. As he exhales, the patient concentrates on releasing the impure, toxic energy out of his body into the Earth, replacing the toxic Qi of the diseased tissue with the clean Qi.

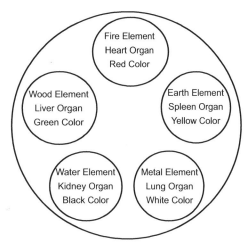

Figure 4.34. The Five Colors of the Five Yin Organs

Exposure to External Color Fields

In certain Five Element Schools of Color Therapy, some patients are required to sit and meditate in special rooms painted in the specific color that relates to their deficient energetic condition. A healthy color is chosen in accordance with either the Five Element Creative Cycle or the Controlling Cycle, depending upon the nature of the patient's disease and which particular Yin organ (or organs) is involved. One example is using the Five Element Creative Cycle to tonify a patient's deficient organ.

According to the theory of the Five Element Creative Cycle, one can stimulate and energize the "Mother" Element in order to strengthen the "Child" Element that follows it. For example, a patient with a Liver imbalance, can be placed in a dark blue room for tonifying the Kidneys (the Liver's "Mother" organ). The Kidney (Mother organ) color indigo (dark blue), is used to nourish the Liver ("Child" organ). For a Liver Excess, the Medical Qigong Doctor would use the Five Element Controlling Cycle and place the patient in a white room, allowing the Lungs' (the "Grandmother") white Metal color to control the Liver Wood (the Child) organ (Figure 4.35).

Additionally, the patient can also be encouraged to wear or surround himself with certain Five Element colors that can be used to initiate healing (e.g., white for Deficient Lung conditions).

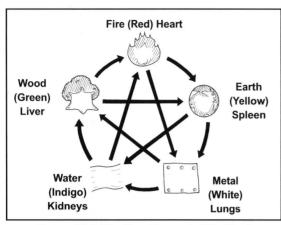

Figure 4.35. The Five Elements (Wu Xing)

Food, Color, and Healing Light

Another Medical Qigong Homework Exercise that emphasizes meditating on specific colors requires the presentation of food (i.e., the patient's diet) as a form of color and light therapy. In this special treatment method, the doctor encouraged the patient to make sure that the Five Element colors are all present within the food that he eats. Each color (i.e., Green/Blue for Liver, Red for Heart, Yellow or Light Brown for Spleen, White for Lungs, and Black or Dark Blue for Kidneys) is chosen to specifically target and tonify a deficient internal organ and its organ system.

Modern nutritional research demonstrates that the presence of specific vitamins and minerals in food is often associated with the color of the food itself. Therefore, when eating the food, the patient is asked to place his intention on also ingesting the specific color, light, and energy of the various types of food being eaten.

Maintaining The Distance & Range, According To Focused Concentration

When using color projection, an important factor is the Medical Qigong Doctor's ability to maintain focused attention. If the doctor becomes distracted or loses visual concentration, the energy of the color resonance being emitted will suddenly become weakened, and the projected color will immediately transform back into non-differentiated white-light energy.

Western Light Therapy

In 1941, Harry Riley Spitler, M.D., O.D., performed extensive research on the way in which light influences the Autonomic Nervous System. Some of his findings are described as follows:

- Light has a regenerative effect on the body, increasing the growth rate of cells.
- Light affects the functioning of the pituitary gland.
- Environmental light can have an effect on the reproductive cycle.
- Light affects the tension between the sympathetic and the parasympathetic nervous system.
- Light influences hormone secretion and neurotransmitters.
- Light affects muscle response (i.e., slowing or speeding up the heartbeat).
- There is a relationship between the frequency of light that enters into the eyes and the perception of pain.
- There is a relationship between the frequency of light that enters into the eyes, the vitamin A content, and the adaptation of the eyes to low degrees of light.
- There is a relationship between environmental light and the affects of the patient's hereditary potential.

Due to Dr. Spitler's extensive research, and the research of his colleagues, Light Therapy is currently being used today in numerous forms by Western Medical Doctors. Some examples of these forms of Light Therapy includes:

- Laser-Light Therapy and Surgery
- Full-spectrum Light Therapy for SAD (Seasonal Affective Disorder)
- Color-Light Therapy for eye problems and various other illnesses
- UV-Light Therapy for "Blue Babies" with hyperbilirubinemia

CHAPTER 4: THE FIVE ENERGIES OF THE HUMAN BODY

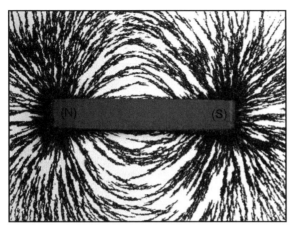

Figure 4.36. The patterns of an Electromagnetic field

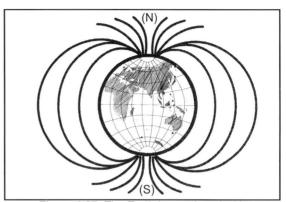

Figure 4.37. The Earth is enveloped with electromagnetic currents, affecting its gravitational fields, weather, and vegetation.

MAGNETIC ENERGY

Magnetic energy is defined as the Qi that is contained within a magnetic field. A magnetic field is generated by the movement of electrical currents. It is difficult to separate the energetic properties of magnetism and electricity, as they are practically two aspects of the same energetic field. However, by establishing different magnetic polarities (Yin and Yang), the Medical Qigong Doctor can influence the energetic flow of electromagnetic Qi within the body.

The Earth, like the body, has both a Yin (Magnetic) field and a Yang (Electrical) charge. These energetic fields are interdependent. In science, an electro-magnetic field is a medium which connects two or more points in space, and is usually represented by ripples or waves of energy (Figure 4.36). These special energetic patterns are traditionally depicted by lines of force, used to indicate direction, shape, and influence.

The Earth's magnetic field (also known as the Geomagnetic Field) is generated by the movement of charged particles, which spans the circumference of the planet, creating a strong electrical field. This electromagnetic current affects the Earth's gravitational fields, weather, vegetation, and all life forms living on the planet (Figure 4.37).

The Earth's Geomagnetic Field contains both strong and weak areas. Generally, the energetic fields within these special areas are fixed and do not move. However, if an energetic field becomes

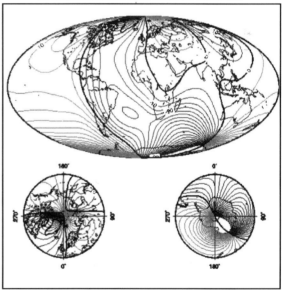

Figure 4.38. The Earth's Magnetic Field, according to US Geologists in 2009

weak due to some type of natural or man-made disaster (e.g., tectonic plate shift, volcanic eruption, nuclear explosion, etc.), then the stronger fields that are nearby will expand, altering the area's overall energetic pattern. This is why, according to modern research, the energetic patterns of the Earth's magnetic field change each year (Figure 4.38).

It is interesting to note, that the ancient Daoists believed that the Earth's energetic fields contained a type of "memory" imprinted within them. Therefore, each geographical area was thought to contain

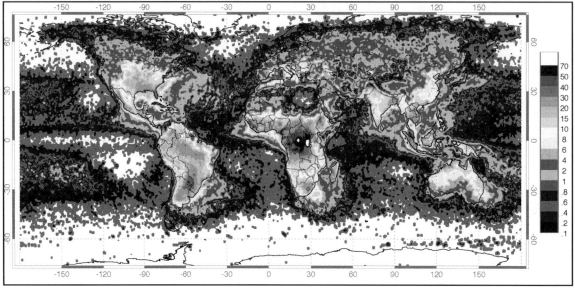
Figure 4.39. The Global map of lightning frequency strikes (Wikipedia 2013)

its own resonant field of ancestral and environmental knowledge. It was originally taught that, because the entire energetic history of any given area was encoded in the subtleties of its present energetic field, this important information could be accessed by the Daoist disciple through special meditation training.

In the Medical Qigong Clinic, it is taught that Magnetism is produced by the body's ever changing energetic patterns, externally manifesting from the various interactions occurring within the tissues. As previously mentioned, the body's cells carry electromagnetic fields containing both positive and negative polarities that both attract and repel each other. This results in a magnetic pull generated between the body's various types of Qi, tissues, organs, and extremities. When viewed as a whole, these tiny electromagnetic fields, govern the body's electromagnetic interaction with the Earth. It is interesting to note, that in the early 1980's, clinical research in China demonstrated that the iron in the hemoglobin of the Blood was attracted to the magnetic pull of the body's tissues, as well as to the magnetic pull of the Earth.

Additionally, the clinical research also revealed that the body's emotional field was connected to the Earth's electromagnetic field, and any shift in the Earth's electromagnetic field influenced an individual's emotional temperament. This unique observation explains the change in moods and behavior historically associated with the phases of the Moon. For example, during the Full Moon, there is a slight expansion and change in the Earth's magnetic field causing a corresponding change and expansion in human emotional fields.

What I find truly fascinating, is the ancient belief that spirit entities exist within the subtle energetic fields that cover the entire surface of the planet. It was believed that these subtle energetic fields were created and supported by lightning striking the Earth. When lightning strikes, its celestial energy was believed to be instantaneously dissipated uniformly over the entire surface of the planet. The continual electrical onslaught of this conductive energetic field created a perpetually dissipating energetic field, that allowed certain spirit entities to exist within the upper realms of these electromagnetic fields. The ancient Daoists believed that it was these subtle energetic fields that enabled certain spirit entities to descend and attach themselves onto unsuspecting victims. What is fascinating, is that in 1997 NASA and The National Space Development Agency of Japan reported that lightning occurs on average of 44 ± 5 times a second over the face of the Earth, for a total of nearly 1.4 billion flashes per year (Figure 4.39). According to modern research, naturally occurring Extremely Low Frequency (ELF) waves are present on the Earth, resonating between the ionosphere and the surface of the planet. These ELF waves are initiated by lightning strikes that make electrons in the atmosphere oscillate.

MODERN RESEARCH ON MAGNETIC FIELDS

Modern researchers in China are convinced that the physical body's internal Channel System charges its magnetic field through movement (i.e., the alternation of positive and negative pressure). This was one of the primary reasons for supporting Medical Qigong Prescription Exercises as clinical homework.

It was further discovered that when Medical Qigong Exercises were continually practiced, the body's internal Channel System created an electrical field that attracted electrons into the center core of the body, allowing for greater tonification of the various internal organs and organ systems.

Through extensive research, Richard H. Lee of The Chi Institute in San Clemente, California, found that the magnetic substances (Yin) stored within the body's water molecules naturally align themselves with the flow of electrical energy (Yang) in the body's channels. When the body's magnetic energy field is low, these channels become weakened and the conductivity is lowered.

Additional research concluded that this magnetic energy could be replenished by either ingesting and transforming energy from food, air, and water, or gathered directly from the Earth's magnetic field. This was because the body's magnetic field is affected by the Earth's magnetic field, through the energetic exchange occurring within both electromagnetic fields (Figure 4.40).

THE ELECTROMAGNETIC EFFECTS OF THE BODY'S TAIJI POLE

According to ancient Daoist teachings, the body maintains its electromagnetic connection with the Earth through the energetic resonance of the center core "Taiji Pole." Within the energetic structure of the body's Taiji Pole are located two major poles of energy. Each pole is located at op-

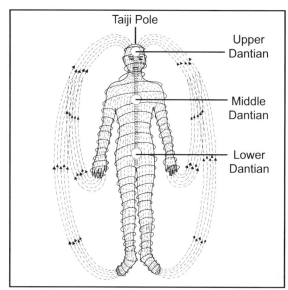

Figure 4.40. The body is enveloped with electromagnetic currents that influence both internal and external organ functions.

posite ends of the Taiji Pole, one is positioned at the top of the head and the other is positioned at the base of the perineum. The purpose of these energetic poles is to absorb Qi from the various universal and environmental fields, and connect and integrate that energy into the body's Three Dantians (i.e., energetic reservoirs).

The magnetic poles of the Upper Dantian (located within the head) and Lower Dantian (located within the lower abdomen) have a different energetic influx. The electromagnetic lines in the human body's biofield begin at the top of the head where the Heaven Qi flows into the body and descends the Taiji Pole, ending at the base of the perineum. Consequently, the Earth energy is drawn upward from the legs and perineum and flows into the Lower Dantian, eventually ending at the top of the head in the Upper Dantian. The bottom pole, located in the Lower Dantian, converts Jing (Essence) into Qi (Energy) and increases the body's overall life-force energy. The upper pole, located in the Upper Dantian, converts Shen (Spirit) into perceptual insight and spiritual light contained within the infinite space of the Wuji.

There are several ways in which the Medical Qigong Doctor can cultivate the electromagnetic

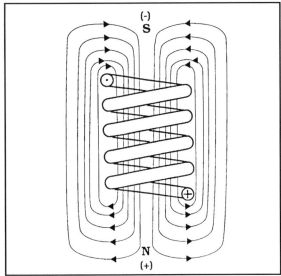

Figure 4.41. Magnetic field around an Electrified Spiral Coil

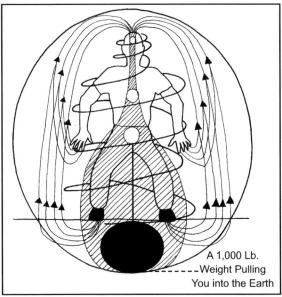

Figure 4.42. Qigong Doctors can create a stronger energetic field by extending Qi into the Earth (like an anchor), increasing and expanding the Weiqi field.

field that surrounds his body. One of the most common Medical Qigong Exercises used for Tonifying the body's Qi and for gathering additional energy into the tissues is known as the "Absorbing Qi From The Five Gates." This special exercise required the doctor to directly absorb the Yang Qi of Heaven (i.e., energy from the Sun, Moon, and Stars) into his body via the top of the head; while simultaneously absorbing the Yin Qi of Earth (i.e., energy from the Soil, Water, and Wind/Air) into his body through the bottom of the feet and center of the palms.

The doctor can also gather and wrap different types of environmental energy around his body through creative visualization, which can increase the thickness and power of his electromagnetic field. This looping action is similar to wrapping a magnet with wire to increase its magnetic field potential (Figure 4.41). Stronger lines of magnetic force will be produced around the body, thus, creating a stronger "energy bubble." The power of this energy bubble can be increased by extending Qi into the Earth via imagining a 1,000 pound weight compressing and pulling the body's Qi under the Earth (Figure 4.42).

The direction of electromagnetic wrapping should be done in accordance with the natural flow of energy in the surrounding environmental fields. Each individual should be sensitive as to which method works best, as there are many techniques available depending on the doctor's intention and belief.

Magnetic Therapy in the Clinic

Medical Qigong Doctors are trained how to stimulate their patient's electromagnetic field by extending emitted Qi into the patient's tissues. This stimulation of the body's magnetic field is extremely effective for regulating the flow of channel energy, and for stimulating the activity of the nervous system.

However, sometimes Magnetic Therapy is used in combination with Acupuncture Therapy in order to increase the effectiveness of the clinical application. For example, an acupuncturist may decide to use Magnetic Patches by placing them over various channel points on the patient's body. This is applied in order to induce energy flow, and stimulate the patient's tissues.

Because the Negative (North) Pole of a magnet is found to have a cooling and calming effect on tissues, it to traditionally placed in contact with the patient's skin when treating conditions of Excess Heat and stagnation. Herbal teas used for Purgation, dispersing, anti-inflammatory, or sedative properties can also be enhanced by placing the tea onto the Negative (North) pole of a magnetized surface for a minimum of one hour before drinking.

Because the Positive (South) Pole of the magnet is said to have a stimulating and warming effect on tissues, it is traditionally placed in contact with the patient's skin when treating deficiencies, Cold, and blockages. Herbal teas used for warming and Tonification can also be enhanced by placing the tea on the Positive (South) Pole of a magnetized surface for a minimum of one hour before drinking.

It is intresting to note that in 1990, Dr. Arthur Trappier submitted a paper entitled "Evaluating Perspectives on the Exposure Risks from Magnetic Fields" to the *Journal of the National Medical Association*. In his article, Dr. Trappier explained that exposing cancer cells to a negative (Yin) magnetic field discourages the growth of the cancer, while exposing cancer cells to a positive (Yang) magnetic field encourages their growth.

Western Magnetic Therapy

In Western clinical terminology, the phrase "Bioelectromagnetics" refers to the study of how electromagnetic fields interact with and influence biological processes. The terms "Electromagnetic Therapy" or "Electromagnetic Field Therapy" refers to clinical therapy involving the use of magnets or electromagnetic energy in medicine to treat disease.

Magnetic Therapy is currently being used in Western Medicine in a variety of clinical modalities. Some of these clinical applications are described as follows:
- Permanent Magnet Therapy for localized pain and inflammation relief
- Super-Magnet Therapy for stimulation of the thymus, and for immune system enhancement in cancer patients
- Pulsed Magnetic Therapy for the treatment of arthritic joints

Heat

When electricity passes through any substance it produces heat. The amount of heat that is generated depends upon the resistance of the substance and the density of the current's flow. Heat is generated at the electron level by the friction created through molecular motion. By increasing the motion of the molecules, more heat is generated.

The molecules in living organisms are in constant motion, increasing or decreasing their rate of acceleration according to the external environmental temperature. In order for heat to have any effect on the body's temperature, enough Qi has to be transferred to increase the movement of the molecules within the tissue's cells.

The heat within the body causes increased electron movement, resulting in more heat being generated on a cellular level. Heat is also created as a by-product of cellular metabolism. The body's metabolism produces 75% of the energy created in the form of heat. Cellular activity is increased through electrical, magnetic, heat, sound, and light stimulation.

The Ancient Daoist Teachings Of The Body's Three Fires

In 1995, when I was completing my clinical studies as a Doctor of Traditional Chinese Medicine at the Hai Dian University in Beijing China, I was introduced to the ancient Daoist alchemical teachings of the body's internal "Three Fires." The unique spiritual properties of these special Fires are quite different in energetic application, than those of the "Triple Burners" ("San Jiao"), traditionally taught in most Western Acupuncture Colleges.

According to the ancient writings of the *Compendium of the Doctrine of the Mean*, heat within the human body is generated from the combined action of the Three Internal Fires (i.e., the "Heart Fire," the "Kidney Fire," and the "Bladder Fire"). These special Fires emanate from three special locations inside the human body (Figure 4.43):

- **The Heart Fire:** This internal fire is located inside the center of the body's chest cavity.
- **The Kidney Fire:** This internal fire is located inside the center of the body's abdominal cavity.

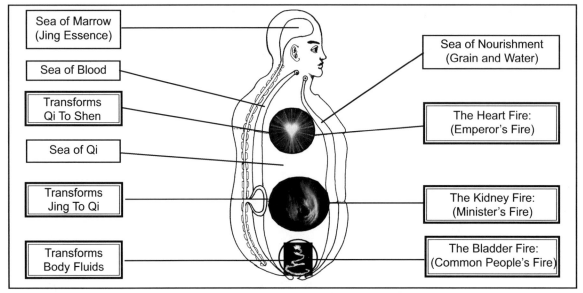

Figure 4.43. The Internal Formation of the Body's True Fire

- **The Bladder Fire:** This internal fire is located inside the center of the body's lower perineum.

When these Three Fires follow their normal course of energetic movement, they lead the body's life-force in the process of creating and sustaining life. There is an ancient Daoist saying which states,

"When the Heart Fire first awakens,
the Kidney Fire responds to it;
When the Kidney Fire moves,
the Bladder Fire follows it."

According to the *Huiming Jing (Scripture on Wisdom and Destiny)*,

"Within the human body,
the "Germinating Vesicle"
is the Heart's Imperial Fire;
At the entrance of the Germinating Vesicle,
is the Kidney's Ministerial Fire;
And within the entire body,
is the Urinary Bladder's Common People's Fire.

When the Heart's Imperial Fire expresses itself,
it is received by the Kidney's Ministerial Fire.
When the Kidney's Ministerial Fire moves,
the Common People's Fire follow.

When the Three Fires express themselves
in this order, a man develops.
However, when the Three Fires return in
reverse order, the True Way of the Dao develops.

This is the main reason why all Daoist Disciples
begin their Alchemical Work within the area of the
Lower Dantian, where outflow has ceased.
If the disciple does not establish this path,
but tries to set up another way,
all his effort will be to no avail."

Traditionally, it is taught that the Three Fires are responsible for regulating the Yin and Yang energy of the body. This is accomplished by fusing the energies of the Five Elements (stored within the body's Wood, Fire, Earth, Metal, and Water organs) with the energy of the Three Dantians.

According to the ancient Daoist teachings contained within the *Nine Levels of Improper Approaches to the Gate*,

"When transporting the Jing and Qi,
the Three Fires return back to the navel.
As the Shen (Heart/Mind) from the Heart Fire is
drawn into the Lower Dantian via the Yi (Intention),
the Bladder Fire fuses with the Kidney Fire
to create heat and form the body's True Fire.

CHAPTER 4: THE FIVE ENERGIES OF THE HUMAN BODY

Figure 4.44. The Heart Fire (Emperor's Fire) Sometimes called the "Commanding Fire"

Figure 4.45. The Kidney Fire (Minister's Fire) "Mingmen Fire" ("Fire of Destiny" - "Fire of Life")

This energetic action causes the body's Jing to transform into Qi within the Lower Dantian. Due to the activation and influence of this special Qi, the Heart Fire then transforms Qi into Shen within the Middle Dantian. Once this transformation is completed, the mind, breath, and body connection becomes regulated."

The Three Fires also represent the regions of vital heat that are responsible for the circulation of vital energy that sustain the human soul. Therefore the energy of the Three Fires is also used for spiritual cultivation and liberation, and can be accessed through Daoist Qigong and Shengong practice, special meditation, and deep prayer.

It is important to remember that, although similar in location, the energetic function of the body's Three Fires is quite different from that of the Triple Burners. The purpose of the Triple Burners is to regulate the ingestion, digestion, and distribution of food and fluids throughout the body. It is considered a completely different energetic system from the Three Fires. The primary purpose of the Three Fires is as follows:
- To transform and transport the energy of Jing, Qi, and Shen throughout the body,
- To transform and transport the energetic natures of the Four Seas (Sea of Blood, Sea of Nourishment, Sea of Qi and Sea of Marrow),
- To provide Heat to the internal organs within the Triple Burner bowl, and

- To assist in evaporating water and transforming Body Fluids.

1. **The Heart Fire (Emperor):** The Heart Fire is located in the center of the chest, and is also known as the "Commanding Fire" or "Emperor's Fire" (Figure 4.44). According to the *Complete Method of the Treasure of the Spirit*, "the Heart is the Emperor's Fire."

   The Heart Fire is responsible for transforming the body's Qi into Shen within the Middle Dantian. It heats the internal organs within the area of the Upper Burner, and energizes the resonating fields of both thought and emotion.
   - **Note:** The energy of the Heart Fire is Not the energy of the Upper Burner. The energetic field of the Upper Burner is formed from the Fire that is created from the combined energies of the Heart, Pericardium, and Lungs. The Upper Burner's energy is housed within the head, throat, and upper chest, extends down to the diaphragm, and is responsible for respiratory and cardiac functions. It moves the body's finer energy, circulating and distributing nutrients and Qi throughout the body like a mist.

2. **The Kidney Fire (Minister):** The Kidney Fire is located in the back of the body, just below the last floating rib, in-between the two Kidneys. It is also known as the "Ministerial Fire," "Prime Minister's Fire," and "Mingmen Fire" (Figure 4.45).

The Kidney Fire is responsible for transforming the body's Jing into Qi, heating the internal organs in the Middle and Lower Burners, and is the "Root" of the body's Yuan Qi (Original Energy). According to the *Classic of Intelligence and Destiny*, "the Ministerial Fire warms the entire body, promotes the functions of the internal organs, and improves their activity."

In ancient China, Daoist masters regarded the Mingmen Fire as the motivating force of the body, and they paid special attention to its training during Qigong exercises. A deficiency of Mingmen Fire may lead to decreased sex-drive, hypogonadism, or impotency. Conversely, if the Mingmen Fire is in excess, increased sex-drive, sexual obsession, or hypergonadism can occur.

Dr. Zhao Xianke, an expert on medicine during the Ming dynasty period, stated, "the Mingmen Fire dominates all Twelve Primary Channels. Without it, the Kidneys would be weak, the Spleen and Stomach could not digest food, the Liver and Gall Bladder would not give any energy to thinking or planning, the urine and feces would not be moved, and the Heart would malfunction, causing dizziness and endangering life."

- **Note:** The energy of the Kidney Fire is Not the energy of the Middle Burner. The Middle Burner is formed from the Fire that is created from the combined energies of the Stomach, Spleen, pancreas, and Gall Bladder. The Middle Burner's energy is housed within the upper abdomen (the diaphragm) and the area of the umbilicus, and is responsible for digestion, fermentation, and the transformation of food and drink into nutrients for distribution.

3. **The Urinary Bladder Fire (Common People):** According to the ancient Daoist text, *The Complete Method of Magical Treasure,* "the Urinary Bladder Fire is located in the lower abdominal area at the base of the perineum." According to Volume Eight of *Looking at the Channels,* "the Urinary Bladder Fire is also known as the "Common People's Fire" and the "Citizen's Fire" (Figure 4.46).

The Urinary Bladder Fire is responsible for heating the internal organs in the Lower

Figure 4.46. The Urinary Bladder Fire "Common People's Fire" or "Citizen's Fire"

Burner, evaporating water, and transforming Body Fluids. It ascends upward in order to assist the Kidney Qi in creating "True Water" ("Zhen Shui"). Then, when the Kidney Water ascends, it interacts with the fluid of the Heart to produce the body's True Qi (Zhen Qi). This energetic action has a minor effect of removing evil spirits and reducing illnesses. It also has a major effect of refining substances and is traditionally used when producing the energetic formation of the Daoist master's Golden Pill (True Alchemical Agent).

- **Note:** The energy of the Urinary Bladder Fire is Not the energy of the Lower Burner. The Lower Burner is formed from the Fire that is created from the combined energies of the Liver, Kidneys, Urinary Bladder, Intestines, and genitalia (in ancient China, the testicles were commonly known as the External Kidneys). The Lower Burner's energy is housed within the area just below the umbilicus and extends down to the lower perineum. It is responsible for the reproductive functions, and for the filtration and elimination of waste products.

THE YIN FIRE AND YANG FIRE CATEGORIES

According to the *Xingming Guizhi (Principles of Nature and Life/Destiny)*, the word "Fire" is traditionally used as a metaphor for the disciple's

"Spirit." Therefore, the energetic characteristics of the body's internal Fires are sometimes distinguished as either existing as a type of Yin (Acquired) or Yang (Original) Fire, described as follows (Figure 4.47):

- **Yin Fire:** This particular category is considered to be the body's "Postnatal Fire," and is often referred to as the "Acquired Emotional Fire." It energetically came into function after the individual's birth. It is energetically responsible for moving the Postnatal Jing, Qi and Shen within the tissues, and for internally and externally manifesting the energetic states of the various acquired emotions (Anger, Rage, Anxiety, Worry, Grief, Sorrow, Fear, Etc).
- **Yang Fire:** This category is considered to be the body's "True Fire," and is often called the "Spiritual Fire" or "Prenatal Fire." This special Spiritual Fire radiates its divine light within the body's center Taiji Pole, and was energetically activated within the body before birth. The Yang Fire radiates its unique light within the spiritually awakened, is responsible for moving the Prenatal Jing, Qi and Shen within the body's tissues, and for internally and externally manifesting the energy of the various Prenatal Spiritual Virtues (Compassion, Inner-Peace, Integrity, Honor, Wisdom, etc.).

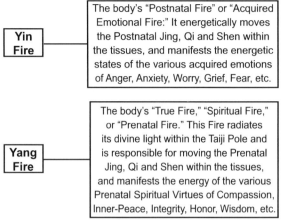

Figure 4.47. In Daoist Alchemy, the body's Fire can be categorized into either a Yin Fire or Yang Fire

FUNCTION OF THE BODY'S SPIRIT FIRES

After many hours of deep cultivation meditation, a Daoist disciple's Lower Dantian Qi will overflow, rise up his spine, and begin to collect inside his brain. Once this happens, the disciple will begin to see a bright White Light shine behind his closed eyes. This special light is traditionally known as the "Mysterious Gate" (Xuan Guan). When activated and manifested, the radiating energy of this special spiritual light can be observed when looking inside a disciple's eyes, as well as seen resonating within his external energy field.

It is important to note, that the refined Prenatal Spiritual Fire of the True Fire, is not internally observed as a White Light shining within the disciple's Yintang (Third Eye) area. Instead, it is observed radiating as a bright Golden Light. Towards the completion of the alchemical training, this Golden Light will eventually be observed glowing inside the energetic field of the White Light, commonly seen inside the Upper Dantian. This advanced mystical state is traditionally known as "the Sun Radiating Within the Moon Light."

This special Golden Light will only appear after the disciple's Middle Dantian has overflown with the Five Colored Vapors. This energetic overflowing naturally occurs after having previously practiced special cultivation meditations, including Divine Virtue Cultivation and spiritual purification (via the body's True Fire). When the True Fire is used in esoteric Alchemy, it is given several names, depending on its specific energetic application. These special applications can be placed into one of three main categories: The Fire Techniques used for Transforming With The Breath, The Fire Techniques used for Transforming With The Mind, and The Fire Techniques used for Manifesting the Original Spirit.

HEAT THERAPY THROUGH EMITTED QI

In the clinic, stimulating the body's tissues through Heat Therapy is extremely effective for treating Deficient and Cold Syndromes. In China, Medical Qigong Doctors traditionally use heat emission into their patients' tissues to regulate the energetic flow of the channels, and to tonify the Qi and Blood.

Figure 4.48. Heaven (Yang) and Earth (Yin) Electricity From the Sky to the Soil

Figure 4.49. Human Electricity: From the Thumb to the Fingers

In the clinic, Heat Therapy is also used in the form of Moxibustion as an adjunct to Acupuncture Therapy (i.e., sometimes Moxa Sticks and/or Cones, are lit and placed over various channel points to induce energy flow, and stimulate the tissues and channel points.

WESTERN HEAT THERAPY

Western Medicine currently uses radiant and conductive Heat Therapy for vasodilation and pain relief. These heat therapies can further be divided and categorized into Dry-Heat Therapy and Moist-Heat Therapy.

DRY-HEAT THERAPY:
- Dry Packs
- Hot Water Bottles
- Heliotherapy-Sun Therapy
- Ultraviolet-Heat Therapy
- Infrared-Heat Therapy
- Diathermy Therapy

MOIST-HEAT THERAPY
- Hot Bath Packs
- Hot Wet Packs
- Hot Foot Baths
- Fomentations
- Poultices
- Vapor and Paraffin Baths

ELECTRICITY

The flow of electrons is called a current. A current produces a magnetic field, and likewise a magnetic field induces an electrical current when it moves in relation to a conductor (Figure 4.48).

In Medical Qigong Therapy, the body's channels are considered to be electrical circuits, and the points existing along each channel can be seen as booster amplifiers (or step-up transformers) that maintain the current's strength.

According to Robert O. Becker, M.D., research scientist and author of the book *Cross Currents*, acupuncture needles have the capacity to act as antennae, drawing charged particles (ions) from the atmosphere and directing them into the body. The acupuncture needle delivers a low-level electrical stimulation to the channel points and can be used to charge up or decrease the energetic potential of these step-up transformers, thus affecting the energetic current flowing along the channel.

While researching the electromagnetic currents within the human body, Dr. Becker found that the human body is an excellent conductor of electricity (Figure 4.49), containing both alternating electrical currents (AC) and direct electrical currents (DC).

- **Alternating Current:** The Alternating Current is responsible for the transformation of the body's magnetic field into the body's electrical field.

- **Direct Current:** The Direct Current is responsible for the body's positive (Yang) and negative (Yin) flow of electrical charges (Figure 4.50).

The friction produced by rubbing the feet on a carpet creates an electrical charge that is stored within the body until it touches another conductor (metal, another body, etc.) which releases the charge. This everyday occurrence demonstrates the storage, conduction, and discharging of electrons from the body. Any time electrons travel, heat or thermal radiation is produced.

According to Swedish physician and medical research scientist, Dr. Bjorn Nordenstrom, the biological circuits of the body are driven by accumulated charges, which, unlike a battery, oscillate between positive and negative. The body's system of channels and Blood Vessels act as insulated cables, while the blood plasma acts as a conductor.

The intercellular fluid in the body's permeable tissue conducts ions. The ion pumps and channels located in the plasma membrane of the cells are a key component of the body's electrical circuits.

Every human thought and action is accompanied by the conduction of electrical signals along the fibers of the nervous system. In fact, life would not exist without this constant flow of ions across the membranes of cells.

The electromagnetic energy in the body's cells is continuously being generated from the biochemical transformation of food and air. It is circulated throughout the body by the electromagnetic fields generated from within the tissues. Perineural cells, or nerve sheaths, carry the direct current of the body's electricity. These cells are responsible for motivating the body to heal, regenerate, and repair itself. Healing is always affected by a change within the body's electromagnetic field.

In the Medical Qigong clinic, the rate and efficiency of healing is based on the strength and polarity of the body's energetic field. This electricity is one of the primary types of energy responsible for maintaining life itself.

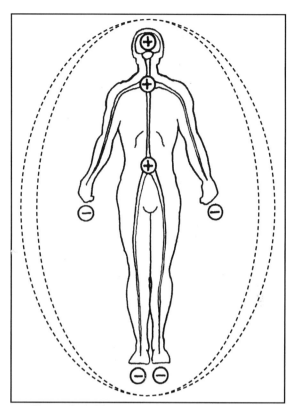

Figure 4.50. The Direct Current is responsible for the body's positive (Yang) and negative (Yin) flow of Electrical Charges.

THE BODY'S PIEZOELECTRIC QUALITIES

Vibratory wave energy is transformed in the human body by the piezoelectric properties (the ability to produce electricity or electrical polarity from the application of mechanical force) of tissues such as Bones and connective tissue containing crystalline structures. The helical molecules such as DNA, keratin, collagen, actin and myosin all have piezoelectric qualities.

Dr. Robert O. Becker conducted extensive research in order to demonstrate that Bones are "piezoelectric," and that when Bones are stressed, mechanical energy is converted into electrical energy. He discovered that running a minute electrical current through a fractured Bone will stimulate the reproduction of the cells, creating a healing current similar to the body's natural healing mechanism.

According to Richard H. Lee of the Chi Institute in San Clemente, California, , electrostatic waves are observed in the body with both EEGs (electro-encephalograms) and EMGs (electro-myograms). Therapies that affect the EEGs include Sound Therapy, Meditation Therapy, Self-Regulation Medical Qigong Therapy, and Light Therapy. By controlling their thoughts, Medical Qigong Doctors can affect the energy currents in their body and thus affect the EEG measurements. Experiments show that EEG measurements in test subjects receiving energy from healers tend to synchronize. Medical Qigong Doctors, when treating patients, can produce voltages as high as 190 volts, which is 100,000 times greater than regular EEG voltages.

The body's natural ability to gather, store, and move Qi increases the body's ability to gather, store, and move electrical charges. The gathering of these electrical charges can cause a gradual buildup of electricity within the tissues and internal organs, and can develop into an excess Qi condition if not properly grounded or rooted.

In the Medical Qigong Clinic, it is observed that Excess Qi conditions often manifest in mood swings, and are responsible for the energetic circuit overloads that occur spontaneously within the body. Excess Qi may manifest as a sudden "explosion" or "release" of emotions such as rage, fear, grief, worry, fright, anxiety, and excitement.

If the treating doctor is not properly grounded or rooted, an excess electromagnetic charge can be released from the patient's internal tissues and become absorbed by the doctor's internal organs. This energetic reaction can cause an already overcharged internal organ to spontaneously release emotions. Sometimes the release can be physiological, sudden sweating, blushing, twitching, jerking, yawning, sighing, burping, are all examples of an internal organ seeking to regain homeostasis by discharging energy.

It is interesting to note, that extensive research conducted on electromagnetic fields revealed that when chronically used, an electric-blanket will diminish the pineal gland's ability to produce melatonin. Since the body uses melatonin to combat cancer, this explains the relationship between the use of electric blankets and increased incidences of leukemia and Alzheimer's disease.

ELECTRICAL THERAPY THROUGH EMITTED QI

The idea that an electric current can stimulate bodily repair, alert defense mechanisms, and control the growth and function of cells is not a new concept in Western Medicine. In fact, the use of bio-electromagnetism dates back at least 200 years.

Electrotherapy has been found to be useful for relieving pain by signaling the brain to activate and alter the body's neurochemicals. The insertion of electrically stimulating needles into a patient's body, for example, causes a release of endorphins and is used for pain management.

Medical Qigong Therapy, Acupuncture, and Chinese Massage likewise stimulate the peripheral and cutaneous nerves that carry sensory information through the spinal cord to the brain. This stimulation of the cutaneous nerves activates the brain's opiates (endorphins) and facilitates the closure of the body's pain-relay gates, stopping pain, and providing the neurological basis for anesthesia.

Because Medical Qigong Therapy also has an analgesic effect on the body's cutaneous tissues, it is increasingly being used in Chinese hospitals for preoperative and postoperative procedures.

WESTERN ELECTROTHERAPY

Western Medicine is currently using electrotherapy in a variety of modalities, some of which are described as follows:
- Giga-TENS therapy for stimulation of healing
- TENS therapy for pain relief
- CES-cranial electro-stimulation therapy, for depression and substance abuse, etc.
- Micro-Stimulation Therapy for micro-current stimulation below the threshold of awareness, to stimulate nonspecific healing, the reduction of inflammation, and the harmonization of tissue polarity.

Chapter 5
The Taiji Pole, Chakras, and Three Dantians

The Taiji Pole

The Taiji Pole is seen as a vertical column of brilliant white light, full of vibration and energetic pulsation. The Taiji Pole roots the Divine Qi into the human body, and is responsible for animating the Eternal Soul (Shen Xian). The energetic pathway of the Taiji Pole, flows from the top of the head (Baihui), through the center core of the body, and physically terminates at the base of the perineum (Huiyin).

The Taiji Pole energetically connects to and empowers all Three Dantians (Figure 5.1). It also "feeds" the Yuan Qi and Yuan Shen of all of the body's organs and tissues, and functions as an energetic highway for the movement of the various life-force energies. According to ancient Daoist Energetic Embryology, the Eternal Soul is drawn into the body at the moment of conception through the Taiji Pole and departs through the Taiji Pole at death. Additionally, the Taiji Pole was also believed to serve as a special energetic portal for the Spirit Body to travel outside the Physical Body.

In Daoist Energetic Embryology, it is taught that, as the father's sperm enters the mother's egg (Figure 5.2), the energetic fusion creates the Upper (or Heavenly) Portal point of the Human Taiji Pole. At this early stage of development, the upper vortex point begins drawing various types of energy into the embryo's forming cells and tissues. This energetic spiralling action is used to create and establish the interconnecting internal foundational structures of the Three Dantians.

During the time of tissue formation, the Taiji Pole energetically roots its column of radiant white light into the newly forming Kidneys and the Mingmen area. In the embryo, this special area is energetically stimulated by the Upper (Heavenly) Vortex, allowing for the growth and development of the Kidney Orb.

It is interesting to note, that in ancient China, the Kidney Orb was also known as the "lotus bulb" or "seed of life," and was seen as the fundamental source for all of the body's Yin and Yang energy. From the lotus seed, the spinal column develops,

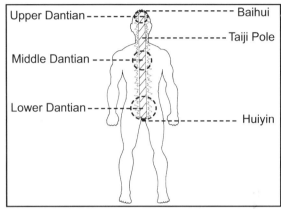

Figure 5.1. The Taiji Pole is ocated in the Center Core of the Body

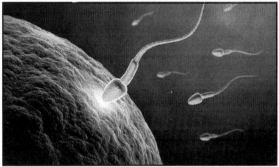

Figure 5.2. The Sperm Penetrates The Egg, and creates the upper energetic portal of Taiji Pole

and extends upward in order to form the Brain. Therefore, in ancient times, the spinal column was sometimes known as the "lotus stem" or "stem of life," and the Brain was known as the "lotus flower."

As the fetus continues to grow and develop around the pulsating energy of the center Taiji Pole, the body's tissues and energetic system continue to alter and change. Eventually, the position of the Taiji Pole transforms from being located at the internal Kidneys and Mingmen area, to being rooted at the base of the lower perineum. This lower location, and its relationship to the Kidney organs, is why in ancient China, the testes were commonly referred to as the "External Kidneys."

Figure 5.3. The Pole Star - Heaven's Taiji Pole

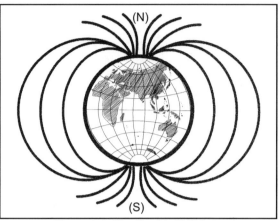

Figure 5.4. The Earth's Taiji Pole

After birth, the Taiji Pole is energetically stabilized inside the body as a vertical column of brilliant white light, surrounded by a spiralling veil of golden light. Its energetic function is to "feed" and animate the internal and external organs and tissues, as well as stabilize and support the individual's Energy Body and Spirit Body.

TAIJI POLE OF HEAVEN, EARTH, & MAN

According to ancient Daoist teachings, the Three Treasures of Heaven, Earth, and Man all contain a central energetic vortex or Taiji Pole. Within the Taiji Pole, the past, present, and future of all time and space energetically converge in order to create a sacred "Still-Point." This special "Still-Point" point can only be spiritually accessed through deep meditation, which allows the disciple's Spirit Body to leave his Energy Body and sojourn into these various energetic realms.

The three Taiji Poles of Heaven, Earth, and Man are traditionally explained to Daoist disciples as follows:

- **The Taiji Pole of Heaven:** To the ancient Daoists, the North Star was seen as the Taiji Pole of Heaven. It is sometimes known as the "Celestial Pole Star," or the "Taiji of Heaven." The original translation of the Chinese character for Taiji means "Supreme Ultimate," and represents the ultimate state of transformation (Yin transforming into Yang, and vice-versa). While the original meaning of the Chinese character for Yin is the shady side of the mountain and Yang depicts the sunny side of the mountain, the center of the mountain's peak is considered a Taiji (the center of Yin and Yang) where the energies of both Yin and Yang meet.

The center core or midline of the Taiji of Heaven is also known as the "Celestial Still-Point." This is because, although all of the Yin and Yang changes continually occur within the Heavens during the course of a day, causing all of the stars to make a 360 degree rotation as the Earth rotates (Figure 5.3), the Pole Star remains stationary, as Heaven's still-point (like the eye of a hurricane).

- **The Taiji Pole of Earth:** The Taiji Pole of Earth is the energetic central axis of the Earth (Figure 5.4). At the extremities of the Earth's Taiji Pole are the North and South Poles, which can be compared to the top of the head (Baihui) and lower perineum (Huiyin) areas of the human body.

According to ancient Daoist teachings, the Earth's center Taiji Pole aligns itself to the "North Star" (i.e., the center "Celestial Pole Star" of Heaven).

- **The Taiji Pole of Man:** The Taiji Pole of the human body is responsible for absorbing the energy from Heaven and Earth, and distributing the collected Qi throughout the body's major internal organ systems (Figure 5.5). The center core of the body's Taiji Pole is viewed as

CHAPTER 5: THE TAIJI POLE, CHAKRAS, AND THREE DANTIANS

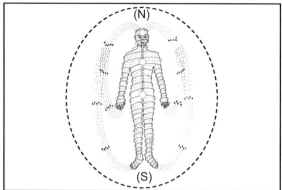

Figure 5.5. The body's center core Taiji Pole is enveloped with electromagnetic currents that influence both internal and external organ functions.

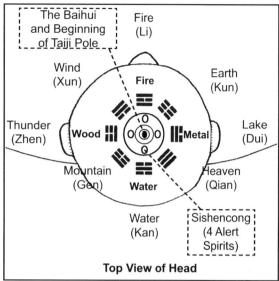

Figure 5.6. The Five Portals of the Heavenly Yang Gate are considered the Gate of the Hun. Celestial Energy is absorbed into the Taiji Pole through the Five Portals of the Heavenly Yang Gate, located at the center of the Baihui and Sishencong areas at the top of the head.

the sacred Still-Point of Man, through which a Daoist disciple is taught to experience all of the energetic changes, transformations, and developments of his life. Consequently, great stillness can be experienced when a disciple meditates, and places the focus of his mind's attention into the center core of his Taiji Pole.

INTERNAL ENERGY INTERACTIONS

Similar to the North (Yang) and South (Yin) magnetic poles of the Earth's central axis, the body's Taiji Pole is divided into Yang (Heaven) and Yin (Earth) energetic polarities. Located in the "North," are the Five Portals of the Heavenly Yang Gate (the Baihui and Sishencong points), positioned at the top of the head. Located in the "South," are the Five Portals of the Earthly Gate (Changqiang GV-1, Huiyin CV-1, etc.), positioned at the perineum. Both of these important areas are described as follows:

- **The Five Portals of the Heavenly Yang Gate:** In Daoist alchemy, the body's Heavenly portals are considered to be the "Celestial Gates of the Hun." During meditation, the Celestial Qi of the Sun, Moon, and Stars are all absorbed into the disciple's body through the Upper Dantian, and Taiji Pole, via these Five Heavenly Yang Gates (Figure 5.6). These special upper gates are located at the top of the head, centered at the Baihui ("One Hundred Meetings") area, and are surrounded by the "Sishencong" ("Four Alert Spirits").

The Sishencong points that surround the Baihui, are also known as the "Four Great Spirits of the Gate." This name signifies the importance of these points as guardians of the human soul, as they control the spiritual access to the body's Taiji Pole. The ancient Daoists believed that only through deep meditation or death could the human soul leave its corporeal residence and travel into the various physical, energetic, and spiritual worlds.

Because of their location above the Niwan Palace (center of the Upper Dantian), it is said that throughout life, the Four Great Spirits of the Gate protect the human soul from spirit possession, and receive Heavenly energy as well as intuitive insights to guide and direct the human soul through the various challenges of life.

239

SPIRITUAL MANIFESTATIONS

In China, the Daoists Abbots say that the body's Taiji Pole is a holy place, one that practically defies all description. Similar to an aquarium which is built to house and contain fish from the deep sea, it is the spiritual container of Divine Light that houses the individual's Eternal Soul (Shen Xian).

The body's Taiji Pole is revered as one of the most sacred of places, as it contains the true essence of the Yuan Shen (Original Spirit), devoid of all ego masks or defense mechanisms. When the body's internal and external energetic wave patterns become synchronized through prayer or meditation, a rhythmic pulsation occurs within the body's Taiji Pole. This energetic pulse of sound and light begins to vibrate deep within the center core of the disciple's body, and resonates outward into infinite space. This sacred energetic pulse is traditionally used in meditation in order to project the Daoist disciple through the infinite space of the Wuji, to eventually fuse with the luminescent pulse and light of the eternal Dao.

If a Daoist disciple penetrates the golden veil that surrounds the center of an individual's Taiji Pole, and extends his intention deep into that sacred light's inner core, he will often experience the sensation of falling into space or dissolving into the infinite space of the Wuji. This special sensation is often followed by seeing flashing colored lights and various moving shapes, as the surrounding core seems to dissolve into infinite space itself. Time and space dissolve and a feeling of being stretched into eternity occurs. This experience is considered to be the "True Connection," in which the Wuji returns back to the eternal Dao.

It is important to note, that the potential for this magical experience exists within everyone, and can also be accessed through deep prayer and meditation. It is considered to be a normal phenomenon within deep spiritual practices. This is why the Taiji Pole is often referred to as the "River of God."

When Daoist disciples become aware of their internal connection to the Divine, it is called a spiritual "Awakening." As we become aware of our deeper self (energetically manifested through the Taiji Pole), we also awaken to a more objective awareness of the energetic and emotional patterns

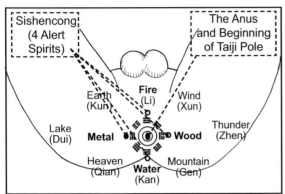

Figure 5.7. The Five Portals of the Earthly Yin Gate are considered the Gate of the Po. The environmental energy of the Earth is absorbed into the Taiji Pole through the Five Portals of the Earthly Yin Gate, located at the center of the anal sphincter, between the Huiyin ("Meeting of Yin") and the Changqiang ("Long Strength") areas, at the base of the perineum.

- **The Five Portals of the Earthly Yin Gate:** In Daoist alchemy, the body's Earthly portals are considered to be the "Terrestrial Gates of the Po." During meditation, the Environmental Qi of the Soil, Wind, and Water is absorbed into the body's Taiji Pole through the tissues, and enters into the Lower Dantian via Five Earthly Yin Gates (Figure 5.7). These special gates are located at the center of the anal sphincter, between the Huiyin ("Meeting of Yin") and the Changqiang ("Long Strength") areas, at the base of the perineum.

According to Daoist Energetic Anatomy, all of the various energies active within the body's internal and external energetic fields, extend directly from the body's Taiji Pole, which supplies Qi to all of the body's organs, channels, and tissues. For example, as the Three Dantians absorb energy from the body's Taiji Pole, they then feed the body's Yin and Yang organs, channels, and Extraordinary Vessels. The energetic system of each individual Dantian is connected to the body's Taiji Pole, and is responsible for a special alchemical transition, used in the process of converting Jing (Essence) into Qi, Qi (Energy) into Shen, Shen (Spirit) into Wuji, and Wuji (Infinite Space) back into the Dao.

contained within the Three Bodies, and to the harmonies and imbalances existing within them.

During a spiritual Awakening, our internal awareness moves from orienting through life via the external social masks and defense mechanisms, to operating from the spiritual guidance of our center core self. Our Yuan Shen (Original Spirit) begins to shine brighter and stronger from within us, as we gradually reorganize various aspects of our internal being to align with our life purpose. Numerous physical, emotional, and energetic adjustments take place throughout this process.

One of my favorite quotes describing the "Awakening" phenomena, comes from Daoist Master Cloud-Chamber's conversation with Lu Dong Bin , and goes as follows:

> **"Fifty years have past and gone
> in a twinkling of an eye!
> What you have gained
> is not worth rejoicing over,
> and what you have lost
> was not worth grieving about!
> Only when people have a great Awakening,
> do they know that the world is but a dream!"**

THE SUBTLE ENERGY OF THE TAIJI POLE

The esoteric energetic aspects, as well as magical and spiritual contents resonating within the Taiji Pole, can best be understood through both metaphysical and mythological perspectives. In ancient China, the subtle energy existing within the Human Taiji Pole was traditionally described as follows:

1. **Metaphysically:** The sacred energy existing within the Taiji Pole contains the following magical and metaphysical aspects:
   - The energy of the Primordial Energetic State that existed before creation
   - The Primordial Energy of Creation
   - The Energetic Principle of Creation Itself
   - The underlying energetic characteristic common to all created things.

   To the ancient Daoists, connecting with the powerful energy resonating within the body's Taiji Pole allowed the disciple to obtain the ability to access, experience, and embody the spiritual state of Primordial Oneness.

Figure 5.8. The Energy From Within the Taiji Pole Radiates Throughout the Physical Body, Energy Body and Spirit Body.

2. **Mythologically:** The sacred energy existing within the Taiji Pole can be understood both as a part of the Divine Energy of Heaven, and as an aspect of the Divine Consciousness contained within each individual, or a combination of the two.

The energy contained within the Taiji Pole is the Divine Energetic Matrix of the Universal Dao (Figure 5.8). Within the human body, the Taiji Pole is primarily identified as the energetic source of the Three Dantians. It is the personification of the central power of life and the universe, expressed as the energetic combination of both spiritual and physical divinity, existing simultaneously on both microcosmic and macrocosmic levels.

MASKS AND DEFENSE MECHANISMS SURROUNDING THE CENTER CORE

According to ancient Daoist teaching, when we are born, we are connected to a divine source of spiritual wisdom and power via our center core Taiji Pole. As we age and seek to establish security in external social relationships, we gradually forget this internal connection. During this process, we create various masks and defense mechanisms that seek to shield us from our pain and self-hatred (shame).

Throughout our lives, any time we repress the flow of feelings connected to an event (especially those that are painful or difficult), we instantly freeze the energy of that particular event and lock it within our cells and tissues. Because the external Weiqi Field is composed of energetic consciousness, a block of frozen psychic energy is formed within both the Weiqi field and the internal tissues at the moment we inhibit any type of feelings, especially those of pain. By walling off our wounds, we also wall off our connection to our deeper core self. We pretend not to feel the pain anymore and we block the memory of the event through denial. Thus, we prevent a natural resolution to the pain and the trauma of the event.

The amount of life-force energy that we are able to feel and experience, is in direct proportion to the exact degree of our internal connection to our center core. When we deny our true feelings, we disconnect from our core self and begin to identify with our created social masks (Figure 5.9). For example, we may smile when we really feel angry, or pretend to be indifferent to our hurts. We lose our creative ability when we deny this deeper connection because creative inspiration comes from our core self. When we attempt to prevent the negative feelings of anger, pain, or fear, we also prevent ourselves from being able to experience a wide spectrum of the positive emotions, and negate the possibility of healing the physical, mental, and emotional aspects of an experience.

During Medical Qigong treatments, patients regress layer by layer through the pain and fear embedded in patterns of blocked energy that give rise to symptoms of disease. Even though the patient's emotional release may cause frightening memories, the pain decreases with the dispersal of the original trauma.

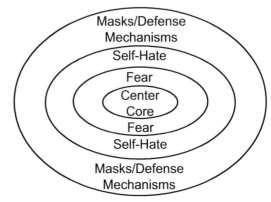

Figure 5.9. The center core self is surrounded by walls of fear, self-hatred, and social masks, which act as trigger mechanisms for the wounded soul.

In clinical practice, most of the patients' pain comes not from the original trauma but from the unconscious belief system in the "story" that was established to protect them from the original trauma. In other words, more pain and illness is created by the avoidance of working through the original trauma (denial) than was present in the original event itself. It requires enormous amounts of energy to suppress our true feelings, and each time we do so we simultaneously exhaust and energetically injure ourselves. Any attempt at healing that does not address the deeper release of these emotional and energetic patterns from the tissues and psyche will ultimately be less effective.

My teacher once explained that the internal process of closing down the human spirit generally proceeds as follows:

1. **The Center Core:** As a young child, coming from a state of wonderment, you choose to experience life by exploring the kitchen cabinets.
2. **Fear:** A parent suddenly enters the room and shouts "No!"
3. **Self-Hate:** Although the parent tries to explain why you are not allowed to experiment with the various items under the sink, as a two year old, you reason that you are bad and unworthy of love.
4. **Masks and Defence Mechanism:** Because you have been asked to act in a certain manner in order to receive approval, you either immediately conform or rebel.

CHAPTER 5: THE TAIJI POLE, CHAKRAS, AND THREE DANTIANS

Normally, this four stage cycle will continue to repeat its patterns throughout an individual's life, continually driving them further away from their true core self by creating various external "Masks" for the sake of acceptance, control, and/or approval.

MEDITATING ON THE TAIJI POLE

The ancient Daoist taught that direct meditation and focused concentration placed onto the body's center core Taiji Pole was paramount in order to return back to the Original Heart/Mind (Yuan Shen) of their true spirit. It was also taught that within the center of the Taiji Pole lay the Supreme Ultimate (Taiji), hence the magical ability to access "Omnipresent Awareness." This secret energetic portal was considered to be the disciple's magical gateway to the entire universe. Through its entryway, the Daoist disciple would be allowed simultaneous perception and control of all the subtle mechanisms of all creation.

The following are seven secret methods of ancient esoteric Shengong practice, used in esoteric Daoist Alchemy. These special meditations were used by priests and disciples in order to awaken the energetic and spiritual consciousness resonating within their center core Taiji Pole. This is a progressive method of "Spiritual Awakening." The disciple will begin with Stage #1, and eventually progress through all seven stages (Figure 5.10):

1. **The Dao, the Three Dantians, and the Taiji Pole:** In this first meditation, the disciple visualizes the divine energy of the Eternal Dao resonating from within his center core and Three Dantians. When mastered, this meditation leads to the eternal survival of the disciple's Yuan Shen (Original Spirit). Even though he experiences the death of the physical body on this Earth, the memories of the disciple's present personality will be preserved by his Yuan Shen.
2. **Dao, the Taiji Pole, and the Postnatal Transformations:** In this second meditation, the disciple will concentrate on feeling the rhythmic Postnatal Transformations of the Three Inner Treasures of Man (Jing to Qi, Qi to Shen, Shen to Wuji, and Wuji to Dao). Consciously awakening to these rhythmic transformations occurring along the

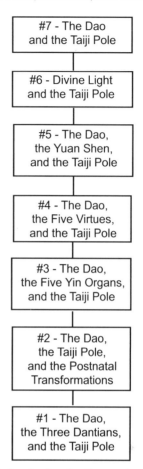

Figure 5.10. Awakening the Energetic and Spiritual Consciousness within the Taiji Pole

Taiji Pole brings about a state of internal and external harmony. When mastered, this awareness will allow the disciple to further refine his Ling Qi (Spiritualized Energy) and Ling Shen (Spiritual Mind), and eventually establish a deep mystical union with the Eternal Dao.

3. **The Dao, the Five Yin Organs, and the Taiji Pole:** In this third meditation, the disciple visualizes the divine energy of the Eternal Dao resonating from within the center core of his body, extending its energy outward into the Five Yin Organs (i.e., Liver, Heart, Spleen, Lungs, and Kidneys). When mastered, this special meditation leads to enhanced physical strength and increases the vitality of the internal organs.

243

4. **The Dao, the Five Virtues, and the Taiji Pole:** In this fourth meditation, the disciple will develop control over his emotions. This is needed in order to house the five spiritual components of his Original Five Element Virtues (Kindness, Inner-Peace, Truthfulness, Integrity, and Wisdom), thereby attaining single-pointedness of mind, and spiritually connecting with the Eternal Dao. When mastered, this special meditation will enhance the dominant spiritual presence of the disciple's Hun. When the Original Five Element Virtues are firmly rooted within the disciple's body, the disciple will manifest a high spiritual state of harmony and compassion, during all activities, even in times of difficulty and misfortune.

5. **The Dao, the Yuan Shen, and the Taiji Pole:** In this fifth meditation, the disciple will obtain control of his thoughts, by surrendering his Shen Zhi (Acquired Personality) to the Dao. This special technique is practiced in order to establish a perfect unity between the spiritual energy of the disciple's Yuan Shen (Original Spirit) and the spiritual energy of the Eternal Dao. When mastered, this special meditation will stabilize the disciple's thoughts, allowing him to obtain limitless energy within his body. This also enables the disciple to transcend physical discomforts (hunger, thirst, pain, etc.), and mental turmoil (anger, worry, fear, etc.).

6. **Divine Light and the Taiji Pole:** In this sixth meditation, the disciple will "awaken" and strengthen the energy flowing within his Taiji Pole, by visualizing the light of the Eternal Dao shining and radiating from deep inside its center core. When mastered, this special meditation will restore a disciple's physical health and ultimately transform his energy into spirit. This will create a mystical union with the eternal light of the Wuji, that exists and extends throughout the entire universe.

7. **The Dao and the Taiji Pole:** In this last meditation, the disciple will visualize the Divine energy of the Eternal Dao resonating from deep within the center of his body. When mastered, this special meditation will lead to the awakening of magical powers within oneself. It will also

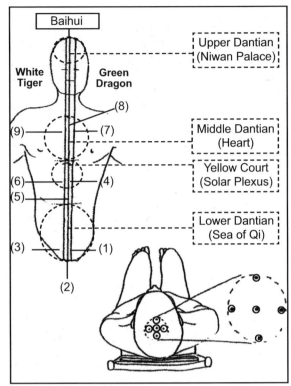

Figure 5.11. Fusing the Qi of the Earthly White Tiger and the Heavenly Green Dragon

enable the disciple to obtain mastery over his environment (e.g., multi-location, invulnerability, spirit travel, and extending his life at will).

ENERGIZING THE TAIJI POLE

This ancient meditation is used to activate the energetic pathways of the body's Thrusting Vessels. It combines the Yin energy of Earth, positioned on the right side of the body (manifesting as a White Tiger), with the Yang energy of Heaven, positioned on the left side of the body (manifesting as a Green Dragon). All three energetic pathways will balance and harmonize the Qi flowing along the center channel of the body's Taiji Pole (Figure 5.11). It is important to note, that the energetic pathways of these special Thrusting Vessels are quite different in location and function than the Chung Mei (Thrusting Vessels) used in post-communist Traditional Chinese Medical Colleges.

This special meditation is traditionally used in ancient Daoist alchemy in order to cleanse, purify, and fuse the energetic fields of the body's Three Dantians, and prepare the disciple for Creating the Immortal Fetus. The Fusing and Energizing the Taiji Pole meditation is divided into three stages. In each stage, three channels are utilized in order to move the Qi up the center core of the body. The three channels are divided into three sections, described as follows:

- **Section 1:** Lower Dantian to the Yellow Court
- **Section 2:** Lower Dantian and Yellow Court to the Middle Dantian (Heart)
- **Section 3:** Lower Dantian, Yellow Court, and Middle Dantian (Heart) to the Upper Dantian (Niwan Palace)

After the energetic fusion has been completed, the disciple will experience the Qi vibrating within his center Taiji Pole. The Fusing and Energizing the Taiji Pole Meditation is divided into three stages, described as follows:

ENERGIZING THE TAIJI POLE: STAGE #1

In the first stage of training, the disciple will begin by using three separate divisions (left, center, and right) of the lower, middle, and upper sections of the Thrusting Vessels, described as follows:

1. Assume a sitting meditation posture. Keep your spine straight, shoulders and chest relaxed, knees positioned lower than your groin, with your tongue placed on the Wood Element tongue position (Figure 5.12).
2. Close your eyes and place your hands naturally on the knees, or place them on your lap with the palms overlapping, and thumbs touching, forming the Radiating Yang Hand Seal (Figure 5.13).
3. Begin by using "Natural Breathing." Inhale and softly expand the abdomen, and focus your mind's intention on filling the Lower Dantian with Qi.
4. Then exhale, and direct your mind to relax the entire body. Softly compressing the abdomen down and inward.
- Next, direct the Qi to flow down into the "Dragons Well" point (Huiyin), located at the center of your lower perineum.
5. Beginning from Section 1, move the Qi from the perineum through the Lower Dantian, up the Thrusting Vessels, to the Yellow Court in the following pattern:

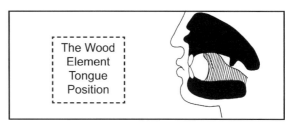

Figure 5.12. The Wood Element Tongue position (Liver). The tongue is placed on the soft palate at the center of the roof of the mouth.

Figure 5.13. Sit with the palms overlapping, and the thumbs touching.

- **Left:** Begin on the left (Yang) side of the Thrusting Vessel, and follow the Heavenly Dragon pathway. Bring the energy from the Dragon Well (lower perineum) through the Lower Dantian to the Yellow Court (via route 1 to 4); then lead the Qi back down through the Lower Dantian into the Dragon Well (via route 4 to 1).
- **Center:** Next, focus on the Center Core Thrusting Vessel. Bring the energy from the Dragon Well, through the Lower Dantian, to the Yellow Court (via route 2 to 5); then lead the Qi back down through the Lower Dantian to the Dragon Well (via route 5 to 2).
- **Right:** Finally, focus on the right (Yin) side of the Thrusting Vessel, and follow the Earthly Tiger pathway. Bring the energy from the Dragon Well through the Lower Dantian to the Yellow Court (via route 3 to 6); then lead the Qi back down through the Lower Dantian to the Dragon Well (via route 6 to 3).

6. After completing Section 1, proceed to Section 2, and move the Qi from the Yellow Court along the Thrusting Vessels to the Middle Dantian in the following pattern:
   - **Left:** Begin on the left (Yang) side of the Thrusting Vessel, and follow the Heavenly Dragon pathway. Bring the energy from the Yellow Court to the Middle Dantian (via route 4 to 7), then lead the Qi back down to the Yellow Court (via route 7 to 4).
   - **Center:** Next, focus on the Center Core Thrusting Vessel. Bring the energy from the Yellow Court to the Middle Dantian (via route 5 to 8), then lead the Qi back down to the Yellow Court (via route 8 to 5).
   - **Right:** Finally, focus on the right (Yin) side of the Thrusting Vessel, and follow the Earthly Tiger pathway. Bring the energy from the Yellow Court to the Middle Dantian (via route 6 to 9), then lead the Qi back down to the Yellow Court (via route 9 to 6).
7. After completing Section 2, proceed to Section 3, and move the Qi from the Middle Dantian along the Thrusting Vessels to the Upper Dantian and Niwan Palace, then to the top of the head (Baihui) in the following pattern:
   - **Left:** Begin on the left (Yang) side of the Thrusting Vessel, and follow the Heavenly Dragon pathway. Bring the energy from the Middle Dantian to the Upper Dantian and Niwan Palace, then to the top of the head (via route 7 to crown); then lead the Qi back down to the Middle Dantian (via the crown to 7).
   - **Center:** Next, focus on the Center Core Thrusting Vessel. Bring the energy from the Middle Dantian to the Upper Dantian and Niwan Palace, then to the top of the head (via route 8 to the crown), then lead the Qi back down to the Middle Dantian (via the crown to 8).
   - **Right:** Finally, focus on the right (Yin) side of the Thrusting Vessel, and follow the Earthly Tiger pathway. Bring the energy from the Middle Dantian to the Upper Dantian and Niwan Palace, then to the top of the head (via route 9 to the crown); then lead the Qi back down to the Middle Dantian (via the crown to 9).

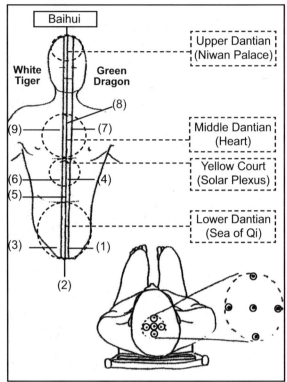

Figure 5.14. Fusing the Qi of the Earthly White Tiger and the Heavenly Green Dragon

ENERGIZING THE TAIJI POLE: STAGE #2

In the second stage, the disciple will continue the practice of using the nine separate sections of the lower, middle, and upper Thrusting Vessels. The meditation continues as follows:

8. Beginning from the Left (1) Section (i.e., the Dragon Side), move the Qi upward, through the entire lower, middle, and upper divisions of the Thrusting Vessels. Then proceed to move the Qi through Sections 2 and 3 (Figure 5.14).

   As you move the energy, imagine and feel the Qi of the Dragon Well moving through the Lower Dantian, up the Thrusting Vessels, past the Yellow Court and Middle Dantian, terminating at the Upper Dantian in the following pattern:
   - **Left:** Begin on the left (Yang) side of the Thrusting Vessel, and follow the Heavenly Dragon pathway. Bring the energy from the Dragon Well (perineum) through the Lower Dantian to the Yellow Court (via route 1 to 4), then to the Middle Dantian (via route 4 to

7), then finally through the Upper Dantian, Niwan Palace, to the top of the head (via route 7 to the crown), located at the Baihui area.

Next, lead the Qi back down from the crown through the same Thrusting Vessel pathway, into the Lower Dantian. This is accomplished by moving the energy from the crown point downward; from the crown through route 7, 7 to 4, and from 4 to 1.

- **Center:** Next, focus on the Center Core Thrusting Vessel. Bring the energy from the Dragon Well (perineum) through the Lower Dantian to the Yellow Court (via route 2 to 5), then to the Middle Dantian (via route 5 to 8), then finally to the Upper Dantian, Niwan Palace, to the top of the head (via route 8 to the crown), located at the Baihui area.

Next, lead the Qi back down from the crown through the same Thrusting Vessel pathway, into the Lower Dantian. This is accomplished by moving the energy from the crown point downward; from the crown through route 8, 8 to 5, and from 5 to 2.

- **Right:** Finally, focus on the right (Yin) side of the Thrusting Vessel, and follow the Earthly Tiger pathway. Bring the energy from the Dragon Well (perineum) through the Lower Dantian to the Yellow Court (via route 3 to 6), then to the Middle Dantian (via route 6 to 9), then finally to the Upper Dantian, Niwan Palace, to the top of the head (via route 9 to crown), located at the Baihui area.

Next, lead the Qi back down from the crown through the same Thrusting Vessel pathway, into the Lower Dantian. This is accomplished by moving the energy from the crown point downward; from the crown through route 9, 9 to 6, and from 6 to 3).

ENERGIZING THE TAIJI POLE: STAGE #3

In the third stage, the disciple will practice using the nine separate sections of the lower, middle, and upper Thrusting Vessels in order to connect with the Heavenly Transpersonal Point, located about a foot above the crown. This special technique is used to strengthen and stabilize the disciple's external energetic fields (Figure 5.15). The meditation continues as follows:

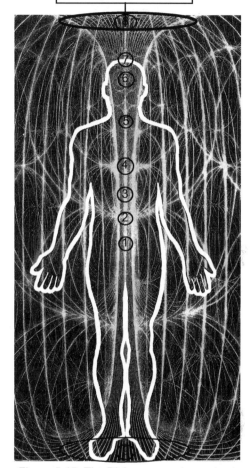

Figure 5.15. The Divine energy is received through the Heavenly Transpersonal Points, which then transform and transfer this subtle information to the disciple's Taiji Pole. The Taiji Pole then radiates this information and "divine inspiration" throughout the disciple's physical, energetic and spirit bodies. (Inspired by the original artwork of Alex Grey)

9. Begin at Section 1, then proceed to Sections 2 and 3, ending at the Heavenly Transpersonal Point. Imagine and feel the Qi of the Lower Dantian move up the Thrusting Vessels, past the Upper Dantian, terminating at the First Heavenly Transpersonal Point, in the following pattern:

- **Left:** Begin on the left (Yang) side of the Thrusting Vessel, and follow the Heavenly Dragon pathway. Bring the energy from the Dragon

Well (lower perineum) through the Lower Dantian to the Yellow Court (via route 1 to 4), then to the Middle Dantian (via route 4 to 7), then to the Upper Dantian, Niwan Palace, to the top of the head (via route 7 to the crown), then extend the energy upward into the divine energetic sphere of the Heavenly Transpersonal point (located one foot above the top of the head).

Then, lead the Qi back down from the Heavenly Transpersonal point, through the crown of the head, past the Lower Dantian, to the Dragon Well. This is accomplished via the Heavenly Transpersonal point to the crown, crown to route 7, 7 to 4, and from 4 to 1.

- **Center:** Next, focus on the Center Core Thrusting Vessel. Bring the energy from the Dragon Well (lower perineum) through the Lower Dantian to the Yellow Court (via route 2 to 5), then to the Middle Dantian (via route 5 to 8), then to the Upper Dantian, Niwan Palace, to the top of the head (via route 8 to the crown), then extend the energy upward into the divine energetic sphere of the Heavenly Transpersonal point (located one foot above the top of the head).

  Then, lead the Qi back down from the Heavenly Transpersonal point, through the crown of the head, past the Lower Dantian, and to the Dragon Well. This is accomplished via the Heavenly Transpersonal point to the crown, crown to route 8, 8 to 5, and from 5 to 2.

- **Right:** Finally, focus on the right (Yin) side of the Thrusting Vessel, and follow the Earthly Tiger pathway. Bring the energy from the Dragon Well (lower perineum) through the Lower Dantian to the Yellow Court (via route 3 to 6), then to the Middle Dantian (via route 6 to 9), then to the Upper Dantian, Niwan Palace, to the top of the head (via route 9 to crown), then extend the energy upward into the divine energetic sphere of the Heavenly Transpersonal point (located one foot above the top of the head).

  Next, lead the Qi back down from the Heavenly Transpersonal point, through the crown of the head, past the Lower Dantian, to the Dragon Well. This is accomplished via the Heavenly Transpersonal point to the crown, crown to route 9, 9 to 6, and from 6 to 3).

THE SIX EXTERNAL TRANSPERSONAL POINTS

The Taiji Pole is the main conduit that allows the resonating energy of celestial sound and light to pass through the core of the body and penetrate into the internal organs. Located within the external energetic field of the Taiji Pole, but still existing several feet outside the human body, are six spiritually oriented external Transpersonal Points; three are located above the head, and three are located underneath the feet (Figure 5.16).

The Taiji Pole is responsible for energetically connecting all of these six external Transpersonal Points into the body's internal Chakra system. This special connection is brought about via the disciple's subtle energetic bodies, which root the energetic and spiritual fields into the physical body via the Three Dantians.

Traditionally, the energetic "Awakening" and secret alchemical training of each of these sacred portals was considered privileged information, taught only to the most trusted senior disciples of esoteric Daoist Magic. Today, much of this secret esoteric knowledge is still traditionally kept hidden from the public.

The reason for this secrecy, is that the inclusion of these Heaven and Earth Transpersonal Points during deep meditation training, allows for a more complete integration of the body's internal and external energetic connections. Because these special Transpersonal Points are energetic portals that transcend the various spiritual realms of the disciple's incarnated personality, they also contain the important teachings needed for obtaining a higher and more powerful spiritual development. Through unveiling and penetrating deep into these sacred energy fields, the disciple may comprehend the subtle energetic dynamics responsible for the manifestation of all creation. This will allow the disciple to manifest such magical skills as the ability to travel beyond the limits of time and space, teleportation, bi-location, telekinesis, and the instantaneous precipitation of thoughts into matter.

All of the body's internal and external chakras are developed and formed from a combination

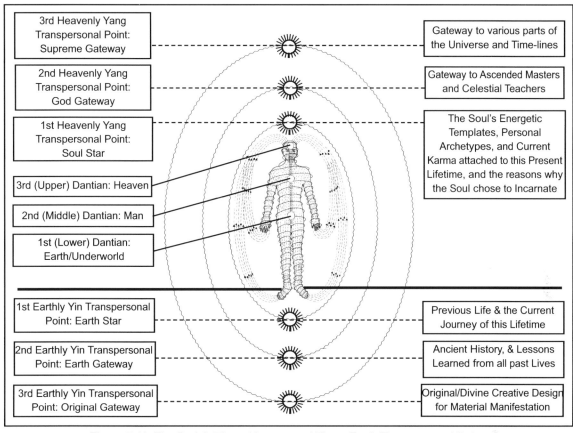

Figure 5.16. The Body's Three Heaven and Three Earth Transpersonal Points

of mental, energetic, and spiritual substances. It is through their subtle energetic fields that a disciple can simultaneously interconnect with both the more dense terrestrial energies of the planet, and with the more subtle energies of the celestial realm. As the disciple continues to grow spiritually, these higher spiritual chakras open, and he is then able to access their subtle energetic fields.

Each time a disciple experiences a personal "death and rebirth," his energetic field changes. Therefore, the specific locations of the Transpersonal Points will vary, depending on the disciple's energetic cultivation practice and spiritual evolution.

When both sets of internal and external chakras are purified, balanced, and energetically fuse as one, they spiritually manifest as a unique alchemical phenomenon known as the "Unification of the Chakras." When experiencing this sacred energetic state, the disciple's Three Bodies are all simultaneously enveloped in divine light and sound, allowing him to experience the "Indestructible Body of Light" (i.e., the "Immortal Body").

The specific locations of the external Transpersonal Points and their energetic functions are described as follows:

- **The First Heavenly Yang Transpersonal Point:** Also known as the "Ling Hun Xing" (Soul Star), the energetic field of the first or lowest Heavenly Yang Transpersonal Point is located about 6 inches to a foot above the top of the head. The Soul Star connects the disciple's Three Bodies with the celestial Qi and Shen of the Heavens, and is considered to be an important spiritual doorway for working with the energies of the upper Spirit Realms.

Because the Soul Star is the energetic bridge that exists between the known and unknown, it works like an energetic transducer to moderate the very high celestial energies and information brought into the disciple's energetic fields via the Spirit Realm (induced by way of the second and third Heavenly Points).

Energetically activating the Soul Star is like securing a powerful Lightning Rod deep into the Heavens. By activating the Soul Star, the disciple is allowed to understand his interconnectedness with all things. This awakened understanding, provides the disciple with a deep feeling of unconditional love and compassion towards all people, places, and things.

The brightness of the Soul Star depends on the disciple's personal spiritual evolution. Although the Soul Star is not the disciple's Soul, as an extension of the Soul, it is considered to be a special energetic vehicle through which the disciple's Eternal Soul (Shen Xian) can do its spiritual work. This includes working with past history and karmic memory. The Soul Star is the source of energetic creation and change. It carries within its energetic matrix, the reasons why the disciple chose to incarnate during this lifetime. Therefore, it is traditionally viewed as the seat of the soul's energetic templates, personal archetypes, and container of the incarnated soul's past and present magical symbols (i.e., all of the individual's sacred spiritual/magical lineage seals).

It is important to note, that the disciple must first activate his First Earth Point (i.e., the Earth Star), before activating his First Heavenly Point (the Soul Star). Otherwise, he will tend to become easily disoriented and ungrounded.

- **The Second Heavenly Yang Transpersonal Point:** Also known as the "Shen Men" (God Gateway), the energetic field of the second or middle Heavenly Yang Transpersonal Point is located about 12 to 18 inches above the head.

This second Heavenly Transpersonal Point is considered to be the disciple's personal spiritual Gateway into the celestial realm. As a special energetic portal into other spiritual dimensions, it is traditionally utilized as the means of making special connections with celestial beings, such as Ascended Masters, Divine Deities, and the Celestial Immortals of the disciple's spiritual lineage.

Once energetically activated, the God Gateway becomes the disciple's direct line to the Divine Source, which gives him access to infinite energy and power. Therefore, before attempting to create this important spiritual connection, the disciple's Three Bodies must be consistently kept pure in order to maintain the highest spiritual exchange that will exist between the disciple and the Divine Beings.

For thousands of years, in many secret magic circles, the God Gateway has been known as the magical portal of the "Radiant Cloud of Knowledge." It was through this secret magical portal that the ancient disciples interconnected with the original language of divine light and sound (the first source of creation).

- **The Third Heavenly Yang Transpersonal Point:** Also known as the "Tai Men" (Supreme Gateway) and the "Xing Men" (Stellar Gateway), the energetic field of the third or highest Heavenly Transpersonal Point is located about 3 feet above the head.

This special chakra is called the "Grand Portal" ("Tai Men"), because it provides the disciple with special access for Soul Travel into other parts of this universe, into alternate universes, to higher planes of existence, and to the past or future history of his own time-line or alternate time-lines. It also allows the disciple to travel forward or backward in time, or to other realms of existence.

It is important to note, that before a disciple attempts to energetically activate and explore his Third Heavenly Yang Transpersonal Point, it is essential that he spend much time cleansing and energizing all the other chakras, especially the body's seven internal chakras. Only when the disciple feels himself energetically and spiritually rooted should he attempt to explore the Grand Portal Point. Otherwise, the disciple will run the high risk of suddenly slipping into an alternate dimension of reality, and not returning.

- **The First Earthly Yin Transpersonal Point:** Also known as the "Di Xing" (Earth Star), the energetic field of the first "Earthly Yin Transpersonal Point" is located below the bottom of the feet, about 6 inches to a foot underneath the ground. This special Transpersonal Point connects and roots the energy of the disciple's Three Bodies into the Earth, and assists the disciple's body in absorbing Earth Qi into his Lower Dantian via the energetic portals located at the bottom of the feet.

  The story of the disciple's current life is recorded inside of the energetic matrix of the Earth Star Point Therefore, this special Point contains the memories of all the experiences, discoveries, and various practices performed during the soul's current journey, while passing through this lifetime.

- **The Second Earthly Yin Transpersonal Point:** Also known as the "Di Men" (Earth Gateway), the energetic field of the second "Earthly Yin Transpersonal Point" is located about 12 to 18 inches below the bottom of the feet. Somtimes known as the Incarnation Point, the Earth Gateway has a special energetic connection to the disciple's personal ancestry, tribe, and clan. It embraces all of the disciple's ancestral history, and all of his current incarnation's family issues and patterns. It is also the record keeper of all past life incarnations and holographic karmic lessons that were learned.

- **The Third Earthly Yin Transpersonal Point:** Also known as the "Yuan Men" (Original Gateway), the energetic field of the third "Earthly Yin Transpersonal Point" is located about 3 feet below the bottom of the feet. Within this sacred energetic orb, is the Original/Divine Creative Design and the reason why the individual manifested in material form.

At the end of the Earthly tour, the disciple's Eternal Soul will disconnect from the Earth Gateway, and begin its energetic ascension through the Taiji Pole, passing through all of the body's internal chakras. Once it arrives at the Niwan Palace, the disciple will suddenly observe the bright radiant light, shining from his Soul Star Point. In the process of this ascension, the disciple will perceive his entire life and existence, from the beginning to the end. These various memories and experiences are all recorded within the various Earthly Yin Transpersonal Points.

Activating The Body's Transpersonal Points

When energetically activating each Transpersonal Point, there are two main objectives. The first and most important is to establish a powerful energetic connection with the chakra. This allows the disciple to create a powerful energetic bridge.

The second objective is to begin the process of purification. By energetically flushing, cleansing, and activating each Transpersonal Point separately, the disciple's Three Bodies will eventually become energetically and spiritually balanced.

There are 72 (9 X 8) Energetic Veils (layers), resonating within each of the disciple's energy fields. The disciple's ability to access these subtle energetic fields, their various magical realms, and their unique spiritual powers will depend primarily on the disciple's spiritual evolution, his personal training, and how clean, clear, and activated his personal Transpersonal Points have become.

My teacher once explained that after I had cleansed and activated all of my Transpersonal Points, whenever I wished to spirit travel, I should first listen for the Inner-Sound of the 1,000 Cicadas Singing. This special hissing sound, sometimes known as the "Hiss of the Dragon," was the vibrational resonance of my body's personal energetic field. By relaxing into it, and allowing my Spirit Body to energetically dissolve into this special sound resonance, I would be able to energetically open a magical portal and spirit travel.

The following is a description of the various energetic properties and functions of the first two of the six external Transpersonal Points that exist within the external energetic field of the body's Taiji Pole.

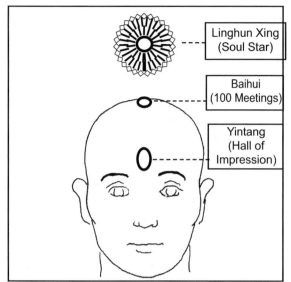

Figure 5.17. The "Ling Hun Xing" ("Soul Star") The First Heavenly Yang Transpersonal Point

THE SOUL STAR (LING HUN XING)

In ancient China, the First Heavenly Transpersonal Point was traditionally known as "Ling Hun Xing" (Soul Star), and was believed to contain the Soul's Energetic Templates, Personal Archetypes, and Current Karma attached to this Present Lifetime, as well as the reasons why the soul chose to incarnate. Located about 6 inches to a foot above the top of an individual's head (Figure 5.17), this special "star" energetically operates within every individual, bringing deep spiritual insights and esoteric perceptions to light. It is considered to exist at a higher level of the divine consciousness, communicating directly with the individual's Yuan Shen (Original Heart/Mind).

The Soul Star nourishes the Yang aspect of the individuals soul, and is responsible for transformations occurring during the Original (Prenatal) spiritual and energetic transitions of Dao to Wuji, Wuji to Shen, Shen to Qi and Qi to Jing.

According to ancient Daoist teaching, it is through the Soul Star that the individual receives and absorbs the various spiritual energies of the Heavenly Five Elements. These subtle energies internally contribute in order to form the developing matrices of the individual's physical, energetic and spirit bodies.

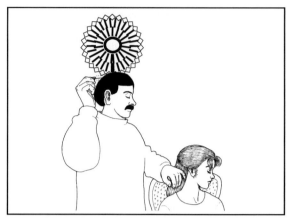

Figure 5.18. The Medical Qigong Doctor imagines Divine Light encircling his head like a sparkling halo. Contained within this halo are the Needles of Light.

The energetic light of the Soul Star is white in color, and corresponds to the Spirit Body. It represents the energetic fusion of all the body's internal chakra colors. It also relates to the spiritual "Realm of Bliss," and the conscious awareness of Complete Enlightenment, which is considered to be beyond the uppermost reach of the human realm.

ENERGETIC AWAKENING

The full energetic awakening of the Soul Star's spiritual potential begins with the purgation of the dysfunctional aspects and imbalances of this particular upper chakra. This energetic cleansing and spiritual releasing allows for the true potential inherent within the Soul Star chakra to gradually manifest, integrating the individual's latent spiritual insights and powers of manifestation into consciousness.

Clinically, it is traditionally from within the external energetic field of the Soul Star Point that the Medical Qigong Doctor will choose to create the "Invisible Needles," that are used in advanced Medical Qigong Therapy (Figure 5.18). These special Needles of Light are imagined energetically existing within the celestial halo of the doctor's Soul Star Point (see Volume 3, Chapter 37) positioned above the doctor's head. To use the energetic needle technique, the doctor will reach above his head and imagine plucking a splinter of light from the celestial halo surrounding the Soul Star. The splinter of light is then transformed into a needle and immediately inserted into the patient's body.

THE EARTH STAR (DI XING)

In ancient China, the First Earthly Transpersonal Point was traditionally known as "Di Xing" (Earth Star), and was believed to contain the memories of all the experiences, discoveries, and various practices performed during the soul's journey, while passing through this current lifetime. Because it connects and roots the energy of the disciple's Three Bodies into the Earth, and assists the disciple's body in absorbing Earth Qi into his Lower Dantian, it is located beneath each individual's feet (Figure 5.19).

The Earth Star nourishes the Yin aspect of the individuals Eternal Soul, and is responsible for transformations occurring during the Postnatal (Acquired) energetic transitions of Jing to Qi, Qi to Shen, Shen to Wuji, and Wuji to Dao.

According to ancient Daoist teaching, it is through the Earth Star that the individual receives and absorbs the various spiritual energies of the Earthly Five Elements that contribute to form the developing matrices of the individual's physical, energetic and spiritual bodies.

The energetic light of the Earth Star is golden yellow in color, and relates to the Energy Body.

ENERGETIC AWAKENING

Full energetic awakening of the Earth Star's spiritual potential begins with the purgation of the dysfunctional aspects and imbalances of this particular lower chakra (i.e., Earthly Karma dragged about like a dead weight). This energetic cleansing and spiritual releasing allows for the true potential inherent within the Earth Star chakra to gradually manifest, integrating the individual's latent spiritual insights and powers of manifestation into consciousness.

Clinically, it is from within the external energetic field of the Earth Star that the Medical Qigong Doctor will choose to root his energetic connection to the various energies of the Earth (Figure 5.20). This is because the Earth Star chakra is the primary spiritual gateway of the Taiji Pole to the Earth, or "The Immortal's Doorway to the Mineral, Plant, and Animal Kingdoms." Once awakened, the Earth Star chakra is said to yield a direct connection to the infinite knowledge of the Dao, contained within the Earthly realms.

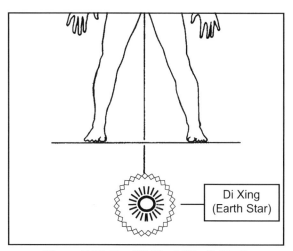

Figure 5.19. The "Di Xing" ("Earth Star") The First Earthly Yin Transpersonal Point

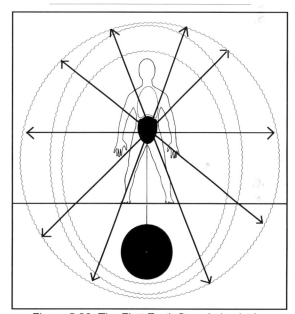

Figure 5.20. The First Earth Star chakra is the primary spiritual gateway of the Taiji Pole to the Earth, it is also known as "The Immortal's Doorway to the Mineral, Plant, and Animal Kingdoms."

It is important to note, that the disciple must first activate his First Earth Point (i.e., the Earth Star), before activating his First Heavenly Point (the Soul Star). Otherwise, he will tend to become easily disoriented and ungrounded.

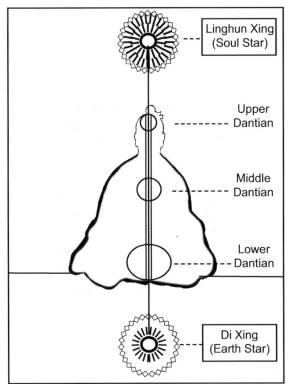

Figure 5.21. Activating the energetic connection between the body's Soul Star, Taiji Pole, and Earth Star

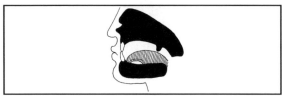

Figure 5.22. Place the tongue onto the Earth Element Position, and look through the center of the body, past the Lower Dantian into the Earth Star.

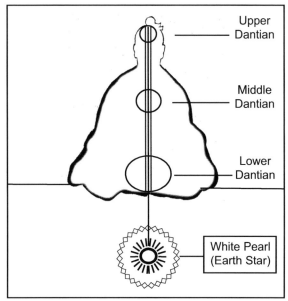

Figure 5.23. Place your Mind onto the White Light Pearl pulsing deep inside the Earth Star

ACTIVATING THE FIRST HEAVENLY AND EARTHLY TRANSPERSONAL POINTS

I was originally introduced to this special meditation from my Nyingma teacher, whom I had been privately studying with for several years. When the Lama explained the activation meditation technique, I immediately recognized its internal connection with the body's Taiji Pole, and how it energetically linked the first Heavenly Yang and Earthly Yin Transpersonal Star points (Figure 5.21).

As in all Shengong (Mind Skill) trainings, this special meditation also includes the unique application of focused images, colors, and sounds, used to captivate the disciple's mind and activate his senses. After some time of continual practice, you will awaken to the subtle intuitions of your Spirit Body. The meditation is described as follows:

- **Preparation:** From a Sitting Meditation Posture, begin by exhaling and squeezing your lower abdomen.
- **Earth Element Tongue Position:** Then, place your tongue behind your lower teeth, onto the Earth Element position (Figure 5.22).
- **The Earth Star:** Tilt your head down, and look through the center of your body, past your Lower Dantian, deep into the Earth Star Transpersonal Point, located about six inches below your body.
- **The White Light Pearl:** Relax and imagine a small radiant White Light Energy Ball, the size of a pearl, pulsing from deep inside the center of the Earth Star (Figure 5.23).
- **Wood Element Tongue Position:** Next, place your tongue onto the center of your upper palate, onto the Wood Element position (Figure 5.24).

CHAPTER 5: THE TAIJI POLE, CHAKRAS, AND THREE DANTIANS

Figure 5.24. Place the tongue onto the Wood Element Position, and look through the center of the body, past the Upper Dantian into the Soul Star.

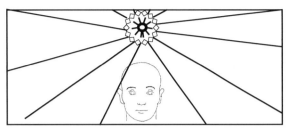

Figure 5.26. Exhale the "Hum" Sound, and imagine a powerful Blue Light Radiating from the "Soul Star"

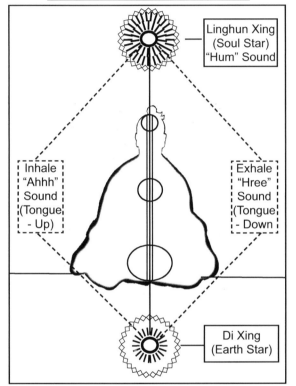

Figure 5.25. Inhale the "Ahh" Sound, and follow the White Light Pearl from the Earth Star, through the Taiji Pole, into the Soul Star

- **The Soul Star:** Straighten your head, roll your eyes upward, and look through the center of your body, past your Upper Dantian, and into the Soul Star Transpersonal Point, located about six inches above your body.
- **Inhale "Ahh:"** Then inhale the "Ahh" Sound, and feel the cold energy of the White Light Pearl flow from the center of the Earth Star, up through the body's lower perineum and enter into the Taiji Pole (Figure 5.25).

Follow this cold energy as it ascends up through the center of the body, passing the Three Dantians, and entering into the Soul Star, located about six inches above your body.

- **Exhale "Hum:"** Once the White Light Pearl enters into the Soul Star, immediately exhale a small portion of your breath, and create the energetic pulse of a short resonant "Hum" Sound.

When speaking the "Hum" Sound, imagine a radiating Blue Light suddenly pulse from the center of the Soul Star, and radiating its powerful celestial rays throughout the entire universe (Figure 5.26).

- **Exhale "Hree:"** Next, imagine that the radiant Blue Light reaches the farthest levels of space, and then immediately rushes back towards its place of origin. As the returning light rushes back into the Soul Star, imagine it immediately creating a bright fiery red pearl.
- **The Red Light Pearl:** Now, place your tongue onto the Earth Element Position (see Figure 5.22), and with the rest of your breath, exhale the "Hree Sound."

As you exhale, follow the fiery red pearl as its warm energy travels through the center of your body via the Taiji Pole, past the Three Dantians, and enters into the Earth Star point, located about six inches below your body.

- Continue to repeat this meditation for several minutes (i.e., Inhale "Ahhh;" Exhale "Hum-Hree"). After about 30-45 minutes of practice, relax into a quiescent state of mind, and allow your Shen (Heart/Mind) to settle back inside your Lower Dantian. Then, end the meditation.

255

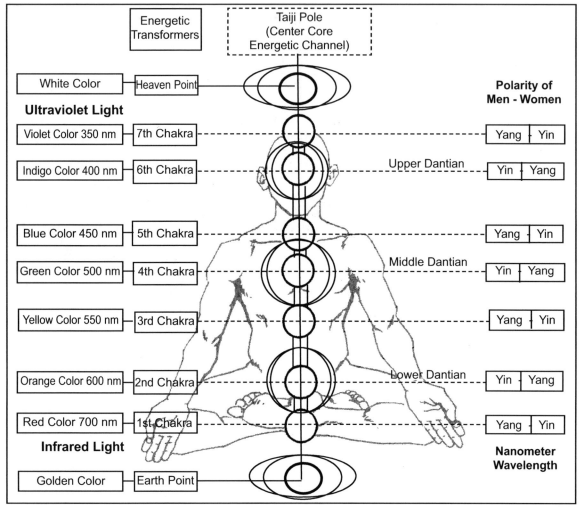

Figure 5.27. The Body's Interconnected Energetic System: The Taiji Pole, Seven Internal Chakras, The Three Dantians, and Two External (Heaven and Earth) Transpersonal Points

THE TAIJI POLE AND THE INTERNAL CHAKRA SYSTEM

The body's major internal energy centers are rooted within the Taiji Pole, which acts as the main channel of the body's energetic network. The Three Dantians are the energetic reservoirs that pool and contain the body's transforming energies. Located within the Taiji Pole, and surrounded externally by the Three Dantians, are the Seven Internal Chakra Centers (Figure 5.27).

The word "Chakra" is Sanskrit for "wheel." The chakras are often described as small colored disks, usually about the size of a silver dollar, resonating from the Taiji Pole at the center of the body. There are differing opinions as to the color correspondences for each chakra. In the mid-seventies, while conducting research at U.C.L.A. on the body's neuromuscular system and its relationship to emotions and energy fields, Dr. Valerie Hunt presented empirical data regarding the energetic frequencies and functioning of the body's chakra system. Specifically, Dr. Hunt's research covered how the chakras affect the body's aura field, state of health and disease, pain, and emotional states.

CHAPTER 5: THE TAIJI POLE, CHAKRAS, AND THREE DANTIANS

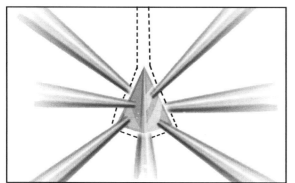

Figure 5.28. Divine Light is refracted by the Upper Transpersonal Point, absorbed into the Taiji Pole, and dispersed into the Seven Chakra Centers

The center Taiji Pole is often compared to the body's main electrical channel, and is considered the primary source of all Yuan Qi (Original/Prenatal Energy), as well as the residence of the human soul (Eternal Soul). The Seven Internal Chakra Centers act as energetic transformers that step-down the Pure Qi radiating from the Taiji Pole into various forms of Qi and Shen. This allows the Eternal Soul the ability to express itself, and interact at the various levels of human experience. The role of the chakra centers and the Taiji Pole can be understood by comparing the Taiji Pole to a prism.

According to ancient Daoist teachings, the Dao (Divine) radiates the infinite light into everything (i.e., the "10,000 Things"). This pure light is absorbed into every individual's body via their Taiji Pole, by way of the upper Heavenly Transpersonal Points, which refract this light into seven internal fields of energy (Figure 5.28). This energetic transformation occurs in the same way that a prism splits a beam of white light into the seven colors of the rainbow.

Light travels in the form of waves. White light is composed of waves of different wavelengths. The different colors of light are due to different wavelengh. The Red colour has maximum wavelength while Violet has minimum. Because of this, the refractive index of the material for violet is greater than red. Rays of different colour are deviated within the body through the prism of the Taiji Pole. This seperation of colors gives rise to dispersion of energy and light that "feeds" the internal organs, channels, and organ systems.

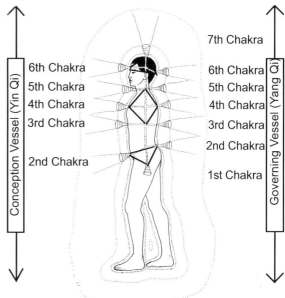

Figure 5.29. The body's Twelve Chakras Gates extend from the Seven Chakra Centers

The Taiji Pole is the primary energetic channel through which the individual connects with the energy of the Divine. It is for this reason that the Taiji Pole is considered to be the residence of the human soul, and the personalized expression of the Divine Light. The energy of the human soul radiates outward from the Taiji Pole to interact with the world on many different levels or dimensions.

In the chakra system, twelve primary dimensions are considered. Each of the chakras projects energy and information from the Taiji Pole into the external world (manifesting as the Yang, active principle of creation). It also receives energy and information from the external world into the Taiji Pole (manifesting as the Yin, receptive principle of assimilation). This constant interaction enables the human soul to engage and experience twelve distinct, though profoundly interrelated, energetic and spiritual dimensions of life.

Each of the seven internal chakra centers is positioned along the Taiji Pole, and manifests externally through twelve major energy gates located along the body's Governing Vessel (Sea of Yang Qi) and Conception Vessel (Sea of Yin Qi) (Figure 5.29). According to ancient Daoist teachings, these

257

12 secret gates energetically correspond to many of the locations of the body's Twelve Earthly Branch points.

Viewed as a compete system, corporately the twelve Chakra Gates also act like an immensely complex hologram, that energetically interacts with the body's Three Dantians. All individuals are continually affected by the energetic patterns resonating from each of the twelve Chakra Gates, whether they are conscious of them or not.

According to one of my teachers, the Divine Light of the human soul is concentrated as a single beam, radiating its bright light within the center core of the disciple's Taiji Pole. This beam is simultaneously split into various beams of energy. All of these beams of light interact to create a complex interference pattern, that manifests as the individual's sumtotal of experiences. As the individual's residual energetic patterns (karma) are stored within each of the seven internal chakra centers, he then experiences the effects of past karma, as they resonate outward into life experiences.

In the process of purifying the chakra centers, it is necessary for an individual to allow these patterns to arise naturally, without attempting to repress or control them. Through consistent practice, the seven internal chakra centers existing within the center core of an individual's body will gradually release their dysfunctional patterns and attachments, thus allowing the light of the soul to resonate unobstructed into every aspect of their life. This internal light is then manifested externally through the individual's twelve Chakra Gates, into his body's energy fields.

Multidimensional Energetic Realms of the Chakra System

Viewed as a complete system, the twelve Chakra Gates, seven chakra centers, Taiji Pole, and the Three Dantian energetic fields together act like an immensely complex hologram, that creates the energetic matrix of an individual's Spirit Body. A hologram is created by taking a single coherent beam of light (analogous to the divine light radiating within the Taiji Pole), and splitting it into two (Yin and yang) equal beams of light using a beam splitter. Both beams of light are then directed to reach an object at the exact same moment, and the resulting interference patterns of light are recorded on a photographic plate (i.e., the body's cells and tissues). When a beam of light is later passed through this photographic plate, the result is the appearance of a three dimensional image, a hologram of the object originally photographed (i.e., the Spirit Body).

Remember that in the chakra system, the divine light of the human soul is concentrated as a single beam of light radiating within an individual's Taiji Pole. This beam of light is simultaneously split into not two, but several distinct beams of energy. All of these beams of light energetically interact in order to create a complex interference pattern, that manifests as the individual's subtotal of experiences. Because an individual's residual energetic patterns (karma) are stored within each of the seven internal chakras, he or she may experience the sudden effects of past karma as they resonate outward from within their energetic field into their personal life experiences. Therefore in the process of purifying the chakras, it is necessary for the individual to allow these patterns to arise naturally without attempting to repress or control them. Through consistent practice, the seven internal chakras existing within the center core of an individual's tissues will gradually release all of their dysfunctional patterns and attachments, thus allowing the light of the Eternal Soul to resonate unobstructed into every aspect of the individual's life. This internal light is then manifested externally through the individual's twelve chakras.

Most people tend to be consciously aware of only the more tangible energetic experiences associated with the lower internal chakras, while remaining unconscious of the subtle energies of the upper internal chakras. This often occurs to such an extent that some people believe these more subtle levels of reality do not even exist. Nevertheless, all individuals are continually affected by the energetic patterns resonating from each of the chakras, whether they are conscious of their energetic influence or not.

Yin and Yang and the Seven Internal Chakras

When I was interning at the Xi Yuan Hospital of Traditional Chinese Medicine in Beijing China, Professor Hsu explained that because the Yin and Yang polarity of the seven internal chakras are generally opposite in men and women, the Medical Qigong Prescriptions must sometimes be modified in order to adjust to the patient's energetic field.

A Woman's Energetic Polarity

The external progression of a woman's energetic polarity starts and ends with a Yin (electronegative) charge. Therefore, a woman is considered to have a Yin energetic nature.

The energetic pathway of a woman's Taiji Pole is traditionally described as follows (Figure 5.30):
- First Chakra: Yin (-) Reproductive Area
- Second Chakra: Yang (+) Navel Area
- Third Chakra: Yin (-) Yellow Court Area
- Fourth Chakra: Yang (+) Heart and Chest Area
- Fifth Chakra: Yin (-) Throat Area
- Sixth Chakra: Yang (+) Yin Tang Area (Third Eye)
- Seventh Chakra: Yin (-) Bai Hui Area (Top of the Head)

A Man's Energetic Polarity

The external progression of a man's energetic polarity starts and ends with a Yang (electropositive) charge. Therefore, a man is considered to have a Yang energetic nature.

The energetic pathway of a man's Taiji Pole is generally described as follows:
- First Chakra: Yang (+) Reproductive Area
- Second Chakra: Yin (-) Navel Area
- Third Chakra: Yang (+) Yellow Court Area
- Fourth Chakra: Yin (-) Heart and Chest Area
- Fifth Chakra: Yang (+) Throat Area
- Sixth Chakra: Yin (-) Yin Tang Area (Third Eye)
- Seventh Chakra: Yang (+) Bai Hui Area (Top of the Head)

Color and Sound

In Medical Qigong Therapy, sometimes emphasis is placed on combining specific colors and sounds with focused concentration placed on stimulating the energy centers existing along the Taiji Pole. The notes of the octaves are said to correspond to the color spectrums of the seven internal chakras. The seven notes, seven colors, and seven chakras are described as follows (Figure 5.31):
- **Do (C):** Red, the 1st Chakra
- **Re (D):** Orange, the 2nd Chakra
- **Me (E):** Yellow, the 3rd Chakra
- **Fa (F):** Green, the 4th Chakra
- **So (G):** Blue, the 5th Chakra
- **La (A):** Indigo, the 6th Chakra
- **Ti (B):** Violet, the 7th Chakra

Taiji Pole Chakra	Polarity		Color & Note	Energetic Influence
	Men	Women	Color	Energy
7th	+ Yang	− Yin	Violet (B)	Shen Knowing
6th	− Yin	+ Yang	Indigo (A)	Shen Seeing
5th	+ Yang	− Yin	Blue (G)	Metal/Space Element
4th	− Yin	+ Yang	Green (F)	Wood/Air Element
3rd	+ Yang	− Yin	Yellow (E)	Fire Element
2nd	− Yin	+ Yang	Orange (D)	Water Element
1st	+ Yang	− Yin	Red (C)	Earth Element

Figure 5.30. The energetic polarity of men & women

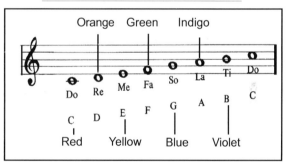

Figure 5.31. The Seven Colors Correlation to the Energetic Pitches

In ancient China, sometimes Daoist Priests and Shaman doctors were taught to play stringed or wind instruments, while focusing on projecting specific colors (with the appropriate sounds) into a patient's body in order to initiate healing. The ancient Daoists observed that different variations in the projected scale could produce combinations of colors and various hues, depending on whether the chord or scale was "carried" using Major or Minor Notes. It was traditionally taught that the three primary colors (Red, Yellow, and Blue) correspond to the three fundamental notes of the scale (the first, third and fifth), which construct the energetic matrix for a major cord.

Awakening The Seven Chakras

In general, all seven internal chakras are continually operating within every individual, though often in an impaired or dysfunctional manner. Full energetic awakening of the spiritual potential of any given chakra begins with the purgation of the dysfunctional aspects and imbalances of that particular chakra. This cleansing and releasing allows for the dormant potential inherent within each chakra to gradually manifest and integrate into the life and consciousness of the individual.

As each chakra is awakened, the individual will release the associated negative emotions and energetic patterns of that chakra in his or her journey to fully manifest the positive patterns and archetypes.

Each chakra contains an energetic storehouse of both positive and negative karma (patterns) which surface during the awakening process and must be released in order to allow the divine light of the individual to fully manifest. Though any or all of the chakras may be accumulating or releasing karma simultaneously, spiritual growth and evolution can be measured by the process of ascending the ladder of the chakras; cleansing, balancing and integrating the potential of each chakra before the one above it.

If an awakening happens too quickly (such as through recreational drug use, bizarre impact trauma to the head or tailbone areas, or the improper practice of psychophysical energetic exercises like Qigong and Yoga), it can cause an explosion of suppressed emotional experiences and latent spiritual and energetic abilities that is too intense for the individual to handle. For this reason, in some systems the individual's 6th Chakra is considered, studied and awakened first. This enables the individual to be better prepared for the energetic and emotional experiences that he or she undergoes during the cleansing and awakening process, maintaining an overall sense of clarity and equanimity.

The Nerve Plexuses of the Seven Internal Chakras

Each internal chakra has a physiological correlation, both with the major nerve plexuses within the spine, and with particular endocrine glands (Figure 5.32).

The three lower chakras are the centers of instinctual energies within the body and are broadly associated with the energy of the Earth and with physical survival. The three uppermost chakras are centers for higher spiritual development and are associated with spiritual evolution and the subtle energies of Heaven. The Heart Chakra rests in between the two Heaven and Earth poles, where the two energies meet and harmonize. The Heart Chakra mediates between the individual's physical and spiritual habits, needs and intentions.

First Chakra

The First Chakra is located in the area of the lower perineum, within the energetic field of the Lower Dantian (Figure 5.33). It corresponds to the Element Earth and the solid state of matter. This chakra is also associated with the sense of smell, and the color red. It energetically roots the Taiji Pole at the base of the perineum, and exits at the top of the head (i.e., the Crown Chakra).

The First Chakra is associated with the control and development of the physical body's external energetic sheath, governs access to the physical (first) plane of reality, and is associated with the kinesthetic, tactile, and proprioceptive senses. This chakra is also energetically connected to both the Conception and Governing Vessels.

CHAPTER 5: THE TAIJI POLE, CHAKRAS, AND THREE DANTIANS

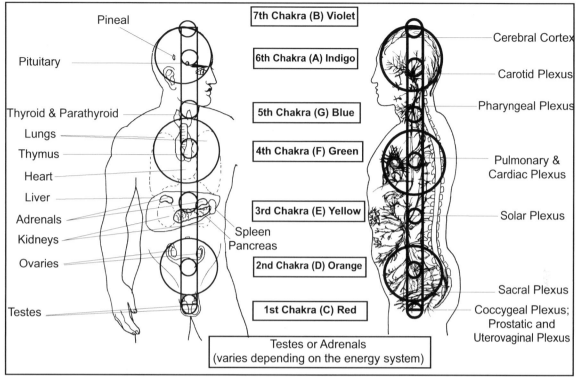

Figure 5.32. The body's Chakra system is connected by the Taiji Pole and extends outward into the body's nerve plexus, affecting the glandular system and both anterior and posterior external energetic fields.

The First Chakra relates to fear, security, and survival instincts (i.e., the "fight, freeze, or flight" response). It also relates to tribal power, group acceptance, and the grounding or "rooting" of the body. It governs the downward and outward movement of energy from the body, especially excretion, orgasm, and exhalation.

PHYSIOLOGICAL ASSOCIATIONS

The First Chakra is associated with the lower limbs and excretory organs. Though it governs much of the energy of the reproductive organs (more so for men than for women), the First Chakra is not usually linked with the emotionally charged energy of sexuality, which is the realm of the Second Chakra. The First Chakra also supplies energy to the spinal column, adrenal glands (in some systems), testicles, ovaries, and Kidneys.

THE FIRST PSYCHIC KNOT

The first of three major psychic knots existing within the human energy system is located in the

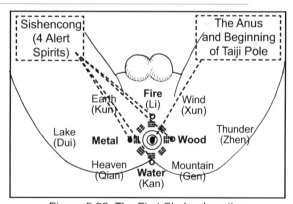

Figure 5.33. The First Chakra Location

First Chakra, and corresponds to the energy of the Lower Dantian. These knots are more substantial than the chakras, and thus require more insight and discipline to work through. According to ancient Daoist teaching, this first knot binds the Human Soul with attachment to physical survival, the desire for procreation, and the fear of death.

In order to release the deeply creative energy that is locked within this lower Chakra area, these attachments must be gradually overcome through discipline, spiritual insight, and surrender.

BALANCED MANIFESTATION

When functioning properly, this chakra ensures the individual's ability to take care of himself while respecting the needs of others, and the needs of the Earth. In the presence of danger or in any emergency situation, this lower chakra will immediately open and release stored information and provide energy needed to ensure survival.

PATHOLOGICAL MANIFESTATION

In its unbalanced state, the First Chakra often creates patterns of chronic fear and victimization, wherein the individual continually feels at the mercy of surrounding influences and is unable to stand on his own.

Energetic malfunctions and stored emotional trauma in this chakra can cause any of the following symptoms: lower back pain, sciatica, constipation, hemorrhoids, rectal tumors and cancer, testicular cancer, knee problems, and varicose veins.

ENERGETIC AWAKENING

This chakra is the seat, or storehouse, of what is known in the Yogic tradition as the "kundalini" energy. The word kundalini is derived from the term "kunda," which means "a pit or cavity." Kundalini is the internal manifestation of the energetic potential of the Human Soul sleeping within the un-awakened Taiji Pole. It is symbolically represented as a serpent coiled three and a half times at the base of the spine. The ancients shamans believed that the entire cosmic experience, from creation to dissolution, is embedded within the folds of the coiled serpent. When the full potential of this stored energy is released, it suddenly travels upward through the individual's spine and central nervous system (in the physical body), and the center of the Taiji Pole (in the energetic body).

When the kundalini energy is initially aroused, the individual is often subject to extreme swings of energy, perception, and emotion. Additionally, some people often report spiritual experiences and sensations of floating or levitation, as the body is beginning to run energy at higher frequencies which in turn causes the Spirit Body to leave the Physical Body.

As the First Chakra awakens, the sense of smell may become extremely acute and strong odors may become unbearable. Other common experiences are feelings of warmth in the coccyx and sacral area, or a creeping sensation, as if something water-like were moving internally up the spine. In working through this chakra, the practitioner descends into the most primitive levels of consciousness, and must fully experience, understand, and integrate them.

SPIRITUAL POWERS

When the First Chakra is fully awakened, the ability of telekinesis begins to manifest, and one feels a strong connection with the energy of the Earth. According to ancient teachings, the control over the First Chakra will manifest certain psychic experiences and spiritual powers, such as the ability to make the body as light as air for levitation and spirit travel.

SECOND CHAKRA

The Second Chakra area is located at the center of the navel or Shenque (Spirit Gateway: CV-8) point (Figure 5.34). This special area is considered to be the spiritual gateway of the body's Lower Dantian. It corresponds to the Water Element and the liquid state of matter. This chakra is associated with the color orange. It is also associated with the sense of taste, the tongue, and the hands (hence palmistry's strength in relating with the subconscious). It is associated with the intermediate plane of spiritual awareness.

The Second Chakra relates to the emotions, sexuality and the unconscious. It is associated with the True Qi and the energy that pervades the entire body. Energetically, the Second Chakra relates to the Lower Burner and corresponds to the first Wei Qi field.

The Second Chakra is the dominant energy center for sexuality and sensuality. It supplies the sexual organs (ovaries and testicles) and the

CHAPTER 5: THE TAIJI POLE, CHAKRAS, AND THREE DANTIANS

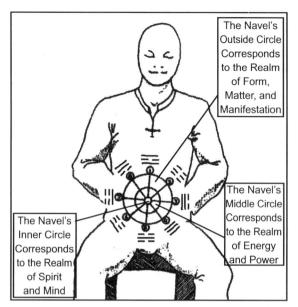

Figure 5.34. The Second Chakra is located at the Shen Que (Spirits Gateway) CV-8 point

immune system with Qi. It is one of the energy centers for empathic perception, through which the individual is able to sense or feel the emotions of others. However, this chakra often manifests in unbalanced patterns characterized by neediness or co-dependency, which limits empathic perception. Instinctual sexual perception, as well as the ability to sense dangerous situations are examples of this level of empathy.

The Second Chakra governs the unconscious mind and the subterranean movement of karma. It is considered the main storehouse of the body's karma and mental impressions, including those accumulated from past lives.

PHYSIOLOGICAL ASSOCIATIONS

The Second Chakra is associated with the prostatic and uterovaginal nerve plexuses, as well as the reproductive organs. It also governs the Kidneys and the area of the lower back.

BALANCED MANIFESTATION

When functioning properly, the Second Chakra allows the ability to fully accept and experience one's feelings. A balanced Second Chakra allows the formation of relationships and communications that are free of emotional neediness or sexual enmeshment. When in balance, this center radiates a full and healthy sense of sexuality.

PATHOLOGICAL MANIFESTATION

In an unbalanced state, energy in the Second Chakra manifests as uncontrolled empathy, or the inability to differentiate one's own feelings from those of others. Unconscious repression of sexuality may give rise to overwhelming or disturbing sexual dreams, desires or fantasies. Feelings of a lack of self-worth and inner emptiness may drive a person into unhealthy or co-dependent relationships or situations. The martyr complex, for example, is rooted in an imbalance of energy in the Second Chakra.

Energetic malfunctions and stored emotional trauma in this chakra can cause lower back problems, frigidity, or impotence. Second Chakra dysfunction can also cause Kidney, ovarian, uterine, and Urinary Bladder, problems

ENERGETIC AWAKENING

In awakening the Second Chakra, individuals often experience extreme sleepiness, or may undergo a crisis when facing the roots of sexual desire. Women may also experience an extremely heightened emotional need to have a child. Relationships are revealed in a new light, and may become temporarily chaotic. When the Second Chakra opens, the individual may feel the release of sexual desires and fantasies, or experience waves of orgasm flowing through the entire body. Additionally, one may go through a period of experiencing an insatiable appetite for food and the process of eating.

SPIRITUAL POWERS

When the Second Chakra is fully awakened, the individual manifests the ability of Clairsentience and the associated ability of psychometry (the ability to touch an object and know its history). The control over the Second Chakra will manifest certain psychic experiences and spiritual powers such as the ability to live for long periods of time without food or water.

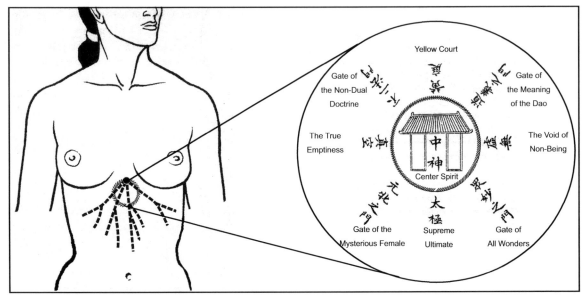

Figure 5.35. The Body's Yellow Court and the Daoist "Yellow Court Graph"
From Liu Yiming's *Huangting Jing Jie (Explanation of the Scripture of the Yellow Court)*

THIRD CHAKRA

The Third Chakra area is associated with the Middle Dantian and is commonly referred to as the "Yellow Court" in Medical Qigong Therapy (Figure 5.35). It relates to the Fire Element and the transformational qualities of Qi. This chakra corresponds to the sense of sight, and its energetic color is yellow. The Third Chakra is the body's main distribution point for psychic energies, and the primary center for personal power and self-image.

This chakra holds the energetic patterns and blueprints for storing issues of responsibility, self-esteem, personal honor and the fear of rejection. It is also a storage chamber for neglected emotional pain and anger. It is associated with the Heavenly plane of existence. It is also associated with the Middle Burner and those aspects of Ying Qi which are responsible for digestion and the Fire of Metabolic Assimilation. It is also the area where the body's Qi transforms into Shen (i.e., energy internally manifests as thoughts and emotions).

The Third Chakra is the place where the energy of inhalation (Yin) meets with the energy of exhalation (Yang). If a Qigong practitioner is able to unify these two energies, an alchemical explosion takes place, that is simultaneously experienced as the full awakening of the Third Chakra, and manifests as the initial rousing of the kundalini. This is why some ancient texts say that the awakening of kundalini actually takes place in the Third Chakra (Yellow Court), and that once it is awakened, this supercharged energy then gathers and drops down to the First Chakra in order to enter into the spinal channel (i.e., Governing Vessel).

PHYSIOLOGICAL ASSOCIATIONS

The Third Chakra is associated with all the organs of the digestive system. It supplies energy to the Liver, Gall Bladder, Stomach, Spleen, pancreas, adrenal glands, and nervous system. Proper diet and fasting helps to purify this chakra, because when the digestive fire is not engaged in assimilating food, it is able to complete its other functions. This is why the ancient Daoists would traditionally practice fasting or eating lightly.

Once the digestive fire is controlled and allowed to turn inward, it immediately begins cleaning and burning all the stagnant undigested foods, thoughts, and emotions trapped and contained within the individual's digestive system. This energetic manifestation accounts for the various feelings of heat and hot purification that are felt when fasting.

BALANCED MANIFESTATION

When in balance, the Third Chakra has the appearance of a radiant sun. The individual experiences abundant physical energy, emotional stability, a strong metabolism and constitution, as well as the ability to work efficiently and complete desired tasks. Dynamic perseverance, energetic achievements, a strong metabolism and/or digestion (including the digestion of thoughts and emotions) are all positive attributes of this special chakra. In the same way that the Sun shines its light onto all of the planets, the Third Chakra (Yellow Court) radiates energy throughout the entire cellular structure of the Physical Body, and supplies power to the vast network of energy channels within the Energy Body.

PATHOLOGICAL MANIFESTATION

When out of balance, the Third Chakra looks like a dying fire or a pile of smoldering embers. This may manifest in symptoms such as poor health, depression, lack of motivation in life and an inability to work or follow through. In its unawakened state, the Third Chakra slowly burns and destroys the essence of the body over time, causing decay, disease, and death.

When the Third Chakra's energy gate opens, feelings of power and waves of anger, rage, fear, greed, jealousy, judgment, or criticism can be released. Because this area is also associated with the desire for power and the ability to manifest one's ideas, sometimes the desire to destroy is also experienced. Energetic malfunctions and stored emotional trauma in this chakra can cause metabolic disorders, indigestion, ulcers, hypoglycemia, diabetes, disorders of the Liver and Gall Bladder, or adrenal problems.

ENERGETIC AWAKENING

Because the Third Chakra is the major distribution center for the physical energy of the body, when this center is energetically awakened, the practitioner is able to greatly (or indefinitely) extend his or her life-span.

When this center is purified, the individual's body also becomes disease free and luminous, and his consciousness does not easily fall back into lower states of expression.

During the "Awakening" process of the lower three chakras, it is often difficult to maintain the quality of energetic focus required to experience the spiritual growth and maturation needed to expand onward towards the next level. Therefore, the practitioner's energy often drops back to the base of the spine, sometimes resulting in feelings of frustration and worthlessness.

However, once the awakening of the Third Chakra is complete, it is naturally easier to harness the Shen's attention. At this stage, the energy of the Heart/Mind will either remain in one place, or continue its upward journey towards the center of the crown.

It is important to note that, when the Third Chakra is finally "freed" from energetic stagnation, there is also a corresponding shift in one's consciousness. This energetic and spiritual freedom can be internally used in order to keep an individual from becoming deeply enmeshed in his or her own mental and emotional problems. It also helps them to be able to more easily comprehend, envision, embody, and manifest their greater spiritual potential.

SPIRITUAL POWERS

It is said that meditation on the Yellow Court and Third Chakra area leads to a deeper understanding of the entire human physical framework and body's energetic system. The psychic powers that come with the awakening of this chakra are naturally lighter than those associated with the lower two chakras, which are still tinged by the darker aspects of the lower mind.

The powers gained by the awakening of the Third Chakra include the ability to create and destroy, the acquisition of hidden treasures, control over the Fire Element, knowledge of one's own body, freedom from disease, and the ability to withdraw one's energy into the central channel at will.

The control over the Third Chakra will also manifest certain psychic experiences and spiritual powers such as allowing the individual to endure strong heat, and empowering them with the ability to consume large amounts of food without gaining weight.

Fourth Chakra

The Fourth Chakra area is associated with the Middle Dantian, the Heart, The Emperor's Fire (Figure 5.36), the Wood/Air Element, and the gaseous state of matter. This special chakra relates to the sense of touch, and the color green.

Energetically, the Fourth Chakra relates to the Upper Burner and Zong Qi (Gathering Qi). It governs the field of mind and emotions, which corresponds to the second Wei Qi field, and to the ever changing energy of the human aura. It is also associated with the first of the Immortal Planes of spiritual awareness.

Traditionally, this energy center is associated with love, compassion, empathy, clairsentience, and intuition. However, it is also responsible for the creative sciences and fine arts such as painting, dance, music, poetry, etc.

Physiological Associations

The Fourth Chakra is connected with the cardiac nerve plexus and it supplies energy to the Heart, Lungs, circulatory system, thymus gland, vagus nerve, diaphragm, and upper back.

Balanced Manifestation

A healthy Fourth Chakra manifests balance and harmony in relationships, and expresses itself in such qualities as affinity, compassion and selfless action. In Fourth Chakra development, an individual is effortlessly defining the external world in his own personal terms; whereas in the Third Chakra development, the individual is struggling to define himself in the terms of the cultural trance established via the external world.

In its positive form, the energy of the Fourth Chakra manifests as creativity, spiritual love, spiritual charity, and spiritual compassion (which is given effortlessly without attachment).

Pathological Manifestation

When out of balance, the energy in the Fourth Chakra can manifest as the inability to feel love for oneself, which then leads to insincerity, co-dependence, insecurity, and isolation. When unbalanced, this chakra is also associated with conditional love and insincere human charity, both of which reflect selfishness and personal attachment.

Figure 5.36. The Fourth Chakra corresponds to the "Heart Fire" ("Emperor's Fire" or "Commanding Fire")

The energetic malfunctions and stored emotional trauma contained within this chakra can also cause Heart and Lung diseases.

The Second Psychic Knot

The second psychic knot is located in the Fourth Chakra, and corresponds to the energy of the Middle Dantian. This knot holds the individual separate from, and therefore dependent on, the social surroundings. It represents the bondage of emotional attachment, co-dependence, and the need to be externally validated as a result of inherent lack of self love and acceptance. Until this knot is released, the individual's thoughts are generally enmeshed with patterns of emotional dependency, such as the fear of being negatively judged by others.

Energetic Awakening

The Fourth Chakra awakens when the individual's ego surrenders into boundless love. During this awakening, the individual's mental and emotional fields are purified and blended as they become aligned with the higher intention of the Eternal Soul.

In the process of awakening the Fourth Chakra, it is important to be in a supportive social environment with "true friends," and to avoid the influences of toxic relationships. At this stage of energetic opening, it is very easy to absorb the surrounding environmental Qi into one's body.

When this energy center opens, and the individual becomes aware of being attached to the personal ego, and the resulting catharsis can be both physically and emotionally painful. The individual may experience chest pain, feelings of a heavy weight on the chest, irregular heartbeat, or the spontaneous release of tears.

As the Fourth Chakra awakens there is a profound sense of peace and emotional ease. The individual's voice becomes subtle, enchanting, and imbued with emotion. Due to the emotional charge developed in both the voice and aura, he or she becomes very attractive and beautiful to others. The individual may also become creatively inspired and will often inspire others. At this state, the ability to heal is greatly increased, and the individual often develops a very sensitive touch. The acceptance of both "good and bad," and a clearer understanding of each also develops.

Spiritual Powers

With the awakening of this chakra, the individual is able to control his or her thoughts and focus with deep mental and emotional concentration, thus effortlessly entering into higher states of meditation. Due to this potential of transcendent focus, the ability to escape preordained fate and to determine one's own destiny now becomes a reality. Voices and sounds originating from other realms are heard. Together with the Fifth Chakra, the Fourth Chakra rules clairaudience. The Fourth Chakra is also said to contain the "wish fulfilling tree," and upon awakening it, the individual is able to manifest and acquire whatever he or she thinks or desires.

Control over the Fourth Chakra will also manifest certain psychic experiences and spiritual powers such as energetically becoming light, soul projecting, and understanding the language of birds.

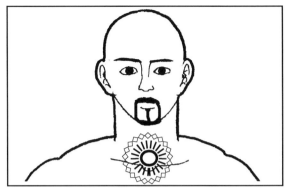

Figure 5.37. The Fifth Chakra corresponds to the area of the Throat (Heaven's Chimney)

Fifth Chakra

The Fifth Chakra area is associated with the Middle Dantian, the throat, and the ancient Daoist "Bridge of Life" used for energetically speaking incantations (prayers) into manifestation (Figure 5.37). The Fifth Chakra area corresponds to infinite space via released sound, and the space in which all the other Elements and their transitions take place (i.e., the space within the space of the Wuji).

This special chakra also relates to the sense of hearing, and governs the upward movement of Qi associated with movements of the head and with facial expressions. Its energetic color is blue.

This energy center is traditionally associated with sound vibration, personal will, divine will, and divine communication. It is the center for clairaudience, and is also the source of the individual's inner voice.

The Fifth Chakra, together with the Sixth Chakra, rules and regulates the intuitive mind. This can be conceptualized as being the perfect harmony between the conditioned (acquired) perceptions and the unconditioned (inherent or intuitive) perceptions of the mind. It is this form of mind that initiates and evolves psychic development. The Fifth Chakra is associated with the fifth or Iimmortal" plane of consciousness.

Physiological Associations

The Fifth Chakra supplies energy to the ears, mouth, throat, vocal chords, thyroid and parathyroid glands, neck vertebrae, , Lungs, and alimentary canal (the digestive tube from the mouth to the anus).

267

Balanced Manifestation

The Fifth Chakra together with the Sixth Chakra, governs the development of intellectual discrimination. Truth and untruth relate to the Fifth Chakra. In its positive form, the energy of the Fifth Chakra manifests as self-expression and the ability to communicate one's own truth to others clearly, honestly and directly. This chakra is the main center for creativity, and when it is balanced one will feel enthusiasm and a genuine interest in life.

Pathological Manifestation

When out of balance, the Fifth Chakra can interfere with the ability of the internal organs to release energy through the throat (voice) and arms, thus upsetting the harmony of Yin and Yang within the upper body.

Heat from Liver Fire sometimes gathers at the Fifth Chakra area, becoming entangled with Phlegm originating from the Lungs. Together, this combination of Phlegm and Fire forms an energetic knot within the throat, often referred to in Traditional Chinese Medicine as "Plum Pit Qi."

Emotionally, an individual may sometimes refuse to communicate or use silence for control and attention. Difficult feelings such as pain, depression, anger, or violence may be suppressed. The individual may feel a lack of creativity, or a mysterious creative weight or block that prevents the feeling of being fully alive. The mind may become cloudy and dull due to a lack of communication, leading to depression and despair.

Energetic malfunctions caused from stored emotional trauma in this chakra area can cause a stiff neck, sore throat, thyroid problems, and swollen glands. The individual can sometimes experience coughing, or laryngitis.

Energetic Awakening

When energetically "Awakened," this chakra is said to be the center at which the "Nectar of Immortality," drips from one of the minor chakras in the head and flows down through the back of the roof of the mouth. This spiritual Nectar is categorized into energetically pure and impure forms. The impure form is discarded as a "poison," while the pure form is cultivated in order to nourish the Three Bodies. In Daoist Alchemy, it is taught that as long as this energy center remains unawakened, the Nectar of Immortality remains undifferentiated, and will flow downward into the Third Chakra (Yellow Court and Stomach area, to be consumed by the body's Digestive Fire.

It is said that Awakening the Fifth Chakra enables one to digest poisons and to overcome the need for food and drink; and by extension, to overcome the aging process. Traditionally, once an individual is able to go beyond consuming food and drink, and has begun to assimilate the Nectar of Immortality, he or she is in essence called an "Earth Immortal."

When the body's internal energy awakens the area of the Fifth Chakra, a spontaneous physical rejuvenation takes place, and sometimes a compulsive urge to sing or chant may arise.

At this awakening stage, the individual may have spontaneous experiences and feelings about the vastness of the infinite space of the Wuji; and their hearing may suddenly become extremely sharp, primarily through their mind, as well as through the ears. Additionally, the individual may also suddenly obtain full knowledge of the past, present, and future.

Spiritual Powers

The "Thread of Creativity" is rooted in the throat, and Fifth Chakra area. This special energetic thread is unique, in that it is energetically created and specifically constructed by each individual, and internally exists as a special energetic bridge, resonating between the Upper Dantian and Middle Dantian. This is why, by meditating on the Fifth Chakra, the mind is said to become pure like infinite space (Wuji). The ability to communicate telepathically initially begins here, and is then refined within the Sixth Chakra.

Control over the Fifth Chakra will manifest certain psychic experiences and spiritual powers, such as the ability to hypnotize and "overshadow" someone's mind, the ability to look into (beyond and before) time, and the ability to dissolve into space. In some systems, the awakening of the Fifth Chakra leads to the ability to manifest the "Eight Supernatural Powers" (see Volume 2, Chapter 14).

Sixth Chakra

The Sixth Chakra area is associated with the Upper Dantian and the "Third Eye" (Figure 5.38), its energetic nature corresponds to light and to "mental seeing" (clairvoyance). Its energetic color is indigo. This special energy center is responsible for psychic intuition (or "knowing without knowing"), clairvoyant seeing (inner vision), and for enabling an individual to see the body's aura fields, chakras, and other energetic images. It is also responsible for energy projection and mental telepathy, sometimes allowing the individual to know another individual's thoughts and feelings.

The Sixth Chakra is considered to be the main chakra of the mind. Intellectual and intuitive, the Sixth Chakra is the root of the plane of duality within human experience. Defining and maintaining boundaries and opposites, this is the center at which the duality of egocentric self-contraction is transcended, and the merger of individual self with the Divine Self takes place.

Along with the Fifth Chakra, the Sixth Chakra rules and regulates the intuition. The Sixth Chakra is associated with the plane of austerity, in which impurities are purified and burned away by means of non-attachment to perceptions of duality.

Physiological Associations

The Sixth Chakra is considered the energetic control center for all the rest of the body. This area of the body supplies energy to the lower Brain, ears, nose, eyes, and nervous system. Physically, this energy center also relates to the pituitary gland and the hypothalamus (which controls the body's endocrine system and the interaction between the body's endocrine system and nervous system).

The Third Psychic Knot

The Sixth Chakra is the home of the uppermost of three major energetic knots within the human energy system, and corresponds to the energy of the Upper Dantian. This knot holds the individual self separate from the divine identity. It is said to effectively block the practitioner's spiritual evolution until attachment to the duality of phenomena is transcended (i.e., pleasure and pain, desire and aversion, life and death etc.).

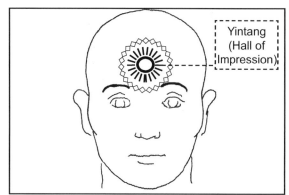

Figure 5.38. The Sixth Chakra corresponds to the area of the Yin Tang (Hall of Impression)

Balanced Manifestation

A balanced Sixth Chakra manifests through the integration of the masculine qualities of discernment, intellectual analysis and clear knowledge, and the feminine qualities of intuition and imagination. This functional integration and its application allows the individual to recognize and ascertain deeper realms of wisdom.

Pathological Manifestation

An imbalanced Sixth Chakra may manifest as over-intellectualization, or even psychic arrogance. One may have very firm views and opinions that he or she is unable to release, or see beyond. There is a tendency to rationalize and theorize one's way through life rather than directly engage in experience.

Blockages in the Sixth Chakra are reflected by very deep and hardened belief structures about the nature of creation itself, these being the root of nearly all other energetic patterns developed and embodied by the individual. Static and inaccurate interpretations of events, and the projections of personal fears and other emotions onto others may also occur. Recurring nightmares and delusional fantasies may further disconnect the individual from the real world.

Energetic Awakening

The process of awakening the Sixth Chakra involves the burning and purification of the "fog of ignorance" that clouds the mind. During this awakening state, energetic releases can manifest through such symptoms as headaches, eye strain, pain around the eyes, distorted or blurred vision, and temporary blindness.

It is important to note, that each of the lower five chakras is associated with a physical sense, whereas the Sixth Chakra is associated with the intuitive sense of the mind itself. In an unawakened individual, the mind gathers and organizes information based only on the five senses; however, when the Sixth Chakra is developed and awakened, the individual will have access to knowledge beyond sensory input. Such knowledge is non-local, being independent of time and space. One aspect of awakening the Sixth Chakra is the true perception, and subsequent interception, of ones own karma.

SPIRITUAL POWERS

Once awakened, the Sixth Chakra is said to manifest clairvoyance, refined telepathy, and a myriad of other minor spiritual powers. Here, the ability to visualize becomes so acute as to involve all five senses (those having been already mastered). One is able to see beyond duality and affect reality directly from the substratum of creation. With these faculties in place, one is able to visit other energetic and spiritual realms and to navigate through a very wide spectrum of consciousness.

SEVENTH CHAKRA

The Seventh Chakra area is associated with the Upper Dantian and crown of the head (Figure 5.39). Its energetic nature corresponds to infinite space (Wuji). Its color is violet. This special energy center is associated with spiritual knowledge, understanding, pure intuition, and ecstasy.

The Seventh Chakra is the primary gateway of the Taiji Pole to the divine, or "the door to kingdom of God." While the other Chakras are considered to be energetic transformers that modify and direct the energy contained within the Taiji Pole, the Seventh Chakra affects the energy of the Taiji Pole by controlling the flow of divine energy into the body.

The Seventh Chakra is associated with totality. It relates to bliss and complete enlightenment, beyond the uppermost reaches of the human realm.

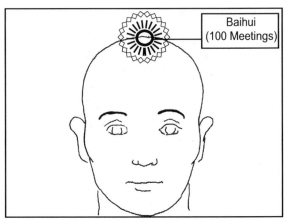

Figure 5.39. The Seventh Chakra corresponds to the area of the Bai Hui (One Hundred Meetings)

PHYSIOLOGICAL ASSOCIATIONS

The Seventh Chakra is located at the highest point of the Taiji Pole and supplies energy to the pineal gland and upper Brain.

BALANCED MANIFESTATION

When the Seventh Chakra is in balance, the individual experiences a strong and continuous connection with the divine, manifesting as a state of spiritual sanctuary, faith and inner peace.

PATHOLOGICAL MANIFESTATION

When this chakra area is blocked or closed, the individual may feel useless or have no meaningful sense of purpose or direction in life. This is often associated with symptoms such as confusion, apathy, alienation, boredom, depression, or varying states of incomprehension.

ENERGETIC AWAKENING

In ancient China, it was believed that when the Seventh Chakra's energetic center opened, it was like a golden flower opening, accompanied by a dazzling bright light and a strong, powerful feeling of connection with the divine.

It is often said that when the Seventh Chakra awakens, the individual transcends all human experiences and enters into the lower divine realms.

SPIRITUAL POWERS

Once the Seventh Chakra has been awakened, an individual will suddenly have access to the infinite knowledge of the Wuji, and is said to be able to exist beyond all time and space.

THE TAIJI POLE, CHAKRAS, AND THE BRIDGE OF LIGHT

This important secret teaching of the Bridge of Light, was originally passed on to me in 1993, by Daoist Master Zhang, in Beijing, China.

The Bridge of Light is an energetically patterned wave frequency, which consists of three main components of the body's energetic field. Its energetic connection to the body's tissues envelops the Conscious Mind, the Subconscious Mind, and the Super-Conscious Mind (i.e., the Divine Mind), resonating within the center core of the disciple's Taiji Pole. It is considered to be the magical bridge existing between the three processes of the Mind, and consists of three separate but intertwining energetic threads: the Thread of Life, the Thread of Consciousness, and the Thread of Creativity, described as follows (Figure 5.40):

1. **The Thread of Life:** This special thread comes directly from the Eternal Soul (Shen Xian) and was originally rooted within the Middle Dantian and Heart area during conception via the Taiji Pole. It is energetically connected to all feelings that stem from the Hun's (Ethereal Soul) influence on the spiritual virtues of the Five Yin Organs (Prenatal Wujingshen), as well as the higher divine energetic fields. It is considered to be the "Stem of Life," and is believed by many to be the "silver cord" that is attached from the individual's Middle Dantian and Heart center to the Spirit Body when an individual is Spirit Traveling.

2. **The Thread of Consciousness:** This special thread also comes directly from the Eternal Soul. However, it is rooted in the Upper Dantian area and Niwan Palace (Pineal Gland), located within the center of the Brain. It embodies portions of the energy of consciousness and is therefore considered to be the "Seat of Consciousness."

3. **The Thread of Creativity:** This thread is rooted in the throat, and is unique in that it is energetically created and specifically constructed by each disciple. It internally exists as a special energetic bridge, resonating between the Upper Dantian and Middle Dantian. The

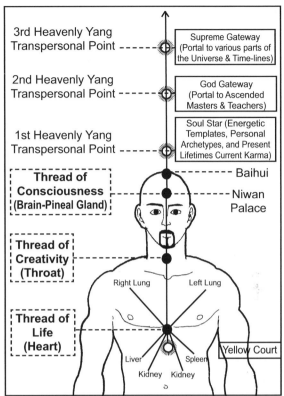

Figure 5.40. The Bridge of Light.
When all three major threads (which together compose the Bridge of Light) are connected as one harmonious cord of light extending upward through the Taiji Pole, a spiritual gateway is opened that enables access to the "Pure Heavenly Sound."

Thread of Creativity is energetically molded by each individual's own personal understanding of his or her spiritual quest (i.e., why they are here). Therefore, it is also considered to be an energetic extension or synthesis of both the Thread of Life and the Thread of Consciousness. The Thread of Creativity is in itself made up of three main energetic branches. These three branches, or additional energetic threads, intertwine as one unified Thread of Creativity and are traditionally explained to Daoist disciples as follows:

- **The First Branch:** This branch of the Thread of Creativity extends from the Heart (Shen: Spirit) to the Spleen (Yi: Intention) and is energized through deep prayer and consistent

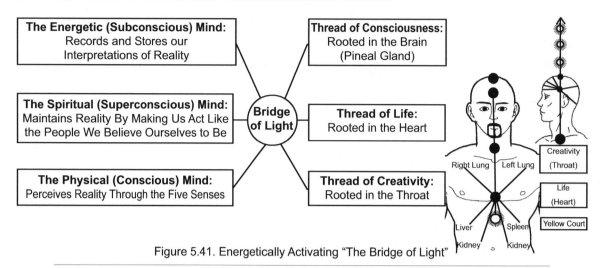

Figure 5.41. Energetically Activating "The Bridge of Light"

meditation. It energetically extends away from the individual's body, and is connected to the first external Weiqi field (existing about an inch away from the skin).

- **The Second Branch:** This branch of the Thread of Creativity extends from the Yellow Court (solar plexus area) to the Heart (Shen: Spirit). It internally responds to any energetic shifting of emotional transitions. It energetically extends away from an individual's body, and is connected to the second external Weiqi field (existing about three feet away from the body).
- **The Third Branch:** This branch of the Thread of Creativity extends from the Yintang (Third Eye) area through the Brain. It ascends out of the body via the Baihui area, through all of the Three Heavenly Transpersonal Points, and beyond. It is responsible for deep spiritual insights and transformations. This energy field is connected to the individual's third external Weiqi field (existing several feet away from the body).

The purpose for training the three components of the Thread of Creativity is to energetically reconnect and spiritually increase the individual's internal awareness of the Original Energy (Yuan Qi) and Original Spirit (Yuan Shen) currently resonating within his center core Taiji Pole. In the clinic, this spiritually awakened awareness allows a Medical Qigong Doctor to progress deeper into the various realms of the Three Worlds, and uncover the "secrets of life" surrounding a patient's diseased state.

After all three Threads of Creativity have been activated, energized, and spiritually cultivated, the next goal is to align and integrate the Qi of the Thread of Life and the Qi of the Thread of Consciousness with the internal energies of the individual's Thread of Creativity.

Because the Thread of Life is connected to the Eternal Soul, the integration of the three threads allows an individual the ability to acquire and obtain a direct connection to their inherent spiritual powers, that currently lie hidden and dormant within their core self. This also allows the individual the ability to consciously access his or her true "Inner-voice" (i.e., the "Voice of the Soul"), and receive important information and spiritual guidance directly from the Divine Source.

Once all of the three major threads that compose the Bridge of Light are internally connected into one harmonious cord of light, they can then be extended upward through the individual's Taiji Pole into the celestial realm. This energetic extension will immediately open a spiritual gateway, that will enable the individual to spirit travel and access the "Pure Heavenly Sound" (i.e., the "Inner-Sound"). This special spiritual state is traditionally embodied in the clinic when constructing a healing circle, creating healing talismans, and speaking healing incantations (i.e., prayers) over the sick.

THE TWELVE CHAKRA GATES

There are 12 important Chakra Gates located on the body's external tissues. These special energetic "pools" look like colorful energetic funnels or vortices of light, extending outward from the front and back of the body's Taiji Pole. Each funnel of light extends its energetic field away from the body's tissues like an subtle mist, expanding its vortex outward as it progresses further into the body's external Weiqi field (Figure 5.42).

As the body's internal Qi travels up and down the center Taiji Pole, it creates an energetic pulse. This energetic pulse resonates from the body's Seven Internal Chakras through the Twelve External Chakra Gates, and can be felt several feet from the body. While the center of each chakra is actually located within the middle of the Taiji Pole, its external energetic field resonates outside the body through these special gates, embedded along the surface of the tissues. Traditionally, these Twelve External Chakra Gates are positioned along the pathways of the body's Conception (Sea of Yin) and Governing (Sea of Yang) Vessels (Figure 5.43).

The First Chakra is located at the perineum and has only one gate, as does the Seventh Chakra located at the top of the head. However, the Second, Third, Fourth, Fifth, and Sixth Chakras all have two gates, one located on the front of the body and the other located on the back of the body, each serving different energetic functions:

1. **The Crown or Seventh Chakra Gate:** This gate is responsible for absorbing the energy and light of the Heavens (i.e., Qi from the Sun, Moon, and Stars) into the body, and for energizing the body's Taiji Pole with Celestial Yang.
2. **The Front Chakra Gates:** The Front Chakra Gates energetically correspond to an individual's Shen (Heart/Mind) and the Qi of the Heart Fire. Because these special gates are responsible for energetically manifesting an individual's feelings and emotions, and are connected to channel points located along the Conception Vessel, they are sometimes used in the clinic in order to remove excess emotions from the patient's tissues.
3. **The Back Chakra Gates:** The Back Gate Chakras energetically correspond to an individual's Zhi and the Kidney Water. Because

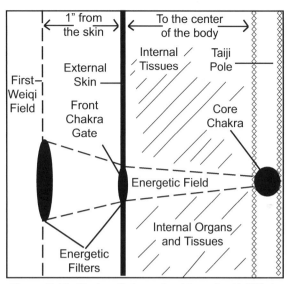

Figure 5.42. Chakra Gates extend from the Taiji Pole

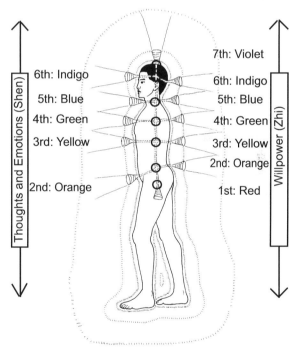

Figure 5.43. The body's Twelve Chakras Gates extend from the Taiji Pole, and expand outward into the body's three external Weiqi Fields

these gates are responsible for energetically manifesting an individual's will and determination, and are connected to channel points located along the Governing Vessel, they are sometimes used in the clinic in order to energetically access and stabilize the patient's emotions and willpower.

4. **The Base or First Chakra Gate:** This gate is responsible for absorbing the energy and light of the Earth (i.e., Qi from the Soil, Water, and Wind) into the body, and for energizing the body's Taiji Pole with Terrestrial Yin.

The Three Dantians system and the Seven Chakra system mutually compliment each other, both in their location of the energy centers and in their associated physical and energetic manifestations.

Energetic Function

Any energy extended by a Medical Qigong Doctor towards an external Chakra Gate will affect the physical body. This is because the Twelve Chakra Gates serve as subtle energetic filters and distributors, that help absorb and deliver environmental Qi to the internal organs, tissues, and major nerve plexus areas located closest to each gate.

Each of the Twelve Chakra Gates also maintains its own energetic potential of psychic perception, interfaces with the body's nervous system, and is associated with a specific endocrine gland.

Opening And Closing A Chakra Gate

When a Medical Qigong Doctor begins to energetically open a patient's Chakra Gate, the external wheel will begin to open and close in half-circle rotations, rhythmically moving with the Taiji Pole's energetic pulse. This action is similar to the centripetal (closing) and centrifugal (opening) action that occurs within the extremities of the body's energetic channels (i.e., tips of the fingers and toes), and is also experienced in the center of the hands and feet, top of the head, and base of the perineum.

If a Chakra Gate becomes stuck open, closed, or tilts out of alignment from the Taiji Pole, Qi Deviations may result due to a distorted or obstructed flow of energy. This type of obstruction may cause physical, as well as psychological stress or trauma, and is one of the main reasons why a trained martial artist will strike the area of an opponent's Yellow Court, along the Center Channel.

Each opening of a Chakra Gate may result in a spontaneous emotional release. Some of these releases can involve painful memories that have been dislodged from the energetic filter that envelops each gate. This energetic filter prevents external emotional traumas from entering into the body.

The release of these emotional traumas can be overwhelming if the patient does not understand the nature of these healing transitions. Releases usually occur after the patient's system has been adequately balanced and energized by the Medical Qigong Doctor. The patient's system then functions with more energy and will effectively seek to release any and all trapped physical, emotional and energetic toxins. Medical Qigong Doctors should be aware of these energetic releases and assist their patients in working through the fears and pain as the Qi Deviations located along the midline of the body are corrected. Sometimes these experiences unwind at a rapid rate, stimulating the patient's central and anterior nervous system; this can release a flood of mental images, emotions, and sensations accompanied by shaking, thrashing, and other unusual movements of the body. The anatomical locations of the Twelve Chakra Gates are described as follows (Figure 5.44):

The Bottom Chakra Gate

- The bottom or First Chakra Gate is located at the "Meeting of Yin" ("Huiyin" CV-1) point (referring to the Earth Yin Qi), located at the perineum in front of the anal sphincter. This special gate is energetically rooted at the "One Hundred Meetings" ("Baihui" GV-20) Crown Chakra point, located at the top of the head.

  The First Chakra Gate controls the reproductive system and the urogenital organs. It accesses the energy of the Lower Dantian and is the Bottom Gate of the Taiji Pole. It is also connected to the Governing, Conception, and Thrusting Vessels, and intersects with the Urinary Bladder and Kidney Channels.

The Second Chakra and Gates

- The center core of the Second Chakra can be accessed through two special energetic gates. The Front Gate is located at the "Spirit's Palace Gate" ("Shenque" CV-8) point, rooted at the navel.
- The Back Gate is located at the "Gate of Life"

("Mingmen" GV-4) point, and is rooted on the lower back.

THE THIRD CHAKRA AND GATES
- The center core of the Third Chakra can be accessed through two energetic gates. The Front Gate is located at the Yellow Court (Solar Plexus area); in this system of chakra correspondence, it is located at the "Spirit Storehouse" ("Shenfu" CV-15) point.
- The Back Gate is located at the "Sinew Contraction" ("Jinsuo" GV-8) point, and is rooted in the middle of the back.

THE FOURTH CHAKRA AND GATES
- The center core of the Fourth Chakra can be accessed through two energetic gates. The Front Gate is located at the "Center Altar" ("Shangzhong" CV-17) point (Heart Center), and is rooted at the center of the breastbone.
- The Back Gate is located at the "Spirit Path" ("Shendao" GV-11) point, and is rooted on the back between the scapulae.

THE FIFTH CHAKRA AND GATES
- The center core of the Fifth Chakra can be accessed through two energetic gates. The Front Gate is located at the "Heaven's Chimney" ("Tiantu CV-22) point (Throat Center), and is rooted just above the hollow of the throat.
- The Back Gate is located at the "Big Vertebra" ("Dazhui" GV-14) point, and is rooted on the back at the base of the neck.

THE SIXTH CHAKRA AND GATES
- The center core of the Sixth Chakra can be accessed through two energetic gates. The Front Gate is located at the "Hall of Impression" ("Yintang" point or "Third-Eye" Center), and is rooted at the middle of the forehead.
- The Back Gate is located on the back of the head between the "Wind Palace" (GV-16) and the "Brain's Door" (GV-17), at the external occipital protuberance.

THE SEVENTH CHAKRA GATE
- The Upper Chakra Gate is located at the "One Hundred Meetings" ("Baihui" GV-20) point at the top of the head. It is rooted at the base of the Root Chakra, located in the lower perineum, at the "Meeting of Yin" ("Huiyin" CV-1) point.

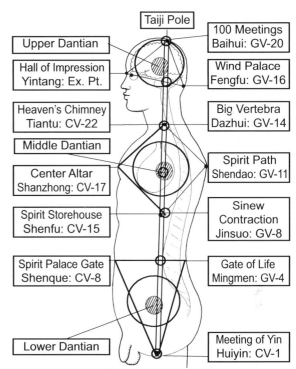

Figure 5.44. The Anatomical Locations of the Twelve Chakra Gates and the Taiji Pole

PRECAUTIONS

It is important to understand when any reaction begins to manifest due to the Opening of a Chakra Gate, that these are "normal" phenomena, that temporarily occur during deep transformational times. Therefore certain precautions such as establishing a support system to process these sudden releases of trapped emotions is essential.

It is important not to allow patients to experience these emotional transitions alone. Because these energy transitions, malfunctions, and deviations are new to the Western mode of thinking, they can easily be misdiagnosed by Western doctors unfamiliar with Energetic Medicine. Therefore patients should be encouraged to find or establish a support group consisting of advanced energy workers familiar with the chakra system. Having a support group of experienced practitioners allows these emotional and spiritual transitions to occur in a safe environment where other experienced practitioners can monitor the patient's feelings and energy, if and when unfamiliar emotions start to emerge.

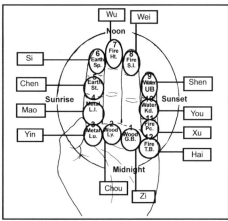

Figure 5.45. The 12 Earthly Branch - 2 Hour Time Period. The left palm of a Daoist priest was traditionally used for gathering and absorbing Qi into the body's Twelve Primary Organs and Postnatal Channels. When the thumb was placed onto a specific finger area of the left hand, the Qi from the external environment was gathered and internally directed to "bathe" and Tonify this deficient organ tissue.

THE TWELVE EARTHLY BRANCHES AND THE TWELVE CHAKRA GATES

The ancient Daoists viewed the human body as a small and complete universe unto itself (a Microcosm within the Macrocosm), with the understanding that the internal organs are continually being energetically influenced by the celestial movement of the Sun, Moon, Five Planets, and 28 Star Constellations. To the ancient Daoists, the body's Sea of Yang Qi (Governing Vessel) and Sea of Yin Qi (Conception Vessel) that energetically supported and maintained the external Twelve Chakra Gates, were also affected by the continual movements of these important Heavenly cycles.

To the ancient doctors of Chinese Energetic Medicine, each day was divided into twelve separate time divisions (Figure 5.45). Each time division encompassed two hours, and was originally named after one of the Twelve Earthly Branches. These twelve time divisions were further organized into 12 months and 4 seasons.

The ancient Daoists also discovered that the body's Qi and Blood mirrored the Earth's seasonal ebb and flow, causing the body's internal energy

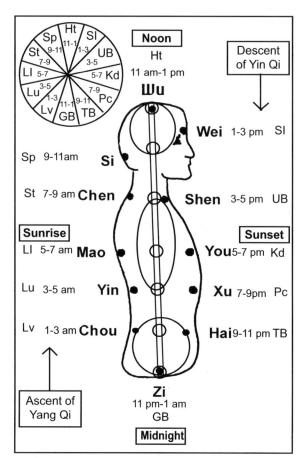

Figure 5.46. The Movement of the Body's Qi as Depicted by the Ancient Daoists "Bright Mirror of Physiological Alchemy" Chart. The Twelve Earthly Branch Relation with the Microcosmic Orbit: the main channels of the back and front of the body correspond to the ecliptic path of the Sun. These twelve special energy points are traditionally associated with the body's Twelve Chakra Gates.

to rise and fall like the lunar tides. Therefore, the rhythmic variations of the waxing and waning of Qi and Blood, were associated with the subtle waxing and waning of the body's Yin and Yang energy, as well as with the circulation of Qi flowing within the body's Sea of Yang Qi (Governing Vessel) and Sea of Yin Qi (Conception Vessels).

Each time period in the Twelve Earthly Branches system, was regarded as having a specific influence on each of the body's seven internal

The Twelve Earthly Branches

子	丑	寅	卯	辰	巳	午	未	申	酉	戌	亥
Zi	Chou	Yin	Mao	Chen	Si	Wu	Wei	Shen	You	Xu	Hai
Rat	Ox	Tiger	Rabbit	Dragon	Snake	Horse	Goat	Monkey	Rooster	Dog	Pig
Nov.	Dec.	Jan.	Feb.	March	April	May	June	July	Aug.	Sept.	Oct.
11-1am	1-3am	3-5am	5-7am	7-9am	9-11pm	11-1pm	1-3pm	3-5pm	5-7pm	7-9pm	9-11pm
Midnight			Sun Rise			High Noon			Sunset		

Figure 5.47. The Twelve Earthly Branches

Chakra Centers and their external Twelve Chakra Gates (Figure 5.46).

The ancient Daoists observed that each of the Twelve Earthly Branches correspond to 12 important energetic stages that naturally occur within nature. For example (Figure 5.47):

- **The 1st Branch "Zi" (11pm-1am):** This Earthly Branch implies that seeds of plants and trees are ready to sprout when absorbing water.
- **The 2nd Branch "Chou" (1am-3am):** This Earthly Branch implies that sprouts are breaking out from the Earth's surface.
- **The 3rd Branch "Yin" (3am-5am):** This Earthly Branch implies that the "Out-of-Earth" grass and plants are stretching upward, toward the sunlight.
- **The 4th Branch "Mao" (5am-7am):** This Earthly Branch implies that all things in Nature are now thickly or densely grown.
- **The 5th Branch "Chen" (7am-9am):** This Earthly Branch implies that the Yang power within all things is being pushed to increase its growth and development.
- **The 6th Branch "Si" (9am-11am):** This Earthly Branch implies that the full power of Yang has arrived, and all things are now in full development.
- **The 7th Branch "Wu" (11am-1pm):** This Earthly Branch implies the full growth of all things on Earth because of the full power of Yang (and the beginning of Yin in Nature). It also implies the blending of Yin & Yang.
- **The 8th Branch "Wei" (1pm-3pm):** This Earthly Branch implies that fruits are ripening and are ready to taste.
- **The 9th Branch "Shen" (3pm-5pm):** This Earthly Branch implies that all things are well formed and developed.
- **The 10th Branch "You" (5pm-7pm):** This Earthly Branch implies that all things are starting to wither after ripening.
- **The 11th Branch "Xu" (7pm-9pm):** This Earthly Branch implies that all things are withering and dying out.
- **The 12th Branch "Hai" (9pm-11pm):** This Earthly Branch implies that all things are exposed to and surrounded by Yin, which now reaches its peak.

Each of the external Twelve Chakra Gates corresponds to one of the Twelve Earthly Branches. These twelve energetic gates extend their Qi outward, through the body's anterior and posterior fields, from the center core Taiji Pole. Beginning at the Bottom Chakra Gate (i.e., the "Zi" Earthly Branch, representing Midnight), the body's energy travels up the spine, following the Governing Vessel. This energetic pathway is considered to be the body's natural "Ascent of Yang Qi."

After the Sea of Yang Qi reaches its peak at the top of the head, the Yin begins to grow. Starting at the Upper Chakra Gate (i.e., the Wu Earthly Branch, representing Noon time), the energy then travels down the front of the chest, following the descending energetic pathway of the Conception Vessel's Sea of Yin Qi.

Reconstructing A Damaged Chakra Gate

The protective energetic grid of a patient's Chakra Gate can sometimes be disfigured, torn, or even completely ripped away from the Chakra Gate itself (Figure 5.48). When the Chakra Gate's protective grid becomes damaged, the patient's energetic field is no longer able to repel the invasion of external pathogens from the body. Neither is the patient able to clearly direct energy out from the chakra, preventing the creative process of expression. In order to repair the damaged energetic grid, the Medical Qigong Doctor must first remove the Chakra Gate from the patient's body. This is accomplished by following the following reconstruction protocol:

- **Removing the Chakra Gate:** With your left palm, use the Qi Compression technique (Volume 3, Chapter 38) and stimulate the tissues several inches above the area of the damaged Chakra Gate. Simultaneously use the Bellows Palm techniques (Volume 3, Chapter 35), with your right palm over the damaged Chakra Gate in a counterclockwise circular direction, to unwind and remove the chakra's gate (Figure 5.49).
- If the Chakra Gate is stuck or frozen within the patient's tissues and becomes difficult to remove from the body, you can remove it by first wobbling it from side to side while applying pressure to the tissue area above the Chakra Gate using the Bellows Palm technique (Figure 5.50).
- Next, pulse White Light into the Chakra Gate area in order to lift and remove the it from its energetic chamber. This rapid energetic pulse should resemble the quick powerful flashing of a Strobe Light.
- Once the Chakra Gate is freed, the energetic filter will reveal a complex root system, that is deeply embedded within the subtle structure of the patient's Energy Body. It is important to note, that this energetic root system has subtle extensions that also extend and connect into the patient's Spirit Body; as well as connecting to the energetic channels that currently travel through the tissue area that supports the external Chakra Gate.

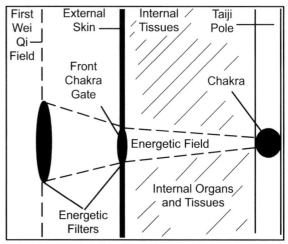

Figure 5.48. The Protective Energetic Grid of a Chakra Gate

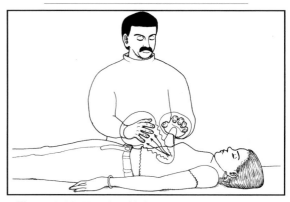

Figure 5.49. Use the Qi Compression and Bellows Palm Techniques over the damaged Chakra Gate

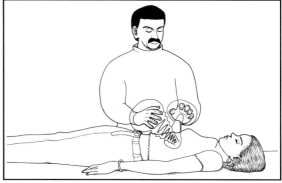

Figure 5.50. Free the damaged Chakra Gate by applying the Bellows Palm technique and wobbling it from side to side

CHAPTER 5: THE TAIJI POLE, CHAKRAS, AND THREE DANTIANS

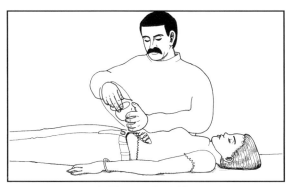

Figure 5.51. The Medical Qigong Doctor will hold the patient's Chakra Gate with his left hand and purge its toxic energy using his right hand.

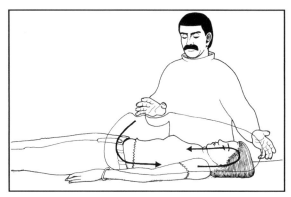

Figure 5.52. After replacing the Chakra Gate, the doctor should place his left hand over the Baihui point to access the patient's Taiji Pole, and then reconnect the Chakra Gate back into the patient's Three Bodies.

The actual size of the Chakra Gate is about the diameter of a silver dollar, therefore it is important to energetically expand its size in order to more effectively clean the filter.

- **Cleaning the Chakra Gate:** In order to clean the chakra filter, hold the energetic body of the Chakra Gate with your left (Yang) palm (like holding an ice cream cone), and begin to clean the Chakra Gate by manually dredging and purging the chakra filter itself (Figure 5.51).

The Chakra Gate can then be energized and reconstructed by connecting its energetic field to a column of Divine White light energy.

- **Replacing the Chakra Gate:** After the Chakra Gate has been cleansed and repaired, it is important to reduce its expanded size back to normal and reconnect it into the patient's body while simultaneously energizing the patient's Taiji Pole. This re-establishes the energetic function of the Chakra Gate by rooting it back into its energetic core. This is accomplished by holding the Chakra Gate with your right Bellows Palm in order to secure it, then mentally commanding it to shrink in size and gently placing it back into its proper residence.

With your right hand still over the area of the replaced Chakra Gate, place your left hand over the top of the patient's head (Baihui), and emit Qi through the Taiji Pole towards the area of the replaced Chakra Gate.

Next, with your left hand, begin to gently and slowly twist the energy of the center core Taiji Pole towards the left and right. This soft twisting action is used in order to engage and integrate the chakra's energetic rhythm, and incorporate it back again with the natural rhythm of the patient's center core Taiji Pole (Figure 5.52).

- **Ending the Treatment:** In order to end the treatment, reconnect with the Divine, and imagine and feel a Divine Cord of White Light envelop the patient's body. Focus on directing this Divine Light through the Microcosmic Orbit (Fire Cycle) for several rotations.

Next, reconnect with the Divine and direct the energy to flow in the Microcosmic Orbit (Water Cycle) for several rotations.

Once you feel the energy of the patient's Three Bodies stabilize, you may end the treatment.

ENERGIZING THE SEVEN CHAKRAS THROUGH STIMULATING THE TWELVE GATES

Vibration, color and sound are all interrelated and are a means of determining or monitoring the frequency of energy within the patient's Twelve Chakra Gates. By projecting the appropriate colors into the Chakra Gates, the Medical Qigong Doctor is able to re-energize the chakras, as well as Tonify their internal organ functions and stimulate the emotional components associated with the specific chakra areas (refer back to Figure 5.43).

Volume 1, Section 1: Foundations of Chinese Energetic Medicine

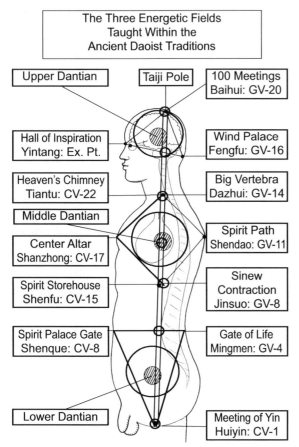

Figure 5.53. The Anatomical Locations of the Three Dantians and Taiji Pole According to Ancient Daoist Teachings

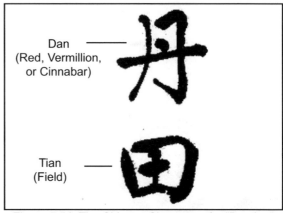

Figure 5.54. The Chinese Characters for "Dantian" (Cinnabar Field)

The Three Dantians

The human body has three important energy centers, that store and radiate Qi similar to the way a battery stores and releases energy. These three powerful energetic centers are called "Dantians" and are located along the center core of the body's Taiji Pole, in the area of the head, heart, and lower abdomen (Figure 5.53).

According to ancient Daoist teachings, these three special areas contain three "Psychic Knots" (called "Granthi" in certain Buddhist and Yogic practices), that were created within the forming tissues during the fetal development. The Three Dantians are connected to each other through the Taiji Pole. The Taiji Pole acts as a passageway for communication between the Three Dantians and as a highway for the movement of the various life-force energies.

The Chinese Character for Dantian

The Chinese word "Dantian," is traditionally translated as "Cinnabar Field," or "Elixir Field," and described as follows (Figure 5.54):

- The first character of the Chinese ideograph "Dan," is generally translated as "red," "vermilion" or "cinnabar." Cinnabar is a bright red (vermilion) mineral, that is chemically known as mercury sulfide, and is the principal ore of Mercury.

  In ancient China, Cinnabar was considered to be an extremely important mineral and was the source material for Red Vermilion Ink, manufactured exclusively for use by the emperors. In ancient Chinese Medicine, Cinnabar was traditionally used in small doses in order to sedate the Heart and calm the patient's Shen (Mind/Spirit), but always for short periods due to its toxic nature. Because it was also discovered to contain an ideal balance of Yin and Yang energetic properties, Cinnabar elixirs and pills were traditionally used in Daoist Alchemy as a part of the body's transformation process.

- The second Chinese character "Tian," is traditionally translated as "field," but can also be translated as "Farmland." In Medical Qigong terms, the word "Tian" is referred to as a "Field of Energy."

The Energetic Functions of the Three Dantians

The primary energetic function of the Three Dantians is to gather, store, and transform life-force energy. The health of the body's tissues and the strength of its energetic fields, all depend on the amount of energy present in the Three Dantians.

The energy reservoirs of the Three Dantians are linked externally through the Governing (Sea of Yang Qi) and Conception (Sea of Yin Qi) Vessels; and are internally connected through the Thrusting Vessels and the body's Taiji Pole.

Each of the Dantians generate heat, light, magnetic fields, and electrical vibrations. The energetic charge and intensity of each Dantian's vibration and magnetic field is dependent upon the ability to discipline and control one's mental focus, posture, and respiration.

Qi moves into the body's Dantians through the body's Taiji Pole. The energy is then absorbed into the body's major organs and surrounding tissues as it flows through the Dantians and into the body's internal and external channels and collaterals (Figure 5.55). Energy can also be absorbed from the external environment through the body's tissues, channels, and internal organs, and be directed to flow directly into the Three Dantians and ultimately into the center core Taiji Pole.

Because each Dantian acts like a reservoir, it collects energy and redistributes it into all of the internal organs. This energy also extends from the surface of the body outward, into the three external "Weiqi" ("Protective Energy") fields (Figure 5.56). In Daoist alchemy, the disciple's cultivated energy is sometimes directed to flow throughout his physical body, purposely stimulating his energy channels, nervous system, and the endocrine glands. Othertimes, this energy is directed to saturate his Blood in order to nourish his entire body.

In ancient China, the movement of Qi flowing within the body's tissues was traditionally visualized by the Daoist disciples as the ever flowing movements of a watercourse, described as follows:

- **Collecting Energy:** Qi flows into the body like rainwater flowing into a large lake. In this example, the body absorbs and collects Qi into the Lower Dantian.

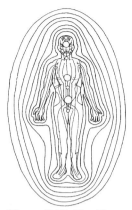
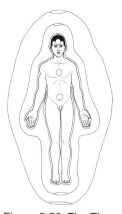

Figure 5.55. The Three Dantians and the Body's Energetic Fields.

Figure 5.56. The Three Dantians and the Three External Weiqi Fields

- **Storing Energy:** The water is then absorbed into the surrounding soil and foliage (the various tissues), before it overflows into its adjacent rivers (vessels and channels).
- **Distributing Energy:** The rivers eventually pour into smaller pools (the organs), which overflow into various streams.

Another popular analogy is to consider the Dantians as batteries, the body's Taiji Pole as a magnetic bar connecting the batteries together, the channels as the wires, and the Three Weiqi Fields as the electromagnetic fields manifesting from the energy contained within the batteries internal structure.

When training esoteric alchemy, any mental or emotional awareness (Shen) contained within a specific tissue area (Jing), can be heightened through increasing the flow of energy (Qi) into that location. When energy fills the tissues, a cellular reaction causes the tissues to either store or release energetic charges, depending on the tissue's energetic excess or deficient condition. For example:

- **Lower Dantian:** If energy is increased inside the Lower Dantian, the result is a heightened feeling of power, stability, and Kinetic Communication.
- **Middle Dantian:** If energy is increased in the Middle Dantian, the result is a heightened feeling of emotional awareness and Empathic Communication.
- **Upper Dantian:** If energy is increased in the Upper Dantian, a heightened sense of Intuitive Communication occurs.

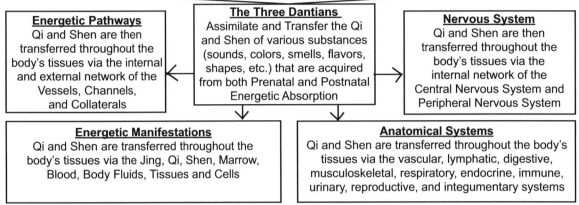

Figure 5.57. In Daoist Internal Alchemy, Qi is dispersed from the Taiji Pole through the Three Dantians

Ancient Daoist Alchemy

In ancient China, Daoist Alchemy was traditionally practiced using two important training methods, External Alchemy (Wai Dan) Training and Internal Alchemy (Nei Dan) Training, described as follows:

- **External Alchemy (Wai Dan) Training:** The ancient Daoist practice of External Alchemy is seen as the ancestor of modern chemistry. The Chinese External Alchemists established various laboratories, and experimented with many substances using mineral, plant, insect, and animal sources. The primary goal being to create powerful long-life elixirs, with the hope of seeking to discover a special magical elixir that would confer immortality (or at least increase one's longevity). Through great experimentation, these ancient sages eventually discovered many exceptionally potent herbal medicines that are still used in Traditional Chinese Medical Clinics today. In addition to the various chemical formulas that were created, one important invention included the discovery of gunpowder.

- **Internal Alchemy (Nei Dan) Training:** The ancient Daoist practice of Internal Alchemy focused on purifying the body's Original Nature (Xing), and transforming a disciple's Original Spirit (Yuan Shen) into its most purified and radiant potential of their life (Ming). As these ancient sages sought to cultivate and circulate the "Inner Elixirs" of the body's Jing (Essence), Qi (Energy), and Shen (Heart/Mind) at various locations within the body, many of the special Medical Qigong Exercises and Meditations were developed (Figure 5.57).

The Internal Alchemists viewed the Three Dantians as inner crucibles or cauldrons, and employed them in the role of gathering and transforming vital substances, energies, and various aspects of awareness. The inner alchemists kept their work hidden by using secret mineral code words such as "gold," "lead," and "cinnabar" in order to describe the movements and transformations of energetic and spiritual substances within the body.

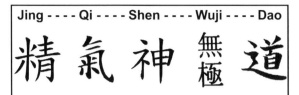

Figure 5.58. The ancient Daoist energetic progression used to create internal Alchemical transformation

The Alchemical Cultivation of Jing, Qi, and Shen

The ultimate goal of the ancient Internal Alchemist, was to obtain "Immortality," by creating a complete energetic transformation of the body's Jing, Qi, and Shen into a body of radiant light (Figure 5.58). These transformations can be compared to the changes of water consistencies, which when heated, can change from solid ice, to liquid, to vapor. These progressive transformations are but one example of the many functions of the Three Dantians as inner crucibles of Jing, Qi, and Shen in the process of internal alchemy (Figure 5.59).

Jing, Qi, and Shen are the three fundamental energies necessary for human life, and are collectively referred to as the "Three Treasures of Man." In order to accomplish "magical transformation," the ancient Daoist Alchemists would traditionally proceed as follows:

- **Jing To Qi:** First they gathered, purified, and transformed their original and acquired Essence into refined Energy. This special transformation process occurred from within the inner cauldron of their Lower Dantian.
- **Qi To Shen:** Then they gathered, purified, and transformed their refined Energy into Yuan Shen (Original Mind/Spirit) from within the inner cauldron of their Middle Dantian.
- **Shen To Wuji:** Next, they gathered, purified, and transformed their Yuan Shen into the infinite space of the Wuji, from within the inner cauldron of their Upper Dantian.
- **Wuji To Dao:** Finally, they would transform their Yuan Shen, and release their Magical Spirit (Ling Shen) through a secret portal located at the top of their head, and sojourn through the infinite space of the Wuji to reconnect with the divine light of the Eternal Dao.

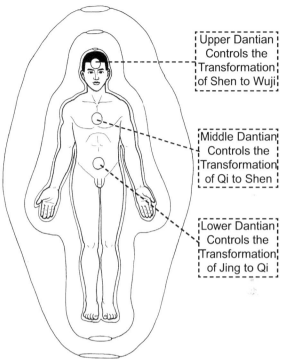

Figure 5.59. The Three Dantians and their relationship to the transformation of Jing, Qi, Shen

Through extensive experimentation in the internal laboratory of their Three Bodies (i.e., the Physical Body, Energy Body, and Spirit Body), the ancient Internal Alchemists were eventually able to become powerful priests, incredible healers, and Immortalized Imperial Augers and Mystics.

The Three Treasures of Man (Jing, Qi, and Shen) are also connected with the Three Outer Forces (or Powers) known as Heaven, Earth, and Man. In the human body, Jing (reproductive essence) is considered to be the most substantial and therefore the most Yin of the Three Treasures, therefore it is closely linked with Earth Qi and gathered into the Lower Dantian. Qi that is closely connected with the atmospheric energy (a blend of Heaven and Earth Qi), and is traditionally gathered into the Middle Dantian. Shen (Spirit) is considered to be the most insubstantial, and therefore, the most Yang of the Three Treasures. It corresponds with Heaven Qi, and is traditionally gathered in the Upper Dantian.

THE LOWER CINNABAR FIELD: (XIA DANTIAN)

The Lower Dantian is the energy center most familiar to martial artists and meditators, as it is the first place on which they are trained to focus their concentration. It is regarded as the center of physical strength and the source of stamina.

The Lower Dantian is located in the lower abdominal area, and its energetic boundary is positioned in the shape of a triangle, formed by drawing a line between the navel, Mingmen (lower back), and perineum (Figure 5.60). These three points form an energetic pyramid, facing downward. This special configuration allows the Lower Dantian to naturally gather and absorb the various Five Element energies from the Earth.

The Lower Dantian's "Brain," is known in Western terms as the Enteric (intestinal) Nervous System. According to modern research, the Lower Dantian sends and receives impulses, records experiences, and responds to emotions. Its nerve cells are bathed in and influenced by the same type of neurotransmitters that exist inside the Brain.

The Lower Dantian's entire nervous system mirrors the body's Central Nervous System, and is a network of 100 million neurons (more neurons than the spinal cord), neurotransmitters, and proteins that can act independently of the body's Brain and can send messages, learn, remember, and produce "gut" feelings (Kinetic Communication).

THE LOWER DANTIAN & POSTNATAL JING

The Lower Dantian collects Earth Qi, is associated with Jing (Essence), and supports the first of three defensive energetic fields, traditionally known as the body's external Weiqi (Protective Energy). This first level of Protective Energy circulates outside the body, extending roughly about one inch beyond the tissues. The more the Lower Dantian gathers and increases its content of energy, the stronger, more expansive, and thicker the body's Weiqi fields become.

The Lower Dantian is the major storage area for the various types of Kidney energies. In ancient China, the "External Kidneys" were traditionally

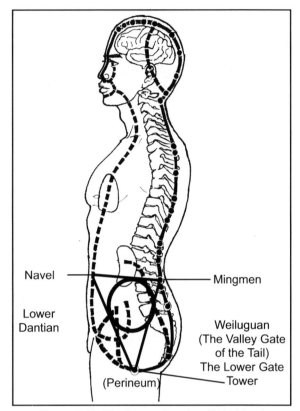

Figure 5.60. The Lower Dantian (Side View)

considered to be the testes, while the "Internal Kidneys" were viewed as the Kidney Organs.

The Kidney energies are closely linked with the Prenatal Qi, and provide the foundation for all other types of energy in the body (Jing, Qi, Yin, and Yang, etc.). When referring to the Kidneys, it is important to note that in certain ancient Daoist, Qigong, and Chinese Medical Literature, the term Kidneys is occasionally used as a synonym for both the testes and the ovaries.

To the ancient Daoists, the Lower Dantian was considered to be an energetic reservoir, used for storing heat and vibration. In Daoist Alchemy, it is taught that after the Earth Qi has been gathered and transformed within the Lower Dantian, it will become a dense, full, thick type of energy. Because the Kidneys control the Water Element within the body, this special type of transformed Jing was said to be analogous to the "water contained within the cauldron."

CHAPTER 5: THE TAIJI POLE, CHAKRAS, AND THREE DANTIANS

Figure 5.61. The Modern Character for Qi

Through focused concentration and meditation, the cultivated Jing (Essence) within the Lower Dantian can be refined and transformed to produce Qi (Energy). When sufficient heat is generated in the Lower Dantian as a result of the Three Fires (Heart Fire, Mingmen Fire, and Bladder Fire) mixing with the Kidney Water, the alchemical transformation of Jing in the Lower Dantian area causes the water of the Jing to transform into steam (Qi). This is one reason why the modern character for Qi is composed of the image of steam rising from rice that is bursting and decomposing (Figure 5.61). This energetic transformation is known as "Changing Jing into Qi" in Daoist Alchemy, and takes place within the Lower Dantian.

THE JING GONG (ESSENCE PALACE)

The Lower Dantian is closely linked to the "Jing Gong" ("Essence Palace"), which serves as a reservoir of the reproductive essence (Postnatal Jing). The Jing Gong is located in the lower perineal area, specifically, the uterus in females and the accessory sexual glands that store semen (i.e., the prostate and seminal vesicles) in males.

One of my Daoist teachers explained that the exact location of the Jing Gong differs in men and women due to the anatomical locations of the male and female reproductive organs. This difference in location affects the production and storage of Jing. The testicles (External Kidneys) in the male cause the transformation of energy to occur lower in the body than in females. In females this transformation takes place in a slightly higher position due to the location of the woman's ovaries (Figure 5.62).

- **Male Jing Gong:** In men, the reproductive essence is located in the prostate and seminal vesicles, known as the Jing Gong (Essence Palace) in Daoist alchemy. This area is located in the center of the body at the level of the superior border of the pubic bone, posterior to the Qugu CV-2 (Crooked Bone) point, level with the superior border of the pubic bone.

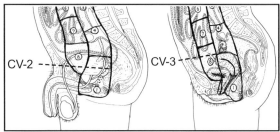

Figure 5.62. The Jing Gong (Essence Palace)

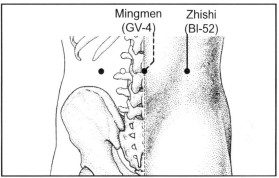

Figure 5.63. The Jing Gong (Back Points)

- **Female Jing Gong:** In women, the Jing Gong area is located higher, centered in the Uterus, about an inch above the superior border of the pubic bone, posterior to the Zhongji CV-3 (Utmost Center) point. Some of the ancient alchemical texts describe the Lower Dantian in women as being located in the "Bao" or Uterus, illustrating the important role of the Uterus in relationship to the function of Jing in a woman's body.

It is interesting to note, that the name "Jing Gong" ("Essence Palace") is sometimes assigned to two different acupuncture points located on the back, both with similar clinical applications. These two areas are the "Mingmen" ("Gate of Life" GV-4) point, and the Zhishi (Will Chamber BL-52) point (Figure 5.63).

According to ancient Daoist teachings, our Prenatal Essence (Yuan Jing) determines our constitutional strengths and vitality and is stored in the Lower Dantian. It interacts with the Kidney energies in order to form Kidney Jing. Jing is the most physical and material form of energy within the body and thus corresponds to Yin and to Earth energy. Therefore the Lower Dantian is the place where the Qi of the Earth is drawn into the body and energetically transformed by heat and vibration.

The Kidney energies are all closely intertwined: Kidney Jing, Kidney Qi, Kidney Yin, Kidney Yang, and Kidney Mingmen Fire. The Mingmen Fire, also called Kidney Yang, helps transform the Jing into steam (Kidney Qi).

Kidney Jing circulates throughout the body via the Eight Extraordinary Vessels, in particular the Governing Vessel, Conception Vessel, and Thrusting Vessels, all of which originate in the Lower Dantian.

Kidney Jing And Reproductive Cycles

Kidney Jing controls the reproductive energies and life cycles of the body. Once a child is born, Acquired Jing is responsible for replenishing Congenital Jing, and starting the first independent "Life Cycle." This important life cycle controls the growth and development of the body's organ systems, and cycles every seven years in girls, and every eight years in boys.

Every new Kidney Jing cycle prompts a new phase of development. For example, according to *The Yellow Emperor's Classic of Internal Medicine*, the body's Life Cycles proceed as follows:

- **(W-1 & M-1):** Prenatal (Congenital) Jing exists from conception, forming the First Cycle from the inherited essence received from the parents.
- **(W-7 & M-8):** In the second cycle, when the child loses its baby teeth, its body begins the "Pre-Adolescence Cycle. A Girl's Kidney Qi becomes abundant, and teeth and hair grow longer; a boy's testes are fully developed, his hair grows longer and his teeth begin to change.
- **(W-14 & M-16):** The next Life Cycle is Adolescence, when Kidney Jing matures and causes the Conception Vessel to open and flow. At this time, part of the Kidney Jing transforms into "Tian Gui." The term "Tian Gui" refers to the Tenth Heavenly Stem (Yin Water Element Qi). In Chinese Medicine it is a component of the Yuan Qi (original/Prenatal Energy) in the Mingmen, which develops and maintains reproductive function (i.e., it is responsible for the production of certain hormones). During this time, a woman begins to menstruate and is able to give birth; the reproductive energy in a man's testicles becomes abundant, he now begins to secrete semen, and is able to father a child.
- **(W-21 & M-24):** The emanations of the Woman's Kidneys are regular, the last tooth has come out, and she is fully grown; the emanations of the Man's Kidneys are regular, his muscles and bones are firm and strong, the last tooth has grown, and he has reached his full height.
- **(W-28 & M-32):** In the next stage physical growth finishes. The woman's muscles and bones are strong, her hair has reached its full length, and her body is flourishing and fertile; the man's muscles and bones are flourishing, his flesh is healthy, and he is able-bodied and fertile.
- **(W-35 & M-40):** The woman's "Yang Ming" ("Sunlight") begins to diminish, her face begins to wrinkle and her hair begins to fall out; the emanation from mans testicles become smaller, he begins to lose his hair, and his teeth begin to decay,
- **(W-42 & M-48):** The energy of the woman's "Upper Three Yangs" begin to diminish, her entire face is wrinkled and her hair begins to turn white; the man's masculine vigor is reduced or exhausted, his face begins to wrinkle and the hair on his temples begins to turn white.
- **(W-49 & M-56):** In the next stage the declining Jing leads to exhaustion of the Tian Gui, thus extinguishing reproductive ability. The woman can no longer become pregnant and the Qi circulation of her Conception Vessel becomes empty and her Thrusting Vessels begin to deteriorate; the power of a man's Liver Qi deteriorates, and his physical strength reaches its end.
- **(W-56 & M-64):** At age 64, the man loses his teeth and hair. In the final stage, the exhaustion of the Tian Gui and the declining of the Kidney Jing inevitably leads to death.

THE LOWER DANTIAN & PRENATAL JING

According to ancient Daoist teachings, the body's "Yuan Jing" ("Original Essence" or "Prenatal Essence") is not "Reproductive Essence," which is considered to be "Postnatal Essence." The body's Yuan Jing is considered to be a primordial energetic substance that was not born from a Postnatal state.

To the ancient Daoists, the body's Original Essence is the innate, true energetic substance, through which a disciple's constitutional makeup, strength, and overall vitality originated and externally manifested within the realm of matter. According to Daoist alchemical teachings,

> "The Original Essence (Yuan Jing)
> is devoid of form and matter.
> As soon as matter is generated,
> it cannot be used in Spiritual Cultivation
> as the Alchemical Mother of the Elixir.
> Only when the Original Essence
> is combined with the energy
> of the Original Breath (Yuan Qi),
> can the Immortal Elixir be created."

In Daoist alchemy, the Original Yang (Yuan Yang) is the same as the Original Essence (Yuan Jing), it has no form, and resides within the Original Breath (Yuan Qi). When the Original Essence receives any type of external stimuli, it moves, separates itself from the Original Breath, transforms from a "Generative Force" ("Jing Qi") into a "Generative Fluid" (Postnatal Jing) and becomes energetically active as the body's Postnatal Essence.

When the Original Essence (Yuan Jing) is in its natural state, it is stored within the body's Yin and Yang Organs, existing as an energetic mist, still, and formless. As soon as a single thought arises from the acquired mind, it immediately transforms itself from a Prenatal energetic state into a Postnatal energetic state.

THE LOWER DANTIAN AND PRENATAL QI

The Lower Dantian is often called "the Sea of Qi." It is the place where Qi is housed, the Mingmen Fire is aroused, the Kidney Yin and Kidney Yang Qi are gathered, and the "Yuan Qi" ("Original Energy" or "Prenatal Energy") is stored.

Also sometimes called "Source Qi" in Traditional Chinese Medicine, the Yuan Qi is the foundation of all the other types of energy and developments occurring within the human body. For example, the Yuan Qi is closely linked with the Yuan Jing (Original or Prenatal Essence). Together, the Yuan Qi and Yuan Jing determine our overall health, vitality, stamina, and life span. Because the Yuan Qi is the true force behind the activity of all the organs and energies in the body, it is closely related to the Mingmen (Gate of Life) and works to sustain the life-force of the body.

In Daoist Alchemy, it is taught that the body's Yuan Qi is the original energy that radiates from the body, and extends into the infinite space of the Wuji in order to reconnect with the celestial realms of the eternal Dao. Therefore, the Yuan Qi is believed to be the original motivational force that energetically links the Prenatal Jing (Yuan Jing) with the Prenatal Shen (Yuan Shen).

The body's Yuan Qi is also the catalytic agent needed for facilitating the production of Blood and for transforming food, air, and drink into Postnatal Qi. Although the Yuan Qi is housed within the Lower Dantian, it also flows to all the internal organs and channels via the Triple Burners (i.e., the Upper Burner, Middle Burner, and Lower Burner).

Yuan Qi is also said to enter into the Twelve Primary Channels (the body's twelve major energetic pathways), and its energy can be accessed and influenced via the channel's Yuan Points.

THE LOWER DANTIAN AND EARTH QI

Of the Three Dantians, the Lower Dantian is the closest to the Earth and is the most Yin; it is therefore the natural center for gathering and storing Earth Qi within the body. In Daoist Alchemy, the body's tissues are viewed as being a living magnet, capable of absorbing energy from people, places, and things like a living sponge. Therefore, once a disciple has learned to absorb life-force energy through his Jing (body and tissues), and conserve and circulate his Qi, he can increase this energy circulation by connecting it to the unlimited reservoirs of Qi existing within the natural environment.

Being the densest and easiest to feel, Earth Qi is the first form of external energy with which the Medical Qigong Doctor will connect with. This energetic connection with the Earth is important for two main reasons:

1. **Energetic Rooting:** The Medical Qigong Doctor needs the Yin grounding power of Earth Qi to counterbalance the more active Yang energy cultivated during prayer, meditation, and Qigong Breathing Exercises. Without this important grounding of Earth Qi, many Medical Qigong Doctors and energetic practitioners develop Qi Deviations in the form of Excess Heat.

2. **Energetic Replenishing:** Each body's supply of Qi is limited. When a Medical Qigong Doctor extends his Qi to perform a healing, because of the massive amount of energy and heat generated, he will inadvertently deplete his body's personal supply of Qi unless he is able to simultaneously replenish this supply from outside sources (i.e., re-hydrating before a treatment begins and connecting/rooting into the Qi of the Earth).

In Daoist Alchemical, absorbing life-force energy through the Earth's Qi (Breath of the Planet) and its energetic fields was essential for cultivation practice. The breath was seen as that which binds together all of the insubstantial vapors. Therefore, the breath was sometimes used like an energetic vacuum, to absorb Earth Qi into the body and create Shen (Mind/Spirit). The Shen was then projected out from the physical body like a net of radiant light, and used to "sip" additional Qi into the disciple's energetic field.

Even people who do not practice Medical Qigong naturally draw Earth Qi into their Lower Dantians as an unconscious action of survival and environmental adjustment. By practicing energetic cultivation with conscious intent, the amount of Earth Qi drawn into the body can be vastly increased.

According to the *Huiming Jing (Scripture of Wisdom and Life,* when Qi (Vital Breath) stirs within the Lower Dantian, its magical "seed" comes into being (i.e., the Yuan Jing is energetically activated).

This special area, harbors the "seed of truth," and is the sacred altar upon which consciousness and life are created. This special area is sometimes called the Dragon's Palace at the Bottom of the Sea."

THE LOWER DANTIAN AND SHEN

Given its Yin nature and close proximity to the Earth, the Lower Dantian itself is considered a center of consciousness. This type of consciousness is more physical and kinesthetic in nature, than the intuitive type of consciousness experienced within the Middle or Upper Dantians.

Additionally, each of the Three Dantians are subject to the energetic influences of both the body's Hun (Ethereal Soul) and Po (Corporeal Soul), which in turn are subject to specific patterns of influence, described as follows:

- **Influence of the Corporeal Soul (Po):** The body's Jing is connected with the Seven Corporeal Souls, which are collectively known as the Po. The Po control our survival instinct and the subconscious physical reflexes associated with survival. For this reason, Daoist disciples and many martial artists spend hours cultivating their Lower Dantian's Qi, in order to create the integration of Jing, Qi, and Shen needed for the split-second clarity of focus required in life-and-death struggles.

- **Influence of the Ethereal Soul (Hun):** The Lower Dantian is the residence of the Lower Hun, called Yu Jing ("Hidden Essence"). This particular Hun is associated with the Earth, and is responsible for encouraging our spirit to appreciate and enjoy life. It also helps our spirit in expressing our gratitude for enjoying the simple pleasures of life.

THE LOWER DANTIAN AND KINESTHETIC AWARENESS

In addition to being the center of physical strength and the source of stamina, the Lower Dantian is also considered the "house" of physical (kinesthetic) feeling, communication and awareness. Kinesthesia is defined as "the sensory experiences mediated by nervous elements within the muscles, tendons and joints, and stimulated by bodily movements and tensions characterized by movement." It is this kinetic state of awareness that allows an individual to naturally feel the internal resonant vibrations occurring within the surrounding environment.

Kinesthetic communication is "the intuition of the physical body," and is stimulated by particular aspects of the subconscious mind. The subconscious mind picks up many signals from the environment that are not processed by the logical mind. Therefore, the subconscious mind may react to these signals with spontaneous body movements, or with subtle but powerful emotional responses sometimes referred to as "gut feelings."

Often, the feelings experienced in the Lower Dantian are very subtle. For this reason, Medical Qigong Doctors are trained to establish a heightened degree of awareness of their own body, and are thus able to pick up subtle variations and energetic shifts occurring within themselves and others.

When a Medical Qigong Doctor collects energy in his Lower Dantian, an increased awareness and sensitivity naturally occurs. Cultivating this ability requires the doctor to pay attention to the subtle sensations occurring within his physical body. A high level of awareness surrounding the physical body and the surrounding environment is required in order to maximize kinesthetic communication. When physical awareness is increased, feeling and kinesthetic body movements happen naturally. These subtle senses allow the Medical Qigong Doctor to feel, smell, or hear energetic phenomena as they are released from a patient's physical body.

THE LOWER DANTIAN AND SCIENCE

The Lower Dantian's "Brain," is known in Western terms as the enteric (intestinal) nervous system. According to research conducted by Dr. Michael Gershon, a professor of anatomy and cellular biology at Columbia Presbyterian Medical Center in New York, the Lower Dantian sends and receives impulses, records experiences, and responds to emotions. Its nerve cells are bathed in and influenced by the same type of neurotransmitters that exist in the Brain.

The entire nervous system mirrors the body's central nervous system and is a network of 100 million neurons (more neurons than the spinal cord), neurotransmitters, and proteins that can act independently of the body's Brain and can send messages, learn, remember, and produce feelings.

Dr. Gershon explains that major neurotransmitters like serotonin, dopamine, glutamine, norepinephrine, nitric oxide, enkephalins (one type of natural opiate), and benzodiazepines (psychoactive chemicals that relieve anxiety) are active within the neural system of the lower abdominal area. The lower abdomen also has two dozen small Brain proteins called neuropeptides. Dr. Gershon's research provides modern scientific verification of what Eastern wisdom has taught for millennia; that centers of consciousness exist at places in the body apart from the organ of the Brain. The abdomen or Lower Dantian, is one of these major centers of awareness.

LOWER DANTIAN ANATOMICAL LOCATION

The Lower Dantian is located under (behind) the umbilicus, inside the lower abdomen. Its boundaries form a downward pointing triangle, and are defined by the three special areas:

1. **The Bottom Gate of the Lower Dantian (Weiluguan - The Valley Gate of the Tail):** The lowest point of the Lower Dantian extends to the Huiyin (Meeting of the Yin CV-1) point at the lower perineum (Figure 5.64), and is located midway between the genitals ("Anterior Yin" or "Qianyin") and anus ("Posterior Yin" or "Houyin"). This special area is traditionally known for gathering and absorbing the Earth (Yin) Qi into the body and Lower Dantian area, via the three Yin leg channels (Liver, Spleen, and Kidney).

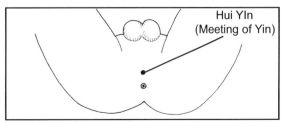

Figure 5.64. The Bottom Gate of the Lower Dantian

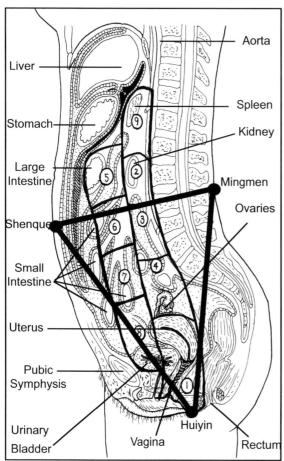

Figure 5.65. The Nine Chambers of the Lower Dantian are shown here in the female body. (Inspired by Dr. Frank H. Netter.)

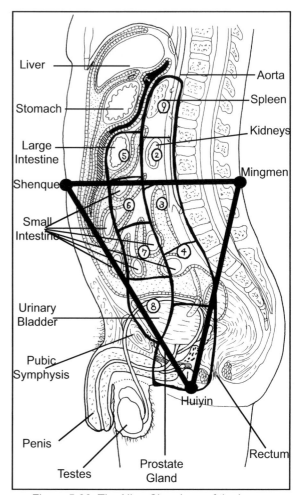

Figure 5.66. The Nine Chambers of the Lower Dantian are shown here in the male body. (Inspired by Dr. Frank H. Netter.)

The Valley Gate of the Tail is also sometimes known in esoteric Daoist Alchemy as the Dragon Well, and is the energetic collection point for the Kidney's Water Element Qi. This special area is also the intersecting point for the Governing, Conception, and Thrusting Vessels, and is the Lower Gate of the Taiji Pole sometimes known as the Bottom Gate of the Lower Chakra Center.

2. **The Front Gate of the Lower Dantian (Shen Que - Spirit's Watch Tower):** The front area of the Lower Dantian is located posterior to the Shenque CV-8 point at the navel (Figure 5.65 and (Figure 5.66). The name refers to the place where the mother's Qi and Shen enter the embryo during fetal development via the umbilical cord. After the umbilical cord is cut, the cord extending out of the navel resembles a tower over the abdomen of the newborn, hence its name "Spirit Watch Tower." The navel is sometimes known as the Front Gate of the Lower Dantian, and Door of Life (Shengmen).

According to secret Daoist teaching, the navel (Shenque CV-8 point) is the Gate of Life that leads straight into the Lower Dantian, and is actually located 2.5 inches "behind" (or deep) into the umbilical area. One of my teachers explained that there has always been a misunderstanding surrounding this particular teaching.

CHAPTER 5: THE TAIJI POLE, CHAKRAS, AND THREE DANTIANS

Figure 5.67. The 28 Star Constellations Spin around the center of the Celestial Pole Star

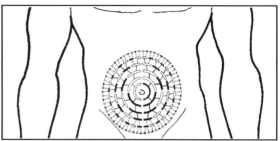

Figure 5.68. The ever-changing energetic form of the 64 Hexagrams of the Yi-Jing

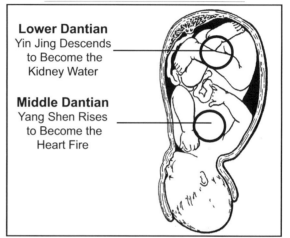

Lower Dantian
Yin Jing Descends to Become the Kidney Water

Middle Dantian
Yang Shen Rises to Become the Heart Fire

Figure 5.69. Once the umbilical cord is cut, the energy of Heaven and Earth separate

In ancient China, it was believed that the twisting of the umbilical cord and the internal coiling of the intestines around it followed the same pattern of the energetic vortex known as the "Taizhong" (Supreme Center). The Taizhong is traditionally known as the body's center core Taiji Pole, and spirals between Heaven (the fetus' head) and Earth (the fetus' lower abdomen). It was through the energetic movement of the Taizhong that all things polarized (becoming either Yin or Yang), and received their energetic form. It was also believed that the Heavenly center of this energetic vortex (within the center of the umbilicus) was equal to the Celestial Pole Star, around which the constellations continually spin (Figure 5.67). Therefore, the area of the umbilicus was sometimes called "Tianshu," the "Pivot of Heaven," or the "Capital of the Spirit."

In ancient Chinese Cosmology, Yin and Yang and the three realms of spirit, energy and matter polarize from the undifferentiated energetic center of the Wuji. As this energetic center begins to polarize, a spinning vortex is created, setting the pattern that forms the energetic template for all things. In ancient Daoism, this energetic interaction sets the foundation for the development of the Prenatal and Postnatal Bagua, the original Eight Trigram formations of the Yi-Jing (Figure 5.68). Due to this internal connection, the area of the navel is considered to be the lair of the Qi and Shen, as energetically both Qi and Shen continually spin and manifest from the umbilical area the same way that the various star constellations spin around the Celestial Pole Star.

The ancient Daoists considered the umbilical area the "root of preserving life," because the energetic treasure of its Qi and Shen flowed inward to connect with all of the internal organs and outward to connect with Heaven and Earth. An ancient Daoist saying states, "When the umbilicus opens, the body's internal organs can interact with the womb of Heaven and Earth."

Once the umbilical cord is cut, Heaven and Earth separate; and the fetus' Yin (Earth: Water Qi) and Yang (Heaven: Fire Qi) polarities divide. The Heavenly Yang Shen rises upward into the chest and Middle Dantian area and becomes the Fire of the Heart; the Earthly Yin Jing descends into the lower abdomen and Lower Dantian area and becomes the Water of the Kidneys (Figure 5.69).

3. **The Back Gate of the Lower Dantian (Mingmen - Gate of Life):** Directly across from the navel, located at the back of the Lower Dantian, is the Mingmen (GV-4 point), positioned inferior to the second lumbar vertebra (Figure 5.70). The Mingmen is located in-between the Kidneys, and in ancient times it was also called by many names, such as: the "Gate of Destiny," the "Door of Fate," the "Golden Portal," the "Mysterious Pass," the "Palace of Essence," the "Mystical Pass," the "Dark Gate," the "Kidney Hall" and the "Door of All Hidden Mysteries."

The ancient Daoists believed that all of creation passed through this special gate, as it emerged from the Eternal Dao to form the individual's Taiji Pole upon conception. The ancient Daoists also believed that one of the spiritual functions of the Mingmen was the ability to empower the disciple with the magical skill of "energetic interpenetration." This special magical ability was said to allow the Daoist disciple to move in-between and within the energetic forms of Yin and Yang, Jing and Shen, as well as the inner aspects of the Pre and Post-Heavenly Realms.

In ancient China, the concept of an individual's Virtue (De) and his Life/Destiny (Ming) were believed to be closely connected. It was also believed that an individual's Life/Destiny was specifically given to him by Heaven at the time of his birth, and that this special knowledge was stored away in the area of his Mingmen Fire, located in-between the Kidneys.

Although the subtle impulses emanating from an individual's Ming are generally hidden from his conscious mind, through special meditations, a deeper realm of understanding of these subtle impulses can be intuitively discovered and accessed. Once awakened, the radiant energy of an individual's Ming becomes the spark of life and the dynamic potential existing behind all of his spiritual thoughts and virtuous actions. Therefore, once activated, it was up to the disciple to consistently act in accordance with his Ming throughout his life.

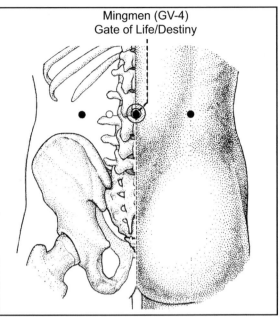

Figure 5.70. The Back Gate of the Lower Dantian

This action is based on the disciple's conscious use of his Intention (Yi). It is through the intention to remain congruent with the "Will and Intent of Heaven" (Zhi Yi Tian) that gives an individual Virtue (De). It is through the development of this Virtue that an individual establishes a healthy relationship with the Dao, Heaven, and the Spirit World.

It is important to note, that the Mingmen provides one third of the body's "True Fire." It is therefore considered to be the root of the body's Yuan Qi (Original Breath/Energy), and the radiant quality of its spiritual energy is what determines the quality of an individual's life and death in the physical realm.

The Mingmen also supplies the heat for the Triple Burners, and is responsible for stabilizing the energy of the Kidneys and the Lower Dantian.

4. **The Center of the Lower Dantian:** The center or middle of the Dantian refers to its position located three inches behind the navel, between the navel, Kidneys, and Mingmen areas (Figure 5.71). Its location corresponds to the point of intersection between the Thrusting Vessels and the Belt Vessel.

Several Daoist schools in China differ in their opinions as to where the center of the Lower Dantian is located. Some schools teach that the center of the Lower Dantian is affected by the different anatomical locations of the male and female reproductive organs. When referring to Daoist alchemical teachings about the energetic location of the Lower Dantian, one ancient text records the following:

"There are Seven Openings [1]
which connect to the Outer-Kidneys. [2]
The Outer-Kidneys can leak
spiritual essence from the penis.

Its orifice is known as the
"Stove of Waning Moon" ("Yan Yuelu"),
and is located in-between
the navel and the two Kidneys.

Lower than the navel,
near the beginning of the Ren Mai
(Conception Vessel),
are Nine Openings [3].

At the "Earth Prison," [4]
we arrive at "Feng." [5]
This area is known as the Qihai (Sea of Qi).

A little lower from this area,
1 cun and 3 fen, is the Jade Pool.
This area is also known
as the Lower Dantian.
It is the place of the Jing (Essence)
of the Zang Organs,
and the place of the collected herb.

At the left of the Jade Pool,
there is an area known as
the "Hall of Brightness" (or "Hall of Light").

At the right of the Jade Pool,
there is an area known as the
"Chamber of the Cave" (Grotto Chamber).

Within the Jade Pool,
there is also an opening,
one cun and two fen in diameter.
There are also two openings
connecting to the Inner-Kidneys.

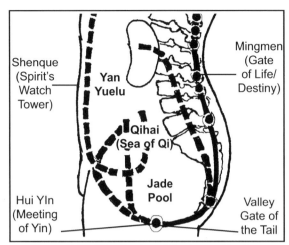

Figure 5.71. The Center of the Lower Dantian

In the middle of the Kidneys,
there is an opening which connects to the
"Weiluguan." ("Valley Gate of the Tail")

Because of this connection,
the Weiluguan can open
to the palaces of both Kidneys;
and can travel further down the body,
below the knees,
to the "Sanli" Cavity (St-36 point),
and the "Yongquan" Cavity (Kid-1 point)."

[(1) Notes: The locations of the Seven Openings will vary depending on the specific teachings being imparted to the disciple (e.g., the eyes, ears, nose and mouth for energetic cultivation). However, in ancient Daoist Alchemy, sometimes the energetic influence of the Mingtang ("Hall of Light" - located behind the Third Eye) was grouped together with the nose, occiput, throat, Heart, spinal column, and coccyx and collectively known as the "Seven Openings" or "Seven Gates" (Qimen)]

[(2) The Outer-Kidneys are the testicles]

[(3) The previously mentioned Seven Openings, plus the penis and anus]

[(4) The "Earth Prison" is commonly referred to as the Underworld (the Realm of the Po); and in this context also refers to the area of the lower perineum]

[(5) Because of the afore mentioned analogy to the "Earth Prison," the word "Feng" in this context refers to "Fengdu," the Underworld city of the dead]

THE 9 CHAMBERS OF THE LOWER DANTIAN

The human body is viewed as a microcosmic replica of Heaven. Just as Heaven is said to be divided into nine different levels, each containing various palaces, the human body is also said to contain various palaces and chambers. The seven stars of the Big Dipper constellation, its Extra Stars, and the Celestial Pole Star (North Star) are said to all energetically correspond to the Nine Chambers located within each of the Three Dantians.

The functional aspects of the body's psyche were described by the ancient Daoists as powerful "spirits" who lived within the various Chambers of the Three Dantians. These powerful "spirits" linked the body's energetic channels and vital internal organs into an organic harmony of life-force energy. The ancient Daoists also believed that as each Dantian became energized, it would initiate specific reactions within the body's energetic system. These various reactions would traditionally manifest certain energetic and spiritual experiences, occurring within the disciple's Three Bodies.

According to ancient Daoist teachings, each of the Nine Chambers is several inches in diameter and is numbered in accordance with its energetic stimulation (Figure 5.72). Traditionally, the vertical abdominal set of Lower Dantian chambers corresponds to many cavities of the body's internal viscera. In Daoist Alchemy, the Nine Chambers of the Lower Dantian are named as follows:

1. **The Palace of Jade:** Also known as the Jade Stem (male) or Jade Cave (female)
2. **The Official Health Monitor:** Kidneys
3. **The Minister of the Orchard Terrace**
4. **The Chamber of Moving Pearls**
5. **The Minister of House Cleaning:** Large Intestine
6. **The Palace of Mystical Spirits:** Small Intestine
7. **The Chamber of Mysterious Elixir**
8. **The Spirit of the Jade Court:** Urinary Bladder
9. **The Spirit of the Yellow Court:** Spleen

TRAINING OF THE LOWER DANTIAN

When starting any type of energetic cultivation meditation, an individual will always begin by directing their mind and breath downward, into the area of their Lower Dantian. The purpose of

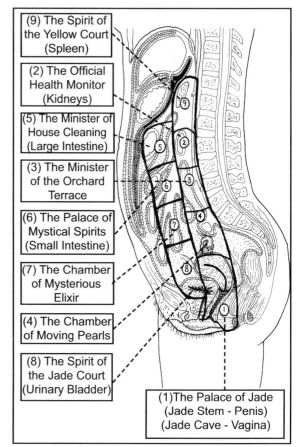

Figure 5.72. The Nine Chambers of the Lower Dantian in the female body.

this cultivation training, is to first gather the body's Yuan Qi (Original Energy) into the Lower Dantian in order to strengthen their Three Bodies. In Daoist Alchemy, this special action is sometimes called "Returning To The Source," and is traditionally taught in order to strengthen an individual's ability to energetically gather and root his body's Qi.

In beginning meditation practice, it is important to gather and balance the Yin and Yang energy contained within the Lower Dantian. In ancient China, the union of Yin and Yang energy within the Lower Dantian was called "Dragon and Tiger Swirling in the Winding River." When the Lower Dantian Qi has been transformed and the energized vital essence energetically "awakened," it always appears as a bright, white light, radiating its energy within the area of the disciple's Upper Dantian.

THE MIDDLE CINNABAR FIELD: (ZHONG DANTIAN)

The Middle Dantian collects Qi, and represents the body's internal reservoir for transforming mental and emotional energy (Figure 5.73). The Heart is the primary organ related to the Middle Dantian, and its secondary organ is the Lungs.

An important energetic process takes place within the Middle Dantian, transforming the Lower Dantian's fluid-like energy into a more refined steam-like energy. This refined energy is then transferred into the Upper Dantian for further energetic processing.

The Middle Dantian transforms Qi into Shen by bathing it with the Heart's Imperial Fire. This alchemical process is commonly called "Changing Qi into Shen," and refers to kinesthetic energy transforming into spiritual consciousness.

The Middle Dantian is connected to the second level of Weiqi (Protective Energy), which extends to about 3.5 feet away from the tissues. As the Middle Dantian fills with Qi, the various colors observed within an individual's middle Weiqi field change, becoming even more radiant and pronounced. The reason for this dramatic change in color is that the Middle Dantian is connected to the Five Agents (i.e., the Hun, Shen, Yi, Po, and Zhi), which in turn govern the Five Yin Organs (i.e., the Liver, Heart, Spleen, Lungs, and Kidneys) as well as the thoughts and emotions stemming from these organs. As an individual begins to experience various stresses and emotional releases, the energy resonating from the internal organ out into the second energetic field changes its color.

Impressions gathered from the Middle Dantian and Heart area are recorded and stored in every cell of the human body, and act as a sort of informational template for the soul. The Heart can literally perceive and react to the external world on its own. According to bio-scientific measurements, the Heart has five thousand times more electromagnetic power than the brain. Therefore, it is considered to be the body's primary generator and transmitter of life-force energy, constantly sending out patterns of energetically "encoded" information that regulates the body's internal organs, tissues, and cells.

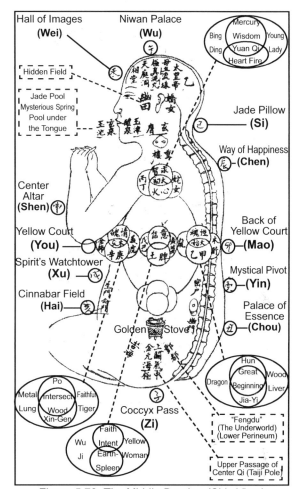

Figure 5.73. The Middle Dantian (Side View)

THE MIDDLE DANTIAN AND JING

The Heart is related to the Fire Element, and derives its Yang Fire from Kidney Yang. Modern research equates the function of the adrenal glands to the traditional function of Kidney Yang. A parallel can be observed in Western physiology, in which the adrenal glands help to regulate the pace of the heart. In order to keep the Heart Fire in balance, the Heart also needs Yin. Heart Yin is derived from Kidney Yin (Jing is one aspect of Kidney Yin).

The Heart governs the Blood. Blood is composed of Ying Qi ("Nutritive Energy" derived from food), Prenatal Kidney Jing (Original Essence), and from Jin and Ye (Body Fluids). Jing, particularly Postnatal Jing, is vital to the Heart's function of governing the Blood.

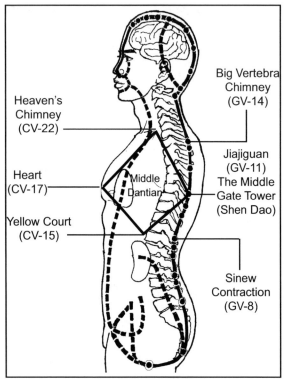

Figure 5.74. The Middle Dantian (Side View)

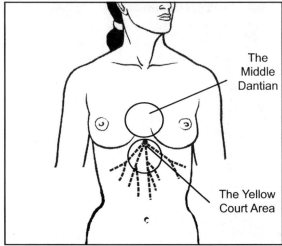

Figure 5.75. Women were encouraged to store their Qi in the Middle Dantian and Yellow Court Area

THE MIDDLE DANTIAN AND QI

Similar to the Lower Dantian, the Middle Dantian is also considered to be a Sea of Qi (Figure 5.74). The Qi of the Middle Dantian is called "Zong Qi," meaning "Ancestral Energy," "Gathering Energy," or "Essential Energy." The Zong Qi nourishes both the Heart and Lungs, controls the speech and the strength of the voice, and interacts with the Kidneys to aid in respiration. The Kidneys assist the Lungs in grasping, holding, and stabilizing the breath during inhalation.

Qi and Blood are closely related. In Traditional Chinese Medicine it is often said, "Qi is the Commander of Blood; Blood is the Mother of Qi." Qi gives the Heart and Blood Vessels the strength to circulate Blood. Qi also gives "life" to the Blood itself.

Blood on the other hand, houses the Qi and carries it to all the cells in the body. When one loses Blood, one also loses Qi. Therefore, Qi and Blood are considered to be inseparable.

The body's Qi is also inseparable from the Shen (Heart/Mind). Through the process of refining the Qi, the mind and spirit are both refined and purified. Therefore, in Daoist Alchemy, the Middle Dantian is considered to be the main focal point for the refinement of energy (Qi) into spirit (Heart/Mind).

WOMEN AND MIDDLE DANTIAN QI

In ancient Daoist teachings, the Middle Dantian was considered the primary location for women to focus on during meditation (the men were encouraged to focus on their Lower Dantian). The ancient Daoists believed that it was harmful for a woman to focus on her Lower Dantian for extended periods of time, especially during menses.

In *The Treatise of Spiritual Alchemy for Women*, the Lower Dantian was considered to be an area for the woman to focus on only in the beginning stages of her practice. For example, after completing the fusion of the Microcosmic and Macrocosmic Orbit meditations, a woman would then focus her attention on the Middle Dantian and Yellow Court area, located at the center of her sternum (Figure 5.75). As the collected energy began to overflow, it would move into her breasts, causing her nipples to become erect, and opening "one hundred energy channels within her body."

The Middle Dantian and Shen

The Middle Dantian houses the Shen (Spirit), defined as being the individual's thoughts and feelings, or "Mind/Heart," located within the energetic structure of the Heart organ. The Heart is also able to control all of the functions of the thoughts and emotions that are attributed to the Five Yin Organs (i.e., Liver, Heart, Spleen, Lungs, and Kidneys). Because of this important energetic function, the Heart is often referred to as the "Heavenly Emperor," who is housed in the Middle Dantian.

The Middle Dantian is also the residence of the Middle Hun named "Shang Ling" or "Pleasant Soul." Shang Ling is situated in the Heart and is considered to be the soul that influences the individual's positive concerns for the well-being of others. The Middle Hun is also associated with the spiritual states of the Original Five Virtues, which produces our desires to be involved in positive social activities and responsibilities.

Throughout the world, people relate the Heart to emotions and feelings. Emotions and feelings are an important aspect of the spirit, therefore all emotions have an effect on the Shen.

The ancient Chinese noted that each individual has two Shen or "Spiritual Natures." These two Heart/Minds are known as the Yuan Shen (Original Heart/Mind) and the Shen Zhi (Acquired Heart/Mind). In Daoist Alchemy, a distinction is continually made between the cultivation and empowering of both, described as follows:

- **The Yuan Shen (Original Mind):** This virtuous spiritual Mind/Heart is traditionally defined as the original divine state that existed before conception. It is energetically influenced by the Hun, and manifests as the dominating Virtues of the Heart, creating a sense of Compassion, Inner-Peace, Truthfulness, Integrity, and Justice. The Hun control the smooth flow of Qi throughout the body and are nourished by the Five Virtues. These Five Virtues give peace and clarity to the Heart, and allow the higher qualities of the Yuan Shen to override the selfish impulses of the Shen Zhi and the Po (Corporeal Soul).

- **The Shen Zhi (Acquired Mind):** These are the emotional traits and survival influences of the acquired personality. Traditionally observed as the "Ren Xin" ("Man Heart"), this state of ego expression is created after birth.

All emotions fall under the influence of the Po (the Seven Corporeal Souls), who are concerned with the body's survival. When the Po dominate the Heart, their overexaggerated self-concern gives rise to a chronic state of fear, sadness, worry, anger, and defensive arrogance. These negative emotions are sometimes called "the Five Thieves," because the chronic states of their negative influence drains the body's life-force.

The Middle Dantian and Empathic Awareness

The Middle Dantian is also considered the "house" of emotional (empathic) feeling, communication, and awareness. Emotional communication is experienced as empathy within the Heart. This empathy is the means by which the Medical Qigong Doctor will most frequently become aware of the hidden emotional components of a patient's energetic blocks and imbalances.

Empathic communication is felt as an emotion and originates in the Heart and Middle Dantian area. When Medical Qigong Doctors focus on the Middle Dantian area, a line of communication is created with their higher self. We are all born with this ability, but as we grow older we tend to override this type of emotional communication with an exaggerated dependence on the logical mind. Through shock, disappointment, denial, and lack of use, impressions slowly diminish, eventually causing us to lose this natural empathic ability of communication.

We generally disconnect from this higher perception as a response to the negative and mixed messages received from our parents and from society. The way to reconnect with the intuitive self is to look inward and become one with the Original Heart/Mind (Yuan Shen) that is connected to the Divine.

THE MIDDLE DANTIAN AND SCIENCE

An important relationship between the Middle Dantian and Shen is found in the Heart's role of governing the Blood. The ancient Daoists state that the Shen (Heart/Mind) resides within the Blood, and pervades the body through Blood circulation. This relationship between Blood and Shen is one reason why anemic patients are often restless and suffer from insomnia. Many forms of spiritual unrest can be treated through nourishing the Heart Blood.

According to Dr. Candace Pert's information on neurotransmitters (stated in *Psychoneuro Immunology*), the brain and white blood cells both contain the same neurotransmitters and biochemical constituents that are prerequisites for the existence of consciousness awareness. The same neurotransmitters and biochemical constituents that are linked to consciousness are synthesized and created by the white blood cells. This correspondence indicates that not only do the brain and abdomen have their own consciousness and nervous systems, but the Blood does as well.

This further implies that consciousness is possible anywhere in the body, substantiating the ancient Chinese understanding that consciousness is pervasive throughout the body via the Shen, which resides in the Blood. According to research conducted by Dr. Paul Pearsall, the history and impressions of the Heart are recorded and stored in every cell of the human body as a sort of informational template of the soul. The Heart can literally perceive and react to the external world on its own.

According to bioscientific measurements, the Heart has five thousand times more electromagnetic power than the brain. It is considered to be the body's primary generator and transmitter of life-force energy, constantly sending out patterns of energetically "encoded" information that regulates the organs, tissues and cells. It beats approximately one hundred thousand times a day and forty million times a year. It propels more than two gallons of Blood per minute and transports about one hundred gallons of Blood per hour throughout the vascular system.

Recent discoveries from research conducted in the new field of neurocardiology (the study of the heart as a neurological, endocrine and immune organ) include the following:

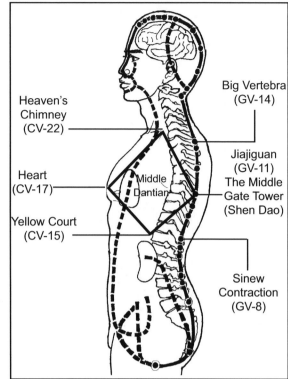

Figure 5.76. The Middle Dantian (Side View)

- Neurotransmitters found in the brain have also been identified within the heart.
- Through hormones, neurotransmitters and "quantum energies" (Qi), the heart exerts as much control over the brain as the brain exerts over the heart.
- The heart requires constant environmental updates from the brain in order to organize the body's bioenergetic fields.
- The heart produces a neurohormone that communicates with the brain and immune system, influencing the thalamus, hypothalamus, pineal, and pituitary glands.

MIDDLE DANTIAN ANATOMICAL LOCATION

The Middle Dantian, having four points, is shaped like a tetrahedron: the top points toward the Upper Dantian and the Heavens, the bottom points toward the Lower Dantian and the Earth, and the sides point toward the front and back. These areas are described as follows (Figure 5.76):

CHAPTER 5: THE TAIJI POLE, CHAKRAS, AND THREE DANTIANS

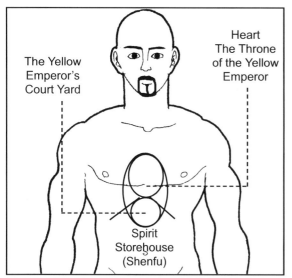

Figure 5.77. The Middle Dantian & Yellow Court Area

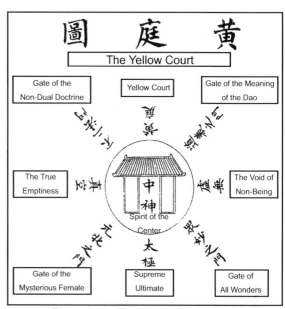

Figure 5.78. The Yellow Court Graph From Liu Yiming's *Huangting Jing Jie* (*Explanation of the Scripture of the Yellow Court*)

1. **The Bottom-Front of the Middle Dantian (Huangting - The Yellow Court):** The front lower point of the Middle Dantian is called the "Yellow Court," also known as the "Golden Palace Garden" and the "Earth Central Cauldron" (Figure 5.77). The Yellow Court is located at the "Spirit Storehouse" (Shenfu) CV-15 point on the midline of the abdomen, just below the xiphoid bone on the sternum (below the "Turtledove Tail").

In Daoist Alchemy, the Yellow Court is the place where Qi (Energy) transforms into Shen (Heart/Mind). This special area is also where the Postnatal Qi flows downward through the Stomach Channels, and the Prenatal Qi flows upward through the Kidney Channels. They converge with the Thrusting Vessels in order to balance the Yang Fire and Yin Water polarities of the Heart and Kidneys.

According to the *Huangdi Neijing Ling Shu* (*The Yellow Emperor's Inner Canon, Magical Pivot*), this special area is the Yuan ("Original") point of the Five Yin Organs, affecting each of the organs Yuan Qi.

The Yellow Court nourishes the Yin Organs, regulates the Heart, and calms the Shen (Heart/Mind). This special area is also the connecting point for the Conception Vessel, the front "Mu" ("Alarm") point of the sex organs, and is the Front Gate of the Third Internal Chakra.

The reason why the Yellow Court (Huangting) is sometimes called the "Spirit Storehouse," is because it energetically "reflects" the various emotions that have been experienced and stored from the Heart (manifesting as "long-term" memories).

In ancient China, the Heart was often referred to as the "Yellow Emperor." The responsibility of the "Heart Protector" (i.e., the Pericardium, or Emperor's "Minister of Council") was to store away the emotional experiences that the Heart was not yet ready to process. These emotions were placed into the Emperor's Courtyard (Figure 5.78), and kept outside the realm of the Heart, until the "Emperor" was ready to receive and/or process the information and experience.

To the ancient Daoists, the transformation of Qi into Shen occurring in the Yellow Court was considered the pivotal stage in Inner Alchemical Training, where the energetic formation of the Golden Embryo takes place.

299

Therefore, the exact location of the Yellow Court was traditionally kept secret from the uninitiated. It was believed that because of the overlap of energies existing between the Heart and Spleen, only a true Daoist initiate would be able to clearly differentiate the exact location of the Yellow Court.

Energetically, the Yellow Court is believed to be a microcosmic replica of the universal Dao, as Yin and Yang energies continually emerge from and return to it. Therefore reuniting the Kan (Yin: Water) and Li (Yang: Fire) of the Five Yin Organs within the secret area of the Yellow Court, reconnected the disciple with the energies of both the Prenatal and Postnatal Heavenly Realms. This energetic reversal enabled the disciple's Shen to "come and go" between the various physical and spiritual realms (Figure 5.79)."

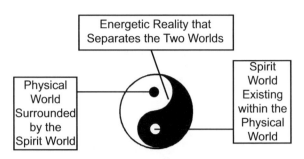

Figure 5.79. In ancient Daoist alchemy, the two circles within the Yin and Yang symbol represented the mysterious existence to the Spirit World existing within the Physical World, as well as the Physical World surrounded by the Spirit World. The center dividing line represented the Energetic World, considered the bridge that separated the two worlds.

2. **The Bottom-Back of the Middle Dantian (Jinsuo - Sinew Contraction):** The back lower point of the Middle Dantian is located at the Jinsuo (Sinew Contraction) GV-8 point (Figure 5.80). Jinsuo refers to this areas relationship to the Liver, and is commonly used to calm the Shen (Heart/Mind). This area is sometimes known as the Back Gate of the Yellow Court.

   Crossing the center of the torso, the horizontal axis located between the front and back gates of the Yellow Court also intersect with the vertical axis of the great vortex of the body's Taiji Pole, which is responsible for connecting the Qi of Heaven and Earth as it flows through the body.

3. **The Center-Front of the Middle Dantian (Shanzhong - Chest Center):** The center front point of the Middle Dantian is located at the Shanzhong (Chest Center) CV-17 point, on the middle of the sternum, at the level of the fourth intercostal space. In Daoist Alchemy, this area is sometimes called the "Central Altar" and the "Place of Worship." It is where the Shen resides, and is sometimes known as the Front Gate of the Fourth Chakra.

4. **The Center-Back of the Middle Dantian (Jiajiguan - Squeeze the Spine Gate):** The center back point of the Middle Dantian is located two inches up from the shoulder blades at the Shendao (Spirit Path) GV-11 point, at the hollow between the fifth and sixth thoracic vertebrae. In Daoist Alchemy, this point is traditionally known as the Jiajiguan (Squeeze the Spine Gate), and is viewed as the "Middle Gate Tower." It is commonly used for obtaining direct access into the thoughts and emotions of an individual's Shen, and is especially used when the front of the body and Heart area is energetically armored. It is also the access point to an individual's "De" (Moral Virtues), and is associated with the Eternal Soul (Shen Xian) and its spiritual connection to the Dao (Divine). This special area is sometimes known as the Back Gate of the Fourth Chakra.

5. **The Upper-Front of the Middle Dantian (Tiantu - Heaven's Chimney):** The upper front point of the Middle Dantian is located at the Tiantu CV-22 point, at the base of the throat. The name refers to the cavity at the base of the throat that "pools" escaped Heaven Qi from the Lungs. It is the intersection point of the body's Six Yin Channels (Liver, Heart, Spleen, Lungs, Pericardium and Kidneys) and Conception Vessel. For this reason, it is considered an influential point in accessing the body's Sea of Yin Qi. This area

is sometimes known as the Front Gate of the Fifth Chakra.

6. **The Upper-Back of the Middle Dantian (Dazhui - Big Vertebra):** The upper back point is located on the Dazhui (Big Vertebra) GV-14 point. The point's name refers to its location above the relatively large first thoracic vertebra and below the much smaller seventh cervical vertebra. It is the intersection point of the body's Six Yang Channels (Gall Bladder, Small Intestine, Stomach, Large Intestine, Triple Burners and Urinary Bladder) and Governing Vessel. Therefore, it is considered an influential point on the body's Sea of Yang Qi. This area is also known as the Back Gate of the Fifth Chakra.

7. **The Center of the Middle Dantian:** The center of the Middle Dantian is located in the right atrium of the Heart, centered between the sinoatrial node (SA node) and the atrioventricular node (AV node). The center of the Heart is considered to be the "Seat of the Soul," and the "throne of all emotions."

THE 9 CHAMBERS OF THE MIDDLE DANTIAN

The Nine Chambers of the Middle Dantian (Figure 5.80) originate around the atria and ventricles of the Heart, particularly the pericardial and pleural cavities. The Middle Dantian regulates the body's Heart-Mind connection. The Heart-Mind connection includes the all pervasive consciousness of the entire body. This connection determines the flow of Yuan Qi (Original Energy) into the various Yin and Yang aspects of both the structure and function of the body, mind, and emotions. The functions within the psyche are controlled by the interaction of the body's "Prenatal Wujingshen" or "Original Five Essence Spirits" (i.e., the Hun, Po, Zhi, Yi, and Shen).

The energy of the Middle Dantian is also associated with the transforming and transporting energies of the Spleen and Stomach.

In Daoist Alchemy, the Nine Chambers of the Middle Dantian are named as follows:

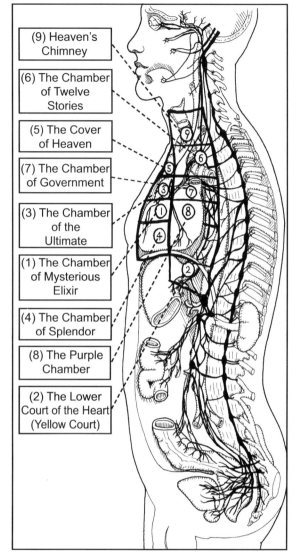

Figure 5.80. The Nine Chambers of the Middle Dantian are identical for men and women.

1. The Chamber of Mysterious Elixir
2. The Lower Court of the Heart
3. The Chamber of the Ultimate
4. The Chamber of Splendor
5. The Cover of Heaven
6. The Chamber of Twelve Stories
7. The Chamber of Government
8. The Purple Chamber
9. Heaven's Chimney

TRAINING OF THE MIDDLE DANTIAN

In Daoist Alchemy, disciples are encouraged to focus their Shen (Heart/Mind) and Qi (breath and energy) onto their Middle Dantian, in order to regulate the energetic functions of their Heart. The following techniques are but a few examples of using the Qi and Shen techniques in order to harmonize the Middle Dantian area:

- **Deficient Conditions:** Techniques that are traditionally used for treating deficient conditions in the Heart and Middle Dantian area, require an individual to inhale and absorb various colored light into the weakened tissues.

    The Middle Dantian's energy field is then regulated (balanced) by using special sounds (spoken incantations) that calm the individual's mind, and soothe their troubled spirit.

- **Excess Conditions:** For treating excess conditions, the disciples are instructed to lead and purge the Excess Qi away from the Heart and Middle Dantian area, releasing it out the body's extremities via sound. The purpose of this special training is to release the toxic Excess Qi that has become energetically stagnant within the disciple's Heart and Yellow Court area.

In Medical Qigong training, all students are traditionally taught how to focus and direct various healing sounds through their Middle Dantian, in order to regulate their Heart and release their own suppressed toxic emotional Qi. Only after sufficiently developing and regulating the energetic fields of their own Middle Dantian, would a Medical Qigong Doctor have the maturity and sensitivity to correctly diagnose and assist others in healing their toxic emotional patterns.

In the clinic, Medical Qigong Doctors strive to gather and balance the Yin and Yang energies flowing within their patient's Middle Dantian. In ancient China, this special union of Yin and Yang energy was called, "The Sun and Moon reflecting on each other in the Yellow Palace." The image of the Yellow Palace was used because the ancient Daoists believed that the "Spirit of Man," who stands between Heaven and Earth as a "mediator spirit," always appears in a Golden Yellow energetic light, and resides within the disciple's Middle Dantian area.

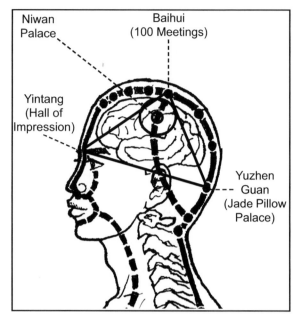

Figure 5.81. The Upper Dantian (Side View)

THE UPPER CINNABAR FIELD: (SHANG DANTIAN)

The Upper Dantian (Figure 5.81), is housed within the brain and is considered to be the root of spiritual (intuitive) communication, awareness, and perception. In Chinese Energetic Medicine, the Brain also controls memory, concentration, sight, hearing, touch, taste, and smell. All of these unique forms of intuitive and sensory awarenesses stay in close communication with the Heart and Shen. Therefore, when the energetic field of the Upper Dantian begins to fill with Qi, the individual's spiritual intuitions and psychic perceptions naturally increase.

The Upper Dantian is also connected to the third field of Weiqi, circulating several yards outside the body. This third external spiritual field, interacts and communicates with the second and first Weiqi field, creating a powerful protective field of awareness for the body (Figure 5.82).

In ancient Daoist Alchemy, the Upper Dantian is the collection point for the Qi of Heaven, and represents the spiritual aspect of Man, and his connection to the Divine. Therefore, the Heaven Qi that is transformed within the Upper Dantian has a radiant, ethereal, vapor-like quality.

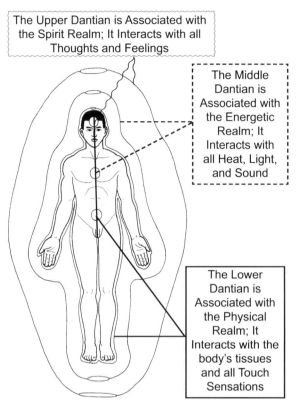

Figure 5.82. The Three Dantians and Their Relationship to the Three External Weiqi Fields

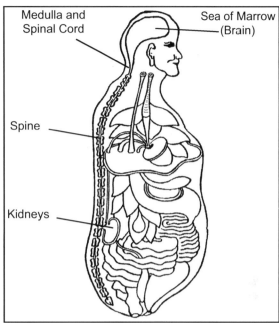

Figure 5.83. The Ancient Daoists "Map" of the Internal Organs - from the "Chart of Inner Lights"

The Upper Dantian and Jing

The Jing (Essence) and Qi (Breath/Energy) form the energetic foundation for the body's Shen (Heart/Mind). In China, the term Shen is nearly always used with the understanding of the close relationship between the mind and spirit, even in the modern medical context. For example, the Chinese term "Jing-Shen" traditionally refers to the "Mind or Consciousness" (although Jing-Shen may sometimes be used to refer to an individual's "Vigor, Vitality, or Drive"). In China, doctors of Western Medicine and Traditional Chinese Medicine both use the term Jing-Shen "Bing" ("Illness") in order to refer to all types of Mental Illness.

In the clinic, the term Prenatal Wu Jing Shen is used by Medical Qigong Doctors to describe the various spiritual energies of the body's Original Five Essence Spirits (i.e., the Hun, Po, Zhi, Yi, and Shen), stored within the Five Yin Organs. The ancient Daoists believed that these five spiritual states combine their congenital energetic essence in order to create the body's innate spiritual consciousness.

The Jing itself, is considered to be the basis for and ruler of the body's Marrow, which is defined in Chinese Medicine as a substance derived from the Kidneys which nourishes the Brain and spinal cord, and also forms the Bone Marrow. In certain ancient Qigong systems of Daoist Alchemy, the body's Jing is intentionally conserved and its energy is drawn upward from the Lower Dantian through the spine to nourish the Brain (Figure 5.83). Such nourishment benefits the mind and enhances spiritual consciousness.

The Brain is considered to be one of the Six Extraordinary Organs, and is called the "Sea of Marrow," because it is considered to be a form of Marrow. The Six Extraordinary Organs are hollow Yang organs that store Yin Jing. A Deficiency of Jing can lead to poor concentration, poor memory, dizziness, and absentmindedness. A Deficiency of Prenatal Jing is related to mental retardation and Attention Deficit Disorder (ADD) in children.

The Upper Dantian and Qi

The ancient Daoists believed that the head is the most Yang aspect of the body, since it is the part of the body closest to Heaven. Therefore, the Qi that operates within the Upper Dantian is considered to be Yang in nature.

The Upper Dantian is also the place where the Daoist disciple connects with the Yang Qi of Heaven. Heaven Qi is composed of the Qi from the celestial bodies: the Sun, Moon, Planets, and Star Constellations. In Daoist alchemical training, disciples consciously absorb Heavenly Qi through the body's "Upper Doorway," traditionally called the Baihui (One Hundred Meetings - GV-20) point.

Anatomically, the Upper Dantian is located in the center of the Brain, in an area that encompasses the pineal, pituitary, thalamus, and hypothalamus glands. The pineal gland (i.e., the Niwan Palace) and the hypothalamus have both been shown to be extremely sensitive to the influence of light, based on a developed sensitivity to the electromagnetic fields of the Earth.

Light, electricity, and magnetism are three forms of energy that the Brain is naturally conditioned to automatically recognize, receive, and respond to. These particular forms of energy stimulate the pineal, pituitary, thalamus, and hypothalamus glands, influencing an individual's mental and emotional state. Although the Brain is also influenced by heat and sound, it does not use or generate them to the degree that it generates light, electricity, and magnetism.

In Daoist Alchemy, we are taught that the Spleen and Kidneys send the transformed Clear Yang Qi (i.e., the internally cultivated pure, clean and radiant energy) upward into the Brain, in order to facilitate deeper spiritual clarity and stronger cognitive mental activity.

The Upper Dantian and Shen

Higher communications, experiences of intense bliss, and perceptions that transcend time and space are associated with the Upper Dantian. These experiences are particularly valuable to Medical Qigong Doctors, who are trained to use these heightened perceptions to diagnose illness. Of particular interest to Daoist alchemists is the opening of the center of the Upper Dantian, called the Niwan Palace (sometimes known as the "Crystal Chamber"). This special area is where psychic perceptions, intuitive awareness, and spiritual transformations outside the body all take place. The efficacy of intuitive cognition is well documented in the works of C. Norman Shealy and Caroline Myss, who use the term "Medical Intuitive" to describe this paranormal ability.

The Upper Dantian is also the place where the Yuan Shen (Original Spirit) dissolves into the infinite space of the Wuji, in order to merge with the radiant light of the eternal Dao. The spiritual awareness associated with this supernatural union is beyond description, as this level of divine unity surpasses conceptual thought and words.

Although the Upper Dantian is responsible for the manifestation of intuitive and psychic perceptions, it is necessary to balance the combined energetic properties of all three Dantians in order to establish a reliable foundation for genuine psychic perception. The steam-like quality of the energy within the Upper Dantian fuses with the radiant light that naturally resides within this energy center. As this combined energy disperses, it travels outward into the infinite space of the Wuji, returning back to the Divine. This interaction (of the refined "steam" and the indwelling light) is also responsible for what the ancient Daoists call "Receiving the Message," which describes the ability of connecting with an individual's subtle energy field to acquire hidden knowledge and images stored within their tissues.

While in a state of tranquility and inner peace, the Medical Qigong Doctor's Upper Dantian intuitively processes information from the environment and the celestial fields of the universe. This intuitive knowledge provides the Medical Qigong Doctor with a greater ability to explore his or her own conscious perceptions, as well as the subtle subconscious patterns contained within a patient's energy field. The ancients Daoists called this special intuitive ability "Knowing Without Knowing."

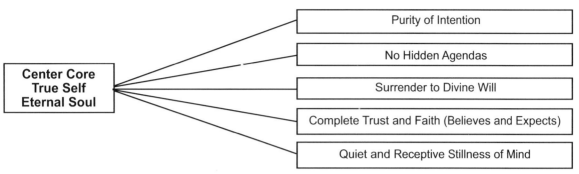

Figure 5.84. The Five Spiritual Principles Required for Open Communication With The Higher Self

THE UPPER DANTIAN AND INTUITIVE AWARENESS

As the Shen is developed and the Upper Dantian is energetically "opened," spiritual communications may reveal themselves in a flash of an image or as a sudden vision within the mind's eye (i.e. the "Heaven's Eye" or "Third Eye" area). These images and visions are sometimes very brief and abstract. Correctly interpreting these images takes practice, as the images streaming from the Yuan Shen (Original Heart/Mind) must be distinguished from the dreamlike wanderings of the subconscious mind, and cannot be interpreted easily by the logical mind.

Medical Qigong Doctors must be able to distinguish between true and false messages reflected through their visions. "True Visions" are received from the doctor's innate spiritual connection to the Dao, experienced through the infinite space of the Wuji; "False Visions" reflect messages from the subconscious mind. The ability to accurately separate these visions is another example of "Knowing Without Knowing."

Although intuitive communication from within is usually felt as a strong impulse, the Medical Qigong Doctor must learn to keep the logical mind from interfering by practicing quiescent meditations. These special meditations involve techniques of establishing and strengthening clear links of communication with the higher self. They should be practiced repeatedly until this connection becomes a natural, recurring phenomenon, replacing the otherwise endless drone of the ego and the logical mind. The more an individual practices quieting and stilling his logical mind and circumventing his ego, the easier it becomes to receive a clear communication from his higher self.

When the higher self initiates a communication, it does not demand or impose itself. If an individual consistently ignores these subtle internal communications from the higher self, they often begin to manifest externally in various messages conveyed through people, animals, and things. These external messages often supersede the individual's own realm of internal intuition.

FIVE SPIRITUAL PRINCIPLES

According to ancient Daoist teaching, five spiritual principles must be in place before communication lines between an individual and his higher self become fully open and operational. These five spiritual principles are described as follows (Figure 5.84):

1. The individual must have purity of intention
2. The individual must have no hidden agendas
3. The individual must surrender to Divine Will
4. The individual must have complete trust and faith in success (believes and expects)
5. The individual must have a quiet and receptive stillness of mind

The lines of communication with the higher self are severed by the logical mind through doubt, fear, and disbelief. Strong faith is required to open this line of communication. Faith requires no logical proof; if proof is needed, then doubts interfere and lead to failure. The logical mind cannot know absolute faith, as genuine faith must come from much deeper within one's True Self (i.e., their Yuan Shen). Any form of cynicism will lead to the stagnation of spiritual growth, for it strikes at the root of faith itself.

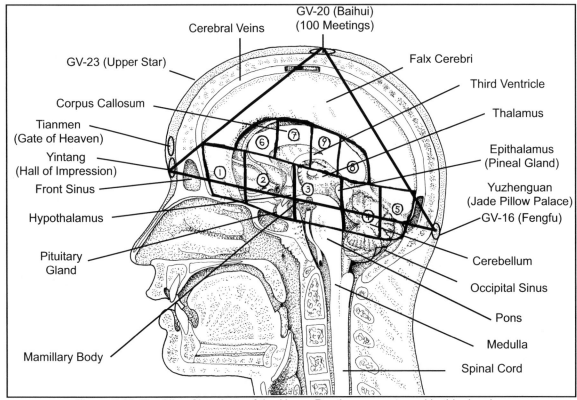

Figure 5.85. The Nine Chambers of the Upper Dantian are portrayed in this drawing. Each number encompasses the entire chamber.

Faith is not something that can be forced. Even after practicing Medical Qigong Therapy for many years, some doctors may still have to struggle with their own questions and doubts. Through deliberate, dedicated practice, however, the seed of faith can be firmly established, allowing faith to grow and blossom. The opposite of faith is a combination of doubt and fear. The suppression and denial of fear builds and armors the Acquired Personality (i.e., the individual's Shen Zhi or "Willful Heart/Mind"), leading to further pain through isolation and confusion. When an individual acknowledges and accepts their fear, he or she can then overcome any obstacle through faith.

THE UPPER DANTIAN AND SCIENCE

Modern research reveals that the Upper Dantian, in particular the Brain, may contain more cellular connections than there are stars in the Milky Way constellation. The Brain never truly falls completely asleep, and it is sustained by different levels of subconscious awareness. Energetically, the Brain is constantly active. It is in a state of perpetual readiness, designed to react, defend, or attack when it senses danger.

UPPER DANTIAN ANATOMICAL LOCATION

The Upper Dantian is centered in the head, approximately three inches posterior to the Yintang (Hall of Impression) point, located between the eyebrows (i.e., the base of the Third Eye). The specific geometric pattern of the Upper Dantian Gates, is shaped like an upright pyramid, facilitating the gathering of energy from Heaven (Figure 5.85). This special energetic reservoir houses radiant light, and is the entry and exit point of the Yuan Shen. The anatomical location of the Upper Dantian points are described as follows:

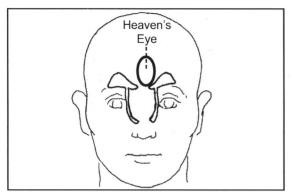

Figure 5.86. The Celestial Eye (Third Eye)

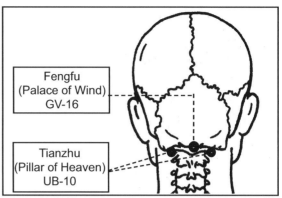

Figure 5.87. Sometimes known as the "Mouth of God," the Jade Pillow Palace is also used to treat seizures, seeing and hearing ghosts, mania, incessant wild talking, and "strange actions" due to spirit possession.

1. **The Front of the Upper Dantian (Yintang - Hall of Impression):** The front point of the Upper Dantian is called the Yintang (Hall of Impression), and is also known as the "Heaven's Eye," or the "Third Eye" (Figure 5.86). Historically, the name "Third Eye" refers to the ancient Buddhist tradition of placing a red mark or "seal" over the "Bright Hall," or "Entrance of the Spirit." The Third Eye is roughly the size and shape of a large almond. Its left and right lids draw apart simultaneously in order to observe the hidden things of the subtle spirit realm, or to illuminate its inner chamber with spiritual light.

   The ancient Daoist text, *Huang Ting Jing* (The Yellow Court Classics), written during the Jin Dynasty (265-420 A.D.), refers to the Yintang point as "the square inch field of the square foot house." The square foot house refers to the human face, the square inch field refers to the chamber of the Bright Hall. The Yintang point represents wisdom and enlightenment, and is sometimes known as the Front Gate of the Sixth Chakra.

2. **The Back of the Upper Dantian (Yuzhenguan - Jade Pillow Palace):** The back point of the Upper Dantian is traditionally called the "Upper Gate Tower," and is located below the external occipital protuberance, on the Fengfu GV-16 (Wind Palace) point. The Jade Pillow Palace is also energetically connected with the UB-10 (Heavenly Pillar) points, positioned on either side slightly below the GV-16 point. When energetically activated, the energy field created by the Jade Pillow Palace may be likened to an antenna receiving messages. It allows the Medical Qigong Doctor to regulate his or her state of consciousness and thereby tune-in to the various frequencies of consciousness existing within the universe.

The ancient Daoists taught that the two Celestial Pillar points (UB-10) that are located on each side of the Jade Pillow point, were also trance-medium channel points (Figure 5.87). In certain esoteric schools of Daoist Magic, these special points, sometimes known as the "Mouth of God," were considered the main areas through which a spirit entity could extend its Qi and Shen into an individual's physical body, and possess them. Therefore, this area was traditionally used in Daoist Magic Rituals for spirit communication (i.e. "Benign Possession" and "Channel Divination").

The Fengfu (GV-16) point is a Sea of Marrow point used to affect the flow of Qi and Blood to the Brain. It is also a "Window of Heaven" point (one of eleven points used for treating Shen Disturbances), as well as one of the "Thirteen Ghost Points" (used for treating Spirit Possession), identified by the famous Daoist physician Sun Simiao. Medical Qigong doctors have observed that individuals with a more prominent occipital protuberance tend to see auras more easily and develop psychic intuition faster. This area is sometimes known as the back gate of the Sixth Chakra.

3. **The Top of the Upper Dantian (Baihui - One Hundred Meetings):** The highest point of the Upper Dantian is located on the vertex of the crown, known as the Baihui point (GV-20). The Chinese name, "Baihui" (One Hundred Meetings) refers to the ancient understanding that a Daoist disciple could access and receive divine messages, spiritual insights, and clairvoyant intuitions through this special point.

The ancient Daoists understood that the Baihui was also one of the esoteric areas responsible for directing the Heavenly Qi into the "Xuan Dangong"("Palace of Mysterious Cinnabar"), sometimes known as "Chamber of Mysterious Elixir;" located just under the Baihui area. Therefore, the Baihui area was sometimes known as the Upper Gate of the Taiji Pole, and was also considered to be the Upper Gate of the Seventh Internal Chakra.

In Daoist Alchemy, all of the body's major energetic channels maintain an important vital connection to the celestial portal of the Three Heavenly Transpersonal Points located above the head, via the Baihui area. Therefore, the ancient Daoists spent much time directing energy into and through this important spiritual gate. This was sometimes practiced so that at the moment of death, the Eternal Soul (Shen Xian) would leave the body through this important upper doorway, and ascend back into the various upper celestial realms.

According to ancient legend, Huang Di would gather and meet with the One Hundred Spirits and Ten Thousand Souls at the "Mingtang" (The Hall of Light), located within the First Chamber of the Upper Dantian, in front of the Celestial Court. In Daoist energetic cosmology, the Yellow Emperor is also believed to represent the Eternal Soul (Shen Xian), located within the inner chambers of the Heart, within the Middle Dantian. As the spirit of the Heart (i.e., the Yellow Emperor) ascends upward through the Taiji Pole, and takes residence within the Niwan Palace, the Baihui begins to radiate internal light. The ancient Daoists believed that the "Primordial Qi" always energetically appeared as a blue-green light,

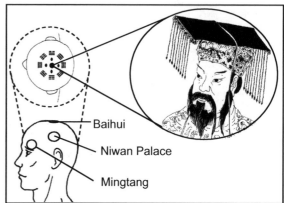

Figure 5.88. The Yellow Emperor (Eternal Soul) Meeting with 100 Spirits at the Baihui

residing as a luminous mist within the Niwan Palace of the Upper Dantian.

According to ancient Daoist teachings, four times a year (i.e., during the Spring and Autumn Equinoxes and the Summer and Winter Solstices), the One Hundred Spirits and Ten Thousand Souls would gather together at the meeting place of the Baihui and Sishencong (located just above the crown of the head). This allowed the Eternal Soul to communicate with the Spirit World via the energy stored within the Mingtang (Hall of Light) area (Figure 5.88). This interaction could be initiated through deep meditation, by rolling the eyes upward and focusing on the Palace of the Celestial Court (the #6 Celestial Palace), and the Shangxing (Upper Star -GV-23) point (Figure 5.89).

It is important to note here, that when training in Daoist Alchemy, the disciple is taught to roll his eyes upward (i.e., joining the celestial lights of the Sun and Moon), and focus on the stored light resonating within his Mingtang (Hall of Light) Chamber. Then, the disciple will open the "Heaven's Eye," located in his Outer Gate (sometimes known as the "Tianmen" or "Gate of Heaven"), in order to see into the Spirit Realm. The joining and crossing of the eyes at the Mingtang Chamber, allows for the convergence and energetic fusion of the disciple's Hun (Ethereal Soul), Po (Corporeal Soul), and Yuan Shen (Original Spirit), with the spiritual energy of the eternal Dao.

CHAPTER 5: THE TAIJI POLE, CHAKRAS, AND THREE DANTIANS

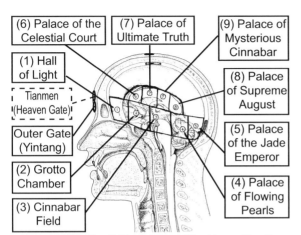

Figure 5.89. The 9 Chambers of the Upper Dantian

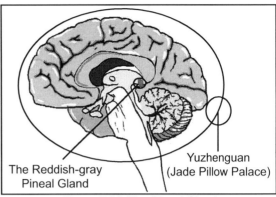

Figure 5.90. The Pineal Gland

4. **The Center of the Upper Dantian**: The center of the Upper Dantian is the Niwan Palace, located within the pineal gland. The pineal gland is a small, reddish-gray colored gland, attached to the base of the third ventricle of the Brain, located in front of the cerebellum (Figure 5.90). The pineal gland is a mass of nerve matter, containing corpuscles resembling nerve cells and small hard masses of calcareous particles. It is larger in children than in adults, and more developed in women than in men.

The pineal gland is the organ of telepathic communication. It receives its impressions through the medium of resonant vibrations created through the thoughts and feelings projected from people, animals, places, and things. Whenever an individual creates a thought, he initiates a series of projected vibrations. This vibrational resonance is released into the surrounding energy field, radiated out from his body as energetic waves and pulses. This projected area of energy is considered to be the space where the individual's Shen transcends the limitations of form, and merges with the infinite space of the Wuji. From the Wuji, the Shen then progresses further, towards reuniting with the Dao.

In ancient Daoist Alchemy, one specific exercise taught to a disciple to "Awaken" the energy "asleep" within his Upper Dantian, was commonly known as "Beating the Heavenly Drum" (Figure 5.91). I was taught

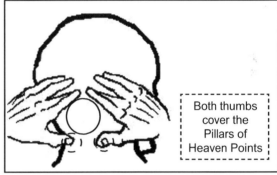

Figure 5.91. Beating The Heavenly Drum is performed in order to activate the Pineal Gland

the following variation in China by one of the priests from the Maoshan Monastery:
- Begin by placing your palms over your ears. As you cover and seal your ears, place both of your thumbs onto the "Pillars of Heaven" (UB-10) points. Your fingers should be facing the back of your head.
- Using a wide stance, bend over and suspend your upper body and head between your legs.
- Now place your index fingers over the "Jade Pillow Palace" area (GV-16), and then put your middle fingers over your index fingers and snap them down onto the indention in your head.
- Use a steady pulse of beating, combined with a relaxed focus. Allow the spirit of your Shen to blend with the rhythmic pulse, and feel the sound of the heart-like beating.
- Tap for 36, 72, or 81 times, and repeat the sequence 3 times a day.

THE 9 CHAMBERS OF THE UPPER DANTIAN

The horizontal set of Nine Chambers located within the Upper Dantian, correspond with the structures and locations of the different ventricles of the Brain. The nine chambers of the Upper Dantian are described as follows (Figure 5.92):

1. **The Hall of Light (Mingtang):** also known as the "Entrance of the Spirit" and the "Bright Hall."
2. **The Palace of the Grotto Chamber (Dongfanggong):** also known as the "Profound Chamber" and the "Chamber of Government."
3. **The Cinnabar Field (Dantian):** also known as the "Hall of the Upper Dantian," the "Upper Medicine Field," and the "Niwan Palace."
4. **The Palace of Flowing Pearls (Liuzhugong):** also known as the "Flowing Pearl Deity."
5. **The Palace of the Jade Emperor (Yuhuanggong):** also known as the "Original Cavity of the Spirit" ("Yuan Shenshi") and the "Ancestral Cavity" ("Zuqiao").
6. **The Palace of the Celestial Court (Tiantinggong):** also known as the "Cover of Heaven" and the "Heavenly Court Palace."
7. **The Palace of Ultimate Truth (Zhizhengong):** also known as the "Palace of the Limitless."
8. **The Palace of the Supreme August (Taihuanggong):** also known as the "Chamber of Splendor."
9. **The Palace of Mysterious Cinnabar (Xuandangong):** also known as the "Chamber of Mysterious Elixir" and the "Chamber of Mystical Medicine."

TRAINING OF THE UPPER DANTIAN

In Medical Qigong, the training of the Upper Dantian is traditionally used for cultivating spiritual intuition and perceptive energetic insight. Upper Dantian training exercises are known as "Shengong" ("Spirit Skill") Meditations, and are the primary methods used for advancing the Medical Qigong Doctor's psychic ability (see Volume 2, Chapter 14).

The Medical Qigong Doctor may absorb Universal Qi and Environmental Qi into his Upper Dantian through either his Baihui (One Hundred Meetings), Yintang (Hall of Impression), or through his Tianmen (Heaven's Gate) points. This cultivated

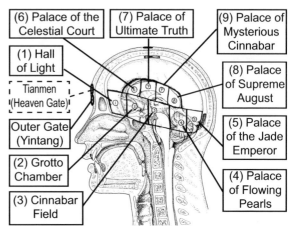

Figure 5.92. The 9 Chambers of the Upper Dantian

Qi is then directed outside the doctor's body as healing energy, emitted into the patient's body through either the doctor's Yin Tang or Tian Men points.

In Daoist Alchemy, the Tianmen (Heaven Gate) is a well guarded secret training point. It is located in the center of the forehead - just above the Yintang area. Its purpose and energetic function is traditionally only taught to senior disciples and trusted apprentices. This was because, the Shen could be trained to both exit and enter the body from the Upper Dantian by way of the Baihui, Yin Tang, or Tian Men (Heavenly Gate) areas.

During cultivation practice, as students of Medical Qigong Therapy strive to gather and balance the Yin and Yang energy within their Upper Dantian, they progress through various stages of transformation. First, the most subtle energies of Ling Qi (Spiritual Energy) and Ling Shen (Spiritual Mind) are gathered into the student's body.

Next, the student's Shen is trained to exit and enter the body at will (e.g., by way of his Baihui, Yintang, and/or Tianmen points). When a student's internal cultivation has reached an advanced stage, the inner apertures of the Upper Dantian's Nine Palaces naturally open. This energetic opening reveals nine small circular spheres revolving around the circumference of a large ball of white light. This large ball of light corresponds to the Sun and the nine smaller balls of light correspond to the Nine Planets, like a miniature version of the solar system (Figure 5.93).

Figure 5.93. The 9 "inner-planets" circle the "Sun"

Daoist Meditations for Energizing the Upper Dantian's Nine Palaces

Throughout all Daoist traditions, meditations that focus on each of the Nine Palaces (Chambers) of the Upper Dantian are extensively used for bringing about enlightenment. The internal principles attributed to the Nine Palaces of the Upper Dantian first appeared in the ancient Daoist text, *Sulingjing*, which states that the Upper Nine Palaces can only be inhabited by Divine Deities, if the disciple practices internal visualization meditations. These internal visualization meditations actualize the presence of the Divine Deities, otherwise the Nine Palaces will remain vacant of divine spiritual power. Each of the Divine Deities not only inhabits a Heavenly Palace, but also governs the physical body in relationship to the specific palace that it occupies within the Brain. These Nine Divine Deities are associated with the Origin of the World and the formation of the human body. They are also responsible for the Celestial Yin functions of specific internal organs, as well as the stages of development at the time of an individual's birth.

The nine cranial palaces measure one square inch in diameter, and are arranged within the Brain in two levels. Each of the Nine Palaces intercommunicates with each other, however, the Upper Cinnabar Field (or Niwan Chamber) also connects with the throat (speaking and sound) and the Heart/Mind of the Middle Dantian. The lower level of the Dantian Chambers extend from the middle of the head (in-between the eyebrows), towards the back of the head, and terminate at the external occipital protuberance, described as follows:

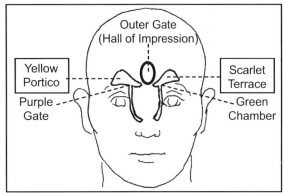

Figure 5.94. The Two Gates to the Inner Passage of the "Hall of Impression" (Heaven's Eye)

- **The Outer Gate (Yintang) Hall of Impression:** The first level includes an Outer Passage or Energetic Gate known as the Hall of Impression, also known as the Heaven's Eye or Third Eye area (Figure 5.94). This special gate exists between the external world (i.e., energy existing outside the body) and the Hall of Light (the Upper Dantian's first Inner Chamber). The Hall of Impression is located three-tenths of an inch inside the head, and has a special magical gateway, positioned on each side of the energetic point. This special passage is sometimes known as the "Entrance of the Spirit," or the "Imperial Canopy," and is where Divine Essence is sometimes breathed into the body.

According to the *Yellow Court Classics*, "the nose is like a high mountain, located in the middle of Heaven; its roots are like a mansion, that hosts the quiet visits of the Jade Emperor (i.e, the King of Heaven). Knowledge advances along this pathway without end. Between the eyebrows, an Imperial Canopy covers a Radiant Pearl, illuminating without interruption, the Nine Hidden Caves of the Upper Dantian."

To the right is the Yellow Portico, which contains a Purple Gate. This energetic half is mainly rose-colored (Yang) light, with a predominantly golden yellow light surrounding it.

To the left is the Scarlet Terrace, which contains a Green Chamber. This energetic half has a predominantly purplish-blue (Yin) light surrounding it.

There are two Gate Guards positioned at the entrance of these two Brain cavities. The ancient Daoists believed that each gate contains a powerful immortal, who holds a small bell of liquid fire in his hand, which he shakes to announce the arrival and departure of spirits.

- **Lower Level, First Palace: Ming Tang (Hall of Light):** The first palace is located behind the Outer Gate (Yintang), and is known as the Hall of Light, Entrance of the Spirit, and the Bright Hall (Figure 5.95). The ancient Daoists believed that the Hall of Light Palace contains three male immortals that hold a red jade mirror in their mouths, and carry a small bell of red jade on their waist. They exhale Red Fire which quenches all those who are spiritually thirsty, and they illuminate the way when the disciple is spirit travelling during the night. The tinkling of their small bells is heard as far away as the celestial North Star. The sound of these bells frightens enemies and causes demons and evil spirits to disappear.

In order to achieve longevity, the disciple must internally inhale, and then exhale the Three Immortals' Red Breaths. This magical Red Breath must then travel throughout the disciple's body, enveloping and immediately transforming all of his tissues into a radiant magical fire. As this internal fire sweeps through the disciple's body, it becomes transformed into a bright radiant light, allowing the disciple to spiritually, energetically and physically transform. In ancient China, this type of Transformation Meditation practice was traditionally known as "The Sun and Moon Purify the Body."

- **Lower Level, Second Palace (Dongfang) Grotto Chamber:** The second palace is located behind the Hall of Light, and is known as the Grotto Chamber, Profound Chamber, and Chamber of Government. The ancient Daoists believed that the Grotto Chamber also contains three male immortals, one of which corresponds to the Liver (Hun, Ethereal Soul) and another corresponding to the Lungs (Po, Corporeal Soul).

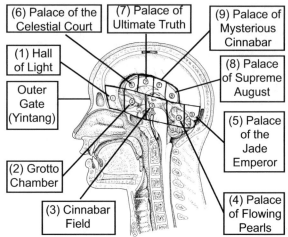

Figure 5.95. The Upper Dantian Nine Chambers

- **Lower Level, Third Palace (Niwangong) Mud Pill Palace:** The third palace is located behind the Grotto Chamber, and is known as the Center of the Upper Dantian, the Hall of the Upper Dantian, the Upper Medicine Field, and the Niwan (Mud Pill) Palace.

According to ancient Daoist teaching, at the Eyebrow's Heart (Heaven's Eye) is Heaven's Gate (Outer Gate). Located one cun deeper is the Ming Tang (Hall of Light); one cun deeper still is the Chamber of the Cave (Grotto Chamber); and one cun deeper is the Niwan (Mud Pill, also known as the Upper Cinnabar Field).

The Niwan Palace is the highest Dantian, and it is located at an area with the circumference of one cun and two fen. The spiritual state of "Complete Emptiness" is required in order to energetically open this special cavity, which hides the dwelling place of the body's Yuan Shen (Original Spirit).

Because the Upper Cinnabar Field is also energetically connected to the throat and Heart, it is one of the primary focal points of concentration used to meditate on while practicing sacred incantations, healing prayers, and the repeating of "sacred sounds."

Once awakened, the ancient Daoists believed that the "Primordial Breath" (Yuan Qi), would always appear as a blue-green light, residing as a luminous mist inside the Niwan Palace.

- **Lower Level, Fourth Palace (Liuzhugong) Palace of Flowing Pearls:** The fourth palace is located behind the Niwan Palace. It is known as the Palace of Flowing Pearls, and the Flowing Pearl Deity. The ancient Daoists believed that the Palace of Flowing Pearls contains male immortals.

After completing meditations that specifically focus on energetically connecting to the masculine (Yang) deities of the first four chambers of the Upper Dantian (i.e., formal introductions, presenting offerings, and requesting assistance in spiritual cultivation and evolution), the disciple will then proceed to practice specific meditations that stimulate the next four chambers of the Upper Dantian, which are all inhabited by feminine (Yin) deities.

It was traditionally taught that only after meditating on the first four masculine deities (attributed to the Yang Trigrams of the Bagua and Yi-Jing) should a disciple attempt to meditate on the four feminine deities (attributed to the Yin Trigrams of the Bagua and Yi-Jing). The combination of four masculine and four feminine deities spiritually establishes the energetic formation of the Prenatal Bagua, responsible for all creation (Figure 5.96). The next four chambers are introduced as follows:

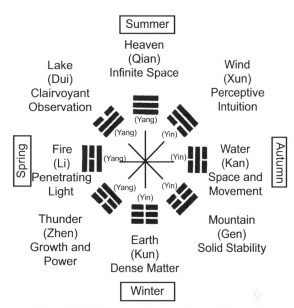

Figure 5.96. The Pre-Heaven Bagua Trigrams

- **Lower Level, Fifth Palace (Yuhuanggong) Palace of the Jade Emperor:** The fifth palace is located on the lower level, behind the Palace of Flowing Pearls. It is known as the Palace of the Jade Emperor, the Original Cavity of the Spirit (*Yuan Shenshi*), and the Ancestral Cavity (*Zuqiao*). It is the last chamber on the first (lower) level of the Nine Chambers of the Upper Dantian. The ancient Daoists believed that the Palace of the Jade Emperor is inhabited by the Holy Mother of the Jade Clarity of Heaven.

Outside the Palace of the Jade Emperor, located on the back of the head, is the area of the "Upper Gate," also known as the Jade Pillow.

- **Upper Level, Sixth Palace (Tiantinggong) Palace of the Celestial Court:** The sixth palace is located above the Hall of Light, one inch above the eyebrows and two inches deep into the Brain. This is the Palace of the Celestial Court, also known as the Cover of Heaven, and the Heavenly Court Palace. Because it is the first Upper Chamber Palace, the ancient Daoists believed that the Palace of the Celestial Court is inhabited by the True Mother of the Great Clarity of Heaven.

- **Upper Level, Seventh Palace (Zhizhengong) Palace of Ultimate Truth:** The seventh palace is located behind the Palace of the Celestial Court. It is known as the Palace of Ultimate Truth, and the Palace of the Limitless. The ancient Daoists believe that the Palace of Ultimate Truth is inhabited by the Imperial Concubine of the Celestial North Star (the Taiji Pole of Heaven).

- **Upper Level, Eighth Palace (Taihuanggong) Palace of Supreme August One):** The eighth palace is located behind the Palace of Mysterious Cinnabar, on the upper level. It is known as the Palace of Supreme August, and the Chamber of Splendor. The ancient Daoists believe that the Palace of Supreme August is inhabited by the Imperial Empress on High.

Only after completing the meditation on the four feminine deities (i.e., formal introductions, presenting offerings, and requesting assistance in spiritual cultivation and evolution), should the disciple attempt to meditate on the final chamber, the Palace of Mysterious Cinnabar, which contains the True Lord of the Great Unity (Taiyi).

- **Upper Level, Ninth Palace (Xuandangong) Palace of Mysterious Cinnabar:** The ninth palace is located behind the Palace of Ultimate Truth, on the upper level. It is known as the Palace of Mysterious Cinnabar, the Chamber of Mysterious Elixir, and the Chamber of Mystical Medicine. The ancient Daoists believed that the Palace of Mysterious Cinnabar is inhabited by the True Lord of Great Unity, Taiyi (Figure 5.97).

Ancient Daoist legends report that Taiyi originally existed before all creation, having formed himself from Pure Qi. He then created Heaven and Earth, and ruled over all creation. Therefore the Daoist Deity Taiyi is sometimes known as "the Supreme One," "Da-yi" ("The Great One"), and "The Supreme Emperor of Heaven."

At some point in time, Taiyi took on an apprentice (the Jade Emperor) so that he could retire from office to work on cultivating Perfect Contemplation. The Jade Emperor later learned the art of Universal Mastery under Taiyi, and eventually became ruler over Heaven and Earth.

According to ancient legend, Tai Yi ruled the Celestial Realm for many Dynasties, prior to the Jade Emperor. He is sometimes called Yuan Shi Tian Zong, the Creator of the Universe, and was popularly worshiped during the Warring States Period (475-221 B.C.), well before the emergence of Daoism as an organized religion.

Eventually Taiyi (or Yuan Shi Tian Zong) relocated to Yu-Qing (the Pure Jade Heaven), in order to continue his spiritual refinement. According to early Han Dynasty texts (206 B.C.-220 A.D.), Taiyi resides in the Central Palace known as Taiwei (Great Tenuity), later known as Ziwei Gong (the Purple Tenuity Palace).

During the Han Dynasty, Tai-yi was venerated as part of the triad of the Three Pure Ones (San-Yi), and became a personified Daoist deity. The Three Pure Ones refer both to the Three Daoist Heavens and the deities ruling them.

Figure 5.97. The True Lord Taiyi

Taiyi is sometimes known as "Jade Pure" or "the Perfect One," and performs his duties in the realm of Yu-Qing. The Jade Emperor, formerly his assistant, is now his co-ruler.

According to ancient Daoist texts, the Northern Dipper was perceived as the instrument of Taiyi, through which he "pours out the Primordial Breath" (Yuan Qi). His followers traditionally believed that he is assisted by Si-Ming, the Ruler of Fate, who resides within the area of the Middle Dantian.

Eventually, Tai-yi became the highest celestial deity, and is said to currently dwell within the Celestial Pole Star, with the Five Legendary Emperors (i.e., the traditional celestial rulers of the five cardinal points) as his subjects. In Daoist rituals, he is sometimes venerated together with the Sun God.

It is interesting to note, that the origin of the Chinese Lantern Festival is attributed to the celebration of Taiyi, as the ancient god of Heaven. It is said that Taiyi had 16 Celestial Dragons and used them to control the destiny of the human world. Therefore Emperor Qin Shi Huang, who first united China, held the first Lantern Festival to ask Taiyi for good weather and for health.

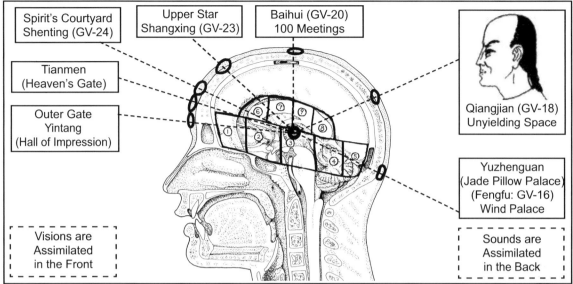

Figure 5.98. The Seven Energetic Portals of the Upper Dantian

THE SEVEN SECRET PORTALS OF THE UPPER DANTIAN

There are seven special energetic portals located on the surface of the head, that are sometimes used in esoteric Daoist Alchemical practices (Figure 5.98). This secret teaching originated from the shamanic influences of the Tibetan Tantra and Bon magical traditions, which were eventually incorporated into the ancient magical practices of the Wu (i.e., the original Chinese shamanic seers, invokers, and conjurers"). According to my teacher, only select disciples are taught this secret information.

Each of these seven cranial energy centers (i.e., four in the front of the head and three in the back), is located along the energetic pathway of the Governing Vessel (Sea of Yang Qi), and are specifically trained during certain times in the disciple's alchemical cultivation practice. These special points are traditionally used in order to enhance the disciple's clairvoyant skills.

Of the four points located on his forehead, the bottom three form a straight line, and correspond to a different aspect of the disciple's "Celestial Eye" ("Third Eye"). Because of their proximity, the energetic field of the bottom three areas are either sometimes linked together, or divided into separate training. The three areas of the Celestial Eye are traditionally described as follow:

- **Yintang (Hall of Impression):** Corresponds to the energy of the "Lower Third Eye"
- **Tianmen (Heaven's Gate):** Corresponds to the energy of the "Middle Third Eye"
- **Shenting (Spirit's Courtyard):** Corresponds to the energy of the "Upper Third Eye"

The back three energetic centers are associated with, and correspond to, the energetic influences of Heaven, Earth, and Man, described as follows:

- **Heaven (Baihui - 100 Meetings):** Corresponds to the energy center located at the top of the skull.
- **Man (Qiangjian - Unyielding Space):** Corresponds to the energy center located towards the back of the head.
- **Earth (Yuzhenguan - Jade Pillow Palace):** Corresponds to the energy center located at the base of the skull.

Positioned in the middle of the three front and three back points, is a special point, known in Daoist Alchemy as the Upper Star (Shangxing):

- **Shangxing (Upper Star):** Corresponds to the Qi of the Celestial Pole Star and Great Luminous Pearl.

The Dantian's Yin and Yang Energetic Chambers

When I was training in China, one of the professors explained that each of the Three Dantians can be divided into Yin and Yang energetic chambers. The Yang chambers relate to the "higher" energetic aspects of each Dantian, and correspond to the spiritual influences of the individual's Hun. The Yin chambers relate to the "lower" energetic aspects of each Dantian, and correspond to the more "carnal" survival based emotions of the individual's Po. The Yin and Yang chambers and their energetic manifestations are described as follows:

The Lower Dantian

1. **The Yang Energetic Chamber of the Lower Dantian** corresponds anatomically to the upper quadrant of the abdomen, located within the area of the small intestine in men and the Uterus in women. When influenced by the Hun, quiescence and serenity are enhanced.
2. **The Yin Energetic Chamber of the Lower Dantian** corresponds anatomically to the lower quadrant of the abdomen, which includes the reproductive organs, the urinary bladder, urethra, and anus. This chamber is responsible for reproduction and sexuality. When influenced by the body's Po, raw physical power and sexual vitality is aroused.

The Middle Dantian

1. **The Yang Energetic Chamber of the Middle Dantian** corresponds anatomically to the upper quadrant of the heart, which includes the left and right atrium, the upper portions of the left and right ventricles, and the atrioventricular node. This chamber is responsible for the spiritual attitudes and virtues associated with the Hun. The Hun are responsible for:
   - gathering and transmitting divine inspirations and spiritual insights
   - giving and receiving unconditional love
   - motivating spiritual growth through prayer, devotion, and commitment
2. **The Yin Energetic Chamber of the Middle Dantian** corresponds anatomically to the lower quadrant of the heart, which includes the left and right ventricles. This chamber is responsible for sensual passions, conquests, and conditional love. It is associated with actions that are based on hidden agendas. These emotions are related to the Po's influence. The influence of both the Po and the Yin energetic chamber of the Upper Dantian activates, energizes, and enhances:
   - biological drives (for food and self preservation)
   - sexuality, lust, and desire
   - sensuality

The Upper Dantian

1. **The Yang Energetic Chamber of the Upper Dantian** corresponds anatomically to the upper quadrant of the Brain, often referred to as the third ventricle or the higher Brain centers. When stimulated, the higher Brain centers manifest spiritual intuition and divine insight related to the influence of the Hun. Such insight is responsible for spiritual growth and maturation. Activation of these higher Brain centers eventually leads to the emergence of extrasensory perceptions (ESP), such as clairvoyance, clairaudience, telepathy, psychokinesis, and eventually to spiritual enlightenment.
2. **The Yin Energetic Chamber of the Upper Dantian** corresponds anatomically to the lower quadrant of the Brain, often referred to as the "reptilian" brain. When stimulated, the reptilian brain activates the thalamus, hypothalamus, cerebellum, and cortex, which awakens the body's intuition, as well as our animalistic and primitive survival instincts. When the Yin energetic chamber dominates, the sensory, animalistic nature of the Po emerges in full force. This phenomenon sometimes occurs when coma patients begin to recover. As energy begins to fill the lower chambers of the Three Dantians, their initial reactions are basic and carnal in nature, i.e., to either engage in sexual activity or strike out in violence. As the Qi begins to fill the upper chambers of the Three Dantians, the energy balances in the patient's Taiji Pole, and the patients' impulses return back to normal.

THE DOCTOR'S PROJECTED AURA FIELDS AND THE THREE DANTIANS

In 1993, while I was interning at the Xiyuan Hospital of Traditional Chinese Medicine, all Medical Qigong Doctors were tested and categorized according to the predominant color of their Qi emissions. The doctor's primary healing color was dependant upon which of the three Dantians was energetically dominant (i.e., the corresponding Lower Dantian, Middle Dantian, or Upper Dantian color). Each doctor was tested, and the energetic strength and healing potential of the doctor was categorized and recorded according to the emitted color that was observed being projected from the doctor's hands (Figure 5.99).

Instances of divine intervention can occur at any stage of the doctor's energetic development and are a testimony to the healing power and love of the divine. Although every Medical Qigong Doctor uses a combination of all Three Dantians when projecting Qi into patients, the color of the aura surrounding the doctor's body reflects which Dantian's reservoir is predominantly used. Through time, patience, and much practice, the doctor will be able to transform from a red to a blue, and eventually to a white-light healer. For example,

- In 1993, I was categorized as a Red.
- In 1995, I was categorized as a Blue
- In 1996, I was categorized as a White

RED QI EMITTED COLOR

Medical Qigong Doctors who have adequately trained their body and mind will emit a red radiant glow around their external energy field. The Qi will overflow from the Lower Dantian area, and the color red will dominate the aura. This is actually a normal aura color observed in most graduating Medical Qigong Doctors who begin their clinical practice.

The radiant energy of the doctor's emitted Qi can be further energized by visualizing Divine Light filling the body's internal core, and extending it outward in order to fill the body's three external Weiqi fields.

GREEN/BLUE QI EMITTED COLOR

Medical Qigong Doctors who have further refined their energy will emit a type of green/

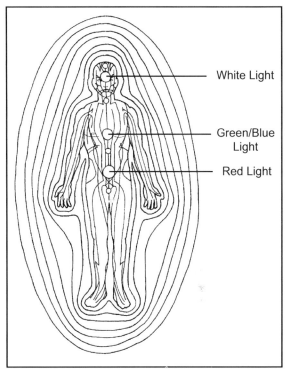

Figure 5.99. The Three Dantians and Their Relationship to the Three External Wei Qi Fields

blue radiant glow around their external energy field. These doctors' Qi will also overflow from the Middle Dantian area, and the color green/blue will dominate their Weiqi field. This special color is observed in more advanced Medical Qigong Doctors.

The radiant energy of the doctor's emitted Qi can be further energized by visualizing Divine Light filling the body's internal core, and extending it outward in order to fill the body's three external Weiqi fields.

WHITE QI EMITTED COLOR

Qi that is emitted directly from the divine is traditionally observed as a multicolored type of white light energy. In the clinic, this powerful type of Qi emission is observed as a sign of divine intervention in the patient's healing process. Therefore, it is considered to be the most powerful form of Heavenly Qi working through "Man," in order to manifest a supernatural energetic transformation (i.e., a healing).

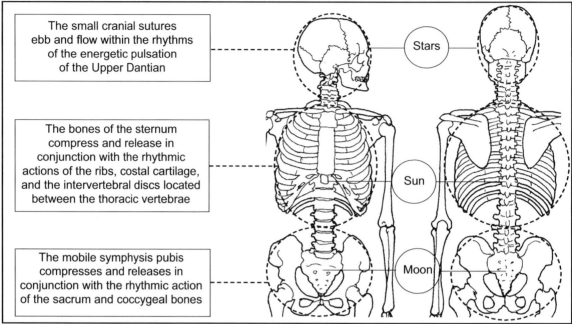

Figure 5.100. The Three Dantians and Their Relationship to the Movable Structure of the Bones

THE MOVEABLE BONES OF THE THREE DANTIANS

When studying the specific anatomical locations of the Three Dantians, a student can observe the structural interactions of the moveable Bones in their relationship to the Dantian's energetic fields. As each Dantian energetically pulses, the surrounding tissues expand and contract with the rising (Yang) and the falling (Yin) rhythm of life. This ebb and flow of the human tissues moves in response to the energetic rhythm radiating from the body's center core. All life is sustained by this rhythmic function (Figure 5.100).

THE LOWER DANTIAN - SACRAL RHYTHM

As the Qi of the Lower Dantian energetically pulses, the mobile joint of the symphysis pubis (interpubic joint) compresses and releases in conjunction with the rhythmic action of the sacrum and coccygeal Bones. This sacral rhythm initiates an energetic pulse that ripples up the spine, also stimulating the vibrational resonance within the Middle Dantian and Upper Dantian.

In ancient Daoist teachings, this special area of the body energetically corresponded to the Celestial Qi of the Moon (i.e., the "Lunar Plexus").

THE MIDDLE DANTIAN - THORACIC RHYTHM

As the energy of Middle Dantian energetically pulses, the manubrium, the sternum body, and the xiphoid bone compress and release in conjunction with the rhythmic action initiated by the ribs and costal cartilage, and the intervertebral discs located between the thoracic vertebrae. This thoracic rhythm initiates an energetic pulse that ripples through the spine, also stimulating the vibrational resonance within the Lower Dantian and Upper Dantian. In ancient Daoist teachings, this special area of the body energetically corresponded to the Celestial Qi of the Sun (i.e., the "Solar Plexus").

THE UPPER DANTIAN - CRANIAL RHYTHM

As the energy of Upper Dantian energetically pulses, the small sutures of the frontal, sphenoid, parietal, temporal, and occipital bones compress and release in conjunction with the rhythmic action initiated by the cerebral spinal fluid, and the dynamic action of the falx cerebri and tentorium cerebelli. This cranial rhythm initiates an energetic pulse that ripples through the spine, also stimulating the vibrational resonance within the Middle Dantian and Lower Dantian. In ancient Daoist teachings, this special area of the body energetically corresponded to the Celestial Qi of the Stars (i.e., the "Stellar Plexus").

Chapter 6
The Eight Extraordinary Vessels

The Body's Eight Extraordinary Vessels

When I was studying at the Hai Dian University of Traditional Chinese Medicine in Beijing, China, students of Medical Qigong Therapy were traditionally introduced to the study of Energetic Anatomy and Physiology. This unique clinical course first began with understanding the Qi extending from the forming fetus's center core Taiji Pole, then the Three Dantians, Eight Extraordinary Vessels, the Six Extraordinary Organs, and finally the Twelve Zangfu Organs. The reason for this unique progression, was because these important energetic systems are believed to be responsible for the "original feeding and supporting" of all of the body's internal organ systems, as well as the external channels and collaterals.

In Chinese Energetic Anatomy and Physiology, the Eight Extraordinary Vessels are considered to be the first vessels to form within the developing fetus, and are also known as the "Eight Ancestral Channels," "Eight Prenatal Channels," "Eight Preheaven Channels," and "Eight Psychic Channels." The ideograph depicting the Chinese characters for the Eight Extraordinary Vessels "Qi Jing Ba Mai," are described as follows (Figure 6.1):

- **Qi:** The first character is the Chinese ideograph "Qi," which is generally translated as "Extraordinary," but can also be translated as "Surprising, Strange, or Marvellous." It is composed of three characters. Positioned on the top is a character "Da," meaning "Big or Great;" positioned on the bottom-right is a character "Ren" depicting a "Person;" and positioned on the bottom-left is a character "Kuo," meaning "Mouth." As a whole, the ideograph depicts the actions of a startled person, having discovered something strange yet wonderful, falling backwards with their mouth open, with the expression of surprise.

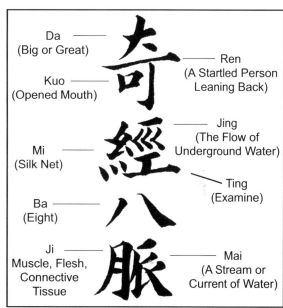

Figure 6.1. The Chinese Ideograph for "Qi Jing Ba Mai" (Eight Extraordinary Vessels)

- **Jing:** The second character is the Chinese ideograph "Jing," which is generally translated as "Channel," but can also be translated as "Meridian, To Pass Through, and The Wrapping of a Silk Fiber or Net." The word Jing carries a multitude of meanings, all of which are reflected within the many components of the character. Positioned to the left is the radical "Mi," used for "Silk, Net or String-like Objects." It depicts threads that have been twisted together to form a net, and refers to a silk rope that is tied around something, pulling and securing it, or the wrapping and enveloping of a silk net.

Positioned on the top right portion of the character is the phonetic "Jing," which is sometimes used to denote "The Flow of Underground Water" (the horizontal line on top represents the ground, while the three curved lines beneath it represent the flow of water).

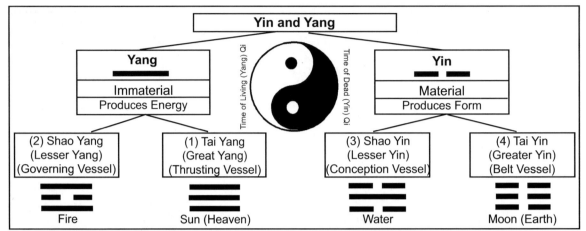

Figure 6.2. The Ancient Daoist Concept of the Yin and Yang of Taiji giving birth to the Four Phases of Universal Energy, and manifesting through the first four foundational Vessels.

Positioned to the bottom-right is a modification of the ancient radical "Ting," meaning to examine the underground veins.

As a whole, this ideograph describes the deep aquatic passageways or subterranean rivers (channels) which energetically knit together the internal fabric of the human body.
- **Ba:** The third character is the Chinese ideograph "Ba," which is generally translated as the number "Eight." The number eight is significant in many areas of ancient Chinese thought, such as:

    1. **Heaven:** The Eight Prenatal (Heavenly Yang) Trigrams; the cycle of energetic creation
    2. **Earth:** The Eight Postnatal (Earthly Yin) Trigrams; the energetic cycle of life
    3. **Man:** The Eight Directions of Perception (i.e., front, back, left, right, above, below, inside and outside the body)
- **Mai:** The fourth character is the Chinese ideograph "Mai," which translates as "Vessel." It is composed of two characters: the character to the left, "Ji" depicts the Chinese ideogram for "Body Tissue, Muscle or Flesh" (all of which are forms of connective tissue); the character on the right "Mai" depicts "A Current of Water, Stream, or Branch of a River. As a whole, the character can be translated as "Arteries, Veins or Pulse," depicting a form of energetic circulation.

The Eight Extraordinary Vessels are given their names because they differ in energetic function from the Twelve Primary Channels. These eight vessels have an extraordinary ability to regulate the deeper energetic reservoirs of the body. These vessels represent the merging of the mother's and father's energy and the linking of the body's prenatal and postnatal energies. They interconnect all of the Twelve Primary Channels and circulate the Jing Qi (Essence Energy) throughout the body.

THE VESSEL FORMATION OF ENERGETIC EMBRYOLOGY

The energetic expansion and contraction of the Eight Extraordinary Vessels affects the creation and development of the baby's tissues up until the time of its birth. In Energetic Embryology (see Chapter 2), the Eight Extraordinary Vessels are subdivided into two groups: The Four Foundational Vessels and the Eight Secondary Formational Vessels, described as follows:
- **The Four Foundational Vessels:** Comprised of the Thrusting Vessel, Governing Vessel, Conception Vessel and Belt Vessel, these four vessels are believed to be responsible for the first cellular divisions (Figure 6.2). The Thrusting Vessel is the oldest of these channels, having originated with the formation of the Taiji Pole when the father's sperm entered the mother's egg. The ancient Daoists believed that the

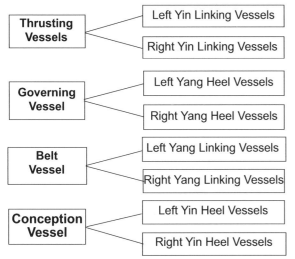

Figure 6.3. The Four Foundational Vessels are Joined to the Eight Secondary Formational Vessels

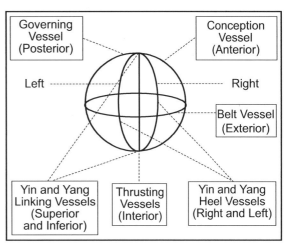

Figure 6.4. A Model of the Flow of the Eight Extraordinary Vessels in Energetic Embryology

Thrusting Vessel was the original "root," allowing the other "branches" to spring forth.

- **The Eight Secondary Formational Vessels:** Comprised of the left and right Yin Linking Vessels, the left and right Yang Linking Vessels, the left and right Yin Heel Vessels and the left and right Yang Heel Vessels, these eight vessels are believed to be responsible for completing the energetic and physical structure of the fetus.

In Traditional Chinese Medicine, it is taught that the Eight Secondary Formational Vessels are joined to the Four Foundational Vessels in the following manner (Figure 6.3):

- The Left and Right Yin Linking Vessels are coupled with the Thrusting Vessels
- The Left and Right Yang Linking Vessels are coupled with the Belt Vessel
- The Left and Right Yin Heel Vessels are coupled with the Conception Vessel
- The Left and Right Yang Heel Vessels are coupled with the Governing Vessel

The Thrusting Vessels, Belt Vessel, Yin Linking Vessels and Yang Linking Vessels are responsible for the organization of the internal embryonic tissues; whereas the Conception Vessel, Governing Vessel, Yin Heel Vessels and Yang Heel Vessels are responsible for both the internal embryonic tissues and the external energy formations.

THE THREE-DIMENSIONAL SPACE OF THE IMPREGNATED EGG

In Chinese Energetic Embryology, the three-dimensional space of the impregnated egg is viewed as an object with eight different surfaces along four axes. Within this unique pattern, each of the Eight Extraordinary Vessels corresponds with one of the following directions (Figure 6.4):

- **Anterior - Posterior:** Governing and Conception Vessels
- **Superior - Inferior:** Yin and Yang Linking Vessels
- **Right - Left:** Yin and Yang Heel Vessels
- **Interior - Exterior:** Thrusting and Belt Vessels

This special circular pattern is seen as the energetic "seed" and living foundation of all human life. It manifests as the sacred energetic space from which all human tissues manifests.

In Western Psychology, the circle is viewed as an geometric archetype of the "psyche." However, in Chinese Macrocosmic Symbology, the image of this circle expresses the "Shape of Heaven," and represents the infinite space of the Wuji through which the Yin and Yang of all creation will begin to manifest within the Earthly realm. In Chinese Energetic Embryology, it is therefore seen as the sacred space through which the circles of time, space, and matter manifest and begin their cycles.

THE ENERGETIC FUNCTION OF THE EIGHT EXTRAORDINARY VESSELS

The Eight Extraordinary Vessels have neither a direct connection nor a clear internal and external relationship with the internal organs. Similar to the Three Dantians' function of distributing the body's energy, these Eight Extraordinary Vessels are reservoirs that regulate the distribution and circulation of Jing and Qi inside the body. When these reservoirs become full, the energy overflows into the center channel or Taiji Pole. This stimulation of the Taiji Pole expands consciousness and increases perception and intuition. Therefore these important vessels are the foundation of the body's energy, bridging the Yuan Qi (Original/Prenatal Energy) with the body's Postnatal Energy.

The Eight Extraordinary Vessels have six main functions: They serve as reservoirs of Qi, store and circulate Jing Qi, circulate the Wei Qi, regulate the body's life cycles, integrate the six primary Yang organs with the Six Extraordinary Organs and the Kidneys, and integrate the Four Seas with the body's internal energy flow. These functions are described as follows (Figure 6.5):

1. **Serve as Reservoirs of Qi:** The Eight Extraordinary Vessels criss-cross the body and weave together the Twelve Primary Channels, strengthening the energetic structure of the Twelve Primary Channels and regulating the flow of Qi and Blood within them. If the Qi and Blood of the Twelve Primary Channels becomes excessive, the overflow is absorbed into the Eight Extraordinary Vessels.

    The Eight Extraordinary Vessels act as Qi reservoirs receiving, storing and distributing the Excess Qi, thus regulating the body's overall energy flow. If the Qi flow of the Twelve Primary Channels becomes deficient, energy can be drawn from the reservoirs of energy stored within the Eight Extraordinary Vessels. In this way, the Eight Extraordinary Vessels maintain internal and external harmony by continually regulating and balancing the body's energy flow.

2. **Store and Circulate Jing Qi:** The Eight Extraordinary Vessels draw their energy from the Kidneys and are responsible for storing and circulating the body's Jing Qi throughout the

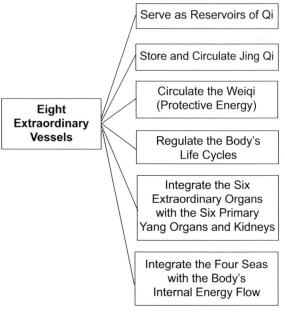

Figure 6.5. The Energetic Functions of the Eight Extraordinary Vessels

tissues, particularly to the skin, hair, and the Six Extraordinary (Curious) Organs. The Six Extraordinary Organs are also known as the Six Ancestral Organs, and include the Brain, Bone, Marrow, Blood Vessels, Gall Bladder and Uterus.

3. **Circulate the Wei Qi:** The Eight Extraordinary Vessels aid in circulating the Wei Qi (Protective Energy), helping to protect the body against the invasion of external pathogens. The Governing, Conception, and Thrusting Vessels are primarily responsible for circulating the body's Wei Qi over the thorax, abdomen, and back.

    The Eight Extraordinary Vessels provide the link between the Kidney Jing and the Wei Qi. Although the Wei Qi is circulated by the Lungs, it has its roots in the Kidneys. Thus the Kidneys play an important role in supporting the Lungs' function of circulating the body's Wei Qi. Due to the Kidneys function in supporting the Wei Qi field, the immune system can also become vulnerable to pathogenic factors, as well as allergies, and asthma. This energetic reaction demonstrates why the Kidneys are always at the root of latent Heat syndromes (chronic fatigue) caused by Kidney Deficiency.

4. **Regulate the Body's Life Cycles:** In the first chapter of *The Yellow Emperor's Classic of Internal Medicine*, it is stated that the life changes of women (every seven years) and men (every eight years) are governed by the Conception and Thrusting Vessels.

   The rhythms and cycles of life are related to the body's Jing and are thus greatly influenced by the Eight Extraordinary Vessels' role in moving and circulating the body's Jing (see Volume 2, Chapter 13).

5. **Integrate the Six Extraordinary Organs with the Six Primary Yang Organs:** The Eight Extraordinary Vessels provide the link between the body's Six Extraordinary Organs (Brain, Bone, Marrow, Blood Vessels, Gall Bladder and Uterus), and the internal energy flow of the body's six primary Yang organs (Gall Bladder, Small Intestine, Stomach, Large Intestine, Urinary Bladder and Triple Burners), in addition to the Kidneys. The integration of this internal connection is described as follows:

   - **The Brain:** This Extraordinary Organ is regulated by the Governing Vessel and the Yin and Yang Heel Vessels.
   - **The Uterus:** This Extraordinary Organ is regulated by the Thrusting and Conception Vessels.
   - **The Blood Vessels:** This Extraordinary Organ is regulated by the Thrusting Vessels.
   - **The Gall Bladder:** This Extraordinary Organ is regulated by the Belt Vessel.
   - **The Marrow:** This Extraordinary Organ is regulated by the Thrusting Vessels.
   - **The Bones:** This Extraordinary Organ is regulated by the Thrusting and Conception Vessels.

6. **Integrate the Four Seas with the Body's Internal Energy Flow:** The *Magical Pivot (Ling Shu)* states, "People have Four Seas: the Sea of Marrow, the Sea of Blood, the Sea of Qi, and the Sea of Grain and Water." The Eight Extraordinary Vessels provide the link between the body's Four Seas and the body's internal energy flow, described as follows:

   - **The Sea of Marrow:** This special "Sea" consists of the Brain and spinal cord, and it is related to the Governing Vessel and the Yin and Yang Heel Vessels. The Sea of Marrow access points (GV-16 and GV-20) are located on the Governing Vessel.

     When the Sea of Marrow is in excess, the patient will show signs of strength and increased power. When the Sea of Marrow is deficient, the patient may experience headaches, tinnitus, blurred vision, dizziness, weak legs, fatigue, or possible physical collapse.

   - **The Sea of Qi:** This special "Sea" is located in the center of the chest and is regulated by the Conception Vessel. The Sea of Qi's access point (CV-17) is located on the Conception Vessel. Some Medical Qigong schools maintain that there are two main reservoirs of Qi in the body: the Middle Dantian, being the Sea of Postnatal Qi; and the Lower Dantian (which is regulated by the Qihai CV-6 point) being the Sea of Prenatal Qi.

     When the Sea of Qi is in excess, the patient may experience a feeling of fullness in the chest, dyspnea (urgent breathing), and a red complexion. When the Sea of Qi is deficient, the patient may experience weakness, energy depletion and insufficient speech.

   - **The Sea of Nourishment:** This special "Sea" is also known as the Sea of Grain and Water. It is considered to be the active energy of the Stomach, and is regulated by the Thrusting Vessels. The Sea of Nourishment's access points (St-30) are located on the Stomach Channels.

     When the Sea of Water and Grain is in excess, the patient may experience a feeling of fullness or bloating in the abdomen. When the Sea of Water and Grain is deficient, the patient may experience a feeling of hunger with a corresponding inability to eat.

   - **The Sea of Blood:** This special "Sea" is also known as the Sea of the Twelve Primary Channels. It is related to the Thrusting Vessels, and the Liver organ. The Sea of Blood access points (Sp-10, St-37, St-39, and UB-11) are located on the Spleen, Stomach and Urinary Bladder Channels.

     When the Sea of Blood is in excess, the patient's mind is constantly thinking and his physical body may feel big and bulky. When the Sea of Blood is deficient, the patient's mind is constantly thinking and his physical body feels small.

The Eight Extraordinary Vessels and Medical Qigong Therapy

The energetic pathways, functions, and use of the Eight Extraordinary Vessels and their associated points are often quite different in Medical Qigong Therapy, than those taught in traditional Acupuncture Colleges, even though they may sometimes bear the same names.

Most Acupuncturists, with the exception of some Japanese practitioners, often pay little attention to the Eight Extraordinary Vessels in diagnosis and treatment. One Medical Qigong Doctor from China has claimed that a Chinese study showed that treatments based on the utilization of the Eight Extraordinary Vessels were far more effective than treatments utilizing standard Traditional Chinese Medical protocols. The results of this study, however, were not released because officials did not want to disturb the credibility of China's already established T.C.M. Universities.

The Eight Extraordinary Vessels have been of special importance to Medical Qigong Doctors for thousands of years, and affect the body on the deepest levels of our basic constitutional energy. They are traditionally viewed as the foundation of the body's energetic system, because they bridge the body's Prenatal and Postnatal Qi.

In the clinic, the reason that Medical Qigong Therapy makes use of the Eight Extraordinary Vessels is because they are relatively easy to access through Qi Emission Therapy and Medical Qigong Self-Regulation Prescription Exercises.

The Eight Extraordinary Vessels And The Medical Qigong Doctor

Traditionally, when performing Daoist Alchemy and certain Medical Qigong Regulation Exercises, opening the flow of Qi through the Eight Extraordinary Vessels is a prerequisite before opening the energy flow in the Twelve Primary Channels.

The major purpose of opening the Eight Extraordinary Vessels is to provide a container for storing the three energetic forces of "Heaven" (i.e., the Sun, Moon, and Star's universal energies), "Earth" (the environmental energies of the Soil, Water, and Wind), and "Man" (the human energies of the body's Essence, Breath, and Heart/Mind).

When practicing personal energetic cultivation, it is essential for the Medical Qigong Doctor to open their Eight Extraordinary Vessels in order to attain mastery of their Energy Body and Spirit Body. This important mastery is essential for clinical diagnosis and treatment. For example, the various energetic patterns of the Microcosmic Orbit (i.e., the Fire Cycle, Water Cycle, and Wind Cycle) are traditionally introduced to the doctor for clinical purgation, tonification, and regulation of the patient's Governing and Conception Vessels. This special exercise is traditionally used in the clinic in order to restore a healthy flow of Qi throughout all of the channels and vessels, creating a balanced energetic system.

Through the refinement of energy achieved by focusing on the development of the Eight Extraordinary Vessels, Medical Qigong Doctors receive more Qi, and the quality of their Blood changes (i.e., its energetic potential contains more Qi). At the advanced stages of energetic transformation, a Medical Qigong Doctor can eventually rechannel the flow of Qi moving through his body's Three Dantians, and stimulate the "Mystical Pass," located in the upper chambers of his Brain.

When the flow of energy is finally directed upward in order to stimulate the Mystical Pass, the Medical Qigong Doctor will suddenly acquire a greater sense of awareness and control over his Three Bodies (i.e., the Physical Body, Energy Body, and Spirit Body). This greater sense of awareness will allow the doctor to enhance his intuitive perceptions, and increase his energetic communication with all of the various realms of Earthly existence (i.e., the Mineral, Plant, Animal, and Human Realms), as well as with the Divine Realm.

Clinical Indications and Uses

In the Medical Qigong Clinic, the general indications for utilizing the Eight Extraordinary Vessels include the following:
- When previous treatment with the Twelve Primary Meridians has failed
- For chronic diseases, especially when the body is extremely depleted of energy
- When there is a multitude of deficiencies
- For endocrine and hormonal problems
- When pulses are balanced, but patient is sick

CHAPTER 6: THE EIGHT EXTRAORDINARY VESSELS

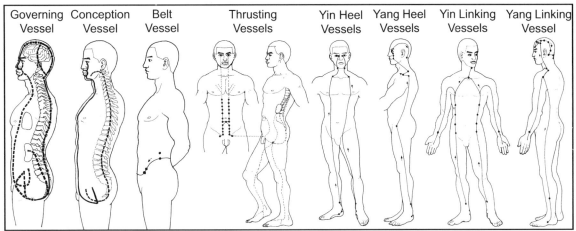

Figure 6.6. The Clinical Functions of the Qi Jing Ba Mai (Eight Extraordinary Vessels)

The Eight Extraordinary Vessels form and establish the energetic patterns for the tissues of the developing fetus, and for the entire body of the adult (Figure 6.6). Their clinical uses can be divided into several different energetic applications, all of which are aimed at changing the energetic patterns within the patient's tissues.

THE VESSELS ENERGETIC LOCATION

One popular clinical approach divides the Eight Extraordinary Vessels into four pairs of Yin and Yang vessels. In this particular clinical application, the Eight Extraordinary Vessels are grouped according to the same polarity, with two pairs of Yin Vessels and two pairs of Yang Vessels. When paired this way, each set of the Yin and Yang Vessels have a common range of energetic action in terms of the patient's body's tissues. These energetic actions and the pairing of the Eight Extraordinary Vessels are described as follows:

1. **The Conception and Yin Heel Vessels:** These affect the flow of energy to the patient's abdomen, chest, Lungs, throat, and face.
2. **The Governing and Yang Heel Vessels:** These affect the flow of energy to the back of the patient's legs, as well as the back, spine, neck, head, eyes, and Brain.
3. **The Thrusting and Yin Linking Vessels:** These affect the flow of energy to the inner aspect of the patient's legs, as well as the abdomen, Stomach, chest, and Heart.
4. **The Belt and Yang Linking Vessels:** These affect the flow of energy to the outer aspect of the patient's legs, as well as the sides of the body, the shoulders, and sides of the neck.

THE VESSELS ENERGETIC FUNCTION

The Eight Extraordinary Vessels can also be categorized according to their energetic functions, which are described as follows:

1. **The Conception, Governing, and Thrusting Vessels:** These are considered the source of all the other Extraordinary Vessels. These three vessels affect the patient's energy at a deep constitutional level. They originate directly from the Kidneys and are connected to the body's Jing.
2. **The Yin and Yang Heel Vessels:** These are mutually complementary in that they both flow from the legs (controlling the condition of the muscles of the legs) into the eyes (controlling the muscles that open and close the eyes). Therefore, the Qigong doctor can treat energetic excess or deficient conditions in either the legs or eyes by simultaneously treating and regulating the Qi of the Yin and Yang Heel Vessels.
3. **The Yin and Yang Linking Vessels:** These Vessels complement each other by linking the body's Yin and Yang Channels.
4. **The Belt Vessel:** This is the only horizontal vessel in the body, encircling and connecting the main channels. For this reason, the Belt Vessel affects the circulation of energy throughout the entire body, especially within the legs and waist.

THE EXTRAORDINARY VESSELS AND THE EIGHT CONFLUENT POINTS

There are Eight Confluent (Meeting) Points that are specifically located where the Eight Extraordinary Vessels and Twelve Primary Channels intersect each other. According to the *Yi Xue Ru Men (Introduction to Medicine)*, "Among the 360 points on the entire body, the 66 points that are located on the four extremities are important; among these 66 points, the Eight Confluent Points are considered to be the most important."

In the clinic, the Eight Confluent Points may be used independently for the treatment of various disease, for example (Figure 6.7):

- **Governing Vessel:** The Confluent point for the Governing Vessel is the "Back Ravine" ("Hou Xi:" SI-3) point. This Wood Element point is used to treat mania-depression, epilepsy, occipital headache, and stiffness or pain of the spinal column. This point is also used to dispel febrile diseases, dispel External Wind Cold or Wind Heat, and to treat diseases of the Small Intestine and Governing Vessel.
- **Conception Vessel:** The Confluent point for the Conception Vessel is the "Broken Sequence" ("Lie Que:" Lu-7) point. This "Ma Dan-Yang Heavenly Star Point is used to treat uterine, reproductive, and urinary organ diseases. This point is also used to treat diseases of the Lung, Large Intestine, and Conception Vessel.
- **Belt Vessel:** The Confluent point for the Belt Vessel is the "Foot Overlooking Tears" ("Zu Lin Qi:" GB-41) point. This Wood Element point is used to treat breast abscesses, pain and distention of the breast, and menstrual disorders. This point is also used to treat diseases of the Gall Bladder, and Belt Vessel.
- **Thrusting Vessel:** The Confluent point for the Thrusting Vessel is the "Yellow Emperor" (Gong Sun:" Sp-4) point. This "Luo" ("Connecting") point is used to treat acute abdominal pain (with cramping), vomiting and edema (especially of the face). This point is also used to treat diseases of the Spleen, Stomach, and Thrusting Vessel.
- **Yang Heel Vessel:** The Confluent point for the Yang Heel Vessel is the "Extending Vessel"

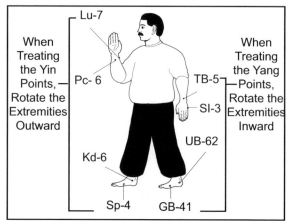

Figure 6.7. The anatomical locations of the body's Master and Couple Points

("Shen Mai:" UB-62) point. This "Ghost Point" is used to treat both External Wind Invasion and Internal Wind Invasion. External Wind invasion usually manifests in symptoms such as headaches and a stiff neck, while Internal Wind Invasion symptoms include insomnia, lockjaw, opisthotonos, Windstroke, epilepsy, upward staring eyes, deviations of the mouth and eyes, or hemiplegia. This point is also used to treat diseases of the Urinary Bladder and the Yang Heel Vessel.
- **Yin Heel Vessel:** The Confluent point for the Yin Heel Vessel is the "Shining Sea" ("Zhao Hai:" Kd-6) point. This point is used to treat tightness and contraction of the inner aspect of the leg, chronic throat disorders (swelling, pain, difficulty swallowing), eye disorders and daytime epilepsy. This point is also used to treat diseases of the Kidneys and Yin Heel Vessels.
- **Yang Linking Vessel:** The Confluent point for the Yang Linking Vessel is the "Outer Pass" ("Wai Guan:" TB-5 point). This "Luo" ("Connecting") point is used to treat temporal, frontal, occipital and vertex headaches, as well as to dispel pathogenic factors located on the Exterior (Yang) portion of the body. This point is also used to treat diseases of the Triple Burner, Pericardium, and Yang Linking Vessel.
- **Yin Linking Vessel:** The Confluent point for the Yin Linking Vessel is the "Nei Guan" ("Nei Guan:" Pc-6) point. This "Luo" ("Connect-

ing") point is used to treat pain in the Heart, chest, and lateral coastal region. This point is also used to treat diseases of the Pericardium, Heart, Triple Burner, and Yin Linking Vessel.

Master - Coupled Point Combination

In Chinese Energetic Medicine, the "Confluent Points are divided into Master and Coupled points (Figure 6.8). Each of the Eight Extraordinary Vessels has both a Master and a Coupled Confluent point on either the upper or lower limbs. The Master Point is the first (primary) point chosen for treatment; while its Coupled Point is the secondary "connecting" point, used to energetically open the targeted Vessel.

Whenever a Medical Qigong Doctor causes Qi to flow from a patient's Master Point to its Coupled point, the targeted Extraordinary Vessel will open. Therefore in the clinic, all of the Eight Extraordinary Vessels can be treated in various combinations according to their specific Master and Coupled point locations, for example:

- **Governing Vessel:** SI-3 is combined with UB-62 in order to treat diseases of the inner canthus, cheek, ear, neck, and shoulder.
- **Conception Vessel:** Lu-7 is combined with Kd-6 in order to treat diseases of the throat, Lung, chest, and diaphragm.
- **Thrusting Vessel:** Sp-4 is combined with Pc-6 in order to treat diseases of the Heart, Chest, and Stomach.
- **Belt Vessel:** GB-41 is combined with TB-5 in order to treat diseases of the outer canthus, cheek, ear, neck, and shoulder.

When treating a patient, after making the Master-Couples Point connection, the doctor will apply a slight traction onto the arm and leg in order to stretch the inner fascia and further stimulate the opening of the channel. This will increase Qi and Blood flow within the targeted Extraordinary Vessel.

When rotating and slightly pulling the limbs, it is important that the doctor focus his mind on energetically opening and increasing the flow of Qi within the Vessel that is being activated.

Channel	Open with Master Point	Complete with Couple Point
Governing	Hand (SI-3)	Foot (UB-62)
Conception	Hand (Lu-7)	Foot (Kd-6)
Thrusting	Foot (Sp-4)	Hand (Pc-6)
Belt	Foot (GB-41)	Hand (TB-5)
Yin Linking	Hand (Pc-6)	Foot (Sp-4)
Yang Linking	Hand (TB-5)	Foot (GB-41)
Yin Heel	Foot (Kd-6)	Hand (Lu-7)
Yang Heel	Foot (UB-62)	Hand (SI-3)

Figure 6.8. The Vessels and their associated Master Points and Couple Points

When stimulating the Yang Vessels, rotate the patient's arms and legs inward, towards the medial aspect of the body; when stimulating Yin Vessels rotate the patient's arms and legs outward, towards the lateral aspect of the body (see Figure 6.7).

When completing the treatment, the doctor must first remove all stimulation applied to the Coupled point; only then should he disconnect Qi stimulation flowing from the Master point.

Same Side and Crossover Treatments

There are two patterns used when applying the Master and Coupled Point combination: Same Side Treatment and Crossover Treatment; described as follows:

1. **Same Side Treatment:** When treating the same side (e.g., the right arm and the right leg), the energetic stimulation will affect the specific side that is being treated. When using the Same Side Treatment, the deficient or stagnant side

is chosen first. The treatment is then immediately followed with the Crossover Treatment. The Same Side Treatment is used to address energetic or physical asymmetries, and initiate a chaotic rhythm used in order to disrupt the established imbalance pattern of the patient's disease. Once the chaotic rhythm has been initiated, the Medical Qigong Doctor will then reprogram the patient's energetic body in order to facilitate a healthy re-patterning of the patient's physical body. Same Side Treatments are used in conditions such as stroke, Multiple Sclerosis, Bells Palsy, and Parkinson's disease.

2. **Crossover Treatment:** When treating with the crossover pattern (e.g., the right arm and the left leg) the doctor will focus on balancing the Qi and Blood within the stimulated Vessel. The crossover pattern is generally used in order to end a treatment, instilling balance and harmony within the patients body.

THE DAOIST MAGIC SQUARE

This special method was originally developed by Master Dou Hanqing, a famous doctor of the Jin and Yuan Dynasties (1115 - 1368 A.D.). The healing system is directly based on the ancient Daoist Yellow River Chart, and became popular after the publication of his book *"Zhen Jing Zhi Nan"* (*"A Guide to Acupuncture & Moxibustion"),"* in 1241 A.D. At that time, this acupuncture system was described as being "Numerical Acupuncture," as opposed to "Astronomical Acupuncture;" and was also referred to as the "Zi Wu Liu Zhu Zhen Fa" ("The Midnight to Noon Ebb and Flow Acupuncture Method") and the "Ling Gui Ba Fa" ("The Eight Methods of the Magic Turtle").

The Ling Gui Ba Fa method ascribes to the theory that all of the Primary Channel Points on the body are dominated by the "Shu" ("Stream") Points, which are in turn dominated by the Eight Confluent Points. The Eight Confluent Points and their trigram correspondences are described as follows (Figure 6.9):

- **The Trigram Kan,** located at Number 1, is associated with the Yang Heel Vessel, and the UB-62 point

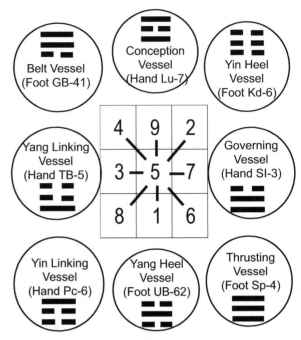

Figure 6.9. The Magic Square and Eight Extraordinary Vessels

- **The Trigram Kun,** located at Number 2, is associated with the Yin Heel Vessel, and the Kd-6 point
- **The Trigram Zhen,** located at Number 3, is associated with the Yang Linking Vessel, and the TB-5 point
- **The Trigram Xun,** located at Number 4, is associated with the Belt Vessel, and the GB-41 point
- **The Bright Hall (Ming Tang),** located at Number 5 on the center of the square, is associated with the Taiji Pole
- **The Trigram Qian,** located at Number 6, is associated with the Thrusting Vessels, and the Sp-4 point
- **The Trigram Dui,** located at Number 7, is associated with the Governing Vessel, and the SI-3 point
- **The Trigram Gen,** located at Number 8, is associated with the Yin Linking Vessel, and the Pc-6 point
- **The Trigram Li,** located at Number 9, is associated with the Conception Vessel, and the Lu-7 point

GOVERNING & CONCEPTION VESSELS: DU & REN MAI

The Governing and Conception Vessels are the main rivers of the body's Yang and Yin energies (Figure 6.10). They are the Yin and Yang polar aspects of the body's internal Sea's of Qi, perfectly complementary, like midday and midnight. In Chinese Energetic Embryology, these two important Vessels are responsible for the structural formation of the holoblastic cleavage, and the first cellular division of the fertilized ovum in embryological development (see Chapter 2).

In ancient China, Doctor Li Shizhen (Figure 6.11), was one of the greatest Chinese Doctors, Scientists, Herbalists and Acupuncturists in Chinese medical history. His major contribution to clinical medicine was 11 books, including the famous text *Bencao Gangmu (Compendium of Materia Medica)*, one of the most important Materia Medica of China. He was the first physician to believe that the Governing and Conception Vessels are two branches of the same source, an inseparable Yin-and-Yang, front-and-back duality. It is recorded that Doctor Li Shizhen remarked that any Chinese Physician who did not use these special Extraordinary Vessels was indeed not truly practicing the highest form of Chinese Medicine.

The Governing and Conception Vessels connect the Uterus with the Kidneys, Heart, and Brain. They originate externally at the Huiyin CV-1 point, ascend the front and back of the torso, and form a small circle when the tip of the tongue touches the upper palate in the mouth and the anal sphincter is closed. Not only does this action complete the balance of Fire (Heart) and Water (Kidney) energy, it also increases the body's protective Weiqi field.

The Governing and Conception Vessels each have energetic pathways on both the anterior and posterior vertical midline of the body. Each vessel's pathway is a complete circle, being composed of an ascending and descending energetic flow. These two medial lines join at the extremes of the torso (the head and perineum), forming one complete circle of energetic current. Therefore regulating the Conception and Governing Vessels is a priority in both Medical Qigong practice and treatment.

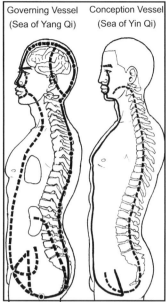

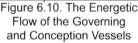

Figure 6.10. The Energetic Flow of the Governing and Conception Vessels

Figure 6.11. The Famous Physician Dr. Li Shizhen

Both vessels are superimposed on each other. The energy of the Governing Vessel is predominant up the back and inferior down the front (interior to the Conception Vessel); the energy of the Conception Vessel is predominant up the front and inferior down the back of the body, where it flows interior to the Governing Vessel. The energetic flow of the Conception Vessel corresponds to Yin, negative polarity, the female aspect, and responds to bass tones. The energetic flow of the Governing Vessel corresponds to Yang, positive polarity, the male aspect, and responds to treble tones.

The direction of the energetic movement of these two vessels explains why there are two opposite methods of directing the flow of energy along the torso in various meditation systems of energy cultivation. One direction follows the Fire Cycle of the Microcosmic Orbit, moving Qi along the Governing Vessel, flowing up the spine and down the chest to energize and regulate the emotions of the acquired mind (Shen Zhi). The other direction follows the Water Cycle of the Microcosmic Orbit, moving Qi along the Conception Vessel, flowing up the chest and down the spine to stimulate spiritual intuition and activate the perceptions of the congenital mind (Yuan Shen).

The Governing Vessel: Du Mai

The Chinese word "Du" translates as "Governing," and it refers to a Governing General, or to someone who controls and is in charge. The character Du can also be translated as: to oversee, inspect, superintend or reprove; a viceroy or governor general; and the center or the middle seam located on the back of a coat. The ideographs for Du Mai are described as follows (Figure 6.12):

- **Du:** The Chinese ideograph Du is composed of two parts. Positioned on the top are three separate characters: "Shang" ("Upper" - on top), "Xiao" ("Small" - bottom left), and "You" ("Again" - bottom right). This three combination upper character is translated as "one's father's younger brother" or "uncle."

    Positioned to the bottom is the character "Mu," depicting "a watchful eye." This ideograph depicts the keen eyes of an inspector who watches and monitors on behalf of someone else; denoting that the Governing Vessel is responsible for overseeing or monitoring the Yang of the body, but is nevertheless subordinate to the Heart (i.e., the Emperor). The authority of the Governing Vessel is therefore not equal to the higher level of the Heart (Emperor), but is that of a "smaller governor" (i.e., Prime Minister) that answers to the Emperor.

- **Mai:** The second character is the ideograph "Mai," generally translated as "Vessel." It is composed of two characters: The character to the left, "Ji" depicts the Chinese ideogram for body tissue, muscle, or flesh, all of which are forms of connective tissue. The character to the right, "Mai" depicts a current of water, stream, or a branch of a river. As a whole, the character can be translated as "Arteries, Veins, or Pulse," indicating a form of consistent energetic circulation.

Development

During the development of the embryo, the Governing Vessel is responsible for the formation of the Medulla Oblongata and Cerebrum (Figure 6.13). It is also responsible for nourishing the Brain and the spinal cord, and for consolidating the Yuan Qi (Original/Prenatal Energy) in the Kidneys.

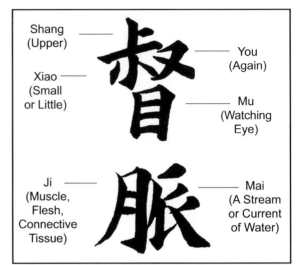

Figure 6.12. Chinese Ideograph for "Du Mai" (Governing Vessel: GV)

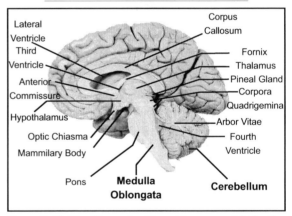

Figure 6.13. The Governing Vessel is responsible for the formation of the Medulla Oblongata and Cerebrum

The Governing Vessel controls all of the Yang energy channels in the body, and is therefore known as the "Sea of Yang." Along its course, it intersects with the three Yang channels of the hands and feet, as well as the Yang Linking (Wei) Vessels several times.

Energetic Pathway

The Governing Vessel originates in the Lower Dantian in both men and women. It is composed of many energetic branches, described as follows:

- **The Primary Channel of the Governing Vessel:** This channel originates in the Lower Dantian (the center of the Uterus in women), emerges at the perineum (bottom gate of the Lower Dantian), and runs posteriorly along the midline of the sacrum (Figure 6.14).

It travels along the interior of the spinal column to the lower back and the Mingmen GV-4 point (back gate of the Lower Dantian). From there it continues to the mid-back and at the Shendao GV-11 point (Back Gate of the Middle Dantian). From the Shendao point it continues to ascend the spinal column to the nape of the neck, where it enters the Brain at the Fengfu GV-16 point (back gate of the Upper Dantian). It further ascends over the head to the vertex at the Baihui GV-20 point (upper gate of the Upper Dantian), from which a branch descends directly into the Niwan Palace of the Brain (Pineal Gland), and then reconnects with the GV-16 point at the base of the skull. From the Baihui point the Governing Vessel progresses along the midline of the forehead, past the Yintang point (front gate of the Upper Dantian) to the bridge of the nose where it terminates at the junction of the upper lip at the gum and joins with the Conception Vessel at the "Corpse Reviver" (GV-28) point.

- **The First Branch of the Governing Vessel:** The first branch originates in the Lower Dantian (the center of the Uterus in women),. From there, it descends to the genitals and perineum (bottom gate of the Lower Dantian), encircles the anus, and ascends up the spinal column slightly internal to the primary channel of the Governing Vessel, entering the Kidneys and Mingmen (Gate of Life) area, located at the back gate of the Lower Dantian.
- **The Second Branch of the Governing Vessel:** This branch also originates in the Lower Dantian (the center of the Uterus in women). It descends to the genitals and perineum (bottom gate of the Lower Dantian), envelops the external genitalia and ascends to the middle of the umbilicus at the Shenque (Spirit Palace Gate) point, located at the front gate of the Lower Dantian.

From the umbilicus it further ascends up the chest, passing through the Yellow Court, Heart, and Middle Dantian, ascending through the throat to circle the mouth. After circling the mouth, it further ascends to the eyes, ter-

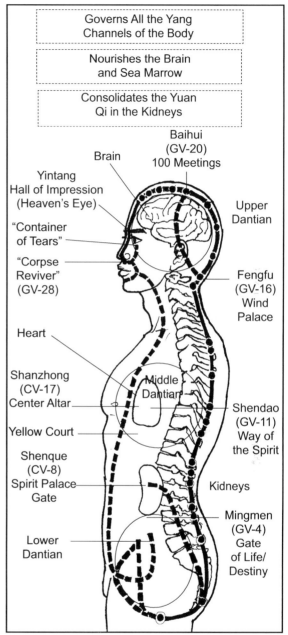

Figure 6.14. The Du Mai (Governing Vessel) Sea of Yang Qi (Side View)

minating just below the middle of the eyes at the Chengqi (Container of Tears: St-1) point.
- **The Third Branch of the Governing Vessel:** This branch originates from the inside of the eyes at the Jingming (Bright Eyes: UB-1) point.

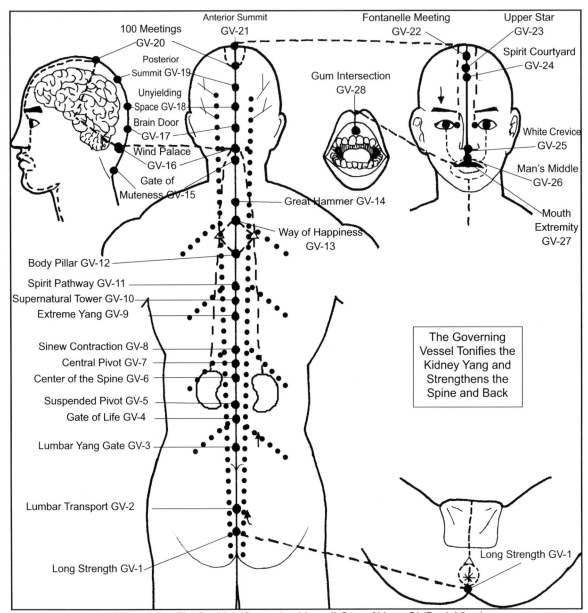

Figure 6.15. The Du Mai (Governing Vessel) Sea of Yang Qi (Back View)

From the UB-1 points, this vessel follows both of the Urinary Bladder Channels along the forehead, converges at the vertex of the Baihui GV-20 point (upper gate of the Upper Dantian), and descends to enter the Brain. From the Brain, the vessel emerges at the Fengfu (Wind Palace) GV-16 point (back gate of the Upper Dantian) and divides into two additional branches which descend down the back. These two branches pass through the Fengmen (Wind Gate: UB-12) points along the sides of the spine before entering into the Kidneys and Mingmen (Gate of Life: GV-4) area (Figure 6.15).

- **The Luo-Connecting Vessel of the Governing Vessel:** This Vessel originates from the Changqiang (Long Strength: GV-1) point at

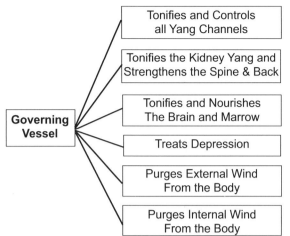

Figure 6.16. The Functions and Clinical Uses Of the Du Mai (Governing Vessel: GV)

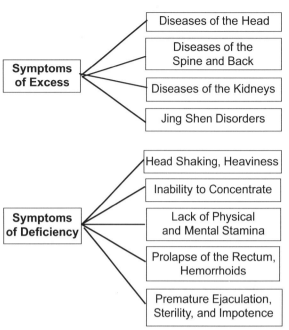

Figure 6.17. Pathological Manifestations of the Du Mai (Governing Vessel)

the perineum (bottom gate of the Lower Dantian) and ascends bilaterally along the sides of the spine to the Fengfu (Wind Palace: GV-16) point (back gate of the Upper Dantian) where it disperses over the occipital region.

Clinical Manifestations

The Governing Vessel tonifies the Kidney Yang and strengthens the spine and back. When the Governing Vessel is in excess, the back becomes stiff; when it is depleted, the head becomes heavy, unstable, and shaky. The functions and clinical uses of the patient's Governing Vessel are described as follows (Figure 6.16):

1. Tonifies and controls all the Yang Channels of the patient's body (particularly in relation to the Kidney Yang and the Brain).
2. Tonifies the Kidney Yang and strengthens the patient's spine and back, especially in cases of chronic lower back pain due to Kidney Deficiency.
3. Tonifies and nourishes the patient's Brain and Marrow and treats such symptoms as poor memory, dizziness, and tinnitus.
4. Treats depression, due to the Governing Vessel's connection to the body's Jing (Kidneys and willpower), Qi (Heart awareness), and Shen (Spirit).
5. Purges External Wind from the patient's body when symptoms such as runny nose, headache, fever, and stiff neck are present.
6. Purges Internal Wind from the patient's body when symptoms such as dizziness, tremors, convulsions, epilepsy, or the condition of Wind Stroke are present.

In men, the Governing Vessel is generally treated by itself, and in women it is combined with the treatment of the Conception Vessel.

Pathological Manifestations

The main diseases associated with energetic malfunctions in the Governing Vessel are described as follows (Figure 6.17):

1. **Symptoms of Excess Qi:** These include diseases of the head (apoplexy, aphasia, epilepsy, headaches, tetany), back, neck, and Kidneys (pain and stiffness in the spinal column), opisthotonos (spastic muscle movement), night sweating, and Jing Shen disorders (such as hyperexcitability, hallucinations).
2. **Symptoms of Deficient Qi:** These include the shaking of the head, feelings of general heaviness, instability, and an inability to concentrate. The patient may lack physical and mental stamina, display weakness of character, and may also experience prolapse of the rectum, hemorrhoids, premature ejaculation, sterility, or impotence.

THE CONCEPTION VESSEL: REN MAI

The Chinese word "Ren" translates as "Conception," and refers to "Pregnancy, Responsibility, and/or Obligation." It can also mean "To Accept or Take Charge." The ideographs for Ren Mai are described as follows (Figure 6.18):

- **Ren:** The Chinese ideograph "Ren" is composed of two parts. Positioned on the left is the radical "Ren" meaning "Person" or "Human." Positioned on the right is the radical for "Ren" that is, etymologically speaking, a "Working Person." It depicts the image of a bamboo pole suspended on the shoulders of one who is walking on the road with a load hanging at each end. This suggests the meaning of "Enduring, Bearing, and/or Taking the Burden of Something." When combined with the previous radical for person, the overall meaning is that of "Bearing the Burden of Being Human."
- **Mai:** The second character is the ideograph "Mai," generally translated as "Vessel." It is composed of two characters: The character to the left, "Ji" depicts the Chinese ideogram for body tissue, muscle, or flesh, all of which are forms of connective tissue. The character to the right, "Mai" depicts a current of water, stream, or a branch of a river. As a whole, the character can be translated as "Arteries, Veins, or Pulse," indicating a form of consistent energetic circulation.

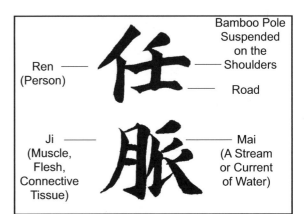

Figure 6.18. The Chinese Ideograph for "Ren Mai" (Conception Vessel: CV)

DEVELOPMENT

The Conception Vessel originates from the Lower Dantian, and specifically in the Uterus for females. It nourishes the Yuan Qi (Original/Prenatal Energy) of all Five Yin Organs (Liver, Heart, Spleen, Lungs, and Kidneys), and governs all the Yin channels of the body. It is for this reason that the Conception Vessel is called the Sea of Yin. It also intersects with the three Yin channels of the hands and feet, as well as the Yin Linking (Wei) Vessels several times.

Functionally, the Conception Vessel can be divided into three quadrants, described as follows:

- **Upper:** The upper third of the Conception Vessel on the sternum controls respiratory functions (Figure 6.19)
- **Middle:** The middle third of the Conception Vessel on the epigastrium controls digestive functions
- **Lower:** The lower third of the Conception Vessel on the abdomen controls the urogenital functions

In women, the Conception Vessel is primarily responsible for nourishing the Uterus and the genital system, and determines her seven-year life cycles. It also links her Yin energy with all aspects of conception and reproduction. The Conception Vessel, along with the Thrusting Vessels, has an important relationship with obstetric diseases that are related to the development of the fetus, delivery, and menstruation.

To the ancient Daoists, the secret "Microcosmic Orbit" Neigong exercises were traditionally developed in order to enhance and augment the sea of energies contained within the disciples Ren Mai (Conception Vessel) and Du Mai (Governing Vessel).

ENERGETIC PATHWAY

The Conception Vessel originates in the Lower Dantian in both men and women. It is composed of many energetic branches, described as follows (Figure 6.20):

- **The Primary Channel of the Conception Vessel:** This channel originates in the Lower Dantian (the center of the Uterus in women) and emerges at the Huiyin CV-1 point of the perineum (bottom gate of the Lower Dantian).

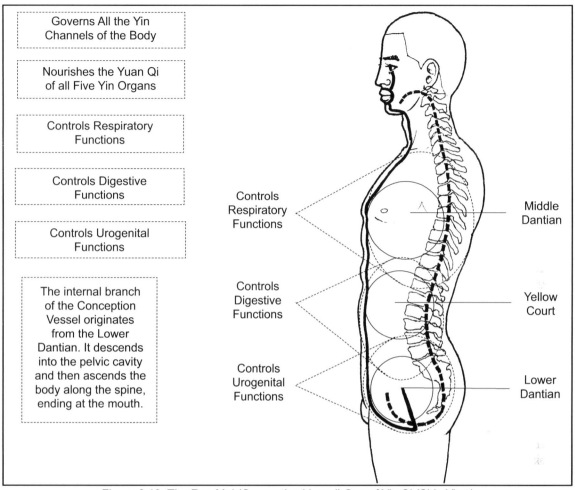

Figure 6.19. The Ren Mai (Conception Vessel) Sea of Yin Qi (Side View)

From the perineum it runs through the anterior aspect of the pubic region, ascends along the middle of the abdomen and passes through the umbilicus at the Shenque (Spirit Palace Gate: CV-8) point, located at the front gate of the Lower Dantian. From the umbilicus it ascends the midline of the chest, passes through the Yellow Court, Heart, and Middle Dantian at the CV-17 point, ascending through the throat and jaw to reach the bottom of the lip and circle the mouth. After circling the mouth, it connects with the Governing Vessel at the top of the lip and gum area, at the "Corpse Reviver" (GV-28) point. From there, it ascends further in two branches toward each of the eyes, terminating just below the middle of the eyes at the Chengqi (Container of Tears: St-1) point.

- **The First Branch of the Conception Vessel:** The first branch originates in the Lower Dantian (the center of the Uterus in women), descends to the genitals and the Huiyin CV-1 point of the perineum (bottom gate of the Lower Dantian), encircles the anus and ascends into the center of the spinal column. Following the spinal column, it ascends through the back gates of the Lower and Middle Dantians, entering into the mouth and the Medulla Oblongata of the Brain.

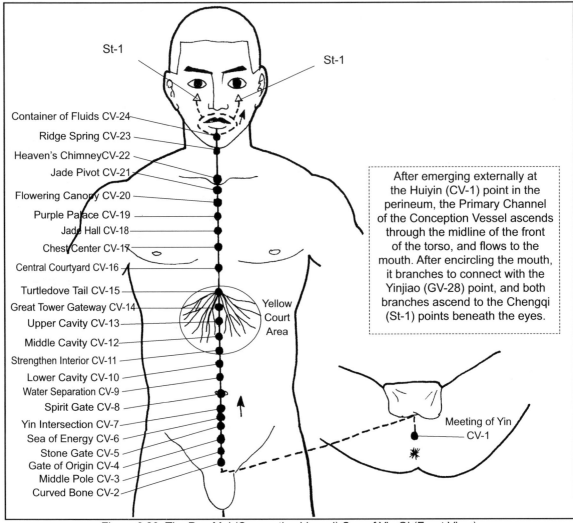

Figure 6.20. The Ren Mai (Conception Vessel) Sea of Yin Qi (Front View)

- **The Luo-Connecting Vessel of the Conception Vessel:** This Vessel originates from the Jiuwei (Turtledove Tail: CV-15) point (Bottom Gate of the Middle Dantian) and disperses over the Yellow Court region.

Clinical Manifestations

In Medical Qigong Therapy, the functions and clinical uses of the patient's Conception Vessel are described as follows (Figure 6.21).

1. Tonifies and nourishes Yin energy (especially in women after menopause) and harmonizes the Lungs and Kidneys.

2. Regulates the energy of the reproductive system, tonifies the Blood and Yin, and reduces the effects of Heart Empty-Heat symptoms (night sweating, hot flashes, anxiety, irritability, insomnia, and dizziness, etc.) developed from Kidney Yin Deficiency after menopause.

3. Promotes Blood supply to the Uterus and regulates Menstrual Disorders (i.e., Dysmenorrhea, Menorrhagia, Amenorrhea, and Metrorrhagia).

4. Moves the Qi in the Lower Burner and treats abdominal lumps, as well as myomas, fi-

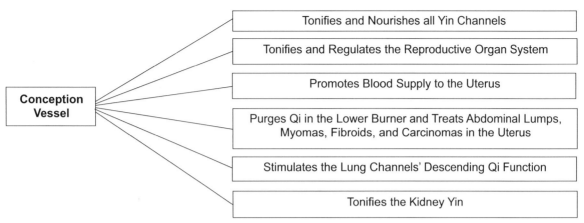

Figure 6.21. The Functions and Clinical Uses of the Ren Mai (Conception Vessel: CV)

broids, and carcinoma in the woman's Uterus, and hernia in men.
5. Stimulates the energetic interaction of the Lung Channels' descending Qi function and the Kidneys' function of receiving and holding the Lung Qi. Asthma, for example, is a common symptom of this type of imbalance.
6. Tonifies and nourishes Kidney Yin

Pathological Manifestations

The main diseases associated with energetic imbalances in the Conception Vessel are described as follows (Figure 6.22):

1. **Symptoms of Excess:** This includes diseases of the reproductive and gastrointestinal systems such as hemorrhoids, diarrhea, decreased urination, abdominal hernia.
 - **In Men:** Problems in the Conception Vessel can lead to impotence and sterility.
 - **In Women:** Problems in the Conception Vessel can cause menstrual difficulties such as Menoxenia, profuse Leukorrhea, and Dysmenorrhea. Other female problems associated with Excess Qi in the Conception Vessel include breast pain, sterility, miscarriage, paralysis after delivery, and emaciation, as well as disorders of the external genitalia, vulva, vagina, and cervix.

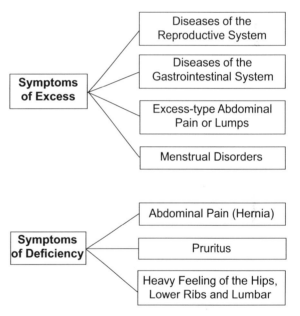

Figure 6.22. Pathological Manifestations of the Ren Mai (Conception Vessel)

2. **Symptoms of Deficiency:** This includes abdominal pains (hernia) and pruritus, as well as a heavy feeling in the hips, lower ribs, and lumbar area.

Thrusting & Belt Vessels: Chong Mai and Dai Mai

The Thrusting (Chong) and Belt (Dai) Vessels balance the energies of the body's external tissues, internal organs, and center core Taiji Pole. The Thrusting and Belt Vessels maintain internal and external energetic balance, and harmonize excess or deficient conditions by evenly dispersing the Qi throughout the body's tissues.

The Thrusting Vessel can be likened to a magnet wrapped with the copper wire of the Belt Vessel. In this way, the body is like an electromagnet, connecting the positive and negative ends of the Taiji Pole to the energetic generators of Heaven and Earth. The power of the human energetic field is thus increased exponentially.

The Thrusting Vessels: Chong Mai

The Chinese word "Chong" translates as "Street," and expresses the idea of "Passing or Penetrating Through Something." In ancient China, the character originally meant "To March, Surge, Rush Against, Clash, Pour Out, Infuse, Flush, and Soar." The ideograph for Chong Mai is described as follows (Figure 6.23):

- **Chong:** The first ideograph is the Chinese character "Chong," it is composed of one radical "Xing," which is divided into two parts. Positioned on the left is the character for "Walking." Positioned on the right is the character "Ren" ("Person" or "Human"). The translation for this character is "To Walk or Step Forward."

   Positioned in the center of the ideograph are the three phonics radicals used to construct the word "Chong," composed of three parts: "Tu" ("Soil, Land, Earth" - on bottom); "Tian" ("Field" - in the middle); and "Gan" ("Dry" - on top). As a whole, the set of characters can be translated to mean "Passing or Penetrating Through a Dry Field."

- **Mai:** The second character is the ideograph "Mai," generally translated as "Vessel." It is composed of two characters: The character to the left, "Ji" depicts the Chinese ideogram for body tissue, muscle, or flesh, all of which are forms of connective tissue. The character

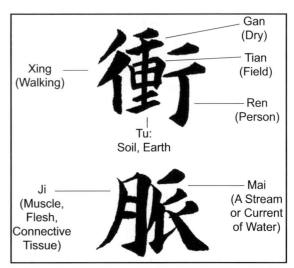

Figure 6.23. Chinese Ideograph for "Chong Mai" (Thrusting Vessels)

to the right, "Mai" depicts a current of water, stream, or a branch of a river. As a whole, the character can be translated as "Arteries, Veins, or Pulse," indicating a form of consistent energetic circulation.

Development

The Qi of the Thrusting Vessels originate in the Lower Dantian, and travel upward towards the head and face, and also penetrates into the lower limbs, irrigating the body's Yin Qi.

The Thrusting Vessels' action of "passing through" refers to their function as the vital pathway for alchemical transformation. To the ancient Daoists, the Thrusting Vessels were the primary channels used to produce the energetic transformations constantly occurring between Jing (Essence), Qi (Energy), and Shen (Spirit/Mind). Therefore the ancient Daoists believed that the Thrusting Vessels also possessed the energetic function of blending the subtle influences of both Heaven (Yang) and Earth (Yin) Qi.

In ancient China, the Thrusting Vessel was also known as the "Penetrating Channel," and was regarded as both the Sea of Blood and the Sea of the Twelve Primary (Regulating) Channels. It regulates (balances) both the Qi and Blood of all Twelve Primary Channels, and energetically ex-

tends to the anterior, posterior, upper, and lower parts of the body. According to some doctors of Traditional Chinese Medicine, all energetic points that have "Chong" ("Penetrating or Rushing Through") in their names relate to the Thrusting Vessels. For example:
- **Qichong (Penetrating Energy):** St-30,
- **Taichong (Great Penetrating):** Liv-3,
- **Shaochong ("Lesser Penetrating"):** Ht-9).

The Thrusting Vessels control all aspects of menstruation, influencing the supply and amount of Blood in the Uterus, as well as nourishing the woman's Jing. They flow along the Kidney Channels and are responsible for tightening the abdominal muscles and the penis.

During the development of the embryo, the Thrusting Vessels are responsible for the development of the adrenal glands and the adrenal cortex. Abnormalities of the Thrusting Vessels during the beginning of pregnancy can result in the spontaneous abortion of the fetus. Abnormalities of the Thrusting Vessels during the end of pregnancy may result in an inability to expel the placenta.

Along with the Conception Vessel, the Thrusting Vessels are responsible for regulating the changes that occur during an individual's Life Cycles. These unique Life Cycles occur every eight years in men and every seven years in women.

Together, the Governing, Conception and Thrusting Vessels are considered to be the energetic gateway to an individual's Ancestry, and the link to his or her ancestral skills and knowledge.

In the early 1980s, one of my Daoist teachers, Master Lu, explained that one unique manifestation of practicing correct Qigong Meditation and deep prayer, is that the Thrusting Vessels will eventually energetically overflow into the eyes. When this energetic phenomenon occurs, the Thrusting Vessels under the eyes will begin to radiate a sparkling white-light energy, which will later extend its radiant glow from out of the center of the practitioners eyes. Master Lu explained that this radiant spiritual light reflects the practitioners Original Spirit (Heart/Mind) that is connected to the energetic pulse of the eternal Dao, and

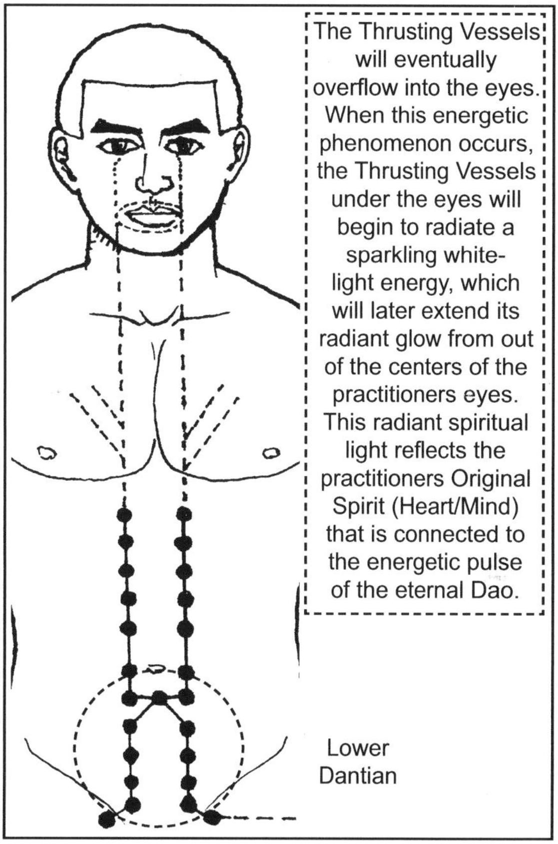

> The Thrusting Vessels will eventually overflow into the eyes. When this energetic phenomenon occurs, the Thrusting Vessels under the eyes will begin to radiate a sparkling white-light energy, which will later extend its radiant glow from out of the centers of the practitioners eyes. This radiant spiritual light reflects the practitioners Original Spirit (Heart/Mind) that is connected to the energetic pulse of the eternal Dao.

Lower Dantian

Figure 6.24. The Chong Mai (Thrusting Vessels) Overflowing into the meditator's eyes

that this is how he was taught to determine if a disciple was truly practicing spiritual cultivation. Throughout the years, I have personally observed this radiant spiritual light shining from several of my spiritual teachers (from different faiths) and from my disciples (Figure 6.24).

To the ancient Daoists, the secret "Fusing and Energizing The Internal Taiji Pole" Neigong exercises were traditionally developed in order to enhance and augment the various energies contained within the disciples Chong Mai (Thrusting Vessels).

ENERGETIC PATHWAY

The Thrusting Vessels originate from the Lower Dantian, and specifically in the Uterus in females. It is composed of five energetic branches, described as follows (Figure 6.25):

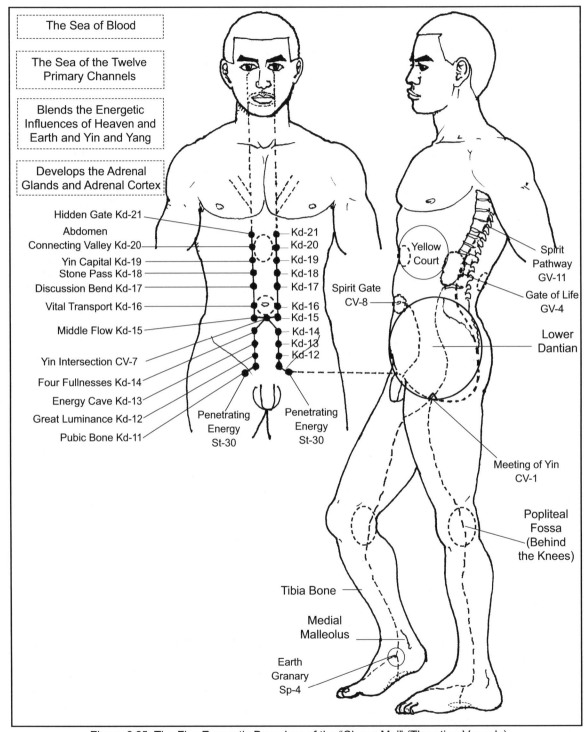

Figure 6.25. The Five Energetic Branches of the "Chong Mai" (Thrusting Vessels)

- **The Primary Channel of the Thrusting Vessels:** This channel originates in the Lower Dantian (the center of the Uterus in women) and emerges at the Huiyin (Meeting of Yin: CV-1) point of the perineum (located on the bottom gate of the Lower Dantian). From the perineum, the Primary Channel ascends the bottom of the abdomen to the top of the inner thighs (level with of the superior border of the pubic symphysis), surfacing at the Qichong (Penetrating Energy - St-30) points.

  From the Qichong, the Primary Channel travels up the chest, alongside the Kidney Channels, doubling its energetic potential. It then surrounds and enters into the "Spirit Gate" (CV-8) located at the umbilicus (front gate of the Lower Dantian). The channel then further ascends up the abdomen alongside the chest, flowing through the area of the Yellow Court. It energetically disperses into the Sea of Qi (i.e., the Middle Dantian) and into the Upper Burner, located in the center of the chest.

- **The First Branch of the Thrusting Vessels:** The first branches originate from the Yellow Court and ascends in two columns upward through the Heart and Middle Dantian areas. They continue to ascend through the throat, encircle the lips and energetically connect with the Governing and Conception Vessels.

  The first branches of the Thrusting Vessels terminate on each side of the nasal cavity. The *Yellow Emperor's Magical Pivot* states that "the energy rising in the Thrusting Vessels emerges from the nasopharynx, and filters into all the Yang, irrigating all of the essences."

  According to ancient Daoist teachings, when these Thrusting Vessels are full and overflowing, as happens through deep prayer and meditation, they radiate a sparkling white-light energy, which extends from the upper chest into the practitioners eyes.

- **The Second Branch of the Thrusting Vessels:** This branch originates in the Lower Dantian (the center of the Uterus in women), and travels to the lower aspect of the Kidneys. From the Kidneys, it descends, fusing into a single channel and terminates into the perineum (bottom gate of the Lower Dantian).

  From the perineum, it again divides into two branches and descends along the medial aspect of the thighs and into the popliteal fossa behind the knees.

  From behind the knees, it buries itself and circulates deep into the tibia bones, where together with the Kidney channels, it descends to penetrate behind the internal aspect of the Medial Malleolus at the ankles.

  At the junction of the ankles it branches again, terminating along the Kidney channels at the bottom of the feet. This detachment, along with the Kidney channels, filters into the three Yin channels of the legs.

- **The Third Branch of the Thrusting Vessels:** This branch originates from the Second Branches along the tibias and obliquely penetrating the malleolus, where they connect and move along the top of the feet, terminating between the big toes.

- **The Fourth Branch of the Thrusting Vessels:** This branch originates from the Primary Channel in the pelvic cavity. It moves backwards along the lower perineum to enter the spinal column, traveling up the back, intersecting with the Mingmen (Gate of Life/Destiny: GV-4) located on the back gate of the Lower Dantian, and the Shendao (Spirit Pathway: GV-11), located on the back gate of the Middle Dantian.

CLINICAL MANIFESTATIONS

The functions and clinical uses of the Thrusting Vessels are described as follows (Figure 6.26):

1. Tonifies, nourishes, and regulates weak constitutions with digestive symptoms (such as abdominal distension, poor appetite, and poor assimilation of food).
2. Moves the Blood of the Heart and relieves symptoms of pain and stiffness of the chest. This function is due to the Thrusting Vessels ability to control all of the Blood in the connecting channels.
3. Purges Abdominal and Chest Qi and Blood Stagnation.

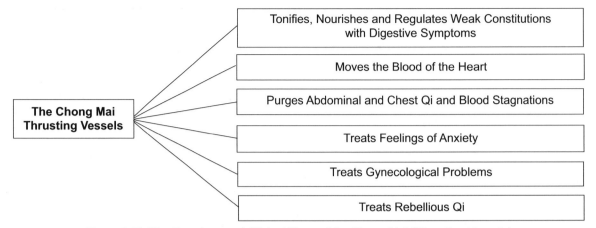

Figure 6.26. The Functions and Clinical Uses of the Chong Mai (Thrusting Vessels)

4. Treats feelings of anxiety (within the chest) caused by Rebellious Qi. One of the Thrusting Vessels' most important pathologies is Rebellious Qi, which is Qi that moves in the wrong direction, going upward instead of downward. Feelings of anxiety that arise in the patient's abdomen and ascend to the chest are especially indicative of this imbalance.

5. Treats gynecological problems (hot flashes), when the Qi of the Thrusting Vessels rises upward. This ascension of Qi can cause the patient's hands and feet to become cold, the face to get hot, and leads to a feeling of fullness in the chest. In such cases, the treatment goal is to regulate the Thrusting Vessels and subdue the Rebellious Qi. If there are accompanying emotional problems and Liver Qi stagnation, then the patient's Lv-3 points are also treated.

6. Treats Rebellious Qi caused by the upward moving energy of the Thrusting Vessels. In this type of condition, the symptoms manifest as oppressive feelings in the chest, as well as dizziness, nausea, and vomiting.

Pathological Manifestations

The main diseases associated with the Thrusting Vessel are described as follows (Figure 6.27):

1. **Symptoms of Excess:** the main diseases associated with the patient's Thrusting Vessels include diseases of the Heart, fullness in the chest and abdomen, gastritis, abdominal pain, and convulsive diseases.

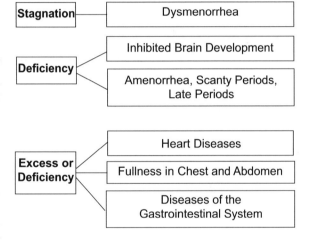

Figure 6.27. Pathological Manifestations of the Chong Mai (Thrusting Vessels)

2. **Symptoms of Deficiency:** If the energy from the Thrusting Vessels to the cortex becomes deficient, it can inhibit the development of the Brain. If a woman's Thrusting Vessels are deficient or empty, she may develop such conditions as amenorrhea, scanty periods, or late periods.

3. **Symptoms of Stagnation:** If there is stagnant Qi and/or Blood in the Thrusting Vessels, a woman may experience dysmenorrhea. Abnormalities of the Thrusting Vessels may also result in the mother having a miscarriage.

THE BELT VESSEL: DAI MAI

The Chinese word "Dai" translates as "A Belt" or "Girdle," and refers to "The Action of Binding and Supporting Something." The ideograph for Dai Mai is described as follows (Figure 6.28):

- **Dai:** The first character is the Chinese ideograph "Dai," which is generally translated as "Belt" or "Girdle." It is composed of two parts: the top radical depicts a "Robe, Cloak or Garment." The lower radical portrays valuable items (usually coins and jade) being held together by a belt, ribbon, or strap. The overall image of valuable items being wrapped and held together within a robe or garment, suggests the meaning of a current of energy binding and covering the body like a coil (Figure 6.29).

This character further communicates the ancient Daoist understanding that this special energetic belt is responsible for securing valuable items within the body (e.g., the various internal organs, energetic vessels and channels, vaporous energies and subtle fluids, etc.).

- **Mai:** The second character is the ideograph "Mai," generally translated as "Vessel." It is composed of two characters: The character to the left, "Ji" depicts the Chinese ideogram for body tissue, muscle, or flesh, all of which are forms of connective tissue. The character to the right, "Mai" depicts a current of water, stream, or a branch of a river. As a whole, the character can be translated as "Arteries, Veins, or Pulse," indicating a form of consistent energetic circulation.

DEVELOPMENT

In Chinese Energetic Embryology, the Belt Vessel is believed responsible for the second cellular division of the fertilized ovum Figure 6.29).

Traditionally, the Belt Vessel's energetic function is to bind, join, and control all of the channels of the body, exerting a powerful influence on the circulation of the body's Governing (Sea of Yang Qi), Conception (Sea of Yin Qi), and Thrusting (blending both Heavenly Yang and Earthly Yin Qi.) Vessels.

According to ancient Daoist teachings, the Belt Vessel was originally believed to "wrap around

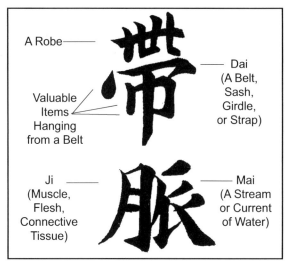

Figure 6.28. The Chinese Ideograph for "Dai Mai" (Belt Vessel)

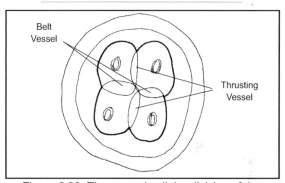

Figure 6.29. The second cellular division of the fertilized ovum is associated with the development of the Belt Vessel and the Thrusting Vessel.

the entire body, like a celestial mist encircling a sacred mountain." It is within this sacred "Breath of the Dao" that the energy of the entire mountain could become contained, united, balanced, concealed from the public, and allowed to manifest its natural internal quiescent state.

The ancient Daoist schools of Qigong training traditionally teach that the Belt Vessel originates from the Lower Dantian (Shenque: CV-8 and Mingmen: GV-4) and wraps the entire body like a silk cocoon or an enveloping whirlpool, flowing from the feet to the head. This was why the secret "Belt Winding" Neigong exercises were traditionally developed in order to enhance and augment the

VOLUME 1, SECTION 1: FOUNDATIONS OF CHINESE ENERGETIC MEDICINE

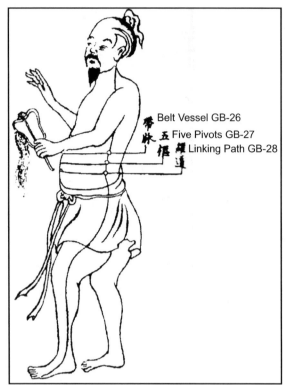

Figure 6.30. The Dai Mai (Belt Vessel), From the *Nei Wai Gong Tushou* (Internal & External Skill Illustrated Instructions).

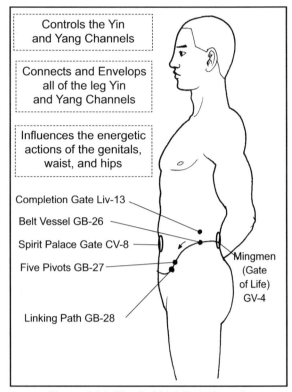

Figure 6.31. The Dai Mai (Belt Vessel), (Modern Depiction)

various energies contained, united, and balanced by the disciples Dai Mai.

During the Han Dynasty (206 B.C. - 220 A.D.) it was taught that the Belt Vessel originated at the Mingmen (Gate of Life: GV-4 point) area, and encircled the waist like a belt, dipping down into the lower abdominal region anteriorly and running across the lumbar region posteriorly. This channel connects with the Dai Mai (Belt Vessel: GB-26), Wushu (Five Pivits: GB-27), and Weidao (Linking Path: GB-28) points, and crosses the Conception Vessel at Guanyun (Gate of Origin: CV-4) point (Figure 6.30).

According to Traditional Chinese Medicine teachings, the Belt Vessel is considered to be a single horizontal vessel circling the body at the waist (Figure 6.31), and is rooted at the Mingmen (Gate of Life/Destiny: GV-4) in the back. Many sources however, also state that the Belt Channel connects with the Zhangmen (Completion Gate: Liver-13) points located at the free end of each 12th rib.

ENERGETIC PATHWAY

The Belt Vessel can be likened to a copper wire wrapping the internal magnet of the Thrusting Vessels (Figure 6.32). In this way, the body is like an electromagnet. Therefore by connecting the positive and negative ends of the Taiji Pole to the energetic generators of Heaven and Earth, the power of the human energetic field is increased exponentially.

At one time, this knowledge of the horizontal energetic flow was a well-guarded secret. The ancient Daoist books on horizontal energetic flow all focused on the alchemical aspects of energetic and spiritual transformation. The main focus of these teachings concentrated on the ability of dissolving the body's Qi and Shen into the various dimensions of infinite space (Wuji) which envelop the energetic fields of Heaven, Earth and Man. These ancient books were nearly all destroyed when the Qin emperor (221 - 206 B.C.) ordered the burning of all writings containing this knowledge.

During the following Han Dynasty, only Confucianism was honored because of its focus on being obedient to the government as a means of obtaining spiritual propriety. Therefore, the "vertical" Confucian classics on energy flow were preserved while the significance of the "horizontal" energetic flow was diminished.

To the ancient Daoists, the body's waist was considered to be the hub of the energetic wheel of the body. The access points of the Belt Vessel's center channel, which circles the waist, are commonly used to control the entire vessel, and thus the entire body. As the energy of the body increases (through Qi and Shen cultivation), the Qi within the entire Belt Vessel increases, wrapping the tissues from feet to head, and increasing the body's Wei Qi fields.

The Belt Vessel exerts an important influence on the body's physiology by encircling the leg channels. This influences the circulation of energy to and from the legs, as well as influencing the energetic actions of the genitals, waist, and hips.

The Belt Vessel also keeps the body's Yin and Yang channels under control, connecting all of the leg Yin and Yang channels as they traverse the body's trunk. As a result, the Belt Vessel is said to assist in regulating the circulation of Qi in all of the Yin and Yang channels of the body, especially those from the waist downward.

The Belt Vessel harmonizes the ascending and descending flow of energy from the Kidneys and Spleen through its connection with the Kidney Divergent Channel. The Belt Vessel also restrains the flow of the body's Liver and Gall Bladder Qi.

In ancient China, meditating on the Belt Vessel was traditionally used for energetically armoring and protecting the body against environmental and emotional pathogenic invasions. The spiritual energy attached to this unique energetic field was also believed to inform the individual when

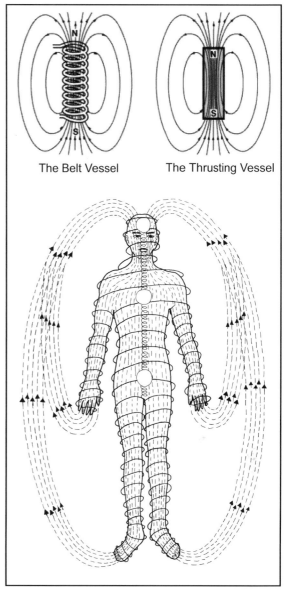

Figure 6.32. The Dai Mai (Belt Vessel) is a current of energy binding and covering the body like a coil

something was "wrong," especially when the individual was out of harmony with the Dao. Therefore, the loss of "Life-Purpose" was originally spiritually and psychologically related to Disorders of the Belt Vessel.

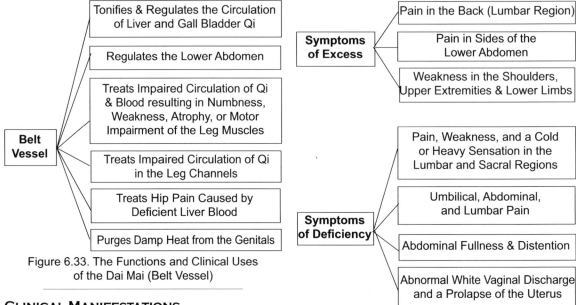

Figure 6.33. The Functions and Clinical Uses of the Dai Mai (Belt Vessel)

Figure 6.34. Pathological Manifestations of the Dai Mai (Belt Vessel)

CLINICAL MANIFESTATIONS

The functions and clinical uses of the Belt Vessel are described as follows (Figure 6.33):

1. Tonifies and Regulates the circulation of Liver and Gall Bladder Qi due to patterns of Excess Liver Qi.
2. Regulates the lower abdomen due to a Belt Vessel imbalance that causes such symptoms as a sagging waist or bloated abdomen.
3. Treats impaired circulation of Qi and Blood that causes numbness, weakness, atrophy, or motor impairment of the leg muscles. This can be due to a Deficiency of Qi in the Stomach and Spleen Channels.
4. Treats impaired circulation of Qi in the leg channels resulting in such symptoms as cold legs and feet or tense leg muscles (gastrocnemius and tibiales). This condition is due to the Liver Blood not moistening the sinews of the legs, and is thus improved through the Belt Vessel's influence on the Liver, as well as its influence on the flow of Qi in the legs.
5. Treats hip pain caused by Deficient Liver Blood (leading to sinew and joint malnourishment and Excess Liver Yang).
6. Purges Damp Heat from the genitals that results in symptoms such as difficulty urinating or burning during urination.

PATHOLOGICAL MANIFESTATIONS

The main diseases associated with the Belt Vessel are described as follows (Figure 6.34):

1. **Symptoms of Excess:** These include pain in the back (lumbar region) and sides of the lower abdomen, as well as weakness in the shoulders, upper extremities, and lower limbs. Symptoms may also include weakness in the opposite side of the body (e.g., eye, breast, ovary, etc.) and a feeling of heaviness in the body and abdomen ("as if carrying 5,000 coins") all due to exposure to Dampness.
2. **Symptoms of Deficiency:** These include physical sensations similar to that of "sitting in cold water" up to the waist. This description generally refers to pain, weakness, and a cold or heavy sensation in the lumbar and sacral regions. Other symptoms include umbilical, abdominal, and lumbar pain, as well as a feeling of something like a stick pressing against the groin. There can also be abdominal fullness and distention. Symptoms in women may include abnormally white vaginal discharge, or a prolapse of the Uterus.

Yin & Yang Heel Vessels: Yin Qiao Mai & Yang Qiao Mai

The word "Qiao" translates as "Heel" or "To Stand on the Toes." It commonly refers to the action of kicking one's foot as high as possible. One medical text from the Shanghai College of Traditional Chinese Medicine states that the word Qiao should be translated as "Nimble."

According to their energetic function, the left Yang Heel Vessel controls the Yang Qi of the left side of the body; and the right Yang Heel Vessel controls the Yang Qi of the right side of the body. Consequently, the left Yin Heel Vessel controls the Yin Qi of the left side of the body, while the right Yin Heel Vessel controls the Yin Qi of the right side of the body (Figure 6.35).

The energy of both Yin and Yang Heel Vessels flow along the medial and lateral aspects of the lower legs and torso, connecting at the inner canthus of the eyes. They are responsible for connecting the energy of the body's Yin and Yang channels and for regulating the movement of all four limbs. They also control the amount of energy used by all the other channels in the body. According to ancient Daoist teachings, once these vessels are energetically full, they naturally relax the body's tissues, enabling all of the limbs to become more dexterous.

The Yin and Yang Heel Vessels are sometimes called "Bridge Channels," because they act like an energetic bridge, linking the areas of the body in which Qi is stored to the areas of the body that are in need of Qi. When any channel uses more than its share of energy, other channels become deficient. Therefore the Heel Vessels seek to ensure that energy is always distributed in a balanced way throughout all of the Yin and Yang channels of the body.

It is intreating to note, that the Yin Heel Vessels are an offshoot of the Kidney Channels at the front of the body; while the Yang Heel Vessels are an offshoot of the Urinary Bladder Channels at the back of the body. Together, the Yin and Yang Heel Vessels can be used to treat structural imbalances and to harmonize the right and left sides of the body.

In ancient China, both the Kidney Channels and Urinary Bladder Channels were jointly re-

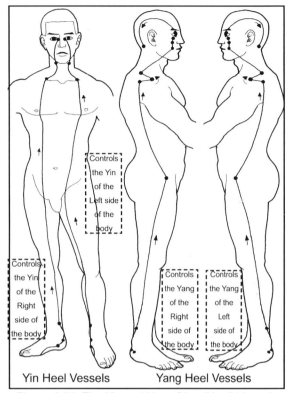

Figure 6.35. The Yin and Yang Qiao (Heel) Vessels

ferred to as the body's "Energetic Vest." This was because the (Yang) Urinary Bladder Channels surround the (Yang) Governing Vessel, and the (Yin) Kidney Channels surround the (Yin) Conception Vessel, similar to an energetic vest.

Because the Heel Vessels cause the motor nerves to develop during the formative stages of the embryo, Traditional Chinese Medicine maintains that the Yang Heel Vessels cause boys to be more physically active (running, jumping, etc.), while the Yin Heel Vessels cause girls to be less physically active. This, in turn, suggests that the Yin and Yang Heel Vessels play a major role in establishing the secondary sex characteristics during the formative years of puberty.

The ancient Daoists believed that the Heel Vessels were thought to psychologically determine "who and what you are in the world." The Yang Heel Vessels relate to how you see the world (external, Yang), while the Yin Heel Vessels relate to how you see yourself (internal, Yin).

The Yin Heel Vessel: Yin Qiao Mai

The ideograph depicting the Chinese characters for "Yin Qiao Mai" ("Yin Heel Vessel") is described as follows (Figure 6.36):

- **Yin:** The first character is the Chinese ideogram "Yin," which is composed of four parts. The character positioned on the left ("Fu") is generally used to describe the shady, Northern watershed of a valley, hill or mound.

  The character positioned to the right of the Fu ideograph is translated as "Yin," and is composed of three parts. The character positioned on the bottom is "Yun" meaning "Clouds." Located at the center is the ancient character for "Qi" meaning "Mist that rises up from the Earth" (also translated as "Energy").

  Positioned at the top is the ancient character "Ji," meaning "a covering used to gather or collect." Etymologically speaking, the ideograph can be translated to mean "the dark, shady side of a hill or river bank."

- **Qiao:** The second character is the Chinese ideogram for "Qiao," which is generally translated as "Heel." It is composed of two parts. The first part positioned on the left, is the character "Zu" meaning "Foot."

  The second half of the character, positioned on the right, is the character "Qiao," which describes "a kind of pavilion (i.e., a large tent used for shelter or entertainment) or a walled town in the middle of a country."

- **Mai:** The third character is the ideograph "Mai," generally translated as "Vessel." It is composed of two characters: The character to the left, "Ji" depicts the Chinese ideogram for body tissue, muscle, or flesh, all of which are forms of connective tissue. The character to the right, "Mai" depicts a current of water, stream, or a branch of a river. As a whole, the character can be translated as "Arteries, Veins, or a Pulse," indicating a form of consistent energetic circulation.

Development

The Yin Heel Vessels control the Yin of the left and right sides of the body, and the motion of the lower limbs. They also nourish the eyes and control the opening and closing of the eyelids.

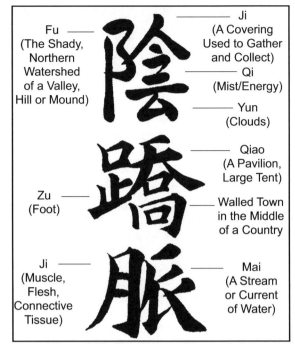

Figure 6.36. The Chinese Ideograph for "Yin Qiao Mai" (Yin Heel Vessel)

The Yin Heel Vessels are an offshoot of the Kidney Channels at the front of the body and influence the reproductive system in both males and females, as well as the entire lower abdominal area in women.

To the ancient Daoists, the secret "Macrocosmic Orbit" Neigong exercises were traditionally developed in order to enhance and augment the sea of energies contained within the disciples Yin and Yang Qiao Mai (Yin and Yang Heel Vessels), and their Yin and Yang Wei Mai (Yin and Yang Linking Vessels).

It is important to note that, according to Professor Li Shizhen, the Yin Qiao Mai (Yin Heel Vessel) is understood as the energetic gateway to "Opening" the other seven Extraordinary Vessels.

Energetic Pathway

The Yin Heel Vessels diverge from the Kidney Channels and begin on the medial side of the foot, distal and inferior to the medial malleolus at the "Rangu" ("Blazing Valley:" Kd-2) points. They flow through the Zhaohai (Shining Sea: Kd-6) and Jiaoxin (Exchange Belief: Kd-8) points before ascending to the inside of the inguinal crease and entering the reproductive organs (Figure 6.37).

CHAPTER 6: THE EIGHT EXTRAORDINARY VESSELS

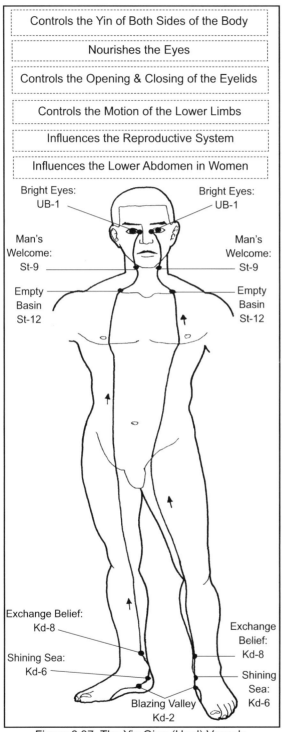

Figure 6.37. The Yin Qiao (Heel) Vessels

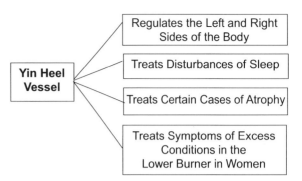

Figure 6.38. The Functions and Clinical Uses of the Yin Qiao (Heel) Vessel

From the reproductive organs, the Yin Heel Vessels continue up the front of the body, through the chest to connect with the Quepen (Empty Basin: St-12) point at the throat before entering into the Renying (Man's Welcome: St-9) points. From the St-9 points the vessels traverse the cheek, flowing alongside the nose to terminate at the Jingming (Bright Eyes: UB-1) points (located on the inner canthus of the eyes), where they join the Urinary Bladder Channel and Yang Heel Vessels.

CLINICAL MANIFESTATIONS

The functions and clinical uses of the Yin Heel Vessels are described as follows (Figure 6.38):
1. Regulates the right and left sides of the body.
2. Treats disturbances of sleep, such as insomnia or somnolence.
3. Treats certain cases of atrophy, when the muscles of the inner aspect of the leg are loose and the outer leg muscles are tight.
4. Treats symptoms of excess conditions in the Lower Burner in women. These conditions manifest as symptoms such as abdominal distension, difficult delivery, retention of the placenta, abdominal masses or lumps, and uterine fibroids.

PATHOLOGICAL MANIFESTATIONS

The main diseases associated with the Yin Heel Vessels are described as follows (Figure 6.39):
1. **Symptoms of Excess of the Yin Heel Vessels:** This occurs when Yang Qi is slowed down in the Heel Vessels and the Yin Qi moves more rapidly. This type of Excess Yin condition

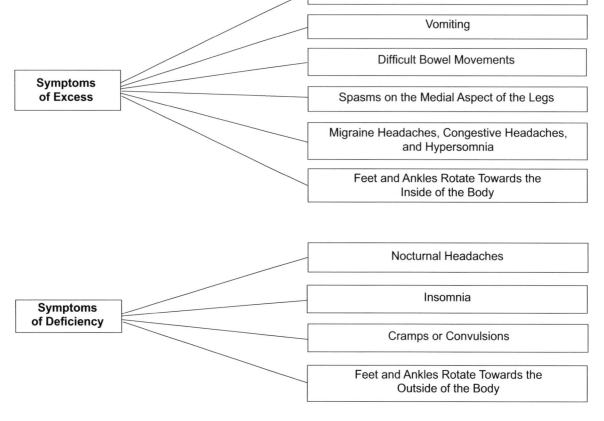

Figure 6.39. Pathological Manifestations of the Yin Qiao Mai (Yin Heel Vessel)

causes the following problems: sleepiness, hypotension, choking, painful urination, stomach rumbling, vomiting, diarrhea, difficult bowel movements, unconsciousness, lower abdominal pain and spasms on the medial aspect of the legs.

Excess energy of the Yin Heel Vessels is also associated with diseases of the eyes, such as watery eyes, heavy sensations of the eyelids or an inability to open the eyes.

Disorders of the Yin Heel Vessels may also result in migraine headaches, congestive headaches, and hypersomnia.

Excess Yin or other abnormalities of the Yin Heel Vessels may cause pregnant women to have difficult labor.

When the Yin Heel Vessels are in excess, the inner leg muscles are tight, while the outer leg muscles are loose.

An excess condition in the Yin Heel Vessels can cause the feet and ankles to rotate towards the inside of the body.

2. **Symptoms of Deficiency of the Yin Heel Vessels:** A Deficient condition may include certain nocturnal aggravations of the symptoms, including nocturnal headaches, insomnia, cramps, or convulsions.

Additionally, weakness in the Yin Heel Vessels can cause the feet and ankles to rotate towards the outside of the body.

THE YANG HEEL VESSELS: YANG QIAO MAI

The ideograph depicting the Chinese characters for "Yang Qiao Mai" ("Yang Heel Vessel") is described as follows (Figure 6.40):

- **Yang:** The first character is the Chinese ideogram "Yang," which is composed of three parts. The character positioned on the left ("Fu") is generally used to describe the shady, Northern watershed of a valley, hill or mound.

  The character positioned to the right of the Fu ideograph is translated as "Yang," and is composed of two parts. On the top right is the character "Tan" meaning "Sun above the horizon at dawn." On the bottom right is the character "Wu" meaning "Sudden Rays or Light." The ideograph can be translated to mean "the bright, sunny side of a hill or river bank."

- **Qiao:** The second character is the Chinese ideogram for "Qiao," which is generally translated as "Heel." It is composed of two parts. The first part positioned on the left, is the character "Zu" meaning "Foot."

  The second half of the character, positioned on the right, is the character "Qiao," which describes "a kind of pavilion (i.e., a large tent used for shelter or entertainment) or a walled town in the middle of a country."

- **Mai:** The third character is the ideograph "Mai," generally translated as "Vessel." It is composed of two characters: The character to the left, "Ji" depicts the Chinese ideogram for body tissue, muscle, or flesh, all of which are forms of connective tissue. The character to the right, "Mai" depicts a current of water, stream, or a branch of a river. As a whole, the character can be translated as "Arteries, Veins, or a Pulse," indicating a form of consistent energetic circulation.

DEVELOPMENT

The Yang Heel Vessels control the Yang of the left and right sides of the body. Abnormalities of the Yang Heel Vessels in newborns can cause vomiting of milk. The Yang Heel Vessels are an offshoot of the Urinary Bladder Channels which flow along the back of the body.

Figure 6.40. The Chinese Ideograph for "Yang Qiao Mai" (Yang Heel Vessel)

To the ancient Daoists, the secret "Macrocosmic Orbit" Neigong exercises were traditionally developed in order to enhance and augment the sea of energies contained within the disciples Yin and Yang Qiao Mai (Yin and Yang Heel Vessels), and their Yin and Yang Wei Mai (Yin and Yang Linking Vessels).

ENERGETIC PATHWAY

The Yang Heel Vessels divide from the Urinary Bladder Channels and begin on the lateral sides of the heels below the lateral malleolus, at the Shenmai (Extending Vessel: UB-62) points. From there, the vessels travel down to the Pushen (Servant's Respect: UB-61) points and then begin to ascend along the external malleolus, passing the Fuyang (Instep Yang: UB-59) point, and ascending the posterior border of the fibula to transverse the lateral aspects of the thighs to connect with the Thigh-Juliao (Stationary Crevice: GB-29) points.

The Vessel then ascends past the posterior aspects of the hypochondrium to the posterior axillary folds and continue to wind over the shoulders, connecting with the Naoshu (Upper Arm Meeting: SI-10), Jianyu (Shoulder Bone: LI-15) and Jugu (Great Bone: LI-16) points.

The Yang Heel Vessels then ascend from the shoulders, passing from the lateral to the medial aspects of the neck, to enter the face where they connect with the Dicang (Earth Granary: St-4), Nose-Juliao (Great Crevice: St-3), and Chengqi (Container of Tears: St-1) points.

From the St-1 points, the Vessels enter the inner canthus of the eyes at the Jingming (Bright Eyes: UB-1) points, where they communicate with the Yin Heel Vessels.

From the UB-1 points at the eyes, they join the flow of the Urinary Bladder Channels, traveling upward to terminate at the forehead and join the Gall Bladder Channels at the Fengchi (Wind Pool: GB-20) points located at the back of the head, below the occiput (Figure 6.41).

Clinical Manifestations

The functions and clinical uses of the patient's Yang Heel Vessel are described as follows (Figure 6.42):

1. Treats acute excess conditions of the lower back, manifesting as symptoms, such as aches due to spasms or invasion of Cold and pain along the Urinary Bladder Channels of the legs.
2. Purges Internal Wind or External Wind from the head, manifesting in symptoms such as facial paralysis, severe dizziness, and aphasia).
3. Purges Wind-Heat and Wind-Cold manifesting as symptoms such as sneezing, headache, runny nose, and stiff neck.
4. In cases of Epilepsy: According to some Traditional Chinese Medical Classics, if Epilepsy occurs during the daytime, Qigong and Moxa are given on the Yang Heel Vessels; however, if Epilepsy occurs at night, Qigong and Moxa are given on the Yin Heel Vessels.

Pathological Manifestations

The main diseases associated with the Yang Heel Vessels are described as follows (Figure 6.43):

1. **Symptoms of Excess in the Yang Heel Vessels** occurs when Yin energy is slowed within the Heel Vessels and the Yang energy moves

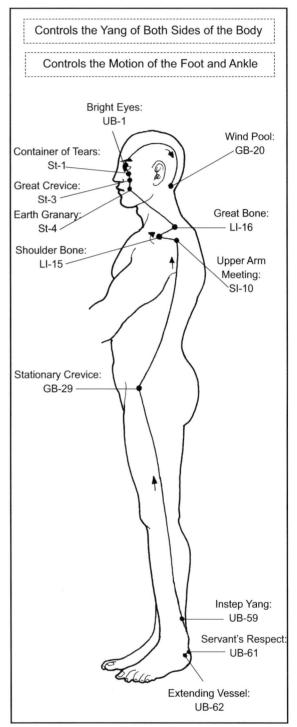

Figure 6.41. The Left Yang Qiao (Heel) Vessel

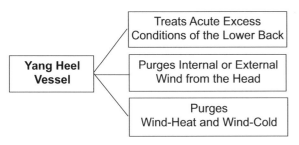

Figure 6.42. The Functions and Clinical Uses of the Yang Qiao (Heel) Vessel

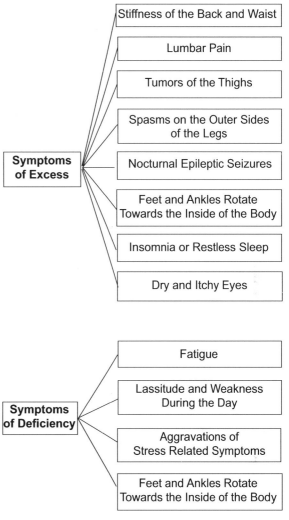

Figure 6.43. Pathological Manifestations of the Yang Qiao (Heel) Vessel

more rapidly. The Excess Yang causes the following problems: hypertension, lumbar pain, spasms on the outer sides of the legs, stiff back and waist (inability to bend down), tumors of the thighs, severe colds, spontaneous sweating, headaches, head sweating, nose bleeding, deafness, nocturnal epileptic seizures, insomnia or restless sleep, swelling of the body, pain in the joints, and paralysis of the arms and legs. Excess energy in the Yang Heel Vessels can also cause the vomiting of milk in infants. The Yang Heel Vessels are also involved with diseases of the eyes such as dry eyes, difficulty in closing the eyes, painful eyes and itchy eyes. When the Yang Heel Vessel is in excess, the inner leg muscles are loose and the outer leg muscles are tight. Excess in the Yang Heel Vessels can cause the feet and ankles to rotate laterally.

2. **Symptoms of Deficiency in the Yang Heel Vessels** include fatigue, lassitude and weakness during the day, and aggravated stress related symptoms during the day. These symptoms improve as the night progresses. Weakness in the Yang Heel Vessels can cause feet and ankles to rotate medially.

Yin & Yang Linking Vessels: Yin Wei Mai & Yang Wei Mai

The Linking Vessels are sometimes called the "Wei Mai" or "Regulator Channels," and are divided into Yin and Yang energetic pathways. The Yin Linking Vessel maintains and communicates with all of the Yin channels of the body; while the Yang Linking Vessel maintains and communicates with all of the Yang channels of the body.

Both Yin and Yang Linking Vessels start at the lower legs and flow upward to the head, along the medial and lateral aspects of the lower legs and torso. When the Yin and Yang Linking Vessels reach the neck and back of the head, they join the Conception and Governing Vessels, respectively.

Secondary vessels, called the "Yu Mai" ("Surplus Vessels"), branch away from each Yin and Yang Linking Vessel to connect the energetic flow of each vessel with the hands.

Instead of serving as streams transporting Qi and Blood, these two important Vessels act as energetic lakes, storing the Qi and Blood that overflow from other Vessels. Together, these important vessels help to regulate the entire body's circulation of Qi and Blood, store the overflowing Qi and Blood, and release the Qi and Blood into the Twelve Primary Channels in the event of a sudden deficiency.

In ancient China, the Yin and Yang Linking Vessels were considered by Daoist Alchemists to be responsible for the energetic and spiritual manifestations of the body's Jing Shen, being reflected in an individual's life.

The Yin Linking Vessel: Yin Wei Mai

The ideograph depicting the Chinese characters for "Yin Wei Mai" is described as follows (Figure 6.44):

- **Yin:** The first character is the Chinese ideogram "Yin," which is composed of four parts. The character positioned on the left ("Fu") is generally used to describe the shady, Northern watershed of a valley, hill or mound.

  The character positioned to the right of the Fu ideograph is translated as "Yin," and is composed of three parts. The character

Figure 6.44. The Chinese Ideograph for "Yin Wei Mai" (Yin Linking Vessel)

positioned on the bottom is "Yun" meaning "Clouds." Located at the center is the ancient character for "Qi" meaning "Mist that rises up from the Earth" (also translated as "Energy").

Positioned at the top is the ancient character "Ji," meaning "a covering used to gather or collect." Etymologically speaking, the ideograph can be translated to mean "the dark, shady side of a hill or river bank."

- **Wei:** The second character is the Chinese ideogram "Wei," which is generally translated as "To Link or Bind." The character "Wei" is composed of two parts:

  Positioned to the left is the radical "Mi," meaning "Silk, Net, or String-like Objects." It depicts threads that have been twisted together to form a net, and refers to a silk rope that is tied around something, pulling and securing it, or the wrapping and enveloping of a silk net.

  On the right is the character "Zhui." This radical was used in ancient China to describe a particular type of bird with a short tail. In ancient

China, this character originally represented the enveloping of a bird caught in a net. Eventually, the expression "Zhui" came to mean "binding the four limbs" or "binding the four directions."

- **Mai:** The third character is the ideograph "Mai," generally translated as "Vessel." It is composed of two characters: The character to the left, "Ji" depicts the Chinese ideogram for body tissue, muscle, or flesh, all of which are forms of connective tissue. The character to the right, "Mai" depicts a current of water, stream, or a branch of a river. As a whole, the character can be translated as "Arteries, Veins, or a Pulse," indicating a form of consistent energetic circulation.

Development

The Yin Linking Vessels (Yin Wei Mai) lie on the medial axis of the body. They help maintain the connection between all of the Yin Channels.

The Yin Linking Vessels are responsible for moving the Yin energy, regulating the Blood, and regulating the internal parts of the body. They connect with all of the body's Primary Yin Channels: Liver, Heart, Spleen, Lung, Kidney, and Pericardium.

To the ancient Daoists, the secret "Macrocosmic Orbit" Neigong exercises were traditionally developed in order to enhance and augment the sea of energies contained within the disciples Yin and Yang Wei Mai (Yin and Yang Linking Vessels) and their Yin and Yang Qiao Mai (Yin and Yang Heel Vessels).

Energetic Pathway

The Yin Linking Vessels originate in the Kidney Channels, and are composed of two main energetic branches, described as follows (Figure 6.45):

- **The Primary Channels of the Yin Linking Vessels:** These Vessels originate in the Kidney Channels, from the medial side of the legs, at the Zhubin (Shining Sea: Kd-9) points.

From there they ascend along the medial aspect of the thighs to the abdomen where they communicate with the Spleen Channels at the Fushe (House of Government: Sp-13), Daheng (Great Horizontal: Sp-15) and Fuai (Abdomen Sorrow: Sp-16) points at the chest. They ascend to the Qimen (Gate of Time: Lv-14) points and move toward the front of the body along the sides of the chest to the

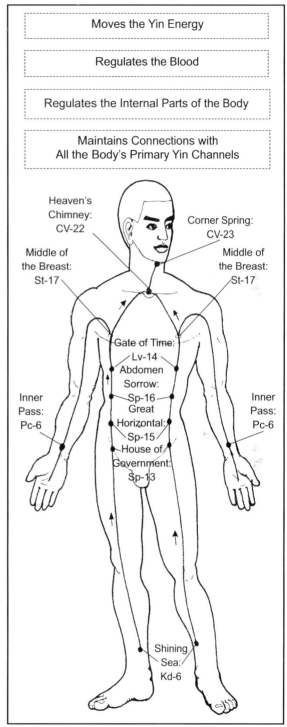

Figure 6.45. The Yin Wei (Linking) Vessels

center of the nipples at the Ruzhong (Middle of Breast: St-17) points where the vessels split into two sets of branches.

The Primary Channels continue to ascend, connecting with the Conception Vessel at the Tiantu (Heaven's Chimney: CV-22) point at the base of the throat, and terminating at the Liangquan (Corner Spring: CV-23) point located on the midline of the neck.

- **The First Branches of the Yin Linking Vessels:** Sometimes called the "Yin Yu Mai" (Yin Surplus Vessels), these important arm Vessels originate at the Ruzhong (Middle of Breast: St-17) points, located at the center of the nipples. They ascend from the chest, winding over the shoulders, and down the inside of the arms following the route of the Pericardium Channels. Each branch energetically pools at the Neiguan (Inner Pass: Pc-6) points just above the wrist folds on each arm, before flowing into the palms. The Neiguan Pc-6 points are therefore considered to be the Master Points for the Yin Linking Vessels.

Clinical Manifestations

The functions and clinical uses of the patient's Yin Linking Vessel are described as follows (Figure 6.46):

1. Tonifies the Heart and is especially effective for symptoms of pain, stiffness, tightness and oppression in the chest, as well as depression, anxiety, apprehension, and nightmares.
2. Treats Deficient Yin and Blood conditions, especially if accompanied by psychological symptoms such as mental restlessness, anxiety, and insomnia.
3. Treats headaches that are located in the back of the neck due to Blood Deficiency.

Pathological Manifestations

The main diseases associated with the Yin Linking Vessel are describes as follows (Figure 6.47):

1. **Symptoms of Excess in the Yin Linking Vessels** occur when the Yin energy is slowed within the Linking Vessels and the Yang energy moves more rapidly. Therefore, if the Yin Linking Vessels become unbalanced, the Excess Yang condition can cause the patient to suffer from diseases of the Heart, such as hypertension, delirium, cardialgia (tightness

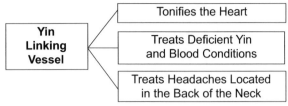

Figure 6.46. The Functions and Clinical Uses of the "Yin Wei Mai" (Yin Linking Vessel)

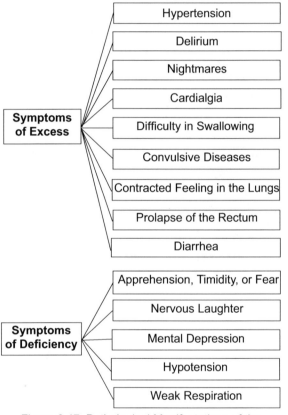

Figure 6.47. Pathological Manifestations of the "Yin Wei Mai" (Yin Linking Vessel)

and oppression in the chest) and nightmares. Imbalances in the Yin Linking Vessels can also lead to dyspnea, difficulty in swallowing, convulsive diseases, contracted feeling in the lungs, prolapse of the rectum, and diarrhea.

2. **Symptoms of Deficiency in the Yin Linking Vessels** include timidity or fear, apprehension, nervous laughter, depression, hypotension, and weak respiration.

THE YANG LINKING VESSELS: YANG WEI MAI

The ideograph depicting the Chinese characters for "Yang Wei Mai" is described as follows (Figure 6.48):

- **Yang:** The first character is the Chinese ideogram "Yang," which is composed of three parts. The character positioned on the left ("Fu") is generally used to describe the shady, Northern watershed of a valley, hill or mound.

  The character positioned to the right of the Fu ideograph is translated as "Yang," and is composed of two parts. On the top right is the character "Tan" meaning "Sun above the horizon at dawn." On the bottom right is the character "Wu" meaning "Sudden Rays or Light." The ideograph can be translated to mean "the bright, sunny side of a hill or river bank."

- **Wei:** The second character is the Chinese ideogram "Wei," which is generally translated as "To Link or Bind." The character "Wei" is composed of two parts:

  Positioned to the left is the radical "Mi," meaning "Silk, Net, or String-like Objects." It depicts threads that have been twisted together to form a net, and refers to a silk rope that is tied around something, pulling and securing it, or the wrapping and enveloping of a silk net.

  On the right is the character "Zhui." This radical was used in ancient China to describe a particular type of bird with a short tail. In ancient China, this character originally represented the enveloping of a bird caught in a net. Eventually, the expression "Zhui" came to mean "binding the four limbs" or "binding the four directions."

- **Mai:** The third character is the ideograph "Mai," generally translated as "Vessel." It is composed of two characters: The character to the left, "Ji" depicts the Chinese ideogram for body tissue, muscle, or flesh, all of which are forms of connective tissue. The character to the right, "Mai" depicts a current of water, stream, or a branch of a river. As a whole, the

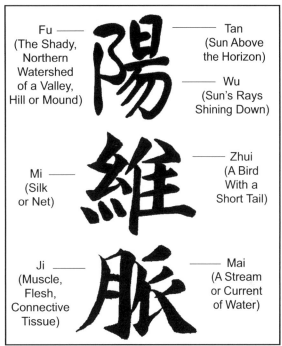

Figure 6.48. The Chinese Ideograph for "Yang Wei Mai" (Yang Linking Vessel)

character can be translated as "Arteries, Veins, or a Pulse," indicating a form of consistent energetic circulation.

DEVELOPMENT

The Yang Linking Vessels lie on the lateral aspects of the body. They serve to maintain and communicate with all of the Yang Channels on the exterior portion of the lateral aspects of the body.

The Yang Linking Vessels are responsible for moving the Yang energy and controlling the Protective (Wei) Qi by regulating its resistance to external infections, and regulating the external parts of the body. They connect with all of the body's Primary Yang Channels: Gall Bladder, Small Intestine, Stomach, Large Intestine, Urinary Bladder, and Triple Burners.

To the ancient Daoists, the secret "Macrocosmic Orbit" Neigong exercises were traditionally developed in order to enhance and augment the sea of energies contained within the disciples Yin and Yang Wei Mai (Yin and Yang Linking Vessels) and their Yin and Yang Qiao Mai (Yin and Yang Heel Vessels).

ENERGETIC PATHWAY

The Yang Linking Vessels originate in the Urinary Bladder Channel. They are composed of two main energetic branches, described as follows (Figure 6.49):

- **The Primary Channels of the Yang Linking Vessels:** These Vessels originate in the Urinary Bladder Channels at the external part of the ankles, just below the lateral malleolus at the Jinmen (Golden Gate: UB-63) points.

From the Jinmen (UB-63) they merge with the leg Gall Bladder Channels, and ascend into the Yangjiao (Yang Intersection: GB-35) points. They continue ascending the lateral aspect of each leg, passing through the outside of the hips, and moving upward along the lateral aspect of the back. From there, the Yang Linking Vessels flow through the hypochondriac and costal regions, to the Naoshu (Upper Arm Meeting: SI-10) points located at the posterior aspect of the axilla to the shoulders. The Naoshu (SI-10) points are the intersecting points of the Yang Linking Vessels and the Yang Heel Vessels (located on the Small Intestine Channels).

From the Naoshu (SI-10) points, the Yang Linking Vessels split into two sets of branches. The Primary Channels flow up the sides of the neck communicating with the Tianliao (Heavenly Crevice: TB-15) points before connecting with the Gall Bladder Channels at the Jianjing (Shoulder Well: GB-21) points. From GB-21, the vessels intersect with the Touwei (Head's Binding: St-8) points above the temples and then continue to follow the Gall Bladder Channels from Benshen (Root of the Spirit: GB-13), Yangbai (Yang White: GB-14), Head-Linqi (Head Governor of Tears: GB-15), Muchuang (Window of the Eyes: GB-16), Zhengying (Upright Nutrition: GB-17), Chengling (Support Spirit: GB-18), Naokong (Brain Hollow: GB-19) and Fengchi (Wind Pool: GB-20) points (located at the lateral aspect of the head).

Here, they join together to communicate with the Governing Vessel at the Back Gate

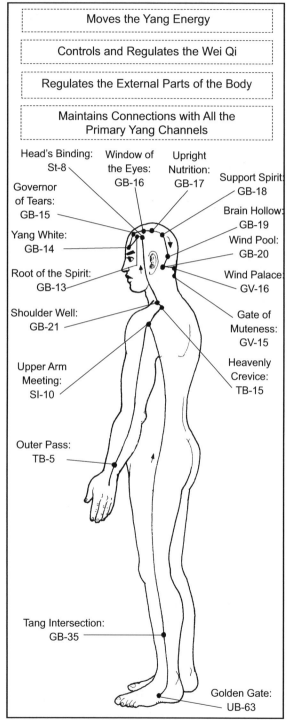

Figure 6.49. The Left Yang Wei (Linking) Vessel

CHAPTER 6: THE EIGHT EXTRAORDINARY VESSELS

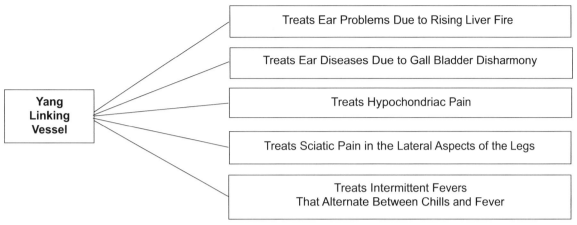

Figure 6.50. The Functions and Clinical Uses of the Yang Wei (Linking)Vessel

of the Upper Dantian located at the Fengfu (Wind Palace: GV-16) point before terminating at the Yamen (Gate of Muteness: GV-15) point located at the lower occipital region of the head.

- **The First Branches of the Yang Linking Vessels:** Sometimes called the "Yang Yu Mai" ("Yang Surplus Vessels"), these important arm Vessels originate at the Naoshu (Upper Arm Meeting: SI-10) points located at the posterior aspect of the axilla to the shoulders. They extend from the shoulders down the back side of the arms following the route of the Triple Burner Channels. Just above both wrists on the outside of each arm, each branch pools at the Weiguan (Outer Pass: TB-5) points before flowing into the back of the hands. The Weiguan (TB-5) points are therefore considered the Master Points for the Yang Linking Vessels.

CLINICAL MANIFESTATIONS

The functions and clinical uses of the patient's Yang Linking Vessels are described as follows (Figure 6.50):
1. Treats ear problems such as tinnitus and deafness due to Liver Fire rising.
2. Treats ear diseases that are caused from a Gall Bladder disharmony.
3. Treats hypochondriac pain.
4. Treats sciatic pain in the lateral aspects of the legs (along the Gall Bladder Channels).
5. Treats intermittent fevers that alternate between chills and fever.

PATHOLOGICAL MANIFESTATIONS

The main diseases associated with disorders of the Yang Linking Vessel are describes as follows (Figure 6.51):

1. **Symptoms of Excess in the Yang Linking Vessels:** This occurs when the Yang Qi is slowed down in the Linking Vessels, and the Yin Qi moves more rapidly. If the Yang Linking Vessels become unbalanced, the Excess Yin condition may cause the patient to catch colds and fevers more easily.

   Symptoms can manifest as alternating chills and fever, and pain in the lateral sides of the head, neck, trunk, and legs.

   Symptoms can also include pain and skin problems that arise or worsen during weather changes, sensitivity to changes in climate (aching muscles, skin rashes, etc.), swelling, pain and fever in the joints, diarrhea, and night sweats.

2. **Symptoms of Deficiency in the Yang Linking Vessels:** This can include coldness, loss of energy, and a lack of physical strength.

   Symptoms can also include cold knees, stiffness, and fatigue (especially during cold or rainy weather).

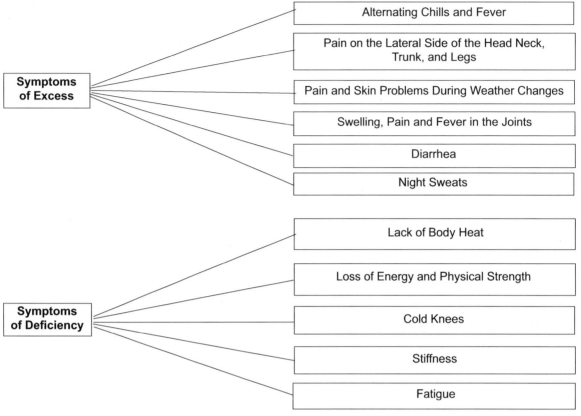

Figure 6.51. Pathological Manifestations of the Yang Wei (Linking) Vessel

THE EIGHT EXTRAORDINARY VESSELS AND TWELVE PRIMARY CHANNELS

The Eight Extraordinary Vessels link together all of the Yin and Yang Channels in the body, and are therefore able to regulate the flow of Qi within these channels in order to maintain a state of energetic balance. The clinical significance of the Eight Extraordinary Vessels manifests through certain pathological indications that are specific to the Vessels' intersection with their particular Primary Channel. Their symptomatology is therefore not distinct from, but rather a composite of, the pathological symptoms associated with their joining primary channel.

A summary of the combined functions of the Eight Extraordinary Vessel Master-Couple Points is listed in Figure 6.52.

The Eight Extraordinary Vessels' energetic pathways used in certain Daoist Qigong meditations are somewhat different from those found in Traditional Chinese Medical texts and Acupuncture Charts. The reason for this uniqueness is that their purposes are different. The goal of Acupuncture is to restore sick people to health. Therefore the energetic points treated by an Acupuncturist must be along the superficial channels, so that they can be activated by the Acupuncture Needles. Medical Qigong exercises and meditations aim to maximize physical vitality and take the individual beyond physical health toward spiritual enlightenment. In Medical Qigong treatment and training, the specific channels and points that one uses can initially be located deep within the body's tissues, since the energy is guided by the mind, postures, and movements, rather than by needles.

Chapter 6: The Eight Extraordinary Vessels

Eight Extraordinary Vessels	Pathologies
Belt (GB-41 - TB-5)	• Pain in the back, lumbar region, and sides of the navel • Weakness in the lower limbs
Conception (Lu--7 - Kd-6)	• Diseases of the reproductive and gastrointestinal systems (hemorrhoids, diarrhea, decreased urination, etc.) • In the male: sterility • In the female: menstruation problems such as leukorrhea and dysmenorrhea, breast pain, paralysis after delivery, emaciation, and sterility. All problems of the reproductive system, including internal and external genitalia (vulva, vagina, and cervix)
Governing (SI-3 - UB-62)	• Diseases of the head (apoplexy, aphasia, epilepsy, headaches, tetanus, etc.), back, neck, and Kidneys • Stiffness in the spinal column, spastic muscle movements of the extremities, night sweating, and circulatory disturbances around the anus
Thrusting (Sp-4 - Pc-6)	• Diseases of the Heart, fullness in the chest and abdomen, gastritis, abdominal pain, convulsive diseases • Brain dysfunctions of physiological origin • In womem: amenorrhea, scanty periods or late periods, dysmenorrhea, spontaneous abortion, inability to expel the placenta, menopause problems
Yang Heel (UB-62 - SI-3)	• Stiffness of the back and waist, lumbar pain, spasms on the outer side of the legs, and tumors of the thighs • Diseases of the eyes • Vomiting of milk (in newborns)
Yang Linking (TB-5 - GB-41)	• Diseases from Cold: fevers resulting in a sensitivity to changes in climate, cold knees, stiffness and fatigue; swelling, pain, and fever in the joints and extremities, and night sweating
Yin Heel (Kd-6 - Lu-7)	• Lower abdominal pain, vomiting, difficult bowel movements, and spasms on the medial side of the legs • Diseases of the eyes • Difficult labor in women
Yin Linking (Pc-6 - Sp-4)	• Diseases of the Heart (cardialgia), tightness of the chest, difficulty swallowing, and convulsive diseases • Prolapse of the rectum and diarrhea

Figure 6.52. Pathologies of the Eight Extraordinary Vessels

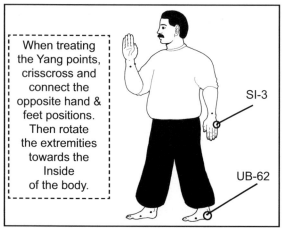

Figure 6.53. Locations of the Body's Governing and Yang Heel Vessel's "Master and Couple" Points

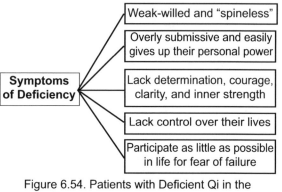

Figure 6.54. Patients with Deficient Qi in the Governing and Yang Heel Vessels

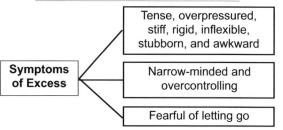

Figure 6.55. Patients with Excess Qi in the Governing and Yang Heel Vessels

Personality Constitutions of the Eight Extraordinary Vessels

In ancient China, another system of identifying a patient's personality traits, was in the observation of the four personality constitutions of the Eight Extraordinary Vessels.

By observing the patient's personality and overall energetic and emotional demeanor, a Medical Qigong Doctor can determine which organ or organ system is Deficient, and which is in a state of Excess. Based on this information, the doctor can establish an appropriate treatment plan.

In this particular system of diagnosis, the Medical Qigong Doctor observes the patient's dominant Yin or Yang emotional characteristics in order to determine which of the Eight Extraordinary Vessels are governing his or her present emotional state. These personality traits can change or appear in different combinations based on the interaction of acquired and congenital organ energy patterns. Therefore, organ patterns and personality traits may change with the patient's age (maturation) and/or situation (environment).

The Pathological Personality Type of the Governing and Yang Heel Vessels

The Governing (Du) and Yang Heel (Yang Qiao) Extraordinary Vessels are located on the back and lateral sides of the body. They affect the Urinary Bladder, Stomach, and Gall Bladder Channels. To access the flow of energy within the Governing and Yang Heel Vessels, the doctor will "crisscross" and stimulate the patient's SI-3 and UB-62 points simultaneously (Figure 6.53).

The pathological personality types of the Governing and Yang Heel Vessels are divided into Yin (Deficient) and Yang (Excess) emotional profiles, described as follows:

1. **Patients with Deficient Qi in the Governing and Yang Heel Vessels:** These patients tend to be weak-willed, "spineless," overly submissive, and easily give up their personal power. They lack determination, courage, clarity, and inner strength, and have no control over their lives. They usually participate as little as possible in life for fear of failure (Figure 6.54).

2. **Patients with Excess Qi in the Governing and Yang Heel Vessels:** These patients tend to be tense, overpressured, stiff, rigid, inflexible, stubborn, and awkward. They are narrow-minded and overcontrolling. Fearful of letting go, they overcompensate by attempting to restrict reality (Figure 6.55).

CHAPTER 6: THE EIGHT EXTRAORDINARY VESSELS

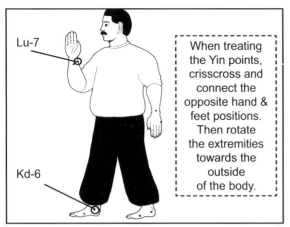

Figure 6.56. Locations of the Body's Conception and Yin Heel Vessel's "Master and Couple" Points

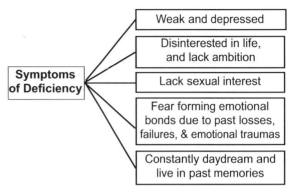

Figure 6.57. Patients with Deficient Qi in the Conception and Yin Heel Vessels

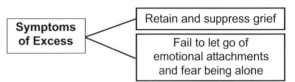

Figure 6.58. Patients with Excess Qi in the Conception and Yin Heel Vessels

THE PATHOLOGICAL PERSONALITY TYPE OF THE CONCEPTION AND YIN HEEL VESSELS

The Conception Vessel (Ren) and Yin Heel (Yin Qiao) Extraordinary Vessels are located on the front and inside of the body. They affect the Lung and Kidney Channels, which in turn affect the Kidneys, Lungs, and Heart organs. To access the energy within Conception and Yin Heel Vessels, the doctor will crisscross and stimulate the patient's Lu-7 and Kd-6 points simultaneously (Figure 6.56). The pathological personality types of the Conception and Yin Heel Vessels are divided into Yin (Deficient) and Yang (Excess) emotional profiles, described as follows:

1. **Patients with Deficient Qi in the Conception and Yin Heel Vessels:** These patients tend to be weak and depressed. They live in the past, are disinterested in life, have no ambition, and also lack sexual interest. It is hard for them to form new relationships because they fear forming emotional bonds due to past losses, failures, and emotional traumas. They constantly daydream and live in their own world of past memories (Figure 6.57).
2. **Patients with Excess Qi in the Conception and Yin Heel Vessels:** These patients tend to participate in life, but hold on to and suppress their grief. They fail to let go of emotional attachments and fear being alone. Female patients with this energetic pattern usually develop Qi Stagnations, resulting in breast cysts, tumors, and cancer, as well as uterine fibroids and cancer (Figure 6.58).

THE PATHOLOGICAL PERSONALITY TYPE OF THE BELT AND YANG LINKING VESSELS

The Belt (Dai) and Yang Linking (Yang Wei) Extraordinary Vessels are located around the waist and on the outside of the body. They affect the Gall Bladder and Triple Burner Channels which in turn affect the Kidneys, Liver, and Gall Bladder organs. To access the energy within the Belt and Yang Linking Vessels, the doctor will crisscross and stimulate the patient's GB-41 and TB-5 points simultaneously (Figure 6.59). The pathological personality types of the Belt and Yang Linking Vessels are divided into Yin (deficient) and Yang (excess) emotional profiles, described as follows:

1. **Patients with Deficient Qi in the Belt and Yang Linking Vessels:** These patients are considered weak, indecisive, and unproductive. They fear criticism and are touchy, snappy, irritable, and hypersensitive. They also have low self-esteem and also lack sexual interest (Figure 6.60).
2. **Patients with Excess Qi in the in the Belt and Yang Linking Vessels:** These patients are aggressive, angry, resentful, bitter, and vindictive. They tend to be opinionated, inflexible, intolerant, domineering, selfish, and frustrated. Their sex life is based on anger or rage (Figure 6.61).

VOLUME 1, SECTION 1: FOUNDATIONS OF CHINESE ENERGETIC MEDICINE

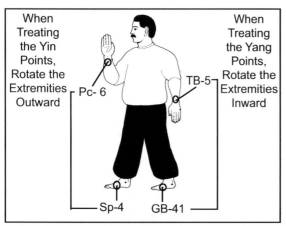

Figure 6.59. Locations of the Belt & Yang Linking - Thrusting & Yin Linking "Master and Couple" Points

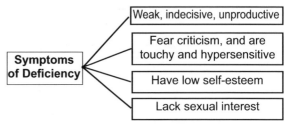

Figure 6.60. Patients with Deficient Qi in the Belt and Yang Linking Vessels

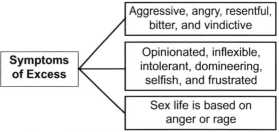

Figure 6.61. Patients with Excess Qi in the Belt and Yang Linking Vessels

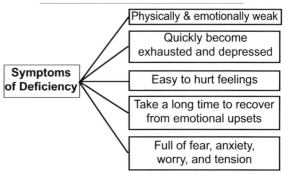

Figure 6.62. Patients with Deficient Qi in the Thrusting and Yin Linking Vessels

Figure 6.63. Patients with an Excess in the Thrusting and Yin Linking Vessels

THE PATHOLOGICAL PERSONALITY TYPE OF THE THRUSTING AND YIN LINKING VESSELS

The Thrusting (Chong) and Yin Linking (Yin Wei) Extraordinary Vessels are located within the center of the body (internally) and on the medial and anterior aspects of the body (externally). They affect the Kidney and Stomach Channels which, in turn, affect the Kidneys, Spleen, and Heart organs. To access the energy within the Thrusting and Yin Linking Vessels, the doctor will crisscross and stimulate the patient's Sp-4 and Pc-6 points simultaneously (see Figure 6.59). The pathological personality types of the Thrusting and Yin Linking Vessels are divided into Yin (deficient) and Yang (excess) emotional profiles, described as follows:

1. **Patients with Deficient Thrusting and Yin Linking Vessels:** These patients are physically and emotionally weak. They quickly become exhausted and depressed. It is easy for them to have their feelings hurt, and they take a long time to recover from emotional upsets. Their internal emotional world is constructed of fear, anxiety, worry, and tension. They do not connect well with the outside world or gain much pleasure from life or relationships (Figure 6.62).

2. **Patients with an Excess in the Thrusting and Yin Linking Vessels:** These patients tend to participate in life but have difficulty expressing their affection and communicating their needs in relationships. They are inclined to have stagnant Qi and Blood in the chest, epigastrium, or Uterus due to fear, anxiety, worry, and sorrow. In their personal relationships, they fear loss of control and cannot make a commitment or a deep emotional connection with others. They also fear surrendering and letting go in their love and sexual relationships (Figure 6.63).

DAOIST ALCHEMY AND THE EIGHT EXTRAORDINARY VESSELS

According to ancient Daoist teachings, cultivation practices that center around the Eight Extraordinary Vessels provide a disciple with one of the secret pathways towards obtaining enlightenment or "Immortality." For example, the ancestral founder of the Daoist Quan Zhen Nan Zong (the Southern Complete Reality School), Master Zhang Ziyang (Figure 6.64) once stated,

> "Those who are able to "Open"
> the Eight Extraordinary Vessels
> will be able to obtain the Dao."

He also stated that the Daoist Alchemist's understanding of the Eight Extraordinary Vessels is by no means identical to the Chinese Physician's understanding of these special energetic seas. This was because, to the Daoist Alchemist, to clinically treat the Extraordinary Vessels was to energetically treat a patient on the level of his or her destiny.

One of Professor Li Shizhen's surviving Ming Dynasty (1368-1644 A.D.) works entitled, *Qi Jing Ba Mai Kao (The Exposition on the Eight Extraordinary Vessels)*, stresses to its readers that the internal cultivation of the Eight Extraordinary Vessels is explicitly linked to quiescent stillness. While in this quiescent state, the ancient Daoist Alchemist, could energetically transform the various Seas of Qi existing within the Eight Extraordinary Vessels into a supernatural gateway into the spirit realm. Each profound depth of dynamic stillness could then become a wellspring of both spiritual development and transformational healing.

Although Professor Li Shizhen never stated that all Doctors of Chinese Medicine must become Daoist Disciples in order to fully comprehend the Eight Extraordinary Vessels, he simply encouraged them to have a sufficient understanding of the energetic principles of internal cultivation, so that the doctor could eventually become skillfully adapted to all medical practices.

The following is a simple breakdown of the Eight Extraordinary Vessels and their energetic

Figure 6.64. Daoist Master Zhang Ziyang
(of the Southern Complete Reality School)

correspondences to some of the more popular ancient Daoist Alchemical Meditation Exercises. For a better understanding and deeper explanation, please see the authors book entitled, *"Daoist Internal Alchemy: Neigong and Weigong Training."*

1. **Training the Qi of the Belt Vessel By Practicing The "Belt Winding" Meditation:** This ancient meditation was used to activate, expand, and increase the energetic size and power of the body's three external Weiqi Fields. It is also designed to create a protective energetic force field around the disciples body, and will allow him to ward off the invasion of any external pathogenic Qi that enters into his Weiqi field.

After creating a white energy ball, all the disciple needs to do is to place his attention onto the Weiqi field and mentally begin to wrap his body's Belt Vessels (like spinning copper coils around a magnet) with the ball of white light.

This energetic wrapping should flow in a clockwise direction from the Lower Dantian to the ground (Earth), then flow upward towards the Heavens in a counterclockwise direction.

The meditation consists of wrapping the body's external Weiqi field in various locations in order to increase its energetic power.

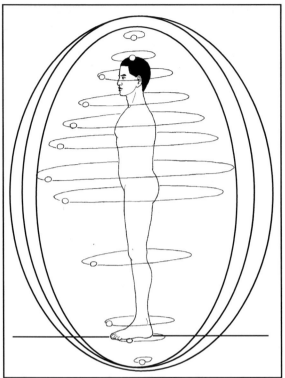

Figure 6.65. Performing the "Belt Winding Meditation" in order to train the Dai (Belt) Mai

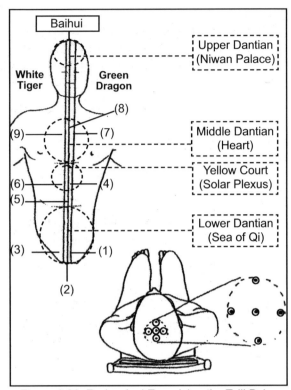

Figure 6.66. Fusing And Energizing the Taiji Pole, to train the Chong (Thrusting) Mai

The disciple will begin at the Lower Dantian, and proceed down to his Huiyin, Knees, Ankles, Bottom of the Feet, and end at the first Earth Transpersonal Point. Then the disciple will pulse the white energy ball and reverse its spiralling direction, moving up the body through the Yellow Court, Heart, Throat, Yintang (Third Eye), Baihui, and end at the First Heaven Transpersonal Point. Finally, the disciple will pulse and reverse the energy ball's direction, moving down the body back into the Lower Dantian. Then, the disciple will expand and fill his external Weiqi Field with radiant white light, and end the meditation (Figure 6.65):

2. Training the Qi of the Thrusting Vessels, By Practicing The "Fusing and Energizing the Taiji Pole" Meditation: This ancient meditation was originally used to activate the energetic pathways of the body's Thrusting Vessels. It combines the Yin energy of Earth, positioned on the right side of the body (manifesting as a White Tiger), with the Yang energy of Heaven, positioned on the left side of the body (manifesting as a Green Dragon). All three energetic pathways will balance and harmonize the Qi flowing along the center channels of the body's Taiji Pole (Figure 6.66).

It is important to note, that the energetic pathways of these special Thrusting Vessels are quite different in location and function than the Chung Mei (Thrusting Vessels) used in post-communist Traditional Chinese Medical Colleges. This special meditation is traditionally used in ancient Daoist alchemy in order to cleanse, purify, and fuse the energetic fields of the body's Three Dantians, and prepare the disciple for Creating the Immortal Fetus.

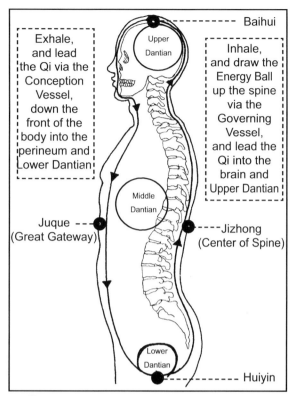

Figure 6.67. The Microcosmic Orbit, to train the Du (Governing) Mai and Ren (Conception) Mai

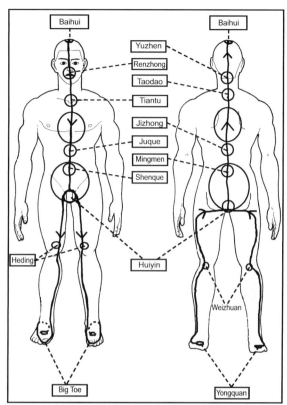

Figure 6.68. The Macrocosmic Orbit Stage #1: Connecting to the Qi of Earth

3. **Training the Qi of the Governing Vessel and Conception Vessel, By Practicing The "Microcosmic Orbit" Meditation:** Once the energy has been cultivated, built up, and securely established within the disciple's Lower Dantian, the next meditation that is traditionally practiced is the circulation of Qi within the Microcosmic Orbit or "Lesser Celestial Circuit" (Figure 6.67).

After energetically filling and overflowing the Lower Dantian, the next level of training is focused on activating the body's primary Yin and Yang Vessels. This is accomplished by circulating the cultivated energy through the Governing Vessel (Sea of Yang Qi) and Conception Vessel (Sea of Yin Qi), using "Reversed Breathing."

It is important to note, that in ancient Daoist Alchemy, it was important that the disciple first clear his Governing and Conception Vessels in order to allow the original energy of his True Breath (Yuan Qi) to freely circulate.

4. **Training the Qi of the Four Leg Vessels By Practicing The "Macrocosmic Orbit" Meditation:** When training the Macrocosmic Orbit, the energetic expansion and contraction of the Eight Extraordinary Vessels will affect and support the creation and development of the disciple's energetic tissues.

The circulation of the Macrocosmic Orbit is used in order to cleanse and regulate the Qi of the Eight Extraordinary Vessels, and is therefore divided into three important stages. The ancient Daoists believed that each stage was necessary, and needed in order to assist the disciple in controlling the first energetic rivers used to form tissue development. Therefore, the Eight Ancestral Channels, or Eight Prenatal Channels were seen as the internal roots of the Great Dao of Prior Heaven, and the Qi of the True Ancestors of the Yiqi (One Energy).

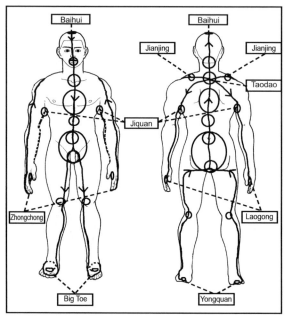

Figure 6.69. The Macrocosmic Orbit Stage #2: Connecting to the Qi of Man

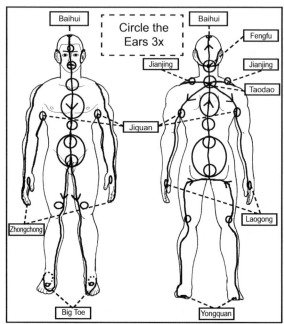

Figure 6.70. The Macrocosmic Orbit (Stage 3): to train the Chong (Thrusting) Mai

To the ancient Daoists, the Eight Extraordinary Vessels all pertain to the disciple's Yin Shen (Yin Spirit), and are usually energetically closed. According to ancient Daoist teaching, only the Divine Immortals are able to open the Eight Extraordinary Vessels by infusing them with Yang Qi. By doing so, the disciple will be able to obtain the True Dao.

Therefore the first meditation begins with the circulation of the Qi of Heaven (i.e., the top of the head- Baihui area) to the Qi of Earth (the base of the feet - Yongquan). According to esoteric Daoist teaching: "Above, the Yin Heel Vessels energetically communicate with the Niwan Palace, located within the center of the Upper Dantian, and Heaven; Below, they energetically communicate with the Bubbling Spring, located within the center of the feet, and Earth. The first stage in the Macrocosmic Orbit meditation is used to energetically open and connect the energy of the body's Governing and Conception Vessels with the Yin Heel Vessels (Figure 6.68). In Daoist alchemy, the Yin Heel Vessels have many names. For example, they are sometimes called "Heaven's Root," the "Door of Death," the "Opening of Life and Death," and the "Barrier of the Return to Life."

If you energetically open and breathe through the Yin Heel Vessels, you will be able to collect and disperse your Original Breath (Yuan Qi) from the Opening of the Barrier (Quanqiao); then the Gate of Heaven (i.e., the Tianmen point) will constantly open for you, and the "Door of Earth" will forever be closed. This is why one ancient Daoist saying states, "the True Man breathes through his heels (considered the circulation of the hidden Prenatal Breath); while the Common Man only breathes through his throat (considered the Postnatal Breath)."

Once stage #1 is completed, the disciple will proceed to stage #2. (Figure 6.69). As the energetic function of the second route of the Macrocosmic Orbit becomes active and established within the body, the disciple will be able to easily project his Qi and Shen out of his body via his hands great distances within the surrounding environment. After he is able to connect with, touch, and feel various objects that are faraway, the disciple should then proceed to Stage #3 of the Macrocosmic Orbit (Figure 6.70).

As the third route of the Macrocosmic Orbit becomes active and established within the body, the energy of the disciple's Shen will be able to be expanded and projected across the cosmos.

Chapter 7
The Six Extraordinary Organs

Introduction To Tissue Formation

According to the teachings of ancient Daoist Alchemy, the Stomach, Large Intestine, Small Intestine, Triple Burners, and Urinary Bladder are all produced by the "Qi of Heaven." These five bowels and their internal energies reflect the "Image of Heaven."

According to the *Yellow Emperor's Inner Canon: Su Wen*, "They (the five bowels) do not store, but make outward flow." In other words, these five "hollow" Yang organs function as temporary repositories where food is transformed, and its essence is internally absorbed as nourishment. The clean, usable essences are then directed towards the five "solid" Yin organs (Liver, Heart, Spleen, Lungs and Kidneys), and the body's internal core; while the turbid wastes are discharged to the exterior of the body. The ancient Daoists believed that the Heavens govern all forms of energetic movement, by controlling the transformation, development, circulation and distribution of Qi. These energetic actions allow for the internal expansion and ascension of Qi within the human body. Once the Qi has reached a crescendo, the Heavens express their energetic form by manifesting "rain and mist" (various forms of Qi), which allows for the internal development and formation of the body's Jing, Qi, and Shen.

According to the *Yellow Emperor's Inner Canon: Su Wen* states, "The Brain, Marrow, Bones, Blood Vessels, Gall Bladder, and Uterus are all produced by the "Qi of the Earth." These six organs store the body's Yin, and reflect the "Image of the Earth;" therefore, they store and do not dispel. These six special "Qi Heng Zhi Fu" ("Extraordinary Organs") function as Yin organs in their capacity to store Jing, Qi, Shen, Blood, Marrow, and Body Fluids. The ancient Daoists believed that the Earth governs all energetic movement by keeping, storing, binding and condensing. The Earth then manifests and expresses its energetic form by releasing Qi, allowing it to rise upward like a mist to form clouds within the Heavens. Similarly, the Six Extraordinary Organs keep, store, bind, and condense the Jing, Qi, Shen, Blood, Marrow and Body Fluids, later distributing them like a mist throughout the body to nourish the tissues.

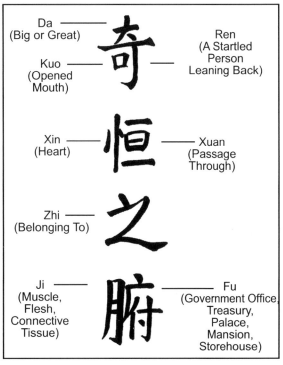

Figure 7.1. The Chinese Ideograph for "Qi Heng Zhi Fu" ("Extraordinary Organs")

Chinese Characters for the Extraordinary Organs: Qi Heng Zhi Fu

The ideographs depicting the Chinese characters for the Extraordinary Organs "Qi Heng Zhi Fu" are described as follows (Figure 7.1):

- **Qi:** The first character is the Chinese ideograph "Qi," which is generally translated as "Extraordinary," but can also be translated as "Surprising, Strange, or Marvellous." It is composed of three characters. Positioned on the top is a character "Da," meaning "Big or Great;" positioned on the bottom-right is a character "Ren" depicting a "Person;" and positioned on the bottom-left is a character "Kuo," meaning "Mouth." As a whole, the ideograph depicts the actions of a startled person, having discovered something strange yet wonderful, falling backwards with their mouth open, in the expression of surprise.

- **Heng:** The second character is the Chinese ideogram "Heng," which translates as "Permanent or Lasting." It is composed of two characters: positioned on the left is the Heart radical "Xin;" positioned on the right is the ancient ideograph "Xuan," depicting "A Passage Through," or "Something crossing between two sides." The combined meaning of these two radicals suggests the Heart's perpetual movement between two things of balance, and is expressed as perseverance.
- **Zhi:** The third character is "Zhi," which can be translated as "Belonging To."
- **Fu:** The fourth character depicts the Chinese ideogram for "Fu," and is composed of two characters: the character to the left, "Ji" depicts the Chinese ideogram for "Body Tissue, Muscle or Flesh" (all of which are forms of connective tissue); the character on the right "Fu" can be translated as "Government Office, Treasury, Palace, Mansion, or Storehouse." Together, both characters represent the body's internal organs as treasure houses within the flesh.

Functions of the Six Extraordinary Organs

The Six Extraordinary Organs are constantly functioning in order to maintain the body's health, and are an essential aspect of the body's energetic matrix. Similar to the Eight Extraordinary Vessels, the Extraordinary Organs (i.e., the Brain, Marrow, Bones, Blood Vessels, Gall Bladder, and Uterus) regulate the specific energetic activities needed to stabilize and harmonize the body's vitality when:
- The body's energetic structures become Deficient
- The body has been attacked by External Pathogenic Factors

The energetic matrix of the Six Extraordinary Organs also function as a entry portal into the body's "original pattern," (i.e., the original DNA blueprint, contained within the body's Yuan Jing). For centuries, the ancient Daoists have used these special energetic structures in order to communicate with the "Original Female," accessing different states of consciousness, that can lead to advanced energetic and spiritual transformations.

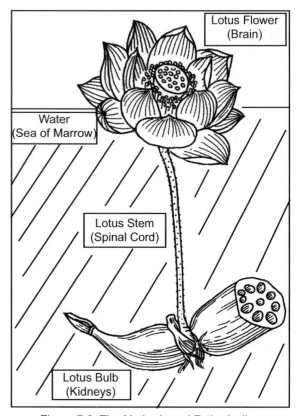

Figure 7.2. The Mother's and Father's Jing (Reproductive Essence) create the formation of the child's Kidneys (Lotus Bulb), Sea of Marrow, Spinal Cord (Lotus Stem), and Brain (Lotus Flower). (Inspired by the original artwork of Lilian Lai Bensky)

The ancient Daoists taught that as the human body forms, two spirits (the composite of the mother's Jing, Qi and Shen and the composite of the father's Jing, Qi and Shen) interlock, uniting to form Prenatal Jing. This Prenatal Essence leads to the formation of the Kidneys (Lotus Bulb), Sea of Marrow, which includes the spinal cord (Lotus Stem) and the Brain (Lotus Flower) (Figure 7.2).

During embryonic development, the Bones form the structural framework of the body, and the Blood Vessels begin to nourish the developing tissues. As the tissues continue to form, the Eight Extraordinary Vessels regulate the energetic structure and function of the body's Six Extraordinary Organs (Figure 7.3).

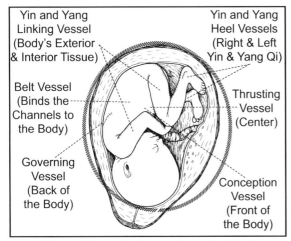

Figure 7.3. As the tissues form, the Eight Extraordinary Vessels regulate the energetic functions of the body's Six Extraordinary Organs.

Because the Eight Extraordinary Vessels are the first energetic rivers to form inside the developing fetus, they are responsible for saturating the Six Extraordinary Organs with the energy of the "Four Seas" (i.e., the Sea of Qi, the Sea of Blood, the Sea of Marrow, and the Sea of Nourishment), and will continue to do so even after the baby is born.

THE EIGHT EXTRAORDINARY VESSELS AND SIX EXTRAORDINARY ORGANS

The body's Eight Extraordinary Vessels (Governing Vessel, Conception Vessel, Thrusting Vessels, Belt Vessel, Yin and Yang Heel Vessels, and Yin and Yang Linking Vessels) integrate the Six Extraordinary Organs with the body's six main Yang organs, and with the Kidneys. The Eight Extraordinary Vessels draw their energy from the Kidneys, and are responsible for storing and circulating the body's Jing Qi throughout the tissues, particularly to the skin, hair and Six Extraordinary Organs.

The Yin aspect of the body's Kidney Jing gives rise to the formation of Marrow. The Marrow flows through the body like a thick sea, pulsating slowly between the lower sacrum and the cranium. Part of the energy of the Sea of Marrow stays within the confines of the Kidney's energetic system, congealing to form the cerebral spinal fluid and Brain. Another portion of the Marrow extends outward

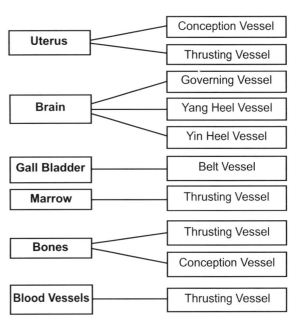

Figure 7.4. The Eight Extraordinary Vessels Regulate the Internal Energy Flow of the Six Extraordinary Organs

from the spine, congealing to form the Bone Marrow, and eventually contributing to the formation of the Blood. Since the Marrow, Bones and Brain are all formed and maintained by the Kidney's Jing, they all are governed by the Kidneys.

The energy of the Six Extraordinary organs is linked to the body's internal energy systems via the Eight Extraordinary Vessels, described as follows (Figure 7.4):

1. **The Uterus:** This Extraordinary Organ is regulated by the Thrusting and Conception Vessels.
2. **The Brain:** This Extraordinary Organ is regulated by the Governing Vessel and the Yin and Yang Heel Vessels.
3. **The Gall Bladder:** This Extraordinary Organ is regulated by the Belt Vessel.
4. **The Marrow:** This Extraordinary Organ is regulated by the Thrusting Vessels.
5. **The Bones:** This Extraordinary Organ is regulated by the Thrusting and Conception Vessels.
6. **The Blood Vessels:** This Extraordinary Organ is regulated by the Thrusting Vessels.

THE UTERUS: BAO

Several classical Chinese dictionaries translate the character "Bao" as "Uterus." However, the word Bao in Chinese Medicine refers to both the physical and also the energetic structure within which the embryo develops.

CHINESE CHARACTER FOR UTERUS

The Chinese character that depicts the ideogram for "Uterus" is "Bao," described as follows (Figure 7.5):

- **Bao:** The Chinese ideogram for "Bao" is composed of two images: the character to the left, "Ji" depicts the Chinese ideogram for "Body Tissue, Muscle or Flesh" (all of which are forms of connective tissue). The character on the right "Bao" means "To Wrap, Surround, and Encase" and refers to "a bag or sack."

Together these characters depict the Uterus and represent an embryo wrapped, protected, and contained inside the mother's abdomen. It is important to note, that in ancient China, the character for Bao was occasionally used to refer to the urinary bladder, placenta, or Uterus.

Figure 7.5. The Chinese character "Bao" ("Uterus")

FUNCTION OF THE UTERUS

The Uterus is shaped like an inverted pear and is anatomically located in the lower abdomen of the female, behind the Urinary Bladder and in front of the rectum. It is a female reproductive organ, with its lower opening connected to the vagina via the cervix (Figure 7.6).

In Chinese Medicine, the term Uterus encompasses the woman's entire internal genital system, including the fallopian tubes and ovaries. Its main physiological functions are that of regulating menstruation, conception, and pregnancy, described as follows (Figure 7.7):

1. **Regulating Menstruation:** The Bao (Uterus) is the organ by which a woman forms her menses. In ancient China, is was believed that a girl's Kidney Qi nourishes the Uterus, increasing the size of her womb into full maturation by the time she reaches the age of 14. Under the influence of "Tian Gui" (the Tenth Heavenly Stem: Yin Water Element Qi), her Conception Vessel flourishes to become more unobstructed, her Thrusting Vessel flourishes, her Sea of Blood becomes fuller, and she begins her menses. It was also believed that at the time when the Kidney Jing became rich in essence, the energetic influence of "Tian Gui" would promote the discharge of the ovum and Blood. To the ancient Daoists, the Tian Gui was the "Yin Water" Heavenly Stem of "Prenatal Heaven." It internally represented the energetic regathering of new life-force associated with Kidney Yin. Tian Gui energetically moves "underground," and is considered to be the Yin Water of the congenital constitution. Being invisibly cultivated, it awaits a new breakthrough. In old age, as the Qi of the Kidneys begins to weaken, the Tian Gui begins to dry up, causing menopause in women.

    The three Yin organs of the Heart, Liver, and Spleen also energetically connect to the Bao (Uterus) through their relationship with the Blood. The Heart governs the Blood. The Liver stores the Blood and regulates the volume of circulating Blood, which is responsible for normal menstruation. The Spleen controls the Blood.

    Generally, when a woman reaches the approximate age of 49 (i.e., her seventh - Seven Year Life-Cycle), her Kidney Qi has weakened because the "Tian Gui" in her body has become exhausted. At this point in her life, both the Ren Mai (Conception Vessel) and Chong Mai (Thrusting Vessel) energetically "close" and become obstructed, creating menstrual irregularities until menopause begins.

2. **Conception and Pregnancy:** Once a woman's Uterus becomes fully developed and she begins her menses, an egg is released from her ovary and she can become pregnant. With

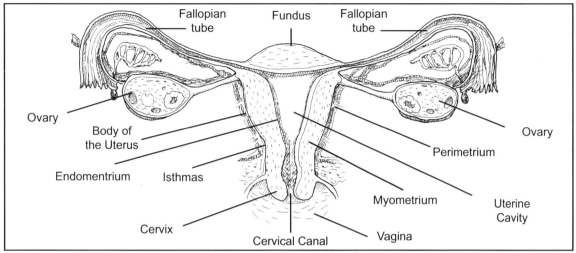

Figure 7.6. The Female Reproductive Organs, including the Uterus, Fallopian Tubes, and Ovaries. (Inspired by the original artwork of Dr. Frank H. Netter)

each ovulation, either the right or left ovary will release a fertile egg. This release generally alternates, with the right ovary releasing an egg one month and the left ovary the next.

The physiological functions of a woman's Uterus are connected to the energetic functions of the Heart, Liver, Spleen, and Kidneys, as well as to the Conception and Thrusting Vessels (Figure 7.8). The Uterus connects to the Kidneys (which provide the Uterus with Jing), the Conception Vessel (which provides the Uterus with Qi and nourishes the fetus), and the Thrusting Channel (which provides the Uterus with Blood).

When the Jing of the Kidneys becomes sufficient, the menstrual period occurs regularly,

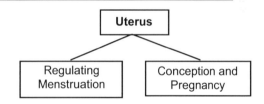

Figure 7.7. The Two Functions of the Uterus

the woman can become pregnant, and her womb is capable of nourishing a fetus. The Qi and Blood of the Twelve Primary Channels pass into the Uterus through the Thrusting and Conception Vessels, affecting the quality and regularity of the menstrual cycle.

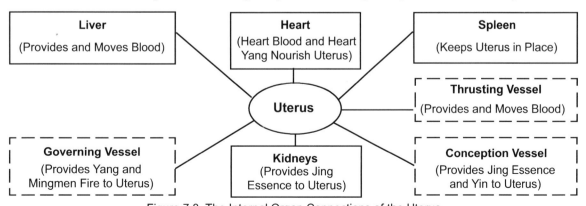

Figure 7.8. The Internal Organ Connections of the Uterus

THE BAO (UTERUS) AND ANCIENT DAOIST INTERNAL ALCHEMY

The Bao and Lower Dantian area is the major storage area for the various types of Kidney energies (i.e., Qi of the ovaries), and it is often called the Sea of Qi. It is the place where Qi is housed, the body's Mingmen Fire is aroused, the Kidney Yin and Yang Qi is gathered, and the Yuan Qi is stored.

As mentioned earlier, Yuan Qi is also known as Source Qi and is the foundation of all the other types of Qi in the body. The Yuan Qi is closely linked with the Prenatal Essence (Yuan Jing). Together, the Yuan Qi and Yuan Jing determine the individual's overall health, vitality, stamina, and life span.

In both Daoist Internal Alchemy (Neigong) and Medical Qigong Training, the Earth Qi is traditionally gathered and cultivated inside the Bao and Lower Dantian area. This is because every individual is originally conceived and began their initial development inside the center of the Bao (Uterus), located in the heart of a woman's Lower Dantian. Therefore in Daoist Alchemy, when a disciple meditates to enter into the infinite space of the Wuji (considered to be the "womb of the universe"), it is a symbolic recreation of the original creative process of his or her prenatal energetic formation.

The Uterus is associated with the development and formation of the fetus' tissues, thereby allowing the Eternal Soul the ability to acquire familiarity with lower vibrational resonances in order to experience life on the material plane. Therefore, within the Physical Realm, the ancient Daoists considered the Bao to be the sacred energetic temple required for the entrance of the human soul into embodied life.

In ancient texts on Daoist Alchemy, both men and women are described as having a Bao (Uterus). In this context, the Bao refers to the area in which the disciple energetically and spiritually grows the "Primordial Embryo" or "Golden Fetus," used for the purpose of entering other

Figure 7.9. The "Golden Fetus" is formed Within the Daoist Disciple's "Lower Bao"

energetic and spiritual realms and for obtaining Immortality.

The ancient Daoists Alchemists used the "Lower Bao" ("Lower Dantian") as the primary internal energetic field through which to nourish and store the "Golden Fetus" (Figure 7.9). The Golden Fetus is constructed of refined Ling Qi (Spiritual Energy) and Ling Shen (Spiritual Mind/Heart), developed through specific "Shengong" ("Spirit Skill") meditations.

To the ancient Daoists, the original quiescent state in which the fetus energetically developed while in the Bao, was considered to be also attainable after birth through prayer, meditation, and deep restful sleep. These three quiescent states formed the true foundation for the internal cultivation and transformation of the disciple's Prenatal Jing, Qi, and Shen.

THE BRAIN: NAO

According to the *Huangdi Neijing Suwen (Yellow Emperor's Inner Classic Simple Questions)*, "The Brain is Yin." Being Yin, it is also the end pool and junction of all of the body's Yang Qi. In other words, the Brain functions like an energetic lid, allowing all the vapors of the Yang Qi and essence to gather and be retained within the Sea of Marrow located inside the head. In ancient China, the Brain was originally viewed as a canopy (Gai) and was believed to attract and receive the subtle external and internal emanations of Heavenly Yang.

The ancient Daoists believed that the body's Jing, Qi, and Shen travel from the Five Zang (Yin) Organs and Six Fu (Yang) Organs into the Brain, allowing the seven upper orifices (eyes, ears, nostrils, and mouth) to perceive and function. The ancient Daoists also believed that the Brain was the "Fu" ("Bowel") of the Yuan Shen (Original Heart/Mind), allowing the energetic influence of the "Spirit of the Heart" and the "Hun of the Liver" to naturally become active within the upper orifices and within the Brain.

The Brain depends on the Heart's Blood for its nourishment. Because the Kidneys store the Jing and the Heart governs the Blood, the Brain depends on a balanced state of the Heart and Kidneys for its vitality.

The Brain is considered to be a chamber of transformation for both Prenatal and Postnatal Essence (Jing) and Energy (Qi). It is regulated by the Governing Vessel, as well as the Yin and Yang Heel Vessels.

CHINESE CHARACTERS FOR BRAIN

The Chinese character that depicts the ideogram for "Brain" is "Nao," described as follows (Figure 7.10):

- **Nao:** The Chinese ideogram for "Nao" is composed of two images. To the left, the first character "Ji," depicts the Chinese ideogram for "Body Tissue, Muscle or Flesh" (all of which are forms of connective tissue).

  The character on the right is composed of two characters. The upper right hand character "Shun" depicts "Head Hair," and reflects the manifestation of the Kidney's Jing.

  The bottom right hand character "Xin," depicts a box with something inside, representing the skull filled with Marrow. Together, these characters are used to represent the Brain. In

Figure 7.10. The Chinese character "Nao" ("Brain")

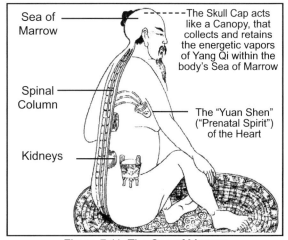

Figure 7.11. The Sea of Marrow

ancient China, the original character for Brain did not have the "Ji" radical on the left, but instead had another radical that depicted the two halves of the symmetrical structure of the Brain.

THE BRAIN AS THE SEA OF MARROW

In Chinese Medicine, "Marrow" is a unique semifluid substance (different from the marrow of Western Medicine), which is the fundamental essence of the Bones, the Bone Marrow, the Brain, and the Spinal Cord. Traditionally, the Brain is considered to be the Sea of Marrow, and extends from the head down through the spinal column, rooting itself within the Kidneys.

There is an old Chinese saying, "The Marrow returns to the Brain." Meaning that Kidney Jing produces Marrow, which generates the spinal cord and "fills the Brain." In Chinese Medicine, it is traditionally taught that the Sea of Marrow flows into the cranial cavity and congeals in order to form the Brain (Figure 7.11).

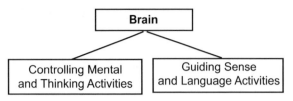

Figure 7.12. The Two Functions of the Brain

MAIN FUNCTIONS OF THE BRAIN

The main functions of the Brain are controlling mental and thinking activities, and guiding sense and language activities, which are described as follows (Figure 7.12):

1. **Controlling Mental and Thinking Activities:** In Chinese Medicine, the Brain is considered to be the house of the innate intelligence (Yuan Shen), and the seat of mental function.

   An individual's thinking ability is strengthened when Qi and Blood in the two hemispheres of the Cerebral Cortex are abundant. This is because the "Memory Zone" and "Thought Center" are also located in the Cerebral Cortex.

   The ancient Daoists believed that the energy of the spine and spinal cord extended an individual's consciousness into their Physical Body from the Brain. According to Energetic Embryology, all of these various regions of the Brain will not develop until the Kidney Channels travel through the spine (along with the Liver Channels) to reach the Cerebral Cortex. This is why, when the Qi of these two channels is abundant the memory function is strong.

2. **Guiding Sense and Language Activities:** Chinese Medicine maintains that the senses and the control of the body's physical movements are related to the Brain. Within the various internal structures of the Brain, there are the following divisions (Figure 7.13):
   - **The Occipital Lobe:** This receives and processes visual information,
   - **The Temporal Lobe:** This receives auditory signals, processing language and the meaning of words.
   - **The Parietal Lobe:** This is associated with the sensory cortex and processes information about touch, taste, pressure, pain, and heat and cold.

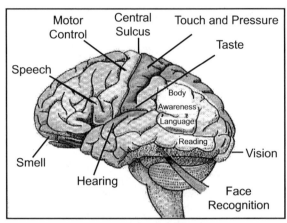

Figure 7.13. The Various Divisions of the Brain

- **The Frontal Lobe:** This is associated with three special functions, motor activity and the integration of muscle activity, speech, and the thought processes.

The Brain is functionally related to the energy of the Kidneys, which are responsible for effecting memory (specifically short term memory) and concentration. The various associations related to hearing, touch, sight, and smell all become especially perceptive when the Sea of Marrow is "full."

THE BRAIN AND DAOIST MYSTICISM

One example of the Kidney's energetic effect on the various functions of the Brain, is reflected in the inner light observed within the center core Taiji Pole. The ancient Daoists believed that with the increase in spiritual activity, a circle of radiant light naturally reflected the internal spiritual light contained within the Taiji Pole. According to the ancient writings of the *Yellow Court Scriptures*,

> "The food of the "Man of Heaven" has no flavor.
> The Immortal Child receives its elixir nourishment straight from the "Center,"
> known as "Gem Soup" or "Jade Frost;"
> and mostly thrives from ingesting
> the Qi of the "Eight Secret Rings of Light"
> used for benefitting the Kidney Essence."

In ancient Daoist teachings, the "Eight Secret Rings of Light" were at one time known as the "Eight White Jades." They secretly refer to the in-

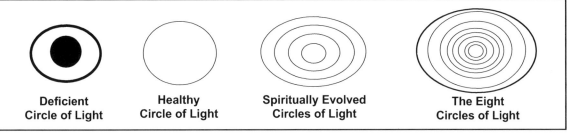

Figure 7.14. The Yuan Shen is reflected in the intensity of the light present in the Taiji Pole. The degree of accumulated spiritual energy can be seen in the number and quality of light circles within the Taiji Pole.

ner spiritual light of the Taiji Pole, projected onto the optic nerves within the Brain, reflecting an image of various circles of radiant light (Figure 7.14).

In ancient Daoist alchemy, this reflected light was considered to be the disciple's innate spiritual energy (Ling Qi), manifesting the level of a disciple's Yuan Shen (Original Spirit). Each level of the disciple's spiritual evolution is represented by the intensity of this special light, and the number of energetic rings that surround the light's resonating core.

When I was first introduced to this particular ancient teaching, I was truly skeptical of my Daoist teacher's explanation. I had trained for many years and had rarely seen such internal light phenomena. However, as I continued to follow my teachers instruction, to my amazement, I eventually began to consistently observe the various rings of light he had previously spoken about.

These circles of light can be best observed upon first awakening after quiescent sleep. By rolling over onto the pillow and placing slight pressure on the external eye lids, the inner light of the Taiji Pole is immediately projected onto the optic nerves, reflecting an image of this circle of light (known as a "Phosphene" in Western Medicine).

If the circle of light is complete, it reflects a strong, healthy condition. If however, the circle of light is dark within its center (similar to that of a doughnut), this reflects a deficient condition. If the circle of light is broken or interrupted, it reflects an extreme deficiency (see Figure 7.14).

Each spiritual "death and rebirth," allows the Ling Shen (Spiritual Heart/Mind) to grow, causing the Ling Qi (Spiritual Energy) to reflect more light and increase the amount of radiant circles observed.

THE BRAIN AND THE MIND

According to Chinese Energetic Medicine, when Kidney Jing is strong it nourishes the Brain and Memory. To understand how the Mind processes and stores different types of memories, the doctor must first understand that the "Mind" and the "Memory" are not completely physical, but exist as energy fields within and around the physical body.

To the ancient Daoists, the physical Brain was believed to act as a type of "transceiver," that interfaces between the Mind and the body, as well as the surrounding environment and all of matter. This is why if the Brains ability to "receive and transmit" becomes damaged, the Mind cannot function and express itself properly.

The Mind is viewed as an energetic field of consciousness, with unknown and potentially infinite boundaries. When teaching this concept to my students, I ask them to "point to where the Mind is," then "point to where the Mind is not." How far the Mind extends as a subtle energetic field is scientifically unknown, however, the ancient Daoists believed that the Mind extended into the farthest reaches of the Universe, as well as into all of the various subtle realms and dimensions. Everything, be it human, animal, insect, plant, or mineral is a point of Mind, a point of consciousness, existing not within the Brain, but within a universal field of all-encompassing Divine Consciousness. Therefore, think of the Mind as not being located within the physical structure of the Brain, but as a discrete unit of subtle conscious energy, enmeshed within a universal field of subtle conscious energy. Imagine an iceberg floating in an ocean. Although it appears to be separate from the water that formed it (until it melts), it has been and will always be a part of the ocean.

The Brain According to Chinese Energetic Medicine

In Chinese Energetic Medicine, the Central Nervous System governs both conscious and unconscious actions. The lower Brain Stem and Spinal Cord are connected to the Yin energetic field, while the Cerebral Cortex is connected to the Yang energetic field.

When a Medical Qigong Doctor attunes his energetic field to a patient's energetic field, and begins emitting Qi, this internally activates the patient's Brain cells responsible for receiving and storing energetic patterns. Once these energetic patterns are accessed, the patient's tissues automatically respond and reproduce an energetic pattern similar to the original pattern used to record the patient's physical, mental, emotional, energetic, and spiritual experiences.

This energetic reaction naturally occurs due to the fact that the patient's tissues and cells conform to the subtle vibrational patterning originally imprinted within his or her Energy Body.

The Brain Receives, Records, and Maintains the Energy of Thought

One set of Brain cells receives, records, and maintains the vibrational patterns that make up thoughts, pictures, actions, and movements of various forms of energy and matter. These vibrational patterns can be perceived and registered within the mind of the Medical Qigong Doctor. Once perceived and registered, these subtle energetic patterns can then be reproduced and projected.

A trained Medical Qigong Doctor can arrange the energetic patterns of his or her cells in such a way as to reproduce the sounds and movements of these subtle energetic forms or objects, and even the thoughts of the individual that sent them. Through these energetically activated cells, the doctor can assist the patient in controlling various toxic thoughts and imaginations.

The Brain's energetic pattern has a direct influence on the external environment, and routinely plays a significant role in one's social interactions. For example, when someone either observes or imagines the occurrence of a specific event (either good or bad), that particular energetic pattern becomes registered and fixed within the individual's cells. When this pattern is energetically fed through consistent focused intention (whether consciously or unconsciously), it develops a powerful energetic charge. The energetic pattern is then projected outside the individual's body to be imprinted on the corresponding cells of another's Brain, which is then projected back until the incident is so fixed and real that the event actually occurs. This is known as a "self-fulfilling prophecy." Similarly, it is thought that accidents and disease are brought into existence through the resonant influence of the cells' energetic patterns.

Another set of Brain cells receives, records, and maintains the energy of the thoughts and activities of the Divine. This Divine energy, pervades everything, and is constantly radiating out its spiritual knowledge in the form of true inspired wisdom. All of the cells within the body naturally receive and project the energy of the "Divine Mind." Therefore, if the Medical Qigong Doctor separates himself from the divine in thought, he will also separate from the Divine in manifestation.

Clinical Pathology and the Brain

When studying the Clinical Pathology of the various energetic influences of the Brain, it is important to note that "Hot" diseases can affect both the Brain and the Sea of Marrow, especially when they are combined with either Wind or Cold Invasion.

Additionally, according to the *Yellow Emperor's Inner Canon: Su Wen,*

> "An Excess of the Sea of Marrow allows one to become alert and robust, with much strength. It also permits the individual to fulfill the number of his or her allotted years.
>
> A Deficiency of the Sea of Marrow causes the Brain to spin (vertigo), the ears to buzz (tinnitus), and the legs to become weak with a form of lower back paralysis (lumbago). It also causes the eyes to lose their sight.
>
> When there is a Deficiency in the Sea of Marrow, the patient also becomes slow and lazy, and desires to lay down quietly."

THE BRAIN DETECTS EMITTED QI

In 1996, while lecturing on "The Emotional Components of Tumor Formation," at the 3rd World Conference on Medical Qigong, Beijing, China (Figure 7.15), I was fortunate enough to meet research scientist Professor Richard Lee. The following is an excerpt from his clinical research based on "Medical Qigong Qi Emission Therapy and its effects on the human brain." This research was originally gathered by Professor Richard Lee, Director of the China Healthways Institute in San Clemente, California, Professor Lu Yan Fang of the National Institute of Electro-Acoustics in Beijing, China, and the Beijing College of Traditional Chinese Medicine.

"I had learned in my many years of research with the Electro-Encephalograph (EEG) that the human Brain responds to even the most subtle of stimuli to the body, so I reasoned that, if there were really any scientific basis to Emitted Qi Therapy, it would show up in the Brain waves of test subjects who were placed in the path of these emissions. I expected to see no difference between the resting states and the Qi Emission states.

What we saw was extraordinary. Within a few seconds after the Medical Qigong Doctor began to emit Qi, the subject's EEG would begin to shift. The EEG power spectrum was enhanced on all channels while the most pronounced increase was in the frontal lobe. Also, there was an enhancement and synchronization of the Alpha rhythm in all channels. When the Medical Qigong Doctor stopped emitting Qi, the EEG would gradually shift back toward the baseline readings.

To determine whether infrasonic energy was a significant part of the Emitted Qi Therapy, we used the Infrasonic Qigong prototypes in the same experiment. The machine was placed 18 inches away from the individual, directly behind the back of the head of the test subject. The EEG electrodes were attached as before. The simulator was activated for short periods of time and the results recorded. We found that the effects on the receiver's EEG were quite similar to those of the Emitted Qi Therapy.

Our further research involved monitoring the various sensory-cortical evoked potentials during

Figure 7.15. Author lecturing on "Tumor Formation" At the World Conference On Medical Qigong

Medical Qigong Meditation, Emitted Qi Therapy, and Infrasonic Qigong stimulation. We again found very similar results from all three stimuli. We found that a large portion of the cerebral cortex was inhibited while other somato-sensory cortex were excited. One of the significant findings of this study is that the inhibition of the cerebral cortex during Medical Qigong Meditation is clearly different from the excitation of the cerebral cortex that is measurable during sleep.

Through Acoustical Brainstem Evoked Response (ABER), it was found that the brainstem structures from the medulla to the hypothalamus were significantly stimulated. The brainstem plays an important role in regulating the functions of the inner organs, motor functions, and emotions.

The implications of these studies were startling. Medical Qigong Doctors can, without touch, voice, eye contact or any other traditional communication means, induce a clear, strong, and highly measurable change in a subject's Brain functioning.

A synchronization of Alpha rhythm indicates deep relaxation, and is closely associated with accelerated healing. Enhanced power spectrum in the frontal lobe is especially significant because the association cortex of the frontal lobe is concerned with higher motor action, higher sensory function, emotional and motivational aspects of behavior, and integration of autonomic function. Stimulation of the brain stem, with its regulation of the internal organs, may be a mechanism by which physical healing is induced or accelerated.

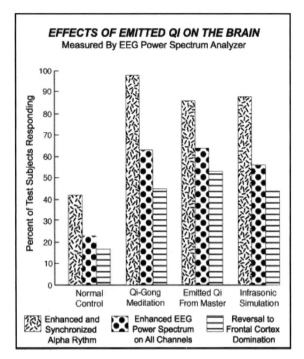

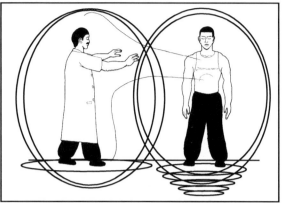

Figure 7.17. In Qi Emission Therapy
The Medical Qigong Doctor emitting Qi into a patient

Figure 7.16. Emitted Qi has a pronounced and repeatable effect on EEG measurements. It enhances frontal and occipital EEG power spectra, and often enhances the frontal to the extent that it becomes the dominant EEG activity (whereas occipital dominance is more common). Emitted Qi also enhances and synchronizes the Alpha rhythm.

Despite these highly significant changes in EEG and evoked potentials, the subjects had felt nothing and had no idea of the profound changes taking place within them.

The findings of these studies are solid evidence that a Medical Qigong Doctor can induce real physiological changes in a subject from several feet away, and further, may help to explain the high rate of recovery from Chronic Degenerative Diseases in groups of hospital patients under the care of Medical Qigong Doctors (Figure 7.16). These studies also show that the Infrasonic Qigong Simulator can induce similar changes in Brain function and that, through Medical Qigong Meditation, a Medical Qigong Doctor can induce these same changes in his own Brain.

SCIENTIFIC CONTROLS

There is much disagreement on how Emitted Qi affects the Brain. Many doctors insist that Brain changes are psychologically induced, and that verbal suggestion, impressive hand motion, and the subject's expectations account for the observed phenomena surrounding Qi Emission Therapy.

To test this, we had several people pretending to be Medical Qigong Doctors treat the test subjects. The subjects were told that all were Medical Qigong Doctors, and all moved their hands in similar ways. We saw no significant changes in Brain wave patterns with the fake Qigong masters. However, when the real Medical Qigong Doctors emitted their Qi, we repeatedly observed highly significant changes (Figure 7.17).

Even this did not satisfy many of the doctors who reviewed our work, so we repeated the study with animals. We monitored EEG in awake rabbits and ABER (Acoustical Brainstem Evoked Response) in anesthetized cats as Medical Qigong Doctors emitted Qi toward them. Even though there was no voice or eye contact between the Medical Qigong Doctors and the animals, and the masters emitted Qi from several feet away, we saw shifts in EEG and ABER similar to those observed in the human subjects. This is a highly convincing result because all kinds of placebo effects are eliminated, yet modification of Brain function at a distance remains constant."

Four Major Changes Occurring in the Brain During Qigong Meditation

According to current research conducted by Dr. Gregg Jacobs of Harvard Medical School, scientists have now discovered that four major changes occur within the Brain during meditation, described as follows (Figure 7.18 and Figure 7.19):

1. **Meditation and the Frontal Lobe of the Cerebral Cortex:** The Frontal Cortex is the most highly evolved part of the Brain. It is responsible for intellectual functions such as reason and abstract thinking, aggressive and sexual behavior, smell, speech, language, and the initiation of movement. During meditation, the normal active processes of the Frontal Cortex shut down.

2. **Meditation and the Parietal Lobe of the Cerebral Cortex:** The Parietal Lobe is concerned with the recognition of specific sensory stimuli concerning the surrounding environment; the ability to use symbols as a means of communication; the ability to develop ideas and the motor responses to carry them out; and the ability to orientate in space and time. During meditation, the activity in the Parietal Lobe slows down.

3. **Meditation and the Thalamus:** The Thalamus is considered to be part of the Diencephalon (i.e., the smaller of the two derivatives of the early forebrain), consisting of several groups of cell bodies and processes that function mostly as a complex relay center. The relay nuclei of the Thalamus receives input indirectly from most of the sensory neurons of the cranial and spinal nerves. Acting as the "gate keeper" of the senses, it primarily focuses the mind's attention by funneling sensory data deeper into the Brain, and stopping other signals from overloading the system. During meditation, the flow of information flowing into the Thalamus is reduced to a trickle.

4. **Meditation and the Reticular Formation of the Brain-stem:** The Reticular Formation is a massive but vaguely defined neural apparatus composed of closely intermingled gray and white matter extending throughout the central

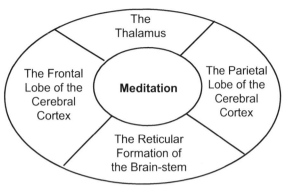

Figure 7.18. Graph of the four major areas in the brain affected during meditation.

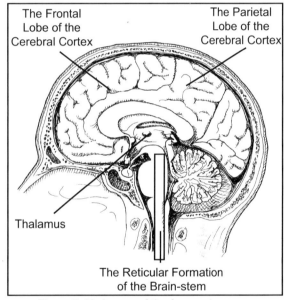

Figure 7.19. Image of the four major areas in the brain affected during meditation.

core of the brain-stem into the Diencephalon. It acts as the Brain's sentry. Always receiving incoming stimuli, it puts the Brain on alert, ready to respond. During meditation, the arousal signals lessen significantly.

The subjects who were studied in the research showed a pronounced change in their brain-wave patterns, shifting from Beta waves (conscious thought wave patterns) to Alpha waves (relaxation wave patterns) after training in meditation for only eight weeks.

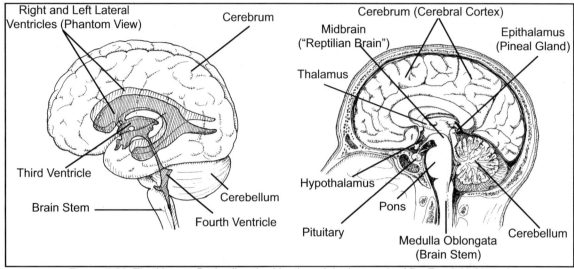

Figure 7.20. The Human Brain. (Inspired by the original artwork of Dr. Frank H. Netter)

Western Medical Viewpoint

The Chinese energetic viewpoint is quite different from the Western approach which views the brain's anatomy as consisting of five regions, including (Figure 7.20):

1. The Cerebral Hemispheres, or Cerebrum (the neocortex, neopallium)
2. The Thalamus, Hypothalamus, and Epithalamus (Pineal Gland)
3. The Midbrain/Mesencephalon (the Colliculi and Cerebral Peduncles)
4. The Pons and Cerebellum
5. The Medulla Oblongata

In Western Medicine, it is taught that the Cerebral Cortex of the brain is divided into two hemispheres, that communicate with each other via a large bundle of fibers known as the Corpus Callosum. The left side of the body is controlled mainly by the right side of the cortex, and the right side of the body is controlled by the left cortex.

- **The Left Hemisphere:** This is predominantly responsible for the individual's analytical and logical thinking, as well as verbal skills, reading, writing, and the ability to make complex mathematical calculations.
- **The Right Hemisphere:** This is predominantly responsible for the individual's artistic and musical abilities, as well as the recognition of faces, body language, nonverbal (symbolic) ideas, and creativity.
- **The Frontal Lobes of the Brain:** This governs the functions of our analytical decision making.
- **The Cerebral Hemispheres:** These are responsible for the body's sense and movement.
- **The Brain Stem:** This controls the heartbeat and breathing.
- **The Cerebellum:** This directs the balance and muscle coordination.
- **The Hypothalamus:** This regulates the body's temperature and the release of hormones.

The Reptilian Brain

In Western Medicine, the oldest part of the brain (evolutionarily speaking), is often called the "Reptilian Brain," because its anatomical formation is similar to that found in lizards, alligators, and turtles. The Reptilian Brain (Brain Stem) is responsible for keeping the heart beating and the respiratory breathing functioning, survival instincts, and reactive impulse movements.

The Mammalian (Limbic) Brain

The Reptilian Brain is situated at the top of the Brain Stem and is surrounded by the Limbic System, which itself is known as the "Mammalian Brain." The Mammalian Brain (Limbic System) regulates the emotions and desires. Its main job is to drive an individual toward the things that maintain the preservation of his or her life.

THE PRIMATE (NEOCORTEX) BRAIN

The third part of the brain wraps itself around the Limbic System, and is called the Primate Brain (Neocortex). The Primate Brain (Neocortex) handles the higher cerebral functions, such as thinking, creating mental maps of the world, and making connections with others.

All three parts of the brain (i.e., the Reptilian, Mammalian, and Primate) are viewed as biologically distinct, both in chemistry and in structure. The older formations of the brain are responsible for the Autonomic Nervous System, whereas the Primate (being the most recent to evolve) is responsible for thinking and voluntary movement (Figure 7.21).

BRAIN-WAVE PATTERNS

Normal brain function involves the continual electrical activity of the neurons. This electrical brain-wave activity is measured in patterns or cycles per second, known as "hertz." Traditionally, Western Medical Science divides brain-wave activity into four main frequency domains: Beta, Alpha, Theta and Delta, described as follows (Figure 7.22):

- **Beta (13-26 Hertz):** The Beta state is associated with an active, waking consciousness, and open eyes.

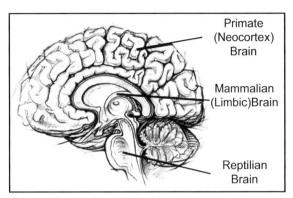

Figure 7.21. The Three Parts of the Human Brain.

- **Alpha (8-12 Hertz):** The Alpha state is associated with a calm, relaxed body, with the eyes closed (or day dreaming with the eyes open).
- **Theta (4-7 Hertz):** The Theta state is associated with a deep relaxation, and drowsiness (the hypnagogic state before sleep). This state is common in children and in adults during the early stages of sleep.
- **Delta (0.5-4 Hertz):** The Delta state is associated with sleep or unconsciousness.

At the borderline between any two states (e.g., between the Beta and Alpha state), the brain-waves generally manifest as a combination of both patterns. Research conducted in England by C. Maxwell Cade on brain-wave patterns revealed a hierarchy of states

Stage	State of Consciousness	Psychological Dimension	Brainwave Pattern	Realm of Expierience
1st	Awake	Conscious Mind	Beta (13-26 Hertz)	Consciousness: waking consciousness, sensory awareness receiving external information
2nd	Prayer, Meditation	Superconscious Mind	Alpha (8-12 Hertz)	Day-dreaming: calm, relaxation, hypnagogic state between being awake and asleep, visionary states, archetypal imagery
3rd	Dreaming Sleep	Subconscious Mind	Theta (4-7 Hertz)	Deep Relaxation: deep relaxation, drowsiness (the beginning hypnagogic state before sleep), and release of suppressed emotions
4th	Deep Sleep	Unconscious Mind	Delta (0.5-4 Hertz)	Sleep or Unconsciousness: the awakening of primal instincts and primitive drives

Figure 7.22. The four main frequencies of an individual's Brain-Wave Patterns

of consciousness, each with physiological correlations. For example, the "fourth" state of consciousness is comparable to the "relaxation response" state, associated with traditional meditation. States of "five" and beyond are considered to be "mystical" states, associated with energy healers, spiritual teachers, and Daoist Mystics (Figure 7.23).

While in these deeper states, Doctor Cade's subjects began to speak like mystics, while others, with no previous artistic talent, produced beautiful drawings or ecstatic poetry. It was noted that the subjects experienced new patterns of neural activity, in these mystical states, which affected both hemispheres of the brain, as well as both parts of the limbic system and brain-stem. The research concluded that mystical states of awareness can be induced by balancing the right and left hemispheres of the brain.

Research involving EEG studies on the brainwaves of children under the age of five has shown that they habitually function in an Alpha mode of consciousness (the first state of altered consciousness), rather than the Beta mode.

Science, the Brain, and Memory

Western Scientists have discovered that the Brain primarily "talks to itself" through the language of wave interference (phase, amplitude, and frequency) and patterns, as opposed to images or chemical impulses. Within this model, we can understand that the electrical and chemical structures and impulses within the Brain are governed by the more subtle energetic wave form patterns of the Upper Dantian. The Brain perceives and analyzes an object by first "resonating" with its energetic wave pattern, then breaking it down into wave frequencies and transmitting this wave-pattern to the rest of the body.

Each set of human Brain cells absorbs and records sets of vibrations. The Brain primarily receives these vibrations through the skin, eyes, ears, nose, and mouth, and it records them as patterns of resonance within its cells. The mind interprets these incoming vibrations as images, sounds, smells, and sensations, and then organizes these into memories. The accuracy and extent of the interpretation of this incoming data

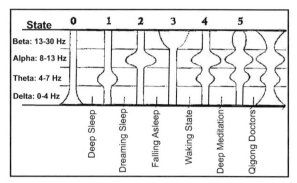

Figure 7.23. Images of Brain-Wave Patterns

depends upon the level of consciousness of the individual at the time of the interaction.

By applying the model of wave interference patterns to the process of memory, it has been conservatively estimated that the average human Brain has the potential to accumulate more than 280 quintillion (280,000,000,000,000,000,000) bits of information during a lifetime. The Brain retrieves "old" information the same way it processes "new" information, through the holographic transformation of wave interference patterns.

The Brain contains a certain mechanism that acts as a highly sensitive frequency analyzer, sorting perceptions and incoming knowledge in order to prevent "information overload." Without this, the infinite waves of information contained within the environment would overwhelm the individual. Normally, the Brain is "tuned in" to only a limited range of frequencies; however, through prayer, meditation, and quiescent relaxation, the receptive areas in the Brain become increasingly more open to the near infinite spectrum of wavelengths existing within the Wuji. In this way, every individual is capable of expanding their Mind into a greater awareness and harmony with the Dao.

Scientists believe that the part of the brain that creates wave-interference patterns might not be located in only one particular area or group of cells, but rather it exists in the spaces between the cells. The Brain simply retrieves and relates the information. What we think of as perception and memory is simply a coherent emission of signals stemming from the Wuji; the stronger memories are but a structured grouping of this type of wave information.

CHAPTER 7: THE SIX EXTRAORDINARY ORGANS

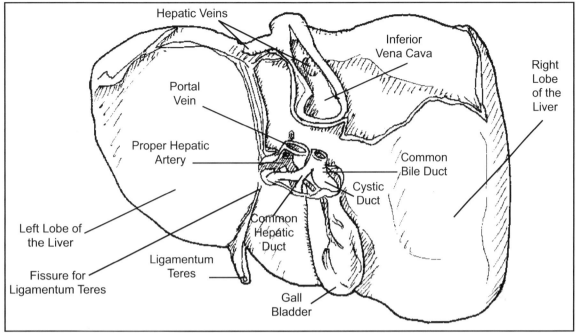

Figure 7.24. The Rear View of the Liver and the Gall Bladder

THE GALL BLADDER: DAN

The Gall Bladder is a green colored, hollow, thin-walled, capsule-shaped Yang organ. It is about three to four inches long, and is located in a shallow fossa on the visceral surface of the liver (Figure 7.24).

It is categorized as an "Extraordinary Organ" because it is the only Yang organ that neither receives "turbid" food and drink nor produces digestive waste products. Instead, it stores a refined "clean" substance (i.e., the bile), thus making it functionally similar to the Yin organs.

Another reason that the Gall Bladder is considered "extraordinary," is that it does not communicate with the exterior directly, as the other Yang organs do, via the mouth, rectum, or urethra. The Gall Bladder Channels, however, travel into the external sensory organs (eyes, ears, nose and mouth) via its trajectories, allowing the sensory organs to become more rooted and grounded.

On a psycho-emotional level, the Gall Bladder is energetically in charge of making the right decisions, and for providing the determination to act accordingly. It therefore has the responsibility of being stable, quiet, tranquil, and unshakable.

Figure 7.25. The Chinese character "Dan" (Gall Bladder)

THE CHINESE CHARACTER FOR GALL BLADDER

The Chinese character that depicts the ideogram for "Gall Bladder" is "Dan," described as follows (Figure 7.25):

- **Dan:** The Chinese "Dan" is composed of three images: the character to the left, "Ji" depicts the Chinese ideogram for "Body Tissue, Muscle or Flesh" (all of which are forms of connective tissue).

The character on the right is composed of two characters. The upper right hand character depicts a person on a steep rocky place bent over and afraid of falling. The bottom right hand character "Yan," meaning "Speech or

385

Words." Together, these characters represent a person in a hazardous position who cannot make a decision, and expresses the Gall Bladder's important role in making difficult decisions and initiating courage.

FUNCTION OF THE GALL BLADDER

The Gall Bladder's associated Yin Organ is the Liver and its element is Wood. In Traditional Chinese Medicine, the Gall Bladder functions the same way as described in Western Medicine, except that in Chinese Energetic Medicine it also incurs some partial functions of the Nervous System. The main functions of the Gall Bladder are described as follows (Figure 7.26):

1. **Stores and Excretes Bile:** Bile is created and secreted by the Liver and is stored and concentrated within the Gall Bladder. The Gall Bladder then releases the bile into the Small Intestines in order to aid in the digestion and absorption of food.
2. **Provides Qi to the Tendons:** The Gall Bladder also helps the Liver control the tendons. The Liver provides Blood to the tendons, while the Gall Bladder provides Qi to the tendons in order to ensure proper movement and agility. These combined functions of the Liver and Gall Bladder ensure that the sinews are soft and pliant and supplied with an abundance of energy.
3. **Psycho-Emotional Aspects:** In ancient China, the Gall Bladder was sometimes called the "Court of Justice," and the "General's Advisor." This is because the Gall Bladder is responsible for making decisions and judgments, overseeing and empowering discernment, as well as providing bravery, courage, confidence, and meeting challenges. Although the Kidneys control drive and vitality, the Gall Bladder provides the capacity to turn this drive and vitality into decisive action.

Weak Gall Bladder Qi can result in timidity, great apprehension, and a lack of courage. In ancient China the term "Da Dan" ("Big Gall Bladder") was commonly used to denote a man with courage; while the phrase "Shao Dan" ("Small Gall Bladder") was used to denote cowardice.

It is important to note, that the Gall Bladder

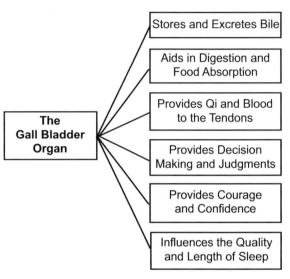

Figure 7.26. The Energetic Functions of the Gall Bladder Organ

(like the Liver), is adversely affected by stress and supressed anger. Pent-up emotions such as anger, frustration, and resentment can cause Stagnation of Liver Qi. If the energy of these suppressed emotions are allowed to build up within the Liver, they can inadvertently produce Toxic Heat, which can affect the Gall Bladder. When toxic Heat begins to rise up within the Gall Bladder Channels, it can give rise to such symptoms as irritability and headaches. In the Medical Qigong Clinic, a "Migrane Headache" is traditionally known as a "Gall Bladder Headache."

4. **Sleeping Patterns:** The Gall Bladder has an energetic influence on the quality and length of sleep. If the Gall Bladder Qi is Deficient, the patient will wake up early in the morning and be unable to fall back to sleep. Additionally, according to the *Yellow Emperor's Inner Canon: Su Wen,*

*"When the Gall Bladder is Deficient
One Dreams of fighting, trials, and sucide."*

THE GALL BLADDER CHANNEL

The Gall Bladder Channels travel into the sensory organs (eyes, ears, nose and mouth), allowing the sensory organs to become more energetically rooted and grounded. They are also responsible for the regulation of hormones and Body Fluids (Figure 7.27).

CHAPTER 7: THE SIX EXTRAORDINARY ORGANS

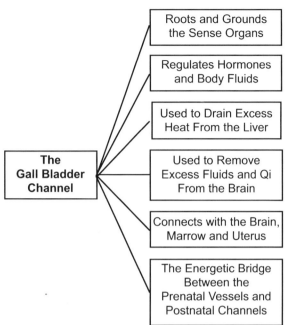

Figure 7.27. The Energetic Functions of the Gall Bladder Channel

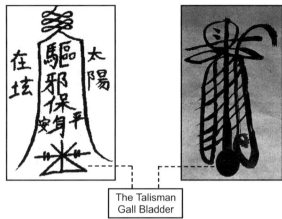

Figure 7.28. Examples of the Talisman Gall Bladder used to contain the priest's magic incantations

The Gall Bladder Channels are often used to drain toxic energy from an overheated or excess Liver condition. The internal flow of the Liver Channel moves Qi into the Brain and Sea of Marrow; consequently, the Gall Bladder Channel can be used to remove excesses (such as fluids and Qi) from the Brain.

The Gall Bladder Channels link to the Brain, Marrow and Uterus and act as an energetic bridge between the Prenatal Eight Extraordinary Vessels) and Postnatal Twelve Primary Channels.

ANCIENT DAOIST MYSTICISM AND THE "GALL BLADDER"

Aside from its medical associations, the ancient Daoists used the "Gall Bladder" as the primary internal organ in which to store the "Qi of Thunder," gathered during the Spring thunder storms. During meditation, the ancient Daoists would dispatch their Hun to gather the power of thunder (considered to be celestial weapons of the Dao) and store them in their Lower Dantian. These "arrows" of Celestial Light were then stored within the "quiver" of the Gall Bladder's energetic field, so as not to disturb the dwelling place of the Hun inside the Liver. The emanation of Yang Celestial Light contained within the thunder was then energetically sealed with a special incantation inside the Gall Bladder (because of its internal connection to the external sensory organs). This powerful energy was later released as a supernatural spiritual weapon (i.e., infused into special talismans or exorcists incantations) for use as protection against the dark, Yin, demonic forces.

Because the "Gall Bladder" internally acted as an energetic container, it was also used as an important reference point in several Daoist rituals. For example, when drawing a Daoist Magical Talisman, the "Talisman Gall Bladder" (sometimes called a "Jie Sha" or "Magic Knot"), refers to a magic seal that is frequently placed at the bottom of a talisman to contain the charms secret activation incantation. The containment image of a Talisman Gall Bladder is always drawn towards the end of the talisman construction. Many times this special container looks either like a black ball of ink, an hourglass with a line through it, or has the image of a double gourd pattern (Figure 7.28). Traditionally, it is said that without this important Gall Bladder containment image, the magic sounds and words imprinted into the talisman paper, cloth, or wood will eventually disperse, ultimately rendering the talisman energetically neutered and ineffective after a certain time period.

The Marrow: Sui

Kidney Jing produces Marrow. In Traditional Chinese Medicine, the term "Marrow" ("Sui") is different from the concept of bone marrow as defined in Western Medicine. In Chinese Energetic Medicine, Marrow is considered to be the substance that produces the Brain (known as the "Sea of Marrow"), the Spinal Cord, and the Bone Marrow.

One of the main functions of the Marrow is to circulate into and irrigate the skull (Brain), the Bones, and the various hollows and orifices, like "water flowing through a riverbed."

Chinese Characters for Marrow

The Chinese character that depicts the ideogram for "Marrow" is "Sui," described as follows (Figure 7.29):

- **Sui:** The Chinese ideogram for "Sui" is composed of two images. To the left, the character on top "Gu" can be translated as "Bone, Spirit," and it depicts the framework of the body's Bones. The bottom left character "Ji," depicts the Chinese ideogram for "Body Tissue, Muscle or Flesh" (all of which are forms of connective tissue).

  The character on the right is comprised of several characters. The "Ji" character appears again, this time below the upper portion of a character that depicts the idea of building a wall or terrace, and something walking beside the wall or terrace.

  Together, these characters are used to represent the movement of the body's Marrow, flowing inside the Bones, and constructing or building something.

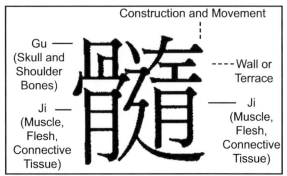

Figure 7.29. The Chinese character "Sui" (Marrow)

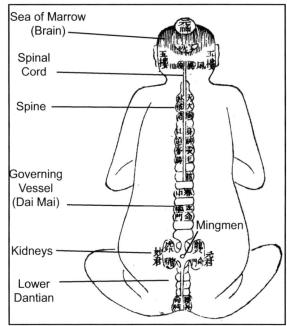

Figure 7.30. Marrow is rooted in the Kidney's Jing, and connected to the Lower Dantian through the Governing Vessel (Dai Mai)

The Marrow and Jing

In ancient Chinese Medical texts, it is stated that the Marrow is rooted in the Kidney's Jing, is connected to the Lower Dantian through the Governing Vessel (Figure 7.30), and is regulated by the energy of the body's Thrusting Vessels.

Kidney Jing is the origin of Marrow. Marrow functions to form the Bone Marrow, as well as to nourish the Brain and spinal cord. When the Mingmen warms and nourishes the body, the Marrow becomes full. This sustains the body's vertical posture and gives strength to both the Brain and the Bones. When the Marrow is full, thinking is also clear and the individual expresses fearlessness.

Energetic Pathology & Marrow

Marrow includes Brain Marrow, Spinal Marrow, and Bone Marrow. The Marrow's energetic constitution is particularly vulnerable to Heat and Dryness. In conditions of Marrow Deficiency, symptoms can manifest such as pain in the Bones and Insomnia may arise.

THE MARROW AND DAOIST MYSTICISM

In Daoist Alchemy, the Marrow is regulated by the Chong Mai (Thrusting Vessel). The ancient Daoists believed that when all of the Postnatal Qi was circulated through the Microcosmic Orbit (i.e., the Du Mai and Ren Mai), the Prenatal Qi stored in the Bone Marrow and Brain become stimulated, and the Ling Shen (Spiritual Consciousness) is "awakened" and enters into the Lower Gate Tower.

It is from this special gate that the body's Marrow flows along its pathway up the spine and into the brain. This special internal pathway was sometimes known as the "Sea of Marrow," the "Water Canal," and the "Yellow River." Once the energy reaches the cranium (Baihui), it indicates that the Governing Vessel, Thrusting Vessel and Sea of Marrow, have reached their full capacity. The energy will then begin to flow down the face and enter into the Conception Vessel, returning back to the Lower Dantian.

When the Microcosmic Orbit training is completed, the disciple may find himself eating and sleeping less. He may also notice a warm energetic current vibrating deep within his bone marrow.

When the disciple feels the Qi penetrate everywhere, and beads of sweat begin to form on the palms of his hands, then the Qi in his Heart is now in harmony with his hands (the external Dragon and Tiger Cavities), and he has established a "closed circuit" within the Microcosmic Orbit.

This circulation of refined spiritual energies is why the brain Marrow is considered to be constructed from the finest and most subtle essences, manifesting the original and hidden power of the Kidneys.

MARROW AND WESTERN MEDICINE

According to Western medicine, the are two types of bone marrow:
- **Red Marrow (Medulla Ossium Rubra):** This marrow consists mainly of hematopoietic tissue. Red blood cells, platelets, and most white blood cells arise in Red Marrow.
- **Yellow Marrow (Medulla Ossium Flava):** This marrow is mainly constructed of fat cells.

At birth, all bone marrow is red. With age, more of the Red Marrow is converted to Yellow Marrow. Eventually, only around half of an adults bone marrow is red.

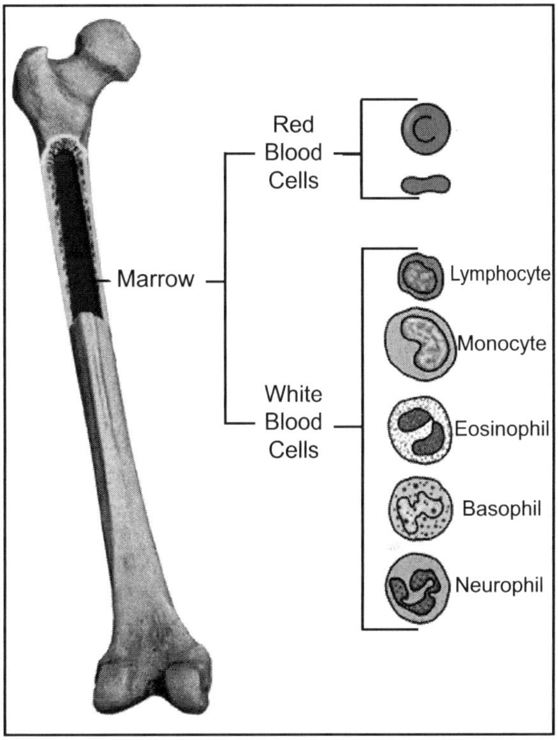

Both types of bone marrow contain numerous blood vessels and capillaries. The specific type of blood cells that are produced inside the body, depends on the type of Marrow that predominates.

Figure 7.31. According to Western Medicine, Bone Marrow is responsible for producing both red and white blood cells.

RED AND WHITE BLOOD CELLS

According to Western Medical Physiology, both the red and white blood cells are produced in the marrow of the bones (Figure 7.31):
- **The Red Blood Cells:** These blood cells are responsible for circulating oxygen and eliminating carbon dioxide. They are produced within the body's long bones (i.e., the Humerus, Femur, Tibia, etc.).
- **The White Blood Cells:** These blood cells are vital to the body's immune system. They are produced within the body's flat bones (i.e., the Skull, Sternum, Scapulae, Pelvis, etc.).

THE BONES: GU

In Chinese Medicine, the Bones are considered to be the structural framework of the body, and are related to the Kidney's Jing.

CHINESE CHARACTERS FOR BONES

The Chinese character that depicts the ideogram for "Bone," is "Gu," and is described as follows (Figure 7.32):

- **Gu:** The Chinese character for "Gu" is composed of several images. The character on the top "Gu" is composed of two ideographs: the upper portion depicts a box with something inside of it, representing a "Skull." The center portion of the box and crossbar represents the "Shoulder Blade." Together, these characters depict the framework of the body's Bones.

  The character on the bottom, "Ji," depicts the Chinese ideogram for body tissue, muscle or flesh (all of which are forms of connective tissue).

BONES AND MARROW

Bones support the body's structure, strength, and mobility, as well as store the Bone Marrow. In Chinese Energetic Medicine, there is an inherent correspondence between the energetic function of Marrow and that of the Bones. The Marrow held within the Bones assures the power, strength, and suppleness of the Bones. The Bones in return, act as internal containers that prevent the dissipation of the essential richness of the Marrow.

Bones are extremely porous and are always "breathing." The porous quality of Bones allows for the absorption and release of Qi and Blood, similar to the way a sponge absorbs and releases water. Energetically, Bones are regulated by the body's Conception and Thrusting Vessels.

PATHOLOGY OF THE BONES

In the Tang Dynasty (618-907 A.D.), the famous Daoist physician Sun Simiao wrote that in cases of Deficient Qi of the Bones, symptoms such as continuous aches and pains will manifest, and the patient will be tired and stiff.

In cases of Excess Qi within the Bones, the patient will have no pain, but will experience uneasiness. This type of agitation is initiated from Heat in the chest.

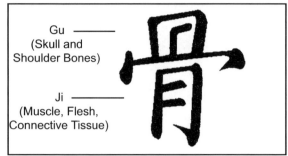

Figure 7.32. The Chinese character "Gu" (Bone)

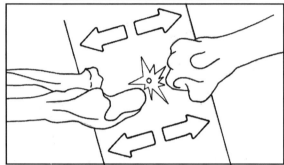

Figure 7.33. Stretching the Tendons and Ligaments while Relaxing the Muscles to Produce Increased Vibrational Resonance

BONES PRODUCE PIEZOELECTRIC CHARGES

Bones are the only substance in the body capable of generating piezoelectric charges. Due to their solid crystalline structure, a piezoelectric charge is created when pressure is applied to the Bones. These electromagnetic charges generate fields of energy that receive and send impulses to the body's cells, tissues, organs, Blood, and channels. The Brain, nervous system, Heart, and lower abdomen also generate electromagnetic fields that resonate with the Bones.

The crystalline structures of the Bones amplify, radiate, and transmit energy and information to the rest of the body. The stretching of the tendons and ligaments while relaxing the muscles also produces increased vibrational resonance within the Bone tissue (Figure 7.33).

The rhythmic oscillation of these Bone-generated electromagnetic fields is further amplified and released through the body due to the tuning fork-like organization of the skeletal structure (Figure 7.34).

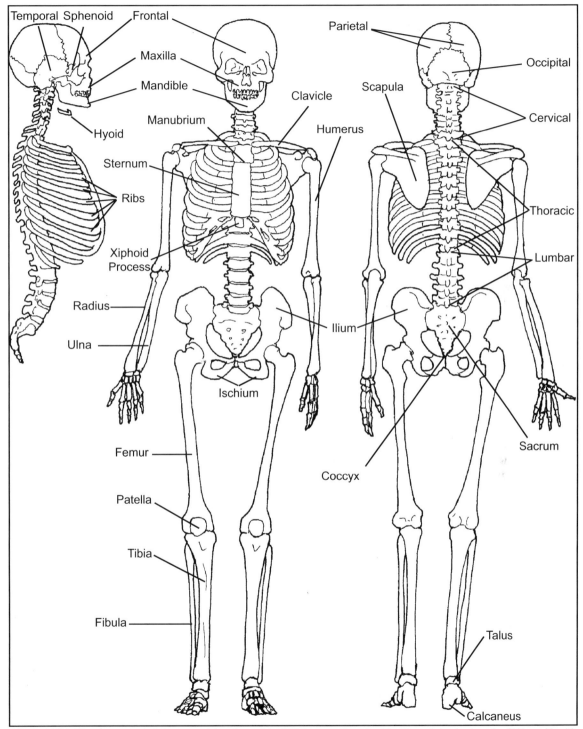

Figure 7.34. The human skeleton consists of roughly 200 bones. (Inspired by the original artwork of Wynn Kapit)

Figure 7.35. The Mountains naturally guide the flow and circulation of water

Figure 7.36. The ancient Daoists considered the human body to be like that of an empty "reed."

BONES AND DAOIST MYSTICISM

The ancient Daoists believed that Bones function within the human body similar to the way that the mountains function on the Earth. Just as the mountains naturally guide the flow and circulation of water (Figure 7.35), the Bones guide the circulation and movement of the body's Jing, Qi, Shen, Blood, Marrow, and Body Fluids.

Additionally, Bones were also believed to internally vibrate like "hollow reeds" (Figure 7.36), especially when the "Divine Wind" ("Spirit of Inspiration") flowed through them. As living reeds, the Bones acted as internal tuning forks, and were thought to be responsible for vibrating celestial and environmental energy throughout the body's entire physical structure.

Because "Bones" internally represent an essential foundational base needed to support the levels of human development, the term "Immortal's Bones" was traditionally used in ancient China in order to reference a Daoist disciples good fortune of meeting and interacting with a celestial god or immortal, who will teach him the hidden secrets of the Daoist Scriptures, which act as the foundational base for developing the "Immortal Body."

During the Tang Dynasty (618-907 A.D.), the ancient Daoist Master Wu Yun wrote in his *Zongxuan Xianshen Wenji (Collected Writings of the Master of Ancestral Mystery)*, that in order for a Disciple to become successful in Alchemical Cultivation practice, he must possess the strong determination to seek after higher spiritual attainments. He must also be ready to embody the sudden shifts in energetic structure, and personal characteristics that this sacred work will bring into his life.

The ancient Daoists attributed these special personality characteristics as having the necessary qualifications for possessing the "Immortal's Bones." The concept of possessing an "Immortal's Bones" is best understood in terms of energetic "family inheritance," experienced through "Karma" ("Yuan").

WESTERN MEDICAL PERSPECTIVE

Bone (osseous) tissue forms most of the body's skeletal system and is the framework that supports and protects the internal organs. The main functions of the skeletal system are:
- To store energy and marrow;
- To allow for mineral homeostasis, blood cell production and physical movement; and
- To provide protection and structural support.

The skeletal system is composed of bone tissue, bone marrow, periosteum (the membrane surrounding the bones), and cartilage. Like other connective tissue, bone tissue contains an abundant matrix of various types of cells, such as osteoprogenitor cells, osteoblasts, osteocytes, and osteoclasts.

Bones are constantly being "remodeled" in order to maintain the integrity of the skeletal system. The Osteoclasts break down the bones, while the Osteoblasts build them up. The Osteoclasts and Osteoblasts signal to each other, via the bone marrow, when to start and stop each action in order to maintain balance.

THE BLOOD VESSELS: MAI

Both Qi and Blood flow within the Channels and Blood Vessels (Mai), continuously circulating throughout the body to nourish, maintain, and moisten the tissues. Qi and Blood flow together, with Qi being both the active force that makes the Blood circulate, and the force that keeps it within the Blood Vessels. Qi is an energetic form, and is considered to be a Yang substance, while Blood is a liquid form of energy, and is considered to be a Yin substance (Figure 7.37).

Through associative diagnosis, observation, and the study of clinical "Bloodletting," the ancient Chinese developed an advanced understanding of the vascular system and Blood Circulation. Much effort was spent in understanding the organizational structure, pathways, and various branches of the internal Blood Vessels.

As the ancient Chinese Physicians studied the body's arterial and venous circulations, they identified the flow of Blood within all of the major Blood Vessels (Mai). Critical junctures, known as "Jie" (meaning "Joint, Node, or Knot") were believed to be formed where the finer branches of the Mai (arterioles, venules, and capillaries) intersected with related nerves and Collateral Vessels. These finer branches of the Mai supplied Blood and nutrients to the various regions of the body.

The ancient Chinese physicians had many reasons for placing great emphasis on understanding the flow of Blood, and the pathways of the body's Blood Vessels. To the ancient Chinese, Blood Circulation was one of the most important physiological manifestations of the body's internal energy.

It was also clinically noted that an impeded Blood flow to any region of the body resulted in pain, tissue dysfunction, and cellular degeneration.

CHINESE CHARACTERS FOR BLOOD

The Chinese word "Xue" translates as "Blood." The ancient character for "Xue" was composed of a pictograph, representing a small, wide-lipped, clay vessel used for collecting Blood. Contained within its bowl was a horizontal line representing Blood (Figure 7.38). During the Shang Dynasty (1600-1028 B.C.) these special Ritual Vessels were crafted out of bronze.

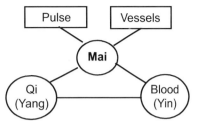

Figure 7.37. Qi & Blood within the Blood Vessels (Mai)

Figure 7.38. The ancient character "Xue" (Blood)

Figure 7.39. The modern character "Xue" (Blood)

Figure 7.40. The character "Mai" (Blood Vessel)

The modern character for "Xue" is composed of two parts: positioned on the top is a line representing the flow of Blood as it pours into a sacrificial vessel; positioned to the bottom is the radical "Min," meaning "A vessel for catching sacrificial Blood" (Figure 7.39).

CHINESE CHARACTERS FOR BLOOD VESSELS

The Chinese character that depicts the ideogram for "Blood Vessels" is "Mai," described as follows (Figure 7.40):

- **Mai:** The Chinese character for "Mai" is composed of two images. The character to the left,

"Ji" depicts the Chinese ideogram for body tissue, muscle or flesh (all of which are forms of connective tissue).

The character on the right depicts a current of water or a stream. In ancient China, the right side of the Mai character was "Yong," meaning "a current of water flowing deep within the Earth." Together, the character can be translated as vein or pulse, depicting a form of energetic circulation.

The word "Mai" has two meanings; it can refer to either the "Pulse," or the "Blood Vessels:"
- **Pulse:** When Mai is used as "Pulse," it refers to the rhythmic, energetic pulsating movement of the "substances" within the Blood Vessels.
- **Blood Vessels:** When the word "Mai" is used to denote "Blood Vessels," it describes the vascular network of the arteries, arterioles, capillaries, venules and veins.

The Energetic Function Of Blood Vessels

The energetic functions and interactions of Qi, Blood, and Mai, are described as follows:
- **Qi (The Commander of Blood):** The Qi provides the dynamic force associated with the movement of the "substances" through the Vessels.
- **Blood (The Mother of Qi):** The Blood provides vital nourishment and moistens the body, thus providing a Yin substance and foundation that allows for the proper functioning of Qi. The Blood also fills the vessels and is the foundation for mental activity. For example, the Five Yin Organs (Liver, Heart, Spleen, Lungs and Kidneys) were believed to store and circulate the refined energetic substances of the body's Five Essence Spirits (Hun, Shen, Yi, Po and Zhi) within the bloodstream.
- **Mai (Pulse and Vessels):** The Mai is both the "Network of the Vessels" and the "Rhythmic Pulsations" from the movement of the "substances" within the vessels.

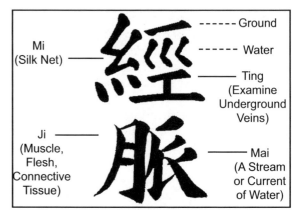

Figure 7.41. The Chinese characters "Jing Mai" (Meridian Channel, Pathway, Streams) The body's Twelve Major Blood Vessels

The Energetic Channels and Streams of the Blood Vessels

In Traditional Chinese Medicine, the concept of Blood is different from the concept of blood in Western Medicine, both in characteristics and in function. In the Chinese model (see Volume 3, Chapter 23), Blood originates from the transformation of food and drink by the Spleen, and from Kidney Jing. The Spleen then transfers this refined food energy upward to be further enhanced by the Heart Qi and Lung Qi, in order to form Blood.

The Lungs are responsible for energizing the Blood; while the Spleen and Kidneys are responsible for assisting in the formation of the basic composition of the Blood. The Blood in its natural form is a precious liquid, composed of Body Fluids and nutrition for the body's tissues.

The ancient Chinese divided the various Blood Vessels into twelve primary pairs of longitudinal arteries and veins. The reason for viewing the Blood Circulation as flowing along a linear pathway of the body, can be explained by understanding the ancient Daoists emphasis of the Yin and Yang energetic aspects of Qi and Blood distribution. The energetic cycle of Yin and Yang, moves from the extremities and superficial regions to the deep internal organs and back, flowing along the energetic pathways of the veins and arteries.

In ancient China, the twelve primary pairs of arteries and veins were known as the "Jing Mai," meaning "Channel Streams" (Figure 7.41). These

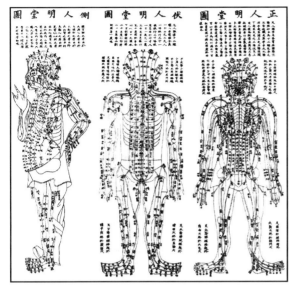

Figure 7.42. The Twelve Primary Channels

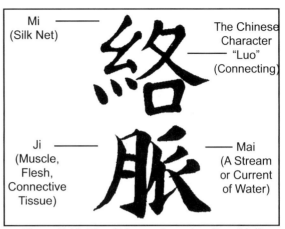

Figure 7.43. The Chinese characters "Luo Mai" (Connecting Streams)

important Channel Systems included six primary pairs of Blood Vessels, positioned on each side of the body; making a total of twelve pairs flowing along the energetic pathways of the Twelve Primary Channels (Figure 7.42).

Additionally, there are also Collateral Branches of the twelve primary pairs of arteries and veins, that supply nutrients to the body's tissues. These Collateral Branches, either surface along the superficial areas of the Twelve Skin Zones, or descend internally into the deeper tissue areas of the body. These important Collateral Branches are known as "Luo Mai," meaning "Connecting Streams" (Figure 7.43).

The names of the twelve primary pairs of arteries and veins (Jing) and their Collateral Branches (Luo) are often combined in order to form the word "Jingluo," used in the modern Traditional Chinese Medical Colleges to describe the vascular system.

The Collateral Branches further divide into the Minute Vessels which comprise the body's arterioles, capillaries, and venules. These Minute Vessels were known as "Sun Mai," meaning "Grandson Streams." The Minute Vessels communicate between the arteries, which direct Blood flow outward, and the veins, which return Blood flow to the Heart. The Minute Vessels are thus the smallest link in the body's continuous flow of Blood circulation.

The Chinese medical understanding of the internal structure and function of the Vascular System is nearly identical to that of Western Medicine. The Chinese system however, places a different emphasis on the deep and superficial branching of the vessels' energetic flow. The Chinese system of Differential Diagnosis relies heavily on understanding the flow of energy within the individual Blood Vessels and the relationship between them.

THE ENERGETIC PATHWAYS OF THE BLOOD VESSELS

The ancient Chinese divided the Twelve Primary Blood Vessels into various out-flowing arteries and returning veins, each being differentiated by the presence of a pulse. The following is a list of the Twelve Primary Blood Vessels and their venous and arterial associations:

1. **Gall Bladder:** Artery (away from the body)
2. **Liver:** Vein (towards the body)
3. **Lungs:** Artery (away from the body)
4. **Large Intestine:** Vein (towards the body)
5. **Stomach:** Artery (away from the body)
6. **Spleen:** Vein (towards the body)
7. **Heart:** Artery (away from the body)
8. **Small Intestine:** Vein (towards the body)
9. **Urinary Bladder:** Artery (away from the body)
10. **Kidneys:** Vein (towards the body)
11. **Pericardium:** Artery (away from the body)
12. **Triple Burners:** Vein (towards the body)

FUNCTION OF THE BLOOD VESSELS

The Blood Vessels serve as the primary reservoir of Blood. In Traditional Chinese Medicine the Heart is considered to be the "Master of the Blood Vessels" (Figure 7.44). The Blood Vessels contain Blood and are indirectly related to the Kidneys in that the Kidney Essence (Jing) produces Marrow, which contributes to the production of Blood.

The function of the Blood Vessels is to transport Qi and Blood throughout the body for nutrition and regeneration. The Blood is held within the Blood Vessels by the energetic "holding" power of the Spleen Qi.

PATHOLOGY OF THE BLOOD VESSELS

The Blood Vessels are regulated by the energy of the body's Thrusting Vessels. The Zong Qi (Pectoral Qi) stored within the chest, incorporates the Lung Qi in order to assist the Heart in moving the Blood through the channel network, nourishing the tissues of the body. According to the *Yellow Emperor's Inner Canon: Su Wen*,

> "The Ying Qi (Nutritive Qi)
> circulates inside of the Blood Vessels,
> and the Wei Qi (Defensive Qi)
> circulates outside the Blood Vessels."

When the circulation of the Blood Vessels becomes impeded, the tissues of the body suffer. According to the *Yellow Emperor's Inner Canon: Ling Shu*:

> "When the Blood is deficient,
> the complexion is pale ,
> and there is insufficient irrigation
> in the layers of the skin,
> the Blood Vessels in this area (of the skin)
> are completely empty."

THE BLOOD VESSELS AND ANCIENT DAOIST MYSTICISM

In ancient China, Red Blood was believed to be the seat of the soul, and that magical powers could be imbued into any object that was ritually smeared with Blood. This is why when statues or pictures of Daoist gods or goddesses are being consecrated, the eyes are painted over with Blood. In this way, the picture or statue is energetically animated and given a soul.

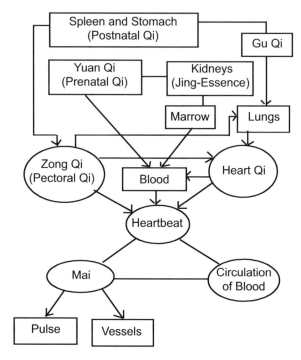

Figure 7.44. The Energetic Connections of the Blood and Blood Vessels

It was also believed that although the Lungs were responsible for the oxygenation of the Blood, and the Spleen and Kidneys have the function of assisting in forming the basic composition of the Blood, Blood in its natural form was only liquid, composed of Body Fluids and nutritive juices. Blood only became "red" because the Heart puts its "Imperial Stamp" onto the liquids, which penetrates the Body Fluids with the power of the Heart's Shen (Spirit/Mind). It was believed that this "imperial" action, transformed the liquids into Blood. Therefore the energetic and spiritual component of the Blood receives its red imperial color from the Heart Fire, which has the ability to bring life to the body, and animate the spirit.

Additionally, male semen was believed to be transformed Blood. Therefore, if too much semen is expended, then the man's health suffered. Likewise, a mother's milk was considered to be Blood transformed into a different energetic state.

It was also believed that during an exorcism, if a demon could be successfully sprayed with Blood, it would be forced to assume its true form.

WESTERN MEDICAL PERSPECTIVE

In Western Medicine, the blood, heart and blood vessels (arteries, capillaries and veins) form the body's Cardiovascular System. The general function of the Cardiovascular System is the circulation of the blood.

As a whole, blood is composed of two components: 55% is formed from Blood Plasma (i.e., a watery liquid containing dissolved substances; while the remaining 45% is formed from cells and cell fragments.

Arteries conduct oxygenated blood away from the heart to the internal organs and the extremities, while the veins circulate the blood back to the heart. The capillaries are simple endothelial tubes from which nutrients and gases diffuse into and out from the tissues. The hollow center through which the blood flows, is called the "Lumen."

The unique structure of the arteries allows them two important properties: elasticity and contractibility. The arterial wall is composed of three layers, described as follows (Figure 7.45):

- **Tunica Intima:** The Tunica Intima is the innermost layer of the arteries, and is composed of a lining of Endothelium (a skin-like tissue that stays in contact with the blood). This is a basement membrane, and contains a layer of elastic tissue called the Internal Elastic Lamina. This is one of the most important layers, as it prevents the adhesion of the blood cells to the wall of the vessel, and also prevents Thrombosis (the formation of blood clots within the vessel).
- **Tunica Media:** The Tunica Media is the middle coating of the arteries, and is composed of both elastic fibers and smooth muscle fibers. It is the thickest layer. The smooth muscles help in increasing and decreasing the calibe of the artery to regulate the Blood Pressure.
- **Tunica Externa:** The Tunica Externa is the outermost coating of the arteries, and is composed of both elastic and collagen fibers. The Tunica Externa helps in maintaining the integrity of the vessel, and provides the tensile strength to the vessel.

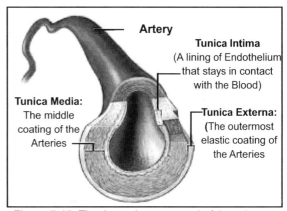

Figure 7.45. The Artery is composed of three layers

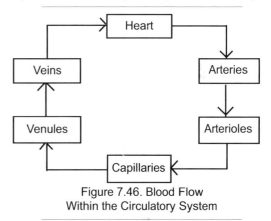

Figure 7.46. Blood Flow Within the Circulatory System

CIRCULATORY SYSTEM

The integrated roles of Qi, Blood, and Mai do not conflict with, but rather augment the Western Medical understanding of the Circulatory System. The Circulatory System includes the Heart, the Blood Vessels, and the Blood. Chapter Eight explains in detail the structure and function of the Heart as a Yin organ, though certain subtle aspects of the pulse that are ascribed to the Heart in Western Physiology are equivalent to aspects of the Blood Vessels in Chinese Energetic Medicine. The term Blood Vessels refers to the entire closed network of vessels that begins and ends at the Heart. The Blood is the essential substance that is energized by the Lungs, pumped outward by the Heart, and distributed throughout the body via the Blood Vessels.

There are over 60,000 miles of Blood Vessels in the average adult human body. The various types of Blood Vessels include arteries, arterioles,

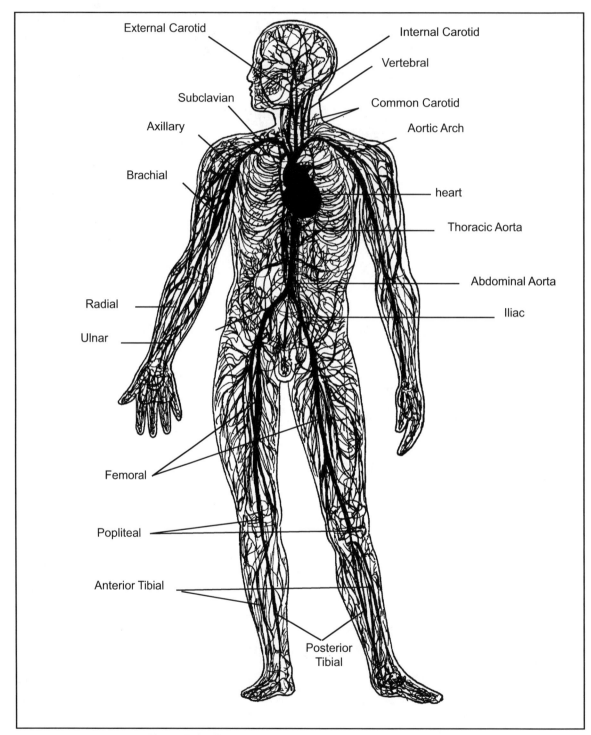

Figure 7.47. The Arterial Network of the Circulatory System

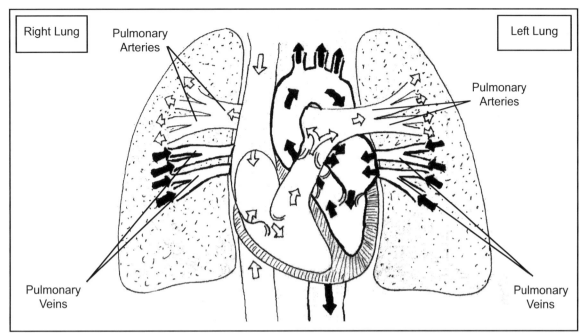

Figure 7.48. Pulmonary Circulation. (Inspired by the original artwork of Wynn Kapit)

capillaries, venules, and veins (Figure 7.46). Blood is carried away from the Heart through a network of vessels called arteries. The arteries distribute Blood throughout the body by branching into smaller vessels, termed arterioles. The arterioles then branch further into tiny vessels, called capillaries, the walls of which are thin enough to allow for the essential exchange of energy and nutrients between the Blood and the individual cells. After distributing Blood through all the tissues of the body, the capillaries begin to merge together, forming into progressively larger vessels called venules. The venules then form the larger vessels, called veins, which return the Blood back to the Heart.

THREE CIRCULATORY ROUTES

Each individual will develop and utilize a total of three circulatory routes: fetal circulation, pulmonary circulation and systemic circulation. The circulatory system of a fetus is slightly different than that of an adult, and is termed fetal circulation. The two circulatory routes within the adult body are termed systemic circulation, and pulmonary circulation. These two routes begin and end at the Heart.

SYSTEMIC CIRCULATION

The systemic circulatory route delivers oxygenated Blood (red) to the entire body by pumping it outward from the left ventricle of the Heart through a vast network of arteries, arterioles, and capillaries. At the level of the capillaries, oxygen and nutrition are delivered to all the tissues of the body, passing from the Blood through the thin capillary walls and into the cells. The capillaries also allow for the Blood to absorb carbon dioxide and other waste products of cellular metabolism from the cells. The Blood (now blue) flows from the capillaries through venules and veins, eventually returning to the right atrium of the Heart (Figure 7.47).

PULMONARY CIRCULATION

Pulmonary circulation refers to the circulatory loop that leads the blood from the Heart into the Lungs to be oxygenated, and then back to the Heart again (Figure 7.48). The pulmonary arteries lead deoxygenated Blood (blue) away from the right ventricle of the Heart and into the right and left Lungs. Arterioles and pulmonary capillaries lead the Blood into contact with the alveoli of the

Lungs, where carbon dioxide and other wastes are released from the Blood, and oxygen is reabsorbed into the Blood. The pulmonary capillaries then gather to form venules and veins, eventually forming the pulmonary veins which return oxygenated Blood (now red) to the left atrium of the Heart. The pulmonary veins are the only postnatal veins that carry oxygenated Blood back to the Heart.

Fetal Circulation

The blood-vascular system of a fetus constantly changes throughout embryonic development and differs functionally from that of an adult. During fetal development, the fetus receives and releases material from its Blood via the vascular network of the placenta (Figure 7.49). Umbilical arteries direct Blood from the fetus along the umbilical cord and into the placenta. The Blood Vessels of the placenta contain tiny villi that allow for oxygen, nutrition, and wastes to be exchanged between the Blood of the fetus and the Blood of the mother. Purified Blood returns into the fetus from the placenta via the umbilical vein.

Fetal Circulation also differs from that of an adult because the gastrointestinal tract, Lungs, and Kidneys of a fetus are nonfunctional, and therefore do not play a role in energizing or detoxifying the Blood. Because the fetus is dependant on the placenta (and not its own internal organs) for the maintenance of its Blood, there are numerous peculiarities to the internal anatomy of the network of Blood Vessels and veins within the fetus, though these peculiarities normally disappear after birth. It is important to note that the Circulatory System of the fetus does not flow directly into the Circulatory System of the mother. The Blood of the mother flows into and out of the placenta via a network of arteries and veins that stems from her Uterus.

The Pulse

The pulse, one meaning of the Chinese word "Mai," can be understood in Western terms as a combined function of the Heart and the arteries. While the left ventricle of the Heart is the primary force for pumping oxygenated Blood throughout the body, the arteries and arterioles create an additional pumping action as the Blood flows outward and into the capillaries. This pump-

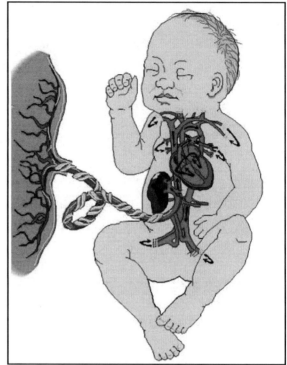

Figure 7.49. Fetal Circulation

ing action is due to the unique structure of the arteries that allows them to expand and contract passively (elasticity), and also to actively contract (contractility).

The arteries have a much more developed layer of smooth muscle than do the veins, allowing for the arteries to play an active role in the distribution of Blood.

As Blood is pumped from the Heart, the arteries passively expand, allowing the extra Blood to flow outward. This is followed by a peristaltic muscular contraction within the arteries that continues to push the Blood outward towards the capillaries. The veins do not have this property of contractility, nor do they have the same degree of elasticity as do the arteries. Instead, the venous network contains numerous one way valves, making return of the Blood along the veins to the Heart relatively passive in comparison to the flow of Blood within the arteries. Venous circulation is thus greatly influenced by the pull of gravity and by the contraction of skeletal muscles.

Chapter 8
The Twelve Primary Organs, Channels and Collaterals

The Internal Organs & Chinese Internal Medicine

In ancient China, various medical graphs and anatomical drawings were used to assist the doctor in clinical practice. The oldest of these detailed charts can be traced back to the Han Dynasty (206 B.C.-220 A.D.). Since that time, textbooks on internal medicine have used two primarily different methods to depict the human body. One method was similar to Western Anatomy in that the internal organs were conceptualized as having shape, form, and function. The illustrations depicting the internal organs in this manner were traditionally known as either the "Charts of Inner Lights" or the "Charts for Visualizing the True Ones" (Figure 8.1). In their most ancient form, such charts would depict the body's internal organ "pools of energy" along with their "energetic presence." The subtle energetic presence of an internal organ was sometimes referred to as the "Radiant One," which was said to reside within the internal organ itself. The internal organs and their associated energetic systems were sometimes known in ancient times as "orbs" or "spheres of influence."

The second common method of illustrating Human Anatomy involves maps which showed the routes of the body fluids, arteries and energetic channels. They were traditionally called the "Charts of the Halls of Light" (Figure 8.2), and focused on the body's "rivers of energy." These ancient maps of the channels of the human energy system are the predecessors of today's modern acupuncture charts. Doctors in ancient China, focused their attention on the circulation and movement of energy and fluids moving throughout the body, rather than just the physical functions of each of the internal organs.

A thorough comprehension of Energetic Anatomy and Physiology is necessary in order to understand the fundamental characteristics of each

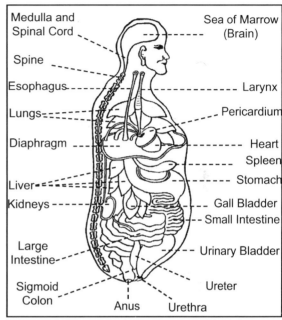

Figure 8.1. The Ancient "Chart of Inner Lights"

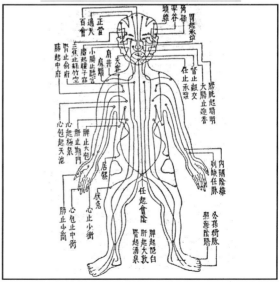

Figure 8.2. The Ancient "Chart of the Halls of Lights"

internal organ and each energy channel, as well as the complex interactions between the two. This understanding is a prerequisite for learning Differential Diagnosis, which is necessary in order to categorize various symptoms into meaningful (clinically useful) Patterns of Disharmony. The ability to categorize various symptoms enables the Medical Qigong Doctor to recognize and treat pathologies unique to specific organs and channel energies.

Energetic Anatomy

In order to gain a deeper understanding of the anatomy of human tissue and the causes of death, ancient Chinese physicians studied the internal formation and structures of the human body through postmortem examination. Initially, the size and weight of all of the body's internal organs were measured and recorded by these ancient physicians. Historians speculate that postmortem autopsies were practiced in ancient China during the Zhou Dynasty (1028-221 B.C.), but were prohibited several hundred years later, because of Confucianistic beliefs.

There are many ancient records in Chinese literature describing dissections. For example, it is recorded that during the Han Dynasty (206 B.C.-220 A.D.), the Emperor Wang Mang ordered his Court Physicians to dissect the body of a captured revolutionary alive. During the procedure, measurements were made of the internal viscera, bowels and vessels by inserting fine bamboo rods into the individual's dissected body.

The *Huangdi Neijing (Yellow Emperors Inner Canon)* contains details on postmortem dissection, and refers to standard procedures for performing Autopsies. In the *Huangdi Neijing Ling Shu*, it states,

> "Upon death, a dissection study can be performed in order to examine, reveal, and disclose the condition of the internal organs.
>
> There are great standard measures used to determine the strength or fragility of the viscera, the size of the bowels, and the contents of the digestive system, being plentiful or sparse.
>
> The length of the vessels can be measured, the Blood examined being either clear or turbid, and the Qi observed being plentiful or sparse."

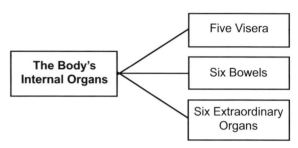

Figure 8.3. The Three Groups of Internal Organs

Energetic Physiology

In Chinese Medical Science, the study of "Energetic Physiology" is called "Zhang Xiang Xue Shou," which literally translates as "The Theory of the Phenomena of Internal Organs." Here, the word "Phenomena" means "Visible External Manifestations." Since all of the major internal organs had already been identified by the postmortem examinations of the past, Chinese Physicians placed little importance on the internal organ's physical structure, focusing instead on each organ's energetic function. While Western Anatomy and Physiology is primarily concerned with the physical body in its most concrete forms (i.e., investigating the structures of the major body organs and organ systems, etc.), Chinese Energetic Anatomy and Physiology focuses mainly on the underlying patterns of energy that animate and sustain the physical form.

The ancient Chinese Physicians noted that when diagnosing illness, all of the body's viscera reflected diseased conditions related to functional disorders that were the result of pathogenic factors. Disruptions within the energetic function of any organ system manifested clinically through various physiological and psychological symptoms.

In Traditional Chinese Medicine, the internal organs are divided into three main groups: the Five Viscera, the Six Bowels, and the Six Extraordinary Organs, described as follows (Figure 8.3):

1. **The Five Viscera (Wu Zang):** These Five Yin Organs include the Liver, Heart, Spleen, Lungs and Kidneys. They internally function to preserve the body's vital substances (Essence, Energy, Mind, Blood, Marrow, and Body Fluids), and are important for their

role in the distribution and dispersion of the body's nutrients. Each of the Five Viscera is capable of containing and storing a particular refined substance known as the body's "Jing Shen" ("Essence Spirit"). Because there is a "spiritual essence" unique to each internal organ's energetic function, when the energies are combined, they are collectively known as the Wu Jing Shen, or "Five Essence Spirits."

It is important to clarify that in modern T.C.M., there are only Five Yin Organs or Viscera (Zang). The Pericardium, which is sometimes categorized as a Sixth Yin Viscera, is not actually considered to be an independent Yin Organ, but rather a protective covering of the Heart.

- **Zang:** The Chinese ideogram for "Zang," is composed of two characters (Figure 8.4). The character to the left, "Ji" depicts the Chinese ideogram for body tissue, muscle or flesh (all of which are forms of connective tissue).

  The character on the right "Cang" can be translated as "To Gather, Store, Collect, Conceal, Hoard and Hide in a Safe Place (as a treasure)." Together, both characters depict the body's internal viscera as the organs that gather and hoard the energetic Jing, Qi and Shen within the flesh.

2. **The Six Bowels (Liu Fu):** These Six Yang Bowels include the Gall Bladder, Small Intestine, Stomach, Large Intestine, Urinary Bladder and Triple Burners. They internally function to transmit and digest food and water, and to eliminate the body's waste products.

   The Triple Burners do not have an anatomical equivalent in Western Medicine. They energetically extend throughout the body's torso, acting as a hollow Yang Organ (Fu), containing the body's "Vapors" (Qi and Shen), "Fluids" (Jing, Blood, Marrow, Jin and Ye), and "Fire" (Heart Fire, Mingmen Fire and Urinary Bladder Fire).

- **Fu:** The Chinese ideogram for "Fu," is composed of two characters (Figure 8.5). The character to the left, "Ji" depicts the Chinese ideogram for body tissue, muscle or flesh (all of which are forms of connective tissue).

  The character on the right "Fu" can be translated as "Government Body, Official Resi-

Figure 8.4. The Chinese character for "Zang," Viscera

Figure 8.5. The Chinese Ideograph for "Fu," Bowel

dence, A Storehouse for Precious Objects, Treasury, Palace, Mansion or Officer." Together, both characters depict the body's internal bowels as treasure house organs within the flesh. In ancient China, the concept of a storehouse or treasury related to short-term storage, since the items were constantly moving in and out.

3. **The Six Extraordinary Organs (Qi Heng Zhi Fu):** The Extraordinary Organs include the Uterus, Brain, Gall Bladder, Marrow, Bones, and Blood Vessels. They energetically function like Yin Organs in storing the body's vital substances, but are hollow and resemble Yang Organs.

Medical Qigong students study the physiological functions and the pathological changes of the internal organs, in addition to their relationship with the universal and environmental energies. Chinese Energetic Medicine, groups the body's Zang/Fu internal organs into five discrete functional systems. Each Zang/Fu system has specific interior (internal organs) and exterior (superficial muscles, tissues, skin and senses) correspondences and is assigned a specific physical, energetic, and spiritual attribute. By observing the physiological features of the internal organs, the ancient Chinese established a consistent model for describing the functions of each organ. This model was then applied to diagnose and treat organ pathologies.

THE ZANG FU ORGANS & YIN AND YANG

To the ancient Daoists, each Zang Fu Organ signified a place where "Human Records" in the form of emotions, thoughts, and experiences were stored. Each of the internal organs were considered to be overseen by spirit "Officials," who were in charge of specific duties in the governing of the human body. The celestial counterparts of these internal organ Officials, were believed to reside within the various realms of Heaven. The job of these organ Officials was to oversee the individual's health and destiny, and to guide the individual in the cultivation of Virtue.

Within the Zang organs, the energy of the Five Agents (i.e., the Virtues of Kindness, Order, Trust, Integrity and Wisdom) internally influences an individual, by providing spiritual insight and inspiration to the body's Hun. This is initiated through the direction of the Yuan Shen (Original Spirit) via the Dao. By acting as a divine vessel of the Dao, the individual is capable of bringing the "Heart of Heaven" into the world, thereby fulfilling his or her personal destiny.

Within the human body, each of the internal Zang Fu organ is paired according to their energetic actions of transforming, transporting, and storing. Each Yin (Zang) organ is therefore paired with a Yang (Fu) organ. The relationship between the Yin and Yang paired internal organs represents an energetic correspondence in both structure and function.

Each of the Yin organs has a corresponding energetic function of storing one of the body's vital substances; while each of the Yang organs corresponds to a particular aspect of the process of transportation and transformation.

The two primary types of Yin and Yang internal organs are described as follows:
- **Yin (Zang) Organs:** These are solid organs and are responsible for storing the pure, refined vital substances (Qi, Blood, Essence, and Body Fluids), which they receive from the Yang (Fu) Organs after the transformation of food.
- **Yang (Fu) Organs:** These are hollow organs and are responsible for receiving, moving, transforming, digesting, and excreting food substances.

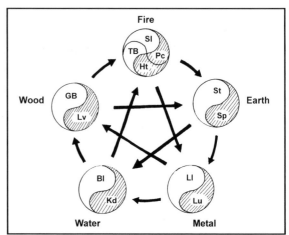

Figure 8.6. The Energetic Movement of the Five Element Correspondences

The paired energetic divisions of the body's Zang (Yin) Fu (Yang) organs are traditionally described as follows:
- The Liver (Yin) Zang Organ is paired with the Gall Bladder (Yang) Fu Organ.
- The Heart (Yin) Zang Organ is paired with the Small Intestine (Yang) Fu Organ.
- The Spleen (Yin) Zang Organ is paired with the Stomach (Yang) Fu Organ.
- The Lungs (Yin) Zang Organ are paired with the Large Intestine (Yang) Fu Organ.
- The Kidneys (Yin) Zang Organ are paired with the Urinary Bladder (Yang) Fu Organ.

THE INTERNAL ORGANS & FIVE ELEMENTS

Traditional Chinese Medicine utilizes the concept of the Five Elements (or Five Phases) as an integral part of both diagnosis and treatment. The Five Element Theory (Chapter 25, Volume 3) was an essential aspect of virtually every discipline in ancient China, including medicine, martial arts, military strategy, politics, painting, poetry, and architecture. This special theory allowed the ancient Chinese to classify tangible and intangible substances, internal organs, and herbs into five interrelating categories for observation and study, as well as for diagnosis and treatment (e.g., five shapes, five colors, five pitches, five senses, five viscera, five emotions, five flavors, etc.).

The complex interaction between the body's internal organs could also be understood and simplified by identifying the various patterns of relationship between the Five Elements.

In Clinical Diagnosis, each internal organ and channel is seen as having either a Yin or Yang energetic characteristic, and is therefore grouped and paired according to its Five Element nature. For example, the Five Element Theory is traditionally applied to the internal organs as follows (Figure 8.6):

- The Liver and Gall Bladder Organs and Channels are associated with the Wood Element, Green-Blue Color, Sour Taste, the "Jue" Sound and "E" Note.
- The Heart and Small Intestine (as well as the Pericardium and Triple Burners) Organs and Channels are associated with the Fire Element, Red Color, Bitter Taste, the "Zhi" Sound, and "G" Note.
- The Spleen and Stomach Organs and Channels are associated with the Earth Element, Yellow Color, Sweet Taste, the "Gong" Sound, and "C" Note.
- The Lungs and Large Intestine Organs and Channels are associated with the Metal Element White Color, Pungent Taste, the "Shang" Sound, and "D" Note.
- The Kidneys and Urinary Bladder Organs and Channels are associated with the Water Element, Black Color, Salty Taste, the "Yu" Sound, and "A" Note.

Internal Organs & the Vital Substances

One of the main functions of the internal organs is to ensure the production, storage, replenishment, transformation and movement of vital substances. Each of the body's vital substances (Qi, Blood, Jing, Body Fluids and Shen) is related to one or more of the internal organs. For example:

- The Liver stores the Blood and is responsible for the body's metabolic process and the dispersal of nutrients.
- The Heart governs the Blood and provides the energetic force for Blood Circulation.
- The Spleen holds the Blood, governs Gu Qi (energy derived from food and drink), and influences Body Fluids. Additionally, the Spleen is also responsible for governing the body's

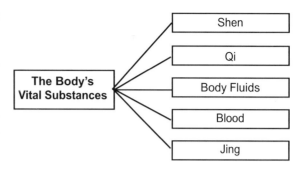

Figure 8.7. The Body's Vital Substances

lymph system, it functions as part of the immune system, and controls Blood coagulation.
- The Lungs govern Qi, influence Body Fluids, and are responsible for the absorption of oxygen and expulsion of respiratory gases.
- The Kidneys store Jing, influence Body Fluids, and are responsible for filtering metabolic waste products from the Blood through the process of urine formation.

In Chinese Energetic Medicine, it is taught that the human body essentially consists of fluids and energy, and that the internal organs are responsible for creating and distributing Jing, Qi, Shen, Blood and Body Fluids (Figure 8.7). In the Medical Qigong Clinic, diagnosis is based on observing these vital substances according to the following:

1. The smooth flow or stagnation of the body's Jing, Qi, and Shen;
2. The Excess or Deficiency of Qi, Shen, Blood and Body Fluids;
3. The Vital Substances influence on internal organ functions.

The external orifices of the body serve as the gates and windows of the Jing and Shen, which are themselves ultimately rooted in the energy of the Blood. The body's Qi and Zhi (Will) serve as the messengers of the Five Yin Organs (i.e., the Five Orbs), and are used for sense reception, respiration, and excretion. The physical and psychological associations of each of the orifices are governed by the Jing and Shen of the internal organ with which they are connected.

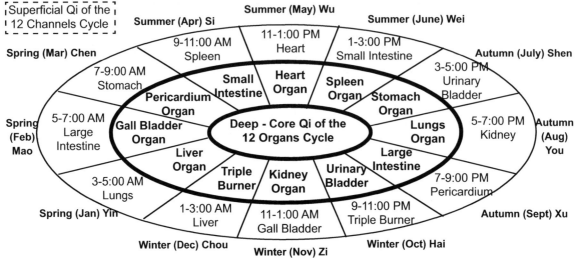

Figure 8.8. The Body's Superficial (External) and Deep (Internal) Energy Cycles

The internal organs create and distribute Qi, Blood, and Body Fluids. These actions occur regularly throughout the body's tissues, and manifest in the Blood-Heat Cycles (Figure 8.8). The Blood Heat Cycle is the alternation of peaks (high-tide) and ebbs (low-tide) of each of the internal organs and channels, which occurs over a 24 hour time period.

In Daoist Alchemy, the skill of mastering energetic cultivation requires the disciple to understand the superficial and deep energetic currents that flow within the body's tissues, and their associated time schedules. For example, the outside circle in the above chart represents the 12 Primary Channels - 24 hour Qi and Blood Cycle, usually studied in all Acupuncture Colleges. In this system, the body's energy moves externally from channel to channel, in a two hour ebb and flow, and displays the high and low energetic "tides," that correspond to the various hours of the day. For example, when the Liver Channel is at "High Tide" (1:00-3:00 A.M.), the Small Intestine Channel is at "Low Tide" (1:00-3:00 P.M.).

In 1995, while training at the Hai Dian University of Traditional Chinese Medicine, in Beijing China, I was introduced to the following "Twelve Hexagram Pattern" as a guide for Medical Qigong Prescription applications. I was taught that the inside circle of this special chart depicted the body's internal organ energy flow, and specifically corresponded to twelve unique Hexagram Patterns (Figure 8.9). These 12 Hexagram Patterns not only corresponded to the ancient *Yijing (Book of Changes)* and the Twelve Earthly Branches, but they also followed a 24 hour Qi and Blood cycle. It is important to note, that this unique energetic correspondence system, originated from the study of the ancient Daoist Lunar Month energy cycles, known as the "Bright Mirror of Spiritual Alchemy."

It was noted that within this special Daoist system of calculating energy movement, the body's Qi and Blood flows internally from organ to organ, in a two hour ebb and flow cycle. This special cycle also displays the high and low energetic "tides" that not only corresponded to the various Lunar months of the year, but also the energy moving along the body's Sea of Yang (Du Mai: Governing Vessel) and Sea of Yin (Ren Mai: Conception Vessel) pathways.

This special 12 Lunar Month cycle is traditionally used in all Daoist Meditation Practices for Internal Qi Cultivation. In the Medical Qigong Clinic, this special chart is traditionally referred to when a doctor prescribes Medical Qigong Exercises and Meditations to his patients.

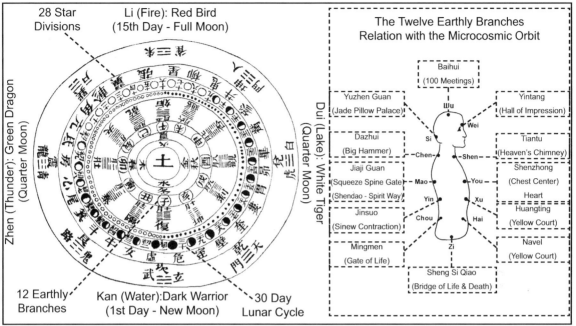

Figure 8.9. The Movement of the Body's Qi as Depicted by the Ancient Daoists "Bright Mirror of Spiritual Alchemy" Chart. The Twelve Earthly Branches Relation with the Microcosmic Orbit: The Main Channels of the back and front of the body correspond to the elliptic path of both the Sun and the Moon. These twelve special energy points are associated with the body's Three Dantians and Twelve Lunar Month Inner-Core Cycle.

THE INTERNAL ORGANS & THE TISSUES

Each internal organ has a direct influence over specific tissues of the body. The health of a particular body tissue is indicative of the state of health of the internal organ with which it is associated. A summary of the internal organs and their associated tissues is described as follows:

- **The Liver:** This organ controls the nerves and tendons, and manifests through the body's fingernails and toenails.
- **The Heart:** This organ controls the Blood and the Blood Vessels, and manifests through the body's complexion.
- **The Spleen:** This organ controls the muscles and flesh, and manifests through the lips.
- **The Lungs:** This organ controls the skin, and manifests through body hair.
- **The Kidneys:** This organ controls the Bones, and manifests through the head hair and eyebrows.

THE INTERNAL ORGANS & THE EMOTIONS

Each of the internal organs is related to a particular psycho-emotional state. These psycho-emotional states are divided into two main categories:

- **"Congenital Spiritual Patterns:"** This internal spiritual state corresponds to the natural influence of the Congenital Wujing Shen (i.e., the Original Five Essence Heart/Mind of the Dao), and the Hun. The congenital spiritual patterns of the Five Yin Organs are representative of an individual's original state of spiritual harmony, manifesting as a calm state of inner-peace, joy, and gratitude.
- **"Acquired Emotional Patterns:"** This internal emotional state corresponds to the influence of the Acquired Wujing Shen (i.e., the emotional states of the Heart/Mind, created via "ego" survival), and the Po. The acquired emotional patterns of the Five Yin Organs are representative of an individual's survival state, manifesting as a need for control, approval, and security. The acquired emotions become a source of imbalance when they are chronic or excessive.

Organ	Jing			Qi			Shen	
	Yin/Yang	Element	Tissue	Sense	Taste	Climate	Color	Spirit
G.B.	Yang	Wood	Nerve/Tendons	Sight	Sour	Wind	Green/Blue	Hun
Lv.	Yin	Wood	Nerve/Tendons	Sight	Sour	Wind	Green/Blue	Hun
Lu.	Yin	Metal	Skin/Body Hair	Smell	Pungent	Dry	White	Po
L.I.	Yang	Metal	Skin/Body Hair	Smell	Pungent	Dry	White	Po
St.	Yang	Earth	Muscles/Flesh	Taste	Sweet	Damp	Yellow/Brown	Yi
Sp.	Yin	Earth	Muscles/Flesh	Taste	Sweet	Damp	Yellow/Brown	Yi
Ht.	Yin	Fire	Blood/Vessels	Touch	Bitter	Heat	Red	Shen
S.I.	Yang	Fire	Blood/Vessels	Touch	Bitter	Heat	Red	Shen
U.B.	Yang	Water	Bones/Head Hair	Hearing	Salty	Cold	Black/Dark Blue	Zhi
Kd.	Yin	Water	Bones/Head Hair	Hearing	Salty	Cold	Black/Dark Blue	Zhi
Pc.	Yin	Fire	Blood/Vessels	Touch	Bitter	Heat	Red	Shen
T.B.	Yang	Fire	Blood/Vessels	Touch	Bitter	Heat	Red	Shen

Figure 8.10. The Internal Organs and their Jing, Qi, and Shen Associations

The energetic state of an internal organ (i.e., balanced, excess, or deficient) will affect an individual's emotions and mental acuity. Likewise, external exposure to certain emotions and experiences will also affect the energetic state of the individual's internal organs. A summary of the psycho-emotional states traditionally correlated with the internal organs is described as follows:

- **The Liver:** Congenital state relates to compassion, patience, and kindness; Acquired state relates to anger, impatience, and rage.
- **The Heart:** Congenital state relates to inner-peace, contentment, and joy; Acquired state relates to nervousness, excitement, and anxiety.
- **The Spleen:** Congenital state relates to truthfulness, acceptance, and honesty; Acquired state relates to worry, remorse, and obsession.
- **The Lungs:** Congenital state relates to integrity, generosity, and righteousness; Acquired state relates to grief, sorrow, and despair.
- **The Kidneys:** Congenital state relates to wisdom and self-understanding; Acquired state relates to fear and insecurity.

The Internal Organs and their Original Spiritual States

The Five Yin Organs (Liver, Heart, Spleen, Lungs, and Kidneys) store and protect the Jing (Essence), and are considered to be the "Command Centers" responsible for the movement of the body's Qi and Shen. These energetic movements are governed and directed by the body's Hun, Shen, Yi, Po, and Zhi, which are energetically housed within the Five Yin Organs.

Each of the internal organs is responsible for creating and maintaining certain spiritual/energetic states. These internal states manifest via a multidimensional correspondence existing between the internal organs and the physical, energetic, and spirit bodies (Figure 8.10). The correspondence between the Five Yin Organ and their original spiritual states is described as follows:

- The Liver stores the Hun (Ethereal Soul)
- The Heart stores the Shen (Spirit)
- The Spleen stores the Yi (Intention)
- The Lungs store the Po (Corporeal Soul)
- The Kidneys store the Zhi (Will)

The Internal Organs and Climate

In Clinical Diagnosis, each internal organ is particularly susceptible to the influence of a different climatic condition, described as follows:
- The Liver is influenced by Wind
- The Heart is influenced by Heat
- The Spleen is influenced by Dampness
- The Lungs are influenced by Dryness
- The Kidneys are influenced by Cold

The Internal Organs and their Sense Organ Openings

Each of the internal organs is functionally related to one of the Five Sense Organs (i.e., the eyes, ears, nose, mouth, and tongue). The physical health and function of a particular sense organ relies specifically on the energetic nourishment that it receives from the internal organ with which it is linked.

Each of the internal organs "Kai" ("Open") into a particular sense organ orifice, allowing for communication between the external and the internal environments. The Chinese character "Kai" (Open) also carries the meaning "to move," suggesting that this movement of energy between the internal organs and external organs is consistent and reciprocal. The internal organs open into the senses, and are described as follows:
- **The Liver "Opens" into the Eyes:** Controlling both the eyes and sight. This allows sight to influence the energetic nature of the Hun (Ethereal Soul).
- **The Heart "Opens" into the Tongue:** Controlling both the tongue and speech. This allows speech to influence the Shen (Heart/Mind).
- **The Spleen "Opens" into the Mouth:** Controlling both the mouth and taste. This allows taste to influence the Yi (Intention).
- **The Lungs "Open" into the Nose:** Controlling both the nose and smell. This allows smell to influence the Po (Corporeal Soul).
- **The Kidneys "Open" into the Ears:** Controlling both the ears and hearing. This allows hearing to influence the Zhi (Will).

The Internal Organs and Taste

Each of the internal organs responds to a certain flavor. In Medical Qigong Treatments, sometimes a moderate amount of the corresponding flavors are prescribed, in order to have a tonifying effect on a particular organ system. The Five Flavors are described as follows:
- The Liver (Yin) and the Gall Bladder respond to the Sour flavor
- The Heart (Yin) and the Small Intestine respond to the Bitter flavor
- The Spleen (Yin) and the Stomach respond to the Sweet flavor
- The Lungs (Yin) and the Large Intestine respond to the Pungent flavor
- The Kidneys (Yin) and the Urinary Bladder respond to the Salty flavor

The Internal Organs and Sound

Each of the internal organs responds to a particular sound. An organ's associated sound will cause a strong resonant vibration within that organ and its organ system, and is generally used in the Medical Qigong Clinic for purgation therapy. The Five Sounds are described as follows:
- The Liver (Yin) and the Gall Bladder respond to the sound "Jue" and the note E
- The Heart (Yin) and the Small Intestine respond to the sound "Zhi" and the note G
- The Spleen (Yin) and the Stomach respond to the sound "Gong" and the note C
- The Lungs (Yin) and the Large Intestine respond to the sound "Shang" and the note D
- The Kidneys (Yin) and the Urinary Bladder respond to the sound "Yu" and the note A

The Internal Organs and Color

Each of the internal organs responds to a particular color, which has a tonifying effect on that particular organ and its internal and external systems, described as follows:
- The Liver (Yin) and the Gall Bladder respond to the color Green/Blue (Qing)
- The Heart (Yin) and the Small Intestine respond to the color Red (Chi)
- The Spleen (Yin) and the Stomach respond to the color Yellow/Light Brown (Huang)
- The Lungs (Yin) and the Large Intestine respond to the color White (Bai)
- The Kidneys (Yin) and the Urinary Bladder respond to the color Black (Hei)

INTRODUCTION TO CHANNELS

According to Chinese Energetic Medicine, a system of "Jing" ("Channels") exists within the human body, that integrates all of its separate parts and functions into a unified organism. The study of these special channels, their energetic functions, and the interaction between them, provides the Medical Qigong Doctor with a foundational basis for understanding the relationships among various physiological and pathological disorders which occur within the body's tissues.

Extensive research conducted by Dr. Kim Bong Han of the University of Pyongang in North Korea, found that the energetic channels are composed of a special type of histological tissue, an association yet to be explored by Western science. Dr. Kim has also discovered that the channels have a thin membranous wall which contains a type of transparent and colorless liquid which provides a pathway for Qi (Figure 8.11)

The study of Chinese Energetic Medicine rests on the understanding of the internal patterns and various cycles of Qi circulation (Figure 8.12). Through the observation and study of these energetic patterns, it becomes apparent that many diseases follow a predictable course of development.

The pathology of an internal organ will often manifest in specific symptoms, which can be diagnosed and linked to the organ or channel of origin through the previously mentioned set of Yin and Yang, Five Element correspondences. Understanding the circulation of Qi flow allows the doctor to control each internal organ's energetic function, and monitor the health of its entire system. By stimulating specific areas on the body's surface, diseases in both the superficial tissues and internal organs can be treated.

A Medical Qigong Doctor is trained to use various techniques in order to facilitate the purgation, tonification and regulation of the body's major energetic pathways, responsible for carrying energy and nutrition to the internal organs. These energetic pathways function as important channels and vessels, that are responsible for connecting the flow of Qi throughout the entire body, in order to transfer energy and nutrition both internally and externally throughout the tissues.

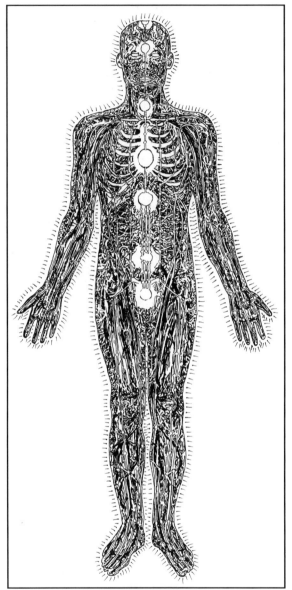

Figure 8.11. The Energetic Matrix of the Human Body (Inspired by the original artwork of Alex Grey)

The Channels are also known as a "Meridian System" or "Jing-Luo." The Chinese character commonly used for this type of "Jing" means "To Move Through" (Figure 8.13), and should not be confused with the Chinese character "Jing" commonly used for "Essence." The character "Luo" (Figure 8.14), means "A Net," and refers to the web-like structure of the body's inner fascia.

Chapter 8: The Twelve Primary Organs, Channels and Collaterals

Channel Name	Yin or Yang	Associated Organ	Element	Blood Heat Cycle	Qi Blood Cycle	Abbreviation
Gall Bladder	Yang	Liver	Wood	11 p.m.–1 a.m.	More Qi Less Blood	G.B.
Liver	Yin	Gall Bladder	Wood	1 a.m.–3 a.m.	Less Qi More Blood	Lv.
Lungs	Yin	Large Intestine	Metal	3 a.m.–5 a.m.	More Qi Less Blood	Lu.
Large Intestine	Yang	Lung	Metal	5 a.m.–7 a.m.	Balanced Qi and Blood	L.I.
Stomach	Yang	Spleen	Earth	7 a.m.–9 a.m.	Balanced Qi and Blood	St.
Spleen	Yin	Stomach	Earth	9 a.m.–11 a.m.	More Qi Less Blood	Sp.
Heart	Yin	Small Intestine	Fire	11 a.m.–1 p.m.	More Qi Less Blood	Ht.
Small Intestine	Yang	Heart	Fire	1 p.m.–3 p.m.	Less Qi More Blood	S.I.
Urinary Bladder	Yang	Kidney	Water	3 p.m.–5 p.m.	Less Qi More Blood	UB.
Kidney	Yin	Bladder	Water	5 p.m.–7 p.m.	More Qi Less Blood	Kd.
Pericardium	Yin	Triple Burner	Fire	7 p.m.–9 p.m.	Less Qi More Blood	Pc.
Triple Burner	Yang	Pericardium	Fire	9 p.m.–11 p.m.	More Qi Less Blood	T.B.

Figure 8.12. The Twelve Primary Channels are divided into Yin Channels (connected to the Solid Organs) and Yang Channels (connected to the Hollow Organs).

Figure 8.13. The Chinese Character "Jing," (Channel, or Passageway)

Figure 8.14. The Chinese character for "Luo," (A Net, or Connecting)

Along these channels are major trunks and lesser branches, that connect internally with the vital organs and externally with the major channels, limbs, sensory organs, and orifices.

The tiny areas where the Qi pools along these channels and collaterals are called "Points" (or "Acupuncture Points"). The ancient Daoists believed that these special Points are the spots where the Qi and Shen enter and leave the body.

When stimulated, these Channel Points cause an energetic response from within the internal organs and channels, thus changing the flow of Qi within the body. In the clinic, the Qi flowing within these channels can be directed to flow from organ to channel, from channel to channel, or from point to point along the same channel.

The channels unite and bind the body into an energetic whole. Channel Theory is therefore related to Organ Theory. Traditionally, the internal organs were not regarded simply as independent anatomical entities. Rather, Chinese Energetic Medicine focuses on the functional and pathological interrelationships between the channel network and the internal organs.

According to basic T.C.M. Theory, a Chinese herbalists will emphasize treating the internal organs, while an Acupuncturists will primarily focus on treating the external channels. When combined, both Acupuncture and Herbs make a powerful internal and external contribution towards healing the patient's disease. This is why acupuncturists will commonly prescribe herbs to further a treatment's healing effect.

Qi travels throughout the physical body along the channels and collaterals in much the same way as water flows through rivers and streams. An ancient Chinese Medical Text explains this concept as follows:

"Heaven is covered with the Constellations, The Earth is covered with the Waterways, and Man is covered with the Channels."

The channels serve as the link between the energies (such as Jing, Qi, Shen) and the ingredients (such as Blood and Body Fluids) that enliven and feed the tissues. The doctors of ancient China paid much more attention to the Body Fluids and energies circulating through the body than to the physical anatomical structures, as the Qi and Body's Fluids were considered to be much more fundamental.

VOLUME 1, SECTION 1: FOUNDATIONS OF CHINESE ENERGETIC MEDICINE

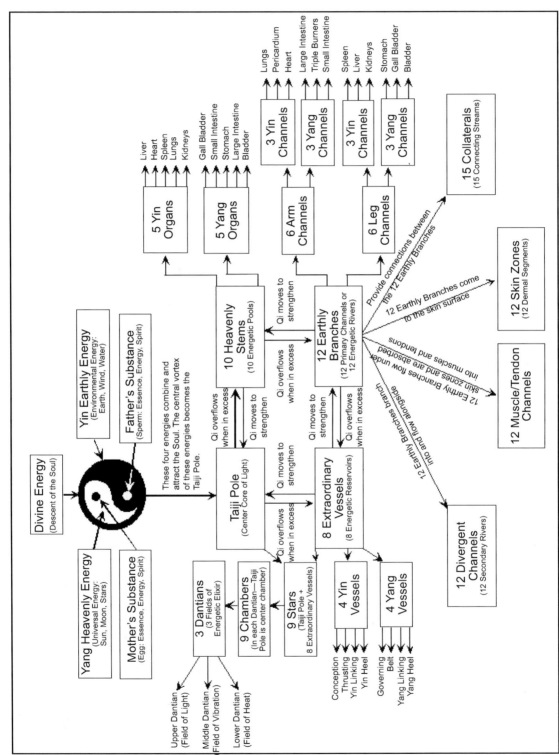

Figure 8.15. The Energetic Connections and Multidimensional Interactions of the Body's Internal Organ and Channel Systems

CLASSIFICATION OF CHANNELS

In Chinese Energetic Medicine, the Channel Network (Jing Luo) of the body is classified into the following four main categories (Figure 8.15):

1. **The Meridian Channels (Jing Mai):** The Jing Mai are the body's main energetic branches. They collectively contain the following Meridian Channels: The Eight Extraordinary Vessels, the Twelve Primary Channels, the Twelve Divergent Channels, and the Huato Channels (these are a set of bilateral points on the lower back, discovered by the famous Daoist Physician Huato in ancient China).
2. **The Collaterals (Luo Mai):** The Luo are the Collateral Channels, sometimes known as "Associated Vessel Collaterals," and the "Connecting Channels." These special Channels include the Fifteen Major Collaterals, the Minute Collaterals, and the Superficial Collaterals.
3. **The Muscle-Tendon Channels (Jing Jin):** The Jing Jin are the twelve special channels that spread through the body's muscles, tendons, and ligaments. They serve as external connections to the major channels (Jing Mai).
4. **The Cutaneous Regions (Pi Fu):** The Pi Fu are the Cutaneous Regions. These regions are the "Skin Zones" where the channels surface on the external tissues.

THE MERIDIAN CHANNELS (JING MAI)

The Jing Mai (Figure 8.16), are the major energetic trunks of the body's circulatory tree, and are considered to be the underlying support of the body's internal organs. They generally flow vertically throughout the body, connecting to all the deep tissues. They traverse the limbs and penetrate the body cavities, in order to connect with the internal organs. They are the body's main interior and exterior rivers of Qi, and are described as follows:

1. **The Eight Extraordinary Vessels:** Sometimes known to the ancient Daoists as the Eight Prenatal (Ancestral) Channels, these special Vessels connect with and regulate the Qi and Blood of the body's tissues and Twelve Primary Channels by either absorbing the energetic overflow in times of channel excess, or by replenishing Qi in times of deficiency.

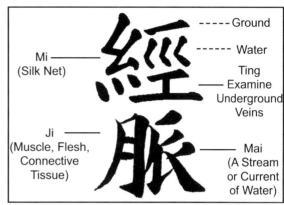

Figure 8.16. The Chinese characters "Jing Mai" (Meridian Channel, Pathway, Streams)

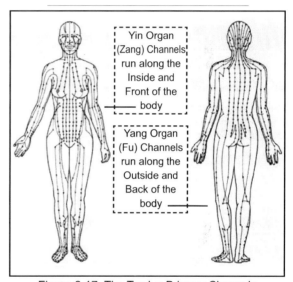

Figure 8.17. The Twelve Primary Channels

2. **The Twelve Primary Channels:** Also known to the ancient Daoists as the "Twelve Postnatal Channels," these energetic pathways run bilaterally and are symmetrical. They can be identified in three specific ways:
   - **Organs:** According to the Yin or Yang organ to which they are connected (Figure 8.17),
   - **Extremities:** By the arms or legs in which the channels originate or end,
   - **Six Divisions:** According to the six divisions of Yin or Yang Qi (i.e., Tai Yang, Yang Ming, Shao Yang, Tai Yin, Shao Yin, and Jue Yin) to which the channels relate.

The Yin Channels run along the medial and anterior aspects of the body. They are associated with the solid Zang Organs, and are paired with the hollow Fu (Yang) Organs. The three Yin Channels of the legs (Kidneys, Spleen, and Liver) flow from the feet to the torso, while the three Yin Channels of the arms (Heart, Pericardium, and Lung) flow from the torso to the hands.

The Yang Channels run along the lateral aspect of the body. They belong to the hollow Fu Organs, and are paired with the solid Zang (Yin) Organs. The three Yang Channels of the arms (Small Intestine, Triple Burners, and Large Intestine) flow from the hands to the head, while the three Yang Channels of the legs (Urinary Bladder, Gall Bladder and Stomach) flow from the head to the feet.

To the ancient Daoists, the Yin/Yang, internal/external, and substantial/insubstantial relationships of the organs and channels allowed for numerous Alchemical interactions, and provide the foundation for the transformation of matter and energy within the body.

3. **The Twelve Divergent Channels:** Commonly known as the "Jing Bie Mai" (Separate Pathway Channels), the Twelve Divergent Channels branch off from the body's Twelve Primary Channels. They are mainly distributed on the chest, abdomen, and head.

    The Divergent channels have the energetic function of connecting various internally and externally related channels, strengthening the connection of the Twelve Primary Channels to their related organs, and serving as extensions of the Twelve Primary Channels.

4. **The Hua Tuo Jia Ji Channels:** Some of the most dynamic Acupuncture Points located on the human body are the Hua Tuo Jia Ji ("Lining the Spine") back points (Figure 8.18).

    Hua Tuo was a famous Daoist Physician of the Han Dynasty (206 B.C.-220 A.D.), and is credited as being the creator of the ancient "Daoist Five Animal Frolics" Qigong Exercise Set. He is specifically known for inventing various herbal anesthetics, and is considered to be one of the most famous successful surgeons of ancient China. During his life, Hua Tuo was called the "Miracle Working Doctor" and "Divine Physician" ("Shen Yi") because of his emphasis on using a small number of acupuncture points or small number of herbs in a prescription in order to attain good results. In the *Chronicles of the Later Han Dynasty*, it is written:

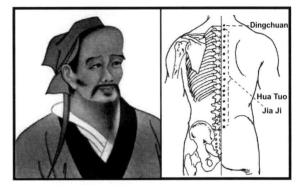

Figure 8.18. Daoist Physician Hua Tuo (110-207 A.D.)

"Knowing well the methods of keeping oneself in good health, Hua Tuo still appeared to be in the prime of his life when he was almost 100, and so was regarded as an Immortal."

In the clinic, the Hua Tuo Jia Ji points are used to treat Somato-Viscero and Musculoskeletal conditions, and are located midline over the vertebral spinous process, half a Cun bilateral to the Du Mai (Governing Vessel), from T-1 through L-5.

Traditionally, there are 17 pairs of back points (34 points total) originally attributed to the Daoist Physician Hua Tuo. However, within the last 2,000 years, these points have been extended, both upward through the cervical spine and downward across the sacrum.

THE COLLATERALS (LUO MAI)

Traditionally known as the "Collaterals," the literal translation of the Chinese term "Luo Mai" is "Connecting Vessels" (sometimes known as "Associated Vessel Collaterals").

The character "Luo" can be translated as "Connecting," and depicts the ideogram of a "Net, Cord, a Fibrous Mesh, or a Fine Silk Thread." The character is composed of two radicals. Positioned to the left is the radical "Mi," used for Silk, Net, or String-like Objects;" the right side of the character is the phonetic sound. The word Luo carries the meaning of energetically enveloping something in a net (Figure 8.19).

The Chinese character "Mai" is generally translated as "Vessel." It is composed of two characters. The character to the left, "Ji" depicts the ideogram for "Body Tissue, Muscle, or Flesh" (all of which are forms of Connective Tissue); the character on the right "Mai" depicts "A Current of Water, Stream, or Branch of a River." As a whole, the character can be translated as "Arteries, Veins or a Pulse, indicating a form of energetic circulation.

The Twelve Primary Channels are interconnected by the Collaterals, which are small inter-linking streams. The Collaterals work as the connecting branches of the energetic circulatory system, and are considered to be the underlying support of the Twelve Primary Channels. They generally flow superficially, in both horizontal and vertical directions. They are viewed as the body's "Secondary Streams of Qi," and form an important intricate network that traverses the body's surface, and interconnects the main energetic rivers, connective tissues, and cutaneous regions (Skin Zones).

There are three types of Collaterals studied in Chinese Energetic Medicine. These special Collaterals are described as follows:

1. **The Fifteen Major Collaterals:** These Fifteen Luo Mai transfer Qi and Blood from the Twelve Primary Channels to all parts of the body. They are sometimes referred to as the "Fifteen Major Arteries," and energetically, they link together the interior and exterior aspects of the body by connecting the body's internal and superficial channels. They also link together the Governing and Conception Vessels and the Great Luo of the Spleen (Figure 8.20).
2. **The Minute Collaterals:** These are the smaller branches of the Fifteen Major Collaterals. They are countless in number.
3. **The Superficial Collaterals:** These are smaller branches of the Minute Collaterals. They are also countless in number.

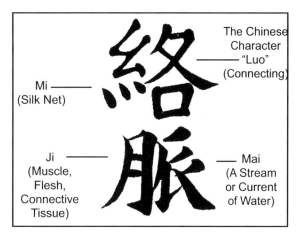

Figure 8.19. The Chinese characters "Luo Mai" ("Connecting Vessel" or "Connecting Streams")

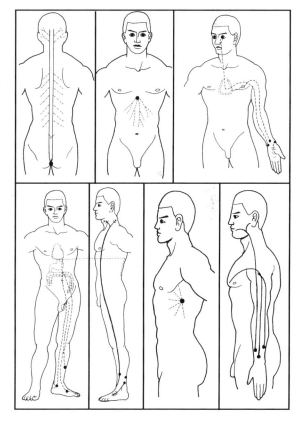

Figure 8.20. The 15 Major Collaterals (Luo Mai) Transfer Qi and Blood from the Twelve Primary Channels

Muscle Tendon Channels (Jing Jin)

The Twelve Muscle and Tendon Channels are the external connections of the major channels. They generally flow superficially along the body's surface and join the main energetic rivers, connective tissues, and Cutaneous Regions. The Twelve Muscle and Tendon Channels are also the regions of the body where the Qi and Blood of the Twelve Primary Channels nourish the muscles, tendons, and ligaments.

The word "Jing" carries a multitude of meanings, reflected by the many components of the character. In Chinese Medicine, the character "Jing," is used to depict the ideogram for "Channel," which can also be translated as "Meridian, To Pass Through, The Wrapping of a Silk Fiber, or a Net." Positioned to the left of the character is the radical "Mi," used for "Silk, Net, or String-like Objects." On the right side of the character is the phonetic "Jing," and is sometimes used to denote the "Flow of Water Underground." The top right of the "Jing" character represents "The Ground," while the three curved lines beneath it represent "The Flow of Water."

Positioned to the bottom-right is the modification for the ancient phonetic "Ting," meaning "To Examine Underground Veins."

Together, the ideograph describes the deep aquatic passageways or subterranean rivers which energetically knit together the internal fabric of the human body.

The bottom character "Jin" depicts the Chinese ideogram for "Sinew, Tendon, or Ligament." One of the earliest Chinese Medical Dictionaries, the *"Shou Wen Jie Zi,"* explains the term "Jin" as "The Strength of the Flesh," and explains that the ancient character is composed of the bamboo radical "Zhu" above two other radicals. The character to the left, "Ji" depicts the Chinese ideogram for "Body Tissue, Muscle, or Flesh" (all of which are forms of Connective Tissue); the character on the right is "Li" meaning "Strength" (Figure 8.21). Therefore, the word "Jin" compares the resilient fibrous qualities of the tendons to the flexible fibrous, intertwining quality of bamboo.

Skeletal muscles and tendons link together and mobilize the Bones of the body, acting on specific joints to provide movement (Figure 8.22).

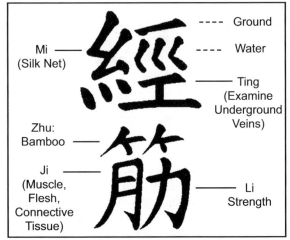

Figure 8.21. The Chinese characters "Jing Jin" ("Muscle-Tendon Channel")

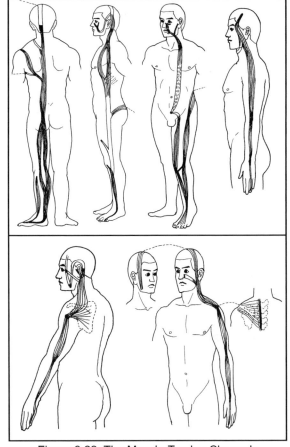

Figure 8.22. The Muscle-Tendon Channels

CUTANEOUS REGIONS: PI FU

In Medical Qigong Therapy, it is taught that because the external tissue represents the energetic base through which all of the body's Twelve Primary Channels, 15 Major Collaterals (Connecting Vessels), and Muscle and Tendon Channels flow, the body's outermost tissue can therefore be an important source for clinical diagnosis and treatment.

In the Medical Qigong Clinic, the body's tissue is traditionally divided into "Twelve Skin Zones" (sometimes known as the "Twelve Cutaneous Regions"). These special areas of the body, are where the Qi and Blood of the Twelve Primary Channels continually surface and connect to the body's skin (Pi Fu). It is through these various skin regions that the internal organs radiate their ever-changing energies outward, into the body's external Weiqi Fields. Conversely, all of the diseases of the Zang (Yin) and Fu (Yang) Organs can therefore be reflected onto the cutaneous regions of the body surfaces.

The Chinese character "Pi" depicts the ideogram for "Skin." The second character "Fu" is composed of two radicals. The character to the left, "Ji" depicts the Chinese ideogram for "Body Tissue, Muscle, or Flesh (all of which are forms of Connective Tissue). To the right side of that character is the phonetic for "Fu." Together the characters Pi Fu translate as "Skin" (Figure 8.23).

In the *Huangdi Neijing Suwen*, it states, "The skin region belongs to the system of regular channels." Because the regions (or zones) of the skin (Pi Fu) are located in the superficial layers of the external derma, they have a continuous and direct contact with the external environment. They are therefore, the areas of the body that are the most sensitive to climactic changes, and must continually adapt to protect the body from external pathogenic factors (Figure 8.24).

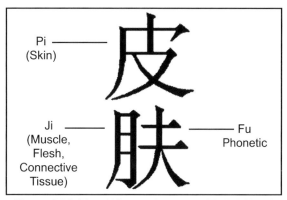

Figure 8.23. The Chinese characters "Pi Fu" (Skin)

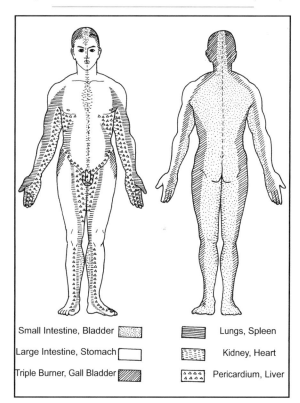

Figure 8.24. The Cutaneous Regions
(The Six Skin Zones)

VOLUME 1, SECTION 1: FOUNDATIONS OF CHINESE ENERGETIC MEDICINE

THE CHANNELS' RELATIONSHIP TO QI AND THE BLOOD HEAT CYCLE

The body resonates in a continuous interplay of Yin and Yang harmony, balancing the energy flow within and between the channels and organs. The Channel Network creates the energetic matrix of the body, giving form and structure to the body's Yin and Yang polarities (internal/external, inferior/superior, etc.). This subtle energetic matrix defines the Qi surrounding and penetrating the physical body, thus providing an energetic foundation for the creation and sustenance of all of the body's tissues.

The channels transport Qi and Blood to nourish, moisten, and vitalize the entire body. Healthy body function depends on the balanced circulation of Qi and Blood, described as follows:

- **Qi is Yang:** Qi provides the energy or force necessary for the body's functional activity (i.e., moving and transporting, warming, containing, transforming, and defending).
- **Blood is Yin:** Blood is the source of the body's moisture, nourishment, and lubrication.

Blood, Qi, and Heat circulate through all of the Twelve Primary Channels within a twenty-four hour cycle. The maximum peak of a Channel's Qi and Blood flow (traditionally known as "High Tide") occurs for a period of two hours during the time of day or night when the energy within that channel is at its fullest. The weakest period of a Channel's Qi and Blood flow (traditionally known as "Low Tide") occurs for a period of two hours during the time of day or night, opposite of its peak time period. In the following chart, the High and Low Tides are observed opposite each other (Figure 8.25).

THE CHANNEL'S QI AND BLOOD RESERVOIRS

From a Traditional Chinese Medical perspective, the Spleen plays two important roles in relationship to Qi and Blood. First, it converts food and drink into Gu Qi which, when further refined by the Liver and Kidneys, becomes Ying Qi (Nutritive Energy). Second, it manages the Blood by keeping it within the channels. Ying Qi nourishes

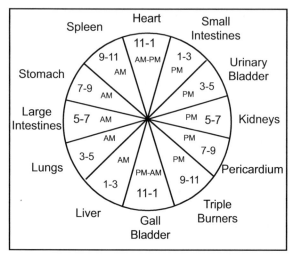

Figure 8.25. The Blood Heat Cycle (24 Hour Cycle) of the Body's Twelve Internal Organs can be divided into High and Low Energetic Tides

Organs & Channels	Qi	Blood
Gall Bladder	More	Less
Liver	Less	More
Lungs	More	Less
Large Intestine	Balanced	Balanced
Stomach	Balanced	Balanced
Spleen	More	Less
Heart	More	Less
Small Intestine	Less	More
Urinary Bladder	Less	More
Kidney	More	Less
Pericardium	Less	More
Triple Burners	More	Less

Figure 8.26. The Body's Organs and Channels Contain Different Proportions of Qi to Blood

the Body Fluids that enter into the Blood Vessels and are transformed into Blood by the Heart. The Heart both creates and governs the Blood; whereas, the Liver stores the Blood and spreads Qi throughout the body. Blood is considered to be a denser, more material form of Qi. Qi and Blood are interdependent: Qi moves the Blood, and the Blood nourishes the Qi. Both flow together.

According to Traditional Chinese Medicine, each of the Twelve Primary Channels has its own individual reservoir of Qi and Blood; however, the energetic quality of each channel varies in accordance with the amount of Qi and Blood available in each organ and its corresponding organ channel (Figure 8.26).

THE CHANNEL SYSTEM & FASCIA NETWORK

There is some speculation that the energy of the channels is transmitted through the body's vast fascial network. The body's connective tissues (also known as fascia) provide a network of semi-flexible structural support for all the tissues of the body.

Nearly every cell and tissue in the body is linked to every other cell and tissue in the body by indirect fascial connection. The inner fascia can be thought of as lubricated layers of living plastic wrap that cover and connect all of the muscles and internal organs, allowing the tissues to slide and move easily while maintaining structural integrity.

The primary channels are woven within the lining of the superficial fasciae, while the deeper channels (e.g., Collaterals, Extraordinary Vessels, and Divergent Channels) exist deeper within the internal fascia matrix. This webbed network conducts energy in the form of electron, proton, and ion transmission, and is also influenced by light and sound.

The fascia is responsible for transmitting a variety of biological energies. When stretched, for example, the fascia creates a Stress Generated Electrical Potential (SGEP). Although the fascia represents the primary physical tissue associated with the body's channels, the channels are also associated with numerous other tissues and their energetic functions.

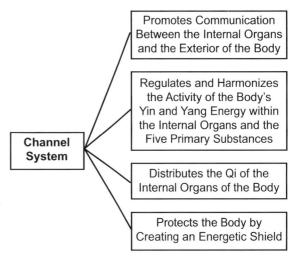

Figure 8.27. The Channel Systems 4 Major Functions

THE FUNCTION OF THE CHANNELS

The body's channel system has four major functions: it promotes, regulates, distributes, and protects, described as follows (Figure 8.27):

1. **Promotes:** The channels promote communication between the internal organs and the exterior of the body, thus connecting the individual to the environmental (Earth) and universal (Heaven) rhythms of life.
2. **Regulates:** The channels regulate and harmonize the activity of the body's Yin and Yang energy within the internal organs and within the Five Primary Substances (Jing, Qi, Shen, Blood, and Body Fluid).
3. **Distributes:** The channels distribute the Qi of the internal organs throughout the body.
4. **Protects:** The channels protect the body by creating an energetic shield, needed in order to deflect foreign pathogens, as well as to fortify the body's internal organ system.

The channels are responsible for reacting to any malfunction that occurs within the human body. However, the very same channels that are used to assist in the healing of the tissues, can also be disseminators of energetic dysfunction and disease as well. This is because disease passes into the internal organs, or from one organ to another, via the channel system. For example, an Exogenous Disease (Wind Cold) will usually progress from

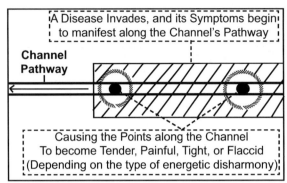

Figure 8.28. The Symptoms of a Disease Manifesting within a Channels Energetic Flow

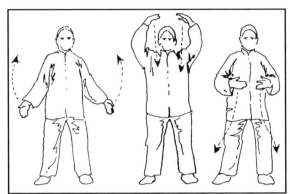

Figure 8.29. Medical Qigong Prescription Exercises are provided after treatment in order to purge, tonify and regulate the patient's organ and channel energy.

the body's Skin Zones (Cutaneous Regions) via the pores, through the Collaterals (i.e., the Superficial, Minute, and/or Major Collaterals). It will then work its way through the Primary Channels, and finally into the internal organs.

In Clinical Diagnosis, it is noted that the channels are affected by and respond to disease in predictable patterns, described as follows (Figure 8.28):

1. **The Channel:** Diseases and symptoms energetically manifest along the channel pathway.
2. **Channel Points:** When there is evidence of any type of energetic disharmony, the points along the channels become tender, painful, tight, or flaccid.
3. **The Weiqi Field:** When in a Deficient State, because there is a weakened Weiqi Field surrounding the tissue area, the electrical resistance and heat tolerance diminishes on the skin at the diseased point(s).
4. **The Shen:** As a disease and its symptoms begin to energetically manifest, the patient's Shen (Heart/Mind) becomes affected, and his or her body's Sensory Organs and perceptive senses (sight, smell, taste, hearing and touch) become affected through channel relationship.

From a Traditional Chinese Medical perspective, the functions and flow of the channels and collaterals, as well as the health of the internal organs, can be influenced by Medical Qigong, Acupuncture, Chinese Massage, and Herbal Medicine. Each of the above ancient Chinese Energetic Modalities utilize the Channel System to disperse excess, to move stagnation, to stimulate and nourish the Qi, to tonify deficiency, and to stimulate the Weiqi field in fighting External Pathogens.

When the body's Channels and Collaterals are continually trained or regulated, they naturally become thicker and filled with more energy. This is one of the reasons why a Medical Qigong Doctor will traditionally provide Medical Qigong Prescription Purgation, Tonification and Regulation Exercises after a clinical treatment (Figure 8.29).

THE CENTRIFUGAL & CENTRIPETAL FLOW OF CHANNEL QI

The energy of the body's channels normally flows in only one direction, while the polarity of the channel's points normally alternates between Yang (centrifugal spirals) and Yin (centripetal spirals) energetic movements. These two energy currents are described as follows:

1. **The Outward Centrifugal Channel Flow:** Some channels possess an outward centrifugal flow of Qi, that moves from the internal organ, through the channel, to the extremities. The Primary Channels with this centrifugal flow of energy are: the Heart, Pericardium, Lung, Stomach, Gall Bladder, and Urinary Bladder.

    This outward flow of energy is expressed or intensified during respiratory "Exhalation" (Figure 8.30). The outward centrifugal flow of energy manifests in points along the channel, or in other areas of the body where there are conditions of Excess.

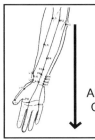

Figure 8.30. The Outward Centrifugal Flow of the Channel moves Qi and Blood from the Internal Organs through the Channel towards the Extremities

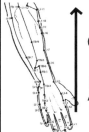

Figure 8.31. The Inward Centripetal flow of the Channel moves Qi and Blood from the Extremities through the Channel towards the Internal Organs

2. **The Inward Centripetal Channel Flow:** Some channels possess an inward centripetal flow of Qi, that moves from the extremities, through the channel, to the internal organ. The primary channels with this centripetal flow of energy are: the Small Intestine, Triple Burner, Large Intestine, Spleen, Liver, and Kidney.

This inward flow of energy is expressed or intensified during respiratory "Inhalation" (Figure 8.31). The inward centripetal flow of energy manifests in points along the channel, or in other areas of the body where there are conditions of Deficiency.

During the channel's energetic movement, once the Qi reaches the fingertips and toes, the energy naturally changes its polarity from Yin to Yang, or vice versa. This change in energetic polarity is due to the body's ever changing Yin to Yang (Zang/Fu) transforming channel system; which allows each combined Zang/Fu Organ and Channel to possess special internal and external energetic patterns and correspondences.

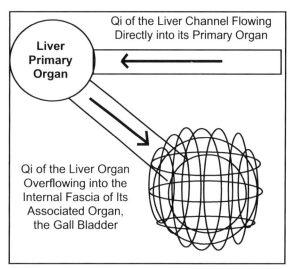

Figure 8.32. The Energetic Interactions Occurring between the Internal Organs and Channels

As the Qi of an internal channel flows into or away from its Primary Organ, it generates an energetic current. In ancient China, this special energetic "pulse" was described as "a river rushing back into the sea" or "a river flowing from the sea into the deep caverns of the Earth."

As the Qi flows through the energetic cavern of an internal channel, it stimulates the energy of its Primary Organ. This reaction initiates a spontaneous energetic connection that is immediately created and felt within the organ's tissues.

However, when the Qi from a primary organ's internal channel flows into its "paired" or "associated organ," the energetic reaction is quite different. Instead of immediately permeating the associated organ, the channel's energy "spirally wraps" the associated organ's tissues through the internal fascia that envelops the associated organ. The tissues of the associated organ then absorb the energy through and from the surrounding fascia (Figure 8.32).

This difference in energetic penetration and absorption rate is an important factor to consider when working with the body's internal energetic channels. When Medical Qigong Doctors extend their energy into a patient's channels, they must be aware that the absorption rate will be immediately felt in the channel's primary organ, and will also have a gradual effect on its associated organ.

Hun and Po Channel Influence

According to ancient Daoist teachings, each of the Twelve Primary Channels correspond to one of the Five Elements, and are additionally aligned within their internal and external channel progressions according to the energetic and spiritual influence of the body's Hun (Ethereal Soul) and Po (Corporeal Soul).

According to Chinese Energetic Embryology, the creation of each channel's internal progression via the Heavenly influence of the Hun and Earthly influence of the Po, occurs in-utero, during Prenatal formation (Figure 8.33).

Each of the Yin Channels have "Jing"("Well") Points located at the tips of either the hands or feet (Figure 8.34). These special points are the first or last point of the Yin Channels, and correspond to the Spiritual Qi of the Wood Element. All of the Yin Jing-Well points are connected to their internal Yin Organ via the energetic influence of the Hun's Heavenly Qi. Because the Hun is the Minister of Council to the Emperor (Heart), these points are traditionally used to treat disorders of the Shen

The Yang Channels Are formed through the Prenatal influence of the Po, and begin with the energetic nature of the Metal Element	The Yin Channels Are formed through the Prenatal influence of the Hun, and begin with the energetic nature of the Wood Element

The Twelve Primary Channels

Figure 8.33. The Energetic Correspondence of the Hun and Po with the body's Channel Flow

(Spirit). The point placement of the Yin Channels progress in a "Five Element Creative Cycle" pattern; starting with Wood, then proceeding to Fire, Earth, Metal, and finally Water.

Likewise, of the Yang Channels also have "Jing"("Well") Points located at the tips of either the hands or feet (Figure 8.35). These special points correspond to the Spiritual Qi of the Metal Element via the Po's Earthly energetic influence; with the point progression starting with Metal, then proceeding to Water, Wood, Fire, and Earth.

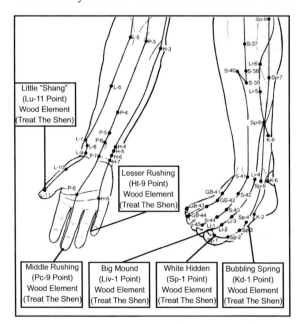

Figure 8.34. The Jing-Well Points on all Yin Channels, correspond to the Wood Element, allowing the Hun (Minister of Council) to influence the Shen (Emperor).

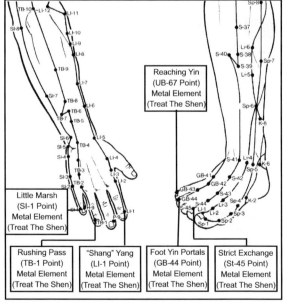

Figure 8.35. The Jing-Well Points on all Yang Channels, correspond with the Metal Element, allowing the Po (Guardian General) to influence the Shen (Emperor).

THE TWELVE PRIMARY ORGANS & CHANNELS

In this special section, I have decided to include the secret teachings of the internal organ energetic patterns, introduced to me by several of my Daoist Teachers. What follows is an explanation as to why this esoteric teaching is so important.

"GODS LIVING IN THE BODY?"

In the early 1970's, I was training in Chinese Internal Martial Arts under a Daoist Master from Taiwan. As my teacher began to explain the deeper "secret" teachings of the Daoist Internal Neigong System, I suddenly found myself in a state of deep internal conflict over something that he had said.

My instructor explained that his teacher Master Ho, had taught all of the senior disciples that inside the human body are various "gods." If you know their Secret Names and their True Forms, and pray to them, you will receive their hidden internal powers and will be able to use this magical energy for both healing applications and combat."

It is important for the reader to understand that up to this point in my life, I had been raised in a strict Christian Household. I had been a pastor of two Half-Way Houses, was a Song-Worship Leader in a "spirit-filled" Pentecostal Church, and was leading Bible-Studies every Wednesday night. Therefore, my immediate "fundamentalist" response was to leave the class and never return.

After a week, I was approached by one of the senior disciples, and questioned as to my absence. I explained to him that I could not accept Master Ho's Theology, and the belief in certain "gods" living within the human body. He suddenly laughed, and then explained, "No, Jerry, that is not what the Master was speaking about. What he meant was simply inside the body are various internal organs. When you understand their energetic form, and speak their proper sounds, these special organs will vibrate. Once they begin to vibrate, you can access and draw upon the Qi and Shen that maintains and supports that internal Organ System." I immediately responded, "Well, why didn't he say that?" To which the senior disciple responded, "He did. It is simply the ancient Chinese custom of repeating esoteric teaching in the exact same way that his master taught him. This is part of the cultural transmission you receive as a disciple of a Daoist lineage." I later discovered that these same organ names and images can be found in the *Huang Ting Nei Jing Wu Zang Liu Fu Bu Xie Tu (Yellow Court Inner Classic Charts of Reinforcing and Reducing Five Zang and Six Fu Organs)* written by the famous Daoist Physician Hu Yin during the Tang Dynasty (618-907 A.D.).

I eventually came to understand that when the imagination begins to construct mental images of certain energetic patterns, the Shen (Heart/Mind) will suddenly be able to access the energy of these forms. For example, once my Tibetan Nyingma teacher was instructing students, when a violent thunder storm suddenly arose and began to quickly approach where he was teaching his disciples. He looked at the storm and told his disciples that the storm was a little child throwing a temper tantrum. Therefore, he immediately gave the storm a "name," and asked his disciples to speak to the child, call it by its name, and simply ask it to calm down. As all of the disciples began to call the storm by its name, and speak gently and lovingly in order to calm the "disruptive child," to their amazement, the storm suddenly vanished.

In the same manner, according to ancient Daoist alchemical teachings, the internal organ energies can be suddenly transformed from a disruptive negative state to a balanced energetic state, depending on how the individual approaches the Qi of the internal organ system. All thought forms, whether benign or malignant, are composed of internal belief structures that create and mold energy. As the energy of the created thought form continues to gather, it begins to coalesce and mold, causing and forming energetic clusters. An energetic thought cluster is considered to be a condensed form of energy. That is, the thoughts and emotions fuse within the cluster, condense, and form an energetic mass.

The belief that formulates the thought form, is created through the emotional charge existing within the individual's mind at the time of its creation, and initiated through conscious or unconscious intention. The initial thought form is then constructed from energy that has been gathered and created within the body's internal energetic fields. The energetic field surrounding the charged belief eventually manifests into "what is and is not" in alignment with the individual's internal belief structure.

Throughout my many years of training, my teachers have always reminded me that, "The imagination leads the Mind, and the Mind leads the Qi. With this esoteric understanding in mind, it is important to note that after performing the "Purification Stages" of Daoist Alchemy (i.e., cleaning and activating the internal channels), a disciple was taught how to energetically fuse with each of the internal organ icon deities. For example, the Essential Spirit of the Brain is known as "Niwan" ("Mud Ball"). According to the *Yellow Court Classics,* all spirits that are expressed on the face have their origin in the "Niwan Palace," which is located in the center of the Upper Dantian and governed by the True Lord Taiyi.

My teacher explained that when the Nine Spirit-Souls of the True Lord Taiyi change form, they become Sacred Spirits (Ling Shen), and have the names "High, Supreme, Great, Void, Immortal, Mysterious, Upper, Spiritual, and Heavenly" (Figure 8.36). They are known as the "Nine Perfected Lords," and symbolically represent the spiritual energies of the Nine Chambers of the Upper Dantian. When energetically combined, they become the

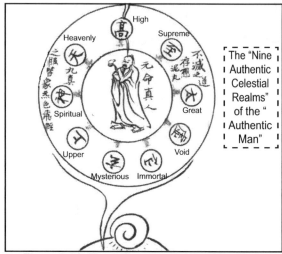

Figure 8.36. The 9 Essence Spirits of the Brain

spiritual form of the True Lord Taiyi, manifesting within the human soul. In ancient China, because each of the internal organs could be energetically manifested as a spiritual form, healing was sometimes addressed to the deity responsible for overseeing that specific organ system (Figure 8.37).

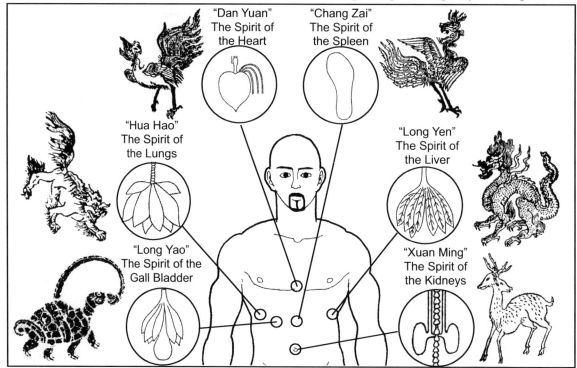

Figure 8.37. The Organ Spirits of the Body

CHAPTER 8: THE TWELVE PRIMARY ORGANS, CHANNELS AND COLLATERALS

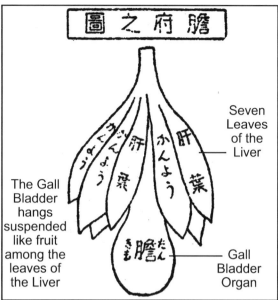

Figure 8.38. The Ancient Chinese Anatomical Diagram of the Gall Bladder (GB) Organ: *"Important Useful Notes on Acupuncture and Moxibustion,"* by Masatoyo Hongo (1718)

Figure 8.39. Spirits of the Gall Bladder (GB) Organ: *Yifang Leiju (Classified Collection of Medical Recipes)*, (Japanese reproduction - 1861)

THE GALL BLADDER: DAN

The Gall Bladder is a Yang (Fu) Organ, belongs to the Wood Element, and its associated paired Yin Organ is the Liver. In ancient Daoist imagery, it was taught that "the Gall Bladder hangs suspended like a fruit among the seven leaves of the Liver Organ" (Figure 8.38).

The Gall Bladder is categorized as being both a Yang Organ and an "Extraordinary Organ." It is the only Yang Organ that does not receive "turbid" food or drink, but instead stores a refined "clean" substance (the bile), similar to the way in which a Yin Organ functions.

Another reason that the Gall Bladder is considered "Extraordinary" is that it does not communicate with the exterior directly (via the mouth, rectum, or urethra), as do the other Yang Organs. Instead, the Gall Bladder Channels travel into the Sensory Organs (i.e., the eyes, ears, nose and mouth) and therefore serve to root and ground the senses.

ANCIENT GALL BLADDER ORGAN TEACHING

The following picture (Figure 8.39) is from the *Yifang leiju (Classified Collection of Medical Recipes),* section on the Five Viscera. The *Yifang Leiju* is a compendium of Chinese Medical Therapy compiled in Korea in the early 1400's. Originally comprised of 365 volumes, it contained over 50,000 prescriptions drawn from 150 medical texts ranging from the ancient Qin Dynasty period (221-206 B.C.) to the early Ming Dynasty (1368-1644). The original text was either lost or destroyed, and is no longer existent. This particular image originates from a Japanese reproduction made in 1861. The ancient text states:

"The Gall bladder is the Essence of Metal,
and carries the Qi of Water (Bile),
and looks like a suspended bottle-gourd.
Its spirit has the form of a Turtle-Snake.

When summoned, its internal energy
is transformed into a Jade Child,
which stands 1 foot tall,
and holds a Halberd in its hand.

This spirit runs swiftly in and out
of the Treasure-House of the Gall Bladder."

Additionally, according to the ancient Daoist teachings of the *Yellow Court Classics,* the energetic function of the Gall Bladder is described as follows:

> "The Deity of the Gall Bladder
> has the shape of a Turtle and Snake,
> whose bodies are fused together.
>
> The Gall Bladder Organ lies underneath
> the Liver's shorter petal,
> and its internal energy resembles
> the shape of a suspended sack."
>
> Although the Spirit of the Gall Bladder
> is called "Long Yao" ("Dragon Glory"),
> according to ancient Daoist texts,
> he is also given the name
> "Wei Ming" ("Majestic Illumination").
>
> The Palace of the Gall Bladder embodies
> the Essence of the Six Yang Organs.
> In the middle of this special area sits a Virgin Boy,
> shining with a powerful brightness.
>
> His Dragon Flag radiates the energy
> of the Fire Bell across the sky.
> Thunder and Lightning and Eight Quakes
> spread the Qi of this magical Jade Banner.
>
> The Virgin Boy masters all of the powerful Qi
> that is absorbed into the body
> by the Tiger's Soldiers (i.e. via the Lungs).
>
> Externally, the Virgin Boy oversees
> the area between the root of the nose
> and the pupils of the eyes.
> Through his influence, the Large Intestine,
> Brain, and the hair are mutually nourished.
>
> The Virgin Boy is clothed
> in a magnificent green gown,
> made of nine-colored brocade and gold,
> with Jade Dragons and Striped Tigers.
>
> He is able to help the disciple survive
> the mighty radiant ride on festive clouds,
> and to control tens of thousands of spirits
> who worship the Three Origins:
> Yuan Jing (Original Essence),
> Yuan Qi (Original Energy),
> and Yuan Shen (Original Spirit)."

Figure 8.40. The Chinese Character "Dan" (Gall Bladder)

CHINESE CHARACTER FOR THE GALL BLADDER: DAN

The Chinese character that depicts the ideogram for "Gall Bladder" is "Dan," described as follows (Figure 8.40):

- **Dan:** The character "Dan" is composed of three images: the character to the left, "Ji" depicts the Chinese ideogram for "Body Tissue, Muscle or Flesh" (all are forms of Connective Tissue).

The character on the right is composed of two characters. The upper right hand character depicts a person on a steep rocky place bent over and afraid of falling. The bottom right hand character is "Yan," meaning "Speech or Words."

Together, these characters represent a person in a hazardous position who cannot make a decision, and expresses the Gall Bladder's important role in making difficult decisions and initiating courage.

THE GALL BLADDER ORGAN IN CHINESE ENERGETIC MEDICINE

The functions of the Gall Bladder Organ described in Traditional Chinese Medicine are similar to those that are described in Western Medicine. In Chinese Medicine, however, the Gall Bladder functions the same way as described in Western Medicine, except that in Chinese Energetic Medicine it also incurs some partial functions of the Nervous System. The main functions of the Gall Bladder are described as follows (Figure 8.41):

1. **Stores and Excretes Bile:** Bile is created and secreted by the Liver and is stored and concentrated within the Gall Bladder. The Gall Bladder then releases the bile into the Small Intestines to aid in the digestion and absorption of food.

2. **Provides Qi to the Tendons:** The Gall Bladder also helps the Liver control the tendons. The Liver provides Blood to the tendons, while the Gall Bladder provides Qi to the tendons in order to ensure proper movement and agility. These combined functions of the Liver and Gall Bladder ensure that the sinews are soft and pliant and supplied with an abundance of energy.
3. **Psycho-Emotional Aspects:** In ancient China, the Gall Bladder was sometimes called the "Court of Justice," and the "General's Advisor." This is because the Gall Bladder is responsible for making decisions and judgments, overseeing and empowering discernment, as well as providing bravery, courage, confidence, and meeting challenges. Although the Kidneys control drive and vitality, the Gall Bladder provides the capacity to turn this drive and vitality into decisive action.

    Weak Gall Bladder Qi can result in timidity, great apprehension, and a lack of courage. In ancient China the term "Da Dan" ("Big Gall Bladder") was commonly used to denote a man with courage; while the phrase "Shao Dan" ("Small Gall Bladder") was used to denote cowardice.

    It is important to note, that the Gall Bladder (like the Liver), is adversely affected by stress and suppressed anger. Pent-up emotions such as anger, frustration, and resentment can cause Stagnation of Liver Qi. If the energy of these suppressed emotions are allowed to build up within the Liver, they can inadvertently produce Toxic Heat, which can affect the Gall Bladder. When toxic Heat begins to rise up within the Gall Bladder Channels, it can give rise to such symptoms as irritability and headaches. In the Medical Qigong Clinic, a "Migraine Headache" is traditionally known as a "Gall Bladder Headache."
4. **Sleeping Patterns:** The Gall Bladder has an energetic influence on the quality and length of sleep. If the Gall Bladder Qi is Deficient, the patient will wake up early in the morning and be unable to fall back to sleep. Additionally, according to the *Yellow Emperor's Inner Canon: Su Wen,*

**"When the Gall Bladder is Deficient
One Dreams of fighting, trials, and suicide."**

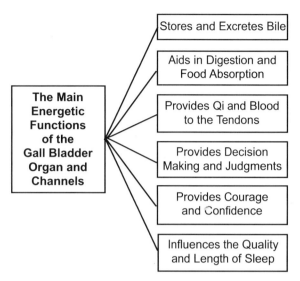

Figure 8.41. The Energetic Functions of the Gall Bladder Organ

THE GALL BLADDER CHANNELS

The Gall Bladder Channels are Yang channels. The external branches flow from the head to the feet on both sides of the body (Figure 8.42).

The internal branches of the Gall Bladder Channels flow from the head to the Gall Bladder. Both the internal and the external branches of these two energetic rivers originate from the outer canthus of the eyes.

- **The External Branches:** The external branches zigzag around the side of the head, and then flow down the sides of the torso. The external rivers then continue to descend the lateral aspects of the torso and legs, ending on the lateral sides at the base of the fourth toenails.
- **The Internal Branches:** The internal branches leave the outer canthus of the eye and descend the neck, entering the supraclavicular fossa where they meet the main channels at the Empty Basin (St-12) and Heavenly Pool (Pc-1) points. From these points, the internal branches pass through the diaphragm, to spirally wrap the Liver, before permeating the Gall Bladder. From the Gall Bladder organ the internal channels descend deep into the lower torso and encircle the genitals, before emerging at the sacrum.

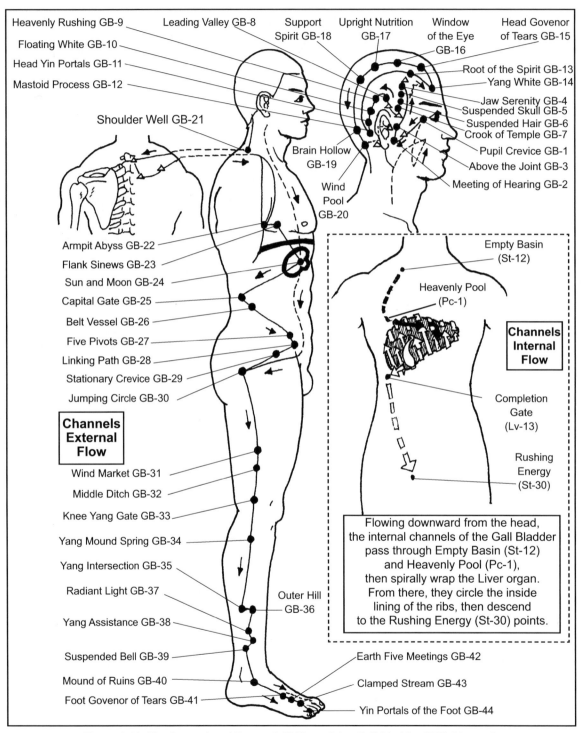

Figure 8.42. The Internal and External Qi Flow of the Gall Bladder (GB) Channels

The Channels' Energy Flow

The Gall Bladder Channels travel into the sensory organs (eyes, ears, nose and mouth) via its trajectories, allowing the sensory organs to become more rooted and grounded. They are also responsible for the regulation of hormones and Body Fluids (Figure 8.43).

The Gall Bladder Channels act on the skin, muscles, and nerves that are found along their pathways. Therefore, the Gall Bladder Channels are often used to drain Heat gathered within the head area, as well as remove Qi Stagnation due to an overheated or excess Liver condition. The internal flow of the Liver Channel moves Qi into the Brain and Sea of Marrow; consequently, the Gall Bladder Channel can be used to remove excesses (i.e., Fluids, Marrow, or Qi) from the Brain.

The Gall Bladder Channels link to the Brain, Marrow and Uterus, and act as a bridge between the Prenatal and Postnatal energetic vessels.

Energetically, the Gall Bladder Channels store more Qi than Blood. This allows them to affect the body's energetic and nervous functions more than they affect the physical substances and the functions of the Blood.

At the High-Tide time period (11 p.m. to 1 a.m.), Qi and Blood abound in the Gall Bladder Organ and within the Gall Bladder Channels. Therefore, at this time period, both the Gall Bladder Organ and Channels can be more easily dispersed and purged.

During Low Tide (11 a.m. to 1 p.m.), both the Gall Bladder Organ and Channels can more easily be tonified.

The Influence of Climate

An External Damp Heat Climate (such as those found in both tropical and sub-tropical regions) can aggravate a Damp Heat Condition existing within the Gall Bladder Organ.

The Influence of Taste, Color, and Sound

- A Sour Taste can be used to tonify both the Gall Bladder and Liver Organs and Channels

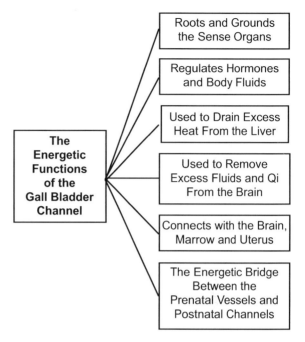

Figure 8.43. The Main Energetic Functions of the Gall Bladder Channel

- A light Green/Blue Color is used to tonify the Gall Bladder and Liver Organs and Channels
- The "Shu" and "Guo" sounds are used to purge both the Gall Bladder and Liver Organs and Channels

Gall Bladder Pathology

The main symptoms associated with imbalances of the Gall Bladder Organ and Channels are described as follows:

- **Pain:** This includes pain in the right and left upper quadrants of the abdomen, abdominal distension, jaundice, hepatitis, cholecystitis, cholelithiasis and digestive disorders including belching, vomiting of sour material, bitter taste in the mouth and flatulence.
- **Disorders of the Head:** This includes the eyes, ears, and face; poor concentration, dizziness and insomnia with tossing and turning.
- **Disorders of the External Sides of the Legs:** Existing along the channel's pathways.

VOLUME 1, SECTION 1: FOUNDATIONS OF CHINESE ENERGETIC MEDICINE

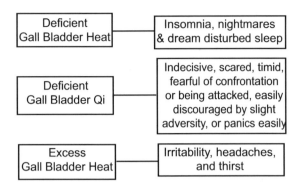

Figure 8.44. Chart of Liver-Gall Bladder Disharmonies

T.C.M. Patterns of Disharmony

In Traditional Chinese Medicine, disharmonies of the Gall Bladder are generally included within the category of Liver Disharmonies. There are, however, minor disharmonies particular to the Gall Bladder Organ such as Deficient Gall Bladder Heat, Deficient Gall Bladder Qi and Excess Gall Bladder Heat, the symptoms of which are described as follows (Figure 8.44):

- **Deficient Gall Bladder Heat:** The Gall Bladder has an influence on the quality and length of sleep. If the Gall Bladder is deficient, the patient will often wake up suddenly, very early in the morning, and be unable to fall asleep again. The Gall Bladder is often treated for insomnia, nightmares and dream disturbed sleep.
- **Deficient Gall Bladder Qi:** Patients who are indecisive, scared, timid, fearful of confrontation or being attacked, are easily discouraged by slight adversity, or who panic easily are said to have a weak Gall Bladder. Conversely, decisive, courageous, and determined patients are said to have a strong Gall Bladder.
- **Excess Gall Bladder Heat:** Like its paired Yin organ the Liver, the Gall Bladder is affected by frustration, anger, rage and resentment. These emotional states give rise to Liver Qi Stagnation, and thus produce heat, which affects the Gall Bladder. When Fire is created within the Liver and Gall Bladder, the symptoms are similar (irritability, headaches, thirst, etc.).

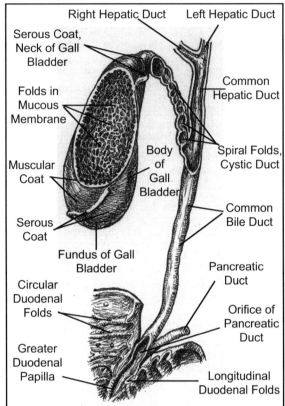

Figure 8.45. The Gall Bladder (GB) Organ

The Gallbladder Organ in Western Medicine

According to Western Anatomy, the gallbladder is a small pear-shaped organ lodged in an indentation (fossa) immediately beneath the right lobe of the liver. It is three to four inches long, and is situated with its widest section (the fundus) slightly beneath and forward to its neck, which is angled upward and slightly to the left (Figure 8.45).

The gallbladder is wrapped in a layer of fascial tissue that is derived from the peritoneum. Within this is a layer of smooth muscle fibers that form the body of the gallbladder; it is the contractions of these fibers that expel bile from the gallbladder into the cystic duct.

Like the stomach, the internal structure of the gallbladder contains many folds (rugae), allowing it to expand and contract as it receives and condenses the bile fluid. Its inner surface is protected by a layer of mucous, which insulates it from the effects of the bile.

Parasympathetic impulses delivered by the vagus nerves have a minor impact on stimulating gall bladder contraction. The major stimulus comes from an intestinal hormone known as cholecystokinin (CCK), which is released into the blood when acidic, fatty chyme enters the duodenum. This also stimulates the secretion of the pancreatic juice into the duodenum.

The gallbladder serves to store and condense bile, which it receives from the liver via the cystic duct. Bile, also called gall, is a bitter yellowish substance secreted from the liver to aid in digestion. It consists mainly of water, bile acids, bile salts, bile pigments, lecithin, cholesterol, electrolytes, and various fatty acids.

Bile is transferred into the duodenum (uppermost portion of the small intestine) via a system of ducts. The bile secretions of the liver are directed through several ducts that ultimately join together to form the hepatic duct, which carries bile away from the liver. The cystic duct connects the gallbladder to the hepatic duct, and is the common duct through which bile enters and exits the gallbladder. The common bile duct flows from the junction of the cystic and hepatic ducts into the duodenum.

When chyme enters the small intestine, a complex system of chemical and nervous impulses directs the gallbladder to contract, expelling bile through the cystic duct, along the common bile duct and into the duodenum to aid in the process of digestion.

When digestion is not taking place, a valve (sphincter of the hepatopancreatic ampulla) closes the connection of the common bile duct to the duodenum, and bile is redirected into the gallbladder for storage.

The gallbladder concentrates the bile by absorbing water and ions from the bile while it is being stored. In some cases the bile released from the gallbladder is ten times more concentrated than the bile secreted by the liver (Figure 8.46).

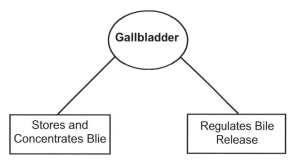

Figure 8.46. The Functions of the Gallbladder (Western Medical Perspective)

Disorders of the Gall Bladder

Gallstones, or biliary calculi, are the result of an imbalance among the components of bile. Bile is the primary vehicle through which the body excretes cholesterol. When the amount or concentration of bile salts contained in the bile is insufficient to dissolve all of the cholesterol within the bile, the remaining cholesterol can crystallize and form into balls, commonly known as gallstones. Large or numerous gallstones can partially or completely obstruct the flow of bile. Gallstones may be composed entirely of cholesterol, entirely of pigment, entirely of minerals, or contain a crystallized mixture of various bile components.

Disorders of the bile duct system include: cholestasis (blockage of bile flow), cholangitis (inflammation of the bile duct system), and cholecystitis (inflammation of the gallbladder wall).

When blockages within the common bile duct prevent the excretion of bile, the excess bile salts and pigments (primarily bilirubin) are absorbed into the blood, giving the body a yellow color. This is known as obstructive jaundice. If the blockage is total, the gallbladder may rupture and leak its contents into the peritoneum, causing peritonitis.

Because it is possible for an individual to survive without the gallbladder organ, the gallbladder is sometimes surgically removed in western medical treatments of gallbladder dysfunction. In patients who have undergone the removal of the gallbladder, the bile is secreted from the liver directly into the duodenum.

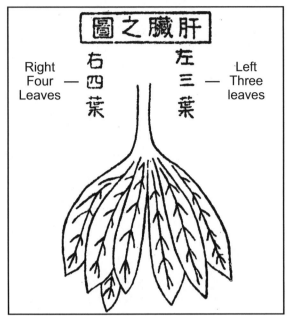

Figure 8.47. The Ancient Chinese Anatomical Diagram of the Liver (Lv) Organ: *"Important Useful Notes on Acupuncture and Moxibustion,"* by Masatoyo Hongo (1718)

Figure 8.48. Spirits of the Liver (Lv) Organ: *Yifang Leiju (Classified Collection of Medical Recipes)*, (Japanese reproduction - 1861)

THE LIVER: GAN

The Liver is a solid Yin (Zang) Organ, belongs to the Wood Element, and stores the Blood. It's associated Yang (Fu) Organ is the Gall Bladder.

In ancient Daoist imagery, it was taught that there are seven "leaves" that internally form the Liver Organ (Figure 8.47). These special leaves are responsible for the circulation and smooth movement of the body's Liver Qi, supporting the movement of the internal energy like an ancient Fan stoking a fire.

The Liver is sometimes referred to as the "Green Emperor," as it governs the Belt (Dai) and Thrusting (Chong) Vessels, and the flow and circulation of Qi moving throughout the body. This smooth flow of Qi ensures balanced mental and emotional activity, and normal bile secretion.

Although the Liver is anatomically situated on the right side of the body, its energetic movements and flow originate on the left side of the body. To understand this energetic function, think of the Liver acting as a bellows, in which the right side compresses, causing the Qi to flow out through the left side.

ANCIENT LIVER ORGAN TEACHING

The following picture (Figure 8.48) is from the *Yifang leiju (Classified Collection of Medical Recipes)* section on the Five Viscera. The ancient text states:

"The Liver is the Qi of Zhen (Thunder Trigram),
It carries the Essence of Wood,
and its Color is Blue/Green.

It looks like a suspended
Bottle-shaped 7 Petal Gourd.

Its spirit has the form
of a Blue/Green Dragon.
The Liver engenders the Hun Soul,
which is transformed into
Two Jade Children,
One is dressed in Blue/Green
and the other is dressed in Yellow.

Each of them is 9 cun tall.
Holding the Jade Syrup,
they emerge from the
Treasure-House of the Liver."

Additionally, according to the ancient Daoist teachings of the *Yellow Court Classics,* the energetic function of the Liver is described as follows:

"The Deity of the Liver
has the shape of a Green Dragon.
According to ancient Daoist teaching,
the internal energy of the Liver Organ
appears like a suspended, Bottle-Shaped Gourd;
that has three petals toward the left
and four petals toward the right.
The Gall Bladder attaches itself
underneath the Liver's shorter petal.

The Eyes are the Officers of the Liver.
The Left Eye is associated with
the "Jia" (Yang Wood Element) Heavenly Stem;
the Right Eye is associated with
the "Yi" (Yin Wood Element) Heavenly Stem.

Although the Spirit of the Liver
is called "Long Yen" ("Dragon Mist"),
according to ancient Daoist texts,
he is also given the name "Han Ming"
("Containing Illumination").

The Palace of the Liver
resembles a thick Emerald Green Province.
Underneath this special province
sits the Spirit of a Virgin Male Child.
To all who pass, he is the key to a bright,
intelligent new beginning.

The Virgin Boy is clothed in a
green brocaded skirt, and carries a Jade Bell.
He mixes and balances the Body Fluids
governed by the Hun (Ethereal Soul)
and Po (Corporeal Soul);
and will externally respond in Eyes that shine
clear like the Sun and Moon.

The Virgin Male Child regulates the Liver function,
so that 100 illnesses will cease to exist,
your life will be renewed, your Po will return,
and your transported Hun will exist forever.

The Liver Qi has great vitality,
is abundantly productive, and everlasting.
Once this energy is gathered
within the Six Fu Organs,
it gives birth to the Three Lights
(i.e., the "Three Ones" who internally reside
within the body's Three Dantians)."

Figure 8.49. The Chinese Character "Gan" (Liver)

Figure 8.50. The ancient Daoist Observation of the Shen (Emperor), Hun (Minister) and Po (General)

CHINESE CHARACTER GAN (LIVER):

- **Dan:** The character "Gan" translates as "Liver" (Figure 8.49). It refers to a general description of the image of the Liver Organ, and is divided into two sections.

  The character to the left, "Ji" depicts the Chinese ideogram for Body Tissue, Muscle or Flesh (all of which are forms of Connective Tissue). The character to the right depicts an ideogram that is a representation of a raised pestle, ready to pound, grind and destroy. Some translators maintain that the raised pestle image is actually an ancient warrior's shield, thrust into the ground in front of foot soldiers, ready to defend, protect, and support, hence the Liver's ability to "control" the body's aggressive "Warrior Spirit."

  My Daoist teacher explained that in ancient China, the Hun of the Liver (i.e., the body's Ethereal Soul) was considered to be the Loyal Minister of Council/Strategy (Figure 8.50). It was his duty to advise the Shen (Emperor of the Heart) on acceptable responses to the various interactions that occurred during the day. There were certain times,

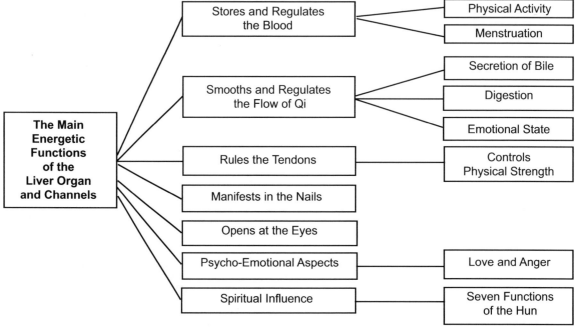

Figure 8.51. The Main Energetic Functions of the Liver Organ and Channels

when the Hun would advise the Emperor to dispatch the fierce Tiger General (i.e., the defensive "animal nature" of the body's Po, Corporeal Soul) in order to fight and protect the "Kingdom." Therefore any obstruction or impairment of the Liver's energetic function, often leads to a "Binding Depression of Liver Qi;" which "frees" the fierce Tiger General, and manifests as Impatience, Impulsive Actions, Hasty Decision Making, and a Hot Temper.

THE YIN AND YANG OF THE LIVER

Traditional Chinese Medicine defines the Liver as having two energetic aspects, Yin and Yang, described as follows:
- **The Yin of the Liver:** This pertains to the material structures of the Liver, including the Blood stored within it.
- **The Yang of the Liver:** This pertains to the Liver's function of heating and moving the Qi.

THE LIVER'S WOOD JING FORMATION

During the Seventh Lunar Month of a woman's pregnancy, the Wood Jing begins to be accepted by the fetus' body. The energy of the Wood Jing supervises the direction of the emotional and spiritual aspects of the fetus. Any faltering of the Wood Jing energy during embryonic formation is associated with serious psychological problems (i.e., Passive-Aggressive Personality Disorder, etc.).

After birth, the Wood Jing can be affected through the Color Green, the Sour Taste, and the "Shu" and "Guo" Sounds.

THE LIVER IN CHINESE MEDICINE

The functions of the Liver described in Traditional Chinese Medicine are similar to those that are described in Western Medicine. In Traditional Chinese Medicine, however, the Liver also assumes other various functions of the Blood, visual organs, Central Nervous System, and Autonomic Nervous System. The Liver also governs various psycho-emotional aspects and has specific spiritual influences.

According to Traditional Chinese Medicine, the main functions of the Liver are to: store and regulate the Blood, smooth and regulate the flow of Qi, rule the tendons, manifest in the nails, open at the eyes, express itself through the psycho-emotional aspects of love and hate, and exert certain important spiritual influences via the Hun (Ethereal Soul). These main functions are described as follows (Figure 8.51):

1. **Stores and Regulates the Blood:** The Liver is the most important organ for storing the Blood and serves as a reservoir to regulate the circulation of Blood volume. The Liver's responsibility of storing the Blood manifests in two ways:
   - **The Liver Stores and Releases the Blood According to Physical Activity:** When the body is active, the Blood flows into the muscles to nourish and moisten the muscle tissues, and to warm and moisten the tendons, allowing them to become more supple. When the skin and muscles are well-nourished by the Blood, the body maintains a stronger resistance to attacks from external pathogenic factors. When the body rests, the Blood flows back into the Liver, allowing the body to restore and recharge its energy.
   - **The Liver Regulates the Blood in Menstruation:** The Liver assists the Uterus, regulates the menses and is responsible for nourishing the growth of the embryo during the first month of pregnancy. The Liver's function of storing Blood also influences the way the Governing and Conception Vessels regulate Blood in the Uterus. During pregnancy, the mother's Blood is transformed into Jing-Essence, which nourishes the mother's body as well as the embryo's. The mother's Liver Channels cause Essence and Blood to coagulate in her womb. This Blood coagulation continues after the initial cellular division.

   An imbalance of the Liver is often reflected in a woman's menstrual cycle. In the Gynecology of Traditional Chinese Medicine, the Liver's function of storing Blood is a major factor in determining the state of a woman's reproductive physiology and pathology. Problems due to malfunctions of Liver Qi and Blood can manifest in symptoms such as Premenstrual Tension, Amenorrhea, Dysmenorrhea, Depression, etc.

2. **Smooths and Regulates the Flow of Qi:** The Liver is responsible for the "free and easy wandering" of Qi throughout the entire body (through all organs and in all directions). This is considered to be the Liver's most important function. The Liver makes the Qi flow smoothly in and around the body. It governs the energy within the Belt and Thrusting Vessels, and is in charge of the circulation of Qi through all of the body's internal organs. An impairment of this function is one of the most common patterns observed in the clinic. The movement of Liver Qi affects the body in three primary ways. It affects the secretion of bile, digestion and the emotional state, explained as follows:
   - **Secretion of Bile:** The smooth flow of Qi ensures normal secretion of bile. If the Liver Qi becomes stagnant, the flow of bile may become obstructed, resulting in symptoms such as belching with bitter taste and jaundice.
   - **Digestion:** The smooth flow of Qi ensures the normal digestive functions of the Stomach and Spleen, thus allowing for a harmonious movement of Qi within the Middle Burner. If the Liver Qi becomes stagnant, or "invades the Stomach or Spleen" it will adversely affect the digestive functions.
   - **Emotional State:** The Liver's function of ensuring the free and easy wandering of Qi has an influence on the body's mental and emotional activity, affecting the emotional states that each organ generates. Impairment of this function can lead to a "binding depression of Liver Qi" associated with impatience, hasty decisions, impulsive actions, and anger.

3. **Rules the Tendons:** The Liver regulates the function and control of the tendons and ligaments via the contraction and relaxation of the muscles, and is the source of the body's physical strength (Figure 8.52). In ancient Chinese Daoist Neigong (Inner-Skill) training, it is said that, "For power, it is better to stretch the tendons half an inch, than to increase the muscles mass three inches."

   In Daoist Martial Gongfu (Skill and Technique) training, the twisting of the tendons (known as "Reeling the Silk) and the stretching of the tendons" (known as "Pulling the Silk"), allows the disciple the ability to increase his

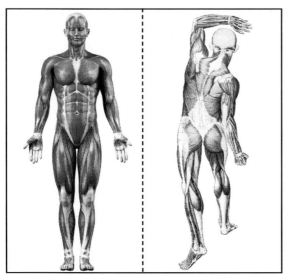

Figure 8.52. The Liver Rules the Tendons

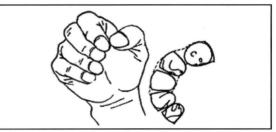

Figure 8.53. The Fingernail Detecting Injury Ancient Method of Clinical Diagnosis

strength, as well as produce a powerful vibrational resonance used to maximize his full striking potential. This vibrational skill is also used in the Medical Qigong Clinic for dispersing energetic stagnation, commonly exemplified in such techniques such as the "Vibrating Palm" and "Crushing Palm" applications.

In the clinic, it is noted that if the Liver Blood becomes deficient, the body will be unable to moisten and nourish the tendons. This often results in symptoms such as muscle cramps, tremors, spasms, numbness of the limbs, impaired extension or flexion ability and an overall lack of strength.

Internal Liver Wind can also adversely affect the tendons, and in some cases cause contraction of the tendons resulting in convulsions and tremors.

4. **Manifests in the Nails:** In Traditional Chinese Medicine, the fingernails and toenails are considered to be an offshoot of the tendons, and as such are also influenced by the flow of Liver Blood. The condition of the nails reflect the quality of nourishment that the tendons are receiving and can be used to determine the state of the Liver Blood. If the Liver Blood is abundant, the finger and toenails will be flexible, smooth and healthy, with no ridges or spots.

The ancient Daoists considered the condition of your fingernails to be an important window into the state of your current physical health. The energetic relationship with the physical changes of the fingernails and diseases of the human body can be traced back to the earliest Chinese Medical text, the *Huangdi Neijing (The Yellow Emperor's Inner Canon)*. However, according to research, the first surviving Chinese Medical Text that focuses exclusively on Fingernail, Blood, and Qi Examination, using the manipulation of the fingernails with pressure, is the book *Shang Ke Hui Zhuan (Compilation of Traumatology)* written by Hu Tingguang of the Qing Dynasty, in 1817.

The fingernail diagnosis that is traditionally used in the clinic, requires observing the abnormalities of the nail's (plate) surface, and studying the surface colors of the nail plate.

One special method of Fingernail Diagnosis originated from ancient Daoist Folk Magic, called "Fingernail Detecting Injury" (Figure 8.53). In this ancient method of diagnosis, the hand is positioned in a curled pattern, exposing the image of the curled body of an infant. Disease patterns are then observed and identified in the similar methods as those currently used in all T.C.M. Clinics for Ear Diagnosis.

This ancient method of diagnosis is currently being further developed by Wen-Hua Wang M.D., who is a Cardiologist and Professor at the Shanghai University of Traditional Chinese Medicine in China.

5. **Opens at the Eyes:** The Liver is connected to the eyes and the sense of sight. The Liver

Blood moistens the eyes and gives them the capacity to see. When the Liver Blood is deficient, there will be blurry vision, dry eyes, Myopia, or Color Blindness.

The images absorbed into the body through the eyes are filtered through the Liver by the spiritual influences of the Hun (Ethereal Souls) or Po (Corporeal Souls), which then generate emotional responses according to the individual's current state of mind.

In ancient Daoist teachings, the Bright Spirit of the Eye is known as "Ying Xuan" ("Profound Mystery")

6. **Psycho-Emotional Aspects:** The Liver is responsible for planning and creating, and is also responsible for instantaneous solutions or sudden insights. It is for this reason that the Liver is sometimes called "The Loyal Minister of Spiritual Council," and "The General in Charge of Strategy."

The Liver's positive psycho-emotional attributes are all influenced by the Hun, and are expressed as love, kindness, benevolence, compassion, and generosity. In normal function, these psycho-emotional aspects of the Hun influence the Liver, allowing the individual to experience love and compassion in thoughts and actions.

The Liver's negative attributes are influenced by the Po, and are expressed as anger, irritability, frustration, resentment, hate, jealousy, rage, and depression. If the circulation of Qi becomes obstructed, the resulting Liver Qi stagnation gives rise to emotional turmoil. This emotional turmoil may sometimes manifest through energetic outbursts of anger (Yang) or sinking into depression (Yin), and is initiated by the Po's effect on the Liver.

7. **Spiritual Influence:** The Liver stores the Three Ethereal Souls, also called the Hun (see Chapter 2). In the context of classical Daoist Theology, the individual's Eternal Soul (Shen Xian) is different from the Three Ethereal Souls (Hun), in that the Eternal Soul is seen as the individual's "Original Spirit" (Yuan Shen); whereas, the Ethereal Souls are seen as more "universal temperaments of the Dao" or

Figure 8.54. The Three Hun (Ethereal Soul), The Liver's Spirit - The Blue-Green Dragon, and the Chinese Character for Hun

"divine archetypes of spiritual propriety."

Ancient Medical Texts state that there are Three Ethereal Souls (Hun) and Seven Corporeal Souls (Po) that symbolize different attributes of the human being. The Hun's spiritual energy is said to be able to leave the body and then return, thus indicating a relationship with out-of-body travel into the Spirit World. This form of Spirit Travel occurs each night during each individual's "Dream State."

Chinese Ideogram of the Hun

The Chinese ideogram for the Hun has two parts. The character to the right represents the word "Gui," meaning "Ghost" or "Earthly Spirit." This character is depicted by the image of a head being suspended above a vaporous body; with an appendage symbolizing the whirlwind accompanying its movements.

The character to the left is the image for Clouds (Yun), seen as vapor rising from the Earth and gathering in the Heavens (Figure 8.54).

Together, the Hun character describes the easy movement of the ethereal spirit, as it freely moves within the tissues; like clouds following the will of the "Heavenly Breath moving within the celestial vault." From this ideogram we also get a distinct picture of the spirit (Hun) rising towards the Heavens.

The ancient Chinese believed that the Hun move within the body as freely as clouds, following the Yi (intent) of the "Heavenly Breath (Eternal Soul), within the celestial vault" (within the Heart, originating within the Taiji Pole).

THE LIVER CHANNELS

The Liver Channels are Yin Channels that flow externally from the feet to the torso (Figure 8.55).

- **The External Branches:** The two external rivers of the Liver Channels originate externally from the lateral side of the big toes, and flow upward on the medial side of the legs to encircle the groin. From there they continue to ascend externally to the lateral aspects of the torso, where they enter internally and penetrate the Liver.
- **The Internal Branches:** Internally, the Liver Channels then connect to, and spirally wrap around the Gall Bladder. From there, they flow to the Lungs, ascend internally through the thorax, and into the head to connect with the eyes, cheeks, and inner surface of the lips.

The Liver Channel then emerges at the forehead and flows upward to connect with the Governing Vessel at the 100 Meetings (Baihui: GV-20) point, located on the top of the head.

CHANNELS' ENERGY FLOW

From both the external and internal energetic pathways flowing from the Liver Organ, the circulating movement of the Qi washes over the whole body, assisting the tissues in storing and distributing the Blood. This allows the energy of the Liver Channels to act on the skin, muscles, tendons and nerves that are found along the channels' pathway.

The Liver Channels contain more Blood than Qi. This allows them to affect the body's physical substances more than affecting its energetic functions.

At the High-Tide time period (1 a.m. to 3 a.m.), Qi and Blood abound in the Liver Organ and Liver Channels. At this time, the Liver Organ and Channels can more easily be dispersed and purged. During Low-Tide (1 p.m. to 3 p.m.), they can be more readily tonified.

The internal energetic flow of the Liver Channel follows the pathway of the Microcosmic Orbit Water Cycle (Figure 8.56). In Daoist meditations, this is the natural energetic pathway used for stimulating the intuitive perceptions of the Hun, and it is traditionally used in advanced meditation practices for cultivating deep spiritual states.

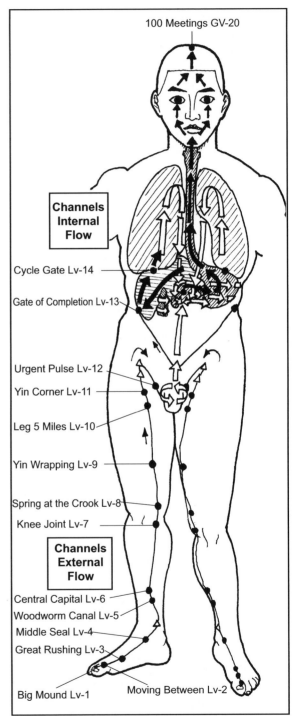

Figure 8.55. The Internal and External Qi Flow of the Liver (Lv) Channels

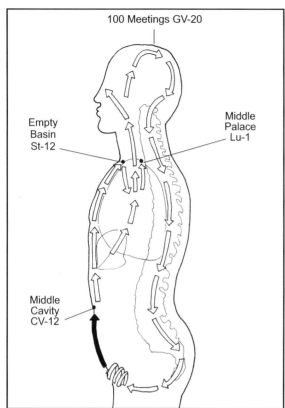

Figure 8.56. Side View of the Liver Channels' Internal Flow of Qi, following the energetic pathway of the Daoist Microcosmic Orbit Water Cycle

The Influence of Climate

In the Springtime, Liver conditions become more pronounced. Therefore, the Liver Qi will become more active in individuals with strong Liver Qi. When the Liver Qi becomes excessive, the patient will become consumed by anger and irritability.

Likewise, the Liver Qi may also become more deficient in those individuals who have weak Liver Qi. When Liver Qi becomes deficient, the patient will become withdrawn and fearful. During the Springtime, the excessive consumption of foods containing preservatives, foods that have been contaminated with pesticides, and the excessive drinking of alcohol can especially deplete the Liver.

Additionally, an external Windy Climate, which is typically stronger during the Springtime, can interfere with the functions of the Liver by aggravating a pre-existing Internal Liver Wind condition. Symptoms relating to an External Wind Invasion aggravating an Internal Liver Wind condition, include headaches, stiff neck, skin rashes that start suddenly and move quickly, as well as Wind Stroke.

The Influence of Taste, Color, and Sound

- A Sour Taste can be used to tonify both the Liver and Gall Bladder Organs and Channels
- A Dark Green/Blue Color is used to tonify the Liver and Gall Bladder Organs and Channels
- The descending "Shu" and "Guo" Sounds are used to purge the Liver and Gall Bladder

Liver Pathology

The main symptoms associated with imbalances of the Liver Organ and Channels are described as follows:

- **Physical Movement:** As the Liver supplies the tendons with the energy and nutrients necessary for the development and maintenance of physical strength. Therefore Liver impairment is sometimes the cause of many disorders of physical strength and movement. These disorders include tremors or spasms of the muscles, tiredness, numbness, and sluggishness in joint movements.
- **Swelling:** Diseases of the Liver Channels can also cause swelling and a distended sensation of the hypochondrium. The Liver Channels also correspond to diseases of the lower abdomen and genital organs.
- **Weakness:** Additionally, the Liver and Kidneys are mutually dependent upon each other. The Liver stores the Blood that nourishes the Kidney Jing; whereas the Kidneys store Jing that helps produce the Blood. Deficient Kidneys may lead to Blood Deficiency, and Deficient Liver Blood may cause weakness of the Kidney Jing due to lack of nourishment from the Blood.
- **Hair Color:** The hair on top of the head is also nourished by the Blood. When the hair turns grey, it is often said to be caused by insufficient Blood stored in the Liver, as well as a Kidney Jing Deficiency.

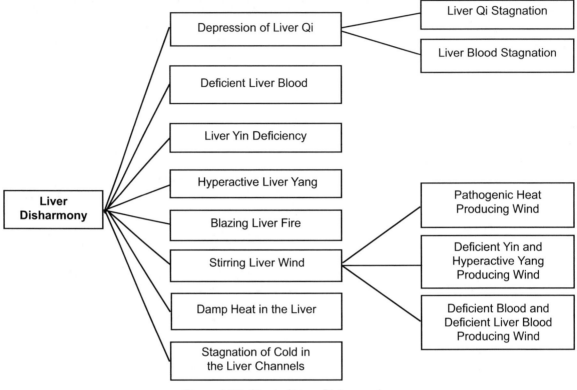

Figure 8.57. Chart of Liver Disharmonies

T.C.M. Patterns of Disharmony

In Traditional Chinese Medicine, Liver disharmonies originate from Deficient Liver Blood, Deficient Liver Yin, Blazing Liver Fire, Internal Liver Wind, or Liver Qi Stagnation. For clinical purposes, Liver Dysfunctions can be categorized into eight major pathological conditions. These pathological conditions are described as follows (Figure 8.57): Depression of Liver Qi, Deficient Liver Blood, Liver Yin Deficiency, Hyperactive Liver Yang, Blazing Liver Fire, Liver Wind, Damp Heat in the Liver and Gall Bladder, and Stagnation of Cold in the Liver Channels.

The following is a brief description of the eight origins of Liver Disharmony (see Figure 8.59):

1. **Depression of Liver Qi:** This is one of the most common patterns of disharmony observed in the clinic. Depression of Liver Qi is usually due to emotional disharmony such as frustration, irritation, anger, or depression. This condition results in the stagnation of both Qi and Blood throughout the body. It can create a disharmony within the patient's digestive system, affect menstruation, and influence the patient's emotional and behavioral patterns (Figure 8.58).

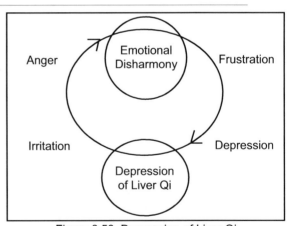

Figure 8.58. Depression of Liver Qi

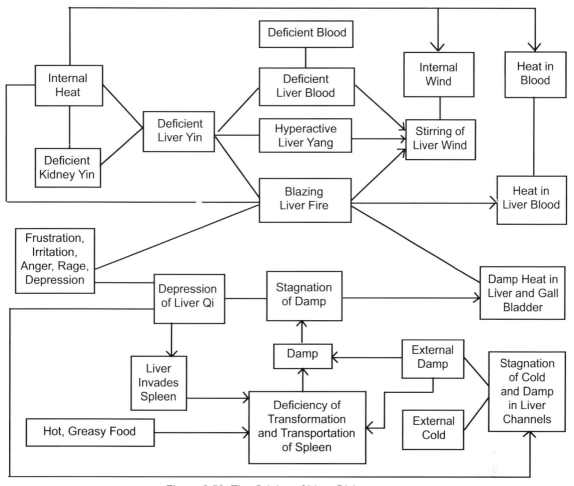

Figure 8.59. The Origins of Liver Disharmony

- **Liver Qi Stagnation:** When Liver Qi is stagnant, it may invade other internal organs and cause further disharmony.

    Symptoms can manifest as irritability, impatience, headaches, plum-pit stagnation in the throat, depression, abdominal pain, abdominal masses, diarrhea, constipation, pain and distension of the hypochondrium, epigastric pain, poor appetite, belching, nausea, vomiting, irregular menses, premenstrual tension, dysmenorrhea and painful urination.

    Stagnant Liver Qi Invading the Stomach can result in epigastric pain, nausea, and vomiting.

    Stagnant Liver Qi Invading the Lungs can cause wheezing and asthma.

- **Liver Blood Stagnation:** Stasis of Liver Blood is usually a consequence of Chronic Liver Qi Stagnation.

    When Liver Blood is stagnant, symptoms can manifest as irritability, impatience, depression, hypochondriac pain, nose bleeds, vomiting blood, abdominal masses, abdominal pain, dysmenorrhea, painful periods, irregular periods, dark blood and clotted menses.

2. **Deficient Liver Blood:** Poor nourishment can weaken the Spleen, resulting in an insufficient production of Blood. When not enough Blood is produced by the Spleen, insufficient Blood is stored by the Liver. Additional pathogenic factors creating Deficient Blood or Liver Dis-

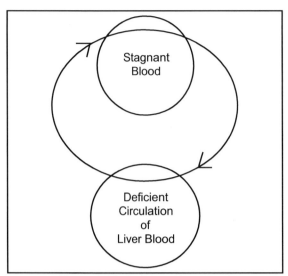

Figure 8.60. Deficient Liver Blood

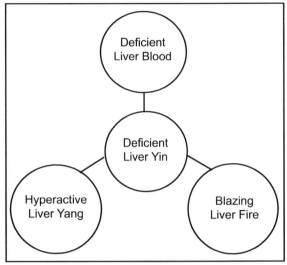

Figure 8.61. Interrelationship of Hyperactive Liver Yang Patterns

harmony can give rise to Deficient Liver Blood (e.g., loss of Blood due to hemorrhage; injury to Yin, injury to Body Fluids, injury to Liver due to Heat caused by fever or Blazing Liver Fire).

Deficient Liver Blood can cause such symptoms as headaches, numbness of the limbs, insomnia, blurry vision, dry brittle nails, tiredness, hypochondriac pain, constipation, irritability, impatience, depression, scanty menstruation, and amenorrhea (Figure 8.60).

3. **Liver Yin Deficiency:** Can cause such symptoms as insomnia, dry eyes, tiredness, irritability, impatience, depression and pain in the hypochondriac region.

4. **Hyperactive Liver Yang:** Deficient Liver Yin can give rise to conditions of Excess Dryness and Heat. Excessive Dryness and Heat can easily lead to conditions of Hyperactive Liver Yang, or the more extreme condition of Blazing Liver Fire (Figure 8.61).

    Liver Yang Rising can cause such symptoms as: irritability, headaches, dizziness, high blood pressure, and tiredness.

    In ancient China, the Liver was sometimes called the "root of resistance to fatigue." This was because, whenever the Liver is not functioning properly (stagnant, deficient, or excessively hot), the patient can experience fatigue and physical weakness.

5. **Blazing Liver Fire:** A chronic condition of Internal Heat or Deficient Liver Yin may predispose the patient to Blazing Liver Fire. Blazing Liver Fire can be caused by suppressed anger or rage, or by excessive consumption of alcohol, tobacco, spicy and greasy food, or drugs. If extreme or chronic in nature, Deficient Liver Blood, and Hyperactive Liver Yang can also result in Blazing Liver Fire. This energetic pattern can also arise from chronic depression of Liver Qi. Stagnation can eventually give rise to Internal Heat and ultimately flare up as Fire.

    Blazing Liver Fire can cause such symptoms as red eyes and face, angry outbursts, tinnitus, temporal headaches, dizziness, dream-disturbed sleep and insomnia.

6. **Stirring Liver Wind:** Deficient Liver Blood, Hyperactive Liver Yang, Blazing Liver Fire or severe fever can result in the stirring of Liver Wind. Liver Wind is considered Yang and light in nature. It generally rises within the body, affecting the upper torso, and especially the head. It manifests through sudden or irregular movements primarily affecting the upper body, and is associated with Liver disharmony. Pathogenic Liver Wind manifests as tics, tremors, spasms, convulsions and stroke, as well as a shaking and vibrating in the tongue. The

upward movement of Liver Wind affects the circulation of Qi and Blood and can cause dizziness or loss of consciousness.

There are three main energetic patterns of Stirring Liver Wind: Pathogenic Heat Producing Wind, Deficient Yin and Hyperactive Yang Producing Wind and Deficient Blood and Deficient Liver Blood producing Wind.

- **Pathogenic Heat Producing Wind:** This is a sudden, acute condition that only occurs in severe febrile diseases. In this condition, the Yin and Blood are damaged by the extreme Heat generated from the fever.
- **Deficient Yin and Hyperactive Yang Producing Wind:** Deficient Yin and Hyperactive Yang, stemming from chronic Liver Yin Deficiency, can cause the rising of Liver Yang. This condition can sometimes give rise to Liver Wind, resulting in such symptoms as weakness, sudden loss of consciousness and mental disorders.
- **Deficient Liver Blood Producing Wind:** Deficient Yin and Deficient Blood result from a lack of nourishment and moisture of the body's muscles and tendons. This pattern of deficiency creates an emptiness within the Blood Vessels, which become "filled" with Internal Wind. This condition of Internal Wind results in such symptoms as blurred vision, dizziness, aphasia, weakness, numbness, trembling, stiffness and spasms of the head and extremities.

7. **Damp Heat in the Liver:** A combination of External or Internal Dampness and Heat (with a tendency towards Liver Stagnation) can result in the condition of Damp Heat in the Liver and/or Gall Bladder. If the transformation and transportation functions of the Spleen are impaired (caused from Liver invasion or External Dampness), Internal Dampness can be produced. If there is depression of Liver Qi, this Dampness may stagnate and create Heat.

Symptoms of Damp Heat in the Liver include: abdominal distension, fullness and pain in the chest and hypochondrium, loss of appetite, bitter taste in the mouth, nausea, vomiting, and a sour taste. Damp Heat in the Liver and Gall Bladder can cause such symptoms as jaundice, headaches, bitter taste in the mouth, nausea, abdominal fullness, leukorrhea, painful and inflamed scrotum, loss of appetite, irritability, impatience, depression, hypochondriac pain, and abdominal pain.

8. **Stagnation of Cold in the Liver Channels:** Stagnation due to Liver Qi Depression in combination with stagnation of Cold can result in stagnation of Cold in the Liver Channels.

Cold concentrates in the lower part of the body, therefore symptoms generated from a stagnation of Cold in the Liver Channels include disharmonies of the lower body, such as hernia, pain and distension in the lower abdomen, testes and scrotum. As these pathologies are due to stagnation of Cold, they are alleviated by movement and warmth.

THE LIVER IN WESTERN MEDICINE

According to Western Anatomy, the liver is situated on the right side of the torso immediately beneath the diaphragm, and is surrounded by the rib cage. It is the largest gland in the body, weighing about 3 pounds in the average adult, and is slightly smaller in women than in men. The liver is also the second largest organ of the human body, with the skin being the largest.

The liver is responsible for a wide range of metabolic and regulatory functions, and is one of the most important organs in the body for maintaining the health of the blood. The bile produced by the liver plays an important role in the digestion of fats and the excretion of wastes.

ANATOMY OF THE LIVER

The liver is roughly a wedge-shaped organ, with its base directed towards the right of the rib cage, and its edge angled to the left (Figure 8.62). Except for the superior aspect of the liver, which is fused to the diaphragm, the entire liver is surrounded by a layer of visceral peritoneum. Within this peritoneum, the liver is enveloped further in a layer of dense irregular connective tissue.

The liver organ is divided into two primary lobes: the right lobe, which comprises the majority of the liver's mass; and the left lobe, which is

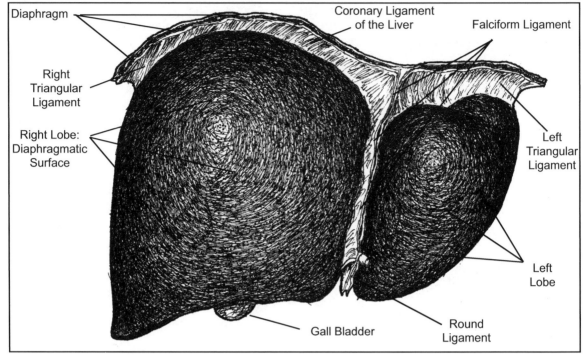

Figure 8.62. The Liver Organ.

smaller and extends slightly across the midline of the body. Two smaller lobes, the caudate lobe and the quadrate lobe, lie along the vertical border of the left and right lobes. The right and left lobes are separated by the falciform (sickle-shaped) ligament, which also connects to the diaphragm above, and to the right rectus-abdominis muscle in front. The round ligament (or ligamentum teres) is a remnant of the fetal umbilical vein, and it spans the distance between the liver and the navel, enmeshing itself into the falciform ligament. The liver is further anchored to the abdomen by the coronary ligament, and by two lateral ligaments.

In the average adult, the liver receives roughly 2 pints of blood every minute, equal to about 28% of the total cardiac output of blood. This blood supply enters the liver through both the hepatic artery and the hepatic portal vein (Figure 8.63). The hepatic artery divides into right and left branches which nourish the tissues of the right and left lobes of the liver respectively. The hepatic portal vein carries venous blood from the abdominal organs into the liver to be processed. It is important to note that the liver is the first internal organ to receive blood that has been exposed to the intestinal capillaries; for this reason the liver is especially susceptible to diseases originating in the digestive tract. Entering the underside of the liver, the hepatic portal vein then quickly divides into a network of capillaries that disperse blood throughout the liver.

The lobes of the liver are composed of numerous sesame seed sized lobules, which are the essential structural and functional units of the liver organ. Each lobule consists of numerous hepatic (liver) cells organized around a central vein. On a horizontal plane, a liver lobule gives the appearance of a roughly hexagonal plate of hepatic cells. These cells are arranged in branching, irregular, interconnected plates which are irrigated by venous capillaries, and which essentially stack together to give the lobule a somewhat oblong vertical dimension.

A portal triad flows vertically along each of the six corners of the lobule, and consists of a branch of the hepatic artery (carrying fresh blood into the liver tissue), a branch of the hepatic portal vein (carrying venous blood from the digestive system),

CHAPTER 8: THE TWELVE PRIMARY ORGANS, CHANNELS AND COLLATERALS

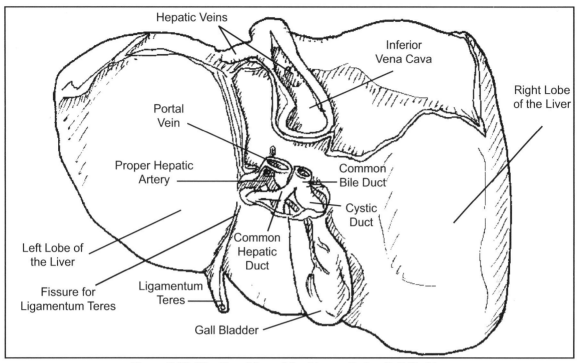

Figure 8.63. The Rear View of the Liver, with the Gall Bladder.
(Inspired by the original artwork of Dr. Frank H. Netter)

and a bile duct. Blood from both the hepatic artery and the hepatic portal vein flow through large capillaries (termed sinusoids) within the liver lobule. These sinusoids are surrounded by hepatic cells that essentially clean the blood as it flows past them. Sinusoids also contain hepatic macrophages (called Kupffer cells) which remove bacteria, old blood cells, and other debris from the blood. Each sinusoid empties into the vein at the center of each lobule. These veins then join together into interlobular veins which eventually flow into the hepatic veins. Cleansed blood is drained from the liver by the hepatic veins, which converge with the inferior vena cava before reaching the heart.

BILE SECRETION

Bile is secreted from the hepatic cells into tiny canals (called bile canaculi) that flow between every other row of cells, such that each row of hepatic cells has a bile canaculi on one side, and a sinusoid on the other. Bile is directed away from the center of the lobule, and on reaching the bile duct at the lobule's corner, it flows downward.

The bile secretions of the liver are directed through several ducts that ultimately join together to form the hepatic duct, which carries bile away from the liver. The cystic duct connects the gallbladder to the hepatic duct, and is the common duct through which bile enters and exits the gallbladder. The common bile duct flows from the junction of the cystic and hepatic ducts, and it is this duct that eventually delivers bile into the duodenum.

PHYSIOLOGY OF THE LIVER

The various functions of the liver can be arranged into the following categories: metabolism of carbohydrates, proteins, and lipids; storage of vitamins and minerals; phagocytosis; removal of poisons, drugs, and certain hormones; and the synthesis and excretion of bile (Figure 8.64). The Liver metabolism has the capacity to convert one nutrient into another nutrient, or to change the form of a nutrient to make it more appropriate for activation, storage, or excretion.

1. **Metabolism of Carbohydrates:** In combination with the pancreas, the liver helps to maintain a steady glucose level in the blood. When blood sugar levels are too high, the liver can draw glucose from the blood and convert it into glycogen (a molecule that is a composition of numerous smaller glucose molecules) for storage. The liver can also convert glucose into triglycerides for storage within the liver or muscle tissue. If there is a decrease in the blood-glucose level, the liver then converts the glycogen (or other available sugars such as lactose and galactose) it has stored back into its glucose form to be used by the cells. In a process known as gluconeogenesis, the liver is also capable of making glucose from lactic acid or from certain amino acids.

2. **Metabolism of Proteins:** The liver alters amino acids so that they can be used for ATP production or changed into fats or carbohydrates. The liver also removes ammonia (produced by bacteria in the GI tract, and also as a by-product of protein metabolism) and other nitrogenous wastes from the system by converting it into the much less toxic urea, which is then later excreted through the urine. Certain enzymes within the liver are capable of converting one amino acid into another, or converting one amino acid into an entirely different nutrient. Liver cells also synthesize heparin and most plasma proteins, such as albumin, alpha and beta globules, fibrinogen (used in blood coagulation), and prothrombin

3. **Metabolism of Lipids:** The liver manufactures cholesterol, some of which is then used in the production of bile. Among other things, cholesterol plays an important role in the creation of certain hormones and is necessary for the production of vitamin D. The liver also synthesizes various lipoproteins, which include both high-density lipoproteins (HDL) and low-density lipoproteins (LDL). Lipoproteins also combine with cholesterol, fatty acids, and triglycerides in order to transport them through the blood. Certain cells within the liver also store triglycerides, which are the body's most concentrated source of energy.

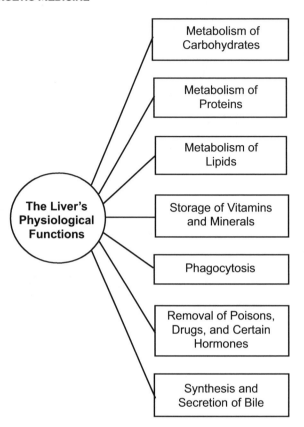

Figure 8.64. The Functions of the Liver
(Western Medical Perspective)

The liver breaks down fatty acids into acetyl coenzyme A, the excess of which is converted into ketone bodies. Other examples of lipids that are metabolized within the liver include phospholipids, steroids, and prostaglandins.

4. **Storage of Vitamins and Minerals:** The liver stores vitamins A, B-12, E, and K, and plays and important role in both the activation and storage of vitamin D. Minerals such as copper, iron (in the form of ferritin), and cobalt are also stored within the liver. These stored nutrients are later released into the bloodstream whenever they are needed by the body.

5. **Phagocytosis:** Within the liver, the Kupffer cells phagocytize (engulf or consume) worn out white and red blood cells as well as some bacteria. This process aids the immune system by removing unwanted material from the blood.

The iron and globulin thus extracted from the breakdown of erythrocytes is recycled, while the bilirubin (derived from heme) is excreted into the bile ducts. Resident bacteria within the GI tract further breakdown bilirubin after the bile is excreted into the intestines, giving the feces their normal brown color.

6. **Removal of Poisons, Drugs, and Certain Hormones:** The liver serves to detoxify the body by chemically altering or excreting certain drugs and organic compounds such as penicillin, sulfonamides, and erythromycin. The liver can also alter or excrete hormones such as estrogen, aldosterone, thyroid hormones, and steroid hormones. Various poisons such as DDT and other pesticides are removed from the bloodstream and stored within the liver. The liver also produces numerous protective, antitoxic substances.

7. **Synthesis and Excretion of Bile:** The liver's only digestive function is the creation and secretion of bile, which is released into the small intestine via the hepatic duct. When considered as a part of the digestive system, both the liver and gallbladder are thus seen as being accessory organs associated with the small intestine.

Bile, is a bitter yellowish substance consisting mainly of water, bile acids, bile salts, bile pigments, lecithin, cholesterol, electrolytes, and various fatty acids. Once delivered into the small intestine, bile salts and acids play an important role in the digestion of fats; though the secretion of bile is also a vehicle for the excretion of unwanted materials from the liver. Nearly one quart of bile is secreted each day by the liver. Secreted bile is stored and concentrated in the gallbladder, and when needed for digestion, it is transferred into the duodenum (uppermost portion of the small intestine) via a system of ducts. The bile secretions of the liver are directed through several ducts that ultimately join together to form the hepatic duct, which carries bile away from the liver. The cystic duct connects the gallbladder to the hepatic duct, and is the common duct through which bile enters and exits the gallbladder. The common bile duct flows from the junction of the cystic and hepatic ducts into the duodenum.

COMMON DISORDERS OF THE LIVER

Impairment of liver function can be at the root of a wide range of symptoms and functional disorders. Some of the most widely recognized disorders of the liver are Jaundice, Hepatitis, and Cirrhosis.

- **Jaundice:** Jaundice is a condition in which there is a buildup of bilirubin in the system, giving the eyes and skin a yellowish discoloration. The three main types of jaundice are: prehepatic jaundice (including neonatal jaundice), in which there is an excess production of bilirubin; hepatic jaundice (due to liver dysfunction); and extrahepatic (or obstructive) jaundice (caused by a blockage of bile drainage).

- **Hepatitis:** Hepatitis, of which jaundice can be a symptom, refers to either an acute or chronic inflammation of the liver. Acute hepatitis is usually non-viral, and can be caused by an overtaxing of the liver due to drug toxicity, oral-fecal contamination, or wild mushroom poisoning. Chronic hepatitis, of which there are now more than a dozen types, is generally attributed to a virus.

- **Cirrhosis:** Cirrhosis is a chronic inflammation and scarring of the liver usually resulting from chronic hepatitis, or from long term alcohol or drug abuse. Eventually, cirrhosis of the liver can lead to liver fibrosis, in which the liver has an excess of scar tissue inhibiting its proper functioning.

Other liver disorders include liver enlargement, portal hypertension, ascites (fluid buildup in the abdomen due to liver leakage), liver encephalopathy (brain deterioration due to blood toxicity), liver failure, and metabolic disorders such as hemochromatosis and Wilson's disease. Hepatocellular adenoma and hemangioma are examples of benign liver tumors, while liver cancers include hepatoma (primary liver cancer), cholangiocarcinoma, hepatoblastoma, and angiosarcoma. Congenital liver disorders include neonatal jaundice, biliary atresia, and choledochal cysts.

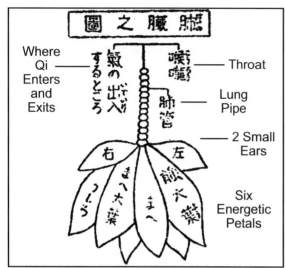

Figure 8.65. The Ancient Chinese Anatomical Diagram of the Lungs (Lu) Organ: *"Important Useful Notes on Acupuncture and Moxibustion,"* by Masatoyo Hongo (1718)

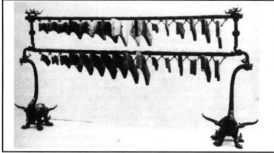

Figure 8.66. Suspended Musical Stones (Warring States Period, Kingdom of Chu)

THE LUNGS: FEI

The Lungs are solid Yin (Zang) Organs, and correspond to the Metal Element. Their associated Yang (Fu) Organ is the Large Intestine. Because the Lungs control the cycle of Qi circulation within the body, and are sometimes referred to as the "White Emperor."

In ancient Daoist imagery, it was taught that since the Lungs are the uppermost organs, they are compared to an eight petaled "Flowery Canopy," that shelters and protects all the other internal organs (Figure 8.65). However, in both the ancient *Yifang leiju* and *Yellow Court Classic* texts, the energetic patterns of the Lung Organs are also compared to "Suspended Musical Stones" (Figure 8.66).

Figure 8.67. Spirits of the Lungs (Lu) Organ: *Yifang Leiju (Classified Collection of Medical Recipes),* (Japanese reproduction - 1861)

ANCIENT LUNG ORGAN TEACHING

The following picture (Figure 8.67) is from the *Yifang leiju (Classified Collection of Medical Recipes)* section on the Five Viscera. The ancient text states:

"The Lungs are the Qi of Dui (Lake Trigram),
It carries the Essence of Metal,
and its color is white.

It looks like suspended
Musical Stones.

Its spirit has the form of a White Tiger.
The Lung engenders the Po Soul,
which is transformed into a Jade Child,
that is 7 cun tall.
It wears a plain garment
and holds a martial rod,
and goes in and out
of the Mansion of the Lung.

The Lung is sometimes said to have
Seven Spirit Children
and Fourteen Jade Women
guarding it."

Additionally, according to the ancient Daoist teachings of the *Yellow Court Classics,* the energetic function of the Lungs are described as follows:

"The Deity of the Lungs
has the shape of a White Tiger.
According to ancient Daoist teaching,
the internal energy of the Lung Organs
appear like Hanging Musical Stones,
which have eight petals total
(6 energetic petals & 2 small ears).

They are positioned on top of the internal organs,
enveloping and covering them like a Canopy.
Therefore, they are traditionally called
"The Flowery Canopy,"
and their deity is sometimes known as
"The Luminous Flower."

Although the Spirit of the Lungs is called
"Hua Hao" ("Brilliant Splendor"),
according to ancient Daoist teachings,
he is also given the name
"Xu Cheng" ("Void Formation").

The Nose is the Officer of the Lungs.
The Left Nostril is associated with
the "Geng" (Yang Metal Element) Heavenly Stem;
the Right Nostril is associated with
the "Xin" (Yin Metal Element) Heavenly Stem.

The Palace of the Lungs
resembles an Imperial Canopy.
Underneath this special canopy is a Boy Child,
who sits on a Jade Watch Tower.

It is here, that the Seven Princes
and 14 Jade Women who guard the Lungs,
transform Qi to externally respond
to the center position of the Nose.

The Boy Child wears
a plain White Brocaded Garment,
with a Yellow Scarf
floating around him like a cloud.
\
If your respiration is not well,
you will be rescued by
the Boy Child and Six Energies.
These immortal spirits
watch over the Lungs,
so that no disaster, harm,
or stagnation takes shape."

Figure 8.68. The Chinese Character "Fei" (Lungs)

CHINESE CHARACTER FOR THE LUNG: FEI

- **Fei:** The character "Fei" translates as "Lungs." It refers to the image of the Lung organs, and is divided into two sections. The character to the left, "Ji" depicts the Chinese ideogram for Body Tissue, Muscle or Flesh (all of which are forms of Connective Tissue).

The character to the right depicts an ideogram that is a representation of a creeping type of plant, branching upward from the soil of the Earth, like a fibrous vine. Together, both ideographs express the idea that the Qi of the Lungs are responsible for connecting into and enveloping the tissues, as well as spreading the Qi (Ying Qi and Weiqi) throughout the interior and exterior of the torso (Figure 8.68).

THE YIN AND YANG OF THE LUNGS

Traditional Chinese Medicine describes the Lungs as having two energetic aspects, Yin and Qi:
- **The Yin of the Lungs:** This pertains to the material structure of the Lungs.
- **The Qi of the Lungs:** This pertains to the physiological function of the Lungs.

THE LUNGS' METAL JING FORMATION

The Metal Jing is established in the fetus' body during the Sixth Lunar Month of pregnancy, and serves to stabilize the sinews and connective tissues. The energy of the Metal Jing is responsible for fetal formation and for the ability to form and maintain emotional bonding with others. Any faltering of the Metal Jing energy is commonly associated with problems of emotional attachment (e.g., autism).

After birth, the energy of the Metal Jing can be affected through the Color White, the Pungent Taste, and the "Shh," "Sss," and "Shang" Sounds.

THE LUNGS IN CHINESE MEDICINE

In Traditional Chinese Medicine, the Lungs function much in the same way as described in Western Medicine. The Lungs are viewed as part of the Respiratory System and are related to Water Metabolism, Blood Circulation, the Autonomic Nervous System, and the Immune System.

Traditional Chinese Medicine, however, expands the role of the Lungs to include the psycho-emotional aspects of integrity, attachment, and grief. The Lungs also exert a powerful spiritual influence on the individual, due to their relationship with the Po (Corporeal Soul).

To the ancient Daoists, the Lungs and its paired organ the Large Intestine energetically corresponded to the continual interactive energies of Heaven and Earth. For example (Figure 8.69):

- **The Lungs:** Within the upper thorax of the chest, the Yin Lung Organs physically as well as energetically surround the Yin Heart Organ. Because the Lungs are located within the Upper Burner, they were viewed as the internal representation of our energetic connection to Heaven, and contain the most rarefied form of our essential Qi.
- **The Large Intestine:** Within the abdomen, the Lungs' associated Yang Organ (the Large Intestine), physically as well as energetically surrounds the Heart's associated Yang Organ (the Small Intestine). Because the Large Intestines are located within the Lower Burner, they are seen as the internal representation of our energetic connection to Earth, and contain the most turbid form of our essential Qi.

In ancient China, it was believed that the tissues of both the Heart (Yin) and its associated organ the Small Intestine (Yang) contained the energy of the Fire Element, and were therefore Hot and Expansive. Because of this energetic pattern, the color "Red" was traditionally ascribed to these two internal organs.

In anatomical placement, the Lungs surround the Heart in the upper thoracic cavity of the chest, while the Large Intestines surround the Heart's associated organ, the Small Intestines in the abdominal region.

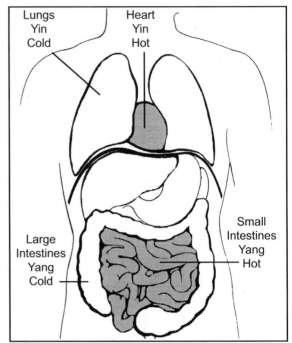

Figure 8.69. The ancient Chinese Yin and Yang relationship between the rhythmical patterns of the body's cardiopulmonary and digestive systems

It was believed that the tissues of both the Lungs (Yin) and its associated organ the Large Intestines (Yang) contained the energy of the Metal Element, and were therefore Cold and Contractive. Because of this energetic pattern, the color "White" was traditionally ascribed to these two internal organs. The continuous Yin and Yang energetic interactions of "Expansion and Contraction" manifesting from the Hot and Cold energetic properties of these internal organ systems, were believed to create the subtle peristaltic rhythmic patterns of both the Cardiopulmonary and Digestive Systems.

Prior to the 19th Century, certain Chinese Medical Texts expressed the belief that the Lungs were the first internal organs to complete their structural formation, occurring when a baby is born (this energetic completion enables the child to breathe and cry). These same texts state that at the end of life, the Lungs are the last internal organ to expire (this is because, if the Brain is dead but the Qi is not interrupted, the respiration will continue, the individual is still considered to be alive).

CHAPTER 8: THE TWELVE PRIMARY ORGANS, CHANNELS AND COLLATERALS

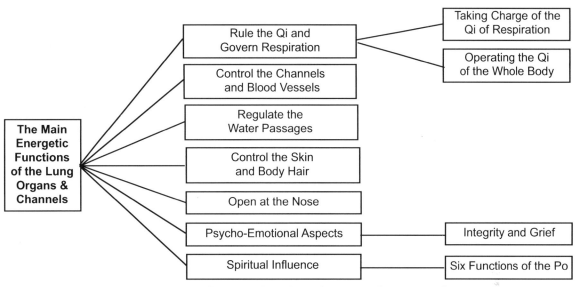

Figure 8.70. The Main Energetic Functions of the Lung Organs and Channels

THE LUNGS' ENERGETIC FUNCTION

According to Traditional Chinese Medicine, the main functions of the Lungs are to: Govern the Qi and Respiration, Control the Channels and Blood Vessels, Regulate the Water Passages, Control the Skin and Hair, Open to the Nose, express itself through the psycho-emotional aspects of integrity and grief, and exert an important spiritual influence via the Po (Corporeal Soul). These main functions are described as follows (Figure 8.70):

1. **Rule the Qi and Govern Respiration:** The Lungs are responsible for controlling the function and movement of Qi and serve in two specific ways: taking charge of the Qi of respiration, and operating the Qi of the whole body.

- **Taking Charge of the Qi of Respiration:** The main function of the Lungs is to regulate breath, controlling both Pulmonary and Cellular Respiration. The Lungs are the main organ responsible for respiration and for the gathering Heaven Qi. For this reason, the chest is sometimes called the "Upper Sea of Qi."

According to the *Huangdi Neijing Ling Shu* (*The Yellow Emperor's Inner Canon, Magical Pivot*),

"The Sea of Qi comes out of the Lungs,
Goes into the throat,
and facilitates inhalation and exhalation."

It is through the action of the Lungs' Respiration, that the Qi (energy) and gases (subtle substances) of the body are exchanged between the interior and exterior of the body. The taking in of fresh oxygen from the air during inhalation, and the expelling of wasted gas in the form of carbon dioxide during exhalation, function to maintain healthy internal organ regulation. This healthy exchange helps to keep the body's energetic and physical metabolism functioning smoothly.

- **Operating the Qi of the Whole Body:** The Lungs operate the Qi of the whole body through two ways: forming Zong Qi (Pectoral Qi), and controlling the ascending and descending, entering and exiting aspects of the body's life-force energy.

- **Forming Zong Qi (Gathering Qi):** When Heaven Qi (i.e., energy of the Sun, Moon, and Stars) and Earthly Qi (Environmental Energy) are absorbed into the body in the form of fresh air and "food essence" (also known as "Gu Qi" or "Food/Grain Energy"), they accumulate within the chest in order to create what is known in Traditional Chinese Medicine as "Zong Qi."

451

Zong Qi is sometimes translated as "Gathering Qi," "Qi of the Chest," "Pectoral Qi" and/or "Ancestral Qi." Its energetic function is to exit the body from the larynx, promoting the Lung's respiratory activities. Zong Qi is also responsible for the heartbeat, assisting the Lungs in the circulation of Qi, and assisting the Heart in the circulation of Blood. It functions to warm the tissues of the torso, including all the Yin viscera and the Yang bowels, and in this way, serves to regulate the physiology of the entire body.

- **Controlling the Ascending and Descending, Entering and Exiting:** The Lungs have the responsibility of causing the Qi and Body Fluids to flow throughout the entire body via the "True Qi" ("Zhen Qi"). The True Qi is formed by the Lungs, and has two main energetic components; "Weiqi" ("Protective Energy") and "Ying Qi" (Nourishing Energy).

    The Weiqi: Also known as "Guardian," or "Defensive" Qi, this special external protective energy flows throughout the muscles and skin, mainly outside the channels; it acts as an energetic custodian, who guards against and removes any and all external pathogenic invasions. There are three Weiqi fields, corresponding to each of the Three Dantians.

    The Ying Qi: This is a special form of Nutritive Energy, that flows internally throughout the body within the Channels and Blood Vessels. Its energetic function is to transform the nutrients gathered from food into nourishment for the Blood to absorb; and helps to provide the sustenance needed for maintaining healthy cells and organ tissues.

    Externally, the Lungs govern the "entering and exiting" of energy to and from the body (a function of the Weiqi). Internally, the Lungs are in charge of the "ascending and descending" movements of Qi and Body Fluids.

    The dispersing action of the Lungs assists in the spreading of the thin Body Fluids (Jin) throughout the skin and muscles via the Weiqi; and the distribution of the thick Body Fluids (Ye) to the Zang Fu Organs, Brain, joints and orifices via the Ying Qi.

- **Circulation of Qi:** The Lungs send Qi downward throughout the body. In particular, Qi is sent from the Lungs to the Heart, which receives and holds onto this Qi, transforming it into Blood and Body Fluids. Qi is also sent down to the Kidneys, which receive and hold onto it in order to maintain and strengthen the inhalation.

- **Circulation of Body Fluid (Jin and Ye):** The Lungs receive the vaporous form of the Body Fluids from the Spleen, and then separate them for circulation throughout the body. The Lungs liquefy the impure fluids and send them to the Heart. The Heart receives and holds these impure fluids, vaporizing and further separating part of the Body Fluids, sending them back to the Lungs. The Lungs then spread the vaporized Body Fluids to the skin in the form of a mist, which moistens the tissues and regulates sweating and the opening and closing of the pores.

- **The Entering and Exiting of Qi:** Like a fog descending from Heaven, the Lungs ensure the free movement of Qi throughout the body. In this aspect, the Lungs ensure that all of the organs receive the nourishment that they need via the distribution of Qi, Blood and Body Fluids. The Lungs also prevent excess or deficient accumulation of fluids.

2. **Control the Channels and Blood Vessels:** There is an ancient Chinese Medical saying, which states, "all Blood Vessels lead to the Lungs," meaning that all of the Blood within the body must pass through the Lungs.

    The Lungs also control the circulation of Qi in both the Blood Vessels and the Channels, in addition to being in charge of the dispersing or spreading of the body's protective energy throughout the Three Weiqi fields.

    According to the *Huangdi Neijing Su Wen (The Yellow Emperor's Inner Canon, Basic Questions)*,

"The Lungs receive the 100 Vessels in the Morning Audience."

In order to understand this statement, the reader should know that in ancient China, every morning, all of the Palace Officials would go to the Court to be assigned specific tasks.

Likewise, in the human body, every morning, the Qi of 100 Blood Vessels must go to the Lungs' "Courtyard," in order to be regulated and recharged to start the new day.

3. **Regulate the Water Passages:** The Lungs regulate the body's "Water Passages" (i.e., Sweat and Body Fluids), the opening and closing of the pores, the skin, and the texture of the body's hair.

   The Lungs receive the vaporous form of the Body Fluids (Jin and Ye) from the Spleen, and further separate them via the Heart for circulation throughout the body organs, tissues, and skin. The Kidneys also receive the Body Fluids from the Lungs and vaporizes a portion of them, sending this refined mist back to the Lungs in order to keep the Lung organs moist.

4. **Control the Skin and Body Hair:** The Lungs are directly exposed to the air through the organs of the Respiratory Tract (i.e., the nose, mouth, larynx, and trachea); and indirectly exposed to the air through their association with the skin (i.e., the pores, sweat glands and body hair).

   The Lungs receive the vaporous form of the Body Fluids from the Spleen, and then separates them for circulation throughout the body. The skin and body hair derive both their nourishment and their moisture directly from this function of the Lungs.

   The ancient Daoist Qigong masters believed that the hair follicles of the body contained both "Fa Men" ("Law Gates") and "Gui Men" ("Ghost Gates"). Each of these Gates are connected in pairs, and find their energetic expression in the respiration (inhalation and exhalation) of the body's pores, described as follows:

- **Fa Men:** In ancient Daoist teachings, there are 84,000 "Fa Men" ("Law Gates") contained within the hair follicles of the body. In Daoist Alchemy, the Fa Men act as special energetic portals, that are traditionally used as a way of absorbing Ling Qi (Spiritual Energy) from the environment into the body's Yuan Shen (Original Spirit), via the tissues, skin, and hair. Therefore, it is by way of these special "Law Gates" that an individual will experience the brighter spiritual aspects and radiant influences of the body's Hun.

   The Fa Men also allow the body's Hun to initiate a more profound spiritual influence on the individual's Yuan Shen (Original Heart/Mind). Once "Open" through deep quiescent meditation practice, the Fa Men naturally act as special talismanic controls, gathering and releasing Ling Qi and Ling Shen within the body's energetic fields, inevitably allowing it to become an "Immortal Body."

- **Gui Men:** In ancient Daoist teachings, there are 84,000 "Gui Men" ("Ghost Gates") contained within the hair follicles of the body. In Daoist Alchemy, the Gui Men act as special energetic portals, that are used as a way of absorbing the dark emotional aspects of the Po into the body's "Shadow Channels." The Shadow Channels are streams of "thought forms" that attach to each internal organ system after the individual is born. This acquired toxic energy is absorbed by the Po into the organ and channel systems in order to assist the Acquired Mind (Shen Zhi) in initiating energetic control over the body, inevitably causing the individual to die, and become a "ghost."

5. **Open at the Nose:** The Lung Qi opens externally at the nose via the throat, and is considered a "phonic-organ," energetically manifesting itself through the voice, for example:

- **Loud Voice:** When the Lung Qi is in excess the voice is too loud;
- **Soft Voice:** When it is deficient the voice is too soft.

   The nose's function of smelling is dependent mainly on the action of the Qi within the Lungs. According to the *Huangdi Neijing Su Wen (The Yellow Emperor's Inner Canon, Basic Questions)*,

> **"Heaven Nourishes Man Through the Five Qi."**

The Five Qi pertain to the following:

- **The Five Qi of Heaven:** Are the Five Climatic Conditions that manifest as Wind, Warmth, Cold, Dampness and Dryness.
- **The Five Qi of Earth:** Are the Five Flavors that manifest as Sour, Bitter, Sweet, Pungent and Salty.

- **The Five Qi of Man:** Are the Five Odors that manifest as Rancid, Scorched, Sweet, Fishy and Rotten.

  These Five Qi enter the body's tissues via respiration and environmental osmosis. Once absorbed into the body, the Five Qi penetrate into the Lungs and expand outward towards the Five Yin Organs, affecting the Qi circulation.

  In ancient Daoist teachings, the Jade Spirit of the Nose Ridge is known as " Ling Jian" ("Clever and Firm")

6. **Psycho-Emotional Aspects:** The Lungs are said to be the "Minister of Heaven," and are responsible for establishing the foundation of Qi for the entire body. The effects of the Hun and Po on the Lungs allow an individual to experience integrity and dignity in thoughts and actions (influenced by the Hun) or healthy grief (influenced by the Po). However, if the circulation of Qi becomes obstructed for long periods of time, the Lung Qi stagnation can give rise to chronic emotional turmoil, sometimes manifesting through energetic outbursts of crying or sinking into despair, (again influenced by the Po).

   The Lungs' positive spiritual attributes, influenced by the Hun, are the internal Virtues of Righteousness, Dignity, Integrity, and High Self-esteem.

   The negative psycho-emotional attributes of the Lungs, influenced by the Po, are the emotional states of Disappointment, Sadness, Grief, Despair, Shame, and Sorrow.

7. **Spiritual Influence:** The Lungs house the body's Seven Corporeal Souls (Po), which are responsible for self-protection and self-preservation. The Po are physical in nature and are attached to the body's Jing and Qi. The ancient Daoists defined the Po as the driving force of the individual's passions, expressed through his or her desires and ambition in life.

   As an internal guardian of the physical body, when the "animal spirit" is released, the energy of the "Po" manifests as the "Fierce Tiger General," whose need for self-protection and self-preservation is ruthless and has no boundaries. (Figure 8.71)

Figure 8.71. As a Guardian of the Physical Body, The "Po" manifest as the "Fierce Tiger General"

Figure 8.72. The Corporeal Spirits of the Seven Po

CHINESE IDEOGRAM OF THE PO

There are two parts to the Po ideogram. The character to the right represents the word "Gui" ("Ghost"), depicted by a head suspended above a vaporous body with an appendage symbolizing the whirlwind that accompanies its movements (Figure 8.72). The character to the left is the image for the color White (Bai). In Daoist Alchemy, the color white represents the Underworld or Realm of the Dead. Similar to the image of dried bones lying on the Earth. The Po are linked with the descending movement of Qi, and with the body's Jing. The Po are also said "to come and go, enter and exit," in association with the body's Jing.

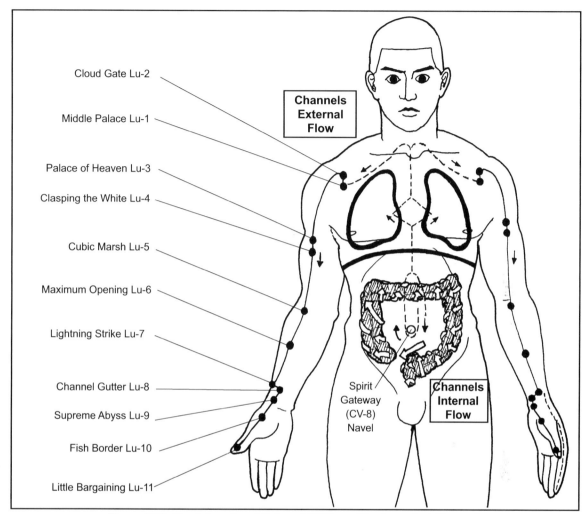

Figure 8.73. The Internal and External Qi Flow of the Lung (Lu) Channels

THE LUNG CHANNELS

The Lung Channels are Yin (Zang) Channels that flow externally from the torso to the hands.

- **The Internal Branches:** The main energetic river originates internally from the Middle Burner, in the middle of the chest. It extends from the navel up to the respiratory diaphragm, then descends downward, connecting with and spirally wrapping the Large Intestine Organ. From there, it ascends along the upper surface of the Stomach and through the diaphragm, where it branches to connect with both Lung Organs (Figure 8.73).

From the Lungs, the two rivers of Qi merge together and ascend into the pit of the throat, where they separate again into two channels. These channels travel beneath the clavicles.

- **The External Branches:** These two main channels then travel externally, descending the arms to end on the lateral side of each thumb.

A small stream of energy branches from each wrist at the Lightening Strike (or "Broken Sequence" "Lie Que") Lu-7 point, and runs directly to the radial side of the tip of the index finger, where it connects with a branch of the Large Intestine Channel.

Channels' Energy Flow

The energy of the Lung Channels acts on the Lungs, bronchi, throat, and larynx, as well as the skin, muscles, and nerves found along the channel pathways.

The Lung Channels store more Qi than Blood. This allows them to have a greater effect on the body's energetic and nervous functions, than on its physical substances and Blood functions.

At the High-Tide time period (3 a.m. to 5 a.m.), Qi and Blood abound in the Lung Organs and Lung Channels. At this time, the Lung Organs and Channels can more easily be dispersed and purged.

During Low-Tide (3 p.m. to 5 p.m.), the Lung Organs and Channels can more readily be tonified.

If the Lung Qi combines with Liver Qi and stagnates in the throat area, a condition known as a "Plum Pit" (i.e., "a knot in the throat") will develop at the "pit of the throat" (i.e., Heaven's Chimney: CV-22).

The Influence of Climate

In the Autumn months, the Lung Qi becomes more pronounced. Therefore, the Lung Qi will become more active in individuals who already possess strong Lung Qi. Likewise, the Lung Qi may also become more deficient in those individuals who have weak Lung Qi.

During the Autumn season, the excessive consumption of Pungent food or beverages and an overexposure to Dryness can further impede and weaken the Lung Qi.

Because the Lungs need a certain amount of moisture to function, they are easily injured by Dryness, which can interfere with the functions of the Lungs. Additionally, an exposure to External Wind Cold, Wind Heat, and Damp Climates can also interfere with the proper functioning of the Lungs.

The Influence of Taste, Color, and Sound

- The Pungent Taste (e.g., garlic, green onions, etc.) can be used to tonify both the Lungs and Large Intestine; although excessive consumption of these flavors can weaken them.
- The White Color is used to tonify the Lungs and Large Intestine Organs and Channels.
- The "Shhh", "Sss" and "Shang" Sounds are used to purge the Lungs and Large Intestine.

Lung Pathology

Dysfunctions of the Lung Organs and Channels can result in diseases of the chest or Lungs, as well as diseases on the radial side of the upper arm and palmar area of the hand. The main symptoms associated with imbalances of the Lung Organs and Channels are described as follows:

- **The Respiration:** The Lungs keep the respiratory passages open and disseminate vital Qi throughout the body. If these functions are impeded, obstructions of the nose, coughing, dyspnea, and fullness of the chest may occur.

   The Lungs also function to cleanse the inhaled air and to keep the Qi flowing downward. If these functions are impeded, coughing, asthma, oliguria (scanty urine production), and edema may occur.

- **The Nose:** Since the Lungs have their external orifice at the nose, stuffy nose, nasal discharge, and impairment of the sense of smell are common symptoms when the Lungs are being attacked by a pathogenic invasion of Wind and Cold.

T.C.M. Patterns of Disharmony

Patterns of Lung Disharmony are divided into Syndromes of Deficient Lung Qi, Deficient Lung Yin, Lung Heat, Invasion of the Lungs by Wind, and the Retention of Phlegm in the Lungs, described as follows (Figure 8.74 and 8.75):

1. **Deficient Lung Qi:** Because the Lungs rule the body's Qi, they play an important role in patterns of Qi Deficiency. Deficient Lung Qi can manifest from a Prenatal (Congenital) Condition, an invasion of the Lungs by Wind, or from the retention of Phlegm in the Lungs.

   Symptoms can manifest as fatigue, weak cough, weak voice, lack of desire to speak, shortness of breath, weak respiration, wheezing, asthma, spontaneous daytime perspiration, slight cough with no phlegm, allergic rhinitis, and enuresis or incontinence.

2. **Deficient Lung Yin:** Deficient Lung Yin may manifest through symptoms such as dry un-

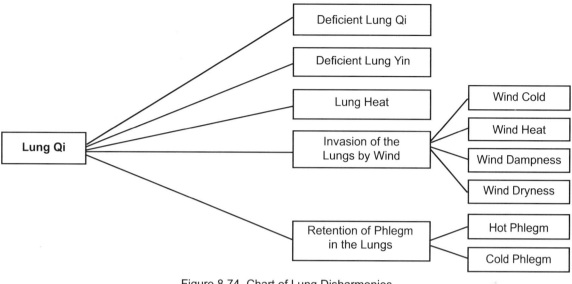

Figure 8.74. Chart of Lung Disharmonies

productive cough, dry cough in short bursts, asthma, emaciation, malar flush, afternoon fever and "Five Palms Heat." In the condition of Five Palms Heat (also known as "Five Center Heat," or "Sweating of the Five Palms") the patient experiences Heat in the palms of the hands and soles of the feet, accompanied by Heat and agitation in the chest or head area.

3. **Lung Heat:** Heat within the Lungs can cause the following symptoms: a feeling of Heat and restlessness, common cold, influenza, cough, sinusitis, breathlessness, and atrophy syndrome.

4. **Invasion of the Lungs by Wind:** Of all the Yin Organs, the Lungs are the most susceptible to the invasion of External Pathogenic Factors. The Lungs are especially vulnerable to Wind, especially Wind Cold and Wind Heat, which can transform into each other.

    Symptoms of Wind Invasion in the Lungs differ according to the specific nature of the invading pathogenic Wind (Cold, Hot, Damp, Dry), but generally include itchy throat, cough, nasal drip, headaches, chills, fever, sweating and aversion to wind.

    - **Wind Cold:** When invading the Lungs, Wind Cold usually enters the patient through the pores of the skin and body hair, both of which are ruled by the Lungs. If the Lungs' energetic field is invaded by Wind Cold, this can cause the Lung Qi to become impure. The impure Lung Qi then ascends, causing obstructions in the pores, resulting in a Wind Cold syndrome. This can cause the following symptoms: headache, cough, aches at the nape of the neck, chills and fever, the common cold, influenza, breathlessness, asthma, allergic rhinitis and an aversion to cold.

    - **Wind Heat:** When invading the Lungs, Wind Heat usually enters the body by way of the mouth and nose. The nose is the orifice of the Lungs and the direct opening into the Lung organ. If the Lungs' energetic field is invaded by Wind Heat, it can cause the Lung Qi to become impure, ascend, and impede the ability of the pores to expel pathogenic evils, resulting in a Wind Heat Syndrome. This can cause the following symptoms: chills and fever, headache, sore throat, cough, the common cold, influenza, asthma, allergic rhinitis, sinusitis, and a slight aversion to cold.

    - **Wind Dampness:** This is a type of Wind Cold Syndrome, which consists of both Wind and Dampness invading either the skin (causing itching and rashes) or the channels and joints (causing painful obstruction syndrome). If the Lungs' energetic field is invaded by Wind Dampness, the following symptoms may

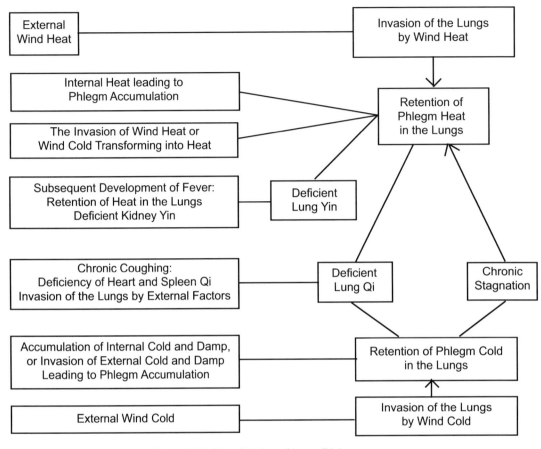

Figure 8.74. The Origins of Lung Disharmony

arise: skin rashes, swollen joints, body aches, headaches, the common cold, and influenza.
- **Wind Dryness:** When invading the Lungs, Wind Dryness can cause symptoms such as dryness, itchy sore throat, dry lips, dry mouth, the common cold, influenza, cough, and nose bleeds.

5. **Retention of Phlegm in the Lungs:** Phlegm is considered a secondary disease factor, derived from either Internal or External Dampness. The Spleen forms the Phlegm, and the Lungs store it. As a Lung disease progresses from a Cold to a Hot condition, the patient's mucus (Phlegm) changes color. The pathological condition of the Phlegm progresses from clear watery, to yellow and thick, to green and pussy, and finally to brown and red as heat increases. Internal conditions leading to the retention of Phlegm in the Lungs can arise due to Chronic Qi Deficiency, Kidney Yang Deficiency, Spleen Deficiency or Lung Deficiency. External conditions leading to the retention of Phlegm in the Lungs can arise from excess conditions that are due to the Invasion of Wind Heat, Wind Cold, or Dampness.

- **Lung Phlegm Heat:** This can cause the following symptoms: influenza, the common cold, cough with yellow or green expectoration, breathlessness, and a sensation of oppression in the chest.
- **Cold-Damp Phlegm invading the Lungs:** This can cause the following symptoms: a feeling of heaviness, cough with clear or white profuse expectoration, wheezing, nausea, poor appetite, and breathlessness.

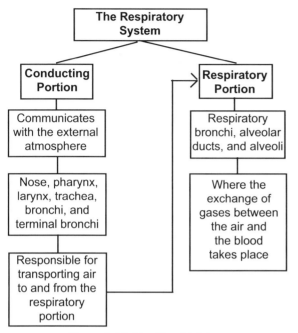

Figure 8.76. The Two Divisions of the Respiratory System

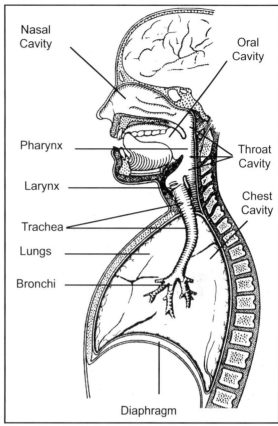

Figure 8.77. The Anatomy of the Respiratory System

ANATOMY OF THE RESPIRATORY SYSTEM

The lungs are the primary organs of respiration. The lungs are paired organs, roughly cone-shaped, located on both sides of the chest and immediately surrounded by the pleural membrane. Between the right and left lung lies the mediastinum, which contains the heart, its main blood vessels, the esophagus, and the bronchi. The lungs have their base at the diaphragm, and extend upward to their apex, which (for each lung) is located just above and deep into the clavicles. The lungs lie closely against the ribs along their lateral, anterior, and posterior surfaces.

The respiratory system can functionally be divided into two portions: the Conducting Portion, and the Respiratory Portion (Figure 8.76). The lungs communicate with the external atmosphere via the Conducting Portion of the respiratory system, which consists of the nose, pharynx, larynx, trachea, bronchi, and terminal bronchi (Figure 8.77). These interconnecting tubes and cavities serve to transport air to and from the Respiratory Portion, which is where the exchange of gases between the air and the blood takes place. The Respiratory Portion consists of the respiratory bronchi, alveolar ducts, and alveoli. Anatomically, the respiratory system is sometimes also divided into the Upper Respiratory System (nose and pharynx) and the Lower Respiratory System (larynx, trachea, bronchi, and lungs) (Figure 8.78).

The entire Respiratory Tract is covered with a thin layer of protective mucous that serves to keep the tissue moist, and to protect it from airborne particles such as dust and bacteria. This mucous contains numerous immune cells (i.e. macrophages and antibacterial enzymes). Pathogens are continuously being swept towards the pharynx (and eventually into the stomach) by the tiny hair-like cilia that line the respiratory passages. Common examples of this mucous movement are sniffling and the clearing of the throat.

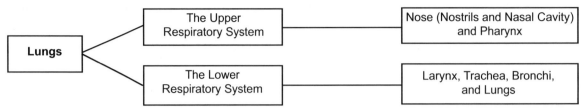

Figure 8.78. The Upper and Lower Respiratory Systems of the Lungs

THE UPPER RESPIRATORY SYSTEM

The upper respiratory system consists of the nose (nostrils and nasal cavity) and the pharynx, which is described as follows:

The Nose: Nostrils and Nasal Cavity

The external portion of the nose connects the nasal cavity to the external atmosphere, and includes the nasal Bones (the bridge of the nose), a supportive and semi-flexible structure of cartilage, and the soft tissue of the nostrils. The internal portion of the nose (also known as the sinuses) is a large cavity in the skull immediately superior to the mouth and inferior to the cranium.

The nasal cavity includes the entire area inside of the external and internal nose, and is divided into right and left sides by a midline nasal septum. The structure of the nasal cavity contains several shelf-like projections (conchae) that serve to create turbulence within the sinuses. The arrangement of these lateral shelves causes the inhaled air to twist and whirl, thus increasing the internal surface area exposed to the air. The tissues of the nasal cavity are richly supplied with blood vessels, and the exposed surface area is covered with countless tiny hairs and lined with olfactory and respiratory mucosa. As the incoming air is directed through the sinuses, nongaseous particles are filtered out by these tiny hairs and trapped in the mucous lining, the excess of which drains downward into the stomach. Every day the nasal cavity produces roughly a quart of this essential mucous.

The internal structure of the nose allows for three important functions:

- Filtering, moistening, and warming the incoming air
- Receiving olfactory stimuli (smell)
- Modifying speech sounds

The Pharynx

The pharynx, commonly called the throat, connects the nasal cavity and the mouth to the larynx. The auditory (eustachian) tubes open from the lateral walls of the pharynx, and serve to equalize atmospheric pressure within the ear. Pairs of tonsils are located throughout the pharynx.

THE LOWER RESPIRATORY SYSTEM

The lower respiratory system consists of the larynx, trachea, bronchi, and lungs, described as follows:

The Larynx: Voice Box

The larynx, or voice box, connects the pharynx with the trachea and has two important functions. The first of these functions is accomplished by the epiglottis, a leaf-shaped flap of cartilage that serves to insure that only the passageway from the throat to the trachea or the passageway from the throat to the esophagus is open at any one time. The second important function of the larynx is voice production, involving the combined action of several pairs of cartilaginous vocal cords. Another cartilage formation within the larynx forms the externally visible "Adam's apple."

The Trachea: Windpipe

The trachea, or windpipe, is a tubular passageway that descends from the larynx. Its structure consists of numerous interconnected C-shaped rings of cartilage, providing a passageway that is both rigid and flexible. The posterior portion of the trachea lies immediately against the esophagus. The trachea ends within the mediastinum, where it splits into the two primary bronchi.

The Bronchi

The right and left primary bronchi are formed by the division of the trachea at the level of the sternum, and are the beginnings of the internal

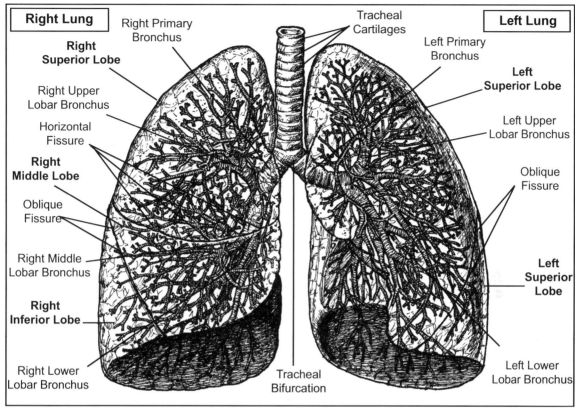

Figure 8.79. The Lung (Lu) Organ

branch-like structures of the right and left lungs. This branching pattern of the lungs is known as the bronchial (or respiratory) tree, and can be effectively compared to the branching pattern of the vascular system.

THE LUNGS IN WESTERN MEDICINE

According to Western Anatomy, the external borders of the lungs are defined by the pleural membrane, which consists of two layers of serous (watery) membrane and the lubricated cavity between them (Figure 8.79). The outer membrane (parietal pleura) is attached to the wall of the thoracic cavity, while the inner layer (visceral pleura) covers the lungs themselves. The space between them is known as the pleural cavity, and is filled with a lubricating substance that decreases the friction between the parietal and visceral pleura as they slide against each other during the expansive and contractive phases of the breathing process. Thus it is the pleural membranes that allow the lungs to move freely within the thorax.

The two lungs differ slightly in both size and shape. The left lung is slightly smaller than the right, as there is a notch-like indentation on the medial aspect of the left lung that is molded to accommodate the heart. Because the diaphragm is higher on the right side (to accommodate the liver), the right lung is shorter than the left lung is. The right lung is also thicker and broader than the left lung, and it consists of three lobes, while the left lung has only two. Within each lung, these lobes are separated from each other by fissures.

Each lung receives a primary bronchus that further divides within the lung into secondary and tertiary bronchi, which themselves divide into bronchioles, terminal bronchioles (smaller), and respiratory bronchioles (microscopic). The respiratory bronchioles further subdivide into alveolar ducts, which lead directly into the alveoli,

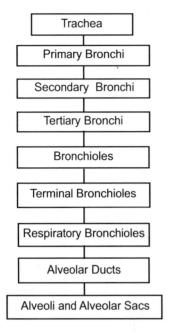

Figure 8.80. The Bronchial Tree

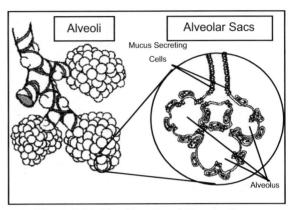

Figure 8.81. The Alveoli and Alveolar Sacs

and alveolar sacs (two or more alveoli that share a common opening) where the bulk of gas exchange takes place (Figure 8.80).

Each lobe of the lungs receives a secondary bronchus and contains a number of pyramid-shaped structures called bronchopulmonary segments. There are ten bronchopulmonary segments in each lung, and each of these receives a single tertiary bronchus. Each of the bronchopulmonary segments has many smaller compartments, termed lobules, that are each fed by a branch from a terminal bronchiole. Each lobule is wrapped in a layer of elastic connective tissue, and also contains an arteriole, a venule, and a lymphatic vessel. It is within these lobules that the smallest bronchioles subdivide into alveolar ducts, which are themselves covered with the essential respiratory structures: the balloon-like alveoli. The alveoli serve to maximize the amount of surface area of the respiratory membrane that is exposed to the incoming air. The average adult has over 300 million alveoli, creating a total respiratory surface area of over 70 square meters.

The alveoli are densely clustered together into sacs which lie along the alveolar ducts, giving the appearance of bunches of grapes opening into a common chamber (Figure 8.81). The alveoli are separated from the capillaries by a very thin membrane known as the respiratory or alveolar-capillary membrane. This respiratory membrane is thin enough to allow for the exchange of oxygen (absorbed from the air by the red blood cells) and carbon dioxide (released by the red blood cells into the air within the alveoli) between the air-filled alveoli and the blood. Trace amounts of other gases and fine particles are also exchanged. Most of the alveoli perform this function of diffusing respiratory gases through the thin alveolar-capillary membrane that defines the border between them and the capillaries. However, a few alveoli (type II alveoli) have the function of secreting a liquid surfactant that prevents the collapse of the other alveoli.

Blood Supply to the Lungs

The lungs receive a double blood supply. One route brings blood into the lungs for the nourishment and maintenance of the lung tissue, while another route brings deoxygenated blood into contact with the alveoli before sending it out to the rest of the body. The tissue of the lungs receives oxygenated blood from the bronchial arteries, while deoxygenated blood flows out primarily by way of the bronchial veins. Blood that is to be oxygenated by the lungs is pumped out from the right ventricle of the heart and is delivered by the pulmonary arteries, which accompany the primary bronchi into the lungs. The pulmonary arteries quickly branch out within each lung, eventually forming the pulmonary capillary networks that surround the alveoli. Oxygen-rich blood is then carried away from the lungs by the pulmonary veins, which lead to the left atrium of the heart. The left ventricle of the heart then pumps this fresh blood throughout the body.

Respiration

The primary purpose of respiration is to deliver oxygen to the cells and to remove carbon dioxide from them. The actual process of respiration can effectively be divided into three stages: pulmonary ventilation, external (or pulmonary) respiration, and internal (or tissue) respiration. Both pulmonary respiration and tissue respiration are intimately connected with the distribution and content of the blood. The three stages of breathing are described as follows (Figure 8.82):

- **Pulmonary Respiration:** This is what is normally referred to as breathing, and consists of the inhalation and exhalation of air arising from the exchange of gases between the inside of the body and the external atmosphere.
- **External Respiration:** This refers to the diffusion of gases across the respiratory membrane. This involves both the oxygenation of the blood, and the diffusion of carbon dioxide (and trace amounts of other material) from the blood into the alveoli of the lungs.
- **Internal (Tissue) Respiration:** This is the exchange of gases between the blood and the cells that takes place throughout the body at the level of the capillaries. In addition to being dependent on the two previous stages of respiration, this last phase of respiration is completely reliant on the ability of the heart and blood vessels to deliver a continuous supply of fresh blood to all areas of the body.

Physiology of Respiration: Inhalation

In order for inhalation to occur, the lungs must expand. This is primarily caused by the contraction of the diaphragm in conjunction with the external intercostals, though numerous other muscles surrounding the rib cage (erector spinae,

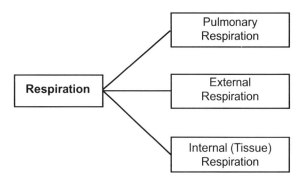

Figure 8.82. The Three Stages of Respiration

sternocleidomastoid, pectoralis minor, and scalenes) are involved to a lesser extent, particularly during abnormally deep or labored breathing. Of all the muscles involved in the breathing process, the diaphragm is the most important. The diaphragm is a dome shaped skeletal muscle that is attached to the inferior portions of the rib cage, thus separating the abdominal and thoracic cavities. The diaphragm exerts a downward pull on the pleural cavity as it contracts, while contraction of the external intercostals pulls the chest upward and outward. The resulting expansion of the thoracic cavity creates a negative internal pressure (relative to the atmospheric pressure outside the body) that causes air to flow in through the respiratory passages and fill the lungs.

Physiology of Respiration: Exhalation

Normal exhalation is a passive process that takes place when the diaphragm and the muscles of the rib cage relax. The passive recoil action of the elastic connective tissues surrounding and supporting the rib cage, in conjunction with the elastic qualities of the lung tissue itself, creates a positive internal pressure (relative to the atmospheric pressure outside the body) while gently pulling the thoracic cavity inward; this causes the lungs to expel air while contracting to return to their resting size.

Forced exhalation (due to obstruction or labored breathing) requires an additional and active muscular contraction that further reduces the size of the thoracic cavity. This contraction involves the action of certain muscles around the ribs (primarily the internal intercostals) that contract to decrease the size of the rib cage, and also the action of various abdominal muscles (rectus abdominis, transverse abdominis, internal obliques, and external obliques) that compress the abdominal viscera and thus exerts an upward force on the diaphragm as they contract.

Diaphragmatic & Costal Breathing

- **Diaphragmatic Breathing,** often called abdominal breathing, involves the near exclusive use of the diaphragm for the process of inhalation. This is almost always associated with the outward expansion of the abdomen that takes place as the diaphragm pushes downward on the abdominal viscera during the process of inhalation.
- **Costal Breathing,** also known as chest (or thoracic) breathing, refers to a breathing pattern that relies primarily on the contraction and release of various intercostals and other muscles surrounding the rib cage.

Respiratory Volumes

The total amount of inhaled or exhaled air varies according to many different factors. In order to describe the capacities in different stages of respiration, several descriptive terms have been developed. About 500 ml of air enters and leaves the respiratory passages with each normal breath; this amount is known as the tidal volume. Nearly 150 ml of this air remains within the anatomically dead space of the respiratory passages, leaving about 350 ml that actually reaches the alveoli.

During deep breathing, the amount of inhaled air can be up to 3100 ml or more above the average tidal volume of 500 ml; this is known as the inspiratory reserve volume. Similarly, a forced exhalation can expel an average of 1200 ml more air than the 500 ml released during a passive exhalation; this amount of exhaled air is known as the expiratory reserve capacity. Even after a forced exhalation, an amount of air known as the residual volume, about 1200 ml on average, remains in the lungs to prevent lung collapse, and to insure that the alveoli stay slightly inflated.

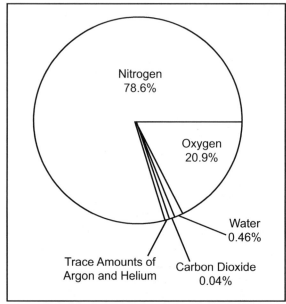

Figure 8.83. The Average Content of Inhaled Air

Respiratory Capacities

The average healthy male has a total lung capacity of about 6 liters, while the capacity of the average female is slightly less due to her smaller size. Because of the differences in atmospheric pressure, an individual living at sea level will develop a relatively smaller total lung capacity than that of an individual living at a high altitude. As noted above, not all of this air can be exhaled at any one time. The vital capacity, about 4,800 ml, represents the maximum amount of exchangeable air. Vital capacity decreases with age, and is decisively less in smokers than in nonsmokers. The inspiratory capacity, about 3,600 ml, refers to the amount of air that can be inhaled after a tidal inhalation. Similarly, the functional residual capacity, roughly 2,400 ml, refers to the amount of air remaining in the lungs after a tidal exhalation.

It is estimated that a normal adult breathes about 12 times a minute, 720 times per hour, 17,280 times per day. This translates as an average exchanged air volume (excluding the air held in the dead air space of the respiratory passages), known as the alveolar ventilation rate, of 4200 ml per minute, 252,000 ml (252 liters) per hour, and 6,048,000 ml (6,048 liters) per day. Rapid shallow breathing does little to increase the alveolar ventilation rate, because of the amount of inspired air that remains in the dead air space within the respiratory passages. Slow deep breathing, on the other hand, can drastically increase the amount of gaseous exchange within the lungs, as the amount of available air increases much further above the 150 ml of dead air space than occurs during tidal or shallow breathing.

The average content of the inhaled air is as follows (Figure 8.83): nitrogen - 78.6%, oxygen - 20.9%, carbon dioxide 0.04%, water - 0.46%. The atmosphere also contains trace amounts of other inert gases such as argon and helium. Exhaled air contains less oxygen (about 16%), and significantly more carbon dioxide (4.5%) and water vapor. About 200 ml of oxygen is diffused across the respiratory membrane and absorbed into the blood each minute.

Common Disorders of the Lungs and Respiratory System

Common disorders of the lungs include: rhinitis (inflammation of the mucous membranes of the nose), sinusitis (sinus infection), sore throat, laryngitis, coryza (common cold), influenza (flu), tuberculosis, cystic fibrosis, pulmonary embolism (the presence of a blood clot that obstructs pulmonary circulation), pulmonary edema (accumulation of interstitial fluid in and around the alveoli), pneumonia, pleurisy (inflammation of the pleura), pneumothorax (air in the plural cavity), hemothorax (blood in the pleural cavity), and atelectasis (collapsed lung). Diseases that involve some degree of obstruction of the air passages, such as asthma, diphtheria (enlarged respiratory mucous membranes), bronchitis, and emphysema (disintegration of the alveolar walls), come under the category of chronic obstructive pulmonary disease, or COPD.

Disorders involving respiratory failure at the level of tissue respiration include various types of hypoxia, a condition in which there is a low level of oxygen available to the cells. The major classes of hypoxia are described as follows: hypoxic (or hypoxemic) hypoxia, in which there is a low relative pressure of oxygen in the arterial blood; anemic hypoxia, caused by the hypofunction of hemoglobin; stagnant hypoxia, in which the blood is unable to deliver oxygen to the cells fast enough; and histionic hypoxia, in which the cells are unable to properly utilize the delivered oxygen. Elevated levels of carbon monoxide in the atmosphere can also lead to hypoxia, as even small amounts of inhaled carbon monoxide (as little as 1%) can drastically reduce the ability of hemoglobin to carry oxygen.

Apnea is a term used to describe the cessation of respiration (such as sleep apnea). Dyspnea refers to any condition in which breathing is painful or difficult, and tachypnea refers to rapid breathing. Respiratory distress syndrome, also called glassy lung disease, is a lung disease that affects newborns. Sudden infant death syndrome (SIDS) has also been linked to several respiratory disorders.

VOLUME 1, SECTION 1: FOUNDATIONS OF CHINESE ENERGETIC MEDICINE

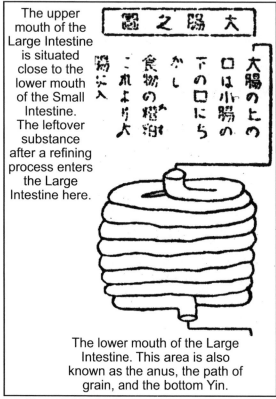

Figure 8.84. The Ancient Chinese Anatomical Diagram of the Large Intestine (LI) Organ: *"Important Useful Notes on Acupuncture and Moxibustion,"* by Masatoyo Hongo (1718)

THE LARGE INTESTINE: DA CHANG

The Large Intestine is a tubular Yang (Fu) Organ (Figure 8.84), belongs to the Metal Element, and its associated Yin (Zang) Organ is the Lungs.

The Large Intestine communicates with the body's skin, and with the anus. During the Han Dynasty, the ancient Chinese believed the Heavenly Hun (Yang souls) and Earthly Po (Yin souls) separated at the time of death. The Hun would leave the body through the Baihui, located at the top of the head; while the Po would stay with the corpse and eventually leave the body through the anus. According to ancient Daoist teachings, the Large Intestine is responsible for controlling the departure of the Po after the death of the body, through the "Po Men" ("Gate of the Po"), which is located at the anus.

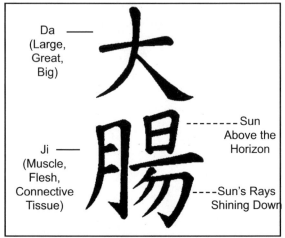

Figure 8.85. The Chinese Characters "Da Chang" (Large Intestine)

CHINESE CHARACTER FOR LARGE INTESTINE: DA CHANG

The Chinese character "Da Chang" translates as "Large Intestine." It refers to a general description of the image of the Large Intestine organ, and is composed of two images (Figure 8.85):

- **Da:** The first character "Da" translates as "Large," "Great," or "Big."
- **Chang:** The second character "Chang" translates as "Intestine," and is divided into two ideographs:

The character towards the left, "Ji" depicts the Chinese ideogram for Body Tissue, Muscle or Flesh (all of which are forms of Connective Tissue).

The character on the right depicts the image of "the Sun above the horizon, with its rays shining downward." This image expresses the Heavenly Yang influence on this particular bowel organ.

The ideograph expresses the image of the Sun enriching and transforming something within the flesh, and conveys the Large Intestines digestive process.

Together, the Chinese characters "Da Chang" can be translated as, "the Large Heavenly Transformation occurring within the Flesh."

The Large Intestines command the body's "Jin" (i.e., the flowing intestinal fluids).

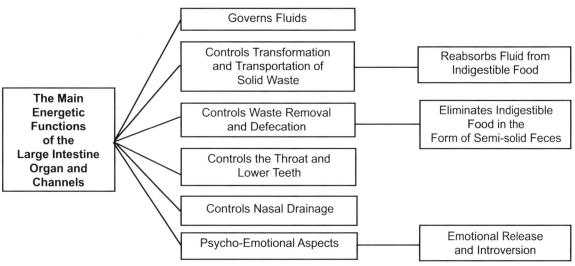

Figure 8.86. The Main Energetic Functions of the Large Intestine Organ and Channels

THE LARGE INTESTINE IN CHINESE MEDICINE

The functions of the Large Intestine described in Traditional Chinese Medicine are similar to those found in Western Medicine. However, some of the functions that are attributed to the Large Intestine in Western Medicine (such as controlling the transformation and transportation of food and fluids throughout the digestive system) are assigned to the Spleen from a Chinese medical perspective.

In Chinese Medicine, the Large Intestine also has a number of psycho-emotional components which exert an influence on the body's functions.

According to Traditional Chinese Medicine, the main functions of the Large Intestine are to: govern fluids, control transformation and transportation of solid waste, control waste removal and defecation, control the throat and lower teeth, control nasal drainage, and express itself through the psycho-emotional aspects of emotional release and introversion (Figure 8.86). These functions are described as follows:

1. **Governs Fluids:** The Large Intestine organ is said to govern Body Fluids (any fluid or semifluid substance in the body). It reabsorbs the fluid from indigestible food, and then eliminates waste from the body in the form of semi-solid feces.

2. **Controls Transformation and Transportation of Solid Waste:** The Large Intestine's main function is to receive the fluid form of food essence from the Small Intestines. After it absorbs this food essence, the Large Intestine is responsible for the transformation and transportation of solid waste in the body, absorbing water and eliminating the waste as fecal matter.

3. **Controls Waste Removal and Defecation:** The Lungs ability to send Qi downward depends on the Large Intestine's role in excreting waste. Consequently, the descending Lung Qi supplies the Large Intestines with the necessary Qi needed for defecation.

4. **Controls the Throat and Lower Teeth:** The Large Intestine controls the throat and lower teeth.

5. **Controls Nasal Drainage:** The Large Intestine controls the drainage of the nose.

6. **Psycho-Emotional Aspects:** The Large Intestine is both energetically and physically associated with letting go of impurity. Emotional imbalances such as unhealthy attachments, or the inability to let go of past people, places and things often have their root in the Large Intestine. Because the Large Intestine is associated with the Lungs, it is equally affected by the emotions of sadness, grief, and worry. An energetic imbalance in the Large Intestine can result in physical weakness and provoke emotional introversion,

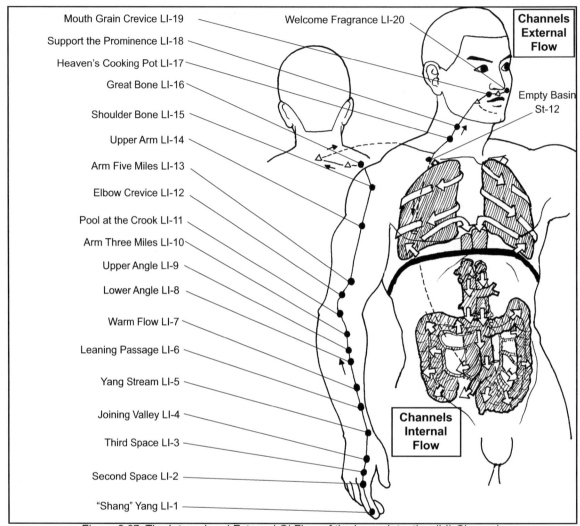

Figure 8.87. The Internal and External Qi Flow of the Large Intestine (LI) Channels

accompanied by feelings of depression, irritability, discouragement, distress, and apathy. Strong emotions of fear or panic can produce an energetic stool reflex reaction in the Large Intestine resulting in a spontaneous defecation.

THE LARGE INTESTINE CHANNELS

The Large Intestine Channels are Yang Channels that flow externally from the hands to the head (Figure 8.87).
- **The External Branches:** The Large Intestine Channels originate externally from the tips of the index fingers, ascending the arms, and crossing the shoulders, where they connect with the 7th cervical vertebra before splitting into two branches.

  One of the two branches ascends externally through the neck and cheek to the gums of the lower teeth. It then curves around the upper lip before flowing to the opposite side of the nose, to connect with the Stomach Channels.
- **The Internal Branches:** One set of branches descends internally and spirally wraps the Lungs, before flowing downward to permeate into the Large Intestine.

Channels' Energy Flow

The energy of the Large Intestine Channels acts on the skin, muscles, and nerves found along the channel pathways.

The Large Intestine Channels contain equally abundant amounts of both Qi and Blood. Therefore the Large Intestine Channels influence both the body's energetic and nervous system functions, as well as the Blood and physical substances of the tissues.

At the High-Tide time period (5 a.m. to 7 a.m.), Qi and Blood abound in the Large Intestine Organ and Channels. Therefore at this time, the Large Intestine Organ and Channels can more easily be dispersed and purged. During Low-Tide (5 p.m. to 7 p.m.), the Large Intestine Organ and Channels can more readily be tonified.

The Influence of Climate

An External Cold, Damp Cold, or Dry Climate can interfere with the proper functioning of the Large Intestine. The Large Intestine requires a certain amount of moisture in order to function efficiently, and is therefore easily injured by Dryness. The Dry Climate (generally active in the Autumn time) can interfere with the functions of the Large Intestine.

The Influence of Taste, Color, and Sound

- The Pungent Taste (e.g., garlic, green onions, etc.) can be used to tonify both the Lungs and Large Intestine; although excessive consumption of these flavors can weaken them.
- The White Color is used to tonify the Lungs and Large Intestine Organs and Channels.
- The "Shhh", "Sss" and "Shang" Sounds are used to purge the Lungs and Large Intestine.

Large Intestine Pathology

Dysfunctions in the Large Intestine organ and channels can result in diseases of the lower part of the face (including the nose, oral cavity, and teeth), throat, and front part of the neck, as well as disease of the back and radial sides of the upper extremities. Tonification of the Large Intestine can be used to eradicate eye pain, toothache, earache, prevent hemorrhages, and greatly reduce excessive menstrual bleeding.

Because of its relationship to the Lungs, the Large Intestine can be purged to treat coughing and asthma caused from excessive Heat in the Lungs. Similarly, replenishing the vital Qi of the Lungs can cure constipation in debilitated patients.

Patterns of energetic imbalances in the Large Intestine generally relate to disturbances in bowel movements. Energetic dysfunctions in the Large Intestine can be categorized as either Excess or Deficient Conditions, described as follows:

1. **Excess Conditions of the Large Intestines:** This can result in symptoms of Heat, Heat obstruction, Damp Heat, or Cold invading the Large Intestine.
2. **Deficient Conditions of the Large Intestines:** This can lead to an invasion of Cold or Dryness, and in severe cases of Deficiency, to the Collapse of the Large Intestine.

T.C.M. Patterns of Disharmony

The Patterns of Disharmony associated with the Large Intestine, are generally related to the conditions of the other internal organs of the Digestive System (i.e., the Spleen, Stomach, and Small Intestine). The most common Large Intestine disharmonies arise from Deficient Qi of the Large Intestine, Damp Cold in the Large Intestine, Damp Heat Invading the Large Intestine, Exhausted Fluid of the Large Intestine and Intestinal Abscesses, described as follows (Figure 8.88):

1. **Deficient Qi of the Large Intestine:** This type of Large Intestine disharmony is often called Deficient Spleen Yang Disharmony.
2. **Damp Cold in the Large Intestine:** This type of Large Intestine disharmony often occurs in conjunction with invasion of the Spleen by Cold and Damp. Cold invading the Large Intestine is considered to be an Excess pattern, and its clinical manifestations include sudden abdominal pain, painful diarrhea, a cold sensation in the abdomen, and a feeling of cold.
3. **Damp Heat Invading the Large Intestine:** This type of Large Intestine disharmony is often associated with Damp Heat accumulating in the Spleen. Damp Heat invading the Large Intestine is considered to be an excess

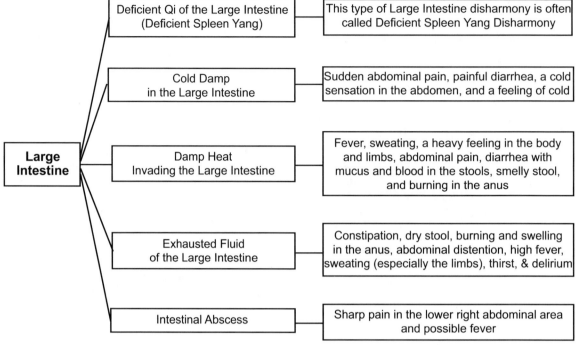

Figure 8.88. Chart of Large Intestine Disharmonies

pattern. Its clinical manifestations include fever, sweating, a heavy feeling in the body and limbs, abdominal pain, diarrhea with mucus, blood in the stool, smelly stool, and burning around the anus.

4. **Exhausted Fluid of the Large Intestine:** This type of disharmony occurs when Heat within the Large Intestine consumes the fluids necessary for the organ to function properly. This can result in constipation, dry stool, burning and swelling in the anus, abdominal distention, high fever, sweating (especially on the limbs), thirst, and delirium.

5. **Intestinal Abscess:** This type of Large Intestine disharmony is similar to the Western syndrome of Acute Appendicitis. It can originate from irregular (or otherwise unhealthy) eating habits, excess physical activity too soon after eating, or an imbalance of Cold and Heat in the abdomen (affecting the Spleen and Stomach's ability to transform and transport). Symptoms include sharp pain in the lower right abdominal area and possible fever.

THE LARGE INTESTINE IN WESTERN MEDICINE

According to Western Anatomy, situated in the lower abdomen, the large intestine is a tubular organ about 5 feet in length that comprises the terminal portion of the gastrointestinal tract. It has the name large intestine due to the fact that it has a greater diameter (2.5 inches) than that of the small intestine (one inch), while the small intestine actually has a greater length (approximately 21 feet). The large intestine is attached to the posterior abdominal wall by its mesocolon of visceral peritoneum.

The walls of the large intestine are also structurally different from the walls of the small intestine, corresponding to the differing functions of each organ. The large intestine stretches from its connection with the small intestine (at the ileocecal valve) to the anus, and is shaped roughly like an upside-down "U". The large intestine can be structurally divided into four parts: the cecum, the colon (ascending, transverse, descending, and sigmoid), the rectum, and the anal canal. These four sections are described as follows (Figure 8.89):

CHAPTER 8: THE TWELVE PRIMARY ORGANS, CHANNELS AND COLLATERALS

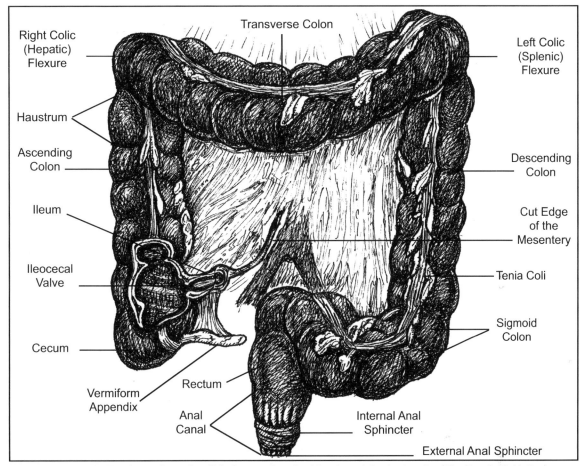

Figure 8.89. The Large Intestine (LI) Organ. (Inspired by the original artwork of Dr. Frank H. Netter)

1. **Cecum:** The cecum is a small pouch about 2.5 inches in length, and is the first part of the large intestine to receive chyme (via the ileocecal valve) from the small intestine. The ileocecal valve (also called the ileocecal sphincter) is a small fold of mucous membrane that acts as a valve between the ileum of the small intestine and the cecum of the large intestine. The vermiform appendix, a small three inch convoluted tube, is attached at the medial portion of the cecum and extends roughly in the direction of the rectum.

2. **Colon:** The colon makes up the majority of the large intestine, and is itself divided into four parts: the ascending colon, the transverse colon, the descending colon, and the sigmoid colon. The colon weaves itself through several layers of the abdomen, though not all of the colon is situated behind the peritoneum. It is anchored to the walls of the abdominal cavity by sheet-like layers of connective tissue called mesentery colons.

- **The Ascending Colon:** This is attached to the open end of the cecum and extends upward on the right side of the abdomen. At about the height of the under-surface of the liver, the colon turns abruptly, forming the right colic (hepatic) flexure that marks the end of the ascending colon and the beginning of the transverse colon.
- **The Transverse Colon:** This begins at the right colic flexure and extends horizontally across the abdomen towards the left. Near the lower left end of the spleen, there is another acute turn in the colon, known as the left colic (splenic) flexure. This marks the end of the transverse colon and the beginning of the descending colon.

471

- **The Descending Colon:** This begins at the left colic flexure and extends downward along the left side of the abdomen. Upon entering the pelvis, the descending colon becomes the S-shaped sigmoid colon.
- **The Sigmoid Colon:** This begins near the iliac crest of the pelvis, extends inward towards the midline, then joins the rectum at the level of the third sacral vertebrae.
3. **Rectum:** The rectum, roughly eight inches in length, is the next to last portion of the gastrointestinal tract. Situated anterior to the sacrum and coccyx, the rectum extends downward from the sigmoid colon to join the anal canal. The rectum has three transverse folds, called rectal valves, that serve to separate feces from flatus. The nature of the location of the rectum allows for a number of lower-abdominal organs to be examined digitally through its anterior wall.
4. **Anal Canal:** The anal canal forms the last inch of the gastrointestinal tract. The anal canal contains an internal sphincter (involuntary - composed of smooth muscle) and an external sphincter (voluntary - composed of skeletal muscle); these lie between the rectum and the anus and control the expulsion or retention of feces. Within the anal canal are longitudinal folds of mucous membranes (anal columns) that contain a number of arteries and veins. It is these veins and the rectal veins that can, when put under excessive pressure, overstretch and cause the condition known as hemorrhoids or piles.

Physiology

The primary functions of the large intestine can be divided into the following four basic categories: Completion of the digestive process, manufacture and absorption of certain nutrients, formation of feces, and the expulsion of feces.

By the time the chyme reaches the large intestine, most of the available water and nutrients have already been absorbed into the bloodstream. Though the large intestine possesses no villi to enable any large scale absorption of nutrients, it plays an important role in maintaining the bodies water balance, absorbing all but 100 to 200 ml of the liter or so of water that it receives. It also absorbs small but essential amounts of various electrolytes. The resident bacteria within the large intestine serve to complete the process of digestion by fermenting and breaking down the proteins and carbohydrates that are still present within the chyme. Once the bacteria have completed the process of breaking down the chyme, the undigested material is now known as feces.

The process of fermenting carbohydrates releases hydrogen, carbon dioxide, and methane gas; while the proteins are broken down and converted into amino acids and their fatty acid components. Protein fermentation in the large intestine also releases indole and skatole, which contribute to the odor of the feces. Bacteria also decomposes the bilirubin released by the liver, giving feces its characteristic brown color. Several vitamins (e.g., vitamin K and some B vitamins) are also created as bacterial by-products, and are absorbed into the body through the colon. Depending on the composition of the chyme, the bacteria in the large intestine may also release large or small amounts of toxic materials; once absorbed into the body, these are generally converted into less toxic substances by the liver and then released in the form of urine.

The large intestine has a thick layer of mucosa to ease the passage of feces towards the end of the digestive tract. This thick mucous layer also protects the walls of the large intestine from the irritating acids and gases produced by the resident bacteria. A gastrocolic reflex, initiated by the introduction of food into the stomach, causes peristaltic waves in the large intestine. While feces travels along the colon by peristaltic contractions, it is also moved along by haustral churning, in which alternate sides (haustra) of the large intestine expand and contract. Mass peristalsis, which begins at the middle of the transverse colon, pushes feces downward and into the rectum. When the rectal wall is adequately distended, stretch receptors then initiate a reflex signal for defecation; in defecation, the rectum is emptied through a combined contraction of the diaphragm, abdominal muscles, and increased peristalsis in the other portions of the colon. If defecation is postponed, due to the voluntary contraction of the external anal sphincter, the feces backs up into the sigmoid colon. Upon the next wave of peristaltic contractions, the intensity of the defecation reflex signal increases.

CHAPTER 8: THE TWELVE PRIMARY ORGANS, CHANNELS AND COLLATERALS

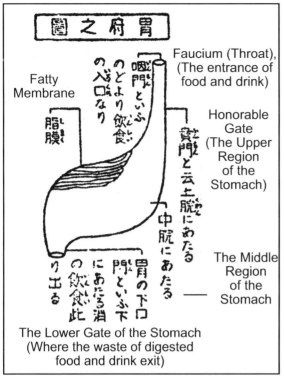

Figure 8.90. The Ancient Chinese Anatomical Diagram of the Stomach (St) Organ: *"Important Useful Notes on Acupuncture and Moxibustion,"* by Masatoyo Hongo (1718)

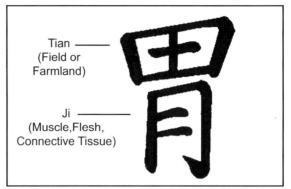

Figure 8.91. The Chinese Character "Wei" (Stomach)

THE STOMACH: WEI

The Stomach is a tubular Yang (Fu) Organ (Figure 8.90), belongs to the Earth Element, and is considered to be the origin of the Body's Fluids. Its associated Yin (Zang) Organ is the Spleen.

The Stomach and the Spleen are the primary organs through which the body acquires Postnatal Qi (i.e., energy gathered into the body through food, water and air). Therefore, the Stomach and the Spleen organs are often called the "Ministers of Food Storage."

Both the Stomach and Spleen Organs internally represent the energetic transformation of the Earth Element, and its natural ability to absorb and transform. In the cycles of Nature, for example, the energy of the Earth continually absorbs the decomposing materials of mineral, plant, insect, animal, and human organic matter, and transforms their energies back into new life. This is observed every Springtime via the manifestation of new plant growth.

When the Stomach Organ takes in food and assimilates it, its tissues naturally expand as the organ stretches in order to absorb the food substance. After the Stomach has internally transformed the food substance, the assimilated energy begins the new creative life cycle, as it manifest internally as an energetic form of nourishment for the body.

CHINESE CHARACTER FOR THE STOMACH: WEI

- **Wei:** The Chinese character "Wei" translates as "Stomach." It refers to the image of the Stomach Organ, and is divided into two separate sections (Figure 8.91).

The character on the top "Tian," represents a "Field or Farmland."

The character on the bottom, "Ji" depicts the Chinese ideogram for Body Tissue, Muscle or Flesh (all of which are forms of Connective Tissue).

Together, both ideographs express the idea that the Stomach Organ is responsible for the harvesting of the "Grains and Liquids."

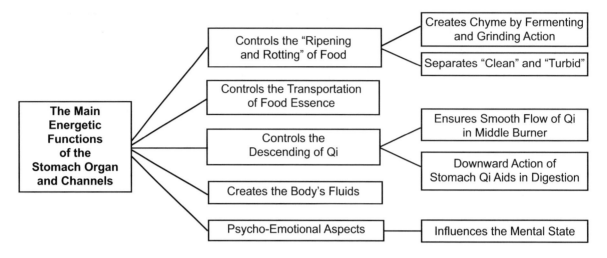

Figure 8.92. The Main Energetic Functions of the Stomach Organ and Channels

THE STOMACH IN CHINESE MEDICINE

The functions of the Stomach described in Traditional Chinese Medicine are similar to those that are described in Western Medicine, except that in Traditional Chinese Medicine the Stomach is also responsible for certain psycho-emotional aspects.

According to Traditional Chinese Medicine, the main functions of the Stomach are to: control the ripening and rotting of food, control the transportation of food essence, control the descending of Qi, create the Body's Fluids, and express itself through the psycho-emotional aspects of influencing mental states. These main functions are described as follows (Figure 8.92).

1. **Controls the Rotting and Ripening of Food:** The Stomach's main function is to receive and decompose food. It receives the ingested food, churns and ferments (rots) it into a "ripe" absorbable liquid, and reduces it into chyme through the fermenting and grinding action.

   The Stomach then separates the "clean" ("pure"), usable portion of the food from the "turbid" ("impure") portion. It then transfers the clean portion to the Spleen (where the food essence is absorbed into the body), while sending the turbid portion to the Small Intestine to be further refined.

2. **Controls the Transportation of Food Essence:** The Stomach ensures the smooth flow of Qi in the Middle Burner. Together with the Spleen, the Stomach is responsible for the transportation of food essences throughout the body.

3. **Controls the Descending of Qi:** The Stomach sends Qi downward, while the Spleen (its paired organ) sends "clean" Qi upward. The downward action of the Stomach Qi aids digestion.

4. **Creates the Body's Fluids:** The Stomach requires a considerable amount of fluids in order to rotten and ripen the ingested food. To create adequate fluids for this function, the Stomach ensures that a part of the ingested food and drink does not go to make food essence, but is condensed to form Body Fluids. The Stomach is closely related to the Kidneys in its role of being the origin of the Body Fluids. The Kidneys are sometimes called the "Gate of the Stomach," because they transform the Body Fluids (which have their origin in the Stomach) in the Lower Burner.

5. **Psycho-Emotional Aspects:** The Stomach also has an influence on the mental state. Stomach Fire or Stomach Phlegm Fire can cause emotional symptoms such as manic behavior, mental confusion, severe anxiety, insomnia, and hyperactivity.

Chapter 8: The Twelve Primary Organs, Channels and Collaterals

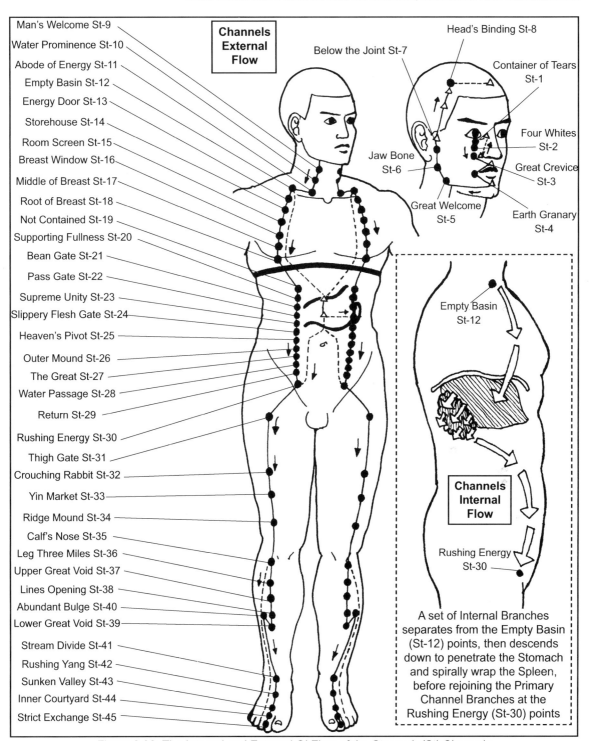

Figure 8.93. The Internal and External Qi Flow of the Stomach (St) Channels

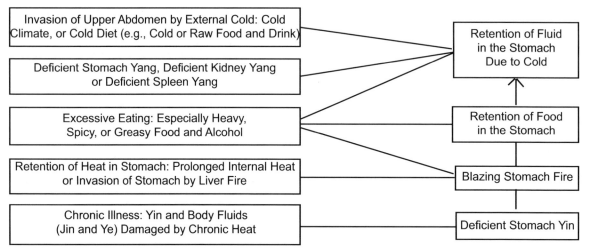

Figure 8.94. The Origins of Stomach Disharmony

THE STOMACH CHANNELS

The Stomach Channels are Yang Channels and flow externally from the head to the feet (Figure 8.93).

- **The External Branches:** The two Stomach Channels originate externally from the lateral sides of the nose (Welcome Fragrance: LI-20), ascending upward to the base of the eye and the bridge of the nose where they communicate with the Urinary Bladder Channels (Bright Eyes: UB-1).

  From the bridge of the nose, they then descend beneath the eyes, down the face, along the angle of the mandible (jaw), and then ascending in front of the ears, following the anterior hairline until they reach the forehead.

  From the Great Welcome (St-5) point (located at the curve of the jaw), the external branches on each side descend the neck and torso. These branches continue to flow externally down the torso and legs to end at the lateral sides of the second toes.

- **The Internal Branches:** Internal branches separate from the Empty Basin (St-12) points and penetrate the Stomach before spiral wrapping the Spleen and joining the primary channel branches at the Rushing Energy (St-30) points.

CHANNELS' ENERGY FLOW

The Qi of the Stomach Channels acts on the skin, muscles, and nerves found along their pathways.

The Stomach Channels contain equally abundant amounts of both Qi and Blood, acting equally on the body's energetic and nervous system functions, as well as on physical substances.

At the High-Tide time period (7 a.m. to 9 a.m.), Qi and Blood abound in the Stomach Organ and Channels. At this time period, the Stomach Organ and Channels can more easily be dispersed or purged. During Low-Tide (7 p.m. to 9 p.m.), the Stomach Organ and Channels can be more readily tonified.

THE INFLUENCE OF CLIMATE

An externally Cold climate can interfere with the functions of the Stomach. The Stomach needs a certain amount of moisture to function, it is easily injured by Cold and Dryness.

THE INFLUENCE OF TASTE, COLOR, AND SOUND

- The taste of Sweet can be used to tonify both the Stomach and Spleen Organ and Channels
- The color of Yellow to Light Brown is used to tonify the Stomach and Spleen
- The "Who" and "Dong" sounds are used to purge the Stomach and Spleen

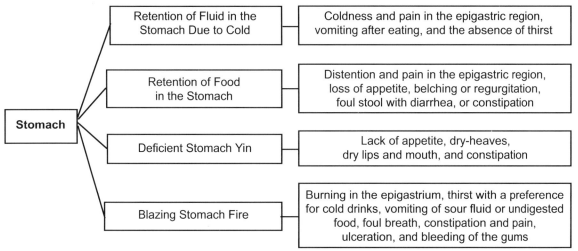

Figure 8.95. Chart of Stomach Disharmonies

Stomach Pathology

In Chinese Energetic Medicine, the Diseases of the Stomach Organ and Channels include the Invasion of Upper Abdomen by External Cold, Deficient Stomach Yang, Deficient Kidney Yang or Deficient Spleen Yang, Excessive Eating, Retention of Heat in Stomach, and Yin and Body Fluids (Jin and Ye) Damaged by Chronic Heat (Figure 55.4).

Also included are Diseases of the Face (i.e., the Nose, Mouth, and Teeth), Throat, Front of the Neck, the Abdomen, the front part of the legs, and Gastrointestinal area (Figure 8.94).

The Stomach has the function of sending the semi-digested food downward. An impairment of this function often causes vomiting.

Diseases of the Stomach Organ are primarily caused by improper diet. To determine the root of a Stomach imbalance, the following five areas are considered:

1. **Constitution:** The patient's Five Element constitution and present state of health.
2. **Foods Ingested:** The type and energetic quality of the foods ingested (Hot or Cold), and whether the food is in season or out of season.
3. **The Scheduling of Meals:** This includes eating meals at regular times, eating balanced meals, allowing adequate time for eating (not eating fast), and not eating too late at night.
4. **The Yin and Yang Food Balance:** This includes evaluating the foods eaten in terms of Yin and Yang, the Five Tastes, and the Five Colors.
5. **The Emotional Factors Surrounding Meal Time:** This includes avoiding emotional distresses (feeling rushed, upset, etc.), and having the proper mental attitude (being relaxed and calm).

The Stomach easily suffers from excess patterns (e.g., Fire or Phlegm Fire), which in turn can agitate the Shen (Heart/Mind). Due to the Stomach's association with the psycho-emotional states of worry and excessive thinking, Stomach disharmonies can often play a primary or supporting factor in numerous emotional or psychological disorders.

When the Shen is disturbed, it can cause manic symptoms such as inappropriate laughter, violent or otherwise inappropriate behavior (e.g., taking off one's clothes in public), pressured speech, unconscious talking, laughing or singing. In milder cases, symptoms may include mental confusion, severe anxiety, obsessive-compulsive thinking, hyperactivity, and hypomania (a milder form of mania).

T.C.M. Patterns of Disharmony

Patterns of disharmony associated with the Stomach generally originate from: Retention of Fluid in the Stomach Due to Cold, Retention of Food in the Stomach, Deficient Stomach Yin and Blazing Stomach Fire, described as follows (Figure 8.95):

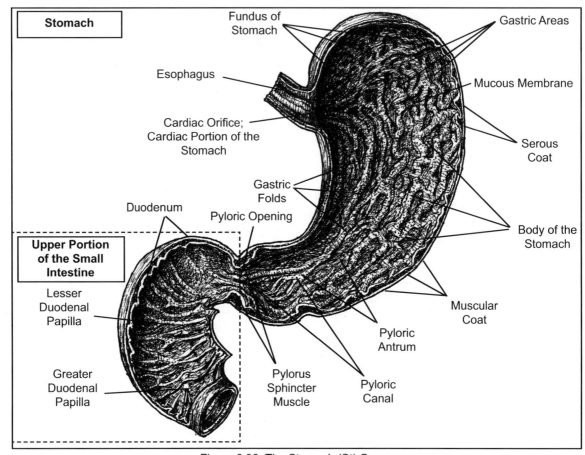

Figure 8.96. The Stomach (St) Organ

1. **Retention of Fluid in the Stomach Due to Cold:** When the Stomach's Yang Qi becomes deficient, it is prone to the accumulation of Cold and Damp. The accumulation of Cold in the Stomach can result in symptoms such as coldness and pain in the epigastric region, vomiting after eating, and the absence of thirst.

2. **Retention of Food in the Stomach:** If the Stomach's functions of receiving, storing and digesting food becomes compromised due to retention of food, the Stomach Qi becomes impaired. This can result in distention and pain in the epigastric region and a loss of appetite. As the retained food begins to rot, the Stomach Qi rebels, resulting in belching or regurgitation, foul smelling stool with diarrhea, or constipation.

3. **Deficient Stomach Yin:** When the Stomach's Yin Qi becomes deficient, it is prone to patterns of Dryness and Heat. The reduction of Body Fluids in the Stomach due to Dryness and Heat can cause symptoms such as lack of appetite, dry-heaves, dry lips and mouth, and constipation.

4. **Blazing Stomach Fire:** Excessive Internal Heat generated from the Fire in the Stomach can create symptoms such as burning in the epigastrium, thirst with a preference for cold drinks, vomiting of sour fluid or undigested food, foul breath, constipation, Stomach pain, ulceration, and bleeding of the gums.

The Stomach in Western Medicine

According to Western Anatomy, the stomach is a "J" shaped organ located under the diaphragm in the epigastric, umbilical, and left hypochondriac region of the abdominal cavity. Its upper opening connects to the esophagus, while its lower opening is at the pylorus, which connects to the duodenum of the small intestine (Figure 8.96).

The adult stomach is approximately 10 inches long. However, the size and position of the stomach constantly changes, depending on the amount of food (chyme) present in the stomach at any given time. When the stomach is empty, the mucosa and submucosa lie in large, longitudinal folds called rugae. When filled with food, the rugae of the stomach unfold, increasing its holding capacity.

The diaphragm pushes the stomach downward during each inhalation; during exhalation, the stomach is pulled upward. The concave medial border of the stomach is called the lesser curvature, while the convex lateral border is called the greater curvature. The stomach can be divided into four main areas: cardia, fundus, body, and pylorus, described as follows.

1. **Cardia:** This part of the stomach surrounds the superior opening of the stomach organ (the cardiac orifice), through which food from the esophagus enters the stomach. Several minutes after food enters the stomach, rippling peristaltic movements known as mixing waves begin to pass over the stomach every 15 to 25 seconds. These mixing waves blend the food with the secretions of the gastric glands, dissolving it into a thin creamy liquid paste called chyme.
2. **Fundus:** The rounded dome-shaped portion of the stomach, located above and to the left of the cardia is called the fundus. The fundus is the storage area for food. When necessary food can remain in the fundus for over an hour without becoming mixed with gastric juice.
3. **Body:** Below the fundus is the large central portion of the stomach called the body of the stomach. During digestion, more vigorous mixing waves begin at the body of the stomach and intensify as they reach the pylorus.
4. **Pylorus:** At the inferior region of the stomach, where it connects to the duodenum, is a funnel-shaped area called the pylorus. The pylorus has two parts: the pylorus antrum, which is connected to the stomach; and the pylorus canal, which leads to the pyloric valve and the duodenum of the small intestine. As food reaches the pylorus, the mixing waves force several milliliters of the chyme into the duodenum through the pyloric sphincter. Most of the food is forced back into the body of the stomach, where it is again mixed with the gastric juices. Each wave pushes a little more chyme into the duodenum, while the remaining chyme continues to mix with the gastric juices of the stomach. The back and forth movements of these mixing waves are responsible for the preliminary digestive process that takes place in the stomach.

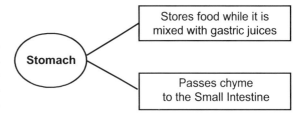

Figure 8.97. The Functions of the Stomach (Western Medical Perspective)

Physiology

The stomach functions both as a reservoir for ingesting food and as a digestive organ (Figure 8.97). The gastric glands of the stomach secrete gastric juice (hydrochloric acid and a few enzymes) for food digestion.

The stomach then passes the resulting mixture, now called chyme, on to the small intestine via the pyloric sphincter. The internal surface of the stomach replenishes its cells every three days, allowing all of the cells of the stomach to be replaced over a time period of one to three months.

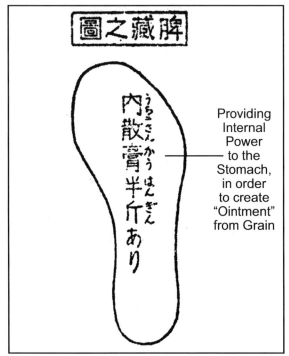

Figure 8.98. The Ancient Chinese Anatomical Diagram of the Spleen (Sp) Organ: *"Important Useful Notes on Acupuncture and Moxibustion,"* by Masatoyo Hongo (1718)

Figure 8.99. Spirits of the Spleen (Sp) Organ: *Yifang Leiju (Classified Collection of Medical Recipes)*, (Japanese reproduction - 1861)

THE SPLEEN: PI

The Spleen is a solid Yin (Zang) Organ, belongs to the Wood Element, and stores and develops the body's Ying Qi (Nourishing Energy). It's associated Yang (Fu) Organ is the Stomach.

The Stomach and the Spleen are the primary organs through which the body acquires Postnatal Qi (i.e., energy gathered into the body after birth, through food, water, and air). Because the Spleen is responsible for absorbing and distributing what the Stomach has stored and digested, the Spleen is sometimes called the "Minister of Grains."

In ancient Daoist imagery, it was taught that the energetic structure of the Spleen Organ maintains the esoteric shape of an "Inverted Bowl." Other ancient texts however often refer to its energetic pattern as having the shape of an "Upside-down Wing" (i.e., the Pancreas) (Figure 8.98).

In ancient Daoist teachings, the Spleen being the "Origin of Blood" provides contentment to an individual's life experience, this is accomplished via the "Yi," which allows each individual to experience a sense of acceptance and completeness.

Additionally, according to the *Yellow Court Classics*, the energy of the Spleen is designed to internally strengthen and build up the Qi of the Middle Palace (i.e., the energy within the Middle Dantian).

ANCIENT SPLEEN ORGAN TEACHING

The following picture (Figure 8.99) is from the *Yifang leiju (Classified Collection of Medical Recipes)* section on the Five Viscera. The ancient text states:

"The Spleen is the Qi of Kun (Earth Trigram),
It carries the Essence of Earth;
And its Color is Yellow.

It looks like an inverted bowl.
Its spirit has the form of the wind.

Spleen engenders Yi (thought),
which is transformed into a Jade Woman.
She is 7 cun tall.
She patrols about the
Treasure-House of the Spleen."

Additionally, according to the ancient Daoist teachings of the *Yellow Court Classics*, the energetic function of the Spleen is described as follows:

"The Deity of the Spleen
has the shape of a Phoenix.
According to ancient Daoist teaching,
the internal energy of the Spleen Organ
has the shape of an upside-down wing.

The Spleen belongs to the Center and Earth,
therefore it radiates its golden light
throughout the Four Seasons,
and corresponds to the Yellow Emperor.

The mouth is the Officer of the Spleen,
and it corresponds to the cheeks.
The left cheek is associated with
the "Wu" (Yang Earth Element) Heavenly Stem;
while the right cheek is associated with
the "Ji" (Yin Earth Element) Heavenly Stem.

Although the spirit of the Spleen
is called "Chang Zai" ("Always Existing"),
and his given name is the "Court of Hun."
According to ancient Daoist texts,
he is also given the name
"Hun Ting" ("Ethereal Soul Pavilion").

The Ministry of the Spleen Palace
is connected to the Wuyi.
In the middle of this special palace
is a Bright Boy, wearing yellow clothes,
dressed in a robe of yellow brocade
with Jade Ornaments, and wearing a Tiger Seal.

He controls the Consumption of Grains,
and the Distribution of Qi absorbed via the teeth.

In this Great Granary, two Bright Boys work
(i.e., the Spleen and Stomach).
They sit at the City Walls'
Nine-Layer Golden Platform,
Who's Gate of Life is 1 inch in circumference.

They are the "Masters of 100 Grains & Five Flavors,"
always adjusting the fragrances
to prevent illness and injury.

Externally, they correspond to the
Qi of complexion, bringing radiant splendor
by means of a bright surface (i.e., glowing skin).

Figure 8.100. The Chinese Character "Pi" (Spleen)

By meditating on these three
(i.e., Hun Ting and the two Bright Boys),
Laozi will help you to gently soar,
and lift you as high as the immortals,
far from the calamity of death."

CHINESE CHARACTER FOR THE SPLEEN: PI

- **Pi:** The Chinese character "Pi" translates as "Spleen." It refers to a general description of the image of the Spleen organ, and is divided into two sections (Figure 8.100).

The character to the left, "Ji" depicts the Chinese ideogram for Body Tissue, Muscle or Flesh (all of which are forms of Connective Tissue).

The character to the right depicts an ideogram that was originally a representation of an ancient drinking vase, provided with a handle on the left side. Later, the character for "Wine Vessel" was taken in the abstract sense, and its meaning was used in order to suggest both noble and vulgar connotations, depending on the context in which it was used.

Together, both ideographs express the idea that the Spleen Organ is responsible for collecting "pure and necessary things" for the body. For example, the collecting of Gu Qi (Food and Grain Energy), and the gathering of ideas.

THE YIN AND YANG OF THE SPLEEN

Traditional Chinese Medicine defines the Spleen as having two energetic aspects: a Yin aspect and a Yang aspect.

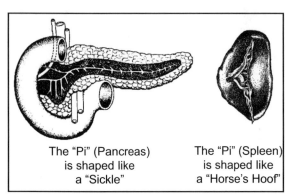

Figure 8.101. The ancient medical description of the "Pi" (Pancreas and Spleen Organs)

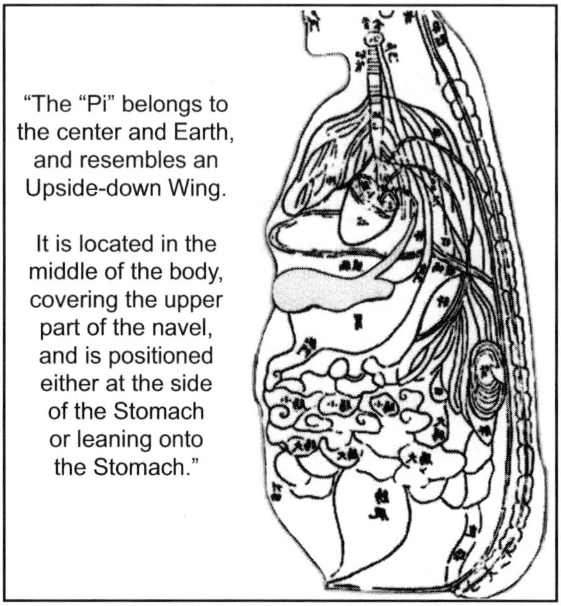

- **The Yin of the Spleen:** This pertains to the material structure of the Spleen, including the Blood stored within it.
- **The Yang of the Spleen:** This pertains to the Spleen's function of heating, transforming, holding, and moving the Qi.

THE SPLEEN'S EARTH JING FORMATION

During the Eighth Lunar Month, the fetus receives the Zong (Essential) Qi from the mother's Spleen. The Zong Qi is the energy collected from Heaven and Earth, and it accumulates within the chest. At this time of tissue formation, the Earth Jing begins to be incorporated into the fetus' body, completing the formation of the skin.

The energy of the Earth Jing also supervises the quality and maturation of the emotional and spiritual bonding and boundaries of the fetus. Any faltering of the Earth Jing energy, is associated with problems of severe psychological disturbances (e.g., schizophrenia). These psychological disturbances may be evident at birth or develop later in life.

After birth, the Earth Jing can be affected through the color Yellow, the Sweet taste and "Who," and "Gong" sounds.

THE SPLEEN AND THE PANCREAS

It is important to note, that in Chinese Medicine today, the major organ responsible for the digestive process is considered to be the Spleen. However, many historical sources in both Chinese Medical and Daoist Alchemical lineages describe the Pancreas as a major organ involved in the digestive process, with the Spleen having an adjunctive part in its energetic transformation process.

According to the *Yixue Rumen (A Primer of Medicine)*, written during the Ming Dynasty (1368-1644 A.D.), the "Pi" organ was originally described as being two individual organs. The text states: "The shape of the Spleen is flat, like a horses' hoof. It is also shaped like a sickle." It is important to note, that as far back as the Northern Song Dynasty (960-1127 A.D.), the term "Pi" has originally been used in ancient Chinese Medicine for describing both the Pancreas ("whose shape is like a sickle") and for the Spleen ("who's shape is like a horse's hoof") organs (Figure 8.101).

The ancient *Daoist Xiuzhen Tu (Chart of the Inner Landscape)*, contains detailed descriptions that are consecutive with the Pi organ being the Pancreas (Figure 8.102), stating:

Figure 8.102. Xiuzhen Tu (Chart of the Inner Landscape) An ancient Chinese graph of the Human Body, with the Pi (Spleen- Pancreas) Organ highlighted.

> "The "Pi" belongs to the center and Earth, and resembles an Upside-down Wing. It is located in the middle of the body, covering the upper part of the navel, and is positioned either at the side of the Stomach or leaning onto the Stomach."

In ancient Chinese Energetic Anatomy, the reason for keeping the two organs joined as "one" was not because the knowledge of ancient Anatomy was defective. Instead, the crucial factor was influenced by the ancient Daoist "Philosophy of Numerology." In ancient China, this special esoteric art was responsible for naming and maintaining the energetic functions of most of the important internal organs within the body. According to the *Huangdi Neijing Su Wen (The Yellow Emperor's Inner Canon, Basic Questions)*,

Figure 8.103. The Ancient Chinese Physician Wang Qingren

> "The ancient people who knew the "Way,"
> Followed Yin and Yang,
> and found Harmony within the Art of Numbers."

The esoteric teachings of Yin and Yang, and the ancient Daoist "Art of Numbers" state that "Heaven is Six and Earth is "Five." Therefore, if the internal organs of the human body were to follow in accordance with the principles of the Way (Dao), the Yin (Zang) Organs must total five (for Earth), and the Yang (Fu) Organs must total six (for Heaven). Consequently, if there were more than five Zang Organs, then certain organs had to be combined or their importance minimized. This is the original reason why the energetic functions of the Spleen and Pancreas organs were joined as "one."

Likewise, if these were less than six "Fu" Organs, then the Yang Organs had to be supplemented. This was the original reason why the "Triple Burners" were added to the Five Fu Organs, in order to create "six."

During the Qing Dynasty (1644-1911 A.D.), Professor Wang Qingren (Figure 8.103) departed from the original thousand year old medical practice of using "Pi" to refer to two different internal organs within the human body. In his book *Yi Lin Gai Cuo (Corrections of Errors Among Physicians)*, Dr. Wang said that "attempting healing without knowing the internal organs is like a blind man walking in the dark." He strongly promoted the idea that many diseases were due to Blood Stasis and by activating blood circulation and clearing away the stagnant blood, one could resolve even the very serious forms of disease. In this ancient text, he also used the term "Pi" to specifically refer

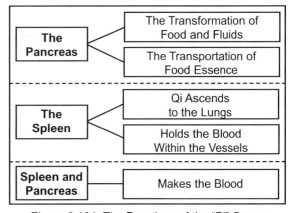

Figure 8.104. The Functions of the "Pi" Organ

to the Pancreas organ, and also included the term "Yi" to specifically refer to the Spleen organ. At that time in China's Medical History however, Professor Wang's book did not receive serious attention from his contemporaries, and the matter was eventually dismissed.

The functions attributed to the Pancreas in Western Medicine, are seen in Traditional Chinese Medicine as being part of the collective functions of the Spleen and Stomach. The Pancreas is an essential energetic component of the Spleen Orb, assisting in the function of processing nutrients, though it is not considered as an independent organ in Traditional Chinese Medicine (Figure 8.104).

The Pancreas also produces insulin, and is energetically connected to the Spleen Orb. The Pancreas also shares certain Blood Vessels with the Spleen and connects with the intestinal tract at the outflow junction of the Stomach.

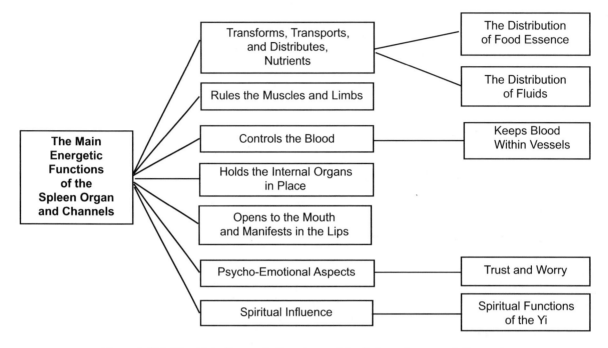

Figure 8.105. The Main Energetic Functions of the Spleen Organ and Channels

The Spleen in Chinese Medicine

In Traditional Chinese Medicine, the functions attributed to the Spleen are completely different than those identified by Western Medicine. From a Chinese energetic perspective, the Spleen is associated with most of the functions of the digestive system, Blood coagulation, and Body Fluid metabolism. It also governs certain psycho-emotional aspects and spiritual influences. Western Medicine, on the other hand, identifies the functions of the Spleen as primarily relating to the body's lymph system.

According to Traditional Chinese Medicine, the main functions of the Spleen are to: transform, transport and distribute nutrients; rule the muscles and limbs; control the Blood; hold the internal organs in place; open into the mouth and manifest in the lips; express itself through the psycho-emotional aspects of trust and worry; and spiritually influencing the individual through the Yi (Intention). These main functions are described as follows (Figure 8.105):

1. **Transforms, Transports and Distributes Nutrients:** The Spleen is sometimes called the "Minister of Grains," as it is responsible for distributing what the Stomach has stored and digested. According to the *Huangdi Neijing Su Wen (The Yellow Emperor's Inner Canon, Basic Questions)*, the distribution of nutrients pertains to two digestive functions originating from the energetic interactions of the Stomach and Spleen: the Distribution of Food Essence, and the Distribution of Fluids.

- **The Distribution of Food Essence:** The Stomach organ is responsible for transforming food essence and separating it into pure (refined) and impure (unrefined) substances. The pure portion (Gu Qi) is absorbed by the Stomach and transported to the Liver, the excess is transported into the tendons and permeates all of the muscles with Qi. The turbid portion (it is important to note that the digestive Qi is only considered turbid in contrast to respiratory Qi) is passed to the Heart. The overflow is transported into the Blood Vessels (Figure 8.106).

CHAPTER 8: THE TWELVE PRIMARY ORGANS, CHANNELS AND COLLATERALS

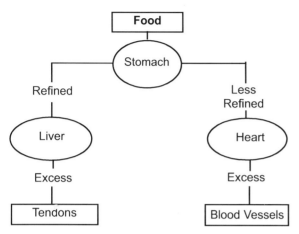

Figure 8.106. The Distribution of Food Essence

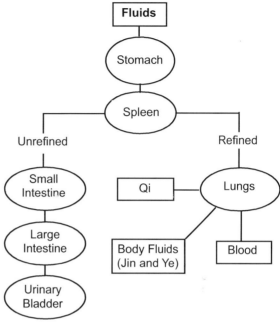

Figure 8.107. The Distribution of Fluids

- **The Distribution of Fluids:** The Spleen Organ is responsible for transforming, separating and distributing the fluid substances received from the Stomach into pure and impure substances. The Pure portion (Gu Qi) is absorbed by the Spleen and transported to the Lungs where it is converted into Qi, Blood, and Body Fluids. The Turbid portion is passed to the Small Intestine, Large Intestine, and Urinary Bladder for further absorption and eventual excretion. The Spleen's main function is to govern or oversee this transportation and transformation of Gu Qi (Figure 8.107).
2. **Rules the Muscles and Limbs:** The Spleen has the function of nourishing and governing the muscles, flesh, and limbs. If the Spleen is invaded by Heat, the patient will experience thirst and his or her muscles will become weak and begin to atrophy. This atrophy occurs because all four limbs are dependent on the Stomach for Qi, and the Ying (Nourishing) Qi transformed by the Stomach can only reach the extremities (via the channels) through the energetic actions of the Spleen. If the Spleen is diseased, it cannot transport the fluids of the Stomach, and thus all four limbs will not receive adequate nourishment.
3. **Controls the Blood:** The Spleen has the function of controlling the Blood by keeping it circulating normally within the Blood Vessels. If the Spleen Qi (especially the Spleen Yang) is deficient, the Blood is not held within the Blood Vessels, and the Blood will leak out, creating various forms of hemorrhaging. The energy of the Spleen, via the Blood, also plays a part in the heat regulation of the body by warming the five Yin organs.
4. **Holds the Internal Organs in Place:** Energetically, the Spleen Yang controls the body's central cavity and holds the internal organs in their places. It is therefore responsible for resisting the downward pull of gravity and controlling the prolapse of the internal organs. The ancient Daoist physicians believed that the Spleen was responsible for influencing the "forms" (the development of the tissues' physical shapes) of the body.
5. **Opens to the Mouth and Manifesting in the Lips:** The Spleen Organ's energy opens externally at the mouth, controlling "taste," and manifests externally at the lips. If the Spleen Qi is abundant, the mouth can differentiate the Five Flavors (Sour, Bitter, Sweet, Pungent and Salty), and the lips will be red and moist. The word "taste" should not be confused with the Western sense of a perceived taste, as it is

used here to denote a flavor's influence on the tissues (via the Spleen's energetic function of digestion and assimilation).

In ancient Daoist teachings, the spirit of the mouth is known as Dan Zhu. Dan Zhu is responsible for spitting filthy Qi out of the disciple's mouth; the Vanguard Spirit of the Teeth is known as "Luo Qian" ("To Catch Thousands"). Luo Qian removes evil, and protects the disciple's internal truth; and the spirit of the throat is Hu Pen. Hu Pen is responsible for "refining the dew" (i.e., improving and perfecting the transformed saliva), and for transforming and transmuting the body's Qi (Energy) and Shen (Mind/Spirit).

6. **Psycho-Emotional Aspects:** In addition to governing physical movement, the Spleen is also responsible for distributing physical, emotional and spiritual nourishment. In this respect, the Spleen digests and assimilates the more subtle aspects of life's experiences, incorporating them into the individual's personality. It houses the body's thoughts and intentions (Yi) and is responsible for analytical thinking, memory, cognition, intelligence, and ideas.

   The Spleen is also responsible for directing memories to the Kidneys for short-term retention. The Kidneys will later transfer these memories to the Heart for long-term memory storage.

   When functioning in harmony, the influences of the Hun on the Spleen allow the individual to experience trust and honesty in both thought and action. If the circulation of Qi becomes obstructed, the resulting Spleen Qi stagnation can give rise to emotional turmoil, sometimes manifesting through obsessions (Yang), or self-doubt (Yin), both of which are influenced by the Po.

   The Spleen's positive psycho-emotional attributes are trust, honesty, openness, acceptance, equanimity, balance, and impartiality. Its negative attributes are worry, excessive thinking, pensiveness, obsessiveness, remorse, regret, obsessions, and self-doubt.

7. **Spiritual Influence:** The Spleen houses the "Yi," which contains the hereditary predisposition towards specific energetic patterns. These unique patterns manifest as specific energetic, biological, mental, emotional, and

Figure 8.108. The Chinese character "Yi" (Idea)

spiritual archetypes and tendencies, that are passed down through the individual's biological and cultural lineages. The Yi codifies the individual's biological and psychic behavior, and permits these unique patterns to be repeated within the individual's lineage.

THE SPLEEN AND THE YI

The Spleen stores the "Yi," one of the spiritual virtues of the Wujing Shen (Prenatal Five Essence Spirits). The Chinese word "Yi" can be translated as Mind, Thought, Opinion, Idea, Sentiment, Inclination, Intention, Intellect, Scholarly Mind, Analytical Thinking, and Memorization."

- **Yi:** The Chinese character "Yi" is depicted by two characters: On the bottom is the "Heart" character "Xin;" on the top is the character for the musical note or sound "Yin." Together, both characters describe the Heart's "Intention" to think, speak or act through sounds, thoughts, or actions (Figure 8.108).

   It is important to note here, that the ancient Daoists believed that the Yi originally represented the "Music of the Heart." Therefore, in ancient China, the Daoist physicians would encourage their patients to "sing" in order to purge the Spleen's acquired emotion of "worry."

The ancient Daoists believed that because the Spleen stores the Yi, it is responsible for the transformation and transportation of all thoughts and ideas on an intellectual level through study, concentration, and memorization. This is different from the creative faculties of the Hun.

It is the interaction between the Yi of the Spleen and the Shen of the Heart that allows an individual to place how he or she thinks, speaks, and acts to sounds, thoughts, and actions. The process of memory retention involves an integrated relationship between the functions of the Spleen (responsible for memory in terms of concentration and studying), the Kidneys (responsible for storing short term memory), and the Heart (responsible for storing the long term memory of past events).

According to Traditional Chinese Medicine, the Postnatal Qi and Blood form the physiological basis for the intellect. For example,

- **A Strong Yi:** An individual with well-developed Yi will have total recall of past events, and is able to memorize things easily.
- **An Excess Yi:** An individual with an excess of Yi will be obsessed with the past,
- **A Deficient Yi:** An individual with Deficient Yi will be absentminded, suffer memory loss, be inattentive, and have problems maintaining concentration and mental focus.

These observations can be especially useful in the Medical Qigong Clinic, when evaluating a patient's internal condition.

The Yi is filled with information from the past, along with current knowledge and sensations. Although all physical pain is registered by the Po, and all psychological pain is registered by the Hun, the memory of the pain is registered by the Yi (Figure 8.109). Therefore, a Deficient Yi condition can often lead to such phenomenon of Transference and Countertransference, defined as follows:

- **Transference:** This refers to the process whereby the patient projects onto the doctor, or any authority figure, past feelings or attitudes toward significant people in his or her life.
- **Countertransference:** This involves the same type of projection of one's feelings, colored by one's own expectations in response. In countertransference, the doctor or therapist is projecting back on to the patient.

It is said that when the Yi is conserved, it will help build the "Zhi" (or "Willpower"). Therefore in ancient Daoist teaching, the term "Yi" also has the meaning of "Divine Purpose," especially when applied to the energy of the Yuan Shen (Original Heart/Mind). This is one reason why the ancient Daoists taught that whenever the body's physical energy was purified by self-cultivation and connection to the Divine, the intention (Yi) of the Shen (Heart/Mind) and the individual's Divine Purpose (Ming) become unified.

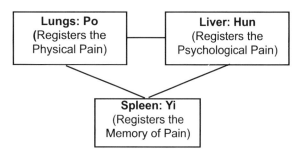

Figure 8.109. Three Ways the Body Registers Pain

THE SPLEEN CHANNELS

The Spleen Channels are Yin Channels that flow externally from the feet to the torso.

- **The External Branches:** These two rivers originate externally from the medial tips of the big toes, ascending upward along the inner thighs, before entering the abdomen (connecting to the CV-3 and CV-4 points) and travelling through the upper torso to connect with the Middle Cavity (CV-12) point. The external Spleen Channels join at the CV-12 point and enter into the body.
- **The Internal Branches:** From the Middle Cavity (CV-12) point, a branch of the Spleen Channel descends internally to flow into the Spleen, and then spirally wraps the Stomach organ. Another internal branch ascends from the CV-12 point into the Heart.

At the CV-12 point, both left and right main external channels meet and separate again to ascend through the diaphragm, up the torso and throat alongside the esophagus, eventually reconnecting at the base of the tongue.

From the Encircling Glory (Sp-20) points, external branches descend along the lateral aspects of the torso and terminate on the mid-axillary line in the 7th intercostal space (Figure 8.110).

CHANNELS' ENERGY FLOW

The Spleen Channels' energy acts on the skin, muscles, and nerves found along their pathway.

The Spleen Channels store more Qi and less Blood, acting more on energetic and nervous system functions, than on physical substance and Blood functions.

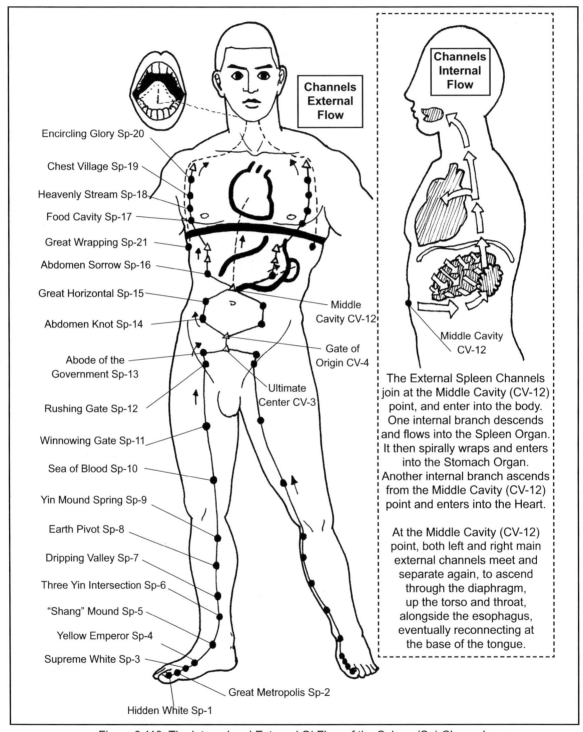

Figure 8.110. The Internal and External Qi Flow of the Spleen (Sp) Channels

At the High-Tide time period (9 a.m. to 11 a.m.), Qi and Blood abound in the Spleen Organ and Spleen Channels. At this time period the Spleen Organ and Spleen Channels can more easily be dispersed and purged.

During Low-Tide (9 p.m. to 11 p.m.), they can be more readily tonified.

The Influence of Climate

In the Late Summer months, Spleen Qi becomes more pronounced. Therefore, during this season, the excessive eating and drinking of sweet foods, greasy foods and overexposure to dampness can weaken the Spleen. Additionally, overexposure to a Damp climate will have a draining effect on the Spleen.

During the Late Summer seasonal time period, the Spleen Qi will become more active in individuals who possess strong Spleen Qi. Likewise, the Spleen Qi may also become more deficient in those individuals who already have weak Spleen Qi.

It is important to note, that an External Damp Climate can interfere with the function of the Spleen's Qi. The Spleen Organ needs a certain amount of Dryness to energetically function. It is therefore easily injured by Damp Heat and Damp Cold. This is why in ancient China, the Spleen Organ was sometimes tonified during the transitional periods that occurred between the four main seasons (Spring, Summer, Autumn, and Winter). This special practice was traditionally used in order to bring the individual's body back into a state of harmony with the Dao of Nature (Figure 8.111).

The Influence of Taste, Color, and Sound

- The Sweet taste can be used to tonify both the Spleen and Stomach Organs and Channels.
- The Dark Yellow to Light Brown color is used to tonify the Spleen Organ and Channels.
- The "Who" and "Gong" Sounds are used to purge the Spleen Organ and Channels.

Spleen Pathology

The main diseases associated with imbalances of the Spleen Organ and Channels include

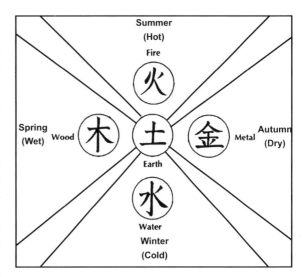

Figure 8.111. In ancient China, the Spleen Organ was traditionally tonified during the transitional time periods that occurred between the four main seasons

Gastrointestinal Dysfunctions (i.e., disturbances of digestion and absorption of food) and diseases of the tongue and throat. Spleen disorders also affect the inner side of the lower extremities along the Spleen's energetic channels.

The main symptoms associated with imbalances of the Spleen Organ and Channels are described as follows:

- **Transporting Food Essence:** The Spleen has the function of sending food essence upward to the Lungs. If this function is impeded, diarrhea or prolapse of the viscera may occur.
- **Keeping The Blood:** The Spleen also has the function of keeping the Blood flowing within the Blood Vessels. Therefore Chronic Spleen Qi Deficiency can lead to hemorrhagic diseases.
- **Nourishing The Flesh:** The Spleen has the function of nourishing the flesh (muscles). A person with a healthy Spleen will usually have a healthy figure and a toned body. A diseased Spleen can lead to a loss of muscle definition.
- **Nourishing The Limbs:** Since the strength of the limbs depends upon the nourishment produced by the normal functioning of the Spleen, a diseased Spleen organ will usually cause a weakness of the limbs.

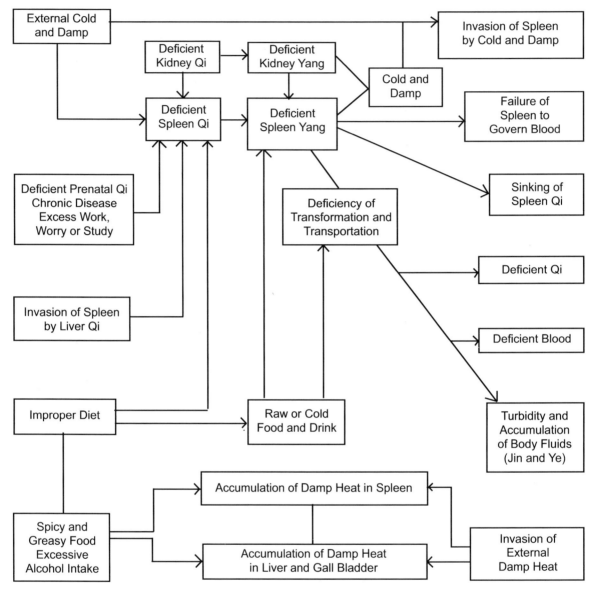

Figure 8.112. The Origins of Spleen Disharmonies

T.C.M. Patterns of Disharmony

The foundation of Spleen Disharmony stems from a tendency of the Spleen to become deficient (i.e., weak Qi and Yang), and its susceptibility to invasion by Damp and Cold. In the clinic, patterns of Spleen Disharmonies include diseases stemming from: Deficient Spleen Qi, Deficient Spleen Yang, Spleen Blood Deficiency, Spleen Yin Deficiency, The Inability of the Spleen to Govern the Blood, The Sinking of Spleen Qi, Invasion of the Spleen by Cold and Damp, Damp Heat Accumulating Within the Spleen and Turbid Phlegm Disturbing the Head. These syndromes are described as follows (Figure 8.112):

1. **Deficient Spleen Qi:** The signs of Deficient Spleen Qi manifest as signs of Deficient Qi, Deficient Blood, Body Fluid Disharmony and a general weakness of the patient's digestive system.

Symptoms of Spleen Qi Deficiency include: slight abdominal pain, abdominal distension, loss of appetite, edema, loose stools with increased frequency, general lassitude, weak limbs and thin muscles. When left unchecked, Deficient Spleen Qi can lead to other functional disorders, the most common of these are failure to transform and transport Qi, sinking Middle Burner Qi, and failure to control Blood circulation.

- **Failure of Transporting and Transforming Qi:** When there is insufficient Qi to support the normal transporting and transforming action of the Spleen, a patient may show symptoms such as a poor appetite, abdominal distension, or loose stools. Turbidity of Body Fluids (Jin and Ye) and their accumulation (such as edema and the retention of Phlegm) may also occur due to the Spleen's inability to "transform and transport water (fluids)."
- **Sinking Middle Burner Qi:** A failure of the Spleen's function of holding the organs in place due to Deficient Spleen Qi may cause the Qi in the Middle Burner to sink. This can result in persistent diarrhea, prolapse of the anus, prolapse of the Urinary Bladder or prolapse of the Uterus, gastroptosis (downward displacement of the Stomach), muscle atrophy, weakness, and sagging of the muscles (such as the eyelids).

Deficient Spleen Qi may also compromise the vessels creating such conditions as mitral valve prolapse, varicose veins and aneurysms.

- **Failure to Control Blood Circulation:** Spleen Qi Deficiency can result in failure of the Spleen to keep the Blood within the vessels and may manifest as the following symptoms: bloody stool, bruising easily, intermittent uterine bleeding, subcutaneous hemorrhaging, bleeding from the nose, Blood in the urine, bleeding from the Lungs, and vomiting of Blood. The patient will also show signs of general weakness due to this deficiency-related type of bleeding.

2. **Deficient Spleen Yang:** This condition is often a progression of Deficient Spleen Qi, and is considered to be a more severe type of deficiency. In addition to the signs of deficiency and weakness, there are also signs of Cold due to Deficient Yang.

Symptoms of Deficient Spleen Yang include: cold limbs, aversion to cold, edema, fatigue transforming into exhaustion, no appetite, retention of urine, undigested food in a loose watery stool, and abdominal pain that is relieved by Heat and pressure.

3. **Spleen Blood Deficiency:** This condition can result in anemia due to insufficient nutrition. The Spleen's inability to transform and transport Gu Qi into Ying Qi makes the body unable to produce Blood.

4. **Spleen Yin Deficiency:** This condition can result in fatigue, emaciation, dry lips, and an inability of the Spleen to deliver nutrients to the cells.

5. **The Inability of the Spleen to Govern the Blood:** This condition results from a deficiency of Spleen Qi and Spleen Yang. This leads to an insufficiency of Qi and Yang which is necessary to hold the Blood in the Blood Vessels, resulting in hemorrhages. This type of hemorrhage is associated with deficiency and signs of Cold, and should be differentiated from the type of hemorrhage associated with excess and Heat.

Symptoms include: hemorrhaging, especially in the lower part of the body, purpura (Blood spots under the skin), Blood in the stool or urine, menorrhagia or metrorrhagia, and shortness of breath.

6. **The Sinking of Spleen Qi:** The Sinking of Spleen Qi results from a failure of the holding function of Spleen Qi and Spleen Yang.

Symptoms of the Sinking of Spleen Qi may be expressed through signs of Deficient Spleen Qi and Deficient Spleen Yang, and can lead to prolapse of the lower body's internal organs. Other symptoms include: severe chronic diarrhea, urinary incontinence and prolapse of the Stomach, Uterus, Urinary Bladder, or anus.

7. **Invasion of the Spleen by Cold and Damp:** External Cold can enter the body through either exposure to a Cold climate or the ingestion of raw or cold food and drink. External

Damp can also enter the body through exposure to a Damp climate, becoming pathological through prolonged or excessive exposure to rain, mists and fog, or from wearing damp clothes after profuse perspiration. Either Cold or Damp can give rise to Deficient Yang, which, can in turn give rise to Internal Cold (due to a lack of Yang to warm the body) or Internal Damp (caused from a deficiency in the function of transformation and transportation by the Spleen, leading to the accumulation of Body Fluids). Deficient Kidney Yang may also accompany Deficient Spleen Yang, both giving rise to Internal Cold and Damp. The patterns of Cold and Damp invasion of the Spleen can be further differentiated according to whether Cold or Damp predominates.

- **Damp:** If Damp predominates, the patterns can be further subdivided according to whether the Damp is from an internal influence (sometimes called Dampness distressing the Spleen) or external influence (sometimes called External Dampness obstructing the Spleen).
- **Cold:** If Cold predominates, there may be an acute aggravation of chronic Yang Deficiency patterns which can result in a temporary Excess Cold condition.

Symptoms arising from an invasion of the Spleen by Cold and Damp include: loss of appetite and sense of taste, lethargy, leukorrhea, a feeling of heaviness in the head and limbs, a feeling of fullness in the chest or abdominal area, copious or turbid secretions, and retention or dribbling of urine and edema.

8. **Damp Heat Accumulating Within the Spleen:** External Heat can enter the body through either exposure to a Hot climate or the ingestion of hot or spicy food and drink. External Damp can also enter the body through exposure to a Damp climate, becoming pathological through prolonged or excessive exposure to rain, mists and fog, or from wearing damp clothes after profuse perspiration. The pattern of Damp Heat accumulating within the Spleen can be subdivided according to whether Dampness or Heat predominates.

- **Damp:** When Dampness predominates, there may be such symptoms as: no thirst, thirst with no desire to drink, loss of appetite, nausea, vomiting, loose stools, leukorrhea, diarrhea with mucous or bad smell, heaviness in the head, a headache that feels as if there is a tight head-band on the head, foggy thinking, edema, oily skin, or rashes with pus and fluid-filled cysts.
- **Heat:** If Heat predominates, there may be such symptoms as: thirst, jaundice, loss of appetite, abdominal distention, yellow leukorrhea, nausea, vomiting, a heavy sensation in the body and mouth sores.

The pattern of Damp Heat can be further subdivided according to whether the Damp Heat originates from an internal imbalance (generally chronic and of gradual onset) caused from a Hot, humid climate, the consumption of contaminated food, or from pathogenic evils. Damp Heat can also emerge from an external influence (generally acute and of sudden onset), caused from excess consumption of greasy foods or alcohol over long periods of time.

Patterns of disharmony created from Damp Heat accumulating within the Spleen give rise to the following symptoms: no appetite, lethargy, feeling of heaviness, stiffness of the epigastrium and lower abdominal area, abdominal distension and pain, yellow leukorrhea, thirst with no desire to drink or with a desire to drink small sips, nausea, vomiting, loose stools with offensive odor, burning sensation of the anus, low-grade fever, headache, and scanty dark-yellow urination.

9. **Turbid Phlegm Disturbing the Head:** This pattern of disharmony is developed from Spleen Dampness. Long term Dampness leads to Phlegm. Because Phlegm is heavier than Dampness, a typical symptom is severe dizziness. Additionally, nodules, cysts, sinusitis, asthma, and copious sputum may also occur.

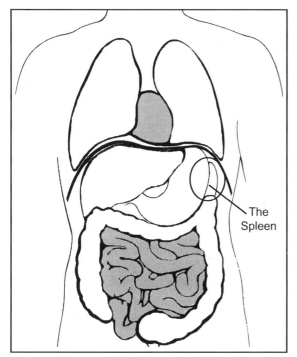

Figure 8.113. The Anatomical Location of the Spleen

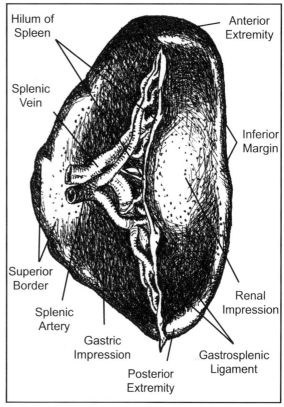

Figure 8.114. The Spleen (Sp) Organ

The Spleen in Western Medicine

According to Western Anatomy, the spleen is a soft oval shaped organ, roughly the size of a fist, located in the left hypochondriac region of the body. With its base at the height of the 11th thoracic vertebrae, the spleen lies behind the fundus of the stomach and below the diaphragm. It also borders with the pancreas, the left flexure of the colon, and with the left kidney (Figure 8.113). The spleen is a secondary lymph organ (as are the lymph nodes), being a place where immune training and response occurs. The primary lymph organs, such as the Bone Marrow and the thymus gland, are where the majority of B and T cells (among others) are actually produced. The spleen is the largest of the body's ductless glands, and is also considered to be the largest mass of lymphatic tissue in the body.

Externally, the spleen is surrounded by a serous coat that is derived from the peritoneum. Immediately within the serous coat lies a fibroelastic coat that encapsulates the spleen while also extending into the organ in numerous tiny fibrous bands called trabeculae. These trabeculae form the primary internal framework of the spleen. The spleen receives blood through the splenic artery which, upon entering into the spleen, quickly divides into a number of smaller convoluted arterial branches that eventually serve to expose the blood to as much spleen tissue as possible. This cleansed blood then leaves the spleen via the splenic vein. Thus, one of the primary functions of the spleen is to bring the blood into contact with the lymphatic tissue contained within it. The inner tissue of the spleen (termed splenic pulp) is sponge-like, and consists of both red and white pulp (Figure 8.114).

Physiology

The spleen serves three primary functions in the adult human body: cleansing the blood, immune response, and storing and releasing blood. These functions are described as follows (Figure 8.115):

- **Cleansing the Blood:** The blood cleansing function of the spleen takes place within the red pulp, which consists of venous sinuses filled with blood and cords of splenic tissue called "splenic cords." These splenic cords contain erythrocytes (red blood cells), macrophages (which serve to phagocytize - or engulf - dead cells and foreign material), lymphocytes (including T and B cells), granulocytes (which contain granules filled with potent chemicals), and plasma cells (which are derived from B cells, and produce antibodies). As blood travels through the venous channels of the spleen, it is exposed to as many of these splenic cords as possible within the red pulp. Thus, the red pulp primarily serves to cleanse the blood through the phagocytosis of bacteria, viruses, and other blood-borne pathogens (including particulate matter present in the blood stream), and also through the recycling of aged or damaged erythrocytes and platelets. As the macrophages breakdown and recycle the hemoglobin of the red blood cells, bilirubin is produced and is released back into the blood plasma to later be removed from the blood by the liver and, to a lesser extent, by the kidneys.
- **Immune Response:** The spleen's role in the immune system is generally considered to be a function of the white pulp of the spleen. The white pulp consists of lymphatic tissue (mostly lymphocytes, with some macrophages) arranged in sleeves or clusters around central arteries. This can give the appearance of islands of white pulp that are surrounded by a sea of red pulp. The spleen's functions of immune surveillance and response (e.g. the generation of antibodies) occur as a result of bringing this lymphatic tissue into contact with the blood. This contact activates the lymphocytes, which then act on any antigens or pathogens present in the blood.
- **Storage and Release of Blood:** Due to its expandable quality and the large amount of blood that passes through the spleen, this organ also serves as a reservoir of blood. When extra blood is needed in the body (as in cases of hemorrhaging), stored blood is released from the spleen through a sympathetic contraction of the smooth muscle tissue of the fibro-elastic layer. Because of its adaptability, the size and weight of the spleen vary dramatically with age. The spleen of an elderly person tends to be about half the size of that of a child or adult based on nutrition, disease status, and other factors. The spleen increases in size during and after digestion, and tends to be relatively large in well-fed animals and small in starved or malnourished animals.

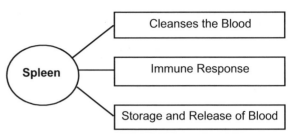

Figure 8.115. The Functions of the Spleen (Western Medical Perspective)

In the fetus, the spleen also serves as a site for red blood cell production. This function normally disappears after birth, but can be reactivated during conditions of extreme erythrocyte depletion.

Common Disorders of the Spleen

Because its walls are very thin and it holds a great deal of blood, the spleen can be relatively easily injured as a result of local impact trauma or severe infection. In Western Medicine as a precaution in certain types of blood (leukemia) or lymphatic (lymphoma) cancers, a splenectomy is generally performed. Under such conditions, the spleen is usually removed (splenectomy) immediately to prevent the occurrence of a life-threatening hemorrhage. Once the spleen has been removed, the body is usually able to adapt quite well, as the bone marrow and the liver take over many of the spleen's previous functions.

CHAPTER 8: THE TWELVE PRIMARY ORGANS, CHANNELS AND COLLATERALS

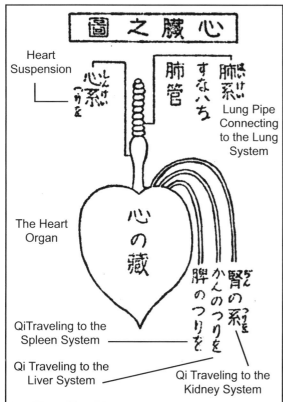

Figure 8.116. The Ancient Chinese Anatomical Diagram of the Heart (Ht) Organ: *"Important Useful Notes on Acupuncture and Moxibustion,"* by Masatoyo Hongo (1718)

THE HEART: XIN

The Heart is a solid Yin (Zang) Organ, belongs to the Fire Element, and energetically paired with the Small Intestine, which is the hollow (Fu) organ in charge of separating the pure and clean energy from the impure Qi.

The Heart controls Blood Circulation, governs all of the viscera (Zang) and bowel (Fu) organs, and is considered to be the most important internal organ of the body. This is why in ancient Daoist teachings, the Heart is sometimes referred to as the "Red Emperor," or as the "Supreme Controller of all Yin and Yang Organs."

In ancient Daoist imagery, it was taught that the energetic structure of the Heart Organ maintains the esoteric shape of an "Hanging Lotus," with closed petals (Figure 8.116).

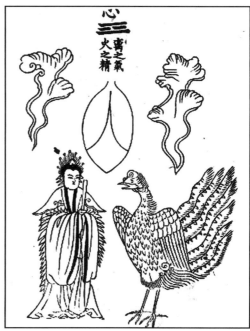

Figure 8.117. Spirits of the Heart (Ht) Organ: *Yifang Leiju (Classified Collection of Medical Recipes),* (Japanese reproduction - 1861)

ANCIENT HEART ORGAN TEACHING

The following picture (Figure 8.117) is from the *Yifang leiju (Classified Collection of Medical Recipes)* section on the Five Viscera. The ancient text states:

**The Heart is Qi of Li (Fire Trigram),
It carries the Essence of Fire;
And its color is Red.**

**It resembles a Hanging Lotus.
Its spirit has the form
of a Red Vermilion Sparrow.**

**Heart engenders the Shen Spirit,
which is transformed into a Jade Woman.
She is 8 cun tall.
She wears brocaded garments,
holds a Jade Flower,
and goes in and out
of the Mansion of the Heart.**

Additionally, according to the ancient Daoist teachings of the *Yellow Court Classics,* the energetic function of the Heart is described as follows:

"The Deity of the Heart
has the shape of a Red Vermilion Bird.
According to ancient Daoist teaching,
the internal energy of the Heart organ
appears like an inverted hanging lotus bud,
with closed petals.

The heart is capable of Transforming
the Kidney Water into Blood.
It is the King of the Five Yin Organs,
and Governs the Laws of the entire body.

The tongue is the Officer of the Heart,
and has a special opening that connects
the Heart and tongue with the ears.
The left ear is associated with
the "Bing" (Yang Fire Element) Heavenly Stem;
while the right ear is associated with
the "Ding" (Yin Fire Element) Heavenly Stem.

Although the Spirit of the Heart is called
"Dan Yuan" ("Elixir Origin"),
according to ancient Daoist texts,
the Primordial Cinnabar Spirit of the Heart
is also given the name
"Shou Ling" ("Guarding the Spirit").

The Palace of the Heart resembles a Lotus Flower,
full of Essence.
Underneath this special flower
sits a Virgin Boy.
He is the Chief of the Red House,
who guards and regulates
the hot and cold harmony of the Elixir.

The Virgin Boy wears Flying Cloths of silk,
brocaded with Jade.
While ringing a Golden Bell,
he playfully dances around with a Red Scarf.

Through continually adjusting the flow of blood to
the ever changing rhythm of life,
the Virgin Boy keeps the body from withering.

He also causes the Heart
to externally respond to the mouth,
and entices the tongue
to pour out the Five Essence.

If you never exhaust him,
your Heart's energy will be revived,
and you will be able to fly within the great
radiance of the Sunrise."

Figure 8.118. The Chinese character "Xin" (Heart)

THE SPIRITUAL EVOLUTION OF THE HEART

According to ancient Daoist teaching, the degree of an individuals spiritual evolution depends on the number of orifices energetically active within his heart. For example:

- **In Men of Superior Wisdom:** There are nine orifices, and the Ling Qi (Spiritual Energy) of the Heart is pervaded with a brilliant radiant light that shines outside the body.
- **In Men of Outstanding Wisdom:** There are seven orifices energetically activated, and the cave of their Heart is connected with the Ling Qi (Spiritual Energy) of the Five Organ Vapors.
- **In Men of Average Wisdom:** There are five orifices energetically activated, and the cave of their Heart is connected with the Ling Qi (Spiritual Energy) of the Five Organ Vapors.
- **In Men of Modest Wisdom:** There are three orifices energetically activated within his Heart.
- **In Men of "Awakened" Clarity:** There are two orifices energetically activated within the Heart of one who barely reaches spiritual clarity.
- **In a Normal Person:** There is one orifice energetically activated within his Heart.
- **In Men of Inferior Person:** There are no orifices energetically active, and the brilliance of the Ling Qi (Spiritual Energy) does not flow through nor radiate from their Heart.

CHINESE CHARACTER FOR HEART: XIN

- **Xin:** The Chinese character "Xin" translates as "Heart." It refers to a general description of the image of a Heart organ, and is divided into three sections (Figure 8.118). The upper half depicts the aorta and major arteries. The Heart itself is depicted in the center, and the lower left part of the character depicts the Pericardium.

In Traditional Chinese Medicine, the character "Xin" also refers as much to the Mind (thoughts and emotions) as it does to the actual Heart Organ.

The Yin and Yang of the Heart

Traditional Chinese Medicine describes the Heart as having two energetic aspects: a Yin aspect and a Yang aspect:
- **The Yin of the Heart:** This pertains to the vital essence of the Heart, including the Blood stored within it.
- **The Yang of the Heart:** This pertains to the Heart's function of heating and moving the Qi and Blood.

The Heart's Fire Jing Formation

During the Fifth Lunar Month, the Fire Jing energy generates, controls, protects, integrates, divides, and harmonizes the fetus' internal energies in order to promote emotional and spiritual well-being. Any faltering of the Fire Jing energy is associated with problems of right (Yin) and left (Yang) Brain communication (e.g., the correct balance of male/rational and female/intuitive energies).

After birth, the Fire Jing can be affected by the color Red, the Bitter taste, and the "Ha," "Ke" and "Zheng" (Jong) Sounds.

The Heart in Ancient Chinese Medicine

In anatomical placement, the Lungs surround the Heart in the upper thoracic cavity of the chest, while the Large Intestine surrounds the Heart's associated organ, the Small Intestines in the abdominal region.

In ancient China, it was believed that the tissues of both the Heart (Yin-Fire) and its associated organ the Small Intestine (Yang-Fire) contained the internal energy of the Fire Element, and were therefore Hot and Expansive. Because of this ancient belief, the color Red was traditionally ascribed to the pulsating energies radiating from these two Fire organs.

It was believed that the tissues of both the Lungs (Yin-Metal) and its associated organ the Large Intestines (Yang-Metal) contained the energy of the Metal Element, and were therefore Cold and Contractive. Because of this ancient belief, the color "White" was traditionally ascribed to the internally absorbing energetic patterns, manifesting via these two internal organs.

The continuous Yin and Yang energetic interactions of "Expansion and Contraction" manifesting from the Hot and Cold energetic properties

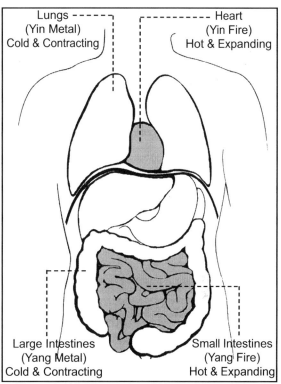

Figure 8.119. The ancient Chinese Yin and Yang relationship between the rhythmical patterns of the body's Cardiopulmonary and Digestive Systems

of these internal organ systems, were believed to create the subtle peristaltic rhythmic patterns of both the body's Cardiopulmonary and Digestive Systems (Figure 8.119).

The Heart in Chinese Medicine

The functions ascribed to the Heart in Traditional Chinese Medicine differ from the functions of the Heart that are described in Western Medicine. Chinese energetic functions of the Heart include the functions associated with the circulatory system, nervous system, the psycho-emotional aspects, and spiritual influences of the Heart.

The main functions of the Heart are to: govern the Blood, control the Blood Vessels, manifest through the complexion, house the mind, open into the tongue, control perspiration, express itself through the psycho-emotional aspects of order and excitement, and exert certain important spiritual influences via the Shen (Spirit). These main functions are described as follows (Figure 8.120).

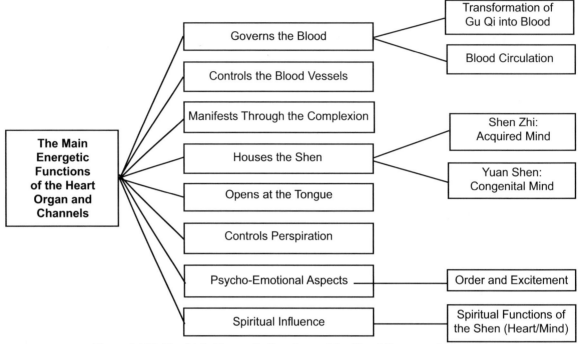

Figure 8.120. The Main Energetic Functions of the Heart Organ and Channels

1. **Governs the Blood:** Within the Heart, Heart Qi and Heart Blood are mutually dependent. The Qi of the Heart is the driving force for the Heart's beat, rhythm, rate and strength. The Heart governs the Blood in two ways: the transformation of Gu Qi into Blood and Blood Circulation.
   - **Transformation of Gu Qi into Blood:** Blood is considered to be a dense, material form of Qi. Within the Heart, the food essence from the Lungs along with the Yuan Qi from the Kidneys is transformed into Blood.
   - **Blood Circulation:** The Heart is responsible for the circulation of Blood. The Lungs, Spleen and Liver also play a role in Blood circulation.
2. **Controls the Blood Vessels:** The Heart distributes the Blood throughout the body through the driving pulse of the Heart. The state of the Blood Vessels depends on the harmony of the Heart's Qi and Blood.
3. **Manifests Through the Complexion:** The Heart has its outward manifestation in the face and complexion, therefore the state of the Heart and the Heart's Blood are reflected in the complexion.
4. **Houses the Shen:** The Heart stores the Mind and Spirit, traditionally called the "Shen." The ancient Daoists believed the Heart's Shen was responsible for mental and emotional activities, intimacy, cognition, intelligent consciousness, and long term memory. The Shen also has the capacity to judge, and influences sleep.

   The energetic functions of the Shen are divided into two main components:
   - **The Shen Zhi (Acquired Mind):** The term Shen Zhi is alternately translated as Postnatal Mind, Willful Mind, Analytical Mind, Acquired Personality, etc. It is used to describe the Heart/Mind that was developed from the ego personalities's analytical senses, and it energetically manifests via the individual's emotional expressions.

   The Shen Zhi is also associated with the Wisdom of the Five Senses and the knowledge acquired through the individual's accumulated experiences. Therefore, in Traditional Chinese Medicine, an individual's conscious mental activities are considered to be a survival function of the Heart's Shen Zhi.

There are five main functions of the Heart's Shen Zhi: Mental Activities, Emotional Activities, Consciousness, Memory, and Sleep.

- **The Yuan Shen (Congenital Mind):** The term "Yuan Shen" is sometimes translated as Prenatal Mind, Prenatal Spirit, Original Mind, Original Spirit, Congenital Mind, Congenital Spirit, Original Personality, etc. It is used to describe the spiritual Heart/Mind that exists as the body's innate intuitive intelligence, and energetically manifests as the spiritual virtues of the individual's True Self.

In Daoist Alchemy, it is taught that there are two ways in which the Shen is Nourished (Figure 8.121). One way is through the Dreams, along with the intuitive or unconscious information that comes from the Hun of the Liver.

The other way is through the thoughts and ideas that stem from the Yi of the Spleen.

Dreaming, Spirit Projection (Traveling Clairvoyance), and Spirit Travel (Astral Projection) are all considered to be functions of the Heart's Yuan Shen.

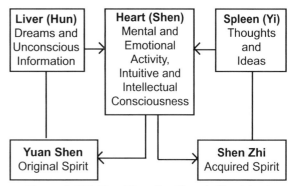

Figure 8.121. Two Ways the Shen is Nourished

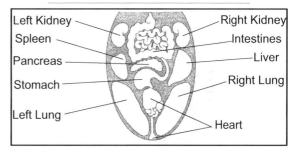

Figure 8.122. The Heart Opens into the Tongue

5. **Opens into the Tongue:** The tongue is said to be the external branch of the Heart and therefore it is seen as a "Mirror of the Heart." The condition of the Heart's Qi manifests through the subtle variations in the color, form, and appearance of the tongue. In tongue diagnosis, the tip of the tongue in particular is said to reveal the state of the Heart (Figure 8.122).

In ancient Daoist teachings, the Magical Spirit of the Tongue is known as "Zheng Lun" ("True Ethics"). Zheng Lun is connected to the disciple's destiny (via the things he says), and is also responsible for cultivating the disciple's spirit.

6. **Controls Perspiration:** Perspiration is considered to be one of the fluids of the Heart. In Traditional Chinese Medicine, Blood and Body Fluids have the same origin, and sweat comes from Body Fluids. Body Fluids are considered to be a very important aspect of Blood. Blood and Body Fluids also mutually interchange; for example, if the Blood is too thick, Body Fluids will enter the Blood Vessels to thin it.

7. **Psycho-Emotional Aspects:** The Heart is sometimes called "The Emperor," or the "Supreme Controller of all Yin and Yang Organs," and it coordinates all of the energetic and emotional functions of the body. When functioning normally, the effects of the Hun on the Heart allow the individual to experience peace and joy in thoughts and actions. If the circulation of Qi becomes obstructed, Heart Qi Stagnation can give rise to emotional turmoil, sometimes manifesting through excitement (Yang), or longing (Yin), both influenced by the Po.

The Heart's positive psycho-emotional attributes are joy, peace, contentment, tranquility, propriety, insight, wisdom, order, forgiveness, and courtesy. Its negative attributes are nervousness, restlessness, excitement, anxiety, panic, shock, longing, craving and guilt.

8. **Spiritual Influence:** The Heart houses the body's Yuan Shen (Original Spirit). An individual's psychic abilities and intuitive faculties are brought about through the influence, cultivation, and training of the Yuan Shen. In Daoist Alchemy, the extraordinary abilities that can be developed from the cultivated spiritual consciousness of the Yuan Shen include: Telepathy,

Figure 8.123. The Chinese character for "Shen," Spirit

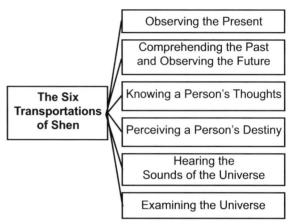

Figure 8.124. The Six Transportations of Shen

Clairvoyance, Clairaudience, Precognition, Time Travel, Levitation, and Teleportation.

Chinese Ideogram of the Shen

The Chinese ideogram for Shen (Spirit) is depicted by two characters. Positioned on the right is a character representing the alternating expression of Natural forces. On the left is a character representing the unfolding of things under the authority and influence of Heaven. The ideograph depicts the Heavenly influence that penetrates and instructs the core of the Heart (Figure 8.123).

The Six Transportations Of Shen

According to the *Huangdi Neijing Su Wen (The Yellow Emperor's Inner Canon, Basic Questions)*,

"The Heart is the Trunk where Life takes Root."

This phrase expresses the ancient Daoist belief that the Eternal Soul (Shen Xian) takes its spiritual residence in the core of the Heart, residing deep within the divine energetic field of the body center Taiji Pole. In this understanding, the Yuan Shen is associated with the congenital spiritual energy of the Shen Xian (Eternal Soul), that descended from the Heavens and possessed the forming body tissues after conception. This universal divine spirit is implanted in each individual, internally connecting each person to the spiritual reality that exists beyond the physical and mental realms. This spiritual state is sometimes referred to as the "Higher-Self."

In Daoist Alchemy, it is taught that each individual's Yuan Shen can be trained to transcend the space-time continuum, as both space and time are multidirectional and interconnected. However, when intuitive perceptions begin to flow, the conscious Analytical Mind (Shen Zhi) automatically begins to act as a filter, seeking to analyze every energetic movement and attempting to identify and categorize each perception. Once the Shen Zhi is engaged, the flow of intuitive perception arising from the Yuan Shen usually stops or becomes unconscious. The ancient Daoist masters explained this process of accessing the Yuan Shen with the following aphorism:

"By rooting the Mind,
The Heart Opens to 10,000 Voices"

This esoteric saying can be best understood to mean: "when the "Chattering Mind" of the Shen Zhi is anchored through focused intention, the Original Heart is able to perceive the various energies of the Three Realms (i.e., the 10,000 voices), and become aware of its connectedness to the multidirectional space-time continuum.

Once the Yuan Shen has been sufficiently cultivated, focused and trained, it naturally reaches a higher level of subtlety and power, and the result is a gradual unveiling of six supernatural diagnostic powers known as the Six Transportations of Shen (Figure 8.124). In the clinic, these six metaphysical abilities enable the Medical Qigong Doctor to evaluate a patient's physical, energetic and spiritual states with accuracy, and by extension, predict the probable future progressions of the patient's life, as well as states or natures of disease. The Six Transportations of Shen are: observing the present, comprehending the past and observing the future, knowing a person's thoughts, perceiving a person's destiny, hearing the sounds of the universe, and examining the universe.

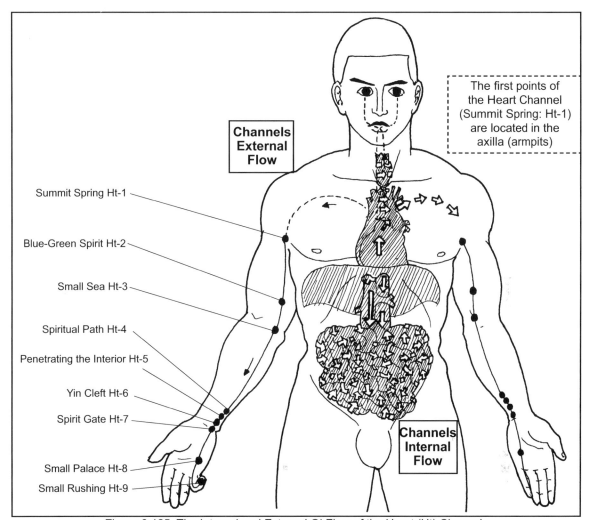

Figure 8.125. The Internal and External Qi Flow of the Heart (Ht) Channels

THE HEART CHANNELS

The Heart Channels are Yin Channels that flow externally from the center of the torso to the extremities of the hands (Figure 8.125).

- **The Internal Branches:** Three rivers originate internally from the Heart on each side of the body. The first pair of these channels ascends from the Heart and flows into the tissues connecting the eyeball.

  The second pair first penetrates the Pericardium, and then descends to connect with and spirally wrap the Small Intestine.

  The third pair of channels flow upward from the Heart into the Lungs, and emerges externally at the armpits.

- **The External Branches:** From the armpit, the Heart Channel then emerges externally, and descends along the medial aspect of the arms, ending on the inside of the little fingers.

CHANNELS' ENERGY FLOW

The Heart Channel's energy acts on the skin, muscles, and nerves found along their pathways, and also provide the energy required for the respiration.

The Heart Channels store more Qi than Blood; that is to say, their dominant action affects the energy of the body. This energetic action controls the emotional temperaments and the spiritual perceptions. The Heart channels also provide the energy required for respiration.

At the High-Tide time period (11 a.m. to 1 p.m.), Qi and Blood abound in the Heart Organ and Channels. At this time, the Heart Organ and Channels can more easily be dispersed and purged. During Low Tide (11 p.m. to 1 a.m.), they can be more readily tonified.

QI & BLOOD FLOW WITHIN THE CHANNELS

Qi and Blood flow within the channels and Blood Vessels (Mai), continuously circulating throughout the body to nourish, maintain, and moisten the tissues. Qi is an energetic form, and is considered a Yang substance; while Blood is a liquid form of energy, and is considered to be a Yin substance (Figure 8.126).

Qi and Blood flow together. Qi is the active energetic force that makes the Blood circulate and keeps it within the Blood Vessels. Blood is a liquid substance that grounds ("roots") the Qi and distributes it along with nutrients to all of the body's tissues. Collectively, the vessels serve as the reservoirs of Blood.

The concept of Blood in Traditional Chinese Medicine is different both in characteristics and in function than the concept of blood in Western Medicine. In Traditional Chinese Medicine, Blood originates from the transformation of food and drink by the Spleen. The Spleen transfers the refined food energy to be further enhanced by the Heart Qi and Lung Qi.

THE INFLUENCE OF CLIMATE

In the Early Summer months, the Heart Qi becomes more pronounced. Therefore, during this season, the Heart Qi becomes more active in individuals who already have strong Heart Qi. Likewise, the Heart Qi may also become more deficient in those individuals who already have weak Heart Qi.

It is important to note that External Climate factors do not affect the Heart directly, but influ-

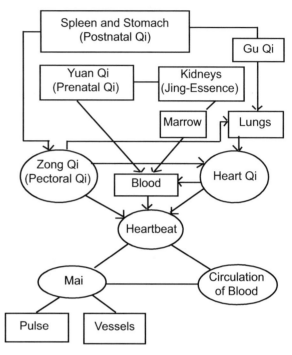

Figure 8.126. The Energetic Functions of the Heart, Blood, and Blood Vessels

ence the Pericardium instead. However, the Heart can be easily injured by Heat and Fire. Therefore, during this season, excessive eating and drinking of bitter food and drink, and the overexposure to Heat will eventually deplete the Heart's Qi. The overexposure to a Hot climate will also have a draining effect on the Heart's Qi.

THE INFLUENCE OF TASTE, COLOR, AND SOUND

- The Bitter taste can be used to tonify both the Heart and Small Intestine, and is also used to drain Excess Heat from the body.
- The dark Red color is used to tonify the Heart.
- The "Ha," "Ke" and "Zheng" Sounds are used to purge the Heart and the Small Intestine.

HEART PATHOLOGY

The main symptoms associated with imbalances of the Heart Organ and Channels are described as follows:

- **Coronary Artery Disease:** The Heart is responsible for governing the flow of Blood through the body's arteries and veins. Coronary Artery Disease (CAD) is a disease in which the patient's coronary arteries begin to harden or impede adequate vascular flow to the myocardium, resulting in an insufficient supply of Qi and Blood throughout the body. This causes such diseases as hypertension, vasculitis, myocarditis, congenital Heart disease, rheumatic Heart disease, nervous malfunctioning of the Heart, organic pathological changes of the Heart, and arteriosclerosis of the Brain.

The main diseases of the Heart organ and channels include diseases that exert pressure on the Brain, eyes, pharyngeal wall, or the lateral sides of the chest, as well as diseases of the Heart itself. The Heart also relates to diseases along the ulnar side of the arms.

The Heart is in charge of mental activities, including consciousness and thinking. Dysfunctions of the Heart can thus lead to insomnia, impairment of consciousness, stuttering, amnesia, and psychosis.

The Heart and Kidneys have a mutual energetic relationship of both supporting and checking each other. The Heart controls the body's Fire, while the Kidneys control the body's Water. Normally, the Fire of the Heart is sent down to warm the Kidneys, and the Water of the Kidneys is sent up to irrigate the Heart. If this balanced relationship breaks down (especially when the Kidney Water is insufficient to check the Heart Fire), a series of Fire symptoms such as hypertension, hyperactivity, palpitations, and insomnia may result.

Since the Heart has its external opening in the tongue, the condition of the Heart is reflected in the tongue. Further distinctions can be made as follows:
- A red-tipped tongue indicates Heart Fire
- A dark purple tongue indicates Blood Stasis of the Heart
- A pale tongue reveals Deficient Blood of the Heart
- An ulcer on the tongue reveals Excess Fire of the Heart or Small Intestine

T.C.M. Patterns of Disharmony

Heart Pathologies have their origin in the Heart's function of ruling the Blood and the Blood Vessels, and of Housing the Shen. The main patterns of Heart Disharmony can be divided into two categories: those associated with Yang Deficiencies (such as Deficient Heart Qi, Deficient Heart Yang, Stagnant Heart Blood and Cold Phlegm Misting the Heart), and those associated with Yin Deficiencies (such as Deficient Heart Blood, Deficient Heart Yin, Blazing Heart Fire and Phlegm Fire Agitating the Heart). These Heart Disharmonies are described as follows (Figure 8.127):

1. **Heart Disharmony Due To Yang Deficiency:**
- **Deficient Heart Qi:** The pattern of Deficient Heart Qi can arise from malnutrition, chronic illness, prolonged hemorrhaging, and can also be caused by various emotional imbalances such as chronic worry or sadness.

    Symptoms of Heart Qi Deficiency can manifest as palpitations, spontaneous sweating, listlessness, facial pallor, fatigue and shortness of breath on exertion.

- **Deficient Heart Yang:** The patterns and pathology of Deficient Heart Yang are similar to, and therefore can arise from, the pathologies of Deficient Heart Qi.

    Symptoms of Deficient Heart Yang include conditions of Cold: aversion to cold, cold limbs, edema and stuffiness in the chest. If the deficiency is severe, the Yang may collapse, manifesting as profuse sweating, extreme cold in the limbs or in the entire body, and loss of consciousness. If the Yin and Yang separate entirely, the patient may die.

- **Stagnant Heart Blood:** Deficient Heart Yang can progress to Stagnant Heart Blood, just as Deficient Heart Qi can progress to Deficient Heart Yang. Sometimes all three conditions can occur together, creating common disease patterns such as angina pectoris and myocardial infarction.

    Other symptoms can manifest as palpitations, shortness of breath, purple facial color, cyanosis of the lips and nails, cold extremities, lassitude, stabbing pain in the chest, tightness in the chest and Heart region, or along the Heart Channel.

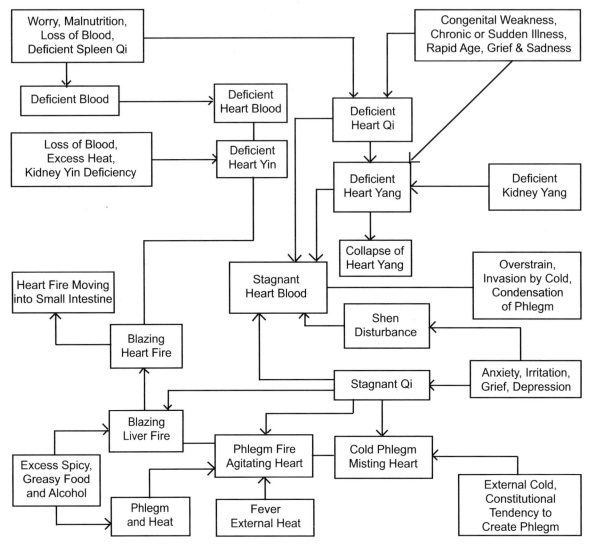

Figure 8.127. The Origins of Heart Disharmony

- **Cold Phlegm Misting the Heart:** This is a Yin Excess pattern in which the Heart is obstructed by Phlegm. However, in this pattern, the Phlegm is associated with signs of Cold rather than with signs of Heat. Seen occasionally in children, the pattern of Cold Phlegm Misting the Heart can cause mental retardation or speech difficulties.

  In adults, the pattern of Cold Phlegm Misting the Heart often occurs after an attack of Wind Stroke. In such cases, the Wind associated with the obstruction of Phlegm can cause aphasia, paralysis and coma.

  The pathological patterns of Cold Phlegm Misting the Heart generally manifest through Yin (inward) imbalances, such as aphasia, depression, muttering to oneself, staring at the walls, lethargic stupor, rattling sound in the throat, or the sudden loss of consciousness.

2. **Heart Disharmony Due To Yin Deficiency:**
- **Deficient Heart Blood:** The pattern and pa-

thology of Deficient Heart Blood can arise from severe hemorrhaging, chronic stress, or a poor diet (i.e., a deficiency of nourishment or lack of Blood producing foods which leads to Spleen Qi Deficiency).

Symptoms of Deficient Heart Blood include palpitations, vertigo, dizziness, insomnia, poor memory, dream disturbed sleep, restlessness, headaches, anxiety, being easily startled, and general tiredness.

- **Deficient Heart Yin:** The pattern of Deficient Heart Yin can arise either from chronic emotional stress or from an invasion of Exterior Heat that consumes the Body Fluids and exhausts the Yin of the Heart.

Symptoms of Deficient Heart Yin can manifest as low fever, palpitations, insomnia, poor concentration, poor memory, fatigue, anxiety, mental restlessness, feelings of heat, malar flush, night sweats, dry mouth and throat, and Five Palms Heat.

- **Blazing Heart Fire:** This is a Yang Excess pattern of Full Heat in the Heart, and can arise from patterns of Deficient Heart Yin. Blazing Heart Fire can form during a severe fever caused by pathological Heat invading the Pericardium. It can also originate from chronic emotional problems that lead to long term Qi Stagnation, which can eventually turn into Fire and disturb the patient's Shen.

The patterns of Blazing Heart Fire are associated with mental depression. Symptoms of Blazing Heart Fire include irritability, restlessness, insomnia, feelings of heat, flushed face, tongue ulcers, bitter taste in the mouth, thirst, palpitations, dark urine, or Blood in the urine.

- **Phlegm Fire Agitating the Heart:** This is a Yang Excess pattern with similar origins to that of Blazing Heart Fire. However, in the pattern of Phlegm Fire Agitating the Heart, the pathogenic Fire and Phlegm obstruct the Heart orifices causing disturbances in the patient's Shen. When severe, these disturbances can result in violent behavior and insanity.

Type of Phlegm	Cold Phlegm Misting Heart	Phlegm Fire Agitating Heart
Yin and Yang	Yin, Cold Signs, Slow Pulse, White Tongue Coat	Yang, Heat Signs, Rapid Pulse, Yellow Tongue Coat
Mental Signs	Introverted, Depressed, Staring at Walls	Extroverted, Laughing & Crying, Incoherent Talking
Disease Patterns	Wind Stroke, Depressive Psychosis	Violent Insanity, Manic Psychosis

Figure 8.128. Difference Between Cold Phlegm Misting the Heart and Phlegm Fire Agitating the Heart

The main manifestations of Phlegm Fire Agitating the Heart are Heart dysfunctions, often occurring in addition to pathological patterns (such as allowing Phlegm to accumulate) that are derived from Spleen Qi Deficiency. The Internal Heat aspect of Phlegm Fire Agitating the Heart, can develop during fevers caused by External Heat invading the Pericardium, or from chronic emotional problems that lead to long term Qi Stagnation. The Qi stagnation turns into Fire and disturbs the patient's Shen. The Excess consumption of spicy greasy foods creates both Heat and Phlegm, and can lead to or exacerbate conditions of Phlegm Fire Agitating the Heart.

The pathological patterns of Phlegm Fire Agitating the Heart generally manifest through Yang (outward) imbalances, such as palpitations, mental restlessness, confusion, agitation, violent behavior (shouting or hitting people), uncontrolled laughter or crying, mental depression, talking to oneself, aphasia, and coma (Figure 8.128).

VOLUME 1, SECTION 1: FOUNDATIONS OF CHINESE ENERGETIC MEDICINE

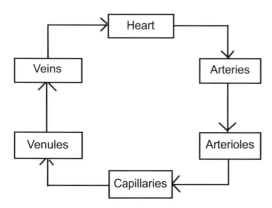

Figure 8.129. The Blood Flow within the Cardiovascular System

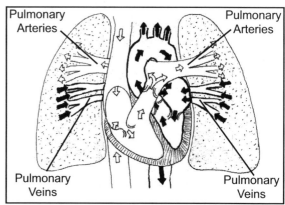

Figure 8.130. The Pulmonary Circulatory Route

THE HEART IN WESTERN MEDICINE

According to Western Anatomy, the heart is a hollow muscular organ, located roughly in the center of the chest, It serves to pump blood throughout the body via the body's vast network of blood vessels. This network of vessels includes all the veins and arteries of the body, and is known as the vascular system (Figure 8.129). Together, the heart and the vascular system are collectively known as the cardiovascular system. The cardiovascular system distributes blood throughout the body so that the blood may deliver nourishment directly to the cells, and remove waste from them. Though it is only about the size of a fist, and weighs an average of ten ounces, the heart is the structural and functional center of the cardiovascular system.

The heart is the hardest working muscle in the human body, beating more than 100,000 times each day. Every minute the heart pumps roughly 10 liters of blood through approximately 96,000 kilometers (60,000 miles) of blood vessels. In trained athletes the amount of blood pumped by the heart in one minute can exceed 70 liters per minute. There are two major circulatory routes in the adult human body, each of which begins and ends with the heart. In the pulmonary circulatory route, the heart delivers deoxygenated venous blood to the lungs, and retrieves oxygenated blood from them (Figure 8.130). The systemic circulatory route then delivers this vitalized blood to all the tissues of the body, and retrieves devitalized blood from them (Figure 8.131). In systemic circulation, the heart is

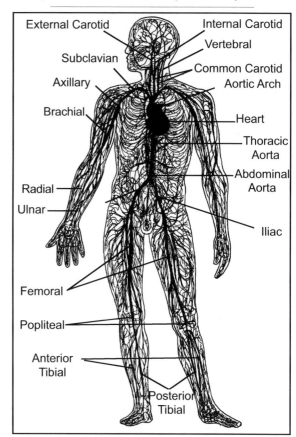

Figure 8.131. The Arterial Flow of the Systemic Circulatory System

responsible primarily for pumping vitalized blood to the cells, while the body must rely mainly on skeletal muscular contractions and gravity for the return of venous blood to the heart.

ANATOMY OF THE HEART

The heart organ is situated in the center of the thoracic cavity, behind and slightly to the left of the sternum, and in front of the vertebral column. Flanked by the lungs, the heart is enclosed in the mediastinum, which also contains the esophagus, the trachea, and the major blood vessels. Vertically, the heart extends from the height of the second rib down to the fifth intercostal space, and it projects horizontally more to the left than to the right, due to the large size of the left ventricle. It is roughly conical in shape, with its base directed upward and to the right, and its apex directed downward and to the left.

The heart is wrapped in a multilayered sac of connective tissue known as the pericardium. The inner layer of the pericardium is called the serous pericardium, and is itself divided into two layers. An inner visceral layer known as the epicardium covers the heart and the initial sections of the major blood vessels and is an integral part of the heart wall. The outer layer of the serous pericardium is called the parietal layer, and it surrounds the epicardium, but is separated from it by a fluid (pericardial fluid) that serves to reduce friction around the heart as it beats. This fluid-filled space between the two layers of the serous pericardium is known as the pericardial cavity. The outer (parietal) layer of the serous pericardium connects into the fibrous pericardium which surrounds it, and which is the pericardium's outermost layer.

The fibrous pericardium is a strong and dense sheath of connective tissue that surrounds the heart and firmly anchors within the thorax. It surrounds the major blood vessels (the superior and inferior vena cava, the right and left pulmonary arteries, the pulmonary veins, and the aorta), which extend outward from superior aspects of the heart, and continue upward to anchor into the cervical fascia. In front, the fibrous pericardium attaches to the internal aspect of the sternum, while it also extends downward to anchor firmly into the diaphragm below.

The wall of the heart is itself composed of three layers. The outer layer of the heart is the epicardium, described above. The myocardium is the middle layer, while the innermost layer of the heart is called the endocardium. The muscular contractions that are the beating of the heart take place at the level of the myocardium. The myocardium forms the bulk of the heart, and is composed mainly of heart muscle tissue. Within the cardiac muscle tissue of the myocardium, crisscrossing bundles of connective tissue wrap around the heart in a dense network that both reinforces the heart internally and provides additional support for the major vessels that connect with the heart. The endocardium is a sheet of endothelial tissue that lines the inside of all the chambers of the heart; the tissue of the endocardium is continuous with the endothelium (inner lining) of the blood vessels.

THE FOUR CHAMBERS OF THE HEART

Structurally, the heart is divided into four chambers: two atria (right and left) that receive blood into the heart, and the two comparatively larger ventricles (right and left) that pump blood away from the heart. Within the heart, blood flows in one direction only. Atrioventricular valves (the tricuspid valve and the bicuspid valve) act as one-way valves that prevent the blood pumped by the atria into the ventricles from flowing backwards into the atria again. Semilunar valves (the pulmonary semilunar valve and the aortic semilunar valve) prevent arterial blood from flowing backwards into the ventricles.

The sequence of blood flow within the heart is as follows: superior and inferior vena cava - right atrium - (tricuspid valve) - right ventricle - (pulmonary semilunar valve) - pulmonary trunk - right and left pulmonary arteries - (lungs) - pulmonary veins - left atrium - (bicuspid valve) - left ventricle - (aortic semilunar valve) - aorta - whole body. The four chambers of the heart are described as follows (Figure 8.132):

1. **Right Atrium:** The right atrium receives deoxygenated venous blood via the superior vena cava, which drains the upper body; and the inferior vena cava, which drains the lower body. The coronary sinus, which drains venous blood from the heart organ itself, also flows into the right atrium. After expanding to receive this blood, the right atrium contracts and pumps the blood into the right ventricle.

2. **Right Ventricle:** the right ventricle receives the deoxygenated blood pumped from the right atrium. As the right ventricle contracts, a valve known as the tricuspid valve prevents blood from flowing back into the right atrium. The right ventricle pumps blood to the lungs via a major vessel known as the pulmonary trunk, which quickly branches into the right and left pulmonary arteries. After contracting, the left ventricle expands, and the pulmonary semilunar valve closes to prevent the back-flow of blood from the pulmonary trunk. The pulmonary arteries are the only arteries in the body that carry deoxygenated (blue) blood.

3. **Left Atrium:** Four pulmonary veins return blood that has been oxygenated by the lungs, delivering it into the left atrium. The left atrium pumps this blood into the left ventricle. The bicuspid (mitral) valve, which is situated between the left atrium and the left ventricle, immediately closes as the left atrium finishes its contraction, and thus serves to prevent a back-flow of blood as the left ventricle contracts.

4. **Left Ventricle:** The left ventricle is the largest and strongest of the heart's four chambers, and it has the function of pumping vitalized blood through the whole body. For this reason, the muscular walls of the left ventricle are thicker than those of the heart's other chambers. After receiving blood from the left atrium, the left ventricle contracts to pump blood out into the aorta. Back-flow into the left ventricle from the aorta is prevented by the aortic semilunar valve. The aorta is the largest blood vessel in the body, and it quickly divides into the other major arteries (left and right subclavian arteries, left and right carotid arteries, descending aorta, and the coronary arteries) that distribute oxygenated blood to the tissues.

THE HEARTBEAT: CARDIAC CYCLE

Each heartbeat, or cardiac cycle, is divided into two phases in which both sides of the heart contract and relax simultaneously. The term systole is used to denote the contractive phase of the

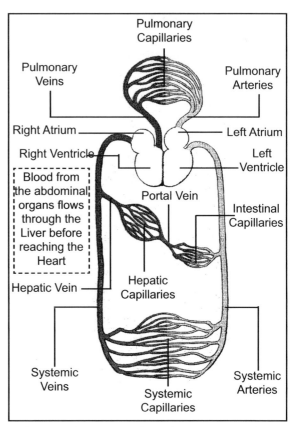

Figure 8.132. The arterial and venous blood flow. (Inspired from the original artwork of H.V. Carter)

cardiac cycle, while the term diastole refers to the relaxation period. The two ventricles contract (ventricular systole) as the atria relax (atrial diastole), then the two atria contract (atrial systole) as the ventricles relax (ventricular diastole).

Listening through a physician's stethoscope, the "lub" sound of the heartbeat is produced as the tricuspid and bicuspid valves snap shut during ventricular contraction; while the "dub" sound is the result of the closing of the aortic and pulmonary semilunar valves during ventricular diastole. Ventricular diastole takes slightly longer than ventricular systole, hence the pause between heartbeats. Heart rate in the average adult is around 72 beats per minute. It is usually about 80 beats per minute in children, while in infants a normal heart rate may be as high as 120 beats per minute.

The Heart's Electrical System

The heart produces its own electrical impulses independent of nervous stimulation from the central nervous system. Communication between the heart and the central nervous system takes place through both the sympathetic and parasympathetic nerve impulses. The electrical stimulus that initiates the contractions of the heart originates within the sinoatrial node (SA node). The SA node is alternately known as the sinus node, or the pacemaker, and it is located in the right atrium of the heart (Figure 8.133). The electrical impulse it produces travels into the atria, causing them to contract, while also continuing through conductive pathways to the atrioventricular node (AV node). Located in the septum between the two atria, the AV node rapidly conducts this charge into the ventricles (via the AV bundle, then the Purkinje fibers), causing them to contract immediately after the atrial contraction. Other areas of the heart contain electrically insulating tissue to insure the proper conduction of this essential electrical impulse. An electrocardiogram (ECG) is the most common method of recording the electrical activity of the heart.

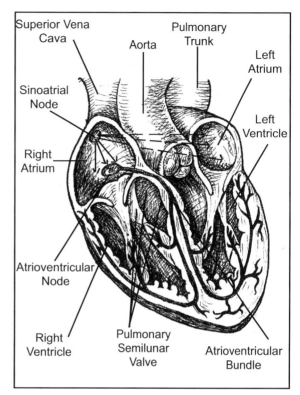

Figure 8.133. The Sinoatrial (SA) Node is located in the right atrium of the heart

Common Disorders of the Heart

Common disorders of the heart include the following: heart failure (inability of the heart to supply adequate blood flow to the tissues), artherosclerosis (hardening or narrowing of the vessels), valve disorders (such as valve prolapse), fibrosis of the cardiac muscle, myocarditis, pericarditis, hypertension, hypotension (low blood pressure), and congenital heart defects. In coronary artery disease, sometimes known as ischemic heart disease, there is inadequate blood flow to the heart tissues, often resulting in hypoxia and angina. A heart attack, or myocardial infarction, generally involves severely reduced blood flow to the heart tissue resulting in irreversible damage to myocardial tissues. Cardiac arrhythmias include dysrhythmia, heart block, heart flutters, atrial or ventricular fibrillation, and ventricular premature contraction. A heart palpitation is a heartbeat that is unusually fast, strong, or otherwise irregular enough to be noticed by a patient. Tachycardia is any abnormally fast heart rate (over 100 BPM), while bradycardia describes an unusually slow heart rate (lower than 60 BPM). The term murmurs refers to unusual or abnormal heart sounds, angina pectoris refers to general chest pain in the area of the heart (usually due to hypoxia), and cardiac arrest refers to the cessation of an effective heartbeat.

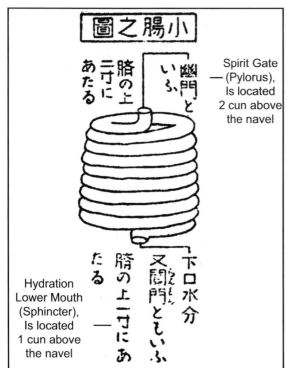

Figure 8.134. The Ancient Chinese Anatomical Diagram of the Small Intestine (SI) Organ: *"Important Useful Notes on Acupuncture and Moxibustion,"* by Masatoyo Hongo (1718)

Figure 8.135. The Chinese characters "Xiao Chang" (Small Intestine)

THE SMALL INTESTINE: XIAO CHANG

The Small Intestine is a tubular Yang (Fu) organ (Figure 8.134), belongs to the Fire Element, and its associated Yin (Zang) Organ is the Heart.

The ancient Chinese understood the role of the Small Intestine in digestion, and observed that the veins of the organ provided the means of absorbing nutrients into the Blood stream.

The Small Intestine is sometimes called "The Official in Charge of Separating the Pure From the Impure," because it separates the "Clean" (usable) Food Essence (Gu Qi) from the "turbid" (unusable) Food Essence.

The Small Intestine is also known as "The Minister who Guards the Emperor's Inner Quarters," because it acts as a filtering lens that focuses the intention of the Heart, helping the Heart to maintain clarity of Mind, and to distinguish right from wrong.

CHINESE CHARACTER FOR SMALL INTESTINE: XIAO CHANG

The Chinese character "Xiao Chang" translates as "Small Intestine." It refers to a general description of the image of the Small Intestine organ, and is composed of two images (Figure 8.135):

- **Xiao:** The first character "Xiao" describes an object that has been split in two, and translates as "Small or Little."
- **Chang:** The second character "Chang" translates as "intestine," and is divided into two ideographs:

The character towards the left, "Ji" depicts the Chinese ideogram for Body Tissue, Muscle or Flesh (all of which are forms of Connective Tissue). The character on the right depicts the image of "the Sun above the horizon, with its rays shining downward." This image expresses the Heavenly Yang influence on this particular bowel organ.

The ideograph represents the image of the Sun enriching and transforming something within the flesh and conveys the Small Intestine's role in the digestive process. Together, the Chinese characters "Xiao Chang" can be translated as, "the Small Heavenly Transformation occurring within the flesh."

The Small Intestines command the "Ye," the thicker aspect of the intestinal fluids.

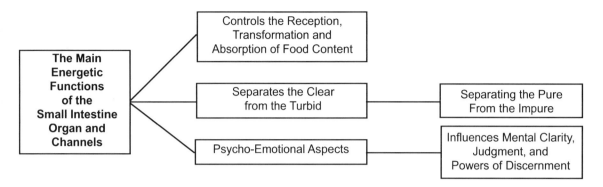

Figure 8.136. The Main Energetic Functions of the Small Intestine Organ and Channels

THE SMALL INTESTINE IN CHINESE MEDICINE

The functions of the Small Intestine described in Traditional Chinese Medicine are similar to those that are described in Western Medicine.

According to Traditional Chinese Medicine, the main functions of the Small Intestine are to: control the reception, transformation and absorption of food content; separate the clear from the turbid; and express itself through the psycho-emotional aspects of mental clarity and powers of discernment. These main functions are described as follows (Figure 8.136):

1. **Controls the Reception, Transformation and Absorption of Food Content:** The Small Intestine temporarily stores partially digested food, allowing for the absorption of the essential substances of the undigested food and a portion of the liquid content. It later transfers the remaining residue (along with a considerable amount of liquid) to the Large Intestine. It is for this reason that the Small Intestine is said to "govern liquid."

2. **Separates the Clear from the Turbid:** The Small Intestine is sometimes called "The Official in Charge of Separating the Pure From the Impure" because it separates the "Clean" (usable) Food Essence (Gu Qi) from the "turbid" (unusable) Food Essence. The Clean Gu Qi is sent to the Spleen, which transports and distributes it throughout the body to nourish the tissues. The waste (turbid) portion is transported to the Large Intestine and Urinary Bladder organs to be further processed. The unwanted liquid is directed into the Urinary Bladder which further refines the liquid into pure and impure portions; the pure portion is sent to moisten the skin and muscles, and the impure portion is excreted from the body in the form of urine.

3. **Psycho-Emotional Aspects:** The Small Intestine is also in charge of sorting the pure from the impure on the level of thoughts and emotions, influencing the individual's mental clarity, judgment, and powers of discernment. Thus, the ability to effectively distinguish between relevant issues with clarity before making a decision is attributed to the Small Intestine.

The Small Intestine is also known as "The Minister who Guards the Emperor's Inner Quarters," and it can act as a filtering lens that focuses the intention of the Heart. The Small Intestine helps the Heart to maintain clarity of Mind, and to distinguish right from wrong. It is believed that sarcasm and sexual perversion may be the result of the Small Intestine not being able to receive or transmit Heart essence properly.

THE SMALL INTESTINE CHANNELS

The Small Intestine Channels are Yang Channels that flow externally from the hands to the head (Figure 8.137).

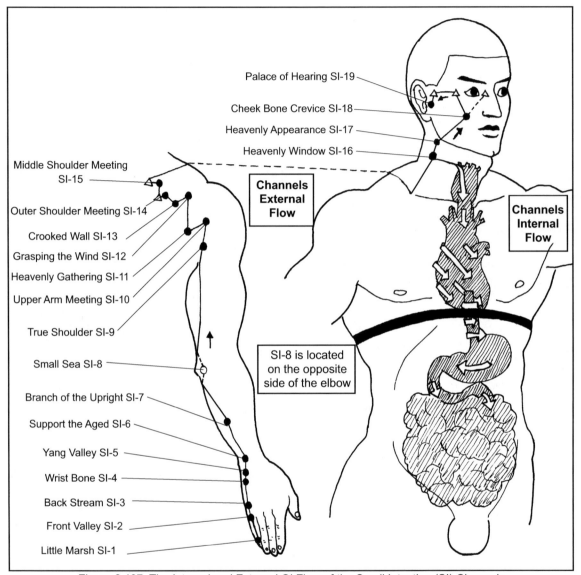

Figure 8.137. The Internal and External Qi Flow of the Small Intestine (SI) Channels

- **The External Branches:** The energetic rivers of the Small Intestine originate externally from the lateral tips (ulnar side) of the little fingers, then ascend the arms to the shoulders where they divide into two pairs of branches.

  The external branch ascends from the Heavenly Window (SI-16) point, travelling externally up the sides of the neck, before dividing into two more pairs of branches at the cheek. One pair of these branches ends at the ears, while the other pair ends at the lateral side of the nose and inner canthus of the eyes.

- **The Internal Branches:** At the Heavenly Window (SI-16) points, the internal branches descend the supraclavicular fossa internally, spiral wraps the Heart, then continues down the esophagus, diaphragm, and Stomach before penetrating the Small Intestine organ.

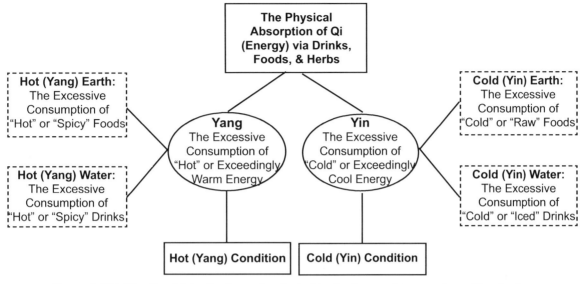

Figure 8.138. The Small Intestine is easily affected by the type and temperature of food eaten

Channels' Energy Flow

The energy of the Small Intestine Channels acts on the skin, muscles, and nerves found along their pathway.

The Small Intestine Channels store more Blood than Qi, and act more on the physical substances and Blood functions than on energy.

At the High-Tide time period (1 p.m. to 3 p.m.), Qi and Blood abound in the Small Intestine Organ and Small Intestine Channels. At this time, the Small Intestine Organ and Channels can more easily be dispersed and purged. During Low-Tide (1 a.m. to 3 a.m.), the Small Intestine Organ and Channels can be more readily tonified.

The Influence of Climate

The Small Intestine can be easily injured by specific types and "temperatures" of food. For example, in Traditional Chinese Medicine, the consumption of drinks, foods, and herbs are categorized as having either Cold (Yin) or Hot (Yang) energetic properties. An excess consumption of Cold or "Raw Foods" can create a Cold Yin Condition within the Small Intestine; likewise, an excess consumption of Hot or "Spicy Foods" can create a Hot Yang Condition within the Small Intestine (Figure 8.138).

The Influence of Taste, Color, and Sound

- The Bitter Taste can be used to tonify both the Small Intestine and Heart
- The light Red color is used to tonify the Small Intestine and Heart.
- The "Ha," "Ke" and "Zheng" Sounds are used to purge the Small Intestine and the Heart.

Small Intestine Pathology

Diseases of the Small Intestine Organ and Channels include diseases of the face, ear, cheek, lower jaw, neck, throat, and the dorsal ulnar side of the upper extremities.

Pathologic Heat in the Heart may be transmitted to the Small Intestine, resulting in urodynia (painful urination) and hematuria (blood in the urine). Herbal prescriptions used to dispel Heat from the Heart are sometimes employed in treating these urinary symptoms when they contribute to a dysfunction of the Small Intestine.

T.C.M. Patterns of Disharmony

Patterns of disharmony associated with the Small Intestine organ and channels are classified as either excess or deficient patterns, described as follows (Figure 8.139):

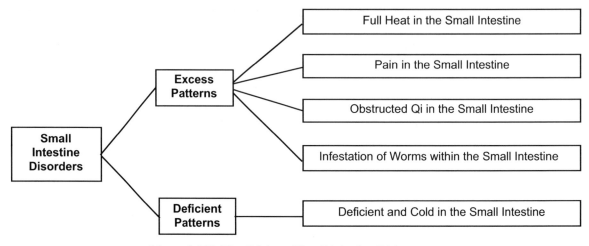

Figure 8.139. The Origins of Small Intestine Disharmony

1. **Excess Patterns of the Small Intestine:**
   - **Full Heat in the Small Intestine:** This pattern is closely associated with Blazing Heart Fire and Internal Full Heat, and can be created through chronic emotional stress.

     Symptoms can manifest as mental restlessness, irritability, abdominal pain, uncomfortable feelings of heat in the chest, thirst, tongue ulcers, painful urination, and Blood in the urine.
   - **Pain in the Small Intestine:** This pattern is a type of Qi Stagnation, and is usually associated with Liver Qi invading the Spleen. This condition can either be acute or chronic.

     Symptoms can manifest as abdominal distension, borborygmus (intestinal rumbling caused by moving gas), flatulence, lower abdominal "twisting" pain (which may extend into the patient's back), and pain in the testes.
   - **Obstructed Qi in the Small Intestine:** This pattern is closely associated with the Western syndrome of acute intestinal obstruction, and can resemble an acute appendicitis. Obstructed Qi in the Small Intestine can be caused from an excessive consumption of Cold or raw foods, which can impede the Small Intestine's function of transforming food essence.

     Symptoms of obstructed Qi in the Small Intestine can manifest as violent abdominal pain, abdominal distension, borborygmus, flatulence, constipation, and vomiting of fecal material.
   - **Infestation of Worms within the Small Intestine:** This type of obstruction of the Small Intestine is due to the infestation of intestinal parasites that cause abdominal pain and distension. According to ancient Chinese medicine, the infestation of worms was believed to be caused by a Cold condition occurring within the Small Intestines and the Spleen, which allows the worms to live.

     Different worms manifest through various symptoms: roundworms can cause abdominal pain, cold limbs, and the vomiting of the roundworm parasites; hookworms may cause the patient to eat unnatural objects such as dirt, leaves, and various uncooked foods; tapeworms often cause the patient to experience a state of constant hunger; and pinworms can cause the patient to experience itching in or around the anus which worsen at night.

2. **Deficient Patterns of the Small Intestine:**
   - **Deficiency and Cold in the Small Intestine:** This is an internal pattern of deficiency (usually of Spleen Yang) and Cold. It can be caused from an excessive consumption of Cold and raw foods.

     Symptoms can manifest as abdominal pain, borborygmus, diarrhea, and a desire for hot drinks.

The Small Intestine in Western Medicine

According to Western Anatomy, the small intestine is a convoluted tube, 1 inch in diameter, with an average length of 21 feet (Figure 8.140). It begins at the pyloric sphincter of the stomach and coils through the central and lower aspect of the abdominal cavity, terminating at the ileocecal valve, which connects to the large intestine. The entire length of the small intestine is anchored to the peritoneum by sheet-like extensions of connective tissues called mesentery.

The small intestine is the body's primary organ of digestion and assimilation. Nearly all of the digestion and absorption of nutrients takes place within the small intestine. In order to facilitate this function, the small intestine is lined with nearly 500 million villi which greatly increases the surface area available for food absorption. These intestinal villi are tiny hairlike projections of epithelium (skin-like tissue) that extend outward from the internal walls of the small intestine. The villi contain a rich network of capillaries that serve to expose the blood to the nutrients available in the chyme contained within the small intestine. Combined with the microvilli, the villi of the small intestine expose about 300 square meters (roughly the size of a tennis court) of surface area to the chyme.

The mucosa and submucosa within the walls of the small intestine are designed to allow for the ability to efficiently digest and absorb chyme. The epithelial cells in the mucosa consist of simple columnar epithelium, and contain absorptive cells, enteroendocrine cells, Paneth cells, and goblet cells. The goblet cells secrete additional mucus.

The small intestine is divided into three segments: the duodenum, the jejunum, and the ileum, which are described as follows:

1. **Duodenum:** Originating from the pyloric sphincter of the stomach, the duodenum is the shortest piece of the small intestine, extending only 10 inches before merging with the jejunum. The duodenum is relatively immovable and mostly retroperitoneal, curving around the head of the pancreas. Within the duodenum, secretions from the liver and pancreas, in addition to certain secretions from the small intestine, are introduced into the chyme, causing it to break down and become more absorbable. The submucosa of the duodenum also contains duodenal glands, that secrete an alkaline mucus that helps to neutralize the gastric acid within the chyme.

2. **Jejunum:** The jejunum is an intraperitoneal (contained within the peritoneum) organ. Originating from the duodenum, the jejunum coils and winds through the abdomen, extending a distance of about 8 feet before it merges with the ileum.

3. **Ileum:** The ileum is also an intraperitoneal organ, and is the longest portion of the small intestine. Originating from the jejunum, the ileum coils and winds through the abdomen, extending for a distance of about 12 feet. It terminates at the ileocecal valve, which separates the small intestine from the large intestine.

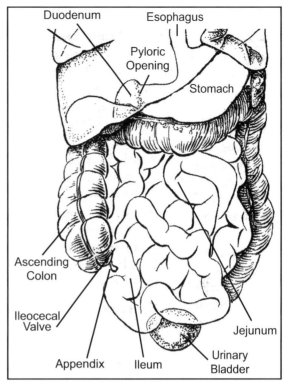

Figure 8.140. The Small Intestine (SI) Organ. (Inspired by the original artwork of Wynn Kapit)

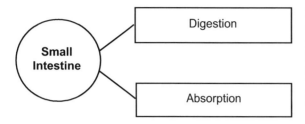

Figure 8.141. The Functions of the Small Intestine (Western Medical Perspective)

Physiology

The small intestine has two primary functions, digestion and assimilation (Figure 8.141). Digestion refers to the process of breaking down the chyme to make it absorbable, while assimilation refers to the process whereby nutrients are absorbed into the blood through the intestinal wall. Wavelike peristaltic contractions ripple along the entire length of the gastrointestinal tract, propelling the food mass through the esophagus, stomach, small intestine, and large intestine. Chyme travels from the stomach and through the small intestine in this way, before being introduced into the cecum of the large intestine via the ileocecal valve.

Chyme from the stomach is released a little at a time into the small intestine via the pyloric sphincter. At this point, the chyme has already been partially broken down by the hydrochloric acid, intrinsic factor, and pepsin that were released into it within the stomach. Secretions of bile (from the liver and gallbladder) are released into the chyme in the duodenum via the bile duct, while the pancreatic duct introduces into the chyme various enzymes (amylase, trypsin, lipase, etc.) secreted by the pancreas. The pancreas also releases sodium bicarbonate into the duodenum to neutralize the acidity of the chyme, changing the PH of the chyme inside the small intestine.

The bile released into the small intestine serves mainly to emulsify (cause large molecules to break down into smaller ones) fats, thereby

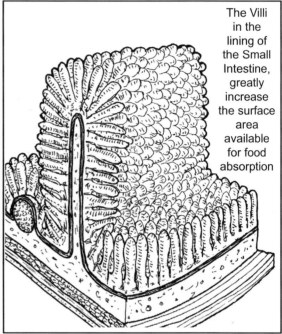

Figure 8.142. The Small Intestine Mucosa (Villi). (Inspired by the original artwork of Wynn Kapit).

making it possible for them to be absorbed into the blood through the thin cell walls of the villi (Figure 8.142). Pancreatic amylase combines starches with water and converts them into the absorbable sugar maltose. Trypsin combines proteins with water to form peptides, which are then absorbed through the intestinal wall. Lipase digests fat droplets and converts them into absorbable glycerol and various fatty acids. The cells of the small intestine also secrete various enzymes (maltase, sucrase, lactase, peptidase, etc.) into the chyme, thus breaking it down still further.

By the time the chyme reaches the ileocecal valve, nearly all available nutrients (e.g., carbohydrates, proteins, and fats) have been absorbed into the bloodstream. The remainder of the food mass then passes into the large intestine, at which point it is referred to as feces.

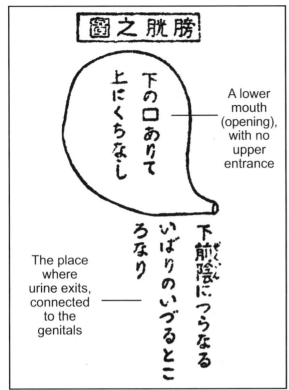

Figure 8.143. The Ancient Chinese Anatomical Diagram of the Urinary Bladder (UB) Organ: *"Important Useful Notes on Acupuncture and Moxibustion,"* by Masatoyo Hongo (1718)

THE URINARY BLADDER: PANG GUANG

The Urinary Bladder is a tubular Yang (Fu) organ (Figure 8.143), belongs to the Water Element, and its associated Yin (Zang) Organ is the Kidneys.

In Daoist Alchemy, the Bladder Fire (also known as the "Common People's Fire"), is located in the lower abdominal area, near the perineum, in the area of the Urinary Bladder. The Bladder Fire is responsible for evaporating water, heating the Lower Burner, and the transforming Jing (Essence) into Qi (Energy). It is also an important aspect of the body's "True Fire," responsible for spiritual transformation.

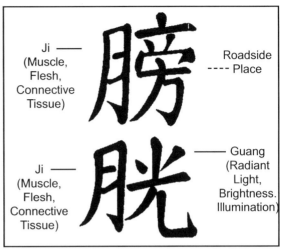

Figure 8.144. The Chinese character for "Pang Guang," Urinary Bladder

CHINESE CHARACTER FOR URINARY BLADDER: PANG GUANG

The Chinese characters "Pang Guang" can be translated as the internal organ that operates as "the Roadside Place of Brightness." This expresses the Urinary Bladder's function as the keeper of the "Bladder Fire" or "Common Peoples Fire," which is responsible for transforming Jing into Qi.

- **Pang:** The first character "Pang" translates as "Urinary Bladder." It is composed of two characters: The character to the left, "Ji" depicts the Chinese ideogram for Body Tissue, Muscle or Flesh (all of which are forms of Connective Tissue). On the right upper half is the radical for "Roadside," the bottom half is the radical for "Place" (Figure 8.144).
- **Guang:** The second character "Guang" is composed of two characters: The character to the left, "Ji" depicts the Chinese ideogram for Body Tissue, Muscle or Flesh (all of which are forms of Connective Tissue). On the right is the radical "Guang" meaning "Brightness, Radiant Light and Illumination." In ancient China, the character Guang was originally composed of two separate characters. The radical for "Twenty" was placed at the top of the ideograph, and the radical of "Fire" was placed at the bottom. Together the characters stood for "The Brightness of Twenty Fires."

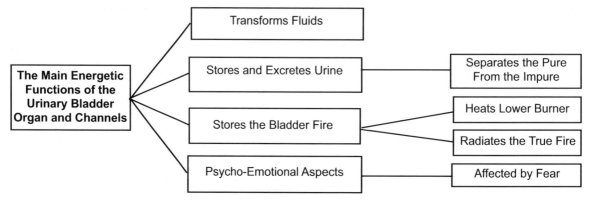

Figure 8.145. The Main Energetic Functions of the Urinary Bladder Organ and Channels

THE URINARY BLADDER IN CHINESE MEDICINE

The functions of the Urinary Bladder in Traditional Chinese Medicine are almost the same as those described in Western Medicine. However, Chinese energetic medicine also considers the functions of the Urinary Bladder to include the transforming of fluids, the storing of the Urinary Bladder Fire, and the governing of various psycho-emotional aspects.

According to Traditional Chinese Medicine, the main functions of the Urinary Bladder are to: store and excrete urine, store the Urinary Bladder Fire, transform fluids, and express itself through the psycho-emotional aspects of fear and lack of decision making. These main functions are described as follows (Figure 8.145):

1. **Transforms Fluids:** One function of the Urinary Bladder is to remove water by Qi transformation. The Urinary Bladder receives the "impure" portion of the fluids that have been separated by the Kidneys from the Lungs, and from the Small Intestine and Large Intestine. The Urinary Bladder temporarily stores and transforms these fluids into urine, and then discharges the urine when the Urinary Bladder is full.
2. **Stores and Excretes Urine:** The Urinary Bladder is sometimes called "the Water District Official (or "Controller") of the Storage of Waste Water." The Urinary Bladder's function of storing and excreting urine is dependent on the Qi and Heat that is provided by the Kidney Yang.

    Because the primary function of the Triple Burner is Body Fluid movement and metabolism, there is a functional link between the Urinary Bladder and the Lower Burner. The Urinary Bladder and the Small Intestine work together to remove fluids from the Lower Burner.
3. **Stores the Urinary Bladder Fire:** The Bladder Fire, also called the Common People's Fire, is located in the lower abdominal area near the perineum. It is responsible for evaporating water, heating the Lower Burner, the transforming of Jing into Qi; it is also an aspect of the body's "True Fire" (see Triple Burners).
4. **Psycho-Emotional Aspects:** The Urinary Bladder stores and utilizes the body's energetic reserves, and like the Kidneys, it is affected by fear. An imbalance in the Urinary Bladder can cause such psychological symptoms as habitual fear, lack of ability to make decisions, and diminished moral character. If the imbalance becomes chronic, it can result in emotional responses such as jealousy, suspicion, and holding on to long-standing grudges.

Chapter 8: The Twelve Primary Organs, Channels and Collaterals

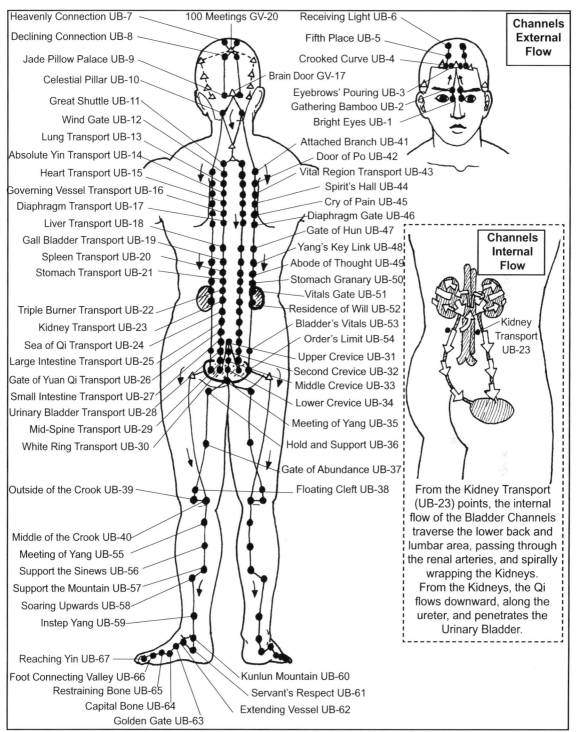

Figure 8.146. The Internal and External Qi Flow of the Urinary Bladder (UB) Channels

The Urinary Bladder Channels

The Urinary Bladder Channels are Yang Channels that flow from the head to the feet (Figure 8.146).

- **The External Branches:** The two rivers of the Urinary Bladder Channels originate externally from the inner canthus of the eyes. From the inner canthus of the eyes they ascend upward over the head to join the Governing Vessel at the 100 Meetings (GV-20) point where they divide into two additional branches that flow into each temple and into the Brain.

From the GV-20 point, the main channels flow down the back of the head to the Celestial Pillar (UB-10) points, where they again divide into two sets of branches that descend the lateral aspect of the back and connect to the Kidneys at the Kidney Transport (UB-23) points.

From the UB-23 points, an internal branch rushes into the lower back, while the main external branches continue to flow down the medial aspect of the thighs, pooling at the popliteal fossa located at the back of the knees.

From the popliteal fossa the main channels further descend the calf and foot, ending on the lateral side of the tips of the little toes.

- **The Internal Branches:** From the UB-23 points, the internal flow of the Urinary Bladder Channels rushes into the lower back and lumbar area, passing through the renal arteries, and spirally wrapping the Kidneys. From the Kidneys, the energy flows downward, along the ureter, and penetrates the Urinary Bladder.

Channels' Energy Flow

The Urinary Bladder Channels regulate the energetic functions of the Kidneys, and act on the skin, muscles, and nerves found along their pathway.

The Urinary Bladder Channels store more Blood than Qi, and act more on the physical substances and the Blood functions than on energy.

At the High-Tide time period (3 p.m. to 5 p.m.), Qi and Blood abound in the Urinary Bladder organ and Urinary Bladder channels. At this time period the Urinary Bladder Organ and Channels can more easily be dispersed and purged. During Low-Tide (3 a.m. to 5 a.m.), the Urinary Bladder Organ and Channels can be more readily tonified.

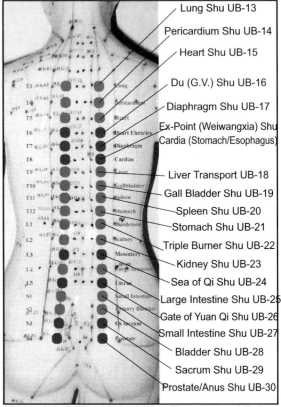

Figure 8.147. The 18 Back Shu (Transporting) Points

The Eighteen Back-Shu Points

The Eighteen Back-"Shu" ("Source" or "Transporting") points are all located on the back, along the Urinary Bladder Channel. They correspond to the Twelve Zang Fu Organs, and are used both for diagnosis and for treatment. These special points are areas on the body that "transport" energy directly into the internal organs, and lie at the same anatomical level as the related organ. In the clinic, they can also be used for treating disorders of their corresponding sense organs.

The Eighteen Back Transporting points are as follows (Figure 8.147): Lungs UB-13, Pericardium UB-14, Heart UB-15, Governing Vessel UB-16, Diaphragm UB-17, Liver UB-18, Gall Bladder UB-19, Spleen UB-20, Stomach UB-21, Triple Burners UB-22, Kidneys UB-23, Sea of Qi UB-24, Large Intestine UB-25, Gate to the Yuan Qi (Guan Yuan) UB-26, Small Intestine UB-27, Bladder UB-28, Sacrum UB-29, and Prostate/Anus UB-30.

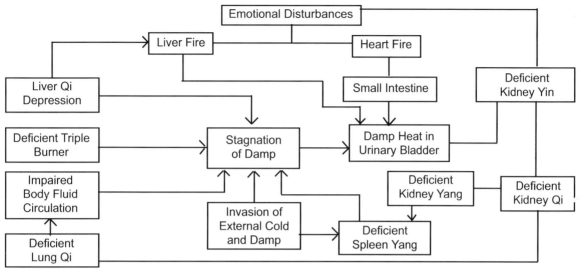
Figure 8.148. The Origins of Damp Heat in the Urinary Bladder Disharmony

THE INFLUENCE OF CLIMATE

The Urinary Bladder can be easily injured by chronic or excessive exposure to Cold and Damp environments. This can lead to the accumulation of Dampness in the Urinary Bladder, which manifests as Damp Cold or Damp Heat syndromes.

THE INFLUENCE OF TASTE, COLOR, AND SOUND

- The Salty taste can be used to tonify both the Urinary Bladder and the Kidneys.
- The Light Blue color is used to tonify the Urinary Bladder.
- The "Chree," "Fuu" and "Yuu" Sounds are used to purge the Urinary Bladder and the Kidneys.

URINARY BLADDER PATHOLOGY

The main diseases of the Urinary Bladder organ and channels include: diseases located at the top of the head, brain disorders, disorders of the neck and back (especially the lumbar and sacral regions), disorders of the back of the legs and thighs, and disorders of the lateral sides of the feet.

Diseases of the Urinary Bladder Organ manifest in changes in urine and urination; these changes will reflect either a deficient or excess condition of the Urinary Bladder, described as follows:
1. **Deficient Conditions** are attributed to a condition of Deficient Kidney Qi which then affects the Urinary Bladder's ability to transform Qi. This dysfunction causes frequent urination, dribbling, or enuresis (involuntary discharge of urine).
2. **Excess Conditions** are attributed to Damp Heat in the Urinary Bladder, and may manifest in symptoms such as: heat and pain during urination, the short release of murky or reddish urine, frequent difficulty in urination, pus or Blood in the urine, and Bladder stones which cause a urinary block and painful distention of the lower abdomen.

Most pathological diseases of the Urinary Bladder organ are due to the accumulation of Dampness (Damp Heat or Damp Cold). The most common pattern of Urinary Bladder disharmony is Damp Heat in the Urinary Bladder.

T.C.M. PATTERNS OF DISHARMONY

Patterns of Urinary Bladder Disharmony are often associated with either Damp Heat in the Urinary Bladder or Damp Cold in the Urinary Bladder, and are described as follows (Figure 8.148):
1. **Damp Heat in the Urinary Bladder:** The pattern of Damp Heat in the Urinary Bladder can be caused from several factors: Depressed Liver Qi, Deficient Lung Qi, Deficient Spleen Qi, Deficient Triple Burner Qi, External Dampness and the invasion of pathogenic evils, or an invasion of External Cold and Damp. Symptoms include frequent and urgent urina-

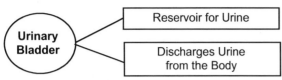

Figure 8.149. The Functions of the Urinary Bladder (Western Medical Perspective)

tion, burning during urination, turbid urine, Blood or "sand" in the urine, fever, and thirst.
- **Depressed Liver Qi:** Depressed Liver Qi can give rise to Liver Fire, which then causes emotional disturbances that aggravate both Liver Fire and Heart Fire. This pathogenic pattern can create Deficient Kidney Yin, Deficient Liver Yin, and Deficient Heart Yin. If the Toxic Heat moves downward, it can affect the Urinary Bladder and aggravate a condition of Damp Heat.
- **Deficient Lung Qi:** Deficient Kidney Qi may interact with Deficient Lung Qi.
- **Deficient Spleen Qi:** Deficient Kidney Yang can contribute to Deficient Spleen Yang and facilitate the invasion of Cold and Damp.
- **Deficient Triple Burner Qi:** Chronic retention of Cold and damp in the Lower Burner can injure Kidney Yang.
- **Invasion of External Cold and Damp:** An invasion of External Cold and Damp may lead to the stagnation of Dampness.
2. **Damp Cold in the Urinary Bladder:** The pattern of Damp Cold in the Urinary Bladder can be caused from excessive exposure to External Dampness and Cold, characterized by the presence of dampness and Cold in the Lower Burner. Symptoms include frequent and urgent urination, heaviness in the hypogastrium and urethra and turbid urine.

THE URINARY BLADDER IN WESTERN MEDICINE

According to Western Anatomy, the urinary bladder is a smooth, collapsible, muscular sac, located on the pelvic floor just posterior to the pubic symphysis. The interior of the urinary bladder has three openings. The upper part of the urinary bladder communicates with the kidneys via the two ureters. Its lower part is connected to the urethra, which opens externally by means of the urinary

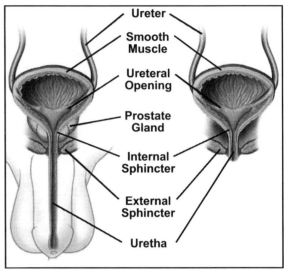

Figure 8.150. The Uribary Bladder (UB) Organ

orifice. In males, the urinary bladder lies immediately anterior to the rectum, and surrounded by the prostate gland before it empties into the urethra. In females, the urinary bladder lies anterior to the vagina and inferior to the Uterus (Figure 8.149).

Though somewhat movable, the urinary bladder is held in position by folds of the peritoneum. Its size and shape fluctuates, depending on how much urine it contains. As the urine volume increases, the urinary bladder expands into a pear-shape and rises inside the abdominal cavity.

The urinary bladder wall has three layers. The innermost coat, known as the mucosa, is a mucous membrane composed of transitional epithelium (which allows the urinary bladder to stretch) and an underlying lamina propria (connective tissue). These inner walls of the urinary bladder are thick, and contain folds known as rugae that allow it to expand and contract (similar to the stomach).

The middle layer of the urinary bladder consists of a muscular layer which itself is composed of three layers of interwoven smooth muscle tissue. The entire urinary bladder organ is surrounded by a protective adventitia that merges with the parietal peritoneum.

Physiology

The bladder is a temporary reservoir for the urine produced by the kidneys; it discharges urine from the body through the urethra (Figure 8.150).

CHAPTER 8: THE TWELVE PRIMARY ORGANS, CHANNELS AND COLLATERALS

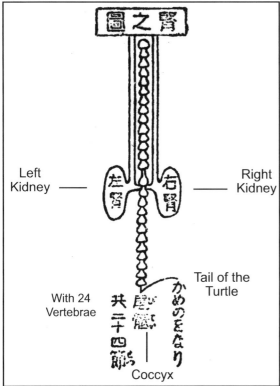

Figure 8.151. The Ancient Chinese Anatomical Diagram of the Kidney (Kd) Organ: *"Important Useful Notes on Acupuncture and Moxibustion,"* by Masatoyo Hongo (1718)

THE KIDNEY: SHEN

The Kidneys are solid Yin (Zang) Organs, belong to the Water Element, and are energetically paired with the Urinary Bladder.

The Kidneys are different from the other Yin organs in that they are the foundation of all of the Yin and Yang energies within the body. They are also said to be the origin of the energies of Fire (Yang) and Water (Yin) within the body (Figure 8.151). Therefore, the spirits of the Kidneys are traditionally "doubled." This is why two animals (i.e., the black turtle and snake, or a Double Headed White Deer) are used to represent Kidney Qi.

According to the *Yellow Court Classics*, the spirit of the two Kidneys is in charge of extending longevity. In ancient Daoist imagery, it was also taught that the energetic structure of the Kidney Organs maintains the esoteric shape of "Egg-Shaped Pebbles."

Figure 8.152. Spirits of the Kidney (Kd) Organ: *Yifang Leiju (Classified Collection of Medical Recipes),* (Japanese reproduction - 1861)

ANCIENT KIDNEY ORGAN TEACHING

The following picture (Figure 8.152) is from the *Yifang leiju (Classified Collection of Medical Recipes)* section on the Five Viscera. The ancient text states:

"The Kidney is Qi of Kan (Water Trigram),
It carries the Essence of Water.
And its color is black.

It looks like Egg-Shaped Pebbles.
Its spirit has the form of
a Mysterious Double-Headed White Deer.

On both sides
it engenders Zhi ("Knowledge);
Which is transformed into a Jade Child,
Who is 1 chi tall.
And goes in and out of the
Treasure-House of the Kidney."

Additionally, according to the ancient Daoist teachings of the *Yellow Court Classics*, the energetic function of the Kidneys is described as follows:

523

The Deity of the Kidneys
has the shape of a Mysterious White Deer
with two heads
that transforms itself into a Jade Youth.

According to ancient Daoist teaching,
the internal energy of the Kidney Organs
appear like egg-shaped pebbles.

The left Kidney is associated with
the "Ren" (Yang Water Element) Heavenly Stem,
and the Mysterious Yang;
while the right kidney is associated with
the "Gui" (Yin Water Element) Heavenly Stem,
the Feminine Yin, and the Gate of Life.

The Ears are the Officers of the Kidneys.
Although the spirit of the Kidneys is called
"Xuan Ming" ("Mysterious Obscurity"),
according to ancient Daoist texts,
he is also given the name "Yu Ying"
("Nourishing the Child").

The Palace of the Kidneys
resembles a Dark Watchtower.
In the center of this special Watchtower
sits a Virgin Boy of profound obscurity
and great mystery.

He is the master of the Six Yang Organs,
the Nine Fluids,
and the source of the two external Ears
that respond to one hundred movements.

The Virgin Boy is clothed
in a Dark Blue brocaded skirt,
that flows like a dragon banner
dancing above the clouds and mist,
reaching the bright radiance
of the Sun and Moon.

Through the assistance of the Water King,
you may cross the Gate of Life,
ascend to the Ninth Heaven,
survive one hundred diseases,
and one thousand disasters."

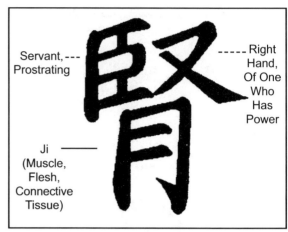

Figure 8.153. The Chinese character "Shen" (Kidney)

CHINESE CHARACTER FOR THE KIDNEY: SHEN

The Chinese character "Shen" translates as "Kidneys," and should not to be confused with the "Shen" character that translates as "Heart/Mind" or "Spirit."

- **Shen:** The character "Shen" refers to the image of a Kidney Organ, and is divided into two sections (Figure 8.153):

  The upper left hand side of the character depicts the radical for "a slave or servant (i.e., minister or general) prostrating and bowing before the Emperor." The upper right hand side of this character depicts the radical for "the right hand," signifying someone who has the power and authority to lead and pull people according to his personal will.

- **Ji:** The character to the bottom, "Ji" depicts the Chinese ideogram for Body Tissue, Muscle or Flesh (all of which are forms of Connective Tissue).

  Together, the Chinese ideograph for "Shen" can be translated as, "that which pushes the organism to the actualization of all its true potentialities."

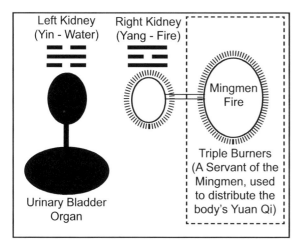

Figure 8.154. The Left Kidney is the "Water of Life," and is connected to the energetic functions of the Urinary Bladder; the Right Kidney is Yang, is connected with the "Fire of Life" and the Mingmen (Gate of Destiny), and is associated with the energetic functions of the Triple Burners.

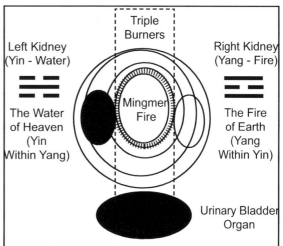

Figure 8.155. After the Ming Dynasty, Chinese doctors no longer saw the Mingmen as being part of the Right Kidney; instead, they believed that it was located in-between both Kidneys.

THE YIN AND YANG OF THE KIDNEYS

Traditional Chinese Medicine describes the Kidneys as an internal organ that can display the energetic manifestations of two main polarities, expressing both Yin and Yang aspects.

- **The Yin of the Kidneys (Primary Yin):** This pertains to the vital essence of the Kidneys, including its material structures. The Kidney Yin is the foundation and fundamental substance of all the Yin in the body, including the Yin of the Liver, Heart, and Lungs. It is responsible for nourishing the tissues and providing them with fluid-like moistening and cooling essences. It also rules the cycles of birth, growth, maturation, and reproduction.

  According to the *Nan Jing: Classic of Difficulties*, the Left Kidney is Yin and is connected with the "Water of Life," and is associated with the Water Metabolism functions of the Urinary Bladder.

- **The Yang of the Kidneys (Primary Yang):** This pertains to the Kidney's function of "Heating and Moving the Qi." The Kidney Yang is the primary motivating force behind all of the body's physiological processes. Kidney Yang is the foundation of all the Yang energies of the body, including the Yang of the Spleen, Heart, and Lungs.

According to the *Nan Jing: Classic of Difficulties*, the Right Kidney is Yang and is connected with the "Fire of Life" and the "Mingmen" ("Gate of Life/Destiny"). It is associated with the energetic functions of the Triple Burners, which act as a servant of the Mingmen to distribute the body's Yuan Qi (Figure 8.154). In ancient China, the Mingmen is the residence of the body's "Shen Jing" ("Spirit's Essence"), where the individual's Yuan Qi (Original Energy) is attached.

It is important to note, that during the time of the Ming Dynasty (1368-1644 A.D.), Chinese doctors reconsidered the energetic location of the Mingmen. Instead of being a part of the right Kidney, they instead believed that the Mingmen was located in-between both Kidneys, continually pulsating under the energetic influence of the individual's Ancestral Qi (Figure 8.155). The understanding of this change was explained to me by my teacher as follows: "From Wuji comes Taiji, and from Taiji comes Yin and Yang. Therefore, from the mysterious opening of the "Gate of Life," comes the Original Yin and Yang manifestations of creation. This sacred Qi creates the body's Four Limbs, Eight Extraordinary Vessels, and the various Zang-Fu Organs and Channels."

The Kidney's Water Jing Formation

The energy of the Water Jing, is the first of the Five Element Jing to be introduced into the body of the forming fetus. This special Qi becomes active during the Fourth Lunar Month of fetal development.

The Water Jing supervises the genetic developmental phase of the fetal growth. This energy also encompasses the fetus' unconscious reservoir of innate and intuitive intelligence, will, and other life-force energies relating to divine love, power, and spiritual perceptions. Any faltering of this energy (e.g., due to the influence of fetal toxins or trauma) is associated with both pervasive and subtle neurological disorders, and with a predisposition to psychological disorders (e.g., schizophrenia). Symptom manifestations of possible Deficient Kidney Jing disorders are described as follows:

- **Signs of Deficient Kidney Jing in Children:** This can energetically manifest as slow physical development, poor bone development, slow mental development, mental dullness, poor memory, retardation, and the late or incomplete closure of the child's cranial fontanels. Deficient Kidney Jing can also lead to Congenital Qi Deficiency (i.e., Deficiency in the Sea of Marrow), which can lead to Down Syndrome, Attention Deficit Disorder (ADD) and learning disabilities.
- **Signs of Deficient Kidney Jing in Adults:** This can include brittle bones, weak knees and legs, loose teeth, poor memory, premature senility, premature graying, premature hair loss, soreness in the lumbar, dizziness, deafness, tinnitus, and a weakness of sexual activity (impotence, infertility, low sex drive, an inability to conceive or carry a baby to full-term, etc.).

After birth, the Water Jing can be energetically affected through the Colors Black and Dark Navy-Blue, the Salty Taste, and through the "Chree," "Fuu" and "Yu" Healing Sounds.

The Kidneys in Chinese Medicine

In Traditional Chinese Medicine, the functions ascribed to the Kidneys are different from those defined in Western Medicine. The Chinese energetic functions of the Kidneys also include the functions of the urinary system, reproductive system, aspects of the endocrine system, the nervous system, production of Bone Marrow, development of Bones, various psycho-emotional aspects, and spiritual influences.

According to Traditional Chinese Medicine, the main functions of the Kidneys are to: store Jing (Essence); provide the foundation of the body's Yin and Yang, produce Marrow, fill the Brain and control the Bones; govern water; control and promote inhalation; open at the ears; manifest in the head hair; control the two lower orifices; house the Gate of Destiny (Mingmen); express itself through the psycho-emotional aspects of wisdom and fear; and exert certain important spiritual influences via the Zhi (Will). These main functions are described as follows (Figure 8.156):

1. **Stores the Body's Jing (Essence):** The Kidneys store both the body's Prenatal (Congenital) Jing and Postnatal (Acquired) Jing.
   - **Storing the Prenatal (Congenital) Jing:** To the ancient Chinese, the Kidneys represented the "trunk where the "Gathered Treasure" (i.e., Prenatal Jing) takes root." Therefore, the Kidneys are traditionally called the "Root of Life." The Prenatal Jing is the body's innate and inherited Original Essence (Yuan Jing), which determines the individual's basic constitutional makeup, strength, and vitality. Before birth, the Prenatal Jing nourishes the fetus. After birth, the Prenatal Jing controls the child's growth, sexual maturation, and development.

   In ancient China, it was believed that at the time when the Kidney Jing became rich in Essence, the energetic influence of "Tian Gui" (the 10th Heavenly Stem) would promote the development of sperm in boys, and initiate the discharge of ovum and the beginning of menstruation in girls. The Tian Gui is known as the "Yin Water" Heavenly Stem of "Earlier Heaven." It represents the energetic regathering of new life-force, associated with Kidney Yin. Within the human body, the energy of Tian Gui moves "underground," and is considered to be the Yin Water of the congenital constitution. Being invisibly cultivated, it awaits a new breakthrough. In old age, as the Qi of the Kidneys begins to weaken, the energy of Tian Gui begins to dry up, causing menopause in women and diminished sexual activity in men.

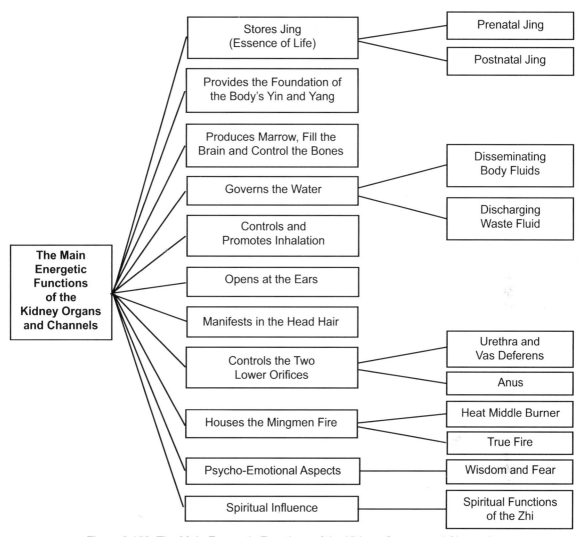

Figure 8.156. The Main Energetic Functions of the Kidney Organs and Channels

- **The Postnatal (Acquired) Jing:** Postnatal Jing (Acquired Essence) is the body's refined essence, extracted from food and drink via the Spleen and Stomach's transformational digestion functions.
2. **Provides the Foundation of the Body's Yin and Yang:** The Kidneys are the root of all the Yin and Yang Qi within the body's organs and tissues.
3. **Produces Marrow, Fills the Brain, and Controls the Bones:** The Kidneys produce Marrow and control the development of the Bones. The Chinese concept of "Marrow" does not correspond to marrow as defined in Western Medicine. In Chinese Energetic Medicine, Marrow is considered a substance which provides the common tissue of the body's Bones, Bone Marrow, Spinal Cord, and Brain. The "Sea of Marrow" is also considered to be the energetic essence that flows from the Kidneys through the spinal cord and into the Brain.
4. **Governs Water:** The Kidneys govern the Body's Fluids and Water Metabolism, and for this reason are sometimes called the "Controllers of Water." They act as a gate, opening and

closing the circulation and flow of Body Fluids in the Lower Burner. The Kidneys' function of governing the body's Water Metabolism has two aspects: Disseminating Body Fluids and Discharging Waste Fluid.

- **Disseminating Body Fluids:** Disseminating the Body Fluids involves dispersing and distributing throughout the body those fluids which have been derived from food essence. The Kidneys are thus responsible for delivering nutritive and nourishing liquid energy to all of the internal organs and tissues of the body.
- **Discharging Waste Fluid:** The Kidneys also separate and discharge from the body all the turbid waste fluid that is produced by the internal organs as a by-product of fluid metabolism.

5. **Controls and Promotes Inhalation:** The Kidneys' Yang Qi has the function of controlling and promoting the inhalation of air, moving the Qi downward and "holding" it. For example, in clinical application, one type of Asthma is associated with Kidney Yang Qi Deficiency.

6. **Opens at the Ears:** The Kidneys energetically open externally through the ears and rely on the nourishment of the Jing for proper hearing.

   In ancient Daoist teachings, the Relaxed Spirit of the Ear is known as "You Tian" ("Serene Field"). Another name also used for the Ear God is "Lovely Lady."

7. **Manifests in the Head Hair:** Although the nutrients for the head hair come from the Blood, its energy originates in the Kidney's Jing. The quality and color of the head hair is related to the state of the body's Kidney Jing. If the Kidney Jing is strong, the head hair and eyebrows will be thick and of good color.

8. **Controls the Two Lower Orifices:** The Kidney Jing controls the function of the lower front and rear Yin Orifices: the Genitalia and the Anus.

- **Genitalia:** Besides the Reproductive Organs, the front Yin Orifice of the genitalia also includes the vas deferens in men and the urethra in women.
- **Anus:** The rear Yin Orifice is the anus. Although the anus is anatomically related to the Large Intestine, it is functionally related to the energy of the Kidneys.

9. **Houses the Mingmen Fire:** The Mingmen is the embodiment of the Fire within the Kidneys. It is the "Root of Yuan Qi," and one of the body's "Three Fires." The Three Fires are all together responsible for creating the "True Fire," needed for warming the body's internal organs and tissues and must be differentiated from the Triple Burner. The Mingmen Fire heats the Qi within the Middle and Lower Burners and assists the body in causing the Jing to transform into Qi (see Triple Burners section).

10. **Psycho-Emotional Aspects:** The Kidneys provide the capacity and drive for strength, skill, and hard work, and for this reason are sometimes called the "Minister of Ingenuity and Vitality." An individual with strong Kidneys can work hard and purposefully for long periods of time.

    The Hun influence the energetic nature of the Kidneys, allowing the individual to experience clear perception and gentleness in thoughts and actions. If the circulation of Qi in the Kidneys becomes obstructed, this Kidney Qi Stagnation can give rise to emotional turmoil, sometimes manifesting as fear (Yang), or loneliness (Yin), influenced by the Po.

    The Kidney's positive psycho-emotional attributes are wisdom, rationality, clear perception, gentleness, and self-understanding. The negative attributes are fear, loneliness, insecurity, and shock (which attacks the Heart then descends into the Kidneys).

    When the Kidneys are in a state of disharmony, the patient can sometimes be driven to a state of obsessive-compulsive working habits (e.g., a workaholic). A patient with weak Kidneys can lack strength, endurance, confidence, and will power.

11. **Spiritual Influence:** The Kidneys house the body's Willpower (Zhi), and also store the individual's inherited ancestral constitutional patterns and innate habits.

    The Chinese term Zhi is translated as "Will," "Ambition" and "Determination." To the ancient Daoists, the Zhi was the Prenatal Spiritual Entity (Jing Shen) that was associated with the Kidneys. It is important to note, that the Willpower of the Kidney's Zhi is not the personal will of the ego that is driven by our desires.

The term Zhi has two common meanings: "Memory" and "Willpower," both of which are primary features of the character Zhi. The character Zhi can also be used to mean "Mind" (i.e., whole body consciousness and awareness).

The five mental aspects of the Spirit include the Hun, Po, Shen, Yi, and Zhi. These Five Jing Shen are sometimes referred to as the "Five Zhi," expressing the fact that each of the Five Yin Organs has its own type of physio-spiritual energetic expression.

Chinese Ideogram of the Zhi

The Chinese ideogram for Zhi is composed of two characters.
- **Xin:** The character on the bottom is "Xin," meaning Heart.
- **Tu:** The character above the Heart is "Tu," meaning Soil or Land. It depicts a plant beginning to rise upward from the soil.

Together, both characters represent the continuous, persistent intention of the Heart, developing towards an intended goal. The plant also represents the process of life's development through the uniting of both "Will and Intention" (Figure 8.157).

The Kidneys and the Willpower

"Willpower" is one of the most important aspects of the Zhi, and includes elements of the individual's mental drive, determination, and the single-minded pursuit of goals and aspirations. It enables the realization of ambitions by providing the focused energy necessary to carry ideas to fruition. A powerful Zhi creates the magnetism and charisma necessary to manifest and materialize our dreams.

Even if a person has acquired all of the information available via the Hun, Po, and Yi, without the Zhi there can be no action. The Hun give an individual the inspiration and goal, but the Zhi is needed to accomplish it (i.e., committing to the decision and following through with consistent action). A person with a well-developed Zhi demonstrates perseverance, determination, and a tenacity to complete personal goals. People with a deficient Zhi can become indecisive, fearful, submissive (often with a blind obedience to authority), and have a tendency to procrastinate. People with excess Zhi often tend to be fanatics, forcing their power, rules or philosophy onto others.

Figure 8.157. The Character "Zhi" (Will-Power)

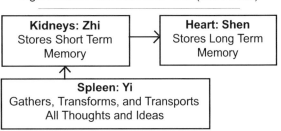

Figure 8.158. Three Ways the Body Stores Memory

In the clinic, the goal of the Medical Qigong Doctor is to reach a level of spiritual atonement, in which his or her personal Will merges with "Heaven's Will" ("Tian Zhi") and the two become one and the same. Tian Zhi is considered to be the movement of the Divine, expressed within man as his personal Virtue (De). The ancient Daoists taught that a man's Virtue is defined as his spiritual righteousness, and the authenticity of his Heart in his actions. It is through the acquisition of Virtue that man finds and possesses his True Nature. If a man's Virtue is initiated into the "Mysterious" (i.e., "Embracing Heaven's Will"), his intuitive spirit will lead him towards limitless perceptions.

Tian Zhi is a Divine inner prompting that guides us on our spiritual quest if we are open to its subtle messages. Tian Zhi is what we can call the Divine Will and also carries within it man's true purpose in this life.

Memory

Memory, another meaning for the word "Zhi," is defined as "the ability to remember information when studying or learning a particular subject or pattern." The Kidneys control Short-Term Memory and store data, whereas the Heart is associated with the Long-Term Memory (Figure 8.158).

The Kidneys help to maintain a determined focus on our goals, and help us to remember where we are going and what we are working to achieve. In other words, the Kidneys maintain a certain vital mindfulness.

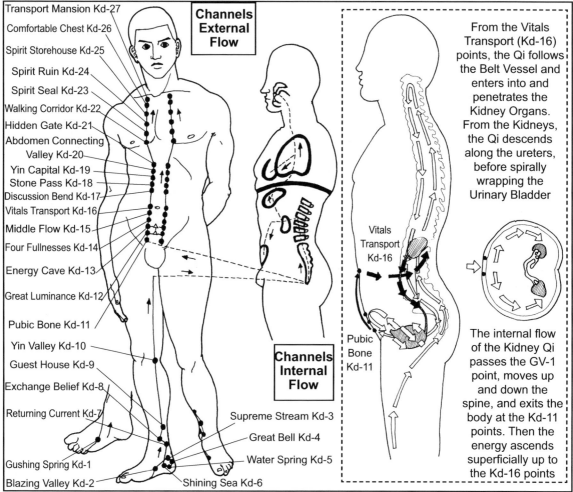

Figure 8.159. The Internal and External Qi Flow of the Kidney (Kd) Channels

THE KIDNEY CHANNELS

The Kidney Channels are Yin Channels that flow externally from the feet to the torso (Figure 8.159).

- **The External Branches:** These two main rivers of Kidney energy originate externally from underneath the little toes before circling the inside of the heels and ascending the medial aspect of the legs, where they then merge and enter into the coccyx and lower lumbar vertebrae.
- **The Internal Branches:** The internal flow of the Kidney Qi passes through the Long Strong (GV-1) point, moving up and down the spine, and exiting the body at the Pubic Bone (Kd-11) points. From the Kd-11 points, the energy ascends superficially up to the Vitals Transport (Kd-16) points.

From the Vitals Transport (Kd-16) points, the Qi follows the Belt Vessel and enters into and penetrates the Kidneys.

At the Kd-16 points, the channels also divide into two branches. One branch penetrates the Kidneys, while the other branch continues to ascend within the spine before entering into the cerebral cortex. From the Kidney organs, two additional pairs of channels emerge internally. One pair descends along the ureters before spirally wrapping the Urinary Bladder. The other set ascends into the Liver, diaphragm, and Lungs. It then spirally wraps the Heart and travels up through the throat, stopping at the root of the tongue.

Channels' Energetic Flow

The Kidney Yin Qi flows to the Liver, Heart, and Lungs. It is responsible for the body's Jing, and rules the cycles of the birth, growth, maturation, and reproduction.

The Kidney Yang Qi flows to the Spleen, Liver, Heart, and Lungs. It supports the Yang of all the body's organs via the energy of the Mingmen (Figure 8.160).

The Kidney Channels store more Qi than Blood, acting more on energetic and nervous functions than on physical substances and Blood functions.

The energy of the Kidney Channels also acts on the skin, muscles, and nerves found along their pathways.

At the High-Tide time period (5 p.m. to 7 p.m.), Qi and Blood abound in the Kidney organ and Kidney channels. At this time period the Kidney Organ and Channels can more easily be dispersed and purged. During Low-Tide (5 a.m. to 7 am.), they can be more readily tonified.

The Influence of Climate

In the Wintertime, Kidney conditions become more pronounced. Therefore, the Kidney Qi will become more active in individuals with strong Kidney Qi. Likewise, the Kidney Qi may also become more deficient in those individuals who have weak Kidney Qi.

Overexposure to a Cold Climate will also have a draining effect on the Kidneys. Additionally, the Kidneys are injured by irregular sleep patterns, fear, excessive caffeine, sex, drugs, alcohol, or smoking.

The Influence of Taste, Color, and Sound

- The Kidneys can be easily injured by excessive exposure to cold and damp weather and environments. This can lead to the accumulation of Dampness in the Kidneys, manifesting as either Damp Cold or Damp Heat syndromes.
- The salty taste can be used to tonify both the Kidneys and the Urinary Bladder. However,

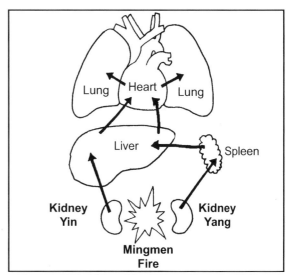

Figure 8.160. Kidney Yin Qi flows from the Kidneys to the Liver, and then to the Heart and Lungs. Kidney Yang Qi flows from the Kidneys to the Spleen, Liver, Heart, and Lungs.

during the Winter Season, the excess consumption of Salty or Cold Foods has a draining effect on the Kidneys.
- The black, dark navy-blue, or purple color is used to tonify both the Kidneys and the Urinary Bladder.
- The "Chree," "Fuu," and "Yuu" Sounds are used to purge both the Kidneys and the Urinary Bladder.

Kidney Pathology

Kidney organ and channel diseases may cause general deterioration of the entire body, weakness in the lower extremities, lumbar pain, or hot sensations deep inside the feet.

The Kidneys open through the ears, urogenital orifices, and the anus. The energetic condition of the Kidneys can be partially reflected by the condition of the patient's urination and defecation; in males this includes the ejaculation process.

Since the Kidneys are responsible for concentration and memory retention, poor concentration and loss of memory are common symptoms of Kidney Deficiency.

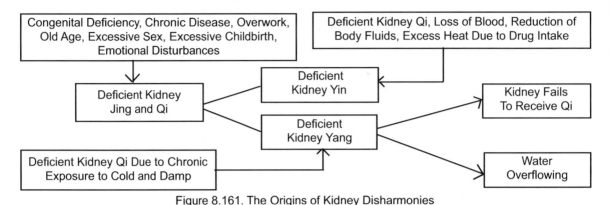

Figure 8.161. The Origins of Kidney Disharmonies

T.C.M. Patterns of Disharmony

Patterns of Disharmony associated with the Kidneys include: Deficient Kidney Jing, Deficient Kidney Yang, Deficient Kidney Yin, The Kidneys Fail to Receive Qi and Water Overflowing (Figure 8.161).

1. **Deficient Kidney Jing:** This can be due to hereditary factors, fetal toxins, or old age. Signs of Deficient Kidney Jing include problems that appear during birth, development, reproduction and aging; especially when these problems relate to the formation and function of the Marrow, Bones, Brain, ears and hair.
   - **Deficient Kidney Jing in Children:** This can be due to hereditary factors or fetal toxins, and will result in a poor congenital constitution. Symptoms of Deficient Kidney Jing can manifest as slow physical development, poor Bone development, slow mental development, mental dullness, poor memory, retardation, and the late or incomplete closure of the child's cranial fontanelles. Deficient Kidney Jing can also lead to Congenital Qi Deficiency (i.e., Deficiency in the Sea of Marrow), which in turn can lead to Down Syndrome, Attention Deficit Disorder (ADD) and learning disabilities.
   - **Deficient Kidney Jing in Adults:** This can develop from an excess of sexual activity, constant stress, chronic exposure to pathogens, or from old age. Symptoms of Deficient Kidney Jing can manifest as brittle bones, weak knees and legs, loose teeth, poor memory, premature senility, premature graying, premature hair loss, lumbago, dizziness, deafness, tinnitus, impotence, infertility, low sex drive, and an inability to conceive or carry a baby to full-term.

2. **Deficient Kidney Yang:** This can be the result of a chronic illness, old age, excessive sexual activity, excess exposure to Cold, or a chronic retention of Dampness that obstructs the movement of fluids. Deficient Yang results in deficient warmth, with symptoms such as a sensation of cold or soreness in the back, cold knees, cold limbs, and aversion to cold. Other symptoms of Deficient Kidney Yang include weak knees and legs, lassitude, edema of the legs, poor appetite, headaches, breathlessness, wheezing, asthma, tiredness, mental and emotional problems, diarrhea, painful urination, enuresis, edema, loose stools, abundant clear urination, impotence, premature ejaculation, menorrhagia, and infertility.

3. **Deficient Kidney Yin:** This can be the result of overwork, excessive Blood loss, chronic illness affecting the Liver, Heart and Lungs, a depletion of Body Fluids due to consumption by Heat after a fever, or an overdose of Chinese medicine used to strengthen Kidney Yang (thus accidentally injuring the Kidney Yin). Symptoms of Deficient Kidney Yin can manifest as dizziness, vertigo, poor memory, tinnitus, deafness, malar flush, night sweating, Five Palms Heat, dry throat and mouth, thirst, tiredness, chest tightness, asthma, breathlessness, mental and emotional problems, sore knees and back, ache in the bones, nocturnal emissions, enuresis, premature ejaculation, menorrhagia, constipation, and dark scanty urine.

4. **Kidneys Fail to Receive Qi:** This pattern of disharmony manifests when the Kidneys fail to hold the Qi that is sent down by the Lungs during respiration. The Qi rebels upward, resulting in difficulty with inhalation, shortness of breath, cough and asthma (aggravated by exertion). This pattern can originate from a long standing chronic disease which inevitably affects the Kidneys, excessive physical strain on the body, or from a hereditary weakness of the Lungs and Kidneys. Symptoms of the Kidneys failing to receive the Qi include rapid and weak breathing, difficulty in inhaling, shortness of breath on exertion, cough, asthma, sweating, cold limbs, cold limbs after sweating, mental listlessness, sore back, and the release of clear urination during an asthma attack.

5. **Water Overflowing:** This is considered to be a severe form of Kidney Yang Deficiency, and can develop from chronic retention of Dampness that interferes with the Kidney's function of transforming the body's fluids. It can also be caused by Spleen Yang Deficiency due to excessive consumption of Cold raw foods, Water overflowing the Heart due to Heart Yang Deficiency, Water overflowing the Lungs due to Lung Qi Deficiency, and a retention of External Cold within the Lungs. Symptoms of Water overflowing include edema in the legs and ankles, feeling cold, lumbago, coldness in the legs and back, and abdominal distension.

THE KIDNEYS IN WESTERN MEDICINE

According to Western Anatomy, the kidneys are paired organs that are located on the sides of the spine, just above the waist and half hidden under the rib cage. The kidneys can be included in a group of organs whose function is to eliminate waste from the body. The other major eliminative organs are the lungs, skin, and gastrointestinal tract.

The primary function of the kidneys is to filter out by-products of cellular metabolism, bacterial toxins, and other wastes from the blood. The kidneys are the major channels through which nitrogenous wastes and drugs are eliminated. In addition to simply filtering the blood, the kidneys also help control the concentration of the various elements (glucose, electrolytes, etc.) contained within the blood. The Kidneys help control blood pressure (through the production of renin), stimulate red blood cell production (through the production of erythropoietin), and regulate the PH of the blood. The kidneys also assist in metabolizing vitamin D, thus allowing the bones and teeth to calcify, while also normalizing the functions of the heart, nervous system, and blood coagulation (Figure 8.162).

FILTERING FLUIDS FROM THE BLOODSTREAM

The kidneys normally filter the entire volume of blood in the body every 45 minutes. To accomplish this, they filter out nearly 48 gallons (180 liters) of fluid every day, though only a small amount of this fluid (1%) actually leaves the body as urine; the rest is reabsorbed into the blood. The function of the kidneys is regulated by the pituitary gland and the hypothalamus.

URINARY SYSTEM

The kidneys are the essential organs of the urinary system. The other organs of the urinary system are the ureters, the urinary bladder, and the urethra. Urine is the end product of the kidneys' function of blood filtration. Urine is composed of various toxic or unneeded materials that are released by the cells into the bloodstream, then extracted from the blood by the kidneys. From the kidneys, urine passes downward along two ureters (one from each kidney) and into the bladder. Situated behind the pubic bone, the urinary bladder stores urine, and then releases it from the body via the pathway of the urethra. Urine is generally slightly acidic, but can range in PH from 4.5 to 8.0, depending on the condition of the blood.

ANATOMY OF THE KIDNEYS

Nestled against the musculature of the back of the body, the kidneys sit behind the peritoneum (abdominal cavity), extending vertically from the height of T-12 down to L-3. Each kidney is approximately the size of a fist, being 4 to 5 inches long, 2 to 3 inches wide, and 1 inch thick. The kidneys are shaped like two beans with their concave edges directed internally towards the spine. The central area of this concave curvature is called the hilus, and the kidneys are open to the rest of the body only through this area.

The kidneys collectively receive about one quarter of the total cardiac output of blood, which

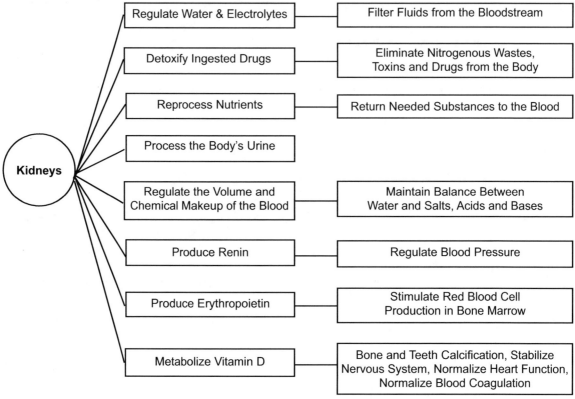

Figure 8.162. The Functions of the Kidney (Western Medical Perspective)

travels into them from the descending aorta via the renal arteries. Purified venous blood flows out of the kidneys into the inferior vena cava via the renal veins. As each renal artery enters the kidney it branches into smaller and smaller arteries and arterioles, which eventually extend into the nephrons in capillary formations that allow for maximum exposure to the filtration membrane. The path of the veins as they leave the kidney are generally side by side with the path of the arteries that bring blood into the kidney. The ureter also exits the kidney at the hilus, before traveling downward to meet with the bladder.

Externally, each kidney is wrapped in three protective layers. The outermost of these is a dense layer of connective tissue, called the renal fascia, that surrounds not only the kidney, but also the adrenal gland located on top of the kidney. The renal fascia anchors itself to the surrounding tissue areas, thus keeping the kidneys in place. The middle protective layer, termed the adipose capsule, is composed primarily of fatty adipose tissue that holds both the kidneys in place and serves to insulate them from impact trauma. The innermost layer, called the renal capsule, is a clear smooth membrane that also wraps the ureter and lines the renal sinus.

THREE REGIONS OF THE KIDNEYS

Internally, each kidney is divided into three distinct parts or regions. From the outermost (convex) portion of the kidney to the innermost (concave) portion, the three regions of the kidney are: the renal cortex, the renal medulla, and the renal pelvis. These three layers are described as follows (Figure 8.163):

Renal Cortex: The renal cortex is the outermost tissue area of the kidney organ; it is immediately deep to the renal capsule described above. The renal cortex lies between the renal capsule and the base of the medullary pyramids, and it also fills the space between one medullary pyramid and the next. The renal cortex and the renal pyramids constitute the functional portions of the kidneys, and are collectively called the parenchyma.

Renal Medulla: The renal medulla is of a reddish brown color and contains eight or more cone shaped medullary (or renal) pyramids. These pyramids have their base directed towards the cortex and their apex pointing towards the center of the kidney. Because they are filled with parallel bundles of straight tubes and blood vessels, the renal pyramids have a striped appearance. Tissue from the renal cortex extends between the medullary pyramids to form what are called renal columns.

Renal Pelvis: The renal pelvis is a funnel shaped structure situated in the central portion of the kidney. It serves to collect the final filtrate of the nephrons (urine) from the calyces and collecting ducts. To accomplish this, the renal pelvis branches to penetrate into the renal pyramids through several major calyces, each of which then branches into minor calyces that enclose the area around the renal pyramids. Peristaltic contractions of the smooth muscles along the length of the calyces, renal pelvis, and the ureter are responsible for propelling the urine out of the kidneys and into the urinary bladder. The renal pelvis is continuous with the ureter, which serves to transport urine downward into the bladder.

Nephrons

The functional units of the kidneys are the microscopic nephrons, which carry out the basic processes of cleansing the blood. Each kidney contains roughly 1 million nephrons, the majority of which (85%) are located in the renal cortex. The three essential functions of nephrons are filtration, secretion, and reabsorption, which take place at different areas within the nephron.

Each nephron is made up of a renal corpuscle and a renal tubule. The renal corpuscle is a convoluted bundle of capillaries (glomerulus) surrounded by a capsule called the glomerular (or Bowman's) capsule. The glomerulus is a looping tuft of capillaries extending from one of the arteriole branches of the renal artery. It is almost completely surrounded by the filtrate-collecting glomerular capsule. The glomerulus and the glomerular capsule meet to form a filtration membrane, the endothelial-capsular membrane, that

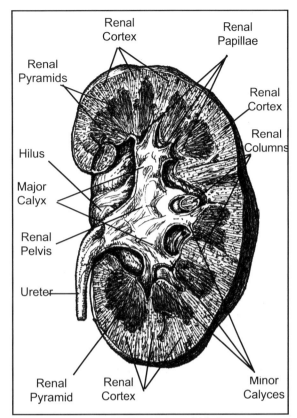

Figure 8.163. The Kidney (Kd) Organ

serves to filter certain materials (e.g. water, salts, glucose, amino acids, vitamins, and nitrogenous wastes such as ammonia) from the blood. This process, called glomerular filtration, takes place because of a unique pressure differential between the glomerular capillaries and the glomerular capsule. Thus in the first stage of urine formation, the filtrate contains both desirable and undesirable materials.

The renal tubule carries this filtrate away and is continuous with the glomerular capsule. Along the length of the renal tubule, the majority of filtrate is reabsorbed into the blood through a series of complex passive and active transport mechanisms including: diffusion, facilitated diffusion, primary active transport, secondary active transport, and osmosis.

Three Main Sections of the Renal Tubule

The three main sections of the renal tubule are the proximal convoluted tubule, the loop of Henle (nephron loop), and the distal convoluted tubule, described as follows (Figure 8.164):

Proximal Convoluted Tubule: Leading away from the glomerular capsule, the proximal convoluted tubule serves to allow the body to reabsorb the desirable portion of the filtrate. The materials recovered into the blood from the proximal convoluted tubule include: water, glucose, amino acids, vitamins, sodium, chlorine, carbonic acid, and potassium, in addition to other substances.

Loop of Henle: The loop of Henle is continuous with both the proximal convoluted tubule and the distal convoluted tubule, and is the connection between them. In the loop of Henle, water, potassium, sodium, and chlorine are reabsorbed into the blood.

Distal Convoluted Tubule: By the time the filtrate reaches the distal convoluted tubule, it is fairly concentrated. Here, nearly all of the remaining water is reabsorbed, along with further amounts of sodium and chlorine.

The distal convoluted tubule empties into a collection tube, which receives this concentrated filtrate from several neurons before emptying into a papillary duct. The last phases of water, sodium, and chlorine reabsorption take place along the collection tube. The resulting filtrate flows down through a papillary duct into one of the minor calyces, then into a major calyce, and eventually into the renal pelvis. The renal pelvis then empties into the urinary bladder via the ureter.

Common Disorders of the Kidneys

Common disorders of the kidneys include: pyelonephritis (kidney infection), pyelitis (inflammation of renal pelvis and calyces), azotemia (caused by excessive waste in the blood), hydronephrosis (obstruction of urine flow due to the enlargement of one or both kidneys), nephritic syndrome (protein lost into the urine), polycystic disease (deformities in the nephrons), kidney tumors (e.g. renal cell carcinoma), acute or chronic renal failure, nephrotosis (floating kidney), diabetes insipidus (excessive glucose secretion), and kidney stones. Kidney stones are composed primarily of calcium salts, uric acid, and various other crystals such as struvite. Anuria is a condition in which the kidneys produce less than 50 ml of urine per day, and can be caused by several internal dysfunctions.

In end-stage renal failure, one of the kidneys may be removed without causing the death of the

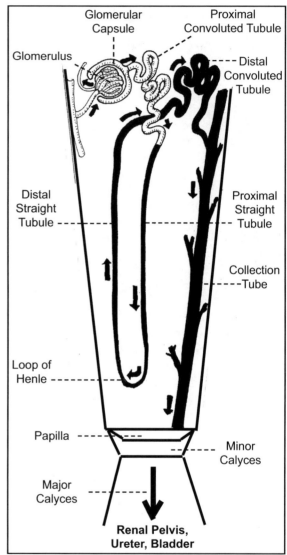

Figure 8.164. Order of Kidneys Filtration Mechanisms: Glomerulus, Glomerular Capsule, Proximal Tubule, Loop of Henle, Distal Tubule, Collecting Tube, Minor then Major Calyces, Renal Pelvis, Ureter, Bladder (storage), and then discharged through the Urethra.

patient. In cases where the remaining kidney is healthy, it may eventually be able to function at 80% of the original combined capacity of both kidneys. If both kidneys are functioning inadequately, kidney dialysis (in which the blood is filtered by a machine outside the body) is often performed. Another increasingly common procedure is a kidney transplant.

CHAPTER 8: THE TWELVE PRIMARY ORGANS, CHANNELS AND COLLATERALS

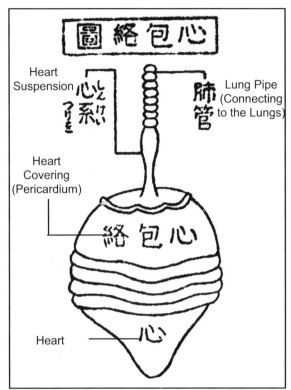

Figure 8.165. The Ancient Chinese Anatomical Diagram of the Pericardium (Pc) Organ: *"Important Useful Notes on Acupuncture and Moxibustion,"* by Masatoyo Hongo (1718)

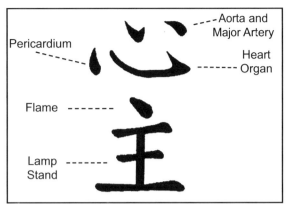

Figure 8.166. The Chinese character "Xin Zhu" Heart Master (Pericardium)

PERICARDIUM: XIN ZHU

The Pericardium is a Yin (Zang) Organ, and its associated Yang (Fu) Organ is the Triple Burner. Its Element is Fire. In Chinese Energetic Medicine, the Pericardium is known as the "Xin Zhu" ("Heart Master") or "Xin Bao Luo" ("Heart Wrapping Connection"). It is not considered to be an independent organ, but rather serves as a protective covering for the Heart (Figure 8.165). Thus the Pericardium's primary responsibility is "to protect the Heart from pathogenic factors."

The energetic function of the Pericardium is to activate, energize, and control the Yin Channel's distribution of the Kidney Yang Qi to the Yin Organs. The Pericardium assists the Heart in Governing the Blood, Housing the Shen, Maintaining the "Emperor's Fire," and for Setting Emotional Boundaries. Therefore, the Pericardium is sometimes known as the "Prime Minister," "The Official Who Protects the Heart," or "The Heart Protector." The Pericardium Channel is also sometimes referred to as the "Circulation-Sex Meridian."

THE CHINESE CHARACTERS FOR PERICARDIUM: XIN ZHU (HEART MASTER)

The ancient Chinese ideograph for the Pericardium ("Xin Zhu"), can be translated as the "Heart Master," which expresses the Pericardium's responsibility of assisting the Heart in Governing the body's Qi and Shen (Figure 8.166).

- **Xia:** The first character "Xin" translates as "Heart." It refers to the image of a Heart organ, and is divided into three sections. The upper half of the character depicts the aorta and major arteries. The Heart itself is depicted in the center. The lower left part of the character depicts the Pericardium.

    In Traditional Chinese Medicine, the character "Xin" also refers as much to the Mind (thoughts and emotions) as it does to the actual internal organ.

- **Zhu:** The second character "Zhu" translates as "Overlord" or "Master." It depicts the image of "a lamp-stand with flames rising upward." The character gives us the image of a man who spreads "light, illumination, and brilliance," expressing the clarity of the Divine Spirit, or the expression of the individual's "Shen Ming." The "Shen Ming" is a special type of spiritual brightness with transformative powers.

ANCIENT PERICARDIUM ORGAN TEACHING

According to ancient Daoist teachings, the Heart Organ is essentially a Spiritual Portal, energetically extending back into the infinite space of the Original Dao. Therefore, each individual's Yuan Shen (Original Spirit) resides within the internal location of their own central Heart Palace. The "Art of Mastering the Heart," is the ancient Daoist "Way" of obtaining access into this most subtle spiritual abode. Obtaining access allows the Original Spirit to commune with the celestial spirits responsible for teaching and guiding each individual, while they exist within the Earthly Realm.

The Pericardium is an energetic filtering system that allows or dismisses ideas in accordance to whether they fit within our catalog of internal beliefs and experiences. Although the energy of the Lung Organs allow for our spontaneous interaction with the world, it is the Pericardium who mediates this experience, and then chooses to either interact or not.

As the "Heart Master" (Xin Zhu), the Pericardium is responsible for "governing and organizing" the Heart's "Shen" (thoughts, beliefs, and feelings) by extending the spiritual "light of awareness" over all things that are encountered. This is why, in ancient China, the purpose of the Pericardium was sometimes viewed as a "Minister of Council," designed to protect the "Emperor" (Heart) and to help create feelings of security, joy, happiness and pleasure. In this respect, an important function of the Pericardium is to energetically intercept strong emotions that may overwhelm the Heart, and then place them in the "Courtyard" (Yellow Court - solar plexus area) until the Heart is ready to deal with such matters (Figure 8.167).

In ancient times, the Heart was also known by the name of the "Yellow Emperor" or "Suspended Gold," and the Courtyard of the Heart (located in the solar plexus area) was known as the "Yellow Emperor's Courtyard," more commonly called the "Yellow Court." The Yellow Court stores the strong emotional experiences such as feelings of being rejected, betrayed, or abandoned. The stored energetic belief structures of these strong emotions are later processed and released, or stored and absorbed by the specific energetic natures of the body's Five Yin Organs (Liver, Heart, Spleen, Lungs and Kidneys).

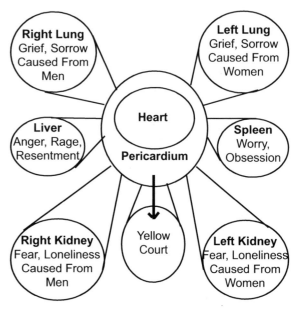

Figure 8.167. The Relationships of the Pericardium

One example of the Pericardium protecting the Heart at the formative years of childhood can be observed when a newborn baby is startled. When startled (as the baby cries), a baby will automatically thrust its chest upward in order to discharge the emotional shock away from the Heart. The emotions are then instinctively released outward through the child's shaking extremities (hands and feet).

Later, as the child continues to grow, the experienced traumatic feelings that are not released from his or her tissues will be immediately stored and suppressed within the Yellow Court area, away from the child's Heart. The energy of these suppressed feelings and memories will eventually be internally distributed according to the corresponding Yin Organ relationships (fear to the Kidneys, anger to the Liver, etc.).

In the clinic, it is common to note that a patient with Deficient Pericardium Qi will have very weak emotional boundaries and will allow their Heart to constantly and indiscriminately connect, bond, and fall in love with other individuals, even when it is not appropriate.

A patient with Excessive Pericardium Qi will be emotionally armored, pushing others away, feeling no need for emotional connection what-so-ever.

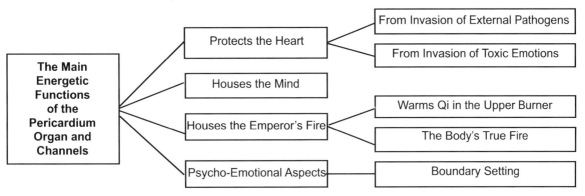

Figure 8.168. The Main Energetic Functions of the Pericardium Organ and Channels

THE PERICARDIUM IN CHINESE ENERGETIC MEDICINE

In Traditional Chinese Medicine, the functions ascribed to the Pericardium are different from the physiological functions described in Western Medicine. Some of the major differences in the Chinese energetic interpretation of the Pericardium are that it also includes certain functions that are ascribed to the nervous system in Western Medicine, and governs important psycho-emotional aspects.

According to Traditional Chinese Medicine, the main functions of the Pericardium are to: Protect the Heart, House the Mind, House the "Emperor's Fire," and express itself through the psycho-emotional aspects of relationships and boundaries. These main functions are described as follows (Figure 8.168):

1. **Protects the Heart:** The Pericardium protects the Heart from external invasion of pathogens and the external invasion of toxic emotions.
   - **External Invasion of Pathogens:** When a pathogenic factor attacks the Heart, it is diverted to the Pericardium instead.
   - **External Invasion of Toxic Emotions:** The Pericardium is considered the Heart's advisor, assisting the Heart in bringing order and peace. It intercepts the emotional discharges directed to the Heart, released from the Zang Fu Organs via respiration. The Pericardium restrains the emotional charge by energetically neutralizing it and temporarily placing it into the Heart's "Courtyard" (also known as the Yellow Court) to be later investigated at a more opportune time, when the individual is ready.
2. **Houses the Mind:** The Pericardium is considered to be the "Center of the Thorax," and it assists the Heart in circulating the Blood and in housing the mental, emotional, and sexual states of the Mind.
3. **Houses the Emperor's Fire:** The Heart Fire is located in the center of the chest, and is also called the "Commanding Fire" or "Emperor's Fire." The Heart Fire is an essential component of the body's True Fire, and is responsible for transforming the body's Energy (Qi) into Spirit (Shen).
4. **Psycho-Emotional Aspects:** The Pericardium is responsible for setting the emotional boundaries for the Heart, and has a powerful influence on the patient's mental and emotional states. It governs energetic circulation, sexuality and intimacy.

THE PERICARDIUM CHANNELS

The Pericardium Channels are Yin channels that flow externally from the torso to the hands.
- **The Internal Branches:** The two main energetic rivers originate internally from the center of the chest, flowing from the Pericardium. They descend through the center of the body, spirally wrapping the Upper, Middle, and Lower Burners.
- **The External Branches:** The two main energetic rivers then surface and branch externally near the nipples before proceeding down the

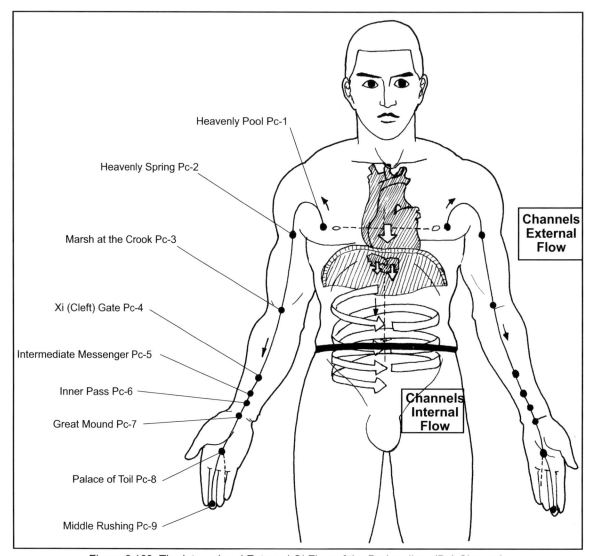

Figure 8.169. The Internal and External Qi Flow of the Pericardium (Pc) Channels

center of each arm to end at the tips of the middle fingers. A second branch arises from the Pc-8 points at the center of each palm and flows into the ring fingers to connect with the Triple Burner Channels (Figure 8.169).

Channels' Energy Flow

The Pericardium Channels affect the body's circulation of Blood. They are considered to be the "Mother of Yin," and are also connected to the Mingmen. The energy of the Pericardium Channel also acts on the skin, muscles, and nerves found along their pathways.

The Pericardium Channels store more Blood than Qi, acting more on the physical substance and Blood functions than on the energy.

At the High-Tide time period (7 p.m. to 9 p.m.), Qi and Blood abound in the Pericardium Organ and Channels. At this time period the Pericardium Organ and Channels can more easily be dispersed and purged. During Low-Tide (7 a.m. to 9 a.m.), they can be more readily tonified.

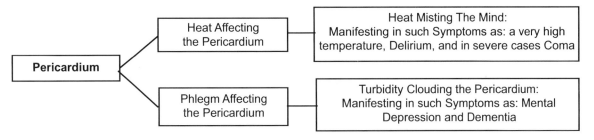

Figure 8.170. Chart of Pericardium Disharmonies

THE INFLUENCE OF CLIMATE

The Pericardium is primarily affected by the invasion of External Pathogenic Heat and Phlegm, which together obstruct the energetic functions of the Pericardium.

THE INFLUENCE OF TASTE, COLOR, AND SOUND

- The Bitter Taste can be used to tonify the Pericardium, or clear Excess Heat.
- The Red Color is used to tonify the Pericardium.
- The "Shee" Sound is used to purge toxic Heat from both the Pericardium and the Triple Burners.

PERICARDIUM PATHOLOGY

The main diseases of the Pericardium organ and channels include Heat and Phlegm affecting the Heart, resulting in symptoms that cause discomfort in the front of the chest, disorders of the major Blood Vessels, and diseases on the midline to upper palmar side of the upper extremities. Mental abnormalities may also manifest.

Disharmonies of the Pericardium are associated with the last two levels, "Ying or Xue," of diagnosis according to the "Four Levels" patterns of disease, and are also associated with the "Upper Burner Phase" of the diagnosis according to the Triple Burners patterns of disease (see Volume 3, Chapter 25).

T.C.M. PATTERNS OF DISHARMONY

There are two main patterns of Pericardium Disharmony, both of which originate from an invasion by external factors: Heat affecting the Pericardium, and Phlegm affecting the Pericardium.

These two patterns have similar symptoms to that of the Heart Disharmony patterns caused from internal disease factors of Phlegm Fire Agitating the Heart and Cold Phlegm Misting the Heart (see Heart Section), which are described as follows (Figure 8.170):

1. **Heat Affecting the Pericardium:** The main pattern of disharmony associated with the Pericardium Organ is that of Heat Invasion. Heat invading the Pericardium is said to "Mist the Mind," and can manifest in symptoms such as a very high temperature, anxiety, insomnia, delirium, and in severe cases coma.
2. **Phlegm Affecting the Pericardium:** This pattern of disharmony is associated with Phlegm Turbidity Clouding the Pericardium. The main symptoms are mental depression, unclear speech, Phlegm Stroke, and dementia.

THE PERICARDIUM IN WESTERN MEDICINE

According to Western Anatomy, the pericardium is a double-walled (triple-layered) fibro-serous sac that surrounds and protects the heart (Figure 8.171).

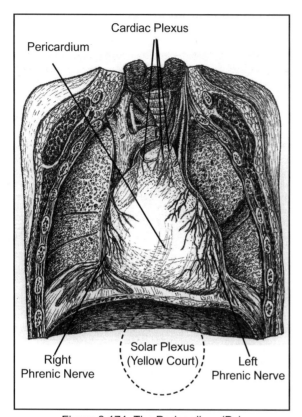

Figure 8.171. The Pericardium (Pc)

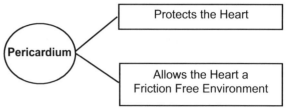

Figure 8.172. The Functions of the Pericardium (Western Medical Perspective)

The pericardium confines the heart to its position in the mediastinum, and also creates a lubricated space that allows sufficient freedom of movement for the heart's vigorous and rapid contractions. The pericardium is divided into two main sections, the fibrous pericardium and the serous pericardium, described as follows:

- **Fibrous Pericardium:** The bag shaped, tough outer layer of inelastic fibrous connective tissue is called the fibrous pericardium. It provides protection and prevents the overstretching of the heart. The fibrous pericardium attaches to the diaphragm and sternum, with its open end fused to the connective tissues of the blood vessels that enter and exit the heart.
- **Serous Pericardium:** The thinner, more delicate serous pericardium forms a double layer around the heart. The outer portion, known as the "parietal layer," is fused with the fibrous pericardium. The inner portion, known as the "visceral layer" or "epicardium," adheres tightly to the outermost layer of the heart. The space between the parietal and visceral pericardium is known as the pericardial cavity, and is filled with a thin slippery film of serous fluid known as the pericardial fluid. The pericardial fluid reduces friction between the serous membranes allowing the heart to move in a relatively friction-free environment.

Physiology

The function of the pericardium is to provide a protective covering for the heart, and reduce the friction caused by the heart's pumping action (Figure 8.172).

Chapter 8: The Twelve Primary Organs, Channels and Collaterals

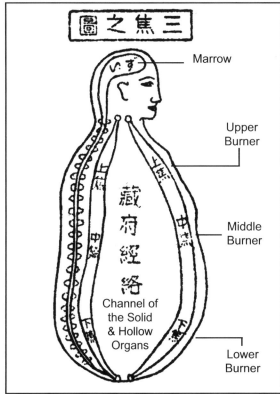

Figure 8.173. The Ancient Chinese Anatomical Diagram of the Triple Burners (TB) Organ: *"Important Useful Notes on Acupuncture and Moxibustion,"* by Masatoyo Hongo (1718)

TRIPLE BURNERS: SAN JIAO

The "Triple Burners" ("San Jiao") are considered a Yang (Fu) Organ, their associated Yin (Zang) Organ is the Pericardium, and their Element is Fire.

The Triple Burners are also known as the Triple Heaters and Triple Warmers, and are called the "Father of Yang Qi," because they are responsible for commanding the circulation of Yang Qi. In ancient China, the Triple Burners were conceptualized as being "a Large Bowel that contained all of the body's internal organs" (Figure 8.173).

CHINESE CHARACTER FOR TRIPLE BURNERS: SAN JIAO

The Chinese characters for Triple Burners, "San Jiao" can be translated as, "Three Fires (or "Ovens") that cook and process food" (Figure 8.174).

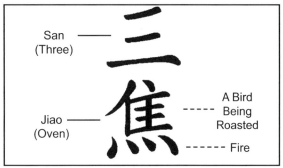

Figure 8.174. The Chinese character "San Jiao" (Three Burners)

Figure 8.175. Doctor Zhang Jiebin

- **San:** The first character "San" translates as the number "Three" or "Triple."
- **Jiao:** The second character "Jiao" translates as "Burners, Cauldrons or Combustion Oven," and is divided into two ideographs. The character on the top is the ideogram of a bird without a tail being cooked by the action of fire. The character on the bottom depicts the small flames of fire rising upward. The ideograph expresses the image of "a bird in the process of being cooked or roasted."

THE TRIPLE BURNERS IN CHINESE MEDICINE

Like the other Yang Organs, the Triple Burners have an "energetic form." In the Ming Dynasty (1368 - 1644 A.D.), the renowned doctor Zhang Jiebin (Figure 8.175) taught that the Triple Burners were in fact the largest Bowel within the body's cavity, and that they existed as an "energetic field" within the body, surrounding and containing the viscera (Zang) and bowels (Fu).

543

The energetic form of the San Jiao is represented by the swirling vortex of Qi that moves from the "Abode of Energy" ("Qi She:" St-11) located at the base of the throat and collar bone, down to the "Spirit Watchtower" (She Que: CV-8) located at the navel.

According to ancient Daoist teaching, life on Earth begins with the first inhalation, and the severing of the umbilical cord. As the child inhales its first breath and swallows, the "Niwan" ("Mud Pill") activates the supernatural substance of Yuan Jing (Original Essence), which immediately flows down to heal the freshly cut tissues of the umbilical area, and reside within the Kidneys. This action creates the internal movement of the San Jiao vortex.

The Niwan area that is responsible for this energetic activation, is associated with the "pineal" gland, and is traditionally "awakened" through a specific tone or sacred sound. It is traditionally associated with Clairvoyance (inner sense of vision), Clairaudience (inner sense of hearing), and Clairsentience (inner sense of touch). Within an individual's life, there are two times that the pineal gland naturally opens: when they are born (previously explained), and when they "crossover" (die).

This is the physical awakening of the body's True Yang, creating the first communication with the external world. Once the first breath and the exposure to the external environment has been initiated, the individual's journey to experience their personal destiny begins.

As the Environmental Qi continues to flow through the Eight Extraordinary Vessels, the Twelve Primary Channels, and Zang/Fu Organs, the energy of the San Jiao vortex creates the energetic connections associated with the body's front "Mu" ("Alarm") and back "Shu ("Transporting") points.

It is important to note, that the main energetic functions of the Triple Burners are derived from clinical observations that are unique to Chinese Energetic Medicine, as they are not described in Western Medicine. Because the Triple Burners relate to the internal organ membrane system of the thoracic, abdominal, and lower abdominal cavities, Modern T.C.M. understands the energetic fields of the Triple Burners as including and influencing the pleura, and both the parietal and visceral peritoneum of the abdominal cavities.

The Triple Burners are regarded as an independent Yang organ. They are assigned to three specific energy areas within the body's cavity, and regulate the general ingestion and digestion of food and fluids throughout the body.

According to Chinese Medicine, the main functions of the Triple Burners are to: control the activities of Qi, transport and transform Qi and food essence, separate clear fluid from turbid, provide an avenue for Yuan Qi, regulate balance and harmonize, regulate the body's aura fields, house the body's True Fire, and manifest through the psycho-emotional aspects of regulating social relations. These main functions are described as follows (Figure 8.176):

1. **Controls the Activities of Qi:** Each of the three Burners controls the movement of specific types of Qi, and various stages of energetic transformation.
   - **The Upper Burner:** Assists in energetically transforming Weiqi (Defensive Energy); it also controls respiration and activates the flow of Qi, Blood, and Body Fluids.
   - **The Middle Burner:** Assists in energetically transforming Ying Qi (Nutritive Energy).
   - **The Lower Burner:** Assists in energetically transforming Body Fluids.
2. **Transports and Transforms Qi and Food Essence:** The Triple Burners are considered to be the "Passage Through Which Water, Food, and Fluid are Transported." The Middle Burner, in particular, plays an essential role in the transportation and transformation of food essence to produce Qi and Blood.
3. **Separates Clear Fluid From Turbid:** In ancient Chinese Medical Texts, the Triple Burners are described as "Opening Up, Discharging Qi, and Letting Qi Out." The Lower Burner separates clear fluid from turbid fluid, discharges urine and stool, and also releases Turbid Qi in the form of gas.
4. **Provides an Avenue For Yuan Qi:** The Triple Burners are considered to be the "Ambassadors For The Body's Yuan Qi." They transport Yuan Qi from the Kidneys to all the other organs of the body, and also provide the internal Heat for digestion. The Conception Vessel brings the Qi to the Triple Burners to assist in this process.

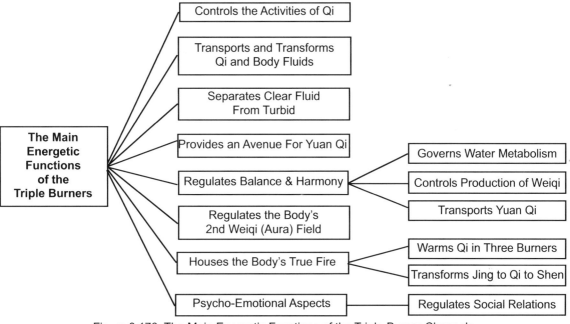

Figure 8.176. The Main Energetic Functions of the Triple Burner Channels

5. **Regulates Balance and Harmony:** The Triple Burners are known as "The Official of Balance and Harmony," because they govern Water Metabolism, control the production of Weiqi, and transport Yuan Qi from the Kidneys to all the other organs of the body. This name also refers to the Triple Burners' role in regulating the body's metabolic functions, and to their production of Qi, Blood, Body Fluids, and waste products.

6. **Regulates the Body's Auric Fields:** The Triple Burners are said to regulate the body's second Weiqi (Auric) field. The Lower Burner is connected to the first and innermost level of Weiqi; the Middle Burner is connected to the second and middle level of Weiqi responsible for aura field movement; and the Upper Burner is connected to the third level and outermost spiritual level of Weiqi.

7. **Houses the Body's True Fire:** One function of the Triple Burners' energy is to produce heat, and thus to regulate the body's temperature like a thermostat. The heat of the Triple Burners can be increased through meditative disciplines such as circulating energy along the Microcosmic Orbit (which connects the Governing and Conception Vessels) or the Macrocosmic Orbit (which connects all Twelve Primary Channels with the Governing and Conception Vessels).

8. **Psycho-Emotional Aspects:** The Triple Burners assist in regulating the emotional interactions of the individual's social relations. On a psycho-emotional level, the Triple Burners can be used to move Qi and lift depression derived from a stagnation of Liver Qi. When the Triple Burners (which regulate the consciousness) are full, the consciousness becomes stable, and the Mind's intent becomes benevolent and kind-hearted. The Triple Burners are especially linked with the Heart and Pericardium and are easily affected by the emotion of joy.

According to ancient Daoist teaching, when the energy of the Heart is strong and pure (e.g., internally consistent and without guilt), and the desires and thoughts of an individual are at peace, then the energy of the body's sexual essence (Postnatal Jing) will spread into the Triple Burners, and the Blood will flourish within the vessels. If the "Fire of Desire" (i.e., sexual passion) is allowed to heat and combine with the energy of the Triple Burners, the energy of the

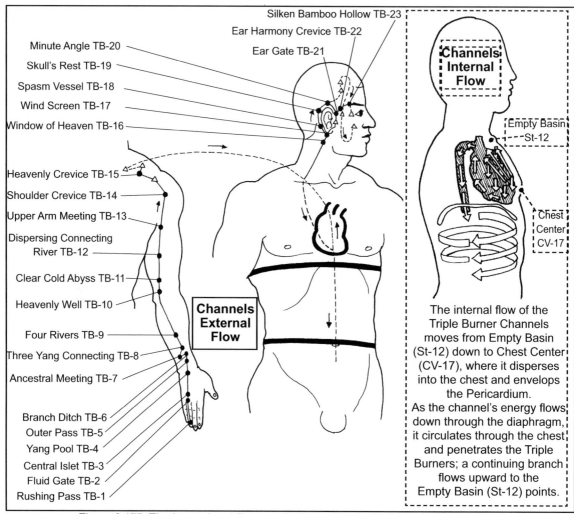

Figure 8.177. The Internal and External Qi Flow of the Triple Burners (TB) Channel

individual's sexual essence will overflow, mix itself with the energy of the Mingmen, and leave the body via the reproductive organs and tissues. This can lead to a depletion of both Jing and Qi.

THE TRIPLE BURNER CHANNELS

The Triple Burner Channels are Yang Channels that flow externally from the hands to the head (Figure 8.177).

- **The External Branches:** The two main channels originate externally from the tips of the ring fingers and ascend along the lateral aspect of the arms, continuing over the shoulders to the clavicles.

- **The Internal Branches:** From the Empty Basin (St-12) points they branch internally, dispersing into the chest to envelop and spiral wrap the Pericardium. They then circle the diaphragm and penetrate the Upper, Middle, and Lower Burners.

A set of branches originate internally from the Chest Center (CV-17) point at the Heart, and the front gate of the Middle Dantian. Flowing upward, these branches return back to the supraclavicular fossa at the Empty Basin St-12 points before ascending up the neck, head, and circling the ears. From the Minute

Angle (TB-20) points, another set of branches flow above the ears towards the outer canthus of the eyes; from the Ear Harmony (TB-22) points, a final set of branches flow downward to the cheek, terminating in the infraorbital region.

Channels' Energy Flow

The energy of the Triple Burner Channels acts on the skin, muscles, and nerves found along their pathways, and also move the body's True Fire.

The Triple Burner Channels store more Qi than Blood, and act more on the energetic and nervous system functions of the body than on physical substances and Blood functions.

At the High-Tide time period (9 p.m. to 11 p.m.), Qi and Blood abound in the Triple Burner Channels. At this time period the Triple Burner Channels can more easily be dispersed and purged. During Low-Tide (9 a.m. to 11 a.m.), they can be more readily tonified.

The Energetic Anatomy of the Triple Burners

The Triple Burners' energy is primarily composed of Zong Qi (Essential Qi). The Zong Qi assists the Heart in the circulation of Blood and assists the Lungs in respiration. The Zong Qi is in charge of distributing the Ying Qi (Nourishing Qi) throughout the body to nourish the Blood, organs, and tissues. Another function of the Zong Qi is to strengthen the Weiqi (Protective Energy) that protects the external body from pathogens (Figure 8.178).

1. **The Upper Burner:**

    The Upper Burner is formed from the Fire that is created from the combined energies of the Heart, Pericardium, and Lungs. The Upper Burner's energy is housed within the head, throat, and upper chest, and extends down to the diaphragm. The Upper Burner is responsible for respiratory and cardiac functions. It moves the body's finer energy, circulating and distributing nutrients and Qi throughout the body like a mist.

2. **The Middle Burner:**

    The Middle Burner is formed from the Fire that is created from the combined energies of the Stomach, Spleen, Pancreas, and Gall Bladder. The Middle Burner's energy is housed within the upper abdomen (the diaphragm) and the umbilicus.

    The Middle Burner is responsible for digestion, fermentation, and the transformation of food and drink into nutrients for distribution. In the Middle Burner area, the Small Intestine connects downward to the Urinary Bladder. The Small Intestine transforms waste, then sends the unusable portion down to the Large Intestine. The Small Intestine also distills the body's fluids before sending them down to the Urinary Bladder.

    The Ying Qi (Nourishing Energy) of the Middle Burner receives its substance from the Stomach and Spleen. The Spleen extracts Gu Qi from the food prepared by the Stomach, churning the food essence into "foam." The Spleen refines this energetic foam, and then sends it as processed Gu Qi to the Lungs. The Lungs (in the Upper Burner) further refine the Gu Qi and send the impure portion to the Kidneys for further refinement of the Gu Qi. The Kidneys return the clean Qi to the Lungs, while sending the turbid portion to the Urinary Bladder to be expelled from the body. In the Lungs, the Qi from the air mixes with the Gu Qi to produce Zong Qi. The Lungs circulate the refined Gu Qi in the form of a vapor (or mist) which is then housed in the Upper Burner. The Heart then utilizes this vapor in the production of Blood.

3. **The Lower Burner:**

    The Lower Burner is formed from the Fire that is created from the combined energies of the Liver, Kidneys, Urinary Bladder, Intestines, and genitalia. The Lower Burner's energy is housed within the area just below the umbilicus and extends down to the lower perineum.

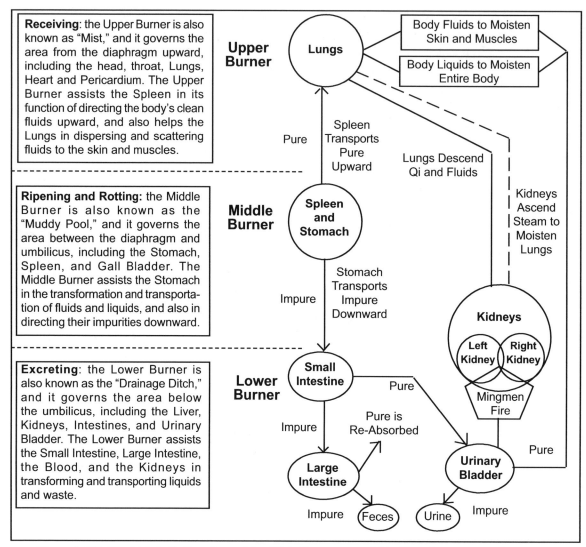

Figure 8.178. The Metabolic Functions of the Triple Burners are divided into three parts or functions: the Upper Burner, Middle Burner, and Lower Burner. These different functions of the Triple Burners control the movement of various types of Qi in the three stages of energy production.

The Lower Burner is responsible for the reproductive functions and for the filtration and elimination of waste products. It moves the body's coarser energy, acting as a "channel for water."

The Triple Burners contribute to the process of the three stages of transformation and aid in the distribution of Ying and Weiqi throughout the body as follows:

- After the Gu Qi (Food Energy) has been separated into clean and turbid Qi, the Upper Burner releases the body's Clean Weiqi (Protective Energy), directing it to the Lungs.
- The Middle Burner releases the body's Clean Ying Qi (Nourishing Energy), directing it to all of the body's organs and tissues.
- The Lower Burner releases the Body Fluids, directing the turbid part to the Urinary Bladder.

Chapter 8: The Twelve Primary Organs, Channels and Collaterals

The Body's Three Fires

According to the ancient Daoist teachings contained within the *Compendium of the Doctrine of the Mean*, heat in the body is generated from the combined action of the Three Fires (i.e., the "Heart Fire," the "Kidney Fire," and the "Bladder Fire"). These special Fires emanate from three special locations inside the human body (Figure 8.179):

- **The Heart Fire:** This internal fire is located inside the center of the body's chest cavity.
- **The Kidney Fire:** This internal fire is located inside the center of the body's abdominal cavity.
- **The Bladder Fire:** This internal fire is located inside the center of the body's lower perineum.

When these Three Fires follow their normal course of energetic movement, they lead the body's life-force in the process of creating and sustaining life. Traditionally it is taught that the Three Fires are responsible for regulating the Yin and Yang energy of the body via the energy of the Three Dantians.

The Three Fires also represent the regions of vital heat that are responsible for the circulation of vital energy that sustain the human soul. Therefore the energy of the Three Fires is also used for spiritual cultivation and liberation, and can be accessed through special meditations and deep prayer.

It is important to remember that, although similar in location, the energetic function of the body's Three Fires is quite different from that of the Triple Burners. The purpose of the Triple Burners is to regulate the ingestion, digestion, and distribution of food and fluids throughout the body. It is considered a completely different energetic system from the Three Fires. The primary purpose of the Three Fires is:

- To transform and transport the energy of Jing, Qi, and Shen throughout the body,
- To transform and transport the energetic natures of the Four Seas (Sea of Blood, Sea of Nourishment, Sea of Qi and Sea of Marrow),
- To provide Heat to the internal organs within the Triple Burner bowl, and
- To assist in evaporating water and transforming Body Fluids.

The physical locations of the Three Fires do however, coincide with the anatomical locations of the Triple Burners (for more information on the Three Fires, please see Chapter 4).

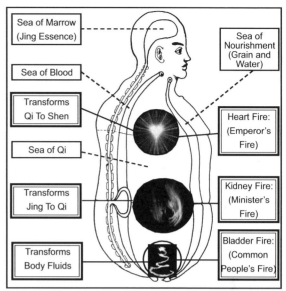

Figure 8.179. The Body's True Fire

The Influence of Climate

The Triple Burners are especially susceptible to the invasion of External Pathogens, such as Wind Heat and Wind Cold in the Upper Burner, and Damp Heat and deficient conditions affecting the Lower Burner.

The Influence of Taste, Color, and Sound

- The Bitter Taste can be used to tonify the Triple Burners.
- The Red Color is used to tonify the Triple Burners.
- The "Shee" Sound is used to purge both the Triple Burners and Pericardium.

Triple Burner Pathology

The main diseases along the Triple Burner Channels involve the face, ear, cheek, larynx, and neck. Diseases of the Triple Burner Channels also include disorders of the back of the upper extremities from the midline to the upper arm and forearm.

When diagnosing problems due to dysfunctions of the Triple Burners, the Medical Qigong Doctor considers the following:

- **A Blockage of the Weiqi in the Upper Burner:** This causes an impairment of the

Lungs' dispersing function. This can result in the invasion of the Lungs by External Evils (e.g., Wind and Heat) that penetrate the Pericardium, corresponding to the initial stage of externally contracted Wind Heat or Wind Cold diseases.

- **A Blockage of the Ying Qi in the Middle Burner:** This causes an impairment of the Spleen's transporting function. This can result in gastrointestinal Heat stagnation and can cause Spleen and Stomach Damp Heat, corresponding to the second stage of externally contracted Heat diseases.
- **A Blockage of the Body Fluids in the Lower Burner:** This causes an impairment of the Urinary Bladder's function of fluid transformation. This results in the deep penetration of Toxic Evils, which weakens the body's Kidney Yin. This in turn can cause Deficient Liver Blood and Wind stirring due to Empty Yin, and corresponds to the advanced stages of externally contracted Heat diseases.

T.C.M. Patterns of Disharmony

Generally, the patterns of disharmony in the Triple Burner are related to the patterns of the internal organs located within the bowels of the Triple Burner, which are described as follows (Figure 8.180):

1. **Patterns of Disharmony in the Upper Burner:** These involve patterns of disharmony that are associated with the Lungs and Heart, and can manifest through symptoms associated with the invasion of External Wind Cold and Wind Heat invasion.
2. **Patterns of Disharmony in the Middle Burner:** These involve patterns of disharmony that are associated with the Stomach and Spleen, and can manifest through symptoms associated with stagnation and Rebellious Qi.
3. **Patterns of Disharmony in the Lower Burner:** These involve patterns of disharmony that are associated with the Urinary Bladder, Kidneys, Small Intestine and Large Intestine. Lower

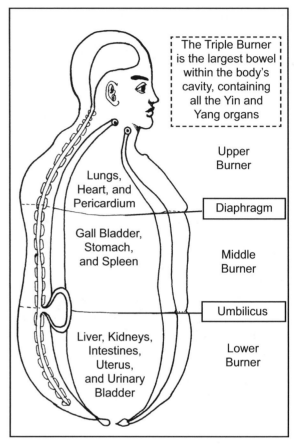

Figure 8.180. The Ancient Chinese Energetic Subdivisions of the Triple Burners

Burner Disharmony can manifest through symptoms associated with Damp Heat in the Urinary Bladder, Damp Cold in the Urinary Bladder, Kidney Yang Deficiency, Damp Heat in the Large Intestine, or Damp Heat in the Small Intestine.

The Triple Burners in Western Medicine

Though some attempts have been made at correlating the Triple Burner with the Western concept of the maintenance of metabolic balance in the body, Western Medicine recognizes no translation of, or reference to, the Triple Burners.

Understanding Internal Organ Pathology

In Chinese Energetic Medicine, the study of Internal Organ Pathology is based on understanding the physiological functions of each of the body's twelve organ systems. This study also includes the internal organ relationships with the energetic function of the body's Jing, Qi, Shen, Blood, and Body Fluids.

The primary goal of an internal organ's metabolic function is to enhance the overall energetic quality of its reserves, while contributing to the support and function of the body as a whole. For example, when healthy, an internal organ will transmute the Qi, Blood, and Shen it consumes, harmonizing its energetic flow within and between the tissues. When in a diseased state, however, an internal organ will consume its source of vitality as it strives to support its own functions.

Understanding Channel Pathology

Channel Pathology is the oldest of all the modes of Pathological Pattern Classification, dating back to the *Huangdi Neijing Ling Shu (The Yellow Emperor's Inner Canon, Magical Pivot)*. In understanding a channel's pathology, the Medical Qigong doctor takes into consideration several aspects of the patient's energy flow (i.e., the Channels are viewed as "Exterior;" whereas, the Organs are viewed as "Interior"). Channel Pathology is often related to Organ Disturbances, but it can also be distinct from Organ Pathology.

The disease of one channel may cause disease in other channels and organs. Likewise, tonification of one channel may cause a tonification of other channels and organs.

The Four Causes of Channel Pathology

There are four main causes of Channel Pathology: Invasion of External Pathogens, Physical Strain, Injuries, and Internal Organ Disharmonies, described as follows (Figure 8.181):

1. **The Invasion of External Pathogens:** The Six External Pathogens of "Fire, Summer Heat, Cold, Wind, Dry, and Damp," can lead to Channel Dysfunction. These External Pathogenic Factors often settle in the joints, causing "Bi" Syndrome ("Painful Obstruction"). Channel Pathology is also closely related to Joint Pathology. In Traditional Chinese Medicine, joints play important roles in the circulation of Qi and Blood.

   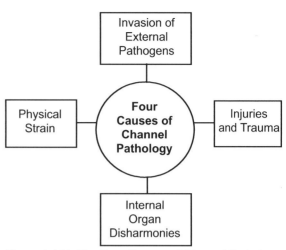

   Figure 8.181. The Four Causes of Channel Pathology

   Both Qi and Blood gather and concentrate in the joints, and Qi enters and exits the channels at the joints. The Five "Shu" ("Source" or "Transporting") Points are usually located on or near the joints (see Chapter 10). It is at these points that the External Pathogenic Influences may enter the body and settle in the joints. These External Pathogenic Influences upset the balance of Yin and Yang, and block the flow of Qi and Blood. Resulting in causing pain and swelling. The body's joints are also affected by Deficient Qi and Blood, causing local weakness and pain from lack of movement.

2. **Physical Strain:** The overuse of joints can cause local stagnation to occur within the Muscle/Tendon Channels, which can manifest as physical pain and tissue weakness.

3. **Injuries and Trauma:** Injuries can cause local Qi and Blood Stagnation. This results in the impairment of channel flow, which can manifest as stiffness, bruising, and pain.

4. **Internal Organ Disharmonies:** Excess or Deficiency occurring within the Yin and Yang organs can also affect the functional relationship of the channels.

DIFFERENTIATION BY CHANNEL FULL/EXCESS AND EMPTY/DEFICIENT

It is important for the Medical Qigong Doctor to differentiate between conditions of Channel Excess and Channel Deficiency. Normal indicators of Channel Dysfunction are described as follows (Figure 8.182 and Figure 8.183):

- **Excess:** When a channel is too full or in an Excess Condition, the symptoms include localized stiffness, contractions, cramps, or intense pain along the channel.
- **Deficient:** When a channel is "empty" or in a Deficient Condition, the symptoms include dull aches, weakness in the muscles, numbness, and muscle atrophy along the channel.
- **Heat:** A red color observed along the channel's pathway indicates Heat.
- **Cold:** A bluish color observed along the channel's pathway indicates Cold.

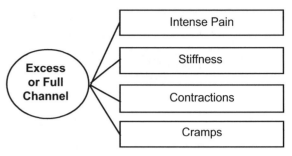

Figure 8.182. Excess or Full Channel Pathology

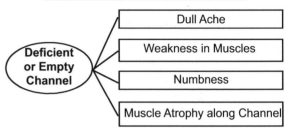

Figure 8.183. Deficient or Empty Channel Pathology

DIFFERENTIATION OF CHANNEL PATTERNS BY SPECIFIC CHANNELS

Channel pathology was originally discussed in the *Huangdi Neijing Ling Shu (The Yellow Emperor's Inner Canon, Magical Pivot)*, and was originally described as follows (see *The Foundations of Chinese Medicine* by Giovanni Maciocia):

1. **Diseases of the Gall Bladder Channels** may cause alternating chills and fever, temporal headaches, acute onset of deafness, pain and distention of the breasts, pain in the hip and on the sides of the body, and pain along the lateral sides of the legs.
2. **Diseases of the Liver Channels** may cause vertex headaches, pain and swelling of the eyes, pain and distention of the breasts, and cramps in the legs.
3. **Diseases of the Lung Channels** may cause fever, aversion to cold, stiffness in the chest, and pain in the shoulders, clavicles or arms.
4. **Diseases of the Large Intestine Channels** may cause a sore throat, toothache, nosebleed, runny nose, swollen and painful gums, swollen eyes, and pain along the channel's pathway.
5. **Diseases of the Stomach Channels** may cause pain in the eyes, nosebleed, neck swelling, facial paralysis, cold legs and feet, and pain along the channel's pathway.
6. **Diseases of the Spleen Channels** may cause vaginal discharge, weakness of the leg muscles, and a Cold feeling along the channel's pathway.
7. **Diseases of the Heart Channels** may cause pain in the eyes, pain along the scapula, and pain along the inner side of the arms.
8. **Diseases of the Small Intestine Channels** may cause pain and stiffness in the neck, and pain along the lateral side of the scapula, elbow, or arms.
9. **Diseases of the Urinary Bladder Channels** may cause fever and aversion to cold, headache, stiff neck, pain in the lower back, pain in the eyes, and pain in the back side of the leg along the channel's pathway.
10. **Diseases of the Kidney Channels** may cause lower back pain, or pain in the soles of the feet.
11. **Diseases of the Pericardium Channels** may cause a stiff neck, contraction of the elbow or hand, and pain along the course of the channel's pathway.
12. **Diseases of the Triple Burner Channels** may cause alternating chills with fever, acute onset of deafness, pain and discharge from the ear, pain at the top of the shoulders, pain in the elbow, and pain along the course of the channel's pathway.

SUMMARY OF THE PRIMARY CHANNELS

The clinical significance of studying the energetic pathways of the Twelve Primary Channels is made evident through observing the association of certain pathological manifestations with specific patterns peculiar to each channel and its associated internal organ. Because the quality, quantity, and proportions of Qi and Blood circulating through each of the Twelve Primary Channels has a vital impact on all the body's organ systems, the conceptual understanding of the "normal" flow of Qi and Blood helps to define the patterns of the reciprocal relationships that exist among the body's internal organs, channels, and energetic points. Some of the most common Twelve Primary Channel Pathologies and their clinical manifestations occurring along the "Roots and Branches" of these channel pathways are categorized in the preceding diagram (see Figure 8.186).

ROOT AND BRANCH

The term "Root and Branch" is used to describe the difference between either the "Medial and Lateral," or between the "Upper and Lower" orientations of the channels, and their points of origin. These terms are also used to describe the progression of a disease, and the priorities and sequence of the Medical Qigong Doctor's treatment. Specifically, the word "Branch" is used to describe the channels' flow of Qi and Blood and the progression and direction of a disease. The word "Root" is used to described the channels' internal organ, or the origin of a disease.

THE DAOIST 12 ORGANS HAND SEAL

The ancient Daoist believed that since the energy of the year is divided into twelve months, likewise, the energy of the human body's twelve internal organs could also be subdivided. These twelve subdivisions were selected as the main focal points for rituals involving the summoning of spirits. That is, the body's twelve internal organs acted as terrestrial living quarters within the microcosm of man, that could be used to initiate and summon the celestial spirits of the Dao. In both auspicious times and in times of trouble, these important celestial spirits could be brought forth to bless or aid the disciple.

Each of the twelve internal organs was also associated with one of the twelve directions of the Lo Pan compass (Figure 8.184). This compass

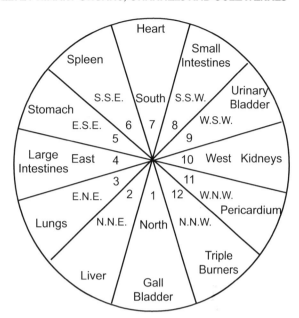

Figure 8.184. The Energy of the Body's Twelve Internal Organs Divided as the Focal Points for Ritual Summoning.

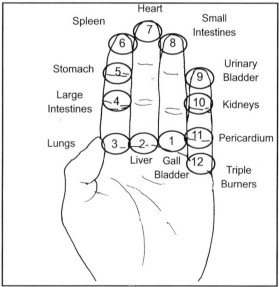

Figure 8.185. The Compass Image was Imprinted as a Hand Seal (Mudra) on the Left Hand.

image was mentally imprinted as a Hand Seal on the left hand of the Daoist disciple, and could be used to summon a specific spirit from within his or her internal organs (Figure 8.185).

Twelve Primary Channels	Channel Pathologies
Gall Bladder	Pain in the upper right and left quadrants of the abdomen Diseases of the head, face, eyes and ears Diseases of the external sides of the lower extremities
Liver	Swelling and a distended sensation of the hypochondrium Diseases of the lower abdomen and genital organs
Lungs	Chest and Lung diseases Diseases on the radial side of the upper arm and palmar area of the hand
Large Intestine	Diseases on the lower part of the face, nose, oral cavity, teeth, throat, and neck Diseases of the back and radial side of the upper extremities
Stomach	Diseases of the face, nose, oral cavity, teeth, throat, and front of the neck Diseases of the abdomen, the frontal part of the lower extremities and gastrointestinal area Certain psychiatric diseases
Spleen	Diseases of the tongue and throat Gastrointestinal diseases (disturbances of digestion and absorption of food) Diseases of the medial side of the extremities
Heart	Diseases that exert pressure on the brain, eyes, or pharyngeal wall Diseases of the Heart and lateral side of the chest Diseases of the ulnar and palmar sides of the upper extremities Insomnia, impairment of the consciousness, amnesia, and psychosis
Small Intestine	Diseases of the face, ear, cheek, lower jaw, neck, and throat Diseases of the back and ulnar side of the upper extremities
Urinary Bladder	Diseases of the top of the head, brain, neck, back, lumbar and sacral region Diseases of the back of the legs and thighs, as well as the lateral side of the foot
Kidneys	Diseases that cause the general deterioration of the entire body Weakness in the lower extremities and lumbar pain Hot sensations deep inside the feet
Pericardium	Diseases of the Heart, front of the chest, major blood vessels Diseases of the midline to palmar side of the upper extremities Mental abnormalities
Triple Burners	Diseases of the face, ears, cheeks, larynx and neck Diseases of the back of the upper extremities from the midline of the torso to the upper arm and forearm

Figure 8.186. Pathologies of the Twelve Primary Channels

Understanding Shadow Organs & Channels

In Chinese Energetic Medicine, the study of Internal Organ and Channel Pathology would not be complete without this final addition. In my studies of Chinese Energetic Medicine, I have traveled the world and have only found a small hand-full of Internal Masters who understood this secret teaching. These are traditionally "Closed Door Teachings," and you must either be taught as an apprentice to a Daoist Exorcist, or train under a disciple under a master of Daoist Transformational Magic in order to gain access to this secret information. Because this esoteric teaching is so rare, I have included it within this chapter for future generations.

Understanding The Shadow

In ancient China, the shadow of an individual was considered to be an important part of his or her immaterial substance. According to my teacher,

> "Ordinary People" view all shadows and reflections as simply being "unreal." According to the uneducated, all shadows and reflections are believed to be things that have form but are without substance. Therefore, the uninformed place no value on shadows or reflections. The intuitive Disciple of the Dao, however, observes these "unreal" shadows and reflections as containers of powerful ethereal forces, which can be energetically manipulated and eventually felt by the human body.
>
> People who have not refined their internal and external energy fields tend to be insensitive to the micro-pulsations of these energetic impressions and remain vulnerable to external manipulation. Through consistent meditation and training, an individual can become "awakened," and develop a sensitivity to the energetic form and micro-pulsations of all shadows and reflections. This is the secret principle underlying the energetic practice of curing illness or creating sickness through influencing an individual's shadow."

In ancient China, it was believed that there was a powerful energetic connection existing between the image of a shadow and the body. To the ancient Daoists, a shadow was "born of light," and was therefore considered to be the external reflection of the individual's internal soul. The energy of a shadow was also believed to be the Yin portion of an individual's soul, and was within itself considered to be a "Mysterious Darkness."

According to ancient Daoist teachings, there are eight energetic aspects that created and maintained an individual's existence within the Physical Realm. These special energetic aspects include:

- **Xing (Shape, Form, Body):** The energetic shape and form of an individual's body,
- **Qi (Energy):** The individual's life-force,
- **Shen (Spirit):** The individual's spirit (Shen),
- **Xin (Heart):** The individual's heart/mind,
- **Zhili (Intellect):** The individual's capacity of retaining knowledge and expressing wisdom,
- **Mingzi (Name):** The sacred sounds and ancestral lineage of an individual's name,
- **Mianju (Mask):** The individual's acquired identity, profession, and social status,
- **Yinying (Shadow):** The energetic shape and form of an individual's shadow.

To the ancient Chinese, after death, the Yin Aspect of an individual's soul survived and existed in a shadow-like form. This surviving energetic form (i.e., ghost or apparition) would sometimes exist in or around tombs and burial sites. Rogue or hostile spirits were sometimes known to take on the appearance of these "Shadow Spirits" in order to "over-shadow" an individual and influence his or her emotional state.

The Shadow Organs and Channels

Similar in effect to the "Shadow Stars" that are prevalent within the night sky, the ancient Daoist were also aware of the existence of Shadow Organs and Shadow Channels located within the body's energetic fields. According to ancient Daoist teachings, each internal organ, channel, and vessel was believed to have its owns energetic shadow (Figure 1.187). Each energetic shadow maintains the delicate Yin and Yang balance that exists within the Jing, Qi, and Shen of each of the body's internal and external organs, channels, and vessels (see Chapter 21, in *The Secret Teachings of Chinese Energetic Medicine: Vol.#3*).

It is said that the body's Hun (Ethereal Soul) continually brings light into the various organs and channels, which are energetically supported and sustained via the individual's spiritual virtues (i.e., compassion, peace, truthfulness, integrity, honor, wisdom, etc). Likewise, the body's Po (Corporeal Soul) brings darkness into the various organs and channels, which are energetically supported and sustained via the individual's emotional state (i.e., anger, anxiety, worry, grief, fear, etc).

Each person has his or her own energetic "dark side." Since "like attracts like," the Shadow Channels are energetically "fed" through their attachments to and assimilation of negative emotional states. Because each internal organ and vessel is energetically coupled with its own "Shadow," it is through these energetic portals that a sorcerer or evil spirit can negatively influence a victim's internal organs and tissues. It was believed that this was one of the reasons why specific types of diseased states were so prevalent in certain individual's medical histories. My teacher further explained,

> "When energetically influenced, the affected Shadow Organ or Channel automatically reduces the electromagnetic field that resonates within the body's channel system. This adverse influence causes the channel's energetic potential to scatter or become stagnant. Once this detrimental type of energetic phenomena occurs, the true channel's energetic amplitude decreases, and the body becomes even more vulnerable to any energetic overshadowing initiated from an evil spirit or malicious sorcerer."

TRAINING TO REMOVE SHADOW ORGAN QI

Traditionally, in Daoist Alchemy we begin training the student's Physical Body in order to eliminate toxic poisons that have stored themselves within the disciple's tissues, and to also strengthen his various internal organs and organ systems. At the same time, we train the disciple's Energy Body in order to remove the toxic energetic states existing within his body as "Shadow Organs and "Shadow Channels." Then, we train the student's Spirit Body by increasing the disciple's divine energy field, and use this subtle spiritual energy to increase the divine heat, light, and vibration currently resonating within the disciple's Three Bodies.

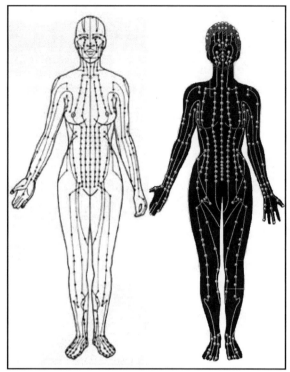

Figure 8.187. The Body's Channel System Has its own corresponding Shadow Channels.

As we train the new disciple to internally connect with the spiritual energy currently existing inside his body, his Original Spirit will begin to "awaken," and he must then go through the process of "Intercepting Karma," needed in order to recognize and eventually eliminate the dominating negative influences of his Acquired Personality, stored within his tissues as "Shadow Organs and Channels."

If the disciple's "Ling Qi" ("Spiritual Energy") is not continually purified, the energy of the forming Spirit Body may energetically mutate, and could transform into what the ancient Daoists call an "Internal Demon" or internal "Shadow Spirit." In Daoist Alchemy, if the "Inner-Breath" is not continually regulated by the disciple's cultivated Divine Virtues, the disciple could develop and "give birth" to states of extreme mental psychosis. This "evil state" is built on the energy of the unprocessed emotional woundings that are still "alive" and active within the disciple's Three Bodies and tissues as "Shadow Organs and Channels."

Chapter 9
The Connecting Vessels, Divergent Channels, Muscle and Tendon Channels and Skin Zones

The Fifteen Connecting Vessels: Luo Mai

The Chinese word "Luo" denotes "A Net or Web," and is translated as "Connecting Vessel" or "Collateral." In Traditional Chinese Medicine this refers to the "passageways" for the circulation of energy through the body's Primary Channels.

The energetic field of the Luo points extends deep into the tissues, beyond the level of the Muscle and Tendon Channels. The body's energy emerges from fifteen primary Luo "pathway" points, thirteen of which are located on the Twelve Primary Channels, while the two other Luo pathway points are located on the Governing and Conception Vessels.

The majority of the body's Luo points are located below the elbows and knees and provide an additional energetic barrier to keep "Evil Winds" from affecting the Primary Channels. The Collaterals are the streams of energy that connect the paired Primary Channel rivers.

Translation of "Luo Mai"

Though often translated as "Collaterals," the literal meaning of the Chinese term "Luo Ma" is "Connecting Vessels" (sometimes known as "Associated Vessel Collaterals").

- **Luo:** The first character depicts the Chinese ideogram for "Luo" ("Connecting"), and is composed of two radicals. Positioned to the left is the radical "Mi," used for Silk, Net, or String-like Objects." The right side of the character is the phonetic sound. The word Luo carries the meaning of "To energetically envelop something in a net" (Figure 9.1).

- **Mai:** The second character is the Chinese ideograph "Mai," which is generally translated as

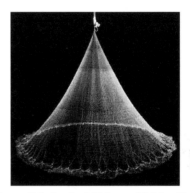

Figure 9.1. Ancient Chinese Fishing Net

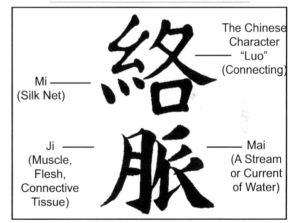

Figure 9.2. The Chinese characters "Luo Mai" ("Connecting Vessel" or "Connecting Streams")

"Vessel." It is composed of two characters: the character to the left, "Ji" depicts the Chinese ideogram for "Body Tissue, Muscle, or Flesh" (all of which are forms of Connective Tissue); the character on the right "Mai" depicts "A Current of Water, Stream, or Branch of a River." As a whole, the character can be translated as "Arteries, Veins or a Pulse, indicating a form of energetic circulation (Figure 9.2).

Energetic Anatomy of the Luo Mai

The Twelve Primary Channels are interconnected by the Collaterals, which are small inter-linking streams. The Collaterals work as the connecting branches of the energetic circulatory system, and are considered to be the underlying support of the Twelve Primary Channels. They generally flow superficially, in both horizontal and vertical directions. They are viewed as the body's "Secondary Streams of Qi," and form an important intricate network that traverses the body's surface, and interconnects the main energetic rivers, connective tissues, and cutaneous regions (Skin Zones).

The Luo distribute Qi and Blood to those areas not directly traversed by the Extraordinary Vessels and Twelve Primary Channels. The Luo Mai are known as the "Interconnecting Passageways" that branch out through the body. They appear in several forms, from deep to superficial, and are usually divided into three levels, described as follows:

- **The Fifteen Connecting Vessels (Shi Wu Luo Mai):** These are also known as the Fifteen Major (or Great) Connecting Vessels (Shi Wu Da Luo Mai). These Fifteen Luo Mai transfer Qi and Blood from the Twelve Primary Channels to all parts of the body. They are sometimes referred to as the "Fifteen Major Arteries," and energetically, they link together the interior and exterior aspects of the body by connecting the body's internal and superficial channels. They also link together the Governing and Conception Vessels and the Great Luo of the Spleen.
- **The Secondary Branches (Minute Collaterals of the Fifteen Connecting Vessels):** These are the smaller branches of the Fifteen Major Collaterals. They are countless in number, and are finer manifestations of the Luo, dispersed throughout the tissues.
- **The Grandson Connecting Vessels (Sun Luo Mai):** These are sometimes called the "Superficial Collaterals" or the "Floating Luo," as they seem to float on the surface of the body. These are the smallest of the Luo, and spread-out into the countless terminal branches of the entire Luo system. The Superficial Collaterals are the subtlest sub-branches of the Luo system. They distribute Qi and Blood directly to the tissues of the body, similar in energetic function to the capillaries of the vascular system.

It is important to note, that both the secondary branches of the Fifteen Connecting Vessels and the Grandson Connecting Vessels, which can be seen beneath the surface as Blood Vessels, are sometimes called "Blood Luo Vessels."

According to ancient Daoist teachings, the Qi of Heaven and Earth is believed to merge and interact with the body's Twelve Primary Channels via the intersecting energy of the Fifteen Collaterals. Therefore, in ancient China, the Fifteen Collaterals were believed to be the intersecting streams of energy existing between the body's Waiqi (External Energy) and Neiqi (Internal Energy) flow.

In order to understand the energetic significance of the Collaterals, it is helpful to think of the body's energy flowing like a "River" (i.e., the Primary Channels) towards the surface of the body, where it transforms into a "Marsh" (Collaterals). The "Marsh" absorbs the universal Qi of Heaven (i.e., the energy of the Sun, Moon, and Stars) and the environmental Qi of Earth (the energy of the Soil, Water, and Wind) before reversing its course and flowing in the opposite direction back toward its original source.

In Daoist Numerology, when the Qi of the 15 Luo Vessels are combined together with the Qi of the 12 Primary Channels, it creates 27 energetic pathways. This energetically corresponds to 9x3, which symbolizes the full diffusion of the life-force energy maintaining command over human life.

Embryological Points of the Luo Mai

The Luo Mai have a functional relationship with the developmental aspects of Ancestral and Embryological Energetic Formation. That is to say, the Luo Mai contain certain "Command Points" that allow a doctor of Chinese Energetic Medicine access to the Eight Extraordinary Vessels, which are responsible for Energetic Embryological Development.

TRANSVERSE & LONGITUDINAL LUO

Flowing from each Primary Channel's Luo point are two Luo Vessels, which are energetically counted as one. The "Transverse Luo Vessel and the Longitudinal Luo Vessel are described as follows:

1. **The Transverse Luo Vessels:** These connect to the "Source" points on the Yin and Yang coupled Primary Channels. They act as energetic safety valves, maintaining balance between the Yin and the Yang Channels by diverting the excess energy of one channel into the Orb (internal organ and energetic field) of its paired Primary Channel.

   When a channel is Deficient (empty) and its paired channel is in Excess (full), for example, the tonification of the Luo point on the Deficient Channel replenishes the deficiency, while simultaneously normalizing the Excess energy of its paired channel.

2. **Longitudinal Luo Vessels:** These flow out from the Luo points, but do not connect with the coupled Primary Channels. The Luo Vessels usually flow proximally toward the channel's organ.

FUNCTIONS OF THE LUO MAI

Located on each Primary Channel are specific Luo points which act as the origins of the branching Luo Vessels (Figures 9.3).

The main function of the Luo Vessels is to transfer Qi and Blood from the Primary Channels to all parts of the body, so as to nourish the tendons, the bones, the skin, and the Five Sense Organs (nose, eyes, ears, lips, and tongue). The Luo Vessels also link the interior with the exterior of the body, connecting the internal channels with the superficial channels.

EXCESS AND DEFICIENT PATHOLOGY

The pathology of the Fifteen Major Collaterals is classified into syndromes of Excess and syndromes of Deficiency, described as follows:

1. **Excessive Conditions of the Collaterals:** This can arise from Exogenous Invasion if the following occurs:

   (A) The internal organ associated with the Luo is in an Excess condition, or

   (B) The body's Weiqi is weak.

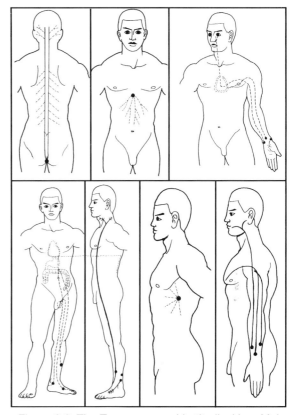

Figure 9.3. The Transverse and Latitudinal Luo Mai

Sometimes Evil Winds can enter the body through the Jing Well or Wind points, and start moving up the channel. In the clinic, the Longitudinal Luo Vessels provide a common route for the diversion of Evil Winds. This is because the Longitudinal Luo Vessels have more Weiqi than the Primary Channels, and can thus fight pathogens more effectively. Sometimes in cases of Wind Cold Invasion, a blue color is visible along the path of the Longitudinal Luo Vessel. If the invasion is due to Wind Heat, there may be a red color noticed along the Vessel.

2. **Deficient Conditions of the Collaterals:** In the clinic, this condition is commonly due to:

   (A) The internal organ associated with the Luo Vessel being deficient, or

   (B) The patient's Qi is deficient due to Exogenous Factors.

LOU MAI COLOR DIAGNOSIS

According to the *Huangdi Neijing Ling Shu (The Yellow Emperor's Inner Canon, Magical Pivot)*, the Luo Mai are a visible manifestation of the Primary Channels, which do not enter into the major joints, and are continually affected by Excess movement, Heat, and Cold. The *Ling Shu* further states that when the Luo Mai are in a diseased state, certain energetic color manifestations will appear. For example:

- **A Strong Color:** Indicates that the Mai is Full, and the Luo Vessels are trying to get rid of a pathogen.
- **A Small/Short Color:** Indicates that there is a Deficiency of Qi within the Vessel.
- **No Visible Color:** Indicates the Mai is Empty.
- **A Red Color:** Indicates Heat and Fever.
- **A Dark (Blue or Green) Color:** A dark color indicates Cold and Pain within the Vessel.
- **A Black Color:** Indicates a chronic condition.
- **A Purple Color:** Indicates that there is a condition known as "Floating Luo Mai." When treating a Purple Colored Vein, Bloodletting the Luo is traditionally recommended; especially in such cases where the Excess Heat is creating mental problems and serious Shen Disturbances (i.e., depression, excessive sorrow, etc.). The Needling Method recommended is quick and shallow, followed with blood letting.

POINT LOCATION OF THE FIFTEEN MAJOR COLLATERALS

1. **The Foot Tai Yin (Greater Yin) Spleen-4 Point:** To the ancient Daoists, this special point was traditionally known as the "Yellow Emperor" (Sp-4) point, because his family name was originally "Gongsun." Today, it is commonly known in the clinic as the "Grandfather-Grandson" (Gong Sun) point. Anatomically, this point is located on the medial side of each foot, just posterior to the base of the first metatarsal bone.

   Although this is the Luo (Connecting) point for the Spleen Channel, it is also the "Xi" ("Confluent") point for the Thrusting Vessel (Chong Mai).

   After energetically branching away from the Spleen Channel, this Luo Mai flows downward to connect with the Stomach Channel on each

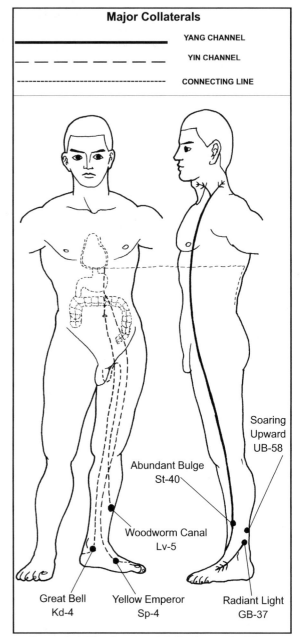

Figure 9.4. The figure at left illustrates the Three Luo points of the Yin Collaterals on the Foot, which are located on the Primary Channels of the Kidneys, Spleen, and Liver. The figure on the right shows the Three Luo points on the Yang Collaterals of the Foot located on the Primary Channels of the Stomach, Urinary Bladder, and Gall Bladder.

foot. A second branch of this Luo Mai flows from the Yellow Emperor (Sp-4) point upward along the medial aspect of the inner thigh, passing the abdomen and connecting with the Stomach and Small Intestine (Figure 9.4).
- Symptoms of Excess in this Luo Mai include sharp intestinal pain, vomiting, and diarrhea.
- Symptoms of Deficiency in this Luo Mai include abdominal swelling.

2. **The Foot Shao Yin (Lesser Yin) Kidney-4 Point:** The "Great Bell" (Kd-4) point is located on the Kidney Channel of each foot, just posterior to the medial malleolus, and is the Luo (Connecting) point for the Kidney Channel.

   The energy of this Luo Mai flows downward, crossing the heel, to connect with the Urinary Bladder Channel by the ankle on each foot. A second branch of this Luo flows upward along the medial aspect of the inner thigh, following the Kidney Channel. It then ascends the abdomen to connect with the Pericardium of the Heart, before descending laterally to connect with the lumbar vertebrae (see Figure 9.4).
- Symptoms of Excess in this Luo include enuresis, emotional irritability, and depression.
- Symptoms of Deficiency in this Luo include lower back pain.

3. **The Foot Jue Yin (Terminal Yin) Liver-5 Point:** The "Woodworm Canal" (Lv-5) point is located on the medial side of each foot, several inches above the medial malleolus, and is the Luo (Connecting) point for the Liver Channel.

   After energetically branching from the Liver Channel, this Luo Mai connects with the Gall Bladder Channel. It then flows upward along the medial aspect of the inner thigh, connecting with the genitals. It terminates at the tip of the penis in males, and the clitoris in women (see Figure 9.4).
- Symptoms of Excess in this Luo include swelling of the testicles.
- Symptoms of Deficiency in this Luo include itching in the pubic region.

4. **The Foot Tai Yang (Greater Yang) Urinary Bladder-58 Point:** The "Soaring Upward" (UB-58) point is located on the lateral side of each foot, several inches above the external malleolus, and is the Luo (Connecting) point for the Urinary Bladder Channel.

   After energetically branching from the Urinary Bladder Channel, the energy of this Luo flows downward to connect with the Kidney Channel on each foot (see Figure 9.4).
- Symptoms of Excess in this Luo include nasal congestion, occipital headache, and back pain.
- Symptoms of Deficiency in this Luo include clear mucus nasal discharge and nosebleed.

5. **The Foot Shao Yang (Lesser Yang) Gall Bladder-37 Point:** The "Radiant Light" (GB-37) point is located on the lateral side of each foot, several inches above the external malleolus, and is the Luo (Connecting) point for the Gall Bladder Channel.

   After energetically branching from the Gall Bladder Channel, this Luo flows downward to connect with the Liver Channel on each foot. It then continues downward to disperse over the dorsum on each foot (see Figure 9.4).
- Symptoms of Excess in this Luo include fainting.
- Symptoms of Deficiency in this Luo include weak and flaccid muscles of the feet.

6. **The Foot Yang Ming (Bright Yang) Stomach-40 Point:** The "Abundant Bulge" (St-40) point is located on the lateral side of each foot, several inches above the external malleolus, and is the Luo (Connecting) point for the Stomach Channel.

   After energetically branching from the Stomach Channel, this Luo flows downward to connect with the Spleen Channel on each foot. A second branch of this Luo ascends along the lateral aspect of the tibia, flowing upward to the top of the head. At the top of the head this Luo branch divides into two smaller branches, one branch connects with the throat, while the other branch converges with all the Yang Channels on the neck and head (see Figure 9.4).
- Symptoms of Excess in this Luo include epilepsy and insanity.
- Symptoms of Deficiency in this Luo include pharyngitis, sudden aphasia, and flaccid or atrophied muscles in the legs or feet.

7. **The Hand Tai Yang (Greater Yang) Small Intestine-7 Point:** The "Branch of the Upright" (SI-7) point is located by the ulnar bone, on the dorsal side of each hand, several inches above the wrist, and is the Luo (Connecting) point for the Small Intestine Channel.

   After energetically branching from the Small Intestine Channel, this Luo flows upward past the elbow and connects with the Large Intestine-6 point (see Figure 9.5).
   - Symptoms of Excess in this Luo include fever, headaches, and blurred vision.
   - Symptoms of Deficiency in this Luo include atrophy of the muscles in the elbow and arm and a looseness in the joints.

8. **The Hand Yang Ming (Bright Yang) Large Intestine-6 Point:** The "Leaning Passage" (LI-6) point is located by the radial bone, on the dorsal side of each hand, several inches above the wrist, and is the Luo (Connecting) point for the Large Intestine Channel.

   After energetically branching from the Large Intestine Channel, this Luo flows upward on each arm to the jaw and pours into the area of the teeth. Another branch of this Luo ascends into each ear, connecting with the Thrusting Vessels which supply energy to the head (see Figure 9.5).
   - Symptoms of Excess in this Luo include deafness and toothache in the lower jaw.
   - Symptoms of Deficiency in this Luo include a sensation of coldness in the teeth, as well as fullness and congestion in the chest.

9. **The Hand Shao Yang (Lesser Yang) Triple Burner-5 Point:** The "Outer Pass" (TB-5) point is located just above the dorsal transverse crease of each wrist.

   Although this is the Luo (Connecting) point for the Triple Burner Channel, it is also the "Xi" ("Confluent") point for the Yang Linking Vessel (Yang Wei Mai).

   After energetically branching from the Triple Burner Channel, this Luo flows upward past the arm and over the shoulder, dispersing into the chest and connecting with the Pericardium Channel (see Figure 9.5).

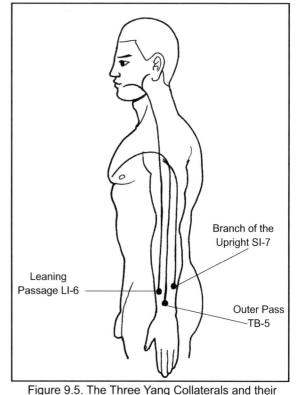

Figure 9.5. The Three Yang Collaterals and their Luo points, located on the Hand; on the Primary Channels of the Large Intestine (LI), Triple Burners (TB), and Small Intestine (SI).

- Symptoms of Excess in this Luo include muscle spasms around the elbow.
- Symptoms of Deficiency in this Luo include flaccid muscles around the arm and elbow joint.

10. **The Hand Tai Yin (Greater Yin) Lung-7 Point:** The "Lightning Strike" (Lu-7) point arises from the cleft of the tendons and bones on the radial side of each wrist.

    Although this is the Luo (Connecting) point for the Lung Channel, it is also the "Xi" ("Confluent") point for the Conception Vessel (Ren Mai), the Gao Wu Command Point, and the Ma Dan-Yang Heavenly Star Point.

    After energetically branching from the Lung Channel, this Luo flows down into the palm before spreading throughout the thenar eminence (see Figure 9.6).

- Symptoms of Excess in this Luo include heat in the palms or wrists.
- Symptoms of Deficiency in this Luo include enuresis and shortness of breath.

11. **The Hand Shao Yin (Lesser Yin) Heart-5 Point:** The "Penetrating the Interior" (Ht-5) point is located on the Heart Channel of each hand, just above the transverse crease of the wrist and is the Luo (Connecting) point for the Heart Channel.

    The energy of this Luo ascends along the Heart Channel, enters the Heart, and then continues up the chest into the head, where it flows into the root of the tongue, then finally ascends to connect with each eye (see Figure 9.6).
    - Symptoms of Excess in this Luo include fullness and pressure in the chest.
    - Symptoms of Deficiency in this Luo include aphasia.

12. **The Hand Jue Yin (Terminal Yin) Pericardium-6 Point:** The "Inner Pass" (Pc-6) point is located on the Pericardium Channel of each hand, just a few inches above the medial transverse crease of the wrist, between the two tendons.

    Although this is the Luo (Connecting) point for the Pericardium Channel, it is also the "Xi" ("Confluent") point for the Yin Linking Vessel (Yin Wei Mai).

    The energy of this Luo Mai follows the Pericardium Channel, and eventually connects with the Heart (see Figure 9.6).
    - Symptoms of Excess in this Luo include chest pain.
    - Symptoms of Deficiency in this Luo include irritability.

13. **The Governing Vessel-1 Point:** The "Long Strength" (GV-1) point is located on the base of the Governing Vessel, at the perineum.

    Although this is the Luo (Connecting) point for the Governing Vessel, it is also the special "Meeting" point where the Qi of the Governing Vessel, Conception Vessel, Gall Bladder Channel, and Kidney Channels all converge. Therefore, the ancient Daoists would some-

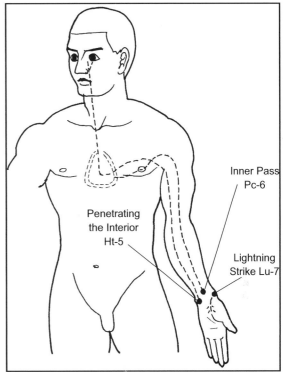

Figure 9.6. The Three Yin Collaterals and their Luo points located on the Hand; on the Primary Channels of the Heart, Pericardium, and Lungs.

times call this special area the "Long Hu Xue" ("Dragon and Tiger Point"), the "Chao Tian Dian" ("Looking at Heaven Summit") point, and the "Shang Tian Ti" ("The Stairway to Heaven") point."

The energy of this Luo flows upward along both sides of the spine, connecting with each of the body's correspondence (Shu) points before reaching the nape of the neck. From the nape of the neck, this Luo's energy spreads to the top of the head, stimulating the Sea of Marrow. From the top of the head, it continues flowing into the scalp region on both sides of the head, eventually connecting with the Urinary Bladder Channel and merging with the spine (see Figure 9.7).
- Symptoms of Excess in this Luo include stiffness along the spine.
- Symptoms of Deficiency in this Luo include dizziness or heaviness in the head.

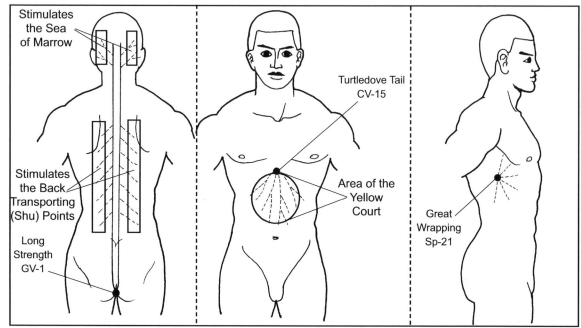

Figure 9.7. The Main Collateral of the Governing Vessel is located on the Long Strength (GV-1) point.

Figure 9.8. The Main Collateral of the Conception Vessel is located on the Turtledove Tail (CV-15) point.

Figure 9.9. The Major Collateral and Luo point of the Spleen is located on the Great Wrapping (Sp-21) point.

14. **The Conception Vessel-15 Point:** The "Turtledove Tail" (CV-15) point is located on the Conception Vessel, just below the xiphoid process of the chest, and is the Luo (Connecting) point for the Conception Vessel.

    The energy of this Luo Mai flows into the Yellow Court and empties downward along the torso, pouring over the abdomen (see Figure 9.8).
    - Symptoms of Excess in this Luo include pain on the surface skin of the abdomen.
    - Symptoms of Deficiency in this Luo include itching on the surface skin of the abdomen.

15. **The Major Luo of the Spleen-21 Point:** The "Great Wrapping" (Sp-21) point is located on the Spleen Channel of the chest, below the axillary fold of each arm, and is the Luo (Connecting) point for the Spleen Channel.

    The energy of this Luo Mai spreads through the chest and hypochondriac region, gathering the Blood like a net (see Figure 9.9).

    In ancient Daoist training, this was the area that was used during the Ren Wu Zang Meditation as an energetic exit portal for releasing the "White Tiger" (Metal Element, Lung Qi, Po- Corporeal Soul) from the right side of the body; and for releasing the Green Dragon (Wood Element, Liver Qi, Hun- Ethereal Soul): Liver Qi from the left side of the body.
    - Symptoms of Excess in this Luo include general aches and pains throughout the entire body.
    - Symptoms of Deficiency in this Luo include weakness in the muscles of the limbs and joints.

THE TWELVE DIVERGENT CHANNELS: JING BIE

The Twelve Divergent Channels comprise an important part of the body's Channel System. These special channels branch off from the Twelve Primary Channels, and share the energetic function of circulating Qi throughout the body. The energetic field of the Twelve Divergent Channels forms an enormous web of complex interconnections within the network of the body's Twelve Primary Channels.

According to the *Huangdi Neijing Ling Shu* (*The Yellow Emperor's Inner Canon, Magical Pivot*), the topic of the Divergent Channels is originally introduced in *Chapert 11: The Separate Channels,* in response to the Yellow Emperor's question:

> "How is the person in tune with
> the Dao of Heaven, and how Internally
> are the Five Zang (Yin) Organs in accord
> and resonate with the Five Tones,
> the Five Colors, the Five Seasons,
> the Five Flavors, and the Five Positions;
> Also, how Externally are the
> Six Fu (Yang) Organs in accord
> and resonate with the Six Pitch Pipes?"

After the Yellow Emperor's question to the great physician Qi Bo, the Divergent Channels are then described in six junctions, starting with the Urinary Bladder and Kidney, and ending with the Large Intestine and Lung Divergent Channels.

During the course of the teaching, the Yin and Yang energetic pathways are described, with the Yang Divergent Channels going through the Zang (Yin) Organs of their associated channel, and reconnecting with their own channel. The energetic pathway of the Yin Divergent Channels however, does not reconnect with their own channel, but rather energetically joins with their Yang-paired Divergent Channel. This reinforces the notion that the Divergent Channels are responsible for "connecting the inner and outer" (e.g., the Yang Divergent Channels move into the Zang and the Heart Organ; while the Yin Divergent Channels move towards their Yang counterparts). In this manner, we can say that the Divergent Channels connect External and Internal in a way that is harmonious with the Dao of Heaven.

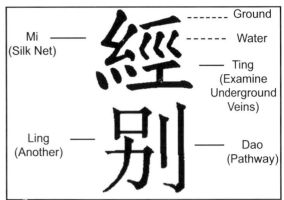

Figure 9.10. The Chinese character "Jing Bie" (Divergent Channel, or Separate Passageway Channel)

TRANSLATION OF "JING BIE"

Also known as the "Separate Pathway Channels," the literal translation of the Chinese term "Jing Bie" is "Divergent Channels" (Figure 9.10).

- **Jing:** The first character depicts the Chinese ideogram for "Jing" ("Channel"), which can also be translated as "Meridian, To Pass Through, and The Wrapping of a Silk Fiber or Net."

  The word Jing carries a multitude of meanings, reflected by the many components of the character. Positioned to the left is the radical "Mi," used for "Silk, Net or String-Like Objects."

  The right side of the character is the phonetic "Jing," and is sometimes used to denote the Flow of Water (the top right character represents the Ground, while the three curved lines beneath it represent the Underground Flow of Water). Positioned to the bottom-right is a modification of the ancient phonetic "Ting," meaning "To Examine the Underground Veins. Together, the ideograph describes the deep aquatic passageways or subterranean rivers which energetically knit together the internal fabric of the human body.

- **Bie:** The second character depicts the Chinese ideogram for "Bie" (divergent) and can be translated as "To Separate From, Difference, and Distinction." The character is composed of two separate ideographs: On the left is the ideograph "Ling," which translates as "Another." On the right is an ideograph "Dao" that describes the following of a straight line or pathway separate from the regular course.

EMBRYOLOGICAL DEVELOPMENT

In ancient China, the Twelve Divergent Channels were believed to be responsible for the Prenatal formation of the body's internal organs, and the internal design and energetic imprinting of the Postnatal Twelve Primary Channels. Some Daoist masters maintain that, due to their interconnection with the body's internal organs, the Twelve Divergent Channels have the deepest energetic flow of all the channels, penetrating deeper than even the Extraordinary Vessels, and are responsible for transporting Ying Qi (Nutritive Energy) and Yuan Qi (Original Energy).

Another essential action of the Twelve Divergent Channels appears to be the activation of the cerebral circulation, which serves to bring the body's Ancestral (Hereditary) Energies and Metabolic Energies to the cranial level.

ENERGETIC ANATOMY OF THE JING BIE

Because the areas governed by the energy of the Twelve Divergent Channels are both detailed and extensive, they are considered to be a separate yet deeper component of the Channel System. They are secondary streams that run parallel to the primary rivers, yet each has its own characteristic functions and unique clinical applications independent of the Primary Channels.

All of the Twelve Divergent Channels (except for the Pericardium Divergent Channel) begin somewhere on the four extremities. The energy runs shallowly at first, then flows deeper into the body before surfacing again at or near the channels' end points. Some Daoist masters believe that the body's Weiqi also flows through the Twelve Divergent Channels, moving from the extremities inward.

The Twelve Divergent Channels have no defined points of their own, although there are intersection points where they cross the major channels. All of the Twelve Divergent Channels separate from the body's main channels at the He-Sea points at the knees and elbows. The energy of the Twelve Divergent Channels travels through the Yellow Court (solar plexus), the Heart, and the throat (connecting through the "Windows of Heaven" points). Therefore, stimulation of these channels will have a profound emotional and spiritual effect on each patient.

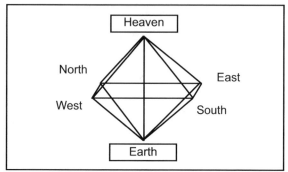

Figure 9.11. The Six Divergent Channel Pairs Correspond to the Six Directions of Space

THE SIX CONFLUENCES

The Twelve Divergent Channels are paired into "Six Confluences" ("Liu He") according to their internal and external relationships. In ancient China, it was believed that the six pairs of Divergent Channels energetically corresponded to the six directions of space: Heaven-Up, Earth-Down, North-Back, South-Front, East-Left and West-Right (Figure 9.11).

It was also believed that specific meditations could stimulate the energy within these six pairs of Divergent Channels, the overflow of which could then be used to stimulate the center body's Taiji Pole. The stimulation of the Taiji Pole would in turn evoke a subtle type of Heavenly resonance, allowing the individual to flow beyond the boundaries of both space and time, into the various spiritual realms.

The Twelve Divergent Channels are divided into six pairs, described as follows:

1. Urinary Bladder Divergent Channel (Foot Tai Yang) and Kidney Divergent Channel (Foot Shao Yin)
2. Stomach Divergent Channel (Foot Yang Ming) and Spleen Divergent Channel (Foot Tai Yin)
3. Gall Bladder Divergent Channel (Foot Shao Yang) and Liver Divergent Channel (Foot Jue Yin)
4. Small Intestine Divergent Channel (Hand Tai Yang) and Heart Divergent Channel (Hand Shao Yin)
5. Large Intestine Divergent Channel (Hand Yang Ming) and Lung Divergent Channel (Hand Tai Yin)
6. Triple Burners Divergent Channel (Hand Shao Yang) and Pericardium Divergent Channel (Hand Jue Yin)

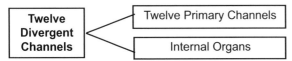

Figure 9.12. The Twelve Divergent Channels intersect with the Twelve Primary Channels and penetrate the internal organs.

ENERGETIC FUNCTION OF THE JING BIE

One of the primary functions of the Twelve Divergent Channels is to integrate all parts of the body with the Twelve Primary Channels, supplementing Qi and Blood to the areas of the body that are not directly traversed by the pathways of the Twelve Primary Channels. They also connect to those internal organs that are either unconnected or only remotely connected by the Primary Channels (Figure 9.12). These internal organ areas are more securely linked by the energetic flow of the Twelve Divergent Channels, which strengthen the bonds between the Twelve Primary Channels and the physical areas that are connected to, or adjoining, their pathways.

YIN & YANG DIVERGENT CHANNELS

The Twelve Divergent Channels facilitate the energetic connection between the linked pairs of Yin and Yang Primary Channels and Organs. Therefore, all Primary Yin and Yang Organs are interconnected by the Divergent Channels. Both Yin and Yang Divergent Channels ultimately connect with the body's Yang Primary Channels (Figures 9.13 through 9.18), which are described as follows:

1. **The Yang Divergent Channels:** These complete a cycle of leaving the Primary Channels (e.g., Gall Bladder Channel) and entering their associated internal organ (e.g., the Gall Bladder Organ) before they resurface on the neck and head to reconnect with their original channels (e.g., the Gall Bladder Channel).
2. **The Yin Divergent Channels:** These leave their Primary Channels (e.g., Liver Channel), to join their associated Yang Divergent Channels (e.g., the Divergent Gall Bladder Channel), which then join with the Yang Primary Channels (e.g., the Gall Bladder Channel). The Yin Divergent Channels influence and are also influenced by the same areas on the body as their Yang Divergent Channel Confluent pair.

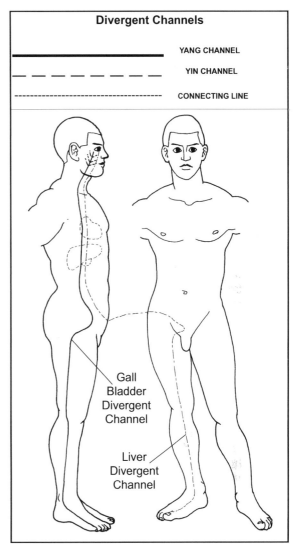

Figure 9.13. The Divergent Channels of the Gall Bladder and Liver

Similarly, within the body's cavities, most of the Twelve Divergent Channels first join with their Primary Yin or Yang Organ, before connecting with the Associated Organ (through its Associated Channel) in the Yin/Yang pair. Through this interaction, the connection between paired Yin and Yang organs and channels is strengthened. Therefore in the Clinic, sometimes a disease affecting a Yang Channel can be treated by selecting certain areas on its associated Yin Channel, and vice versa. The same theory holds true for the treatment of diseases of the internal organs.

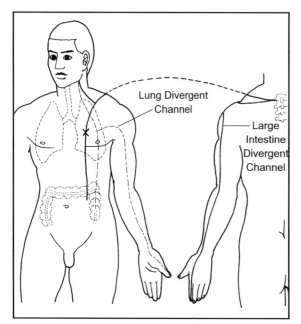

Figure 9.14. Lungs and Large Intestine Divergent Channels

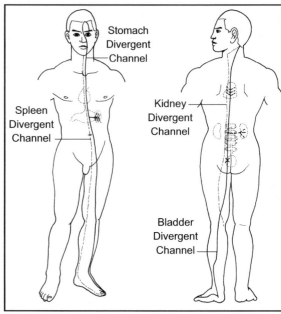

Figure 9.15. Stomach and Spleen Divergent Channels

Figure 9.16. Bladder and Kidney Divergent Channels

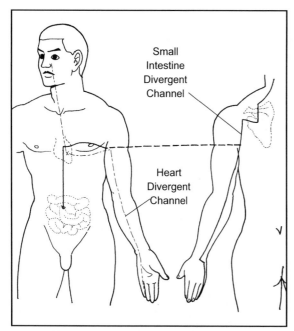

Figure 9.17. Heart and Small Intestine Divergent Channels

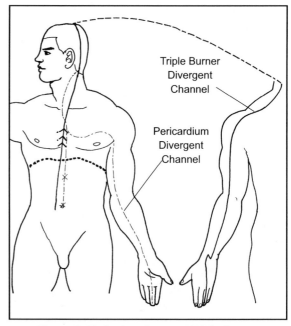

Figure 9.18. Pericardium and Triple Burner Divergent Channels

THE TWELVE MUSCLE AND TENDON CHANNELS: JING JIN

Skeletal muscles and tendons link together and mobilize the Bones of the body, acting on specific joints to provide movement. The Twelve Jing Jin (Muscle and Tendon Channels) are the muscle and soft tissue regions of the body where the Qi and Blood of the Primary Channels nourish the skin, muscles, and tendons. They are very superficial in relation to the Primary Channels, and they form a capillary network that travels in the depressions and planes between muscles and tendons. The Twelve Muscle and Tendon Channels subsequently spread over the whole of the epidermis, through their close connection with the cutaneous tissues.

TRANSLATION OF "JING JIN"

Long before the Zhou Dynasty (1028-221 B.C.), the ancient Chinese had already identified all of the body's muscles and their attachments to specific Bones. When observing the longitudinal organization of the muscular system, the ancient Chinese Physicians described its energetic flow as being similar to that of a "Valley" (where the larger muscles gathered) or a Stream (where the smaller muscles gathered). The spaces between the striated muscles were viewed as the "Meeting of the Valleys and Streams."

Commonly known as "the Tendino-Muscular Meridians" and "the Ligamentous Meridians," the literal translation of the Chinese term "Jing Jin" is "The Muscles of the Channels" or "The Muscles within the Channels" (Figure 9.19).

- **Jing:** The first character depicts the Chinese ideogram for "Jing" ("Channel"), which can also be translated as "Meridian, To Pass Through, and The Wrapping of a Silk Fiber or Net." The word Jing carries a multitude of meanings, reflected by the many components of the character. Positioned to the left is the radical "Mi," used for "Silk, Net or String-Like Objects."

The right side of the character is the phonetic "Jing," and is sometimes used to denote the Flow of Water (the top right character represents the Ground, while the three curved lines beneath it represent the Underground Flow of Water). Positioned to the bottom-right is a modification of the ancient phonetic "Ting," meaning "To Exam-

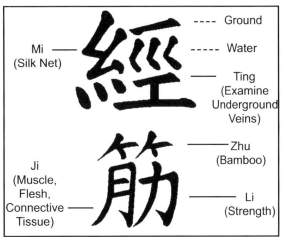

Figure 9.19. The Chinese characters "Jing Jin" ("Muscle-Tendon Channel")

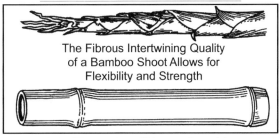

Figure 9.20. The ancient Chinese viewed the strong and resilient quality of the tendons as being similar to the fibrous and flexible structure of bamboo. (Inspired from Lilian Lai Bensky)

ine the Underground Veins. Together, the ideograph describes the deep aquatic passageways or subterranean rivers which energetically knit together the internal fabric of the human body.

- The bottom character "Jin" depicts the Chinese ideogram for "Sinew, Tendon, or Ligament." One of the earliest Chinese Medical Dictionaries, the *"Shou Wen Jie Zi,"* explains the term "Jin" as "The Strength of the Flesh," and explains that the ancient character is composed of the bamboo radical "Zhu" above two other radicals. The character to the left, "Ji" depicts the Chinese ideogram for "Body Tissue, Muscle, or Flesh" (all of which are forms of Connective Tissue); the character on the right is "Li" meaning "Strength." Therefore, the word "Jin" compares the resilient fibrous qualities of the tendons to the flexible fibrous, intertwining quality of bamboo (Figure 9.20).

Embryological Development

The Twelve Muscle and Tendon Channels have their Embryological Origin separate from the Twelve Primary Channels. Because of their connection to the Liver and the mesenchymal formations in the body, the Twelve Muscle and Tendon Channels are associated with the formation of the Skeletal System, Muscle-Tendon System, and the early development of the limbs.

The Twelve Muscle and Tendon Channels are also associated with the embryological formation of the diaphragm and the thoraco-abdominal serous membranes: Specifically the pleura, the peritoneum and the Pericardium.

Each of the Twelve Muscle and Tendon Channels appears to regulate and govern a definite number of muscle fasciculi, with each muscle spindle covering a certain amount of the body's fibrous or membranous casings.

The function of the Twelve Muscle and Tendon Channels is also associated with the body's Weiqi, barring access to the deeper channels.

Energetic Anatomy of the Jing Jin

Originating in the extremities, the Twelve Muscle and Tendon Channels ascend to the head and torso. They coordinate the movement of the Bones and limbs but do not enter into the internal organs. They are connected to the inner fascial structure of the body's muscles, tendons, and ligaments, as well as to the fascial structure of other connective tissues.

The Twelve Muscle and Tendon Channels are affiliated with the network of Primary Channels and Collaterals (Luo) on the exterior of the body and also serve as mediators between any energetic reactions (trauma, stress, etc.) that vibrate from the body's exterior into the deep internal organs.

These channels are found along the four extremities on the surface of the body, as well as along the head, neck, back, chest, and abdomen.

The name of each Muscle and Tendon Channel comes from the Twelve Primary Channels whose external energy flow they follow. They also receive the Blood and Qi nourishment necessary for their proper functioning activity through the Twelve Primary Channels.

Yin (Flexion) and Yang (Extension)

In Chinese Energetic Medicine, the muscles and tendons are described in relation to their Yin (flexion, contraction, internal rotation, etc.) and Yang (extension, expansion, external rotation, etc.) energetic actions, which seek to continually balance each other.

When the Yin and Yang energetic actions of the muscles and tendons fail to balance and regulate each other, Muscle Channel Dysfunction results. For example, when exposed to cold, the muscles and tendons become tense and over-contract. Conversely, when exposed to heat, muscles and tendons become loose and overextend.

Clinical Application

There are connecting and intersecting points found all along the Twelve Muscle and Tendon Channels. Treatment of these points can create a favorable response, allowing for successful purgation and tonification techniques. Therefore, the Medical Qigong Doctor can effectively apply "Jing Point Therapy" (Channel Point Applications) to specific areas and points along the Twelve Muscle and Tendon Channels in order to apply purging and tonifying tissue stimulation (Figure 9.21 through 9.32).

The Twelve Muscle and Tendon Channels are the external connections of the major channels. They generally flow superficially along the body's surface and join the main energetic rivers, connective tissues, and Cutaneous Regions. The Twelve Muscle and Tendon Channels are also the regions of the body where the Qi and Blood of the Twelve Primary Channels nourish the muscles, tendons, and ligaments. Because these channels are also responsible for extending and flexing the muscles, tendons, ligaments and joints, their pathology is reflected in symptoms of impaired movement (i.e., pulled, twisted, strained, cramped or atrophied muscles, flaccid muscles, spasms, etc.).

The pathology of the Muscle and Tendon Channels is also reflected in symptoms of dysfunction in corresponding groups of muscles and other associated connective tissues. The connective tissues are divided into three groups: the large, the small, and the membranous connective tissues.

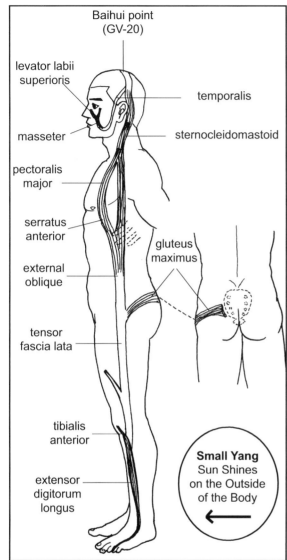

Figure 9.21. Gall Bladder Muscle Tendon Channel
(The Foot Shao Yang Muscle and Tendon Channel).
High Tide is 11p.m. to 1 a.m.
Pathological symptoms include:
strained muscles from the fourth toe to the knee upon lateral rotation, with an inability to bend the knee; muscle spasms or stiffness within the popliteal fossa; strained muscles of the sacrum, pelvis, and lower ribs; pain in the hypochondria, chest, and clavicle region; muscle spasms (facial tics) occurring around the outer edges of the eyes, and an inability to turn the eyes to the left or right.

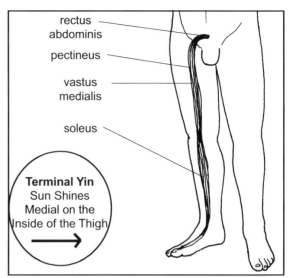

Figure 9.22. Liver Muscle Tendon Channel
(The Foot Jue Yin Muscle and Tendon Channel).
High Tide is 1 a.m. to 3 a.m.
Pathological symptoms include:
strained muscles of the big toe; pain in the anterior internal malleolus of the ankle; pain at the medial aspect of the knee and thigh; and dysfunction of the reproductive organs, i.e., impotence.

A local Muscle and Tendon Channel symptom can be treated by stimulating an area located next to the origin of the pain. For example, if the area is Yang (lateral) and overactive, then the Yin (medial) will be underactive, and vice versa. Treatment is thus directed towards restoring balance between the Yin and Yang Muscle and Tendon Channels.

The Twelve Muscle and Tendon Channels, being superficial, contain and circulate Weiqi. They thus provide the body's third line of defense against any unfavorable exogenous influence.

The body's first line of defense is the external Weiqi field, and second line of defense is the Weiqi stored within the skin. Only after overcoming the resistance of the body's Muscle and Tendon Weiqi can the Exogenous pathogens travel down the length of the channel to penetrate the corresponding primary channel at the Jing-Well point. Jing-Well points are points of energetic union, connecting primary channel points together with the points where the Muscle and Tendon Channels have their origin.

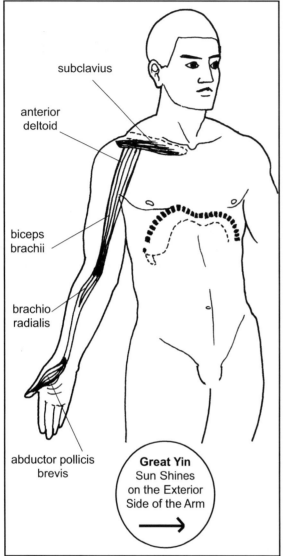

Figure 9.23. Lung Muscle Tendon Channel (The Hand Tai Yin Muscle and Tendon Channel). High Tide is 3 a.m. to 5 a.m. Pathological symptoms include: strained muscles of the thumb; stiff, strained muscle or muscle spasms, and/or pain along the course of the Lung Channel. In more serious cases, there will be muscle spasms over the rib area & spitting of blood.

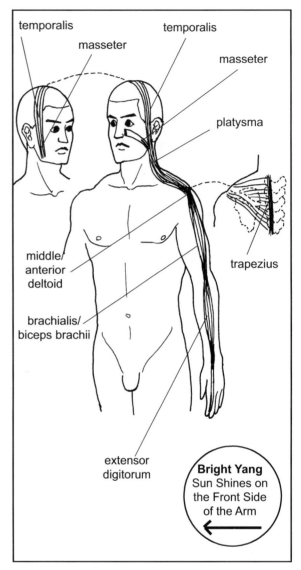

Figure 9.24. Large Intestine Muscle Tendon Channel (The Hand Yang Ming Muscle and Tendon Channel). High Tide is 5 a.m. to 7 a.m. Pathological symptoms include: strained muscles of the index finger; stiffness, strained muscles, or muscle spasms along the course of the channel, resulting in frozen shoulder; and an inability to rotate the neck from side to side.

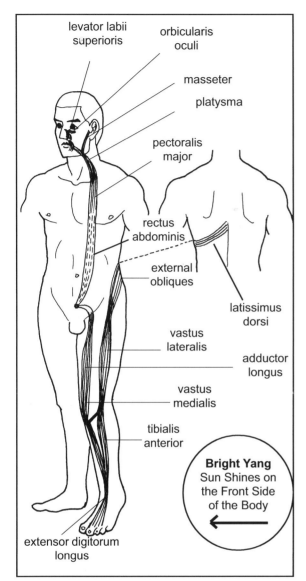

Figure 9.25. Stomach Muscle Tendon Channel
(The Foot Yang Ming Muscle and Tendon Channel).
High Tide is 7 a.m. to 9 a.m.
Pathological symptoms include:
strained muscles of the big toe; spasms or hardening of the muscles in the foot; knotted or twisted muscles in the lower leg and thigh; swelling in the anterior pelvis region; hernia; spasms of the abdominal muscles; spasms or stiffness of the neck and cheek muscles; and eye spasms.

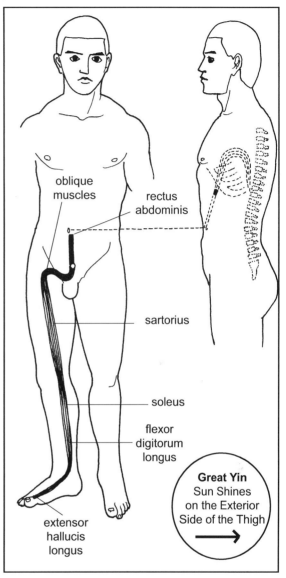

Figure 9.26. Spleen Muscle Tendon Channel
(The Foot Tai Yin Muscle and Tendon Channel).
High Tide is 9 a.m. to 11 a.m.
Pathological symptoms include:
strained muscles of the big toe; pain in the internal malleolus of the ankle upon rotation; pain along the medial aspect of the knee and adductor muscles of the thigh; groin strain; and pain due to strained upper abdominal muscles and mid-thoracic vertebrae.

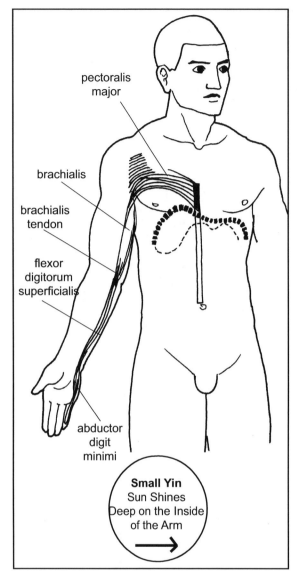

Figure 9.27. Heart Muscle Tendon Channel (The Hand Shao Yin Muscle and Tendon Channel). High Tide is 11 a.m. to 1 p.m. Pathological symptoms include: strained muscles of the little finger; stiff or strained muscles with spasms and/or pain along the course of the Heart Channel, including internal cramping within the diaphragm and upper abdominal area.

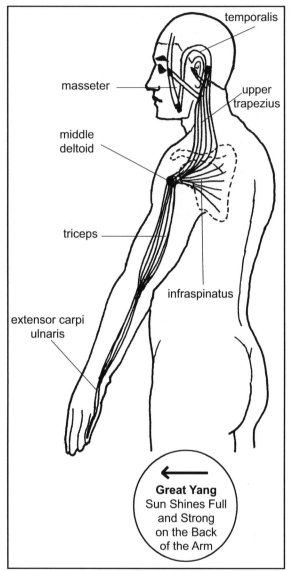

Figure 9.28. Small Intestine Muscle Tendon Channel (The Hand Tai Yang Muscle and Tendon Channel). High Tide is 1 p.m. to 3 p.m. Pathological symptoms include: strained muscles of the little finger; pain along the medial and posterior aspects of the elbow; pain in the posterior aspect of the axilla, neck, and scapula region; tinnitus related to ear ache; and poor vision.

CHAPTER 9: THE CONNECTING VESSELS, DIVERGENT CHANNELS, MUSCLE/TENDON CHANNELS AND SKIN ZONES

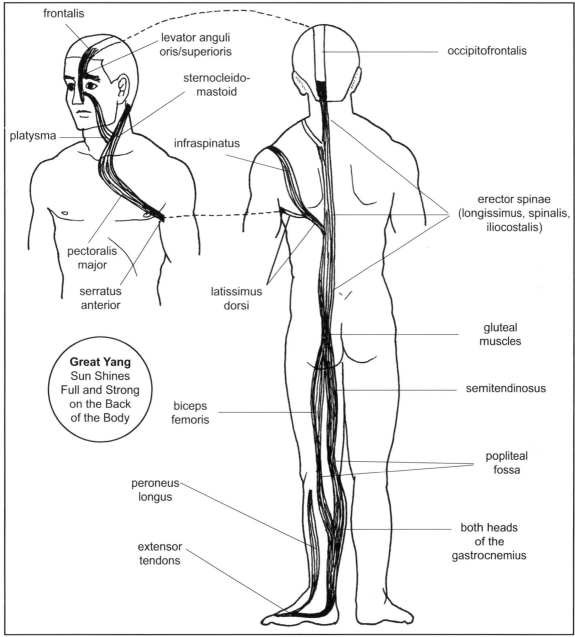

Figure 9.29. Urinary Bladder Muscle Tendon Channel (The Foot Tai Yang Muscle Tendon Channel). High Tide is 3 p.m. to 5 p.m. Pathological symptoms include the following: strained muscles of the small toe; swelling and pain in the heels; stiffness or spasms along the spine and back area; frozen shoulder; and stiffness or spasms in the axillary and clavicle regions.

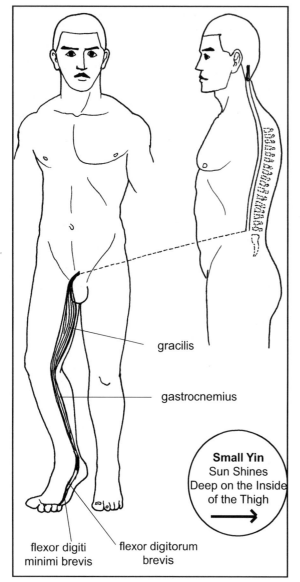

Figure 9.30. Kidney Muscle Tendon Channel
(The Foot Shao Yin Muscle and Tendon Channel).
High Tide is 5 p.m. to 7 p.m.
Pathological symptoms include:
strained muscles on the bottom of the foot;
spasms or stiffness along the channel resulting in
an inability to bend forward (Yang disorder)
or backward (Yin disorder), with difficulty in flexing
or extending the head.

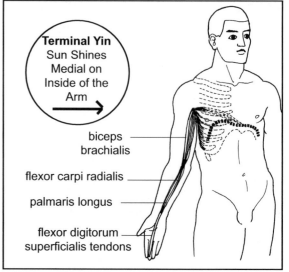

Figure 9.31. Pericardium Muscle Tendon Channel
(The Hand Jue Yin Muscle and Tendon Channel).
High Tide is 7 p.m. to 9 p.m.
Pathological symptoms include:
strained muscles of the middle finger; stiff or
strained muscles, or spasms and/or pain along the
course of the channel; and chest pain and spasms.

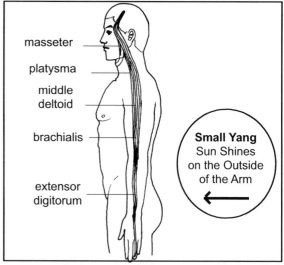

Figure 9.32. Triple Burner Muscle Tendon Channel
(The Hand Shao Yang Muscle and Tendon Channel).
High Tide is 9 p.m. to 11 p.m. Pathological symptoms
include: strained muscles of the ring finger; stiff or
strained muscles, or spasms and/or pain along the
course of the channel.

Diagnosis and Treatment Using The Muscle Tendon Channels

The Muscle and Tendon Channels are considered to be the "energetic conduits" of the body's Weiqi. Therefore, because the Weiqi warms, protects, and energetically supports the body's posture and its movements, it is through the "reading" of the Muscle and Tendon pathways that a Doctor of Chinese Energetic Medicine can confirm the exact location of Qi Stagnations and/or energetic depletions existing within the body's Channel System.

Problems corresponding to the Weiqi flowing within the body's Muscle and Tendon Channels, can result from the sudden or extreme exposure to temperature changes. This external "shock" to the tissues can result in the sudden onset of such conditions as Wind-Cold, Wind-Heat, or Wind-Damp Invasion; which can manifest through such acute symptoms as Skin Conditions (i.e., acute dermatological problems), headaches, and muscular problems.

If the patient is experiencing acute muscular problems, one way to evaluate the condition is to identify the specific "zone" where the problem functionally resides. For example:

1. **Tai Yang:** The Tai Yang Channels are involved when there is pain experienced when extending the limb away from the centre line of the body:
   - **The Small Intestine (Hand Tai Yang) Muscle Tendon Channel:** Pain is felt when extending a straight arm forward, away from the centre line of the body.
   - **The Urinary Bladder (Foot Tai Yang) Muscle Tendon Channel:** Pain is felt when extending a straight leg forward, away from the centre line of the body.
2. **Shao Yang:** The Shao Yang Channels are involved when there is pain on rotation:
   - **The Triple Burner (Hand Shao Yang) Muscle Tendon Channel:** Pain is felt when rotating a straight arm forward or backward.
   - **The Gall Bladder (Foot Shao Yang) Muscle Tendon Channel:** Pain is felt when rotating a straight leg forward or backward.
3. **Yang Ming:** The Yang Ming Channels are involved when there is pain bringing the limb back towards the centre line of the body:
   - **The Large Intestine (Hand Yang Ming) Muscle Tendon Channel:** Pain is felt when bringing a straight arm back towards the centre line of the body.
   - **The Stomach (Foot Yang Ming) Muscle Tendon Channel:** Pain is felt when bringing a straight leg back towards the centre line of the body.
4. **Tai Yin:** The Tai Yin Channels are involved when there is pain experienced when moving a bent limb in towards the centre of the body:
   - **The Lung (Hand Tai Yang) Muscle Tendon Channel:** Pain is felt when moving a bent elbow in towards the centre of the body.
   - **The Spleen (Foot Tai Yang) Muscle Tendon Channel:** Pain is felt when moving a bent knee in towards the centre of the body.
5. **Shao Yin:** The Shao Yin Channels are involved when there is pain experienced when moving a bent limb away from the centre of the body:
   - **The Heart (Hand Shao Yin) Muscle Tendon Channel:** Pain is felt when moving a bent elbow away from the centre of the body.
   - **The Kidney (Foot Shao Yin) Muscle Tendon Channel:** Pain is felt when moving a bent knee away from the centre of the body.
6. **Jue Yin:** The Jue Yin Channels are involved when there is a lack of movement or paralysis:
   - **The Pericardium (Hand Jue Yin) Muscle Tendon Channel:** When there is a lack of movement or paralysis experienced within the arm.
   - **The Liver (Foot Jue Yin) Muscle Tendon Channel:** When there is a lack of movement or paralysis experienced within the leg.

Because these unique diagnostic patterns reveal the specific Muscle and Tendon Channel that is involved, regardless of the exact location of the pain, it provides the Medical Qigong Doctor with another method of working with injured tissues. Therefore, when treating the condition, the doctor can release the muscle tension within the injured sinews by stimulating the Jing-Well point of the involved channel.

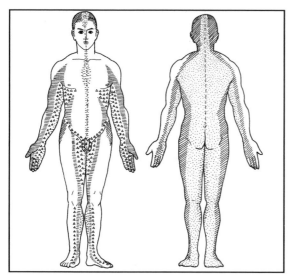

Figure 9.33. The Body's Pi Fu (Skin Zones)

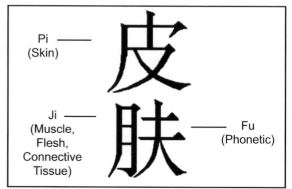

Figure 9.34. The Chinese characters "Pi Fu" (Skin)

THE SKIN ZONES: PI FU

Based along the body's Twelve Primary Channels, Connecting Vessels, and Muscle and Tendon Channels, the body's outermost tissue is divided into Twelve Skin Zones (also known as the Twelve Cutaneous Regions). These skin zones are the surface contact areas for the body's Channel System (Figure 9.33).

The regions (or zones) of the skin (Pi Fu) are located in the superficial layers of the external derma and have continuous and direct contact with the external environment. They are, therefore, the areas of the body that are the most sensitive to climactic changes and must adapt to protect the body from external pathogenic factors.

ORIGIN OF NAME

The literal translation of the Chinese term "Pi Fu" is "Skin" (Figure 9.34).
- **Pi:** The first character "Pi," depicts the Chinese ideogram for "Skin."
- **Fu:** The second character "Fu," also depicts the Chinese ideogram for skin. It is composed of two radicals. The character to the left, "Ji," depicts the Chinese ideogram for "Body Tissue, Muscle, or Flesh (all of which are forms of Connective Tissue). To the right side of that character is the phonetic for "Fu." Together the characters Pi Fu translate as "Skin."

THE ENERGETIC PATTERNS OF SKIN

One of the subjects Developmental Biologists are interested in is the development of patterns. There are the obvious externally visible patterns (i.e., the stripes of a tiger, a leopards spots, etc.), and internal energetic patterns.

Everything about most multi-cellular organisms is about these energetic patterns. Without these important genetic configurations, the physical body would simply end up being an amorphous blob of cells and tissues. These important "invisible" patterns are structural aspects of the process of genetic assembly, formulating little compartment boundaries where disparate pieces of the organism are stitched together during fetal development.

THE SKIN PATTERNS OF BLASCHKO'S LINES

Throughout the life of the human tissue development, the skin patterns transform to genetically induced formations due to normally invisible lines and stripe formations of subtle molecular differences, running across our bodies, which are occasionally exposed by human mosaicism. These special marks are called the "Lines of Blaschko," named after the doctor who first reported a common set of patterns in patients with dermatological disorders in 1901 (Figure 9.35).

One popular theory is that, a patch of tissue that follows a Blaschko patterned line represents a clone of cells derived from a single cell in the early embryo. These clones follow stereotypical expansion and migration patterns depending on their position in the embryo. For example, as a cell located in the middle of the back of a tiny embryo continues to grow larger during fetal development, it would tend

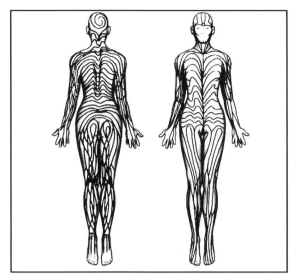

Figure 9.35. Skin Patterns of Blaschko' Lines

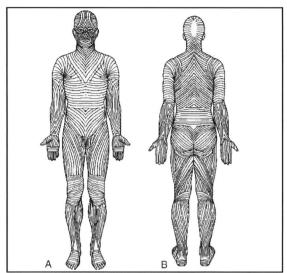

Figure 9.36. Skin Patterns of Langer's Lines

to expand first upward towards the head and then sweep backward and around to the front of the body.

THE SKIN PATTERNS OF LANGER'S LINES

Langer's Lines (also known as "Cleavage Lines"), are specifically patterned topological lines, that are observed like a map on the human body (Figure 9.36). They energetically correspond to the natural orientation of collagen fibers located within the dermis, and are generally parallel to the position of the underlying muscle fibers.

Historically, Langer Lines were originally defined by the direction in which the skin of a human cadaver would split when it was struck with a spike. The study of the body's Langer's Lines have an important relationship to Forensic Science, and in the development of Surgical Techniques.

THE SKIN PATTERNS OF DERMATOMES

A Dermatome is an area of skin supplied by sensory neurons that arises from a spinal nerve ganglion. Within the human body, there are several Dermatomes (Figure 9.37):
- 8-Cervical Nerve Zones (C)
- 12-Thoracic nerve Zones (T)
- 5-Lumbar Nerve Zones (L)
- 5-Sacral Nerve Zones (S)

Each of these Nerve Zones relay sensations (including pain) from a particular region of skin to the brain. Although the Nerve Zone patterns

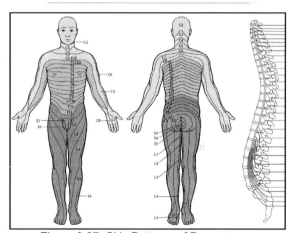

Figure 9.37. Skin Patterns of Dermatomes

differ along the arms and the legs, as compared to those observed along the thorax and abdomen, the precise areas of innervation are slightly different and unique to each individual.

Clinical Symptoms (e.g. like a pain or rash) that follow a Dermatome Skin Pattern may indicate a pathology that involves the related Nerve Root. Examples include somatic dysfunction of the spine or viral infection. Viruses that lie dormant inside the Nerve Ganglia (e.g. Chickenpox and Herpes Zoster) often cause either pain, rash or both in a pattern defined by a Dermatome. However, the symptoms may not expand across the entire Dermatome region.

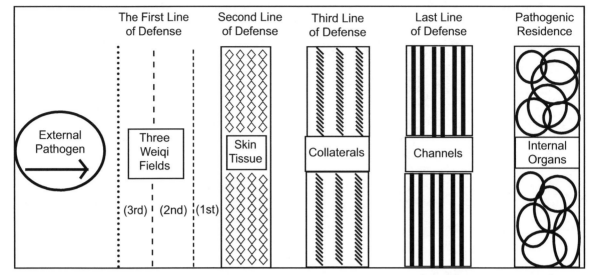

Figure 9.38. The body utilizes multiple lines of Energetic Defense, In order to prevent Invading Pathogens from reaching the Internal Organs.

Energetic Function of the Skin

The Qi and the Blood of the Twelve Skin Zones receive their nourishment via the Connecting Vessels. The Twelve Skin Zones circulate Weiqi, which in addition to having a defensive function, is also in charge of opening and closing the pores. The skin relies primarily upon the strength of the Weiqi for its ability to resist the invasion of external pathogenic influences. Any harmful influences must first penetrate the skin before they can affect the body's internal tissues and organs. Since the Lungs rule the skin, weak Lung Qi can allow pathogens to penetrate the skin and affect the Lungs.

Pathological Symptoms

Pathological symptoms associated with the Twelve Primary Channels and Connecting Vessels manifest along the surface of the Twelve Skin Zones before progressing deeper into the body's connective tissue. The early stages of disease are called exterior conditions; if the exterior Weiqi is strong enough, pathogens will be stopped at the external level. The progression of Pathogenic Invasion is described as follows (Figure 9.38).

1. **The Body's Weiqi:** The body's external energetic field is the human tissues first line of defense. A healthy body will naturally project three strong, protective, external energetic fields, which can maintain an effective capable defensive boundary.
- The body's first Weiqi Field is closest to the tissues and surface channels, and energetically corresponds to Jing and the Lower Dantian.
- The body's second Weiqi Field is about three feet from the tissues and surface channels, and energetically corresponds to Qi and the Middle Dantian.
- The body's third Weiqi Field is beyond three feet from the tissues and surface channels, and energetically corresponds to Shen (Heart/Mind) and the Upper Dantian.

If the patient becomes weak, tired, or stressed, the three external Weiqi Fields can also become weak, allowing External Pathogens to advance into the patient's skin. Once the tissues have become vulnerable to invasion, a disease causing agent may begin to attack an individual's health.

2. **The Skin:** The energy that supports and maintains the Skin tissues is the body's second line of defense.

   If the body's Three Weiqi Fields are not strong enough to resist an external pathogenic attack, and the skin is also not capable of warding off the invading toxic energy, then the pathogens will attack and enter into the tissues of the skin. This can also cause the sweat pores to open, allowing the pathogens to advance towards the patient's internal Collaterals.

3. **The Collaterals (or Connecting Vessels):** The internal Collaterals are the body's third line of defense.

   If the body's Collaterals are unable to redirect or purge the advancing pathogens, the toxic energy will then advance deeper into the tissues, and enter into the Primary Channels.

4. **The Channels (including the Twelve Primary Channels, Eight Extraordinary Vessels, and Twelve Divergent Channels):** The Channels are the body's last line of defense, before the advancing external pathogens invade the patient's internal organs.

   If the body's main Channels are unable to redirect or purge the invading pathogens, and the toxic energy is allowed to continue in its progression, it will advance further into the body's internal organs.

5. **The Internal Organs:** The internal organs are affected by pathogenic invasion only after the toxic energy has penetrated through all of the outer defenses. Once the pathogens have reached the internal organs, they can begin establishing a residence within the body's inner most tissues, causing and contributing to a chronic disease state.

Pathologies associated with the Primary Channels may manifest diagnostically through various symptoms, affecting the body's skin, channels, and points. For example, pimples, moles, skin discolorations, and changes in electro-conductivity of the body's external energetic fields, are all signs of External Pathogens, or toxic energetic obstructions invading the skin.

When caught early, certain diseases of external origin that first lodge within a patient's skin may be effectively treated by the Medical Qigong Doctor. In this type of situation, a doctor of Chinese Energetic Medicine will stimulate the patient's external Weiqi in the affected Skin Zone. This is accomplished through External Qi Projection, and used in order to purge or disperse the pathogen before it progresses further into the body's connective tissue.

Another common clinical treatment used in order to stimulate the Weiqi of the skin and disperse pathogens, is the external application of Herbal Ointments and/or Moxa Therapy.

THE CONNECTIVE TISSUE OF THE TWELVE SKIN ZONES

From a Traditional Chinese Medical perspective, the Qi circulating within the body's inner fascial connective tissue can be accessed with the external energy stimulation of the Twelve Skin Zones.

The ancient Daoist physicians noted that the body's underlying connective tissue always responds to the external stimulation of the Twelve Skin Zones. Because the body's vast network of connective tissue begins just below the skin, it is regarded as one of the largest, most extensive tissue organs in the body. The connective tissue simultaneously fulfills the functions of supporting, connecting, containing, and transmitting Jing, Qi, Shen, Blood, and Body Fluids. It is a continuous structural network that binds tissues into their organ shape. It also supplies the internal organ's with vessels and ducts, and securely fastens each organ within the body cavity.

This important connective tissue surrounds and anchors the vessels within the muscles, Bones, and organ tissue. Its fluid nature supports the entire body structurally by transmitting and absorbing hydrostatic pressure. Any stimulation of one of the body's Twelve Skin Zones will directly affect the body's connective tissue and will stimulate the corresponding internal organ associated with that particular zone (Figure 9.39).

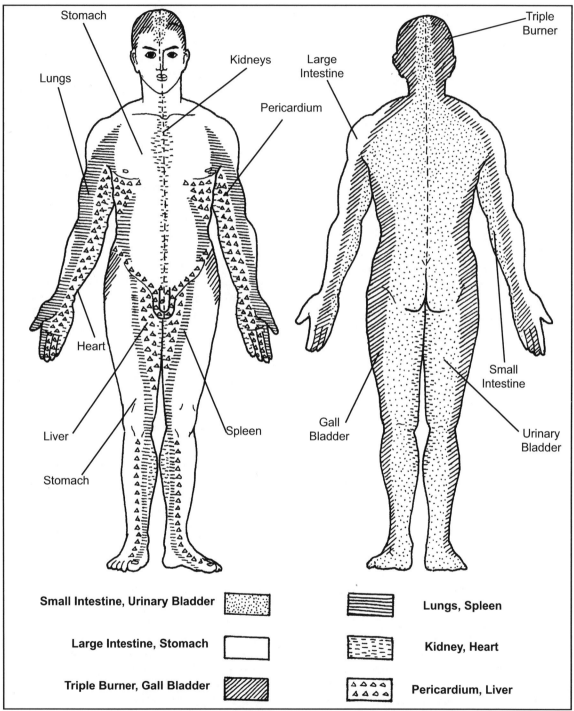

Figure 9.39. The Body's Twelve Cutaneous Regions (Skin Zones), are based on the external flow of Qi from the Twelve Primary Channels and their Fifteen Collaterals

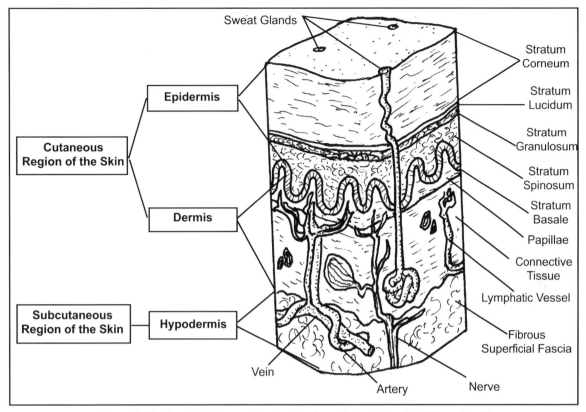

Figure 9.40. The Skin Tissue (Inspired by the original artwork of Wynn Kapit)

The skin tissue is composed of two regions: the Cutaneous Tissue Region (containing the Epidermis and the Dermis), and the Subcutaneous Tissue Region (containing the Hypodermis or Superficial Fascia) (Figure 9.40).

The Superficial Fascia is the connective tissue just under the skin. It divides into a top and bottom layer. The top layer is the fatty layer, which constitutes the main fatty tissue of the outer surface of the body and fascia. This fatty layer acts as an insulator, helping to maintain a constant body temperature. It is metabolically significant, in that it is responsible for: storing fat as fuel, and releasing it in response to nerve and hormonal stimuli. It also corresponds to the greasy layer where the Weiqi circulates throughout the body's surface tissues. It is important to note, that the deeper layer of the superficial fascia envelops the nerves, veins, arteries, lymph vessels, and nodes.

Heat and physical movement help maintain the health of the body's connective tissue's base fluids, increasing flexibility, and further enabling the conduction and release of energy. Any obstruction occurring in or on the body's surface tissues can result in the binding or thickening of the connective tissue beneath it, thus causing adhesions. This obstruction decreases physical strength and range of motion, slows the metabolic process, and compromises the body's immunity.

If the integrity of the connective tissue is compromised, the health of the body's Immune System declines. Compartments of connective tissue influence the spread of toxins, diseases, infections, and tumors. The fibrous walls of connective tissue, as well as the chemicals present in the fluid of the connective tissue, help to prevent the spread of pathogens from one area of the body to another.

CLINICAL DIAGNOSIS AND THE TWELVE SKIN ZONES

In ancient China, the clinical diagnosis and treatment techniques relating to the use of the Twelve Skin Zones were quite extensive. Traditionally, the skin along the various zones was examined for evidence of discoloration or tissue obstruction. All changes in skin color and tissue formations were observed and categorized according to the following patterns (Figure 9.41):

- **A Darkish Hue:** This color reflects an obstruction of Qi and Blood.
- **White or Pallid Skin Tone:** This signifies a Deficiency or a Cold condition.
- **Reddish-Purple:** Indicates internal infection.
- **Bluish-Purple Color:** Indicates local pain.
- **A Change in Color:** When the color changes from Yellow to Red, it shows the evidence of Heat; the more the Red, the greater the amount of Heat within the organ system.
- **Skin Formations:** Boils, Pimples (especially on the back), Hives, and Eczema, as well as hard lumps or nodules beneath the surface of the skin, indicate diseases associated with the Twelve Primary Channels (manifesting through the Twelve Skin Zones).

A palpable lump can develop from a variety of sources, including congealed or stagnant Blood. There are generally eight types of lumps observed in Chinese Energetic Medicine:

1. **The Shrimp Lump:** This lump is shaped in the form of a "C" curled formation.
2. **The Turtle Lump:** This shape often has multiple lump formations.
3. **The Green/Blue Lump:** This unique colored lump derives its name from the superficial Blood Vessels originating within its tissues.
4. **The Single Lump:** This lump appears to be isolated, and is differentiated from multiple lump formations.
5. **The Dry Lump:** This type of lump indicates a form of Heat Obstruction.
6. **The Blood Lump:** This type of lump relates to congealed and stagnant Blood.
7. **The Abdominal Lump:** This type of lump is named for its physical location.

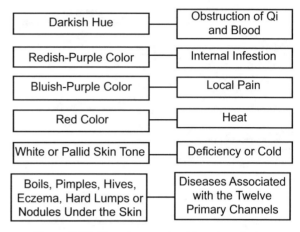

Figure 9.41. The changes in skin color, shape, and texture are observed and categorized.

8. **The Yellow Lump:** This type of lump is named because of the yellow color located within the specific region of its tissue formation.

PALPATING THE PATIENT'S SKIN

Before palpating and diagnosing the patient's skin, a doctor of Chinese Energetic Medicine will first energetically scan the body, in order to feel the temperature, moisture, and texture of the patient's tissues.

1. **Temperature:** The doctor scans and palpates the patient to diagnose the condition according to temperature:
   - If the skin feels hot to the touch, it often indicates the presence of a Damp-Heat condition.
   - When first touching the patient with light pressure, if the skin feels immediately hot, and as the pressure is maintained the feeling of heat increases, this indicates an invasion of exterior Wind-Heat, with a pathogenic factor still present on the surface of the tissues.
   - If the skin over a blood vessel feels hot on medium pressure, it indicates interior Heat.
   - If the skin feels hot on deep, heavy pressure, it indicates a Deficient Heat condition from a Yin Deficiency.
   - If the skin feels cold to the touch, it often indicates a Cold Condition. This condition is often manifested in the lower back and lower abdominal region, indicating a Deficiency of Kidney Yang.

2. **Moisture:** The doctor scans and palpates the patient to diagnose the condition according to the amount of moisture present on the skin:
   - A moist feeling of the skin may indicate an External Invasion of Wind-Cold or Wind-Heat.
   - If the skin feels moist due to spontaneous sweating, it indicates a Deficiency of Lung Qi (in the absence of exterior symptoms).
3. **Texture:** The doctor scans and palpates the patient to diagnose the condition according to the texture of the skin:
   - If the skin feels dry, it indicates either a Yin Condition of the Lungs, or a Blood Deficiency.
   - If the skin is scaly and dry, it indicates an exhaustion of the Body's Fluids.
   - If the skin is swollen and a visible indentation remains after applying pressure, it indicates Edema (called "Water Swelling").
   - If the skin is swollen and no visible indentation remains after applying pressure, it indicates a Retention of Dampness (called "Qi Swelling").

CHANNEL & COLLATERAL THERAPY

Because the Qi of the Yin and Yang Organs flows along the body's internal and external surfaces, all of the internal and external Channels and Collaterals, Five Tissues (i.e., the tendons, blood vessels, muscles, skin, and bones), and Five Sense Organs (eyes, ears, nose, mouth, and tongue), link together in order to create a powerful energetic network. Patients and practitioners of Chinese Energetic Medicine can become aware of the circulation of Qi within the body's Channels and Collaterals by practicing Sitting Meditations. The awareness of what the Qi feels like enables the meditators to feel the flow and function of each channel, as well as the Blood and Heat cycles in each Skin Zone. This subtle energetic awareness, eventually makes it possible for the individual to control Qi circulation through the use of mental intention and imagination.

In ancient Daoist Alchemy, energetically balancing the Qi of the Conception and Governing Vessels was one of the most important Qigong Regulation practice. It allowed the Daoist disciple to energetically draw the body's Yang Fire and Yin Essence, up and down the center line of the torso, energetically fusing together the Water and Fire Qi. This important energetic fusion is also initiated within each patient's body, by the doctor during every Medical Qigong treatment. Its clinical application is that it naturally maintains the proper balance of the patient's Yin and Yang energy.

When training to obtain this special energetic perception, the doctor's awareness of subtle Qi flow within the tissues usually develops in three distinct stages, described as follows:

1. In the First Stage, energy is felt flowing along the surface channels of the body, especially within the areas of the extremities. Usually at this stage, Heat and tingling sensations are perceived and experienced flowing within the body's skin and surface muscles.
2. In the Second Stage, energy is felt flowing deeper within the tissues, especially along the tendons, deeper muscles, and visceral organs. Usually at this stage, mild electric shocks and pulsating vibrations are perceived and experienced within the muscles, bones, and internal organs.
3. In the Third Stage, the Qi of Heaven and Earth is perceived and experienced penetrating deep into the body; flowing from the outside channels and internal organs, connecting into the center Taiji Pole, and then flowing outward again. Usually at this stage, the meditator will feel their entire energized body vibrate. This subtle vibration may be triggered through either universal or environmental changes, as the practitioner becomes hypersensitive to any form of external energetic disturbance.

QI EXTENSION AND THE BODY'S CHANNELS

Before clinical practice is encouraged, a Medical Qigong Doctor must first be able to control his or her own energy circulation; causing it to flow in or out, expand or contract at will, before beginning to extend energy for the treatment of any patient. This energetic control is gained through specific imagination and visualization techniques. The fundamental premise for these techniques is reflected in the Daoist saying, "the imagination leads the Mind, the Mind leads the Qi."

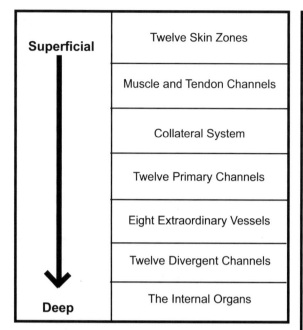

Figure 9.42. The Body's Energetic Flow According to Traditional Chinese Medicine

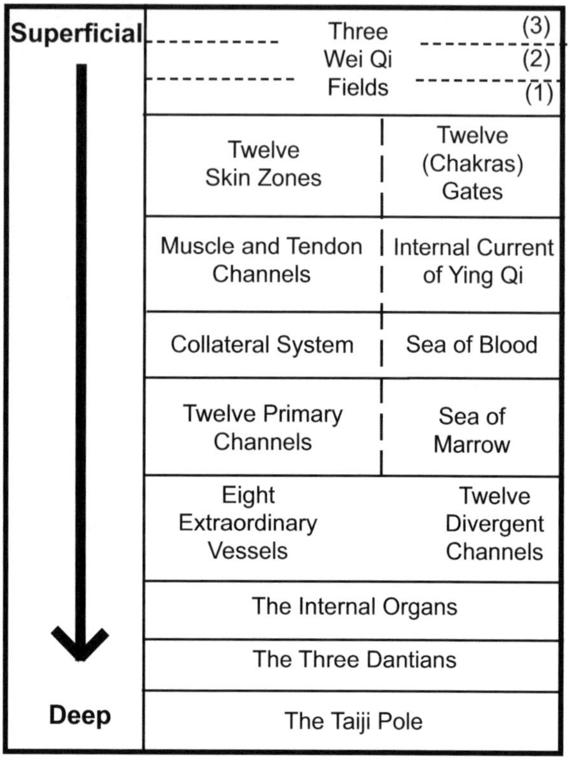

Figure 9.43. The Body's Energetic Structures According to Ancient Chinese Medicine

The doctor must also be able to utilize energy from the natural environment in order to replenish his own depleted energy. By drawing in Heavenly Qi and combining it with already gathered Earthly Qi, the doctor uses powerful energies beyond himself to mobilize and activate the Qi of the patient. This method of combining Heaven and Earth energies establishes a powerful healing field. This sacred healing field then responds to the Medical Qigong Doctor's own Qi circulation, the energy of the natural environment, and the energy of the patient.

This ability to energetically gather and blend must first be achieved in order to activate the Qi of the patient's channels and internal organs. It then allows the doctor to regulate the patient's body by purging excess Qi, dredging the channel Qi, replenishing deficient Qi, and guiding the Qi back to its origin.

THE DEPTH OF THE BODY'S CHANNEL FLOW

According to most modern acupuncture colleges of Traditional Chinese Medicine, the energetic flow of the body's channel system begins superficially along the Twelve Skin Zones of the body. Next, the energy flows deeper into the body along the Muscle and Tendon Channels. After the Muscle and Tendon Channels, the energy of the Collateral System is considered deeper still. Next is the flow of the Twelve Primary Channels, then the Eight Extraordinary Channels. Deeper than the Eight Extraordinary Channels is the network of the Twelve Divergent Channels. Deeper still is the energetic matrix of the Zang Fu Organs (the six viscera and five bowels) (Figure 9.42).

According to ancient Chinese Energetic Medicine and the various Medical Qigong Colleges that were in China up until the year 2000, the body's energetic system also includes the following: the Three Weiqi Fields, the Twelve (Chakra) Gates, the Internal Current of Ying Qi, the Sea of Blood, the Sea of Marrow, the Three Dantians, and the center core Taiji Pole (Figure 9.43).

Chapter 10
The Body's Energetic Points

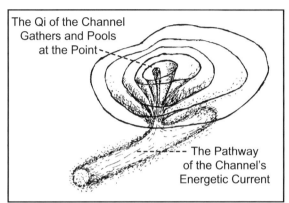

Figure 10.1. The energetic points can be seen as small energetic pools lying along the body's channels.

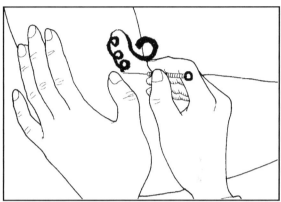

Figure 10.2. After drawing a special Talisman, the doctor would insert the Needle into a patient's Channel Point to stimulate the movement of Qi.

Introduction to Energetic Points

Channel Points (also known as "Acupuncture Points"), are specific areas located within the body's tissues where Qi flows towards the surface of the skin and forms energetic pools (Figure 10.1). These special pools collect Qi from deep within the body's internal organs, channels, and tissues, and are traditionally used in Chinese Energetic Medicine for diagnosis and clinical treatment.

As the Qi moves along its various pathways, it manifests the current condition of the internal organ and organ system. This is why in Chinese Energetic Medicine, in order to stimulate the Qi flowing within their body's channel system, needles must sometimes be inserted into the skin of patients who are not energetically sensitive, or because of trauma need to be physically "stimulated" because of the serious degree of disassociation with their body.

In ancient China, before an apprentice was allowed to insert any type of needle into a channel point (Figure 10.2), he was first required to master the art of "De Qi" ("Reaching and Feeling Energy"). Once the Apprentice could feel the energy flowing within the patient's channels, he was then required to stimulate this flow of energy through, breath, sound, heat, light, and thought. Only then, was the Apprentice taught to insert needles. Eventually, the Apprentice was taught how to create special energetic patterns with the needle, used to increase, decrease, or balance the Qi moving within the patient's body. These esoteric clinical patterns were always accompanied with special prayer incantations (Intoned Words of Power), used to increase the energetic stimulation of the patient's Three Bodies (i.e., the Physical Body, Energy Body, and Spirit Body).

In Chinese Energetic Medicine, each Channel Point is considered to be a reflexive component of its original channel system. Acting as a Microcosm, each energetic point reflects the Qi (Energy), and Shen (Mind/Heart) of the internal organ and channel system it represents. This is why the energetic fields of the Channel Points are always changing.

In order to understand the Channel System better, a doctor of Chinese Energetic Medicine must first investigate the point's individual location and specific energetic function. According to the *ZhenJiu Da Cheng (The Great Compendium of Acupuncture-Moxibustion)*, written by the famous physician Yang Jizhou in the Ming Dynasty (1386-1644A.D.),

> "Whether on the face, the sides,
> the front or the back, Qi and Blood have
> more than 600 Guardians of the Frontiers.
> This means that Qi and Blood
> circulate within the body
> through the Channels and Luo Mai,
> by moving across hollow spaces;
> This occurs regardless
> of the posture the person assumes.
>
> The Internal Yin (Qi and Blood)
> circulating inside the Vessels
> passes into more than
> 300 Guardians of the Frontiers.
> The External Yang Qi
> circulating outside the Vessels
> passes into more than
> 300 Guardians of the Frontiers."

The body's energetic points that have been identified and categorized in Traditional Chinese Medicine, are almost always located on prominent depressions or hollows in the patient's physical structure. These points lie all over the body, and many (but not all) of them are located along the major channels and vessels. Sometimes when touching a point, it feels as if one's fingertip has found the entrance of a small cave or opening that is hidden by the skin covering it.

In the human body, our living Qi gathers and pools within these protected hollows (Figure 10.1). For this reason, some writers have preferred to translate Xue as "Vital Hollow," rather than "point." Because of its popular acceptance, however, the term "point" is used throughout this textbook series.

THE TRANSLATION OF "XUE"

Although the Chinese word "Xue" is usually translated into English as "Point" or "Acupoint," it is valuable for the non-Chinese speaking student to understand the word's different connotations. The Chinese ideograph for "point" ("Xue" or "Xue

Figure 10.3. The Chinese character "Xue" (Cave)

Wei") is translated as "Cavity Place, Cave, Den, Hole, or Hollow." The word Xue also implies "a den or lair." Thus, it is not only a "Cave," but a home for some type of powerful life form.

- **Xue:** The character for "Xue" is divided into two parts. The top of the character represents a "roof" or "covering." The bottom part of the character is the word "Ba," and in ancient times originally represented the "division of two parts." The literal interpretation of this character could be "a dwelling place that results from dividing or opening up."

The character was later changed to mean "eight," referring to the "Eight Treasures" (Viscera, Bowels, Qi, Blood, Sinews, Vessels, Bone, and Marrow). Together, the translation reveals a hidden space which contains passage to the "Eight Treasures," accessible only after removing or uncovering its entry portal (Figure 10.3).

HISTORIC USE OF ENERGETIC POINTS

Though the therapeutic use of point stimulation is most often associated with Traditional Chinese Medicine (acupuncture and massage), numerous other cultures around the world have been treating illness and disease with point therapy for many thousands of years.

The first references to point therapy in Chinese Medicine are from the Shang era (1600-1028 B.C.). It is quite possible, however, that the use of the human body's energetic points for healing arose at a much earlier time in human history, perhaps independently in different cultures around the globe. There is some debate as to the original discovery of the energetic points used in ancient (and modern) Chinese Energetic Medicine. Some scholars claim that these points were first discovered through a trial and error process of random tissue stimulation by ancient Chinese shaman healers, while others believe that energetic points (and energetic channels) were first "seen" by shamans in altered states of consciousness.

The human body naturally seeks a state of health and balance (homeostasis), and the first discovery of point therapy may have been made by an individual - or individuals - unconsciously or inadvertently stimulating an area that felt tender or blocked. This principle can also be observed in the modern Medical Qigong Clinic. When describing a headache, for example, a patient may be observed to touch the same energetic points that, when stimulated, can bring about a release of the very condition from which he or she is suffering. This kinesthetic observation is an important part of Medical Qigong Diagnosis, as it can provide important clues as to the best strategy for point stimulation. However, this diagnostic observation must be integrated with the Medical Qigong Doctor's ability to see the patient's energetic field directly, a skill that is developed with diligent practice of Qigong Self-Regulation Exercises.

Though it may be impossible to know for certain where point therapy first originated (if indeed there was a single place of origin), we can be fairly certain that Acupuncture and other forms of Point Therapy were practiced throughout the ancient world. If extended to include the laying on of hands, the origin of Point Therapy would most certainly date back tens of thousands of years, if not more.

India's indigenous medical system of Ayurveda traditionally incorporates the stimulation of various energy points called "Marma" on the body, through the use of therapeutic pressure, needling, and moxibustion. This special system of healing is known as "Marmapuncture." A "Marma" is defined as "secret, hidden, or vital energy," therefore a "Marma Point" is a receptor or reflex point on the skin which has a high concentration of "Prana" (Qi). A Marma is also a junction where flesh, veins, arteries, tendons, bones and joints meet. In India, there are thousands of Marmas located all over the body, 365 of which are considered essential points.

The Marma Points and locations are measured in "Anguli" which are finger units relative to the individual. Additionally, the Marmas are located along the Nadis (Channels) which link the Marmas to each other and to the organs.

Indian Acupuncture stems from an ancient Indian branch of surgery, which used the knowledge of the Marma points so as not to cause harm during surgical procedures, or when treating scar tissue. Knowledge of Marma points is also drawn from Kalari, an ancient Indian martial art form used for self defense, which used 107 lethal Marma Points to cause extreme pain, unconsciousness, or even death.

References dating as far back as 4000 B.C. to the use of Indian Acupuncture as a healing modality have been found in the *Vedic* texts of ancient India, leading some scholars to believe that the knowledge of the healing use of the body's energetic points traveled to China from India along with the theory of the Five Elements (see Volume 3, Chapter 24).

Similar references to Acupuncture have surfaced in the relics of the ancient Egyptian culture, also dating back several thousand years.

Point Therapy is also traditionally utilized by shamans and healers in such geographically separated locations as Sri Lanka, Africa, Peru, and the Amazon basin. Today, Acupuncture and Point Therapy are widely practiced throughout Asia, though the systems that are utilized are almost exclusively derived from Chinese Energetic Medicine. Examples of other modern derivatives of Chinese Point Therapy include: Acupressure, Shiatsu, Auriculotherapy, Jin Shin Jyutsu, Reflexology, and Trigger Point Therapy.

THE THREE LEVELS OF POINTS

In Traditional Chinese Medicine, studying the flow and energetic nature of the body's Channel Points is essential. The ancient Chinese believed that the points along the channels allowed the individual's Spirit Qi to flow in and out of the body, unhampered by physical tissues such as skin, flesh, muscle, and bone.

In ancient times, the interior of the Channel Points were divided into three energetic levels: Heaven, Earth and Man. Each energetic point contains three progressively subtle aspects or

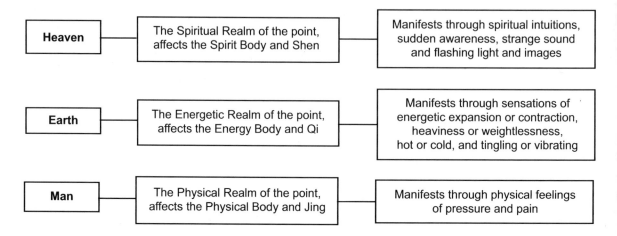

Figure 10.4. The energetic points can be seen as small energetic pools lying along the body's channels.

dimensions, affecting an individual's physical, energetic and spiritual bodies. These subtle influences also correlate to the physical, energetic and spirit realms, described as follows (Figure 10.4):

- **The Physical Nature of a Point:** This is expressed through an individual's sensory perceptions, and manifests through feelings of pressure and pain.
- **The Energetic Nature of a Point:** This is expressed through an individual's subtle sensory perceptions, manifesting through feelings of energetic expansion or contraction, heaviness or weightlessness, hot or cold, and tingling or vibrating.
- **The Spiritual Nature of a Point:** This is expressed through the individual's most subtle intuitive perceptions, manifesting through such experiences as flashing lights and images, strange sounds, and sudden awareness and inspirations.

In ancient China, when diagnosing the conditions of the disease, the clinical doctor was required to ascertain at which level the pathogen was residing. For example, sometimes the Righteous Qi is flowing within the Heavenly level, while Turbid Qi is subtly active within the patient's Earthly level. If these subtle energy flows are not clearly distinguished, then it is impossible to use the needle properly in order to balance internal disharmony.

THE FORMATION OF ENERGETIC POINTS

Generally, Energetic Points are formed in one of four different ways, described as follows:

1. **Intersect or Overlap:** The first type of point occurs when two or more muscles, tendons, or ligaments intersect or overlap in a way that creates a small depression at the area of convergence. To form the depression, the two muscles either come together, separate, overlap, or run parallel to each other. Usually the channels lie under a protective layer of muscle, but at the aforementioned junctures the channels may be exposed, and thus lie closer to the surface. Examples of this type of point include:
   - Liver 8 point
   - Kidney 10 point
   - Triple Burner 4 point
2. **Exposed Nerve:** The second type of point occurs when a nerve is exposed in an area with relatively little muscle tissue to cover and protect it. Because the nerve is exposed, such points are especially sensitive, and when stimulated may cause the patient to experience a sharp pain or a sensation like an electric shock. Examples of this type of point include:
   - Large Intestine 4 point
   - Pericardium 6 point
   - Small Intestine 8 point

3. **Under a Muscle:** The third type of point lies under a protective superficial layer of muscle. It can however, still be stimulated due to its natural sensitivity and because the overlying layer of muscle is thin. Examples of this type of point include:
   - Gall Bladder 1 point
   - Urinary Bladder 16 point
   - Urinary Bladder 46 point
4. **Natural Depression:** The fourth type of point is located in the natural depressions on the surface of the bones and cartilage. These depressions may take the form of grooves, pits, hollows, indentations, fissures, or crevices. Examples of this type of point include:
   - Governing Vessel 20 point
   - Gall Bladder 20 point
   - Kidney 1 point

THE FOUR CATEGORIES OF POINTS

Points are divided into four categories: Channel Points, Extra Points, New Points, and Ahshi Points, described as follows (Figure 10.5):

1. **Channel Points:** These are the primary points that are distributed along the Twelve Primary Channels and the Conception and Governing Vessels. If you count the number of Channel Points located on each of the 12 Primary Channels, the total comes to 309 points. Then, if you include the number of points located on the Governing Vessel (28 Points) and Conception Vessel (24 Points), the total increases to 361 Channel Points. It is important to note that in ancient China, a total of 365 Channel Points was traditionally used in order to coincide with the number of days in a Solar year.
2. **Extra Points:** Sometimes known as "Miscellaneous Points," the Extra Points are not regarded as having a specific origin in the Twelve Primary Channels. However, they are still named in Classis Texts, and have definite locations.
3. **New Points:** This includes a fairly large group of points that have been "discovered" since the Communist "Liberation" of 1949. In many cases, these New Points were discovered through Electronic Point Detection. Because of this, these points generally have no energetic description. However, they do have clinical indications. There are more than 700 New Points, when counted to include the Extra Points.
4. **Ahshi Points:** These special points are tender or painful spots near a diseased or injured area, and can be located anywhere on the body. They function like Trigger Points, as they are points of tension or pain. Ahshi Points differ according to each patient and condition, and are often not given specific names or definite locations. They are most commonly used for Pain Syndromes.

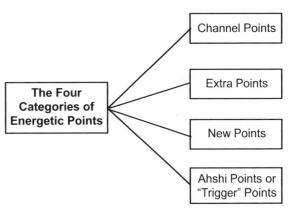

Figure 10.5. The Four Categories of Energetic Points

A POINTS ENERGETIC GATE

It is useful to further categorize the points into two types commonly used by Medical Qigong Doctors in the clinic. These two types of Energetic Gates are specific areas where the Medical Qigong Doctors concentrate their intention and focus their Qi Emission.

The locations of these special points have a greater amount of accumulated Qi, than do the surrounding channels or tissues. They are therefore specifically chosen for purging and tonifying the body's organ energy, and for promoting the balanced circulation of Qi and Blood.

These two types of points, are known as the Outer Qi Gate Points and the Inner Qi Gate Points, described as follows:

1. **The Outer Qi Gate Points:** These are special points through which the patient's Qi and Shen enter and leave their body. The Medical Qigong Doctor or his patient may gather

healing energy from the external environment through these special gates. They may also choose to use them in order to purge the body of internal excesses or stagnations.

It is important to note, that these special points are especially vulnerable to the Six External Pathogens (i.e., Cold, Hot, Wind, Damp, Dry, and Fire), which tend to enter the body through these gates (see Volume 3, Chapter 22). However, these same external pathogens may also be expelled through these special gates. For this reason, many of these Outer Qi Gates have the word Feng (Wind) in their names, such as
- Fengchi GB-20 (Wind Pool),
- Fengmen Bl-12 (Wind Gate) and
- Fengfu GV-16 (Wind Palace).
2. **The Inner Qi Gate Points:** These are special points through which the Qi of the Yin and Yang Organs and Channels is transported back and forth internally and externally, from deep to superficial, and back again.

These special points are more involved with the movement of Qi within the body, and are less involved in the exchanging energy with the outer environment. In this way, the Inner Qi Gate Points enable the Qi to communicate between the different parts of the body.

When stimulating the patient's energetic tissues and treating either of the two gates, the Medical Qigong Doctor can initiate the healing potential of a specific point by using various modalities, such as Qi Projection, Energetic Point Therapy, Jing Point Therapy, or Invisible Needle Therapy.

Energetic Functions of Points

The use of energetic points has three important clinical functions: Diagnosis, The Manipulation of Qi and Blood, and To Serve as Pathways for the Elimination of Disease. These three clinical functions are described as follows (Figure 10.6):
1. **Diagnosis:** Diagnosis through point palpation and inspection is an important tool in all branches of Chinese Energetic Medicine. If a point hurts when touched with light pressure,

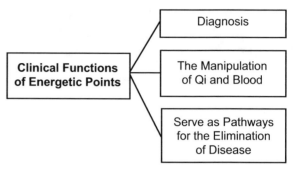

Figure 10.6. The Three Clinical Functions of Energetic Points

is hard or swollen, or is purple, black and blue, or red, this indicates an excess condition. If the point hurts on deep pressure, is soft to the touch, lacks resilience, or is sallow in color, it indicates an underlying deficiency.

The skin over points often feels sticky, in contrast to the slippery or smooth quality of the skin surrounding the point. When passing the fingers over a point, the doctor generally feels the energetic pulse of the channel. When touched, the point responds like an energetic echo, vibrating through the channel into the organ and then back again to the doctor's finger. The doctor can use this energetic response for diagnostic evaluation by sending a pulse into the organ itself along the flow of the channel (for those channels that flow inward), or against it (for those channels that flow outward). Once sufficient stimulation is applied to the point, its organ or region is "reminded" of its normal function. In this way, diagnosis and treatment are accomplished simultaneously.

Once the point and energy flow of the channel to be treated is diagnosed, the doctor must take into consideration that each patient will react differently according to the severity of the presenting symptoms, and the individual's basic constitutional type.

Before beginning a treatment, the doctor should extend Qi into the point to the depth of the energetic space that exists between the Wei and Ying energy fields. Once contact is made, the doctor uses either the tips of his

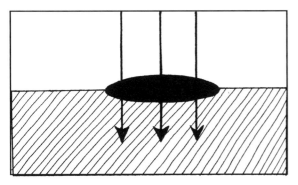

Figure 10.7. Weak or Deficient tissue will naturally pull and absorb Qi into the surrounding areas.

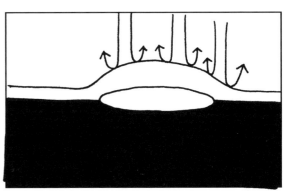

Figure 10.8. Strong, Excess, or Armored tissue will naturally repel Qi from the surrounding areas.

or her fingers or the palm of the hand like a barometer to detect if there is any soreness or distention at that particular point. This form of diagnosis determines the condition of the channel and the area needing treatment. Although the feelings and sensations will vary with each patient, correct diagnosis depends on recognizing energetic patterns that reveal the nature of the disharmony, for example:

- **Weak or Deficient Areas:** The energetic points in these deficient tissue areas will often feel like an empty hole or a deep well. Deficient Blood or Qi will actually pull energy into the deficient area and may feel something like a subtle vacuum suction (Figure 10.7).

If the area attacks the doctor's Qi and begins to absorb it, the doctor should tonify that area immediately. This reaction is like that of a dry house plant that is starving for water. The minute the water touches the soil, the plant immediately absorbs it into its roots.

- **Strong or Excess Areas:** The energetic points in these excess tissue areas will immediately repel the doctor's Qi (Figure 10.8). If the diseased area repels the doctor's Qi, he or she must immediately dredge the excess energy from the tissues.

First, the doctor should focus on the region surrounding the excess to drain the additional energy away from the damaged points. Once the excess is removed, the doctor then dredges the excess energy away from the original trauma area. This technique is excellent for treating damaged or sprained joints. When dredging, the doctor should focus on the patient's breathing in order to maximize the efficacy of the treatment.

As the patient inhales, the doctor exhales and vice-versa. As the patient exhales, he or she releases pathogenic factors; by inhaling when the patient exhales, the doctor facilitates this process, and prevents the depletion of his or her own Qi.

2. **Manipulation of Qi and Blood:** Qi and Blood can be manipulated through accessing the body's energetic points, in order to purge excess conditions, to tonify deficient conditions, or to regulate and balance restoring internal harmony.

- **To Purge or Disperse an Excess Condition:** A Medical Qigong Doctor will energetically envelop a specific tissue area, and begin to purge or disperse, the Toxic Qi from the body. Purging involves the removal of toxins directly from the organ, whereas dispersing is to lead the energy out of the tissue area via the channels. The goal of this treatment is to remove any excess, particularly stagnant Qi and Blood.

A dull, moving pain is characteristic of Qi Stagnation. If the blockage is primarily due to Blood Stagnation, the patient will experience a sharper pain that does not move. This distinction, however, is more clinically significant in Chinese Herbology than it is for Medical Qigong Therapy, Acupuncture, or

Chinese Massage. It is stated in the Chinese medical classics that, "Qi is the commander of Blood," therefore, moving the Qi will also move Stagnant Blood.

- **To Tonify a Deficient Condition:** In order to strengthen a weak condition, the Medical Qigong Doctor will emit Qi over a specific tissue area with the intention of tonifying and strengthening the patient's Qi, Blood, Yin, Yang, or specific channel and organ system. The doctor may also choose to use a variety of techniques according to the patient's needs. For example, in order to prevent discomfort, the doctor can tonify a weak patient by slowly emitting Qi into the Kd-1 points, and direct the energy to flow up the Kidney Channels to fill the patient's Lower Dantian, using the Sword Finger technique.
- **To Regulate:** In order to balance the patient's Yin and Yang energy, the doctor can emit Qi over a specific tissue area and allow the body's natural homeostasis to take over, and restore its healthy function. This type of treatment may be used when a patient has a combined excess or deficiency syndrome (such as Stagnant Qi in the chest due to Qi Deficiency in the Lungs and Kidneys).

3. **Serve as Pathways for the Elimination of Disease:** Through the energetic flow of the Channel Points, the doctor can effectively eliminate pathogens from the patient's tissues caused from the invasion of External Pathogenic Qi (Wind, Fire, Summer Heat, Damp, Dry and Cold).

Some of the body's points are especially vulnerable to Exogenous Invasions, particularly the invasion of External Wind. Wind-susceptible points, for example, usually have the word Feng (Wind) in their names. Some examples of Wind susceptible points include (Figure 10.9): Bingfeng (Grasping the Wind) SI-12, Fengchi (Wind Pool) GB-20, Fengmen (Wind Gate) Bl-12, Yifeng (Wind Screen) TB-17, and Fengfu (Wind Palace) GV-16. Due to their susceptibility to Wind penetration, these specific points may also be used to purge Wind invasion, or used to release other types of toxic energy from the body.

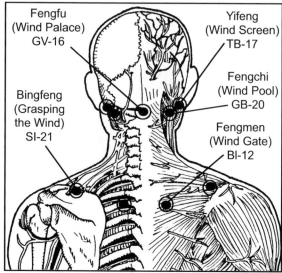

Figure 10.9. Points on the back of the neck that are especially vulnerable to external Wind invasion.

CENTRIFUGAL AND CENTRIPETAL ENERGY FLOW

All of the body's points are capable of energetically spiraling in two opposite directions: Centrifugally spiralling away from the body, or Centripetally spiralling into the body. Each point's capacity to energetically spiral in either direction is independent of whether the primary flow of its associated channel is moving from the extremities into the center of the body, or moving away from the center of the body towards the extremities.

The energy of a channel normally flows in only one direction, while the polarity of the body's points normally alternates between Yang (centrifugal spirals) and Yin (centripetal spirals) movements. The polarity of these two energy currents are described as follows:

1. **The Point's Outward Centrifugal Flow of Qi:** Qi moves from the channel, to the point, to the external environment. This outward flow of energy is expressed or intensified during the exhalation. The outward centrifugal flow of energy manifests in points along the channel, or in other areas of the body where there are conditions of excess. These points have a positive polarity, and repel Qi from the surrounding tissue area.

2. The Point's Inward Centripetal Flow of Qi: Qi is drawn from the external environment, through the point, and into the channel. This inward flow of energy is expressed or intensified during the inhalation. The inward centripetal flow of energy manifests in points along the channel, or in other areas of the body where there are conditions of deficiency. These points have a negative polarity, pulling and absorbing Qi from the surrounding tissue area.

The stimulation of channel points has two important clinical results. Centrifugally, the stimulation of channel points informs the doctor of impending internal disorders by discharging excess energy. Centripetally, they transmit the energy and intention placed on them back to their source organ or tissue, absorbing energy to remedy and counteract the body's internal deficiencies.

POINT NAMES

Each point has a traditional name, which either describes its location, its energetic function, or both. In addition, modern Acupuncture texts have assigned a name and a number for each point, according to the channel on which it is located and its order along the natural course of that channel.

Sometimes a point may have several different traditional names, varying according to whether they are being used by Medical Qigong Doctors, Acupuncturists, Martial Artists, or Daoist Religious and Folk Magic practitioners. For example, GV-1 is called Changqiang (Long Strength) in Traditional Chinese Medicine, and Weilu (Tail Gate) in Daoist Alchemy.

The history of point naming and the different terminologies used can usually be traced back to different Buddhist and Daoist temples in ancient China. Each religious sect gave its own particular names to certain points, in accordance with the temple's spiritual and energetic needs. Giving different names to common points was also used as a form of secret code to keep the system pure, and to prevent the esoteric knowledge from falling into the hands of the unscrupulous or uninitiated.

Because the names of the various Channel Points describe its unique energetic application, in ancient China the name descriptions would sometimes differ from region to region, and monastery to monastery. Therefore, certain points are sometimes referred to by several names.

- **Anatomical Location:** Some of the names reflect the anatomical location of the point. For example, the Large Intestine 4 point is called "Hegu," meaning "the Joining Valley." It is given this name because the point is located in the "valley" formed in-between the thumb and first (index) finger.

- **Channel Application:** Some of the names reflect the energetic application attributed to the point. For example, the Kidney 7 point is called "Fu Liu," meaning "Returning Current." It is given this name because the point stimulates Kidney secretions.

- **Common Applications:** Some of the names reflect the common application attributed to the point. For example, the Lungs 11 point is called "Shaoshang," meaning "Little Bargaining." It is given this name because the point, located on the outside edge of the thumb, describes the ancient Chinese custom of raising the thumb to indicate the minimum sum asked for during merchant bargaining.

- **Energetic Application:** Some of the names reflect the energetic application attributed to the point. Functionally, each point either "Opens" in order to release information and energy; or "Closes" in order to store information and energy. Therefore, certain names include the descriptions of specific "Gates, Doors, and Passes." For example, the Governing Vessel 4 point is called "Mingmen," meaning the "Gate of Life/Destiny." It is given this name because the point, located by the midline of the lower back, is the energetic access portal to the body's Mingmen Fire, Reproductive Jing Qi, the Sea of Marrow, and the Sea of Yang Channels.

Points	Yin Channel Elements (Ethereal Soul—Hun)	Yang Channel Elements (Corporeal Soul—Po)
Jing-Well Points	Wood	Metal
Ying-Spring Points	Fire	Water
Shu-Stream Points	Earth	Wood
Jing-River Points	Metal	Fire
He-Sea Points	Water	Earth

Figure 10.10. The Five Shu Points and their Correspondence to the Five Elements

CLASSIFICATION OF ENERGETIC POINTS

Points in similar locations (i.e., ankles and wrists) often have similar actions, therefore many points are further classified into groups of similar energetic potential. This classification is used to assist the doctor of Chinese Energetic Medicine in choosing the right point or points during a treatment. The following is a list of energetic point classifications.

THE FIVE SHU POINTS

Like the internal organs and channels, some points have a more powerful influence on the body than others. Each point has an action on the quality and quantity of energy of an organ. Along each of the Twelve Primary Channels lie five specific points below the elbow or the knee called "Shu ("Transporting") points. These special points belong to the oldest classification of points, and are described using water as a metaphor. Each section of the channel is compared to the course water takes as it emerges from the ground and makes its way to the ocean.

In this unique system, points are identified as follows: Jing (Well), Ying (Spring), Shu (Stream), Jing (River), and He (Sea). These five points exist on each of the Twelve Primary Channels, and are located sequentially between the patients hands (or feet) and elbows (or knees). Flowing from distal to proximal, the points progress from superficial to deep, as follows: Well, Spring, Stream, River, and Sea.

THE 5 SHU POINTS, YIN AND YANG CHANNELS, AND THE FIVE ELEMENTS

Each of the Five Shu Points correspond to one of the Five Elements, and are identified in the Five Element Creative Cycle's energetic progression (Figure 10.10).

- **Yin Channel Points:** Each Yin Channel will begin with the Hun (Ethereal Soul) progression, starting with Wood, Fire, Earth, Metal, and Water (Figure 10.11).
- **Yang Channel Points:** Each Yang Channel begins with the Po (Corporeal Soul) progression, starting with Metal, Water, Wood, Fire, and Earth (Figure 10.12).

Similar to the eyes' energetic relationship to Wood (Hun) and Metal (Po) in Daoist Alchemy, the beginning points on the Twelve Primary Channels also have a relationship to either a Wood (Ethereal Soul) or Metal (Corporeal Soul) energetic pattern. Hence, in Meditation exercises, when specific finger tip points are connected while forming special Daoist Hand Seals (known as "Mudras" in Buddhist energetic practice), it facilitates a specific blending of the Hun and Po energies. This is why, in ancient China, the practice of connecting specific finger tip points was sometimes referred to as "the fusion of the body's Ethereal and Corporeal Souls."

The Five Shu Points energetically flow from superficial to deep and are susceptible to external pathogens and climatic changes. The distal points

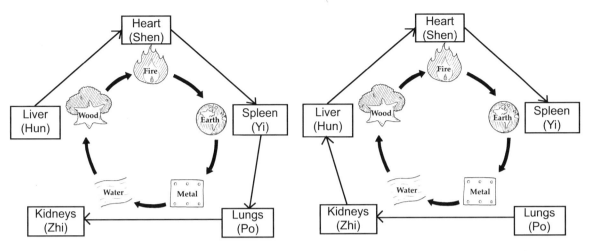

Figure 10.11. The Hun Progression of the Five Element Creative Cycle

Figure 10.12. The Po Progression of the Five Element Creative Cycle

on the feet tend to be more powerful than those on the hands. Therefore, after the manipulation of the patient's distal points, the local channel points are used according to their feeling of tenderness. The Five Shu Points, are described as follows (Figure 10.13 and 10.14):

1. **Jing (Well) Points:** These are the first points along the extremities of the channels and are located at the tips of the fingers and toes. These pools of energy are where the channel is at its thinnest and most superficial.

   These are the points from which the energy of the channels leaves the body when moving outward centrifugally. At the end of the fingertips and toes, the channel's energetic polarity changes from Yin to Yang or vice versa. Due to this shift in polarity, the energy at the channel's extremities tends to be unstable, and is therefore more easily influenced.

   Due to their outward movement of energy, the Well Points can be used by the doctor to eliminate the patient's pathogenic factors quickly, especially when the Yin Organs are affected.

   The Well Points will also have a strong effect on the patient's mental state, and can be used to quickly change the patient's mood. In treating mental disorders, the Jing-Well points are commonly used for irritability, mental restlessness, anxiety, hysteria, mania, and insomnia.

   In the clinic, these points are generally used for resolving acute disorders, expelling exogenous pathogens, and for relieving mental disorders. They are sometimes used as "Revival Points" for loss of consciousness due to fainting and heat stroke; and, they can also be used to treat convulsions, local neuropathy (tingling, numbness, burning pain), or a feeling of fullness below the Heart.

2. **Ying (Spring) Points:** These are the second set of points along the channels, and are located in the second position of the channels' energetic progression up the arms or legs just above the Well Points. The Ying-Spring Points are where the channel's energetic flow quickens its progression of Qi into the body.

   At the location of the Spring points, the energy in the channels is very dynamic and powerful, and can change quickly, slipping and gliding like the swirling movements of cascading water.

   In the clinic, the Spring Points are generally used to eliminate both internal and external pathogenic factors (especially Heat) from the patient's body. They are also used when a disease effects a color change in the patient's complexion.

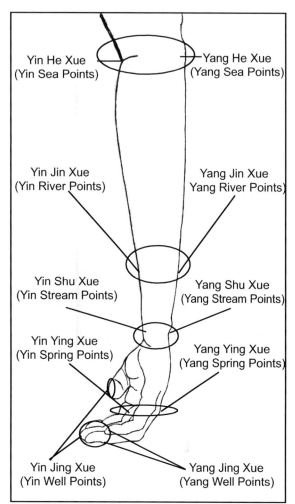

Figure 10.13. The Five Shu Points and their Arm Channel Flow Correspondences

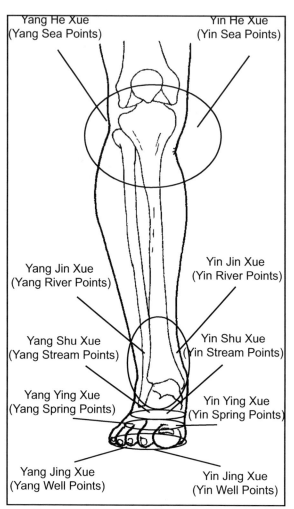

Figure 10.14. The Five Shu Points and their Leg Channel Flow Correspondences

In the Yin Channels, this point corresponds to the Fire Element. Purging the Spring Point in the Yin Channels reduces Heat and clears Fire.

In the Yang channels, the Spring Point corresponds to the Water Element. The doctor can reduce Heat in the patient's Yang Channels by tonifying this Water point.

3. **Shu (Stream) Points:** These are the third set of points along the channels, and are located in the third position in the channels' energetic progression up the arms or legs, just above and next to the Spring Point (except for the Gall Bladder Channel where it is located at the fourth point).

The Shu-Stream Points are where the channel's energy rapidly pours through and slightly deepens its flow into the body. Therefore, at the Shu-Stream Points, the external pathogenic factors may penetrate deep into the channels, and can then be "transported" into the body's interior.

In the clinic, the Shu-Stream points are used to clear Wind and Dampness from the patient's channels, and are also used when a disease manifests intermittently.

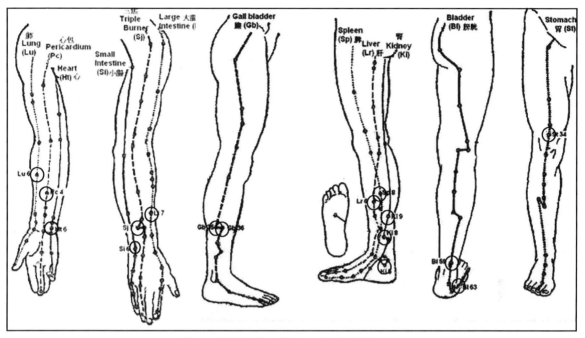

Figure 10.15. The Sixteen Xi (Cleft) Points

4. **Jing (River) Points:** These are the fourth set of Transporting Points; though they are not always located on the fourth point along the channel. The points are, however, always located in-between the wrist and elbow on the arms, or in-between the ankle and knee on the legs. The Jing-River points are where the channels broaden, and the energy flow continues to increase.

At the Jing-River points, the energy current flows wider, deeper, and more irregularly, like a large river, directing the energy (or the invasion of external pathogenic factors) inward, towards the body's tendons, joints, and bones.

In the clinic, these points are generally used when there is stagnation of Qi and Blood in the patient's channels. They are also used for treating such symptoms as coughing, asthma, dyspnea, sore throat, and upper respiratory diseases.

5. **He (Sea) Points:** These are the fifth set of Five Element Transporting points. In all cases, these points are located at the elbows and knees, and are where the energy of the channels is vast, and plunges deep into the body.

The Qi at the He-Sea points moves centripetally inward, flowing relatively slowly, while joining, collecting, and fusing with the general circulation of the body's energy the way a mighty river flows into the sea.

In the clinic, the He-Sea points are generally used for all Stomach and intestinal diseases and for internal disorders of the organs.

THE 16 XI-CLEFT (ACCUMULATION) POINTS

The Sixteen "Xi" ("Cleft") Points are where the Qi and Blood gather and plunge deeply into the body. They are used for purging acute conditions of excess in the channels and organs. There is one Xi-Cleft point on each of the Twelve Primary Channels, plus one point on each of the Yin and Yang Heel Vessels, and one point on each of the Yin and Yang Linking Vessels (Figure 10.15).

- **Yin Points:** The Yin Channel Accumulation points are Lu-6, Pc-4, Ht-6, Sp-8, Lv-6, Kd-5, Yin Heel Kd-8, and Yin Linking Kd-9.
- **Yang Points:** The Yang Channel Accumulation points are LI-7, TB-7, SI-6, St-34, GB-36, UB-63, Yang Heel UB-59, and Yang Linking GB-35.

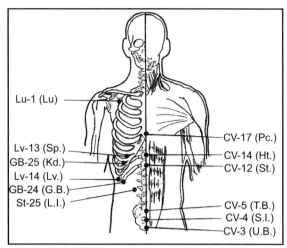

Figure 10.16. The 12 Front "Mu" ("Alarm") Points

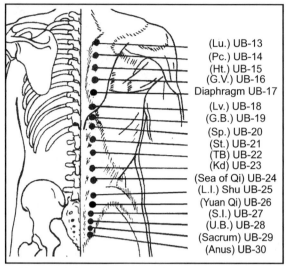

Figure 10.17. The 18 Back (Transporting) Points

THE 12 FRONT-MU (ALARM) POINTS

The Twelve Front-Mu Points are located on the chest and abdomen. Because the energy of the internal organs collects at these points, they can therefore be used for both diagnosis and treatment. These points are palpated for diagnosis and may feel tender to the patient, either with light touch or with the application of pressure.

- **Excess Condition:** If they respond to a light touch or feel tight or swollen, the patient has an excess condition.
- **Deficient Condition:** If the points respond to deep pressure, or feel hollow or deflated, the patient has a deficient condition.

The Twelve Front Alarm points are listed as follows (Figure 10.16): Lungs Lu-1, Pericardium CV-17, Liver Lv-14, Spleen Lv-13, Gall Bladder GB-24, Kidneys GB-25, Heart CV-14, Stomach CV-12, Large Intestine St-25, Triple Burners CV-5, Small Intestine CV-4, and Urinary Bladder CV-3.

THE 18 BACK-SHU (TRANSPORTING) POINTS

The eighteen Back-Shu points are all located on the back along the Urinary Bladder Channel. They correspond to the twelve Zang Fu organs and are used both for diagnosis and for treatment. These points transport Qi very effectively and directly to the internal organs. They can also be used for treating disorders of the corresponding sense organs.

The Eighteen Back Transporting points are listed as follows (Figure 10.17): Lungs UB-13, Pericardium UB-14, Heart UB-15, Governing Vessel UB-16, Diaphragm UB-17, Liver UB-18, Gall Bladder UB-19, Spleen UB-20, Stomach UB-21, Triple Burners UB-22, Kidneys UB-23, Sea of Qi UB-24, Large Intestine UB-25, Gate to the Yuan Qi (Guan Yuan) UB-26, Small Intestine UB-27, Urinary Bladder UB-28, Sacrum UB-29, and Anus UB-30.

THE 15 LUO (CONNECTING) POINTS

The Fifteen Luo points are used in treating channel pathologies. There is a Luo-Connecting point located on each of the Twelve Primary Channels, as well as on the Governing and Conception Vessels (Figure 10.18). The Fifteenth Luo point is clinically known as the Great Luo point of the Spleen. The Fifteen Connecting points are divided into Yin and Yang Channel Points, described as follows:

- **Yin Points:** Yin Channel points include: Lu-7, Pc-6, Ht-5, Sp-4, Lv-5, Kd-4, CV-15, and the Great Luo Channel Sp-21.
- **Yang Points:** The Yang Channel points include LI-6, TB-5, SI-7, St-40, GB-37, UB-58, and GV-1.

THE TWELVE ENTRY POINTS

The Twelve Entry Points are where each Primary Channel connects with and receives energy from the channel immediately preceding it in the 24 hour Blood-Heat cycle (Figure 10.19). The Entry Point is the first point on each channel in all cases except for the Large Intestine Channel, which is

CHAPTER 10: THE BODY'S ENERGETIC POINTS

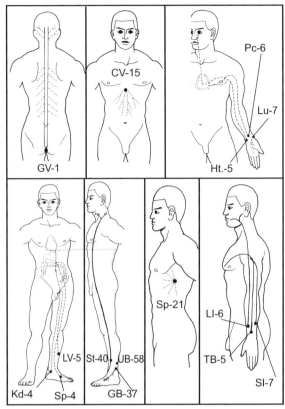

Figure 10.18. The 15 Luo (Connecting) Points

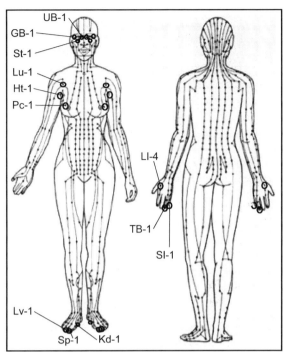

Figure 10.19. The Twelve Entry Points

LI-4. The Twelve Entry Points are divided into Yin and Yang Channel Points, described as follows:
- **Yin Points:** The Yin Channel Entry points include: Lu-1, Pc-1, Ht-1, Sp-1, Lv-1, and Kd-1.
- **Yang Points:** The Yang Channel Entry points include: LI-4, TB-1, SI-1, St-1, GB-1, and UB-1.

THE TWELVE EXIT POINTS

The Twelve Exit Points are where the energy of each Primary Channel exits to connect with the channel immediately following it in the 24 hour Blood-Heat cycle (Figure 10.20). The Twelve Exit Points are divided into Yin and Yang Channel Points, described as follows:
- **Yin Points:** The Yin Channel Exit points include: Lu-7, Pc-8, Ht-9, Sp-21, Lv-14, and Kd-22.
- **Yang Points:** The Yang Channel Exit points include: LI-20, TB-23, SI-19, St-42, GB-41, and UB-67.

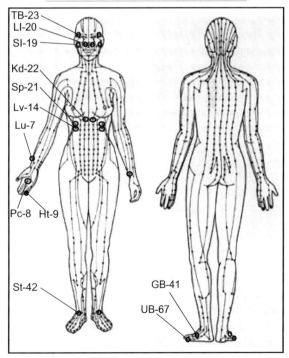

Figure 10.20. The Twelve Exit Points

601

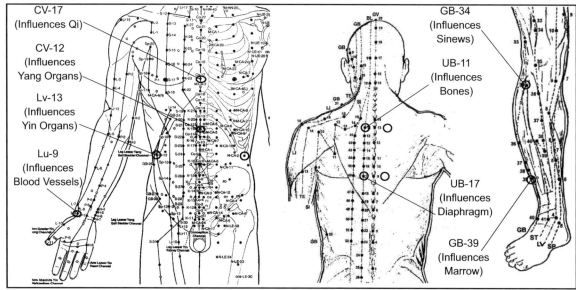

Figure 10.21. The 8 Influential Points

THE EIGHT INFLUENTIAL POINTS

The Eight Influential points have specific effects on their respective organs, substances, and tissues. They affect the body's Qi, Blood, sinews, Blood Vessels, Bones, and Marrow, as well as the Yin and Yang Organs.

The Eight Influential points and their respective influences are listed as follows (Figure 10.21):

- Lv-13 (Gate of Completion) - Yin Organs
- CV-12 (Middle Cavity) Yang Organs
- CV-17 (Chest Center) - Qi
- UB-17 Diaphragm Transport) - Blood
- GB-34 (Yang Mound Spring) - Sinews
- Lu-9 (Supreme Abyss) - Blood Vessels
- UB-11 Great Shuttle) - Bones
- GB-39 (Suspended Bell) - Marrow

THE EIGHT CONFLUENT POINTS

The Eight Confluent points communicate with the Eight Extraordinary Vessels. The Confluent points are divided into Master points and Coupled points. The Master point is the primary point chosen for treatment, and its Coupled point is the connecting or secondary point that is used in conjunction with the Master point to open the specific Vessel. Each of the Eight Extraordinary Vessels has both a Master and Coupled Confluent point on the upper or lower limbs (Figures 10.22 and 10.23).

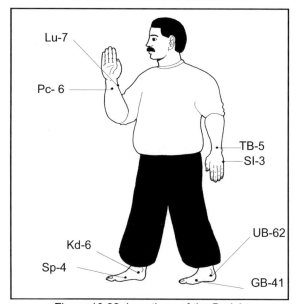

Figure 10.22. Locations of the Body's Master and Couple Points

The Eight Confluent points are listed as follows: Governing Vessel SI-3, Conception Vessel Lu-7, Belt Vessel GB-41, Thrusting Vessel Sp-4, Yang Heel Vessel UB-62, Yin Heel Vessel Kd-6, Yang Linking Vessel TB-5, and Yin Linking Vessel Pc-6.

Channel	Open with Master Point	Complete with Couple Point
Governing	Hand (SI-3)	Foot (UB-62)
Conception	Hand (Lu-7)	Foot (Kd-6)
Thrusting	Foot (Sp-4)	Hand (Pc-6)
Belt	Foot (GB-41)	Hand (TB-5)
Yin Linking	Hand (Pc-6)	Foot (Sp-4)
Yang Linking	Hand (TB-5)	Foot (GB-41)
Yin Heel	Foot (Kd-6)	Hand (Lu-7)
Yang Heel	Foot (UB-62)	Hand (SI-3)

Figure 10.23. The Vessels with their Associated Master Points and Couple Points

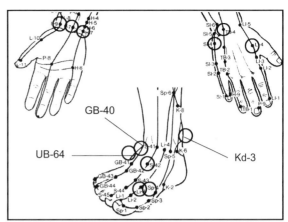

Figure 10.24. The 12 Yuan (Source) Points

In the Medial Qigong Clinic, all of the Eight Extraordinary Vessels can be energetically accessed and treated in various combinations, according to their specific Master and Coupled point locations. For Example, if the Medical Qigong Doctor emits Qi into the Governing Vessel Master Point on the patient's right hand (SI-3), and directs it to flow to its Coupled point (UB-62) on the patient's left foot, then the Qi in the patient's Governing Vessel will suddenly "Open" and fill.

In order to complete the treatment, the doctor must first remove stimulation from the Coupled (UB-62) point located on the patient's left foot, then he is free to disconnect his energy from the Master point on the right hand (SI-3).

THE 12 YUAN (SOURCE) POINTS

Each of the Twelve Primary Channels has a special "Yuan" ("Source") Point, where the body's Original Qi surfaces and energetically pools (Figure 10.24). The Yuan Qi originates and resides within the Lower Dantian area, it is first dispersed to the Yin and Yang Organs and then to the limbs via the energetic function of the Triple Burners.

- **Yin Points:** On the Yin Channels, the Yuan (Source) Points are always the Shu (Stream) Points. These are the primary points on the Yin Channels used for tonifying and regulating their respective Yin Organs.

  In the clinic, the Yuan (Source) Points can be used for diagnosis of the Yin Organs. For this, the Medical Qigong Doctor will examine the various points, by both palpation and visual diagnosis.

- **Yang Points:** On the Yang Channels, the Yuan (Source) Points are separate points located between the Shu (Stream) and the Jing (River) Points. These points are usually the fourth point from the distal end of the channel, except in the case of the Gall Bladder Channel where the Yuan-Source point is the fifth point.

  The Yuan (Source) Points of the Yang Channels have different energetic functions and clinical applications than do the Yin channels' Source points. These points generally have a small tonifying effect on their related Yang Organs and comparatively little Qi regulating effect. Their main functions are to expel various pathogenic factors, and to treat disorders along their channel pathways.

The Twelve Yuan points are as follows: Gall Bladder GB-40, Liver Lv-3, Lungs Lu-9, Large Intestine LI-4, Stomach St-42, Spleen Sp-3, Heart Ht-7, Small Intestine SI-4, Bladder UB-64, Kidney Kd-3, Pericardium Pc-7, and Triple Burners TB-4.

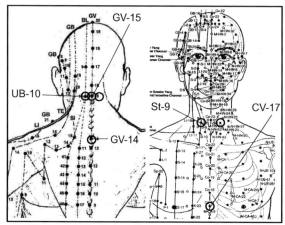

Figure 10.25. Points To Access The Sea of Qi

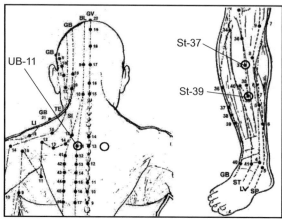

Figure 10.26. Points To Access The Sea of Blood

THE POINTS OF THE FOUR SEAS

In Chinese Energetic Medicine, the human body is seen to have Four Seas: the Sea of Qi, Sea of Blood, Sea of Marrow, and the Sea of Nourishment (literally "Sea of Water and Grain"). The Medical Qigong Doctor can energetically access these special seas by stimulating the following points:

1. **Points For Accessing The Sea of Qi:** These special points include UB-10, St-9, CV-17, GV-14, and GV-15 (Figure 10.25).
   - **Excess in the Sea of Qi:** This condition manifests in symptoms such as fullness in the chest, flushed complexion, and dyspnea.
   - **Deficiency in the Sea of Qi:** This condition manifests in symptoms such as fatigue, low energy, or an inability to speak.
2. **Points For Accessing The Sea of Blood:** These special points include UB-11, St-37, and St-39 (Figure 10.26).
   - **Excess in the Sea of Blood:** This condition manifests in symptoms such as anxiety, uneasiness, unrest, and a feeling of the body being too big.
   - **Deficiency in the Sea of Blood:** This condition manifests in symptoms such a feeling that the body is too small for no apparent reason.
3. **Points For Accessing The Sea of Marrow:** These special points include GV-15, GV-16, GV-17, and GV-20 (Figure 10.27).
   - **Excess in the Sea of Marrow:** This condition manifests in symptoms such as specific

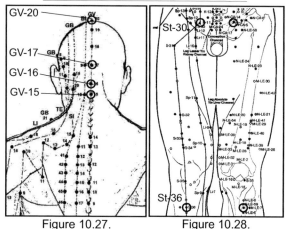

Figure 10.27. Points To Access The Sea of Marrow

Figure 10.28. Points To Access The Sea of Nourishment

sensations relating to that of Excess Qi (i.e., lightness, feelings of strength and vitality).
   - **Deficiency in the Sea of Marrow:** This condition manifests in symptoms such as fatigue, vertigo, dizziness, tinnitus, pain in the lower legs, impaired vision, and a desire to sleep.
4. **Points For Accessing The Sea of Nourishment:** These special points include St-30 and St-36 (Figure 10.28).
   - **Excess in the Sea of Nourishment:** This condition manifests in symptoms such as abdominal distension.
   - **Deficiency in the Sea of Nourishment:** This condition manifests in symptoms such as hunger with an inability to eat.

THE THIRTEEN GHOST POINTS

The 13 Ghost Points have a particularly powerful effect on a patient's overall mental, emotional, and spiritual balance. This is why in ancient China, they were traditionally used in the clinical treatment of Spirit Possession, Mania Disorders, and Epilepsy.

Since the creation of Traditional Chinese Medicine in the People's Republic of China, the notion of spirits and demons has been down-played. However, educated Daoist priests understand and teach the causes, effects, and treatments of demon and spirit possession. These following Thirteen Ghost Points (Shi San Gui Xue) are listed in the *Qian Jin Yao Fang (Thousand Ducat Formulas)*, prescribed by the famous physician and esoteric Daoist Alchemist, Dr. Sun Simiao (Figure 10.29). In 7th century China, these special points were once used for the treatment of Demonic Oppression and Demonic Possession.

Today in the People's Republic of China, these points are still used in the Traditional Chinese Medical Clinics for the treatment of Shen (Mind/Heart) Disorders, Manic Disorders, Severe Mental Depression, and for treating Epilepsy.

In extreme Manic cases (with Heat) the doctor will bleed all of these points, as well as all Twelve Jing (Well) points on the patient's hands. When bleeding, the blood can also be extrapulated from the tissues by inserting an acupuncture needle into each point and then immediately withdrawing it. The Thirteen Ghost points are listed as follows:

Figure 10.29. Daoist Master Sun Si Miao (590-682 A.D.)

1. **The Guigong (Ghost's Palace) Point:** This point is also known as the Renzhong GV-26 (Middle of Man) point. It is a major influential point that affects the entire chest area.
2. **The Guixin (Ghost's Faith) Points:** These points are also known as the Shaoshang Lu-11 (Little Bargaining) points. They are located on both thumbs, and are treated to calm the Shen and restore Collapsed Yang.
3. **The Guilei (Ghost's Fortress) Points:** These points are also known as the Yinbai Sp-1 (Hidden Clarity) points. They are located on the medial aspects of the big toes and are treated to calm the Shen, clear Heat, clear the brain, and instill clarity of thought and mind.
4. **The Guixin (Ghost's Heart) Points:** These points are also known as the Daling Pc-7 (Big Mound) points. They are located at the center of the wrists, and are treated to calm the Shen and clear the brain.
5. **The Guilu (Ghost's Path) Points:** These points are also known as the Shenmai UB-62 (Extending Vessel) points. They are located under both outside ankles (the Master Point for the Yang Heel Vessel), and are treated to calm the Shen.
6. **The Guizhen (Ghost's Pillow) Point:** This point is also known as the Fengfu GV-16 (Wind's Palace) point. It is located just below the occiput, and is treated to clear the brain.
7. **The Guichuang (Ghost's Bed) Points:** These points are also known as the Jiache St-6 (Jaw Vehicle) points. They are located on both sides of the jaw and are used to treat neurological and psychological problems, as well as to dispel Wind and Cold, and to clear Heat.
8. **The Guishi (Ghost's Market) Point:** This point is also known as the Chengqiang CV-24 (Receiving Liquid) point. It is located under the lower lip and is stimulated to treat mental disorders, dispel Wind and Cold, clear Heat, and to transform Dampness and Phlegm.
9. **The Guicu (Ghost's Cave) Points:** These points are also known as the Laogong Pc-8 (Palace of Labor) points. They are located at the center of the palms and are stimulated to treat mental disorders and to clear the brain.

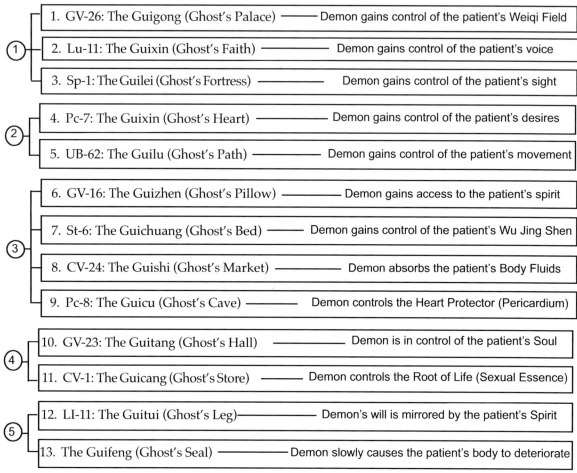

Figure 10.30. Using the 13 Ghost Points to diagnose the progression of Spirit Possession

10. **The Guitang (Ghost's Hall) Point:** This point is also known as the Shangxing GV-23 (Upper Star - Polaris) point. It is treated to brighten the Shen and clear Heat.
11. **The Guicang (Ghost's Store) Point:** This point is also known as the Huiyin CV-1 (Meeting of the Yin) point. It is used to treat mental disorders. In ancient Daoism this area of the body was known as Yumentou (Jade Gate) located at the opening of the vagina in women, and Yinxiafeng (Below the Hidden Seam) located below the scrotum in men.
12. **The Guitui (Ghost's Leg) Points:** These points are also known as the Quchi LI-11 (Pool at the Bend) points. They are treated in order to drain the pathogenic influences from the Lungs, remove Heat, and calm the Po (Corporeal Soul).
13. **The Guifeng (Ghost's Seal) Points:** These points are also known as the Haiquan (Sea Spring) and She Xia Zhong Feng (Under Tongue Middle Frenulum) points. These two Extra points located below the tongue are stimulated in order to treat mental disorders.

A summary of using the Thirteen Ghost Points to diagnose the progression of the spirit or demonic influence is listed in the following chart (Figure 10.30).

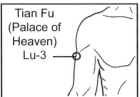

Tian Fu (Palace of Heaven) Lu-3

Figure 10.31. Patient is disoriented, sees/hears floating corpse ghosts, or hears crying ghosts

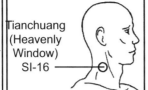

Tianchuang (Heavenly Window) SI-16

Figure 10.32. Patient is manic-depressed, sees and hears ghosts talking

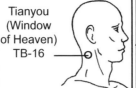

Tianyou (Window of Heaven) TB-16

Figure 10.35. Patient experiences chronic nightmares, confused dreaming, & restless sleep

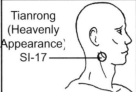

Tianrong (Heavenly Appearance) SI-17

Figure 10.36. "Oppressive Sensation" felt within the chest at night, with an inability to breathe

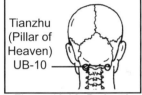

Tianzhu (Pillar of Heaven) UB-10

Figure 10.33. Patient is having seizures, sees and hears ghosts talking

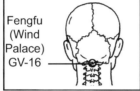

Fengfu (Wind Palace) GV-16

Figure 10.34. Patient is manic and suicidal with incessant wild talking and actions

Ren Ying (Man's Welcome) St-9

Figure 10.37. Patient has headache and dizziness, with a sudden panic attack

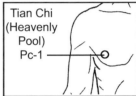

Tian Chi (Heavenly Pool) Pc-1

Figure 10.38. Patient is disoriented, has headache, blurred vision, weak limbs, and fever with no sweat

THE TEN WINDOW OF HEAVEN POINTS

These ten special "Window of Heaven" Points have a powerful calming effect on the patient's Shen (Heart/Mind). Therefore, they are traditionally used when treating emotional disorders.

According to one of my Daoist teachers, many of these special points were originally used in ancient China in order to treat Shen Disturbed patients who were delusional, and experienced hallucinations of seeing demonic spirits and ghosts.

The Ten Window of Heaven points and their ancient clinical application are listed as follows:

- Lu-3 (Tian Fu) Palace of Heaven: Patient is disoriented, sees and hears floating corpse ghosts, or hears crying ghosts (Figure 10.31).
- SI-16 (Tian Chuang) Heavenly Window: Patient is manic-depressed, sees and hears ghosts talking (Figure 10.32).
- UB-10 (Tian Zhu) Pillar of Heaven: Patient is having seizures, sees and hears ghosts talking (Figure 10.33).
- GV-16 (Feng Fu) Wind Palace: Patient is manic and suicidal with incessant wild talking and actions (Figure 10.34).
- TB-16 (Tian You) Window of Heaven: Patient experiences chronic nightmares, confused dreaming, and restless sleep (Figure 10.35).

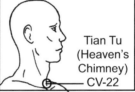

Tian Tu (Heaven's Chimney) CV-22

Figure 10.39. Heart pain, with an inability to breathe and a shortness of breath

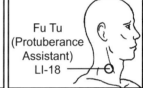

Fu Tu (Protuberance Assistant) LI-18

Figure 10.40. Patient is Vomiting white foam, followed by a sudden loss of voice

- SI-17 (Tian Rong) Heavenly Appearance: "Oppressive Sensation" felt within the chest at night, with an inability to breathe (Figure 10.36).
- St-9 (Ren Ying) Man's Prognosis: Patient has headache and dizziness, with a sudden panic attack (Figure 10.37).
- Pc-1 (Tian Chi) Celestial Pool: Patient is disoriented, has headache, blurred vision, weak limbs, and fever with no sweat (Figure 10.38).
- CV-22 (Tian Tu) Heaven's Chimney: Patient has Heart pain, with and inability to breathe and a shortness of breath (Figure 10.39).
- LI-18 (Fu Tu) Protuberance Assistant: Patient is vomiting white foam, has a sudden loss of voice (Figure 10.40.)

SUMMARY OF POINTS

Understanding the origin and function of the body's energetic points, as well as the Qi flow along the energetic channels, allows the Qigong doctor to emit energy through these energetic cavities in order to easily and directly access the tissues and internal organs of the patients body. This understanding also enables the Qigong doctor to purge the toxic or pathogenic Qi (which has become stagnant or detrimentally active within the patient's body) away from the diseased organs, through specific channels, and out the body.

The preceding chart (Figure 10.41) is a basic categorization of the body's points and their descriptions.

SCIENTIFIC RESEARCH OF ACUPOINTS

In the early 1970's, shortly after President Nixon's historic visit to China, Dr. Robert O. Becker, M.D., a Syracuse University Orthopedist, received a grant from the National Institute of Health to research how Acupuncture works. Dr. Becker reasoned that the channels were electrical conductors that existed independent of the nervous system yet somehow communicated with it. He theorized that these channels carried an injury message to the brain, which then responded by sending back the appropriate level of direct current (DC) that would stimulate healing in the troubled area.

Becker also suggested, in his book *The Body Electric*, that "any current grows weaker with distance, due to resistance along the transmission cable. The smaller the amperage and voltage, the faster the current dies out. Electrical engineers solve this problem by building booster amplifiers every so often along a power line to get the signal back up to strength. For currents measured in nanoamperes and microvolts (such as those generated in the human body), the amplifiers would have to be no more than a few inches apart—just like the acupuncture points."

Dr. Becker and his assistant Maria Reichmanis, herself a biophysicist, designed special equipment to measure and map the electrical conductivity along the channels. They found the predicted electrical characteristics along the channels charted in Traditional Chinese Medicine and at half of the known points. These same points showed up consistently on all the people tested. Because they were able to measure only half of the traditionally charted points, Becker and Reichmanis suggested that the other points may simply be weaker, or of a different kind, than the ones that their instruments detected.

Each point that they found was electrically positive in comparison to its surrounding tissue, and each point had an electrical field surrounding it with its own characteristic shape.

Later research in China, France, and the United States has demonstrated that not only do these points and channels have electrical properties, but they also emit and absorb light and sound, both of which are vital to healthy biological functions.

Chapter 10: The Body's Energetic Points

Category	Points	Description
Five Shu Points	Jing-Well, Ying-Spring, Shu-Stream, Jing-River, He-Sea	Transporting and Command Points
Sixteen Xi Cleft Points	Yin: Lu-6, Pc-4: Ht-6, Sp-8, Lv-6, Kd-5, Yin Heel Kd-8, and Yin Linking Kd-9 Yang: LI-7, TB-7, SI-6, St-34, GB-36, UB-63, Yang Heel UB-59 and Yang Linking GB-35	Accumulation Points
Twelve Front Mu Points	Lungs Lu-1, Pericardium CV-17, Liver Lv-14, Spleen Lv-13, Gall Bladder GB-24, Kidneys GB-25, Heart CV-14, Stomach CV-12, Large Intestine St-25, Triple Burners CV-5, Small Intestine CV-4, and Urinary Bladder CV-3	Alarm, Collecting Points
Eighteen Back Shu Points	Lungs UB-13, Pericardium UB-14, Heart UB-15, Governing Vessel UB-16, Diaphragm UB-17, Liver UB-18, Gall Bladder UB-19, Spleen UB-20, Stomach UB-21, Triple Burners UB-22, Kidney UB-23, Sea of Qi UB-24, Large Intestine UB-25, Gate to the Original Qi (Guan Yuan) UB-26, Small Intestine UB-27, Urinary Bladder UB-28, Sacrum UB-29 and Anus UB-30	Associated, Transporting Points
Fifteen Luo Points	Yin: Lu-7, Pc-6, Ht-5, Sp-4, Lv-5, Kd-4, CV-15, the Great Luo Channel Sp-21 Yang: LI-6, TB-5, SI-7, St-40, GB-37, UB-58 and GV-1	Connecting Points
Twelve Entry Points	The first point on each channel except for the Large Intestine Channel in which it is LI-4	Qi enters Channel
Twelve Exit Points	Yin: Lu-7, P-8, Ht-9, Sp-21, Lv-14 and Kd-22 Yang: LI-20, TB-23, SI-19, St-42, GB-41 and UB-67	Qi exits Channel
Eight Influential Points	Yin Organs Lv-13, Yang Organs CV-12, Qi CV-17, Blood UB-17, Sinews GB-34, Blood Vessels Lu-9, Bones UB-11 and Marrow GB-39	Influence Internal Organ Function
Eight Confluent Points	Governing Vessel SI-3, Conception Vessel Lu-7, Belt Vessel GB-41, Thrusting Vessels Sp-4, Yang Heel Vessels UB-62, Yin Heel Vessels Kd-6, Yang Linking Vessels TB-5 and Yin Linking Vessels Pc-6	Master and Couple Points
Twelve Yuan-Source Points	Gall Bladder GB-40, Liver Lv-3, Lungs Lu-9, Large Intestine LI-4, Stomach St-42, Spleen- Sp-3, Heart Ht-7, Small Intestine SI-4, Urinary Bladder UB-64, Pericardium Pc-7, and Triple Burners TB-4	Source of Original Qi Points
Four Seas Points	Sea of Qi Points: UB-10, St-9, CV-17, GV-14 and 15 Sea of Blood Points: UB-11, St-37 and 39 Sea of Marrow Points: GV-15, GV-16, GV-17, and GV-20 Sea of Nourishment Points: St-30 and St-36	Give Access to the Four Seas
Upper He-Sea Points	Stomach LI-10, Large Intestine LI-9 and the Small Intestine LI-8	Affect the Yang Organs
Lower He-Sea Points	Stomach St-36, Large Intestine St-37, Small Intestine St-39, Triple Burners UB-39, Urinary Bladder UB-40, and Gall Bladder GB-34	Affect the Yang Organs
Thirteen Ghost Points	GV-26, Lu-11, Sp-1, Pc-7, UB-62, GV-16, St-6, CV-24, Pc-8, GV-23, LI-11, CV-1, and She Xia Feng	Affect the Mind, Emotion, and Spirit
Ten Windows of Heaven Points	Lung 3, Large Intestine 18, Triple Burners 16, Urinary Bladder 10, Stomach 9, Conception Vessel 22, Governing Vessel 16, Small Intestine 16, Small Intestine 17, and Pericardium 1	Affect the Mind, Emotion, and Spirit

Figure 10.41. Point Review Chart

Appendix 1
Chronology of Chinese Dynasties

Introduction

The following Appendix has been added in order to assist the reader in comprehending the chronology of the Chinese Dynasties. It is important to note that the years of the dynasties were not always the same in all regions of China. Some dynasties overlap in time, and there were also various periods of political upheaval where no specific emperor or ruling family was in control.

China's Pre-Dynasty Myths

The Reign of Fu Xi: 5000-4000 B.C.
The Blue/Green (Qing Di) Emperor of the East
Founder of Family and Music

The Reign of Shen Nong: 4000-3000 B.C.
The Red Emperor (Chi Di) of the South
Founder of Farming and Herbology

The Reign of Huangdi: 2697-2599 B.C.
The Yellow Emperor (Huang Di) of the Center
Founder of Magic and Medicine

Fu Xi (East)   Shen Nong (South)   Huang Di (Center)

According to Han Dynasty texts, the "Three Sovereigns" (i.e., "Three August Ones" in Daoist Alchemical practice), were said to be god-kings who used their magical powers to improve the lives of their people. According to *The Book of Lineages*, the Three Sovereigns are the first three Emperors Fuxi, Shennong, and Huangdi.

The Reign of Shaohao: 2598-2514 B.C.
The White Emperor (Bai Di) of the West
Founder of Burial and Afterlife Rites

The Reign of Zhuanxu: 2514-2436 B.C.
The Black Emperor (Hei Di / Xuan Di) of the North
Founder of Martial Arts and Exorcism
(God of the Celestial Pole Star)

Shao Hao (West)   Zhuan Xu (North)

The Three Rulers Period

The Reign of Yao: 2357-2258 B.C.
Heaven appointed ruler because of his virtue

The Reign of Shun: 2257-2208 B.C.
Appointed Yao's successor because of his virtue

The Reign of Yu the Great: 2207-2197 B.C.
Controlled the Floods, Xia Dynasty begins

Yao   Shun   Yu the Great

Dynasties of China

Xia Dynasty:	2207-1766 B.C.
Shang Dynasty:	1765-1122 B.C.
Zhou Dynasty:	**1121-222 B.C.**
Western Zhou Dynasty:	1121 - 771 B.C.
Eastern Zhou Dynasty:	770 - 256 B.C.
Spring & Autumn Period:	722 - 481 B.C.
Warring States Period:	403 - 222 B.C.
Qin Dynasty:	**221-206 B.C.**
Han Dynasty:	**206 B.C.-220 A.D.**
Western Han Dynasty:	206 B.C. - 8 A.D.
Xin Dynasty:	9 A.D. - 25 A.D.
Eastern Han Dynasty:	25 - 220 A.D.
Three Kingdoms Period:	**220-280 A.D.**
Wei Dynasty:	220 - 265 A.D.
Shu Dynasty:	221 - 263 A.D.
Wu Dynasty:	222 - 280 A.D.
Jin Dynasty:	**265-420 A.D.**
Western Jin Dynasty:	265 - 316 A.D.
Eastern Jin Dynasty:	317 - 420 A.D.
Northern Dynasties:	**386-581 A.D.**
Northern Wei Dynasty:	386 - 534 A.D.
Eastern Wei Dynasty:	534 - 550 A.D.
Western Wei Dynasty:	535 - 557 A.D.
Northern Qi Dynasty:	550 - 577 A.D.
Northern Zhou Dynasty:	557 - 581 A.D.
Southern Dynasty:	**420-589 A.D.**
Song Dynasty:	420 - 479 A.D.
Qi Dynasty:	479 - 502 A.D.
Liang Dynasty:	502 - 557 A.D.
Chen Dynasty:	557 - 589 A.D.
Sui Dynasty:	**581-618 A.D.**
Tang Dynasty:	**618-907 A.D.**
Five Dynasties Period:	**907-960 A.D.**
Later Liang Dynasty:	907 - 923 A.D.
Later Tang Dynasty:	923 - 936 A.D.
Later Jin Dynasty:	936 - 946 A.D.
Later Han Dynasty:	947 - 950 A.D.
Later Zhou Dynasty:	951 - 960 A.D.
Ten Kingdoms Period:	**902-979 A.D.**
Song Dynasty:	**960-1279 A.D.**
Northern Song Dynasty:	960 - 1127 A.D.
Southern Song Dynasty:	1127 - 1279 A.D.
Liao Dynasty:	**907-1202 A.D.**
Western Xia Dynasty:	**1032-1227 A.D.**
Jin Dynasty:	**1115-1234 A.D.**
Yuan (Mongol) Dynasty:	**1277-1367 A.D.**
Ming Dynasty:	**1368-1644 A.D.**
Qing (Manchu) Dynasty:	**1644-1911 A.D.**
The Republic of China:	**1912-1949 A.D.**
People's Republic of China:	**1949-Present**

Yu the Great, First ruler of the **Xia Dynasty**

Cheng Tang, First ruler of the **Shang Dynasty**

Wu of Chou, First ruler of the **Zhou Dynasty**

Qin Shihuang, First ruler of the **Qin Dynasty**

Gaozu (Liu Bang), First ruler of the **Han Dynasty**

Appendix 2
Medical Qigong Therapy Instruction

 **International Institute of Medical Qigong
Overseas Medical Qigong College of the
Henan University of Traditional Chinese Medicine**

Introduction

Chinese Medical Qigong Therapy is attracting interest from Energetic Healers, Acupuncturists, Allopathic Doctors, Psychotherapists, Chiropractors, Naturopathic Doctors, and Physical Therapists from all around the world.

The titles "Medical Qigong Practitioner" (M.Q.P.), "Medical Qigong Therapist" (M.Q.T.), "Master of Medical Qigong" (M.M.Q.), and "Doctor of Medical Qigong" (D.M.Q.) were originally introduced to the public by Professor Jerry Alan Johnson and the International Institute of Medical Qigong (I.I.M.Q.) in 1985, for the purpose of promoting and regulating Chinese Medical Qigong Therapy in the West. Today, these clinical titles have become world renown.

For over 30 years the I.I.M.Q. has been consistently educating Westerners in Chinese Energetic Medicine, and currently have hundreds of graduates operating clinics throughout the United States, Bermuda, Belgium, Brazil, Canada, Guatemala, Ireland, Sweden, and the United Kingdom.

Originally fashioned after the Medical Qigong College at the Hai Dian University of Traditional Chinese Medicine in Beijing, China, the I.I.M.Q. is known internationally for maintaining the highest standards in Medical Qigong instruction and clinical therapy. Because of these consistent high standards, the Chinese Ministry of Health honored Professor Johnson and the I.I.M.Q. early in 2005 for meeting and exceeding the People's Republic of China's Medical Standards for Academic and Clinical Instruction.

The Institute's achievements in providing strict academic and clinical instruction have also been recognized by the Medical Qigong Department at the Xi Yuan Hospital (Beijing, China) as well as the Henan University of Traditional Chinese Medicine (Henan, China).

Professor Johnson's Academic License to Teach Chinese Medicine & Clinical License to Treat Patients

Due to the overwhelmingly positive response to the academic standards and clinical qualifications established by the International Institute of Medical Qigong (I.I.M.Q.), the following appendix includes information on the current history of the Medical Qigong Programs offered by several U.S. Colleges of Traditional Chinese Medicine.

At the International Institute of Medical Qigong, it is our policy that all our Medical Qigong Programs maintain these same teaching standards, syllabi, and clinical hours for certification. This way, prospective students may feel confident in attending the specific college or institute of their choice, knowing that each Medical Qigong educational facility will teach and maintain the same clinical format and strict standards established by Professor Johnson and the International Institute of Medical Qigong.

Medical Qigong Therapy Classes

Traditionally, all of the I.I.M.Q. courses entail two to six year programs in Medical Qigong Therapy, plus Clinical Internship. The programs include classes, labs, and seminars on Traditional

Chinese Medical Theory, and the Foundations of Chinese Medicine for Internal Diseases according to the *Yellow Emperor's Inner Canon: Spiritual Pivot, Essential Questions*, and the *Canon of Perplexities*.

Classes also include Energetic Anatomy and Physiology, Energetic Diagnosis and Symptomatology, Energetic Psychology, Qigong Pathology and Medical Qigong Therapy, as well as a survey of other related medical modalities. Other related modalities include: a basic understanding of Herbal Medicine, Acupuncture Therapy, and Chinese Massage. Classes in Western Anatomy and Physiology, Western Internal Diseases, and Health and Recovery are also required

The Certification Programs offered by the I.I.M.Q. is based upon the curriculum that was originally established by the Medical Qigong College at the Hai Dian University in the early 1990s, and was implemented at the Xi Yuan Medical Qigong Hospital in Beijing, China.

In the 1990s, some of the most common diseases that were treated in the Medical Qigong Clinics in China included the following:
- Diabetes
- Arthritis
- High-Blood Pressure
- Breast and Ovarian Cysts and Tumors,
- Brain Tumors and certain types of Cancer
- Migraine Headaches
- Fibromyalgia
- Insomnia
- Prostatitis
- Irritable Bowel Syndrome
- Muscle Atrophy
- Stroke
- Coma Retrieval

The Medical Qigong Therapy also focused on relieving pain, detoxifying the body of suppressed emotions (e.g., anger, fear, worry, etc.), correcting internal organ dysfunctions, and balancing excess or deficient Qi and Blood conditions.

MEDICAL QIGONG PHILOSOPHY

The ancient philosophical principles that underlie the medical teachings introduced to students at the International Institute of Medical Qigong, is simply living in harmony with the Dao (the Natural Way of the Universe) and following the Natural Laws of Heaven. We believe that through this simple yet profound teachings, we can support and inspire our students and patients to live in harmony with their True Nature, and utilize their talents to maintain balance within their lives.

In ancient China, practitioners of Medical Qigong first train to enhance their own life-force energy (Qi), and later learn to sense and directly influence the Qi of another person in order to bring about a state of health and vitality. Medical knowledge exists in order to alleviate the pains of humanity, whether physical, mental, emotional, or spiritual. While the I.I.M.Q.'s principle purpose is to enable students to obtain the academic and clinical knowledge to be a successful practitioner of Chinese Energetic Medicine, it does not stop there. The curriculum encourages the philosophy that through the healing of oneself, one can understand how to heal others. The emphasis is placed on the cultivation of one's True Self and the comprehension of human nature.

Medical Qigong Therapy consists of simultaneously treating and eventually harmonizing the patient's Three Bodies (i.e., the Physical Body, Energy Body, and Spirit Body). This is why the IIMQ classes also include special instruction that focuses on various Daoist Medical Neigong (Internal Skill), Qigong (Energy Skill), and Shengong (Spirit Skill) training.

Over the past two millennia, many doctors of Tradition Chinese Medicine, Daoist and Buddhist Monks and Priests, and Internal Martial Arts Masters have contributed to the expansion of Chinese Medical Qigong Therapy.

To the ancient Chinese, Medical Qigong Therapy is where the medical skills of treating patients and the energetic and spiritual intuitive skills of Shamanism united, creating a complete and balanced form of Energetic Medicine. For example, ancient Chinese Medical Qigong Therapy was originally divided into three levels of treatment, corresponding to the Qi of Heaven, the Qi of Earth, and the Qi of Man. Which of the various clinical methods and applications that were used to treat a patient depended on the healer's own personal internal cultivation and understanding of these energetic and spiritual principles.

In 1999, the International Institute of Medical Qigong Operated the Medical Qigong Clinic at the Five Branches T.C.M. College

Medical Qigong Doctors combine their energies in order to treat a cancer patients.

In the main treatment area, patients are categorized according to the severity of their condition.

Students at the Five Branches Medical Qigong Clinic in 1999

The 1999 Medical Qigong Courses at the Five Branches T.C.M. College

In the Spring of 1999, Professor Jerry Alan Johnson accepted the position of Dean of Medical Qigong Science and Director of the Medical Qigong Clinic from the Five Branches Institute, College and Clinic of Traditional Chinese Medicine, in Santa Cruz, California.

At that time, Professor Johnson established a 200 hour Medical Qigong Practitioner (M.Q.P.) certification program, and an ongoing Medical Qigong Clinic.

The Five Branches T.C.M. Medical Qigong Therapy program consisted of two years (i.e., 4-Semester) of 128 Academic Hours, plus an additional 72 hours of Clinical Internship.

MEDICAL QIGONG INSTRUCTION

1999 - MEDICAL QIGONG PRACTITIONER CLASSES TAUGHT AT THE FIVE BRANCHES T.C.M. COLLEGE IN SANTA CRUZ, CALIFORNIA

The Five Branches Institute:
College and Clinic of Traditional Chinese Medicine

Pictured from left to right are the Five Branches President and CEO Ron Zaidman, M.B.A., M.T.C.M.; the Academic Dean and Clinical Medical Director Dr. Joanna Zhao L.Ac., Dipl. Ac (NCCA), D.T.C.M. (China); and the Dean of Medical Qigong Science and Director of the Medical Qigong Clinic Professor Jerry Alan Johnson, Ph.D., D.T.C.M., D.M.Q. (China).

In addition to Clinical Applications and Prescription Exercises, the Five Branches Medical Qigong Students were also taught Energetic Psychology, and how to handle the Toxic Emotional Discharges released from their patients during treatment.

In 1999, during the First Semester, the Medical Qigong Students at the Five Branches Institute learned and experienced basic applications of Medical Qigong Purgation, Tonification and Regulation Exercises. They were also taught the underlying principles for each Medical Qigong Prescription Exercise and its Contraindications.

2003 Students at the Medical Qigong Clinic at the Academy For Five Element Acupuncture, in Hallandale, Florida

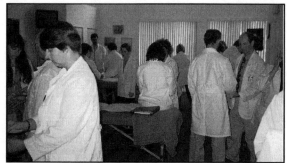

Preparing for another day at the clinic, the Five Element Medical Qigong students take time to share and support each other.

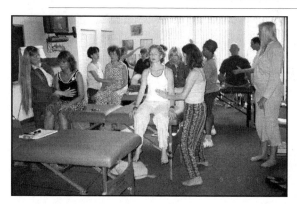
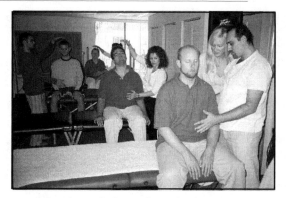

The Five Element Medical Qigong students take turns practicing the technique of treating hypertension.

The 2003 Medical Qigong Courses at the Five Element T.C.M. College

In May of 2003, Professor Jerry Alan Johnson accepted the position of Dean of Medical Qigong Science from The Academy For Five Element Acupuncture, in Hallandale, Florida.

At that time, Professor Johnson established four Medical Qigong Therapy programs at the Academy For Five Element Acupuncture. These programs included: A 200 hour Medical Qigong Practitioner (M.Q.P.) certification program; A 500 hour Medical Qigong Therapist (M.Q.T.) certification program; A 1000 hour Master of Medical Qigong (M.M.Q.) certification program; and an ongoing Medical Qigong Clinic.

MEDICAL QIGONG INSTRUCTION

2003 - MEDICAL QIGONG THERAPIST CLASSES WERE TAUGHT AT THE ACADEMY FOR FIVE ELEMENT ACUPUNCTURE, IN HALLANDALE, FLORIDA

The Academy For Five Element Acupuncture: College and Clinic of Classical Chinese Medicine

Pictured from left to right is the Dean of Medical Qigong Science and Director of the Medical Qigong Clinic Professor Jerry Alan Johnson, Ph.D., D.T.C.M. (China) and The Academy For Five Element Acupuncture C.E.O. and President Dorit Reznek, M.Ac., A.P.

In addition to clinical modalities and energetic prescriptions, the Academy For Five Element Acupuncture students are also taught energetic psychology and how to handle the toxic emotional discharges released from their patients.

During the first semester, the Medical Qigong students at the Academy For Five Element Acupuncture have learned and experienced basic applications of Medical Qigong purgation, tonification and regulation exercises. They are taught the underlying principles for each Prescription exercise and its contraindications.

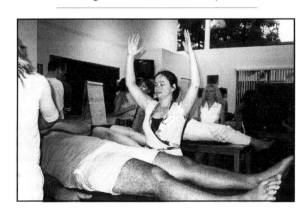

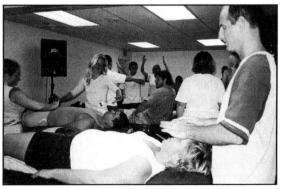

THE 2005 MEDICAL QIGONG COURSES AT THE HENAN T.C.M. UNIVERSITY

In August 2005, the Henan University of Traditional Chinese Medicine, in Zheng Zhou China appointed Professor Jerry Alan Johnson as the Overseas Director of Medical Qigong Therapy.

At that time the university invited Professor Johnson to join the facility as Professor of Medical Qigong Therapy, and he was issued an official Government Seal authorizing his post as Overseas Director. Historically, Professor Johnson was the first official representative of the Henan University of Traditional Chinese Medicine for the United States of America.

At that time, the Henan University recognized and supported the International Institute of Medical Qigong (I.I.M.Q.) as a "sister school" of the university, and adopted the I.I.M.Q.'s Medical Qigong Practitioner (M.Q.P.), Therapist (M.Q.T.), Master (M.M.Q.), and Doctorate (D.M.Q.) curriculum as part of the Universities Oversees Medical Qigong Therapy Academic and Clinical Program.

The Henan T.C.M. University operates three different hospitals for their medical interns (i.e., a hospital for Oncology, Neurology, and Pediatric Care). Therefore, at that time, Professor Johnson and his senior student Dr. Bernard Shannon also demonstrated for the doctors at the Henan University's Oncology Hospital several Medical Qigong clinical protocols used for treating cancer patients.

Additionally, at that time Professor Johnson presented his five volume textbook series entitled, *Chinese Medical Qigong Therapy: A Comprehensive Clinical Text*, to the Director of the Henan University's Medical Library.

After the signing of official government documents, Professor Johnson and Dr. Shannon of the I.I.M.Q. pause for a photo with the President of Academic Programs of the Henan University of T.C.M.

Professor Johnson is appointed to the position of Overseas Director of Medical Qigong Therapy for the United States, from the People's Republic of China's Ministry of Health and the Ministry of Education; this official document authorizes him to represent the Henan University of T.C.M. in the field of Medical Qigong Therapy and Clinical Application

MEDICAL QIGONG INSTRUCTION

(R) The Henan University of T.C.M. Official Logo
(L) The Official Seal of Professor Johnson
"Overseas Director of Medical Qigong Therapy;"
Authorized by the People's Republic of China's
Ministry of Health and the Ministry of Education

A Welcome Banner was displayed for Dr. Johnson, Dr. Shannon, and the International Institute of Medical Qigong, at the front of the Henan University's Administrative Entrance

Dr. Johnson presenting his five volume Medical Qigong Textbook series to the Director of the Henan University's Medical Library

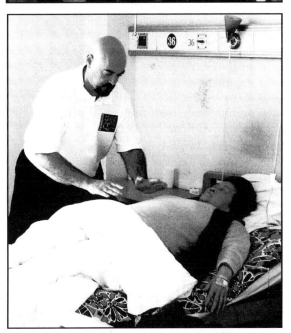

Dr. Johnson Demonstrating Medical Qigong techniques used for treating cancer patients at the Henan University's Oncology Hospital

INTERNATIONAL INSTITUTE OF MEDICAL QIGONG
OVERSEAS COLLEGE OF MEDICAL QIGONG,
HENAN UNIVERSITY OF TRADITIONAL CHINESE MEDICINE

DOCTOR OF MEDICAL QIGONG THERAPY
GRADUATE DIRECTORY

DOCTOR OF MEDICAL QIGONG THERAPY GRADUATING CLASSES

For the last 15 years, the Doctorate of Medical Qigong (DMQ) Certification Program has provided students with an opportunity to pursue advanced specialization in Medical Qigong Oncology. Students who completed this specialized clinical program received a diploma from the International Institute of Medical Qigong, the Overseas Medical Qigong College of the Henan University of Traditional Chinese Medicine, and from the Western District Medical Qigong Science and Traditional Chinese Medicine Research Institute in Beijing, China.

Students, who had prior training in Chinese Energetic Medicine and Acupuncture, and had previously received their Master of Traditional Chinese Medicine (M.T.C.M.) from a qualifying Acupuncture College, also received their clinical license from the People's Republic of China's Ministry of Health as Doctors of Traditional Chinese Medicine (D.T.C.M.).

THE MEDICAL QIGONG DOCTOR QUALIFICATIONS

In order to qualify as a Medical Qigong Doctor from the International Institute of Medical Qigong, each student had to complete a 2,000 hour program in Chinese Energetic Medicine. This special program includes the following studies:
- 936 hours of lecture, lab, and internship
- 72 hours of Supervised Clinical Theatre
- 818 hours of Clinical Externship
- 174 hours of Additional Course Related Material

All of which was based upon the academic and clinical curriculum established at the Medical Qigong College at the Hai Dian University in Beijing China, and supervised by Professor Jerry Alan Johnson, under the International Institute of Medical Qigong, the Overseas Medical Qigong College of the Henan University of Traditional Chinese Medicine.

The Emphasis placed on this ancient medical teaching focused on both the analytical/deductive and the intuitive approaches to comprehending and utilizing the body, energy, and mind for cultivation, regulation, and clinical application.

This unique training program in Chinese Energetic Medicine, included the study of:
- Chinese Energetic Anatomy and Physiology
- Energetic Embryological Development
- Introduction to Traditional Chinese Medicine Theory and Clinical Application
- The Pathologies of Tissue, Blood, Energy, and Spirit
- Introduction to Clinical Foundations & Formulating Treatment Plans
- Introduction to Medical Qigong Theory and Clinical Application
- The Pathologies of the Human Bodies Energetic Matrix
- Clinical Examination and Diagnosis
- Sensory, Intuitive, and Perceptual Diagnosis
- Self-Regulation Prescription Therapy
- Foundations of Chinese Medicine for Internal Diseases
- Energetic Diagnosis and Symptomatology
- Energetic Psychology
- Treatment of Internal Organ Diseases and Prescription Exercises

MEDICAL QIGONG INSTRUCTION

- Advanced Traditional Chinese Medicine Theory
- Differentiation of Psycho-Emotional Disorders
- Differential Diagnosis of Energetic Principles
- Qi Deviations and Dao Yin Therapy
- Distance Qi Emission Therapy
- Herbal Medicine
- Five Element Massage Therapy
- Qigong Massage Therapy
- Acupressure Point Therapy
- Cupping and Moxa Therapy
- Sound, Light, and Mineral Therapy
- Medical Qigong Therapy for Pediatrics, Geriatrics, Gynecology, and Neurology
- Clinical Oncology #1
- Clinical Oncology #2
- Clinical Oncology and Herbal Therapy
- Western Anatomy and Physiology
- Western Internal Diseases
- Pharmaceutical Terminology
- Plus – A Doctoral Thesis based on the students extensive Clinical Experience.

The following is a list of students who have fulfilled all academic and clinical requirements, and have received special certification as a Doctor of Medical Qigong Therapy (D.M.Q.) from the International Institute of Medical Qigong:

1997 DMQ Graduating Class
Dr. Seth Lefkowitz, DC, DMQ
Dr. Arnold E. Tayam, DMQ

2003 DMQ Graduating Class
Dr. Lois Brunner, MS, DMQ
Dr. Janette Lillian Carver, DMQ
Dr. Ted J. Cibik, ND, DMQ
Dr. Dennis Martin Earnest, DMQ
Dr. Gideon Enz, DMQ
Dr. L. Francesca Ferrari, L.Ac., M.T.C.M., DMQ
Dr. Suzanne B. Friedman, L.Ac., M.T.C.M., DMQ
Dr. Louis B. Frizzell, DMQ
Dr. Thomas Katsabekis, DMQ
Dr. Michelle Ann Katsabekis, DMQ
Dr. Elizabeth M. Marcum, MA, DMQ
Dr. Deneen C. Seril, DMQ
Dr. Eric W. Shaffer, BA, DMQ

After a full day at the clinic, the 2003 Doctor of Medical Qigong Graduating Class pauses to take a photo

2004 DMQ Graduating Class
Dr. Bernard Shannon, DMQ
Dr. Jade Goldstein Stewart, DMQ
Dr. Lisa Van Ostrand, DMQ

2006 DMQ Graduating Class
Dr. Dennis Alexander, DMQ, PhD
Dr. Harry Haryanto, DMQ
Dr. Thomas Leichardt, DMQ
Dr. Keyes Lloyd, DMQ
Dr. Kelly Loos, DMQ
Dr. Margaret McDonald, DMQ
Dr. Krista Merrimac, DMQ
Dr. Veronica Ramirez, DMQ
Dr. Jennifer Talyor, DMQ
Dr. Mary Wallis, DMQ

2009 DMQ Graduating Class
Dr. Michael M Ackerman, DMQ
Dr. Fern Alexander, DMQ
Dr. Isaac Goren, DMQ
Dr. Jo McCauley, DMQ

2012 DMQ Graduating Class
Dr. Hannibal Abera, DMQ
Dr. Pat Bardone, DMQ
Dr. Francis Bottone, DMQ
Dr. Barbara Branaman, DMQ
Dr. Tyler Cole, DMQ
Dr. Matthew W Cook, M.D., DMQ

Students of 2012 Medical Qigong Doctor Program prepare for Clinical Exams
At the International Institute of Medical Qigong in Monterey, California

Dr. John DeAnzo II, DMQ
Dr. Daniel Devine, DMQ
Dr. Amba Ann Dryg, DMQ
Dr. Julie Endsburg, DMQ
Dr. Marcy Estudillo, DMQ
Dr. Harris Frank, DMQ
Dr. Mara Frank, DMQ
Dr. Doug Gallant, DMQ
Dr. Sean Lee Gardner, DMQ
Dr. Phil Garrison, DMQ
Dr. Sri Srikanth Gopalaswami, DMQ
Dr. David Haro, DMQ
Dr. Chris Holder, DMQ
Dr. Justin Howell, DMQ
Dr. Danny Hull, DMQ
Dr. Zen Heijin Hwang, DMQ
Dr. Erika Rosa Johnson, DMQ
Dr. Bob Joyce, DMQ
Dr. Kelly Lake, DMQ
Dr. Chad Lanphear, DMQ
Dr. Kristen Lansdale , DMQ
Dr. Chad Laughlin, DMQ
Dr. Genady Leyfman, DMQ
Dr. Keyes Lloyd, DMQ

Dr. Ariel Ma'ayan, DMQ
Dr. Mairam Mansy, DMQ
Dr. Laura Johnson McCreary, DMQ
Dr. Marty Morgenrath, DMQ
Dr. Eve Yvette Payan, DMQ
Dr. Word Ramirez, DMQ
Dr. Victor Bowman Rivera, DMQ
Dr. Chunīyo Yvonne Rodriguez, DMQ
Dr. Sundar Tomas Sanchez, DMQ
Dr. Christine Sanmiquel, DMQ
Dr. Diego Sanmiquel, DMQ
Dr. Rodney Sasaki, DMQ
Dr. Vladi Starkov, DMQ
Dr. Chrissy Suits, DMQ
Dr. Dawn Sullivan, DMQ
Dr. Michael Sweeney, DMQ
Dr. Takashi Tamasu, DMQ
Dr. Natalie Trees, DMQ
Dr. Lishanna Tryllium, DMQ
Dr. Daniele Uzes, DMQ
Dr. Mary VanTran, DMQ
Dr. William Welch Jr., DMQ
Dr. Billy Weltch, DMQ

INTERNATIONAL INSTITUTE OF MEDICAL QIGONG
OVERSEAS COLLEGE OF MEDICAL QIGONG,
HENAN UNIVERSITY OF TRADITIONAL CHINESE MEDICINE

MASTER OF MEDICAL QIGONG THERAPY GRADUATE DIRECTORY

MASTER OF MEDICAL QIGONG THERAPY GRADUATING CLASSES

The following is a list of students who have fulfilled all academic and clinical requirements, and have received special certification as a Master of Medical Qigong Therapy (M.M.Q.) from the International Institute of Medical Qigong:

1997 MMQ GRADUATING CLASS
Shannon K. Brown, M.M.Q.
Anne Elderfield, M.M.Q.
Pamela Lee Espinoza, N.C.T.M.B., M.M.Q.
Carole Marie Kelly, Ed.D., M.M.Q.
Dr. Seth Lefkowitz, D.C., M.M.Q.
Shifu Arnold E. Tayam, C.M.T., M.M.Q.
Dr. Stephanie Taylor, M.D., Ph.D., M.M.Q.

1999 MMQ GRADUATING CLASS
William H. De Groat, M.M.Q.
Diane De Terra, Ph.D., M.M.Q.
Dennis M. Earnest, M.M.Q.
Brooks M. Fiske, C.P.A., M.M.Q.
Michael J. Finch, M.M.Q.
Madeleine H. Howell, M.F.T., M.M.Q.
William H. Lewington, B.Sc., P.H.M., L.Ac., M.M.Q.
Paul E. Miller, M.M.Q.
Katy Reed, M.M.Q.
Shifu Matthew B. Weston, M.M.Q.
Jean R. Vlamynck, L.Ac., M.T.C.M., M.M.Q.

2000 MMQ GRADUATING CLASS
Adam Atman, L.Ac., M.T.C.M., M.M.Q.
Louis Frizzell, C.P.A., M.M.Q.
Shifu Todd Mathew Gedryn, M.M.Q.
Geoffrey Greenspahn, M.M.Q.
Layth Hakim, M.M.Q.
Luc Arnauld Logan, M.M.Q.
Maria Pepe, L.Ac., M.T.C.M., M.M.Q.
Rose Mary Stewart, M.M.Q.
Amos Ziv, L.Ac., M.T.C.M., M.M.Q.

After a full day at the clinic, some of the Medical Qigong Doctors of the 2001 Graduating Class relax and share encouraging experiences.

2001 MMQ GRADUATING CLASS
Sue Angulo, M.M.Q.
Eddie L. Bates, M.M.Q.
Robert B. Bates, D.C., M.M.Q.
Robert C. Bawol, M.A., N.M.S.U., M.A., M.M.Q.
Shifu Reginald Cann, L.Ac., M.T.O.M., M.M.Q.
Janette L. Carver, C.M.T., M.M.Q.
Ted J. Cibik, N.D., M.M.Q.
Francesca Ferrari, L.Ac., M.T.C.M., M.M.Q.
Emma Deepa Gleason, R.N., L.Ac., Dipl.Ac., M.T.C.M., M.M.Q.
Robert C. Grant, M.M.Q.
Robert W. Haberkorn, D.C., M.M.Q.
Carla Hughett, L.Ac., M.T.C.M., M.M.Q.
Harvey D. Jennell, M.M.Q.
Wendy A. Lang, M.M.Q.
Dia Lynn, B.A., L.M.T., M.M.Q.
Elizabeth M. Marcum, M.Ed., M.M.Q.
Celestine McMahan, Ph.D., M.M.Q.
Mark L. Rappaport, M.M.Q.
Ryan M. Rrusuelas, M.M.Q.
Deneen C. Seril, M.M.Q.
Joyce Thom, MMQ

2002 MMQ Graduating Class
Jeff Tukum Barnard, E.M.T., M.M.Q.
Donna Bell, R.N., M.M.Q.
Mitchell Blank, D.C., M.M.Q.
Alan C. Fischer, L.Ac., M.T.C.M., M.M.Q.
Suzanne B. Friedman, L.Ac., M.T.C.M., M.M.Q.
Myrt Hawkins, M.D., M.M.Q.
Ann-Sofie Gustavsson Hobbs, M.M.Q.
Leah Ann Johnson, M.M.Q.
Nora Kim, M.M.Q.
Kelly Loos, M.M.Q.
Stuart Loyd, M.M.Q.
Ti Pence, M.M.Q.
Judy Pruzinsky, L.Ac., M.T.C.M., M.M.Q.
Ijaz Rasool, B.Sc., M.Sc., M.M.Q.
Eric W. Shaffer, M.M.Q.
Shifu Bernard Shannon, M.M.Q.
Joyce Thom, M.M.Q.
Camille Vardy, L.Ac., M.T.C.M., M.M.Q.
Nadezhda Zoe Wein, C.M.T., M.M.Q.
Gary S. Weinstein, M.D., M.M.Q.
Catherine Zimmerman, D.C., M.M.Q.

2003 MMQ Graduating Class
Lois Brunner, M.M.Q.
Joy Li Duremdes, BA, M.M.Q.
Gideon B. Enz, M.M.Q.
Calvin Fahey, M.M.Q.
Anna Belle Fore, M.M.Q.
Bradley M. Gilbert, B.A., M.M.Q.
Harry Asoka Haryanto, M.S.C., M.M.Q.
Mark Frederick Herro, M.M.Q.
Michele Ann Katsabekis, M.M.Q.
Thomas Katsabekis, M.M.Q.
Rana C. A. De Keczer, O.T.R./L, L.C.M.T., A.A.M.T., M.M.Q.
Tomas C. Leichardt, N.C.B.T.M.B., M.M.Q.
Francesca Marie O'Dona, B.S., M.M.Q.
Dermot A. O'Connor, Dip. Ac., M.M.Q.
Lisa Van Ostrand, M.M.Q.
Keiko Pence, M.M.Q.
Paul Pheasey, B.A., M.M.Q.
Lucy M. Roberts, L.Ac., M.T.C.M., M.M.Q.
James Bryant Seals, Jr., M.S., M.M.Q.
Jade Goldstein Stewart, M.M.Q.
J. Michael Wood, PBMC, OBDS, M.M.Q.

2004 MMQ Graduating Class
Stephen Armstrong, M.M.Q.
V. Daniel Azcarate, M.M.Q.
Caroline Deery, M.M.Q.
Denise Douglass-White, M.M.Q.
Eddie Dowd, M.M.Q.
Jan Eeckhout, D.O., Dipl.Ac., M.T.C.M., M.M.Q.
Jose E. Gonzalez, M.M.Q.
Allison L. Harter, M.M.Q.
Cathriona Hillery, Lic. Ac., Dipl.Ac., M.M.Q.
Matthew Jones, M.M.Q.
Brian McKenna, D.O.M., Lic. Ac., M.M.Q.
Stephen McNamee, Lic. Ac., Dipl.Tuina, M.M.Q.
Paula S. Medler, D.V.M., M.M.Q.
Ted O'Brian, L.Ac., M.M.Q.
Edwin T. Pickett, Jr., M.M.Q.
Rodney G. Sasaki, M.M.Q.
Stephen D. Steidle, M.M.Q.
Sara R. Storm, L.Ac., M.M.Q
Allen Wentland, M.M.Q.
Catherine A. White, M.M.Q.
Vic Wouters, Dipl.Ac., Tuina, M.T.C.M., M.M.Q.
Myles Wray, Lic. Ac., Dipl.Ac. & Tuina, M.M.Q.

2005 MMQ Graduating Class
Maryann Allison, M.M.Q.
Christopher Michael Axelrad, L.Ac., M.M.Q.
Dr. Mona A. Boudreaux, M.M.Q.
Joseph V. Bozzelli, MMQ
Lou Eberle, M.S.O.M., M.M.Q.
Maria Sal Eberle, M.M.Q.
Layth Hakim, M.M.Q.
Matthew Hayat, Ph.D., MMQ
Mollie Kelleher, M.M.Q.
Rebecca Pope, PhD, MMQ
Zhanneta Raskin, M.M.Q.
Gregory D. Sparkman, M.M.Q.
Sifu William L. Welch Jr., M.M.Q.
Douglas K. Womack, J.D., M.M.Q.
Robert Youngs, R.M.T., Ac., M.M.Q.

2006 MMQ Graduating Class
Leah Anderson, MMQ
Mariano Ardissone, R.Y.T.,M.M.Q.
Victoria Cannon, M.M.Q.
Hila Davidson, B.Ed., M.M.Q.
Joanne Epstein, M.Ac. A.P., M.M.Q.

Jason H. Gordon, M.Ac., L.M.T., M.M.Q.
Isaac Goren, M.Ac., M.M.Q.
M. Lourdes Gonzalez, M.Ac., L.Ac., M.M.Q.
Rachel Hebden Harrison, M.Ac., L.Ac., M.M.Q.
David Herman, L.Ac., M.M.Q.
Susan T. Kropff, M.Ac., L.M.T., M.M.Q.
Jo McCauley, B.S.N., R.N., M.Ac., L.Ac., M.M.Q.
Dawn Eileen Meltzer, M.Ac., L.Ac., M.M.Q.
Dava Joyce Michelson, M.Ac., L.M.T., M.M.Q.
Christina J. Romo, M.M.Q.
Teresa Saragga, M.M.Q.
Sherwood S. Swartz, A.P., D.O.M., M.M.Q.

2007 MMQ Graduating Class
Dr. Fern Alexander, MMQ
Dr. Terri Audino Dluhy, MMQ
Shifu Charles Ganzon, MMQ

2008 MMQ Graduating Class
Dr. Marie Conrad, PhD, MMQ

2010 MMQ Graduating Class
Laara Jansen, MMQ
Bonnie Jang, MMQ
Michael Lines, MMQ
Noel Taylor, MMQ
Aum Song Troughton, MMQ
Rommy Verlaan, MMQ
Arlene Wilkinson, MMQ

2011 MMQ Graduating Class
Thomas Dicklin, L.Ac., MMQ
Christian "Fa Jun" Real MMQ

Glossary of Terms

A

Abdominal Breathing - to breathe from the abdomen (expand with inhalation, contract with exhalation).

Acupuncture - one of the Four branches of Traditional Chinese Medicine, which involves treating patients through the use of needling, cupping, Bloodletting, moxa and magnets in order to stimulate energy flow.

Acupuncturist - a doctor of acupuncture therapy.

Acquired Essence - also called Postnatal Jing, is acquired energetic tissue substance, developed after birth.

Acquired Force - energy pertaining to the earth and surrounding environment.

Acquired Qi - also called Postnatal Qi, is the body's energy derived from food, air and drink, acquired after birth.

Acquired Rational Mind - also called Postnatal Mind, are thoughts and feelings derived from the acquired experiences of one's environment.

Acute - a rapid onset and short duration of a particular condition.

Adenoma - a neoplasm (abnormal formation of tissue) of glandular epithelium.

Adenocarcinoma - a malignant tumor arising from a glandular organ.

Affirmation - a word, phrase or sentence that is repeated frequently to influence, or change, a belief held deeply within the unconscious mind.

Agoraphobia - fear of places or situations from which escape might be difficult or embarrassing. Symptoms include panic like symptoms and a precondition towards panic attacks.

Akashic Records - a Sanskrit term used to describe the detailed knowledge of all the historical events of the world recorded within the "all-pervasive space of the universe" or "Wuji," also called the "knowledge of the infinite Void."

Alchemy - internal transformation of body and energy brought about by: Nei Dan (inner alchemy) through internal Qigong training, and Wai Dan (external alchemy) using herbal formulas.

Amenorrhea - the absence or suppression of menstruation.

Ancestral Channel - a term used to describe one of the Eight Extraordinary Vessels.

Ancestral Qi - energy inherited from both parents at the time of conception, responsible for innate talents and skills.

Ancestral Traits - pertaining to the ancestral spiritual influence which affects the patient's body. Ancestral traits are developed according to the geographic location at the time of conception.

Anemia - a reduction in the number of circulating red Blood cells.

Angina Pectoris - severe pain and a sensation of constriction about the Heart.

An Jing - see Hidden Power.

Ankylosing Spondylitis - inflammation of the vertebrae, giving rise to stiffness of the back and neck.

An Mo Therapy - a tissue manipulation therapy that focuses primarily on the treatment of internal organ disorders.

Anorexia - loss of appetite.

An Sound Resonation - hidden or inaudible sound resonation.

Antibody - any of the numerous proteins produced by the immune system that defend against antigens.

Anxiety - emotional distress, resulting in Heart palpitations, inability to concentrate, muscle tension causing muscle aches.

Aphasia - the absence or impairment of the ability to communicate through speech, writing, or signs, due to a dysfunction within the Brain center.

Aplastic Anemia - anemia caused by deficient red cell production, due to Bone marrow disorders.

Apoptosis - the disintegration of cells into membrane-bound particles that are then phagocytosed by other cells.

Archetypes - a term coined by the psychiatrist Carl G. Jung to describe the collective unconscious images and motifs (e.g., warrior, healer, priest, etc.). An inherited idea or mode of thought derived from the experiences of the race which is present in the unconscious of the individual.

Arrhythmia - an irregularity or loss of rhythm pertaining to the Heart.

Arteriosclerosis - term pertaining to a number of pathological conditions in which there is a thickening, hardening, and loss of elasticity of the artery walls.

Arthralgia - pain in the joints.

Arthritis - pain and inflammation of the joints, followed by progressive stiffness.

Arthropathy - pertaining to any joint disease.

Ascariasis - infestation of ascaris lumbicoides parasite (pinworm).

Ascending Qi - the action and flow of energy moving upward.

Ashi Points - also called "Trigger Points" are places on the body which are tender spots or painful areas near diseased or injured tissue.

Asthma - a disease caused by increased responsiveness of the tracheobronchial tree within the Lungs, due to various stimuli, causing severe difficulty in breathing.

Astral Body - also called the soul body, describes the energetic vehicle in which the eternal soul can journey outside of the physical body. The astral body is connected to the Middle Dantian by a silver "cord of life."

Astral Matter - the energetic substance located within the second field of the body's external Wei Qi and attributed to the emotional energy body.

Astral Plane - an energetic and spiritual plane of existence parallel to the physical plane.

Astral Travel - also called soul travel (or astral projection) describes the condition of the eternal soul journeying outside of the physical body, connected to the Middle Dantian by a silver "cord of life."

Astringent - any substance or agent that causes tissues to contract or that inhibits secretion of Body Fluids such as mucus or Blood.

Antigens - any substance able to provoke an immune response in the human body.

Atelectasis - pulmonary collapse.

Atrophic - pertaining to atrophy.

Atrophy Syndrome - a disorder characterized by flaccidity and weakness of the limbs and a progressive loss of strength and muscle tone.

Attention Deficit Disorder - a learning disorder manifesting through the following symptoms: habitual failure to pay attention, easily distractible, inability to organize, extreme impulsiveness, difficulty in studying, often accompanied by hyperactivity.

Aura - the energetic field which radiates light and circulates around the second field of the body's external Wei Qi

Aura Colors - the body's energetic luminous colors ranging from red, orange, yellow, green, blue, violet to white.

Auspicious Powers - the energy potential contained within the Five Yin Organs.

B

Ba Gan - eight diagnostic principles used in Traditional Chinese Medicine in order to differentiate symptoms.

Bai Dai - leukorrhea or white vaginal discharge.

Baihui Point (One Hundred Meetings) - the Governing Vessel point at the top of the head (GV-20).

Bellows Palm Technique - a palm technique in which the thumb and little finger compress and release like a bellows.

Bells Palsy - unilateral facial paralysis of sudden onset.

Benign - gentle or kindly, not aggressive, the opposite of malignant.

Bile - a secretion stored in the gall bladder released into the duodenum as a digestive juice.

Bio-Rhythm - three distinct cycles and energy flow that pertain to the body's physical, emotional and intellectual rhythms.

Bipolar Personality Disorder - formerly known as manic depressive personality disorder, a state of extreme euphoria or pervasive irritability, with racing thoughts, inability to sleep, and impulsive behavior (that may last for days or months), that alternate with morbid depression with suicidal ideation or attempts at suicide (see depression). During the manic phase there may be hallucinations.

Bird's Bridge - pertaining to the energetic connection between the tongue and the upper "hard" palate, behind the teeth.

Birth Energetic Patterns - pertaining to the energetic patterns developed according to the influence of the time and geographic location of the patient's birth.

Blended Originals (Hun Yuan) - the body's "internal combined energy" fused into the Lower Dantian area.

Bloated and Expanded Stagnation - stagnation with a characteristically expansive or bloated appearance, can be caused from an accumulation of phlegm and Body Fluids (in addition to Qi and Blood) in the adjacent tissue areas of the body.

Blood (Xue) - the dense fluid which nourishes the body, transmits Qi, and provides the material for the mind and emotions.

Blood Heat - a condition categorized by Heat and Blood signs (retching of Blood, expectoration of Blood, Bloody stool or urine, nosebleeds, and menstrual irregularities).

Bloodletting - a technique used in acupuncture therapy which entails pricking the skin to release and remove Blood Heat and Blood stagnation.

Blood Stagnation - the impairment or cessation of normal Blood flow.

Blood Stasis - the impairment or cessation of normal Blood flow.

Blood Vessels - the body's transportation system for Qi and Blood nutrition and regeneration. The Blood Vessels are one of the Eight Extraordinary Organs, its function is to moisten the body's tissues.

Body Fluids (Ye) - these are clear, light, and watery. They originate from food and drink and are transformed and separated by the Spleen (aided by the Kidneys) and dispersed by the Lungs and Triple Burners. (i.e., perspiration, tears, saliva, and mucus.)

Body Liquids (Jin)- these are a heavier, denser form of Body Fluids, compared to the Body Fluids (Ye). Their function is to nourish the joints, spine, Brain, and Bone marrow. They lubricate the orifices of the sensory organs.

Bone - the body's skeletal material related in essence to the Kidneys. The Bones are one of the Eight Extraordinary Organs, its function is to store the body's Marrow.

Bone Marrow - sustains and nurtures the Bones, composed of Kidney Jing (Essence) and Marrow. The Marrow is one of the Eight Extraordinary Organs.

Book of Commentaries - consisting of ten commentaries from Confucius and his disciples, pertaining to the study of the eight Trigrams, sixty-four hexagrams, and the Yi-Jing.

Book of Oracles - written by King Wen and the Duke of Zhou, pertaining to the study of the eight Trigrams, sixty-four hexagrams, and the Yi-Jing.

Borborygmus - a gurgling, rumbling sound heard over the Large Intestine, caused by the passing of gas through the liquid contents of the intestines.

Borderline Personality Disorder - a psychological disorder characterized by a pervasive pattern of intense, unstable relationships, and an unstable self-image. Such patients suffer from chronic feelings of emptiness stemming from abandonment issues. They exhibit self-destructive behavior and transient paranoia, or dissociative symptoms.

Brain - pertaining to the Sea of Marrow issuing from the Kidneys that collects within the cranium. The Brain is one of the Eight Extraordinary Organs.

Brain Tumor Point - Shihmien Point located on the heel of each foot.

Bronchial Asthma - asthma caused by a hypersensitivity to an allergen.

Bronchiectasis - chronic dilatation of a bronchus or bronchi, with a secondary infection (usually involving the lower portion of the Lungs).

Bronchitis - inflammation of mucous membrane of the bronchial tubes.

C

Caduceus - medical insignia picturing double snakes wrapping a winged staff.

Calculi - the plural of calculus or stones, usually composed of mineral salts.

Cancer (Carcinoma) - an obstruction of Qi and Blood circulation resulting in stagnation and the formation of a malignant tumor that tends to spread.

Carbuncle - a circumscribed inflammation of the skin and deeper tissues.

Carcinogens - any substance or agent that produces or increases the risk of developing cancer.

Carcinoma (Cancer or Tumor) - a malignant growth or tumor that occurs in the epithelial tissue (the outer surface or first layer of tissue that lines the body's cavities, as well as the principal tubes and passageways leading to the exterior of the body)

Catatonic - totally withdrawn, almost unconscious, frozen and unable to move.

Celestial Stems - see Ten Celestial Stems.

Center Core - pertaining to either the core of light within the Taiji Pole which joins the body's three Dantians through the center of the body, or the True Self (the essence of a person's spirit).

Cerebral Embolism - a condition which occurs when an embolus (bubble of air, or piece of a thrombus) detaches from a thrombus and obstructs a cerebral artery.

Cerebral Hemorrhage - bleeding caused from a rupture of a sclerosed or diseased vessel in the Brain.

Cerebral Thrombosis - an obstruction of a cerebral artery by a thrombus (Blood clot).

Cerebro-Vascular Accident (CVA) - in the clinic, conditions referred to as stroke (or Wind-stroke) include cerebral hemorrhage, cerebral thrombosis, cerebral embolism, and cerebrovascular spasm. These four conditions are termed in Western Medicine as "Cerebro-Vascular Accident."

Cervical Spondylosis - a degenerative arthritis (osteoarthritis) of the cervical vertebrae and related tissues.

Chakra - an energetic vortex, spiraling out from the body's center Taiji Pole, and extending through the external field of Wei Qi.

Chakra Gates - the twelve major energy gates located on the center line of the anterior and posterior aspects of the body, as well as at the lower perineum and the top of the head.

Chakra System - the seven major Chakra or energy centers that connect to the Taiji Pole. Five Chakras extend to the front and back of the torso, with one located at the top of the head and the other located on the perineum.

Channels - the body's energetic rivers responsible for transporting Qi, also called "meridians."

Channel Points - areas or points (similar to small pools of Qi) found along the streams of a Channel, through which energy of the Yin and Yang (Zang/Fu) organs and channels are transported internally and externally.

Channel Qi - pertaining to the Qi found within the energetic flow of a channel.

Cholangioles - pertaining to small terminal portions of the bile duct.

Charts of the Hall of Light - ancient diagram depicting the body's internal organs and channels.

Chemotherapy - the application of chemical agents that have a specific and toxic effect upon the disease-causing microorganism, as well as the patient's tissues, energetic fields and immune system.

Chicken Pecking Palm Technique - a palm technique wherein the doctor's hand resembles the head of a chicken while manipulating the energy flow of the Invisible Needle.

Chi Dai - red vaginal discharge.

Child Element - pertaining to the Five Element Creative Cycle of Traditional Chinese Medical, the primary organ is considered the Mother and its sequential organ is considered the Child.

Chinese Massage - one of the four branches of Traditional Chinese Medicine, which involves treating patients through the use of tissue manipulation, including Jie Gu Therapy for Bone disorders, Tui Na Therapy for muscle disorders, Gua Sha Therapy for febrile diseases and Blood Stagnation, An Mo therapy for internal organ disorders, and Jing Point Therapy for channel and internal organ regulation.

Cholecystitis - inflammation of the Gall Bladder.

Cholelithiasis - formation of calcium, i.e., bile stones in the Gall Bladder.

Cholestasis - an infection of the biliary tract.

Chronic - the long duration of a specific disease or condition, showing slow or little improvement.

Chronic Fatigue Syndrome - debilitating fatigue that is not the result of physical or mental exertion, and is not relieved by resting.

Chrono-biology - the science that deals with the study of the body's biological clocks and fluctuations in accordance with the cycles of the sun, moon and nature's rhythms.

Chyluria - the passing of fat globules in the urine.

Circle of Willis - the union of the anterior and posterior cerebral arteries, forming an anastomosis at the base of the Brain.

Circulating Energy Technique - this method refers to rotating Qi in a circular pattern (clockwise or counterclockwise) to move Qi and Blood stagnation, or to gather energy for tonification.

Cirrhosis - Cirrhosis is a generalized Liver disease marked by hepatic lesions, characterized by the formation of dense lobular connective tissue, degenerative changes in the parenchymal cells, structural alterations in the Liver lobules, and sometimes fatty and cellular infiltration within the Liver.

Clairaudience - the ability to hear sounds, music, and voices not audible to normal hearing (for example, receiving Messages and/or inspirations from the divine).

Clairasentience - the ability to perceive smells, taste, touch, emotions and physical sensations that contribute to an overall psychic and intuitive impression.

Clairvoyance - the ability to perceive current objects, events and/or people that may not be discerned through the body's normal senses. Both time and space are perceived on a clairvoyant spiritual dimension.

Clean Qi - Energy which has been purified.

Clinical Ethics - the moral principles and standards governing the doctor's conduct with patients in or away from the clinic.

Coccyx Pass (Wei Lu Guan) - is located on the lowest segment of the spine just posterior to the anus, near the Chang Qiang (GV-1) point.

Colitis - the inflammation of the colon.

Cold - one of the Six Evils

Cold Constitution - pertaining to a physical body innately prone towards coldness.

Collapsed Qi - this is considered a subcategory of Deficient Qi, and is regarded as the third and most severe type of Deficiency.

Collaterals (Luo) - the body's energetic streams that branch off the Twelve Primary Channels and the Conceptional and Governing Vessels.

Collective Unconsciousness - concept of psychiatrist Carl G. Jung pertaining to the memories of mental patterns that are experienced and shared by all mankind.

Coma - an abnormal deep state of unconsciousness with some possible awareness of surroundings, but a total inability to communicate with the outside environment. Comas result from a Qi obstruction to the Brain caused by illness or injury.

Common People's Fire - pertaining to the generated Heat originating from the Urinary Bladder Fire, located in the perineal area of the body.

Compressed Stagnation - a type of stagnation caused by the patient's energy contracting (externally moving inward); Compressed Stagnation feels energetically armored and hollow.

Conception Vessel - one of the Eight Extraordinary Vessels, also known as the "Sea of Yin"

Concentrative Meditation - keeping the mind focused and under control.

Congealed - when Qi and/or Blood become thick and solid within the body's tissues, energetic fields, or both.

Congenital Qi (Prenatal Qi) - energy existing before the fetus is born, acquired from the mother's, father's energies, as well as from the environmental and universal energies. It is sustained through prayer, meditation and sleep.

Conscious Mind - acquired mental reasoning, created through learning via the five senses and interactions with other people.

Constipation - difficulty or infrequent defecation, with the passage of unduly hard and dry fecal material.

Constitutions - see Five Elemental Constitutions.

Contracted Stagnation - stagnation caused by the patient's energy pulling inward, feels armored and solid.

Contraindications - any symptom or circumstance indicating the inappropriateness of a form of treatment that would be otherwise advisable.

Controlling Cycle - pertaining to the Five Element Cycle, where one elemental organ controls the second elemental organ in the Five Elements' Circle.

Corporeal Soul - associated with the Lungs, see Po.

Coryza - the inflammation of the respiratory mucous membranes.

Cosmology - the study of the universe.

Countertransference - this is the process whereby a doctor loses objectivity and unconsciously projects feelings, thoughts, beliefs and patterns of behavior onto the patient.

Couple Point - the Master Point's secondary point of connection affecting the Eight Extraordinary Vessels.

Cranio-Sacral Rhythm - Western term given to the fluctuating rhythm of the Sea of Marrow flowing from the Kidneys.

Creative Cycle - pertaining to the Five Element Cycle, where one organ creates the energy for the next.

Creative Subconscious Mind - the part of the mind that maintains the patient's reality by making him or her act like the person they believe themselves to be.

Creative Visualization - the process of using visualization as a tool for transforming energy and spirit.

Crown Center - the name given to the Baihui Point (GV-20) and Upper Chakra Gate, at the top of the head.

Crystal Palace - the energetic field of Qi located within the third ventricle of the Brain.

Cupping - a technique used in acupuncture therapy in which wooden, clay, or glass cups adhere to the patient's skin by suction, to drain or remove pathogenic Qi from the body's pores.

Curious Organs - the body's Six Extraordinary Yang Organs which function like Yin Organs as they store Yin Essence (i.e., Blood, Marrow, or Kidney Essence), but look like Yang Organs (because they are hollow). These organs consist of the Uterus, Brain, Marrow, Bones, Blood Vessels and Gall Bladder.

Cycle of Disharmony - an emotional state which induces a vicious cycle of physical, mental, emotional, energetic and spiritual disharmony.

Cyst - a closed sac that forms in tissue or a body cavity.

Cystitis - inflammation of the Urinary Bladder, usually occurring secondary to ascending urinary tract infection.

Cytotoxic Treatments - treatment containing toxins which attack the cells of the body (for example: radiation, chemotherapy and toxic herbs).

D

Dacryorrhea - excess tear flow.

Damp - a internal pathogenic condition relating to the storage of Damp or Wet toxins; Damp is one of the Six Evils; long-term Dampness may lead to Phlegm.

Dantians - the body's three main energetic pools, or reservoirs of Qi located in the head, chest and lower abdominal areas.

Dantian Regulation - the principle of balancing the energy governing the body's Three Dantians.

Dao - pertaining to God or divine consciousness.

Daoist - a student of the "Dao" or way of life, pertaining to living in harmony with the universe and environment.

Dao Yin - energy regulation exercises consisting of training the body, mind, and breath.

De - pertaining to an individual's personal Virtue.

Defence Mechanisms - see Ego Defence Mechanisms.

Deficiency (Xu) - a condition relating to the inadequate degree of a particular substance, e.g., Qi, Blood, Yin, Yang, Heat, etc.

Delusions - refers to the occurrence of a mental derangement in the patient resulting in a false belief based on incorrect inference about external reality. Regardless of the evidence to the contrary, the belief is strongly maintained.

Demon or Spirit Oppression - the condition of having a foreign spirit attach to a patient's external Wei Qi field, resulting in emotional disharmony.

Demon or Spirit Possession - the condition of having a foreign spirit invade and inhabit the patient's body, mind, emotion, and spirit.

Denial - a conscious refusal of an impulse-evoking fact, feeling or memory.

Depersonalization Disorder - persistent, recurring episodes of depersonalization, characterized by a feeling of detachment, or estrangement from one's self.

Depression (Major) - a psychological disorder resulting in major sadness and pessimism, feelings of worthlessness, helplessness and hopelessness. Symptoms include overeating or under-eating, insomnia or hyper-insomnia, difficulty concentrating, and fatigue. In Traditional Chinese Medicine, depression often emanates from Liver Qi Stagnation.

Descending - the action of energy moving downward.

Diabetes - a general term used to describe diseases characterized by excessive urination and a sugar imbalance in the Blood.

Diaphoresis - profuse sweating.

Diastolic - the resting phase of the Heart.

Diathermy - the therapeutic use of a high-frequency current to generate Heat within a certain area of the body.

Di Qi - Earth (Environmental) Energy.

Disharmony - pertaining to a lack of adequate balance of energy.

Disorder - an abnormal state of physical, mental, emotional, energetic or spiritual disharmony.

Dispersing - the spreading of Qi to other parts of the body, or purging of pathogenic energy from the body.

Displacement - the shifting of impulses aroused by one person, or situation to a safe target.

Dissociated Identity Disorder - new terminology used for multiple personality disorder.

Distance Therapy - also called External Qi Therapy, Qi Emission and Outgoing Qi Therapy, is defined as extending or projecting energy into a patient from a distance.

Divergent Channels - twelve secondary channels that parallel the Twelve Primary Channels.

Divine - pertaining to God.

Divine Center - referring to the North Star's stable position in the sky.

Divine Hook-Up - the Qigong doctor's initial preparation for therapy, wherein he or she connects with the divine for guidance.

Divine Therapy - long distance Qigong healing.

D.M.Q. - a licensed Doctor of Medical Qigong Therapy, presently only obtainable in China.

Dong - the Yang method of dynamic Postural Dao Yin training.

Dragon's Mouth Palm Technique - hand technique wherein the thumb touches the other four fingers of the hand, forming an image of the head of a dragon. This hand manipulation is used for leading and pulling the Qi.

Draining Qi - drawing off or releasing pathogenic energy from a specific organ area or channel of the patient's body.

Dredging - a type of energetic purging, used to clean the patient's energetic fields and channels.

Drilling Energy Technique - this method refers to rotating Qi in a spiraling pattern (clockwise or counterclockwise) to access the energy deep inside the patient's body.

Dry - one of the Six Evils

Dryness - a internal pathogenic condition relating to the storage of Dry toxins (i.e., dry mucus membranes resulting from a lack of Body Fluids).

Dynamic Qigong - energy gathering which utilizes active movements of the body.

Dysmenorrhea - painful menstruation.

Dyspepsia - painful digestion.

Dyspeptic - one afflicted with dyspepsia.

Dysphagia - difficulty in swallowing.

Dysphoria - exaggerated feeling of depression, anxiety and unrest.

Dysplasia - the abnormal development of tissue.

Dyspnea - air hunger, resulting in difficult breathing, shortness of breath, sometimes accompanied by pain.

Dysthymia - a chronic, form of depression (lasting at least two years), for children and adolescents the mood can be irritable rather than sad.

E

Earth Element - one of the Five Elements, pertaining to the Spleen and the Stomach.

Earth Energy (Qi) - Energy pertaining to the Earth and surrounding environment.

Earth Jing - energy that supervises the maturation phase of the fetus's ability for emotional and spiritual bonding during the seventh month of pregnancy.

Earthly Branches - twelve energies of the Earth represented in the human body as the Twelve Primary Channels.

Earth Transpersonal Point - pertaining to the body's energetic connection to the Earth, located several feet beneath the feet.

ECG (or EKG) Eletrocardiogram - a graphic record made by an instrument that measures the Heart's electrical activity; usually used to confirm a diagnosis of a Heart condition.

Eclampsia - coma and convulsive seizures (between the 20th week of pregnancy and first week postpartum). Symptoms result in edema of the legs and feet, puffiness of the face, hypertension, severe headaches, dizziness, epigastric pain, nausea, sudden convulsive seizures and coma.

Eczema - an acute or chronic inflammation of the skin.

Edema - an acute or chronic cutaneous inflammatory condition.

EEG Electroencephalogram - a graphic record made by an instrument that measures the brain's electrical activity and records it as patterns of fluctuating waves.

Ego - the ego is the mediator between the id and the superego. According to Dr. Sigmund Freud's psychoanalytical theory, the superego combines the critical inner parent aspect with the idealistic aspect of the individual's conscience; the id consists of unconscious drives and instincts. The ego as meditator is responsible for ensuring rational behavior.

Ego Defense Mechanisms - according to Dr. Sigmund Freud's psychoanalytical theory, the ego defence mechanisms include: Repression, Displacement, Projection, Intellectualization, Regression, Fixation, Denial, Reaction-Formation, and Sublimation.

Eight Confluential Points - the areas where the Eight Extraordinary Vessels and Twelve Primary Channels intersect with each other.

Eight Energetic Principles (Eight Principle Theory) - a system of differential diagnosis using four pairs of opposites (Yin and Yang, Cold and Hot, Deficient and Excess, Internal and External).

Eight Energetic Touches - pertaining to the somatic tissue response to energy stimulation (tingling, sensations of Heat, coldness, expansiveness, contracted, heaviness, lightness, and vibration).

Eight Extraordinary Vessels (Ancestral Channels)- the primary channels responsible for the formation of the fetus, which after birth, are considered the body's reservoirs for collecting the overflow energy from the Twelve Primary Channels.

Eight Miscellaneous Factors - eight factors that can off set the patient's Yin and Yang balance (diet, overexertion, excessive sex, child bearing, traumatic injuries, exposure to poisons, parasites, and iatrogenic disorders).

Eight Trigrams (Bagua) - eight cosmological patterns of three lines (solid and/or broken), called Yaos, used to diagnose as well as predict future transitions.

Emaciation - the state of being malnourished and extremely lean.

Embolus - a plug, composed of a thrombus or vegetation, mass of bacteria, or other foreign body obstructing a vessel.

Embolism - the obstruction of a Blood Vessel by foreign substances or a Blood clot.

EMG Electromyogram - a graphic record made by an instrument that measures the muscle's electrical activity and records its function.

Emitting Qi - the Qigong doctor extending energy outside the body for the purpose of treating a patient.

Emotional Energy Body - is the external energy existing in the body's second field of Wei Qi, which is attached to the internal organs.

Emotional Spirit - pertaining to the Emotional Energy Body.

Empathic Communication - the doctor's ability to experience the feelings and thoughts of his/her patients.

Empty Qi - a serious weakness or Deficiency of the body's Qi.

Encephalomyelitis - acute inflammation of the Brain and spinal cord.

Endometrial Hyperplasia - excessive proliferation of the cells within the lining of the Uterus.

Energetic Armoring - a condition resulting from the patient protecting specific tissues, organs, or areas of the body. Energetic armoring is initiated when the patient freezes certain emotional feelings to maintain the denial system.

Energetic Barriers (Energetic Boundaries) - the protective barriers existing within and outside of the body's tissues.

Energetic Complications - pertaining to energetic imbalances within the patient's tissues (e.g., compressed energy stagnation, energetic armoring, migrating Qi deviations, etc.)

Energetic Cords - energetic bands of light and vibration which form an emotional attachment, connecting the patient to certain people, places, or things.

Energetic Grids - an energetic net covering the surface of Heaven, Earth or the human body.

Energetic Leakage - a condition resulting from the leaking of Qi from the joints, due to an injury or unconscious sabotage.

Energetic Medicine - any and all medicine having to do with the stimulation, cultivation, tonification, purgation, balance and maintenance of the body's Qi.

Energetic Point Therapy - Emitting Qi into specific channel points or vessels on the body.

Enteric Nervous System - pertaining to the nervous system of the Small Intestine.

Enuresis - the involuntary discharge of urine.

Environmental Energy (Qi) - Energy pertaining to the Earth and surrounding environment.

Environmental Force - energy pertaining to the Earth and surrounding environment.

Epigastric Pain - pain in the region over the pit of the Stomach.

Epileptiform - having the form of epilepsy.

Epistaxis - bleeding of the nose.

Epithelial Hyperplasia - excessive proliferation of the cells within the outer surface of the body, including the secreting portions of the glands and ducts.

Essence (Jing) - referring to either Prenatal and Postnatal energetic tissue mass.

Eternal Soul - the individual's True Self, which is always connected to the divine. It is absorbed into the mother's egg at the time of conception, and is rooted within the body's Taiji Pole.

Ethereal Souls - associated with the Liver, see Hun.

Etiology - the causes of a disease.

Eustachian Tubes - the auditory tube, extending from the middle ear to the pharynx.

Evil Embryo - pertaining to a toxic formation in the form of a tumor or cancer mass.

Evil Influences - pathogenic factors that can be either physical, mental, emotional, energetic or spiritual.

Evil Qi (Xie Qi) - also called Pathogenic Qi, Perverse Qi, Toxic Qi, and Heteropathic Qi, is energy that causes disease or harmful effects to the body.

Evil States - a condition wherein the patient experiences mental delusions, obsessions, infatuations with the doctor, spiritual oppression or possession.

Evil Wind - toxic Wind that invades the body, tissues or organs.

Excess - a condition relating to the over abundance of a particular substance. (e.g., Heat, Wind, Damp, Cold, etc.).

Exopathogenic - a disease or pathogen originating outside of the body.

Extended Fan Palm Technique - hand technique where the fingers separate like a Chinese fan, used for extending energy through the doctor's palm.

External Pathogenic Factors - an external invasion of Heat, Damp, Cold, Dryness, or Wind, or a combination thereof.

External Qi Therapy - a technique used in Medical Qigong therapy which pertains to Qi being emitted onto a patient.

Extraordinary Organs - also called Curious Organs, these six organs are shaped like Yang (Hollow) organs but function like Yin organs. The Brain stores Marrow, the Marrow stores Kidney Jing, the Bones store Marrow, the Blood vessels store the Blood, the Gall Bladder stores the bile, and the Uterus stores Kidney Jing, Blood, and Qi.

Extraordinary Vessels - secondary channels that flow in conjunction with the body's Twelve Primary Channels.

Extra Point - a point with a definite location, but not originating on the fourteen main channels.

F

False Cold (Pseudo Cold) - a clinical condition wherein Heat has become stagnated within the Interior of the body and the patient experiences symptoms of cold in the extremities.

False Heat (Pseudo Heat) - a clinical condition wherein an overabundance of Cold is transformed into Heat within the Interior of the body and the patient experiences symptoms of Heat in the extremities.

False Self - pertaining to the dark emotional side of the self, i.e., the masks and defence mechanisms that serve to protect the individual from dealing with his or her issues.

Fascia - a fibrous membrane covering, supporting, and separating the muscles, as well as uniting the skin with the body's underlying tissues.

Febrile Diseases - any and all diseases which cause the body to produce a fever.

Feng Shui (Wind and Water) - the study of harmonizing the energetic flow of Wind and Water, and the healing art of adjusting the person's environment to create improvements in the person's health and life.

Fetal Education - regulating the mother's behavior to improve her child's physical, emotional, and mental health is called "fetal education" in Traditional Chinese Medicine, and is important in the development of the child's Prenatal Essence, Energy, and Spirit.

Fetal Leakage - after conception, if a small amount of Bloody fluid discharges from a woman's vagina, it is known as Tai Lou or fetal leakage.

Fibroadenoma - a tumor with fibrous tissue, forming a dense covering.

Fire - one of the Five Elements, pertaining to the Heat and can be transformed into a pathogenic condition

Fire Element - one of the Five Elements, pertaining to the Heart, Small Intestine, Pericardium, and Triple Burners.

Fire Jing - energy that controls the development phase of the fetus's emotional and spiritual well-being during the fifth month of pregnancy.

Five Agents - the five energies that are linked to the moral qualities of a person's inner characteristics (the five virtues stored within the body's Wood, Fire, Earth, Metal and Water elements).

Five Elements - Wood, Fire, Earth, Metal and Water.

Five Element Animals - Green Dragon, Red Phoenix, White Tiger, Black (Indigo) Turtle, and Yellow Phoenix.

Five Elemental Constitutions - physical constitutions based upon the observation of the Five Elemental formations within the human body.

Five Element Organs - the organs related to the Five Elements, including: Wood - Liver and Gall Bladder; Fire - Heart and Small Intestine (Pericardium and Triple Burners); Earth - Spleen and Stomach; Metal - Lungs and Large Intestine; Water - Kidneys and Urinary Bladder.

Five Energetic Fields - pertaining to the body's five levels of energy, including: The External

Wei Qi Fields, Internal Ying Qi Field, Sea of Blood, Sea of Marrow, and Center Core of Light (Taiji Pole).

Five Flavors (Five Tastes) - sour, bitter, sweet, pungent, and salty.

Five Major Yang (Fu) Organs - also called the Five Bowels, they are the body's five hollow organs: Gall Bladder, Small Intestine, Stomach, Large Intestine, and Urinary Bladder.

Five Major Yin (Zang) Organs - are the body's five solid organs: Liver, Heart, Spleen, Lungs and Kidneys.

Five Orbs - pertaining to the 5 Yin internal organs (Liver, Heart, Spleen, Lungs and Kidneys), their complete organ system, and the surrounding areas that they influence.

Five Palms Hot - a condition in which the patient feels a hot sensation in the palms and soles of the feet, accompanied by Heat and agitation of the chest and/or head area.

Five Passes - five important gates on the Governing Vessel located at the coccyx, Mingmen, Shendao, occiput and Baihui, where energy tends to stagnate.

Five Portals of the Earthly Yin Gate - pertaining to the five points at the bottom of the perineum through which the Qi of Earth enters into the body.

Five Portals of the Heavenly Yang Gate - pertaining to the five points at the top of the head through which the Qi of Heaven enters into the body.

Five Sense Organs - eyes, tongue, mouth, nose and ears.

Five Thunder Fingers Technique - hand manipulation technique wherein the fingers and thumb are rapidly extended from a closed soft fist, to strike with Qi for dispersing stagnations.

Five Thrusting Channels - see Thrusting Channels.

Five Tissues - tendons, Blood vessels, muscles, skin and Bones.

Five Zhi - in connection with the five mental aspects of the Mind, the Hun (Ethereal Soul), Po (Corporeal Soul), the Shen (Spirit), the Yi (Intellect), and the Zhi (willpower) are sometimes referred to as the Five Zhi.

Fixation - has the same result as regression, but the person becomes fixated at a particular stage of mental and emotional development.

Flat Palm Detection - an extended palm technique used for sensing and diagnosing.

Four Bigs - pertaining to severe excess of fever, sweating, thirst, and pulse.

Four Doors - the center of each palm and foot.

Four Winds - pertaining to the Energy of the four compass points. (North - back, South - front, West - right, and East - left.)

Fu Organs - Yang or hollow organs (Gall Bladder, Small Intestine, Stomach, Large Intestine, and Urinary Bladder). The Fu Organs operate primarily to relieve the Zang (Yin) Organs of toxic energies and wastes.

G

Gallow's Syndrome - laughing at a very painful experience instead of grieving or crying.

Gastritis - the inflammation of the Stomach.

Gastroptosis - the downward displacement of the Stomach.

Gate of Access - the passageway between life and death, believed to be related to the stars of the Big Dipper.

Gate of the Moon - the western energetic region, which the sun must pass through in order to create Autumn.

Gathering the Immortal's Water (Juice of Jade) - pertaining to the energetic production of the saliva used to create the "Immortal Pill."

Gathering Qi - also called Respiratory Qi, Collection Qi, Chest Qi, Pectoral Qi, and Big Qi of the Chest. It is derived from the conversion of the purest and most potent forms of the body's Jing (particularly sexual fluids, hormones, and neurochemicals).

Ghosts (Gui) - disembodied spirits.

Ghost Points - points used for the treatment of emotional and spiritual disorders.

Gland - an organ that produces a hormone or other secretion.

Golden Gate in the East - the Eastern energetic region, which the sun must pass through in order to create Spring.

Gong - meaning skill or study.

Gout - sudden intense pain in a joint, usually the big toe or ankle, followed by swelling, inflammation and Heat in the joint (in extreme cases alternating chills and fever are experienced).

Grandmother Element - pertaining to the Five Element Creative Cycle of Traditional Chinese Medical, the primary organ is considered the Mother and its previous organ is considered the Grandmother.

Grain Qi (Gu Qi, Nutritive Energy) - Energy derived from food and drink and processed by the Spleen and Stomach.

Grounding - see Rooting.

Gua Sha Therapy - an external "surface" tissue scraping technique commonly used to clear Excess Heat from the body and remove stagnation.

Guiding Qi - the technique of leading Qi.

Gu Qi (Grain Qi, Nutritive Energy) - Energy derived from food and drink and processed by the Spleen and Stomach.

Gui - ghosts or spirits.

H

Hai - means sea.

Healing Tones - resonant sounds used to purge the body of pathogens.

Heart Fire - pertaining to the energy of the Heart, which is responsible for transforming the body's Energy into Spirit. This occurs in the chamber of the Heart's courtyard (the Yellow Court).

Heaven Qi - also known as Heavenly Qi, this energy pertains to the Heavens, the divine and the celestial influences.

Heavenly Stems - the ten energies of Heaven represented in the human body as the Yin and Yang aspects of the Five Elements or ten major internal organs.

Heavenly Transpersonal Point - pertaining to the body's energetic connection to the Heavens, located two to five feet above the head.

Hei Xia - dark brown or black vaginal discharge.

Hematuria - Blood in the urine.

Hemiparalysis - paralysis on one side of the body

Hemiplegia - paralysis on only one side of the body.

Hemoptysis - the expectoration of Blood.

Hepatitis - inflammation of the Liver.

Hepatolithiasis - calculi or concretions in the Liver.

Hepatomegaly - enlargement of the Liver.

Hepatosplenomegaly - the enlargement of both the Spleen and Liver.

Herbal Therapy - one of the four branches of Traditional Chinese Medicine, which involves treating patients through the use of formulas created through teas, soups, tinctures, wines, oils, balms, liniments and pills to stimulate energy flow.

Herbalist - a doctor of Herbal Therapy.

Herpes Simplex I - an infectious disease caused by the herpes simplex virus. This disease is characterized by thin-walled vesicles that occur in the skin, usually at a site where the mucus membrane joins the skin, above the waist area.

Herpes Simplex 2 - an infectious disease caused by the herpes simplex virus. This disease is characterized by thin-walled vesicles that occur in the skin, usually at a site where the mucus membrane joins the skin, below the waist area.

Hexagram - a six line symbol representing the function and flow of Yin and Yang energy, formed by stacking two Trigrams on top of each other.

Hibernation Breathing - a breathing method which includes inhaling and exhaling through every pore on the body's surface, from the body's Center Core (Taiji Pole).

Hidden Power (An Jing) - techniques that emphasize stretching and twisting the tendons and ligaments (known as Reeling and Pulling the Silk) to cultivate resonant vibration within the body for striking and breaking up energetic stagnations or tissue masses.

Hollow Organs - the body's Yang organs, which consist of the Gall Bladder, Small Intestine, Stomach, Large Intestine, Urinary Bladder. Also included in this list are the Triple Burners.

Hologram - pertaining to the body's energetic three dimensional image.

Hook-Up - see divine Hook-Up.

Hostile Forces - dark spiritual forces which seek to influence the physical, mental, emotional, energetic and spiritual life of an individual.

Hot Constitution - pertaining to a physical body innately prone towards Heat.

Hot Evil - also known as Evil Heat, a pathogenic condition causing Excess patterns that are Hot and Yang in nature.

Hou Tian Zhi Qi (Postnatal Qi) - translates to mean "after the baby sees the Heavens."

Hua Jing - see Mysterious Power.

Huang - any membranous tissue.

Hua Sound Resonation - Mysterious or Spiritual Sound Resonation.

Huang Dai - yellow vaginal discharge.

Hui Yin Point (CV-1) - Conception Vessel point located between the scrotum (or vagina) and the anal sphincter.

Human Force - the energy or force manifesting from inside of the human body, as well as the within the human energetic field.

Humor - any fluid or semifluid substance in the body.

Hun (Ethereal Soul) - the Three Ethereal Souls which are the spiritual part of man that ascends to Heaven upon the death of the body. The Hun is stored in the Liver.

Hunter Killer Cells - the body's neutrophils and macrophages, as well as the interferons and antibodies.

Hun Yuan - the body's internal energies that has been combined and fused into the Lower Dantian area.

Hyperbilirubinemia - excessive amounts of bilirubin (the orange-colored or yellowish pigment in bile) in the Blood.

Hyperhidrosis - excessive sweating due to an over-activity of the sweat glands.

Hypertension - high Blood pressure.

Hyperthyroidism - a condition caused by excessive secretions of the thyroid glands, resulting in an increased metabolic rate and the consumption of food to support this increased metabolic activity.

Hypertrophy - the increase in the size of an organ or structure that does not involve tumor formation.

Hypochondriac Pain - pain in the upper lateral region on each side of the body below the thorax and beneath the ribs.

Hypomania - a milder form of mania and excitement with moderate change in behavior.

Hyposmia - a deficient sense to smell.

Hypotension - low Blood pressure.

I

Iatrogenic Disorders - any adverse mental or physical disorder induced in a patient from the treatment by a doctor or surgeon.

I-Ching - see Yi-Jing

Id - Dr. Sigmund Freud's terminology for one of the three divisions of the psyche in Psychoanalytic Theory that is the unconscious source of psychic energy responsible for the body's drives and instincts.

Immortal's Pill - pertaining to the energetic production of Heaven and Earth Qi, in conjunction with the saliva.

Immortal's Water - when meditating, another word for energized saliva.

Incontinence - an inability to control urination, involuntary urination when coughing, laughing, sneezing, running, or performing some other physical activity. This condition can also refer to involuntary defecation.

Indole - A solid, crystalline substance found in feces. It is the bases of many biologically active substances formed in degeneration of tryptophan and is largely responsible for the odor of feces.

Infatuations - refers to the patient feeling intensely amorous towards the doctor.

Influenza - an acute contagious respiratory infection, characterized by a sudden onset, with chills, fever and headache.

Inner-vision - the skill of observing images of the internal organs, and energetic fields relating to the body, mind, emotion and spirit, and their transition stages.

Insight Meditation - focusing on sensual stimuli (sounds, smells, colors, etc.) while meditating.

Insomnia - a sleeping disorder resulting in the inability to sleep.

Insulting Cycle - pertaining to the Five Elemental Cycle, wherein the Child Element counter attacks the Grandmother Element.

Intellectualization - an elaborate rationalization of a naked impulse, to justify it.

Interferons - a group of proteins released by the white Blood cells and fibroblasts, responsible for fighting infection.

Interjection - the insertion or interpose the energetic pattern.

Internal Dialogues - internal conversations, which are part of the patient's personal belief structure.

Internal Pathogenic Factors - pertaining to diseases originating from the body's internal organs and emotions (e.g., anger, fear, grief, worry, etc.).

Internal Viewing - technique used by the Qigong doctor to view the patient's internal organs.

Interpersonal Relationships - close personal relationships, relating to self and others.

Invading Cycle - pertaining to the Five Elemental Cycle, wherein the Grandmother Element overcontrols the Child Element.

Invisible Needle Therapy - the insertion of invisible energetic needles into the patient's body to stimulate energy flow.

Invisible Needle Palm Technique - Qi emission in which energy is emitted in a very fine line, to stimulate specific channel points.

J

Jaundice - a condition due to deposition of the bile, characterized by the yellowing of the skin, eyes, mucous membranes and Body Fluids.

Jia Ji Guan (Spinal Pass) - two points located on the lateral sides of the Mingmen (GV-4) where Qi can become stagnant.

Jie Gu Therapy - a tissue manipulation therapy that focuses on the adjustment of Bones and ligaments.

Jin - Body Fluids whose function is to moisten.

Jing - the human body's Essence, divided into Prenatal and Postnatal Essence.

Jing Luo - the body's channels and collaterals.

Jing Point Therapy - the original term for Channel Point Therapy or Acupressure.

Jing Shen Bing - pertains to all types of mental illness.

Jiu Wei (Yellow Court) - located in the center of the diaphragm, below the xiphoid process of the sternum. Its function is that of being the access point to release emotional memories from the body's internal organs. Its location is attributed to the 3rd Chakra.

Jue Yin (Reverting Yin) - associated with the most severe diseases, indicates Yin Qi developing its final stage and then reverting into

Yang. Jue Yin is categorized with the Liver and Pericardium Channels.

Juice of Jade - Energized saliva produced in meditation practices.

K

Karma - the manifestation of consequences to our actions and beliefs: "As you sew, so shall you reap."

Karmic Related Illness - pertaining to spiritual illnesses, which can be either congenital or acquired.

Ketheric Matter or Substance - pertaining to the spiritual energy located within the third external field of Wei Qi.

Kidney Fire (Mingmen Fire) - the energy that heats the body's Essence (Jing), and dominates all Twelve Primary Channels. It is the motivating force of the body.

Kinetic Communication - the intuition of the physical body, felt by the Qigong doctor as a movement in or of his or her own body.

Kneading Tiger Palm Technique - hand manipulation technique resembling the movement of a tiger kneading the ground, used for dispersing Qi stagnations.

Kyphotic - the exaggeration or angulation of the normal posterior curve of the spine (humpback).

L

Laogong (Pc-8) - Pericardium Channel point located at the center of each palm.

Large Heaven Cycle (Macrocosmic Orbit) - Qigong Meditation which connects the Qi of the extremities to the Qi within the Governing and Conception Vessels.

Leading Qi - technique of manipulating the patient's Qi by using a guiding gesture with the hands.

Leukocyte - the body's white Blood corpuscles, which included lymphocytes and other immune system cells.

Leukorrhea - an acute or chronic disease caused by the unregulated clonal proliferation of stem cells within the Blood forming tissues.

Ley Lines - the energetic pathways that connect energy spots on the planet.

Life Force Energy - Qi.

Light Energy Therapy - color, light projection and visualization used for healing.

Light of the Dao - divine healing light energy.

Lipid Bilayers - the outer membrane of most cells, includes two layers of lipid molecules.

Lithotripsy - crushing of a calculus in the Urinary Bladder or urethra.

Liver Wind - terminology used to describe excess Heat generated from a toxic Liver condition which can cause pathogenic symptoms. Liver Wind often stems from Liver Blood and Yin Deficiency.

Lobular - composed of small lobes.

Lords of the Three Dantians - three spiritual energies used to describe the energetic aspects of the human soul (Tai Yi, Si Ming and Xia Tao Kang).

Lo Scroll (Magic Square) - a tool used for diagnosis and treatment of disorders through number configurations, which correspond to the Late-Heaven sequence of the Trigrams of the Yi-Jing (I-Ching).

Lower Burner - area of the body in the Lower Dantian, responsible for the separation of Clean and Dirty Fluids. It also facilitates the production of urine.

Lower Dantian - area in the center of the lower abdomen, attributed to the body's chamber of Heat and physical power. The Lower Dantian is also known as the Sea of Energy, Pill of Immortality, Root of life, Source of Generating Qi, Five Qi Collection Seat, Progenitor of Life, Stove of Spirit, Root of Heaven, and Cinnabar Field.

Lower Unconsciousness - pertaining to the acquired mind which is connected to the primal senses.

Lumbago - dull, aching pain in the lumbar region of the lower back.

Luo - translates as "a net or web," and in Traditional Chinese Medicine it refers to the Connecting Vessels (i.e., the Fifteen Collaterals). These vessels are the major "passage ways" for the circulation of the body's channel energy, emerging out of the Luo (pathway) points on the Twelve Primary Channels (plus the Governing and Conception Vessels).

Luo Points - are the major intersecting points of the Fifteen Collaterals. The Luo points are located below the elbows and knees and provide an additional energetic barrier to keep Evil Winds from affecting the Twelve Primary Channels, being somewhat deeper then the Muscle/Tendon Channels.

Lymphocytes - immune cells present in the Blood and lymphatic tissue.

Lymphoma - a group of malignant solid tumors of the lymphoid tissue.

Lymphosarcoma - a sarcoma of the lymphatic system.

M

Macrocosmic Orbit - Qigong Meditation which connects the Qi of the Governing and Conception Vessels with the extremities of the body.

Macrophages - the major phagocytic cells of the immune system (also known as Hunter Killer Cells).

Magic Square - also known as the Lo Scroll, a tool used for diagnosis and treatment of disorders through number configurations corresponding to the Late-Heaven sequence of the Trigrams of the Yi-Jing (I-Ching).

Magnetic Energy Therapy - magnetic energy affecting the body's channels and points via electromagnetic field stimulation.

Malar Flushes - pertaining to flushed skin along the cheeks.

Malignant - detrimental; growing worse; threatening to produce death.

Man Qi - general term used to describe the energy relating to the body, mind, emotion, energy and spirit of both men and women. In the body, the area between the navel and the lower sternum correspond to "Man."

Manic Depressive Personality Disorder - see Bipolar Personality Disorder

Mantra - a Sanskrit word, meaning a spiritual phase or sound repeated internally or externally, used as a tool in meditation to induce an altered state of consciousness.

Marrow - derived from the Kidneys, nourishes the Brain, spinal cord and forms the Bone Marrow.

Master Point - the main point of energy interaction on a specific channel, used to affect another organ system or channel energy flow.

Mastitis - inflammation of the breast.

Medical Qigong - one of the four branches of Traditional Chinese Medicine.

Menorrhagia - excessive bleeding during the time of menstruation.

Menoxenia - the pathological changes of menstruation occurring in a woman's cycle, affecting the color, quantity and quality of Blood flow.

Mental Delusions - the occurrence of mental derangement in the patient resulting from a false belief based on an incorrect inference regarding external reality. This belief is firmly sustained despite incontrovertible evidence to the contrary.

Meridians - the body's channels or rivers of Energy.

Mesenchymal - a diffused network of cells forming the embryonic mesoderm, and eventually creating the connective tissues, Blood and Blood Vessels, lymphatic system and the cells of the reticuloendothelial system.

Message (Xin Xi) - knowledge stored within the Wuji or the Void.

Metal Element - one of the Five Elements, relating to the Lungs and Large Intestine.

Metal Jing - Energy that supervises the development phase of the fetus's ability for emotional attachment and bonding during the sixth month of pregnancy.

Metrorrhagia - bleeding from the Uterus.

Microcosmic Orbit - energetic orbits that circulate the Qi within the body's energetic channels; divided into Fire, Water and Wind pathways.

Micturition - discharging urine.

Middle Burner - area of the body pertaining to the body's digestive system, responsible for transporting Gu Qi (derived from food and drink).

Middle Dantian - area in the center of the chest, attributed to the body's chamber of emotional and vibrational power. The Qi of the Middle Dantian is called Zong Qi. Zong Qi is translated as Gathering Qi, Ancestral Qi, Genetic Qi, or Essential Qi. The Middle Dantian is also known as Middle Field of Elixir, Scarlet Palace, Central Altar, Middle Sea of Energy, Courtyard of the Heart, Opening of Suspended Gold, and the Seat of Emotion.

Middle Emotional/Mental Barrier - the second and middle energetic barrier of the Wei Qi fields.

Mind Regulation - the principles governing the conduct, action or functions of the mind.

Ming Jing - see Obvious Power.

Mingmen (Gate Of Life, GV-4) - area in the lower back responsible for heating the body, in particular the Kidneys and Lower Dantian.

Mingmen Fire (also known as Kidney Fire, Advisor Fire, or Ministerial Fire,) - the Energy that heats the body's Essence (Jing), and dominates all Twelve Primary Channels. It is the motivating force of the body.

Ming Sound Resonation - Obvious or Audible Sound Resonation.

Ministerial Fire - pertaining to the Energy responsible for heating the Middle Burner.

Monocytes - A mononuclear phagocyte white Blood cell derived from the myeloid stem cells.

Moon Essence - energy gathered during meditation from the moon's Essence in the form of cool light.

Morphogenic Field - pertaining to the form of the energetic field of Jing.

Mother and Child Therapy - the Traditional Chinese Medical description of the primary organ (Mother) and its sequential organ (Child) in the Five Elemental Creative Cycle.

Mother Element - pertaining to the Five Element Creative Cycle, the primary organ is considered the "mother."

Moxa Therapy (Mugwart, Ai Ye) - herb heated and applied in a clinical setting for tonification of Yang.

Multiple Personality Disorder - also called Identity Disorder, is a mental state in which the patient develops "alter" personalities as a coping mechanism in dealing with severe emotional traumas.

Multiple-Sclerosis (MS) - an inflammatory disease of the central nervous system in which infiltrating lymphocytes degrade the myelin sheath of nerves.

Muscle/Tendon Channels - channel connections to the body's muscles, tendons, ligaments and other connective tissues.

Myalgic Encephalomyelitis - acute inflammation of the Brain and spinal cord.

Myocarditis - the inflammation of the cardiac muscle (located in the middle layer of the walls of the Heart).

Myoma - a uterine tumor that is a solid benign growth in the myometrium, often called a fibroid, containing muscle tissue.

Myophagism - a condition where the macrophages destroy (eats) muscular tissue.

Mysterious Pass - the space between Yin and Yang where infinite space and time (Wuji) exists.

Mysterious Power (Hua Jing) - techniques which emphasize training and conditioning the mind's imagination and intention, to project and utilize the power of the individual's Shen (Spirit).

N

Nebula - a translucent fog-like opacity of the cornea.

Necrosis - part of an area of tissues or Bone that is dying or dead and may spread to healthy tissues or Bones.

Nei Dan Shu - internal elixir cultivation, that focuses on cultivating Qi from within the individual's body.

Nei Gong (Internal Skill) - the training of the body's tendons, Bone, breath, mind, emotion, and spirit to facilitate internal power.

Nei Guan (Internal Viewing) - see inner vision.

Nei Jing - the Yellow Emperor's classics on Chinese internal medicine.

Neoplasm - a new or abnormal formation of tissue, as in a tumor growth.

Nephritis - inflammation of the Kidneys.

Neurasthenia - unexplained chronic fatigue and lassitude.

Neutrophils - the most common type of granulocytic white Blood cell, responsible for fighting infection.

Nine Dantian Chambers - the nine internal cavities established within the energetic matrix of each Dantian.

Nine Palaces - the Later-Heaven sequence of the Trigrams of the Yi-Jing (I-Ching), represented in the human body as the Eight Extraordinary Vessels and the Taiji Pole.

Nine Star System - pertaining to the total development of the three periods of life and the three star developmental sequence.

Noxious Qi (Turbid Qi) - coarse, Toxic, Evil, unrefined, polluted, or dirty Energy.

O

Objective World - pertaining to the spiritual world existing outside an individual's thoughts or feelings.

Obstructed Qi - Energy that is immobile.

Obstruction - the inhibition of the flow of Qi or Blood, caused by Cold, Damp, Heat and Wind, etc.

Obvious Power (Ming Jing) - techniques that emphasize the training and conditioning of the muscles, strengthening the Bone structure, and increasing the individual's overall stamina. This school also includes such techniques as pounding the body (arms, hands, legs, and torso) to strengthen and toughen the tissues.

Occipital Pass (Yu Zhen Guan) - the area located just inferior to the occipital Bone where the Brain originates (according to energetic embryology), known as a specific point where Qi often stagnates.

Oliguria - diminished amount of urine formation.

Omniscient Sight - the ability to see 360 degrees simultaneously.

One Finger Skill Technique - clinical modality involving Energy extension employed through a single finger.

Ontology - the study of the historical development of an individual.

Opening and Closing - the method of leading Qi into and out of specific internal organs, the Triple Burners areas, or one of the Three Dantians, via the hands.

Opisthotonosis - a form of spasm in which the patient's head and heels are bent backwards, and the body is bowed forward.

Organ Dysfunction - the impaired or abnormal function of an internal organ.

Organ Regulation - technique for balancing the action or functional principles of the internal organs.

Organ Qi - Energy of the body's Yin and Yang organs.

Original Spirit (Yuan Shen) - see Prenatal Spirit.

Original Qi (Yuan Qi) - pertaining to the body's Prenatal Qi acquired from both parents at conception, and from the mother during gestation.

Original Force - pertaining to the Heavenly energy, manifesting as the energy of the entire cosmos.

Original Yang - pertaining to the body's Prenatal Kidney Yang.

Original Yin - pertaining to the body's Prenatal Kidney Yin.

Osteoarthritis - a chronic disease involving the joints and the deterioration of the articular cartilage.

Osteoporosis - a general term used for describing any disease process that results in the reduction of Bone mass.

Osteosarcoma - a sarcoma of the Bones.

Outer Spiritual Barrier - the third and furthermost energetic barrier of the Wei Qi fields.

Overcontrolling Cycle - pertaining to one of the Five Elemental Cycles, where one organ overcontrols the second elemental organ in the Five Elements' Circle.

P

Palace of Eternal Frost - the northern energetic region, which the sun must pass through in order to create Winter.

Palace of Universal Yang - the southern energetic region, which the sun must pass through in order to create Summer.

Palpitations - an abnormal rapid, throbbing, or fluttering of the Heart.

Pancreatitis - inflammation of the pancreas.

Panic Attack - overwhelming panic and sense of impending doom, resulting in hyperventilation (breathlessness), Heart palpitations and visual distortions.

Papillary Masses - small, nipple-like protuberances or elevated tissue masses.

Paraplegia - paralysis on both sides of the body.

Parenchymal Cells - the essential parts of an organ's cells that are concerned with the organ's function.

Parkinson's Disease - a chronic nervous disease characterized by muscular weakness, rigidity and a fine, slow tremor.

Past Life Regression - pertaining to the patient's exploration and experiences of previous lives.

Pathogenic (Evil) - disease-causing; see Internal Pathogenic Factors and External Pathogenic Factors.

Penetrating Wind - pertaining to the external pathogen of Wind invading the tissues.

Peptones - pertaining to the term applied to intermediate polypeptide products, formed in partial hydrolysis of proteins, that are soluble in water, diffusible, and not coagulable by Heat.

Peribronchial - surrounding the windpipe (bronchus).

Perineural Cells - the sheath of cells around a bundle of nerve fibers within the perineurium.

Peristalsis - a progressive wave like movement that occurs involuntarily in the hollow tubes of the body.

Peritonitis - inflammation of the abdominal cavity.

Pernicious Influences (Evil) - pertaining to the Six External Factors that cause disease.

Personal Subconscious Mind - part of the mind associated with the recording and storing of personal interpretations of reality.

Peyer's Patch - an aggregation of lymph nodes found chiefly in the ilium.

Phagocytes - cells that have the ability to destroy and ingest bacteria, protozoa, unhealthy cells and cell debris.

Phantom Embryo - an energetic thought form in the shape of an embryo created through the woman's feelings of grief, guilt or remorse after a surgical abortion.

Phantom Organ - the energy of a particular organ which still exists, even after surgical removal.

Phantom Pain - the feeling of pain relating to a particular organ which still energetically exists, even after surgical removal.

Phlegm - pathogenic factor responsible for the formation of diseases including tumors.

Physical Barrier - the first level and closest to the body of the three Wei Qi energetic barriers.

Piezoelectric - pertaining to the electricity created from pressure, especially pressure on or within the Bones.

Po (Seven Corporeal Souls) - sometimes called the Seven Turbid Demon Natures, this spiritual energy manifests as the physical or material soul of the human body that returns to the Earth at death. The Po are associated with the Lungs.

Points - specific areas on the body where energy can intersect to travel externally to internally, or visa versa.

Point Respiration - exercise which requires breathing into a specific channel point, organ, or area of the body.

Polarity - opposite negative and positive qualities of power.

Polergeists - malevolent spiritual entities. Parapsychology research indicates that poltergeist activity is often the manifestation of a psychokinetic ability.

Polydipsia - excessive thirst.

Polyphagia - eating abnormally large amounts of food at a meal.

Polyuria - the excessive secretion and discharge of urine.

Portal Hypertension - the increased pressure in the portal vein resulting from an obstruction of the Blood flow through the Liver.

Postnatal Essence (Postheaven Jing) - sometimes called the Acquired Essence, it is the Essence acquired after birth from food, air and drink.

Postnatal Qi (Postheaven Qi) - sometimes called the Acquired Qi, it is the Energy acquired after birth from food, drink, and air.

Postnatal Spirit (Zhi Shen) - also called the body's Mental Spirit, Acquired Spirit, and Conscious Spirit. This spiritual essence is acquired after birth through the refinement of one's Qi.

Post Traumatic Stress Disorder - characterized by the reexperiencing of an extremely traumatic event or events, accompanied by symptoms of increased arousal, and by avoidance of stimuli associated with the traumas. This includes the general numbing of the patient's emotional responsiveness.

Prenatal Essence (Yuan Jing) - also called Pre-heavenly Essence, Original Essence, Inherited Essence, Congenital Essence, Primordial Essence, and Ancestral Essence. It is the Original Essence existing before the fetus is born, acquired from the mother and father.

Prenatal Qi (Yuan Qi) - sometimes referred to as Congenital Qi, Pre-Heaven Qi, Inherited Qi, Source Qi, Ancestral Qi, Primordial Qi, Genuine Qi, and Kidney Qi. It is energy existing before the fetus is born, acquired from the mother's, father's, environmental and universal energies, and sustained through prayer, meditation and sleep.

Prenatal Spirit (Yuan Shen) - also called the Intuitive Spirit, Perceptual Spirit, Primordial Spirit, Congenital Spirit, and the Original Subconscious. It is the Spirit essence existing before the fetus is born, acquired from fusing the mother's, father's, environmental and universal energies. The Prenatal Spirit also relates to the individual's ability to perceive and intuit information.

Prescriptions - directions given to the patient with regard to the manner of Medical Qigong exercises and meditations that must be practise after the initial Medical Qigong treatment.

Primal Senses - pertaining to the gross physical, animalistic survival senses (seeing, hearing, feeling, smelling, etc.).

Primary Channels - the body's twelve main channels, containing six Yin and six Yang rivers of Energy.

Primary Posture - the main posture, in a series of Medical Qigong prescriptions, that the patient focuses on.

Primitive Unconsciousness (Lower Unconsciousness) - pertaining to the acquired mind and related to the primal senses.

Projection - the attribution of unacceptable impulses within oneself to other people.

Proliferative Arthritis - the rapid reproduction and growth of arthritis.

Prostatitis - the inflammation of the prostate.

Protective Qi (Wei Qi) - the body's external field of defensive, protective energy (divided into three external fields of Qi).

Pruritus - severe itching.

Psychogenic - a condition developed from the beliefs originating within the mind.

Psychogenic Polyuria - pertaining to the belief that one must frequently secrete and discharge urine.

Psychometry - the act of sensing the thoughts, images and so on, with which the object has been imprinted.

Psychoneurosis - emotional disfunction caused from unresolved unconscious conflicts.

Psychosexual Qi Deviation - a condition resulting from an immediate energetic tissue over-stimulation of the sexual organs. Patients with this condition experience intense sexual undulations and orgasms when being treated in a safe clinical environment.

Psychosis - a term formerly applied to any mental disorder, but now generally restricted to those conditions resulting from personal disintegration and loss of contact with reality.

Psychosomatic - pertaining to the relationship between the physical tissues and the emotions.

Pulling Down the Heavens - an opening and closing meditation used to energize and clear the body from the top of the head to the bottom of the feet, with breath, mind and hand movements.

Pulmonary Emphysema - a chronic disease of the Lungs characterized by a destructive increase in the normal size of air spaces distal to the terminal bronchiole.

Purpura - a condition characterized by hemorrhages of the internal organs, skin, mucous membranes and other tissues, with various manifestations and diverse causes.

Purgation (Purging) - technique used in order to reduce Excess and expel pathogenic Evils located within the energetic fields and tissues of the body.

Pyelonephritis - the inflammation of the Kidneys and pelvis.

Q

Qi - the energetic medium existing between matter and spirit (also known as Life Force Energy, when pertaining to the physical body).

Qi Collapse - pertaining to the complete absence (void) of either Yin or Yang Qi.

Qi Compression - using the Qi to press the tissues.

Qi Deviations - an alteration of energetic patterns and flow of energy that affects the body, mind, emotion and spirit, resulting in disease.

Qi Dysfunction - the impaired or abnormal function of the body's energy.

Qi Extension - the emission of energy from the body.

Qigong (Energy Skill) - pertaining to exercises and meditations that cultivate Life Force Energy. There are three primary schools of Qigong training - Martial, Medical and Spiritual.

Qigong Clinic - a facility for diagnosis and treatment of outpatients with Medical Qigong therapy.

Qigong Doctor - in China, a person who medically treats patients for mental or physical disorders using Qi.

Qigong Massage - soft tissue regulation wherein the Doctor's hand lightly skims the patient's body. This gentle surface tissue stimulation is used to energize, stimulate or dredge the patient's Wei Qi fields. It is used with purging and tonifying techniques.

Qigong Therapy - one of the four branches of Traditional Chinese Medicine, which involves treating patients through the use of Energetic Point Therapy, Qigong Massage, Distance Therapy, Self-Regulation Therapy, and Invisible Needle Therapy, to stimulate energy flow.

Qigong Therapist - in North America, a person who medically treats patients for mental or physical disorders using Qi.

Qi Hai - Sea of Qi point (CV-6).

Qi Manipulations - techniques used to treat or influence the flow of energy in the body.

Qing Dai - green-blue vaginal discharge.

Qi Projection (Energy Extension) - the emission of energy from the body.

Qi Regulation - energetically balancing the action or functions of the body's Yin and Yang energies.

Qi Stasis - the total stagnation of energy.

Quiescent - a meditative state wherein the individual's mind and body becomes quiet and peaceful.

R

Rachialgia - spinal inflammation.

Reaction-Formation - the conversion of one feeling into its opposite, typically seen in love turning into hate, or vice versa.

Rebellious Qi - energy that does not follow the correct flow or current, acting recklessly.

Reconstructive Qi Therapy - pertaining to the reconstruction and energizing of the body's energetic fields and organ systems (especially after surgery).

Reducing Qi - to lessen or decrease an organ or channel's energy.

Reflexology - the skill of pressing specific areas of the body's hands and feet to initiate internal energetic movement.

Regression - the return to an earlier childhood stage of behavior to reduce the demands on the ego.

Regulating - pertaining to the balancing of the body's Yin and Yang Energies.

Reinforcing Qi - to strengthen and support the body's organ or channel Energy.

Repression - the pushing down of unwanted ideas and emotions into the unconscious.

Respiratory Qi - Energy of the chest.

Restrictive Cycle - pertaining to the Five Elemental Controlling Cycle, where one organ restricts the energy of another organ (as depicted in the pentagram drawing).

Retrobulbar Neuritis - inflammation of the nerves behind the eyeball.

Returning To The Origin - see Rooting the Lower Dantian.

Reverse Breathing - opposite of abdominal breathing, wherein the patient will contract the abdomen with the inhalation, and expand the abdomen with the exhalation.

Rhabdomyosarcoma - a sarcoma of the muscles.

Rheumatic - pertaining to a rheumatism (a general term used to describe an acute or chronic condition characterized by inflammation, soreness and stiffness of the muscles, and pain in the joints and associated structures.

Rheumatoid Arthritis - a form of arthritis, characterized by inflammation of the joints, swelling, stiffness, cartilaginous hypertrophy, and pain.

Rheumatoid Spondylitis - a chronic, progressive disease, characterized by inflammation of the joints between the articular processes, costovertebral joints, and sacroiliac joints.

Rheumatosis - an acute or chronic condition characterized by inflammation, soreness and stiffness of the muscles, and pain in the joints.

Rhinitis - the inflammation of the nasal mucosa.

Righteous Qi (Zheng Qi) - is also called Upright Qi and Correct Qi. It is energy that heals the body and fights disease.

Rigor - a sudden, chill with high temperature, followed by Heat and profuse perspiration.

Can also be referred to a state of hardness and stiffness, as in the muscles.

Root - the original cause of a disease; or to energetically secure into the Earth by extending the body's Energy deep into the ground, as if growing tree roots.

Rooting - the process of extending the body's Qi into the Earth to either establish a solid energetic foundation, or if need be, disperse Toxic Qi.

Rooting the Lower Dantian (Returning to the Origin) - returning the body's collected Qi back into the Lower Dantian.

S

San Bao (Three Treasures of Man) - pertaining to Jing (Essence), Qi (Energy) and Shen (Spirit).

San Jiao (Triple Burners) - corresponding to three main body cavities, responsible for heating the body and transporting the Body Fluids. The Triple Burner Channels are considered one of the Twelve Primary Channels.

Sarcoma - a malignant growth, or tumor, that occurs within the connective or mesenchymal tissue. It may affect the muscles, Bones, fat, Blood Vessels, lymph system, Kidneys, Bladder, Liver, Lungs, Spleen, and/or parotid glands.

Schizophrenia - a mental disorder, that induces hallucinations - usually auditory - through can also be visual, accompanied by very disordered thinking, delusions, disorganized speech, irrational or catatonic behavior, such as stupor, rigidity, or flaccid movement of the limbs. The ability to interact with others is greatly impaired.

Sclera - a tough white fibrous tissue that covers the white of the eyes.

Sea of Blood (Sea of the Twelve Channels) - pertaining to the Energy located in the Thrusting Vessel.

Sea of Energy - Energy located in the Lower Dantian, or Qi Hai area.

Sea of Grain and Water (Sea of Nourishment) - pertaining to the Energy located in the Stomach.

Sea of Marrow - pertaining to the Energy flowing in the spinal column and Brain, originating from the Kidneys.

Sea of Qi - the chest center. Some Medical Qigong schools maintain that there are two reservoirs of Qi: the Middle Dantian, being the Sea of Postnatal Qi, and the Lower Dantian, being the Sea of Prenatal Qi (which is regulated by the Qihai CV-6 point).

Sea of Yang Channels - pertaining to the Governing Vessel.

Sea of Yin Channels - pertaining to the Conception Vessel.

Secondary Gains of Disease - pertaining to the subconscious psychological empowerment of a patients disease and its sabotaging potential.

Self Regulation Therapy - pertaining to the patient's Qigong prescriptions (meditations and/or exercises).

Seven Emotions - see Seven Internal Factors.

Seven Essential Stars - the Sun, Moon, Mars, Venus, Mercury, Saturn and Jupiter, associated with the body's seven orifices.

Seven Internal Factors - pertaining to the seven emotional pathogenic factors that cause disease, when in an Excess condition (Joy, Sorrow, Worry, Grief, Fear, Fright, and Anger).

Seven Material Souls - pertaining to the seven Earthly spirits that reside in the body as the Po.

Seven Orifices - ears, eyes, nostrils, mouth, anus and urethra, which are considered the gates and windows of Essence, Energy and Spirit.

Seven Turbid Demon Natures - see Po.

Shaman - an ancient Tungus term meaning "between the worlds." A Shaman is a tribal priest or priestess who heals the physical, mental, emotional, energetic and spiritual aspects of the patient.

Shao Yang - Small Yang, also called Lesser Yang, Minor Yang, or Young Yang, is affiliated with the sunrise and the waxing-moon phase. Modern physicists associate the Lesser Yang with a light force and electromagnetism.

Shao Yin (Small Yin) - also called Lesser Yin, Minor Yin, or Young Yin, is affiliated with the sunset and the waning-moon phase. Modern physicists associate the Lesser Yin with a heavy force, and gravity. Shao Yin is associated with the Kidney and Heart Channels.

Shen - meaning Spirit; when speaking about physical development, it is derived from Qi, and can be divided into both Prenatal and Postnatal Shen.

Shen Deviations - mental and emotional disorders which have caused the Three Ethereal Souls (Hun) to leave the patient's body.

Shengong - training of the spirit through meditation and visualization.

Shening Out - terminology used to describe the Ethereal Soul (Hun) wandering away from the body.

Shi Qi (Turbid Qi) - also known as Evil Qi, Toxic Qi, and Pathogenic Qi, it is coarse, unrefined, polluted or dirty energy.

Shou Zhen (Hand Diagnosis) - a form of diagnosis, wherein, the doctor assess the "energetic blueprint" of the patient's body transformed onto the doctor's left hand.

Shu Points - five specific points below the elbows and knees identified as the Well, Spring, Stream, River and Sea points. Each point has an affect on the quantity of the energy of an organ.

Sishencong (Four Spirit Hearings) Points - also known as the "Four Alert Spirit Points," they are a group of four points located at the top of the head (surrounding the Baihui point), used for absorbing Heavenly Qi into the body through the Taiji Pole.

Six Evils (Six External Factors) - also known as the Six Pernicious Influences, these factors pertain to the six climatic changes (Wind, Summer Heat, Heat, Damp, Dryness, Cold, and Fire).

Six Extraordinary Organs - also called Curious Organs, these six organs are shaped like Yang (Hollow) organs but function like Yin organs. The Brain stores Marrow, the Marrow stores Kidney Jing, the Bones store Marrow, the Blood vessels store the Blood, the Gall Bladder stores the bile, and the Uterus stores Kidney Jing, Blood, and Qi.

Six Storage Areas - the body's Yang organs constantly fill and empty, and include the Urinary Bladder, Gall Bladder, Stomach, Large Intestine, Small Intestine, and Triple Burners.

Skatol - Beta-methyl indole, formed in the intestine by the bacterial decomposition of L-tryptophan and found in fecal matter, to which it imparts its characteristic odor.

Skin Zones - twelve dermal-zones, based upon the surface location of the body's Twelve Primary Channels.

Soaring Dragon Technique - hand technique for Qi emission, where the energy is emitted through the middle finger bent and pointing downward, while the other fingers are extended straight outwards.

Solid Organs - the body's Yin organs, which include the Liver, Heart, Spleen, Lungs, and Kidneys (also included in this list is the Pericardium).

Soul - immaterial Spiritual Essence of an individual's life, stored within the Heart and Middle Dantian.

Soul Body - see Astral Body.

Soul Extensions - the Shen develops and contains Twelve Soul Extensions. These Twelve Soul Extensions contain the body's different personality characteristics.

Soul Loss - the loss of parts of the Eternal Soul.

Soul Retrieval - to spiritually search for and bring back one's forgotten memories (soul), which have been isolated from consciousness due to trauma and shock.

Soul Travel - see Astral Travel.

Sound Energy Therapy - sound projected as audible and inaudible tone resonation, used for healing.

Sound Resonation - healing tones used for tonifying or dispersing the patient's Energy.

Spider Nevus - a branched growth of dilated capillaries on the skin, that resemble a spider.

Spinal Pass (Jia Ji Guan) - two points located on the lateral sides of the Mingmen (GV-4), where energy has a potential to stagnate.

Spinous Process - the single midline posterior projection arising at the junction of each vertebra.

Spiraling Energy Technique - hand manipulation, that extends and spirals the doctor's projected energy.

Spirit - the energetic manifestation of the Eternal Soul.

Spirit Body - the energetic vehicle in which the body's Shen can travel throughout the Astral Plane. The Spirit Body can manifest through many forms (Body of Light, animal forms, etc.).

Spirit Demons - see Demon Possession and Oppression.

Spirit Soul - the Three Ethereal Souls, accompanied by the individual's consciousness, acting as one unit for spirit travel.

Spirit Travel - the spirit (Hun) journeying outside of the physical body.

Splenomegaly - the enlargement of the Spleen.

Squamous Metaplasia - the conversion of tissue into a form of scalelike cells, that is abnormal for that tissue.

Stacking the Bones - allowing the Bones to stack upon each other from the bottom of the feet to the top of the head.

Stagnation (Yu - Stasis) - not moving, inactive; pertaining to Qi, Blood, or thought patterns.

Static Qigong - the process of stationary, quiescent Energy gathering.

Stroke (Wind Stroke) - caused by the buildup of Excess Liver Fire creating Internal Wind. This Internal Wind causes Qi and Blood to rebel upwards causing Phlegm to form and obstruct the cavities and vessels, creating Penetrating Wind or Stroke.

Subarachnoid Hemorrhage - bleeding internally, within the spaces at the base of the Brain, between the pia proper and arachnoid contain the cerebrospinal fluid.

Subconscious Mind - part of the mind associated with the recording and storing of personal interpretations of reality (not readily accessible to the conscious mind).

Sublimation - the channeling of unacceptable impulses into acceptable, refined social forms and is the only defence mechanism considered to be a healthy reaction.

Substances - pertaining to the body's essential parts of physical and energetic material.

Sui - Marrow.

Summer Heat - one of the Six Evils.

Super Ego - Dr. Sigmund Freud's terminology for the division of the psyche in psychoanalytic theory, responsible for the psychic reward and punishment system.

Sun's Essence - energy gathered from the sun, ingested as warm light.

Sword Fingers Technique - hand manipulation that emits Qi through the extended index and middle fingers.

Symptoms - a subjective manifestation of a pathological condition, reported by the patient.

Syndromes - a grouping of signs and symptoms, based on their frequent reoccurrence, that may suggest a common underlying pathogenesis.

Systemic - affecting the entire body.

Systolic - vascular Blood pressure relating to the contraction of the Heart.

T

Taiji Pole - the Center Core of light which joins the body's three Dantians and the Eternal Soul together originating at the Baihui at the top of the head and extending through the center of the body, terminating at the Huiyin, located at the base of the perineum.

Tai Yang - Great Yang, also called Strong Yang, Major Yang, or Old Yang, is affiliated with high noon and the full-moon phase. Modern physicists associate the Strong Yang with a strong nuclear force. Associated with the Urinary Bladder and the Small Intestine Channels.

Tai Yi - meaning Great Divinity or God.

Tai Yin - Great Yin, also called Strong Yin, Major Yin, or Old Yin, is affiliated with midnight and the new-moon phase. Modern physicists associate the Great Yin with a weak nuclear force. Associated with the Spleen and the Lung Channels.

Ten Heavenly Stems - the ten energies of Heaven that rule the changes of the Five Elemental seasonal transitions, and are represented in the human body as the Yin and Yang aspect of the Five Elements (represented in the human body as the ten major internal organs).

Ten Thousand Voices - pertaining to the state of open receptivity of the Qigong doctor's Heart, after rooting the mind.

Ten Wings - consisting of ten commentaries from Confucius and his disciples, pertaining to the study of the eight Trigrams, sixty-four hexagrams, and the Yi-Jing.

Tenesmus - spasmodic contraction of the anal or vesical sphincter combined with pain.

Third Eye Point (Yin Tang- Extraordinary Point) - located in the center of the forehead, between the eyebrows, responsible for spiritual intuition and communication.

Thought-forms - images of concentrated thought patterns that manifest on the vibrational resonance of the Astral Plane.

Three Ethereal Souls (Hun) - pertaining to the three heavenly spirits that reside in the body.

Three Fires - the Heat in the body, generated from the energy radiating from the Heart Fire, Kidney Fire, and Urinary Bladder Fire.

Three Outer Forces - pertaining to the three natural powers of Heaven, Earth and Man.

Three Parts Wisdom - knowledge obtained through the doctor's connection and communication with his or her Upper, Middle, and Lower Dantians.

Three Periods of Life - the developmental stages of the patient's Jing, Qi and Shen divided into the womb, childhood and adulthood.

Three Stars - pertaining to the three periods of life, each period is divided into three stages of development, known as the Three Stars.

Three Treasures of Earth - pertaining to the energy of Soil, Water and Wind, and the study of Feng Shui (Wind and Water).

Three Treasures of Heaven - pertaining to the energy of the sun, moon and stars, and the study of Chinese astrology.

Three Treasures of Man - pertaining to the energetic interaction of the body's Essence, Energy and Spirit, and the study of the Yi-Jing (I-Ching or Book of Changes).

Three Wonders - Clinical manifestations of Qi, categorized as Subtle, Mysterious and Incredible Wonders.

Thrombosis - the formation and development or existence of a Blood clot (thrombus) within the walls of the vascular system.

Thrusting Channels - the Five Energy Channels which surround and penetrate the body's center core via the Taiji Pole.

Thrusting Vessels (Chong Mai) - they are the Five Energy Vessels which originate from the center of the body and internally transverse the legs and torso. The Thrusting Vessels are responsible for the connection between the Conception and Governing Vessels.

Ti - referred to as the Divine Center.

Tian Qi (Heavenly Energy) - the transformed energy of the Yuan Qi and the divine.

Tian Shen (Heavenly Spirit) - the transformed energy of the Yuan Shen and the divine.

Tie Bi (Iron Wall) - the areas of the body where it is most difficult for the energy to pass through when circulating the Microcosmic Orbit.

Tinnitus - a ringing, tinkling, or buzzing sound in the ear. In Traditional Chinese Medicine, tinnitus can originate from either an Excess or Deficient condition.

Toe Raised Stepping - pertaining to energetic walking therapy, wherein the toes are stretched when stepping in order to facilitate the increase of Qi flowing into the body via the leg channels.

Tonification (Tonify) - to supplement the insufficiency and strengthen the body's resistance.

Traditional Chinese Medicine - Chinese Energetic Medicine, divided into four branches of healing modalities (Acupuncture, Herbal Therapy, Medical Qigong Therapy, and Tissue Regulation Therapy (Chinese Massage).

Transference - the process whereby a patient unconsciously transfers feelings, thoughts, beliefs and patterns of behavior that had been previously experienced with others onto the doctor.

Transient Ischemic Attacks (TIA) - temporary interference with the Blood supply to the Brain. Multiple TIA can lead to a stroke.

Treatment - the medical care given to a specific condition.

Trigger Points (Ashi Points) - places on the body which are tender spots, or painful areas near diseased or injured tissue.

Trigram - pertains to three Yao lines stacked upon one another forming a specific symbol, which represents certain characteristics.

Triple Burners (San Jiao) - also known as the Triple Heaters and Triple Warmers, they correspond to three main body cavities (perineum to navel, navel to base of solar plexus, solar plexus to throat), and are responsible for heating the body and transporting Body Fluids.

True Fire - the original Heat or Fire Energy that regulates the body's Yin and Yang Qi, created from the radiating energy of the Heart's Fire, Kidneys' Fire and Urinary Bladder's Fire.

True Nature - one's innate nature in harmony with life.

True Qi - the energy that circulates in the body's channels and collaterals which nourishes the Yin and Yang organs and fights disease.

True Self - one's true nature, connected to the subconscious mind.

True Spirit - pertains to the spiritual nature of the True Self. The Hun and Po are expressions of the body's True Spirit.

Tsou Hou Ru Mo ("the Spirit leaves and the Demon enters") - describes self induced psychosis, pertaining to improper Qigong training, wherein the patient's Hun leave the body and the Po take over.

Tui Na Therapy - a tissue manipulation therapy that focuses on the adjustment and/or stimulation of the muscles and tendons.

Tumor - an abnormal growth, either benign or malignant, caused by a retention of mass due to stasis of Qi, Blood and Phlegm, etc.

Turbid Qi - also called Evil Qi, is coarse, unrefined, polluted, and dirty energy.

Twelve Pi Hexagrams - the twelve symbols pertaining to the twelve time periods of the day and year.

Twelve Primary Channels - the body's twelve main energetic rivers (Liver, Lungs, Large Intestine, Stomach, Spleen, Heart, Small Intestine, Urinary Bladder, Kidneys, Pericardium, Triple Burners, and Gall Bladder).

Twelve Earthly Branches - twelve energies of the Earth that determine the six Qi factors of the seasonal transitions (represented in the human body as the Twelve Primary Channels).

Two Breathings - pertaining to the abdominal breathing method of holding the breath.

U

Umbilications - a depression resembling a navel.

Universal Qi - energy pertaining to the Heavens, the divine and the celestial influences.

Upper Burner - pertaining to the body's complex system of Fluid distribution via the Lungs and located within the upper chest cavity.

Upper Dantian - area within the center of the head, attributed as the body's chamber of light and door to psychic and intuitive powers. The Upper Dantian is also known as Seal Palace, Ancestral Opening, Calm Fountain, Heaven's Valley, Inner Source, and Clay Pill Palace.

Urinary Bladder Fire - also called Common Peoples' Fire, or Perineal Fire, is located in the lower abdomen by the perineum, and is responsible for evaporating water.

Urodynia - painful urination

Uterus - female reproductive organ, one of the Eight Extraordinary organs.

V

Vasculitis - the inflammation of a Blood or lymph vessel.

Vertigo - the sensation of moving in space, resulting in such symptoms as dizziness and light-headedness.

Virtue (De) - pertaining to the function of the divine in man.

Virtue of Dao - pertaining to the commendable quality of the divine.

Viscera - the body's internal organs.

Void - also called Wuji, it pertains to the infinite space between matter and energy.

W

Wai Dan Shu - external elixir cultivation, that focuses on cultivating Qi from outside the individual's body.

Wai Qi - external, extended energy.

Walking Therapy - Postoral Dao Yin walking exercises and dynamic "moving" meditations used for the treatment of organ Deficiencies.

Wandering Bi - migrating pain within the body's cavities.

Waning - to grow smaller.

Water Element - one of the Five Elements, pertaining to Kidneys and Urinary Bladder.

Water Jing - energy that controls the genetic development phase of the fourth fetal month.

Waxing - to grow larger.

Wei Lu Guan (Coccyx Pass) - located on the lowest segment of the spine just posterior to the anus, near the Chang Qiang (GV-1) point.

Wei Qi - the body's external field of Defensive and Protective energy, which is subdivided into three fields of Qi.

Wen Huo - pertaining to the gentle breathing method of Respiratory Dao Yin training.

White Blood Cell - any of a group of Blood cells that have no hemoglobin and migrate into tissues to fight infection and digest cell debris.

Wind - one of the Six Evils.

Wind Bi - pain in the body created by toxic Wind invasion.

Wind Stroke - Stroke caused by the buildup of Excess Liver Fire creating Internal Wind. This Internal Wind causes Qi and Blood to rebel upwards causing Phlegm to form and obstruct the cavities and vessels, thus creating Penetrating Wind or Stroke.

Windy Breathing Method - pertaining to the method of breathing through the nose.

Wood Element - one of the Five Elements, pertaining to the Liver and Gall Bladder.

Wood Jing - energy that controls the development phase of the direction of the fetus's emotional and spiritual aspects during the seventh month of pregnancy.

Wu Guan (Five Passes) - five important gates on the Governing Vessel located at the coccyx,

Mingmen, Shendao, occiput, and Baihui areas where energy tends to stagnate.

Wu Huo - pertaining to the vigorous breathing method of Respiratory Dao Yin training.

Wuji - pertaining to infinite space or the formless Void.

Wuji Posture - a quiet standing posture used in meditation to allow the practitioner to return to a state of tranquility.

Wu Jing Shen (Five Essence Spirits) - the spiritual energy radiating from the core of the Five Yin Organs. Combined, these energies create the foundation of the body's Shen (Spirit).

Wu Se Dai - pertaining to the five colors of vaginal discharge - white, yellow, red, green-blue, and dark brown or black.

Wu Wei - a state of "no mind," i.e., no thoughts.

Wu Zang - the Five Yin Organs. Wu translates to mean "five," Zang translates to mean "to store or hold."

X

Xie Qi (Evil Qi) - energy that causes disease or harmful effects to the body.

Xin Xi (The Message) - knowledge stored within the Wuji or the Void.

Xiphoid Process - the lowest part of the sternum Bone (sometimes referred to as the Doves Tail).

Xue - Blood.

Y

Yang - the positive charged energetic polarity, opposite of its companion Yin, pertaining to man, hard, light, hot, etc.

Yang Channels - the body's Yang energetic rivers, consisting of the Governing Vessel, Belt Vessel, Yang Linking Vessels, Yang Heel Vessels, Large Intestine Channels, Triple Burner Channels, Small Intestine Channels, Stomach Channels, Gall Bladder Channels, and Urinary Bladder Channels.

Yang Fire - also called Emperor's Fire, energy of the Heart Fire.

Yang (Fu) Organs - also known as Hollow Organs, that consist of the Gall Bladder, Small Intestine, Stomach, Large Intestine, Urinary Bladder. Also included is this category are the Triple Burners.

Yang Shen Disturbances - an emotional Yang state of energetic dysfunction.

Yang Ming (Yang Brightness) - indicates Yang Qi developing its final stage and then reverting into Yin. Associated with the Stomach and Large Intestine Channels.

Yao - a solid or broken line which is representative of either Yang or Yin energy, used in combination of three as Trigrams or six as Hexagrams.

Yao Cycles - the progression of twelve hexagrams (six Yang and six Yin) flowing in a waxing and waning cycle.

Ye (humor) - thick, turbid Body Fluids; its function is to nourish the tissues.

Yellow Court - located in the center of the diaphragm, just below the xiphoid process of the sternum. Its function is that of being the access point to releasing the body's internal organ emotional memories. Its location is also attributed to the 3rd Chakra.

Yi - the intention or thought (the cognitive mind).

Yi Jing - Chinese "Book of Changes," pertaining to the natural transitions of life.

Yin - the negative charged energetic polarity, opposite of its companion Yang, pertaining to woman, soft, dark, cold, etc.

Yin Channels - Yin energetic rivers, consisting of the Conception Vessel, Thrusting Vessel, Yin Linking Vessels, Yin Heel Vessels, Lung Channels, Pericardium Channels, Heart Channels, Spleen Channels, Liver Channels, and Kidney Channels.

Yin (Zang) Organs - also known as the Solid Organs, that consist of the Liver, Heart, Spleen, Lungs and Kidneys. Also included in this category is the Pericardium.

Yin Shen Disturbances - an emotional Yin state of energetic dysfunction.

Yin Tang (Third Eye Point) - located in the center of the forehead between the eyebrows, responsible for projecting the Spirit for psychic intuition and communication.

Yu (Stagnation) - an obstruction.

Ying Qi (Nutritive Qi) - the body's nourishing energy.

Yu (Surplus) Vessels - secondary vessels that branch away from the energetic flow of the major Linking Vessels (at the chest and back), connecting the Linking Vessels energetic flow to the hands.

Yuan Jing (Original Essence) - the Original Kidney or Prenatal Essence.

Yuan Shen (Original Spirit) - the Original Prenatal Spirit.

Yuan Qi (Original Energy) - the Original Kidney or Prenatal Qi.

Yun - the Yin method of dynamic postural Dao Yin training.

Yu Zhen Guan (Occipital Pass) - the area located just inferior to the occipital Bone where the Brain originates, known as a specific point where Qi often stagnates.

Z

Zang Organs - Yin or solid organs (Liver, Heart, Spleen, Lungs, Kidneys and Pericardium).

Zang/Fu Organs - the body's Yin and Yang organs.

Zhang Xiang Xue Shou - in Chinese medical science, the study of energetic physiology.

Zhen Qi - see True Qi

Zheng Qi - Righteous Qi, pathogenic fighting Energy.

Zhi - the Will power, mental drive and determination.

Zhong Qi - Center Qi, Energy of the chest.

Zhou Qi - Turbid Qi, Evil Qi, Impure Qi

Zong Qi - Gathering Qi, and/or Respiratory Qi.

Zygomatic Facial Regions - pertaining to the sides of the cheeks below the eyes.

BIBLIOGRAPHY

A Barefoot Doctor's Manual
    A Guide To Traditional Chinese and Modern Medicine
    A Cloudburst Press Book
    Madrona Publishers, 1977 Seattle, Wa

Agrippa, Henry Cornelius
    Occult Philosophy or Magic
    Ernest Loomis and Company, 1897 New York

Allen, James
    As a Man Thinketh
    Grosset and Dunlap, 1940 New York

Ames, T. Roger and David L. Hall
    Daodejing "Making This Life Significant"
    Ballantine Books 2003, New York

Anodea, Judith
    Wheels of Life
    Liewellyn Publications, 1990 St. Paul, Mi

Atteshlis, Dr. Stylianos
    The Esoteric Teachings: A Christian Approach to Truth
    The Stoa Series, 1992; Strovolos, Cyprus

Bai, Jingfeng
    Episodes in Traditional Chinese Medicine
    Panda Books
    Beijing, China 1998

Bao, Fei et al.
    Application of Acupuncture in the
    Treatment of malignant Tumors
    Medical Research Bulletin; Beijing, China 1997

Bandler, Richard, and John Grinder
    The Structure of Magic: A Book About Language and Therapy
    Science and Behavior Books, Inc. 1975 Palo Alto, Ca

Bardon, Franz
    Initiation into Hermetics: The Path of the True Adept
    Merkur Publishing, Inc.
    Madrona Publishers, 2001
    Salt Lake City, Utah

Bardon, Franz
    The Practice of Magical Evocation: A Complete Course in Instruction in Planetary Spheric Magic
    Merkur Publishing, Inc.
    Madrona Publishers, 2001 Salt Lake City, Utah

Beaulieu, John
    Music and Sound in the Healing Arts: An Energy Approach,
    Station Hill Press 1987, Barrytown, New York

Becker, Robert O., M.D. and Gary Selden
    The Body Electric
    Electromagnetism and the Foundation of Life
    Quill - William Morrow and Co., 1985
    New York City, New York 10016

Becker, Robert O., M.D
    Cross Currents
    The Perils of Electropollution: The Promise of Electromedicine
    Jeremy P. Tarcher, Inc., 1990 Los Angeles, Ca.

Beer, Robert
    The Encyclopedia of Tibetan Symbols and Motifs
    Shambhala, 1999, Boston, Mass.

Beinfield, Harriet, L.Ac. and
    Efrem Korngold, L.Ac., O.M.D.
    Between Heaven And Earth: A Guide To Chinese Medicine,
    Ballantine Books, 1991 New York, New York

Bensky, Dan and Andrew Gamble with Ted Kaptchuck
    Illustrations Adapted by Lilian Lai Bensky
    Chinese Herbal Medicine Materia Medica - Revised Edition
    Eastland Press, Inc., 1993 Seattle, Washington

Berkow, Robert, M.D., Andrew J. Fletcher M.B.
    The Merck Manual of Diagnosis and Therapy
    17th Edition, Merck Research Laboratories
    Merck & Co. Inc., 2000 Rahway, N.J.

Blofeld, John
    The Secret and Sublime: Taoist Mysteries and Magic
    E.P. Dutton & Co., Inc
    George Allen & Unwin Ltd., 1973 New York

Bokenkamp, Stephen R.
   Early Daoist Scriptures
   E.P. Dutton & Co., Inc
   University of California Press, 1997 Berkely, Ca

The Brain Workshop Handbook
   The Brain Company, Inc., 1984
   Burlington, Mass. 01803

Brennan, Barbara Ann
   Hands of Light: A Guide to Healing Through the Human Energy Field
   Bantam Books Publishing, 1988 New York

Bryant, Darren A.
   Ancestors and Ghosts: The Philosophic and Religious Origins of the Hungry Ghost Festival
   Asian Studies, 2003 Hong Kong

Burnham, Sophy
   A Book of Angels
   Ballantine Books New York City, New York

Carlo, George and Martin Schram
   Cell Phones
   Invisible Hazards in the Wireless Age
   Carroll & Graf Publishers, 2001
   New York City, New York

Carus, Paul
   Chinese Astrology: Early Chinese Occultism
   Open Court Publishing, 1989 La Salle, Ill.

Cao, Guangwen et al.
   Current Biological Treatment of Cancer
   People's Military Press, 1995 Beijing, China

Castleman, Michael
   The New Healing Herbs
   Rodale Press, Inc., 2001 Emmaus, Pa.

Ce, Jin and Hu Zhanggui, with Jin Zhenghua
   Practical Chinese Qigong for Home Health Care
   Foreign Languages Press, 1996 Beijing, China

Chang, Stephen T., Dr.
   The Complete System of Self-healing Internal Exercises
   Tao Publishing, 1986 San Francisco, Ca. 94132

Chang, Minyi
   Anticancer Medical Herbs
   Hunan Science and Technology Pub. House
   Beijing, China 1992

Charles, George
   Le Rituel du Dragon
   ILes sources et les racines des Arts Martiaux
   Editions, Chariot d'Or, 2003 France

Chen, Kaiguo and Zheng Shunchao
   Opening the Dragon Gate
   The Making of a Modern Taoist Wizard
   Translated by Thomas Cleary
   Charles E. Tuttle Co., Inc., 1998 North Clarendon, Vt.

Chen, Yan-Feng, Dr.
   Pre-Natal Energy, Mobilizing Qigong
   China Taoist Ancient Qigong
   Chinese Kung Fu Series, 1992
   Guandong Xin hua Printing House

Chen, Yaoting
   Origin of the Big Dipper
   Translated by Luo Tongbing 2002
   Taoist Culture and Information Center
   www.eng.taoism.org.hk/

Chen, Zeming
   Complete Effective Prescriptions for Women's Diseases
   Jin Dynasty, China 1237

Chinese Qigong
   Publishing House of Shanghai, 1990
   College of Traditional Chinese Medicine
   Shanghai, China

Chinese Qigong, Outgoing - Qi Therapy
   Shandong Science and Technology Press,
   1992 Shandong, China

Chinese Qigong Therapy
   Shandong Science and Technology Press,
   1995 Shandong, China

Choa, Kok Sui, Dr.
   Pranic Healing
   Samuel Weiser, Inc., 1990 York Beach, Maine

Chogyal, Namkhai Norbu
   Dream Yoga and the practice of Natural Light
   Snow Lion Publications, 1992 Ithaca, New York

Cleary, Thomas
   Immortal Sisters: Secret Teachings of Taoist Women
   North Atlantic Books, 1996 Berkeley, Ca.

BIBLIOGRAPHY

Cleary, Thomas
    The Inner Teachings of Taoism: Chang Po-Tuan,
    Commentary by Liu I-Ming
    Shambhala Press, 2001 Boston & London

Cleary, Thomas
    The Secret of the Golden Flower
    Harper Collins Publishers 1991 New York

Cleary, Thomas
    Understanding Reality: A Taoist Alchemical Classic
    by Chang Po-tuan with a Concise
    Commentary by Liu I-ming
    University of Hawaii Press 1987 Honolulu, Hi

Cleary, Thomas
    The Taoist Classics Volume Two
    The Collected Translations of Thomas Cleary
    Shambhala Publications, Inc. 2003 Boston, Ma

Cohen, Kenneth S.
    The Way of Qigong
    Ballantine Books 1997 Random House, New York

Concise
    English-Chinese, Chinese-English Dictionary
    Second Edition
    Oxford University Press, 1999 Oxford, New York

Cooper, Primrose
    The Healing Power of Light: A Comprehensive Guide to
    Healing and the Transformative Powers of Light
    Weiser Books, Inc. 2001 York Beach, Me

Cunningham, David Michael
    Creating Magickal Entities
    Egregore Publishing 2003 Perrysburg, OH

Davis, Edward L.
    Society and the Supernatural in Song China
    University of Hawaii Press 2001 Honolulu, Hawaii

Deadman, Peter
    Selected Articles from the
    Journal of Chinese Medicine
    England

Deadman, Peter & Maazin Al-Khafaji with Kevin Baker
    A Manual of Acupuncture
    Journal of Chinese Medicine Publications 1998 England

DeGroot, J.J.M., Ph.D., LL.D.
    Religion in China: Universalism: A Key To The Study of
    Taoism and Confucianism
    G.P. Putnam's Sons, 1912 New York and London

DeGroot, J.J.M., Ph.D., LL.D.
    The Religious System of China: Book 1, Volume l
    Its Ancient Forms, Evolution, History and Present Aspect
    Manners, Customs & Social institutions Connected Therein
    Disposal of the Dead,
    Part 1 - Funeral Rites; Part 2 - The Ideas of Resurrection
    Ch'eng Wen Publishing Co., 1976 Taipei, Taiwan

DeGroot, J.J.M., Ph.D., LL.D.
    The Religious System of China: Book 1, Volume ll
    Its Ancient Forms, Evolution, History & Present Aspect
    Manners, Customs & Social Institutions Connected Therein
    Disposal of the Dead,
    Part 3 - The Grave (First Half)
    Ch'eng Wen Publishing Co., 1976 Taipei, Taiwan

DeGroot, J.J.M., Ph.D., LL.D.
    The Religious System of China: Book 1, Volume lll
    Its Ancient Forms, Evolution, History & Present Aspect
    Manners, Customs & Social Institutions Connected Therein
    Disposal of the Dead,
    Part 3 - The Grave (Second Half)
    Ch'eng Wen Publishing Co., 1976 Taipei, Taiwan

DeGroot, J.J.M., Ph.D., LL.D.
    The Religious System of China: Book 2, Volume IV
    Its Ancient Forms, Evolution, History & Present Aspect
    Manners, Customs & Social institutions Connected Therein
    On the Soul and Ancestral Worship
    Part 1 - The Soul in Philosophy
    Ch'eng Wen Publishing Co., 1976 Taipei, Taiwan

DeGroot, J.J.M., Ph.D., LL.D.
    The Religious System of China: Book 2, Volume V
    Its Ancient Forms, Evolution, History & Present Aspect
    Manners, Customs & Social institutions Connected Therein
    Disposal of the Dead,
    Part 2 - Demonology
    Part 3 - Sorcery
    Ch'eng Wen Publishing Co., 1976 Taipei, Taiwan

DeGroot, J.J.M., Ph.D., LL.D.
    The Religious System of China: Book 2, Volume VI
    Its Ancient Forms, Evolution, History & Present Aspect
    Manners, Customs & Social institutions Connected Therein
    Disposal of the Dead,
    Part 4 - The War against Spectres
    Part 5 - The Priesthood of Animism
    Ch'eng Wen Publishing Co., 1976 Taipei, Taiwan

DeSchepper, Luc, M.D., Ph.D., C.Ac.
Acupuncture for the Practitioner
Santa Monica, California 91403

DeVita, Vincent T., Jr., Samuel Hellman, & Steven A. Rosenberg
Cancer Principles and Practice of Oncology
Fifth Edition - Vol 1
Lippincott - Raven Publishers, 1997 New York

DeVita, Vincent T., Jr., Samuel Hellman, & Steven A. Rosenberg
Cancer Principles and Practice of Oncology
Fifth Edition - Vol 2
Lippincott - Raven Publishers, 1997
Philadelphia - New York

Diagnostics of Traditional Chinese Medicine
Publishing House of Shanghai, 1990
College of Traditional Chinese Medicine
Shanghai, China

Ding, Li, Professor
Acupuncture, Meridian Theory,
and Acupuncture Points
China Books & Periodicals, Inc., 1992
Foreign languages Press, Beijing

Dong Paul and Thomas Raffill
Empty Force
Element Books, Inc., 1996 Rockport, Mass. 01966

Duan, Shizhen
A Modern Chinese-English Dictionary
Hai Feng Publishing Co., Ltd. Oxford University Press

Eberhard, Wolfram
A Dictionary of Chinese Symbols
Hidden Symbols in Chinese Life and Thought
Routledge, 2003 New York City, New York

Eckman, Peter, M.D., Ph.D., M.Ac. (UK)
In the Footsteps of the Yellow Emperor
Tracing the History of Traditional Acupuncture
Cypress Book Company, Inc. 1996 San Francisco, Ca

Ellis, Andrew, Nigel Wiseman, Ken Boss
Grasping the Wind: An exploration into the meaning of
Chinese acupuncture point names
Paradigm Publications, 1989 Brookline, Massachusetts

Essentials of Chinese Acupuncture
Beijing College of Traditional Chinese Medicine
Foreign Languages Press, 1980 Beijing, China

Evola, Julius
The Yoga of Power, Tantra, Shakti, and The Secret Way
Inner Traditions International, 1992 Rochester, Vt

Feit, Richard and Paul Zmiewski
Acumoxa Therapy: A Reference and Study Guide
Volume II The Treatment of Diseases
Paradigm Publications, 1990 Brooklyn, Ma

Flaws, Bob and James Lake, M.D.
Chinese Medical Psychiatry: A Textbook & Clinical Manual
Blue Poppy Press, 2001
Boulder, Colorado

Flaws, Bob
Curing Headaches Naturally with Chinese Medicine
Blue Poppy Press, 1998 Boulder, Colorado

Gao, Bingjun
A Collection of Expieriences in the Treatment of Sores
Qing Dynasty, China 1808

Gao, Qiyun
Questions and Answers in External Diseases
Ming Dynasty, China 1517

Gerber, Richard, M.D.
Vibrational Medicine
Bear and Company, 1988 Santa Fe, New Mexico

Goldman, Jonathan
Healing Sounds: The Power of Harmonics
Healing Arts Press, 2002 Rochester, Vt

Gordon, James S., M.D. and Sharon Curtin
Comprehensive Cancer Care: Integrating Alternative,
Complementary, and Conventional Therapies
Perseus Publishing, 2000 Cambridge, Ma

Gore, Belinda
Ecstatic Body Postures: An Alternate Reality Workbook
Bear and Company Publishing, 1995 Santa Fe, NM

Govinda, Anagarika, Lama
The Inner Structure of the I-Ching
The Book of Transformations
A Wheelwright Press Book, 1981 Tokyo, New York

Graham, Donald H, Jr.
Bronze Mirrors From Ancient China
Techpearl Printing, Ltd., 1994 Hong Kong

BIBLIOGRAPHY

Graves, Tom
Needles of Stone Revisited
Gothic Image Publications, 1986
Glastonbury, Somerset, England

Gray, Henry F.R.S.
Gray's Anatomy
Barnes & Noble Books, 1995 America

Grof, Stanislav, M.D. with Hal Zina Bennett
The Holotropic Mind
Harper Collins Publishers, Inc., 1993 New York

Guiley, Rosemary Ellen
Harper's Encyclopedia of
Mystical and Paranormal Experiences
Harper Collins Publishers Inc., 1991, New York

Guo, Liang Cao, Dr.
Essentials Of Tuinaology
Chinese Medical Massage and Manipulation
Cao's Fire Dragon, 1983 Hilo, Hawaii

Guo, Shuping, Dr.
Selections from Gao's Medical Works on Tumor
Treatment using Traditional Chinese Medicine
China Press of Traditional Chinese Medicine, 1997
Beijing, China

Hai Dian University, Medical Qigong Textbook
The Cultivation of the Innate and the Destines
White Cloud Monastery, 1988 Beijing, China

Hall, Manly P.
Magic: A Treatise on Esoteric Ethics
Philosophical Research Society, 1998 Los Angeles, Ca.

Hammer, Leon, M.D.
Dragon Rises and Red Bird Flies
Psychology and Chinese Medicine
Staton Hills Press, Inc., 1990 Barrytown, New York

Han, Rui
Chemical Drugs & Preparations in the Treatment of Tumors
Beijing Medical University and Peking
Union Medical University Joint Press
Beijing, China 1992

Harper, Donald
Early Chinese Medical Literature
The Mawangdui Medical Manuscripts
Kegan Paul International, 1998 London & New York

Hawk, Ambrose
Exploring Scrying
New Page Books, 2001 Franklin Lakes, N.J.

Ho, P.Y. and F.P.Lisowski
A Brief History of Chinese Medicine, 2nd Edition
World Scientific Publishing Co., 1997 Singapore

Holmes, Peter
The Energetics of Western Herbs Volume 1
Snow Lotus Press, Inc., 1997 Boulder, Colorado

Holmes, Peter
The Energetics of Western Herbs Volume 2
Snow Lotus Press, Inc., 1997 Boulder, Colorado

Huang, Jane and Wurmbrand, Michael
The Primordial Breath, Volume 1
Original Books Inc., 1998 Torrance, Ca. 90509

Huang, Jane and Wurmbrand, Michael
The Primordial Breath, Volume 2
Original Books Inc., 1990 Torrance, Ca. 90509

Illustration of Channels and Points For
Acupuncture and Moxibustion and Qigong
Hunan Science and Technology Press, 1992
Hunan, China

Jahnke, Roger, D.O.M.
The Healer Within
Harper Publishing, 1997 San Francisco, Ca.

Jarrett, Lonny S.
Nourishing Destiny
The Inner Traditions of Chinese Medicine
Spirit Path Press, 2000 Stockbridge, Mass.

Jarrett, Lonny S.
The Clinical Practice of Chinese Medicine
Spirit Path Press, 2003 Stockbridge, Mass.

Jiao, Guo Rui, Dr.
Qigong Essentials for Health Promotion
China Reconstruction Press, 1990

Johnson, Jerry Alan, C.Ac.
Chi Kung Correspondence Course, Vol. 1-6
Ching Lung Martial Arts Association, 1988 P.G., CA

Johnson, Jerry Alan, C.Ac.
The Essence of Internal Martial Arts, Vol. 1
Esoteric Fighting Techniques and Healing Methods
Ching Lien Healing Arts Center, 1994, Pacific Grove, CA

Johnson, Jerry Alan, C.Ac., *The Essence of Internal Martial Arts,*
Vol. 2: Energy Theory and Cultivation
Ching Lien Healing Arts Center, 1994 Pacific Grove, CA

Johnson, Jerry Alan, Ph.D., D.M.Q. (China)
The Emotional Components of Tumor Formations
Doctoral Theses - Beijing Western District
Qigong Research Institute, 1995 Beijing, China

Johnson, Jerry Alan, Ph.D., D.T.C.M. (China)
Chinese Medical Qigong Therapy:
A Comprehensive Clinical Text
The International Institute of Medical
Qigong, 2000, Pacific Grove, CA

Johnson, Jerry Alan, Ph.D., D.T.C.M. (China)
The Treatment of Cancer With
Chinese Medical Qigong Therapy
The International Institute of Medical
Qigong, 2001, Pacific Grove, CA

Johnson, Jerry Alan, Ph.D., D.T.C.M. (China)
Chinese Medical Qigong Therapy Vol 1:
Energetic Anatomy and Physiology,
The International Institute of Medical
Qigong, 2002, Pacific Grove, CA

Johnson, Jerry Alan, Ph.D., D.T.C.M. (China)
Chinese Medical Qigong Therapy Vol 2: Energetic Alchemy,
Dao Yin Therapy and Qi Deviations
The International Institute of Medical
Qigong, 2002, Pacific Grove, CA

Johnson, Jerry Alan, Ph.D., D.T.C.M. (China)
Chinese Medical Qigong Therapy Vol 3:
Differential Diagnosis, Clinical Foundations,
Treatment Principles and Clinical Protocols
The International Institute of Medical
Qigong, 2002, Pacific Grove, CA

Johnson, Jerry Alan, Ph.D., D.T.C.M. (China)
Chinese Medical Qigong Therapy Vol 4: Prescription Exercises
and Meditations, Treatment of Internal Organ Diseases,
Pediatrics, Geriatrics, Gynecology, Neurology and
Energetic Psychology
The International Institute of Medical
Qigong, 2002, Pacific Grove, CA

Johnson, Jerry Alan, Ph.D., D.T.C.M. (China)
Chinese Medical Qigong Therapy Vol 5:
An Energetic Approach to Oncology
The International Institute of Medical
Qigong, 2002, Pacific Grove, CA

Johnson, Jerry Alan, Ph.D., D.T.C.M. (China)
Daoist Internal Alchemy: Neigong & Weigong Training
The International Institute of Medical Qigong
Publishing House, 2013 Pacific Grove, Ca.

Johnson, Jerry Alan, Ph.D., D.T.C.M. (China)
Daoist Magical Talismans
The International Institute of Medical Qigong,
2010 Pacific Grove, Ca.

Johnson, Jerry Alan, Ph.D., D.T.C.M. (China)
Daoist Magical Transformation Skill: Dream Magic,
Shape-Shifting, Soul Travel and Sex Magic –
The International Institute of Medical Qigong,
2008 Pacific Grove, Ca.

Johnson, Jerry Alan, Ph.D., D.T.C.M. (China)
Daoist Weather Magic and Feng Shui –
The International Institute of Medical Qigong,
2007 Pacific Grove, Ca.

Johnson, Jerry Alan, Ph.D., D.T.C.M. (China)
Daoist Mineral, Plant, and Animal Magic -
The International Institute of Medical Qigong,
2006 Pacific Grove, Ca.

Johnson, Jerry Alan, Ph.D., D.T.C.M. (China)
Daoist Exorcism: Encounters With Sorcerers,
Ghosts, Spirits, and Demons
The International Institute of Medical Qigong,
2006 Pacific Grove, Ca.

Johnson, Jerry Alan, Ph.D., D.T.C.M. (China)
Magical Tools and the Daoist Altar
The International Institute of Medical Qigong,
2006 Pacific Grove, Ca.

Johnson, Jerry Alan, Ph.D., D.T.C.M. (China)
Daoist Magical Incantations, Hand Seals, & Star Stepping
The International Institute of Medical Qigong,
2006 Pacific Grove, Ca.

Johnson, Jerry Alan, Ph.D., D.T.C.M. (China)
Absorbing the Riches of the Profound
The International Institute of Medical Qigong,
2006 Pacific Grove, Ca.

Johnson, Yanling Lee
A Woman's Qigong Guide
Empowerment Through Movement, Diet, and Herbs
Y.M.A.A. Publication Center, 2001 Boston, Mass

Jou, Tsung Hwa
The Tao of Meditation: Way to Enlightenment
Tai Chi Farm, 1986 Warwick, New York 10990

Jurasunas, Serge, Dr.
> *Orthomolecular Treatment of Cancer*
> Townsend Letter for Doctors and Patients
> The Examiner of Medical Alternatives 2002
> February/March 1999

Kapit, Wynn and Lawrence M. Elson
> *The Anatomy Coloring Book*
> Harper Collins Publishers, 1977 New York,

Kaplan, Aryeh
> *Meditation and Kabbalah*
> Samuel Weiser, Inc., 1982 York Beach, ME 03910

Kaptchuk, Ted J., O.M.D.
> *The Web That Has No Weaver*
> Congdon and Weed, Inc., 1983 New York

Kendall, Donald E.
> *Dao of Chinese Medicine*
> *Understanding An Ancient Healing Art*
> Oxford University Press, Inc. 2002 New York

Keville, Kathi, with Peter Korn,
> *Herbs for Health and Healing*
> Rodale Press, Inc., 1996 Emmaus Pennsylania, p. 109

Kohn, Livia and Harold D. Roth
> *Daoist Identity History, Lineage and Ritual*
> University of Hawaii Press, 2002 Honolulu, Hawaii

Kohn, Livia & Yoshinobu Sakade
> *Taoist Meditation and Longevity Techniques*
> Center for Chinese Studies, 1989 University of Michigan

Komjathy, Louis
> *Scripture on the Hidden Talisman*
> Wandering Cloud Press, 2003 Seattle, Washington

Komjathy, Louis
> *Book of Master Celestial Seclusion*
> Wandering Cloud Press, 2003 Seattle, Washington

Konstantinos
> *Summoning Spirits: The Art of Magical Evocation*
> Liewellyn Publications, 2001 St. Paul. MN 55164-0383

Lade, Arnie, Dr., D.O.M.
> *Acupuncture Points, Images & Functions*
> Eastland Press, 1989 Seattle, Washington, 98111

Larre, Claude and Elisabeth Rochat de la Vallee
> *The Seven Emotions Psychology & Health in Ancient China*
> Monkey Press, 1996 Cambridge, CB4 3PU

Larre, Claude and Elisabeth Rochat de la Vallee
> *The Eight Extraordinary Meridians*
> Monkey Press, 1997 Spider Web, London N7

Larre, Claude and Elisabeth Rochat de la Vallee
> *Essence Spirit Blood and Qi*
> Monkey Press, 1999 Spider Web, London N7

Larre, Claude and Elisabeth Rochat de la Vallee
> *The Extraordinary Fu*
> Monkey Press, 2003 Spider Web, London N7

Larre, Claude and Elisabeth Rochat de la Vallee
> *Heart Master - Triple Heater*
> Monkey Press, 1998 Spider Web, London N7

Larre, Claude and Elisabeth Rochat de la Vallee
> *The Lung*
> Monkey Press, 2001 Spider Web, London N7

Larre, Claude and Elisabeth Rochat de la Vallee
> *The Liver*
> Monkey Press, 1999 Spider Web, London N7

Larre, Claude and Elisabeth Rochat de la Vallee
> *The Kidneys*
> Monkey Press, 2001 Spider Web, London N7

Larre, Claude and Elisabeth Rochat de la Vallee
> *Essence Spirit Blood and Qi*
> Monkey Press, 1999 Spider Web, London N7

Larre, Claude and Elisabeth Rochat de la Vallee
> *Rooted in the Spirit: The Heart of Chinese Medicine*
> Station Hill Press, Inc., 1992 Barrytown, New York,

Larre, Claude, Jean Schatz, and
> Elisabeth Rochat de la Vallee
> *Survey of Traditional Chinese Medicine*
> Institut Ricci, Paris and Traditional Acupuncture
> Institute, 1986 Columbia, Maryland

Lee, John R., M.D., David Zava, Ph.D., and Virginia Hopkins
> *What Your Doctor May Not Tell You About Breast Cancer*
> Warner Books, 2002 New York City, New York,

Lee, Mariam, Dr., D.O.M.
> *Insights of a Senior Acupuncturist*
> Blue Poppy Press, 1992 Boulder, Colorado

Lee, Richard H.
> *Qi and Kirlian Photography*
> China Healthways Institute, 1996 San Clemente, Ca

Legeza, Laszlo
> *Tao Magic: The Secret Language of Diagrams & Calligraphy*
> Thames and Hudson, 1975 New York

Li, Gang
> *Ancient Shamanism*
> Translated by David Palmer 2002
> Taoist Culture and Information Center
> www.eng.taoism.org.hk/

Li, Yan
> *Essentials of Clinical Pattern Identification of Tumors*
> People's Medical Publishing House,
> 1998 Beijing, China

Li, Zhongzi
> *Required Readings for Medical Professionals*
> Ming Dynasty, China 1637

Liang, Shou-Yu, Master and Wen-Ching Wu
> *Qigong Empowerment, A Guide to Medical, Taoist,*
> *Buddhist and Wushu energy Cultivation*
> The Way of Dragon Publishing, 1997
> East Providence, Rhode Island 02914-0561

Lieberman, S.
> *Maitake, King of Mushrooms*
> Keats Publishing, 1991 Los Angeles, Ca., p. 16-19.

Lin, Henry B.
> *The Art & Science of Feng Shui*
> *The Ancient Chinese Tradition of Shaping Fate*
> Llewellyn Publications, 2000 St. Paul, Min.

Lin, Huo Sheng, Dr. & Dr. Luo Pei Yu
> *Three Hundred Questions on Qigong Exercises*
> Guandong Science and Technology Press,
> 1994 Guandong, China

Liu, Hong, Dr. with Paul Perry
> *Mastering Miracles*
> Warner Books Inc., 1997 New York

Liu, Zheng-Cai and Hua Ka
> *A Study of Daoist Acupuncture*
> Blue Poppy Press, 1999 Boulder, Colorado

Liu, Zhongyu
> *Divine Incantations*
> Translated by Ginny Yue 2002
> Taoist Culture and Information Center
> www.eng.taoism.org.hk/

Liu, Zhongyu
> *The Origin of Talismans*
> Translated by Ginny Yue 2002
> Taoist Culture and Information Center
> www.eng.taoism.org.hk/

Liu, Zhongyu
> *The Structure of Talismans*
> Translated by Ginny Yue 2002
> Taoist Culture and Information Center
> www.eng.taoism.org.hk/

Liu, Zhongyu
> *The Underworlds (of Chinese Mythology)*
> Translated by David Palmer 2002
> Taoist Culture and Information Center
> www.eng.taoism.org.hk/

Loo, May
> *Pediatric Acupuncture*
> Churchill Livingston, 2002 Printed in China

Lu, Ke Yun
> *The Essence of Qigong*
> *A Handbook of Qigong Therapy and Practice*
> Abode of the Eternal Tao, 1998 Eugene, Oregon

Lu, K'uan Yu
> *Taoist Yoga, Alchemy & Immortality*
> Weiser Books, 1973 Boston, Ma 02210

Maciocia, Giovanni
> *Tongue Diagnosis in Chinese Medicine*
> Eastland Press Inc., 1987 Seattle, Washington

Maciocia, Giovanni
> *Obstetrics & Gynecology in Chinese Medicine*
> Churchill Livingstone Inc., 1998 New York

Maciocia, Giovanni
> *The Foundations of Chinese Medicine*
> Churchill Livingstone Inc., 1989 New York

Maciocia, Giovanni
> *Diagnosis in Chinese Medicine: A Comprehensive Guide*
> Churchill Livingstone Inc., 2004 New York

Maclean, Will with Kathryn Taylor
> *The Clinical Manual of Chinese Herbal Patent*
> *Medicines: A guide to ethical and pure patent medicines*
> Pangolin Press, 2000 Sydney, Australia

MacGregor, Mathers, S.L.
The Book of the Sacred Magic of Abramelin the Mage
Dover Publications, Inc. 1975 New York

MacRitchie, James
Alive With Energy The Chi Kung Way
Harper-Collins Publishers, 1997 San Francisco, Ca.

Marieb, Elaine N., R.N., Ph.D.
Human Anatomy and Physiology
Second Edition
The Benjamin/Cummings Pub. Co., Inc., 1992
Redwood City, California, 94065

Markides, Kyriacos C.
Homage to the Sun: The Wisdom of the Magus of Strovolos
Arkana: Penguin Books, 1987
New York City, New York, 10014

Markides, Kyriacos C.
Fire in the Heart: Healers, Sages and Mystics
Arkana: Penguin Books, 1990 New York

Matsumoto, Kiiko & Stephen Birch
Extraordinary Vessels
Paradigm Publications, 1986 Brookline, Ma

Matsumoto, Kiiko and Stephen Birch
Hara Diagnosis: Reflections on the Sea
Paradigm Publications, 1988 Brookline, Ma

Melchizedek, Drunvalo
The Ancient Secret of the Flower of Life, Vol.1
Light Technology Publishing, 1998 Flagstaff, Az 86003

McAfee, John
Beyond the Siddhis:
Supernatural Powers and the Sutras of Patanjali
Woodland Publications, 2001 Woodland Park, Co.

McTaggart, Lynne
The Field, The Quest For The Secret Force Of The Universe
Harper-Collins Publishers, 2002 New York

McTaggart, Lynne
The Cancer Handbook
Vital-Health Publishing, 1997 Bloomingdale, Ill 60108

Moss, Ralph W., Ph.D.
The Cancer Industry - New Update Edition
The Classic Expose on the Cancer Establishment
Equinox Press, 1999 Brooklyn, New York, 11217

Milne, Hugh
The Heart of Listening
A Visionary Approach to Craniosacral Work
North Atlantic Books, 1995 Berkeley, California

Needham, Joseph, F.R.S., F.B.A.
Science and Civilization in China
Volume 5 Chemistry and Chemical Technology
Part V: Spagyrical Discovery and Invention:
Physiological Alchemy
Cambridge University Press, 1986 Cambridge, London

Netter, Frank H., M.D.
The CIBA Collection of Medical Illustrations
Volume 1 Nervous System
Part II - Neurologic and Neuromuscular Disorders
CIBA Pharmaceutical Co., 1986 West Caldwell N.J.

Netter, Frank H., M.D.
The CIBA Collection of Medical Illustrations
Volume 2 Reproductive System
CIBA Pharmaceutical Co., 1965 West Caldwell N.J.

Netter, Frank H., M.D.
The CIBA Collection of Medical Illustrations
Volume 3 Digestive System, Part I Upper Digestive Tract
CIBA Pharmaceutical Co., 1989 West Caldwell N.J.

Netter, Frank H., M.D.
The CIBA Collection of Medical Illustrations
Volume 3 Digestive System Part II Lower Digestive Tract
CIBA Pharmaceutical Co., 1959 West Caldwell N.J.

Netter, Frank H., M.D.
The CIBA Collection of Medical Illustrations
Volume 3 Digestive System
Part III Liver, Biliary Tract and Pancreas
CIBA Pharmaceutical Co., 1964 West Caldwell N.J.

Netter, Frank H., M.D.
The CIBA Collection of Medical Illustrations
Volume 5 Heart
CIBA Pharmaceutical Co., 1978 West Caldwell N.J.

Netter, Frank H., M.D.
The CIBA Collection of Medical Illustrations
Volume 6 - Kidneys, Ureters, and Urinary Bladder
CIBA Pharmaceutical Co., 1979 West Caldwell N.J.

Netter, Frank H., M.D.
The CIBA Collection of Medical Illustrations
Volume 7 Respiratory System
CIBA Pharmaceutical Co., 1980 West Caldwell N.J.

Ni, Hua Ching, Master
   The Book of Changes and the Unchanging Truth
   The Shrine of the Eternal Breath of Tao, 1983 Malibu, CA

Ni, Hua Ching, Master
   Mysticism Empowering the Spirit Within
   The Shrine of the Eternal Breath of Tao, 1992 Malibu, CA

Niranjanananda, Saraswati Swami
   Prana Pranayama Prana Vida
   Shi Panchdashnam Paramahamsa
   Alakh Bara, 2002 Deoghar, Bihar, India

Niranjanananda, Paramahamsa
   Dharana Darshan Empowering the Spirit Within
   Shi Panchdashnam Paramahamsa
   Alakh Bara, 1993 Deoghar, Bihar, India

O'Connor, John and Dan Bensky
   Acupuncture, A Comprehensive Text
   Shanghai College of Traditional Medicine
   Eastland Press, 1981 Chicago, Illinois

Olsen, Cynthia
   Essiac A Native Herbal Cancer Remedy
   Kali Press, 1996 Pagosa Springs, Colorado

Omura, Yoshiaki, Sc.D., M.D.
   Acupuncture Medicine
   Japan Publications, Inc., 1982 Tokyo, Japan

Panchadas, Swami
   Clairvoyance and Occult Powers
   Fujian Science and Technology
   Yogi Publication Society, 1916 Chicago, Illinois U.S.A.

Pan, Mingji, M.D. (China)
   How to Discover Cancer Through Self-Examination
   Fujian Science and Technology
   Publishing House, 1992 Beijing, China

Pan, Mingji, M.D. (China)
   Cancer Treatment with Fu Zheng Pei Ben Principle
   Fujian Science and Technology
   Publishing House, 1992 Beijing, China

A Modern Chinese-English Dictionary
   Hai Feng Publishing Co., Ltd.
   Oxford University Press, 1997 Oxford, New York

Pearsall, Paul, Ph.D.
   The Heart's Code Tapping the Wisdom and Power of Our Heart Energy
   Broadway Books, 1998 New York City, New York,

Peoples Republic of China
   The Cultivation of the Innate and the Destined
   White Cloud Monastery 1988 Beijing, China

Pereira, M. A., et al
   Effects of the Phytochemicals, Curcumin and Quercitin, upon Azoxymenthane- Induced Colon Cancer and 7, 12- DimenthybenzA Chinese Traditional Therapeutic Skill
   Shandong Science and Technology Press, 1990
   Shandong, China

Pidwirny, Michael, Dr.
   Introduction to the Hydrosphere
   Department of Geography
   Okanagan University College, 2004

Rago, D. Scott
   Leaving the Body: A Complete Guide to Astral Projection
   Prentice-Hall, Inc., 1983 Englewood Cliffs, NJ

Ramacharaka, Yogi
   Fourteen Lessons in Yogi Philosophy and Oriental Occultism
   Yogi Publication Society, 1903 Chicago, Illinois U.S.A.

Ramacharaka, Yogi
   Science of Breath A Complete Manual of The Oriental Breathing Philosophy of Physical, Mental, Phychic and Spiritual Development
   Yogi Publication Society, 1904 Chicago, Illinois U.S.A.

Ramacharaka, Yogi
   Raja Yoga or Mental Development
   Yogi Publication Society 1906 Chicago, Il.

Ramacharaka, Yogi
   The Science of Phychic Healing
   Yogi Publication Society, 1909 Chicago. Il

Ramacharaka, Yogi
   The Life Beyond Death
   Yogi Publication Society, 1909 Chicago, Il.

Ramacharaka, Yogi
   The Hindu Yogi Practical Water Cure
   Yogi Publication Society, 1909 Chicago, I.

Reid, Daniel
   The Complete Book of Chinese Health and Healing
   Shambhala Publications, Inc., 1994 Boston, Ma

Reid, Daniel
   A Complete Guide to Chi-Gung Harnessing the Power of the Universe
   Shambhala Publications, Inc., 2000 Boston, Ma

Requena, Yves
Character and Health
The Relationship of Acupuncture and Psychology
Paradigm Publications, Inc., 1989 Brookline, Ma

Rinpoche, Tenzin Wangyal
Healing with Form, Energy and Light: The Five Elements in Tibetan Shamanism, Tantra and Dzogchen
Snow Lion Publications, 2002 Ithaca, New York,

Robinet, Isabelle
Taoist Meditation
The Mao-shan Tradition of Great Purity
State University of New York Press, 1993 Albany, NY

Ros, Frank, Dr.
The Lost Secrets of Ayurvedic Acupuncture
Lotus Press, 1994 Twin Lakes, Wisconsin

Ross, Elisabeth Kubler, M.D.
On Death and Dying
Collier Books, 1969 Macmillan Pub. Co., New York

Ross, Jeremy, C.Ac. (Nanjing), B.Ac. (M.B.Ac.A.), C.Ed.
Zang Fu, The Organ Systems of Traditional Chinese Medicine Functions, Interrelationships and Patterns of Disharmony in Theory and Practice
Churchill Livingstone, 1985 New York

Sabetti, Stephano
The Wholeness Principle Exploring Life Energy Process
Life Energy Media, 1986 Sherman Oaks, Ca

Sagar, Stephen M., M.D.
Restored Harmony An Evidence Based Approach for
Menlo Park, California

Sancier, Kenneth M., Ph.D.
Anti-Aging Benefits of Qigong
Qigong Institute, 1986 Menlo Park, California

Sankey, Mikio, Ph.D., L.Ac.
Esoteric Acupuncture Gateway to Expanded Healing Vol.1
Mountain Castle Publishing, 1999 Los Angeles, Ca.

Saso, Michael
The Gold Pavilion Taoist Ways to Peace, Healing and Long Life
Charles E. Tuttle Co., 1995 Boston, Mass. 02109

Saso, Michael
Taoist Master Chuang
Sacred Mountain Press, 2000 Eldorado Springs, Co.

Satyananda Saraswati, Swami
Sure Ways to Self Realization
Yoga Publications Trust, 1980 Bihar, India

Satyananda Saraswati, Swami
Taming the Kundalini
Yoga Publications Trust, 1982 Bihar, India

Satyananda Saraswati, Swami
Yoga Nidra
Yoga Publications Trust, 1998 Bihar, India

Satyananda Saraswati, Swami and
Muktibodhananda Saraswati, Swami
Swara Yoga Tantric Science of Brain Breathing
Satyananda Ashram, 1983 Australia

Satyasangananda, Swami
Tattwa Shuddhi
Yoga Publications Trust, 2000 Bihar, India

Scambia, G., et al
Antiproliferative Effects of Silybin on Gynaecological Malignancies: Synergism with Cisplatin and Dororubien
European Journal of Cancer, 1996. 32A (5): 877-882

Scanlan, Michael T.O.R., Randall J. Cirner
Deliverance From Evil Spirits
A Weapon for Spiritual Warfare
Servant Books, 1980 Ann Arbor, Mi

Schneider, Michael S.
A Beginner's Guide to Constructing the Universe
The Mathematical Archetypes of Nature, Art and Science
Harper Collins Publishers, 1994, New York

Schwark, Jack
Human Energy Systems
The Aletheia Foundation 1980 New York

Sheldrake, Rupert
The Presence of the Past
Morphic Resonance &the Habits of Nature
Park Street Press, 1995 Rochester, Vt

Sha, Zhi Gang (Xiao Gang Guo)
Zhi Neng Medicine Revolutionary Self-Healing Methods from China
Zhi Neng Press, 1997 Vancouver, B.C. Canada

Sha, Zhi Gang, Dr.
Power Healing: The Four Keys to Energizing Your Body, Mind and Spirit
Harper Collins Publishers Inc., 2002, New York

Shi, Lanling
>   *Experience In Treating Cancers
>   with Traditional Chinese Medicine*
>   Shandong Science and Technology Press,
>   1992 Shandong, China

Shih, Tzu Kuo, Dr.
>   *Qigong Therapy The Chinese Art of Healing With Energy*
>   Station Hill Press, 1994 Barrytown, New York

Sivapriyananda, Swami
>   *Secret Power of Tantrik Breathing*
>   Abhinav Publications, 1996 New Delhi, India

Small, Eric, et al.
>   *Journal of Clinical Oncology*
>   Vol 18, November 2000

Smith, Jia Yin
>   *The Application of Talisman in Feng Shui*
>   Translated by K.C. Goh 2002
>   Taoist Culture and Information Center
>   www.universalfengshui.com/

Stedman's Medical Dictionary.
>   Vol 18, 2000

Stewart, Goldstein Jade, D.M.Q. (China)
>   *Oncology, Traditional Chinese Medicine & Clinical case Studies*
>   International Institute of Medical Qigong,
>   September, 2004 Monterey, Ca.

Strickmann, Michel
>   *Chinese Magical medicine*
>   Stanford University Press, 2002 Stanford, Ca.

Sun, Jiyuan
>   *A Probing into the Treatment of leukemia
>   with Traditional Chinese Medicine*
>   Hai Feng Publishing Co., 1990 Hong Kong

Svoboda, Robert E.
>   *The Art of Sacred Speech*
>   Yoga International Vol. No.69, January 2003

Svoboda, Robert, and Arnie Lade
>   *Chinese Medicine and Ayurveda*
>   Motilal Banarsidass Publishers, 1998 Delhi, India

Svoboda, Robert E.
>   *Aghora: At the Left Hand of God*
>   Brotherhood of Life, Inc., 1986 Albuquerque, NM

Svoboda, Robert E.
>   *Aghora II: Kundalini*
>   Brotherhood of Life, Inc., 1993 Albuquerque, NM

Svoboda, Robert E.
>   *Aghora III: The Law of Karma*
>   Brotherhood of Life, Inc., 1997 Albuquerque, NM

Talbot, Michael
>   *The Holographic Universe*
>   Harper Collins Publishers, 1991 New York,

Taylor, Kylea
>   *The Ethics of Caring*
>   Hanford Mead Publishers, 1995 Santa Cruz, Ca

Textbook of Medical Qigong Therapy
>   Haidian Qigong University Medical Qigong College
>   White Cloud Monastery, 1988 Beijing, China

Thomas, Clayton L., M.D., M.P.H.
>   *Taber's Cyclopedic Medical Dictionary*
>   F.A. Davis Company, 1993 Philadelphia, Pa.

Thornes, D., et al
>   *Prevention of Early Recurrence of High
>   Risk Malignant Melanoma by Coumarin.*
>   Irish Melanoma Group,
>   1989 European Journal of Surgical Oncology
>   15 (5): 431- 435.

Tierra, Michael, L.Ac., N.D., A.H.G.
>   *East West Master Course In Herbology*,
>   1981 Santa Cruz, California

Tierra, Michael, L.Ac., N.D., A.H.G.
>   *Treating Cancer with Herbs An Integrative Approach*,
>   Lotus Press 2003 Twin Lakes, Wi

Torisu, M., et al
>   "*Significant Prolongation of Disease-free Period Gained
>   by Oral Polysaccharide K (PSK) Administration
>   after Curative Surgical Operation of Colorectal Cancer*"
>   Cancer Immunology and Immunotherapy,
>   1990 31 (5): 261-268.

Tortora, Gerard J. and Sandra R. Grabowski
>   "*Principles of Anatomy and Physiology Seventh Edition*
>   Harper Collins College Publishers, 1993 New York,

Tyson, Donald
>   *The Power of the Word The Secret Code of Creation*
>   Llewellyn Publications, 2004 Saint Paul, MN

Tyson, Donald
>   *Scrying for Beginners*
>   Liewellyn Publishers, 2004 St. Paul, Mi

Tyson, Donald
Familiar Spirits
Liewellyn Publishers, 2004 St. Paul, Mi

The University of Rochester School of Medicine
Clinical Oncology A multidisciplinary Approach,
1978 Rochester, New York

Unschuld, Paul U.
Medicine in China Nan-Ching The Classic of Difficult Issues
University of California Press 1986 Berkeley, California

Unschuld, Paul U.
Forgotten Traditions of Ancient Chinese Medicine
A Chinese View of the Eighteenth Century
Paradigm Publications 1998 Brookline, Ma

Van Ostrand, Lisa, D.M.Q.
Treating Cysts, Tumors and Cancer
Using a Medical Qigong Approach
International Institute of Medical Qigong,
Florida Branch, 2004

Van Buskirk, Patricia, L.Ac.
Anatomy of a Stroke
Journal of Oriental Medicine in America,
Summer 1997, Volume 1, Number 4, Ca.

Veith, Ilza
The Yellow Emperor's Classic of Internal Medicine
University of California Press, 1966 Berkeley, Ca.

Vieira, Waldo, M.D.
Projections of the Consciousness
A Diary of Out-of-Body Experiences
International Institute of Projectiology
and Conscientiology, 1997 Rio De Janerio, Brazil

Walker, Martin J.
Dirty Medicine
Science, big business and the assault on natural health care
Slingshot Publishing, 1993 London, England

Walters, Derek
The Complete Guide to Chinese Astrology
Watkins Publishing, 2005 London, England

Walters, Derek
Ming Shu: The Art and practice of Chinese Astrology
Kim Hup Lee Printing Co. 1989 Singapore

Weed, Susan S.
Breast Cancer? Beast Health! The Wise Woman Way
Ash Tree Publishing, 1996 Woodstock, New York.

Welch, Holmes
Taoism: The Parting of the Way
Beacon Press, 1972 Boston, Mass.

Weil, Andrew, M.D.
Spontaneous Healing
Fawcett Columbine
Published by Ballantine Books, 1995, New York

Whitcomb, Bill
The Magician's Companion A Practical &
Encyclopedic Guide to Magical & Religious Symbolism
Llewellyn Publications, 2002 St. Paul, MN

Wieger, L. Dr., S.J.
Chinese Characters: Their origin, etymology, history,
classification and signification
Dover Publications, Inc., 1965, New York

Wilber, Ken, Carol McCormick, Alex Grey
Sacred Mirrors: The Visionary Art of Alex Grey
Inner Traditions International, 1990 Rochester, Vt

Willmont, Dennis
The Twelve Spirit Points of Acupuncture
Willmountain Press, 1999 Roslindale, Ma

Wing, R. L.
The I Ching Workbook
Doubleday Dell Publishing Group, 1979 New York,

Wiseman, Nigel and Feng Ye
A Practical Dictionary of Chinese Medicine
Second Edition
Paradigm Publications, 1998 Brooklyn, Ma

Wiseman, Nigel and Feng Ye
Chinese Medical Chinese Grammar and Vocabulary
Paradigm Publications, 2002 Brooklyn, Ma

Wong, Eva
Teachings of the Tao
Shambhala Press, 1997 Boston & London

Wong, Eva
The Shambhala Guide to Taoism, A complete introduction
to the history, philosophy, and practice of an ancient
Chinese spiritual tradition
Shambhala Press, 1997 Boston & London

Wu, Baolin, Dr. and Jessica Eckstein
Lighting the Eye of the Dragon
Inner Secrets of Taoist Feng Shui
St. Martin's Press, 2000 New York

Wu, Henry S., D.C.
Differentiation of Syndromes
California Acupuncture College, 1982 Los Angeles, Ca.

Wu, Jing-Nuan
Ling Shu or The Spiritual Pivot
Asian Spirituality, Taoist Studies Series
The Taoist Center University of Hawaii Press,
1993 Honolulu, Hawaii

Wu, Qian
The Goldem Mirror of Medicine
Qing Dynasty, China 1742

Wu, Zhongxian
Ba Zi - Chinese Astrology
Qi The Journal of Health and Fitness
Volume 14, No. 2 Summer 2004

Xiao, Qian
Observations on the Therapeutic Efficacy of the Treatment of 38 cases of Acute Leukemia with a Combination of Chinese Medicines and Chemotherapy, 1998 Zhong Yi Za Zhi (Journal of Chinese Medicine), #5, p.283-285.

Xie, Wenwei
Cancer = Death
New World Press Beijing, China 1997

Xu, Rui-rong et al.
The Treatment of 50 Cases of Acute Nonlymphocytic Leukemia with a combination of Chinese Medicine Pattern Discrimination & the HA Program,
Zhong Guo Zhong Xi Yi Jie He Za Zhi
(Chinese National Journal of Integrated Chinese-Western Medicine), 1995, #5, p 302-303.

Yan, De-Xin
Aging & Blood Stasis
A New TCM Approach to Geriatrics
translated by Tang Guo-shun & Bob Flaws
Blue Poppy Press, 1995 Boulder, Co.

Yance, Donald R., Jr. with Arlene Valentine
Herbal Medicine, Healing & Cancer
Keats Publishing, 1999 Los Angeles, Ca. p.116

Yang, D. A., S. Q. Li, X. T. Li,
Chinese Journal of Surgery
Hua Wei Ko Tsa Chih, July 1994, p. 434.

Yang, Jwing Ming, Ph.D.
The Root of Chinese Qigong The Secrets of Qigong Training
Yang Martial Arts Association, 1989 Jamaica Plain, Ma

Yang, Li
Book of Changes and Traditional Chinese Medicine
Beijing Science and Technology Press,
1998 Beijing, China

Yang, Qiyuan
Chinese Yuanbao Qigong
New World Press, 1998 Beijing, China

Yeung, Him-che, L.Ac, O.M.D., Ph.D.
Diseases of the Colon and Rectum
Institute of Chinese medicine, 1993 Rosemead, Ca.

Yin, Hui He
Fundamentals of Traditional Chinese Medicine
Foreign Languages Press, 1995 Beijing, China

Yu, Gong Bao
Chinese Qigong Illustrated
New World Press, 1995 Beijing, China

Zhao, Ruan Jin, Dr.
The Origin of Cancer and Phlegm
Traditional Chinese Medicine World
March 2002 - Vol.3. No. 4, New York

Zhang, Enqin
Basic Theory of Traditional Chinese Medicine
Publishing House of Shanghai College of
Traditional Chinese Medicine, 1988 Shanghai, China

Zhang, Yu Huan & Ken Rose
A Brief History of Qi
Paradigm Publications, 2001 Brookline, Ma

Zhang, Yu Huan & Ken Rose
Who Can Ride the Dragon? An Exploration of the Cultural Roots of Traditional Chinese Medicine
Paradigm Publications, 1999 Brookline, Ma

Zhu, Danxi
Danxi's Experiential Therapy
Revised by Cheng Yun
Ming Dynasty, China 1481

Clinic References

American Cancer Society- Cancer Facts and Figures
www.cancer.org. 2002

American Cancer Society- Melanoma Skin Cancer
www.cancer.org. 2002

Fey, John, Master
Clinical Notes from Lectures Medical Qigong Therapy
Reference: Differential Healing Modalities
Los Angeles, CA 1984 to 1987

Gershon, Michael, M.D.
Professor of Anatomy and Cell Biology
Columbia Presbyterian Medical Center
Research presented by Sandra Blakeslee
New York Times, New York   1996

Gill, Jason L.Ac.
Lectures on Traditional Chinese Medicine
Clinical Notes on Differential Diagnosis
Pacific Grove, CA 1994 to 1997

Gill, Jason L.Ac.
Clinical notes and Lectures
Reference: Dr. Jeremy Ross Lectures
on Traditional Chinese Medicine
Pacific Grove, CA. 1994 to 1997

Guo Xian He, Dr., Dr. Zhou Jun Jie
Clinical notes from Orthopedic Traumatology
Clinic of the Hu Guo Si Hospital of T.C.M.
on Medical Qigong Therapy and Anmo Therapy:
Internship specializing in Chinese bone-setting,
traumatology, and tissue manipulation Sept. 1993

Hong, Lu Guo, Dr., Dr. Niu Yu Hua, Dr. Li Fu Dong
Clinical notes from Hai Dian Medical University on
Medical Qigong Therapy and Differential Healing
Modalities Beijing, China 1993 - 1996

Integrative Medicine Communications
Skin Cancer
www.ivillagehealth.com. 2001

Johnson, Jerry Alan, Ph.D., D.T.C.M., D.M.Q. (China)
Clinical notes from the First World Conference on
Medical Qigong Therapy and Differential Healing
Modalities, Reference Conference No. 1, Sept. 1988

Johnson, Jerry Alan, Ph.D., D.T.C.M., D.M.Q. (China)
Clinical notes from the International Symposium on
Chinese Qigong Health Preservation and Qigong
Techniques Medical Qigong Therapy and Differential
Healing Modalities Reference Symposium, Nov. 1990

Johnson, Jerry Alan, Ph.D., D.T.C.M., D.M.Q. (China)
Clinical notes from the Second World Conference on
Medical QigongTherapy and Differential Healing
Modalities, Reference Conference No. 2, Sept. 1993

Johnson, Jerry Alan, Ph.D., D.T.C.M., D.M.Q. (China)
Clinical notes from Xi Yuan Hospital on Medical
Qigong Therapy and Differential Healing Modalities
Internship July 1993 through Sept. 1995

Johnson, Jerry Alan, Ph.D., D.T.C.M., D.M.Q. (China)
Clinical notes from Orthopedic Traumatology Ward
of the Hu Guo Si Hospital of T.C.M.on Medical Qigong
Therapy and AnmoTherapy: Internship specializing
in Chinese bone-setting, traumatology, and tissue
manipulation, Sept. 1993

Johnson, Jerry Alan, Ph.D., D.T.C.M., D.M.Q. (China)
Clinical notes from Hai Dian Medical University
on Medical Qigong Therapy and Differential Healing
Modalities, July 1993 through Sept. 1995

Johnson, Jerry Alan, Ph.D., D.T.C.M., D.M.Q. (China)
Clinical notes from the Third World Conference on
Medical QigongTherapy and Differential Healing
Modalities, Reference Conference No. 3, Sept. 1996

Johnson, Jerry Alan, Ph.D., D.T.C.M., D.M.Q. (China)
Clinical notes from the Second World Congress on
Medical Qigong Therapy and Differential Healing
Modalities, San Francisco, California, Nov. 1997

Johnson, Jerry Alan, Ph.D., D.T.C.M., D.M.Q. (China)
Clinical notes from the Fourth World Conference on
Medical Qigong Therapy and Differential Healing
Modalities, Reference Conference No. 4, Sept. 1998

Johnson, Jerry Alan, Ph.D., D.T.C.M., D.M.Q. (China)
Clinical Notes from Medical Qigong Clinic
Pacific Grove, CA., from 1988 - 2004

Johnson, Jerry Alan, Ph.D., D.T.C.M., D.M.Q. (China)
: Clinical Notes from The Five Branches Acupuncture and Medical Qigong Clinic, Santa Cruz, CA, 2000 - 2004

Johnson, Jerry Alan, Ph.D., D.T.C.M., D.M.Q. (China)
: Clinical Notes from The Academy of Five Element Acupuncture and Medical Qigong Clinic, Hallandale, Fl, from 2003 - 2004

Johnson, Mark, Sifu
: Clinical Notes in Geriatric Medical Qigong Therapy and Esoteric Daoist Studies of the Yi-Jing & Feng Shui, Mill Valley, CA 1998 - 1999

Krieger, Lisa M.
: *Full-body X-ray scans boost cancer risk*
San Jose Mercury News, Tuesday, August 31, 2004

Li, Fudong, D.M.Q., Lu Guohong D.M.Q., Niu Yuhua D.M.Q.
: Clinical notes from Hai Dian Medical University on Medical Qigong Therapy and Differential Healing Modalities, July 1993 through Sept. 1995

Lu, Dr. and Dr. Xu Zong Wei
: Clinical Notes from Xi Yuan Hospital Medical Qigong Therapy and Differential Healing Modalities, Beijing, China 1993

Meng, Xiantong, D.T.C.M., and Tara Peng, D.M.Q.
: Clinical notes from the Beijing Chengjian Clinic of Integrated T.C.M. and Western Medicine, Sept. 1998

Milne, Hugh, Dr.
: Clinical Notes from Cranial-Sacral Therapy Level 1 through 6, 1990-1995 Monterey, Calif.

National Cancer Institute
: What You need To Know About Skin Cancer www.nci.org. 1998

National Women's Health Resource Center
: Skin Cancer www.ivillagehealth.com 2000

Pang, Jeffrey, L.Ac., M.D. (China)
: Clinical Notes from class on Traditional Chinese Medical Treatment for Oncology, Five Branches Institute Feb. -June 2003 Ca

Pang, Jeffrey, L.Ac., M.D. (China)
: Clinical Notes from class on Traditional Chinese Medicine: Dietetics Five Branches Institute Feb. -June 2002 Santa Cruz, California

Pereira, M. A., et al Effects of the Phytochemicals, Curcumin and Quercitin, upon Azoxymenthane-Induced Colon Cancer and 7, 12-Dimenthybenz (a) anthracene-Induced Mammary Cancer in Rats Carcinogenesis 17 (6): 130 5-11 1996.

Ren, Shun Tu, Dr. & Dr. Xu Hong Tao
: Clinical Notes from Xi Yuan Hospital Medical Qigong Therapy and Differential Healing Modalities Beijing, China 1995

Sun, Dr., and Dr. Tu
: Clinical notes from Xi Yuan Hospital on Medical Qigong Therapy and Differential Healing Modalities Internship July 1993 through Sept. 1995

Sun, Shuchun, D.T.C.M., Dr. Fan
: Clinical notes from Orthopedic Traumatology Ward of the Hu Guo Si Hospital of T.C.M. on Medical Qigong Therapy and Anmo Therapy: Internship specializing in Chinese bone-setting, traumatology, and tissue manipulation, Sept. 1993

Turk, Michael, L.Ac.
: Clinical Notes from CSOMA International Expo & Comvention 2002 Seminar: Healing Chronic Pain and Disability, San Francisco, California 2002

Teng, Ying Bo, Dr.
: Clinical Notes from Beijing Medical Qigong Science and Research Institute; Medical Qigong Therapy and Differential Healing Modalities, Beijing, China 1995

Xu, Hongtao, D.M.Q., Ren Shuntu, D.M.Q., and Xu Zongwei
: Clinical Notes from Xi Yuan Hospital Medical Qigong Therapy and Differential Healing Modalities Beijing, China 1995

Zheng, Zhan Ding, Master
: Clinical Notes on Medical Qigong Diagnosis, Therapy and Differential Healing Modalities Beijing, China 1993 - 1998

Zhong, Jiang Gui, Dr. and Dr. Cai Chang Rong
: Clinical Notes from Hu Guo Hospital Medical Qigong Therapy, An Mo Therapy and Differential Healing Modalities, Beijing, China 1993

Zhou, Fang, D.M.Q.
: Clinical Notes on Medical Qigong Therapy, An Mo Therapy and Differential Healing Modalities, Hai Dian University Clinic, Beijing, China 1993-95

About the Author

Medical Background

Professor Jerry Alan Johnson is one of the few internationally recognized non-Chinese Grand Masters, practicing doctors, and Director/Professor of Medical Qigong Therapy. Having studied Chinese Energetic Medicine for more than forty-two years, he is recognized both in China and the West as America's leading authority on Medical Qigong Therapy, and is considered to be the "Father of Medical Qigong Therapy to the West."

Professor Johnson is licensed as a Doctor of Traditional Chinese Medicine (D.T.C.M.) in Beijing, China, by the People's Republic of China's Ministry of Health, and has served on national and international committees to promote and encourage the practice of Medical Qigong Therapy.

Professor Jerry Alan Johnson, Ph.D., D.T.C.M., (China)

He is the President and Founder of the International Institute of Medical Qigong, in Monterey, California, and has designed several Medical Qigong programs which have been implemented into various T.C.M. Colleges and Medical Qigong Institutes throughout the United States, Belgium, Bermuda, Brazil, Canada, Central America, England, France, Germany, Ireland, South Africa, and Sweden.

To date, Professor Johnson has presented many papers on clinical research utilizing Medical Qigong Therapy. He has also written and published over six Clinical Textbooks on the practice of Medical Qigong Therapy. These special textbooks are currently used in many T.C.M. Colleges and universities throughout the world for the purpose of studying Chinese Energetic Medicine.

He has also produced 19 Instructional DVDs on Medical Qigong Therapy, including an Interactive Instructional CD-ROM using Medical Qigong Therapy for the Prevention and Treatment of Breast Disease; as well as 2- Meditation CDs

History

Professor Johnson began his initial training in Chinese Energetic Medicine in 1972, in Monterey, California. In 1974, he started formal studies in Traditional Chinese Medicine (T.C.M.), focusing on Acupuncture, Herbology, Medical Qigong Therapy, Traumatology, and Chinese Massage from his Northern Shaolin Kungfu instructor.

In 1978, he entered into an Acupuncture Tutorial Program, and began working as an assistant to a Buddhist Monk named Dr. Hyun Huh. Upon completing a 4,000 hour clinical internship in 1981, he was awarded an Acupuncture and Herbology Certification of Completion.

Professor Johnson then moved to Colorado Springs, Colorado, and began operating an Acupuncture Clinic (1981-84), working as a medical consultant and associate in Acupuncture, Herbs, and Medical Qigong Therapy to Western Medical Doctors, Naturopaths, and Chiropractors.

In 1993, Professor Johnson traveled to China and furthered his clinical studies at the China Beijing International Acupuncture Training Center and at the Acupuncture Institute of China, Academy of T.C.M. He was the first foreigner from the Acupuncture Institute of China invited to treat patients in the Medical Qigong Clinic at the Xi Yuan Hospital of T.C.M. (featured in Bill Moyer's special "Healing and the Mind"). There he interned as a Doctor of Medical Qigong Therapy, specializing in the treatment of cancer, tumors, and cysts, and in treating Atrophy Syndromes (kidney "wasting-away" diseases).

In 1993, Professor Johnson also interned as a Doctor of Anmo Therapy at the Orthopedic Traumatology Clinic of the Hu Guo Si Hospital of T.C.M. (in Beijing, China). There he specialized in Chinese bone-setting, traumatology, and tissue manipulation. His training in somatic regulation also includes Neuromuscular Therapy, Psychophysical Integrational Therapy, Advanced Visceral Manipulation, and Advanced Cranio-Sacral Therapy.

In 1995, Professor Johnson obtained his Masters Degree in Medical Qigong Therapy from the Medical Qigong College at the Hai Dian University in Beijing, China. He then received his clinical license as a "Doctor of Traditional Chinese Medicine" (D.T.C.M.), specializing in Medical Qigong Therapy and Anmo Traumatology.

In 1995, Professor Johnson also received his License of Academic Qualifications needed to teach Chinese Medicine, as well as a License of Clinical Qualifications needed to practice Chinese Medicine. Both licenses were awarded from the Beijing Bureau of Public Health and The People's Republic of China, Ministry of Health.

After completion of both academic doctoral thesis and numerous clinical field studies, the Beijing Western District Medical Qigong Science and Traditional Chinese Medicine Research Institute (China) also awarded Doctor Johnson an academic license as "Professor of Medical Qigong Science and Philosophy."

1996

An active member of the World Academic Society of Medical Qigong (W.A.S.O.M.Q.), Professor Johnson was a key speaker at the 1996 Third World Conference on Medical Qigong Therapy, held in Beijing, China, lecturing on "The Psychophysical Components Associated With Tumor Formation."

In 1996, Professor Johnson taught a seminar on "Traumatology, Chinese Massage, and Herbal Healing" at the Emerge International Tai Chi Chuan and Qigong Meditation Arts in Toronto, Canada.

In 1996, Professor Johnson additionally lectured on "The Healing Benefits of Medical Qigong Therapy" at the Monterey Institute of International Studies, in Monterey California; and also lectured on "Healing Emotional Traumas With Medical Qigong Therapy" at the Psychology Department at the Monterey Peninsula College, in Monterey California.

1997

In 1997, Professor Johnson became the first Medical Qigong Doctor allowed to assist in surgery at the Community Hospital of the Monterey Peninsula in Carmel, California.

Professor Johnson also lectured and taught seminars on "Treating Patients with Medical Qigong Therapy," to Nurses, Acupuncturists, the faculty and students of the University of California San Francisco, and the American College of Traditional Chinese Medicine, in San Francisco, California.

In 1997, he lectured at the Second World Congress on Medical Qigong and the First American Qigong Association Conference held in San Francisco, California.

In 1997, Professor Johnson was also elected to the Board of Directors of the National Qigong Association (N.Q.A.), in the United States.

Additionally, in 1997, Professor Johnson was interviewed in Newsweek Magazine, and was the focus of a documentary filmed for the Discovery Channel, on the use of Medical Qigong Therapy for the treatment of internal organ diseases.

1998

In 1998, Professor Johnson lectured at the Northern California Society of Radiation Therapists on "The Use of Medical Qigong Therapy to Rectify the Side Affects of Radiation Therapy" at the Queen of the Valley Hospital in Napa, California.

In 1998, Professor Johnson was also appointed to the National Qigong Association's Chairman of the Medical Qigong Committee, responsible for establishing the guidelines and national standards for Medical Qigong Practitioners (M.Q.P.) working in clinical settings.

In 1998, Professor Johnson lectured on the "Utilization of Medical Qigong Therapy and Surgery" at the Fourth World Conference on Medical Qigong held in Beijing, China, and was elected to the Board of Directors of the World Academic Society of Medical Qigong (W.A.S.O.M.Q.) centered in Beijing, China. He served as one of four Council Board Members that represented the United States at the W.A.S.O.M.Q. Conferences.

Additionally, in 1998, the status of Professor Johnson's Clinical License was elevated to the position of "Physician in Charge" (Clinical Director) and he was licensed as a "Doctor of Traditional Chinese Medicine" from the Beijing Bureau of Medical Science in Beijing, China.

1999

In 1999, Professor Johnson was interviewed in Health and Fitness Magazine on "The Healing Power of Medical Qigong Therapy."

He also lectured on "Correcting Qi Deviations with Medical Qigong Therapy" at the National Qigong Gathering held in Baltimore, Maryland.

In the Spring of 1999, Professor Johnson accepted the position of Dean of Medical Qigong Science from the Five Branches Institute, College and Clinic of Traditional Chinese Medicine, in Santa Cruz, California. At the Five Branches Institute, Professor Johnson developed two programs: a 200 hour Medical Qigong Practitioner (M.Q.P.) program and a 500 hour Medical Qigong Therapist (M.Q.T.) program. Both programs included specific instruction and training gathered from his popular medical textbook entitled: *Chinese Medical Qigong Therapy, A Comprehensive Clinical Text*. The two courses also included the study of specific Medical Qigong Therapy, such as Pediatrics, Geriatrics, Gynecology, Neurology, Psychology, Oncology, and Surgery.

2000

In 2000, Professor Johnson lectured on "Healing Qi Deviations" at the National Qigong Gathering held in Portland, Oregon; the Fourth World Congress on Medical Qigong, and the Fourth American Qigong Association Conference, held in San Francisco, California.

He was also interviewed in a film documentary featured by the Seoul Broadcasting System (S.B.S.) of Korea entitled: "Qi-into the World of the Unknown." The focus of his interview was placed on "The Effects of Medical Qigong Therapy and the Treatment of Patients."

In the Spring of 2000, Professor Johnson implemented within the Five Branches Institute the first Medical Qigong Clinic at a T.C.M. College in North America, facilitating the combined use of acupuncture, herbs, and Medical Qigong therapies to the general public.

2001

In May 2001, Professor Johnson presented to the White House Commission on Complementary and Alternative Medicine Policy (W.H.C.C.A.M.P.) the government standards established by The Peoples Republic of China. These strict standards have currently been implemented into several T.C.M. Colleges in the U.S. through Professor Johnson's own International Institute of Medical Qigong (I.I.M.Q.) organization. These standards were presented to the W.H.C.C.A.M.P. to be incorporated in the future, integrating Complementary and Alternative Medical (CAM) policies for health care for the United States.

In August 2001, Professor Johnson joined with colleagues to establish the Educational Competency of Medical Qigong Therapy for the California State Acupuncture Board (C.S.A.B.). At that meeting, the Educational Competency and Outcomes Task-force of the California State Acupuncture Board was formed.

In September 2001, Professor Johnson was approved as a Continuing Education Provider for the Board of Behavioral Sciences (PCE 2272), authorized to issue C.E.U.s for Marriage Family Therapists (M.F.T.) and Licensed Clinical Social Workers (L.C.S.W.).

Also in September 2001, Professor Johnson began teaching a two year 250-hour intensive study course on Chinese Medical Qigong Therapy and Chinese Clinical Oncology. The focus of this course entailed several Medical Qigong therapeutic modalities for the treatment of various types of cancer, as well as primary Medical Qigong prescription exercises and meditations used in China for the treatment of cancer and the side effects of radiation and chemotherapy. This course was offered through the International Institute of Medical Qigong in Pacific Grove, California.

In October 2001, Professor Johnson lectured on "The Healing Practice of Medical Qigong Therapy" at the California State Oriental Medicine Association's International Expo and Convention, held in San Francisco, California.

In November 2001, Professor Johnson was approved as a Continuing Education Provider for the California State Acupuncture Board (CEP

369), and authorized to issue C.E.U.s for Licensed Acupuncturist (L.Ac.).

2002

In February 2002, Professor Johnson was included in the "Who's Who in the 21st Century" for his "Outstanding Contribution in the Field of Chinese Medicine and Medical Qigong Therapy," through the International Biographical Center in Cambridge, England.

In May 2002, Professor Johnson was approved as a A.O.B.T.A. Certified Instructor in Medical Qigong by the American Organization for Bodywork Therapies of Asia, allowing graduate students from the I.I.M.Q. and several T.C.M. Colleges to qualify in taking the 500 hour National Certification Examination developed for graduate students of Medical Qigong Therapy, by the National Certification Commission for Acupuncture and Oriental Medicine (NCCAOM).

In 2002, Professor Johnson lectured on "Treating Cancer with Chinese Medical Qigong Therapy," at the Academy of Oriental Medicine at Austin, in Austin Texas.

In 2002, Professor Johnson lectured on "Chinese Medical Qigong Therapy and the Treatment of Cancer," at the International Healing Center, in Carracas, Venezuela.

In 2002, Professor Johnson lectured on "Medical Qigong Therapy and the Treatment of Breast Cancer," at the California State Oriental Medicine Association's International Expo and Convention, held in San Francisco, California.

2003

In January 2003, Professor Johnson began reviewing case reports and providing editorial reports on research articles on Medical Qigong Therapy for the Journal of Alternative and Complementary Medicine.

In March 2003, Professor Johnson was nominated as the "2003 International Health Professional of the Year." He was also honored for his outstanding achievements and leadership in the International Medical Community, by the International Biographical Center, Cambridge, England.

In April 2003, Professor Johnson met with the Accreditation Commission for Acupuncture and Oriental Medicine (A.C.A.O.M.) to secure Educational Competency of Medical Qigong Therapy standards as taught at the Five Branches T.C.M. College for the California State Board of Education, as well as other T.C.M. Colleges throughout the United States.

In May of 2003, Professor Johnson accepted the position of Dean of Medical Qigong Science from The Academy For Five Element Acupuncture, Inc., in Hallandale, Florida. At the Florida acupuncture college, Professor Johnson developed two Medical Qigong programs: a 200 hour Medical Qigong Practitioner (M.Q.P.) and a 500 hour Medical Qigong Therapist (M.Q.T.) program.

In 2003, Professor Johnson lectured on "The Effective Treatment of Migraine Headaches using Medical Qigong Therapy," at the Asian Organization for Bodywork Therapists of America (A.O.B.T.A.) National Convention, Boston, Massachusetts.

In 2003, Professor Johnson was interviewed by the Nirvana Magazine in Paris, France, and lectured on "The Treatment of Emotional Disorders with Chinese Medical Qigong Therapy."

He was also honored for his outstanding contributions to the American way of life and his leadership role in implementing Traditional Chinese Medicine with Allopathic (Western) Medicine, and nominated in the 2003 American Biography Profile, by the American Biographical Institute, Raleigh, North Carolina, USA.

2004

In February of 2004, Professor Johnson implemented within the Academy For Five Element Acupuncture, Inc., in Hallandale, Florida, an active Medical Qigong Clinic. This was the second T.C.M. College within the United States to facilitate the combined use of Acupuncture, Herbs, and Medical Qigong Therapy to the general public.

In February of 2004, Professor Johnson began teaching a six month 186-hour intensive study course on Chinese Medical Qigong Therapy and Chinese Clinical Oncology in Houston, Texas. The focus of this course entailed several Medical Qigong therapeutic modalities for the treatment of various types of cancer, as well as primary Medical Qigong Prescription exercises and meditations used in China for the treatment of cancer and the side effects of radiation and chemotherapy. This course was made possible to the public by a grant from the Fant Foundation, and offered through the International Institute of Medical Qigong, sponsored by the Institute for Regenerative Medicine in Houston, Texas.

In August of 2004, Professor Johnson implemented within the Belgium College of Traditional Chinese Medicine an active 200 hour Medical Qigong Practitioner (M.Q.P.) program.

2005

In January of 2005, Professor Johnson was invited to serve on the External Advisory Committee for the Department of Palliative Care & Rehabilitation Medicine at the M.D. Anderson Cancer Center, in Houston, Texas. His responsibilities included advising the specific research using Medical Qigong Therapy for the treatment of various types of cancer.

Also in January of 2005, another 200 hour Medical Qigong Practitioner (M.Q.P.) certification program and ongoing Medical Qigong Clinic was started at the Acupuncture and Integrative Medicine College, in Berkeley, California.

Founded in 1985 and currently having branches in 10 countries and 23 states, the International Institute of Medical Qigong is known for maintaining the highest standards in Medical Qigong instruction and therapy. Because of the consistent high standards, in March of 2005 the Chinese Ministry of Health honored Dr. Johnson and the International Institute of Medical Qigong for exceeding the Chinese academic and clinical standards for clinical instruction and practice.

In July 2005, Professor Johnson's Biography was included in the column "Great Minds of the 21st Century," by the American Biographical Institute, Raleigh, North Carolina.

2006

By February 2006, the International Institute of Medical Qigong had been appointed as the Overseas College of Medical Qigong for the Henan University of Traditional Chinese Medicine, and was empowered to represent the University in all matters of Medical Qigong Clinical Therapy in the United States. As the Overseas Director, Professor Johnson was granted an official stamp from the University, which acknowledged his student's skill level and certified their exceptional academic and clinical training. Additionally, as a sister school, I.I.M.Q. was exclusively authorized to conduct Medical Qigong Clinical Residency programs at the H.U.T.C.M. and its three national hospitals.

In May of 2006, Professor Johnson was invited by the President of the Acupuncture Commission to teach the Medical Qigong Practitioner (MQP) program in Montréal, Canada. These courses were taught to 65 acupuncturists, under the supervision of the Université du Québec à Trois-Rivières. This was the first time in the history of Canada, that the Canadian government officially sponsored a Medical Qigong Therapy course.

In June of 2006, Professor Johnson attended the 4th General Assembly and 5th World Conference on Medical Qigong, and was nominated and elected Vice-President (U.S.A.) of the World Academic Society of Medical Qigong (W.A.S.O.M.Q.), in Beijing China. He also chaired the academic presentations and was later assigned to a special committee along with W.A.S.O.M.Q President Feng Lida to establish academic and clinical standards of Medical Qigong training. During the conference, Professor Johnson lectured on the "Medical Qigong Approach to Cancer Prescriptions."

2009 - 2012

In February 2009, Professor Johnson came out of "retirement," and began teaching a 3-year intensive Doctor of Medical Qigong Therapy course. All of the students were required to complete a 2,000 hour Clinical Program, including:

- 936 hours of lecture, lab, and internship
- 72 hours of Supervised Clinical Theatre
- 818 hours of Clinical Externship
- 174 hours of Additional Course Related Material
- and a Doctoral Thesis

This unique program was based on the original curriculum established by the Medical Qigong College at the Hai Dian T.C.M. University in Beijing China, and was supervised by the Overseas Medical Qigong College of the Henan

University of Traditional Chinese Medicine via the International Institute of Medical Qigong, in Monterey, Ca.

As in all Medical School Programs, there is always some degree of attrition occurring during the time-line of a course. This was especially true during the 3 years of intensive Medical Qigong training, as no breaks were given in-between the student's studies.

The beginning of the Medical Qigong Doctoral Program started with over 110 candidates. However, at the end of the course, only 52 students qualified for the title of "Doctor of Medical Qigong" (D.M.Q.),. These graduates were officially acknowledged by the People's Republic of China's Ministry of Health as "Doctors of Traditional Chinese Medicine" (D.T.C.M.).

Author and Publisher

Professor Johnson was a contributing author, selected to write the Medical Chi Kung section for the book *The Complete Illustrated Guide to Chi Kung*, a cooperative project between Element Books (UK) and author James MacRitchie.

Additionally, he was also one of the selected contributing authors for the book *Qigong-Essence of the Healing Dance*, a cooperative project between P.B.S. and Documentary Producer/Director Garri Garripoli.

Professor Johnson has been interviewed many times on local radio programs and has been featured in numerous local and international newspapers and magazines, including:
Newsweek Magazine (The International Journal),
The World Medical Qigong Quarterly,
Qi-The Journal of Traditional Eastern Health & Fitness,
The Empty Vessel Magazine,
Internal Arts Magazine,
The Mystical World of Chinese Martial Arts,
Inside Kung Fu Magazine,
Combat Karate Magazine,
Black Belt Magazine,
The Pa Kua Chang Journal, and
Inside Karate's Master Series Magazine,
Self Magazine,
Billboard Magazine,
Penthouse Magazine,

His televised interviews included some of the following special programs:
NBC News "Dateline,"
CBS/Channel 46 "Eye on America,"
The David Letterman Show
Discovery Channel
S.B.S. (Seoul Broadcasting Service)
K.P.B.S. Documentry

In 1988, Professor Johnson created and published a six level "Pa Kua Chang Chi Kung Correspondence Course," and in 1989, founded the "Pa Kua Chang News Letter," which later became known as the "Pa Kua Chang Journal," and was distributed worldwide.

As a master of several styles of Chinese Internal Martial Arts, Professor Johnson has written and published five Martial Arts Books, entitled:
- *The Secrets of the Eight Animals,*
- *The Masters Manual of Pa Kua Chang,*
- *Classical Pa Kua Chang Fighting Systems and Weapons,*
- *The Essence of Internal Martial Arts Vol. 1: Esoteric Fighting Techniques and Healing Methods, and*
- *The Essence of Internal Martial Arts Vol. 2: Energy Theory and Cultivation.*

From 1984 to 1986, Professor Johnson produced and directed six Baguazhang instructional videos entitled:
- *The Eight Animal School of Pa Kua Chang*
- *The Original Form of Pa Kua Chang*
- *The Eight Circular Pa Kua Staff*
- *The Eight Circular Pa Kua Broadsword*
- *The Dragon School of Pa Kua Chang, and*
- *The Fighting Techniques of Pa Kua Chang.*

In 1994, he was featured in two videos on Taijiquan, as well as one Qigong video narrated by the famous movie-star John Saxon, entitled:
- *Tai Chi-The Empowering Workout,*
- *Power Tai Chi- Total Body Workout,*
- *Chi Kung-The Healing Workout.*

In 1994, Professor Johnson additionally created two Meditation CD/cassette tapes with composer John Serri entitled:
- *Tai Chi Meditation - [1] Life Force Breathing,* and
- *Tai Chi Meditation - [2] Eight Direction Perception.*

In 1999, Professor Johnson produced 10 Medical Qigong Instructional Videos and DVD's as a compendium to his soon to be released Medical Qigong textbook. These nstructional Videos and DVD's were entitled:
- *Gathering Energy from Heaven and Earth,*
- *Stationary and Dynamic Medical Qigong Posture Training,*
- *Treating Patients with Medical Qigong Therapy (Vol.1),*
- *Treating Patients with Medical Qigong Therapy (Vol.2),*
- *Medical Qigong Energy Techniques and Qi Emitting Methods,*
- *Medical Qigong Invisible Needle Technique, Five Element Qigong Massage, and Energetic Point Therapy,*
- *Medical Qigong Healing Sound Therapy and Prescriptions,*
- *Treatment of Internal Organ Diseases with Medical Qigong,*
- *Treatment of Cysts, Tumors, and Cancer with Medical Qigong Therapy,* and
- *Soul Retrieval.*

In May 2000, Professor Johnson finally released his famous 1066 page tome on Chinese Energetic Medicine, which was happily received and highly praised by his contemporaries at that time. The extremely large textbook was entitled:
- *Chinese Medical Qigong Therapy, A Comprehensive Clinical Text.*

In September 2000, Professor Johnson produced the first in a series of new Medical Qigong videos and Interactive CD-ROMs. The featured topic for the first CD-ROM was entitled:
- *Medical Qigong for Understanding, Prevention & Treatment of Breast Disease (CD-ROM).*

- *Medical Qigong for Treating Breast Disease (Instructional Video).*

In August 2001, Professor Johnson composed and published a series of five new textbooks. This unique work was based on the previous information introduced in his Medical Qigong Textbook. The names of the five new books are entitled:
- *Chinese Medical Qigong Therapy Vol 1: Energetic Anatomy and Physiology,*
- *Chinese Medical Qigong Therapy Vol 2. Energetic Alchemy, Dao Yin Therapy and Qi Deviations*
- *Chinese Medical Qigong Therapy Vol 3: Differential Diagnosis, Clinical Foundations, Treatment Principles and Clinical Protocols*
- *Chinese Medical Qigong Therapy Vol 4: Prescription Exercises and Meditations, Treatment of Internal Organ Diseases, Pediatrics, Geriatrics, Gynecology, Neurology and Energetic Psychology*
- *Chinese Medical Qigong Therapy Vol 5: An Energetic Approach to Oncology*

In September 2004, Professor Johnson began producing a new series of six Medical Qigong Oncology DVD sets. This new series accompanies the clinical textbook entitled: *Chinese Medical Qigong Therapy Vol 5: An Energetic Approach to Oncology,* and contains four to five DVDs in each set. The name of the six new DVD sets are entitled:
- *Houston Cancer Seminar #1 - Introduction to Medical Qigong Therapy and Cancer Treatment:*
- *Houston Cancer Seminar #2 - An Energetic Approach to Oncology*
- *Houston Cancer Seminar #3 - Medical Qigong Treatment Protocols Used for Breast, Cervical, Prostate, Ovarian, and Uterine Cancer*
- *Houston Cancer Seminar #4 - Medical Qigong Treatment Protocols used for Brain, Skin, and Bone Cancer, Leukemia, Malignant Lymphoma, and Multiple Myelomas*
- *Houston Cancer Seminar #5 - Medical Qigong Cancer Prescription Exercises and Meditations*
- *Houston Cancer Seminar #6 - Medical Qigong Treatment Protocols Used For Radiation and Chemotherapy*

In May 2005, Professor Johnson composed and published a series of 3 new books based on his extensive training in ancient Chinese Daoist Mysticism. The names of the three new books were entitled:
- *Introduction to Daoist Mysticism #1: Lighting the Eyes of the Dragon*
- *Introduction to Daoist Mysticism #2: Journey into the Infinite Void*
- *Absorbing the Riches of the Profound*

From 2006 to 2012, Professor Johnson composed and published a series of 8 new books based on his extensive training in ancient Chinese Daoist Mysticism. The names of these eight special workbooks are entitled:
- *Daoist Internal Alchemy: Neigong and Weigong Training*
- *Magical Tools and the Daoist Altar*
- *Daoist Magical Talismans*
- *Daoist Magical Incantations, Hand Seals, and Star Stepping*
- *Daoist Mineral, Plant, and Animal Magic*
- *Daoist Weather Magic and Feng Shui*
- *Daoist Magical Transformation Skills: Dream Magic, ShapShifting, Soul Travel, and Sex Magic*
- *Daoist Exorcism: Encounters With Sorcerers, Ghosts, Spirits and Demons*

In June 2014, Professor Johnson revised and expanded his five *Chinese Medical Qigong Therapy* Textbook series. These new versions were published under the new title:
- *The Secret Teachings of Chinese Energetic Medicine Vol 1: Energetic Anatomy and Physiology*
- *The Secret Teachings of Chinese Energetic Medicine Vol 2: Energetic Alchemy, Dao Yin Therapy, Healing Qi Deviations, and Spirit Pathology*
- *The Secret Teachings of Chinese Energetic Medicine Vol 3: Developing Intuitive and Perceptual Awareness, Energetic Foundations, Treatment Principles, and Clinical Applications*
- *The Secret Teachings of Chinese Energetic Medicine Vol 4: Prescription Exercises, Healing Meditations, And The Treatment of Internal Organ Diseases*
- *The Secret Teachings of Chinese Energetic Medicine Vol 5: An Energetic Approach to Oncology, Gynecology, Neurology, Geriatrics, Pediatrics, and Psychology*

Professor Johnson's books, video tapes, meditation C.D.'s and cassette tapes have been translated into other languages and are currently being sold around the world.

For more information about the author, the reader can connect to his two web sites at:

www.qigongmedicine.com

www.daoistmagic.com